A Handbook of Corporate Governance and Social Responsibility

Corporate Social Responsibility Series

Series Editors:
Professor Güler Aras, Yildiz Technical University, Istanbul, Turkey
Professor David Crowther, DeMontfort University, Leicester, UK

Presenting applied research from an academic perspective on all aspects of corporate social responsibility, this global interdisciplinary series includes books for all those with an interest in ethics and governance, corporate behaviour and citizenship, regulation, protest, globalization, responsible marketing, social reporting and sustainability.

Recent titles in this series:

Creating Food Futures
Trade, Ethics and the Environment
Cathy Rozel Farnworth, Janice Jiggins and Emyr Vaughan Thomas
ISBN: 978-0-7546-4907-6

Spirituality and Corporate Social Responsibility
Interpenetrating Worlds
David Bubna-Litic
ISBN: 978-0-7546-4763-8

Global Perspectives on Corporate Governance and CSR
Güler Aras and David Crowther
ISBN: 978-0-566-08830-8

Looking Beyond Profit
Peggy Chiu
ISBN: 978-0-7546-7337-8

Corruption in International Business
Sharon Eicher
ISBN: 978-0-7546-7137-4

Wealth, Welfare and the Global Free Market
I. Ozer Ertuna
ISBN: 978-0-566-08905-3

A Handbook of Corporate Governance and Social Responsibility

Edited by

GÜLER ARAS and DAVID CROWTHER

Routledge
Taylor & Francis Group

LONDON AND NEW YORK

First published in paperback 2024

First published 2010 by Gower Publishing

Published 2016 by Routledge
4 Park Square, Milton Park, Abingdon, Oxon OX14 4RN

and by Routledge
605 Third Avenue, New York, NY 10158

Routledge is an imprint of the Taylor & Francis Group, an informa business

Gower Applied Business Research
Our programme provides leaders, practitioners, scholars and researchers with thought provoking, cutting edge books that combine conceptual insights, interdisciplinary rigour and practical relevance in key areas of business and management.

British Library Cataloguing in Publication Data
A handbook of corporate governance and social
   responsibility. -- (Corporate social responsibility series)
   1. Corporate governance. 2. Social responsibility of
   business.
   I. Series II. Aras, Guler. III. Crowther, David.
   658.4'08-dc22

Library of Congress Cataloging-in-Publication Data
A handbook of corporate governance and social responsibility / [edited] by
G|ler Aras and David Crowther.
       p. cm. -- (Corporate social responsibility)
   Includes index.
   ISBN 978-0-566-08817-9 (hardback) 1. Corporate
governance. 2. Social responsibility of business. I. Aras,
G|ler. II. Crowther, David.
   HD2741.H357 2009
   658.4--dc22
                                                                 2009029713

ISBN 13: 978-0-566-08817-9 (hbk)
ISBN 13: 978-1-03-283807-6 (pbk)
ISBN 13: 978-1-315-56479-1 (ebk)

DOI: 10.4324/9781315564791

Contents

List of Figures

List of Tables

About the Editors

Professor Dr Güler Aras, BA, MBA, PhD, CPA

PROFESSOR OF FINANCE & ACCOUNTING, YILDIZ TECHNICAL UNIVERSITY, ISTANBUL, TURKEY

Güler Aras is Professor of Finance and Director of the Graduate School at the Yildiz Technical University, Istanbul, Turkey and Visiting Professor at De Montfort University, UK as well as various other institutions throughout the world. Her qualifications are in the area of finance where much of her research and teaching is located. She serves as advisor to a number of government bodies and is also a member of a number of international editorial and advisory boards.

Güler has published 15 books and has contributed over 150 articles to academic, business and professional journals and magazines and to edited book collections. She has also spoken extensively at conferences and seminars and has acted as a consultant to a wide range of government and commercial organisations. Her research is into financial economy and financial markets with particular emphasis on the relationship between corporate social responsibility and a firm's financial performance.

Professor Dr David Crowther, BA, MBA, M.Ed., PhD, DSocSc, DSc, PGCE, FCMA, CPFA, MCMI

PROFESSOR OF CORPORATE SOCIAL RESPONSIBILITY, DE MONTFORT UNIVERSITY, UK

David Crowther is a qualified accountant who worked as an accountant, systems specialist and general manager in local government, industry and commerce for 20 years before moving in to the higher education arena. His teaching has been focused upon the use of accounting as a management technique while his research is interdisciplinary. He is Visiting Professor at Yildiz Technical University and various other institutions throughout the world.

David has published over 25 books and has also contributed more than 250 articles to academic, business and professional journals and to edited book collections. He has also spoken widely at conferences and seminars and acted as a consultant to a wide range of government, professional and commercial organisations. His research is into corporate social responsibility with a particular emphasis on the relationship between social, environmental and financial performance.

Their joint research is concerned with sustainability, sustainable development and with governance issues and is reflected in their recent (2009) research book, *The Durable*

Corporation: Strategies for Sustainable Development. Together they run the Social Responsibility Research Network an informal network of scholars (both academic and professional) concerned with issues of social responsibility – and also edit its official journal, Social Responsibility Journal, and organise its annual conference, the International Conference on Corporate Social Responsibility.

About the Contributors

Maria Aluchna is Assistant Professor at Department of Management Theory, Warsaw School of Economics, Poland. She specializes in corporate governance (ownership structure, board, executive compensation, transition economies) as well as in strategic management. She was awarded the Deutscher Akademischer Austauschdienst (DAAD) scholarship for research stay and the Universität Passau and Polish-American Fulbright Commission scholarship for the research stay at Columbia University. She received the Polish Science Foundation award for young researchers (2004, 2005). Currently Maria Aluchna teaches 'Comparative Analysis of Corporate Governance' (both in Polish and English), 'Transition in Central and Eastern Europe' (in English) and 'Foundation of Management' (in Polish). She serves on two boards (as Vice-Chairman and Secretary). Since January she has been the Editor in Chief of Warsaw Stock Exchange portal on corporate governance best practice (www.corp-gov.gpw.pl).

Jane Andrew is a Senior Lecturer in the School of Accounting and Finance, Faculty of Commerce, University of Wollongong and is currently the School's Research Director. She teaches in Accounting Theory to postgraduate students. Her research interests include the relationship between social and environmental issues and accounting. She has publications on environmental ethics as well as the privatisation of prisons.

Bokhodir Ayupov graduated from University of Surrey (UK) with an M.Sc. Management in 2004. Soon after that he was employed as a lecturer at Westminster International University in Tashkent. Currently Bokhodir Ayupov is a senior lecturer and holds the position of Course Leader in Certificate of Foundation Studies. The areas of his research interest include project management, management of education, organisational behaviour and marketing. He has also been providing professional training for various organisations. His training expertise includes subjects of Project Management, Developing People Internationally, Business Communication, Time Management, Teambuilding and Working in Teams, Presentation Skills.

Dominique Bessire is a Professor at Orleans University (France) She started her career as an auditor by KPMG and then spent six years as a controller at Darty, the leading retail French firm in household equipment. Her teaching and research fields cover management control, organisation theory, epistemology, corporate governance, corporate social responsibility and ethics. She has published articles in leading French and Anglo-Saxon academic journals and has presented papers in numerous international conferences. She has been the chair of the *Laboratoire Orléanais de Gestion* (LOG) for four years and now is in charge of a research project on SME.

David Birch has been Professor of Communication since 1997 and was the Founding Director of the Corporate Citizenship Research Unit (1998–2005), Deakin University,

Melbourne, Australia. He was previously Professor of Media and Communication at Central Queensland University (1993–1997), Senior Lecturer in the School of Human Communication, Murdoch University (1985–1992), and Lecturer in English Language and Linguistics, National University of Singapore (1980–1985). He has been General Editor of *The Journal of Corporate Citizenship* and also of *Social Semiotics*. He is currently on the Editorial Boards of several international Journals, including *Journal of Corporate Citizenship; Asian Business and Management; Asia Pacific Public Relations Journal; International Journal of Business Governance and Ethics; Corporate Social Responsibility and Environmental Management; The Journal of Social Responsibility; Social Semiotics; Social Identities; Continuum The Australian Journal of Media and Culture* and *Critical Journal of Media Studies*. David was Adjunct Professor in Corporate Citizenship at Southern Cross University (2000–2003) and Visiting Research Professor at the International Centre for Corporate Social Responsibility, University of Nottingham (2001–2004) and has published widely in linguistics, communication, media, cultural studies, corporate citizenship, corporate social responsibility, governance and accountability. He is currently teaching a Masters course in Accountability and CSR (Deakin University).

Muzaffer Bodur is a Professor of Marketing and International Business at the Management Department of Boğaziçi University in Istanbul, Turkey. She received her doctoral degree from Indiana University and acted as a visiting professor at George Mason University of USA, Uppsala University of Sweden and Odense University of Denmark. Her teaching topics include global marketing management and multivariate data analysis methods at graduate level and marketing research for the executive MBA program. She has been a member of Academy of International Business (AIB) and a founding member of Consortium for International Marketing Research (CIMAR) group. She served as the editor of *Bo aziçi Journal: Review of Social, Economics and Administrative Studies* and on the editorial board of *Journal of International Marketing* for several years. Her publications focus on business cultures and internationalisation of firms, marketing strategies of multinational firms in emerging markets, cross cultural studies on societal and organisational practices and values, and consumer satisfaction, dissatisfaction and complaining behaviour.

Stephen Brammer is Deputy Director of the Centre for Business Organizations and Society at the University of Bath in the UK. His research addresses the links between organisational strategy and social responsibility with a focus on how organisations build effective relationships with stakeholders including employees, communities and suppliers. Currently, he is collaborating with colleagues around the world on projects that (a) explore socially and environmentally responsible procurement in private sector organisations with a focus on international purchasing, and (b) examine the community involvement activities of firms in a range of different countries. His research has been published in leading scholarly and practitioner journals including *Business & Society*, the *Journal of Management Studies*, and the *Journal of Business Research*.

Álvaro de Regil Castilla is Executive Director of The Jus Semper Global Alliance, a coalition of societal, trade union and academic organisations dedicated to the promotion of living wages throughout the world as a core element of sustainability, democracy and business accountability and based in California, USA. He holds a degree in Business Administration from Universidad La Salle, Mexico City and an MBA in Marketing and

International Business Management from George Washington University, Washington, D.C. He specializes on living wage equalisation analysis and has written several position and assessment papers on the social responsibilities of business, business and human rights, fair trade and consumer responsibility.

Pavel Castka is Senior Lecturer in Operations Management and former MBA Director at the University of Canterbury, New Zealand advising Ph.D. and MBA students as well as teaching MBA and undergraduate courses in Operations and Quality Management. Pavel's research interests in quality management and corporate social responsibility focus on management frameworks and aspects of standardisation. His work has received numerous international awards and has been published in many refereed journals. Pavel is a leading author of the CSR framework published by BSi. As a consultant, he works closely with businesses to improve their management systems; he serves as nominated expert on ISO/TMB/WG Social Responsibility (responsible for the development of ISO 26000) and is a member of ISO/TC 176/SC2 (ISO 9000) within the International Organisation for Standardization (ISO). Pavel often speaks at global events related to quality management and CSR.

Céline Chatelin-Ertur is Associate Professor in Organizational Strategy and Finance and Assistant Director of the *Laboratoire Orléanais de Gestion* at Orleans University. Her research activities focus on three topics of corporate governance: managerial decision-making process, cognitive and stakeholder approach of corporate governance, principles of corporate governance. Her recent papers analyse the dynamics of corporate governance systems and the process of standardisation of corporate governance rules. Her papers have been published in French and Canadian academic journals, and discussed in international conferences.

Stuart Cooper is a Senior Lecturer in Finance and Accounting at Aston Business School. After graduating from Exeter University with a first class honours degree in Economics and Statistics, he qualified as a Chartered Accountant and gained several years' audit experience. In 2002 he successfully completed a Ph.D. in Management at Aston University. His publications and research interests are in the areas of social and environmental accounting and reporting, stakeholder management and the Operating and Financial Review.

Mirella Damiani is Professor of Economics in the Department of Economics, Finance and Statistics at the University of Perugia, Italy. Mirella's main research interests are in corporate governance and the changing nature of the modern firm, incentives and employee participation in profits and enterprise results, labour market rigidities and macroeconomic policy questions. Most of her work, published in books and journals, deals with micro as well as macroeconomic issues related to the role of labour market institutions. She has both explored the theoretical grounds of labour markets, and evaluated the contemporary relevance of theoretical models in a comparative perspective.

Wallace N. Davdison III is a Rehn Professor of Finance at Southern Illinois University. His teaching area is corporate finance. He has published over 150 papers in referred journals, including papers in the *Journal of Finance*, *Journal of Financial and Quantitative*

Analysis, Financial Management, Journal of Banking and Finance, Journal of Corporate Finance, Financial Review, Journal of Financial Research, Academy of Management Journal, and *Strategic Management Journal*. Dr. Davidson has authored numerous continuing education seminars and on-line continuing education classes for the Professional Development Institute and American Institute of CPAs. He has presented these seminars across the country and has twice been named an 'Outstanding Discussion Leader' by the AICPA and has received numerous awards for teaching and research. His recent awards include 'Excellence Through Commitment' and 'Outstanding Research Honor Roll' in 2007 at SIU. Two of his papers are among the most downloaded papers on the Social Science Research Network.

Douglas DeJong is the John F. Murray Professor of Accounting at the Tippie College of Business, University of Iowa, USA. He holds a Ph.D. in Accounting from the University of Michigan. His research interests include corporate governance and capital markets, and experimental economics and its application to strategic and market settings. Douglas's work appears in the leading academic journals in accounting, economics and finance.

Charles Elad is a Reader in Accounting and Finance at the University of Westminster. He received a Masters degree in International Accounting & Financial Management, and a Ph.D. in Accountancy from the University of Glasgow. He was formerly a Lecturer at the University of Aberdeen. Charles has served as a consultant to a number of international organisations and has also held competitive research grants from the UK Economic and Social Research Council (ESRC), the French *Centre National de la Recherche Scientifique* (CNRS), the Research Committee of the University of Aberdeen, the Chartered Institute of Management Accountants, and the Institute of Chartered Accountants of Scotland. His publications include a book on accounting for sustainability and articles in: *European Accounting Review, Management Accounting Research, Critical Perspectives on Accounting, Advances in International Accounting, Advances in Public Interest Accounting, Research in Accounting in Emerging Economies, Socio-Economic Review*, among others. He has served as an ad hoc referee for many scholarly journals.

Deniz Erden is a Professor of International Business at the Department of Management of Boğaziçi University in Istanbul, Turkey. She received her doctoral degree from the University of Massachusetts, Amherst. Her teaching topics at the graduate level include the political and economic interrelations among key global actors, the institutional framework of international trade, investment, production, flows, foreign direct investment theories, the internationalisation process of firms and the social responsibilities of multinational corporations. She is a member of the Academy of International Business. Her publications cover the human resource, export, joint-venture and social responsibility strategies of multinational corporations in emerging economies. She has conducted the first country survey of foreign direct investment firms operating in Turkey.

Bengi Ertuna is an Associate Professor of Finance at Bogazici University, Istanbul. She obtained her Ph.D. in Finance at Boğaziçi University in 1995 and she has taught in the Tourism Administration Department of Bogazici University since then. Her research interests include corporate governance, initial public offerings and small business finance. She has published articles on family ownership and initial public offerings in Turkey.

Ozer Ertuna teaches in Okan University and part time in Bosphorous University, Istanbul. He has served in the Boards of some private and public companies and provided consultancy services to many others. He was a member of the Board of Directors of Sumer Holding, which was one of the major State companies, which assumed significant roles in economic development in Turkey. Ozer has provided consultancy services to various Ministries of Turkish Government. He served as advisor to Ministry of Enterprises, Ministry of Labor and Ministry of States. He also served as chief advisor to the Prime Minister of Turkey in 1992–1993. He joined the Nigeria Mission of the Wold Bank as an expert. He also served the World Bank as an expert in the management evaluation team of ICARDA. Ozer has published more than 100 scholarly articles and more than 20 books. His book on *The Liberalization of Turkey's Gold Market* was published by World Gold Council as Research Study No. 7, in 1995.

Marc Goergen holds a BA in Economics from the Free University of Brussels, an MBA from Solvay Business School, Brussels, and a DPhil in Economics from Oxford University. Marc holds a chair in finance at Cardiff Business School, Cardiff University. His previous appointments have been at UMIST, the University of Manchester, Reading University and the University of Sheffield. Marc's research interests are in corporate finance, in particular initial public offerings (IPOs), corporate governance, mergers and acquisitions, managerial compensation, private equity and insider trading. His research has been published in various academic journals including *European Financial Management*, the *Journal of Corporate Finance*, the *Journal of Finance* and the *Journal of Law, Economics and Organization*. He is also a research associate of the European Corporate Governance Institute (www.ecgi.org).

Kimberly Goetz is the Financial Assurance Officer for the Washington State Department of Ecology's Hazardous Waste and Toxics Reduction Program. She is responsible for handling corporate finance, economic, policy, and legislative issues for the program. Kimberly also oversees the implementation of financial assurance programs for facilities handling hazardous or dangerous waste. She was actively involved in the development of Ecology's Sustainable Washington program and managed the development of financial and economic incentives for the project. She currently manages quality assurance and data analysis for the Sustainable Washington pilot. Kimberly's BA in Political Science (International Relations) and Global Studies (Development and Social Justice) is from Pacific Lutheran University in Tacoma, Washington and her MPA (Public Policy) is from The Evergreen State College in Olympia, Washington.

Suzanne Gregory holds an honours degree in Business Studies from The University of Sunderland in 2005. She works as a KTP Associate for Durham Business School, where she is currently involved in a research project regarding the economic impact on the North East of England of trading locally, encompassing procurement and CSR.

Stephan Heblich is a Senior Research Fellow at the Max Planck Institute of Economics in Jena, Germany. He holds a Diploma and a Ph.D. in Economics from the University of Passau. In his Ph.D., he started connecting the fields of CSR and Regional Economics. Before Stephan joined the Max Planck Institute, he worked on two studies with a regional economics perspective. One project was for the European Social Fund (2004–2006) dealing with adjustment problems of the labor market in the Bavarian objective two regions at the Czech Republic's border. The other project was for BMW's production plant in Regensburg (2006) dealing with its economic and social impact on the region. His current research is focused on modern location factors that foster regional development and growth. Such modern location factors cover intangible assets like knowledge, social ties and entrepreneurial capacities.

Wang Hong is a Lecturer at Shanghai University, College of International Business and Management, China, where she also researches on environmental management. Currently she is also a doctoral candidate of Tongji University, School of Economics and Management, China.

Jenke Ter Horst is Associate Professor of Finance at Tilburg University. He obtained his Ph.D. from Tilburg University. His research interests include financial econometrics, mutual fund and hedge fund behaviour.

Kumba Jallow is a Principal Lecturer in the Department of Accounting and Finance at De Montfort University, Leicester, UK. Her research interests include corporate social responsibility and accounting for sustainability, and the mechanisms, both verbal and imagery, that companies use to communication their CSR activities. This is reflected in her teaching, which is to both post- and under-graduate students in the Business School and in other Faculties across the University. She has publishes internationally and is the Founding Editor of *The Journal of Applied Accounting Research*.

Abe de Jong is Professor of Corporate Finance at RSM Erasmus University, The Netherlands and member of ERIM. He holds a Ph.D. in Finance from Tilburg University. His research interests include corporate finance and corporate governance. His work has been published in, among others, the *Journal of Corporate Finance*, *Financial Management*, *Journal of Banking & Finance* and the *Journal of Management & Governance*. His current research is in the field of capital structure choice, behavioral corporate finance and the history of corporate governance in the Netherlands.

Mary Kaidonis is Associate Professor and currently Head of School of Accounting and Finance, Faculty of Commerce, University of Wollongong, NSW, Australia. Mary has over 20 years experience as an academic in financial accounting and accounting theory at undergraduate and post-graduate levels. She has supervised students completing Ph.D.s in Environmental Accounting and Accounting for the Extractive Industries. She has developed a nexus between teaching and research which culminated in winning the Vice Chancellor's Outstanding Contribution to Teaching and Learning 2000 team award. The interdisciplinary feature of her work has lead to collaborations between accounting and taxation law and has resulted in international publications on environmental tax. Mary has also led teaching education projects overseas which complement her research in accounting and its role in developing countries.

Iroda Komilova graduated from University of Surrey (UK) with an M.Sc. Management in 2004. Soon after that she was employed as a lecturer at Westminster International University in Tashkent. Currently Iroda Komilova is a Senior Lecturer and holds the position of Course Leader for Undergraduate Business Programme. The areas of her research interest include project management, management accounting, corporate strategy and audit. She has also been providing professional training for various organisations. Her training expertise includes subjects of Project Management, Financial and Management Accounting.

Cubie Lau (Lau Lai Lai) received her undergraduate education in Hong Kong, followed by graduate study in the UK (MBA, Kent) and Hong Kong (MA, Hong Kong Baptist University). She worked in marketing and the hospitality industry, then several academic posts in Hong Kong. In 2007 Cubie returned to school to pursue a Ph.D. in Management at the Smurfit Business School at University College Dublin, Ireland. She has delivered papers at many academic conferences on these topics and has published in *Social Responsibility Journal* and in *The Chinese Economy*, and has already taught universities business courses in Hong Kong, Singapore and Ireland. She is interested in cross-cultural aspects of management and leadership as well as corporate social responsibility.

Gerard Mertens is Professor of Financial Analysis at RSM Erasmus University, Chair of the Department of Accounting & Control, and Research Fellow of ERIM, the RSM Erasmus University Research Institute, The Netherlands. He received his Masters degree in Applied Economics from Radboud University and holds a Ph.D. in accounting from Maastricht University. His research interests include financial reporting and disclosure strategies, earnings management and corporate governance. His work has been published in the *Journal of Corporate Finance, Journal of Accounting and Public Policy, European Accounting Review, International Journal of Accounting* and the *Journal of Management & Governance*. He has also contributed chapters to various books on financial reporting and corporate governance.

Kurtay Ogunc is a Managing Partner of Stowbridge Partners and a faculty member at Texas A&M University – Commerce. He acts as the Chairman of the Board in two portfolio companies, Alpha Dynamics Group and RiskFusion. In addition, he is an external advisor of the International Center for Decision and Risk Analysis (ICDRiA) at the University of Texas at Dallas. Kurtay also heads up the efforts of the strategic alliance between Stowbridge Partners and Mcube Investment Technologies, Inc., which recently won the prestigious Global Pensions Award as the best software provider in investment management. Kurtay obtained an MBA in Finance from Western Michigan University, and the Master of Applied Statistics and a Ph.D. in Decision Sciences from Louisiana State University. Currently, he works on the conceptual and theoretical development of Flexibility Theory™, as well as a monograph, entitled Transformational Portfolio Management for Institutional Investors.

Stéphane Onnée is Professor of Finance and Dean of the Faculty of Law, Economics and Management at Orleans University. His researches focus on corporate governance, social responsibility and financial communication. His recent papers study discourses of managers and economic-social-governance (ESG) ratings. He has published several papers in French academic journals and presented several communications in international congresses.

Stephen Pavelin is a Reader in Economics at the University of Reading in the UK. His current research agenda focuses upon the application of economic analysis to key issues relating to corporate social responsibility, such as the effect of corporate social performance on the reputations and financial performance of firms. Recent publications include articles in the *Journal of Management Studies*, the *Journal of Business Research*, the *International Journal of Industrial Organisation*, the *Journal of Business Ethics*, *Financial Management*, the *Journal of Business Finance and Accounting*, *Business Ethics: A European Review* and the *European Management Journal*.

Rob Peddle is a passionate advocate of 'System Thinking' – especially the capability this gives organisations to deliver the broad range of business requirements now demanded by stakeholders. He has co-developed a number of innovative tools that support organisations in their application of this philosophy. A Chartered Mechanical Engineer by training, Rob has wide experience across many different business sectors. This broad view of many organisations and what makes them effective is the foundation of his strong belief that process management starts in the boardroom. Rob is a director of The High Performance Organisation Group (www.the-hpo.com) in the UK and has authored and co-authored a number of books on the subject, such as *'Implementing Effective Corporate Social Responsibility and Corporate Governance - A Guide'* published by Bsi.

Luc Renneboog is Professor of Corporate Finance at Tilburg University. He graduated from the Catholic University of Leuven with degrees in Management Engineering (M.Sc.) and in Philosophy (BA), from the University of Chicago with an MBA, and from the London Business School with a Ph.D. in Financial Economics. He held appointments at the Universities of Leuven and Oxford, and visiting appointments at LBS (London), EUI (Florence), HEC (Paris), Venice University and CUNEF (Madrid). He has published in the *Journal of Finance, Journal of Financial Intermediation, Journal of Law and Economics, Journal of Corporate Finance, Journal of Banking and Finance, Cambridge Journal of Economics,* and others. He has co-authored and edited several books with Oxford University Press. His research interests are corporate finance, corporate governance, dividend policy, insider trading, law and economics, and the economics of art.

Juliane Riese is an Assistant Professor at the Department of Organization Science at the Free University in Amsterdam. She studied economics and management in Greifswald (Germany), Oxford and Bremen (Germany) after spending her gap year working as a volunteer for Greenpeace Nordic in Stockholm. She received her Ph.D. in the Social Sciences from the University of Bremen in 2008. Her thesis, which seeks to contribute to systems theory as founded by Niklas Luhmann, includes a systems-theoretic case study of Greenpeace's anti-whaling campaign in Norway.

Riham Rizk gained a joint honours degree in Accounting and Marketing from Simmons College in Boston, Massachusetts in the USA. She then went on to complete her MBA at the Arab Academy for Science and Technology in Alexandria, Egypt where she was a Lecturer in Accounting. Dr Rizk joined Durham Business School in the UK in 2000 as a Ph.D. candidate and later started teaching for the Department of Economics and Finance. She now leads the BA Accounting and Finance Course and teaches Management Accounting,

Financial Planning and Control, Business Accounting and Finance and Managing Finance and Microperspectives in Business on undergraduate and postgraduate programmes.

She is a member of the Finance and Accounting Research Group at Durham and of the Center for Social and Environmental Accounting Research and the Social Responsibility Research Network. Her particular research interests include CSR and Disclosure, Corporate Governance, The Influence of Culture and Religion on Accounting. Riham has authored and co-authored papers in the *Social Responsibility Journal*.

Peter Roosenboom is Associate Professor of Corporate Finance at RSM Erasmus University, The Netherlands and member of ERIM. He holds a Ph.D. in Finance from Tilburg University. His research interests include corporate governance, private equity and initial public offerings. His work has been published in the *Journal of Corporate Finance, Contemporary Accounting Research, International Journal of Accounting, International Review of Financial Analysis, European Financial Management Journal, Applied Economics, Pacific-Basin Finance Journal* and the *Journal of Management & Governance*. He is the co-editor of the book 'The Rise and Fall of Europe's New Stock Markets' that has appeared in the book series Advances in Financial Economics. He has also contributed book chapters to various books on initial public offerings, mergers and acquisitions, venture capital and corporate governance.

Ian Rosam has extensive knowledge of creating process-based management systems linked to best practice 'System Thinking' that led organisations from ISO9001:2000 to CSR. This experience has been gained from working in organisations from many different sectors. He has co-developed the 360 degree behavioural assessment techniques needed for Auditing in the 21st Century. These have been delivered online and/or onsite reporting organisational effectiveness against drivers of real performance, as well as compliance. This has greatly enhanced ISO 9001, internal process audits, customer satisfaction assessment activity for many organisations. Ian is well published having written a number of books on System Thinking including providing significant 'real world' experience for a CSR book entitled: *Implementing Effective Corporate Social Responsibility and Corporate Governance – A Guide*, published by the British Standards Institution (Bsi).

Sameh Sakr is an assistant professor of finance at Sultan Qaboos University in Muscat, Oman. He has published papers in areas of corporate governance; mergers and acquisitions; and the effect of regulation. Other areas of interest include country governance of MENA region, contagion among financial markets, and banks' efficiency.

Henry Schäfer is holder of the Chair of Finance at the University of Stuttgart. His main focus in research is on the valuation of assets, in particular regarding real options and non-financial parameters. Other research fields are project finance, behavioral corporate finance and the valuation of real estate projects. Particular relevance is given to research regarding 'Sustainability & Finance'. Henry is one of the leading German research capacities in SRI and CSR. He has also published several text books in finance and is consulting several major well-known global firms.

Hillary Shaw is a Senior Lecturer at Harper Adams University College, Newport, Shropshire, UK, since October 2006. His main area of academic interest is into the global food system, and food retailing in particular. His research areas include food access by disadvantaged consumers, food deserts, the globalisation of food retailing and the CSR of food retailers, global and local, towards the community they operate within. Hillary was awarded a Ph.D. on his research into the extent and classification of food deserts from the University of Leeds in 2004. He has also undertaken a research project with the School of Geography, University of Southampton, UK, on the societal and economic effects of supermarkets opening local outlets in small towns in Hampshire.

Julia Shaw began her academic career at the University of Lancaster, where she held her first full-time lectureship and completed a jurisprudential doctoral thesis on Kant's moral philosophy and its application to ethical dilemmas arising in a formal legal context. Her Ph.D. was awarded in December 1998. Accepting a post at Aston University's Business School, she became Director of Legal Studies and published in legal ethics and legal philosophy, also in business ethics and corporate governance. Following a visiting lectureship at Nantes University in France and as external examiner at Beijing University in China, Julia now holds a post at De Montfort Business and Law School in Leicester, UK. Maintaining an active interest the theory of moral responsibility and political philosophy, her research activities are mostly in the areas of socio-legal theory and CSR.

Natalie Stoianoff is a Professor in the Faculty of Law at the University of Technology, Sydney, NSW Australia and the Director of the Master of Industrial Property Program. Her interdisciplinary research is concerned with the legal, ethical and commercial aspects of biotechnology. In particular, Natalie's research interests range from the patenting of living organisms, technology transfer and environmental taxation. Natalie has been the recipient of a number of research fellowships and is a regular participant in the annual Global Environmental Taxation conference series publishing on the impact of taxation concessions for mine site rehabilitation and conservation covenants.

Antonio Tencati is an Assistant Professor of Management at the Institute of Innovation and Technology Management, Department of Management-CSR Unit, and a Senior Researcher at SPACE, the European Research Centre on Risk, Security, Occupational Health and Safety, Environment and Crisis Management, at Bocconi University, Milan, Italy. He is also member of the Business Ethics Faculty Group of the CEMS-MIM (Community of European Management Schools – Master in International Management) Programme. His research interests include management of sustainability, CSR, environmental management and innovation and operations management.

Wim Vandekerckhove is Assistant Professor of Practical Ethics with the Center for Ethics and Value Inquiry at Ghent University Belgium and a post-doc researcher with the Fund for Scientific Research Flanders. He has published *Whistleblowing and Organizational Social Responsibility* with Ashgate as well as chapters and articles in books and journals on whistleblowing, business ethics, philosophy of management, socially responsible investment and global ethics.

Stella Vettori is Professor at the University of South Africa (UNISA). She specialises in labour law and social security law. She completed her doctoral thesis entitled 'Alternative means to protect legitimate employee interests in the changing world of work' in 2005. She has more than fifteen years practical experience in labour law. She advises numerous companies on labour law issues such as retrenchments and dismissals, affirmative action policies and various codes of conduct. She acts as mediator in labour disputes. She has published extensively both locally and abroad. She has also presented at numerous international conferences. She recently published a book entitled *The Contract of Employment and the Changed of Work* (Ashgate). She is editor and co-author of an international book concerning the effects of ageing populations on the labour market and labour laws.

Antonio Vives is Principal Associate of Cumpetere, a CSR consulting group. Previously he was Manager of Sustainable Development at the Inter-American Development Bank. He is the author of numerous articles on private participation in infrastructure, financial markets development and CSR. Antonio has published several books and it is at work on one book on CSR in developing countries. He created the Inter-American Conferences on Corporate Social Responsibility and is Chair of the organising committee and editor of the six editions of the Proceedings. He has been Adjunct Professor at George Washington, Virginia Tech and Carnegie-Mellon Universities in the United States and was Professor at the Graduate School of Business, IESA, in Venezuela. He is currently consulting professor at Stanford University. He is a frequent lecturer in international conferences on CSR and holds a Masters degree in Industrial Administration (MBA) and a Ph.D in Corporate Finance from Carnegie Mellon University.

Sandra Waddock is Professor of Management at Boston College's Carroll School of Management and Senior Research Fellow at BC's Center for Corporate Citizenship. She holds the MBA and DBA degrees from Boston University and has published over 100 articles on corporate responsibility, corporate citizenship and inter-sector collaboration in journals. Author of *The Difference Makers*, *Leading Corporate Citizens*, and co-editor of *Unfolding Stakeholder Thinking* and *Learning to Talk*, among others, she is a founding faculty of the Leadership for Change Program, co-founder (with Stephen Lydenberg and Brad Googins) of the Institute for Responsible Investing, initiated Business Ethics' 100 Best Corporate Citizens ranking with co-author Samuel Graves and editor Marjorie Kelly, and edited the *Journal of Corporate Citizenship* from 2003–2004. She received the 2004 Sumner Marcus Award for Distinguished Service from the Social Issues in Management Division of the Academy of Management, and the 2005 Faculty Pioneer Award for External Impact by the Aspen Institute Business in Society Program and the World Resources Institute. She has been a visiting scholar at the Harvard Kennedy School of Government (2006–2007) and University of Virginia Darden Graduate School of Business (2000).

Rowan E. Wagner is currently a Senior Lecturer and Subject Area Leader of Management Studies in the Department of Business Administrative Studies at Westminster International University in Tashkent, Uzbekistan. In addition to this job he frequently works as a consultant for community capacity development, social marketing, behaviour change communication and health project/program development and implementation in Central and South Asia. Rowan has worked in the past as the Project HOPE TB Program Manager in Uzbekistan, the Central Asia Regional Health Delegate for the American Red Cross and the IFRC, and Technical Advisor for an Abt. Associates/AIHA/MOH Kazakhstan/Uzbekistan health system reform project in Kazakhstan and Uzbekistan which involved the development and implementation of family practice primary health centres. In his free time, Rowan enjoys spending time assisting his wife Dilnoza with her small but growing lifestyles' businesses (cosmetics/perfumes and catering) and playing games and watching cartoons with his rapidly growing daughter Yasmeen.

Hongxia Wang is an assistant professor of finance at Ashland University. Her teaching interests are corporate finance and personal finance. Her research areas include corporate finance, CEO turnover and succession and corporate control and governance.

Ian Worthington is Professor of Corporate Sustainability in the Leicester Business School, De Montfort University, Leicester, UK. His teaching and research interests centre around CSR and environmental issues in business and he has published in a variety of journals including *Long Range Planning*, the *Journal of Business Ethics*, *Public Administration*, *Environment and Planning 'C': Government and Policy and Sustainable Development*. He is co-author of several books on the external context of business and is currently writing a book on 'Greening Business' for Oxford University Press.

Wang Xiaoli is a Professor of Tongji University, School of Economics and Management, China and a Visiting Scholar of Humboldt-University zu Berlin, Germany. His research interests are in the area of enterprise culture and system theory.

Chendi Zhang is Assistant Professor of Finance at the University of Warwick. He obtained his Ph.D. from Tilburg University. His research interests include corporate finance, behavioural finance and ethical investments.

1 *Overview*

GÜLER ARAS AND DAVID CROWTHER

Introduction

National governance has been defined by the World Bank as the exercise of political authority and the use of institutional resources to manage society's problems and affairs. This is a view of governance which prevails in the present, with its assumption that governance is a top down process decided by those in power and passed to society at large. In actual fact the concept is originally democratic and consensual, being the process by which any group of people decide to manage their affairs and relate to each other. Such a consensual approach is, however, problematic for any but the smallest of groups and no nation has actually managed to institute governance as a consensual process. With the current trend for supra-national organisation[1] then this seems even more of a remote possibility; nor is it necessarily desirable. Thus a coercive top down form of governance enables a society to accept leadership and to make some difficult decisions which would not otherwise be made.[2] Equally, of course, it enables power to be usurped and used dictatorially – possibly beneficially[3] – but most probably in a way in which most members of that society do not wish.[4]

Governance is however an issue which has come to the fore recently as a direct cause of problems associated with the financial and economic crisis. This applies to governance in general but to corporate governance in particular. Corporate governance can be considered as an environment of trust, ethics, moral values and confidence – as a synergic effort of all the constituents of society – that is the stakeholders, including government; the general public and so on; professional/service providers – and the corporate sector. One of the consequences of a consideration of the actions of an organisation, and the consequences of those actions, has been an increasing awareness of corporate governance (Hermalin 2005). Corporate governance is therefore a current buzzword the world over. It has gained tremendous importance in recent years. Two of the main reasons for this upsurge in interest are the economic liberalisation and deregulation of industry and business and the demand for new corporate ethos and stricter compliance with the law of the land. One more factor that has been responsible for the sudden exposure of the corporate sector

---

1   Such as, for example, the European Community.

2   For example, the decision to abolish capital punishment in the UK in 1969 could not have been made consensually; nor too could the decision to invade Iraq in 2003.

3   The ancient Greeks favoured beneficial dictatorship as a means of running their city states.

4   Most people would disagree that, for example, power was usurped in the USSR by Stalin because of a centrally imposed governance; equally few would suggest that this power was used beneficially or in a way which most members of the society were happy about.

to a new paradigm for corporate governance that is in tune with the changing times in the demand for greater accountability of companies to their shareholders and customers (Bushman & Smith 2001). There is a considerable body of literature which considers the components of a good system of governance and a variety of frameworks exist or have been proposed. We must stress also that we have taken a broad view of the definition of corporate governance both in terms of the aspects of corporate behaviour with which it is involved and also regarding the types of organisation with which it is concerned. Thus the term corporate governance has become ubiquitous in considering the governance of every type of organisation – corporate or not – in order to distinguish this from societal or civic governance. It is this broader interest with organisational governance which is the focus of this book.

Good governance is essential for good corporate performance and one view of good corporate performance is that of stewardship and thus, just as the management of an organisation is concerned with the stewardship of the financial resources of the organisation so too would management of the organisation be concerned with the stewardship of environmental resources. The difference, however, is that environmental resources are mostly located externally to the organisation. Stewardship in this context, therefore, is concerned with the resources of society as well as the resources of the organisation. As far as stewardship of external environmental resources is concerned then the central tenet of such stewardship is that of ensuring sustainability. Sustainability is focused on the future and is concerned with ensuring that the choices of resource utilisation in the future are not constrained by decisions taken in the present (Aras & Crowther 2007a). This necessarily implies such concepts as generating and utilising renewable resources, minimising pollution and using new techniques of manufacture and distribution. It also implies the acceptance of any costs involved in the present as an investment for the future.

A great deal of concern has been expressed all over the world about the operation of systems of corporate governance in operation – and the attendant problems – and its organisation and operation has been a major concern of business managers, academics and government officials all over the world. Often companies' main target is to become global – while at the same time remaining sustainable – as a means to get competitive power. But the most important question is concerned with what will be a firms' route to becoming global and what will be necessary in order to get global competitive power. There is more then one answer to this question and there are a variety of routes for a company to achieve this. Corporate governance can be considered as an environment of trust, ethics, moral values and confidence – as a synergic effort of all the constituents of society – that is the stakeholders, including government; the general public and so on; professional/service providers – and the corporate sector.

Of equal concern is the question of corporate social responsibility – what this means and how it can be operationalised (Aras & Crowther 2007b). Although there is an accepted link between good corporate governance and corporate social responsibility the relationship between the two is not clearly defined and understood. Thus many firms consider that their governance is adequate because they comply with The Combined Code on Corporate Governance, which came into effect in 2003. Of course all firms reporting on the London Stock Exchange are required to comply with this code, and so these firms are doing no more than meeting their regulatory obligations. Many companies regard corporate governance as simply a part of investor relationships and do nothing more regarding such governance except to identify that it is important to investors/potential investors and to flag up that they have such governance policies. The more enlightened recognise that there is a clear link between governance and corporate social responsibility and make efforts to link the two. Often this is no more than making a claim that good governance is a part of their Corporate Social Responsibility CSR policy as well as a part of their relationship with shareholders.

Globalisation and Corporate Governance

Two features describe the modern world – globalisation and the free market. It is widely accepted – almost unquestioningly – that free markets will lead to greater economic growth and that we will all benefit from this economic growth. Around the world people – especially politicians and business leaders – are arguing that restrictions upon world economic activity caused by the regulation of markets are bad for our well-being. And in one country after another, for one market after another, governments are capitulating and relaxing their regulations to allow complete freedom of economic activity. So the world is rapidly becoming a global market place for global corporations, increasingly unfettered by regulation. We have seen the effects of the actions of some of these corporations within the United States itself – the champion of the free market. We have seen the collapse of the global accounting firm Anderson; we have seen the bankruptcy of major corporations such as Enron and World.com with thousands of people being thrown out of work and many people losing the savings for their old age which they have worked so long and hard to gain.

One way to describe why this has happened is to acknowledge that there are problems with accounting, with auditing, and with peoples' expectations. We must remember that the myth of the free market is grounded in classical liberal economic theory,[5] as propounded by people such as John Stuart Mill in the nineteenth century, which, briefly summarised, states that anything is OK as long as the consequences are acceptable. The regulatory regime of accounting has been increasingly changed over time to serve the interests of businesses rather than their owners or society. Thus no longer is it expected that the accounting of a business should be undertaken conservatively by recognising potential future liabilities while at the same time not recognising future profit. Instead profit can be brought forward into the accounts before it has been earned while liabilities (such as the replacement of an aging electricity distribution network) can be ignored if they reduce current profitability. A study of the changes made in accounting standards over the years shows a gradual relaxation of this requirement for conservatism in accounting as these standards have been changed to allow firms to show increased profits in the present. This of course makes the need for strong governance procedures even more paramount.

---

5   Furthermore, the whole of the economic system upon which capitalism functions is predicated in the Utilitarian philosophy developed from Liberalism by such people as John Stuart Mill and Jeremy Bentham.

Scandals, Failures, Problems

Every time society faces a new problem or threat then a new legislative process of some sort is introduced which tries to protect that society from a future reoccurrence (Romano 2004). The crisis which started in 2008 is resulting in much discussion of changes which are needed. Recently we have seen a wide range of problems with corporate behaviour, which has arguably led to prominence being given to corporate social responsibility (see, for example, Boele, Fabig & Wheeler 2001; Aras & Crowther 2007a). Part of this effect is to recognise the concerns of all stakeholders to an organisation, and this has been researched by many people (for example, Johnson & Greening 1999; Knox & Maklan 2004) with inconclusive findings. Accordingly, therefore, corporations, with their increased level of responsibility and accountability to their stakeholders, have felt that there is a need to develop a code for corporate governance so as to guide them towards appropriate stakeholder relations.

A great deal of concern has been expressed all over the world about shortcomings in the systems of corporate governance in operation: Britain, Australia, most other Anglo-Saxon and English-speaking countries, and many other countries, have a similar system of governance. Conversely, Germany is a good example of where the distance between ownership and control is much less than in the United States, while Japan's system of corporate governance is in some ways in-between Germany and the United States, and in other ways different from both (Shleifer & Vishny 1997). By contrast, in India, the corporate governance system in the public sector may be characterised as a transient system, with the key players (namely, politicians, bureaucrats and managers) taking a myopic view of the system of governance. Such international comparisons illustrate different approaches to the problem of corporate governance and the problem of ensuring that managers act in their shareholders' interest. Recently of course much attention to this issue has been paid by institutional investors (Cox, Brammer & Millington 2004).

Good governance is, of course, important in every sphere of society whether it be the corporate environment or general society or the political environment. Good governance levels can, for example, improve public faith and confidence in the political environment. When the resources are too limited to meet the minimum expectations of the people, it is a good governance level that can help to promote the welfare of society. And, of course, a concern with governance is at least as prevalent in the corporate world (Durnev & Kim 2005).

The Relationship Between Governance, Social Responsibility and Business Success

Often the more significant the power that multinational corporations and some groups of stakeholders in a firm have, the more is spoken about corporate social responsibility. Thus a concept that was some kind of luxury some years ago, nowadays has reached the forefront of public opinion and discussion – often of a cynical nature – of CSR abounds in every public arena. Some steps taken in the corporation's development, in the environment and in the human values can be the guilty causes of this CSR fashion. If in the beginning firms were small and there was no distinction between ownership and management, the economic development made that there was a necessity to attract more capital to set up bigger enterprises. Thus, there were owners who gave the funds and there were experts in management, who managed the company and were paid by the owners. Agency Theory establishes this relationship between the principal (the shareholder or investor) and the agent (the manager) bearing in mind that the goals of the principal must be achieved through the management of the agents. But when considering what are the shareholders´ objectives then the obvious answer is that they are mainly to increase the enterprise value through the maximisation of profits.

The agency relation of course creates its own problems and, some would argue, has been the cause of some of the corporate scandals referred to. This is a matter which is addressed in this book. At this point however we would like to emphasis that – just as we have taken a broad definition of corporate governance to really encompass organisational governance – we have taken a broad definition of corporate social responsibility to encompass the social responsibility of all organisations. It is unfortunate that the word corporate has become attached to the concepts of governance and of social responsibility as in some ways it provides a misleading picture of the issues. Nevertheless the terms, including the word corporate, have entered common parlance and therefore have been used in this book.

Corporate governance is fundamental to the continuing operating of any corporation; hence much attention has been paid to the procedures of such governance. A significant part of the reason for this is due to the developments brought about through globalisation. The phenomenon known as globalisation is a multidimensional process involving economic, politic, social and cultural change. However the most important discussion about globalisation is related to the economic effect it has upon countries and the corporations operating within and across these countries. There has been much written about globalisation – either positive or negative – and the effects which it is having. One consequence of globalisation though is manifesting itself in the structure and organisation of corporations. This is concerned with the harmonisation procedures and structures which will manifest itself through the emergence of global norms for corporate governance. We will see through the preceding chapters a variety of issues concerned with corporate governance. Equally we have seen examples of the central message of this book concerning the overwhelming importance of cultural issues in the operation of whatever systems of governance are introduced. Nevertheless some form of commonality and harmonisation continues to be a subject of debate. This chapter takes this debate and the arguments from the chapters in this book in order to consider what the future might hold for corporate governance procedures and mechanisms.

The relationship between good governance and business performance is, however, clearer. As shown in various chapters of this book, investors are increasingly willing to pay a premium for good governance in a business because of the expected improvements in sustainable performance which will, over time, be reflected in future dividend streams. And the relationship between social responsibility and governance is similarly clear and described by us previously (see Aras & Crowther 2007b, 2008a). In an attempt to satisfy the necessities of the stakeholders other conflicts can appear between the interests of the different groups included in the wider concept of stakeholders. Sometimes, because of this conflict of interests and its own specific features, the company tries to establish different levels between the stakeholders, paying more attention to those ones that are most powerful, but are there some goals more socially responsible than others? In the end the hierarchy will depend on the other goals of the company, it will give an answer to those stakeholders that can threaten the performance of the economic goals.

The difficulties in measuring the social performance of a company are also due to the ownership concept. This is because the concept of corporate social responsibility is really comprehensive. There are companies whose activities are really different but all of them have to bear in mind their social responsibility, and this applies not only to companies, but also to people in whatever activity they do. From a politician to a teacher: ethics, code of conducts, human values, kindness to the environment, respect to the minorities (which should not be understood as a dictatorship of the minorities) and so on, are values that have to be borne in mind and included in the social responsibility concept. A good example of this diversity can be seen in this book where experts discuss a variety of different topics such as 'building and construction' and 'auditing', although each has got a deep relationship with the others. The same can be said about the regions; besides the classification according to topics in the directory, another classification of CSR in accordance with regions has been included. The point of view of the concept can vary depending on the country or the region, because some important problems linked to basic human values are more evident in some countries than in others. These social problems cannot be isolated because they have an important relationship with the degree of development of the country, so in the end it is the economy that pushes the world. Capitalism allows the differences between people, but what is not so fair is that these differences are not only due to your effort or work but are also due to having taken advantage of someone else's effort. And this can be the case with multinational corporations, which sometimes abuse their power, closing factories in developed countries and moving them to developing countries because the wages are lower, or, for example, because the security and health conditions are not so strict and so are cheaper to maintain for the company. Then the same companies obtain large profits to expense them in philanthropic ways.

Development conditions of regions can determine the relationship between governance and business success, as we have highlighted elsewhere,[6] if it is allowed, in some developing countries, to damage the environment or there are no appropriate labour unions and so on. Because of a lack of requirement of government attention, the global players use these facilities to obtain a better economic performance although they can be aware of their damaging policies. But it is not only the development degree that affects governance social responsibility, countries or regions are also deeply associated with human values through education and culture. The values are so deep inside us that it is said that people from different regions of the world who have shared the same education, for example, ethics courses at the university, do not share the same human values, because they are marked by their origins. Perhaps it should be understood that the inclusion of an ethics course as part of a university degree is useless because, ultimately, people will go on thinking what they thought at the beginning, depending on the values of their origin culture. But not everything is so simple, because there has been evidence of situations where different values have been imported from one culture to another and accepted as their own values without any problem. So, it shows that the questions related to CSR are complicated and not as simple as they can seem at a first glance.

---

6   See particularly Aras & Crowther 2008b, 2009.

This complexity can be argued as a disadvantage to take into account when speaking about the creation of global standards of socially responsible behaviour for companies: there are so many different cases that to establish a general regulation may be very difficult. But at the same time, this diversity can be argued to require this regulation because there have been different initiatives, most of them private, and they have added diversity to the previous one and the subject requires a common effort to try to tackle the problem of its standards and principles. The latest financial scandals have proved that it is not enough for companies to have their own codes or human values, but that it is necessary to reach an agreement to establish a homogeneous regulation, at least at the level of global players and multinational corporations.

The Gaia Hypothesis

While the discourse of accounting was developing the notion of greater accountability to stakeholders during the 1970s, other developments were also taking place in parallel. Thus, in 1979, Lovelock produced his Gaia Hypothesis (Lovelock 1979, 2000) in which he posited a different model of the planet Earth; in his model the whole of the ecosphere, and all living matter therein, was co-dependant upon its various facets and formed a complete system. According to this hypothesis, this complete system, and all components of the system, was interdependent and equally necessary for maintaining the Earth as a planet capable of sustaining life. This Gaia Hypothesis was a radical departure from classical liberal theory which maintained that each entity was independent and could therefore concentrate upon seeking satisfaction for its own wants, without regard to other entities. This classical liberal view of the world forms the basis of economic organisation, provides a justification for the existence of firms as organs of economic activity and provides the rationale behind the model of accounting adopted by society. The Gaia Hypothesis, however, implied that interdependence, and a consequent recognition of the effect of ones actions upon others, was a facet of life. This consequently necessitates a different interpretation of accountability in terms of individual and organisational behaviour and reporting.

Given the constitution of economic activity into profit-seeking firms, each acting in isolation and concerned solely with profit maximisation, justified according to classical liberalism, it is inevitable that accounting developed as organisation-centric, seeking merely to measure and report upon the activities of the firm insofar as they affected the firm. Any actions of the firm which had consequences external to the firm were held not to be the concern of the firm. Indeed enshrined within classical liberalism, alongside the sanctity of the individual to pursue their own course of action, was the notion that the operation of the free market mechanism would mediate between these individuals to allow for an equilibrium based upon the interaction of these freely acting individuals, and that this equilibrium was an inevitable consequence of this interaction.[7] As a consequence, any concern by the firm of the effect of its actions upon externalities was irrelevant and not, therefore, a proper concern for its accounting.

---

7   This assumption of course ignores the imbalances in power between the various parties seeking to enact transaction through the market.

The Gaia Hypothesis stated that organisms were interdependent[8] and that it was necessary to recognise that the actions of one organism affected other organisms and hence, inevitably, affected itself in ways which were not necessarily directly related. Thus the actions of an organism upon its environment, and upon externalities, were a matter of consequence for every organism. This is true for humans as much as for any other living matter upon the planet. It is possible to extend this analogy to a consideration of the organisation of economic activity taking place in modern society and to consider the implications both for the organisation of that activity and the accounting for that activity. As far as profit-seeking organisations are concerned, therefore, the logical conclusion from this is that the effect of the organisation's activities upon externalities is a matter of concern to the organisation, and hence a proper subject for accounting in terms of organisational activity.

While it is not realistic to claim that the development of the Gaia Theory had a significant impact upon organisational behaviour, it seems perhaps overly coincidental to suggest that a social concern among business managers developed at the same time that this theory was propounded. It is perhaps that both are symptomatic of other factors which caused a re-examination of the structures and organisation of society. Nevertheless organisational theory has, from the 1970s, become more concerned with all the stakeholders of an organisation, whether or not such stakeholders have any legal status with respect to that organisation. At the same time, within the discourse and practice of accounting there has been a growth in concern with accounting for externalities and for the effects of the actions of the firm upon those externalities. One externality of particular concern is that of the environment; in this context the environment has been defined to include the complete ecosphere, rather than merely the human part of that ecosphere. These concepts form part of the foundations of a concern with environmental accounting.

International Standards

Governance is concerned with both the rights of shareholders and, increasingly, the rights of other stakeholders. This extended concern has been paralleled in the developments of regulations concerning financial reporting. At the start of the twentieth century it was generally accepted that accounting served the purpose of facilitating the agency relationship between managers and owners of a business through its reporting function, but that the general public had no right to such information (Murphy 1979). Thus as far as the UK is concerned, but paralleled in many other countries throughout the world (Crowther 2000), the Companies Act 1906 stated that there was no requirement for companies to produce financial statements, although the Companies (Consolidations) Act 1908 amended this to require the production of a profit and loss account and balance sheet. This was further amended by the Companies Act 1929 which required the production of these, together with a directors' report and an auditors' report for the AGM. Subsequent legislation has extended the reporting requirements of companies to the format seen today.

---

8   In actual fact Lovelock claimed in his hypothesis that the earth and all its constituent parts were interdependent. It is merely an extension of this hypothesis to claim the interrelationship of human activity whether enacted through organisations or not.

Thus there was at this time a general acceptance that corporate reporting should be provided for the knowledgeable professional rather than the individual investor or potential investor, who was assumed to be financially naive (Mauntz & Sharif 1961), and in order to satisfy the needs of these professionals corporate reports became more extensive in content with greater disclosure of financial and other information. This pressure for greater disclosure was not however new, and Mitchell (1906) argued that the accounts produced did not give an adequate basis for shareholder judgement. All that has changed is the perception of who the reporting should be aimed at with a widening of the perceived intended audience from managers and shareholders to include other professionals. There was at this time little questioning of the assumed knowledge that the financial information is the most important part of the corporate report. The importance of the financial information contained in the reports has changed however and Lee & Tweedie (1977) claimed that the most important financial information contained in the report was the detail concerning profits, earnings and dividends. They equally claimed that the economic prospects of the firm are the most important information contained in the report (Lee & Tweedie 1975) but were dismissive of the private shareholder in recording that the majority read the chairman's report but nothing else (Lee & Tweedie 1977).

This focus upon the development of the financial reporting aspects of corporate reporting of course ignores the development of the semiotic of such reporting and the changing nature of this semiotic. This lack of recognition is despite the acceptance that such reporting had changed over time to become more forward looking, to include more non-financial information including the chairman's report, and to become used by a wider range of people. It has been argued (Crowther 2002; Crowther, Carter & Cooper 2006) that this semiotic of corporate reporting is the most important use of such reporting and the prime vehicle for developing an understanding of such reporting and the changed nature of the reporting itself. Indeed the function of the semiotic is to aid social construction of corporate activity in a way which is mediated through the semiotic (Vygotsky & Luria 1994) in such a way that the interpretation of the reader is controlled from without by the creators of the semiotic. It is further argued that the lack of recognition of the semiotic of corporate reporting has also led to a lack of exploration of the dialectics inherent in such reporting.

The most recent stage in the development of reporting is epitomised by the most dramatic changes in corporate reporting. No longer is the firm seeking to communicate internally – to members or potential members – but rather the focus is upon the external environment. Indeed, no longer do results matter, although still contained in the report but relegated to semi-obscurity, and it is only prospects that matter. Thus the report now becomes predominantly forward looking and, perhaps more significantly, the forward orientation is not upon the economic prospects of the firm but upon the prospects for the shareholder community in terms of rewards – both dividends and share price increases. Additionally the report now acknowledges the rest of the stakeholder community and seeks to demonstrate corporate citizenship by commenting upon relationship with, and benefits accruing to, employees, society, customers and the local community. Indeed the report has tended to become not a communication medium but rather a mechanism for self-promotion. Thus the actual results of the firm's past performance no longer matter but rather the image of the firm is what matters and the production of the report is the event itself, rather then merely a communication mechanism. And of course the availability of this reporting has increased dramatically as all companies[9] now publish their reports on the Internet as well as on paper, thereby making them potentially accessible to everyone.

Structure of This Book

The big corporate scandals of a decade ago have been superseded by the much greater problems associated with the financial crisis of 2008 onwards. This in turn has meant that corporate governance has become central to most companies. After the recent big corporate scandals corporate governance has become central to most companies. It is understandable that investors' protection has become a much more important issue for all financial markets after the tremendous firm failures and scandals. Investors are demanding that companies implement rigorous corporate governance principles in order to achieve better returns on their investment and to reduce agency costs. Most of the time, investors are ready to pay more for companies to have good governance standards. Similarly a company's corporate governance report is one of the main tools for investor decisions. Because of these reasons, companies cannot ignore the pressure for good governance from shareholders, potential investors and other markets actors.

On the other hand, banking credit risk measurement regulations are requiring new rules for a company's credit evaluations. New international bank capital adequacy assessment methods (Basel II) necessitate that credit evaluation rules are elaborately concerned with operational risk which covers corporate governance principles. In this respect corporate governance will be one of the most important indicators for measuring risk. Another issue is related to firm credibility and riskiness. If the firm needs a high-rating score then it will have to pay attention to corporate governance rules also. Credit-rating agencies analyse corporate governance practices along with other corporate indicators. Even though corporate governance principles have always been important for getting good rating scores for large and publicly-held companies, they are also becoming much more important for investors, potential investors, creditors and governments. Because of all of these factors, corporate governance receives high priority on the agenda of policymakers, financial institutions, investors, companies and academics. This is one of the main indicators that the link between corporate governance and actual performance is still open for discussion. In the literature a number of studies have investigated the relation between corporate governance mechanisms and performance. Most of the studies have shown mixed results without a clear-cut relationship. Based on these results, we can say that corporate governance matters to a company's performance, market value and credibility, and therefore that every company has to apply corporate governance principles. But the most important point is that corporate governance is the only means for companies to achieve corporate goals and strategies. Therefore companies have to improve their strategy and effective route to implementation of governance principles. So, companies have to investigate what their corporate governance policy and practice needs to be.

---

9   It is accepted that not all companies throughout the world do this yet, but the number of companies which do not report via the Internet is shrinking rapidly. Moreover, it is a requirement in an increasing number of countries.

Management can be interpreted as managing a firm for the purpose of creating and maintaining value for shareholders. Corporate governance procedures determine every aspect of the role for management of the firm and try to keep in balance and to develop control mechanisms in order to increase both shareholder value and the satisfaction of other stakeholders. In other words, corporate governance is concerned with creating a balance between the economic and social goals of a company including such aspects as the efficient use of resources, accountability in the use of its power and the behaviour of the corporation in its social environment. The definition and measurement of good corporate governance is still subject to debate. However, good corporate governance will address such points as creating sustainable value, achieving the firm's goals and keeping a balance between economic and social benefit. Also, of course, good governance offers some long-term benefits for a firm, such as reducing risk and attracting new investors, shareholders and more equity.

Although there is an accepted link between good corporate governance and corporate social responsibility the relationship between the two is not clearly defined and understood. Thus many firms consider that their governance is adequate because they comply with The Combined Code on Corporate Governance, which came into effect in 2003. Of course all firms reporting on the London Stock Exchange are required to comply with this code, and so these firms are doing no more than meeting their regulatory obligations. Many companies regard corporate governance as simply a part of investor relationships and do nothing more regarding such governance except to identify that it is important to investors/potential investors and to flag up that they have such governance policies. The more enlightened recognise that there is a clear link between governance and corporate social responsibility and make efforts to link the two. Often this is no more than making a claim that good governance is a part of their CSR policy as well as a part of their relationship with shareholders.

The purpose of this handbook is to provide a series of chapters concerning the practice of governance and of social responsibility, which have been written by experts from all over the world. In doing so it is our intention to highlight examples of practice, both good and bad, and to show international and cultural similarities and differences while at the same time intending to further the debate regarding the relationship between good governance and social responsibility. In doing this we recognise the different traditions alluded to earlier, although we also recognise the international interest in this topic. Furthermore we recognise that different groups have different perspectives on the subject and that practitioner experience and academic theorising do not always coincide. We have tried to take all of these into account in the development of this handbook as a truly international compendium with contributions from leading academics and leading practitioners. We have therefore structured the book into a logical sequence and represented here the latest in research together with case studies and practical applications in order to make the book accessible to researchers and practitioners. We have organised the book into five parts, each covering a different aspect of this topic:

- Part 1 – Theoretical Overview
  In this section we deal with a range of issues of general significance and look at some of the broader theoretical perspectives which underpin the governance and social responsibility concepts.

- Part 2 – Applying Corporate Governance
  A number of particular governance issues relating to organisations are dealt with in this section, as well as a review of the state of understanding of this area.
- Part 3 – Applying Corporate Social Responsibility
  There are an equally diverse range of issues concerned with social responsibility and in this part we focus upon a range of these issues.
- Part 4 – Dealing with Stakeholders
  One of the most important aspects of both governance and social responsibility is concerned with the relationship between the organisation and a range of its stakeholders. This part, therefore, is devoted to a consideration of aspects of this relationship.
- Part 5 – Experience in Practice
  It is always helpful to consider practical applications of issues and this final section is devoted to just that. A variety of contexts are used to consider some of the issues discussed in the previous sections, but in terms of actual organisations.

In this book we do not claim to provide all of the answers. We do not even claim to have dealt with all of the issues connected to governance and social responsibility – corporate or organisation. To deal with all of the issues would require a book at least twice as long, while to provide the answers would require a lifetime's work. We do believe however that we have provided, through the experts involved in contributing to this book, a number of theoretical and practical insights into important issues which will both be of assistance to practitioners and have theoretical benefit to researchers. If any issues are of particular interest and you wish to pursue further, then either contact the publisher or make contact with the Social Responsibility Research Network (www.socialresponsibility.biz).

References

Aras G & Crowther D (2007a); Is the global economy sustainable?; in S Barber (ed), *The Geopolitics of the City*; London; Forum Press, 165-194.

Aras G & Crowther D (2007b); The Development of Corporate Social Responsibility; *Effective Executive*; Vol X No 9, September, 18-21.

Aras G & Crowther D (2008a); Corporate Sustainability Reporting: A Study in Disingenuity?; *Journal of Business Ethics*, 87 (supp 1) 279-288.

Aras G & Crowther D (eds) (2008b); *Culture and Corporate Governance*; Leicester; Social Responsibility Research Network.

Aras G & Crowther D (eds) (2009); Global Perspectives on Corporate Governance and Social Responsibility; Aldershot; Gower (forthcoming).

Boele R, Fabig H & Wheeler D (2001); Shell, Nigeria and the Ogoni. A Study in Unsustainable Development: II. Corporate Social Responsibility and 'Stakeholder Management' versus a Rights-based Approach to Sustainable Development; *Sustainable Development*, 9, 121-135.

Bushman R M & Smith A J (2001); Financial Accounting Information and Corporate Governance; *Journal of Accounting and Economics*, 32, 237-333.

Cox P, Brammer S & Millington A (2004); An Empirical Examination of Institutional Investor Preferences for Corporate Social Performance; *Journal of Business Ethics*, 52, 27-43.

Crowther D (2000); Corporate Reporting, Stakeholders and the Internet: Mapping the New Corporate Landscape; *Urban Studies*, 37 (10), 1837-1848.

Crowther D (2002); *A Semiology of Corporate Reporting*; Escola Superior de Tecnologia e Gestao da Guarda Working Paper no 04/02; Guarda, Portugal.

Crowther D, Carter C & Cooper S (2006); The Poetics of Corporate Reporting; *Critical Perspectives on Accounting*, 17 (2) 175-201.

Durnev A & Kim E H (2005); To Steal or not to Steal: Firm Attributes, Legal Environment, and Valuation; *Journal of Finance*, LX (3), 1461-1493.

Hermalin B E (2005); Trends in Corporate Governance; *Journal of Finance*, LX (5), 2351-2384.

Johnson R A & Greening D W (1999); The Effects of Corporate Governance and Institutional Ownership Types on Corporate Social Performance; *Academy of Management Journal* 42 (5), 564-576.

Knox S & Maklan S (2004); Corporate Social Responsibility: Moving Beyond Investment Towards Measuring Outcomes; *European Management Journal*, 22 (5), 508-516.

Lee T A & Tweedie D P (1975); Accounting Information: An Investigation of Private Shareholder Understanding; *Accounting & Business Research*, Autumn 1975, 280-291.

Lee T A & Tweedie D P (1977); *The Private Shareholder and the Corporate Report*; London; ICAEW.

Lovelock J (1979); *Gaia*; Oxford; Oxford University Press.

Lovelock J (2000); *Homage to Gaia*; Oxford; Oxford University Press.

Mauntz R H & Sharif H A (1961); *The Philosophy of Auditing*; American Accounting Association.

Mitchell T W (1906); Review of Corporate Reports: The Report of the American Locomotive Company; *Journal of Accountancy*.

Murphy G J (1979); The evolution of corporate reporting practices in Canada; in E N Goffman (ed), *Academy of Accounting Historians Working Paper Series* Vol 1 pp 329-368.

Romano R (2004); The Sarbanes-Oxley Act and the Making of Quack Corporate Governance; *European Corporate Governance Institute Finance Working Paper* No 52/2004.

Shleifer A & Vishny R W (1997); A Survey of Corporate Governance; *Journal of Finance*, 52 (2), 737-783.

Vygotsky L & Luria A (1994); Tool and symbol in child development; in R Van Der Veer & J Valsimer (eds), *The Vygotsky Reader* pp 99-173; Oxford; Blackwell.

I *Theoretical Overview*

Thomas Hobbes is well known for discussing the concept of the social contract. In his work citizens would agree to vest absolute power in a sovereign power as the only way to avoid anarchy. In doing so, citizens give up their individual rights, including control of liberty and property, and possibly life. He argued that human self-interest is such that we would be willing to wage war on each other, the end result being a short and unpleasant life for all. This tradition accords with a utilitarian position: the pursuit of maximum welfare, and this can be considered to provide the basis for the capitalist system and its reliance upon the market and individual endeavour. This, therefore, provides the test for whether corporate behaviour is morally right or wrong. Utilitarianism regards corporate activity as morally good if it maximises human welfare, and collective welfare may override individual welfare.

The concept of Utilitarianism was developed as an extension of Liberalism in order to account for the need to regulate society in terms of each individual pursuing, independently, his or her own ends. It was developed by people such as Bentham and John Stuart Mill who defined the optimal position for society as being the greatest good of the greatest number. They argued that it was government's role to mediate between individuals to ensure this societal end. In Utilitarianism it is not actions which are deemed to be good or bad but merely outcomes. Thus any means of securing a desired outcome was deemed to be acceptable and if the same outcomes ensued then there was no difference, in value terms, between different means of securing those outcomes. Thus actions are value neutral and only outcomes matter. This is, of course, problematical where the actions of firms are concerned because firms only consider outcomes from the point of view of the firm itself. Indeed accounting, as we know, only captures the actions of a firm insofar as they affect the firm itself and ignores other consequences of the actions of a firm. Under Utilitarianism, however, if the outcomes for the firm were considered to be desirable, then any means of achieving these outcomes was considered acceptable. In the nineteenth and early twentieth centuries this was the way in which firms were managed[1] and it is only in more recent times that it has become accepted that all the outcomes from the actions of the firm are important and need to be taken into account. The development of Utilitarianism led to the development of Economic Theory as a means of explaining the actions of firms. Indeed the concept of Perfect Competition is predicated in the assumptions of Classical Liberal Theory – and the

---

1   It is arguably the way that the Russian plutarchs have usurped economic power in that country, and legitimated that usurption.

arguments for the unregulated Free Market are based upon the concept of such Perfect Competition.[2] From Economic Theory, of course, both Finance Theory and accounting developed as tools for analysis to aid the rational decision making assumed in Economic Theory.

During the era of individualism in the 1980s, however, a theoretical alternative was developed in the USA, which became known as Communitarianism, although the concept goes back to the earlier work of such people as Tonnies (1957) and Plant (1974). Communitarianism is based upon the argument that it is not the individual, or even the State, which should be the basis of our value system. Thus the social nature of life is emphasised alongside public goods and services. The argument is that all individuals, including corporations, have an obligation to contribute towards the public nature of life rather than pursuing their own self-interests. Underpinning the theories of Communitarianism is the assumption that ethical behaviour must proceed from an understanding of a community's traditions and cultural understanding. Exponents (see Crowther & Davila Gomez 2006) argue that the exclusive pursuit of private interest erodes the network of social environments on which we all depend, and is destructive to our shared experiment in democratic self-government. A Communitarian perspective recognises both individual human dignity and the social dimension of human existence and that the preservation of individual liberty depends on the active maintenance of the institutions of civil society where citizens learn respect for others as well as self-respect where we acquire a lively sense of our personal and civic responsibilities, along with an appreciation of our own rights and the rights of others.

The twenty-first century has seen an explosion of interest in the concept of corporate social responsibility as a means of conducting business. Corporate social responsibility is based upon the concepts of transparency and accountability and the adoption of these concepts into business practice has led to an increasing level of disclosure and a more firmly defined basis for the governance of organisations. Hence the concept of corporate governance has become as ubiquitous as the concept of corporate social responsibility within both business practice and academic investigation. Early work was concerned with critique of business practice but more recently the concern has been with finding a theoretical basis to underpin this current concern. The theories which have been adopted primarily consist of stakeholder theory, social contract theory and political economy theory. Other theories have also been used which provide valuable insights and understandings and in this first part we consider a variety of these theories.

In the first chapter, therefore, Riese makes use of Niklas Luhmann's theory of autopoietic social systems to explore the workings of corporate social responsibility. She argues that moral and rational motivations for corporate social responsibility are necessarily limited and they do not deliver a guideline for organizations as to what should actually be included in their Corporate Social Responsibility CSR strategies and programmes. She argues that the value of the systems-theoretic observation of CSR which she adopts lies in an improved understanding of the problems connected to it, and therefore that the importance of organizational observantness and reflexivity for sensible corporate social responsibility is emphasised.

---

2   This is despite the fact the that concept of Perfect Competition is an elementary assumption in foundation level economics which is recognised as never existing and is an assumption which is speedily relaxed in more advanced economics.

In the next chapter Bessire, Chatelin and Onnée consider the meaning of good corporate governance. They use Utilitarianism as their starting point but their consideration of the theoretical positions encompasses such diverse theories and concepts as stakeholder theory, Tonnies' view of communities and the idea of the firm as a nexus of treaties. The essence of their argument is that the assumption that people are utility-maximising individuals is fundamentally flawed and that we are actually free and responsible individuals who combine together for many purposes but who seek to ensure the common good in our endeavour – a quite different view to the norm.

Aras and Crowther are concerned with sustainability which they consider to be one of the most over-used words in business at the present time – such that the meanings attached to its use are so varied and vague as to render it effectively meaningless. They therefore start by identifying an appropriate meaning for the concept before considering how sustainability can be applied in business. In doing this they set the concept within the current debates about sustainability and sustainable development, before extending their analysis to develop their own definition of sustainability and its four aspects. This is further extended then to show that sustainability must be applied in a global environment to both the operational activities of a company and to the distributional decisions which are made.

Waddock considers the social contract between business and society, which she contends has always existed but has evolved in terms of the meaning and understanding attached to it. She sees considerable change (development?) during the twentieth century and the beginning of the twenty-first century. Waddock considers that the changes have largely been reactive to the forces affecting business practice such as regulation/deregulation and globalization, and that firms have adapted their understanding of their social contract to compensate for the changed environment. In this chapter she traces the history of this evolution, which is valuable in situating the current debates concerning Social Contract theory.

Kaidonis, Stoianoff and Andrew, in the next chapter, also take a historical perspective and also consider sustainability. They concur with Aras and Crowther concerning the ubiquity of the concept, tracing its importance back to the Brundtland Report which is credited with first referring to sustainability as having three of the necessary and coexisting components of environmental, economic and social sustainability. Essentially they argue that the sustainability concept has been commandeered by organisational accounting which has focused on the economic – in terms of market-adjusted returns – and which gives prominence and privilege to economic markets. In doing so they consider that the emphasis has shifted away from the environmental and social aspects of sustainability, to the detriment of future actions.

In the next chapter, Cooper focuses on accounting and its relationship to corporate social responsibility. From an argument that CSR goes beyond economic and legal responsibilities to shareholders and incorporates ethical and voluntary considerations to a broader set of stakeholders, he considers how accounting systems can, and have, been used to measure, analyse and communicate information of a broader nature than has been traditionally the case. He considers also developments in CSR reporting practice that now augment more traditional financial reporting before concluding by discussing the possible future of CSR and accounting.

In the final chapter in this part Vives relates theory and practice to an important but often neglected part of the global business arena – namely that of small and medium-sized enterprises (SMEs). In this chapter Vives presents the case for fostering responsible practices in SMEs by describing the characteristics that make these enterprises good candidates, offering suggestion on those practices, suggesting measures to enhance their adoption and presenting the results of several surveys in developed and developing countries to illustrate the extent of those practices and the need for supporting actions. He argues that this is desirable, not only for the contribution that they make to the betterment of society and the environment, but also because such practices can better economic produce performance for the firm itself.

References

Crowther D & Davila Gomez A M (2006); I will if you will: risk, feelings and emotion in the workplace; in D Crowther & K T Caliyurt (eds), *Globalisation and Social Responsibility*; Cambridge; Cambridge Scholars Press, pp 166-184.

Plant R (1974); *Community and Ideology;* London; Routledge & Kegan Paul.

Tonnies F (1957); *Community and Society*; Trans. Loomis C P; Harper & Row; New York.

2 A Luhmannian in the Playground: Corporate Social Responsibility from a Systems-Theoretic Perspective

JULIANE RIESE

Introduction[1]

This chapter of the Handbook reviews ethical and rational arguments for practising Corporate Social Responsibility (CSR) in the context of Niklas Luhmann's theory of autopoietic social systems. While this theory is notorious for its degree of abstraction, the attempt here is to make some intuitive and pragmatic inroads into it so that practitioners may also profit.

According to Luhmannian theory, ethics and morals cannot have an integrating function in modern, functionally differentiated society. Organizational rationality, on the other hand, is always limited, because no organization possesses requisite variety to exert comprehensive control over its environment. From the point of view of Luhmannian theory, this means that the power of both moral and rational motivations for practising CSR is necessarily limited. Moreover, they do not deliver a guideline for organizations as to what should actually be included in their CSR strategies and programmes.

Yet CSR must work, because, according to Luhmann, we cannot rely on the political or any other functional system to solve modern society's pressing problems. The value of a systems-theoretic observation of CSR lies in improved understanding of the problems connected to it. As a derived lesson, the importance of organizational observantness and reflexivity for sensible CSR is emphasized.

Scholars of the theory of autopoietic systems as founded by Niklas Luhmann are something like the Martians in the playground of organizations and organization studies. Not that managers and scholars exactly *dislike* them. But their theoretical world seems to be a universe which is separate from, and maybe not really aware of, the rest of the stuff that is going on.

---

1   I would like to thank the editors, Tore Bakken and Oliver Dehne for their valuable help in developing this piece.

Niklas Luhmann (1927–1998) was a sociology professor in Bielefeld in Germany and conceptualized a 'supertheory' (general theory) of modern society, using concepts from philosophy, biology, and other disciplines and treating a wide range of problems (Hernes & Bakken, 2003). Seidl & Becker (2005:10) say that when starting to read Luhmann it takes a hundred or two hundred pages before one understands anything. (Much of the original Luhmann literature is still only available in German, which doesn't help.) And when it comes to practical questions, it seems to be pretty hard for scholars to actually *apply* Luhmann's theory to anything happening in the real world. (Notable exceptions, all published during the last few years, are: Weinbach, 2004; Vogd, 2005; Czarniawska, 2005; Nollmann, 2007.)

But let us, just for the fun of it, imagine a coincidental and unexpected meeting between the average manager, who, for whatever reason, went to look for some ideas on CSR, and the average Luhmannian. What might the Luhmannian say? I suspect it might be something like the following:

1. *I'm really sceptical of the ethical argument for CSR.* Our functional systems, like the economic, juridical or political system, process information according to their own codes, and these codes have nothing to do with morals. In fact, morals are *equidistant* from all the functional systems. The economic system is interested in the binary code 'payment/non-payment' – but 'good/ bad'? That's none of their business.

2. *I'm not so sure organizations will take CSR measures for rational reasons, either.* Sure, it's rational for organizations to reflect on how the consequences of what they do to their environment affect themselves in return, just in order to stay alive themselves. But frankly, I don't believe that organizations are that rational most of the time. And apart from that, I think it's perfectly possible to act rationally in the said sense without taking any CSR measures whatsoever.

3. *Speaking of consequences – it is my belief that organizations miss most of the stuff that is going on around them.* I see organizations as self-reproducing, closed systems of communication, which are highly receptive for some specified impulses and unreceptive for others. So – CSR as insurance against future criticism from some as-yet-unnamed NGO is unlikely to work also.

4. *I'm really worried about the state we're in though.* I mean, look at all those social and environmental problems our functional systems produce. There's just no central authority in modern society any more to tell them to stop it. Nobody seems to be *managing* it all, you know?

5. *As a matter of fact, I believe organizations are the only social systems in modern societies that can be addressed as collective actors.* Societal functions must be parcelized and assigned to specific organizations. There's just no one else who can do the job, you know? It's probably a good idea if you get going with your CSR. What was that? Tell you what exactly you should be doing for CSR? Tough question, really… I'd suggest that you try to enhance your organization's responsivity and reflexivity…

The remainder of this chapter may be read as a translation of the words of the Luhmannian for the manager.

Niklas Luhmann was very much aware of the fact that modern society faces enormous and complex social and environmental problems. He did discuss the fact that these problems may even become life-threatening for society as such (Luhmann, 1990; Bakken,

2000:300). Luhmannians can thus be assumed to be very interested in possible solutions, including CSR. It's just that they, looking from their theoretical perspective, are sceptical about our chances of finding quick and powerful solutions.

As a working basis, let's adopt the following definition of CSR from the Green Paper of the European Commission:

> *Most definitions of corporate social responsibility describe it as a concept whereby companies integrate social and environmental concerns in their business operations and in their interaction with their stakeholders on a voluntary basis. Being socially responsible means not only fulfilling legal expectations, but also going beyond compliance and investing 'more' into human capital, the environment and the relations with stakeholders.*

(Commission of the European Communities, 2001:6)

The Ethical Argument for Corporate Social Responsibility

We start with the idea that organizations may take CSR measures for ethical or moral reasons. With regard to this idea, it must be noted that Luhmann's theory is sceptical that morality can have an *integrating function* in modern society and its subsystems.

SOME BASICS

Functional differentiation is a term for what Luhmann sees as characteristic of modern society. There is no such thing anymore as a universal 'ethos' for the whole of society, an 'integrated' society. There is no, say, king or queen who could determine across-the-board what rules apply for doing business, for fashion, for punishment of crimes and so on.

Rather, we now see different functional systems, which each serve one particular function for society. They do this using function-specific, binary codes. Thus, the economic system uses the code 'Payment/Non-Payment'; the juridical system, the code 'Legal/Illegal'; the scientific system, the code 'True/Not True'; and so forth. And these codes are badly integrated among each other in the sense that what is positive in one system, say, 'True', need not necessarily be positive in another code, say, 'Legal', or, 'Economically Good' (Luhmann, 1990).

If we accept this description, a major problem of modern society becomes immediately and intuitively clear. The economic system can only observe payments or deficits of payments (think of it as profit or no profit, if that's easier for you). It will not pay attention to, for example, environmental destruction, if the destruction is not expressed in terms of money. This is just one example of the general problem that 'the functional systems do not see what they do not see'.

If a certain problem, or side effect, of modern society is not 'seen' in the functional systems (or only in parts), because it cannot be completely or sufficiently processed with the help of any of the codes, then society will have a problem processing, or internalizing, or integrating, or solving that problem or side effect (Luhmann, 1990). Organizations partake in many of the systems. To the extent that they are economic organizations, they have to operate according to the economic code. To the extent that they are legal organizations, they have to operate according to the juridical code. And so on. But the problems produced by our functional systems are often insufficiently integrated into the functional systems. One might therefore argue for a moral responsibility of individuals or organizations with regard to these problems.

MORALITY'S DISTANCE FROM THE FUNCTIONAL SYSTEMS

But morality, Luhmann says, cannot (re)integrate the functional systems. This is because the functional codes cannot be equivalent to the moral code, which is 'Regard/Disregard'. Imagine the consequences if the government in the political system was declared to be morally good and the opposition morally bad (or vice versa), or if all legal things were declared to be morally good and all illegal things morally bad (or vice versa). This would in all probability make the functional systems collapse. Morality is equidistant from all functional systems.

Instead, morality is a special kind of communication, which indicates regard or disregard for a *person* (or in our case, an organization). Morality is slightly pathological: It is activated in times of crisis, as an alarm function, at points where urgent societal problems can seemingly not be solved inside the functional systems. Moral communication seems to be present especially where practices sabotage the binary coding of functional systems, for example when corruption sabotages the coding legal/illegal.

But this does not lead to practical advice. The problems cannot be solved via morals and ethics; but again, have to be solved by the functional systems. Ethics (the description or reflection theory of morality) can question and alarm society, but society's problems must be solved by society. And so we are back at starting point (Luhmann, 1997:396ff; Luhmann, 1990; Luhmann, 1990a; Luhmann, 1993).

This leaves organizations in a position where a moral conviction that they should take social responsibility is possible. The adopted working definition tells us that being socially responsible means going beyond compliance. But over and above respecting the codes of the functional systems, what do morality or ethics tell you to do? Build kindergartens in Africa? Pay a certain amount of money for every unit of CO_2 you produce? In some cases, you might even argue that morals and ethics tell you to *ignore* the codes of the functional systems, because it is these that cause irresponsible behaviour in the first place! Where does this leave your organization?

Moral communication remains vague and is mostly limited to cases where socially *irresponsible* corporate behaviour resulting in big societal problems is blatantly obvious, such as treatment of workers in the textile industry in developing countries (see, for example, Zadek, 2004). Moral communication just isn't a very probable path to everyday CSR.

It is tempting to argue (using moral communication) that just like a king and queen in earlier times, the political system should now shoulder the responsibility of solving social problems. This would include legislating on how corporations have to be socially responsible. But according to Luhmann, this can't be the solution. The code of the political system is the holding or not-holding of positions of political power. Again, this is intuitively convincing: The political system operates with the help of the code 'Power/ No Power'. Something which did not operate under the rule of this code would not be recognized as a political event and connected inside the system in the first place.

If politicians are socially interested, and (or: because they) can gain power when emphasizing social issues, this increases the political system's ability for resonance towards social issues. But because of this precondition, the political system cannot be the centre of society when it comes to negative side effects and their internalization, either. It may well solve some problems by legislating on them and then CSR is not necessary with respect to these problems any more. But it may just as well not manage to react to certain problems (Luhmann, 1990; Luhmann, 1984:645).

IS LUHMANN A FRIEDMAN?

Note that the systems-theoretic scepticism of morally motivated CSR is not the same as saying that business organizations *should not* do CSR because 'the business of business is business'. This is an argumentation which rests on the neoclassical model of the firm, in which its primary if not sole purpose is to maximize wealth for its shareholders. Any CSR projects are therefore seen as instances of misappropriation (of shareholders' money) and misallocation (because firms are seen to advance social welfare most by doing what they are there for, which is making profit for shareholders). Milton Friedman is probably the most famous representative of this view. (For discussion of this argument against the ethical argument for CSR, see Margolis & Walsh, 2003 or Mintzberg, 1983.)

Bakken (2000:281) says that there is something 'cynical and Friedman-ish' about Luhmann's argumentation when he says that when operating in the economic system, one operates according to the economic code, not a moral one, and that morals are so removed from 'daily life', so to speak. This is a feeling many people will have when following Luhmann's argumentation. But it is important to note that Luhmann's systems theory does not argue that moral communication is *wrong*, or superfluous, or any of the sort, or that people *should not* take ethical stances. In fact, Luhmann says that moral inclusion and exclusion of individual *people* is still happening. To the extent that organizations are perceived as person-like actors (see Drepper, 2005, below), moral inclusion and exclusion of organizations is also happening in modern society. But this doesn't result in the moral integration of *society* (Luhmann, 1990a).

The Rational Argument for Corporate Social Responsibility

Can there be a rational argument for CSR? The CSR literature offers several possible rational arguments:

CSR might work as a (social) insurance against criticism, boycotts and so on. This is also discussed under the headings of 'retaining your license to operate' or 'avoiding interference by pressure groups'. (For discussion, see Porter & Kramer, 2006; Mintzberg, 1983.) Doing business the socially responsible way might actually increase profits. This is because reputable firms may find it easier to attract able employees and sell their products, and because the business community as a whole may benefit from a socially stable business environment (for discussion, see Porter & Kramer, 2006; Mintzberg, 1983; Waddock & Graves, 1997; McWilliams & Siegel, 2000; Hillman & Keim, 2001; Vogel, 2005). Doing business the socially responsible way may reduce costs, because responsible firms are seen as less risky investments and their cost of capital is lower (Mintzberg, 1983). These arguments can be presented in many ways and under different headings. The underlying argument in all cases is that you do not need an ethical argument to practise CSR, because CSR is good from an economic perspective and thus, a rational decision for a business organization.

This section will not deal with the question to what conclusion about these hypotheses the empirical evidence points. Rather, it will explain why systems theorists are sceptical about the whole notion of 'rational organizational behaviour' in the first place.

SOME BASICS

Autopoietic systems theory conceptualizes organizations as self-reproducing systems of *communication*. The elements of social systems are communications. The communication concept is a central and complex one in Luhmannian theory, but for the purposes of this chapter, suffice to say that communications are inherently social. They are *always* produced between people. The condition for the emergence of communication is that there are systems of consciousness which can communicate. In the case of the specific social system 'organization', communications take the form of *decisions*. These decisions are produced inside the organization system and connected to one another.

The term *autopoiesis* is used to describe the idea that the elements the system consists of are produced inside the same system, that is, the system reproduces *itself*. Such systems are *operationally closed* because the operations leading to the productions of new elements in the system are always dependent on earlier operations of the same system and cannot be carried out outside the system. Every decision in the organizational system thus forms a premise for its further decisions.

Luhmann refuses the idea that organizational decisions are taken by individual people. Decisions are produced by the organization. As communications, they are inherently social things. Communicational systems and systems of consciousness in Luhmann's theory are quite independent of each other (see, for example, Luhmann, 2006 or Baraldi et al., 1997).

This basic conceptualization is quite hard to grasp at first sight (so no wonder Luhmannians always get a parcel of the playground to themselves where they stick together). It breaks new ground compared to older theories of action or theories on the interplay of system and actors (macro- and micro-level) (Nollmann, 2007; Bakken & Hernes, 2003). What especially bewilders people about it is that the social system organization is conceptualized seemingly independently of the people inside it.

But the Luhmannian conceptualization is really quite intuitively convincing, if you think about it for a bit. Anyone who has ever worked inside an organization will know that organizational communication and what individual people think about it can be two very different things. There is the communication, the decisions, the projects and the planning, and there are the free thoughts inside systems of consciousness which can completely disagree with all of it. Sometimes this disagreement does not become part of communication at all. Sometimes the disagreement is voiced, but the dominant organizational communication wins.

Social systems and systems of consciousness do depend on each other for their existence. And it does matter what people think, because it will probably influence communication (Luhmann is also aware of the question of power, for example).

But if any one individual system of consciousness tries to exert direct control over organizational communication or even radically change it, there may be a few surprises. This is true even for the bosses. And we all know situations where nobody knows anymore where a particular decision came from, and situations where a past decision gives rise to a host of new decisions although nobody is very happy with the starting decision any more. Organizational communication does seem to have an *eigen*-momentum.

Operational closure of organizations is also quite plausible once you think about it. This is because organizational decisions cannot be produced anywhere but in the organization itself. Of course, decisions taken elsewhere can *influence* organizational communication. But it will always be clear to everybody that they are not organizational decisions. Organizational decision making can only happen on the basis of the organizational decision making which has been going on so far.

What happens, Luhmann says, is that the world around us is so enormously complex that there is no chance of one single organization referring to all of it. What an organization does, instead, is to reconstruct world complexity internally, but in a less complex way, which is known under the term complexity reduction.

The organization constructs an internal picture of the world around it, *according to the meaning of the organization*. And then the organization observes its environment according to that internal reconstruction. The organization as an operationally closed system is thus still *cognitively open*. But it observes according to its own structure (Luhmann, 1984, Ch.1; Baraldi et al., 1997; as a forerunner see March & Simon, 1976:153).

Apart from the technical terms, this is again something everybody knows. An oil-producing multinational corporation will observe a world of competition, petrol stations, stock prices or issues of political instability, but it will probably not be very interested in prices for children's clothing or who is going to be the next Booker prize winner. Greenpeace observe their environment as a world of big bad corporations and too-slow political processes. And so on.

The internal reconstruction of the environment depends on the meaning of the organizations: The oil company operates according to the meaning of a reliable fuel-provider in an unstable world, making money for their shareholders. Greenpeace operate according to the meaning of rubber boat-riding David against plump and evil Goliath. And what belongs inside an organization and what doesn't depends on the meaning of the organization as well: organizational boundaries are meaning boundaries (Luhmann, 1984, Ch.2).

Anybody who has ever worked in an organization will know that organizations do this. But it's also obvious there is a rub in it. The internal reconstructions of the organizational environment are under-complex. They depend on how the organization observes its world. That means they might be flawed, or *too* under-complex. The organization has its blind spots. A famous example for under-complexity, operational closure, and communication's *eigen*-momentum is Nike.

EXAMPLE: NIKE

Zadek (2004) describes how '[i]n the 1990s, the [Nike] company was blindsided [*sic!*] when activists launched an all-out campaign against it because of worker conditions in its supply chain'.

> *The company's first reaction was defensive. 'We said, "Wait a minute; we've got the best corporate values in the world, so why aren't you yelling at the other folks?"' one of Nike's senior managers recalls. […] [I]n 1996, Nike 'went professional' in creating its first department*

specifically responsible for managing its supply chain partners' compliance with labor standards. [...] By the turn of the millennium, Nike's labor-compliance team was more than 80 strong. The company had also hired costly external professionals... Even so, new revelations about Nike's failure to adhere to its own labor codes constantly came to light. [...] Those inside Nike's walls were incredibly frustrated by their failure to move past this ongoing crisis. After a particularly painful documentary on Nike aired in the United Kingdom, the CEO assembled a team of senior managers and outsiders led by Nike's vice president for corporate responsibility [...]. The team's review didn't focus on the behaviours of factory managers and workers, as many previous studies did; the group considered issues at the factory level symptoms of a larger systemic [sic!] problem. [...] After six months, it concluded that the root of the problem was not so much the quality of the company's programs to improve worker conditions as Nike's (and the industry's) approach to doing business.

(Zadek, 2004:128f.)

The approach to doing business – global outsourcing – was one where demands on price, quality and delivery times dominated the corporate responsibility efforts throughout the entire supply chain.

You can dismiss the defensive attitude and early solution strategies as hypocrisy and argue that what mattered for Nike was maximum profit. You can believe they just didn't want to admit in public that they didn't care about working conditions, and hoped that the protests would peter out. For a Luhmannian, however, the interesting bits of this judgment are the idea that they didn't pay attention to working conditions, and the question why that was.

From a Luhmannian perspective, it is plausible that the realization process inside the organization took this long. The organization constructed its environment in a similar way as other organizations in the same industry did. 'Labor activists ... targeted Nike because of its high-profile brand, not because its business practices were any worse than its competitors.' (Zadek, 2004:128). So the organization was surprised when something showed up that meant the construction had been insufficient.[2]

Note that a Luhmannian interpretation, based on Zadek's analysis published in the *Harvard Business Review*, is not, at its core, contradictory to the brilliant and highly critical analysis Naomi Klein delivers in her book *No Logo!* (2002). Klein's argument is that Nike became a 'product-free brand'. What was important was not the product as such, or where and how it was produced; it was the brand, the lifestyle, the marketing.

Klein would agree with Zadek that Nike was attacked because their brand was so enormously visible, not because their business practices were more visible or outrageous than that of others. (See also Oxfam Australia, 2006 on this.) No matter what your normative judgment on a Nike-style business model and corporate culture may be, it is quite imaginable that for a corporation thinking along these lines, the protests *were* surprising.

---

2   It is not surprising, but in my view not justified, that Niklas Luhmann by many was seen to be endorsing conservative, even right-wing views, affirming the status quo. See for example his interview with Kai-Uwe Hellmann in Luhmann (1997a).

The organization produced its own decisions (communications) and connected these to the decisions that had been going on so far. Organizational decisions can never be taken outside the system.

> *An external observer may not be satisfied with this, especially when he gets the impression that an organization has failed to do something.... [...] In this way the futility [...] of system-external expectations and appeals which do not find access to the internal network of decisions [...] becomes understandable.*

(Luhmann, 1992:168, my translation)

Activist groups can demand change as much as they like. If this does not fit with the meaning of the closed system, if it does not even make sense inside the organization, then it will not be translated into *organizational communication*. Nike operated according to a certain meaning ('We've got the best corporate values in the world', 'We produce according to industry logic: outsourcing', 'What is important is not the shoe as such') which meant that the pressure groups' demands were decidedly un-connectable inside the system.

Even when some of the appeals did register with Nike (and for profit-oriented companies, loss in profits will be a signal that is taken up inside the closed system), they were still processed internally *according to the meaning of the organization*. Thus, labour codes were imposed on suppliers but the basic supply chain logic remained intact. The existing organizational communication's *eigen*-momentum still dominated.

It is perfectly possible that individuals working for the organization realized where the problems lay. It is even possible that some Nike employees sympathized with the pressure groups. But organizations are not just the sum of the people working there, as Luhmann tirelessly points out. Organizational communication produces a meaning which can be quite independent of what employees think. It is the *organization as a communicational system* which needs to change if real change is going to happen. (On inertia of individual apparel companies and of the industry in general, again see Oxfam Australia, 2006.)

THE REQUISITE VARIETY PROBLEM

Vos (2005) criticizes well-known strategic management approaches for obscuring, or not taking into account the systems-theoretic insight that organizations are closed systems which construct their own world-view. He says that the paradigm underlying strategic thinking in general is adaptation to the environment. The environment is out there for all to see, and you should observe what is going on and take measures accordingly. (Vos' criticism is directed at outside-in as well as inside-out approaches.)

> *From a systems-theoretical point of view, this solution is conceptually based on 'The Law of Requisite Variety' or 'Ashby's Law' [...]. This law states that in order to be in control, a system needs at least as many control measures as there are external variations [...]. This 'requisite variety' ultimately implies that organizations need to establish a point-to-point correspondence to their environment [...]. However, since the environment is much more complex than any organization can be, such a point-to-point correspondence is impossible [...]. This leads to the crucial question: what are companies ultimately supposed to adapt to? It cannot be the*

environment as such because of its incomprehensibility, and it cannot be the organizational construction of the environment because then organizations would just adapt to themselves. [...] This paradoxical indecision is obscured by the 'Law of Requisite Variety'... because the observation of the environment is not regarded as being problematic.

(Vos, 2005:368f.)

The upshot is that *it becomes very hard to define what rational behaviour is for organizations at all*. Nike was a successful company. It acted as other companies in the industry did (only more successfully so, maybe). Was this *irrational*? Should Nike have seen the problems and acted on them even before the protests started?

You could even interpret it as 'bad luck' (for Nike) that it was just Nike that was singled out as the baddie by protest organizations. With hindsight, it is easy to claim that it was rational to take the protests very seriously, because failing to do so entailed major losses in profits. But could you have known that when the protests started?

Of course, limitations to rational behaviour are researched extensively, the most famous concept in the field probably being Simon's 'bounded rationality' (Simon, 1978). So it's not that the topic is exclusive to systems theory, it's just that systems theory is very fundamentalist in listing the problems with our ideas of rational behaviour. Complexity reduction according to the meaning of the organization constrains rationality and strategic decision making inside that organization. Organizations are highly receptive to specific impulses from the outside, but unreceptive to those which take a form they don't understand.

To the extent that organizations take part in the juridical system, they have to respect its code 'legal/illegal'. To the extent that they take part in the economic system, they have to operate according to the code 'payment/non-payment'. But this is not sufficient as guideline for rational behaviour (Luhmann, 2006:26ff).

This corresponds to what has been stated above: Today's problems seemingly can't be solved inside society's functional systems. If that was possible, of course it would suffice for organizations to simply respect the functional codes, and everybody would be happy. But the way things are, it is not very obvious, for a Luhmannian, what the guidelines for organizations – beyond respect for functional systems' codes – might be. The dilemma remains that organizations can't see everything, and can't know in advance what will become important, but they still have to choose what to concentrate on.

RATIONALITY RECONSIDERED

Rationality, in Luhmann's theory of social systems, is *reference to the difference between the system and its environment – considering the unity of that difference*. This definition, like other systems-theoretic concepts, might seem hard to swallow, but can be understood intuitively.

Remember that the social system produces its own meaning. (Both Nike and Greenpeace do this.) This meaning, inside the social system, always takes the form of 'that what the environment is not'. (Would it make sense for Greenpeace to reproduce their communications if there were no evil, environmentally destructive Goliaths around any more? Would the Nike culture continue to exist if Nike thought all competitors were just like Nike, or that there were enough shoes in the world already?) Remember also that how the social system perceives the environment depends on the system's structure. (We perceive ourselves as that what the environment is not, so the environment is what we are not.) Rationality means reflecting on this 'what they are not – what we are not' construction – bearing in mind that one side of it cannot exist without the other. The meaning difference is produced inside the system – and the system can reflect on this production (Luhmann, 1984: Ch.11).

This means that the social system looks at itself, but at the same time bears in mind that the idea it has of itself isn't necessarily the idea the environment has of it.

'Translated into the language of causality, this idea decrees that a system must control its effects on the environment by checking their repercussions upon itself if it wants to behave rationally. A system that controls its environment in the end controls itself.' (Luhmann, 1995:475).

If we take it that organizations want to continue to reproduce themselves, then it is rational to do what will secure your ability to self-reproduce also in the future. This means paying attention to the effects you have on your environment, because if they rebound upon you, this will impair your ability to self-reproduce. Another way of putting it is 'always try to act so as to increase the number of choices', a famous statement by cyberneticist Heinz von Foerster (Von Foerster, 1992; Bakken, 2000:388).

CSR is rational for organizations to practice if it secures their ability to make decisions also in the future. This may be so if, for example, CSR 'heads off' critical NGOs, or includes care for resources the organization will need in the future. The question is whether, from the point of view of Luhmann's theory, this is a strong argument for the belief that sensible CSR will be done at all.

Firstly, Luhmann is sceptical that the described kind of reflexivity and rationality will be found in organizations most of the time. This is because it makes it very hard for organizations to continue their day-to-day business. Imagine a person walking, while at the same time reflecting about each individual step (Luhmann, 2006:471). Organizations are mostly busy trying to find 'the next step' rather than reflecting on the repercussions of that step and all that, simply because without the next step they won't get into the future (Luhmann, 1990:38). (Fascination for 'business ethics', according to Luhmann, stems partly from the hope to escape the tricky reflection problem [Luhmann, 1993; Luhmann, 2006:471].)

Secondly, even if organizations are rational in the said sense, it is perfectly possible to imagine situations where you secure your ability to reproduce for the future without acting socially responsibly at all. You could secure access to resources you need by force, for example. (This is a point where we can see very well how Luhmann tried to be descriptive instead of normative.) It may be rational to 'insure' yourself against a possible attack by practising CSR. But it may also be rational to do something else to secure your autopoiesis and not hope for the doubtful success of heading off an as yet unspecified NGO/stakeholder criticism in the vague future.

If we use the above definition of rationality very broadly, we could of course say, that if the whole world is going to hell (climate change being the buzzword of the hour), it would be rational for organizations to reflect on this and act accordingly. But this, in a systems theoretical perspective on organizations, is too broad to promise success. Organizations cannot develop a point-to-point-correspondence with their environment. So they only refer to, or reflect on, some points of everything. And 'everything is going to hell' is definitely too many points for one organization to refer to (Cp. also Drepper, 2005).

So then, again, we would have to hope that the supra-systems do something (for example, tell organizations what to do). But we have seen above that that is problematic. Functional systems *can* realize that they themselves are threatened, but they might as well not.

Coporate Social Responsibility Must Work: Organizations As Actors

To sum up: ethical appeals, rational arguments pro CSR... all seem too simplistic to the Luhmannian, because of the Dazzling Complexity of All Things in General. This does not mean, however, that the Luhmannian takes the social and ecological 'side effects' of modern society lightly (just see Luhmann, 1990 and 1997a).

According to Drepper (2005), organizations are the only social systems in modern society that can be addressed in communication processes as collective actors. This is because:

> *Luhmann characterizes organizations as the only social systems that are structurally equipped for external communication, that is, for crossing their boundaries by communication. Neither the heterogeneous modern society as a unit nor interactions as simple systems have the capacity to communicate with their environments, so they cannot be addressed as collective actors.*

> (Drepper, 2005:182)

If there is no central authority in society, then of course our best hope lies with organizations, in a general sense. So surely, the Luhmannian would not be *against* CSR, as in the above working definition. Can organizations practise reasonable, sensible CSR? Can they do something about the problems of modern society?

Practical Lessons for Practising Corporate Social Responsibility

We have discussed the problematic side of the fact that organizations react to their environment according to their own structure and meaning. However, you can also look at it from a different perspective: 'The extent to which organizations are capable of transforming external stimuli into events for which they are designed to respond is almost too great to comprehend.' (Salancik, 1979:645). Much of what is going on in the world *can* be interpreted in the meaningful system organization, *according to the interpretation scheme of the organization*.

This capability of corporations, by the way, is also discussed by Klein in her book *No Logo!* Klein describes the depression civil society activists feel when they realize that corporations are able to incorporate so much of popular culture into their marketing machine, even the protests directed against them. Yet Klein suggests boldly: why not use this particular form of responsivity as a weapon against these corporations? From a more business-friendly perspective, we might ask: why not use the responsivity of your organization more consciously for the ends of CSR?

The second positive message is that, while reflection in the systems-theoretic sense (reference to the difference between the system and its environment, observing yourself in your environment) is deemed to be unlikely, or at least a special achievement, Luhmann does believe that social systems' reflective ability can be trained. Systems theoretic concepts are today successfully used in family therapeutic practice (Luhmann, 2006:472; Bakken, 2000:287; Simon, 2000 and 2000a). Vos puts it thus:

> *... Ashby's 'Law of Requisite Variety' should be reformulated as the 'Law of Requisite Reflexivity' [...]: in order to stay in control, an organization needs to be able to deal with its inabilities by means of self-observation. This law states that social systems should be able to develop new ways of observing their environment and themselves, depending on the situation at hand'.*

(Vos, 2005:371, emphasis in original)

The Luhmannian thus offers two pieces of advice to the CSR manager: (1) Train the responsivity – you can also call it observantness, or power of observation – of your organization. (2) Train the reflexivity of your organization. As I will show in this section, this advice derived from Luhmannian theory has much in common with the advice given by stakeholder theory (recall that the definition of CSR quoted in the introduction explicitly refers to stakeholder relations).

As for responsivity, the point of departure here is – quite in accordance with the EU Commission's definition of CSR – that compliance with the conditions of the functional systems of society is a minimum condition, rather than a maximizing imperative or even the only goal. Thus, an economic organization must be profitable to survive – but not necessarily more than that (Bakken, 2000:273f.; Wieland, 2007).

There is, of course, the question whether this is a practicable instruction for big listed corporations. (For a discussion from an organization theory perspective see, for example, Ortmann, 2004.) The radical point of view is that the structure of our economic system and the structure of the (major) players inside it preclude truly responsible behaviour (Mintzberg, 1983). A comprehensive discussion would exceed the limits of this piece. My only remark is that it may be wiser to use systemic latitude today than wait for revolution.

Over and above the minimum condition of observation of functional codes, it should be integrated into the *decision premises* of the organization that we face the problem of requisite variety, the fact that we live in a 'society of observers of systems' (Czarniawska, 2005:142). This humbles managers and organizations. The Luhmannian believes that is a good thing. It means that organizations must constantly strive for better awareness of their environment. They must *go look* for signals, impulses they have missed.

This, of course, is exactly what stakeholder dialogue is about: understanding 'stakeholder behaviours, values, and backgrounds/contexts including the societal context' (Freeman, 2004:231; see also Freeman et al., 2004). Systems theorists just make it very clear that nothing, not even the best stakeholder management, can produce a point-to-point correspondence with the environment. They adamantly repeat that we live in a society that is forced 'to resign from authority and to espouse ignorance' (Czarniawska, 2005:142). *All* constructions are under-complex.

Integrating such humbleness into the decision premises of the organization (and according to Luhmann, organizational culture is part of organizational decision premises [Luhmann, 2006:145]) also means that there can be no 'quick CSR fix', no fail-safe, simple, end-of-pipeline CSR programme. As Mintzberg (1983:13) points out, standard tick-off approaches to CSR can desensitize the issue, which *de*creases organizational responsivity: 'Socially responsible behaviour will infuse the organization not through procedures but through attitudes'. Integrating the need for responsivity into organizational decision premises means integrating CSR into the organizational way of doing business, building up CSR as an integral part of overall strategy. Assigning the job to a few specialized individuals won't do the trick. The Nike case is illustrative of that. (See also the report of Oxfam Australia, 2006.) And indeed, stakeholder theory comes to the same conclusion: It recommends defining stakeholders widely and integrating their concerns into the business processes, which makes a separate CSR programme superfluous (Freeman, 2004; Freeman et al., 2004).

Not only must the solution be truly *organizational*; it is also clear that each organization must find *its own* solution (Porter & Kramer, 2006; Waddock & Graves, 1997). Each organization will be responsive in a different way. Or, in the words of stakeholder theory: 'There may be many particular "stakeholder narratives" [...]. Surely there are lots of ways to run a firm.' (Freeman, 2004:232).

The ideal conception, to be followed but never quite reached, of this kind of integration of CSR may be rationality in a Luhmannian sense translated into the language of causality – integrate the concerns of your social and natural environment because they may rebound upon you. In this point, Luhmann is again not far from stakeholder theory instruction: 'No matter what you stand for, no matter what your ultimate purpose may be, you must take into account the effects of your actions on others, as well as their potential effects on you.' (Freeman, 2004:231).

'To approximate what we want to call rationality here, the system possesses self-correcting mechanisms. It tries to realize and avoid "errors".' ([Luhmann, 2006:463; my translation.)

Bear in mind however that this is not necessarily rational in a classic sense, as in increasing profits. (See Freeman, 2004, Freeman et al., 2004, and Donaldson & Preston, 1995, on the 'stakeholder versus shareholder' debate. Again, stakeholder theory, starting from a different point of departure, comes to a conclusion similar to Luhmann's.) Note also that 'integrate the concerns of your environment', in the eyes of Luhmannians, is not simply an ethical appeal (as Mintzberg, 1983:13, would have it). Ethics, Luhmannians say, will only take you so far in observing your organizational environment.

But it's not only about observing your environment, but also about self-observation, which leads us to reflexivity.

More ambitious methods could try to realize and avoid self-referential 'projections'. Self-correcting mechanisms are expanded to become self-accusing mechanisms. The system observes itself with the help of the distinction normal/ pathologic. It psychiatrizes itself, kind of, often with the help of consultants, to realize whether its own structures (programmes, interests and above all of course: organizational culture) lead to a distorted perception of 'reality'. [...] The system [can] carefully generalize its projection awareness, normalize its self-psychiatrization and, thus, become self-critical in a strict sense [...], without pulling the rug of reality from under itself. It can use the rug for walking carefully feeling its way, without the illusion that you could reach the right standpoint....

(Luhmann, 2006:463f.; my translation)

The attentive reader will have noticed that responsivity and reflexivity blend into one another, and interact. Responsivity means you pay attention to the ideas of the environment, which then force you to reflect. Reflexivity requires that you bear in mind that others can think differently, which in turn enhances responsivity. For Freeman, understanding stakeholders and answering the question 'What do we stand for?' also go together. It's the *relationship* which is in focus: '[S]takeholders are about the business, and the business is about the stakeholders.' (Freeman, 2004:231) We need to embrace the paradox of 'the environment is what the system is not, and the system is what the environment is not' construction. Instead of seeing paradoxes as 'the cloven-hoofed foot of the devil stuck in the door of orthodoxy' (Von Foerster, 1992), and obscuring them as has been criticized above we need to accept and deal with the fact that the observation depends on the observing system.

Conclusion

As I see it, the value of including some systems theoretic thoughts in a Handbook on CSR lies not in delivering ready-made solutions. The value lies in going over the problems you thought you knew already in a new frame of mind, making you understand them better. Systems theory expands your capacity of looking at things from different angles. What it doesn't do is save you from 'the danger of flying from reflection' – '[n]ot that it is possible, according to Luhmann' (Czarniawska, 2005:142).

From a systems theoretic perspective, we have to be sceptical of both moral and rational arguments for CSR. Morals and ethics cannot reintegrate a functionally differentiated society. And organizations will never be able to develop requisite variety to be in control of their environment, which means that 'perfect' rationality is impossible. Organizations should integrate into their decision premises the fact that we live in a 'society of observers of systems' (Czarniawska, 2005:142). They should strive for increased observantness and responsivity, and increased reflexivity. From a systems theoretic perspective, these would be the preconditions for integrating social and environmental concerns in business operations. The emphasis, here, is on process not on outcome.

Importantly, systems theory stubbornly reminds you that you need to address the communicational system not blame individuals. Each organization must devise its own CSR strategy, and the strategy must be truly organizational.

Bibliography

Bakken, T. (2000). System og iakttagelse. Teorien om Autopoietiske Systemer og dens Implikasjoner for Moral og Etikk. Oslo: Det historisk-filosofiske fakultet, Universitetet i Oslo.

Bakken, T. & Hernes, T. (2003). The Macro-Micro Problem in Organization Theory: Luhmann's Autopoiesis As a Way of Handling Recursivity. In T. Bakken & T. Hernes (Eds), Autopoietic

Organization Theory. Drawing on Niklas Luhmann's Social Systems Perspective (pp. 53-74). Copenhagen: Abstrakt Liber Copenhagen Business School Press.

Baraldi, C., Corsi, G. & Esposito, E. (1997). GLU: Glossar zu Niklas Luhmanns Theorie sozialer Systeme. Frankfurt am Main: Suhrkamp Verlag.

Commission of the European Communities (2001). Green Paper: Promoting a European Framework for Corporate Social Responsibility. Brussels, COM (2001)366final, 18.7.2001.

Czarniawska, B. (2005). On Gorgon Sisters: Organizational Action in the Face of Paradox. In D. Seidl & K. H. Becker (Eds), Niklas Luhmann and Organization Studies (pp. 127-142). Malmö: Liber & Copenhagen Business School Press.

Donaldson, T. & Preston, L. E. (1995). The Stakeholder Theory of the Corporation: Concepts, Evidence, and Implications. Academy of Management Review, 20 (1), 65-91.

Drepper, T. (2005). Organization and Society. On the desideratum of a society theory of organizations in the work of Niklas Luhmann. In D. Seidl & K. H. Becker (Eds), Niklas Luhmann and Organization Studies (pp. 171-190). Malmö: Liber & Copenhagen Business School Press.

Freeman, R. E. (2004). The Stakeholder Approach Revisited. Zeitschrift für Wirtschafts- und Unternehmensethik, 5 (3), 228-241.

Freeman, R. E., Wicks, A. C. & Parmar, B. (2004). Stakeholder Theory and "The Corporate Objective Revisited". Organization Science, 15 (3), 364-369.

Hernes, T. & Bakken, T. (2003). Introduction: Niklas Luhmann's Autopoietic Theory and Organization Studies – a Space of Connections. In T. Bakken & T. Hernes (Eds), Autopoietic Organization Theory. Drawing on Niklas Luhmann's Social Systems Perspective (pp. 9-22). Copenhagen: Abstrakt Liber Copenhagen Business School Press.

Hillman, A. J. & Keim, G. D. (2001). Shareholder Value, Stakeholder Management, and Social Issues: What's the Bottom Line? Strategic Management Journal, 22 (2), 125-139.

Klein, N. (2002). No Logo! 2. Aufl., Riemann Verlag.

Luhmann, N. (1984). Soziale Systeme: Grundriß einer allgemeinen Theorie. Frankfurt/Main: Suhrkamp.

Luhmann, N. (1990). Ökologische Kommunikation: Kann die moderne Gesellschaft sich auf ökologische Gefährdungen einstellen? 3. Aufl., Opladen: Westdeutscher Verlag.

Luhmann, N. (1990a). Paradigm lost: über die ethische Reflexion der Moral: Rede anläßlich der Verleihung des Hegel-Preises 1989/ von Niklas Luhmann. Niklas Luhmanns Herausforderung der Philosophie: Laudatio/ von Robert Spaemann. Frankfurt am Main: Suhrkamp.

Luhmann, N. (1992). Organisation. In W. Küpper & G. Ortmann (Eds), Mikropolitik. Rationalität, Macht und Spiele in Organisationen (pp. 165-185). 2., durchges. Aufl. Opladen: Westdeutscher Verlag.

Luhmann, N. (1993). Wirtschaftsethik – als Ethik? In J. Wieland (Eds), Wirtschaftsethik und Theorie der Gesellschaft (pp. 134-147). Frankfurt am Main: Suhrkamp Verlag.

Luhmann, N. (1995). Social Systems. Stanford, Calif.: Stanford University Press.

Luhmann, N. (1995a). Konzeptkunst. Brent Spar oder Können Unternehmen von der Öffentlichkeit lernen?. Frankfurter Allgemeine Zeitung, 19.07.1995.

Luhmann, N. (1997). Die Gesellschaft der Gesellschaft. Frankfurt/Main: Suhrkamp.

Luhmann, N. (1997a). Protest. Systemtheorie und soziale Bewegungen. Hrsg. und eingeleitet von Kai-Uwe Hellmann. 2.Aufl., Frankfurt/Main: Suhrkamp.

Luhmann, N. (2006). Organisation und Entscheidung. 2. Aufl., Wiesbaden: VS Verlag für Sozialwissenschaften.

March, J. G. & Simon, H. A. (1976). Organisation und Individuum: Menschliches Verhalten in Organisationen. Wiesbaden: Gabler-Verlag.

Margolis, J. D. & Walsh, J. P. (2003). Misery Loves Companies: Rethinking Social Initiatives by Business. Administrative Science Quarterly, 48 (2), 268-305.

McWilliams, A. & Siegel, D. (2000). Corporate Social Responsibility and Financial Performance: Correlation or Misspecification? Strategic Management Journal, 21 (5), 603-609.

Mintzberg, H. (1983). The Case for Corporate Social Responsibility. The Journal of Business Strategy, 4 (2), 3-16.

Nollmann, G. (2007). Geschlecht als sozialpsychologische, sozialstrukturelle und differenzierungstheoretische Kategorie. Zur Erforschung von Geschlechtszurechnungen und ihren Konkurrenten – mit Ergebnissen aus einer Umfrage. In C. Weinbach (Eds), Geschlechtliche Ungleichheit in systemtheoretischer Perspektive (pp. 109-137). Wiesbaden: VS Verlag für Sozialwissenschaften.

Ortmann, G. (2004). Als Ob. Fiktionen und Organisationen. Wiesbaden: VS Verlag für Sozialwissenschaften.

Oxfam Australia (2006). Offside! Labour Rights and Sportswear Production in Asia. www.oxfam.org.au/campaigns/labour/06report/.

Porter, M. E. & Kramer, M. R. (2006). Strategy & Society: The Link between Competitive Advantage and Corporate Social Responsibility. Harvard Business Review, December, 78-92.

Salancik, G. R. (1979). Field Stimulations for Organizational Behavior Research. Administrative Science Quarterly, 24 (December), 638-649.

Seidl, D. & Becker, K. H. (2005). Introduction: Niklas Luhmann and Organization Studies. In D. Seidl & K. H. Becker (Eds), Niklas Luhmann and Organization Studies (pp. 8-18). Malmö: Liber & Copenhagen Business School Press.

Seidl, D. & Becker, K. H. (Eds) (2005a). Niklas Luhmann and Organization Studies. Malmö: Liber & Copenhagen Business School Press.

Simon, H. A. (1978). Rational Decision-Making in Business Organizations. Nobel Memorial Lecture, http://nobelprize.org/economics/laureates/1978/simon-lecture.pdf.

Simon, F. B. (2000). Meine Psychose, mein Fahrrad und ich. Zur Selbstorganisation der Verrücktheit. 8. Aufl., Heidelberg: Carl-Auer-Systeme Verlag.

Simon, F. B. (2000a). Name Dropping. Zur erstaunlich großen, bemerkenswert geringen Rezeption Luhmanns in der Familienforschung. In H. De Berg & J. F. K. Schmidt (Eds), Rezeption und Reflexion. Zur Resonanz der Systemtheorie Niklas Luhmanns außerhalb der Soziologie (pp. 361-386). Frankfurt/Main: Suhrkamp Verlag.

Vogd, W. (2005). Systemtheorie und rekonstruktive Sozialforschung: Eine empirische Versöhnung unterschiedlicher theoretischer Perspektiven. Opladen: Verlag Barbara Budrich.

Vogel, D. (2005). Social Responsibility: The Low Value of Virtue. Harvard Business Review, June, 26.

Von Foerster, H. (1992). Ethics and Second-Order Cybernetics. Cybernetics & Human Knowing, 1 (1).

Vos, J. (2005). Strategic Management from a Systems-Theoretical Perspective. In D. Seidl & K. H. Becker (Eds), Niklas Luhmann and Organization Studies (pp. 365-385). Malmö: Liber & Copenhagen Business School Press.

Waddock, S. A. & Graves, S. B. (1997). The Corporate Social Performance-Financial Performance Link. Strategic Management Journal, 18 (4), 303-319.

Weinbach, C. (2004). Systemtheorie und Gender: Das Geschlecht im Netz der Systeme. Wiesbaden: VS Verlag für Sozialwissenschaften.

Wieland, J. (2007). Die Ethik der Governance. 5. Aufl., Marburg: Metropolis Verlag.

Zadek, S. (2004). The Path to Corporate Responsibility. Harvard Business Review, December, 125-132.

KEY REFERENCES FOR FURTHER READING

Bakken, T. & Hernes, T. (Eds.) (2003). Autopoietic Organization Theory. Drawing on Niklas Luhmann's Social Systems Perspective. Copenhagen: Abstrakt Liber Copenhagen Business School Press.

Baraldi, C., Corsi, G. & Esposito, E. (1997). GLU: Glossar zu Niklas Luhmanns Theorie sozialer Systeme. Frankfurt am Main: Suhrkamp Verlag.

Freeman, R. E. (2004). The Stakeholder Approach Revisited. Zeitschrift für Wirtschafts- und Unternehmensethik, 5 (3), 228-241.

Seidl, D. & Becker, K. H. (Eds.) (2005). Niklas Luhmann and Organization Studies. Malmö: Liber & Copenhagen Business School Press.

3 *What is 'Good' Corporate Governance?*

DOMINIQUE BESSIRE, CÉLINE CHATELIN AND
STÉPHANE ONNÉE

Introduction

The definition of what is 'good' corporate governance depends on the paradigm to which the answer refers. The theoretical as well as empirical limits of the prevailing paradigm, which is based on utilitarianism (Mill, 2001) and defines enterprises as nexus of contracts, are more and more obvious. An epistemological break is necessary. In this perspective we propose to define enterprises as communities of free and responsible persons, engaged in a project directed to the common good, and to draw a few directions for future research in corporate governance.

What is 'good' corporate governance? This question became very real for us when we were asked by a well-known European social rating agency to make a critical evaluation of the grid they used to rate companies in the domain of corporate governance. We discovered that this grid was based on principles underpinned by a strict disciplinary shareholder-oriented perspective. This situation seemed to us inconsistent with the concept of social rating, which is supposed to take into account the interests of all stakeholders. We came to the conclusion that the answer to the question 'what is "good" governance?' differs according to which paradigm it refers.

The prevailing paradigm today gives the primacy to shareholders' interests and is embedded in a disciplinary perspective. This domination is largely correlated with the rise of investment funds and has been enforced through a circular process which involves rating agencies, standard-setters and scholars. However, there are more and more signs which indicate that this paradigm is becoming exhausted. From an empirical point of view, the multiplication of more and more detailed and constraining codes and acts goes hand in hand with the proliferation of scandals on an unseen scale (Enron, Worldcom, Parmalat, Vivendi, EADS and so on). On a theoretical level, a multiplication of new developments can be observed: from a shareholder perspective to a stakeholder perspective, from a disciplinary approach to a cognitive approach, from an agency vision to a stewardship vision. This inflation of regulatory devices and of theoretical additions appear more and more as sterile attempts to caulk a vessel which is leaing at every seam.

We believe that if we are looking for relevant answers to questions of corporate governance, we have to achieve an epistemological rupture and to break off with the prevailing paradigm. The essence of this rupture lies in the anthropological assumption.

In the prevailing paradigm, human beings are seen as enslaved to the pursuit of their self-interest; opportunism is the leitmotiv and monitoring, surveillance, alignment, conflicts, competition are the keywords. In the paradigm which we advocate, man is considered as a free and responsible person and the keywords are trust, self-achievement, concurrence and responsibility. It is important to underline that only the adoption of such an approach enables us to take into account the ethical question; in the utilitarian perspective, this question cannot even be asked.

Glory and Misery of a Paradigm

The paradigm of corporate governance prevailing today has developed through a process of circular reinforcement which makes it not easy to contest. However, more and more signs of exhaustion can be detected, which call for an epistemological rupture.

THE INSTALLATION OF THE PREVAILING PARADIGM: A PROCESS OF CIRCULAR REINFORCEMENT

Since the beginning of the 1990s, throughout the world, codes of corporate of governance have multiplied. They appear to have mainly emerged as an attempt to satisfy growing demand expressed by investment funds, especially American funds, and to reassure public opinion, unsettled by the numerous financial scandals of the past decades (Enron, Worldcom, Parmalat, Vivendi and so on). Most influential codes have been elaborated in Anglo-Saxon countries. But even countries which have different traditions (such as France or Germany), not only in the legal field (a regime of Roman law instead a regime of common law) but also in the economical field (regulation through banks and States instead of regulation through financial markets), tend to elaborate codes which adopt similar principles because they fear that in the absence of such codes most powerful investors would invest in other countries.

One of the first and most influential of these codes, known as the Cadbury Report (1992) seems to have been used as a matrix for the elaboration of most other codes at the national or international level (Wirtz, 2005). It must be noticed that Sir Adrian Cadbury appears at the head of the list of the persons who are acknowledged for their contribution to the *OECD Principles of Corporate Governance* (2004, a revision of the 1999 version), which are explicitly presented as a synthesis of most important codes and which are used by rating agencies as a major reference.

However different these codes may appear, all of them seem in fact to share the same perspective. They usually present detailed mechanisms to protect shareholders and to control managers, through a variety of devices, namely the composition of the Board and the constitution of specialised Committees, such as the Audit Committee, with an emphasis on the role of non-executive directors. These codes appear therefore to be underpinned, more or less explicitly, by agency theory, which assumes a divergence of interests between shareholders and managers. Many of the devices which have been proposed by the normative branch of agency theory in order to limit managers' opportunistic behaviour are now incorporated in these codes. The international comparison of national models of corporate governance made by Labelle and Raffournier (2000, p. 12) shows, in spite of minor differences, 'a convergence of norms which give legitimacy to the OECD's efforts to develop internationally accepted norms in this field'.

Academic papers and books on agency theory and its implications for corporate governance form a huge bulk of literature which has acquired since the end of the 1970s the status of mainstream literature. Agency theory can indeed be considered as having gained the status of 'normal science' (Kuhn, 1970). The dominant paradigm becomes very difficult to contest. Davis et al. (1997, p. 21), who advocate another vision of corporate governance, for instance, insist on the fact that 'stewardship theory fits in the theoretic landscape, relative to agency theory, rather than opposes to it'. The agency-theory literature provides theoretical legitimacy for the codes which incorporate its recommendations. In their turn, these codes provide the theory with some form of social recognition (in a way a little similar to the phenomenon of the Chicago School of Economics when its supporters were trying to implement its recommendations in underdeveloped countries, notably South America).

These codes have gained a boost to their legitimacy when their recommendations were incorporated, at least partially, in legal devices such as the Sarbanes Oxley Act in the United States of America or the *Loi de sécurité financière* (Law for financial security) in France. Even in the countries where norms of corporate governance have kept their voluntary nature, the diffusion of the principle 'complain or explain' makes it very difficult for a company to adopt divergent principles: it faces the risk of downgrading.

Rating agencies have indeed significantly contributed to the installation of the disciplinary and shareholder-oriented paradigm as a prevailing paradigm. These agencies have progressively developed extra-financial ratings to assess the quality of companies' systems of corporate governance. The ratings are delivered according to the degree of compliance with criteria which have been picked up in well accepted codes such as the above mentioned *OECD Principles of Corporate of Governance* (2004). These ratings are used by asset managers to make decisions, since 'good' corporate governance is assumed to have a positive influence on shareholders' wealth. These ratings are also used for the construction of indexes. For companies, to be included in such indexes becomes an objective since it demonstrates their commitment to 'good' corporate governance. Finally, rating agencies, index diffusers and asset managers appear to constitute the industrial side of the dominant paradigm which is expressed through theoretical discourses and regulation devices. As a consequence, the agency-based paradigm has been solidified through a process of circular reinforcement and has become hegemonic. Investors exert a pressure which is legitimated by the academic world and which is embedded in codes and instrumented through ratings. In other words, the disciplinary paradigm has acquired the status of 'normal science' (Kuhn, 1970).

SIGNS OF EXHAUSTION

In spite of (or maybe because of) this process of circular reinforcement, the prevailing paradigm is more and more undermined by facts as well as by academic research. More and more signs of a crisis as implied by Kuhn (1970) can be observed: discrepancies between theory and fact, changes in social/cultural climates, scholarly criticism of existing theory.

Discrepancies between theory and fact

On an empirical level, the growing diffusion of codes has been unable to prevent the outbreak of huge financial scandals. Indeed, the more the codes are diffused and allegedly implemented in companies' practices, the huger the financial scandals seem to be. A recent example has been provided by EADS.

On the academic level, empirical studies on the effectiveness of the devices which are underpinned by agency theory and implemented in companies through compliance with the detailed prescriptions of codes of corporate governance do not provide convergent results. There is no evidence that compliance contributes to value creation (Dedman, 2002). Wirtz (2005) demonstrates indeed that these codes are elaborated to prevent a process of value destruction, but that they remain silent on the process of value creation.

Proliferation of theoretical additions

Concurrently a proliferation of theoretical additions can be observed. Drawing on Freeman's approach (1984), the focus on the relationship between managers and shareholders has been extended to the relationship between managers and other stakeholders such as customers, suppliers, employees and communities (Charreaux and Desbrières, 1998). The disciplinary perspective has been complemented by a cognitive dimension. More recently stewardship theory (Davis et al., 1997) questions the priority given to the opportunistic assumption. On both empirical and theoretical levels, the lack of consistency, even contradictions, between approaches in the field of corporate governance and corporate social responsibility are coming under increasing criticism. As a consequence, the theoretical landscape which formerly exhibited a kind of self-evidence is becoming more and more confused. The process observed has many points in common with the description of the response to a crisis in normal science given by Kuhn (analysis drawn on the outline and study guide prepared by Pajares, http//www.des.emory.edu/mpf/Kuhn.htmpl): normal science continually strives to bring theory and fact into closer agreement whereas the prevailing paradigm becomes more and more blurred. As this process develops, scientists express discontent, competing articulations of the paradigm proliferate, scholars may turn to philosophical analysis and debate.

THE NECESSARY RUPTURE WITH THE 'ORTHODOX' PARADIGM: HUMANISM VERSUS OPPORTUNISM

The limits and the adverse effects of a strictly disciplinary and shareholder-centred approach in corporate governance have been pointed out briefly here above. This failure invites a break with the old paradigm (Bessire and Meunier, 2000) and development of a new one. Do the recent theoretical developments suggest such a paradigm? The answer, from our point of view, is negative. In spite of some assertions, as different as they seem to be at first view, these theoretical developments remain underpinned by the same fundamental anthropologic assumption: man as a human being enslaved to his own interest. All these approaches remain, more or less, embedded in an utilitarian approach, which gives no room for the question of ethics. The only theoretical development in which premises of a new paradigm might be identified is stewardship theory, although in some aspects, it does not totally depart from the old paradigm. The objective is therefore to draw new perspectives based on a radically different anthropological assumption, that is, man as a free and responsible person.

It might be believed, considering the abundant literature related to the utilitarian paradigm, which proposes a pessimistic and reductive vision of human nature and in which contract-based theories (agency, property rights, transaction costs theories) are embedded, that the opportunistic assumption has always reigned triumphantly in management sciences. It is far from the truth. As the defenders of stewardship theory remind us, other theories have placed in the first rank of human motivation the need for self-achievement. The size of this chapter does not allow us to describe in detail examples of this epistemological posture, but there is a long line of authors, from Schumpeter (1989) to contemporary Canadian authors, such as Pauchant et al. (1996 and 2000) or Chanlat et al. (1990), who advocate another vision. Davis et al. (1997, p. 27) note for instance that Argyris (1973a and b) advocated a model of man as self-actualising, drawing in the early work of McGregor (1960) and the later work of Maslow (1954). However the kind of imperialism conveyed by the 'orthodox' paradigm tends to disqualify their works, at least with regards to the dimensions which are related to a humanistic approach.

In their defence, the supporters of principal-agency approaches contend that opportunism keeps the status of simple assumption and that it does not exclude other behaviours. Davis et al. (1997, p. 23) reply to this objection by underlining the fact that 'the model of the agent remains inherently opportunistic, in that there is an ever-present possibility of opportunism, unless it is curbed through controls; moreover, because controls are imperfect, some opportunism will remain'. Besides the theoretical debate, it must also be noticed that codes of corporate governance are specifically designed mainly to prevent managers' opportunistic behaviour. Referring to Argyris (1964), Davis et al. (1997, p. 27) point to the devastating effects of such an assumption: 'when humans are placed in organisations that are designed on this economic view, they tend to suppress their level of aspirations, thereby creating a self-fulfilling prophecy. [...] for those individuals who are unable to suppress their aspirations, frustration with the organizational structures may lead to withdrawal and aggressive behaviours'.

Even more worrying, the opportunistic assumption intrinsically excludes the question of ethics. Prevailing theories in corporate governance stage individuals who are enslaved to their self-interest. But without freedom, there is no room for ethics. The ethical intention according to Ricoeur (2002) can be founded indeed only on the recognition of human freedom. The French philosopher contends that without this recognition, the whole question of responsibility, and with it of ethics, is invalidated. To escape the general amorality to which codes of corporate governance lead us, it is absolutely necessary to adopt another assumption, the assumption of man as a free and responsible person. Responsibility and freedom are paired. Ethics in this perspective is not something which is added; it comes first.

The Enterprise as a Community of Free and Responsible Persons

A different vision of human nature leads to a different conception of enterprises, which, in its turn, has implications in the field of corporate governance, since it implies questioning enterprises' mission and taking into account their political dimension.

We advocate a vision of man as a responsible person. However, responsibility does not exist for itself; it always exists in relation to others. In prevailing discourses on corporate governance, managers have to report to shareholders (narrow approach of agency theory) or to stakeholders (enlarged vision of agency theory); in discourses on corporate social responsibility, enterprises are responsible towards their stakeholders.

In the perspective which is advocated here and which draws on approaches developed by ethics philosophers such as Ricoeur (2002), responsibility is shared; every person or group of persons has to take their part of responsibility, to the extent of the mission and means which have been assigned to them. Shareholders' responsibility (Pérez, 2002), which is extremely seldom mentioned in the professional or academic discourses, has to be taken into account. Davis and al. (1997, p. 29) adopt a similar point of view: 'according to stewardship theory, the principal would expect to be accountable to the collective for his or her contributions as much as the steward would be'. This is more necessary if we want to fill the gap within the field of management sciences between corporate governance and corporate social responsibility (Bhimani and Soonawalla, 2005).

Simon (1993) accepts as his own the thesis developed by Ricoeur (2002). He, however, insists on a specific dimension: he considers that responsibility cannot be reduced to the relation with others and that it necessarily includes an intervening third party. Responsibility requires institutions and laws, what Levinas calls *justice*. Political institutions have therefore to play a role. The development of 'soft' law (Thibierge, 2004), which has given birth to most codes of corporate governance, is not necessarily an evil, but its generalisation, beyond the control of any kind of democratic process, should be firmly countered. Pesqueux (2006) expresses the same point of view and describes the present phenomenon as a process of 'desinstitutionalisation of institutions'.

In short, in the question of corporate governance, we have the confrontation of a multitude of subjects, all responsible to some extent: shareholders, managers, customers, suppliers, employees, institutions... How to take into account this multitude of persons and groups with divergent interests? Our answer to this question is to define enterprises as *communities of free and responsible persons*, in opposition to the prevailing paradigm which considers them as nexus of contracts. Etzioni (1998, p. 679) adopts the same perspective: 'all those involved in the corporation are potentially members of one community: while they clearly have significantly divergent interests, needs, and values, they also have some significant shared goals and bonds'.

This definition has many important implications for the conception of corporate governance. However, the term community which was made popular in sociology and philosophy by Tönnies (1977), who has contrasted community (*Gemeinschaft*) with society (*Gesellschaft*) has a lot of meanings (Guérin, 2003–2004; Vattimo éd., 2002). In order to define it, it may be useful to refer to etymology. The word community is made of two Indo-European roots (Grandsaignes d'Hauterive, 1994): *kom* which means together (which has given the Latin word *cum*, with) and *mei* which means charge (which has given in Latin *munis*: the one who assumes his charge). If we keep to this etymology, two questions arise: *kom*, how to conceive and to organise a sense of togetherness; *mei*, what is the nature of this charge?

LIVING TOGETHER (KOM-)

The enterprise is not an isolated and monolithic community: it is composed of communities and it interacts with other communities. Its intrinsically political dimension must be recognised. The question of democracy as a consequence has to be asked. Constructive conflict could be a means to address it.

Community and communities

First, as with any community, enterprises are characterised by both their universal dimension (their humanity), and their singular dimension: they have a history, they are rooted in a specific space, a specific period of time and a specific culture; they rely upon a specific system of values which makes sense for their members (Nifle, 2004a and b). A SME is different from a multinational corporation, a mining company from a high-tech company, a French firm from an English or an Egyptian firm. In the field of corporate governance, this implies that the application of uniform rules is nonsense and is to be avoided; only a few general principles (in the proper sense of the word) should be defined, instead of developing a never-ending list of extremely detailed specifications; this would facilitate taking into account the specific context of each country and of each company.

Secondly, enterprises, as with any community, are made up themselves of a multiplicity of persons and sub-communities of persons (Cohendet and Diani, 2003; Crozier and Friedberg, 1981): managers and shareholders, but also men and women, young and old people, employees of the financial department and of the sales department, Muslims and Christians, chess players and basketball players. In contrast with a totalitarian vision which considers any person only in the relation to their membership of such and such specific and unique community, the perspective we propose puts the emphasis on the necessity to consider every person in their multidimensional adherences. In the field of corporate governance, the problem therefore is no more how to align interests, mainly of managers' on shareholders', but how to facilitate the emergence of shared meanings between the firm's different stakeholders. Finally, as with any community, enterprises are entrenched in larger communities, local, regional, world communities and they interact with other communities, NGO's, political institutions.. Corporate governance regulations therefore must be conceived at these different levels and take into account the articulation between all these communities. Such a vision could provide the means for developing the missing link between corporate governance and corporate social responsibility and take into account the question of common good.

Politics, participation and trust

We contend that enterprises, as with any community, have necessarily a political dimension since they participate into the fabrication of our society (Sainsaulieu et al., 1983; Denis, 2007). It will therefore be possible to establish a continuum between governance at a State level and governance at the enterprise level.

This dimension has been forgotten in management science. However, up to the beginning of the 1980s, that was not the case. Jarniou, for instance, published in 1981 a book entitled *L'entreprise comme système politique* (*The enterprise as a political system*), which had a great success. In a former book (1975), Tabatoni and Jarniou had already insisted on the political dimension of management systems.

De Woot, in his book, *Pour une réforme de l'entreprise* (*For a reform of the enterprise*, 1968), helps us to understand why it is so important to take into account the political dimension in management. Without political participation, individuals are to behave as passive agents and are unable to assume their function as creators and entrepreneurs. Only full and multi-dimensional participation can lead them to use their capacities for the benefit of the community to which they belong, because participation is the means for self-achievement (p. 208).

Participation has several dimensions: operational (the individual provides the enterprise with resources: labour force, competencies, funds...), functional (the individual identifies himself with his work) and finally political (the individual integrates the enterprise's mission). Political participation demands 'participation in power or in its control' (p. 211). Trust makes the link between functional participation and political participation because 'the success of functional participation demands trust from people who are asked to assume this functional participation and in return, trust on their side depends mainly on political participation' (p. 215).

To accept trust as the directing principle leads also to a more positive, but also more realistic conception of managers' entrenchment (Shleifer and Vishny, 1989). Managers are persons who are entrusted by shareholders, but also by other stakeholders. In order to assume their specific charge, these managers must regain some latitude. It seems indeed paradoxical on one hand to encourage empowerment among employees and on the other hand to limit as strictly as possible managers' autonomy. Trust also plays a central role in stewardship theory. Instead of considering it, as Williamson (1993) does, as the residue of a sophisticated calculus, Davis et al. (1997, p. 33) define it as 'a willingness to be vulnerable in the context of a relationship'. Our postulation does not deny the existence of possible opportunistic behaviour, but rather establishes a new hierarchy: what makes life together possible is in the first place trust (Gomez, 1995; Bidault, 1998; Hirigoyen and Pichard-Stanford, 1998); if we permanently feared opportunistic behaviour, life would become a hell.

If the political dimension of management is to be recognised, this necessarily implies redefining modes of governance. An autocratic governance (shareholders as absolute monarchs – the orthodox paradigm of corporate governance; or enterprises as enlightened sovereigns conceding their favours to stakeholders they have carefully selected –the prevailing paradigm of corporate social responsibility) is no more possible; corporate governance must become democratic.

From democracy to constructive conflict

The question of corporate governance, as indicated above, has to deal with the integration of multiple subjectivities (shareholders, managers and others stakeholders). How to construct this inter-subjectivity? Husserl 'explains in a text written in 1932 that even an empathy which has been actively experienced by "I" and "Thou" allows nothing more than a mere being-together of subjects', because 'to provoke the emergence of an actual inter-subjectivity, [...] we also need [...] a project and the will to communication' (Mutelesi, 1998, our free translation). As communication appears to be central, we have turned our reflections towards discourse ethics and the analyses conducted by Apel and

Habermas in order to propose a few pathways. The two philosophers suggest transcending the paradigm of subjectivity by the paradigm of communication. 'Whereas Kant allots to the individual the task of applying the universality principle in order to discover what actually are his obligations [...], discourse ethics gives this determination to practical and actual discussions with all the persons who are affected; [...] as soon as we accept to discuss, we have already tacitly accepted a normative and ethical principle which requires us to submit any disagreement to argument in order to achieve a consensus' (Desjardin, 2004, in his comments on Apel's writings, our free translation). In other words, Habermas and Apel, who have developed the concept of deliberative (or participative) democracy, give a central role to discussion in the functioning of democracies and the definition of ethical choices.

Similarly, a satisfying mode of corporate governance should open spaces for discussion between individuals, within the enterprise and with outside stakeholders. But Habermas' and Apel' posture has arisen some criticisms, namely from Mouffe, a scholar in politics (1994). She agrees on the necessity to open spaces for discussion, but she thinks that the philosophy of discussion ethics is too obsessed by the search for consensus and that since it emphasises the dimension of living together (*polis*), it tends to neglect the dimension of antagonism and conflict (*polemos*) and therefore is not capable of fully understanding the specificity of the politics of democracy (p. 5, our translation). She therefore suggests the concept of pluralist democracy (Walzer, 1997) whose objective is not to eradicate power but 'to multiply spaces where power relations are open to democratic contestation' (id., p. 19) and 'to stage conflicts according to agonistics devices which enhance the respect of pluralism (ibid.).

We find a similar idea in a lecture by Follett (1942) entitled 'Constructive Conflict'. For Follett, conflict should not be considered as warfare but as difference, difference of opinions, of interests (p. 30). She thinks that 'instead of condemning it, we should set it to work for us' (ibid.). She identifies 'three main ways of dealing with conflict: domination, compromise and integration. Domination, obviously, is a victory of one side of the other. This is the easiest way of dealing with conflict but not usually successful in the long run' (p. 31). Compromise 'is the accepted, the approved, way of ending controversy. Yet no one really wants to compromise, because that means a giving up of something' (p. 32). With compromise, 'the conflict will come again and again in some other form, for in compromise we give up part of our desire, and because we shall not be content to rest there, sometime we shall try to get the whole of our desire' (p. 35). In the orthodox paradigm of corporate governance, which puts the emphasis on the alignment of interests, most of the time for the sole benefit of shareholders, domination and compromise are obviously the means which are privileged. The other method of ending conflict in a constructive and sustainable way is, according to Follett, integration: 'when two desires are *integrated* (underlined by Follett), that means that a solution has been found in which both desires have found a place, that neither side has had to sacrifice anything' (p. 32). In contrast with compromise which 'does not create, [which] deals with what already exists, integration creates something new' (p. 35). Follett believes that 'only integration really stabilizes' (ibid.). But by stabilisation, she does not 'mean anything stationary. Nothing ever stays put' (ibid.). She means only 'that a particular conflict is settled and the next occurs on a higher level' (ibid.). Again her opinion is in opposition to the prevailing paradigm of corporate governance which appears to be embedded in an illusory quest for some ideal state and does not take into account any dynamical dimension.

Further, Follett thinks that we can often measure our individual as well as our social progress by watching the nature of our conflicts. 'We become spiritually more and more developed as our conflicts rise to higher levels' (p. 35). Once more, it must be noted that the orthodox paradigm of corporate governance stages conflict at a purely static level, mainly as a conflict of financial interests. Only the cognitive approach suggests that conflicts could happen at another level, the cognitive level.

Follett suggests bases for dealing fruitfully with conflict in order to obtain integration. The first step is 'to bring the differences into the open. We cannot hope to integrate our differences unless we know what they are' (p. 37). She explains that 'one of the most important reasons for bringing the desires of each side to a place where they can be clearly examined and valued is that evaluation often leads to revaluation' (p. 38). She makes a comparison with 'the evolution of our desires from childhood, through youth, etc.' (ibid). 'The baby has many infantile desires which are not compatible with his wish for approbation; therefore he revalues his desires. We see this all through our life' (ibid.). If the first step is 'to put our cards on the table', 'the next is step is to take the demand of both sides and break them up into their constituent parts' (p. 40). This 'involves the examination of symbols [...], that is the careful scrutiny of the language used to see what it really means' (p. 41). 'One often has to find [...] the real demand, which is being obscured by miscellaneous minor claims or by ineffective presentation' (p. 42): the emphasis must be put rather on significant features than on dramatic ones. Moreover, people should develop efforts to anticipate conflicts. 'The anticipation of conflict [...] does not mean necessarily the avoidance of conflict, but playing the game differently. That is, you integrate the different interests without making all the moves' (p. 43), like in a chess game. Then the response must be prepared, in the awareness that this response does not take place in one-way process but in a circular and dynamic process, in a way similar to what we can observe for instance in a game of tennis. 'A serves. The way B returns the ball depends partly on the way it was served to him. A's next play will depend on his original serve plus the return of B, and so on and so on.' (p. 44).

ASSUMING A CHARGE (-MEI)

If the community has a mission to achieve, is engaged in a project, it has therefore a dynamic, a teleological dimension, a vision which is quite opposite to the static vision of the firm as a nexus of contracts. What is the nature of this mission? How is it related to common good?

Contract-based approaches see enterprises as organisations devoted to specific interests; an ethical approach demands building a bridge between enterprises' mission and common good, that is a good which is not the simple addition of specific interests without any reference to the historical, geographic or cultural context, but a good defined with a reference to communities which are embedded in a specific cultural space to be defined and with reference also to a value scale.

In French law, the notion of *intérêt social* (social interest) already recognises the necessity of transcending peculiar interests for the benefit of enterprises as a whole. Ph. de Woot (1968) again makes a few fruitful propositions in this direction. He demonstrates that it is not possible to define the enterprises' mission, either by referring only to the peculiar interests of its members, or in terms of submission to general interest. Enterprises have 'a specific purpose distinct from the purposes of the individuals who compose them and from a general interest which transcends them' (p. 185, our translation). It is only when enterprises achieve their specific mission that they contribute to the common good and that they enable individuals to achieve themselves. For De Woot, economic creativity is the specific mission devoted to enterprises. Creativity here does not mean the creation of a wealth which would be purely quantitative and static, it means dynamic and qualitative value creation. Enterprises exist 'to create, to progress, to produce something better' (p. 189). Here the difference between producing *more* and producing *better*, especially in reference to sustainable development, must be underlined. Creativity is the means through which to achieve the integration of social and individual interests which themselves are respectively situated up and downstream of the entrepreneurial action (Bréchet, 1994). Through creation, enterprises contribute to the common good, since 'creativity is the lever for social progress and [...] simultaneously gives the necessary means to achieve it' (De Woot, 1968, p. 192). Through creativity, individuals can also satisfy their highest ambitions and make sense of their work (p. 191).

This vision of enterprises and of the role of persons who contribute to their functioning leads De Woot to question the relation between ownership, decision and risk in a way which differs from the 'orthodox' paradigm. If managers have a specific charge – to give an orientation to enterprises – all other members have also 'to some extent to assume a piece of the entrepreneur's role' (p. 112). Risk is no more located within a specific group, because the achievement of the enterprises' mission depends on a great variety of resources. Owners of these resources (not only shareholders, but also managers, employees, customers, suppliers, other communities and so on) face a risk when they decide to cooperate with an enterprise, because they decide to use them 'in a specific way which excludes other alternatives. This choice exposes them to a loss if the option which has been chosen is less profitable or less sustainable than the options they have renounced' (p. 111). Etzioni (1998) shows moreover that the concept of 'private property' is a social construct, that is a concept 'which reflects the particular values, interests, and needs of the society in which [this concept is] recognized in a given historical period. [It is] not an expression of some kind of 'natural', self-evident, absolute or inalienable right' (p. 680). He therefore contends that 'corporations are the Property of ALL (underlined by Etzioni) who invest in them' (p. 681) and that 'all stakeholders invest some resources in the corporation; all do so in expectation of a return; that return is not guaranteed; and hence all are entitled to form a relationship with the users of their resources to help ensure that the usage will be in line with their interest and values' (p. 683). Etzioni then develops his demonstration as regards with different kinds of stakeholders: employees, communities, creditors, clients. He also illustrates the fact that 'for all these stakeholders, all other things being equal, the *longer* (underlined by Etzioni), the larger the investment' (p. 685). Therefore all 'have the right to participate in the governance of a corporation' (pp. 681–682). Here Etzioni, as we did above, points to the political dimension of corporate governance.

What is at stake, in this perspective, is therefore no more the simple alignment of interests of some individuals with the interests of other individuals, but the contribution that everyone brings to the common work: concurrence instead of competition.

Conclusion

The prevailing paradigm of corporate governance leads to a theoretical and empirical cul-de-sac; indeed attempts to enlarge or even to transcend it are sign posts for its incapacity to account for the actual functioning of enterprises and to propose efficient, effective and acceptable mechanisms; the multiplication of codes and their never-ending revision go along with a limitless quest to secure investment. Within the 'orthodox' paradigm, in spite of what is repeated everywhere, the aim is not to restore trust: 'control-oriented systems are designed to avoid vulnerability and therefore to avoid the need for trust' (Davis et al., 1997, p. 33); it is to create a situation where, through a strict surveillance of managers, trust would become useless, as it is in the case of a prisoner in his jail.

To escape this cul-de-sac, it is necessary to depart from the underpinning anthropological assumption which present man as an individual who maximises his/her utility function and to develop a new approach of corporate governance which would rely on the assumption of man's freedom and responsibility. On this basis, it becomes possible to develop a new vision of enterprises, no longer as nexus of contracts between individuals enslaved by their own interests, but as communities of free and responsible persons, engaged in a creative project, able to contribute to the common good. In this perspective, 'good' governance is no longer understood as blind compliance with a static system of detailed and codified rules, which are applied in an uniform way, without consideration of the specific attributes of each enterprise and each country. It must be seen as a never-ending process which progresses through conflicts, under the condition that these conflicts are solved, as far as possible, through integration and not through domination or compromise. 'Good' corporate governance therefore does not lie any more in the mythical quality of an organisational architecture, deprived of any political dimension, but in the quality of entrepreneurial democracy, which systematically questions the enterprise's mission and its relation to the common good.

References

Argyris C. (1964), Integrating the individual and the organization, Wiley, New York.

Argyris C. (1973a), 'Organization man: Rational and self-actualizing', Public Administration Review, vol. 33, July-August, pp. 354-357.

Argyris C. (1973b), 'Some limits of rational man organizational theory', Public Administration Review, vol. 33, May-June, pp. 253-267.

Bessire D. & Meunier J. (2000), 'Conceptions du gouvernement des entreprises: une grille de lecture épistémologique', XVèmes Journées Nationales des I.A.E., Bayonne-Biarritz, 6-8 septembre.

Bhimani A. & Soonawalla K. (2005), 'From conformance to performance: The corporate responsibilities continuum', Journal of Accounting and Public Policy, vol. 24, pp. 165-174.

Bidault F. (1998), 'Comprendre la confiance: la nécessité d'une nouvelle problématique', Economies et Sociétés, série 'Sciences de gestion', numéro spécial XXe anniversaire Confiance et gestion, no. 8-9, pp. 33-46.

Bréchet J.-P. (1994), 'Du projet d'entreprendre au projet d'entreprise', Revue Française de Gestion, juin-juillet-août, pp. 5-14.

Chanlat J.-F., dir. (1990), L'individu dans l'organisation: les dimensions oubliées, Presses de l'Université Laval, Québec; Eska, Paris.

Charreaux G. & Desbrières P. (1998), 'Gouvernance des entreprises: valeur partenariale contre valeur actionnariale', Finance-Contrôle-Stratégie, vol. 1, no. 2, juin, pp. 57-88.

Coehndet P. & Diani M. (2003), 'L'organisation comme une communauté de communautés', Revue d'Economie Politique, vol. 113, no. 5, pp. 697-721.

Crozier M. & Friedberg E. (1981), L'acteur et le système, les contraintes de l'action collective, Editions du Seuil, collection 'Points Politique' (1ère édition, 1977).

Davis J.H., Schoorman F.D. & Donaldson L. (1997), 'Towards a stewardship theory of management', Academy of Management Review, vol. 22, no. 1, pp. 20-47.

Dedman E. B. (2002), 'The Cadbury Committee recommendations on corporate governance – a review of compliance and performance impacts', International Journal of Management Reviews, vol. 4, December, pp. 335-352.

Denis J.-Ph. (2007), 'L'exercice du corporate control: un objet politique en quête de projet gestionnaire?', XVIème Conférence Internationale de Management Stratégique, Montréal, 6-9 juin.

De Woot P. (1968), Pour une doctrine de l'entreprise, Editions du Seuil.

Desjardin A. (2004), 'Karl-Otto Apel, la réponse de l'éthique de la discussion', http://www.ac-amiens.fr/academie/pedagogie/philosophie/lectures/Apel.htm

Etzioni A. (1998), 'A communitarian note on stakeholder theory', Business Ethics Quarterly, vol. 8, n 4, pp. 679-691.

Follett M.P. (1942), 'Constructive conflict' in Metcalf H.C. & Urwick L. (1942), Dynamic administration. The collected papers of Mary Parker Follett, Harper & Brothers Publishers, New York.

Freeman E.R. (1984), Strategic management: a stakeholder approach, Pitman, Boston.

Gomez P.-Y. (1995), 'Agir en confiance', in F. Bidault, P.-Y. Gomez et G. Marion, éd., Confiance, entreprise et société, collection 'Essais', Eska.

Grandsaignes d'Hauterive R. (1994), Dictionnaire des racines des langues européennes, Larousse (reprint of the 1948 issue).

Guérin F. (2003-2004), 'Le concept de communauté, une illustration exemplaire de la production de concepts en sciences sociales?', Cahier de recherche du CESAMES, n° 48, Groupe ESC Rouen.

Hirigoyen G. & Pichard-Stamford J.-P. (1998), 'La confiance, un outil de la finance organisationnelle : une synthèse de la littérature récente', Economies et Sociétés, série 'Sciences de gestion', numéro spécial XXe anniversaire Confiance et gestion, no. 8-9, pp. 219-234.

Jarniou P. (1981), L'entreprise comme système politique, Presses Universitaires de France.

Kuhn T.S. (1970), The structure of scientific revolutions, University of Chicago Press, Chicago, 2nd edition.

Labelle R. & Raffournier B. (2000), 'Comparaison internationale en matière de gouvernement d'entreprise', Cahier du CETAI, vol. a.2000, no. 2.

Maslow A. (1954), Motivation and personality, Harper, New York.

McGregor D. (1960), The human side of enterprise, McGraw Hill, New York.

Mill J.S. (2001), L'utilitarisme, Flammarion, collection 'Champs Flammarion', no. 201 (1st edition, 1861).

Mouffe C. (1994), Le politique et ses enjeux. Pour une démocratie plurielle, La Découverte/M.A.U.S.S., collection 'Recherches'.

Mutelesi E. (1998), Subjectivité comme auto-organisation. Une étude du constructivisme radical au départ de Husserl, dissertation doctorale à l'Institut Supérieur de Philosophie, Université Catholique de Louvain, Louvain-La-Neuve, Belgique, http:///www.univie.ac.at/constructivism/books/mutelesi/4html, 02/04.

Nifle R. (2004a), 'Qu'est-ce qu'une communauté humaine?', www.coherences.com, 25/07.

Nifle R. (2004b), 'Mondes et communautés humaines', www.coherences.com, 21/07.

OECD (2004), Principles of corporate governance, www.oecd.org/dataoecd/32/18/31557724.pdf.

Pauchant T. et collaborateurs (1996), La quête du sens, Les Editions d'Organisation.

Pauchant T. et collaborateurs (2000), Pour un management éthique et spirituel. Défis, cas outils et questions, Editions FIDES – Presses HEC, Montréal, Canada.

Perez R. (2002), 'L'actionnaire socialement responsable: mythe d'hier ou réalité de demain?', Revue Française de Gestion, vol 28, no. 141, pp. 131-151.

Pesqueux Y. (2006), 'Organisation et institution', Congrès de l'Association Francophone de Comptabilité, Tunis, 10-12 mai.

Ricoeur P. (2002), 'Ethique', Encyclopaedia Universalis, version 8 (DVD).

Sainsaulieu R., Tixier P-E. & Marty M-O. (1983), La Démocratie en organisation, Librairie des Méridiens.

Schumpeter J.A. (1989), Essays: on entrepreneurs, innnovations, business cycles, and the evolution of capitalism, Addison Wesley, New Brunswick (USA) et Oxford (UK), 1st edition, 1951.

Shleifer A. et Vishny R.W. (1989), 'Management entrenchement: the case of managers specific investments', Journal of Financial Economics, vol. 25, pp. 123-139.

Simon R. (1993), Ethique de la responsabilité, Editions du Cerf.

Tabatoni P. et Jarniou P. (1975), Les systèmes de gestion, politiques et structures, Presses Universitaires de France.

Thibierge C. (2004), 'Le droit souple: réflexions sur les textures du droit', RTD Civ., pp. 599-628.

Tönnies F. (1977), Communauté et société, Catégories fondamentales de la sociologie pure, Presses Universitaires de France, collection 'Les classiques des sciences humaines' (translated from Gemeinschaft und Gesellschaft, Darmstadt, 1887).

Vattimo G. éd. (2002), 'Communauté', Encyclopédie de la philosophie, Le Livre de Poche.

Walzer M. (1997), Pluralisme et démocratie, Esprit.

Williamson O.E. (1993), 'Calculativeness, trust, and economic organization', Journal of Law and Economics, no. 36, pp. 453-486.

Wirtz P. (2005), 'Meilleures pratiques de gouvernance et création de valeur: une appréciation des codes de bonne conduite', Comptabilité Contrôle Audit, tome 11, vol. 1, pp. 141-159.

4 Redefining Sustainability

GÜLER ARAS AND DAVID CROWTHER

Introduction

Sustainability is one of the most overused words in business in the present time. And the meanings attached to its use are so varied and vague as to render it effectively meaningless. In this chapter therefore we start by identifying an appropriate meaning for the concept before considering how sustainability can be applied in business. In doing so we set the concept within the current debates about sustainability and sustainable development. We then extend this to develop our definition of sustainability and its four aspects. This is further extended then to show that sustainability must be applied in a global environment to both the operational activities of a company and to the distributional decisions which are made.

The term sustainability appears in all corporate reports, is frequently in the media and also in academic writing. It is apparent however that different meanings are attached to the term so some would argue that it is an empty phrase. Nevertheless the term sustainability currently has a high profile within the lexicon of corporate endeavour. Indeed it is frequently mentioned as central to corporate activity without any attempt to define exactly what sustainable activity entails. This is understandable as the concept is problematic and subject to many varying definitions – ranging from platitudes concerning sustainable development to the deep green concept of returning to the 'golden era' before industrialisation – although often it is used by corporations merely to signify that they intend to continue their existence into the future.

The ubiquity of the concept and the vagueness of its use mean that it is necessary to re-examine the concept and to consider how it applies to corporate activity. In this chapter therefore we do just this – examining what is meant by sustainability – and looking at the various aspects of sustainability. For us there are two aspects to this – corporate actions and their consequences; and the distribution of the benefits accruing from such corporate activity. Furthermore both have to be set not just within the sphere of the corporation itself, or even the wider context of its stakeholders, but also within the widest geospatial context – that of the global environment.

Many people talk about *the triple bottom line* as if this is the panacea of corporate social responsibility and therefore inevitably concerned with sustainability. We regard it as self-evident that corporations needs to be concerned with these three aspects of Corporate Social Responsibility (CSR) and equally self-evident that all corporations are so concerned. This is not new and is not really what CSR is all about. Instead we focus our concern differently and reuse *the going concern principle* of accounting to argue that what really matters for a corporation's continued existence is the notion of sustainability. For us this is the cornerstone of both CSR and of corporate activity.

One problem is the fact that the dominant assumption by researchers is based upon the incompatibility of optimising, for a corporation, both financial performance and social/environmental performance. In other words financial performance and social/environmental performance are seen as being in conflict with each other through this dichotomisation. Consequently most work in the area of corporate sustainability does not recognise the need for acknowledging the importance of financial performance as an essential aspect of sustainability and therefore fails to undertake financial analysis alongside – and integrated with – other forms of analysis for this research. We argue that this is an essential aspect of corporate sustainability and therefore adds a further dimension to the analysis of sustainability.

The Social Contract

A growing number of writers over the last quarter of a century have recognised that the activities of an organisation impact upon the external environment and have suggested that such an organisation should therefore be accountable to a wider audience than simply its shareholders. Such a suggestion probably first arose in the 1970s[1] and a concern with a wider view of company performance is taken by some writers who evince concern with the social performance of a business, as a member of society at large. This concern was stated by Ackerman (1975) who argued that big business was recognising the need to adapt to a new social climate of community accountability, but that the orientation of business to financial results was inhibiting social responsiveness. McDonald & Puxty (1979) on the other hand maintain that companies are no longer the instruments of shareholders alone but exist within society and so therefore have responsibilities to that society, and that there is therefore a shift towards the greater accountability of companies to all participants. Implicit in this concern with the effects of the actions of an organisation on its external environment is the recognition that it is not just the owners of the organisation who have a concern with the activities of that organisation. Additionally there are a wide variety of other stakeholders who justifiably are concerned with those activities, and are affected by those activities. Those other stakeholders have not just an interest in the activities of the firm but also a degree of influence over the shaping of those activities. This influence is so significant that it can be argued that the power and influence of these stakeholders is such that it amounts to quasi-ownership of the organisation. Indeed Gray, Owen & Maunders (1987) challenge the traditional role of accounting in reporting results and consider that, rather than an ownership approach to accountability, a stakeholder approach, recognising the wide stakeholder community, is needed.[2] Moreover Rubenstein (1992) goes further and argues that there is a need for a new social contract between a business and its stakeholders.

---

1   Although philosophers such as Robert Owen were expounding those views more than a century earlier.

2   The benefits of incorporating stakeholders into a model of performance measurement and accountability have however been extensively criticised. See for example Freedman & Reed (1983), Sternberg (1997, 1998) and Hutton (1997) for details of this ongoing discourse.

Central to this social contract is a concern for the future which has become manifest through the term sustainability. This term sustainability has become ubiquitous both within the discourse globalisation and within the discourse of corporate performance. Sustainability is of course a controversial issue and there are many definitions of what is meant by the term. At the broadest definition, sustainability is concerned with the effect which action taken in the present has upon the options available in the future (Crowther, 2002). If resources are utilised in the present then they are no longer available for use in the future, and this is of particular concern if the resources are finite in quantity. Thus raw materials of an extractive nature, such as coal, iron or oil, are finite in quantity and once used are not available for future use. At some point in the future, therefore, alternatives will be needed to fulfil the functions currently provided by these resources. This may be at some point in the relatively distant future but of more immediate concern is the fact that as resources become depleted then the cost of acquiring the remaining resources tends to increase, and hence the operational costs of organisations tend to increase.[3]

Sustainability therefore implies that society must use no more of a resource than can be regenerated. This can be defined in terms of the carrying capacity of the ecosystem (Hawken, 1993) and described with input-output models of resource consumption. Thus the paper industry for example has a policy of replanting trees to replace those harvested and this has the effect of retaining costs in the present rather than temporally externalising them. Similarly motor vehicle manufacturers such as Volkswagen have a policy of making their cars almost totally recyclable. Viewing an organisation as part of a wider social and economic system implies that these effects must be taken into account, not just for the measurement of costs and value created in the present but also for the future of the business itself.

Such concerns are pertinent at a macro level of society as a whole, or at the level of the nation state but are equally relevant at the micro level of the corporation, the aspect of sustainability with which we are concerned in this work. At this level, measures of sustainability would consider the rate at which resources are consumed by the organisation in relation to the rate at which resources can be regenerated. Unsustainable operations can be accommodated for either by developing sustainable operations or by planning for a future lacking in resources currently required. In practice organisations mostly tend to aim towards less unsustainability by increasing efficiency in the way in which resources are utilised. An example would be an energy efficiency programme.

Sustainability is a controversial topic because it means different things to different people. Nevertheless there is a growing awareness (or diminishing naivety) that one is, indeed, involved in a battle about what sustainability means and, crucially, the extent (if at all) it can be delivered by MNCs in the easy manner they promise (United Nations Commission on Environment and Development (Schmidheiny, 1992). The starting point must be taken as the Brundtland Report (WCED, 1987) because there is explicit agreement with that Report and because the definition of sustainability in there is pertinent and widely accepted. Equally, the Brundtland Report is part of a policy landscape being explicitly fought over by the United Nations, Nation states and big business through the

---

3   Similarly once an animal or plant species becomes extinct then the benefits of that species to the environment can no longer be accrued. In view of the fact that many pharmaceuticals are currently being developed from plant species still being discovered this may be significant for the future.

vehicles of the WBCSD and ICC, (see for example, Beder, 1997; Mayhew, 1997; Gray & Bebbington, 2001).

There is further confusion surrounding the concept of sustainability: for the purist sustainability implies nothing more than stasis – the ability to continue in an unchanged manner – but often it is taken to imply development in a sustainable manner (Marsden, 2000; Hart & Milstein, 2003) and the terms sustainability and sustainable development are for many viewed as synonymous. Ever since the Bruntland Report was produced by the World Commission on Environment and Development in 1987 there has been a continual debates concerning development (Chambers, 1994; Pretty, 1995) and this has added to the confusion between sustainability and sustainable development. For us we take the definition as being concerned with stasis; at the corporate level if development is possible without jeopardising that stasis then this is a bonus rather than a constituent part of that sustainability.

Most analysis of sustainability (for example, Dyllick & Hockerts, 2002) only recognises a two-dimensional approach of the environmental and the social. A few (for example, Spangenberg, 2004) recognise a third dimension which is related to organisation behaviour. We argue that restricting analysis to such dimensions is deficient. One problem is the fact that the dominant assumption by researchers is based upon the incompatibility of optimising, for a corporation, both financial performance and social/environmental performance. In other words financial performance and social/environmental performance are seen as being in conflict with each other through this dichotomisation (see Crowther, 2002). Consequently most work in the area of corporate sustainability does not recognise the need for acknowledging the importance of financial performance as an essential aspect of sustainability and therefore fails to undertake financial analysis alongside – and integrated with – other forms of analysis for this research.[4] We argue that this is an essential aspect of corporate sustainability and therefore adds a further dimension to the analysis of sustainability. Furthermore we argue that the third dimension sometimes recognised as organisational behaviour needs to actually comprise a much broader concept of corporate culture. There are therefore four aspects of sustainability which need to be recognised and analysed, namely:

- **Societal influence**, which we define as a measure of the impact that society makes upon the corporation in terms of the social contract and stakeholder influence.
- **Environmental impact**, which we define as the effect of the actions of the corporation upon its geophysical environment.
- **Organisational culture**, which we define as the relationship between the corporation and its internal stakeholders, particularly employees, and all aspects of that relationship.
- **Finance**, which we define in terms of an adequate return for the level of risk undertaken.

These four must be considered as the key dimensions of sustainability, all of which are equally important. Our analysis is therefore considerably broader – and more complete – than that of others. Furthermore we consider that these four aspects can be

---

4   Of course the fact that many researchers do not have the skills to undertake such detailed financial analysis even if they considered it to be important might be a significant reason for this.

resolved into a two-dimensional matrix along the polarities of internal versus external focus and short-term versus long-term focus, which together represent a complete representation of organisational performance this can be represented as the model shown in Figure 4.1.

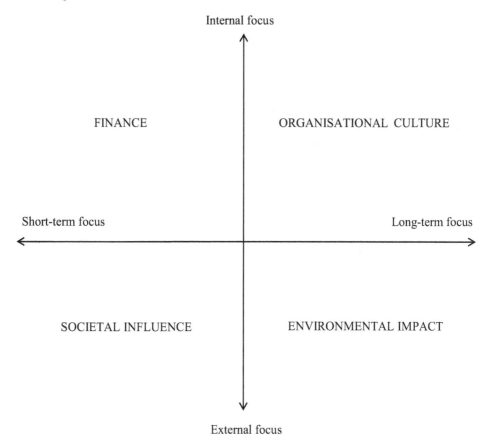

Figure 4.1   Model for evaluating sustainability

This model provides both a representation of organisation performance and a basis for any evaluation of corporate sustainability.

In order to achieve sustainable development[5] it is first necessary to achieve sustainability and there are a number of elements to this. What is important for sustainability is not just addressing each of these elements individually but also paying attention to maintaining the balance between them. It is the maintenance of this balance which is the most challenging – but also the most essential – aspect of managing sustainability. There are a number of elements which must be addressed but these can be grouped together into four major elements, which map exactly on to the model for evaluating sustainability outlined earlier. These four major elements of sustainability therefore are:

1. Maintaining economic activity, which must be the central *raison d'etre* of corporate activity and the principle reason for organising corporate activity. This of course maps on to the finance aspect.
2. Conservation of the environment, which is essential for maintaining the options available to future generations. This maps on to the environmental impact aspect.
3. Ensuring social justice, which will include such activities as the elimination of poverty, the ensuring of human rights, the promotion of universal education and the facilitation of world peace. This maps on to the societal influence aspect.
4. Developing spiritual and cultural values, which is where corporate and societal values align in the individual and where all of the other elements are promoted or negated; sadly at present they are mostly negated (see Davila-Gomez & Crowther, 2007; Crowther & Davila-Gomez, 2006a, 2006b, 2006c). This maps on to the organisational culture aspect.

Often theorists attempt to prioritise these but our argument is that it is the balancing of them equitably which is essential to developing sustainability, and hence we maintain that most considerations of the concept are unworkably simplistic. It can therefore be seen that the representation of corporate activity is considerably more complex than simply managing the stakeholder versus shareholder dichotomisation which is ever present in organisational theory.

The Conflation of Financial, Social and Environmental Performance

One view of good corporate performance is that of stewardship and thus just as the management of an organisation is concerned with the stewardship of the financial resources of the organisation so too would management of the organisation be concerned with the stewardship of environmental resources. The difference, however, is that environmental resources are mostly located externally to the organisation. Stewardship in this context therefore is concerned with the resources of society as well as the resources of the organisation. As far as stewardship of external environmental resources is concerned then the central tenet of such stewardship is that of ensuring sustainability. Sustainability is focused on the future and is concerned with ensuring that the choices of resource utilisation in the future are not constrained by decisions taken in the present. This necessarily implies such concepts as generating and utilising renewable resources, minimising pollution and using new techniques of manufacture and distribution. It also implies the acceptance of any costs involved in the present as an investment for the future.

Not only does such sustainable activity, however, impact upon society in the future; it also impacts upon the organisation itself in the future. Thus good environmental performance by an organisation in the present is in reality an investment in the future of the organisation itself. This is achieved through the ensuring of supplies and production techniques which will enable the organisation to operate in the future in a similar way to its operations in the present and so to undertake value creation activity in the future much as it does in the present. Financial management also, however, is concerned with the management of the organisation's resources in the present so that management will be possible in a value creation way in the future. Thus the internal management of the firm, from a financial perspective, and its external environmental management coincide in this common concern for management for the future. Good performance in the financial dimension leads to good future performance in the environmental dimension and vice versa. Thus there is no dichotomy (Crowther, 2002) between environmental performance and financial performance and the two concepts conflate into one concern. This concern is of course the management of the future as far as the firm is concerned.[6] The role of social and environmental accounting and reporting and the role of financial accounting and reporting therefore can be seen to be coincidental. Thus the work required needs be concerned not with arguments about resource distribution but rather with the development of measures which truly reflect the activities of the organisation upon its environment. These techniques of measurement, and consequently of reporting, are a necessary precursor to the concern with the management for the future – and hence with sustainability.

Similarly the creation of value within the firm is followed by the distribution of value to the stakeholders of that firm, whether these stakeholders are shareholders or others. Value, however, must be taken in its widest definition to include more than economic value as it is possible that economic value can be created at the expense of other constituent components of welfare such as spiritual or emotional welfare.[7] This creation of value by the firm adds to welfare for society at large, although this welfare is targeted at particular members of society rather than treating all as equals. This has led to arguments by Tinker (1988), Herremans et al (1992) and Gray (1992), amongst others, concerning the distribution of value created and to whether value is created for one set of stakeholders at the expense of others. Nevertheless if, when summed, value is created then this adds to welfare for society at large, however distributed. Similarly good environmental performance leads to increased welfare for society at large, although this will tend to be expressed in emotional and community terms rather than being capable of being expressed in quantitative terms. This will be expressed in a feeling of well-being, which will of course lead to increased motivation. Such increased motivation will inevitably lead to increased productivity, some of which will benefit the organisations, and also a desire to maintain the pleasant environment which will in turn lead to a further enhanced environment, a further increase in welfare and the reduction of destructive aspects of societal engagement by individuals.

Thus increased welfare leads to its own self-perpetuation. In the context of welfare also therefore financial performance and environmental performance conflate into a general concern with an increase in welfare.

---

6   Financial reporting is of course premised upon the continuing of the company – the going concern principle.

7   See for example Mishan (1967), Ormerod (1994) and Crowther, Davies & Cooper (1998). This can be equated to the concept of utility from the discourse of classical liberalism.

The Ownership of Performance

Agency theory suggests that the management of an organisation should be undertaken on behalf of the owners of that organisation, in other words the shareholders. Consequently the management of value created by the organisation is only pertinent insofar as that value accrues to the shareholders of the firm. Implicit within this view of the management of the firm, as espoused by Rappaport (1986) and Stewart (1991) amongst many others, is that society at large, and consequently all stakeholders to the organisation, will also benefit as a result of managing the performance of the organisation in this manner. From this perspective, therefore, the concerns are focused upon how to manage performance for the shareholders and how to report upon that performance (Myners, 1998).

This view of an organisation has however been extensively challenged by many writers (for example, Herremans et al., 1992; Tinker, 1985) who argue that the way to maximise performance for society at large is to both manage on behalf of all stakeholders and ensure that the value thereby created is not appropriated by the shareholders but is distributed to all stakeholders. Others such as Kay (1998) argue that this debate is sterile and that organisations maximise value creation not by a concern with either shareholders or stakeholders but by focusing upon the operational objectives of the firm and assuming that value creation and equitable distribution will thereby follow.

Adherents to each of these conflicting philosophies have a tendency to adopt different perspectives on the evaluation of performance. Thus good performance for one school of thought is assumed to be poor performance for the others. Thus performance maximising philosophies are polarised in the discourse and this leads to a polarisation of performance reporting and the creation of the dialectic considered earlier. Almost unquestioned within the discourse however is the assumption that good performance from one aspect necessitates the sacrificing of performance from the other, despite the ensuing distributional conflicts being hidden within the discourse. Indeed Kimberley et al (1983) have argued that some areas of performance which are important to the future of the business are not even recognised let alone evaluated. It is argued in this chapter that the future orientation of performance management necessitates the creation of value over the longer term for all stakeholders and moreover that this value creation must be manifest in the way in which the value created in the organisation is distributed among the various stakeholders. It is only in this way that the continuing temporal existence of the organisation can be ensured.

It can readily be seen that the differing needs of different parties in the evaluation process causes tensions within the organisation as it seeks to meet its internal control, strategy formulation and accountability functions and produce a reporting structure to meet these needs. While the basic information required to satisfy these needs is the same organisational information, or at least derives from the same source data, the way in which it is analysed and used is different, which can lead to conflict within the organisation. Such conflict is exacerbated when a measure is adapted for one need but only at the expense of a deterioration in its appropriateness for another purpose. It is for this reason that accounting and information systems in organisations are in a constant state of development and enhancement as the systems are designed to meet perceived needs and adapted to meet newly identified needs. One such source of conflict in an organisation therefore is caused by the different stakeholders seeking to access and use information differently, and this conflict tends to have a dysfunctional impact upon organisational cohesiveness and ultimately performance. Performance therefore can also be viewed deterministically in that it can be considered to be as good as it is evaluated to be, and Fish (1989) argues that contextually, truth and belief are synonymous for all practical purposes.

One factor of importance in performance evaluation is the concept of sustainability as far as performance is concerned. It is therefore important for all stakeholders to be able to ascertain, or at least project, not just current performance but its implications for the future. Performance evaluation must therefore necessarily have a future orientation for all evaluations. The appropriate measures are likely to facilitate a better projection of the sustainability of performance levels and the future impact of current performance. This is because the addressing of the needs of all stakeholders is likely to reveal factors which will impact upon future performance and which might not be considered if a more traditional approach was taken towards performance evaluation. An example might be the degree to which raw materials from renewable resources have become significant to many industries recently but were not considered at all until recently by any stakeholders of an organisation other than community and environmental pressure groups.

Sustainability Reporting

There have been many claims (see Crowther, 2000) that the quantification of environmental costs and the inclusion of such costs into business strategies can significantly reduce operating costs by firms; indeed this was one of the main themes of the 1996 Global Environmental Management Initiative Conference. Little evidence exists that this is the case but Pava and Krausz (1996) demonstrate empirically that companies which they define as 'socially responsible' perform in financial terms at least as well as companies which are not socially responsible. It is accepted however that different definitions of socially responsible organisations exist and that different definitions lead to different evaluations of performance between those deemed responsible and others. Similarly in other countries efforts are being made to provide a framework for certification of accountants who wish to be considered as environmental practitioners and auditors. For example the Canadian Institute of Chartered Accountants is heavily involved in the creation of such a national framework. Azzone, Manzini and Noci (1996) however suggest that despite the lack of any regulatory framework in this area a degree of standardisation, at least as far as reporting is concerned, is beginning to emerge at an international level, one of the central arguments of this paper.

Growth in the techniques offered for measuring social impact, and reporting thereon, has continued throughout the last 25 years, during which the concept of this form of accounting has existed. However the ability to discuss the fact that firms, through their actions, affect their external environment and that this should be accounted for has often exceeded within the discourse any practical suggestions for measuring such impact. At the same time as the technical implementation of social accounting and reporting has been developing, the philosophical basis for such accounting – predicated in the transparency and accountability principles – has also been developed. Thus some people consider the extent to which accountants should be involved in this accounting and argue that such accounting can be justified by means of the social contract as benefiting society at large.

Others have argued that sustainability is the cornerstone of social and environmental accounting and that auditing should be given prominence.

An examination of the external reporting of organisations gives an indication of the extent of socially responsible activity. Such an examination does indeed demonstrate an increasing recognition of the need to include information about this and an increasing number of annual reports of companies include some information in this respect. This trend is gathering momentum as more organisations perceive the importance of providing such information to external stakeholders. It has been suggested however that the inclusion of such information does not demonstrate an increasing concern with the environment but rather some benefits – for example tax breaks – to the company itself. One trend which is also apparent in many parts of the world, however, is the tendency of companies to produce separate social and environmental reports.[8] In this context such reports are generally termed CSR reports or sustainability reports, depending upon the development of the corporation concerned. This trend is gathering momentum as more organisations realise that stakeholders are both demanding more information and are also demanding accountability for actions undertaken. Equally the more enlightened of these corporations are realising that socially responsible activity makes business sense and actually assists improved economic performance.

This realisation obviates any need for regulation and calls into question the standards suggested by such bodies as accountability. The more progressive corporations have made considerable progress in what they often describe as their journey towards being fully socially responsible. In doing so they have developed an understanding of the priorities for their own business – recognising that CSR has many facets and needs to be interpreted differently for each organisation – and made significant steps towards both appropriate activity and appropriate reporting of such activity. The steps towards CSR can be likened to increasing maturity as all organisations progress towards that maturity by passing through the same stages (see below), although at different paces. The most mature are indeed recognising that nature of globalisation by recognising that the organisational boundary is permeable (see Crowther & Duty, 2002) and that they are accountable also for the behaviour of other organisations in their value chain.

All businesses[9] recognise the business benefits of CSR activity in their reporting. Equally all business recognise that sustainability is important and it features prominently in their reporting. Indeed it is noticeable that extractive industries – which by their very nature cannot be sustainable in the long term – make sustainability a very prominent issue. Any analysis of these statements regarding sustainability, however, quickly reveals the uncertainty regarding what is meant by this sustainability. Clearly the vast majority do not mean sustainability as defined in this chapter, or as defined by the Brundtland Report. Often it appears to mean little more than that the corporation will continue to exist in the future. Our argument is not just that this focus upon such a vague notion of sustainability is misleading and obfuscates the need for a rigorous debate about the meaning of sustainability. Our argument is that this treatment of sustainability is actually

---

8   Originally these were called environmental reports. Now they are normally known either as CSR reports or as sustainability reports.

9   We base our assertion regarding *all businesses* upon our study of the FTSE100 businesses, and so recognise that our claim may not have universal truth.

disingenuous and disguises the very real advantages that corporations obtain by creating such a semiotic of sustainability.

Sustainability and the Cost of Capital

It is recognised in the financial world that the cost of capital which any company incurs is related to the perceived risk associated with investing in that company – in other words, there is a direct correlation between the risk involved in an investment and the rewards which are expected to accrue from a successful investment. Therefore it is generally recognised that the larger, more established companies are a more certain investment and therefore have a lower cost of capital. This is all established fact as far as finance theory is concerned and is recognised in the operating of the financial markets around the world. Naturally a company which is sustainable will be less risky than one which is not. Consequently most large companies in their reporting mention sustainability and frequently it features prominently. Indeed it is noticeable that extractive industries – which by their very nature cannot be sustainable in the long term – make sustainability a very prominent issue. The prime example of this can be seen with oil companies – BP being a very good example – which make much of sustainability and are busy redesignating themselves from oil companies to energy companies with a feature being made of renewable energy, even though this is a very small part[10] of their actual operations.

Just as a company which is sustainable is less risky than one which is not then one which can claim sustainable development is even less risky and many companies mention this concept and imply that it relates to their operations. Such a company has a rosy future of continued growth, with an expectation of continued growth in profitability. An investigation of the FTSE100 for example shows that 70 per cent make a feature of sustainability while 15 per cent make a feature of sustainable development. So the cost of capital becomes lower as the certainty of returns becomes higher. We have shown in this article that the concept of sustainability is complex and problematic and that the idea of sustainable development is even more problematic. It is our argument that companies are not really addressing these issues but are merely creating an image of sustainability.[11] The language of the statements made by corporations tends therefore to be used as a device for corrupting thought (Orwell 1970) by being used as an instrument to prevent thought about the various alternative realities of organisational reality. Significantly it creates an image of safety for investors and thereby reduces the cost of capital for such corporations. Such language must be considered semiotically (Barthes 1973) as a way of creating the impression of actual sustainability. Using such analysis then the signification is about inclusion within the selected audience for the corporate reports on the assumption that those included understand the signification in a common way with the authors. This is based upon an assumed understanding of the code of signification used in describing corporate activity in this way. As Sapir (1949: 554) states:

'... we respond to gestures with an extreme alertness and, one might almost say, in accordance with an elaborate and secret code that is written nowhere, known by none and understood by all'.

---

10   It needs a very careful reading of the annual report to discover this.

11   See Crowther 2002 for a full discussion of image creating in corporate reporting.

Risk Reducing

It is our argument that the methodologies for the evaluation of risk are deceived by this rhetoric and are deficient in their evaluation of risk – particularly environmental risk. In order to fully recognise and incorporate environmental costs and benefits into the investment analysis process the starting point needs to be the identification of the types of costs and revenues which need to be incorporated into the evaluation process. Once these types of costs have been identified then it becomes possible to quantify such costs and to incorporate qualitative data concerning those less tangible benefits which are not easily subject to quantification. The completion of an environmental audit will enhance the understanding of the processes involved and will make this easier. In considering environmental benefits, as distinct from financial benefits, it is important that an appropriate time horizon is selected which will enable those benefits to be recognised and accrued. This may imply a very different time horizon from one which is determined purely by the needs of financial analysis.

Once all the data has been recognised, collected and quantified it then becomes possible to incorporate this data, in financial terms, into an evaluation which incorporates risk in a more consistent manner. It is important to recognise benefits as well as costs, and it is perhaps worth reiterating that many of these benefits are less subject to quantification and are of the less tangible and image related kind. Examples include:

- enhanced company or product image – this in itself can lead to increased sales;
- health and safety benefits;
- ease of attracting investment and lowered cost of such investment;
- better community relationships – this can lead to easier and quicker approval of plans through the planning process;
- improved relationship with regulators, where relevant;
- improved morale among workers, leading to higher productivity, lower staff turnover and consequently lower recruitment and training costs;
- general improved image and relationship with stakeholders.

Many of these benefits are not just intangible but will take some time to realise. Hence the need to select an appropriate time horizon for the evaluation of the risk and associated effects. This time horizon will very likely be a longer one than under a traditional financially based evaluation. Obviously cash flows need to be considered over that period and an appropriate method of evaluation (for example, a discounted cash flow technique) needs to be used in the evaluation. None of this will change with the incorporation of environmental accounting information, except for assessment of risk and its associated impact upon the cost of capital, which can be expected to rise as the true extent of the environmental impact is fed into the calculation.

The steps involved in the incorporation of environmental accounting into the risk evaluation system can therefore be summarised as follow:

- identify environmental implications in term of costs and benefits;
- quantify those costs and incorporate qualitative data regarding less tangible benefits;

- use appropriate financial indicators;
- set an appropriate time horizon which allows environmental effects to be fully realised.

The Distributional Problem

It is apparent however that any actions which an organisation undertakes will have an effect not just upon itself but also upon the external environment within which that organisation resides. In considering the effect of the organisation upon its external environment it must be recognised that this environment includes both the business environment in which the firm is operating, the local societal environment in which the organisation is located and the wider global environment. This effect of the organisation can take many forms, such as:

- the utilisation of natural resources as a part of its production processes;
- the effects of competition between itself and other organisations in the same market;
- the enrichment of a local community through the creation of employment opportunities;
- transformation of the landscape due to raw material extraction or waste product storage;
- the distribution of wealth created within the firm to the owners of that firm (via dividends) and the workers of that firm (through wages) and the effect of this upon the welfare of individuals.

It can be seen from these examples that an organisation can have a very significant effect upon its external environment and can actually change that environment through its activities. It can also be seen that these different effects can in some circumstances be viewed as beneficial and in other circumstances be viewed as detrimental to the environment. Indeed the same actions can be viewed as beneficial by some people and detrimental by others.[12] This is why planning enquiries or tribunals, which are considering the possible effects of the proposed actions by a firm, will find people who are in favour and people who are opposed. This is of course because the evaluation of the effects of the actions of an organisation upon its environment are viewed and evaluated differently by different people.

An organisation therefore is completely embedded into its environment as the actions it takes have such wide-ranging effects. Thus one of the key aspects of sustainability is concerned with distribution of the effects of its actions. The traditional approach to this was to record profit as internal to the organisation and treat everything else as an externality to be ignored. Thus the sole discussion was concerned with the distribution of the profit resulting from corporate activity: to owners as their return for bearing risk; to managers as their reward for creating profit; and to be retained for future profitability enhancement.

---

12   See Child (1984) and Crowther (1996) regarding the different dimensions of performance.

Such an approach of course ignores two aspects of corporate activity:

1. it is possible to earn an increase in profit (as recorded by accounting) simply by externalising costs;
2. it is not realistically possible to earn profit without the cooperation – active or passive – of the other stakeholders to the organisation.

Thus the social accounting approach is to recognise all costs and benefits resulting from an organisation's activities and to focus upon a distribution of these to ensure that all stakeholders are satisfied – a satisficing approach common within the social accounting literature.[13] The underlying principle is that if all stakeholders are satisfied then conflict between them will cease and all will cooperate for mutual benefit.

Thus the performance of businesses in a wider arena than the stock market and its value to shareholders has become of increasing concern. Fetyko (1975) considered social accounting as an approach to reporting a firm's activities and stressed the need for identification of socially relevant behaviour, the determination of those to whom the company is accountable for its social performance and the development of appropriate measures and reporting techniques. Klein (1977) also considered social accounting and recognises that different aspects of performance are of interest to different stakeholder groupings, distinguishing, for example, between investors, community relations and philanthropy as areas of concern for accounting. He also considered various areas for measurement, including consumer surplus, rent, environmental impact and non-monetary values. While these writers considered, by implication, that measuring social performance is important without giving reasons for believing so, Solomons (1974) considered the reasons for measuring objectively the social performance of a business. He suggested that while one reason is to aid rational decision making, another reason was of a defensive nature.

Unlike other writers, Solomons not only argued for the need to account for the activities of an organisation in term of its social performance but also suggested a model for doing this, in terms of a statement of social income. His model for the analysis of social performance is shown in Figure 4.2

This approach however still fails to recognise the realities of the global environment (see Aras & Crowther, 2007a; 2007b) insofar as the company is firmly embedded into a global environment which necessarily takes into account the past and the future as well

---

Analysis of Social Performance

£

Statement of Social Income:

Value generated by the productive process	xxx
+ unappropriable benefits	xxx
- external costs imposed on the community	xxx
Net social profit / loss	xxx

Figure 4.2   Analysis of social performance

---

13   See for example Crowther (2000); Gray & Bebbington (2001).

as the present. This effectively makes a stakeholder out of everything and everybody both in the present and in the future. This is illustrated in Figure 4.3.

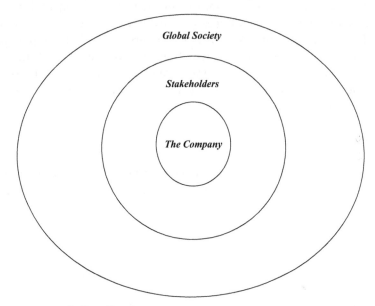

Figure 4.3   Aspects of distribution

Sustainability therefore requires a distribution of effects – positive and negative – in a way which eliminates conflict between all of these and pays attention to the future as well as the present. Thus a short-term approach is no longer acceptable for sustainability and Figure 4.4 represents such an approach to sustainability.

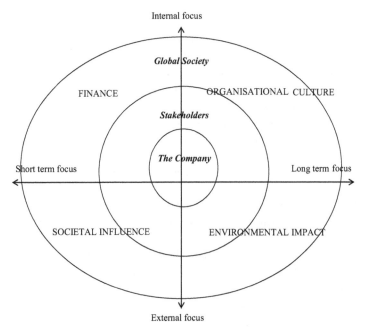

Figure 4.4   Model of sustainable distribution

Conclusion

Sustainability is, of course, fundamental to a business and its continuing existence. It is equally fundamental to the continuing existence not just of current economic activity but also of the planet in a way which we currently understand. It is a complex process, as we have discussed. Moreover it is a process which must recognise not just the decision being made in the operational activity of the organisation but also the distributional decisions which are made. Only then can an organisation be considered to be sustainable.

References

Ackerman R W (1975); *The Social Challenge to Business*; Cambridge, MA; Harvard University Press.

Aras G & Crowther D (2007a); Is the global economy sustainable?; in S Barber (ed), *The Geopolitics of the City* pp 165-194, London; Forum Press.

Aras G & Crowther D (2007b); Sustainable corporate social responsibility and the value chain; In M M Zain & D Crowther (eds), *New Perspectives on Corporate Social Responsibility* pp 119-140, Kuala Lumpar; MARA University Press.

Azzone G, Manzini R & Noel G (1996); Evolutionary Trends in Environmental Reporting; *Business Strategy and Environment*, 5 (4), 219-230.

Barthes R (1973); *Mythologies*; trans A Lavers; London; HarperCollins.

Beder S (1997); *Global Spin: The Corporate Assault on Environmentalism*; London; Green Books.

Chambers, R (1994); The Origins and Practice of Participatory Rural Appraisal; *World Development*, 22 (7), 953-969.

Child J (1984); *Organisation: A Guide to Problems and Practice*; London; Harper & Row.

Crowther D (1996); Corporate Performance Operates in Three Dimensions; *Managerial Auditing Journal*, 11 (8), 4-13.

Crowther D (2000); *Social and Environmental Accounting*; London; Financial Times Prentice Hall.

Crowther D (2002); *A Social Critique of Corporate Reporting*; Aldershot; Ashgate.

Crowther D, Davies M & Cooper S (1998); Evaluating Corporate Performance: A Critique of Economic Value Added; *Journal of Applied Accounting Research*, 4 (3), 2-34.

Crowther D & Davila-Gomez A M (2006a); Is Lying the Best Way of Telling the Truth; *Social Responsibility Journal*, 1, (3 & 4), 128-141.

Crowther D & Davila-Gomez A M (2006b); Stress in the Back Office; in *Proceedings of India - the Processing Office of the World*; Kochi, January 2006, pp. 27-38.

Crowther D & Davila-Gomez A M (2006c); I will if you will: risk, feelings and emotion in the workplace, in D Crowther & K T Caliyurt (eds), *Globalization and Social Responsibility*, Newcastle, UK; Cambridge Scholars Press, pp. 163-184.

Crowther D & Duty D J (2002); Operational Performance in Post Modern Organisations - Towards a Framework for Including Time in the Evaluation of Performance; *Journal of Applied Finance*, May, 23-46.

Davila-Gomez A M & Crowther D (2007); Psychological violence at work: where does the Human Dignity lie?; in A M Davila Gomez & D Crowther (eds), *Ethics Psyche and Social Responsibility*; Aldershot; Ashgate, pp. 15-34.

Dyllick T & Hockerts K (2002); Beyond the Business Case for Corporate Sustainability; *Business Strategy & the Environment*, 11, 130-141.

Fetyko D F (1975); The Company Social Audit; *Management Accounting*, 56 (10), 645-647.

Fish S 1989; *Is There a Text in this Class? The Authority to Interpret Communities*; Cambridge, MA; Harvard University Press.

Freedman R E & Reed D L (1983); Stockholders and Stakeholders: A New Perspective on Corporate Governance; *California Management Review*; XXV (3) 88-106.

Gray R (1992); Accounting and Environmentalism: An Exploration of the Challenge of Gently Accounting for Accountability, Transparency and Sustainability; *Accounting, Organizations & Society*, 17 (5), 399-425.

Gray R H & Bebbington K J (2001); *Accounting for the Environment*; London; Sage.

Gray R, Owen D & Maunders K (1987); *Corporate Social Reporting: Accounting and Accountability*; London; Prentice-Hall.

Hart S L & Milstein M B (2003); Creating Sustainable Value; *Academy of Management Executive*, 17 (2), 56-67.

Hawken P (1993); *The Ecology of Commerce*; London; Weidenfeld & Nicholson.

Herremans I M, Akathaparn P & McInnes M (1992); An Investigation of Corporate Social Responsibility, Reputation and Economic Performance; *Accounting, Organizations & Society*, 18 (7/8), 587-604.

Hutton W (1997); *Stakeholding and its Critics*; London; IEA Health and Welfare Unit.

Kay J (1998); Good Business; *Prospec,t* 28, March, 25-29.

Klein T A (1977); *Social Costs and Benefits of Business*; Englewood Cliffs, NJ; Prentice-Hall.

Kimberley J, Norling R & Weiss J A (1983); Pondering the performance puzzle: effectiveness in interorganisational settings; in Hall R H & Quinn R E (eds); *Organisational Theory and Public Practice*; Beverly Hills; Sage; pp 249-264.

Marsden C (2000); The New Corporate Citizenship of Big Business: Part of the Solution to Sustainability; *Business & Society Review*, 105 (1), 9-25.

Mayhew N (1997); Fading to Grey: the use and abuse of corporate executives' 'representational power'; in R. Welford (ed), *Hijacking Environmentalism: Corporate Response to Sustainable Development*; London; Earthscan; pp 63-95.

McDonald D & Puxty A G (1979); An Inducement - Contribution Approach to Corporate Financial Reporting; *Accounting, Organizations & Society*, 4 (1/2), 53-65.

Mishan E J (1967); *The Costs of Economic Growth*; Harmondsworth; Pelican.

Myners P (1998); Improving performance reporting to the market; in A Carey & J Sancto (eds), *Performance Measurement in the Digital Age*; London; ICAEW; pp 27-33.

Ormerod P (1994); *The Death of Economics*; London; Faber and Faber.

Orwell G (1970); *Collected Essays, Journalism and Letters Vol 4*; Harmondsworth; Penguin.

Pava M L & Krausz J (1996); The Association between Corporate Social Responsibility and Financial Performance: The Paradox of Social Cost; *Journal of Business Ethics*, 15 (3), 321-357.

Pretty, J.N. (1995); Participatory Learning for Sustainable Agriculture; *World Development*, 23 (8), 1247-1263.

Rappaport A 1986; *Creating Shareholder Value*; New York; The Free Press.

Rubenstein D B (1992); Bridging the Gap between Green Accounting and Black Ink; *Accounting Organizations & Society*, 17 (5), 501-508.

Sapir E (1949); The Unconscious Patterning of Behaviour in Society; in D G Mendelbaum (ed), *Selected Writings of Edward Sapir*; Berkley, CA; University of California Press.

Schmidheiny S (1992); *Changing Course;* New York; MIT Press.

Solomons D (1974); Corporate social performance: a new dimension in accounting reports?; in H Edey & B S Yamey (eds), *Debits, Credits, Finance and Profits*; London; Sweet & Maxwell; pp 131-141.

Spangenberg J H (2004); Reconciling Sustainability and Growth: Criteria, Indicators, Policy; *Sustainable Development*, 12, 76-84.

Sternberg E (1997); The Defects of Stakeholder Theory; *Corporate Governance: An International Review*, 6 (3), 151-163.

Sternberg E (1998); *Corporate Governance: Accountability in the Marketplace*; London; IEA.

Stewart G B III (1991); *The Quest for Value*; New York; Harper Collins.

Tinker T (1985); *Paper Prophets: A Social Critique of Accounting*; London; Holt, Rinehart & Winston

Tinker T (1988); Panglossian Accounting Theories: The Science of Apologising in Style; *Accounting, Organizations & Society*, 13 (2), 165-189.

WCED (World Commission on Environment and Development) (1987); *Our Common Future* (The Brundtland Report); Oxford University Press; Oxford.

KEY READING

Aras G & Crowther D (2007); Sustainable corporate social responsibility and the value chain; In D Crowther & M M Zain (eds), *New Perspectives on Corporate Social Responsibility*, pp 119-140, Kuala Lumpur; MARA University Press.

Aras G & Crowther D (2008); *The Durable Corporation: Strategies for Sustainable Development*; Aldershot; Gower.

Crowther D & Capaldi N (2007); *Research Companion to Corporate Social Responsibility*; Aldershot; Ashgate.

Hart S L & Milstein M B (2003); Creating Sustainable Value; *Academy of Management Executive*, 17 (2), 56-67.

Marsden C (2000); The New Corporate Citizenship of Big Business: Part of the Solution to Sustainability; *Business & Society Review*, 105 (1), 9-25.

Welford R (ed) (1997); *Hijacking Environmentalism: Corporate Response to Sustainable Development*; London; Earthscan.

5 The Social Contract of Business in Society

SANDRA WADDOCK

Introduction

The social contract between business and society is constantly evolving. Business's social contract has evolved from one of simply doing business with little regard to the consequences, to an era in the 1930s in which businesses were much more highly regulated, followed by an era of managerialism in which separation of ownership from control occurred. More recently, forces of globalization have placed multinational corporations in the position of being the most powerful institutions on the planet, and simultaneously companies have faced criticism about their roles and impacts. In response, companies have evolved their corporate responsibility stances, from a reactive corporate social responsibility stance that mostly involved reacting to external crises and offering charitable contributions, to a more responsive stance that involved the development of specific boundary-spanning functions. As these responses proved inadequate to calls for greater transparency, responsibility, and accountability, companies and other institutions evolved a voluntary system of responsibility assurance that emerged in the late 1990s and early 2000s, along with critiques of the corporate form itself and calls for change that continue today. This entry briefly traces this history.

In January 2008 something unusual happened. One of the richest capitalists in the world, a man who had made billions building a company that had become a world-class company, top of its field, by using some of the most aggressive competitive tactics known to capitalism, made a remarkable speech. In that speech Microsoft founder and CEO Bill Gates, speaking to the World Economic Forum in Davos, Switzerland, calling himself an 'impatient optimist,' called for a new 'creative capitalism' that would shift in a fundamental way the relationship of modern business to society.

In making his speech, Gates argued that, 'The great advances in the world have often aggravated the inequities in the world. The least needy see the most improvement, and the most needy get the least—in particular the billion people who live on less than a dollar a day.' He further noted, 'The genius of capitalism lies in its ability to make self-interest serve the wider interest. The potential of a big financial return for innovation unleashes a broad set of talented people in pursuit of many different discoveries. This system, driven by self-interest, is responsible for the incredible innovations that have improved so many lives.'

In calling for a new creative capitalism, Gates was arguing, as others have, for a new relationship of business to society, a relationship that goes well beyond the accepted maxim, popularized by the late Nobel Prize-winning economist Milton Friedman that the purpose of business is to maximize shareholder wealth. Ironically, from the perspective of someone who has created an aggressive, no-holds-barred giant of its industry, Gates' current view is that capitalism needs to be more collaborative and generative in its approach: 'I like to call this idea creative capitalism,' he said, 'an approach where governments, businesses, and nonprofits work together to stretch the reach of market forces so that more people can make a profit, or gain recognition, doing work that eases the world's inequities.'

Gates' call for a more creative capitalism echoes the call for a new 'global compact' between business and society issued to the World Economic Forum, a gathering of business leaders, by former UN Secretary Kofi Annan in 1999. In his speech, Annan challenged business leaders to give a more 'human face to the global market.' He stated, 'We have to choose between a global market driven only by calculations of short-term profit, and one which has a human face. Between a world which condemns a quarter of the human race to starvation and squalor, and one which offers everyone at least a chance of prosperity, in a healthy environment. Between a selfish free-for-all in which we ignore the fate of the losers, and a culture in which the strong and successful accept their responsibilities, showing global vision and leadership.'[1]

Kofi Annan's speech resulted in the launch two years later of the United Nations Global Compact (UNGC), today the world's largest corporate citizenship initiative. The UNGC sets forth ten core principles related to human rights, labor rights, environmental sustainability, and anti-corruption, all based on global treaties, which businesses agree to uphold in their strategies and operating practices. The UNGC has become part of the changing roles and expectations for businesses in society that have come with the advent of the twenty-first century, with companies increasingly expected not only to tout but to actually operationalize their corporate responsibilities in practice.

As the conservative magazine *The Economist* admitted in January 2008, three years after it had panned the whole corporate responsibility movement, 'Corporate social responsibility [CSR], once a do-gooding sideshow, is now seen as mainstream. But as yet too few companies are doing it well.'[2] *The Economist* admitted that despite the fact that it still believed that too much of CSR is still 'misguided or worse,' nonetheless 'in practice few big companies can now afford to ignore it.'[3]

The shifts noted above, along with many others that might be named, highlight the shifting set of roles and expectations that businesses today have in society, or the shifting social contract between business and society. In addition, they highlight the responsibilities associated with doing business in a world where issues of climate change and ecological sustainability, social equity, conflict and violence, human and labor rights, and transparency are among an emerging set of urgent issues facing businesses and have become paramount to the way that the social contract is being defined. In what follows

---

1   Kofi Annan, Business and the U.N.: A Global Compact of Shared Values and Principles, January 31, 1999, World Economic Forum, Davos, Switzerland. Reprinted in *Vital Speeches of the Day*, February 15, 1999, 65 (9): 260-261. For further information on The Global Compact, see http://www.unglobalcompact.org/.

2   Daniel Franklin, 'Just Good Business,' *The Economist*, January 17, 2008, Lead Story.

3   Franklin, 'Just Good Business,' ibid.

we will briefly trace the evolution of expectations of businesses in society, looking at the attendant shift in the social contract.

The Changing Social Contract

The social contract that exists between business and society, or more accurately with respect to business *in* society, for businesses are intricately and inextricably embedded *in* societies, helps to define what are considered be the appropriate roles, responsibilities, and relationships on both sides of the so-called contract. The notion of a social contract implies an agreement that is understood and acted upon by both parties, in this case between business and society. The nature of the particular relationship between business and society, however, has shifted over time as new challenges have arisen on both sides and different sets of expectations have emerged.

In one sense, the social contract can be thought to be formally expressed in the corporate charter, which grants companies certain rights and imposes certain obligations on them, but there is also a more informal social charter that is much more subject to shifting social interests, needs, and expectations to which corporations are subject. Below, we will first briefly discuss the formal charter; then we will move to the less formal set of social expectations that constitute the shifting social contract, and finally look at an initiative called Corporation 2020, which has generated conversation about how the purpose of the corporation should potentially be redefined in the twenty-first century.

The relationship of business to society, particularly the corporation, has been thorny right from the inception of the corporation, although of course forms of businesses, usually owner-operated, have existed for millennia. Corporations in their modern form represent a relatively new breed of organization, in that for the past couple of centuries they have been officially sanctioned or chartered by nations, typically with the idea that they will undertake certain types of business activities. In return for this corporate charter, a form of contract, companies, depending on the national origin of their charter or papers of incorporation, assume certain rights and duties. For example, they are self-governing entities, who can hire and fire people, engage in business activities and relevant contractual agreements, and have a form of legal personhood that grants them certain rights, including limited liability, and the ability to continue in existence even when the original owners are no longer present. Typically, corporations are said to be 'owned' by shareholders, who purchase a certain percentage of the ownership rights in the firm and expect a return on their investment as a product of that purchase.

Because of fears that they would grow too powerful, the earliest corporate charters were written so that companies were expected to be in existence only so long as they continued to do the business for which they were being chartered and—importantly—continued to serve the public interest (Derber, 1998). Some of these fears were realized during early days of industrialization when corporations grew enormously and made industrialists wealthy, some might say, on the backs of their workers. By the late-1900s, wealthy capitalists were becoming philanthropists in efforts to salvage their reputations and ensure their legacies. In that era what philanthropy was given came from the individuals who had grown wealthy, not the companies themselves. As companies grew in size and power, they were ultimately subjected to a movement to unionize workers who demanded gain rights with respect to their employers and to trust-busting activities by the US government in the early 1900s, which attempted to scale companies back to more manageable sizes. The 1929 stock market crash in the United States, followed by a global depression, and the ensuing New Deal by the US government, put into place new regulations that supported workers and provided some constraints on corporate behaviors.

Managerialism and Philanthropy

In their earliest days, the shares that corporations issued were owned by those who also ran the corporation, but as Berle and Means (1932) pointed out, as corporations grew both larger and more powerful, there was a separation between ownership and control with 'ownership' going to shareholders. Executives and managers, often with little formal ownership in the firm, were generally the ones actually in control of the firm and its activities. This separation of ownership and control, which Berle and Means called managerialism, combined with a 1919 court case in the US called *Dodge v. Ford*, focused the attention of company leaders on shareholders in what has become the accepted norm of 'maximizing shareholder wealth.' According to *Dodge v. Ford*, 'A business corporation is organized and carried on primarily for the profit of the stockholders.'

Yet legal scholars (for example, Greenfield, 2005; Stout, 2006) have recently argued that *Dodge v. Ford* does not in fact define the sole or only purpose of the corporation. Stout concludes that despite the apparent simplicity of an imperative for corporations to maximize shareholder wealth, it is a legal fiction to assume that corporate purpose is actually that simple. She notes that, '...simplicity is not a virtue when it leads to misunderstanding and mistake. ...Corporations seek profits for shareholders, but they seek other things as well, including specific investment, stakeholder benefits, and their own continued existence. Teaching *Dodge v. Ford* as anything but an example of judicial mistake obstructs understanding of this reality' (Stout, 2006, p. 12).

According to legal scholar Kent Greenfield, in the US the *Dodge v. Ford* case has meant that there is an 'unyielding' duty for managers to benefit shareholders, which is interpreted as wealth maximization (Greenfield, 2005, p. 11). This imperative is balanced by the 'business judgment rule,' which allows managers to make decisions that are in the long-term interests of the corporation, but even so the primary corporate objective is profit maximization (Greenfield, 2005, p. 11). In the US, notes Greenfield, some states have made efforts to relax this imperative by passing stakeholder laws, which explicitly allow managers to take into their consideration stakeholders other than shareholders. Despite the dominance of this logic—and the explicit social contract that it implies, Greenfield later argues, agreeing with management thinker Charles Handy (2002) that, 'shareholders are not owners in any traditional sense of ownership. They are not owners in any other meaningful way either, if one means that there is something that distinguishes their contribution to the firm from that of other stakeholders' (Greenfield, 2005, p. 88).

Englander and Kaufman (2004) note that managerialism combined with self interest and desire on the part of managers to hold on to their power during the mid-1980s, an era of hostile take-overs, down and 'right' sizings, and resistance to more stakeholder-oriented policies, coupled with the Reagan-Thatcher revolution, which emphasized laissez-faire government with respect to businesses and a free-market ideology, managerialism focused attention on wealth maximization for shareholders with little attention to consequences of corporate decision making for other stakeholders, signaling a shift in the social contract of business towards a narrow shareholder orientation.

During the late 1980s and into the 1990s, pay scales for executives were tied to fiduciary duties to a single stakeholder—the shareholder—through options and related financial packages, all based on share price. This emphasis neatly coincided with growth in wealthy families' participation in equity markets, which as Englander and Kaufman note, 'hardly made for a shareholder democracy' (p. 428). Complimented by ERISA's (Employee Retirement Income Security Act) definition of pension fund trustees' responsibilities as being solely to funds' beneficiaries 'made it impossible for these trustees to consider the corporation, in which they had invested, as anything other than an instrument for enhancing their funds' beneficiaries' (p. 430).

Thus, despite these relatively recent re-conceptualizations, many judicial decisions, and rulings have created a context in which perhaps the most common understanding of the purpose of the firm with respect to its social contract is that of the late neoclassical economist Milton Friedman. Friedman argued repeatedly that the purpose of the firm is singular: to maximize shareholder wealth. According this conservative neoclassical economics perspective, promulgated by Friedman and other economists of the so-called Chicago School, markets should be built upon free trade, leaving businesses largely unfettered by other types of responsibilities, or by government regulations, so that it can work toward the maximization of profits with the shareholders' interests kept firmly in mind.

The neoclassical economics view of the firm has dominated much executive and economic thinking, particularly in the United States, since the early-1980s during the era of President Ronald Reagan and UK Prime Minister Margaret Thatcher's so called Reagan-Thatcher revolution. But since the 1950s, corporations have actually been involved in society in a variety of different ways that began with corporate philanthropy and have continued to evolve as corporate responsibility and stakeholder-oriented thinking have emerged and become more sophisticated, changing the basis of the business-society contract.

The Informal Contract: Corporate Social Responsibility Emerges

Perhaps the first stage of what today can be called corporate citizenship or corporate responsibility, began with an emphasis on the social—corporate social responsibility——during the 1950s. As noted above, early industrialists had begun giving away some of their riches, often through what are today well-known foundations, such as the Rockefeller, Ford, Kellogg, and Carnegie Foundations, but these foundations were not directly associated with corporations except that the money that was used to build them had been generated for the owners by firms. During the 1950s, however, a court case called *A.P. Smith Manufacturing Company v. Barlow* (1952) established the right of companies' managers to legally make charitable contributions in the name of the company without facing legal recriminations from shareholders (Campbell, Gulas, & Gruca, 1999).

With this court decision, companies became able to make philanthropy a part of their strategy for dealing with their communities and other stakeholders, and this practice has grown steadily since. During the 1960s companies faced a great deal of social activism directed at them with the rise of the consumer and environmental movements. The criticisms by social activists put some companies on the defensive during the 1960s and into the 1970s, and one of the responses was an increase in charitable giving, as well as some efforts on the part of more progressive firms to work with communities, for example, on job training programs, the problems of cities, or education of the less advantaged. These activities were largely reactive, coming as a result of the criticisms companies were receiving, and resulted in a set of practices that ultimately gave birth to corporate social responsibility in its first phase, or what business ethicist William Frederick (2006) called CSR1.

CSR1 emerged somewhat as a defensive posture on the part of companies reacting to the criticisms being directed at them, who were attempting to demonstrate that they played a constructive role in society through their philanthropic and related community-based activities. The major orientation of CSR1 was reacting to criticisms, such as Ralph Nader's attacks on corporations or the emerging environmental movement, and in a positive way towards making charitable contributions, and many companies began establishing their own foundations during this period, in an effort to put forward a good public face around issues that seem to matter to various constituencies.

As sophistication about corporate social responsibility began to evolve, in the 1970s some companies began establishing various functions that we would now call boundary-spanning or stakeholder-engagement functions. Among the earliest of these functions was the public affairs or business-government relationships function. Other functions today include investor relations, community relations, employee relations, and customer relations, as examples. This evolution was what Frederick called corporate social responsiveness, labeled as CSR2, a more proactive stance compared to the reactive stance that CSR1 represented. Companies moving into CSR2 were attempting to scan their external—or stakeholder—environments (although this period began before stakeholder terminology became popular) so that they could avoid unpleasant surprises and deal more proactively with possible issues that were arising before they became problematic. In a sense the emergence of these functions reflected a shifting social contract between business and society, in which businesses felt that they had to deliberately put forward a positive face by engaging proactively with different constituencies to avoid the kinds of criticisms that they had received in the 1960s.

Two important signifiers of the need to enhance corporate responsibility occurred in the 1980s. First was the 1984 industrial accident in Bhopal, India, in which a pesticide plant owned and operated by Union Carbide spilled tons of toxic chemicals into the air, killing nearly 4,000 people and injuring tens of thousands of others in which was one of the worst chemical spills in history. The second major event that drew public attention to issues of corporate responsibility was the 1989 Exxon Valdez 11 million gallon oil spill in Prince William Sound, Alaska's formerly pristine waters. As a result of the publicity associated with these disasters, both companies were put into the spotlight and issues of their responsibility were brought to the surface. These disasters made clear in a highly public forum that whatever progress had been made in implementing CSR programs, more work needed to be done.

Concurrently with these major events, a series of defense industry contractor scandals around issues of corruption and bribery during the 1980s focused public and company attention on issues of ethics. This attention coincided with an influx of scholars into management from philosophy and resulted in the development of the field of business ethics. On the company side, many companies began implementing codes of conduct, typically dealing relatively narrowly with anti-corruption and anti-bribery mechanisms, along with the institution of compliance and ethics officers, to help them avoid future scandals. Noting this development Frederick developed the concept of CSR3 (corporate social rectitude, terminology that never became popular), by which he meant a focus on integrating consideration of ethics into business decision making.

Although the CSR3 terminology did not catch on, the notion of having a code of ethics in business gained a foothold and many business ethics scholars began writing both from philosophical and managerial perspectives, and a good deal of attention was focused on how businesses could be more responsible and more ethical in their actions. With respect to the social contract of business in society, the implication of this new thinking about business ethics was that business activities and their impacts could no longer be considered separately. Although it would be years until a more integral perspective emerged, these early codes of ethics and the early thinking about business ethics planted seeds that would later grow.

Corporate Stakeholder Relationships

Simultaneously with the emergence of business ethics and the new understanding of business's need to operate ethically in society, another stream of work began to emerge in the mid-1980s, following publication of the seminal book by R. Edward Freeman, *Strategic Management: A Stakeholder Approach*. Stakeholder theory, as argued by Freeman, suggested a managerial approach to thinking not specifically about the responsibilities or ethics of businesses as they operated in society, but very practically about how businesses might better manage themselves to be more effective by paying closer attention to the needs, demands, and interests of important stakeholders. Like the interpenetrating systems model of Preston and Post (1975), which had placed business in its societal context in the mid-1970s, stakeholder thinking placed businesses in the context of a network of stakeholders with which, if it were to be successful, it had to have interactive and engaged relationships.

Stakeholder theory implies a much more interactive and engaged set of relationships between businesses and other social actors than did corporate social responsibility framings, which imply a more or less one-way relationship of business operating 'on' society. At least conceptually, stakeholder thinking implies a two-way relationship with stakeholders themselves having some degree of claim or power over what companies do, although in practice companies mostly maintained the dominant role over their stakeholders. As stakeholder thinking began to take hold, companies entered into an era during the late-1980s and early-1990s of corporate restructurings, mergers and acquisitions, and increased emphasis on shareholder value, which brought even more public attention to their responsibilities, now expressed as responsibilities to stakeholders and the natural environment, which is a different way of phrasing the business-society interface. All of this combined with the power of the Internet to increase demands on companies for greater accountability, responsibility, and transparency coming from a wide range of stakeholders.

By the mid-1990s, some companies had begun to think in terms of relating to or engaging with their stakeholders (including those representing the natural environment). In 1995 two seminal events happened to Royal Dutch Shell, one of the world's largest oil companies. First, the company ran into a buzzsaw of protest from Greenpeace, the activist organization, when it attempted to dispose of its Brent Spar oil rig, which had outlived its usefulness, in the North Sea. Second, the company became associated with the execution of social activist Ken Saro-Wiwa and his associates in Nigeria, because of the company's involvement in oil extraction in that country. Facing significant external criticism and public pressure, Shell launched itself into efforts at corporate transformation that would provide both a better public face for the firm and enable it to better engage with its stakeholders—and, it was hoped, avoid future reputational problems. Issuing its first 'triple bottom line' report, focused on 'people, planet and profits,' or more generically, social, ecological, and economic issues.

During this era, globalization proceeded apace and many other companies began developing their own multiple bottom line reporting schemes in their efforts to put forward a good public face in society. Anti-corporate and anti-globalization activism exploded in 1999 when the World Trade Organization (WTO) attempted to meet in Seattle, Washington, protests that were followed by others around the planet whenever the WTO tried to meet. Companies had, in many respects, become the most powerful institutions in the world, as government powers had slowly eroded over the past 20 years and free market ideology, fostered by the so-called Brettan Woods organizations formed after World War II (the World Trade Organization, International Monetary Fund, and World Bank), had taken firm hold in the minds of executives, economists, and many others.

A Responsibility Infrastructure Puts Pressure on Corporate Responsibilities

The increasing power of companies combined with intensifying anti-corporate activism, particularly for multinational corporations, fostered a need, particularly on the part of MNCs, to put forward a good public face to ensure that what some called their 'license to operate' in society would be continued. This need manifested in growing attention to corporate responsibilities to stakeholders and the natural environment, expressed variously as corporate social responsibility, corporate responsibility, corporate citizenship, and, increasingly, using the language of sustainability. By the mid-1990s, although the dominant logic about corporations was and continues to be that they should maximize shareholder wealth, other stakeholder considerations had begun to make their way into corporate thinking in the form of a wide range of corporate responsibility initiatives. Some of these are still of the philanthropic or deliberately 'social good' variety, while others were increasingly being linked to corporate strategies and practices in what Porter and Kramer (2006) characterized as strategic CSR.

In part these shifts began to occur because of a growing external infrastructure surrounding companies that focused more attention on the responsibility inherent in their strategies and practices. For example, the social investment movement, which focused broadly not just on negative products or services offered by companies, but increasingly on both positive and negative aspects of stakeholder-related practices, with information becoming more widely available, had been steadily building since the anti-Apartheid movement in the 1980s had focused attention on corporate divestment from that country.

By the late-1990s and into the early-2000s, when a wave of corporate scandals brought attention to corporate governance as well as fraudulent practices in some large companies, this infrastructure also included a responsibility assurance framework. The responsibility assurance framework included emerging new sets of standards or codes, such as the UN Global Compact, or the OECD Guidelines for Multinational Enterprises, or any number of other sets of codes that had been promulgated to provide a set of standards of practice or behavior to which companies were increasingly expected to adhere. Another element of the responsibility infrastructure was a growing array of organizations that not only set standards for company practices, but also were willing to audit the companies to ensure that those standards were being met. Such certification, monitoring, and verification services provided companies with social audits from an independent, albeit company-paid, perspective and had somewhat more credibility and expertise than would internal audits have had.

The third element of the responsibility infrastructure is a structure similar to Generally Accepted Accounting Principles (GAAP) in the accounting world, a standardized reporting framework for non-financial matters that were reported in increasingly popular triple or multiple bottom line reports issued more commonly by large firms as a way of establishing their credentials as good corporate citizens. The emerging global standard for non-financial reporting is the Global Reporting Initiative, a multi-stakeholder alliance that provided a framework for consistent reporting on Ecological, Social, and Governance (ESG) issues.

The relationship between business and society was also being framed differently by activists and Non-Governmental Organizations (NGOs), who were frequently highly critical of corporations, and whose numbers had grown rapidly. To deal with these groups, many companies began engaging in multi-stakeholder dialogues, social partnerships and other forms of collaboration, and social enterprises aimed at producing profits through business activity focused on dealing with a social or ecological problem. Companies and other social actors also gathered frequently in an emerging array of convenings and conferences dealing with issues of corporate responsibility and sustainability, some business only (such as the World Business Council for Sustainable Development), and others involving multiple types of entities. Added pressure was being placed on companies by various ranking and rating schemes that generally focused attention on particular company practices, such as their treatment of employees or their environmental performance.

Integrative Social Contracts Theory

The emergence of codes of conduct and set of principles during the 1990s and well into the 2000s created somewhat of a new context for business, in that the specific aspirational standards that were expected to be met were being laid out. The UN Global Compact (UNGC) had become the world's largest corporate citizenship initiative by 2008, with nearly 5,000 signatories, 3,700 of which were companies, to its ten principles. Because the UNGC was based on globally agreed treaties signed by the nations of the world, its ten relatively simple and aspirational principles had some degree of moral authority. Companies that signed the UNGC explicitly agreed to uphold these principles, as did companies that signed similar codes or principles of which there was a proliferation.

Business ethicists Thomas Donaldson and Thomas Dunfee explicitly focused on the notion of business's social contract with their Integrative Social Contract Theory (ISCT) and attempted to determine whether there were underlying norms of behavior that provided an ethical foundation for business practice that could be set forth in principles like the UNGC. Drawing from the work of earlier philosophers including Locke and Rawls, these scholars argued that ISCT links two streams of thinking, a hypothetical or 'macro' social contract that exists that ties community members to each other and an 'extant' or 'micro' contract, which specifies actual, though sometimes informal, agreements in communities (Donaldson & Dunfee, 1999, p. 19). The more macro agreement is an implicit or informal understanding of the relationship of individuals (or organizations) to the broader society, while the micro agreements are far more specific to individual entities, more like explicit contracts or agreements between parties.

Underpinning both the formal and informal social contracts, according to Donaldson and Dunfee, is a set of what they termed hypernorms—universal principles by which other principles, including social contracts, can be judged—combined with 'moral free space,' which constitutes the macro social contract. At the global level, ISCT provides this moral free space so that local economic communities can generate their members' ethical norms through more specific micro social contracts, grounded in individual rights to exit and use their voice, and when legitimate compatible with broader hypernorms (Donaldson & Dunfee, 1999, p. 47).

In earlier work, Donaldson (1996, p. 6) had identified respect for core human values, local traditions, and the belief that context matters when deciding what is right and wrong as useful for helping find hypernorms. In turn, these aids would help focus on what Donaldson and Dunfee claimed were three basic values: respect for human dignity, respect for basic rights, and respect for good citizenship, which involves working together to support and improve the institutions on which the community depends. Like the UNGC, hypernorms (to the extent that they exist) are transcultural and apply to all, hence derive from widely accepted sources.

Donaldson & Dunfee (1999, p. 68) report ten basic rights that Donaldson himself had earlier identified, the right to: freedom of physical movement, ownership of property, freedom from torture, fair trial, nondiscriminatory treatment, physical security, freedom of speech and association, minimal education, political participation, and subsistence. This type of thinking, without the philosophical trappings, underpins much of the emergence of codes of conduct, principles, and standards that corporations acting in society now face.

The application of principles like those of the UNGC or the set identified by Donaldson and Dunfee or others means that companies' responsibilities to stakeholders in society are beginning to be conceived more broadly than the narrow conception embedded in the shareholder wealth maximization maxim suggests. At the same time, as Robert Reich pointed out in his book *Supercapitalism*, expectations of the modern corporation are still very much dominated by demands for wealth generation by shareholders, most of which today are institutional owners, rather than individual shareholders, and by consumers who demand high quality at reasonable prices. Indeed, he argues that without greater and different regulatory mechanisms to control the behavior and practices of firms in society, corporate responsibility initiatives alone are unlikely to achieve the social benefits that increasingly are at the center of attention: ecological sustainability (and dealing with climate change), social equity (in the face of a growing gap between rich and poor), and conflict reduction, to name just a few.

Shifting Relationships Between Business and Society

These issues surrounding businesses' roles in society create some degree of tension. As issues of ecological sustainability have gained public attention, so too has attention been directed at the role that processes of industrialization—and the corporation in particular—have played in creating the problems. The regulatory framework surrounding business has shifted over time from at first having business beholding to society for producing some public good to then being criticized and regulated during the early part of the twentieth century to a wave of deregulation that took place in the late-1970s and early-1980s with the emergence of free market ideology. Since the mid-1990s in particular the mostly voluntary corporate (social) responsibility movement has created, as noted above, a new responsibility assurance framework intended in part to place new kinds of pressures on businesses for greater responsibility. There is a constant interplay of efforts to regulate business activities and control the corporation with countervailing efforts to free the firm from restraints and let the market do its work.

Externalities created by over-reliance on market mechanisms (for example, pollution, possibly climate change, sweatshops, deforestation, desertification, and growing inequity) ultimately create a need for different or new regulations and with the advent of the Internet have also brought far greater visibility—and a degree of transparency earlier not possible—to corporate activities. The emergence of the voluntary responsibility approaches by corporations and related institutions represents at one level a set of initiatives designed to forestall further regulatory moves by governments, and at another level a set of corporate-led initiatives designed to foster greater peer pressure and responsibility. Many activists, however, deride these efforts as mere window dressing that fails to deal with the fundamental issues of power and wealth distribution at the heart of growing corporate dominance in society.

Whether a voluntary set of initiatives can significantly change business's role in society and rebuild what some, including Reich (2007), claim are faltering democratic institutions that result from increased interlinkages between businesses and government, is yet unclear. What does seem clearer is that critiques of the corporation are likely to continue as long as this form maintains its current dominance in society. Because there is inherently greater transparency in a world where instant communications are possible, companies will continue to have to respond to the changing expectations of society. One set of possible changes will be briefly explored below.

The Future of the Corporation—the Corporation of the Future

Given the tension that exists around business's social contract, it is not surprising that some thinking about the nature and purpose of the corporation in the twenty-first century has begun to evolve. Anti-corporate sentiment has found its way into numerous movies and books (including the fairly radical book and movie called *The Corporation* by Joel Bakan, but also many others) as well as into initiatives to take away the corporate personhood in the law in the United States that has formed the foundation for many of the rights claimed by corporations. As noted earlier, recent legal scholarship has begun questioning the premise that the purpose of the firm is to maximize shareholder wealth, and one legal scholar (Greenfield, 2005) argues for a set of five new principles for US corporate law, which if implemented would be quite radical. Those principles are:

1. The ultimate purpose of corporations should be to serve the interests of society as a whole.
2. Corporations are distinctively able to contribute to the society good by creating financial prosperity.
3. Corporate law should further principles one and two.
4. A corporation's wealth should be shared fairly among those who contribute to its creation.
5. Participatory, democratic corporate governance is the best way to ensure the sustainable creation and equitable distribution of corporate wealth.

Another initiative that has begun asking fundamental questions about the nature of the corporation has been started in Boston by the think tank Tellus Institute. Corporation 20/20 is a multi-stakeholder initiative that seeks to answer the question, 'What would a corporation look that was designed to seamlessly integrate both social and financial purpose?'

The goal of Corporation 20/20 is to develop and disseminate corporate designs where social purpose moves from the periphery to the heart of future organizations. The idea is premised on the view that polarized choices about the future of the corporation as either free market or strict regulation are flawed and counterproductive. Corporation 20/20 posits a third path: *system redesign*. This path is grounded in recognition that the existing corporate forms characterized rooted in shareholder primacy, directors duties to shareholders, capitalization oriented to short-term profits, minimal accountability to non-shareholder interests are in urgent need of redefinition.

While the corporate responsibility and governance movements have achieved some notable progress, a more systemic, integrated transformation is both needed and plausible at this moment in history. Redesign aims at such transformation by shifting the focus from the 'what' and 'how' of corporate wealth creation to the nature and purpose of the corporation itself. The initiative has developed six Principles of Corporate Redesign that are used to inspire the proposed redesign:

1. The purpose of the corporation is to harness private interests to serve the public interest.
2. Corporations shall accrue fair returns for shareholders, but not at the expense of the legitimate interests of other stakeholders.
3. Corporations shall operate sustainably, meeting the needs of the present generation without compromising the ability of future generations to meet their needs.
4. Corporations shall distribute their wealth equitably among those who contribute to its creation.
5. Corporations shall be governed in a manner that is participatory, transparent, ethical, and accountable.

6. Corporations shall not infringe on the right of natural persons to govern themselves, nor infringe on other universal human rights (www.corporation2020.org).

Whatever comes of initiatives like Corporation 2020 or the proposal for new principles of corporate law, it is clear that the tension that exists between business and society will continue to shift and evolve over time as companies attempt to establish their proper role in society and as societies attempt to determine the basis of legitimacy on which corporations rest. The heart of the matter is one of control—control of the corporation or by the corporation, and these are questions that are fundamental to the long-term health and well-being of societies, the natural environment, and those who live within them.

The continuing evolution of the social contract between business in society is apparent when successful entrepreneurs like Bill Gates call for a more 'creative capitalism.' Or when the CEO of the world's largest retailer Wal-Mart, subject to numerous criticisms for its social policies, calls for an emphasis on sustainability and drives that through its supply chain as the retail giant is now doing. Or when Klaus Schwab, executive chair of the World Economic Forum, states that, 'a new imperative for business, best described as "global corporate citizenship," must be recognized. It expresses the conviction that companies not only must be engaged with their stakeholders but are themselves stakeholders alongside governments and civil society' (Schwab, 2008).

References

Berle, A., and Means, G. (1932). *The Modern Corporation and Private Property*. New York: Macmillan.

Campbell, L., Gulas, C.S. and Gruca T.S. (1999). Corporate Giving Behavior and Decision-Maker Social Conscience. *Journal of Business Ethics*, May, 19 (4): 376-382.

Derber, C. (1998). *Corporation Nation: How Corporations Are Taking Over Our Lives and What We Can Do About It*. New York: St. Martin's Press.

Donaldson, T. (1996). Values in Tension: Ethics Away from Home. *Harvard Business Review*, September-October, Reprint # 96402, 1-12.

Donaldson, T. and Dunfee T.W. (1999). *Ties that Bind: A Social Contracts Approach to Business Ethics*. Boston: Harvard Business School Press.

Englander, E. and Kaufman A. (2004). The End of Managerial Ideology: From Corporate Social Responsibility to Corporate Social Indifference. *Enterprise & Society*, 5 (3): 404-531.

Frederick, W.C. (2006). *Corporation, Be Good: The Story of Corporate Social Responsibility*. Indianapolis, IN: Dog Ear Publishing.

Freeman, R.E. (1984). *Strategic Management: A Stakeholder Approach*. Boston: Pitman.

Greenfield, K. (2005). New Principles for Corporate Law. *Hastings Business Law Journal*, May, 1: 87-118.

Handy, C. (2002). What's a Business For? *Harvard Business Review*, December, 49-55.

Porter, M.E., and Kramer M.R. (2006). Strategy and Society: The Link Between Competitive Advantage and Corporate Social Responsibility. *Harvard Business Review*, December, 78-92.

Preston, L.E., and Post J.E. (1975). *Private Management and Public Policy*. New York: Prentice-Hall.

Reich, R.B. (2007). *Supercapitalism: The Transformation of Business, Democracy, and Everyday Life*. New York: Knopf.

Schwab, K. (2008). Global Corporate Citizenship: Working with Business and Society. *Foreign Affairs*, January/February, http://www.foreignaffairs.org/20080101faessay87108/klaus-schwab/global-corporate-citizenship.html, accessed April 15, 2008.

Stout, L.A. (2006). 'Why We Should Stop Teaching Dodge v. Ford' . UCLA School of Law, Law-Econ Research Paper No. 07-11 Available at SSRN: http://ssrn.com/abstract=1013744.

KEY REFERENCES FOR FURTHER READING

Freeman, E.R., Harrison, J., and Wicks A. (2007). *Managing for Stakeholders: Business in the 21st Century*. New Haven: Yale University Press.

Donaldson, T. and Preston L.E. (1995). The Stakeholder Theory of the Corporation: Concepts, Evidence, and Implications. *Academy of Management Review*, January, 20: 1, 65-91.

Greenfield, K. (2007). A New Era for Corporate Law: Using Corporate Governance to Benefit All Stakeholders. 2007 Summit on the Future of the Corporation, paper series, 19-28.

Marens, R. and Wicks A. (1999). Getting Real: Stakeholder Theory, Managerial Practice, and the General Irrelevance of Fiduciary Duties Owed to Shareholders, *Business Ethics Quarterly*, April, 9 (2): 273-293.

Waddock, S. (2006). *Leading Corporate Citizens: Vision, Values, Value Added*, 2nd edition. New York: McGraw-Hill.

White, A.L. (2007). Is It Time to Rewrite the Social Contract? Business for Social Responsibility White Paper, http://www.bsr.org/reports/bsr_aw_social-contract.pdf (accessed April 15, 2008).

6 *The Shifting Meaning of Sustainability*

MARY A KAIDONIS, NATALIE P STOIANOFF AND
JANE ANDREW

Introduction

Sustainability, as a concept, gained momentum as international non-government organizations developed the term. The United Nations' Brundtland Report is credited with first referring to sustainability as having three necessary and coexisting components being, environmental, economic and social sustainability. International accounting professional institutions also responded to this momentum, at first with an in principle adoption of the term. As sustainability reporting accompanied financial reporting, the concepts of business were also imposed on the term. The objective of global equity was surpassed by financial terminology which also prioritized concepts of risks and opportunities to explore market potentials.

There is no doubt that we are in 'the age of sustainability' and it will be hard to 'escape the pressures of the global sustainability movement' (Newson, 2003, p. 1). The use of the term sustainability has been equated with 'good environmental management' (Bebbington, 2001, p. 128) and its meaning has been adapted and 'moulded' (Bebbington, 2001, p. 128; Bebbington and Gray, 2001) so that it has been used in a variety of contexts and referred to as 'sustainable business, sustainable development, sustainable growth, environmental sustainability [and] social sustainability' (Bebbington, 2001, p. 129). Indeed the term 'sustainability' has become a popular and persuasive marketable concept.

In this chapter we consider how the meaning of sustainability has shifted. We argue that the shift has been facilitated by some prominent international Non-Government Organizations (NGOs) and their uses of the term. NGOs' role in shifting the meaning of the term is important for a number of reasons. First, NGOs have a unique and important role in society in general and in particular, the societies which form them also implicitly support and affirm the NGOs' actions and commentary. Secondly, international NGOs can have a huge global reach and hence, influence. Indeed '(t)oday's NGOs are skilful communicators, mediators, managers and intermediaries. They are proficient … international information exchange networks' (Global Environment Facility, 2002, p. xiii). Therefore NGOs can perpetuate the use of the term sustainability, but also influence the meaning of the term, even if this influence is inadvertent.

We begin by looking at international NGOs which have published reports on sustainability. We then address international accounting institutions and their responses to sustainability. A term such as sustainability may have different meanings in different contexts and these contexts can be associated with assumptions which need not be explicit. There are a number of international efforts which reflect the importance of sustainability. We discuss three of these and start with the Brundtland Report 1987, not because there were not earlier references to social and environmental concerns, but because of its influence on subsequent United Nations' reports and conferences (see Bebbington, 2001).

Global Equity

In 1987 the World Commission on Environment and Development published 'Our Common Future' which is also known as the Brundtland Report. This report is widely credited as 'a pivotal document' (Bebbington, 2001, p. 131) and refers to sustainable development as 'development that meets the needs of the present without compromising the ability of future generations to meet their own needs' (United Nations World Commission on Environment and Development, 1987, p. 64). The term therefore had a vast perspective of accountability for and to future generations. Further, it was expected that the term sustainable development would also incorporate economic and ecological issues which would impact on how future decisions are made (United Nations World Commission on Environment and Development, 1987). Therefore it can be argued that intergenerational responsibility of the economy and the environment was an important feature of sustainable development whether it was by organizations or nations. The United Nations represents an international institution which had an instrumental role in drawing attention to the concept of sustainability. The Brundtland Report highlighted three components of sustainable development being: environmental protection, economic growth and social equity and collectively these components would work towards 'securing global equity' (Brundtland Report, 2006).

In 1992, the United Nations Conference on Environment and Development in Rio de Janeiro was another global event having an impact on the sustainability movement. This conference (commonly referred to as the Earth Summit) has 'heralded an unprecedented era of environmental awareness' (Global Environment Facility, 2002, p. xiii). The Earth Summit produced a plan of action, referred to as Agenda 21. The principles of Agenda 21 have been adopted by 178 Governments (United Nations Division for Sustainable Development, 2004). This number of nations engaging with Agenda 21, reinforces the extensive global reach that a NGO such as the United Nations can have.

Agenda 21 refers to both sustainable development and sustainability, and uses these as interchangeable terms as well as to connote specific meanings. For example, there are references to 'sustainable development in developing countries', as well as, 'sustainable human settlement' (United Nations Division for Sustainable Development, 2004). When reference is made to 'sustainable agriculture' it is under the heading of conservation and management of resources for development (United Nations Division for Sustainable Development, 2004). Agenda 21 also has specific reference to '(g)lobal action for women towards sustainable and equitable development' as well as reference to '(c)hildren and youth in sustainable development' (United Nations Division for Sustainable Development, 2004). Agenda 21 therefore provides more detail about the extent to which sustainable development can impact the lives of people in order to achieve social and environmental global equity. Agenda 21 also recognizes explicitly that social and environmental global equity needs to be supported by financial resources from 'national and international cooperation and capacity-building' (United Nations Division for Sustainable Development, 2004). Therefore the economic component of sustainability is to enable social and environmental needs rather than limit or delineate such needs.

Business Conceptions of Sustainability

In this section we have focused on accounting institutions which have membership from many countries and which have specifically responded to issues of sustainability. Another NGO, an international accounting association, the European Federation of Accountants (FEE), produced and commissioned reports or discussion papers and also referred to the Brundtland Report. The 2002 report, in particular, commented that, 'the Brundtland definition relates to the macro level and is not directed to individual entities' (European Federation of Accountants, 2002, p. 13), which can be taken to mean that global equity is only a broad goal for society. The FEE also added a qualifying sentence stating, '(h)owever, progress towards sustainability at an individual level or organizational level is a necessary part of this' (European Federation of Accountants, 2002, p. 13). Organizations or businesses have progressed towards sustainability, and in so doing, have also shifted the meaning of sustainability.

As well as the FEE, the Association of Chartered Certified Accountants (ACCA) and the International Federation of Accountants (IFAC) were noteworthy in responding to the call for sustainability. The ACCA has offices in over 30 countries as well as members and students in 160 countries and accordingly can claim to have a vast 'global reach' (ACCA, 2004a, p. 3; ACCA 2004b). It has produced and/or commissioned reports related to sustainability. The first of these reports was on 'business conceptions of sustainability and the implications for accountancy' (Bebbington and Thomson, 1996). In interviews of environmental managers and accountants, it was noted that the definition and the goal of sustainable development was 'not in question' (Bebbington and Thomson, 1996, p. 2-3) even if the definition itself was 'not clear' (Bebbington and Thomson, 1996, p. 1). Hence business managers supported the concept of sustainability in principle, even if business 'is not sustainable at present' (Bebbington and Thomson, 1996, p. 3). It seems business managers acknowledged that 'human activity, especially in the West, is also not sustainable' (Bebbington and Thomson, 1996, p. 3). These comments point to an interpretation of sustainability which acknowledges environmental and social concerns, or 'eco-efficiency issues ... and ...eco-justice issues (Bebbington and Thomson, 1996, p. 3). The report did reveal that sustainability for business was still not a consistent or a well-formed idea (Bebbington and Thomson, 1996). As such, it seems inevitable that the meaning of sustainability would shift to one with which businesses could engage.

This business engagement offered opportunities for accounting and accountants to play a role in the meaning of sustainability. More importantly, it was recognized that since accounting is 'a powerful driver of current organizational behaviour, [it] is going to be part of any future drive towards sustainability' (Bebbington and Thomson, 1996, p. 3). Initially accountants' role was limited to the domains of full costing of sustainability (Bebbington and Thomson, 1996) at least in the first instance of engaging with sustainability. The domain of full costing implied including the costs of sustainability in the organization's costs. This means that concepts which are familiar with the discipline of accounting would be invoked with the effect of sustainability being couched in financial terms. Therefore, the ideas of social and environmental sustainability, as well as concepts of global equity, need to fit into specific financial concepts. By definition, financial concepts require quantifiable components to which monetary values are assigned. The potential problem with such quantification is that aspects of sustainability which may not be readily quantifiable, such as global equity, can be left out or not adequately represented. Further, financial language is also associated with principles of business and can invoke the imperative of organizational profit, particularly, if the organization participates in capital markets. We contend that expressing sustainability in financial terms can have a limited connection to the ethos of sustainability.

A contrasting view to this is given by Chambers and Lewis (2001) in their ACCA report titled 'Ecological Footprinting Analysis: Towards a Sustainability Indicator for Business'. This report considered that businesses were 'essential partners in delivering both the social and environmental dimensions of sustainable development' (Chambers and Lewis, 2001 p. 1). It concentrated on indicators, using Ecological Footprint Analysis (EFA), to assess the environmental impact of businesses, recognizing that they were not addressing the social and economic dimensions of sustainability. Whilst their aims to capture the 'overall carrying capacity of the planet' (Chambers and Lewis, 2001, p. 2) were on a macro level, they recognized the problems that such indicators can have, including problems of aggregation and related assumptions, as well as limited or unreliable data (Chambers and Lewis, 2001). However, the acknowledgement of 'philosophical boundary issues' (Chambers and Lewis, 2001, p. 2), suggests to us a recognition of the problems associated with imposing financial criteria on concepts which exacerbate such intentions. Since accounting presents the financial implications of decisions related to an organization's operations, then any efforts to represent concepts of sustainability will be represented using known financial calculations. Therefore only those operations which can be accurately and reliably measured would be presented. Further, this has the potential for operations or activities which have social and environmental impact but are not readily reflected in financial terms, not to be counted. The impact of not counting can be that the organization's accountability for a particular issue of sustainability simply does not get visibility or attention. A condition of the business perspective of sustainability may be to insinuate rational decision making for sustainability as is expected of organizations' normal operations. If sustainability has a caveat, subject to economic imperatives, then its expression in financial terms may distort meanings of sustainability intended to promote protecting the planet for present and future generations.

Another ACCA Report (No 86), emphasizes that organizations have a role to play in achieving sustainability. Indeed this report asserts that organizations need to 'take responsibility for their social, environmental and economic impacts' (Zadek and Raynard, 2004, p. 1). Further, it is recommended that the extent to which responsibility is taken needs to be conveyed to the organization's stakeholders and a level of assurance of such responsibility is essential (Zadek and Raynard, 2004). In reporting the responsibility which an organization has taken means that the reporting should 'capture the entirety of a company's impacts' (Zadek and Raynard, 2004, p. 4). However, this report advocated that such assurance can only be given by a range of providers including the audit professional and civil society organizations, not a single assurance provider (Zadek and Raynard, 2004). In any case, there would need to be a set of 'Generally Accepted Accounting Principles for Sustainability (GAAPS) and Generally Accepted Assurance Standards for Sustainability (GAASS)' (Zadek and Raynard, 2004, p. 3). As the term of sustainability was meant to be all encompassing, it created confusion and attempts to report on it were inconsistent. This inconsistency in reporting triggered efforts to operationalize sustainability reporting. Accompanying such efforts for clarity, were further shifts in the term sustainability.

Standardization, Guidelines and Indexes

The Earth summit also stimulated efforts to standardize operational guidelines. The International Organization for Standardization's ISO 14000 on Environmental Management in 1992 'grew out of support of ISO's commitment to support the objective of sustainable development' (International Organization for Standardization, 2003). Later efforts to standardize or provide a framework reporting on sustainability were reflected by the Global Reporting Initiative (GRI) 1997 which produced a report and GRI Guidelines (Global Reporting Initiative, 2004). The GRI Guidelines are for voluntary disclosures on management performance by a firm and provides a framework to report on economic performance, environmental performance and social performance (Global Reporting Initiative, 2002). According to the GRI website, Sir Mark Moody-Stuart, a GRI board director and retired chair of Royal Dutch/Shell, considered the GRI Guidelines to be 'the most comprehensive and credible set of sustainability disclosure standards ever produced' (Global Reporting Initiative, 2006, p. 1). This claim will be put to the test in the next few years as more corporations report according to the GRI Guidelines.

As a framework the GRI considers sustainability reporting can be 'parallel' to financial reporting (Global Reporting Initiative, 2002, p. 17). The GRI goes further to suggest that the two reports together can 'enrich each other' (Global Reporting Initiative, 2002, p. 17) despite the fact that the financial reports are compulsory and sustainability reports are voluntary. In any case, the association of sustainability reporting with financial reports provides an opportunity for accounting and its related institutions to engage in the term sustainability. As well as the GRI Guidelines the term sustainability was incorporated by the Dow Jones Index, marking another shift in its meaning.

The FEE 2002 report quotes The Dow Jones Sustainability Index definition of corporate sustainability (European Federation of Accountants, 2002) and indicates a more than subtle shift in the meaning of sustainability. In the first instance the term 'corporate sustainability' may suggest how the corporation survives, and not how a corporation upholds the ethos of sustainability. The Dow Jones Sustainability Index explicitly refers to 'embracing opportunities and managing risks deriving from economic, environmental and social developments' (European Federation of Accountants, 2002, p. 13). There is a shift in the language and hence meaning of sustainability, since now corporate responsibility to social and environmental issues is replaced by opportunities and risks.

Further, this shift is underscored by The Dow Jones Sustainability Index definition requiring leaders to 'harness the market's potential for sustainability products and services' (European Federation of Accountants, 2002, p. 13). It may be appropriate for a market index to exploit a market potential, however, the point here is that in this FEE report, the definition of sustainability shifts from the Brundtland Report's definition to the Dow Jones Sustainability Index without recognizing any potential contradiction in meaning.

The FEE 2004 report is also noteworthy because it refers to another international accounting institution, namely the International Federation of Accountants (IFAC), noting that its membership 'consists of 158 professional accountancy bodies in 118 countries, representing 2.5 million accountants in public practice, industry and commerce, government and education' (European Federation of Accountants, 2004, p. 16). It can be inferred that reports from such institutions have the potential for the proliferation and the shifting meaning of sustainability.

The IFAC also responded to sustainability. The IFAC linked the international attention to sustainability to the 'unprecedented growth in population and consumption, global resource depletion, and broadening expectations regarding social and environmental accountability' (International Federation of Accountants, 2006, p. 1). In this reference, the meaning of sustainability is taken back to a more macro or global perspective. However, at the same time the IFAC recognized the importance of the GRI proposed Sustainability Reporting Guidelines (G3) and aimed to attract comment from professional accountants 'with some familiarity with sustainability assurance' (International Federation of Accountants, 2006, p. 1). There is an implicit assumption that the role of accountants is significant as assurance providers. Early Australian accounting responses also focused on assurance services.

Triple Bottom Line

CPA Australia expressed its commitment to 'demonstrating transparency and accountability beyond the domains of financial performance' (CPA Australia, 2004, p. ii) in a summary report of the *Triple Bottom Line – a study of assurance statements worldwide*. The report and the summary focused on assurance statements on publicly released documents about an organization's social, environmental and economic performance, that is, an organization's Triple Bottom Line (TBL) (CPA Australia, 2004, and Deegan et al., 2004). Although this report does not explicitly refer to sustainability, it does refer to the three aspects of sustainability. In studying 161 organizations worldwide, it was found that there was no consensus or generally accepted framework for undertaking TBL assurance engagements (CPA Australia, 2004).

The CPA Australia 2005 report investigated 'current sustainability/Triple Bottom Line (TBL) reporting practices in Australia' (Jones et al., 2005, p. 1). They noted an 'inability or reluctance of organizations to modify or develop tools, processes and frameworks through which they can report their direct and indirect economic, social and environmental impacts to stakeholders' (Jones et al., 2005, p. 19). The project refers to TBL and sustainability reporting as synonymous and recognizes that these have become 'catch-phrases to capture the notion of entities reporting to stakeholders not only on their economic performance, but also on their performance in relation to the environment and society' (Jones et al., 2005, p. 3). The research report considered private sector and public sector entities against the GRI Guidelines and described the GRI as 'an internationally recognized framework for reporting on sustainability issues that is used by many entities throughout the world' (Jones et al., 2005, p. 72). The researchers found that there were 'low levels of sustainability reporting' (Jones et al., 2005, p. 19). Further, of the entities which did report, they identified a lack of consistency and range of responses as a challenge for the accounting profession (Jones et al., 2005).

For instance, the CPA Australia 2005 report provided an analysis of financial performance of companies reporting on sustainability, an analysis of financial performance of socially responsible investment funds, as well as considering market-adjusted returns and sustainability (Jones et al., 2005). Whilst this analysis not only highlights a range of expressions, it also demonstrates how accounting can prioritize financial aspects and in so doing can distort the meaning of sustainability. It seems inevitable that accounting would analyze sustainability from financial and market perspectives. This analysis can therefore influence an organization to use criteria based on economic rationality alone to address sustainability issues.

Conclusion

If sustainability issues are couched in terms of business or financial perspectives, then this can usurp the environmental and social imperative. Accordingly, considering sustainability or sustainability reporting in terms of market-adjusted returns by accounting professions may not be surprising since these are concepts with which the accounting profession is familiar. However, the accounting institutional responses have been demonstrated to engage in a language which gives prominence and privilege to economic markets. If accounting persists in viewing and understanding sustainability from a business perspective, it can be complicit in organizations merely to perpetuate the status quo. Given the professions vast global reach, the potential for the business perspective to override the intention of sustainability should not be underestimated. In accounting or business and corporations' enthusiasm to embrace sustainability, we draw attention to the shifting meaning of sustainability where the emphasis shifts from global social and environmental equity.

References

Association of Chartered Certified Accountants (ACCA), 2004a, 'ACCA's membership reaches 100,000', *Teach Accounting*, ACCA, Issue 4, p. 3.

Association of Chartered Certified Accountants (ACCA), 2004b, *Your route to success*, ACCA, Glasgow.

Bebbington, J., 2001, 'Sustainable Development: A Review of International Development, Business and Accounting Literature', *Accounting Forum* 25, 2: 128-57.

Bebbington, J., and Gray R., 2001, 'An Account of Sustainability: Failure, Success and a Reconceptualization', *Critical Perspectives on Accounting* 12, 557-87.

Bebbington and Thomson, 1996, 'Business Conceptions of Sustainability and the Implications for Accountancy', *ACCA Research Report* No. 48, pp. 1-3.

Brundtland Report, 2006, The Brundtland Report (http://www.ace.mmu.ac.uk/eae/Sustainability/Older/Brundtland_Report.html accessed 10 February 2006).

Chambers and Lewis, 2001, 'Ecological Footprinting Analysis: Towards a Sustainability Indicator for Business', *ACCA Research Report* No 65, pp. 1-3.

CPA Australia, 2004, *Summary report on Triple Bottom Line: a study of assurance statements worldwide*, CPA Australia.

Deegan, C., Cooper B. and Shelly, M., 2004, *Triple Bottom Line: a study of assurance statements worldwide*. CPA Australia's Audit and Assurance Centre of Excellence.

European Federation of Accountants (FEE), 2002, *FEE discussion paper providing assurance on sustainability reports*, European Federation of Accountants (FEE).

European Federation of Accountants (FEE), 2003, *Benefits of sustainability assurance*, European Federation of Accountants (FEE).

European Federation of Accountants (FEE), 2004, *FEE Call for action: assurance for sustainability* European Federation of Accountants (FEE).

Global Environment Facility, 2002, *The Challenge of Sustainability, an action agenda for the global environment*, Global Environment Facility, Washington.

Global Reporting Initiative, 2002, *Sustainability reporting guidelines*, Global Reporting Initiative, Boston.

Global Reporting Initiative, 2004, *Building sustainability into the fabric of the Global Reporting Initiative, Sustainability Report 1 July 2003-30 June 2004*, Global Reporting Initiative.

Global Reporting Initiative, 2006, *About G3*, (http://www.grig3.org/aboutg3.html accessed 14 February 2006).

International Federation of Accountants (2006) IFAC consultation paper explores assurance aspects of proposed sustainability reporting guidelines, IFAC, (http://accountingeducation.com/index.cfm?page=newsdetail&id=142345 accessed 20 February 2006).

International Organization for Standardization, 2003, 'ISO and the environment' (http://www.iso.org/iso9000-14000 accessed 14 July 2003).

Jones, S., Frost G., Loftus, J. and van der Laan, S., 2005, *Sustainability reporting: practices, performance and potential*, CPA Australia.

Newson, M., 2003, 'The age of sustainability', a PriceWaterhouseCoopers *Briefings* publication, June 2003, http:www.pwcglobal.com?Extweb/manissue.nsf/docid/D4CBD9628DEEF46CA256. accessed 14/07/2003.

United Nations World Commission on Environment and Development, 1987, *Our Common Future (The Brundtland Report)* Oxford University Press, Oxford.

United Nations Division for Sustainable Development, 2004, Agenda 21, http://www.un.org/esa/sustdev/documents/agenda21/index.htm, accessed 12 March 2006)

Zadek, S, and Raynard, P., 2004, 'The Future of Sustainability Assurance', *ACCA Research Report* No 86, pp. 1-8.

7 Corporate Social Responsibility and Accounting

STUART COOPER

Introduction

Traditionally accounting as a discipline has been associated with 'the process of measuring, analysing and communicating economic information' (American Accounting Association, 1966). In this traditional accounting the economic, or financial, information has been communicated through two primary statements, namely: the income statement (or profit and loss account); and the balance sheet. The balance sheet is designed to provide an indication of a business' financial position (or strength) at a particular point in time. The income statement reports the financial performance of a business for a period of time and results in the bottom line of retained profit (the profit that is retained for the owners of the business).

These traditional financial statements may appear to have little to do with Corporate Social Responsibility (CSR) and this is largely true, although in 1962 Friedman famously suggested that:

> 'there is one and only one social responsibility of business – to use its resources and engage in activities designed to increase profits'.

Friedman continued that the only check on increasing profits should be to engage 'in open and free competition, without deception or fraud'. Many other definitions of CSR have since been provided and Carroll (1999) provides an informative history of the evolution of the concept of CSR. Carroll provided a four-part definition of CSR in 1979 and in 1983 this was further elaborated as follows:

> 'In my view, CSR involves the conduct of a business so that it is economically profitable, law abiding, ethical and socially supportive. To be socially responsible ... that means that profitability and obedience to the law are foremost conditions to discussing the firm's ethic and the extent to which it supports the society in which it exists with contributions of money, time and talent. Thus, CSR is composed of four parts: economic, legal, ethical and voluntary or philanthropic.'

(Carroll, 1983, p. 604, as cited in Carroll, 1999, p. 286)

Carroll's definition is broader than Friedman's in that it suggests going beyond what is required by the rules of the game and identifies ethical and voluntary dimensions to CSR. In fact Carroll's definition does not explicitly require corporations to increase, or maximise, profit, but rather requires some level of profitability to be present, as a condition for the furtherance of the more ethical and voluntary aspects of CSR. Carroll (1999) also provides alternative CSR definitions from the 1960s that corporations have 'certain responsibilities to society' (McGuire, 1963, p. 144) and emphasises the effect of their actions 'on the whole social system' (Davis, 1967, p. 46). Carroll refers to his own 1991 paper, which argues that 'the term 'social' in CSR has been seen by some as vague and lacking in specificity as to whom the corporation is responsible' (1999, p. 290). He continues that the value of Freeman's (1984) stakeholder concept is that it 'personalizes social or societal responsibilities by delineating the specific groups or persons business should consider in its CSR orientation and activities'. Although Freeman's 'Strategic Management: A Stakeholder Approach' text is a seminal text in this area he actually refers to an internal memorandum at the Stanford Research Institute in 1963 as an earlier use of the 'stakeholder' term, and Preston and Sapienza (1990) traced the approach, as opposed to the term, back a further 30 years. Even within Carroll's history of CSR we can see that what we now conceive as a stakeholder approach was in existence before 1984, as evidenced by Johnson's (1971, p. 50) definition:

> *A socially responsible firm is one whose managerial staff balances a multiplicity of interests. Instead of striving only for larger profits for its stockholders, a responsible enterprise also takes into account employees, suppliers, dealers, local communities, and the nation.*

Certainly within the accounting literature that considers CSR it is now common to see a link between CSR and stakeholder accountability (see for example: Gray et al., 1996; and O'Dwyer, 2003).

There is, therefore, an alternative, broader conception of CSR that goes beyond economic and legal responsibilities to shareholders. Rather it incorporates ethical and voluntary considerations to a broader set of stakeholders. It is this broader conception of CSR that will be used in this chapter. This chapter considers how accounting systems can, and have, been used to measure, analyse and communicate information of a broader nature than has been traditionally the case.

The remainder of this chapter is divided into three main sections. Firstly, there is a section that considers the performance measurement systems that have been developed to augment the traditional financial measures used by corporate managers. These performance measurement systems are used internally and are therefore equivalent to, or replacing, more traditional management accounting systems. This is then followed by a section that considers developments in CSR reporting practices that now augment more traditional financial reporting. Finally, the chapter concludes by discussing the possible future of CSR and accounting.

Performance Measurement Systems

The primary purpose of management accounting is to provide information to assist managers in managing their business. Traditionally the information provided has been financial in nature and performance has been measured through profitability, efficiency and financial stability as measured through profit and loss accounts, balance sheets and derivative measures thereof. The appropriateness of these traditional performance measures, however, has been called into question. A particularly influential critique was published by Johnson and Kaplan (1987) and entitled 'Relevance Lost: The Rise and Fall of Management Accounting'. They argued that performance measures, which draw upon traditional accounting information, are inadequate in that they are backward looking and that they do not adequately reflect all of the perspectives of a corporation's performance (see Brignall, 2007, for a more detailed consideration of this discussion). Subsequently, a number of multi-dimensional performance measurement systems have been developed that implicitly, or explicitly recognise relationships that corporations have with stakeholders other than shareholders. Furthermore, these multi-dimensional performance measurement systems do not focus solely on financial performance measurement, but also consider non-financial measures. Such performance measurement systems include: the 'results and determinants framework' (Fitzgerald et al., 1991); the 'performance pyramid' (Lynch and Cross, 1991); the 'balanced scorecard' (Kaplan and Norton, 1992, 1993); and the 'performance prism' (Neely, Adams and Kennerley, 2002). Whilst the creators of these performance measurement systems did not identify them as CSR performance measurement systems, the fact that they are not completely focused upon financial performance for shareholders does suggest a relevance to CSR. The best known and most widely used of these is Kaplan and Norton's balanced scorecard and we shall therefore now consider its CSR potential.

CORPORATE SOCIAL RESPONSIBILITY AND THE BALANCED SCORECARD

Originally the balanced scorecard, as the name suggests, aimed to balance the competing needs of a corporation. It was to do this by allowing 'managers to look at the business from four important perspectives', which were the:

- Financial perspective – how does the firm look to shareholders?
- Customer perspective – how do customers perceive the firm?
- Internal business perspective – what must the firm excel at?
- Innovation and learning perspective – can the firm change and improve to make its vision come true?

Within the early conception of the balanced scorecard the four perspectives were depicted as being equally important, each effected by a corporation's vision and strategy and suggested that the relationships between the four perspectives were many and could be in any direction. For example, Kaplan and Norton (1996a) suggests that the customer perspective affects and is affected by both the financial perspective and the learning and growth perspective. In the introduction to this chapter it was decided that a broader conception of CSR, which goes beyond the economic, or financial, perspective for shareholders would be used. It is for this reason that the balanced scorecard appears to be of more relevance to CSR than traditional management accounting. Firstly, the balanced scorecard considers perspectives beyond the financial, but is it truly a stakeholder model? Shareholders and customers are clearly identified within the financial and customer perspectives respectively. Other stakeholders can be argued to be important within the other perspectives. For example, the work processes and development of employees will be part of the internal business and learning and growth perspectives. Also, it can be argued that relationships with suppliers could be incorporated within the internal business process perspective.

Kaplan and Norton (1996b), however, state that they 'don't think that all stakeholders are entitled to a position on a business unit's scorecard'. The actual development of the balanced scorecard both in practice and in later publications by Kaplan and Norton (see 2000 for an example) does suggest that it is a tool that is not necessarily used to further the CSR practices of organisations. For example, Stringer (2005) reporting on a case study of the implementation of a balanced scorecard discusses the different weightings given to different perspectives within the case. She identifies the fact that, in this case, the organisation effectively puts an 85 per cent weighting on the financial measures within the (balanced?) scorecard. In such a case it appears that the balance has been lost and rather we see that the scorecard is very much biased towards more traditional financial measures of performance. In this example it is hard to see that the implementation of this scorecard can have truly broadened the organisation's objectives beyond one that is narrowly focused on financial, or shareholder, imperatives.

If we now consider the development of the balanced scorecard concept by Kaplan and Norton (2000) we see that a change from the balanced scorecard to the 'Balanced Scorecard Strategy Map'. Even in 1996 Kaplan and Norton (1996c) had started to discuss the 'cause and effect relationships' within 'a scorecard'. Effectively they suggested that within a scorecard some measures would relate to outcomes whilst others would be concerned with 'the performance drivers of those outcomes'. The strategy map takes this idea further and identifies causal relationships between the four perspectives of the balanced scorecard. Kaplan and Norton (2000, p. 168) provide an example of what a strategy map could look like for an organisation. The map appears very different to earlier conceptions of the balanced scorecard. In earlier versions the four perspectives were located at equal distances around the central vision and strategy of the organisation. Also, as mentioned earlier, the relationships between the different perspectives were many and reciprocal. In the strategy map there is a clear hierarchy of perspectives. At the bottom is the learning and growth perspective that affects the internal process perspective that affects the customer perspective that affects the financial perspective. The relationships identified in the strategy map are one way, upwards, and all, either directly or indirectly, are pointing towards an overarching objective, which is to 'Improve Shareholder Value'. This conception of a strategy map appears to have little to do with balance and conceptualises the other perspectives as simply a means to the shareholder value ends. It certainly appears to have little to do with the broader ethical and voluntary aspects of CSR that this paper is interested in.

The balanced scorecard strategy map has been criticised within the academic literature. Nørreklit (2000) provides a 'critical analysis' of the balanced scorecard strategy map and identifies two research questions. The first question relates to whether the cause and effect relationships identified by Kaplan and Norton actually exist. Nørreklit suggests that if the relationships are truly causal, then the strategy map should incorporate a time dimension. This is to say that there should be a lag between the observation of the cause and the subsequent observation of the effect. The time dimension is not clearly conceptualised in Kaplan and Norton's strategy map. Furthermore, Nørreklit also suggests that the relationships between the different perspectives could be causal, but could equally be circular or interdependent, either of which would more accurately reflect the original conception of the balanced scorecard. The second question relates to the validity of the strategy map as a strategic management control tool. Here the criticism relates to how the strategy map fails to 'monitor the competition or technological developments' (p. 78) and how the implicit top-down approach to control within the strategy map could create tension for relationships with internal stakeholders, most obviously employees.

Irrespective of these criticisms of the development of the balanced scorecard it is still possible that such a multi-dimensional performance measurement model could be of use within the CSR practice of an organisation. The use of multiple perspectives of performance could easily be adapted to incorporate the legal, ethical and voluntary issues identified within Carroll's CSR definition. Clearly questions of priority and causality would need to be considered, but this should be possible. In fact, in some ways this has already been attempted by Figge et al. (2002) with their 'sustainability balanced scorecard' and it is to this that we now turn our attention.

THE SUSTAINABILITY BALANCED SCORECARD

Figge et al. (2002) suggest that their concern with the balanced scorecard is that the logic of all of the four perspectives (as suggested by Kaplan and Norton and discussed above) are 'almost exclusively in the economic sphere' (p. 274). They suggest that in so doing the balanced scorecard fails to incorporate environmental and social aspects of an organisation. This conception of three aspects of an organisation, namely: economic, environmental and social, is one which is used widely in the field of reporting and we will therefore return to this in section 3 of this chapter. Clearly this identification of the social aspects of a corporation is in line with the CSR concerns of this chapter. Also, the environmental aspects of a corporation are, to my mind, also a fundamental part of CSR. From a stakeholder perspective environmental pressure groups are significant within society and there are clearly ethical issues concerning how a corporation affects the environment. The importance of corporations' environmental impacts has certainly become an important part of the accounting literature and this will be reflected in the remainder of this chapter.

Figge et al. (2002) suggested that there are three different ways in which social and environmental aspects could be incorporated into a balanced scorecard. Firstly, one could integrate social and environmental aspects into the four perspectives that have been developed by Kaplan and Norton. For example, the environmental impacts, possibly in terms of pollution, could be incorporated into the internal processes perspective or social aspects, such as affordability and availability, could be incorporated into the customer perspective. This approach would result in a balanced scorecard that is easily recognisable and would not involve too great a change.

The second alternative would be to maintain the four original perspectives and add a fifth perspective that dealt with the social and environmental aspects. This approach would mean that the social and environmental aspects were more visible within the scorecard, as they are clearly identified within this new perspective. This approach could be adopted in a balanced way. This is to say that the five perspectives could be seen to be of equal importance and the purpose of the scorecard would be to assist managers in making balanced decisions when there is a conflict between the different perspectives. One can see that the fact that there is only one social and environmental, also called non-market, perspective in contrast to four economic, or market, perspectives could already suggest a lack of balance. Figge et al. (2002, p. 277) do, however, also provide an example of a sustainability balanced scorecard as a strategy map. This strategy map again shows causal relationships between the Kaplan and Norton's four perspectives will all arrows pointing towards the financial perspective. The main difference in this visualisation is that the non-market perspective surrounds the four traditional perspectives, but, to reiterate, it is not the case that the non-market perspective is considered to the primary goal of the corporation. This version of the sustainability balanced scorecard strategy map does not appear balanced, but this does not mean to say that it is impossible to design one that is.

The final way to incorporate social and environmental aspects into a balanced scorecard would be to develop a specific environmental and/or social scorecard. Actually it is possible to imagine three scorecards, one for each of the economic, social and environmental aspects of a corporation's activities. An economic scorecard could most simply adopt a version of the balanced scorecard as developed by Kaplan and Norton. A social scorecard could be developed with specific perspectives to deal with social issues of relevance to a particular corporation. For example, human rights or local community could be identified as perspectives for a social scorecard. An environmental scorecard would again require development from the specific environmental issues that impact upon and are impacted by the corporation. Clearly again the perspectives could involve issues such as greenhouse gas emissions or water usage along with many more.

This suggestion of different scorecards for the different aspects resonates with the GRI sustainability reporting guidelines that will be considered in the reporting section that comes later in this chapter. As an internal approach the use of multiple scorecards may be useful to corporations in that it would ensure that the social and environmental aspects are not easily lost within a single, possibly economically driven, scorecard. There is a danger, however, that such an approach would still result in the primacy of the economic scorecard and there is a potential complexity to the prospect of managing multiple perspectives within two or three scorecards that could be extremely challenging in practice.

ENVIRONMENTAL MANAGEMENT ACCOUNTING

As mentioned in the previous section there has been a significant interest in accounting for the environment and environmental management accounting is element of this. The interest is both in terms of the academic accounting literature and its growing use in practice. There are a number of possible reasons for this interest and these include the actual environmental pressures that the planet currently faces (see Gray and Bebbington, 2001, p. 302, for one list of these pressures) including ozone depletion, species extinction, desertification, deforestation and many more. Other possible reasons suggested by Soonawalla (2006, p. 380) include 'disastrous industrial accidents', 'public awareness', 'media attention', and that 'the environment began to see a powerful and influential lobby group acting on its behalf'. Certainly studies have provided some evidence that media attention setting (see Brown and Deegan, 1998) and the activities of environmental pressure groups (see Tilt, 1994) do potentially influence corporations. The response to these pressures has not been uniform. On the one hand Gray and Bebbington (2000, p. 11) suggest that in Northern Europe there was a 'more engineering focus' and this 'led to exploration of how to most accurately and precisely measure the physical flows – of energy, materials, wastes etc. – and their associated costs.' In contrast they suggest that in 'the Anglo-American community, the emphasis is most clearly on seeking ways in which to exploit the so-called "win-win situations".' In this regard the accounting system was integral to the response, as it could be used to identify potential financial savings from reductions in uses of resources and waste. Therefore for Anglo-American corporations the primary motivator can appear to be financial, or economic, rather that environmental, although as win-win situations are identified so there is also a reduction in environmental impacts.

This section will now consider two competing environmental management systems, namely: Eco-Management and Audit System (EMAS) and the ISO 14000 series. EMAS was recommended by the European Council in 1993, but, unusually, corporations are not required to adopt it. Instead corporations are allowed to choose to implement EMAS if they want to. There are three key elements to EMAS and these are that:

- EMAS insists on corporations setting targets for environmental performance and further that these targets are improved, environmental impact reduced, over time.
- EMAS requires that the targets are set on a site by site basis. This ensures that poor performing sites are not hidden or compensated for by other improving or high performance sites.
- Corporations following EMAS are required to disclose their targets and performance against them. Furthermore, this disclosure must be verified.

According to Gray and Bebbington (2001) these key elements make EMAS a relatively stringent system for corporations that voluntarily adopt it and suggest that this may well explain the relatively low uptake of this system. They continue that the ISO14000 series is less demanding in that it does not require target performance, disclosure or rigorous verification. Instead, as documented by Gray and Bebbington (2001, p. 108), ISO 14001 states that an environmental management system must comprise:

- an environmental policy;
- an assessment of environmental aspects and legal and voluntary obligations;
- a management system;
- a series of period internal audits and reports to top management; and
- a public declaration that ISO 14001 is being implemented.

Furthermore ISO 14010 requires that there is an environmental audit to confirm whether, or not, ISO 14001 is being complied with. We can see from these requirements that in particular performance is not targeted. Gray and Bebbington (2001) suggest that the concern within the ISO 14000 series is with a management system being in place rather than performance. Having said this, however, within the series, specifically ISO 14031, a number of environmental indicators are identified. These are separated into three broad categories: environmental condition indicators; operational environmental indicators; and management of environmental performance indicators (see Bennett and James (1999) for more details).

Both of these environmental management systems can be applied at the level of the site or the corporation. Therefore they are consistent with the traditional view that a corporation has a boundary and that certain activities and impacts are internal to the corporation and some are external. An alternative approach is the life cycle assessment that is product-based and takes account of a product's impacts irrespective of whether the impacts would traditionally be considered to be internal or external to the corporation. In these terms the life cycle of a product stretches back to the extraction of the relevant raw materials and follows it through to its use and final disposal. Gray and Bebbington (2001) suggest that there are three major stages to a life cycle assessment and these: review the product in order to identify all of the resources and emissions it makes; to where possible quantify the product's impacts; and to analyse the product to attempt to improve its environmental impact as far as is possible.

Activities involved within the field of management accounting are now much more diverse than previously was the case. The budgeting for and control of the profit and loss of a corporation is now only a small part of the management accountant's role. The broadening of management accounting to multi-dimensional performance measurement frameworks that include non-financial measures offers scope for CSR to be incorporated within this fundamentally important management control system. This section has shown that social and environmental aspects of a corporation's activities can be incorporated through some form of balanced scorecard or environmental management accounting system. There have also been significant developments within corporate reporting that has relevance for CSR and the next section of this chapter considers these.

Corporate Social Responsibility Reporting

Corporations and their management are powerful bodies within society that control vast resources and as such it seems reasonable that they are held accountable for how this power and these resources are used. According to Laughlin (1990, p. 95):

> *Accountability can be seen as a relationship involving the 'giving and demanding of reasons of conduct'... It is usually assumed that some individual has certain rights to make these demands [a principal]... and another has some responsibility to supply this information [an agent].*

There is therefore a question as to whom a corporation and their management is to be held accountable. Benston (1982, p. 88) suggests that three possible principals are: shareholders, stakeholders and the general public/society. The more liberal/traditional view is that corporations and their management are primarily accountable to shareholders (see Benston, 1982 and Watts and Zimmerman, 1986). This is a narrow view of the corporation that is not consistent with the broader conception of a CSR corporation that we have followed in this chapter. A more consistent and broader conception of the corporation is provided within the growing field of accounting literature that is concerned with social and environmental reporting. This literature is, in the main, premised on the belief that the corporate accountability should extend beyond the provision of a financial account to shareholders. In the words of Gray, Owen and Adams (1996, p. 3): 'Such an extension is predicated on the assumption that companies do have wider responsibilities than simply to make money for shareholders.' This literature calls for a reporting on the social and environmental impacts of a corporation that would inform stakeholders or general members of society. The need for such reporting has been justified from a stakeholder approach (Gray, 1998), social contract theory arguments (see Mathews, 1995) and accountability requirements (Cooper and Owen, 2007) as well as others. Perhaps the most widely used theoretical lens within the social and environmental reporting literature is legitimacy theory. This has been used to try and explain the social and environmental reporting (SER) actually undertaken by corporations either in their annual report and accounts or in stand-alone reports. From a legitimacy theory perspective it has been argued that companies provide social and environmental disclosures to ensure that they repair, maintain or enhance their legitimacy within society (see, for example, Deegan, 2002; and O'Dwyer, 2002, as well as many others).

There have been a number of more practical developments in the area of SER and for the purposes of this chapter two development periods are distinguished: the 1970s and the 2000s. In the 1970s two interesting developments were 'The Corporate Report' (Accounting Standards Steering Committee, 1975) and Social Audit Ltd. The Corporate Report was an attempt by a professional accounting body to redesign the scope of reporting for wider stakeholder groups. Specifically, it sought to 'seek to satisfy, as far as possible, the information needs of users'. With this aim in mind the following user groups were identified and their information needs considered:

1. the equity investor group;
2. the loan creditor group;
3. the employee group;
4. the analyst advisor group;
5. the business contact group (including customers, suppliers, competitors...);
6. the government; and
7. the public (including taxpayers, consumers and special interest groups).

The Corporate Report also identified a total of 15 specific contributions to user information needs, which would enable user groups to evaluate the performance, effectiveness and efficiency of both the corporation and its management. Furthermore the Corporate Report suggested that the traditional financial statements, the income statement and the balance sheet, were insufficient to provide the necessary information and so a number of alternative reports were suggested. These additional reports included value added statements and employment reports. The value added by an organisation, as measured by turnover less purchased materials and services, is used to pay the contributing factors in terms of employee wages and benefits, dividends and interest, taxation, and amounts retained for reinvestment. According to Burchell, Clubb and Hopwood (1985) there are two strands to value added. Firstly, it reports on the overall performance of a corporation and can assist in calculations of efficiency and productivity. Secondly, it is suggested that value added puts profits into 'proper perspective'. In that it can 'reveal something about the social character of production' as it is created by a combination of efforts from different stakeholders cooperating. Therefore an important part of the rationale for value added was that it would make for a 'harmonious', 'democratic', 'cooperative' and 'efficient' corporation. The Corporate Report also suggested that corporations should provide employment reports. Recommendations for the content of employee disclosure were summarised by Hilton (1978) and include employment, pay, conditions, productivity, plans and financial information. Both value added statements and employment reports were popular aspects of corporate reporting in the late 1970s. Such reporting in the UK went into decline with the election of the Conservative government in 1979. Burchell, Clubb and Hopwood (1985) argue that this was due to a shift in economic and industrial relations policy. Therefore stress was placed on competition, training and 'shedding "surplus" labour', and the previous moves towards industrial democracy were not central to this.

Social Audit Ltd was an organisation that was set up for the explicit motivation of 'undertaking social audits of different companies and different industries' (Social Audit Ltd, 1973a). The quarterly publication 'Social Audit' contained investigations into Tube Investments Ltd (Social Audit Ltd, 1973b), Cable and Wireless and Avon Rubber Company Ltd, as well as other more general issues such as the 'social costs of advertising'. The reporting of these audits was argued to be important, as it would provide information, which 'although insufficient to correct all failings', would be an 'indispensable' part of the interaction between corporations and society. Certain groups 'most affected by what a company does' were identified. These include shareholders who need additional information on a corporation's 'social policy' to inform their actions. It was suggested that employees would require information on areas such as redundancies, minority hiring, and health and safety. It was also argued that consumer sovereignty was failing, as 'big business' has too much control over a market and therefore the consumer is left relatively powerless. Therefore it was argued that consumers need information with regard to products and price, innovation, disposability and consumer representation. Also the corporation's relationship with the community within which it operates and its environmental impact, in terms of the use of natural resources, restoration, recycling and pollution, were identified as important. The Social Audit experiment was relatively short lived, but demonstrated how accounting could critically consider a corporation's activities and, to some extent, hold them accountable to broader society (Medawar, 1976).

SER levels decreased after this high point in the 1970s, but have had a significant resurgence more recently. This resurgence started with a relatively small number of corporations producing environmental or health and safety reports, but this has expanded to the extent that more recently many larger corporations are producing reports that cover their broader social and environmental impacts. In the last decade a number of social accounting standards or guidelines have been developed and these include the Global Reporting Initiative (GRI), AccountAbility 1000 (AA1000) and Social Accountability 8000 (SA8000). Perhaps the best known of these is the GRI, which provides reporting guidelines for corporations 'reporting on the economic, environmental and social dimensions of their activities, products and services'. The guidelines are voluntary, but hope to provide a consistent and clear format for 'sustainability' reporting. The use of the term sustainability by the GRI is interesting and the exact meaning of sustainability and its relevance to CSR will be considered in the concluding section of this chapter. The GRI prescribes a set content for sustainability reporting that includes vision and strategy, governance structures and performance indicators. The performance indicators fall into the three areas of economic, environmental and social indicators and these are provided at www.globalreporting.org. It has been suggested by the GRI organisation itself that the environmental indicators are the more advanced than the economic and especially the social indicators.

Both AA1000 and SA 8000 specifically state that they are 'accountability standards'. AA1000 is a foundation standard that provides a set of principles and processes for planning, accounting, reporting, auditing, and embedding social and ethical accounting within corporations. Part of the aim of the standard is to provide a way for corporations to identify appropriate social and environmental measures through 'stakeholder engagement'. SA8000 is a standard that is primarily concerned with a corporation's dealings with its employees and the need for corporations to comply with national and international labour law. The specific areas of concern are child labour, forced labour, health and safety, collective bargaining, discrimination, disciplinary practices, compensation and management systems.

This section has considered a number of developments within corporate reporting that have sought to extend the information provided to be of greater relevance to a broader set of stakeholders and society more generally. Traditional financial accounting is a requirement of company law and the inclusion of specific financial information is mandatory and must be in line with appropriate (international) accounting standards. In contrast the SER standards that have been discussed here are very much voluntary and therefore corporations do not have to report this information. In fact many empirical have suggested that most SER is biased towards the reporting of good news and has a tendency to not report items where a corporation has created a negative social or environmental impact.

Discussion and Conclusions

This chapter has considered the role that accounting could have in the CSR activities of a corporation. It started by specifically selecting a broad definition of CSR that included economic, legal, ethical and voluntary aspects. Using this definition it then considered some of the developments within performance measurement and corporate reporting that have been or could be used in the auspices of CSR. Internally corporations could adopt a balanced scorecard approach or apply environmental management accounting techniques to aid their CSR activities. Furthermore, a number of reporting standards and guidelines have been discussed that could be used by corporations to inform stakeholders or society more generally about its CSR activities. One point of clarification is that none of these approaches are in any way legally required and so corporations adopting these approaches are doing so voluntarily. Therefore corporations that do adopt these approaches could well do this to signal to external parties that they are serious about CSR. Even for those corporations that do publicise their adoption of one of these approaches a degree of caution is required. For example, a corporation that signs up to the GRI can do so and then only partially implement the recommendations. Without a mandatory requirement of, for example EMAS and GRI, there will be companies that do not adopt these principles or choose to only adopt aspects that reflect well upon their operations.

Finally, this chapter will now briefly discuss the concept of sustainability and how this is being considered within the accounting literature. Sustainability is concerned with the ability of our planet to support life. In reality this is an incredibly complex concept, but one that we would expect a socially responsible corporation to, at the very least, consider. Much of the interest in sustainability stems from the release of 'Our Common Future' (also referred to as the Brundtland report, WCED, 1987). From this report comes a commonly quoted definition of sustainable development:

Humanity has the ability to make development sustainable to ensure that it meets the need of the present without compromising the ability of future generations to meet their own needs.

The concept of sustainable development does imply limits – not absolute limits but limitations imposed by the present state of technology and social organization on environmental resources and by the ability of the biosphere to absorb the effects of human activity. (paragraph 27)

Sustainability is often considered to be primarily an environmentally focused concern, but even here the question is whether environmental considerations should constrain economic and social matters or, alternatively, whether the environment can, in some way, be traded off against them (Ball and Milne, 2005). Much of the business led thinking on sustainability (including the World Business Council on Sustainable Development) believes that such a trade off is necessary and this is referred to as weak sustainability (Ball and Milne, 2005). This weak sustainability emphasises eco-efficiency – where corporations seek opportunities for economic and social benefits to be achieved through more efficient use of resources in the production process. Under this weak definition of sustainability corporations would be expected to undertake environmental improvements only where there are also economic benefits – a win-win scenario. A stronger form of sustainability is one where eco-efficiency is not sufficient for sustainability to be achieved. Gray and Bebbington (2001) suggest that eco-justice and eco-effectiveness are equally important if sustainability is to be achieved. Eco-justice issues incorporate issues such as income inequality and poverty that many might see as social issues, but in this conception they are considered to be part of sustainability. Therefore, this strong form sustainability is broader than environmental issues alone. Eco-effectiveness considers the total global impact of human activity. Production processes may become more efficient, but if there is a greater proportional rise in production then the total impact will continue to increase. As Ball and Milne (2005, p. 327) state 'a tenfold reduction in material inputs per computer is of little use if it is accompanied by a greater than tenfold increase in the consumption of the product.'

As suggested above it is hard to conceive of a responsible corporation that does not, at the very least, consider the issue of sustainability or sustainable development. In its strongest form sustainability would require corporations to subordinate economic and social issues to environmental considerations. Such a shift in priorities is difficult to envisage given the capitalist structures within which modern corporations operate. If such a shift were to occur it would quite clearly require a whole new conception of accounting and CSR. There have been some developments in terms of measuring environmental impacts and perhaps the best known are ecological (or more narrowly carbon) footprints.

'Ecological footprint analysis is an accounting tool that enables us to estimate the resource consumption and waste assimilation requirements of a defined human population or economy in terms of a corresponding productive land area.'

(Wackernagel and Rees, 1996, p. 9)

At present there can be only a very small minority, if any, corporations that are sustainable in this sense. This author is much persuaded by the arguments offered by Ball and Milne (2005) that one of the problems that exist is with the prevalent performance measures (including accounting profit), as they 'fail to capture the realities of environmental damage and the quality of many people's lives, in many cases they positively encourage destructive acts against nature and people' (p. 319). Therefore, one part of the solution would be to change the performance measures and this chapter has discussed some developments in the areas of corporate performance measurement and reporting that move some way towards doing this. Whether the reader believes that the developments to date, such as EMAS and GRI, are sufficient will depend upon their view as to the sustainability of current human, and corporate, activity. If, as is very possible, it becomes more and more apparent that current activities are not sustainable then more dramatic and innovative changes to human, and corporate, behaviour will be required. Even if this is the case it is likely that there will be a role for some (very different) form of CSR accounting in the future.

References

American Accounting Association (1996), *A Statement of Basic Accounting Theories*, AAA, New York.

ASSC, (Accounting Standards Steering Committee) (1975) *The Corporate Report,* London.

Ball, A. and Milne, M. J. (2005) 'Sustainability and management control' in A. J. Berry, J. Broadbent and D. Otley (eds) *Management control: Theories, Issues and Performance*, Palgrave MacMillan, London.

Bennett, M. and James, P. (1999) 'ISO 14031 and the future of Environmental Performance Evaluation' in M. Bennett, P. James and L. Klinkers (eds) *Sustainable Measures: Evaluation and Reporting of Environmental and Social Performance*, pp. 76-97, Greenleaf, Sheffield.

Benston, G. J. (1982) 'Accounting and corporate accountability', *Accounting, Organizations and Society*, 7(2), pp. 87-105.

Brignall, T. J. S. (2007) 'A financial perspective on performance management', *Irish Accounting Review*, 14(1), pp. 15-29.

Brown, N and Deegan, C. (1998) 'The public disclosure of environmental performance information – a dual test of media agenda setting theory and legitimacy theory', *Accounting and Business Research*, 29(1), pp. 21-41.

Burchell, S., Clubb, C., and Hopwood, A. G. (1985) 'Accounting in its social context: Towards a history of value added in the United Kingdom' *Accounting, Organizations and Society*, 10(4), pp. 381-413.

Carroll, A. B. (1983) 'Corporate Social Responsibility: Will industry respond to cut-backs in social program funding?' *Vital Speeches of the Day*, 49, pp. 604-608.

Carroll, A. B. (1999) 'Corporate Social Responsibility: Evolution of a Definitional Construct', *Business and Society*, 38(3), pp. 268-295.

Cooper, S. M. and Owen, D. L (2007) 'Corporate social reporting and stakeholder accountability: The missing link', *Accounting, Organizations and Society*, 32, pp. 649-667.

Davis, K. (1967) 'Understanding the social responsibility puzzle: What does the businessman owe to society?' *Business Horizons*, 10, pp. 45-50.

Deegan, C. (2002) 'The legitimising effect of social and environmental disclosures - a theoretical foundation', *Accounting, Auditing and Accountability Journal*, 15(3), pp. 282-311.

Figge, F., Hahn, T., Schaltegger, S., and Wagner, M. (2002) 'The sustainability balanced scorecard – linking sustainability management to business strategy', *Business Strategy and the Environment*, 11, pp. 269-284.

Fitzgerald, L., Johnston, R., Brignall, T. J. S., Silvestro, R., and Voss, C. (1991) *Performance Measurement in Service Businesses*, CIMA, London.

Freeman, R. E. (1984) *Strategic Management: A Stakeholder Approach,* Pittman, Boston.

Friedman, M. (1962) *Capitalism and Freedom,* University of Chicago Press, Chicago.

Gray, R. (1998) 'Imagination, a bowl of petunias and social accounting', *Critical Perspectives on Accounting,* 9, pp. 205-216.

Gray, R. and Bebbington, J., (2000) 'Environmental accounting, managerialism and sustainability', *Advances in Environmental Accounting and Management,* 1, (pp. 1-44).

Gray, R. and Bebbington, J. (2001) *Accounting for the Environment,* 2nd edition, Sage Publications, London.

Gray, R., Owen, D. and Adams, C. (1996) *Accounting and Accountability: Changes and Challenges in Corporate Social and Environmental Reporting,* Pearson, London.

Hilton, A. (1978), *Employee Reports: How to Communicate Financial Information to Employees,* Woodhead-Faulkner, Cambridge.

Johnson, H. L. (1971) *Business in Contemporary Society: Framework and Issues,* Wadsworth, Belmont, CA.

Johnson, H. T. and Kaplan R. S. (1987) *Relevance Lost: The Rise and Fall of Management Accounting,* Harvard Business School Press, Cambridge, MA.

Kaplan, R. S. and Norton, D. P., (1992) 'The balanced scorecard - measures that drive performance', *Harvard Business Review,* January / February 1992, pp. 71-79.

Kaplan, R. S. and Norton, D. P., (1993) 'Putting the balanced scorecard to work', *Harvard Business Review,* September / October 1993, pp. 134-147.

Kaplan, R. S. and Norton, D. P., (1996a) 'Using the balanced scorecard as a strategic management system', *Harvard Business Review,* January / February 1996, pp. 75-85.

Kaplan, R. S. and Norton, D. P., (1996b) *The Balanced Scorecard: Translating Strategy into Action,* Harvard Business School Press, Harvard.

Kaplan, R. S. and Norton, D.P., (1996c) 'Linking the balanced scorecard to strategy', *California Management Review,* Fall, 4, pp. 53-79.

Kaplan, R. S. and Norton, D.P., (2000) 'Having trouble with your strategy? The map it', *Harvard Business Review,* September / October, pp. 167-176.

Laughlin, R. C. (1990) 'A model of financial accountability and the Church of England', *Financial Accountability & Management,* 6(2), pp. 93-114.

Lynch, R. L. and Cross, K. F. (1991) *Measure Up! Yardsticks for Continuous Improvement,* Blackwell, Oxford.

McGuire, J. W. (1963) *Business and Society,* McGraw-Hill, New York.

Mathews, M. R. (1995) 'Social and environmental accounting: A practical demonstration of ethical concern?' *Journal of Business Ethics,* 14(8), pp. 663-670.

Medawar, C. (1976) 'The social audit: a political view', *Accounting, Organizations and Society,* 1(4), pp. 389-394.

Neely, A., Adams, C. and Kennerley, M. (2002) *The Performance Prism: The Scorecard for Measuring and Managing Business Success,* Financial Times Prentice Hall, London.

Nørreklit, H. (2000) 'The balance on the balanced scorecard – a critical analysis of some of its assumptions', *Management Accounting Research,* 11, pp. 65-88.

O'Dwyer, B. (2002), 'Managerial perceptions of corporate social disclosure: An Irish story', *Accounting, Auditing and Accountability Journal,* 15(3), pp. 406-436.

O'Dwyer, B. (2003) 'Conceptions of corporate social responsibility: the nature of managerial capture', *Accounting, Auditing & Accountability Journal,* 16(4), pp. 523-557.

Preston, L. E. and Sapienza, H. J. (1990) 'Stakeholder management and corporate performance', *Journal of Behavioral Economics,* 19, pp. 361-375.

Social Audit Ltd (1973a) 'The case for social audit', *Social Audit Quarterly*, 1(1), pp. 5-26.

Social Audit Ltd (1973b) 'Tube investments', *Social Audit Quarterly*, 1(3), pp. 4-66.

Soonawalla, K. (2006) 'Environmental Management Accounting', in A. Bhimani (ed.), *Contemporary Issues in Management Accounting*, pp. 380-406, Oxford University Press, Oxford.

Stringer, C. (2005). 'Performance management practice', in A. J. Berry, J. Broadbent and D. Otley (eds), *Management Control: Theories, issues and performance*, 2nd edition, pp. 122-136, Palgrave Macmillan, London.

Tilt, C. A. (1994) 'The Influence of External Pressure Groups on Corporate Social Disclosure: Some Empirical Evidence', *Accounting, Auditing & Accountability Journal*, 7(4), pp. 47-72.

Wackernagel, M. and Rees, W. (1996) *Our Ecological Footprint: Reducing Human Impact on the Earth*, New Society Publishers, Gabriola Island, BC.

Watts, R. and Zimmerman, J. (1986) *Positive Accounting Theory*, Prentice-Hall, Englewood Cliffs, NJ.

World Commission on Environment and Development (WCED) (1987) *Our Common Future*, Oxford University Press, Oxford.

8 *Responsible Practices in Small and Medium Enterprises*

ANTONIO VIVES

Introduction

Is the relative neglect of corporate social responsibility in small and medium enterprises justified? Aren't those firms after all a small part of economic activity? Should we bother about the responsible practices of SMEs? This chapter presents the case for fostering responsible practices in SMEs by describing the characteristics that make these enterprises good candidates, offering suggestion on those practices, suggesting measures to enhance their adoption and presenting the results of several surveys in developed and developing countries to illustrate the extent of those practices and the need for supporting actions.

There are as many definitions of corporate social responsibility as there are authors and we will not add yet another one. In this chapter, in the context of SMEs as opposed to large firms, we prefer the term 'responsible practices' as more illustrative and less controversial. By responsible practice, we mean the day-to-day business practices that avoid harm and try to do good to employees, the environment, the surrounding communities, providers of financial and non-financial inputs and consumers, obeying the laws and regulations of the countries, and where these are considered by managers to be insufficient, go beyond in order to achieve the objective of being considered a good and proud company. Unlike the case of large firms, where the issues of philanthropy on one extreme (give money) and contribution to social and economic development at the other extreme (concern for the advancement of the quality of life), for SMEs we are concerned with what lies mostly but not exclusively between those extremes: practices that do not harm and insofar as possible, contribute to do good. For large firms, the controversy lies normally in the extent of practices within those extremes. Is philanthropy a responsibility? What is their responsibility to contribute to development? We will avoid these controversies by concentrating the discussion on the core responsible practices. Also, we prefer not to emphasize the term 'corporate social responsibility', as the vast majority of SMEs is not familiar with the concept. Their involvement tends to be in some specialized area and rarely do they embrace the overall concept as a strategy. They react better to terms like 'responsible business practices'. Many of them are not 'corporations' and the term 'social' is too narrow.

SMEs Characteristics Conducive to Responsible Practices

For many readers it may come to a surprise that SMEs constitute more than 90 percent of business worldwide and account for between 50 and 60 percent of employment and more than half of GDP. In the case of Latin America over 60 percent are SMEs providing between 40 and 50 percent of jobs. If we include micro-enterprises, the numbers go to 99 percent and over 70 percent respectively.[1] In member countries of the European Union (as of 2007) it is estimated that there are more than 24 million SMEs (with employees up 250) providing over 90 million jobs. In the United States they provide close to 60 percent of employment with a definition of a small firm of up to 500 employees. Regardless of the accuracy of these statistics, it is clear that the vast majority of enterprises in the world are SMEs and have a significant contribution to employment and production.

Even if the impact of SMEs on the amount of goods and services is not as much as that of large firms, SMEs Corporate Social Responsibility (CSR) practices can have a larger impact on society as they tend to be more labor intensive than larger enterprises. Furthermore, they tend to contribute more to the equitable distribution of income, as they provide employment and living means for the less well off, they contribute to provide social cohesion and stability. Also, given the relatively local concentration in the sourcing of inputs and the provision of goods and services, they tend to have a bigger impact in the communities where they operate. These are even more reasons to be interested in promoting responsible SMEs.

But to promote these practices, we must realize the special characteristics of these enterprises, which are very different from the larger ones, for which most of the concepts and methodologies on CSR have been developed. While some of the fundamentals of the enterprise may be the same, SMEs are subject to very different stakeholder signals. In particular many will be family owned firms, or at least privately held firms within a small group of shareholders, particularly in emerging economies.[2]

The generalized assumption that larger firms have as one of the major objectives profit maximization may not be true for most SMEs. As a consequence, promotion of CSR practices rely less on the business case, that is, that CSR is good for the bottom line, either now or later, tangibly or intangibly. While most SMEs would like to have profits as large as possible, they may not have profit maximization as their foremost goal and may have other objectives. This is not to say that SMEs are not concerned with profits, if they are not, they will probably have short lives. It means that besides seeking to make money, they may be willing to forego some of those profits, knowingly or unknowingly, to achieve other objectives, like producing products that owner/managers find satisfying, giving back to society, helping others less fortunate, and so on. The point being that they are not driven only by the pursuit of 'maximum profits,' and many times are satisfied with 'satisfactory profits' and are willing to trade off some profit for other goals. Unlike large

---

1   These statistics are very hard to aggregate as countries have different definitions and different dates of reporting. For smaller economies it is up to 60 employees, for the middle-sized economies it is up to 200 and for some of the largest countries it can go up to 250 employees.

2   For the case of Europe, 85 percent of SMEs describe themselves as owner-managed, 60 percent as family business, 90 percent are privately owned or are partnerships, and 74 percent operate out of one single location (see the 2002 European Business Survey of Grant Thornton, an accountancy firm in the U.K.). It must be kept in mind that in the case of Europe, SMEs include up to 250 employees, although the vast majority of respondents were under 100 employees. If we were to limit the definition to a smaller number, as is the case in emerging economies, all these proportions would probably be larger.

enterprises, their 'cost-benefit' analysis of responsible practices will tend to be subjective, it will be enough to see that costs and/or benefits go in the right direction, not necessarily that they are as favorable as they can be. This has implications for the strategies used to promote CSR practices in SMEs: the business case may be important, but it may not be critical as they will also react to enlightened self-interest, to social conscience stimuli and altruistic reasons.

In terms of markets, the majority of SMEs tend to serve local markets and are not exposed to international pressure or incentives. Civil society will not be very concerned with their actions, preferring to devote their limited resources to the 'big fish,' to the larger corporations that have a greater impact. Nevertheless there are some SMEs that tend to sell to larger corporations, many of which are concerned about the responsible practices of their suppliers.

SMEs by their very nature are, in general, local institutions, which depend on customers that live around the enterprise, the few workers are likely to also live close by and the owners are likely to be involved in the community. SMEs may stay in the same location for a long time. Community development, concern for the environment and for social issues is closer to their nature.

SMEs are normally struggling to survive under adverse economic conditions and any regulations tend to be more burdensome than for larger corporations that have the resources to deal with them. SME managers are very likely to be concerned by the implications of social and environmental issues and regulations. They will perceive them to be an additional burden, unless the business case is made in a language and in a form that can be understood. As in the case of larger enterprises, it must be shown that it can be a competitiveness tool, for the same reasons, but with very different emphasis. It will be less a matter of education and more an issue of awareness and changing perceptions over the implications of CSR for the enterprise.

A caveat: While SMEs share of the characteristics described above, there are also significant differences between them. Depending on the country definition, they cover companies from ten to 100 employees and in some cases up to 250 employees. And what are small companies in one country may be deemed large companies in another. There is a wide diversity in such a group, within a country and much more across countries, particularly between developed and developing countries. Furthermore, SMEs in commerce are very different from those in manufacturing and will react to different drivers. A large part of the discussion that follows is based on generalizations, and they must be taken as such and contrasted and validated with the local reality and needed adjustments made. Below we discuss the different drivers of responsible practices.

The Case for Corporate Social Responsibility in Small and Medium Enterprises

The business or performance case is as valid for SMEs as it is for large enterprises, although it may not be as critical for their adoption of CSR practices. While many SMEs engage in responsible practices as a natural consequence of their beliefs and intuitions, it is also important to consider the impact that these practices can have in the performance of the enterprise. As we will see later, the financial impact of these practices may not be the main reason why firms engage in them, as they increasingly face competitive pressure, for the practices to be sustainable in the long run, some benefits, tangible or intangible may need to be shown. To guide these practices it is important that management be aware of what drives them.

RESPONSIBILITY DRIVERS

While one of the most important drivers for larger enterprises is likely to be the protection and enhancement of reputation or the brand name, for SMEs it may be the desire or need to be a good citizen in the community. Large firms feel the impact of the actions of *consumers* very strongly, particularly those selling in mass markets, where adverse publicity on irresponsible practices can have an immediate, large and lasting impact on revenues. For SMEs this may be a lesser issue, and one that can be managed more easily, as they do not tend to sell in mass markets and there is less public information associated with their products and services. In relatively developed markets an important driver, particularly for larger firms, are the existence of independent certifications, whereby institutions certify that the firm's products and services have been producing using responsible practices.[3] This applies to SMEs to a much lesser extent. While all firms can capitalize on the positive aspects of responsible practices, it will depend on the actions of consumers willing to act on the available information.

Nevertheless, CSR can be practiced by SMEs and reap many of the same benefits that larger corporations do. The level of involvement will certainly be different. There are many responsible practices that SMEs can do as a matter of routine and without having to develop extensive or expensive engagement strategies. Actually, they may turn their smaller scale to their advantage. Areas like reducing environmental impact, waste reduction and recycling, skill development and concern for the health and well-being of staff, are issues that can be handled relatively easy, and can yield tangible returns.

Ethical behavior is more visible in the geographical area of influence and hence tends to be more pronounced in SMEs than in the case of distant, impersonal big business. Relations with customers, suppliers and competitors are more based on trust than in the case of larger corporations, which rely on legal contracts or their business power to elicit response. In the case of SMEs there are many cases where credit is extended to customers or received from suppliers with little documentation. They are so well known in the community and with whatever stakeholders they may have, that it is harder for an SME to be visibly irresponsible. Nevertheless, they can be more responsible and reap the benefits.

Also, SMEs, having fewer employees and having the owners closer to the business, in many cases as managers, are more influenced by a few individuals, *employees and managers*, and for this reason it is easier to transmit a responsible ethic. Also, lately a new generation of SMEs is coming into force, younger, more educated, that has been born after the surge of interest in sustainability issues, which will be more responsive to responsible practices. This is the case in developed and developing countries alike. The problem of creating a *corporate ethic* is less of a problem for SMEs, as there are fewer independent decision makers and it is easier to develop a collective ethic. Also, the *agency problem* of the divergence of objectives between managers and shareholders or owner is

---

3   Examples of certifications are those related to fair labor practices, payment of fair prices to producers in less developed countries, sustainability of the forestry and agricultural practices, among others.

a much lesser problem. Managers of larger firms have incentives normally tied to short-term performance that may lead to compromising the 'investment' in CSR, which many times involves short-term tangible cost in exchange for long-term (tangible or intangible) gains. In the case of SMEs, gains, if sought, tend to be reaped in the shorter term and the goals of managers and owners are more aligned, as they tend to be the same persons.

Given the relatively local character of SMEs, where employees and owners are known in the community and many times are the community leaders, SMEs have a strong *identification with the community*. As a consequence the drivers for CSR for SMEs will tend to come from the community and the major external CSR activities will tend to be community related, in particular related to sports, health, and education support. By the nature of SMEs, these CSR activities grow out of philanthropy or, at best, strategic philanthropy (philanthropy on matters related to the success of the business). CSR activities outside its core are seldom practiced as SME managers do not have time and the company does not have ample resources to invest. This means that CSR activities tend to vary with economic conditions and may fluctuate depending on the fortunes of the corporation.

Nevertheless, this discussion does not mean that CSR activities are limited to these external manifestations. There are a host of CSR practices that are suitable for SMEs that can reap benefits, particularly related to internal management of people and processes, as we discuss below.

Another important driver for SMEs is the *demand from larger firms*, and in some cases from enlightened government buyers, for responsible practices in their SME suppliers, precisely to maintain the reputation for responsibility. SMEs selling to larger firms, particularly to those selling into consumer markets, will need to adopt responsible practices in order to keep their clients. These responsible practices transmitted through the supply chain tend to be concentrated in environmental and human resources issues.[4] Some of these affected supplier firms may, in turn, influence other SMEs in their market, for instance their competitors selling in the local market, and, through example, other unrelated SMEs. The impact on the firms that do sell to large buyers in developed and developing countries is indeed a very important driver, sometimes, like the case of textile or sporting good suppliers, the most critical driver.

But this driver must be put in the proper perspective. Only a very small fraction of SMEs do sell to firms that have responsible practices requirements in their supply chain, particularly in developing countries. Most SMEs in developing countries sell only to local customers or to other SMEs and even when selling to large firms, these firms may not yet have those requirements. This is a case where the diversity of SMEs makes generalizations very risky and each case must be analyzed separately. While important, the driver of responsible practices of the supply chain does not yet affect many SMEs, although it is one of the practices that has the fastest growth in recent times.

Nevertheless, some SMEs in emerging economies are also the ones that stand to lose the most as they are rather vulnerable, as they may become dependent on these buyers. As has been pointed out, you may not gain a contract by being responsible (competition

---

4   Not all pressures on the supply chain tend to enhance responsible practices. Sadly, there are many multinationals that in their efforts to maintain their competitiveness in developed markets will outsource their purchases to less developed countries, pressuring their suppliers to forgo their responsibility or ignoring their irresponsible practices in order to get the products as cheaply as possible. These practices will eventually surface and all involved may end up paying for it.

on price continues to be important), but you may lose it by being irresponsible.[5] With the requirements for good behavior from the buyers must come support, in particular training and advice from the larger firm, to produce responsibly. To be effective in promoting responsibility, social and environmental standards must be used in a positive manner.[6]

While SMEs are subject to the same *environmental and social regulations*, few see them as opportunities and most consider them as costs of doing business. SMEs have substantially lower capacity to cope or influence regulations than larger firms and many see regulations only as a burden and in some less developed countries, as a source of irresponsibility, paving the way for corruption to overcome inefficient regulation or its enforcement. But as the discussion of the business case below shows, environmental regulation can be a source of cost savings and provide opportunities to develop new products and services. It is precisely SMEs, with their flexibility and capacity to adapt to changing conditions, that are the type of firms that can capitalize in new products and markets resulting from the increased awareness of society on social and environmental concerns.

Media and civil society pressures (monitoring institutions) tend to be less important drivers, as SMEs are less visible and fragmented. These stakeholders will most likely concentrate their resources in larger corporations or issues that command national or international attention. Only local media and local NGOs may be interested in the responsibility of local SMEs, and if they are, they can be a powerful driver. Local reporting of misbehavior, say pollution of a stream or mistreatment of workers, can galvanize a community against a local firm. Nevertheless, these cases are rare, as media, if they are concerned at all, will be more concerned with larger firms.

Providers of financial resources are also less important as drivers for SMEs than for larger firms. As mentioned above, most are privately owned firms with little access to the financial system, financed with owner, family and friend's resources and with retained earnings. In developing countries access to finance is even more difficult. Furthermore, SMEs are more likely to be customers of rather smaller local banks. Even if they are public corporations, the market for their shares is likely to be very thin. Their relationship with the financial system is also likely to be rather narrow and of a small magnitude, such that these institutions will not bother to demand socially responsible behavior, nor will the SMEs reap any cost of funds advantage by being responsible. If any cost advantage is realized, it is most likely a result of financial transparency (corporate governance) and not from environmental and social responsibility. Recall for instance, that the Equator Principles,[7] adopted by rather large banks, applies for *project finance* and in this case, for projects with cost over US$10 million. Even though the major financial institutions are extending the concepts to *corporate finance*, it may take a while before the application reaches small loans, which have high enough transactions costs already. This is not to say that some enlightened financial institutions will not look at the environmental and social risks and responsibility of SMEs, but it will not be the norm, much less in emerging economies.

---

5   See Vogel (2005) for a comprehensive discussion of supply chain issues.

6   In some cases developed countries may use the demands for responsible behavior as a protectionist tool. This is a very important issue in public policies, especially in the negotiation of free trade agreements.

7   Equator Principles are voluntary agreements by signatory institutions to apply social and environmental safeguards and monitoring and reporting procedures in the financing of large projects. As of late 2007, there were a little over 50 signatory banks, mostly large institutions (www.equator-principles.com).

The driver of financial markets may affect innovative, high-growth or larger SMEs in developed countries that may have access to the financial and capital markets, particularly if they have to access specialized funds. This would certainly be the case for up and coming SMEs that want to tap into the market for sustainable products like energy efficiency, environmental products and services, and the like.

Other drivers of CSR in large corporations, like *internal codes of conduct* are also less likely to have an impact in SMEs, as the objectives of employees, executives, and owners tend be more closely aligned and there are fewer of them. They work better by example than by written rules. Codes of conduct, properly enforced, tend be more effective in impersonal firms with large number of employees. External codes of conduct tend to be relatively unknown to SMEs. Again, not all SMEs are alike and for larger SMEs in developed countries, codes of conduct may be an important factor particularly if they are part of supply chain requirements, enforced by large buyers.

Table 8.1 summarizes the discussion on the impact of drivers. The reader must bear in mind the extreme differences between SMEs depending on size, on relative country development, and on sector of activity. This table is only illustrative of the differences between large and small and medium firms, on a generalized basis.

Table 8.1   Relative impact of CSR drivers in SMEs and large corporations

DRIVERS	SMEs	LARGE
Laws and regulations	Important but not determinant	Very important
Civil society	Somewhat less important	Critical for consumer goods and extractive industries
Financial and capital markets	Little importance, except for selected firms with access to these markets	Important in developed markets, more so for the larger firms
Educated consumers/large buyers (supply chain)	Consumers have some influence. Large buyers can be critical for a small number of SMEs	Very important when the final product is a consumer good (as opposed to a commodity or an industrial product)
Media and monitoring institutions	Relatively unimportant. Unlikely to be concerned with smaller firms	Very important in selected cases, particularly for multinationals in developing countries where environment and human rights are exposed
Employees	Very important, some responsible activities originate with employees	Lesser importance as they are impersonal
Exposure to competition and globalization	Important if and when consumers and buyers can appreciate the value of responsibility	Critical, both in a positive way (capture competitive advantage of being responsible) and in a negative way (race to the bottom to avoid costs). Balance will depend of industry sector and structure

Table 8.1   *Concluded*

DRIVERS	SMEs	LARGE
Managers/Board of directors	Important drivers. Many times initiatives originate with enlightened managers	Important also, but tends to be overshadowed by other drivers. Some company leaders are realizing the competitive advantages of responsibility, including new products and markets
Owners/shareholders	Critical for family and owner/ manager firms. Sometimes are the original and most important driver	Only important for very well-developed financial markets where responsible investment is mainstreamed

IMPACT OF RESPONSIBLE PRACTICES ON COMPETITIVENESS

Even if SMEs are involved in responsible practices for altruistic or ethical reasons, the increasing competitive pressures and the economic situation of the marketplace make the issues of the impact on these practices on the competitiveness of the firm more and more relevant. This section considers the performance case of responsible practices and how can the SME do good by doing good.

The impact of responsible practices on the competitiveness of SMEs will depend on the extent that the drivers mentioned above apply to the firm, the industry, and the country. A careful analysis of the impact of responsible practices must start with an assessment of the applicability of those drives to the situation at hand.

Perhaps motivated by the lack of time and resources to look at the bigger picture, most of the involvement of SMEs tends to be of an internal nature, that is, towards its own employees and inside the company, which is a natural way to start, one that it is highly visible and has tangible returns. Many of the SMEs in developing countries are family owned and as such the concern for the welfare of the employees is almost like an extension of family. For instance, in many countries of Latin America, there was and still exists to some extent, a predominance of SMEs related to immigration, which makes the owners even more sensitive to the welfare of its employees, having felt the need for caring concern.

The external involvement tends to emphasize impact on the community and it is also driven by their impact on their employees or the pressure put on by employees and to a lesser extent by clients. Involvement in environmental matters tends to be limited to the larger segment of the SMEs and concentrated on internal actions, like recycling, energy and water consumption, and the like. Consideration for the impact of operations on the external environment tends to be in response to regulations or by some large buyers that are exposed to the behavior of their suppliers.

While the business case may not be as strong, as generalized, or as critical as it is for larger corporations, the case for SMEs can be shown effectively in the following three areas:

- increased revenues;
- costs savings;

- productivity improvements;
- risk reduction and asset values.

This is not to say that other areas are not likely to yield net benefits, but are less likely to be managed capably by SMEs.[8] Table 8.2 illustrates in a schematic form some of the major areas of impact.

Table 8.2   Business case arguments for better SMEs*

	ECOLOGY AND ENVIRONMENT	HEALTH/ WELL-BEING	DIVERSITY	COMMUNITIES
SAVING MONEY	Energy savings Waste disposal costs down	Staff stay longer, so lower training costs	Lower recruitment costs Wider sources new staff	Insurance and security costs less because less crime and vandalism
IMPROVING PRODUCTIVITY	Better waste disposal	Healthier and happier employees Less absenteeism	Less downtime as new staff learn	Better motivated staff
GETTING MORE SALES	Eligible for corporate tender lists Customer of choice for eco-consumers	More continuity in customer service	Better understanding of diverse markets Representative of markets served	Raised profile Active in networks, which help identify new business opportunities

*   Taken from Grayson and Hodges (2001).

Increased revenues

As a consequence of strong community identification, major benefits of responsible behavior tend to be consumer loyalty and reputation within the community and other stakeholders. Both may translate into increased revenues, either through sales volume and/or the ability to charge higher prices, depending on the extent of the competition. If the firm is consumer oriented, that is, deals with the final user of the product or service, it may be able to attract a larger customer base or keep the loyalty of the existing one. It may also be able to pass on cost increases with less resistance. If the firm sells to other firms, this impact will depend on the corporate responsibility practices of the buyers, and may go from being critical to accessing the clients to irrelevant if the clients do not care.

Another road to increased revenues may come from marketing the responsible characteristics of the product. For instance, if the product is recyclable, energy efficient, or produced using recycled materials with less energy, more healthy, organically produced or produced with fair wages, and so on, the SME may properly emphasize these

---

8   For some examples see SustainAbility (2002) and companion volume (2007).

characteristics in marketing the product. In this sense, it may also be able to attract a customer/client base that it was not able to attract before.

While there is no space to be comprehensive, some examples will suffice. For instance, activities that may enhance the goodwill of local customers and potential employees include: involvement in community affairs, employee and executives volunteering time, donation of surplus inputs and products to local assistance institutions, purchasing from local suppliers, support for local sports and local schools (very common, everywhere you go you a see a picture of the sports team sponsored by the local small business), among others.[9] Some of these activities have very little cost for the company and may provide enhanced returns.

As consumers and clients become more educated in the value of corporate responsibility and start incorporating their preferences into buying decisions, a market opens for responsible products. Nevertheless, it must be emphasized that this is no panacea. There are many customers that state they would buy responsible products, sometimes even pay a premium; nevertheless these stated preferences do not materialize in practice. There is huge gap between intentions and actions.[10] The reader can contrast this with their own behavior when buying goods. Furthermore, in many cases consumers do not know and even have no way of knowing about the responsible practices that went in the product. Under these conditions it is even harder to express preferences and for those preferences to have an impact on revenues. This is even more problematic in developing countries, where there is less access to information on responsible practices. SME managers must inform markets about their responsible practices for these to have an impact. The communication strategies described below are critical to achieve these impacts.

Furthermore, with the movement towards more responsible products, SMES, with their capacity to adapt and innovate, are very well placed to take advantage of new market opportunities. Good examples are SMEs engaged in the production of business and personal gifts using recycled materials. In large firms a good example is the Ecomagination strategy of General Electric, seeking to capture the market for more efficient production of energy and reduction of greenhouse gas emission. Wal Mart decided to push the sales of energy efficient bulbs as part of their corporate responsibility and ended up with a very profitable business line, with sales exceeding the most optimistic expectations. A whole new industry on sustainable tourism is being developed, where SMEs are normally the major suppliers of goods and services to the large providers and can take advantage of the new demand. New markets are opened through the increased concern with social and environmental responsibility.

Cost savings

This is probably the most effective area for SMEs, as there are myriad of possibilities to do good and save money.[11] The most accessible ones are in resource consumption, for instance, the consumption of energy, water and paper, of packaging materials, waste reduction,

---

9   For more examples, see Grayson (undated).

10   This is what retailers call the '30:3 phenomenon' where 30 percent of buyers say they have responsible production in mind when buying and 3 percent actually act on it. See the article by Michael Shapinker in the Financial Times issue of September 11, 2007.

11   Green Business (2001) contains suggestions and references to more suggestions.

recycling of materials, among others. Some responsible actions may not save costs, but may nevertheless contribute to enhance the reputation of the firm or the motivation of employees, which in turn may translate into increased sales or increased productivity (for example, the use of recycled paper or recycled printer and copier cartridges).

There are many ways to reduce energy consumption and while an energy audit is to be recommended, one should not use its cost or its timing as an excuse. One can start by raising consciousness of employees as to the importance of energy savings, encouraging them to turn off lights, computers, machines, and so on, when they are not in use, especially overnight and over the weekends. Check for heating or air conditioning losses and consider changing the regulated temperature, install automatic switches to turn lights, heating, and air conditioning off at specified times, change light bulbs to reduce consumption and save on air conditioning to reduce the extra heat generated by lighting (fluorescent versus incandescent), when replacing any energy consuming equipment investigate the possibility of buying more energy-efficient ones, maintain equipment to insure efficient operation. There are energy savings also in the proper maintenance and use of vehicles, including using more fuel efficient ones.

Similar suggestions can be made for water consumption. Start by checking for leaks, reducing consumption in non-essential uses, installing water efficient fixtures, recycle water if at all possible.[12] Other savings in resource consumption can be had in the use of paper, by installing printers and photocopiers with two-sided capabilities, when replacing old equipment, or using paper already printed on one side to print or photocopy on the other side non-essential documents (saving waste at the same time).

For SMEs selling packaged items, savings may be possible by analyzing the use of materials. For example, using less expensive materials, for instance recycled ones, or designing the packaging to minimize the use or maximize the possibility of reusing the materials. This may save transportation and waste disposal costs and save money in the purchase of packaging materials.[13] Also, eliminating non-recyclable elements in the packaging may increase recyclability and reduce costs. Use of environmentally-friendly inks in printing may not reduce costs, but may enhance the reputation of the company.

In waste disposal the major savings come from reducing the amount of waste, but also from a reduction in environmental risk. Reputation can be enhanced with proper disposal of waste.[14] Some waste reduction can come from redesign of the product and the packaging, but also from process analysis. By analyzing the manufacturing process, the byproducts may be reduced or may be produced in such a way that they are useful to the firm or can even be sold or recycled.

---

12   By installing waterless men urinals in a building housing 1,700 employees, the Inter-American Development Bank (not an SME!) saves 6 million gallon of water a year, besides being much more healthy. The investment has a very short payback period and can be replicated in SMEs.

13   WalMart (not an SME either!!) is moving into an extensive program of reducing packaging materials in its program of 'zero waste'. It estimates that by reducing packaging by 5 percent '....it will equal to removing 213,000 trucks from the road and saving about 324,000 tons of coal and 67 million gallons of diesel fuel per year...our supply chain alone could save US$3.4 billion.' (see www.walmartfacts.com) Granted, savings in an SME will probably very small, but this example shows that these savings cannot be ignored, as packaging has a significant impact in materials and energy consumption (in production and transportation) and contributes to waste.

14   One of the most egregious examples is the one of plastic bags in supermarkets, which are not biodegradable. Many may have seen the unsightly views in many developing countries of plastic bags hanging on trees for years. A supermarket in Spain is offering reusable, recyclable, biodegradable bags made from potato starch, which are significantly more environmentally friendly than bags made out of fossil fuels or made out of trees.

In relatively more advanced financial markets, responsible practices may allow the firm access to finance in better terms. Slowly but surely, financial institutions, including insurance companies, are evaluating those practices and are willing to offer coverage on better terms if the risk perception is lower. Responsible practices may not yet offer SMEs access to finance where the market is rather underdeveloped, but it may avoid denial of access in those markets where SMEs do have access to finance. It may not open the door, but it may prevent it from closing.

Productivity improvements

Actions on human resources management and the working environment are the most likely to lead to productivity improvements. Most of the of the activities discussed in this section related to human productivity are the result of good human resources management tools, which can be further enhanced when placed in the context and strategy for responsible practices.

Some of these management practices that can have a further impact on productivity are those related to some benefits, like providing access to education, training, and health care for the employee and the family. Also, counseling on addictions and domestic violence, which can reduce absenteeism. Many SMEs do not go this far. Also, in-house training programs, access to outside training, or at the very least time off for training can also enhance productivity. Mentoring is another responsible activity that can pay dividends in terms of employee retention and enhanced productivity.

A responsible firm will also look to have other benefits that do not necessarily have a tangible short-term impact on productivity but that may have a longer-term impact or no impact at all, and do it as solidarity to the employees. This would be the case of paying wages above the minimum wage, it this is deemed to be insufficient for decent living.

An overlooked activity in SMEs is that of job enrichment. Many SMEs have jobs which are quite repetitive and managers are content with optimizing the process to enhance productivity. Sometimes including variety as the possibility of learning other skills on the job can be a good investment.

Conciliation of work-family demands can also yield benefits, for instance, through the use of flexible working hours or even working from home. Adequate vacation, even beyond industry norms, may help attract and retain qualified personnel. The provision of exercise facilities or adapting the work schedule to allow it can be beneficial. For some SMEs this may mean pooling with other SMEs in the area.

SMEs must take full advantage of the benefits provided by non-discrimination, both in terms of gender and race. Non-discrimination of young women of child-bearing age can also yield loyalty and enhance productivity in the long run. In some less developed areas, there may even be a need to provide some level of positive discrimination in order to contribute to the development of the community and to attract goodwill.

Good working conditions, for instance, in terms of proper lighting, comfortable working spaces, clean restrooms, adequate rest periods, the proper use and pay for overtime are also part of responsible practices. SMEs are sometimes under pressure to cut costs and these are unfortunately areas that tend to suffer.

Something relatively uncommon in SMEs is making employees participate in the decision making, even if it is only at the tactical level. Their input could contribute to bettering working processes. Also, SMEs should consider the possibility of involving some employees in revenue sharing programs. Obviously this may not be suitable for some types of SMEs.

These responsible practices enhance the capacity to attract and keep good employees and the motivation of existing ones as they see the responsiveness of the firm to issues of concern. There is evidence that employees prefer to work with firms that have a good reputation for concern with the environment, community, and employees. This may allow the firms more choice in selecting from the pool of qualified employees and may help in retaining them.

Risk reduction and asset values

While not as critical as for large enterprises, responsible practices can lead to risk reduction. For instance, by employing sound human resources, environmental, and corporate governance practices, the firm can avoid future problems related to litigation for damages or fines imposed by regulators. Respect for the rights of workers and care for their welfare can avoid or mitigate labor actions like strikes or work stoppages.

These practices can also lead to increases in the value of assets, particularly intangible assets like reputation that, while not accounted for in most financial statements, may be incorporated in the share valuations for those firms that quote in stock exchanges or at the time of a takeover by another firm. It may allow them access to capital on better terms. For large firms, reputation can be one of the most important assets, particularly for those firms that sell consumer products. Reputation in turn can enhance business opportunities, allowing the firms to enter into partnerships with other reputable partners, attracting better employees, and accessing markets among others.

Closing remarks

One of the most responsible practices is to offer long-term gainful employment and fair wages, for which the long-term sustainability of the firm is critical. Responsible practices can provide impetus to the virtuous circle of performance enhancement, which in turn facilitates the process of investing in responsible practices. It must be remembered that SMEs in less developed markets are very likely competing on price with other firms that may not have a high regard for responsible practices. Jeopardizing the competitive position of the firm may be irresponsible to the many workers that depend on the firm. But responsible practices can enhance their competitiveness, when properly managed.

The business case must be sold carefully, as some responsible activities do have real tangible costs in the short term that can impact the finances of the firm. Many of the benefits may be intangible and may only be realized over longer terms. The firms must develop a careful strategy for involvement, taking into account the values of the firms, the competitive environment in which it operates, the prospects of the firms, the possibility of capturing benefits, among others. The firm may get involved in responsible practices just because it is the 'right thing to do'. This is perfectly valid, but the extent of the involvement must be part of the business strategy. For this, education of managers and employees are important ingredients, as is the communication strategy that we discuss below.

Communication Strategies for Small and Medium Enterprises

To reap the benefits of competitiveness, communication, as for larger firms, is important, as the realization of some of the benefits requires that others be aware and act, in particular consumers and buyers (to increase revenues) and employees (to reduce costs and enhance productivity). While many of the responsible practices of SMEs may be done for altruistic, ethical, or religious reasons, the sustainability of those practices, their extent and intensity can be enhanced if the company receives some benefits. Actually some argue that the company should engage in responsible practice, only to the extent they are profitable. The responsible practices of the company must be made known for stakeholders to act and provide potential benefits. In order to act, they must know. 'If a tree fell in the forest and nobody heard it, did it fall?'

As the CSR activities of SMEs are rather natural and informal, it is unlikely that these firms would think it is a priority to report these activities and many would not even see a need. Nevertheless, if these activities are going to become part of the strategy, or at least enhanced and systematized, they need to produce some long-term return and a good strategic communication can be of help. The communication can also help the firm reflect on its own responsible practices and help enhance and focus them. Furthermore, these communication efforts may stimulate other firms to also undertake or deepen CSR activities.

As the major stakeholders of SMEs are the employees and the communities (which for many SMEs is almost synonymous with consumers), and in some cases suppliers and large buyers, the strategic communication should be directed to these groups. To some extent, civil society and local government institutions will also be interested, although to a lesser extent than in large firms. There is much less need to produce formal sustainability reports for the public at large, which are probably unaffordable anyway for many SMEs. For SMEs, targeted interventions are a must and they should be targeted to these four audiences:[15]

- **workplace**: employees, including trade unions;
- **community**: local organizations like community organizations and schools;
- **marketplace**: customers and buyers, including consumer associations and providers of financial resources; and
- **surrounding Environment**: local government and civil society.

Good communication may lead the firm to enhance consumer loyalty, be known to responsible buyers (some of which may even require a report from the firm on their CSR activities to make it eligible), improve the reputation of the firm or the brands, enhance the pride of employees in working for the firm, among other things. These effects can reinforce some of the benefits of the CSR activities themselves.

This is not to say that SMEs should start 'marketing' their responsible activities, in the sense of prioritizing the impact of the communication over the activity that it is being reported. The idea is to report the good that the firm is doing, not to have the publicity used as an end, it must be a mean. It is not a matter of making a contribution

---

15   Following the 'Guide to communicating about CSR' included in the Toolkit of the European Commission for SMEs. See European Commission (2004).

to the community in order to have the picture taken and displayed in the papers, it is a matter of doing good for the community and eventually letting it be known. *Reporting on responsibility must be done responsibly.*

Table 8.3 presents an illustrative view of the communication strategy. It does not pretend to be all-inclusive and each SME will have to tailor its strategy to their situation and, especially, their means.

Table 8.3   Strategies for communicating with stakeholders

AUDIENCE	INSTRUMENTS	CONTENT
Marketplace (Consumers/buyers)	Website Special reports/brochures TV/radio/press advertisements	Responsible activities in: environment (resource consumption, waste, pollution, protection), quality of workplace, human resources, community support, purchasing criteria, product quality and safety, consumer education and the like
Community	Website Live presentations in meetings Press releases	Responsible activities in: community support, social inclusion (race, gender, age, handicapped), environment
Workplace (Employees)	Intranet Newsletters/bulletins Personal meetings E-mails/e-bulletins Posters/banners/videos	Responsible activities in: fair wages, work-life balance, health and safety policies, counseling, social inclusion, quality of workplace, training and career development, job enrichment, benefits, environment
Surrounding environment (Public/third sectors)	Website Special reports Press releases Interviews	Taxes, transparency, environment, social inclusion, quality of workplace

Corporate Social Responsibility and Small and Medium Enterprises in Europe and in Latin America

The observations presented above on responsible practices in SMEs are the results of empirical observations and many of them derive from several surveys that have been conducted to analyze those practices. To illustrate the extent of the adoption of those practices in SMEs and to derive lessons for promoting those practices, in this section we discuss the results of two interesting surveys, one carried out in a set of developed countries in Europe and the other, asking similar questions, carried out in the developing countries of Latin America. A recent third survey sheds lights on questions not covered by the other two surveys. Analyzing the similarities and differences yields important lessons for fostering of responsible practices in diverse economic environments.

RESULTS FOR EUROPE

For the case of *Europe* there is a comprehensive survey on the external social and environmental responsibility practices of small and medium firms carried out for the European Observatory on SMES.[16] Unfortunately the report did not address issues of CSR internal practices (that is, responsible practices on the working environment, training, participation, work-family balance, management of human resources, and corporate governance), which could have shown even more significant involvement and benefits, as it is one of the more tangible areas of concern and one where the benefits are more easily perceived, even if not measured. The survey covered external practices related to community involvement (health, education, culture, sports, diversity, and the like) and environmental practices related to use of resources (water, energy, and so on), recycling, use of byproducts, and environmental management policies and systems.

One of the major conclusions of the report is that SMEs are not yet defining social and environmental responsibility as an issue to be incorporated into the enterprise's core business activities, so in most cases these activities are occasional and unrelated to business strategy. The key motivation for involvement is related to 'ethical reasons'. Nevertheless, CSR behavior and communication are increasingly becoming an advantage for those SMEs that are effectively addressing these activities.

In terms of *external social involvement*, the main findings are:

- Half of the SMEs are involved and the involvement is directly related to the size of the enterprise (48 percent for micro, 65 percent for small, and 70 percent for medium), it is not sector specific, tends to be local and it tends to be larger in the northern countries, where enterprises are more aware of benefits on the business.
- Activities are concentrated in four main fields: sports, cultural and health/welfare, education and training (not aimed at SMEs' own employees) in the community and it occurs in the form of donations, either in cash or in kind, conducted on an *ad hoc* or irregular basis.
- Three-quarters of the firms involved are able to identify benefits and the two main ones include an improvement in the loyalty of customers and better relations with the general community/public authorities.
- The major explanation for lack of involvement is lack of awareness, this being more important than lack of resources. This would suggest that local campaigns to increase awareness may be effective in increasing engagement.

Regarding involvement in *environmental* responsibility activities, the main findings are:

16   European Commission (2002). The size definition used was up to 50 employees for a small-sized firm and up to 250 employees for a medium-sized firm.

- The majority of those involved in environmental responsibility activities do so in relation to their own operations, very few are concerned with sector-broad issues. But even the number of these firms is rather limited, concentrated in larger SMEs and in the northern countries.
- The main reasons for getting involved are market demands (basically from customers and through subcontracting relationships), as well as some other more proactive reasons such as the desire to obtain a competitive advantage. Ethical considerations do not seem to be a relevant driving force.
- Most remain unaware of both the environmental impacts derived from their business activities and the programs and resources available to them.
- Most of the lack of involvement is a consequence of lack of awareness and resources (technical, financial, and human), skepticism as to the benefits and a negative company culture.

Time and again, studies of CSR practices in SMEs in developed countries[17] tend to show that the main impediments are lack of awareness of what they could do, of the benefits of engagement, fear of bureaucracy, time and cost, but interestingly, these problems are not actually experienced by those SMEs engaged, so these barriers may be more a matter of perception rather than reality.[18] Nevertheless, as everybody tends to act on perceptions, they become a reality and this reinforces the need to act on the perceptions of SMEs.

RESULTS FOR LATIN AMERICA

A similar study to the one described above for Europe was commissioned by the Inter-American Development Bank, with the survey carried out during 2004. The *Latin America* study, unlike the one done in Europe, did include internal activities. The questions asked and the definition of the size of the enterprises utilized were the same as the Europe survey (even though a size of 250 employees in Latin America makes a rather large firm).[19]

The survey found that a significant number of firms were engaging in responsible practices, without calling them CSR. As a matter of fact, the survey never referred to CSR and the questions were rather specific regarding practices. As was to be expected, the more intense level of activity was on internal activities, as these are more related to traditional good management practices and have a more tangible impact on results.

In terms of *internal activities*, the main findings were:

- Almost 60 percent of the medium-sized enterprises and 40 percent of the small firms declared a high level of involvement, with the most involvement in respect for working hours, time off for training, and space for dialogue with management. Among the least developed are health exams, in-house training, flexible working hours, and corporate governance issues (auditing, anticorruption policies, suppliers supervision).
- Main reasons for involvement were to enhance worker satisfaction, to increase profits, for ethical/religious beliefs, and to comply with the law, in that order.

---

17   See also Department of Trade and Industry (2002).

18   Grayson (2003).

19   Full results are included in Vives et.al. (2005).

In terms of *external activities*, the main findings were:

- About 22 percent and 11 percent of the medium and small firms respectively declared high levels of involvement. These are significantly lower percentages than for internal activities, as the impact is not tangible. The major activities were in support for the disadvantaged and for education, although with low levels of involvement (only 44 and 39 percent of firms reported involvement in these two areas). Most of the involvement is through donations and to a much lesser extent by sponsorships and management/employee involvement. For SMEs, these activities are more philanthropic than strategic.
- Main reasons for involvement were ethical/religious beliefs and to build community relationships.

In terms of *environmental activities*, the main findings were:

- About 35 percent and 22 percent of the medium and small firms respectively declared high levels of involvement. This level of activity is between the levels of internal and external activities. The main activities are on energy consumption and on recycling, activities that presumably will bring reductions in costs. A mid level of activity was reported in water use reduction and in utilization of byproducts.
- Main reasons for involvement are to increase profits, ethical/religious beliefs, and to comply with the law.

One of the reasons to be responsible which is remarkably absent is that of pressure from stakeholders that was reported only as a significant factor in environmental issues and a small number at that. Only 17 percent reported some pressure to get involved in environmental issues, but much less in external activities (4 percent) or internal activities (5 percent). Stakeholders do not seem to be a factor for SMEs to pursue responsible practices. Ethical/religious beliefs, performance, and compliance with the law are more significant drivers.

The cited obstacles to a more active participation in external and environmental responsibility are rather concentrated: lack of knowledge and lack of resources. Lack of knowledge is cited by about 30 percent of the firms in each category of responsibility and lack of finance is cited mostly as an obstacle for external responsibility. This is consistent with other results that show this activity as mostly altruistic, done through philanthropy and unrelated to the business, obviously reflecting a lack of knowledge of the potential impact on the welfare of the firm. Additionally, an obstacle for non-involvement in environmental responsibility is the perceived lack of impact. This perception may also be a reflection of lack of knowledge, because while it may be true that some firms may not have direct measurable environmental impact, all use resources and produce waste that may be optimized. Rather surprisingly, lack of human resources and lack of time are not mentioned as obstacles by most firms.

In terms of public support, SMEs think of it as almost non-existent as is information regarding responsible practices. Half of the firms would like the government to support the adoption of these practices through recommendations and financial support. 35 percent support regulation and ten percent prefer to be left alone. In general they would prefer that these practices be voluntary, but with facilitation and encouragement from the public sector.

A more recent, complementary, survey carried out by the Inter-American Development Bank over 5,100 small, medium, and large enterprises in ten countries in Latin America found some other interesting results regarding their responsible practices.[20] While this survey was extensive in the breadth of questions and the number of firms questioned, it was only able to include a limited number of questions on CSR, as it was part of a larger survey on the business climate for enterprises in developing countries (Enterprise Surveys), carried out jointly with the World Bank.[21] The major findings were:

- 41 percent claim that they have formal policies related to responsible practices (63 percent of the large firms, over 100 employees, 45 percent for medium sized firms with between 20 and 99 employees, and 30 percent of the small firms with between 5 and 19 employees). These results seem rather optimistic.
- 47 percent believe that responsible practices positively affect competitiveness (67 percent of large firms, 51 percent for medium-sized and 36 percent of small firms).
- 74 percent of large firms and 36 percent of small ones have programs to conserve energy. 69 percent and 33 percent respectively for conserving water. 62 percent and 31 percent for recycling (results for medium-sized are in between)
- 75 percent and 31 percent have programs in place to control air and water pollution.
- 62 percent and 34 percent have community involvement programs (health, education, sports, community development, donations). On this item the gap between large and small firms is the narrowest of all questions asked.
- As in the earlier survey, stakeholders are not perceived to be critical drivers: Only 13 percent of the firms report feeling pressure from stakeholders (buyers, customers, society, financiers, and so on) to act responsibly. 20 percent of large, 15 percent of medium-sized, and 10 percent of small firms. In developing countries, not even large firms feel pressures from stakeholders.

This last result is indicative of the policies that must be followed in order to promote the adoption of responsible practices. It seems as if most of the impetus comes from inside the firms (managers and employees). The strengthening and education of stakeholders is a critical issue, at least in developing countries. Most of the literature is on what the behavior of stakeholders should be, not on what it is.

A caveat: as in most surveys of this type, the results reflect the perceptions of respondents and have not been independently corroborated. Some responses may be considered too optimistic (respondent wants to look good in front of the interviewer) and some may reflect the lack of expertise of the respondent on the issue at hand.

COMPARISON EUROPE/LATIN AMERICA

From these surveys we can conclude that the behavior of SMEs in Europe and Latin America are surprisingly similar, although the involvement is relative more intense (in

---

20   Here the size definitions were more adapted to developing countries: up to 50 employees for small firms and up to 100 employees for medium-sized, above 100 employees were called large.

21   The survey on the CSR part was only carried out in 2006 in Latin America and the results are unpublished. The rest of the results for 55 countries can be found on the website http://www.enterprisesurveys.org/.

the comparable items of external and environmental activities) in Europe (although the countries of Latin Europe (Portugal, Spain, Italy, and France) tend to have levels closer to those of Latin American countries. The reasons for engaging in responsible behavior are very similar, only the relative importance is different. All give credit to ethical and religious beliefs and to the need to enhance performance. The obstacles to engage are also similar, in both cases lack of knowledge, although in the case of developing countries lack of financial resources is relatively more of a hindrance.

A major difference between both groups of countries is the support given by governments and business associations to promote and facilitate the adoption of responsible practices. In Europe most countries have a well-developed public and private network of support, including at the supranational level, in the European Commission, while in Latin America the support systems are less developed, especially the public sector, which are basically non-existent. Most business associations supporting responsible practices cater to the larger segment of firms, although there is a movement towards supporting SMEs and several business associations and NGOs have developed toolkits for SMEs, although the penetration is still relatively low.

At the level of detail, there are some more visible differences. For instance, in terms of external activities, European SMEs prefer to support sport, cultural, and health activities, through sponsoring and donations, while in Latin America they prefer to support education and disadvantaged groups (poor and marginalized), but adding the participation of managers and employees to their donations. In terms of environmental responsibility, compliance with the law seems to be relatively more important for European firms.

The differences are probably sharper for the case of larger enterprises that in Europe tend to feel the pressures of stakeholders, while in developing countries are much less developed. This is reflected in the relatively larger importance of environmental activities, of communicating responsible behavior, and of better corporate governance, given the more developed financial markets. Also, in developing countries large firms are expected to contribute more to the solution of social problems, even if it is not their responsibility.

Fostering responsible practices in Small and Medium Enterprises[22]

The approach of SMEs to CSR activities will be conditioned by the characteristics described above and the fact that there may be more personal reasons for their existence, for instance to make a living, to apply entrepreneurial skills, to become rich, to exploit a product or service idea, and so on. This produces a more personal and less institutional approach to CSR activities.

While for larger firms some important elements of a CSR strategy are the full-fledged Sustainability Reports, where the firm reports on all their responsible practices, many of them reporting progress on self-devised or international indicators, this is less relevant for smaller firms, as they do not have the resources, in particular the information and

---

22 See, for instance, the publication of the Department of Trade and Industry of the United Kingdom cited in the references.

managements systems, to produce such formal and comprehensive reports.[23] For large firms these reports are a way to capture competitive advantage by showing responsibility, but as the reports are scrutinized by stakeholders, they become a source of feedback to enhance those practices.

The most important barrier to overcome is the perception by many SME managers that being responsible is expensive, takes time and money and does not yield commensurate returns. This is associated with the lack of awareness of the potential benefits and the realization that a responsible strategy involves more than occasional philanthropy, responding to demands from the community.

In order to engage SMEs, especially the smaller ones, it may even be counterproductive to try to promote an integral CSR concept and may be better to build upon what they are already doing, deepening or widening their activities. For the SME it may not be a case of integrating CSR into the firm's strategy (even if it were to have one), as is the case for the larger corporation, but will be more of a piece-meal, gradual, approach to responsible practices. Many SMEs are engaged in what we would call CSR but they do not call it by that name, they may not even know about CSR, they may not even think that they are explicitly engaged. Their involvement is *informal*, gradual, one thing at a time, almost without noticing it. It need not involve large investments or recurring cost. Many of these activities have been developed naturally, as a result of demands from the employees and the community. Sometimes the best way to start is by appealing to the altruism of the managers/owner, using the 'feel good' argument, as many of them may have been low-level employees themselves and understand the value of solidarity.

The comprehensive concept as it is traditionally presented for larger firms is alien to most SMEs in developed countries and much more in developing countries. The engagement in CSR is more of a natural part of doing business, than a conscious effort to engage in something of strategic value. One of the best ways to enhance the adoption of CSR practices is precisely to develop an appreciation of this strategic value, that CSR is more than philanthropy and that it can have business benefits, as described above.

How should SME involvement be promoted? As SMEs are a lot closer to the community and more dependent on associations or networks with similar businesses, the most useful sources of influence would be local governments, industry and commerce associations, and large buyers. The preferred method should be persuasion, through encouragement and support. SMEs must be shown the business case, but care must be exercised not to overstate it, as many of the actions taken by these firms may not have a direct or measurable impact on the bottom line. Recall that the information systems of SMEs are not as well developed and may not be able to detect causality. As a matter of fact, many SMEs admit that their responsible practices do yield benefits, but are not able or do not bother to quantify these benefits. They may be content with a subjective or perceived relationship.

The tools they need must be rather simple and come naturally. For instance, one of the most effective tools is the dissemination of examples from their peers. Also, the availability of guidelines, checklists and cases[24] prepared and presented by institutions

---

23   There internationally accepted guidelines for reporting prepared by the Global Reporting Initiative, GRI, that are used mostly by very large firms, although they have produced a supplement for smaller firms. See the GRI website at www.globalreporting.org.

24   Examples of these guidelines and checklists are those produced by the Canadian Manufacturers and Exporters (undated) and the one produced by Green Business (2003). Cases, only from European SMEs, can be found on the

and individuals that think like them that do not attempt to sell them the tools of big corporations. For SMEs, which in some cases are not sophisticated and do not have the resources or talent to devote to CSR issues, the most important recommendation is to make the advice and strategy of engagement as simple as possible, trying to promote one achievement at a time. It is important to avoid frustration to set in. In all of this process, it must be kept in mind that there are many barriers to engagement mostly related to lack of resources, especially the time of the owner or managers, and knowledge or awareness of the opportunities afforded by these practices.

While it is desirable for business and local associations to try to engage new business, it is also important and more effective in the short run to widen the involvement of those already engaged by showing them the business benefits. As far as possible, the impression of obligation must be minimized in order to develop the conviction, which is more sustainable in the long run.

The discussion above has assumed, implicitly, that all responsible actions are of a voluntary nature and that all that it is needed are measures to stimulate their desires to act responsibly. There are many areas (particularly in labor and environment) that cannot be left to voluntary actions and to be 'promoted' they must be mandated by laws and regulations. Nevertheless, care must be exercised that these regulations do not impose a heavy burden that forces SMEs to forego other responsible practices. SMEs have much less capacity to deal with regulations than larger firms, which can devote significant resources to fighting or complying.

In Summary: Is Corporate Social Responsibility Possible in Small and Medium Enterprises?

Not only are responsible practices possible in SMEs, but they are also desirable, not only for the contribution that they make to the betterment of society and the environment, but also because they can yield performance improvements to the firm. The reasons for engaging in responsible practices are different for SMEs than for large firms, as they are less subject to the pressures of stakeholders and rely more on owners, managers, and employees motivations. Those firms are much less aware of the potential benefits of responsible practices and are content with the perception of those benefits, unlike larger firms that may need to see tangible evidence. While SMEs are aware of the potential of some practices, to deepen their involvement, managers need to be educated on many of the possibilities and shown with examples and cases the value of involvement. Programs must be put in place by governments and business associations to support this process.

In order to have a manageable discussion, we have made many generalizations. It must be borne in mind that there is extreme variety within the term SMEs that encompasses small firms and some quite large ones, manufacturing and commerce, innovative and growth firms and family firms, even subsistence firms, operating in developed and developing markets. Even the simple concept of responsible practices involves an extremely wide variety of activities. Responsible practices must take into account the characteristics of

---

SMEKey and the Business in the Community websites (see references). Cases for Latin America can be found in Vives and Peinado-Vara (2004) and Flores et. al (2007), although several of the firms highlighted are relatively large.

the firm and the environment in which they operate. Definitely one size does not fit all. We have attempted to present the discussion to cover those differences.

References

PUBLICATIONS

Canadian Manufacturers and Exporters, *'Gaining the Competitive Edge: An Environmental Guidebook for Small and Medium Enterprises'*, undated, available at www.cme-mec.ca/on/documents/Environmental_Guidebook.pdf.

Danish Commerce and Companies Agency, *'People and Profits: A Practical Guide to Corporate Social Responsibility'*. Danish Commerce and Companies Agency, Copenhagen 2006.

Department of Trade and Industry, *'Engaging SMEs in Community and Social Issues'*, available in the website of Business in the Community', May 2002. Available in www.bitc.org.uk/docs/SMEs_1.pdf

European Commission, *'European SMEs and Social and Environmental Responsibility'*, European Commission, Brussels, 2002. Available in the web site of the commission, http://ec.europa.eu/enterprise/enterprise_policy/analysis/doc/smes_observatory 2002 report4_en.pdf.

European Commission, *'Introduction to Corporate Social Responsibility for Small and Medium-Sized Enterprises'*, European Commission, Brussels, 2004. Toolkit available in www.europa.eu.int/comm/enterprise/csr/campaign/documentation/index_en.htm.

European Commission, *'Opportunity and Responsibility: How to Help More Small Businesses to Integrate Social and Environmental Issues into What They do'*, European Commission, Brussels, 2007. Available in the web site of the commission, http://ec.europa.eu/enterprise/csr/documents/ree_report.pdf.

Flores, J.; Ogliastri, E.; Peinado-Vara, E. y Petry, I. *'El argumento empresarial de la RSE: 9 casos de América Latina y el Caribe'*. Inter-American Development Bank, Washington, 2007. Available in www.csramericas.org.

Grayson D., *'40 Practical Things that a Small Firm can do: Drawn from Real Life Examples of what Small Businesses are Actually Doing'*, undated. Available in www.smallbusinessjourney.com/output/Page220.asp.

Grayson, D., *'Inspiration: Successfully Engaging Europe's Smaller Businesses in Environmental and Social Issues'*, The Copenhagen Centre, Copenhagen, March 2003. www.copenhagencentre.org.

Grayson, D. and Dodd T. *'Small is Sustainable (and Beautiful!) – Encouraging European Smaller Enterprises to be Sustainable'*, Cranfield School of Management, UK, 2007. www.som.cranfield.ac.uk/som/research/centres/ccr/downloads/Small_is_Sustainable.pdf.

Grayson D., and Hodges, A., 'Everybody's Business: Managing Risks and Opportunities in Today's Global Society', Dorling Kindersley Publishing, London, 2002.

Green Business, *'Greening your Business: A Primer for Smaller Companies'*, 2001. Available in www.greenbiz.com/greenbizchecklist.pdf.

Journal of Business Ethics, Vol 67, No. 3, Spring 2006. Issue devoted to Responsibility in SMEs.

Skapinker, M., *'There is Good Trade in Ethical Trade'*, Financial Times, September 11, 2007.

SustainAbility, International Finance Corporation and Ethos Institute, *'Developing Value: The Business Case for Sustainability in Emerging Markets'*, SustainAbility, London and Washington, 2002. Available in www.ifc.org.

SustainAbility and International Finance Corporation, *'Market Movers: Lessons from a Frontier of Innovation'*, SustainAbility, London and Washington, 2007. Available in www.ifc.org.

UNIDO, 'Corporate Social Responsibility: Implications for Small and Medium Enterprises in Developing Countries', UNIDO, Geneva, 2003.

Vives, A., 'Social and Environmental Responsibility in Small and Medium Enterprises in Latin America', Journal of Corporate Citizenship, Issue 21, Spring 2006.

Vives, A., Corral A., and Isusi, I., 'Responsabilidad Social de la Empresa en las PyMEs de Latinoamerica', Inter-American Development Bank, 2005. Book available in www.csramericas and www.cumpetere.com.

Vives, A. and Peinado-Vara, E., eds. *'Proceedings of the Inter-American Conference on Corporate Social Responsibility: CSR as an Instrument of Competitiveness'*, Inter-American Development Bank, 2004. Available at www.csramericas.org and www.cumpetere.com.

Vogel, D., 'The Market for Virtue: The Potential and Limits of Corporate Social Responsibility', Brookings Institution, Washington, 2005

WEBSITES

SME Key, www.smekey.org, a website devoted to promote CSR practices in SMES. Includes downloadable software to guide the firm through the process of planning CSR activities and assessing progress, based on the business case. It also includes a database of cases and best practices. Available in English, Dutch, French, Italian and Spanish.

Business in the Community is a website for the United Kingdom promoting the improvement of the positive impact of business in society. It includes a channel for SMEs, with cases and other materials. www.bitc.org.uk/small_businesses.

The Corporate Social Responsibility site of the *European Commission* contains extensive materials, including cases and toolkits for SMEs. http://ec.europa.eu/enterprise/csr/.

Applying Corporate Governance

Corporate governance has become an issue which has been raised in popular consciousness in recent years. This has been heightened since 2008 by the financial crisis and the apparent failures in governance. In the UK there have been a succession of codes on corporate governance dating back to the Cadbury Report in 1992. Currently all companies reporting on the London Stock Exchange are required to comply with the Combined Code on Corporate Governance, which came into effect in 2003. It might be thought, therefore, that a framework for corporate governance has already been developed but the code in the UK has been continually revised while problems associated with bad governance have not disappeared. So clearly a framework has not been established in the UK and an international framework looks even more remote.

One of the problems with developing such a framework is the continual rules versus principles debate. The American approach tends to be rules based while the European approach is more based on the development of principles – a slower process. In general, rules are considered to be simpler to follow than principles, demarcating a clear line between acceptable and unacceptable behaviour. Rules also reduce discretion on the part of individual managers or auditors. In practice, however, rules can be more complex than principles. They may be ill-equipped to deal with new types of transactions not covered by the code. Moreover, even if clear rules are followed, one can still find a way to circumvent their underlying purpose – this is harder to achieve if one is bound by a broader principle.

There are of course many different models of corporate governance around the world. These differ according to the nature of the system of capitalism in which they are embedded. The liberal model that is common in Anglo-American countries tends to give priority to the interests of shareholders. The coordinated model, which is normally found in Continental Europe and in Japan, recognises in addition the interests of workers, managers, suppliers, customers and the community. Both models have distinct competitive advantages, but in different ways. The liberal model of corporate governance encourages radical innovation and cost competition, whereas the coordinated model of corporate governance facilitates incremental innovation and quality competition. However there are important differences between the recent approach to governance issues taken in the USA and what has happened in the UK.

In the USA a corporation is governed by a board of directors, which has the power to choose an executive officer, usually known as the chief executive officer (CEO). The CEO has broad power to manage the corporation on a daily basis, but needs to get board approval for certain major actions, such as hiring immediate subordinates, raising money, acquiring another company, major capital expansions or other expensive projects. Other duties of the board may include policy setting, decision making, monitoring management's performance or corporate control. The board of directors is nominally selected by and responsible to the shareholders, but the articels of many companies make it difficult for all but the largest shareholders to have any influence over the makeup of the board. Normally individual shareholders are not offered a choice of board nominees among which to choose, but are merely asked to rubberstamp the nominees of the sitting board. Perverse incentives have pervaded many corporate boards in the developed world, with board members beholden to the chief executive whose actions they are intended to oversee. Frequently, members of the boards of directors are CEOs of other corporations – in interlocking relationships, which many people see as posing a potential conflict of interest.

Corporate governance principles and codes have been developed in different countries and have been issued by stock exchanges, corporations, institutional investors or associations (institutes) of directors and managers with the support of governments and international organisations. As a rule, compliance with these governance recommendations is not mandated by law, although the codes which are linked to stock exchange listing requirements[1] will tend to have a coercive effect. Thus, for example, companies quoted on the London and Toronto Stock Exchanges formally need not follow the recommendations of their respective national codes, but they must disclose whether they follow the recommendations in those documents and, where not, they should provide explanations concerning divergent practices. Such disclosure requirements exert a significant pressure on listed companies for compliance.

There are a lot of aspects of corporate governance which we have alluded to here. The contributors to this part pick up many of these issues as some other important ones. In doing so the intention is to show both the diversity of the topic and the way in which it continues to evolve. In the first chapter of this section therefore Davidson, Sakr & Wang provide an overview of corporate governance and the current situation regarding such governance. As they state, in order to understand the current trends in corporate governance, it is essential to understand corporate problems and the mechanisms that control or mitigate such problems. In this chapter therefore they discuss and investigate the governance issues and current trends, mainly based on theories and evidence in the USA. They focus their attention upon governance as being concerned with managing the decision-making process in the organisation itself and relations with shareholders – the narrow definition of corporate governance which some later chapters will deviate from. Nevertheless they make the important point that one size does not fit all and a universal approach to dealing with issues is problematic.

In the following chapter Aluchna reinforces the message concerning the importance of the Board of Directors in setting and enforcing procedures for a high standard of corporate governance. Her aim in this chapter is to present the functions of the board in line with the current problems and challenges caused by first of all the waive of corporate scandals and frauds that resulted in reform actions introducing increased transparency and accountability as well as the worldwide processes of globalisation and internationalisation of capital markets and corporate governance initiatives, and to consider the impact of regulatory reforms, codes of best practice, public pressure and investors' expectations

---

1   Such as, for example, the UK Combined Code referred to earlier.

addressed to board results in significant change in the attitude of board members, board responsibilities and accountability.

One of the sources of debate in governance is the different approaches taken by the Anglo Saxon and the European countries and this is something which Damiani addresses in the next chapter. She takes a perspective of employees and considers governance taking into account this most significant stakeholder grouping, primarily from a European perspective. In doing so she provides an analysis which recognises the power of stakeholder groupings which can result in small shareholders being disadvantaged – a different perspective to that normally adopted which considers only the primacy of the shareholder. She advocates paying attention to informal understandings as an essential complement to formal governance mechanisms.

The next chapter sees Shaw concerned with the legal and regulatory framework of corporate governance. In his words, the increasing scale of operations and global reach of many corporations has both heightened the need for fair and efficient regulation of corporations and widened the range of agencies that have a stake in such regulation. After discussing many of the issues he then identifies areas where closer cooperation between the various regulatory agencies could bring about a more sustainable economy and society, which would benefit both the stakeholders in a company and the corporation itself.

A perennial problem with business is that of the agency problem which examines the relationship between the managers of a business and its owners and investors, and this is the subject of the next chapter by Aras & Crowther. They argue that in the past this has been attempted by seeking to ensure the alignment of objectives through manipulations of the rewards structures with little success and that therefore more recent efforts have been concerned with procedural changes through the development of strong systems of corporate governance. In this chapter, therefore, they consider the relationship between governance procedures and the agency problem.

In the following chapter Elad is concerned with the proliferation of product certification and labelling schemes that are designed to signal to consumers that goods have been produced in a sustainable manner. In this chapter, therefore, he reviews the development of audit certification schemes by the Fair Trade Labelling Organisation (FLO) and the Forest Stewardship Council (FSC) in order to set the scene for an assessment of their role as tools for managing stakeholder dialogue and corporate social responsibility. Then he examines the concept of corporate social responsibility, and highlights some of the contrasts between financial audits and the audit certification models established by the FSC and the FLO, and their implications for corporate governance.

The next chapter focuses upon an area of increasing importance and, as Ogunc points out, this has normally been approached in terms of mathematical modelling. This has the problem of giving spurious legitimacy to the modelling and obscuring the problems in that data could be flawed or simply wrong and that rare events are very difficult to predict. He argues that risk is not a by-product of the corporate decision making but rather must be considered as the starting point of the strategic management process. He then proposes a new form of risk management for corporations.

In the final chapter in this part Aras & Crowther take the broadest possible definition of corporate governance by considering the relationship between such governance and corporate social responsibility – the other theme of this handbook. They take a position which has been taken by other contributors to this part in stating that it is clearly accepted that good corporate governance is fundamental to the successfully continuing operating of any corporation – and hence much attention has been paid to the procedures of such governance – but that often what is actually meant by the corporate governance of a firm is merely assumed without being made explicit, and moreover it is assumed that the concept is simply connected to the management of investor relationships – the narrow definition of such governance. They therefore examine the relationship between governance and social responsibility.

9 *Trends in Corporate Governance*

WALLACE N. DAVIDSON III, SAMEH SAKR AND
HONGXIA WANG

Introduction

In the past three decades, corporate governance research has experienced a tremendous evolution. Interest in corporate governance in general is growing given the changes in the business environment and the recent worldwide governance reforms in the new millennium. Empirical studies document that poor governance hurts stock market performance (Gompers, Ishii, and Metrick, 2003) and operating performance (Core, Guay, and Rusticus, 2006). Recent studies and the popular press have noted several trends in corporate governance, such as more independent boards; more incentive-based pay for outside directors; more public, exchange, and government scrutiny; and increased institutional stock ownership (Huson, Parrino, and Starks, 2001). Using a theoretic model, Hermalin (2005) further finds trends toward more diligent boards, more outside CEOs, short CEO tenure, more efforts/less perquisite consumption by CEO's, and greater CEO compensation. Research in areas of corporate boards, CEO turnover, and compensation provides extensive empirical evidence supporting the trends predicated by the Hermalin Model.

To understand the current trends in corporate governance, it is essential to understand corporate problems and the mechanisms that control or mitigate such problems. This chapter discusses and investigates the governance issues and current trends, mainly based on theories and evidence in the United States, because of the generally high-standard corporate governance system in the United States (Holmstrom and Kaplan, 2003).

Governance Problems and Corporate Governance

Corporate governance has been defined as 'the structure and the functioning of corporate policies' (Eells, 1960) and as 'the mechanism by which corporations and managers are governed' (Holmstrom and Kaplan, 2001). Corporate governance includes both internal and external governance mechanisms. Internal mechanisms address issues such as how the board of directors, board committees, and executive compensation contracts are used to align the interests between shareholders and managers. External mechanisms deal with the market forces for corporate control, such as takeover offers and proxy contests.

Since the two categories of governance mechanisms interact with each other, we do not make clear distinctions between the two in the following discussion.

In his survey paper, Denis (2001) summarizes the literature in corporate governance and points out that it is commonly believed that corporate governance problems are associated with the separation of ownership and control in modern corporations. Shareholders own stocks and are owners. They do not have direct control over their firms. They delegate control of the corporation to management. The major benefit of delegating day-to-day operations to management is professional management. However, the different incentives between managers and shareholders can lead to agency problems, that is, managers may not work in the best interests of shareholders, but instead may work toward their own interests. Denis (2001) argues that the conflicts of interest may take the form of managerial shirking, managerial consumption of perquisites, managements' desire to remain in power, managerial risk aversion, and misuse of free cash flow.

Separation of ownership and control comes at a cost. Jensen and Meckling (1976) note that once an owner-manager owns less than 100 percent of the corporation, the costs of providing the manager with pecuniary and non-pecuniary benefits are partially borne by shareholders. According to Jensen and Meckling (1976), agency costs include: i) costs incurred by the agent to bond him with the principle, ii) costs incurred by the principle to monitor the agent, and iii) residual loss resulting from the agent's pursuance of non-value-maximizing behaviors. Alchian and Demsetz (1972) note that because monitoring and policing management are costly, it may be in management's best interest to engage in non-value-maximizing behaviors, also labeled shirking, as this will cause their realized rate of rewards to be greater than their promised rate. Shirking drives down the productivity of the whole team and not just the slacking member of the management team. The finance literature is rich in research on the agency costs resulting from the separation of ownership and control in publicly traded corporations, first noted by Berle and Mean (1932).

Governance problems may be compounded when the ownership is dispersed. The question is why corporations with dispersed ownership exist. In other words, what are the benefits and costs of corporations with dispersed ownership? According to Alchian and Demsetz (1972), people organize themselves in production teams when their marginal output from joining forces exceeds the costs incurred in managing and disciplining team members. Demsetz (1967) argues that corporations are formed when the costs of internalizing a process are less than the costs of dealing across markets. Given the large size of modern corporations, it is impossible for any individual to own 100 percent of a corporation. Most shareholders only own a small fraction of a relatively large corporation. Monks and Minow (1995) argue that it makes little sense to consider any of the shareholders an 'owner,' given that there are so many owners in large corporations. A large number of shares deprives shareholders of the power attached to ownership (Berle and Means, 1932). As a consequence, none of the shareholders have the incentive and ability to monitor managers, not only because their ownership is too small to justify such efforts, but also because the benefits of such monitoring will accrue to all shareholders and will not be limited to any one person. This free rider problem gives managers some leeway in perquisites over consumption, since managers will only bear a fraction of such costs, which is commensurate with their fractional ownership, which is usually small.

In respect to the problems that corporate governance target, we redefine corporate governance as mechanisms used to coordinate the relationships among shareholders, managers, the board of directors, and the other forces in the market. We discuss the mechanisms in the following sections.

The Board of Directors, Subcommittees, and Executive Compensation

THE BOARD OF DIRECTORS

Corporate boards and board committees are important components of internal governance. Demsetz (1967) notes that corporations are an efficient organizational structure because of the presence of the board of directors. The delegation of authority from shareholders to the board of directors is among the reasons cited for the sheer existence of a corporation. Fama and Jensen (1983) note that delegation of decision management functions to management, and delegation of decision control functions to boards allows both specialization benefits and efficiencies to accrue to shareholders. The separation of ownership from control necessitates decision systems to separate among risk bearing, decision management, and decision control functions.

Empirical studies document profound evidence that board composition, structure, and activities matter to corporate governance. Fama and Jensen (1983) and Jensen (1993) claim that the ineffective corporate governance in monitoring top management is due to lack of independent leadership and to CEO/Chair duality. The basic logic underlining this argument is that the independent status of outside directors and of the chairman is less likely to be dominated by the management. The impact of board independence (the proportion of outside directors on the board) and board structure (CEO/Chair duality) on board decision is extensively examined in finance literature. For example, Weisbach (1988) argues that outsider-dominated boards are more likely to dismiss CEOs in response to poor performance; Goyal and Park (2002) document that the sensitivity of CEO turnover to firm performance is significantly lower for firms with CEO/Chair duality. Hermalin and Weisbach (2001) argue that outside director-dominated boards and small boards tend to make better decisions in acquisitions, poison pills, CEO turnover, and CEO compensation.

According to agency theory, small boards can be more effective monitors than large boards because small boards lessen free rider problems (Jensen, 1993; Lipton and Lorsch, 1992). Yermack (1996) finds empirical evidence that board size and firm value are negatively related. However, Cheng (2008) discovers that larger boards of directors are associated with lower performance variability. Cheng (2008) explains this notion by pointing to the necessity of compromises by the increased number of members in large boards. This in turn leads to decisions that are less extreme, and shareholders bear relatively less risk. Given the inconsistent empirical results on board size, Coles, Daniel, and Naveen (2007) posit and show that one board size does not fit all. They find evidence that Tobin's Q increases with board size for complex firms. In any event, board size does play an important role that determines the strength of the board of directors, and consequently the board's monitoring effectiveness. The argument in Coles et al. (2007) appears to be more practical. Board size should be determined by the business and other specific factors of a firm.

Another measure of board effectiveness is board activities, which are usually proxied by the number of times that the board meets in a year. Conger, Finegold, and Lawler (1998) argue that effective board decisions require that directors have 'sufficient, well organized periods of time together as a group' (p. 7). Empirical studies also provide profound evidence that supports this notion. Vafaes (1999) shows that boards that meet more often can improve firm performance. Xie, Davidson, and DaDalt (2003) show that more active boards are associated with lower levels of earnings management.

BOARD SUBCOMMITTEES

Audit, compensation, and nomination committees have been found to have the highest qualifications and to be the most powerful committees. The 2002 governance rule in the United States reflects the importance of these committees. The Sarbanes Oxley Act requires that the audit committee be independent. This act also requires that each corporation disclose whether the audit committee is composed of at least one financial expert. New York Stock Exchange and NASDQ also require that independent directors play a large role in the compensation and nominating committees. Research focuses on both the independence and activities of these committees. The general conclusion of the extant research is that more independent and more active committees provide close monitoring of the management.

Only high-quality boards can effectively monitor the management and mitigate the potential conflicts between the management and the shareholders. In the mid-1980's, scholars advocated change in the director selection process. Lorch and MacIver (1989) posit that directors be selected by a nominating committee rather than the CEO. This makes sense because of the collective wisdom of a committee. Moreover, using a nominating committee can also mitigate the potential problems of packing the board with the CEO's friends. Intuitively, the nomination committee determinates the quality of the board. Vafeas (1999) examines the nature of board nominating committees and their role in corporate governance, and finds that nominating committees can influence the independence of outsiders. Meanwhile, the findings of the determinants of committee composition also reflect the important role of the board of directors in corporate governance. Specifically, the independence of nominating committees is positively related to the quality of the board (Vafeas, 1999).

The corporate scandals in early 2000 in the United States puts audit committees in an extremely important position to discipline and monitor corporate management. The Sarbanes Oxley Act increases the power and responsibility of the audit committee. The audit committee composition and function has been examined by Klein (2002), who finds that the audit committee's independence is directly associated with board size and independence, and negatively associated with growth opportunities, the presence of other corporate control mechanisms, and the information sought from the corporation's financial statements. Xie, Davidson and Dadalt (2003) and Ebrahim (2007) examine boards of directors and audit committees from the susceptibility of the corporation to engagement in earnings management. Board and audit committee independence and activities (proxied by the number of meetings) have been found to be associated with decreased incidence of earnings management. Also, board members' financial sophistication was negatively associated with firms engaging in earnings management.

Conyon and Peck (1998) find no effect of the percentage of outsiders on the board or on remuneration committees, and CEO/Chair duality on the level of management pay for a sample of UK corporations. In boards with a higher percentage of outsiders, however, they found more alignment of top management pay and corporate performance. However, Elsaid and Davidson (2007) argue that the composition of the compensation committee of a firm influences the board's bargaining power in CEO compensation negotiation.

EXECUTIVE AND DIRECTOR COMPENSATION

CEO compensation design has long been viewed as a contractual device that the board of directors uses to resolve agency conflicts between managers and shareholders (Brander and Poitevin, 1992; and Dybvig and Zender, 1991 among many). Well-designed CEO compensation can attract the talented, motivate the CEO to align their interest with those of shareholders, and enhance firm value. Agency theory assumes that the board acts fully on behalf of shareholders and develops optimal compensation contracts that maximize shareholders' wealth. In this contract, both CEO pay level and pay structure should be carefully designed. Compensation solution dictates not only how much the CEO gets paid, but also how they get paid. Both the level and the form of compensation affect CEOs' decision. For example, Bliss and Rosen (2001) find that CEOs with stock-based compensation were less likely to make an acquisition.

The principal-agent model provides a theoretical guideline for designing CEO compensation. The principal-agent model states that a manager should be paid relative to a benchmark which factors out the effects from elements beyond a CEO's control, such as general economic conditions. In other words, agency theory suggests that an agent be evaluated on a relative basis. Gibbons and Murphy (1990) document that a CEO's pay is negatively and significantly related to industry and market performance, and CEO performance is more likely to be evaluated relative to aggregate market movement rather than relative to industry performance, which supports the Relative Performance Evaluation (RPE hereafter) view. Bertrand and Mullainathan (2001) provide evidence that well-governed firms fit the predictions of the contracting view in which shareholders use pay to align the managers' interests with those of their own. However, the evidence for determining CEO compensation based on RPE is sparse (Janakiraman, Lambert and Larcker, 1992; Aggarwal and Samwick, 1999). Academics conduct a lot of research on the phenomenon of the lack of RPE in CEO compensation practice. Researchers provide a lot of explanations which can be grouped in two categories: rent extraction (Bebchuk and Fried, 2004; Bertrand and Mullainthan, 2001; Garvey and Mibourn, 2006) and non-optimal contracts which state that RPE is not optimal, but costly (Aggarwal and Samwick, 1999; Garvey and Milbourn, 2003; Gibbons and Murphy, 1990; Rajgopal, Shevlin, and Zamora, 2006; among many).

Equity-based pay, including stocks and options, increased tremendously in the US during the 1990s. The underlying rationale is that owners are more concerned about firm values. If managers are made owners, they may then be motivated to maximize firm value and shareholder wealth. An increase in managerial ownership provides some explanation for the executive compensation trend toward equity-based pay. However, managers may have a different goal from that of the board of directors. Ofek and Yermack (2000) examine the impact of stock-based compensation on managerial ownership, and find that equity-based compensation increases the incentives for lower-ownership managers, but not for higher-ownership managers. These findings suggest that equity-based pay has a limited ability to align shareholders' interests with those of managers. Such agency conflict results from managerial risk aversion. Ofek and Yermack's (2000) findings may have important implications for boards of directors. Boards should work out ways to prevent executives from unloading their shareholdings and thus their incentive to increase the value of the firm and the wealth of the shareholders.

Directors are also agents. Director compensation also plays a role in effective monitoring. Hoi and Robin (2004) offer advice on the best practice with regards to designing the incentive compensation plan for directors. While part of the compensation could be in the form of cash, most of the compensation should be in the form of equity. The director ought to have a substantial equity exposure, and should not be allowed to offset such an exposure through selling or through the use of derivatives contracts. Last but not least, the compensation package should not only include an incentive package for future performance, but also a reward for past performance.

Kang, Kumar, and Lee's (2006) results point to the relationship between the corporation's compensation package, its investment opportunity set, and the extent of agency conflict within a corporation. The equity-based compensation is an important determinant of the long-term capital investment of major United States' corporations. Also, equity-based compensation is used to alleviate agency conflicts. The more susceptible the corporation is to agency conflict, the larger the proportion of equity-based compensation in the director's total compensation. Along the same line, Cyret, Kang, and Kumar (2002) have similar findings. They show that the board of directors (as a part of the internal control mechanisms) and the takeover market (as a part of the external market of corporate control) substitute for each other in limiting management's perverse behavior of self dealing through overpaying themselves in the form of equity compensation.

In sum, both governance theories and empirical evidence show that independent and active boards and board subcommittees provide effective monitoring to the management, which helps mitigate agency problems. As for board size, it depends on the specific factors of a firm. There is no wonder that the Sarbanes Oxley Act, New York Stock Exchange, and NASDAQ require the independence of the board of directors and other related changes in board structure.

Direct monitoring from the board of directors is one solution to the potential conflicts between managers and shareholders. Giving executives and board directors incentives to align their interest with those of shareholders provides an alternative to strengthen the accountability of managers to shareholders. Incentives and bonding can be achieved by using executive compensation contracts. Equity-based pay, if properly designed, can help to reduce agency conflicts.

Blockholders and Corporate Governance

Researchers have defined blockholders as shareholders who hold 5 percent or more of a corporation's common stock. Blockholders can be individuals, corporations, and institutional investors. Due to their large stake held in a corporation, blockholders have an incentive to monitor and control management and the board of directors. Moreover, blockholders also have better influence over the company than shareholders with smaller holdings and they may also have greater resources and abilities to be more effective monitors. As a result, blockholders are an important internal governance mechanism. One way for blockholders to influence management decision is to sit on the board or serve as officers, which entitles them the power to influence management decisions (Holderness, 2003). Studies suggest that restructurings and the replacement of the CEO increase significantly after the acquisition of a block of stocks by outside investors (Peck, 2004; Denis and Serrano, 1996, among many). Shliefer and Vishny's (1986) model shows that benefits accruing from the presence of blockholders are not only from their monitoring of management because of their holdings' size, but also from facilitating takeovers that benefit themselves and the remaining shareholders in the process. Actually, corporations' dividend policy may be designed to accommodate the preferences of blockholders and go against that of the remaining shareholders since dividends are taxed as regular income rather than deferred capital gains tax. Such management decisions reflect the significant impact of blockholders on management.

The presence of blockholders also affects both executive pay level and pay structure. In his survey paper on blockholders and corporate control, Holderness (2003) states that the literature is consistent with the role of external blockholders in monitoring executive compensation. For example, Mehran (1995) provides evidence that the use of incentive-based pay declines with blockholder monitoring as a substitute for incentive-based compensation (Mehran, 1995). However, Peck (2004) finds evidence that blockholders do not have a significant role in increasing executive incentive pay, which may be explained by the short block holding period. According to Peck (2004), the majority of professional investors sell their block holdings within one year.

The effectiveness of blockholders in mitigating agency costs depends on both the nature of agency problems and type of blockholders (Chen and Yur-Austin, 2007). Chen and Yur-Austin (2007) find that outside blockholders are more vigilant about managerial extravagance, while the inside blockholders are more effective in improving firm asset efficiency. Sun (2005) classifies blockholders on the basis of how informed the blockholders are. Sun (2005) argues that same-industry blockholders are better informed than blockholders outside the industry, and hence better monitors. Recent research has also indicated that not all blockholders have the same effect on the firm's cash flow performance (Cornett, Marcus, Saunders, and Tehranian, 2007) or on the quality of acquisition announcements (Chen, Harford, and Li, 2007). Cornett et al. (2007) show that the positive effect of institutional holdings on operating cash flow occur only when the blockholder is pressure insensitive. In other words, institutional investors who have a business relationship with the firm (pressure sensitive) are not as good at monitoring as those who do not have a business relationship with the firm. Chen et al (2007), on the other hand, show that institutions with large shareholdings with a long-term orientation are better monitors than institutions that lack such qualities. The monitoring of these institutions benefits all other shareholders rather than benefiting themselves only through trading for short-term profits.

Based on the above analysis, given the large stake of blockholders in a corporation and their ability to monitor the board and management, we believe that blockholders will continue to play their role in influencing the board and management decisions and the firm value. Their contribution not only benefits themselves, but also other shareholders. However, the role of blockholders in corporate governance has its limit. As pointed out by Peck (2004), the majority of professional investors do not hold their blocks long enough to exert changes in governance policies. The short block holding period does not improve the independence and effectiveness of the board of directors (2004).

Who Monitors the Board?

Shareholders delegate to the board of directors the responsibility of running the corporation. Theoretically, board directors must fulfill their duties with loyalty and care, meaning that directors must demonstrate unyielding loyalty to their shareholders and exercise due diligence in making decisions (Monks and Minow, 1995). Among the most notable of these responsibilities is hiring, rewarding, disciplining, and even firing management. In other words, the board monitors management. However, board directors are selected, compensated, and informed by management (among many, Monks and Minow, 1995; Bebchuk and Fried, 2004). Such a relationship between the board and the management casts doubt on whether the board members can effectively exercise their duties. Directors are agents themselves (Hermalin and Weisbach, 1991). In addition, research on board directorship shows that directors are too busy to fulfill their monitoring duties because of their multiple directorships (for example, Fitch and Shivdasani, 2006; Perry and Peyer, 2005; Jiraporn, DaDalt., Ning, Davidson, 2007). To ensure that the board of director fulfills its fiduciary duties to its shareholders, there must be some forces that can monitor the board effectively. The question is, who monitors the board?

This question has puzzled the corporate finance field—for example, Berle and Mean (1932) and Jensen and Meckling (1976), among several others—and constitutes a main research topic in finance literature. When boards (as agents to shareholders) fail to carry out their responsibility of disciplining inefficient management, forces outside the firm step in. Bebchuk and Cohen (2005) identify two ways that boards may be removed: one is proxy fight, and the other is takeover. In addition to these proxy contests and takeovers, current research shows that shareholder proposals also play a significant role in monitoring the effectiveness of the board of directors. The role of the managerial labor market cannot be ignored. We discuss each of these as follows.

PROXY FIGHT

Proxy fight, or proxy contest, is defined as a 'solicitation in opposition' of the incumbent management, and requires special disclosures by the dissident and the incumbent whenever such solicitation occurs. Proxy fight is initiated by dissidents who actively and formally solicit votes to oppose incumbent management (Alexander, Chen, Seppi, Spatt, 2006). In a proxy contest, the incumbent management proposes to re-elect a slate of directors, while the dissident offers a different slate of directors to a vote by the shareholders (Edelman and Thomas, 2005).

Proxy fight may not only provide a way to remove boards, but also have a direct effect on incumbent management (Huang and Yen, 1996; Yen and Chen, 2005) and shareholder value implications (IKenberry and Lakonishok, 1993). Yen and Chen (2005) document empirical evidence of the highest turnover rate of top management in firms in which the dissidents win majority seats, and the lowest management turnover rates in firms in which the dissidents win no seats. Ikenberry and Lakonishok (1993) find negative abnormal returns and deteriorating operating performance prior to the announcement of proxy contests.

However, the problems of proxy fight are the costs involved and the unproven leadership of dissidents. This may provide an explanation for the rare use of proxy contests. As indicated by Bebchuk and Hart (2002), rival teams that initiate proxy fights face great impediments. Staggered boards add more difficulties to the challengers because the dissents have to win two elections, which require more resources and time. In other words, staggered boards provide incumbent management with protection from being removed.

THE MARKET FOR CORPORATE CONTROL

Demsetz (1967) notes that it is the control rights attached to the physical property being exchanged that determines the ultimate value of the exchanged property. When shareholders designate a board of directors to run the firm, they retain ownership of part of the firm's assets (stocks), but they hand over the control rights to the board of directors. Jensen and Ruback (1983) define corporate control as 'the rights to determine the management of corporate resources—that is the right to hire, fire, and set the compensation level of top level management' (p. 8).

Shareholders do not monitor management directly because of the widely dispersed ownership. In the absence of shareholders' direct monitoring, another device used in disciplining management and the board is takeovers of the market for corporate control. In takeover bids, raiders offer to purchase the shares from the targets' shareholders if they see profit opportunities. Shareholders are more likely to vote in favor of selling their stock if the price is high enough (Edelman and Thomas, 2006). Raiders in takeovers gain control of the corporation's assets, fire inefficient management, and realize stock price appreciation.

Corporate market control literature documents that poorly-performing firms are more likely to become the takeover targets, the managers in such firms are more likely to be fired, and the takeover is more likely to create value, on average (for example, Denis, 2001; Holmstrom and Kaplan, 2001; Haan and Riyanto, 2006). Takeover has a significant effect on target directors. According to Harford (2003), target directors not only lose their current board seats, but also hold fewer directorships in the future following a complete takeover offer.

However, Gravey and Swan (1994) argue against the effectiveness of takeovers as a disciplinary mechanism due to their cost, and also because takeovers are absent in some places, such as Japan and Germany, where corporations are doing well. In the survey paper, Denis (2001) also recognizes the limitation of takeover as a corporate governance mechanism in regard to the costs and time involved in takeover, and potential conflicts caused by the takeover. One obvious problem is that the majority of acquirers pay too much for the targets and cause their own shares to fall, which Denis (2001) calls negative net present value project. From the perspective of target shareholders, the premium paid by the acquiring firm is another source for target shareholders to gain value. Haan and Riyanto (2006) show that a takeover threat decreases managerial effort. To provide entrenchment to the board and management, staggered board and poison pills are the most commonly used anti-takeover techniques

SHAREHOLDER PROPOSALS

Securities and Exchange Committee (SEC) Rule 14a-8, adopted by SEC in 1934, provides a relatively cheap and simple channel for shareholders to express their views on corporate management. The purpose of rule 14a-8 is to 'strengthen shareholders' voice in corporate affairs' (Thomas and Cotter, 2007). Under Rule 14a-8, owners with 1 percent of shares of publicly-traded companies with the market value of $2,000 have the right to offer shareholder proposals. Shareholder proposals' subjects are limited and are generally in the form of a recommendation to the board. Proposals are placed in corporations' annual proxy statements, to be voted on by all stockholders. Shareholder proposals cover two areas in which shareholders request the board of directors to take actions: corporate governance and social responsibility. Empirical studies document the frequent presence of shareholder proposals in underperforming firms, indicating the poor governance in such firms and shareholders' intention of change (Black, 1998; Karpoff, 2001; and Romano, 2001). For our purpose, we focus on the proposals relating to corporate governance.

Proposals relating to corporate governance target issues that have direct effects on shareholder wealth, such as issues of executive compensation, director selection, CEO/ Chair duality, classified boards, independence of key committees, voting, and other anti-takeover defenses. Shareholder proposals address both the internal and external governance problems perceived.

Historically, shareholder proposals receive little support from shareholders (Karpoff, Maltesta, Walking, 1996; Gordon and Pound, 1993) and are generally ignored by corporate boards (Black, 1998). Based on the empirical evidence, earlier studies conclude that the approach of shareholder proposals is marginally effective at best. However, with the increased shareholder activism in recent years, shareholders tend to vote in favor of these proposals, starting in the 1990s (Black, 1998; Gillan and Starks, 2000). Ertimur, Ferri, and Stubben (2006) argue that it is costly to ignore majority-voted proposals for both the firm and individual directors. Directors may lose their jobs under the pressure of shareholders if they continuously fail to respond to the shareholders' call. Factors which may hurt the firm and individual directors include lower ratings from governance services, negative press coverage, radical change pressure, reputation loss, and 'vote no' campaigns caused by directors' failure to implement shareholder proposals (Ertimur, Ferri, and Stubben, 2006).

Given that more and more proposals are gaining support from shareholders and the changed business environment in the post-Enron period, boards are under pressure to take actions on shareholder proposals. The pressure comes not only from shareholders, but also from peer firms and the new governance environment in the post-Enron period (Ertimur, Ferri, and Stubben, 2006). Proposal initiators, proposal type, ownership structure, and recommendations by third-party voting advisory services affect the level of support for proposals, and hence the likelihood of implementation by boards of directors. Proposals brought up by unions and institution investors gain more favorable votes and exert more pressure on corporate boards and management in recent years (Gordon and Pound, 1993; Gillan and Stark, 2000). Insider ownership and director ownership are negatively related to favorable votes (Gordon and Pound, 1993; Romano, 2001). Institutional investors' use of the service provided by proxy advisors has experienced tremendous growth in the past few years (Alexander et al, 2006). Empirical studies show that boards increasingly implement shareholder proposals. Using data in the Standard and Poor's 1500 index,

Ertimur, Ferri, and Stubben (2006) find that the frequency of implementation has more than doubled from the late 1990s to the period of 2003–2004, and the likelihood of implementation is positively related to the degree of voting support. In other words, voting outcome determines, to some degree, whether the board of directors acts on the shareholder proposals or not. Similarly, Thomas and Cotter (2007) provide empirical evidence that many more proposals are receiving majority shareholder support and boards are more responsive to those majority-favored proposals. In particular, they find that boards are increasingly willing to remove anti-takeover defenses such as classified boards and poison pills. Thomas and Cotter (2007) conclude that shareholder proposals are becoming an emerging force in corporate governance.

From the above discussion, there is no doubt that shareholders are increasingly using the channel of shareholder proposals to request change, and management and the board of directors have to reconsider their attitude and decisions on majority-approved proposals. Obviously, shareholder proposals are becoming an important governance mechanism.

MANAGERIAL LABOR MARKET

The ex-post settling-up of the managerial labor market with inefficient managers was first noted by Fama (1980) to counter the argument that disciplining inefficient management is the responsibility of the takeover market and outside shareholders (Manne, 1965; Jensen and Meckling, 1976). The disciplinary role of the managerial labor market has spurred a stream of research that is still flowing to date.

Fama (1980) argues that shareholders are more concerned with an efficient capital market that correctly prices different management teams rather than with disciplining a particular inefficient management team. Accordingly, an efficient managerial labor market would discipline inefficient management ex-post because of their deviations from ex-ante contract specifications. Harford (2003) and Farrell and Whidbee (2000) document the ex-post settling by the labor market. Harford (2003) finds that all directors hold fewer seats post-takeover, except for the less experienced ones who gain experience from the takeover; and directors who facilitate a merger benefit more in the future by holding more seats than other directors. Also, Farrell and Whidbee (2000) find that after the forced removal of the CEO, there was a higher probability for outsiders to remain on the boards and to hold more directorships in the future when they are independent of the sacked CEO, when they have substantial equity holdings, and when their performance rises after the departure of the CEO, signaling a good replacement decision. Arthaud-Day, Certo, and Dalton (2006) investigate the executive and director turnover following corporate financial restatement in the pre-SOX period, and find that directors and audit committee members were about 70 percent more likely to exit in financial restatement firms. These results support that argument that directorship is not always safe if the directors do not fulfill their fiduciary duties.

Moreover, competition among management teams occurs for teams both inside and outside the corporation. Fama (1980) notes that the price of a management team affects all of the management team. Therefore, there is pressure from managerial levels above and below the management team inside the corporation, as well as from management teams outside of the corporation (Alchian and Demsetz, 1972). However, outside management teams will face the problem of identifying which management teams engage in non-value maximizing behavior, and the extent of such behavior.

Gravy and Swan (1994) and Amihud and Lev (1981) argue against the role of managerial reputation in disciplining management. Gravy and Swan (1994) undermine the role of reputation in the case of directors who are close to retirement. In addition, there is also the Berle and Mean (1932) argument that what is important is the board member's talent contribution to the incumbent management, not to the shareholders' benefit. Amihud and Lev (1981), on the other hand, present the following reasons why the labor market does not make managers bear full responsibility for their actions: i) welfare lost by shareholders might be greater than welfare gained by management; ii) noise surrounding management performance results in managerial contracts that depend on stochastic variables; and iii) full monitoring of managerial actions is not possible.

Other Forces in Corporate Governance

Denis (2001) posits that the most basic corporate governance mechanisms exist in the system of laws and regulations that govern the firm. La Porta, Lopez-de-Silanes, Shleifer, and Vishny (1997, 1998, and 2000) find evidence that English common-law origins provide stronger protection for investors, and that French civil law origins provide weaker protection. They show the association between the capital market and the character of legal rules and the quality of law enforcement, and argue that better legal protection for shareholders can reduce the risk of expropriation by management, and allow more separation between ownership and control.

Legal systems affect corporate governance. La Porta et al. (1997) argue that strong investor protection creates an environment that fosters good corporate governance. A good example is the 2002 governance rules, including the Sarbanes Oxley Act and NYSE and NASDAQ governance rules in the United States. Declining stock prices, corporate fraud, and unethical corporate behaviors at the turn of this century became headline stories in the media. High-profile corporate failures led to the passage of the Sarbanes Oxley Act and amendments to the United States' stock exchanges which targeted corporate governance. The major changes of the 2002 governance rules include provisions on accurate financial reporting, requirements for the independence of corporate board and key subcommittees, individual responsibilities, prohibition of personal loans to executives and directors, and whistle blowing systems. Under the new rules, both corporate boards and executives are under the scrutiny of regulators, the media, and the public. A number of empirical studies have been conducted on the effects of the Sarbanes Oxley Act, and there is extensive evidence that the 2002 governance rules have had a significant influence on corporate behaviors. For example, using a sample of 7,000 firms from 1990 to 2004, Linck, Netter, and Yang (2006) find that SOX significantly increases the costs and monitoring function of corporate boards. Following SOX, board size increases by adding non-employee (outsider) directors, director compensation increases substantially, director work load and risk increase, board committee (especially audit committees) meet more often, and CEO/Chair duality decreases. Moreover, they find the director pool also changes; specifically, they find that the numbers of retired executives, financial experts, and lawyers/consultants increase.

In general, firm-level governance is positively related to country-level investor protection, but that is not always the case. Klapper and Love (2004) find a wide variation in firm-level governance, but the differences are not explained by differences in country-level legal systems (there are well-governed firms in countries with poor legal systems and vice versa). Klapper and Love (2004) further find that firm-level corporate governance provisions matter more in countries with weak legal systems.

In addition to the previously-discussed mechanisms in corporate governance, the monitoring role of creditors cannot be ignored. Agency problems can also come from free cash flow. Debt obligation can reduce such problems. It is argued that privately-held debt (bank debt) and short-term debt are two important corporate governance devices (Florack and Ozkan, 2004). The reasons cited are that banks are better informed, and short-term debt may be more useful in reducing free cash flow problems.

Concluding Remarks

In this chapter, we provide a brief review of corporate governance problems and mechanisms for the past 30 years and of the current trends in corporate governance. The root of governance problems is the separation of ownership from control. As a corporation grows larger, ownership becomes more dispersed. Governance problems may become more serious due to the compounding effect of the lack of incentives and abilities of each small individual shareholder to monitor managers. Governance mechanisms are developed to deal with governance issues.

There are a lot of factors, related to widely-dispersed ownership that may magnify governance problems. Such factors include: the age of key executives, the degree of information asymmetry, technology advancement, political change, the general business environment, and the existence of other stakeholders. Given the complexity of those forces that either cause or magnify the agency problems, we argue that governance problems are dynamic, not static.

Corporations face different problems at different times; dynamic problems need dynamic solutions. The past three decades have witnessed the dynamic nature of both governance problems and solutions. Sometimes internal governance mechanisms are in a controlling position, while other times, external governance mechanisms are dominant. In addition, effective governance mechanisms may differ from firm to firm. For example, in the 1980s and 1990s, institutional shareholders and equity-based pay served to reinforce the bond of common interest between managers and shareholders (Holmstrom and Kaplan, 2003). However, the design of equity-based pay may have some serious problems. On the one hand, equity-based pay may not lead to the expected incentives. Ex-post outcome may deviate far from the ex-ante expectations. Ofek and Yermack (2000) point out that the board of directors and the CEO may have different goals, where the board wants to give the CEO incentives to increase firm value, while the CEO wants to diversify by selling ownership. On the other hand, a possible solution may also create new problems. It is argued that the corporate scandals of the early 2000's may have some connection to equity-based pay (Holmstrom and Kaplan, 2003). Improperly designed pay may give managers incentives to be involved in activities that benefit themselves, but hurt shareholders.

A governance mechanism that is good for one corporation may not solve agency problems in another company. As the saying goes, one hat does not fit all. Therefore, governance issues present a never-ending challenge to corporations, regulators, and scholars. However, many of the problems can be avoided or mitigated if the involved parties collaborate to find solutions ahead of time.

References

Aggarwal. R., Samwick, A., 1999, Executive compensation, strategic competition, and relative performance evaluation: Theory and evidence. *Journal of Finance* 54 (6), 1999-2043.

Alchian, A., Demsetz, H., 1972. Production, information costs and economic organization. *American Economic Review* 62 (5), 777-795.

Alexander, C., Chen, M., Seppi, D., Spatt, C., 2006. The role of advisory services in proxy voting. Unpublished working paper. Office of Economic Analysis, Securities and Exchange Commission.

Amihud, Y., Lev, B., 1981. Risk reduction as a managerial motivation for conglomerate mergers. *The Bell Journal of Economics* 12, 607-617.

Arthaud-Day, M., Certo, S., Dalton, C., Dalton, D., 2006. A changing of the guard: executive and director turnover following corporate financial restatements. *Academy of Management Journal* 49 (6), 1119-1136.

Bebchuk, L., Cohen, A, 2005. The costs of entrenched boards. *Journal of Financial Economics* 78 (2), 409-433.

Bebchuk, L., Fried, J., 2004. Pay without performance: the unfilled promise of executive compensation. Harvard University Press.

Bebchuk, L., Hart, O., 2002. Takeover bids vs. proxy fights in contests for corporate control. NBER Working Paper No. 8633.

Berle, A., Means, G., 1932. The modern corporation and private property. Macmillan, New York.

Bertrand, M., Mullainathan, S., 2001. Are CEOs rewarded for luck? The ones without principals are. *The Quarterly Journal of Economics* 116 (3), 901-932.

Black, B., 1998. Shareholder activism and corporate g overnance in the United States. In: Newman, Peter (Ed), The New Palgrave Dictionary of Economics and the Law.

Bliss, R., Rosen, R., 2001. CEO compensation and bank mergers. *Journal of Financial Economics* 61, 107-138.

Brander, J., Poitevin, M.,1992. Managerial compensation and the agency costs of debt finance. *Managerial and Decision Economics* 13, 55-64.

Chen, X., Harford, J., Li, K., 2007. Monitoring: Which institutions matter? *Journal of Financial Economics* 86, 279-305.

Chen, X., Yur-Austin, J., 2007. Re-measuring agency costs: The effectiveness of blockholders. *The Quarterly Review of Economics and Finance* 47, 588-601.

Cheng, S., 2008. Board size and the variability of corporate performance. *Journal of Financial Economics* 87, 157-176.

Coles, L., Daniel, N., and Naveen, L., 2008. Boards: Does one size fit all? *Journal of Financial Economics* 87, 329-356.

Conger, J., Finegold, D., Lawler III, E., 1998. Appraising boardroom performance. *Harvard Business Review* 76, 136-148.

Conyon, Martin J., Peck, S., 1998. Board control, remuneration committees, and top management compensation. *Academy of Management Journal* 41 (2), 146-157.

Core, J., Guay, W., Rusticus, T., 2006. Does weak governance cause weak stock returns? An examination of firm operating performance and investors' expectations. *Journal of Finance* LXI (2), 655-687.

Cornett, M., Marcus, A., Saunders, A., Tehranian, H., 2007. The impact of institutional ownership on corporate performance. *Journal of Banking and Finance* 31, 1771-1794.

Cyret, R., Kang, S., Kumar, P., 2002. Coporate governance, takeovers, and top management compensation: theory and evidence. *Management Science* 48 (4), 453-469.

Demsetz, H., 1967. Toward a theory of property rights. *American Economic Review* 57, 347-359.

Denis, D. K., 2001. Twenty five years of corporate governance research ... and counting, *Review of Financial Economics* 10, 191-211.

Denis, D., Serrano, J., 1996. Active investors and management turnover following unsuccessful control contests. *Journal of Financial Economics* 40, 239–266.

Dybvig, P., Zender, J., 1991. Capital structure and dividend irrelevance with asymmetric information. *Review of Financial Studies* 4, 201-219.

Ebrahim, A., 2007. Earnings management and board activity: An additional evidence. *Review of Accounting and Finance* 6 (1), 42-58.

Edelman, P., Thomas, R., 2006. Corporate voting and the takeover debate. Working paper, Vanderbilt University Law School.

Eells, R., 1960. The meaning of modern business: An introduction to philosophy of large corporate enterprise. New York: Columbia University Press.

Elsaid, E., Davidson, W.N., 2007. What happens to CEO compensation following turnover and succession. Working paper, Southern Illinois University Carbondale.

Ertimur, Y., Ferri, F., Stubben, S., 2006. Board of directors' responsiveness to shareholder proposals: Evidence from majority-vote shareholder proposals. Working paper, Duke University.

Fama, E., 1980. Agency problems and the theory of the firm. *Journal of Political Economy* 88, 288-307.

Fama, E., Jensen, M., 1983. Seperation of ownership and control. *Journal of Law and Economics* 26, 301-325.

Farrell, K., Whidbee, D., 2000. The consequences of forced CEO succession for outside directors. The *Journal of Business* 73 (4), 597-627.

Fitch, E., Shivdasani, A., 2006. Are busy boards effective monitors? *Journal of Finance* LXI (2), 689-724.

Florack, C., Ozkan, A., 2004. Agency costs and corporate governance mechanism: Evidence for UK firms. Working paper, University of York, UK.

Garvey, G., Milbourn, R., 2003. Incentive compensation when executives can hedge the market: evidence of relative performance evaluation in the cross section. *Journal of Finance* 58 (4), 1557-1581.

Garvey, G., Mibourn,T., 2006. Asymmetric benchmarking in compensation: Executives are rewarded for good luck but not penalized for bad. *Journal of Financial Economics* 82, 197-225.

Gibbons, Murphy, 1990, Relative performance evaluation for chief executive officers. *Industry and Labor Relation Review* 43, 30-51.

Gillan, S., Starks, L., 2000, Relationship investing and shareholder activism by institutional investors. *Journal of Financial Economics* 57, 275-305.

Gompers, P., Ishii, J., Metrick, A., 2003, Corporate governance and equity prices. *Quarterly Journal of Economics* 118, 107–155.

Gordon, L., Pound, J., 1993. Information, ownership structure and shareholder voting: evidence from shareholder sponsored corporate governance proposals. *Journal of Financial Economics*, 48 (2), 697-718.

Goyal, V., Park, C., 2002. Board leadership structure and CEO turnover. *Journal of Corporate Finance* 8 (1), 49-66.

Gravey, G., Swan, P., 1994. Economics of corporate governance, beyond the Marshallian firm. *Journal of Corporate Finance* 1, 139-174.

Haan, M., Riyanto, Y., 2006. The effects of takeover threats on shareholders and firm value. *Journal of Economic Behavior & Organization* 59 (1), 45-68.

Harford, J., 2003. Takeover bids and target directors' incentives: the impact of a bid on directors' wealth and board seats. *Journal of Financial Economics* 69, 51-83.

Hermalin, B., 2005. Trends in corporate governance. *The Journal of Finance* LX(5), 2351-2384.

Hermalin, B., Weisbach, M., 1991. The effects of board composition and direct incentives on firm performance. *Financial Management* 20 (4), 101-112.

Hermalin, B., Weisbach, M., 2001. Boards of directors as an endogenously determined institution: A survey of the economic literature. National Bureau Economic Research.

Hoi, C., Robin, A., 2004. The design of incentive compensation for directors. *Corporate Governance* 4 (3), 47-53.

Holderness, C., 2003. A survey of blockholders and corporate control. *FRBNY Economic Policy Review*, April, 51-64.

Holmstrom, B., Kaplan, S., 2001. Corporate governance and merger activity in the United States: Making sense of the 1980s and 1990s. *Journal of Economic Perspectives* 15 (2), 121-144.

Holmstrom, B., Kaplan, S., 2003. The State of U.S. Corporate Governance: What's Right and what's wrong? NBER working paper.

Huang, W., Yen, G., 1996. The impact of proxy contests on managerial turnover: a test of the job security hypothesis. *Managerial and Decision Economics* 17, 551–558.

Huson, M., Parrino, R., Starks, L., 2001. Internal monitoring mechanisms and CEO turnover: A long-term perspective. *Journal of Finance* 55, 2265–2297.

IKenberry, D., Lakonishok, J., 1993. Corporate governance through the proxy contest: evidence and implications. *Journal of Business* 66 (3), 405-435

Janakiraman, S., Lambert, R., Larcker, D., 1992, An empirical investigation of the relative performance evaluation hypothesis. *Journal of Accounting Research* 30 (1), 53-69.

Jiraporn, P., DaDalt.P., Ning, Y., Davidson,W., 2007. Too busy to show up? An analysis of directors' absence. Working paper.

Jensen, M., Meckling, W., 1976. Theory of the firm: Managerial behavior, agency costs, and ownership structure. *Journal of Financial Economics* 3, 305-360.

Jensen, Michael C, 1993, The Modern industrial revolution, exit and the failure of internal control systems. *Journal of Finance* 48, 831-880.

Jensen, M., Ruback, R., 1983. The market for corporate control: The scientific evidence. *Journal of Financial Economics* 11, 5-50.

Kang, S., Kumar, P., Lee, H., 2006. Agency and corporate investment: the role of executive compensation and corporate governance. *Journal of Business* 79 (3), 1127-1147.

Karpoff, J., 2001. The impact of shareholder activism on target companies: A survey of empirical findings. Working paper, University of Washington.

Karpoff, J., Malatesta, P., Walking, R., 1996, Corporate governance and shareholder initiatives: Empirical evidence. *Journal of Financial Economics* 42 (3), 365-395.

Klapper, L., Love, I., 2004. Corporate governance, investor protection, and performance in emerging markets. *Journal of Corporate Finance* 10 (5), 703-728.

Klein, A., 2002. Economic determinants of audit Committee independence. *The Accounting Review* 77 (2), 435-452.

La Porta, R., Lopez-de-Silanes, F., Shleifer, A., Vishny, R., 1997. Legal determinants of external finance. *The Journal of Finance* 52, 1131-1150.

La Porta, R., Lopez-de-Silanes, F., Shleifer, A., Vishny, R., 1998. Law and finance. *Journal of Political Economy* 106, 1113–1155.

La Porta, R., Lopez-de-Silanes, F., Shleifer, A., Vishny, R., 2000. Investor protection and corporate governance. *Journal of Financial Economics* 58, 3-27.

Linck, J., Netter, J., Yang, T., 2006. Effects and unintended consequences of the Sarbanes-Oxley Act on corporate boards. Working paper, University of Georgia.

Lipton, M., Lorsch, J., 1992. A modest proposal for improved corporate governance. *Business Lawyer* 48 (1), 59-77.

Lorsch, J., Maclver, E., 1989. Pawns or Potentates, Harvard Business School Press.

Manne, H., 1965. Mergers and the market for corporate control. *Journal of Political Economy*, April, 110-120.

Mehran, H., 1995. Executive compensation structure, ownership, and firm Performance. *Journal of Financial Economics* 38 (2), 163-84.

Monks, R., Minow, N., 1995. Corporate Governance. Blackwell Publishers Ltd.

Ofeck, E., Yermack, D., 2000. Taking stock: Equity-based compensation and the evolution of managerial ownership. *The Journal of Finance* 55 (3), 1367-1384.

Peck, S., 2004. Do outside blockholders influence corporate governance practice? Corporate Governance. *Advances in Financial Economics* 9, 81-101.

Perry, T, Peyer, U, 2005. Board seat accumulation by executives: A shareholder's perspective. *The Journal of Finance* 60 (4), 2083-2123.

Rajgopal, S., Shevlin, T., Zamora, V., 2006. CEOs' outside employment opportunities and the lack of relative performance evaluation in compensation contracts. *Journal of Finance* 61, 1813-1842.

Romano, R., 2001. Less is more: Making institutional investor activism a valuable mechanism of corporate governance. *Yale Journal on Regulation* 18, 174-251.

Shleifer, A., Vishny, R., 1986. Large shareholders and corporate control. *Journal of Political Economy* 94 (3), 461-488.

Sun, J., 2005. Information asymmetry and internal monitoring: which blockholders monitor managers more effectively? Working paper, University of Southern California.

Thomas, R., Cotter, J., 2007. Shareholder proposal in the new millennium: Shareholder support, board response, and market reaction. *Journal of Corporate Finance* 13, 368-391.

Vafees, N., 1999. Board meetings frequency and firm performance. *Journal of Financial Economics* 53, 113-142.

Weisbach, M., 1988. Outside directors and CEO turnover. *Journal of Financial Economics* 20, 431-460.

Xie, B., Davidson, W., Dadalt, P., 2003. Earnings management and corporate governance: the role of the board and the audit committee. *Journal of Corporate Finance* 9, 295-316.

Yen, G., Chen, C., 2005. Proxy contest, board reelection, and managerial turnover-yes, the proxy contest outcome matters. *Managerial and Decision Economics* 26, 15-23.

Yermack, D., 1996. Higher market valuation of companies with a small board of directors. *Journal of Financial Economics* 40 (2), 185-211.

10 *Corporate Governance – Responsibilities of the Board*

MARIA ALUCHNA

Introduction

This chapter discusses the role and importance of the board in the corporate governance structure. More precisely, it analyses the duties and responsibilities of board referring to the dynamics of its process and to two existing models of control (unitary and dual board). The main aim of this chapter is to present the functions of the board in line with the current problems and challenges, caused first of all by the waive of corporate scandals and frauds that have resulted in reform actions, introducing increased transparency and accountability as well as the worldwide processes of globalization and internationalization of capital markets and corporate governance initiatives. The impact of regulatory reforms, codes of best practice, public pressure and investors' expectations addressed to the board results in significant change in the attitude of board members, board responsibilities and accountability. Under the conditions of severe competition, as well as crisis control, the board and its experienced, responsible and honest members play a crucial role in restoring confidence in capital markets, assuring sound governance and corporate efficiency.

The comparative analysis of corporate governance reveals significant changes in control structures applied in different countries, delivering a starting point for research in efficiency of the mechanisms used. Such analysis shows differences in ownership structure, compensation policy, corporate disclosure standards, investor protection, legal regime and the court system, and models of capital markets. Although national differences can also be depicted in the board model, its structure, composition and practice, the comparative analysis indicates the great importance of a board in each corporate governance system. According to all national approaches, the board should represent the interest of the company and look after the shareholder interests of corporate performance, generated profit and realized dividend. The board becomes a platform for balancing shareholders and stakeholders expectations, for discussing corporate strategy, for resolving shareholder conflicts and fights, for electing executives and formulating compensation policy. The board is also perceived as a liaison between shareholders and their general shareholder meeting and top management, having access to company data, detailed financial statements, corporate strategy plans and results, reports on performance and company problems. Hence, the collectively responsible board has responsibilty for monitoring, control as well as counsel, and advice on its meeting's agenda. Moreover, worldwide discussions provide evidence for the common understanding that board members should be highly skilled experienced professionals with high morale and that they are responsible and accountable, since the performance and even existence of the company lies in the board members' hands, more precisely in the work and advice they deliver and monitoring they exert.

This chapter analyzes the key role and importance of the board in the corporate governance structure depicted in national systems. It attempts to discuss the duties and responsibilities of the board referring to two existing models of control – the one-tier system (board of directors) and the two-tier system (supervisory and management boards). The aim is to present not only the immanent responsibilities and tasks of the board, but also to track the current challenges caused by corporate scandals, worldwide-adopted corporate governance reforms and globalization and internationalization processes, as well as to discuss future tendencies for the work of the board and tasks. The chapter is organized as follows – the first section presents the board within the corporate governance system, stressing its crucial role for protecting shareholder interests. It refers to a change in board position after 1960 and differences in the control approach in the case of a board of directors and supervisory board. The second section analyzes board duties which constitute the legal accountability of its members towards shareholders including fiduciary duty, duty of loyalty and duty of fair dealing, duty of care, duty not to entrench and duty of supervision. Responsibilities of the board, main tasks which need to be fulfilled and challenges that have to be addressed in the work of the board, are discussed in the third section. The conclusion section summarizes the discussion.

The Board within the Corporate Governance System

THE ROLE OF THE BOARD

The board is a crucial element of the corporate governance structure and its efficiency and performance determines the success of monitoring and the operation of the company. As noticed by Monks and Minow (2004) boards 'are the link between the people who provide capital (the shareholders) and the people who use that capital to create value (the managers)'. In other words, boards become the liaison between concentrated or dispersed shareholders of different identities (individuals, funds, companies, banks and so on) who exert the residual rights and executives who, as a matter of fact, constitute the powerful group that runs and controls the company (Roe, 1994). The organization form of a joint stock company, characterized by separation of ownership and control or, using other words, of finance and management, (Jensen and Meckling, 1976) was questioned already by Adam Smith due to the huge discretionary power left in the hands of executives and marginal control capabilities of the capital owners. According to Smith investors 'seldom pretend to understand anything of the business of the company' whereas 'being the managers of others people's money rather than of their own, it cannot well be expected that they should watch over it with the same anxious vigilance with which the partners in a private co-partnery frequently watch over their own (Smith, 1937 as quoted in Monks and Minow, 1996). These severe problems rooted in moral hazard were identified as principal-agent conflict leading to substantial agency costs in companies characterized by separation of ownership and control and dispersed ownership structure (Shleifer and Vishny, 1997). Shareholders face the information asymmetry of hidden action and hidden information that results from the opportunistic behaviour of managers who are acting within the framework of incomplete contracts, primarily in their own interests (Fama and Jensen, 1983a; Fama and Jensen, 1983b). Research and analyses delivered evidence that interests of executives are opposed to those of shareholders due to the issues of choice, effort, differential risk exposure or differential horizon of activity (Jensen and Smith, 1985). Business practice and numerous examples of frauds or corporate scandals provide vast evidence for the real risk of expropriation of shareholders and hence their need to form a control and monitoring body within the company. As stated by Fama and Jensen (1983a) the residual risk, meaning the risk of the difference between stochastic inflows of resources and promised payments to agents, is borne by those who contract for the rights to net cash flows, that is, the shareholders. Thus, shareholders must have incentives to monitor contracts with agents. The central hypothesis provides that the separation of residual risk bearing from decision management leads to decision systems that separate decision management from decision control. Residual claims are distributed amongst many agents that provide for unrestricted risk-sharing. This situation reflects perfectly the conditions and organization form of large, open, common stock corporations, mostly referring to public listed companies (Fama and Jensen, 1983a). These companies are characterized by the specific knowledge and diffusion of decision functions and diffuse residual claims and delegation of decision control. Therefore, in order to provide efficiency and mitigate the principal-agent problem, so severe under the condition of separation of decision management (initiation and ratification) and decision control (implementation and monitoring), strong decision hierarchies such as boards are necessary. In other words, the board ensuring effective monitoring is described as one of many efforts that are meant to reduce agency costs and to align the interests of non-owner management to the interests of shareholders in modern public corporations (Fisch, 2004).

Corporate governance of joint stock companies, and particularly public listed companies, encompasses different governance mechanisms that form sets of characteristics for respective national systems. As shown in Figure 10.1, governance mechanisms include mechanisms of monitoring and control as well as motivation and binding mechanisms. The other perspective delivers the typology of the internal mechanism known as hierarchies, such as ownership structure, board, creditor or internal monitoring and external mechanisms such as markets of debt, products, executives and corporate control (Weston et al., 2001).

It is important to stress that the board functions within a corporation and within its structure, by-laws and constraints. Since the corporation involves different parties that contribute capital, expertise and labour (Monks and Minow, 1996) in order to achieve the corporate goal and maximize shareholder value, the board becomes a platform where all these parties debate and compromise for the direction of company activity. Most recently, the efforts of worldwide reforms and initiatives introducing improvement of monitoring standards as well as the globalization process based on increased capital mobility, flexibility and market transparency, drew a lot attention to corporate governance practices. Moreover, control problems revealed in corporate scandals place boards in the centre of governance structure indicating the need for its work improvement,

Figure 10.1 Governance mechanisms

Source: Wolf (1999), p. 17.

strengthening monitoring function and increasing the moral and ethical standards of its members (Fisch, 2004; MacAvoy and Millstein, 2003).

MAIN TASK OF THE BOARD

The board and its function within the company should address the problematic issues mentioned in the section above. Therefore, the board should responsd to challenges of separation of ownership and control and act towards mitigating agency problems, aligning the goals of managers with the interest of shareholders. Hence, the main board task is to represent, formulate and realize the interests and expectations of shareholders as the owners of the companies (see also, Hambrick and Jackson, 2000; John and Senbet, 1998). It is the board which holds the ultimate accountability and bears the final responsibility for corporate success or failure (Ibrahim and Angelidis, 1994). As formulated in the OECD Corporate Governance Principles (2004) 'board members should act on a fully informed basis, in good faith, with due diligence and care and in the best interest of the company and the shareholders'. The board should provide for balancing 'two distinct powers: the power of those who own the corporation and the power of those who run it' (Monks and Minow, 1996). The board functions as the result of empowering shareholders, providing for the representation of their interest that is rooted in the shares they possess, as the title of invested capital and right for exerting influence of the corporation (Monks and Minow, 2004; Fisch, 2004). The construction of joint stock companies is based on the assumption that shareholders delegate substantial powers to management and therefore there is a need to assure that these powers will not be abused at their cost. Hence, the board plays the control function over the vast discretionary power which was given to executives as the fundament for the joint stock company and separation of ownership and control. However, representing the interests of shareholders, the board has to keep in mind that limiting the activity of top managers and incurring substantial constraints on them to prevent them from expropriating shareholder value may have the reverse effect. Researchers and business practice reveal that managers need to hold significant power, technical capabilities and shareholders' trust for efficient work towards maximizing shareholder wealth and realizing shareholder goals. Too restrictive control exerted over executives limits their abilities, power and creativity, which leads to poorer corporate performance and lower shareholder value. Hence, the board needs to provide balance between mechanisms of monitoring and control versus motivation and binding as shown in Figure 10.1.

It is also important to mention that, looking at fulfilling the interests and expectations of shareholders, the board has to take into account the interests of the company as a whole. Hence, the orientation of the board should be based on the long-term perspective, not pushing exclusively for short-term goals. This requirement places a high responsibility on the board, demanding from the board members a balanced approach, objectivity and wise policy of assets accumulation, investment and consumption. Thus, as stated in the mentioned above OECD Corporate Governance Principles (2004), the board has to be very careful when making decisions that affect shareholder groups and should always provide for equal and fair treatment of shareholders.

UNITARY VERSUS DUAL BOARD

Discussing the role and responsibilities of the board requires the mention of two board models – the one-tier system and the board of directors and the two-tier system and supervisory board and their specificity (Mallin, 2004). The characteristics, work organization, advantages and constraints of both types of boards are crucial for the analysis since it has a significant impact on the main task, responsibilities and structure supporting realization of the board goals.

The board of directors (Kojima, 1997) known also as the unitary board, is dominant in corporate governance systems and can be found in Anglo-Saxon countries (United States, UK, Ireland, Australia, Canada) as well as in others (Japan, Russia). The board of directors consists of executives (managers of the company) and non-executives who can be appointed out of affiliated or gray members and independent directors with no ties related to the company. The biggest advantages of the board of directors include the possibility of dialogue and better communication between executives and non-executives (monitoring, counsel, advice, reprimand) and the access to corporate data and information by non-executive directors. The board of directors proves to be flexible and relatively inexpensive, representing the interests of shareholders as well as allowing for a quick decision-making process and efficient information flow. The negative aspects of the unitary board refers to the very powerful position of the CEO who, in 90 per cent of American public listed companies, holds the Chairman function at the same time (it is important to mention that both functions are separated in 85 per cent of boards of UK companies) fully controlling the work, agenda and directions of the board. The presence of executive directors and the directors' appointment process dependence on the CEO impacts the board's work and responsibilities and more precisely affects 1) building coalition between executives and independent directors and outside directors' support for CEO policy; 2) evaluation of board work; 3) resisting hostile takeover; and 4) formulating compensation policy for top management. As a matter of fact, the risks of these negative aspects are mitigated by the formulation of different committees (compensation, audit and nominating) which should be dominated by independent directors. Moreover, latest recommendations suggest the separation of the CEO and Chairman roles, introducing the function of 'leading' or 'presiding' directors to conduct board meetings or to call meetings exclusively of independent directors.

As shown in Table 10.1, the dual board system (Mallin, 2004) is based on two main bodies, that is, the supervisory board and the management board (executives), and is provided by Corporate Law in Germany, Austria and Poland. The supervisory board includes exclusively non-executive directors who should provide for their objectivity, or at least independence from, the executives representing different shareholders (families, banks, individual investors) or stakeholder groups (employees) or have the status of independent directors. The mandates of supervisory and management boards have to be kept separately (Kojima, 1997). The supervisory board plays monitoring functions, appoints the CEO and structures executive compensation, selects the auditor and follows corporate strategy issues. The strong independence of board directors provides for a better balancing of the roles of Chairman and CEO, as well as a high objectivity for accessing corporate policy, top management evaluation and setting executive compensation. The major weakness of the dual model lies in its limited access to corporate data and information which has to be delivered by the management board. The relative separation of board members and executives is mitigated by joint meetings and specialized committees (compensation, audit and nominating). The threat of the dominance of the board work by representatives of controlling shareholders, particularly in the area of dividend policy, is attempted to be reduced by the presence of independent directors. The dual board is also often criticized for its higher costs of functioning and the lack of direct contact between executives and outside directors. Table 10.1 summarizes the pros and cons of unitary and dual boards.

Table 10.1 Comparative analysis of board of directors and supervisory board

	Board of directors (unitary board)	Supervisory board (dual board)
Advantages	Capability to represent shareholders interests Flexible and relatively inexpensive form Direct contact between executives and non-executives that enables sound monitoring and counselling Efficient information flow and non-executives' access to corporate data	Capability to represent shareholders interests All members are non-executives Balancing the power of CEO and board Chairman Higher objectivity and independence, particularly in the process of management evaluation, compensation policy No personal connections enable sound monitoring and counselling
Disadvantages	Powerful position of CEO who holds Chairman function Dependence on CEO policy, lack of objectivity Risk of building a coalition between CEO and outside directors (evaluation of board work, resisting to takeovers)	Higher costs of board functioning Poorer information flow and non-executives' access to corporate data Lack of direct contact between executives and non-executives Risk of dominating the board by majority shareholder

Source: Own analysis.

The ongoing debate on efficiency of board types often delivers more positive arguments for a board of directors, indicating higher flexibility, better information flow and lower costs. Moreover, proponents of the unitary board point at countries such as France and Italy where corporate law allows for both board models leaving the choice to corporations. Moreover, the company decision can be reversed. The analysis shows that approximately 85 per cent of French companies and aproximately 90 per cent of Italian companies adopted the board of directors as the main control and monitoring corporate body. However, recent reforms and initiatives introduced in both board systems indicate common directions of increasing the number of independent directors and creating respective committees for detailed tasks. The emergence of a unified board still remains in purely theoretical debate, but the recent reforms deliver the harmonization of board best practice.

Referring to the main task, the board of directors provides an undoubtedly stronger representation of shareholder versus stakeholder interests, focusing primarily on creating value. Although the composition of the unitary board reveals strong representation of independent directors, ranging from 30 per cent to even 75 per cent, it does not show real participation of stakeholder representatives. The supervisory board reveals in this matter higher participation of contingency directors representing not only shareholders, but also employees or communities (for example, the codetermination rule in German boards). Therefore the dual board is often perceived as the corporate body which becomes a wider platform for balancing interests of different stakeholder groups and presenting a long-term orientation.

INCREASING BOARD RESPONSIBILITIES

As corporate governance is currently an extensively researched topic, many analyses concerning its work procedures, composition and efficiency of functioning provide understanding for board role and responsibilities. However, despite the impressive number and quality of articles, papers and reports on board functioning, the topic is far from being fully analyzed. Moreover, in line with recent corporate scandals (WorldCom, Enron), identified governance shortcomings (inefficient independent directors, limited information for board members) as well as responding to emerging business challenges and major changes in the corporate environment (growing importance of IT, e-commerce, e-business, deep changes in economic systems), the analysis of the board still remains at the centre of management research. Recommendations for board work constitute a significant part of the best practice code formulated either on the regional (OECD, EU), national (United States, UK, Germany, France) or corporate levels (Allianz, ING, GM). More interestingly, newly formulated guidelines are heavily rooted in the former hints and suggestions, although, as seen from the today's perspective, provide a deeper meaning and understanding for board role and functioning referring to its fundamentals. The research and analysis on board efficiency that used to address the form now seems to focus on the substance.

The change in perceiving board role and functions becomes a response to reforms in corporate governance system and a substantial shift in powers, which today lies in the hands of aware and strong investors. MacAvoy and Millstein (2003) refer to the 'broken engine' of companies that failed to create value for shareholders and focus on the misinterpreted or misused role of the board saying that 'between 1960 and 1990 this system was, in general, disoriented, with the board serving as a source of support in the pursuit of management's goals. The CEO dominated both management and the board, serving as the board chairman, and appointing the board of directors to assist. It was the CEO, not the board, who determined corporate strategy as well as how earnings were to be distributed among employees, customers, community groups and investors'. Thus in that system, the board was not functioning as an agent for investors and was not pursuing the main goal of protecting shareholder interest. Figure 10.2 presents the original structure of governance as well as the twisted system of 1960–1990.

As shown in the figure, the original system provides the structure that enables the board to fulfil its role and responsibilities, and the board becomes a control, monitoring and motivating mechanism over management. The board acts in the interest of shareholders and through this system profits generated by company are returns on investment for investors. However, the system after 1960 substantially reduced the control and monitoring power of the board that led to the 'strong managers, weak owners' problems. The executives dominated the decision-making process, referring to the distribution of generated earning which, according to the figure, were not paid out as dividends for shareholders but became tools for aggressive mergers and acquisition policy. In result, the system led to 'expansive diversification, increased executive compensation and, last, discretionary dividends' (MacAvoy and Millstein, 2003:9). The abovementioned corporate governance shortcomings, as well as devastating corporate scandals and loss of the confidence to companies and capital markets, imposed the necessity to return to the original construction of a board of directors and its role and place within the corporate governance system, particularly versus management.

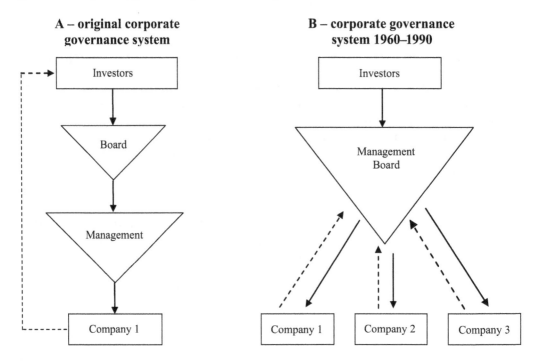

Figure 10.2 Board role in two systems

Source: MacAvoy and Millstein (2003), p. 8.

It must be mentioned that the previously discussed problems of the 1960–1990 corporate governance system refer predominantly to the United States, and to some extent, to the UK. However, a different picture can be depicted from companies operating in continental Europe and south-east Asia, particularly in Japan. The major problems of boards functioning in continental Europe refer to the dominance by the controlling shareholder as the result of the concentrated ownership structure. Therefore, instead of – as presented in Figure 10.2 – the influence and the power exerted by management, the controlling shareholder was able to dominate the board and literally take over the decision process. Problems such as these are now solved by (or attempted to be solved by) the recommendation of independent directors sitting on the board. The Japanese version of these issues referred to the necessity of operating within a group of companies (keiretsu). This led to high interest rates imposed by keiretsu banks on that group companies. As a result, companies tended to lower the proportion of external capital (bank loans) which led to a reduction of the monitoring executed by banks (and the Japanese corporate governance is known as the bank-based), created a control vacuum and provided high discretionary power for managers who engaged themselves in expansive diversification and investment policy.

Board Duties

The work of a board includes not only certain responsibilities that will be outlined in the next section, but also becomes a legal construct based on contract between directors and shareholders. The directors are to fulfill given set of tasks which assume 'the obligation to represent the interest of owners who cannot represent themselves, undertaking a serious fiduciary responsibility' (Colley at al., 2003). Therefore the board directors, before engaging in tasks of monitoring, control and counseling, have to be aware of the set of duties that are imposed on them. These duties place board directors in a special professional group referring to high ethical and moral standards and include:

- **The fiduciary duty** that means that 'a director must demonstrate unyielding loyalty to the company's shareholders' (Monks and Minow, 2004) which translates into being trustworthy in acting in the best interests of those whom the director represents (Colley at al., 2003; Wallace and Zinkin, 2005). The main function here is enhancing the stockholder gain and simultaneously pursuing creation of firm value in the long term. However, directors have to keep in mind their obligation to act in the interest of the company as a whole at the same time. Moreover, while being appointed to the board, the director has to represent all shareholders, not only the group that elected them, as the board is a collective body based on team work and collective responsibility.
- **The duty of loyalty and duty of fair dealing** – duty of loyalty refers to the supremacy of shareholders' interests and means that the interests of shareholders must prevail over any individual director's interests or benefits. As a result, directors cannot use their position, power resulting from this position or information in order to make personal profits or gain private advantages. The duty of fair dealing constitutes a component of the duty of loyalty requiring all transactions with the corporations to be handled forthrightly and in an open manner fair to the interests of

the corporations. Moreover, the duty of fair dealing refers to disclosure of any existing conflict of interest and rejection of taking advantage of opportunities for receiving personal gains.

- **The duty of care** – which means that 'a director must exercise due diligence in making decisions' (Monks and Minow, 2004) and assumes that directors act carefully in carrying out their responsibilities referring to the possible best performance of directors in dealing with board functions (Colley at al., 2003). Hence, the board directors have to act in the interests of the company using their skills, experience and knowledge to provide for best monitoring, control and counselling. This may include, particularly these days, the director's personal responsibilities of accepting the workload and, for instance, limiting themselves from serving on too many boards which could lower their performance. From the perspective of the whole board, duty of care would include delegating some functions or using the expertise of respective specialists (lawyers, accountants) when organizing the work of the board. Additionally, it is crucial to mention that the practical interpretation of the duty of care imposes high standards of independence in terms of business relations to the company, strong requirements towards directors' skills and experience, as well as the appropriate and efficient organization of board work.
- **The duty not to entrench** – which refers to the needs of the objective assessment of the company situation, openness to possible solution and the board readiness to undertake crucial decisions, particularly in the cases of poor economic performance. The business practice reveals that poor corporate performance quite often results in creating certain coalition between the board and management. The entrenched board blocks the decisive movements and shareholders initiatives (for example, replacing executives), does not address the main problems and as a result does not fulfill its responsibilities.
- **The duty of supervision** – is an element of duty of fair dealing with effectiveness with which directors exercise their oversight responsibilities (Colley at al., 2003). This translates into the best performance of the primary board function of supervision over management and assumes the care of collecting all necessary data, information and documents required for effective oversight. The predominant rules of duty of supervision are based on the highest standards of ethics and disclosure referring both to board directors as well as to executives.

The set of directors' duties presented in Table 10.2 concludes this section.

Table 10.2 Duties of directors

Categories	Detailed duties
Primary duties	
Looking after the company's best interests as a whole	acting in good faith in the best interest of the company as a whole exercising the level of care, skill and diligence that can be reasonably expected exercising the powers granted by the company's constitution for a 'proper purpose' refraining from or prevent any act that would adversely affect decision making concerning the company activities

Table 10.2 *Concluded*

Categories	Detailed duties
Primary duties	
Avoiding conflict of interest	declaring fully to the board all dealings in company shares recording material-relevant interests in any transaction for the register avoiding improper use of his or her position or the use of any information obtained through that position for personal gain or to harm the company ensuring that his or her remuneration is fair to the company
Dealing with shareholders	determining and certifying what is fair and reasonable consideration for the issue of shares or the repurchase of shares on issue responding appropriately to written shareholder requests for information ensuring that the company does not carry out businesses in a manner that is harmful to creditors and shareholders
Others	maintaining the company's solvency and reputation fulfilling specific duties in the event of takeovers (see also Colley at al., 2003)
Secondary duties	
Ensuring the quality of company information	taking all reasonable steps to prevent falsification of accounting records providing proper explanations to external auditors to help them to interpret the information correctly making sure that any overseas documentation is properly recorded checking the accuracy and completeness of any statements that are made by the company ensuring that the financial statements comply with the appropriate financial reporting standards ensuring that these financial statements are audited whenever audits are required
Providing documentation	ensuring that shareholders receive a copy of the annual report or the financial statements at least a set number of working days before the AGM ensuring that the annual return is filed with the Registrar within the time required ensuring that the following documents are available for inspection by the public: certificate of incorporation, constitution of the company, share register, register of directors and address for servicing documents
Ensuring that shareholders can inspect shareholders' minutes, written communications to shareholders, and directors' certificates and the interest register (see also Fisch, 2004)	dealing with Registrar to ensure: the board notifies the Registrar of any changes of the constitution, issue of shares, acquisition of own shares or changes in the directors; and the board delivers a copy of share certificate to the Registrar, having certified that the consideration for a share, option or convertible securities or financial assistance to buy company's shares recording for register any relevant interest in shares issued by the company or any interest in any transaction or proposed transaction involving the company having previously notified the board

Source: Wallace and Zinkin (2005), p. 263-264.

Responsibilities of the Board

OUTLINE OF BOARD RESPONSIBILITIES

The work of the board is placed within a strong and stable framework of legal standards as well as ethical and moral requirements. Having in mind these requirements, positive postulates (the board should) and negative warnings (the board should not) and being aware of examples of corporate scandals and frauds, the board has to be very careful in fulfilling its responsibilities. The sets of board responsibilities may differ slightly in the importance placed on given issues, but all of them include: (Monks and Minow, 2004; Carter and Lorsch, 2004) 1) the aspects of review of strategic, financial and investment decisions; 2) providing accountability, monitoring and counsel to top managers; 3) selection, evaluation, replacement of CEO and review of succession planning; 4) providing highest moral and performance standards of board; and 5) review the adequacy of the company's systems with all applicable laws/ requirements. One of the examples of the comprehensive and complete set of board responsibilities is formulated in the OECD Corporate Governance Principles (2004). According to OECD board functions include the following (see also Alexander et al., 1993; Sherdian, 2001):

- Reviewing and guiding corporate strategy, major plans of action, risk policy, annual budgets and business plans; setting performance objectives; monitoring implementation and corporate performance and overseeing major capital expenditures, acquisitions and divestitures.
- Monitoring the effectiveness of the company's governance practices and making changes as needed.
- Selecting, compensating, monitoring and when necessary replacing key executives and overseeing succession planning.
- Aligning key executive and board remuneration with the longer-term interests of the company and its shareholders.
- Ensuring a formal and transparent board nomination and election process.
- Monitoring and managing potential conflict of interest of management, board members and shareholders, including misuse of corporate assets and abuse in related party transactions.
- Ensuring the integrity of the corporation's accounting and financial reporting systems, including the independent audit and that appropriate systems of controls are in place, in particular, systems for risk management, financial and operational control and compliance with the law relevant standards.
- Overseeing the process of disclosure and communication.

Additionally, the board should also take care of its structure, composition, procedures, cooperation and communication that respect all appropriate laws and requirements as well as provide the highest efficiency and performance in the best interests of shareholders. Therefore, the board should have access to accurate, relevant and timely information which becomes the basis for its discussion and decision. The most crucial board functions are discussed in detail below.

REVIEW OF STRATEGIC, FINANCIAL AND INVESTMENT DECISIONS

The review of strategic, financial and investment decisions can be generally understood as the review of a company's strategic direction which is the primary responsibility of the board that allows to protect shareholders' and companies' interests and provide for long-term growth and development. The board controls and influences the dividend payout process. According to the agency theory, board members representing the companies' and shareholders' interest should have a longer time horizon for the investment and strategy as compared to executives who always calculate the threat or the possibility of changing their job and leaving for another company. Therefore the time perspective becomes crucial. The review of strategic direction requires the board members to have knowledge, experience and awareness of the business characteristics, structure, complexity and 'rules of the game'. Discussing the state-of-the-art of the board position in the strategic process, it is important to refer to the two models of corporate governance described above where, following the framework of MacAvoy and Millstein, the change of the board role is noticeable. From the 'twisted' corporate governance model of 1960–1990, characterized by weak board position and its coalition with top management, the board currently gains 'original' importance and role and is powerful enough to exert real control over management and review the strategic direction. This change, along with the requirements towards board knowledge, gains importance under current market turbulence, dramatic economic and social challenges and the growing role of Internet technology and globalization. This requirement is heavily rooted in the developing internal management technologies, business to business transactions and dealing with customers that are themselves creating new market choices and opportunities worldwide (Carter and Lorsch, 2004). Additionally, the growing importance of intellectual capital and intangible assets, as well as the development of a knowledge-based economy, produces new challenges for companies and their boards. Yesterday, solutions and business strategy that turned out to be outdated may lead to market share loss and even to corporate failures. Therefore the review of a company's strategic direction, particularly corporate strategy, investments and divestures, are on the one hand an extremely difficult task and, on the other hand, constitute the essentials of board responsibilities which are to be evaluated by markets and shareholders with no sentiments whatsoever.

PROVIDING ACCOUNTABILITY, MONITORING AND COUNSEL TO TOP MANAGERS

Providing accountability and monitoring to executives remains the core of board responsibilities as it is rooted in the primary goal of board functioning, that is, protecting shareholder interest. The control exerted over the work of top managers remains the most crucial source for the evaluation of company performance, also related to competitors and market trends. It is suggested that the board prepares some points of reference, using the benchmarks of other companies as well as widely recognized measures that provide effective evaluation. The fulfilling of this responsibility requires a complex set of corporate materials and reports, presenting to top managers the goals achieved, corporate performance and financial results. Therefore, the content of this responsibility includes providing a formal procedure to determine the quality of the materials received from top managers and to ensure a complete approach to monitoring corporate performance. Some elements of the recommended procedure and content of reports are suggested by the Best Practice Code or stipulated by hard law. It is important to mention that several crucial changes in this area were introduced by the Sarbanes-Oxley Act. Although requirements stipulated by SOX refer only to companies listed on United States markets, its analysis from the perspective of increased accountability proves to deliver interesting insights. For instance SOX requires 'board members to know not only cash flow versus earnings, but also how and from which information system these estimates were derived, as well as the roles played by internal and external auditors in valuation of the information from which the estimates were derived' (MacAvoy and Millstein, 2003:101). Moreover, SOX stipulates that top executives sign financial statements, guaranteeing that the provided information is reliable. The monitoring of executives by the board assumes that its members should react to warning signals, poor performance results or negative symptoms, referring to either corporate efficiency or corporate governance practices. This should then prevent the question frequently asked after the Enron and WorldCom scandals: 'Where was the board?' (Carter and Lorsch, 2004; Wearing, 2005).

The second component of this responsibility requires the board members to be able and willing to provide counsel and advice for executives, reply to their questions and respond to their needs and expectations with reference to company operating, business rules or corporate governance practices. Apparently, board members can neither delegate their responsibilities to executives nor make decisions about the company management. However, the board counsel is often perceived as of huge importance and high value by top managers (Carter and Lorsch, 2004; Demb and Neubauer, 1992).

SELECTION, COMPENSATING, EVALUATION, REPLACEMENT OF THE CEO. REVIEW OF SUCCESSION PLANNING

The responsibilities discussed above remain in strong interdependence with the selection of the CEO out of the most appropriate candidates, evaluating the CEO's job as well as structuring the compensation package for them. The selection of the CEO, which may seem an easy task, proves to be one of the most difficult and complicated responsibilities to fulfil as this decision always has far reaching and long-term results determining *de facto* the company's fate. More and more management research indicates the key role of the CEO in corporate success and failure, stressing additionally the impact of the compensation package (structure, particularly the proportion of variable component referred the fixed pay) for the CEO's working attitude and motivation towards increasing shareholder value. Board tasks of selection and compensating the CEO are gaining more attention both from board members and powerful investors, who expect improved performance and increase of shareholder value. The fact that we now have the highest turnover rate of CEOs in corporate history remains an indication of today's turbulent times and investors' pressure. Additionally, in response to CEO turnover, as well as retirement, the succession planning and the process of preparation of the new CEO to take over the top function gains more importance from the perspective of assuring managerial continuity. What is more, the believed to be optimal compensation scheme, based mostly on stock options, turned out to be not only inefficient but also a path to fraud and substantial shareholder loss in the case of corporate scandals. Hence, current efforts aim at identifying the balance between fixed pay and performance-based components in order to provide both high motivation and long-term managerial perspective.

PROVIDING HIGHEST MORAL AND PERFORMANCE STANDARDS OF BOARD

Providing highest moral and performance standards of the board refers mostly to two aspects. First, the board should take care of its composition of the highly qualified members whose education, experience, objectivity, morale as well as availability (time for reading corporate reports and for participating in meetings) meet the company's needs and requirements, and ensure the high performance of the collective body. It must be emphasized that these requirements strongly demand that directors truly know the business of the company they monitor relating to the main competitors, customers, suppliers, market rules, threats and regulatory framework (Monks and Minow, 1997, 2004; MacAvoy and Millstein, 2003). These requirements often also refer to the suggested proportion or number of independent directors. As the examples of companies engaged in corporate scandals show, the quality of board members, particularly their knowledge about the business and the morale and ethical standards, become crucial aspects, not only for the board performance, but also for the success or failure of the company (problems of conflict of interest, dependence on CEO, low skills and low morale). Apparently the composition of the board remains the decision of the general shareholder meeting but board members also have some influence and, more importantly, they are able to assess the quality of the given member. The issue of high moral standards includes avoiding conflict of interests, providing the best possible monitoring, careful reading of corporate materials, efficient communication with other members, active participation in board meetings, readiness and ability to objective evaluation of management as well as fulfilling all board duties (fiduciary duty, the duty of loyalty and duty of fair dealing, duty of care, the duty not to entrench and duty of supervision). High morale refers also to refraining from leaving the board if this should be costly or negative for the company. However, some examples indicate that members leaving the board because of its poor performance can serve as the signal for conflicts or inefficiencies of the board (for example, Robert Monks in Tyco). The second group of responsibilities in this point includes all aspects related to the board procedures, structure and work organization, either perceived as a formal requirement or best practice code recommendation or known as a tool for efficient performance (Colley et al., 2003). The board should select a chairman (or leading or presiding director), vice-chairman and secretary, and form board committees (audit, nominating and governance, remuneration, executive and committee of outside directors). The board itself should formulate or fulfil the existing role of the board function, organization of board meetings (time, place, frequency, information about the meeting) and discussing the agenda, approving procedures for voting, communicating with executives, disclosure policy and meetings with shareholders, as well as the formal procedure for evaluating its functions. Concluding this point it must be emphasized that the work of the board and its efficiency relies to a large extent on board resources and capabilities, therefore board responsibilities should include ensuring the best inputs.

Conclusions

This chapter presents in depth analysis of the board responsibilities and duties referring to aspects of the board role within the corporate governance system, board model and future challenges of emerging new business sectors and economic phenomena. However, despite expansive analysis that undoubtedly ensures impressive numbers and quality articles and papers, the aspects of the work of the board, its responsibilities and decision process still remains a challenging area of further research and study. The dynamics of board process, confronted with the emerging new business characteristics rooted in Internet technology, market turbulence, structural changes and finally globalization, provide a complex set of challenges for companies and their boards. Moreover, the dynamic market situation, as well as inpatient shareholders that become a crucial source of external financing for companies, push boards for higher efficiency, stricter evaluation procedures, tougher accountability and threat of shareholder litigation, as well as more disclosure. The board, protecting the interests of shareholders and the company, becomes the ultimate stage of review of strategic planning, monitoring of executives, evaluation and compensation, succession policy, addressing of all legal requirements, ensuring integrity for corporate communication and disclosure. In summary, the board facing these challenges, and addressing all the demands and needs directed at it, has to carefully manage its infrastructure, including skilled, experienced and objective members, resources and capabilities to ensure it functions at its best. The complexity of the work of the board, its position within the company, its accountability and responsibilities under the pressure of investors and market situation create a fascinating research area for both academics and business practitioners and will surely remain the centre of corporate governance analysis.

References

Alexander J.A., Fennell M.L., Halpern M.T (1993). 'Leadership instability in hospitals: The influence of board-CEO relations and organizational growth and decline', *Administrative Science Quarterly*, no. 38, issue 1, p. 74-93.

Carter C.B., Lorsch J.W. (2004). *Back to the drawing board*, Harvard Business School Press, Cambridge, MA.

Colley J.L., Doyle J.L., Logan G.W., Stettinius (2003). *Corporate governance*, McGraw-Hill.

Demb A., Neubauer F.F. (1992). *The corporate board: Confronting the paradoxes*, Oxford University Press.

Fama E.F., Jensen M.C. (1983a). 'Separation of ownership and control', *Journal of Law and Economics*, Vol. XXVI.

Fama E.F., Jensen M.C. (1983b). 'Agency problems and residual claims', *Journal of Law and Economics*, Vol. XXVI.

Fisch J.E. (2004). 'Taking boards seriously' in Joo T. (eds.) *Corporate Governance. Law, theory and policy*, Carolina Academic Press, pp. 329-337.

Hambrick D.C., Jackson E.M. (2000). 'Outside directors with a stake: The linchpin in improving governance', *California Management Review*, no. 42, issue 4, s. 108-127.

Ibrahim N.A., Angelidis J.P. (1994). 'Effect of board members' gender on corporate social responsiveness', *The Journal of Applied Business Research*, Vol. 10, issue 1, s. 35-42.

Jensen M.C., Meckling W.H. (1976). 'Theory of the firm: managerial behavior, agency costs and ownership structure', *Journal of Financial Economics*, Vol. 3, No. 4, pp. 305-360.

Jensen M.C., Smith C.W. (1985). 'Stockholder, manager and creditor interests: applications of agency theory', *Recent Advances in Corporate Finance*, E. Altman, M. Subrahmanyam (eds), Dow-Jones Irwin.

Kojima K. (1997). *Japanese corporate governance. An international perspective,* Research Institute for Economics and Business Administration, Kobe University.

MacAvoy P.W., Millstein I. (2003). *The recurrent crisis of corporate governance,* Palgrave Macmillan, Basingstoke.

Mallin Ch. A. (2004). *Corporate governance,* Oxford University Press, Oxford.

Monks R.A., Minow N. (1996). *Watching the Watchers,* Blackwell Business, Cambridge, MA.

Monks R.A., Minow N. (2004). *Corporate Governance,* Blackwell Publishing, Malden, MA.

OECD (2004). *Corporate Governance Principles,* www.oecd.com

Roe M. (1994). *Weak Owners, Strong Managers,* Princeton Univeristy Press, Princeton.

Sheridan A. (2001). 'A view from the top: women on the boards of public companies', *Corporate Governance,* Vol. 1, issue 1, s. 8-14.

Shleifer A., Vishny R.W. (1997). 'A survey of Corporate Governance', *Journal of Finance,* Vol. 52, pp. 737-783.

Smith A. (1937). *The Wealth of nations,* New York, Random House edition, pp. 699-700.

Wearing R. (2005). *Cases in corporate governance,* SAGE Publications, London.

Wallace P., Zinkin J. (2005). *Mastering business in Asia. Corporate governance,* John Willey & Sons, Singapore.

Weston F.W., Siu J.A., Johnson B.A. (2001). *Takeovers, restructuring and corporate governance,* Prentice Hall, Upper Saddle River, NJ.

Wolf J. Benedict (1999). *The effects of agency problems on the financial behavior, performance and efficiency of German industrial stock corporations,* Peter Lang Europäischer Verlag der Wissenschaften.

KEY REFERENCES FOR FURTHER READING

Murray A. (2007). *Revolt in the boardroom. The new rules of power in corporate America,* Collins, New York.

11 Shareholder Rights and Stakeholder Rights in Corporate Governance*

MIRELLA DAMIANI

Introduction

Two main issues have animated the debate on corporate governance: the role of ownership and control concentration, on one side, and, on the other side, investor protection and legal institutions. All the debate has been driven by an intense research devoted to examining the distinct or complementary role of these variables in creating firm value and in explaining cross-country differentials. But this intense research has left partly unexplored how industrial relations, and thus the conflict between workers and management, interact with the divergence of interest between shareholders and management. Actually – as recently observed – 'these two conflicts are present simultaneously and interact' (Pagano and Volpin, 2005, p. 841).

For a long time, a central concern of corporate governance literature has been a comparative evaluation of two different systems prevailing in industrialized countries: the *market* or *outsider oriented system*, well represented by the Anglo Saxon economies, and the *insider-bank oriented system*, mainly typified by the European Continental countries.[1]

In the outsider system, companies are widely held and largely financed through equity issues. In this context small shareholders have little power and incentive for active governance and the *agency* relationship between many dispersed owners and management is the main critical issue, as shown in the pioneering work of Berle and Means (1932).

In the insider system, fewer companies are listed on stock markets; moreover, families, banks and other companies hold a majority of equities or exert control thorough pyramids or cross-shareholding links. 'Strong' managers and 'strong' block-holders typified, respectively, the different scenarios but in both systems what it is relevant, and well explored by this literature, is the basic problem of a *divergence of*

*   My greatest debt is to Alberto Chilosi who has helped me with valuable suggestions and accurate corrections. I am also indebted to Milica Uvalic for her precious comments. However I bear full responsibility for the contents of the present paper.

1   Some surveys examine the main differences between the various systems of corporate governance; see, among others, Prowse (1995), Maher and Andersson (1999); Allen, Gale (2000), Becht, Bolton and Röell (2003), Damiani (2006).

interests and the main remedies to solve it (Shleifer and Vishny, 1997). At the root of this issue there is the problematic concern that shareholders have equity claims whose nature is intrinsically *residual*. Thus, as reminded by Baums and Scott (2003, p. 4), 'this makes them highly vulnerable to exploitation by those in control of the firm'. Different forms of exploitation are recorded around the world as different 'actors' are in control.

On the other side, a second more recent strand of literature, originated by the contribution of La Porta et. al. (1998), has focused on legal determinants of corporate finance by showing that owners' residual claims can be better enforced in environments where good legislative measures provide investor protection. In this framework, a restricted protection of shareholders' interests, which spans mainly countries with civil law codes, causes concentration of ownership and illiquid capital markets. Hence, as this literature suggests, the main causality link is that between 'law and finance' which makes strictly endogenous the degree of concentration or dispersion of ownership rights one can observe around the world. They maintain that if insufficient shareholder protection causes concentration and a low degree of capitalization, legal reforms to protect investors and to increase insufficient financing of firms (La Porta et al., 2000) should be called for.

But how to reconsider these issues when a third actor, besides owners and managers, that is, the employee, comes to the forefront? Principal or agent? Claimant of residual rights or exploiter of these rights? These questions gain relevance in the contemporary debate since new theories of the firm suggest 'an alternative view in which the relationship among the people who participate in the production activity of firms are at the heart of the definition of the firm itself' (Blair, 1995). This novel view which calls for a full answer to the above questions is a challenge for further research and for an exploration of a third dimension of corporate governance.

The next section reviews cross-national differences in both investor and labour regulation with the main intent of discovering systematic linkages that qualify distinct patterns of corporate governance. The hypothesis to be tested is that finance and labour regulation may be complementarily arranged in different ways and that the various dimensions have to be taken into account in comparing national patterns. This review is performed by considering new measures of legal protection of minority shareholders against expropriation by corporate insiders provided by Djankov et al. (2008) and labour regulation indexes collected by Botero et al. (2002). Moreover, in the same section, some insights on the most important differences, as well as on some converging trends towards a market shareholder system are pointed out.

The section entitled 'Incentives and labour relationships in a stakeholder model' further explores institutional diversities by a deeper investigation of incentives and also of informal labour practices. As fully analyzed in corporate governance literature, managerial incentive mechanisms may mitigate the moral hazard problems affecting corporations (Shleifer and Vishny, 1997). These mechanisms interact with labour incentives and various coalitions, as we shall see in this section, are conceivable: employees and shareholders may form alliances to monitor poorly performing executives, but 'insiders' (workers and managers) may also act in opposition to capital ('outsiders') and impede restructuring processes by erecting takeover barriers (Jackson 2005, Pagano and Volpin 2005). In the final section some conclusions are offered.

Investor and labour protection

As a first step one may obtain some preliminary insights from an overall picture where labour regulations, as well as ownership and investor protection, are explicitly taken into account. Indeed, the legal origin hypothesis, firstly adopted for financial legal institutions by La Porta et al., has recently been applied to labour regulation by Botero et al., 2002, whose main statement dictates that 'the historical origin of a country's laws shapes its regulation of labour and other markets' (Botero et al., 2002, p. 1340).

In our perspective, what is relevant is the role of complementarities between legal and economic institutions, since labour regulations may either exacerbate or cure some of the distortions arising from asymmetric information in contexts where a separation between investors and managers exists. For instance, returns to human capital investments, and thus the wage setting rules, or employment laws, governing the continuity of employment relation, may influence the acquisition of firm specific skills and thus have a role in creating firm value. Furthermore, conferring upon employees the right to oblige managers to pay out dividends or make other choices in terms of investment strategies produces a new 'balance' effect on the conflict between owners and executives. Hence, incentives and legal rights assigned to employees end up interacting with the various forms of self dealing, adopted by 'strong managers' and 'strong block holders', and recently computed by Djankov et al. (2008).

The indices used to measure the strength and weakness of legal financial and labour rules are shown in Table 11.1, which refers to a representative sample of industrialized economies:

Table 11.1 shows a comparison by countries in terms of ownership structure, investor protection and finally labour regulation.

More precisely, shareholder rights are measured in terms of legal provisions that are directly aimed at the control of self-dealing, as recently examined by Djankov et al. (2008).[2] The authors offer 'a key contribution' and elaborate new indexes of the strength of minority shareholder protection against self-dealing by the controlling block-holder (*anti-self-dealing* index) (Djankov et al., 2008, p. 6). Hence, according to their new data base, legal restraints to limit the pursuit of private benefits are carefully evaluated and compared by countries; for instance, indexes of disclosures required before transactions are approved or indexes that measure the ease in rescinding transactions concur to determine, respectively, ex-ante and ex-post private control of self dealing. These two groups of indicators, which compound the (private) anti self-dealing index, have to be considered along a public enforcement index, which measures the real effectiveness of all the provisions.[3]

Moreover, three main aspects of labour rules are caught: an index for those norms that shape the individual employment relationship, a second one for collective rules that discipline unionized actions and, finally, a third indicator that measures various social security provisions. Indeed, workers' position inside the firm is dependent on those norms that regulate hiring, working time and dismissal conditions (the Employment Laws Index), but also on employees' contractual strength, empowered by collective actions (the collective relations laws index). Finally, it cannot be left out of the scene the role of social

---

2   The research covers a sample of 72 countries and refers to legal rules prevailing in 2003.

3   For a methodological explanation of these new indicators, see Djankov et al. (2008) Tab. I.

Table 11.1 Ownership concentration, investor protection, employment regulations

Country	Ownership concentration	Ex-ante private control of self dealing	Ex-post private control of self dealing	Anti-self dealing Index	Public enforcement Index	Empl. law Index	Collective relations laws index	Social Security laws index
	(a)	(a)	(a)	(a)	(a)	(b)	(b)	(b)
France	34	0.08	0.68	0.38	0.5	0.7443	0.6667	0.7838
Belgium	54	0.39	0.7	0.54	0.5	0.5133	0.4226	0.624
Italy	58	0.17	0.68	0.42	0	0.6499	0.631	0.7572
Finland	37	0.14	0.78	0.46	0	0.7366	0.3185	0.7863
Denmark	45	0.25	0.68	0.46	0.75	0.5727	0.4196	0.8727
Netherlands	39	0.06	0.35	0.2	0	0.7256	0.4643	0.6282
Austria	58	0	0.43	0.21	1	0.5007	0.3601	0.7139
Norway	36	0.42	0.43	0.42	1	0.6853	0.6488	0.8259
Ireland	39	0.78	0.8	0.79	0	0.3427	0.4643	0.7144
Sweden	28	0.17	0.5	0.33	1	0.7405	0.5387	0.8448
Switzerland	41	0.08	0.45	0.27	0.75	0.452	0.4167	0.8151
Japan	18	0.22	0.78	0.50	0.00	0.1639	0.628	0.6417
United Kingdom	19	1	0.9	0.95	0	0.2824	0.1875	0.6915
Canada	40	0.33	0.95	0.64	1	0.2615	0.1964	0.7869
Germany	48	0.14	0.43	0.28	1	0.7015	0.6071	0.6702
United States	20	0.33	0.33	0.98	0.65	0.2176	0.2589	0.6461
Mean	38.4	0.285	0.617	0.489	0.509	0.518	0.452	0.738
Median	39	0.195	0.68	0.44	0.575	0.543	0.44345	0.736
Min	18	0	0.33	0.2	0	0.1649	0.1875	0.624

Source: (a) Djankov et al. (2008, Tab. V); the indexes for investor protection are elaborated on legal rules prevailing in 2003; see the detailed description in Djankov et al. (2008, Tab. I); ownership concentration is the average percentage of common shares owned by the top three shareholders in the ten largest non-financial, privately-owned domestic firms in a given country.[a] (b) Botero et al. (2002, Tab. III, p. 1362-1363).[b] The employment laws index is the average of four different measures: 1) alternative employment contracts; 2) cost of increasing hours worked; 3) cost of firing workers; 4) dismissal procedures. The collective relations laws index is an average based on two indicators: 1) labour union power; 2) collective disputes. The Social security index is an average based on three indicators: 1) pension and disability benefits; 2) sickness and health benefits; 3) unemployment benefits (see Botero et al. 2002, pp. 1348-1349).

[a] The authors consider a firm privately-owned 'if the State is not a known shareholder in it' (Djankov et al., 2008, Tab. I).
[b] The authors precise that they 'collect data on employment collective relations, and social security laws as of 1997 for the Djankov et al. (2008) sample of 85 countries, and code them to measure worker protection' (Botero et al. 2004, p. 1341).

security provisions. After all, a basic concern of payment schemes is the intrinsic trade-off between optimal incentives and optimal risk sharing (Hart and Holmstrom, 1987). Thus, a good governance system has to adopt a performance-related payment scheme which also properly allocates risk. This allocation may be conditioned by some public provisions, such as unemployment benefits, which can influence the ex-post division of firm's surplus.

Now, by considering this entire dataset, the picture one obtains is enriched. From Table 11.1 it is possible to see that in market or outsider systems, belonging to the Common Law families, such as the United States and the United Kingdom, ownership is widely held, small shareholders have little power and incentive for active governance, investor protection is high, while less pronounced is the protection afforded to employees and more limited are the social security provisions. In sum, in these economies a clear orientation towards a shareholder view seems to emerge.

On the opposite side, one finds countries such as Germany, where concentration is above average values of the sample, while lower ex-ante and ex-post shareholders protection is coupled with strong employment and collective bargaining safeguards. Less homogenous are, in any case, the patterns for finance and employment rules of Continental Europe and Japan. For instance, in Nordic countries, and Denmark is a good point in case, concentrated ownership is accompanied by limited protection of investors and employees, but by strong law enforcement and generous social security benefits. One plausible interpretation is that it is the absence of *state rules* that may explain the adoption of *company rules* 'to fill the void', and as suggested by a recent and vast report on corporate social responsibility (The Economist, 2008, p. 4), setting labour standards at a firm level is a good example in that sense. On the other side, the various indicators for Japan confirm that its stakeholder model relies on informal rules, quite different from the legal basis that shapes, through co-determination devices, the industrial relations in Germany.

A more synthetic description of correlations between institutional variables is offered by Table 11.2.

As seen so far, the polarization between two opposite situations, the Anglo Saxon shareholder model and the stakeholder German model, seems still valid. This distinction

Table 11.2 Correlations of labour regulations protection and corporate governance indexes

	Ex-ante private control of self-dealing	Ex-post private control of self-dealing	Anti-self-dealing index	Public enforcement index
Employment laws index	-0.3564*	-0.4416*	-0.4685*	0.2248
Collective relations laws index	-0.2571*	-0.3836*	-0.3687*	0.1099
Social Security index	-0.0652	-0.0119	-0.0497	0.2464*

Source: Our elaborations on Djankov et al. (2008) and Botero et al. (2002; the correlations are computed for a sample of 69 countries; * significant at the 5% level.

reflects some well known differences between two distinct regimes of corporate governance that a huge literature has compared in many surveys, but that some studies have recently contested. It seems a remarkable step in the ongoing debate on convergence issues, where, for the Renanian model, qualified sweeping changes towards a shareholder orientation have been widely stressed, as recently recalled by Beyer and Hassel (2002).

Additional and prominent deviations between the two polar systems arise in terms of financial and employment outcomes, as can be easily ascertained by Figure 11.1 and Table 11.3, where German and British corporations are compared.

As Figure 11.1 and Table 11.3 suggest, differences in ownership and management priorities mirror deviations in outcomes. Indeed, as shown by information concerning performances, even if current profitability, measured by real returns on equities, is quite similar in Germany and the UK, stock market capitalization and valuation (price book ratio and market value) are definitely higher in the Anglo-Saxon country.[4] On the other

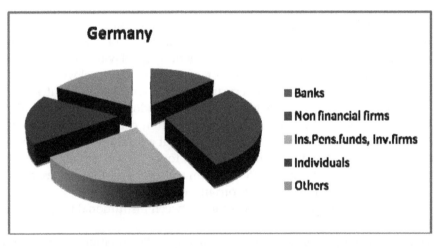

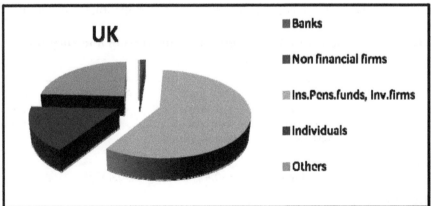

Figure 11.1 Ownership structure: German and British firms, 2000

---

4   It must be added, however, that market capitalization may depend on various determinants; for instance it can be related to the size structure of firms (in relation to the nature of the production processes according to sectoral specialization), and on the response to different normative structures and different propensities to internationalization. On some of the linkages between sectoral fields of specialization and institutional varieties of capitalism see Hall and Soskice (2001b).

Table 11.3   British and German companies: Aims and outcomes

	Germany	UK
Management board priorities (1998)		
Meeting financial goals	53	72
M&As, joint ventures	28	46
Reducing costs	36	15
Improving productivity	36	15
Performances (2000)	**$**	
Real returns on equity	18.2%	20.4%
Market valuation:		
Price book ratio	2.5	4.6
Market value (mill. euros)	20,754	42,337
Sales and employment:		
Return on sales	9.4%	19.2%
Employees	138,072	60,676

Source: Jürgens and Rupp, (2002, Tab. 5, p. 17); Höpner and Jackson (2004, Tab. 2, p. 13).

side, German companies give less importance to meeting financial goals (see the first rows of Table 11.3) and sustain nearly double the number of employees with respect to the British firms, as the volume of the workforce hired in the two different countries (last row of Table 11.3) seems to indicate.

However, additional evidence shows that the relevance of two of the traditional cornerstones of the German system, the monitoring function of banks and of employees has been eroded in the last decades. As well known, bank monitoring may be a relevant element in *relational financing*. For instance, in Germany, banks and client firms maintain long-term relationships and have access to information on firm's financial conditions (Edwards and Fischer, 1994). Thus, they are able to distinguish between good and bad projects and may renegotiate with failing, but efficient, firms in difficulties, thus avoiding their premature liquidations and favouring their restructuring. However, in the last years the monitoring role of German banks has diminished dramatically and, as signalled by Beyer and Hassel (2002), 'between 1992 and 1999 the share of bank representatives as chairmen of supervisory boards fell from 44 per cent to 23 per cent in 40 large companies in Germany'.

Notice also, as shown in Table 11.4, the declining relevance of banks' long-term loans, in the past a crucial complement of a strong internal finance, and the falling influence of employees, as disclosed from the Report on 'Co- Determination and New Company Results', performed in 1998 (Bertelsmann and Hans-Böckler).

Table 11.4 Convergence towards a shareholder model?

The declining role of banks in Germany

	1994	2000
External financing	42.6	64.4
of external financing:
Banks:	16.3	13.5
short-term loans	0.5	3.5
long-term loans	15.8	10.0

The declining role of employees in Germany

	1984	1994/1995
Supervisory boards and works council	30.5%	24.5%
Works council only	18.9%	15%
None	50.6%	60.5%

Source: Jürgens, Rupp, (2002, Tab. 8, p. 3 and Tab. 13, p. 46).

On this last issue it is remarkable that there have been a growing number of companies where neither supervisory board nor works council are present and this group of companies counts, in the mid-1990s, for more than 60 per cent of all the German firms.

Summing up, recent trends in terms of convergence towards a market-oriented system can be undeniable and 'the stereotypical view of German finance' (Jenkinson and Ljungqvist 2001, p. 397) has to be abandoned. However, there is also supportive evidence that some fundamental differences are still significant (Goergen, Manjon and Renneboog, 2004).

The distinctive functioning of the Renanian model of corporate governance motivates us to better understand the main qualitative features of a stakeholder economy and to evaluate if the recent trends towards its abandoning should be continued.

Incentives and Labour Relationships in a Stakeholder Model

In the Anglo-Saxon *shareholder system*, where the single small shareholder has limited incentive to monitoring activities,[5] the main issue of corporate governance is the optimal design of incentives to implement strategies that maximize the return on equity capital.

---

5   The role of monitoring activity is relevant when managerial conduct and investment opportunities are not perfectly observable. See, among the main theoretical references for the observability issue, Holmstrom (1979).

Here the narrow view of the firm impinges on a single agency conflict, the one between managers and owners.[6]

In the *stakeholder economy*, where the interest of other actors, including employees, as well as creditors, suppliers and customers, are taken into account, the existence of various conflicts arises. But in this context, how do incentive mechanisms work in aligning the interests of a *multiplicity* of stakeholders and those of their agents? And how does the alignment motivation, behind the endorsement of a stakeholder society, concealinstead of mitigatingmanagerial misconduct and moral hazard problems?

Indeed, reliable measures of stakeholders' welfare are difficult to find, and the problem of providing explicit incentives to pursue the interests of a multiplicity of stakeholders seems to fit well, as noticed in Tirole (2001), with the *multitasks* agency model suggested by Holmstrom and Milgrom (1991). In this model, a well-designed incentive system has to balance the distortions that may induce effort in one task but indifference and suboptimal strain in some other occupations. These considerations gain relevance in a stakeholder perspective, since management may rationalize any action by invoking its impact on the welfare of some stakeholders, even if these actions worsen the welfare of some others. Since this balance is difficult, a *flat* compensation system may be preferable, while variable incentive rewards may generate misallocation of efforts, that is, the achievement of welfare of some stakeholders, at the expense of some others. In this perspective, 'there is some consistency between lenient views in the French, German, and Japanese populations toward the stakeholder society and the low power of the managerial incentive schemes in these countries' (Tirole, 2001, p. 26). Table 11.5 shows that in the United States, that is, in the more shareholder-oriented system, the CEOs 'compensation is less flat than in the other countries'. However, it must be noticed that the figures related to the UK do not confirm a homogenous reward system in the Anglo-Saxon economies,

Table 11.5 Flat CEO's compensation and stakeholder society: Variable remuneration as percentage of total remuneration in some countries

Countries	Variable CEOs' remuneration component			
	1996	2001	2003	2005
France	29%	26%	29%	41%
Germany	12%	36%	51%	52%
Italy	24%	33%	30%	35%
Japan	8%	18%	19%	22%
UK	30%	30%	34%	35%
US	47%	61%	63%	62%

Source: Towers Perrin, 2001–2002, 1997, 2005 'Worldwide Remuneration Data

---

6   On the agency problem between owners and managers see Jensen and Meckling (1976) and Fama and Jensen (1983).

as well analyzed by Conyon and Murphy (2000),[7] the authors who name the CEOs in the United States and the United Kingdom the 'prince and the pauper'.

In any case, even by adopting a flat remuneration system, some critical objections on the feasibility of the stakeholder view remain and the existing literature seems to present two opposite views.

In a first view, grounded on the Alchian and Demsetz' (1972) classical approach to the private firm, all property rights should be uniquely assigned to the firm's owner, and all the devices that split these rights perturb the efficient allocation of resources that is associated with the maximization of shareholders' value. In the same vein, as suggested by Jensen (2001), it may be argued that corporate governance arrangements that give 'voice' to employees, as codetermination in Germany, increase agency costs because they dilute board's power, promote collusion between management and employees and impede the emergence of a dispersed ownership.[8]

These claims have found some empirical support. Indeed, as Gorton and Schmid (2004) have shown by studying a sample of the 250 largest Germany public companies for the years 1989–1993, employees wield enough power to obtain private benefits of control and pursue this strategy by altering managerial remuneration, as confirmed by the weaker link, in cases of more extensive labour participation, between executive managerial compensations and company results. Moreover, employees' representatives aim at maintaining a high staffing level and wield resistance to corporate restructuring.

Analogous conclusions are reached for the same United States' experience by Bertrand and Mullainathan (1998, 2003). The authors prove on empirical grounds, by studying the years 1976–1995 that an increased attention to employees does not improve the efficiency of the American firms, especially those firms incorporated in states with anti-takeover laws. On the contrary, it is exactly the approval of state-level anti-takeover provisions that permits an increase in average wages up to the figure of 4 per cent for white collars, without positive impacts on labour productivity nor on investments and firm size. In sum, stakeholder protection does not 'pay for itself', a result which should call for a better regulation of hostile bids and for company laws more oriented to prevent the adoption of anti-takeover devices, sometimes hidden under the umbrella of stakeholders' interests.

For the United States' experience another important study by Chaplinsky and Niehaus (1994) which considers a whole decade (1980–1990), shows the use of Employees Ownership Plans (ESOPs) as a deterrent to takeovers; the rationales behind these results is that employees who hold ESOP shares have a high reservation price for tendering a bidder and thus play an effective role in lowering the likelihood of hostile bids; at the same time, the same reason can explain why the negotiated tender offers that are successfully completed produce higher returns for all the selling shareholders. In any case, all mismanagement failures, which would need high turnover rates of executives, cause more serious problems when employees holding ESOP shares hinder an active market for corporate control.

---

7   The authors, in a very largely quoted article, have shown that in British companies executive rewards have remained far behind payment levels obtained by the CEOs in the US.

8   A critical analysis of stakeholder theory is also offered in Sternberg (1997).

In the same European scenario, some prominent examples teach a lot.[9] For instance, in Italy, trade unions have rejected labour shedding and restructuring conditions asked by the potential bidders to buy the Italian flag carrier (Forbes, 2007); in fact, the Alitalia case well exemplifies that collusive alliances between employees, government and management may be relevant since 'requirements to maintain bloated staffing levels (cabin crew work less than 10 hours a week)' has been a serious obstacle to its privatization and not by chance the selling of a company 'which loses about €1m a day' (The Economist, 2006) has been postponed several times along the years and it must still be accomplished.

Now consider the second more optimistic perspective, where the potential strength of a 'broad' view of the firm is advocated. In this alternative view 'the multiple and hard-to-measure missions of management' (Tirole, 2006, p. 59) are obtained by the same institution of a supervisory board, where owners and employees exert their monitoring function on management. This emerges as particularly relevant in the modern firm, where new needs to attract firm-specific inputs from other participants in the enterprise, such as skilled employees, require new pillars of corporate governance (Blair, 1995, Blair and Roe, 1999).

Even this thesis finds an empirical support from the German case, as shown by Fauvera and Fuerst (2006). The authors precise that their study integrates that of Gorton and Schmid (2004) as their sample consists 'of all publicly traded (AG) German corporations as of 2003, including firms with varying degrees of labour representation (from zero to more than one-half) and firms for which labour representation is both optional and mandatory' (p. 677). What Fauvera and Fuerst find, using their sample, is that 'prudent levels of employee representation on corporate boards can increase firm efficiency and market value. This result contrasts with that of Gorton and Schmid (2004)' (Fauvera and Fuerst, 2006, p. 703).

A selection of their findings is reported in Table 11.6, where accounting performances for firms with or without employee representation are compared and tests for the statistical differences are shown.

Let us read these results. First of all, it must be noticed that employee representation is more diffuse not only in firms significantly larger with respect to sales and assets, but also relatively more profitable. Moreover, it is relevant that capital expenditure and R&D efforts (computed as ratios to sales) are lower in companies with employee representation, a finding that the authors interpret as a confirmation that workers' *voice* intervenes against poor investment choices. Further, there is some evidence, as shown from Table 11.6, that employee representation reduces the agency cost of free cash flows: dividend yields and payout ratios are significantly greater (more than double) for firms with employee representation. Additional estimates performed by the authors corroborate the hypothesis of diminishing marginal returns after a threshold level of employees representation, around one third of seats, thus suggesting that 'judicious use of labour representation can increase firm value' (p. 677).

It must be noticed that, to date, the studies that test on empirical grounds benefits and costs of labour involvement in corporate governance are very few.

However, some additional insights that complement micro-econometric evidence may be obtained by an overall picture of labour regulation and wage-setting rules, as

---

9   Among other case studies of strategies and collusive alliances against takeovers see the use of ESOP plans to prevent the hostile bid of Gucci, as shown in Chilosi and Damiani (2007).

Table 11.6 Employee representation and accounting performances in a sample of all publicly traded German corporations – 2003

Firm characteristics	No employee Representation mean	Employee representation mean	Difference p-value mean
Sales (Eu MM)	129.3	393.6	0.000
Assets (Eu MM)	222.6	1,320.0	0.000
Capital Exp./sales	0.208	0.067	0.160
R&D/sales	0.033	0.011	0.007
Dividend yield	0.012	0.025	0.000
Dividend payout ratio	0.089	0.229	0.000
Ownership concentration	0.197	0.407	0.000

Source: Fauvera and Fuerst (2006, Tab. 2, p. 685). The p-values for differences in means are from a standard t-test. Dividend yield is defined as dividends per share over the year-end market price. Dividend payout ratio is defined as dividends per share divided by earnings per share.

can be ascertained not only by formal rules but also by informal labour practices. For example – as stressed by Ahlering and Deakin (2006, p. 19) – 'the mandatory requirement that companies bargain with unions or works councils shapes a great deal about the labour environment in Germany, while the lack of this particular written law may be less significant to shaping the labour environment in Japan, where a different style of consensual company politics prevails, making it less necessary for the formal law to intervene'.

Indeed, when 'de jure' regulations of labour, as those discussed by Botero et al. 2002, and overviewed in the above section, are complemented with new indices of 'de facto' labour practices, some additional insights can be reached. Let us consider the 2004 Global Labour Survey (GLS) performed for 33 countries and aimed at surveying practitioners and experts who have direct knowledge of both regulations and de facto practices (Chor and Freeman, 2005, p. 4).[10] One relevant indicator is the frequency of labour unrest and conflicts. According to this index, the frequency of labour disputes has the lowest score in a shareholder country, such as the United States. By contrast, in countries where unions and labour organizations are more powerful, such as France, Belgium and Italy, the indicator for employer-employees conflicts reaches the highest levels. But an interesting and unexpected result arises: the frequency of labour strikes and the nature of labour conflicts qualify the German case as one of the less 'confrontational' environment in terms of labour management, as shown in Figure 11.2.

---

10   The GLS survey is an Internet-based survey aimed at gathering information from labour experts and practitioners of 33 countries and addressed to evaluate de jure labor regulations. Chor and Freeman explicitly compare the GLS measures with data on the legal provisions for regulation of labor from Botero et al. (2004). What they find is an insignificant correlation between formal and informal real regulation, for instance for bargaining setting rules (Chor and Freeman, 2005, pp. 21-22).

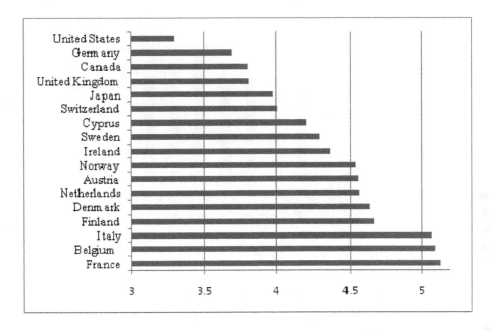

Figure 11.2 Labour disputes in some industrialized countries, 2000

Source: Chor and Freeman (2005, Tab. 5, p. 37). The indicator scores from 1 to 7 and it is obtained from the responses to 12 questions related to threats, frequency and features of strikes. See Chor and Freeman (2005, Module 4, pp. 49-50).

A parallel dimension of industrial relations climate is obtained by the bargaining governability, an indicator that, as clarified in OECD (2004, p. 152), 'addresses the governance capacity of the bargaining system, *i.e.* the ability of the employer and trade union associations to control the behaviour of their constituency or *rank and file'*. Here it comes out that Germany is one of the nine cases, out of 20 countries, that exhibit high bargaining governability. It means that contractual clauses have a strong legal enforceability and that during the validity of an agreement there is an automatic peace obligation (OECD, 2004, p. 152).

In sum, the above comparative evidence shows that the German economy becomes again a benchmark model, but in this more optimistic perspective, its experience confirms the success of the 'stakeholder' system of corporate governance, as evaluated in Hall and Soskice (2001a). A success that may be attributed, in a more comprehensive analysis, not only to the *sole* device of a two-tier board, but also to the crucial role played by some *institutional complementarities*, as we will see below.

It must be premised that in coordinate market economies, as in the German case, extensive relational and incomplete contracting entails more reliance on collaborative relationship and on the exchange of private information.

In Germany, this design is mirrored in moderate wage differentials across firms and industries that reduce the propensity of employees to change jobs, thus contributing to a compressed wage structure and to long employment tenure. The employment stability is implemented, at least at a first glance, through the functioning of two relevant labour market institutions. The first one is the industry-level wage bargaining that prevents intra-industry wage differentials and generates low spreads by firm

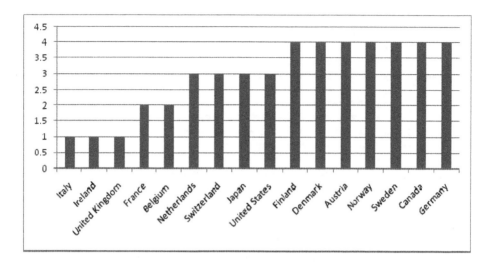

Figure 11.3 Bargaining Governability in some Industrialized Countries, 2000

Source: OECD (2004, p.152). The governability indicator ranges from 4 to 1:4 = when collective agreements are legally enforceable and there is an automatic peace obligation during validity of the agreement. 3 = when collective agreements are legally enforceable and there are widespread (but optional) peace obligation clauses in agreements. 2 = where there is legal enforceability, but no effective tradition or practice of peace obligation clauses. 1 = where neither of the above conditions are effectively present.

size, thus lowering voluntary separation rates. The second one is the legal institution of codetermination at the level of the supervisory board and works councils. These arrangements, as shown in Freeman and Lazear (1994), enhance the efficiency of the firm by permitting the flows of communications between management and workers, but give *voice* to employees in their demand for lower layoffs and lower labour shedding in case of adverse shocks.

A potential drawback could be a higher bargaining power over the distribution of the company results, with suboptimal outcomes.[11] It has been well clarified by Freeman and Lazear (1994). The authors observe that a potential trade off arises since owners realize that a higher works council power may enhance productivity and rents (a larger pie), but reduces their own share (a smaller slice). The owners' choice is a lower sub-optimal level of codetermination since they cannot fully appropriate all the benefits from collaborative labour relations. An escape and solution to the dilemma is to separate the factors that affect the magnitude of the surplus from those that have an impact on its division. Thus, the predominant "sectoral" level of collective bargaining is a crucial device that makes easier to separate wage setting from all aspects of codetermination. In this framework, adopted in the German case where an implicit empowerment of labour is provided, the interplay of *sectoral* wage setting rules and *firm level* employment decisions reveals a crucial and successful factor' (FitzRoy and Kraft, 2005).

---

11   Indeed, as the study of Milgrom and Roberts (1990) has shown in a general context, insiders' involvement may generate lobbying and 'influence' costs, with negative side effects that outweigh the efficiency gains obtained from better communication.

This implies that corporate governance concerns induce to reconsider in a new light the role of the degree of centralization of wage bargaining, one of the main determinants of labour market performances, carefully explored by the OECD in its Employment Outlooks. For years a common view, along the lines suggested by Calmfors and Driffill (1988), has been that the intermediate, sectoral level of negotiations, as that adopted in the German case, produces the worst outcomes, while both the centralized and decentralized levels perform better. The rationale of this claim is that in both the extreme polar cases forces operate which can moderate wage growth: in the centralized system, it is the cooperative union behaviour and the internalization process which can determine real wage restraint; in the decentralized one it is the competitive forces operating in the product and labour markets which tend to induce wage moderation. On the contrary, in cases of intermediate levels of bargaining, unions do not cooperate at a central level in wage setting and do not internalize the benefits by adopting a real wage restraint; at the same time, they have sufficient market power to inhibit the competitive pressures that moderate wage policies, as those of decentralized systems. Thus the relation between the degree of centralization and economic performance should be depicted as a hump-shaped relation, an inverse U, between the degree of centralization and unemployment, with both decentralized and centralized bargaining systems outperforming intermediate systems.

Empirical evidence, up to present, provides only ambiguous results and as recently stressed in its 2004 Employment Outlook, the OECD reports that 'more than a decade of research has failed to provide decisive evidence either for or against the Calmfors and Driffill hypothesis, illustrating the difficulties researchers have encountered in obtaining robust results or even in agreeing how best to characterize the effective degree of co-ordination in bargaining' (OECD, 2004, p. 134).[12]

The disappearing 'inverse U' has been recently stressed by Freeman (2007) and can be evaluated in a broader perspective: the coexistence of industry-level wage bargaining with inter-firm relations, long-term oriented strategies, small wage dispersions are all significant aspects of *varieties of capitalism,* where there are relevant forces capable of implementing long-term relationships and the interests of a group of stakeholders.

Thus, a synthetic representation of the different wage and employment setting rules in coordinated market economies, such as in Germany and Japan, in comparison to those adopted in liberal market economies (United States and United Kingdom), may prove that institutional complementarities, as suggested by Aoki (1994), reveal to be decisive.

As shown in Table 11.7, in coordinated economies, such as Germany, where more than 40 per cent of total shares of companies are owned by other non-financial enterprises, sectoral bargaining level is desirable for its 'peace-keeping function': it is a useful device that transfers 'the distributional conflict between management and the workforce to a level above that of the firm' (Hassel and Rehder, 2001, p. 5). Furthermore, the German and Japan model of a 'patient capitalism' is assured via long-term labour contracts, and thus longer-term jobs and higher employment tenures, something that can contribute to lower the intra-firm conflicts related to selection and retain policies of skilled employees. Further, as shown by Table 11.7, wage inequalities are more moderate, as is indicated not

---

12   A detail comparison of wage structures and bargaining setting rules for the European Union is offered in European Commission (2003, chapter 3).

Table 11.7 Bargaining, stability of labour relations and comparative features of Coordinated Market Economies (CME) and Liberal Market Economies (LME)

	Bargaining level (dominant form(a)	Employment Tenure (average tenure years) (b)	Inter-firm relations (percentage of common stocks owned by other non financial enterprises (c)	Ratio of pay of manual workers to CEO* (%) (d)	Earnings dispersion** (a)
CME					
Germany	Sectoral	9.7	42	8.8	2.87
Japan	Sectoral	11.3	22	9,5	2.99
LME					
US	Company	7.4	0	3.2	3.45
UK	Company	7.8	1	5.4	4.59

Source: (a) OECD (2004); (b) OECD, Employment Outlook (various years c); (c) OECD (2003); (d) Towers Perrin (2005), 'Worldwide Remuneration Data', (*) manufacturing; 90-10 percentile ratios for the gross earnings of full-time employees.

only by lower earning dispersions, but also by a flatter compensation structure that offers temperate premiums to managers and top executives.

Conclusion

What complementary institutions are necessary to implement the stakeholders-labour governance? Are only the labour regulation rules sufficient to explain the functioning of German and Japanese firms?

The above analysis has shown that institutional linkages and complementarities offer a fruitful line of research and further progresses call for an integration of comparative institutional studies where financial and labour rules are contemporaneously explored (Djankov et al. 2008; Botero at al. 2002). Furthermore, 'an understanding of more formal institutions, including the legal framework, must be complemented by an appreciation of how they interact with informal norms, social conventions and tacit understandings in shaping behaviour' (Ahlering and Deakin, 2006, p. 4). An effort quite appreciable at a time of intense debate over the role of labour market institutions, as noticed by Chor and Freeman (2005), and when legal formal determinants are increasingly at the centre of the scene.

Preliminary steps along the lines of institutional complementarities have suggested that cross-national diversities, and thus *varieties of capitalism*, are still present, not withstanding the indisputable converging trends in a shareholder and market direction. Indeed, in coordinated market economies, long-term employment relationships call for a 'financial system capable of providing capital on terms that are not sensitive to current profitability' (Hall and Soskice, 2001a, p. 18). Also, the option *voice*, which sustains long-term relationships, is related to concentrated ownership which permits to overcome the free-riding problem of dispersed ownership, since large investors are able and motivated to exercise control by obtaining significant gains by their monitoring activity. In addition inter-firm relations are relevant and are achieved by cross-shareholdings and bargaining coordination. Additionally, an overall picture of labour regulation and wage-setting rules has shown that some European countries outperform the Anglo Saxon economies on the grounds of collaborative relations and bargaining governability.

Finally, some remarks concern the 'convergence' issue, a topic still controversial and open to debate. The above analysis confirms that 'the diffusion of shareholder value has not undermined the core institutions of German industrial relations, namely codetermination and collective bargaining' (Jackson, Höpner and Kurdelbusch, 2006, pp. 117-118). In any case, what each reform programme should achieve is not the attainment of a world-wide convergence aim in itself, but effective improvements grounded on a new perception of the complex web of coalitions on which each variety of capitalism is founded.

But among the various forms of coalition, one should discover those corporate governance arrangements that conceal natural alliances of managers and employees, new accomplices of misconduct and opportunistic behaviour. Thus, as shown by the misfunctioning of the market for corporate control (Chaplinsky and Niehaus, 1994, and Bertrand and Mullainathan, 1998, 2003), interests of employees may be invoked as deterrent to hostile bids, and labour relationships may conceal new powerful anti-takeover devices (Pagano and Volpin 2005).

In sum, when a conflict between *strong* insiders (management, employees, block-holders) and *weak* outsiders (small shareholders) arises, market-based evolutions and 'institutional conversions' that discourage and punish rent-seeking behaviour could have beneficial effects, while the 'broad view' of the firm is no more a defensible alternative.

References

Ahlering B., Deakin S. (2006), Labour Regulation, Corporate Governance and Legal Origin: A Case Of Institutional Complementarity?, ECGI Working Paper, n. 72.

Alchian A., Demsetz H. (1972), Production, Information Costs, and Economic Organization, *American Economic Review*, vol. 62, n. 5, pp. 777-795.

Allen F., Gale D. (2000), Comparing Financial Systems, Cambridge, MIT Press.

Aoki M. (1994), The Japanese Firm as a System of Attributes: a Survey and Research Agenda, in Aoki, M., Dore R. (eds), The Japanese Firm: Sources of Competitive Strength, Oxford, Clarendon Press, pp. 11-40.

Baums T., Scott K. E. (2003), Taking Shareholder Protection Seriously? Corporate Governance in the United States and Germany, EGCI Working Paper, n. 17.

Becht M., Bolton P., Röell A. (2003), 'Corporate Governance and Control', in Costantinides George M., Harris M., Stulz R.M. (eds), Handbook of the Economics of Finance, Amsterdam, North Holland, pp. 4-109.

Berle, A., A., Means G. C., (1932), The Modern Corporation and Private Property, New York, McMillan.

Bertelsmann S., Hans-Böckler S. (eds) (1998), Co-Determination and New Company Cultures, Mitbestimmung und neue Unternehmenskulturen – Bilanz und Perspektiven, Bericht der Kommission Mitbestimmung, Gütersloh.

Bertrand M., Mullainathan S. (1998), Executive Compensation and Incentives: The Impact of Takeover Legislation, NBER Working Paper, n. 6830.

Bertrand M., Mullainathan S. (2003), 'Enjoying a Quite life', Journal of Political Economy, vol. 111, no. 5, pp. 1043-1075.

Beyer J., Hassel A. (2002), 'The Effects of Convergence: Internationalization and the Changing Distribution of Net Value Added in Large German Firms', Economy and Society, vol. 31, n. 3, pp. 309-332.

Blair M. (1995), Ownership and Control. Rethinking Corporate Governance for the Twenty First Century, Washington D.C., The Brookings Institution.

Blair M., Roe M. J. (eds) (1999), Employees and Corporate Governance, Washington, D.C., The Brookings Institution.

Botero J. C., Djankov S., La Porta R., Lopez-de-Silanes F., Shleifer A. (2002), 'The Regulation of Labor', Quarterly Journal of Economics, vol. 119, n. 4, pp. 1339-1382.

Calmfors, L. Driffill J. (1988), 'Bargaining Structure, Corporatism and Macroeconomic Performance', Economic Policy, vol. 3, n. 6, pp. 13-61

Chaplinsky S., Niehaus G. (1994), 'The Role of ESOPs in Takeover Contests', The Journal of Finance, vol. 49, n. 4, pp. 1451-1470.

Chilosi A., Damiani M. (2007), 'Stakeholders vs. Shareholders in Corporate Governance', Icfai Journal of Corporate Governance, vol. 6, n. 4, pp. 7-45.

Chor D., Freeman R. (2005), The 2004 Global Labor Survey: Workplace Institutions and Practices around the World, NBER Working Paper, n. 11598.

Conyon, M. J., Murphy, K. J. (2000), 'The Prince and the Pauper? CEO Pay in the US and UK', The Economic Journal, vol. 110, n. 467, F640-71.

Damiani M. (2006), Impresa e Corporate Governance, Roma, Carocci.

Djankov S., La Porta R., Lopez-de-Silanes F., Shleifer A.(2008), 'The Law and Economics of Self Dealing', Journal of Financial Economics, forthcoming.

Edwards, J., Fischer, K., (1994), Banks, Finance and Investment in Germany, Cambridge, Cambridge University Press.

European Commission (2003), Employment in Europe, 2003 – Recent Trends and Prospects, Directorate General for Employment and Social Affairs.

Fama E.F., Jensen M.C. (1983), 'Agency Problems and Residual Claims', Journal of Law and Economics, vol. 26, n. 2, pp. 327-349.

Fauvera L., Fuerst M.E. (2006), 'Does Good Corporate Governance Include Employee Representation? Evidence from German corporate boards', Journal of Financial Economics, vol. 82, n. 3, pp. 673-710.

Fitzroy F.R., Kraft K. (2005), 'Co-determination, Efficiency and Productivity', British Journal of Industrial Relations, vol. 43, n. 2, pp. 233-247.

Forbes, (2007), 'Alitalia Trade Unions Reject Air One Labour Conditions to Buy Airline – Report', 07.09.07, electronic edition.

Freeman R.B. (2007), Labor Market Institutions around the World, NBER, Working Paper n. 13242.

Goergen M., Manjon M.C., Renneboog (2004), Recent Developments in German Corporate Governance, Finance Working Paper, n. 41.

Freeman R. B., Lazear E. P. (1994), An Economic Analysis of Works Councils, NBER Working Paper, n. 4918.

Gorton, G., Schmid, F., (2004), 'Capital, Labor and the Firm: A Study of German Codetermination', *Journal of the European Economic Association*, vol. 2, n. 5, pp. 863-905.

Gospel H., Pendleton A. (eds) (2006), Corporate Governance and Labour Management, Oxford, Oxford University Press.

Hall P.A., Soskice D. (2001a), 'Introduction', in Hall P.A., Soskice D. (eds) (2001b), pp. 1-68.

Hall P.A., Soskice, D., (2001b), Varieties of Capitalism, Oxford, Oxford University Press.

Hart O.D., Holmstrom B. (1987), 'The Theory of Contracts', in Bewley T.F. (ed.), Advances in Economic Theory, Cambridge, Cambridge University Press pp. 71-155.

Hassel A., Rehder B. (2001), Institutional Change in the German Wage Bargaining System – The Role of Big Companies, MPIfG Working Paper, n. 01/9.

Holmstrom, B., (1979), Moral Hazard and Observability, *Bell Journal of Economics*, vol. 10, n. 1, pp. 74-91.

Holmstrom, B., Milgrom, P., (1991), 'Multitask Principal-Agent Analyses: Incentive Contracts, Asset Ownership, and Job Design', *Journal of Law, Economics, and Organization*, vol. 7, n. 1, pp. 24-52.

Höpner M. Jackson G. (2004), An Emerging Market for Corporate Control? The Mannesmann Takeover and German Corporate Governance, Max-Planck-Institute fur Gesellschaftsforschung, 01/4.

Jackson G. (2005), 'Stakeholders under Pressure: corporate governance and labour management', *Corporate Governance: An International Review*, vol. 13, n. 3, pp. 419-427.

Jackson G., Höpner M., Kurdelbusch A. (2006), 'Corporate Governance and Employees in Germany: Changing Linkages, Complementarities, and Tensions', in Gospel H., Pendleton A. (eds), pp. 84-121.

Jenkinson, T., Ljungqvist A. (2001): 'The Role of Hostile Stakes in German Corporate Governance', *Journal of Corporate Finance*, vol. 7, n. 4, pages 397-446.

Jensen, M. C., (2001), 'Value Maximization, Stakeholder Theory, And The Corporate Objective Function, *European Financial Management*, vol. 7, no. 3, pp. 297-317.

Jensen M.C., Meckling W.H. (1976), 'Theory of the Firm: Managerial Behaviour, Agency Costs and Ownership Structure', *Journal of Financial Economics*, vol. 3, n. 4, pp. 305-360.

Jürgens U., Rupp J., (2002), The German System of Corporate Governance Characteristics and Changes, Veröffentlichungsreihe der Abteilung Regulierung von Arbeit des Forschungsschwerpunkts Technik-Arbeit-Umwelt des Wissenschaftszentrum Berlin für Sozialforschung, FS II, n. 02-203.

La Porta R., De Silanes F.L., Shleifer A., Vishny R. (2000), 'Investor Protection and Corporate Governance', *Journal of Financial Economics*, vol. 58, n. 1-2, pp. 3-27.

La Porta R., Lopez-de Silanes F. Shleifer A., Vishny R. (1998), 'Law and Finance', *Journal of Political Economy*, vol. 106, n. 6, pp. 1113-1155.

Maher M., Andersson T. (1999), Corporate Governance: Effects on Firm Performance and Economic Growth, OECD, Paris.

Milgrom, P., Roberts, J., (1990), 'Bargaining Cost, Influence Costs, and the Organization of Economic Activity', in Alt, J., Shepsle K. (eds), Perspectives on Positive Political Economy, Cambridge, Cambridge University Press, pp. 57-89.

OECD (2003), Survey of Corporate Governance Developments in OECD Countries, Paris.

OECD (2004), Employment Outlook, Paris.

Pagano, M., Volpin, P. F., (2005), 'Managers, Workers and Corporate Control', *Journal of Finance,* vol. 60, n.2, pp. 841-868.

Prowse, S., (1995), 'Corporate Governance in an International Perspective: A Survey of Corporate Control Mechanisms among Large Firms in the U.S., U.K., Japan and Germany', *Financial Markets, Institutions and Instruments*, vol. 4, n. 1, pp. 1-63.

Shleifer, A., Vishny, R., (1997), 'A Survey of Corporate Governance', *Journal of Finance*, vol. 52, n. 2, pp. 737-783.

Sternberg. E. (1997), 'The Defects of Stakeholder Theory', *Corporate Governance: An International Review*, vol. 5, n. 1, pp. 3-10.

The Economist (2006), 'The Italian exception', 10/14/2006, vol. 381, n. 8499, electronic edition.

The Economist (2008), 'A Special Report on Social on Corporate Social Responsibility', 1/19th-25th/2008, vol. 386, n. 8563, pp. 1-14.

Tirole J., (2001), 'Corporate Governance', *Econometrica*, vol. 69, n. 1, pp. 1-35.

Tirole J., (2006), The Theory of Corporate Finance, Princeton, Princeton University Press.

Towers Perrin, Worldwide Total Remuneration, various years.

12 *The Regulatory and Legal Framework of Corporate Governance*

HILLARY SHAW

Introduction

The increasing scale of operations and global reach of many corporations, coupled with the legal autonomy granted to limited companies at a time when businesses were much smaller and generally manageable within one national jurisdiction, has both heightened the need for fair and efficient regulation of corporations and widened the range of agencies that have a stake in such regulation. However there is no consensus as to the definition or scope of corporate governance. Different regulatory agencies have different agendas, and many institutions currently involved in such regulation do so independently of the other bodies. In particular, organisations' constraints may militate against cooperation in some cases. For example, the legal duty of directors to make best use of shareholder money may conflict with both the self-interest of the company board and the desire to enhance Corporate Social Responsibility (CSR). Employees may be torn between safeguarding their livelihoods and pushing their corporate employer towards more ethical policies. This chapter identifies areas where closer cooperation between the various regulatory agencies could bring about a more sustainable economy and society, which would benefit both the stakeholders in a company and the corporation itself.

The Need for Good Corporate Governance

The efficient, fair and transparent regulation of corporations is increasingly important, not just to lawyers and governments, but to every private individual. The unprecedented financial size and geographical scope of today's largest corporations has created entities whose profits exceed the GDPs of many smaller countries. Wal-Mart, and the larger oil and car-related corporations such as Exxon, Royal Dutch Shell, BP and General Motors, regularly achieve annual profits in the region of US$10 to 40 billion.[1] This exceeds the GDP of nations like Belarus, Bulgaria, Kenya and Uruguay. The total revenues of the

---

1   Figures derived from Fortune 500 – world's largest 100 companies. Profits especially for the oil companies vary widely depending on world oil price.

world's 12 largest corporations in 2007, US$ 2.8 trillion, are comparable to the GDP of Germany and exceed the GDP of China or the UK. Accountants talk of corporate profits as the 'bottom line'; as if that were the financial conclusion. In GAAP[2] terms it may be; in societal terms there are many lines below. Who gets these profits, how are they distributed, how, if at all, are losers from corporate activities compensated? Without a distribution framework, the large companies of the twenty-first century may become not so much generators as concentrators of economic wealth. That could lead to a loss of legitimacy of the corporation, a damaging prospect for all, investors included, even when things are going right for the business.

When things go wrong they may do so on an appalling scale. The Union Carbide explosion at Bhopal is often cited as the world's worst industrial accident; the total death toll came to 15,000, and a further 120,000 continue to live with the effects of gas poisoning. In 1993 hundreds of workers were burnt to death or died from falling when the Kader toy factory, Bangkok, caught fire. There were no sprinklers, the fire exits were locked and the fire spread rapidly as the building collapsed. Several major US and European toy corporations sourced their toys from Kader. Globalised food chains also have the potential to cause casualties on this scale. In 2006 the confectionery giant Cadbury was forced to recall one million chocolate bars due to possible contamination with salmonella. In the event 'only' 30 people reportedly fell ill, with no fatalities; although the vast majority of food poisoning comprises 'low-level' illness for a day or two, with the victim unaware of the exact cause. Cadbury had altered its testing system to allow 'safe' levels of salmonella contamination as far back as 2003.[3]

Even when corporations are not negligent, they are dependent, in an era of globalised supply chains, on stable social, economic and environmental conditions in countries far beyond the governmental reach of the UK or the EU. The BP website's 'good governance' section[4] significantly points out that the UK is dependent on developing countries for long-term energy supplies so 'we have a clear interest in our host countries' development'. A recent example of this was the threat to western European gas supplies in winter 2006/7 caused by an economic dispute between Russia and the Ukraine. A third economic threat that has been magnified by globalisation is the potential disruption that can be caused by one lone protestor against a corporation. It only takes one bomb threat or contamination scare to frighten consumers around the world, and ironically, the better known, more profitable, the company is, the more vulnerable to such threats it is (Hussain, 2007).

However even as the increasing scale of firms has highlighted the need for them to be accountable to a wide range of stakeholders, the law has given owners of these firms considerable protection from legal sanctions against any misdeeds perpetrated by such corporations. The Companies Act 1844 and the Limited Liability Act 1855 gave companies their own legal identity (Cadbury, 2002, p. 4), a principle confirmed by *Salomon vs. A Salomon & Co Ltd* (1897). Introduced to protect investors in a company, this gives them, or rather their directors, considerable power to act in self-interest; legally immune from

---

2   Generally Accepted Accounting Principles.

3   Report from Guardian unlimited, http://www.guardian.co.uk/society/2007/jul/14/health.lifeandhealth, accessed 3 January 2008.

4   Details at http://www.bp.com/sectiongenericarticle.do?categoryId=9015663&contentId=7028911, accessed 13 September 2007.

many of the checks and balances that constrain a real person as against the 'legal person' that is a limited company. This effectively grants a company near-immortality.

Many of the legal sanctions, such as prison, that constrain a flesh and blood person, cannot be applied to a company. Lord Denning, in 1954, attempted to anthropomorphise the corporation, likening the directors to the controlling brain of a human body (Shaw, 2006, p. 187). However the legal view of a corporation today is still not so different from the view expressed by Lord Edward Baron Thurlow (English jurist, 1731–1806); 'Did you ever expect a corporation to have a conscience, when it has no soul to be damned, and no body to be kicked?' The only legal sanctions a corporate 'person' can face are fines, or the 'death penalty', closure. Fines ultimately impact innocent shareholders who are only very indirectly connected with any malfeasances by the board of directors,[5] and as the 2007 Northern Rock debacle showed, public interest may militate against the application of corporate capital punishment. Partly in response to two fatal rail accidents, at Southall in 1997 and at Ladbroke Grove in 1999, the UK enacted the Corporate Manslaughter and Corporate Homicide Act 2007, but this legislation also specifies no more than unlimited fines, along with a publicity order and a remedial order to force the guilty corporation to address the causes of the fatalities. In practice, it may be the publicity order that causes the corporation most concern. The one sanction companies may truly fear is a form of 'starvation'; that is, loss of market share through bad publicity, a sanction often invoked when unethical corporate conduct comes into public view.

Seeking good publicity, rather than simply avoiding the bad, has become a key part of corporate strategy in the twenty-first century. With a public increasingly aware of social and environmental issues this entails an explicit engagement with ethical matters, via CSR, and with issues of good corporate governance. Defining corporate governance, both in terms of *how* it is done and *who* is affected by it or has input into it, is therefore crucial for the survival, financial and social, of the modern global business. Indeed, is good corporate governance even possible, given that corporations represent a fundamental split between ownership of and control of financial assets? This must be one of the few areas where Karl Marx and Adam Smith would agree; that it may not be possible (Monks and Minnow, 2004 p. 195). Adam Smith, the economist so admired by many company directors, was opposed to 'joint-stock companies', now called corporations (Galbraith, 1977, p. 26), for the same reason as Karl Marx; namely because people are less careful and vigilant when operating assets that they don't own, than in overseeing their own money.

The Scope of Corporate Governance

Economists, especially of the neo-liberal persuasion, may define corporate governance narrowly as 'being concerned with the institutions that influence how business corporations allocate resources and returns', or more widely as 'a set of relationships between a company's board, its shareholders, and other stakeholders' (Wojcik, 2006). From this perspective, the purpose of a business is solely to make money for its owners. However the actions of a company, any company, will inevitably affect a much wider range of actors. These include national governments, other companies, the managers and

---

5   As affirmed in *Short and Another vs. Treasury Commissioners*, Court of Appeal, 1947.

employees, the suppliers and customers of that business, and through the externalities[6] they may suffer at the hands of a corporation, the general public also.

A wider definition of corporate governance was offered by Sir Adrian Cadbury. He is quoted in 'Global Corporate Governance Forum', World Bank 2000, as stating, 'Corporate Governance is concerned with holding the balance between economic and social goals and between individual and communal goals. The corporate governance framework is there to encourage the efficient use of resources and equally to require accountability for the stewardship of those resources. The aim is to align as nearly as possible the interests of individuals, corporations, and society.'[7] There is similar disagreement over the scope of CSR, and even of its relevance to business. The Confederation of British Industry stated, in 2001, that, 'CSR is highly subjective and therefore does not allow for a universally applicable definition.' However the Commission for the European Communities, also in 2001, defined CSR as, 'a concept whereby companies integrate social and environmental concerns in the business operations and in their interactions with stakeholders on a voluntary basis' (Jones et al., 2007, p. 583). CSR has also been defined as, (Crowther, 2005a, p. 31) 'The obligation of a firm, *beyond that required by law or economics*, to pursue long term goals that are good for society.'

The variance between the definitions is as instructive as the definitions themselves and serves to highlight the different agendas of the agencies involved. Ernst and Young (2002)[8] notes the influence of investors, peer pressure, stakeholders and an internal 'sense of social responsibility' within the corporation, as agents promoting an increase in CSR as a regulatory factor in corporate governance. The identity and role of investors (shareholders) in a company is often clear, and corporations may well feel pressure, either from competitors (peer pressure) or from within the corporation (internal sense) to adopt a socially responsible form of governance, but who are the 'stakeholders'? The term 'stakeholder' is generally defined as anyone affected by the corporation's activities. In the case of smaller companies or companies in sectors with limited environmental/ social impact, the identity of stakeholders may be clear. A local building company has 'stakeholders' in the immediate area of its building works and road traffic routes, as well as the customers who buy its houses, and the local council who collects the council tax and has to provide municipal services to those houses. A large insurance company has 'stakeholders' in the form of premium payers and loss payment beneficiaries, as well as its employees, re-insurers and the government which receives tax from it. But who are the stakeholders for a company like Tesco, whose supply chains reach around the world to garment makers in Bangladesh, customers in China and beef producers in Argentina? Who are the stakeholders in Shell Plc, whose oil is extracted from Alaska and the Middle East, and when the end result of using its product may be global climate change? Companies like Ben and Jerry's (ice cream) and Stride Right (shoes) defined their stakeholders very widely including entire disadvantaged neighbourhoods and even countries; trying for example to keep their jobs where they were socially needed rather

---

6   'Externality' is an economic term used to describe an economic, social or environmental effect, positive or negative, experienced by a third party C due to an economic transaction between parties A and B in which C has played no part. Example; householder A drives to garden centre B and buys some flowers for her front garden. Passer-by C gains a positive externality from the beauty of the flowers, but suffers a negative externality from the car exhaust fumes emitted by A during the journey to B.

7   Source, www.mhcinternational.com/glossary.htm, accessed 9 November 2007.

8   Available at www.ey.nl/download/publicatie/doemload/c0rporate_social_responsibility.pdf.

than where was most economical for the company. Corporate history suggests that this strategy failed, as both companies were forced to adopt a more 'hard-headed' commercial strategy concerning the sourcing of labour and raw materials (Shaw, 2007, p. 15). A key question to be resolved is therefore, how ethical is it to use shareholder's money for social ends (Crowther, 2005b, p. 136). There is even a Kantian argument that firms should *not* be involved in CSR because this is using shareholders as means to a social end, not as 'ends in their own right'. The contrary argument is that such social ends bring benefits back to the company and its owners.

Nevertheless a broad view of CSR can be profitable, according to recent data from the journal *Marketing* (13 September 2006, pp. 30-31). This publication reports that 80 per cent of FTSE 100 companies now employ CSR directors, and that the UK market for ethical goods was worth £24.7 billion in 2004 and growing at 15 per cent per annum. However building a CSR commitment with customers can be a long-term process, and in today's fast changing and crowded advertising world that may not always appeal to the marketers. When a consumer spending downturn looms, corporations, especially large global corporations heavily reliant on economies of scale, may be tempted to re-focus on price cuts rather than quality and green issues. This was the route Tesco, Britain's largest grocery retailer, appeared to be taking in 2007.[9]

Conflicts Arising from Corporate Governance

Conflicts over the exact scope of CSR and of corporate governance may therefore arise over several dimensions:

- over time, as booms and busts in the economy make CSR more or less profitable;
- over space, as a broader definition of 'stakeholders' conflicts with the need to focus production in least-cost regions;
- pver the agency framework, as different agencies/actors offer competing definitions of the true scope of shareholder-funded CSR; and
- over competing philosophical perspectives as to what is the true function of a company and what constitutes ethical use of its owners' money.

In the absence of clear, transparent, guidelines, such conflicts may be resolved in a makeshift, improvised, manner that is likely to be influenced more by immediate financial pressures than by long-term societal goals. The UK paper manufacturer Elliot Baxter has, creditably for a smaller company, an environmental policy page on its website.[10] This states in part (italics added), 'We have successfully achieved accreditation to FSC and PEFC in May 2006, and will *so far as is reasonably practicable*: comply with all relevant environmental laws and regulations both locally and nationally. Ensure that sub-contractors and suppliers apply equivalent environmental standards.' Although their website goes on to say 'good environmental policy at work is good business,' the wording suggests that the 'business' part may well take priority over the 'environmental' part.

---

9   The Times, 'Tesco sets aside green issues to focus resources on a price war', 13 July 2007, p. 44.

10   Details at http://www.ebbpaper.co.uk/environment.php, accessed 9 November 2007.

There may also be a power and knowledge imbalance between the fragmented body of shareholders and the small but influential group of directors making company decisions (Hoffman et al., 2001, p. 191). The board of directors may decide that the CEO is paid partially in shares or share options, to incentivise them to run the company efficiently. Few shareholders may understand the arcane world of shares options, and it is open to a CEO near retirement to take short-term action to boost the shares price that is not in the long-term interests of the company. For example, they may make redundancies that, short term, lower the price to earnings ratio of the shares and so boost their price. In the longer term, the company loses experience and skills and may do worse. For the CEO it is *après moi le deluge*. In the infamous case of Enron there was outright fraud. The directors hid the true financial position of the company from both investors and employees, persuading the former to invest and the latter to contribute to a doomed pension scheme; Enron subsequently went bankrupt in December 2001 with the loss of 4,000 jobs.

The power of the directors over the shareholders in the USA was confirmed in the case of *Shlensky v. Wrigley*, 1968.[11] Here, a shareholder of the Chicago Cubs holding company sued the Cubs president, Philip Wrigley, because Wrigley had refused to install lights for night games at the baseball pitch. Chicago Cubs were the only Major League ground without lights, and so could not play lucrative night games, which would have commanded high TV fees at peak viewing times (Monks and Minnow 2004, p. 2). Wrigley maintained that baseball was a daytime sport and that night games would lead to a deterioration of the neighbourhood. The court ruled that as there was no fraud or breach of good faith, there could be no legal intervention in the internal affairs of corporations. Cases such as *Roth v. Robertson* (1909) or *Miller v. AT&T Co* (1974) show that even where an illegal act was committed to further the business interests, the court will not sanction it.

Moral conflicts may also arise, especially for those who maintain a wider definition of corporate governance and CSR. By 1998 all legal liabilities arising from the Bhopal tragedy were wound up, and in 2001 the Dow Corporation bought Union Carbide, having checked on the legal situation. Yet many Indians have ongoing severe disabilities arising from Bhopal 1984. Does the Dow Corporation have a moral responsibility towards these victims? If so, what about their families, their dependants, in a land with rudimentary State support for those who cannot work? There are companies still trading today that traded with the Nazis in the 1930s and 40s, although directorships, employees and shareholder ownership have changed, perhaps many times, since then. Does any liability remain to compensate descendants of the (uncompensated) victims of the Nazi regime? Corporations are theoretically immortal, and this is the disadvantage of immortality (Hoffman et al., 2001, p. 229). If employees are made redundant, the effects on them and their families may linger on (Darley et al., 2001, p. 6[12]); entire UK districts remain economically depressed today because of the closure of major industries decades ago.

---

11   Full reference *Shlensky v. Wrigley*, 237 N.E.2d 776 (Ill. App. 1968).

12   This refers to a wide-ranging study on the effects of downsizing in the Russian military in the 1990s. Further described in Chapter 7 of this book.

Who Should be Involved in Corporate Governance?

Such conflicts of corporate governance can probably only be solved with the intervention of a wide range of stakeholders. A number of players are already involved in corporate regulation, and these eight categories of agency are listed below:

1. supranational organisations, for example, EU, UN;
2. national governments, for example, UK;
3. self-regulation by the corporations themselves, to ensure a good image and so more sales;
4. shareholders;
5. employees;
6. suppliers;
7. customers;
8. indirect participants, for example, public/media/Non-Government Organisations (NGOs). This category comprises parties not part of the corporate supply chain and with no formal legal regulatory influence over the corporation. However they may well be affected by externalities[13] caused by corporate activities.

1. SUPRANATIONAL ORGANISATIONS

Since World War Two a number of supranational organisations have emerged across the globe, notably North American Free Trade Agreement (NAFTA), the European Union (EU) and Association of South East Asian Nations (ASEAN). A common aim of these blocs is to build prosperity by providing a large, stable, integrated and prosperous, trading area for corporations to trade within. The EU lacks the population (market size) of India or China, and has a lower per capita GDP than the USA; however the EU's growth potential and current wealth make it an irresistible target for global corporations. The EU is leader amongst supranational organisations in one respect; its keenness for environmental and social regulation. Brussels is now 'emerging as the regulatory capital of the world'.[14] Hoffman et al. (2001, p.223) notes how even by the 1990s Europe was the leader in establishing a compliance and regulatory framework for corporations.

There are two mechanisms whereby the EU is becoming corporate-regulatory standard-bearer to the world. One is the way in which non-EU states such as Japan have adopted 'western'[15] (that is, European) laws; governments worldwide look to European legal systems as a model of an equitable system. The other is that corporations know that if they satisfy stringent EU standards on, for example, product safety or antitrust rules, they have also satisfied standards enabling them to trade in any country or bloc. However the EU may not always assume corporate innocence, but rather the opposite. Under the EU's REACH laws, companies have to prove that many of the chemicals they may use are harmless, reversing the burden of proof from innocent until proved guilty.[16] Other large

---

13   The idea of CSR as a mechanism to reduce negative externalities and enhance positive ones was posited by Mallenbaker (http://www.mallenbaker.net/csr/CSRfiles/definition.html) who defined CSR as 'how companies manage the business process to produce an overall positive impact on society'.

14   *Financial Times*, 'Standard Bearer', 10 July 2007, p. 13.

15   *Financial Times*, ibid.

16   *The Economist*, 'Brussels rules OK', 22 September 2007, p. 52.

trade blocs and their economic sectors, such as the US and its biotechnology firms, may be concerned that EU standards against GM foods may spread outside Europe, but this has not stopped a government delegation from California visiting Brussels to link with the EU carbon emissions trading scheme.

However the EU is not totally unblemished concerning the ethical regulation of companies. The UN, as well as some of the EU's own MEPs, and some EU member states, have criticised Brussels for signing a treaty with Morocco allowing EU boats to fish the waters off Western Sahara.[17] Western Sahara was a former Spanish colony, invaded by Morocco in 1975; its legal independence is recognised by 70 states worldwide. The EU is here behaving rather like many corporations, embracing those CSR initiatives which suit them but ignoring the initiatives which might seriously impact on their finances. Overall the EU seems keen to adopt CSR or environmental measures which improve standards within the EU territory, but is less keen to restrict corporate activities having a negative social or economic impact on peoples and territories beyond its boundaries.

2. NATIONAL GOVERNMENTS

National governments frequently find their policy towards promoting ethical behaviour by corporations compromised by the economic power of large multinationals, who can threaten to relocate investment and jobs. However in 2006 the UK government enacted the Companies Act, hailed as the most significant redrafting of company law in 20 years. The Act will require UK publicly listed companies to 'report on their environmental and social impacts, as well as obliging all company directors to take stock of all their business activities' effects on employees, communities and the environment'.[18] However, the Corporate Responsibility Coalition (CORE) maintains that the 2006 Act rather lets companies off the hook, requiring them only to demonstrate that they have 'considered' CSR issues, regardless of the final corporate plan.[19] With increasing concern amongst the electorate in many developed countries about global environmental threats, as well as growing awareness of less-developed-world social issues, western governments may feel compelled to enact socio-environmental legislation that would not necessarily be welcomed by corporations. Across the Atlantic, more than half of US states have passed 'stakeholder laws', permitting or even requiring directors to consider the interests of stakeholders other than shareholders; including employees, customers, suppliers and the wider community (Monks & Minnow, 2004, p. 50).

However government regulation needs to be carefully framed or it may have the opposite effect to that intended. Two examples from the UK food industry illustrate this. There is concern in the UK, as in other countries, that processed foods are too high in salt, fat and sugar (Shaw, 2006, p. 233). The Food Standards Agency had set a standard 100g 'portion' of various foods and then evaluated these for high levels of salt and so on.[20] This had the perverse result of marking out foods such as cheese and marmite (which are eaten in relatively small daily amounts but are healthy in terms of calcium, vitamins) as unhealthy; yet Diet Coke passed this 100g test as wholesome. A similar case of regulations

---

17   Details from www.fishelsewhere.org, accessed 9 November 2007.

18   Details from www.waronwant,org, media centre, archive entry 1 October 2007, accessed 8 November.

19   The Times Focus Report, Corporate Social Responsibility, 24 July 2007, p. 4.

20   The Grocer, 'Weigh it up', 3 February 2007, accessed 15 November 2007 at www.thegrocer.co.uk.

backfiring occurred with rules intended to minimise the number of 'junk food' television advertisements seen by British children. Junk food adverts in programmes with a high proportion of child viewers were restricted; yet this took no account of the total number of children exposed to these advertisements. For example *The Simpsons* had 163,000 child viewers, compared to 442,300 children watching *The X Factor*. Yet because the latter programme had a lower percentage of young viewers, it escaped junk food advertising regulations.[21] Unethical corporations concerned only at maximising sales and profits are liable to exploit the slightest chink in seemingly watertight rules.

Unfortunately the governmental regulatory environment is often very different in the case of less developed countries, with civil unrest, weak governmental territorial and economic control, a hazardous environment for international observers, and yet a large resource base attracting strong multinationals. Such is the Congo, where the transitional government which took power after a shaky peace deal in 2003 signed several secret deals with mining companies. Joseph Kabila's Congolese government appeared to be heeding calls for more transparency of these mining contracts following 2003[22] but numerous corporate excuses seem to have thwarted this. China, a government rather less committed to CSR-compatible corporate governance, has moved into the Congo, and mining has recommenced with a vengeance following the recent rise in world commodity prices. Record world highs for copper have also encouraged mining development in Peru, where a coalition of environmentalists, Catholic priests, NGOs, farmers and local mayors, have protested against river pollution and a lack of development that benefits local people. The Peruvian President has vilified these protesters as 'Communists', an interesting example of what Bourdieu (1991) calls the power of naming. Mining companies are attempting to clean up their developed-world image, and pacify local protestors, by giving money for local development, but 'local governments often make a bad job of spending this money'.[23]

The examples above show that government regulation, 'command and control' by 'experts', may have little or no impact on the problem being addressed; it may even exacerbate the situation. A further complication is that large corporations can capture a feedback channel to the government and influence the laws and regulations supposedly being passed to moderate corporate behaviour. The UK supermarkets have had a major role in modifying UK law, including getting Sunday trading legalised and in securing the abolition of Resale Price Maintenance, a move which enabled major undercutting of independent small retailers by large supermarkets. Obesity is a major problem in the UK, yet the UK government stands accused by the Children's Food Campaign of allowing its School Food Trust, a government body with a remit to secure healthier food in UK schools, to be influenced by companies such as Coca Cola and Dairy UK.[24] These food producers have secured access to schools for their sweetened products on the grounds that calcium and fruit intake will be boosted; healthy-food campaigners are less sure of the benefits.

In such situations, corporate self-regulation, or regulation by shareholders or other NGO agencies, may be the only way to curb corporate excesses. Hughes et al. (2007) assert

---

21   *The Guardian*, 'New rules fail to stop children seeing adverts for unhealthy food on TV', 12 November 2007, p. 14.

22   *The Economist*, 'Who benefits from the minerals', 22 September 2007, p. 70.

23   *The Economist*, ibid.

24   *The Guardian*, 'U-turn over healthier drinks in school canteens', 12 September 2007, p. 3.

that where corporate supply chains cross national borders, and so are beyond the control of any one government, corporations now take prime responsibility for labour standards at sites of production.

3. SELF-REGULATION BY THE CORPORATIONS

As noted earlier, a good brand image, which may well include excellent CSR credentials, is an important part of a successful corporation. Nevertheless, the fierce price competition generated by globalisation may, especially in leaner economic times, erode both consumer and corporate concerns about ethical production and trade. The role of branding in maintaining good corporate governance and a socially responsible code of conduct was recently illustrated by the supply-chain deficiencies in China which led to the US company Mattel having to recall toys it had sourced from Chinese subcontractors.[25] *The Economist*, contrasting the relationship of Japanese subcontractors (for example, Matsushita) to retail electronics companies such as Panasonic in the 1950s, noted how upstream companies in the supply chain then maintained a good 'brand image' themselves so as to ensure continued custom from the retailers. By contrast, Chinese subcontractors are 'inscrutable and transient, with no brand or reputation to speak of'.[26] This facilitates the Chinese manufacturers in dealing with several competing Western retailers simultaneously. It also suits the retailers themselves; *The Economist* (ibid) notes that the distinction in the consumer's mind between Hewlett Packard, Dell and Apple would collapse if they knew that a firm called Hon Hai produced for all of them. Similarly a company called Yue Hen produces shoes for Adidas, Nike and Puma. Yet as events of 2007 showed, it also means few safeguards against unsafe products being passed down the supply chain to the consumer. As the Chinese economy develops, and moves to more value-added goods, *The Economist* speculates whether pressure will emerge for Chinese suppliers to raise their profile, and become more socially responsible, to distinguish themselves from other suppliers still producing unsafe goods.

The three biggest grocery supermarkets in the UK, Tesco, Asda and Sainsbury, have all deemed it necessary to take on 'Directors of Corporate Social Responsibility', as CSR has emerged as a competitive edge in this sector. Since around 2000, the position of CSR director has risen from a mere corporate backwater into a high-profile position reassuring the shopping public that a particular company is doing all it can to help the environment, from using less plastic bags to promoting renewable energy and even helping fight child obesity.[27] The supermarket chain Asda announced in 2006 that it was to voluntarily raise the minimum age for purchasing cigarettes from 16 to 18.[28] However some corporate policies dressed up as CSR may in fact be commercial policies to reduce costs (Shaw, 2007, pp.16-17). Tesco CSR emphasises low price,[29] value for money, as CSR; but is this really CSR or just astute competition policy? Marks and Spencer has also 'greened' its stores, by using, for example, only free-range eggs and Fairtrade cotton in its product range. However

---

25   In 2007 the United States toy retailer Mattel was forced to recall over 10 million Chinese-made toys because they contained lead-based paint, also small components that children might swallow.

26   *The Economist*, 'Face value | China's toxic toymaker', 18 August 2007, p. 57.

27   *The Guardian*, 'Asda, Sainsbury's and Tesco looking for green crusaders', 20 August 2007, p. 21.

28   *Daily Mail*, 'We'll raise the age for cigarette buying from 16 to 18 says Asda', 20 July 2006, p. 28. The legal minimum age for buying cigarettes in the UK is currently 16.

29   On Tesco Ireland CSR site, http://www.tesco.ie/csr/index.html, accessed 9 November 2007.

there are extra costs here and these are being passed on to environmentally conscious consumers. Again, a policy presented under a green CSR light may in fact be a judicious commercial move upmarket in order to capture a higher-income consumer segment. Corporate self-directed CSR has an important place in the realm of corporate governance, but alone it is all too easily twisted into SCR (Strategic Commercial Reasoning).

4. SHAREHOLDERS

According to USA Supreme Court Judge Louis Brandeis, there is no such thing as 'innocent ownership' (Monks and Minnow, 2004, p.127). Ownership of anything brings responsibilities, and shares are no exception. In fact the responsibility of shareholders is a double one; investment in a corporation, however small, implies tacit acceptance of its acts, and the same shares give access to a key avenue of influence over that company, at least at its AGM. 'Shareholder activism', where members of the public buy just a share or two for a few pennies, simply to gain access to the AGM and present their views or put forward a resolution, is becoming more common. At the 2003 AGM of Glaxo Smith Kline, over half the shareholders voted against a remuneration scheme that would have rewarded the Chief Executive, Jean-Pierre Garnier, with millions of dollars should he ever be dismissed; shareholder concerns were that this would leave the company with insufficient monies to fulfil its pension obligations.[30] Shell is no stranger to shareholder activism, having faced protests over climate change, the 1990s disposal of the Brent Spar oil platform in the North Sea, and civil rights in Nigeria focussed on the execution of the poet and activist Ken Saro-Wiwa in 1995. The website www.karmabanque.com even informs its visitors, 'You don't need money. *Hedge funds* will attack a company's stock price for you with short-sales if you bait them correctly with boycotts' (italics added). This represents an interesting subversion of a financial-markets instrument that was intended to facilitate greater corporate profits. It is possible that the system of shareholder ownership of firms, so disliked by Karl Marx and Adam Smith, may actually be a portal towards greater public accountability of these enterprises.

5. EMPLOYEES

Employees are often in rather a weak position to force changes to corporate governance, unless they also become shareholders. However a company with a poor CSR image may face problems in attracting new graduates. Crucial in many areas from marketing to design and production, graduate company staff may be in the best position to force changes before they actually join the organisation, simply by the possibility of their boycotting it. As with shareholders, graduates tend to be well connected in cyberspace and are often keenly aware of global social issues, which improves their (pre-employment) bargaining position with the corporation. By slight temporal extension backwards, one might include here student 'anti-sweatshop' activism (Silvey, Featherstone, Cravey, Russell, 2004). As noted later in this chapter, employees can gain considerably more bargaining strength by allying with Trade Unions and then by creating further links with NGOs.

---

30   Guardian II, 'Is it OK to own shares', 16 May 2006, p. 26.

6. SUPPLIERS

Suppliers may also take action against perceived unethical conduct by their corporate customers. Fashion designer Katherine Hamnett cut supplies of her 'Choose Love' organic clothes range to Tesco in 2007[31] because she believed the supermarket lacked true commitment to the environment. This commercially bold move (Tesco had a market share, 2007, of the UK clothing market of approximately 10 per cent) was prompted by fears that Tesco might get free, undeserved, green credentials from stocking her range. Generally, the retailer industry is far more concentrated than the supplier industry, so supplier power over retailers is limited; only when the supplier has a strong ethical dimension to their brand, which appeals direct to the public 'over the retailer's head', can this type of suasion work.

7. CUSTOMERS

Customers of large corporations may also desire a more ethical standpoint from their retailer, even if this means the customers paying higher prices at the till. An ICM poll commissioned to mark the launch of AsdaWatch found that 83 per cent of shoppers wanted tougher rules on ethical trading for supermarkets, with 75 per cent of those polled believing that supermarkets should pay their staff, and suppliers in less-developed countries, a fair wage. It is ironic that advances in information technology, which have greatly facilitated the globalisation of many corporations, have also given their customers and other members of the public a key tool to force moderations of corporate governance and policy, for example the Internet (Jones et al., 2006). The Internet has the potential to become an important channel of communication utilised by corporations to promote their CSR credentials on their websites, and equally by activists to achieve social gains in corporate policy.

8. INDIRECT PARTICIPANT ACTION

Many thousands of NGOs are monitoring unethical conduct by corporations, exposing in detail the sometimes perverse economics of globalised supply chains. To give one example, the 2007 Report, 'Lets Clean Up Fashion',[32] noted how garment workers in Bangladesh, supplying UK stores, were paid as little as 13 pence an hour. This wage is so low that Dhaka has to aid its workers with food parcels; effectively the Bangladeshi Government is subsidising both western multinational corporations and UK consumers. The Multinational Monitor publishes a 'league table' of the world's ten worst corporations, which may induce these corporations to improve their conduct. Chiquita, a large banana producer and importer into Europe, was named and shamed in 1995. Since then it has improved and developed a comprehensive CSR policy (Prieto-Carron, 2006, p. 97). However the resultant improvements in conditions for banana workers may be at risk because banana retailing is so competitive. Bananas are a 'Known Value Item', meaning

---

31   Details from http://www.forbes.com/facesscan/2007/10/02/hamnett-tesco-organic-face-cx_ll_1001autofacescan02.html, Forbes website, accessed 9 November 2007.

32   More details at http://www.labourbehindthelabel.org/images/pdf/letscleanupfashionsummary.pdf, accessed 15 November 2007.

supermarkets sell them cheaply to give the illusion that the entire store offers competitive pricing. In 2003 Wal-Mart signed a contract with Del Monte reducing the retail price of bananas from £1.08 per kilo to 85 pence per kilo. This reduction was achieved by shifting sourcing from the Windward Islands to Ecuador, where labour conditions are poorer, forcing other supermarkets to follow suit (Prieto-Carron, 2006, pp. 100-101). As with other corporations noted earlier, a downturn in the world economy, an intensification of price competition, and many recent gains in corporate governance and CSR begin to look rather fragile.

The durability and effectiveness of gains in corporate governance and CSR may be bolstered where different agencies work together. The globalisation of corporations may have increased their remoteness from those affected by their actions. It has however exposed these corporations to scrutiny by a wider range of agencies who can act together to monitor corporate ethical standards. Hoffman et al. (2001, p. 207) lists key groups who can cooperate in ensuring corporate accountability and democracy, such as employees, NGOs, governments and shareholders. The examples given below illustrate how both NGOs and corporations have cooperated with others, but also exposes 'deserts of cooperation' where there may be potential for further advances in CSR policies.

Inter-agency Cooperation

CORPORATIONS AND OTHERS

Companies are starting to get together with their suppliers to share ethical information within their industry sector. The Daily Telegraph reported in 2006 on an initiative by the global oil and gas companies, BP Shell, Statoil and Norsk Hydro, to pilot a database called Achilles.[33] Likewise, clothing retailers such as Nike and Gap have set up the Suppliers Ethical Data Exchange to list and regulate the ethical practices of clothes manufacturers in the global South. Employees, although weak against corporations on their own, can achieve significant gains when organised into unions, particularly with help from outside NGOs. In cooperation with War on Want and the Ethical Trading Initiative,[34] companies like Tesco are working with local trade unions in production sites such as Bangladeshi clothing factories to ensure minimum wage and working conditions are maintained.[35] Customer opinion is of course extremely important to corporations; in the food industry, rising obesity levels have sparked health consumer concerns. High Fructose Corn Syrup (HFCS), whilst useful both for preserving and for sweetening foods, has been labelled as 'The Newest Health Villain'.[36] Eurofood reports that 'a handful of smaller companies' were leading the way in eliminating HFCS from their food stuffs. However by 2006 this combination of customer wants and smaller companies had created enough pressure to force giant corporations like Kraft Foods, Danone and Del Monte to similarly remove HFCS from their products This is one example of what Korten (2000) terms 'consumer democracy'. It is the power to 'vote' for certain corporations, in a sort

---

33   *Daily Telegraph Jobs*, 'Global suppliers feel ethical pressure', 20 July2006, p. 1.

34   More details at www.ethicaltrade.org, accessed 15 November 2007.

35   *The Guardian*, 'Top fashion brands accused over failure to ensure living wage', 14 September 2007, p. 9.

36   Eurofood, 'Food giants ditch sweetener amid health concerns', 19 September 2007 p. 11.

of ongoing referendum where the cash register represents the ballot box. Given that consumer democracy is continuous, it usually presents a wide choice of 'candidates' and is closely geared to 'voter' desires; this form of 'democracy' is in many ways superior to conventional political democracy.

Corporations may also attempt to link with NGOs, especially those with an environmental flavour, to improve their green or CSR credentials. The journal *Marketing* reported that Coca Cola, concerned about accusations that its activities were leading to water shortages in India, was to link with the World Wildlife Fund (WWF). The WWF will advise Coca Cola on conservation and replenishment of freshwater resources, and also on sustainable production of sugarcane. There are moral perils for both parties here. Coca Cola may be accused of cosmetic spin; the US$20 million being spent on environmental initiatives is of the order of 1 per cent of corporate profits. Meanwhile the WWF might be tainting its reputation by allying with a global corporation with environmental accusations against it.

Corporations, therefore, have linked with suppliers, employees (unions), customers and NGOs to achieve significant social gains in corporate governance. NGOs have also linked with a number of other agencies in this field.

NON-GOVERNMENT ORGANISATIONS AND OTHERS

Significant pressure on corporations can be achieved when trade unions ally with NGOs. Within the UK, the Ethical Trading Initiative[37] (ETI) was set up in 1998 to improve conditions for clothing manufacturing workers. Unannounced visits are made to production sites to check on conditions. The ETI encourages companies to join its alliance of NGOs and trade unions; corporate members have to sign up to an ethical code of behaviour. This code can then become an important part of the corporate brand; Marks and Spencer, Next, Debenhams and Asda/Wal-Mart are members of the ETI (Hughes et al., 2007). Similar organisations to the ETI exist in other countries; for example, the Fair Labor Association and the Worldwide Responsible Apparel Production, both based in the USA. However corporate membership of the ETI sometimes takes second place to commercial concerns. The UK supermarket chain Somerfield has been suffering commercial problems including loss of market share since it took over another chain, Kwik-Save, in 1998.[38] In 2006, a year before the Kwik Save fascia finally ceased trading, Somerfield announced[39] it was to pull out of the ETI, along with other cost-saving measures including redundancies. Somerfield reaffirmed its commitment to CSR but said it would monitor this in-house in future. Likewise, *Marketing Week* reported[40] on cuts in commitment to CSR by the bank Co-operative Financial Services in 2007, as the world financial climate worsened.

NGOs can also exert pressure on national governments. In 2006 a coalition of religious organisations, human rights and development organisations lobbied the UK Church Commissioners, a group including the British Prime Minister and the Royal Family, to divest from shareholdings in Caterpillar. Caterpillar stands accused of helping Israel to build the Separation Wall, cutting off Arabs from their farms and destroying their

---

37   More details at www.ethicaltrade.org, accessed 15 November 2007.

38   More details at www.fooddeserts.org.

39   Eurofood, 'Job cuts loom at Somerfield depot', 18 May 2006, p. 16.

40   Marketing Week, 'The fall of the ethical bank', 26 July 2007, pp. 20/21.

homes.[41] NGOs may also become involved in shareholder activism. The UK supermarket chain Tesco faced an 'unprecedented revolt by shareholders' at its 2007 AGM.[42] A coalition of shareholders and poverty-related NGOs, led by the company secretary for the charity War on Want, Ben Birnberg, condemned the decision to pay the company's chief executive, Sir Terry Leahy, more than £11 million, whilst Tesco was selling garments made by workers in Bangladesh earning 5 pence an hour. Amongst the shareholders of Tesco participating in this revolt was the Joseph Rowntree Charitable Trust, owning one million Tesco shares. Furthermore, NGOs can facilitate improvements in relations between corporations and their suppliers. An example of this is the ongoing scrutiny by the UK's Competition Commission into the power imbalance between British supermarkets and their suppliers.

Legislative and Democratic Influences on Corporate Governance

The legislative influence of governments and of supranational legislative bodies, such as the EU, upon corporations is entwined with the democratic process; legislation representing in theory the actions of government in response to the electorate's wishes. A complicating factor is that corporations may also have considerable influence as to what legislation is enacted. At a European level, industrial pressure groups have influenced, *inter alia*, the emergence of a common currency and the development of EU transport links. At a national level, the major supermarkets have persuaded UK governments to legalise Sunday trading and remove Resale Price Maintenance. Of course, elections are seldom fought mainly on ethical corporate issues. However occasionally a major media issue coincides with a government initiative and forces it through to a conclusion. Public opinion both forms and is formed by the media publicity and this in turn may influence government action.

A recent example of these factors working together to produce corporate legislation occurred in 2004, when trade unions were becoming increasingly concerned about the use of low-paid gangmaster labour, especially in the UK food and agriculture sector. This issue was taken up by Labour MP Jim Sheridan, on behalf of the TGWU. By January 2004 Sheridan's proposed Gangmasters (Licensing) Bill had reached the second reading stage in Parliament, where many Private Members Bills fail due to lack of government support. However on 5 February 2004, 21 Chinese cockle-pickers working under a gangmaster drowned in Morecambe Bay. The resultant media spotlight on the entire gangmaster system ensured that the Gangmaster (Licensing) Bill did receive Royal Assent, on 8 July 2004 (Pollard, 2006, p. 125).

Other areas where public concern coupled with the media spotlight is driving regulation of corporate governance include food and health, energy conservation, and perhaps less prominently, excessive pay awards for directors along with poor pay and conditions in the less developed world. Economists like Amartya Sen have noted how a free press can be a crucial factor in linking democracy with government action, and in curbing potential excesses by either government or corporations (Stiglitz, 2003, p. 115). There are therefore numerous checks and balances in place on corporate governance,

---

41   Details from www.waronwant.org, media centre, archive entry 11 April 2006, accessed 8 November 2007.

42   Eurofood, 'Shareholder revolt at Tesco', 11 July 2007, p. 21.

conducted by a wide range of agencies from national governments down to local NGOs, from corporations and their suppliers down to the customers and employees. Nonetheless, there are areas where the regulation of corporate governance could be improved; 'deserts' where no regulation takes place even though the relevant agencies are in a prime position to create and monitor such regulation.

Corporate Governance: The Regulatory 'Deserts'

Based on the eight categories of agency proposed earlier, from supranational organisations to the public and NGOs, it is possible to draw a 'map' showing where the regulation and scrutiny of corporate governance is now taking place, and where it is not. This is shown in Figure 12.1 opposite.

All 36 possible areas of regulation are shown in Figure 12.1. The solid black areas represent agencies acting alone; examples of all eight are given in the text. The top left of the diagram shows 'regulation' as a joint effort between national governments, supranational organisations and the corporations affected by such regulation. This may be regarded as a joint venture because of the input corporations have into such legislation. Political democracy is a joint effort between citizens and governments, including the EU; Korten's consumer democracy represents feedback between corporations and their customers. As represented by the grey column under 'corporations', many companies also liaise with employees, suppliers, customers and NGOs concerning improvements in CSR and corporate governance. Outsiders to the economic process, the public/NGOs/ media, those affected by corporate externalities, also act together with many parties, from the corporations themselves to government, suppliers and customers, to achieve gains in corporate governance.

There are two areas in Figure 12.1 where little or no cooperation between agencies occurs. One area, labelled 'L', represents governmental (and supranational-governmental) collaboration with those closest to the corporations; those most affected by them, namely shareholders, employees, suppliers and customers. Although most developed economies operate under a form of neo-liberalism where regulation of the market is largely left to economic forces, the government has superior information regarding the entire economy that corporations cannot have. Therefore gains in corporate governance should be possible by combining the unique insider information possessed by shareholders, employees and so on, with the unique insight possessed by government. To avoid excessive input of government effort, that is, taxpayers' money, the government could set up a channel, a department whereby those closest to corporations could take the initiative to approach and make representations about corporate governance matters. This would be a type of policing of the corporations, and could operate on a national scale similar to the localised neighbourhood drop-in centres operated by many police forces, where citizens can call in anonymously to report matters of concern. Unfortunately the current neo-liberal ethos directing relations between corporations and government militates against such an arrangement, therefore this regulatory 'gap' may be termed a neo-liberal desert, in the same way that Wacquant spoke of 'organisational deserts'.

Wacquant (1996, p. 257) wrote of 'organisational deserts' as areas abandoned by the apparatus of local urban governance and economy, in sectors from government and education to retailing and jobs. Wacquant was using as an example the poor Black areas

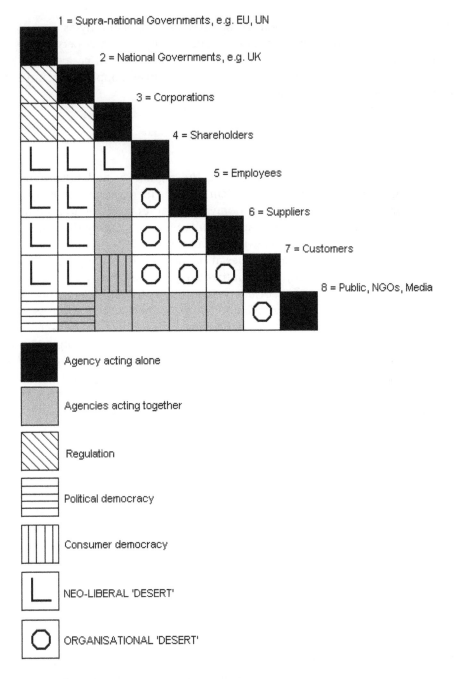

Figure 12.1 Areas of regulation of Corporate Governance

of Chicago, but by extension the idea of an 'organisational desert' may apply to any area or group that is isolated and does not have access to the levers of power that control its livelihood. As in the 'neo-liberal desert', there is little liaison between the workforce, suppliers and the customers of a corporation, or between customers of a corporation and the media or NGOs monitoring that corporation. Yet, just as the government has superior economic information about companies and the economy as a whole, so the workers, suppliers and users of corporate products enjoy a unique perspective on that corporation's activities not shared by corporate activists. Lack of cooperation between parties in the 'organisational desert' likely represents a missed opportunity in the field of corporate governance and regulation.

Conclusion

The array of agencies involved in managing the regulatory and legal framework of corporate governance has expanded in tandem with the increasing complexity and range of corporate activities in a globalised economy. Companies have had to become adept at managing the very small and the very large simultaneously; running the global economy of the firm along with directing the everyday affairs of a local branch. Consumers are increasingly seduced by the local manifestation of the global corporation; the Tesco Express, the town bank branch, the familiar-place branded foodstuff (Shaw, 2008, p. 19). To maintain the pressure for socially responsible corporate governance, the range of agencies involved must also manage and integrate their activities across a range of spatial scales, from the local to the global. The need for cooperation between grassroots neighbourhood groups, global NGOs and supranational governmental organisations such as the EU and the United Nations is important to maintain a sustainable corporate agenda. If there is any possibility of curbing the excesses of the monolithic multinationals, it can only succeed by joint endeavour at all levels (Shaw, 2004, p. 69). Achieving this would benefit not only society but the corporations themselves, and result in a more stable and affluent social order.

References

Bourdieu P (1991), *Language and Symbolic Power*, 1991, Polity, Cambridge.

Cadbury A (2002), *Corporate Governance and Chairmanship*, Oxford University Press, UK.

Crowther D, Jatana R (2005a), International Dimensions of Corporate Social Responsibility Vol. I, ICFAI University Press, India.

Crowther D, Jatana R (2005b), International Dimensions of Corporate Social Responsibility Vol. II, ICFAI University Press, India.

Darley J, Messick D, Tyler T (2001), *Social influences on Ethical Behaviour in Organisations*, Lawrence Erlbaum, New Jersey.

Galbraith J K (1977), *The Age of Uncertainty*, BBC, London.

Hoffman W, Frederick R, Schwartz M (2001), *Business Ethics*, McGraw Hill, New York.

Hughes A, Buttle M, Wrigley N (2007), *Organisational geographies of corporate responsibility: a UK-US comparison of retailers' ethical trading initiatives*, Journal of Economic Geography, Vol. 7, No. 4, pp. 491-513.

Hussain H (2007), *They're out to get you – so be ready*, The Grocer, 21 July 2007, p. 27.

Jones P, Comfort D, Hillier D (2006), *Anti-corporate retailer campaigns on the internet*, International Journal of Retail Distribution and Management, Vol. 34, No. 12, pp. 882-891.

Jones P, Comfort D, Hillier D (2007), *Marketing and corporate social responsibility within food stores*, British Food Journal, Vol. 109, No. 8, pp. 582-593.

Korten D (2000), *The Post-Corporate World: Life after Capitalism*, Kumarian Press, Connecticut, USA.

Monks M, Minnow N (2004), *Corporate Governance* 3rd edn, Blackwell Publishing, Oxford.

Pollard D (2006), The Gangmaster System in the UK: Perspective of a Trade Unionist, in *Ethical Sourcing in the Global Food System*, ed by S Barrientos and C Dolan, Earthscan, London, 2006.

Prieto-Carron M, (2006), Central American Banana Production: Women Workers and Chiquita's Ethical Sourcing from Plantations, in *Ethical Sourcing in the Global Food System*, ed by S Barrientos and C Dolan, Earthscan, London, 2006.

Shaw H J (2006), *Food desertification: towards the development of a new classification*, Geografiska Annaler Vol. 88 B, No. 2, pp. 231-248.

Shaw H J (2007), *The Role of CSR in Re-empowering Local Communities*, Social Responsibility Journal, Vol. 3, No. 2, 2007, pp. 11-20.

Shaw H J (2008), *Resisting the Hallucination of the Hypermarket*, International Journal of Baudrillard Studies, Vo. 5, No. 1, pp. 1-30.

Shaw J J A (2004), Giants and freaks: understanding the challenges of social responsibility in a context of oppression, in *Stakeholders and Social Responsibility*; eds D. Crowther and K.Tunca Caliyurt, Ashgate, pp. 57-74.

Shaw J J A (2006), *The European Constitution and CSR; Consensus or Conflict*, Social Responsibility Journal, Vol. 2, No. 2, September 2006, pp. 186-193.

Silvey R, Featherstone L, Cravey A J, Russell J (2004); papers in 'Antipode', Vol. 36, No. 2.

Stiglitz J (2003), On Liberty, the Right to Know, and Public Discourse: The Role of Transparency in Public Life, pp. 115-156 in *Globalizing Rights*, ed. Matthew J Gibney, Oxford University Press, UK.

Wacquant L J D (1996), Red Belt, Black Belt: Racial Division, Class Inequality and the State in the French Urban periphery and the American Ghetto, pp. 234-274 in *Urban Poverty and the Underclass*, ed. Enzio Mingione, Blackwell, Oxford.

Wojcik (2006), *Convergence in corporate governance: evidence from Europe and the challenge for economic geography*, Journal of Economic Geography, Vol. 6, No. 5, pp. 639-660.

13 *The Agency Problem and Corporate Governance*

GÜLER ARAS AND DAVID CROWTHER

Introduction

A perennial problem with the management of a business is the relationship between the managers of a business and its owners and investors, which is, of course, known as the agency problem. It is generally accepted that the information asymmetry which inevitably exists in this situation cannot readily be overcome and so attention has been devoted to the minimisation of any risk associated with the asymmetric information. In the past this has been approached by attempting to ensure the alignment of objectives through manipulations of the rewards structures, but many would argue that this has merely resulted in increasing information asymmetry and the passing of control – and an element of ownership – to the managerial hierarchy. However viewed, the desired results have not been achieved. More recent attempts therefore have been concerned with procedural changes through the development of strong systems of corporate governance. Such systems of governance have become enshrined in codes with universal application but cannot be considered to be fully effective and are under continual development and modification. In this chapter, therefore, we consider the relationship between governance procedures and the agency problem.

In order for the economy – either national or international – to function satisfactorily, 'trust' is important. Informal unwritten guarantees are preconditions for all trade and production (Akerlof, 1970). On the other hand, international rules and principles may be necessary to protect investors and stakeholder from the uncertainty in the market. Loosely speaking these arrangements – either formal or informal – can be described as governance.

Corporate governance and Agency Theory are both characterised by conflicts of interests. Businesses attempt to realise profits[1] as a primary goal on one hand while they face issues of social responsibility and stakeholder rights on the other. Corporate governance is about fair conduct and management by a business and its representatives in all of its relations. In business behaviour, corporate governance principles have been set out with a view to minimising uncertainty and developing an atmosphere of confidence in a web of

---

[1] We use the term to realise profits deliberately. n doing so we imply that a business does not necessarily seek to maximise profits – at least not short-term profits – but does at least seek to make a return which is adequate for the risk undertaken.

emerging complex relations. With the impact of these developments, it is very important for financial markets operating within these countries and markets to accommodate and implement good governance. The reason for this is the quality of transactions and instruments in the financial markets. This area contains riskier transactions and complex instruments. The uncertainty created by this situation makes it difficult for organisations to create confidence in the segments concerned. Legal provisions and control mechanisms and sanctions introduced by them alone are not sufficient to ensure sound operation of the system and create confidence. Therefore, the introduction of corporate governance rules and principles is aimed at increasing compliance with legal provisions and also in creating an atmosphere of confidence by securing the interests of all parties. To achieve its goals, a firm or organisation should have (as a whole) firm governance rules. Corporate governance is not a sacrifice, but a part of the behavioural processes of management and its organisation. Corporate governance should not be altered depending on circumstances and countries, but harmonised in accordance with them.

Corporate governance principles help to resolve any conflict of interest problems by considering a balance between competing and often incompatible corporate goals. They also help businesses to meet global challenges while improving organisational competitiveness and safeguarding stakeholders' interests. Adhering to corporate governance principles ensures long-run viability, more efficient resource allocation and elimination of the uncertainties facing companies. In many ways, corporate governance principles are an attempt to alleviate the agency problem inherent in all organisations except, perhaps, the very smallest.

Our argument is based upon the importance of the Organisational Failure Framework which was developed. Firstly, however, it is necessary to briefly review the origins of the existence of the firm in terms of Classical Liberalism.

CLASSICAL LIBERAL THEORY

Classical Liberal Theory started to be developed in the seventeenth century by such writers as John Locke as a means of explaining how society operated, and should operate, in an era in which the Divine Right of Kings to rule and to run society for their own benefit had been challenged and was generally considered to be inappropriate for the society which then existed. Classical Liberalism is founded upon the two principles of reason and rationality: reason in that everything had a logic which could be understood and agreed with by all, and rationality in that every decision made was made by a person in the light of what their evaluation had shown them to be for their greatest benefit. Classical Liberalism therefore is centred upon the individual, who is assumed to be rational and would make rational decision, and is based upon the need to give freedom to every individual to pursue their own ends. It is therefore a philosophy of the pursuance of self-interest. Society, insofar as it existed and was considered to be needed, was therefore merely an aggregation of these individual self-interests. This aggregation was considered to be a sufficient explanation for the need for society. Indeed, Locke argued that the whole purpose of society was to protect the rights of each individual and to safeguard these private rights.

There is however a problem with this allowing of every individual the complete freedom to follow their own ends and to maximise their own welfare. This problem is that in some circumstances this welfare can only be created at the expense of other individuals. It is through this conflict between the rights and freedoms of individuals that problems occur in society. It is for this reason therefore that de Tocqueville argued that there was a necessary function for government within society. He argued that the function of government, therefore, was the regulation of individual transactions so as to safeguard the rights of all individuals as far as possible.

Although this philosophy of individual freedom was developed as the philosophy of Liberalism it can be seen that this philosophy has been adopted by the Conservative governments throughout the world, as led by the UK government in the 1980s. This philosophy has led increasingly to the reduction of State involvement in society and the giving of freedom to individuals to pursue their own ends, with regulation providing a mediating mechanism where deemed necessary. It will be apparent, however, that there is a further problem with Liberalism and this is that the mediation of rights between different individuals only works satisfactorily when the power of individuals is roughly equal. Plainly this situation never arises between all individuals and this is the cause of one of the problems with society. This problem will be returned to periodically throughout this book in the context of the role of accounting in maintaining this inequilibrium in power relationships.

While this philosophy of Liberalism was developed to explain the position of individuals in society and the need for government and regulation of that society, the philosophy applies equally to organisations. Indeed, Liberalism considers that organisations arise within society as a mechanism whereby individuals can pursue their individual self-interests more effectively that they can alone. Thus firms exist because it is a more efficient means of individuals maximising their self-interests through collaboration than is possible through each individual acting alone. This argument provides the basis for the Theory of the Firm, which argues that through this combination between individuals the costs of individual transactions are thereby reduced.

THE DEVELOPMENT OF UTILITARIANISM

The concept of Utilitarianism was developed as an extension of Liberalism in order to account for the need to regulate society in terms of each individual pursuing, independently, their own ends. It was developed by people such as Bentham and John Stuart Mill who defined the optimal position for society as being the greatest good of the greatest number and argued that it was government's role to mediate between individuals to ensure this societal end. In Utilitarianism it is not actions which are deemed to be good or bad, but merely outcomes. Thus any means of securing a desired outcome was deemed to be acceptable and if the same outcomes ensued then there was no difference, in value terms, between different means of securing those outcomes. Thus actions are value neutral and only outcomes matter. This is, of course, problematical when the actions of firms are concerned because firms only consider outcomes from the point of view of the firm itself. Indeed accounting as we know only captures the actions of a firm insofar as they affect the firm itself and ignores other consequences of the actions of a firm. Under Utilitarianism, however, if the outcomes for the firm were considered to be desirable then any means of achieving these outcomes was considered acceptable. In the nineteenth and early twentieth centuries this was the way in which firms were managed and accounting information was used purely to evaluate actions and potential actions from the point of view of the firm itself. It is only in more recent times that it has become accepted that all the outcomes from the actions of the firm are important and need to be taken into account.

The development of Utilitarianism led to the development of Economic Theory as means of explaining the actions of firms. Indeed the concept of Perfect Competition is predicated in the assumptions of Classical Liberal Theory. From Economic Theory, of course, accounting developed as a tool for analysis to aid the rational decision making assumed in Economic Theory.

The Organisational Failure Framework

While the Theory of the Firm explains why firms come into existence and the role of accounting in firms as a tool to aid rational decision making, it does not sufficiently explain the workings of a firm. Thus the role of accounting within a firm cannot be considered without a consideration of the people involved in that firm. A firm, of course, consists of a collection of people who are involved, The people involved in the firm are affected by the accounting systems of that firm as well as affecting those accounting systems, and this will be considered in greater details in future chapters. The main people involved in the control of a firm are, of course, its managers and Williamson (1970) argues that because in any large organisation the management of the firm is normally divorced from its ownership, then this is a factor which hinders its control and decision making. This leads to internal efficiencies within the firm and conflicts of interests which mean that organisations do not operate efficiently as a means of transaction cost minimisation and value-creating maximisation. From this analysis, Williamson developed what is known as the Organisational Failure Framework.

Thus Williamson (1975) develops this analysis and considers organisations to be complex due to their size, which leads to uncertainty, bounded rationality and information impactedness. He argues that the extent of these factors determines the likelihood of organisational failure from organisations becoming the principle means of resource allocation and decision making. Thus, he argues that there are organisational limits to the size of a firm brought about by such factors as diseconomies of scale, communication distortion and bureaucratic insularity. Furthermore, he argues that the market as a mediating mechanism cannot itself overcome these inefficiencies brought about through the organisation of productive activity into firms. He states that multidivisionalism is a method of overcoming this but that there are still limits to size because of difficulties of communication, resource allocation and lack of entrepreneurial opportunities. He argues, therefore, that organic growth beyond a certain size leads to failure, thereby limiting the size of a firm. While this theory has a certain logic to it, practical examples of such activity are lacking and there do appear to be some very large firms in existence in the world. Perhaps, however, current trends towards downsizing and returning to core business aims is evidence of the validity of this theory, but some empirical testing seems to be needed which is beyond the scope of this chapter.

These factors together are described as the Organisational Failure Framework. In its simplest form this framework can be summarised as follows:

- people are not perfect and managers are unlikely to ignore their own self-interest in pursuing the interests of the owners of the firm;

- organisations as resources allocation mechanisms are not perfect and inefficiencies arise as the size of firms increases;
- markets are not perfect and cannot by themselves compensate for the other inefficiencies inherent in the organising of productive activity into firms.

Upon this premise, Agency Theory was founded as a way of defining and addressing the problems.

The Agency Problem

The general agency problem can be characterised as a situation in which a principal (or group of principals) seeks to establish incentives for an agent (or group of agents) who takes decisions that affect the principal to act in ways that contribute maximally to the principal's own objectives. In business this means the relationship between the owner of the business and other investors – as principal – and the managers of the business – as agents. The difficulties in establishing such an incentive structure arise from either divergence of the objectives of principals and agents or the asymmetric information between principals and agents (Vickers and Yarrow, 1988), and very often from both of these factors.

As stated by Lambert (2001), Agency Theory evaluates the impact of the conflict of interest between principals and agents because of (1) shirking by agent; (2) diversion of resources by the agent for private consumption; (3) differential time horizon of the agent and the principal; and (4) differential risk aversion of the agent and the principal. Jensen and Meckling (1976) developed Agency Theory in the context of the conflicts of interest between corporate managers and outside equity and debt holders. Agency Theory starts with the assumption that people act unreservedly in their own narrowly defined self-interest with, if necessary, guile and deceit. The firm is usually seen as a set of contracts between the various parties involved in the production process including the owners, managers, workforce and creditors among others. Agency Theory switches the centre of attention from the firm to the set of contracts that define each firm. It is primarily concerned with the contracts and relationships between principals and the agents under asymmetric information.[2]

---

2   Information asymmetry has two separate, though related elements: moral hazard and adverse selection. Moral hazard arises where it is difficult or costly for owners to observe or infer the amount of effort exerted by managers. In such a situation, there is an inevitable temptation for managers to avoid working to the terms of the agreed employment contract, since owners are unable to assess the 'true picture'. Managers may also have the incentive as well as the means to conceal the 'true picture' by misrepresenting the actual outcomes reported to the owners. Accounting provides one such means for misrepresentation through its ability to represent outcomes from any course of action in more than one way – a point which we will return to in subsequent chapters.

Whereas moral hazard relates to the 'post-decision' consequences of information asymmetry, adverse selection is concerned with the 'pre-decision' situation. Since all the information that is available to the manager at the time a decision is made is not also available to the owner, then the owner cannot be sure that the manager made the right decision in the circumstances. In addition, the manager has no incentive to reveal what they know since this will then make it easier for the principal to properly assess their actions in the future. This is known as 'information impactedness'.

The existence of 'information asymmetry' means that for owners to obtain relevant information concerning the manager's effort, they must either rely on the communications received from the managers themselves, or must incur monitoring costs. An example of monitoring costs would include the annual audit of the firm's financial statements; indeed such auditing of financial statements was instituted as a means of safeguarding such investments in firms made by those who had no part in the operational activity of the firm. In the context of the agency relationship between top management and divisional management, such monitoring costs would include the cost of employing head office staff

Agency costs are defined as the costs associated with cooperative efforts by human beings. The agency costs within the organisation occur when one entity, the principal, hires another, the agent, to act for them. According to the financial theory, rational shareholders will recognise the incentives facing managers to shirk, to diversify their interests and to underinvest their time and effort and resources in the business. Therefore, the firm would suffer losses from these decisions, and these losses would represent the agency costs of outside equity financing. Agency costs are defined as the sum of the contracting, monitoring and bonding costs undertaken to reduce the costs associated with conflicts of interest plus the 'residual loss' that occurs because it is generally impossible to perfectly identify the agents' interests and align them with those of the principal. Markets are assumed to be potent forces to help control agency costs.[3]

Ethical behaviour that is either altruistic, which is concerned for the welfare of others or by the desire to feel good by helping others, or utilitarian, which is concerned with the compliance with rules in the individual's self-interest, is essential for efficient functioning in the economy; this has many implications in Agency Theory (Noreen, 1988). Unwritten agreements, trust and mutual understanding constitute the core of the relationships within the firm. Written contracts, which are the foundation of the Agency Theory, 'hit only the high spots of agreements' (McKean, 1975: p. 31). Therefore, if unconstrained opportunism pervades the economy, contracting, monitoring and bonding costs, and therefore, agency costs, increase. Conversely, 'altruism economizes on the costs of policing and enforcing agreements' (Hirshleifer, 1977: p. 28).

Constraining Managers – Agency Theory

Given that managers have both the ability to commit the organisation to whatever contracts and transactions they feel appropriate and a responsibility towards the owners of the business, there was a need to ensure that this responsibility took place. It is normally accepted that Agency Theory provides a platform upon which this can be ensured. Agency Theory suggests that the management of an organisation is undertaken on behalf of the owners of that organisation, in other words the shareholders. Consequently the management of value created by the organisation is only pertinent insofar as that value accrues to the shareholders of the firm. Implicit within this view of the management of the firm, as espoused by Rappaport (1986) and Stewart (1991) amongst many others, is that society at large, and consequently all other stakeholders to the organisation, will also benefit as a result of managing the performance of the organisation in this manner.[4] From this perspective therefore the concerns are focused upon how to manage performance for the shareholders and how to report upon that performance (Myners, 1998).

---

to monitor the performance of divisions. One approach to this problem is to get managers to commit to acting in the best interests of the owners, but in this situation the owners will incur a bonding cost to effect this relationship. Even in this situation, however, since managers may not share the same beliefs and preferences as the owner, there may still however, be a 'residual loss'.

3   Agency costs are of course as aspect of transaction costs – the costs of firms engaging in collaborative ventures (through treaties) with others (for example, managers) – and the proponents of markets maintain that they optimise the efficiency of these treaties through the minimsation of transaction costs.

4   Such assumptions are made regardless of evidence – there is little evidence to support or deny such assertions. Instead they are based upon the dogma of market liberalisation grounded in Utilitarianism.

This view of an organisation has, however, been extensively challenged by many writers,[5] who argue that the way to maximise performance for society at large is to both manage on behalf of all stakeholders and to ensure that the value thereby created is not appropriated by the shareholders but is distributed to all stakeholders. Others such as Kay (1998) argue that this debate is sterile and that organisations maximise value creation not by a concern with either shareholders or stakeholders but by focusing upon the operational objectives of the firm and assuming that value creation and equitable distribution will thereby follow.

The shareholder theory of the firm is often also referred to as Agency Theory because the role of the management of a firm is to act as the agents of the shareholders (the principals). The separation of ownership and control that is apparent in large modern-day (joint stock) companies, presently the most common way for a business to be organised, is one of the most significant changes since the days of Smith and Mill.[6] It is this separation that leads to what is known as the principal-agent relationship. It is also argued that within this role it is only appropriate for managers (the agents) to use the funds at their disposal for purposes authorised by shareholders (the principals) (Hasnas, 1998; Smith and Hasnas, 1999). Furthermore, as shareholders normally invest in shares in order to maximise their own returns then managers, as their agents, are theoretically also obliged to target this objective. In fact this is tantamount to arguing that as an owner a shareholder has the right to expect their property to be used to their own benefit. Donaldson (1982; 1989) disagrees and suggests that it can be morally acceptable to use the shareholder's money in a particular way if it is to further public interest.[7] The ethical and moral acceptability of this suggestion is questionable and Smith and Hasnas (1999) point out that such an act would contravene Kant's (1804) principle. This principle states that a person should be treated as an end in their own right rather than as a means to an end. By using shareholders' money for the benefit of others it is argued that the shareholders are being used as a means to further others ends. This defence of shareholder theory is as ironic as it is compelling given that the exact same principle is often cited to defend stakeholder theory.

Assumed within Agency Theory is that there exists a lack of goal congruence between the principal and agent and that it is costly or difficult to confirm the agent's actions (Eisenhardt, 1989). In saying this it is suggested that, left to their own devices, the agent will prefer different options to those that would be chosen by the principal. This assumes that the agent would make decisions and follow courses that further their own self-interest as opposed to that of the principal. This assumption that an agent's behaviour will be driven by their own self-interest and nothing else has been criticised as being an overly simplistic conception of human behaviour (Williamson, 1985). It is argued that in addition to self-interested motives, such other factors as altruism, irrationality, generosity and a genuine concern for others must also be taken to characterise what is actually a multi-faceted human behaviour. Sen (1987) agrees and states that 'to argue that anything other than maximising self-interest must be irrational seems altogether extraordinary'.

---

5   For example, Herremans (1992), Tinker (1985).

6   Adam Smith and John Stuart Mill are often seen to provide a philosophical basis for modern capitalism.

7   Essentially this can be taken to mean that long-term objectives must outweigh short-term objectives and that the manager must resolve this conflict in the long-term best interests of the owner.

It has been argued that shareholders should have rights to determine how their property be used, as should an owner of any asset under private property rights. Etzioni (1998) suggests that this view of shareholders' property rights, which are both moral and legal, is 'widely embedded in the American political culture' and therefore needs no further introduction. Taking a step back, Etzioni observes that such property rights are essentially a social construct, as opposed to natural or inalienable rights, and as such society has the opportunity and the ability to change them if it is considered to be necessary. A closer consideration of what is meant by private property, as it has been socially constructed in present day Western societies, has been undertaken. Thus Donaldson and Preston (1995) argue that the philosophy of property 'runs strongly counter to the conception that private property exclusively enshrines the interests of owners'. They specifically note the work of Pejovich (1990) as recognising that ownership does not entail unrestricted rights as they cannot be separated from human rights. In addition, Honore (1961) suggests that these rights are restricted where their use would be harmful to others. Donaldson and Preston (1995) suggest that as property rights are restricted then they need to be founded on distributive justice. Interestingly, Sternberg (1998), a proponent of shareholder theory, because 'it alone respects the property rights that are so essential for protecting individual liberty', also suggests that ethical business must also be based on 'distributive justice' along with 'ordinary decency' (Sternberg 1994; 1998). Donaldson and Preston (1995) follow Becker's (1992) suggestion that the 'three main contending theories of distributive justice include Utilitarianism, Libertarianism and social contract theory'. Utilitarianism and Classical Liberalism must be taken to provide the philosophical foundation and therefore the historical roots of the shareholder theory considered above.

Within the legal systems of the UK, the USA and most Western countries the managers of a business have a fiduciary duty to the owners of that business. This duty to shareholders is 'more general and proactive' than the regulatory or contractual responsibilities to other groups (Marens and Wicks, 1999; Goodpaster, 1991). These more general duties have also been used as a justification of the appropriateness of shareholder theories of the firm. The purpose and meaning of fiduciary duty were considered by Marens and Wicks (1999) who suggest that in actual fact this duty does not limit managers to a very narrow shareholder approach. They argue that the purpose of the fiduciary duty was originally designed to prevent managers undertaking expenditures that benefited themselves rather then the owners (Berle and Means, 1933). Additionally, Marens and Wicks (1999) suggest that fiduciary duties simply require that the fiduciary has an honest and open relationship with the shareholder and does not gain illegitimately from their office. Therefore the tension between fiduciary responsibility and the responsibility to other stakeholder groups, the so-called stakeholder paradox (Goodpaster, 1991), is not as apparent as is often assumed. Further support for this argument is provided from the United States courts. When shareholders have challenged management's actions as being too generous to other stakeholder groups then the court has almost without exception upheld the right of management to manage.[8] Management's justification or defence has often been on rational business performance grounds, such as efficiency or productivity, and the accuracy of such claims is difficult to prove. As such Marens and Wicks (1999) suggest

---

8   Recent evidence form the era of the Bush junior presidency however suggests that this view is certainly not immutable and there have been recent findings demonstrating the opposite.

that 'virtually any act that does not financially threaten the survival of the business could be construed as in the long-term best interest of shareholders'.

Thus Agency Theory argues that managers merely act as custodians of the organisation and its operational activities[9] and places upon them the burden of managing in the best interest of the owners of that business.[10] According to Agency Theory, all other stakeholders of the business are largely irrelevant and if they benefit from the business then this is coincidental to the activities of management in running the business to serve shareholders. This focus upon shareholders alone as the intended beneficiaries of a business has been questioned considerably from many perspectives, which argue that it is either not the way in which a business is actually run or that it is a view which does not meet the needs of society in general. Conversely stakeholder theory argues that there are a whole variety of stakeholders involved in the organisation and each deserves some return for their involvement. According to stakeholder theory therefore, benefit is maximised if the business is operated by its management on behalf of all stakeholders and returns are divided appropriately amongst those stakeholders, in some way which is acceptable to all. Unfortunately a mechanism for dividing returns amongst all stakeholders which has universal acceptance does not exist, and stakeholder theory is significantly lacking in suggestions in this respect. Nevertheless this theory has some acceptance and is based upon the premise that operating a business in this manner achieves as one of its outcomes the maximisation of returns to shareholders, as part of the process of maximising returns to all other stakeholders. This maximisation of returns is achieved in the long run through the optimisation of performance for the business to achieve maximal returns to all stakeholders.[11] Consequently the role of management is to optimise the long-term performance of the business in order to achieve this end and thereby reward all stakeholders, including themselves as one stakeholder community, appropriately.

These two theories can be regarded as competing explanations of the operations of a firm which lead to different operational foci and to different implications for the measurement and reporting of performance. It is significant, however, that both theories have one feature in common. This is that the management of the firm is believed to be acting on behalf of others, either shareholders or stakeholders more generally. They do so, not because they are the kind of people who behave altruistically, but because they are rewarded appropriately and much effort is therefore devoted to the creation of reward schemes which motivate these managers to achieve the desired ends. Similarly, much literature is devoted to the consideration of the effects of reward schemes on managerial behaviour (see, for example, Briers and Hirst, 1990; Child, 1974; 1975; Coates, Davis, Longden, Stacey and Emmanuel, 1993; Fitzgerald, Johnston, Brignall, Silvestro and Voss, 1991) and suggestion for improvements.

Critiquing Agency Theory

The simplest model of Agency Theory assumes one principal and one agent and a modernist view of the world merely assumes that the addition of more principals and

---

9   See for example Emmanuel, Otley and Merchant (1985).

10   Such owners are of course the legal owners of the business, that is the shareholders.

11   See for example Rappaport (1986).

more agents makes for a more complex model without negating any of the assumptions. In the corporate world this is problematic as the theory depends upon a relationship between the parties and a shared understanding of the context in which agreements are made. With one principal and one agent this is not a problem as the two parties know each other. In the corporate world, however, the principals are equated to the shareholders of the company. For any large corporation, however, those shareholders are an amorphous mass of people who are unknown to the managers of the business.[12] Indeed there is no requirement, or even expectation, that anyone will remain a shareholder for an extended period of time. Thus there can be no relationship between shareholders – as principals – and managers – as agents – as the principals are merely those holding the shares – as property being invested in[13] – at a particular point in time. So shareholders do not invest in a company and in the future of that company; rather they invest for capital growth and/or a future dividend stream and shares are just one way of doing this which can be moved into or out of at will. This problem is exacerbated, particularly in the UK, by the fact that a significant proportion of shares are actually bought and sold by fund managers of financial institutions acting on behalf of their investors. These fund managers are rewarded according to the growth (or otherwise) of the value of the fund. Thus shares are bought and sold as commodities rather than as part ownership of a business enterprise.

If the principal and agent relationship has ceased to exist then this leaves managers without any great degree of accountability[14] and able to act on their own in seeking to meet their own needs. It is therefore argued that the role of management in shaping the organisation, determining its performance and reporting upon that performance is much more central to an understanding of organisational behaviour than is a study of managerial reward schemes in the context of Agency Theory. The sole vehicle for communication – and no longer for accountability therefore – has become the annual report and concomitant annual general meeting. Thus managers at the centre of an organisation are the authors of the script which becomes the corporate report (see Crowther, 2002). Thus as authors they shape that script and decide its contents. Furthermore, they determine the image of the organisation which they wish to be portrayed to the readers of the script. They are then able to operationalise the production of that image through the corporate reporting mechanisms which are instituted within the organisation and through determining the format of the report actually produced. The purported nature of that corporate report is to inform shareholders, and other interested parties (who are thereby considered to be readers of the script and consequently stakeholders to the corporate reporting process), of the actions which have been taken by management in the preceding period on behalf

---

12   Indeed many shares are held in trust by investment funds and the connection between the actual owners and the managers is even more tenuous, being established through these funds and their managers. And of course fund managers are most certainly trading in commodities – buying and selling shares to optimise income and/or capital growth according to the stated objective of the particular fund that they manage. Moreover their performance is determined according to these objective which gives a very short-term perspective to share ownership.

13   Effectively therefore shares become commodities – comparable to oil or metals on other markets – and the connection with owenership (and associated responsibilities) has been completely severed.

14   Evidence to support this assertion is provided in the UK by the near impossibility of the shareholders – whose only opportunity comes at the annual general meeting – being able to remve the Board of Directors, or any member thereof, against the wishes of the board themselves. Indeed it is becoming commonplace that a minimum sharehlding is required in order to be able to even attend the annual general meeting. Although various reasons are cited for this is nevertheless shows complete contempt by managers for the oweners – or by the agents for their principals.

of the shareholders, and the outcomes of those actions in terms of performance (see Crowther, 2000).

This report is intended to be forward looking and to signal to the readers of the script that the future will be an improvement on the present. Indeed, an examination of corporate annual reports shows that the past has continually been dismissed as almost an irrelevance and certainly no basis for judgement concerning the future. Instead the future will be an improvement upon that past and this improved future will be brought about by the skills of the management team, who best know how to manage the resources of the business, despite overwhelming evidence to the contrary from the results of the preceding years.

This kind of statement is common throughout all the annual reports of the organisations and indicates the general ability of management to reconstitute itself and determine its own succession without reference to anyone else. Thus observation of corporate endeavours reinforces the argument that reference to the past has no place in determining the future of the organisation. Instead the future is all that matters. If management truly believed that they acted as agents for others, either shareholders exclusively or a combination of stakeholders, then admissions of failure would cause them to tender their resignations or at the very least seek reaffirmation of their role in managing the organisation. This behaviour therefore provides one clue in the consideration of the role of management in any organisation.

The Limitations of Agency Theory

While Agency Theory offers a number of advantages in the way in which it explains managerial behaviour in organisations, it is necessary to recognise that it also suffers from a number of limitations:

- It is based on a single-period model. In other words, it is not a dynamic model, and may not be applicable in more realistic multi-period settings.
- Its assumption that both principal and agent are rational utility maximisers is questionable.
- The analysis is limited to one principal and one agent, and therefore the results may not be applicable in multi principal and multi agent settings.

The reasons for considering Agency Theory of importance to an understanding of management accounting can be illustrated by the following quotations:

'While top management cannot keep lower-level managers from defining problems and formulating solutions in ways coloured by their situational contexts, they can influence that context by careful attention to organisational design and the measurement/ reward system employed.' (Caves, 1980: p. 76).

In circumstances where managers' effort cannot be directly observed, the role of the accounting system is to promote optimal risk-sharing.

Thus we can see that an understanding of Agency Theory is of importance to both the understanding of managerial behaviour in organisations and to the understanding of the use of management accounting information for evaluating and rewarding performance. Both will be returned to in subsequent chapters. At this point, however, we will turn to the other aspect of the Organisation Failure Framework which we mentioned earlier. This is Transaction Cost theory.

INTRODUCTION TO TRANSACTION COST THEORY

As far as the activities of a firm are concerned, accounting adopts an entirely internal perspective and fails to recognise that the effects of the actions of the firm have effects outside the organisation. As we stated earlier, these are considered to be irrelevant to the firm operating under the assumptions of Classical Liberalism. Moreover, accounting, as practised by firms, is based upon the product or service provided by the firm as the basic unit of cost. In working in this manner, accounting has been designed to capture the costs that are incurred in the provision of these products or services and to simply measure the costs that are accumulated in the production process. These cost accumulations form the basis of accounting information which is used for the multiple purposes for which management accounting is used within the firm. These uses of course will include:

- operational planning and control;
- decision making;
- performance measurement and reporting;
- the evaluation and rewarding of managerial performance.

The implications from the use of accounting in this way by firms is that the key to successful management of the firm is the understanding of cost behaviour and so extensive techniques have been developed to understand the behaviour of costs in the operational processes of the firm. Equally many techniques have been developed for the allocation of costs and their absorption into the product costs which are the outcome of the accounting process. There is an implicit assumption, therefore, that cost minimisation is the key to operational success for a firm. This is of course untrue and the key to sustainable success by a firm is the maximisation of value creation. This is achieved through an understanding of the transformational process of the firm. The transformational process can be depicted thus:

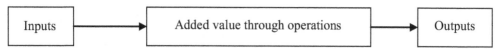

Transaction Cost theory adds to accounting theory through an understanding of the transformational process. The starting point for the theory is that all activities of the firm are transactions. This is true whether these activities are carried out within the firm or are carried out by an interaction between the firm and a part of its external environment. Thus there is no difference in principle between internal activities and external activities as far as the firm is concerned as they are all transactions. The only difference is that when these transactions take place externally to the firm then a price can be determined for the transactions through the operation of the market mechanism. When they occur entirely within the firm, the no market mechanism exists to set a price for the transactions and hence we have to develop accounting techniques to compensate for this deficiency and to simulate the operation of the market mechanism. Such techniques would include for example the transfer pricing systems used by firms.

As well as a price for the exchange all transactions have a cost associated with them. This is the cost of engaging in the transaction itself and examples include the cost of acquiring raw materials, which is included into the accounting cost of those raw materials, or the cost of creating a Pareto optimal principal-agent contract. In theory, firms exist because the cost of engaging in these transactions is reduced when they are carried out within the firm rather than through the market as mediated through the price mechanism. In practice all firms carry out some transactions entirely within the firm and some are carried out through the market mechanism. This is theoretically because the cost of each individual transaction is minimised either by internalising it within the firm or by externalising it to the market. For optimal value creation in the transformational process these transaction costs need to be minimised and, therefore, this theory turns the focus of organisational activity upon the transaction costs associated with the transformational process. Minimising the costs of all transaction will inevitably achieve the following:

- the maximising of the efficiency of operational activity through optimising the source of all transactions;
- the maximising of the profitability of the firm through the minimising of the costs of the products or services provided;
- the minimising of the costs of the transformations undertaken and hence the maximising of value created within the firm.

If a firm understands the transaction costs associated with its transformational process then it will be able to decide whether transactions are more efficiently accommodated within the firm or through the market. If transactions are reduced in cost through accommodating them within the firm then they should be carried out within the firm and this could imply a firm engaging in vertical integration as a means of reducing its transaction costs. Another way of reducing the cost of any particular type of transaction is by ensuring that economies of scale lead to a reduction in unit transaction costs and this could lead to horizontal integration. On the other hand, an understanding of these transaction costs may lead to a firm externalising transactions and engaging in them through the market. This would lead to a firm downsizing and divesting certain activities while engaging in the outsourcing of such transactions as the need arises. In such a way the performance of any individual firm would be optimised and this implies that there is an optimal size for any particular firm and an optimal set of activities in which it should engage.

An observation of the economy of any country will show that firms are engaging in the changing of the source of their transactions through integration and through divestment at all times. The assumption to be drawn from this is that the managers of these organisations understand their transaction costs and are reacting accordingly. The Organisational Failure Framework, however, argues that this is not the case and that communication distortions and bureaucratic mechanisms prevent this from happening efficiently. One problem which firms face, however, which interferes with this process, is the use of accounting information itself. Accounting as cost accumulation does not, however, measure these transaction costs and so does not provide a means of measurement which will facilitate transaction cost minimisation. This therefore reveals one problem with the use of accounting information to manage the value creation process of the firm and this is that accounting does not even measure this key determinant of operational performance.

Transaction Cost Theory therefore provides a different perspective upon the operation of a firm and shows that accounting fails the managers of the firm in determining its transaction costs. It argues that accounting differently would help a firm optimise its performance.

THE PROBLEMS OF TRANSACTION COST THEORY

This sounds intuitively logical and these arguments accord with those of strategic management which focus upon the value chain. There are, however, problems with the use of this theory in practice. These problems stem from the points made earlier in this chapter which stem from the Organisational Failure Framework, which are that firms are not efficient allocators of resources and that markets themselves do not operate efficiently. It is to these points that we now turn.

Organisations as resource allocators

Traditionally, organisations base their resource allocation decision on the information available to them from their accounting systems. We have already identified, however, that accounting information does not provide the information necessary to base decisions concerning the allocation of resources upon the transaction costs associated with individual transactions in the transformational process. Thus such decision tend to be made based upon incomplete information and it is logical, therefore, to accept that the optimum allocation of resources within a firm will not be achieved through the use of traditional accounting information as a decision-making tool. Furthermore, we have considered the behaviour of managers in the context of Agency Theory and this makes it apparent that these managers do not necessarily have the incentive to allocate resources in a way which is optimum for the organisation itself. The behaviour of managers in organisations is further complicated by the way in which accounting information is used to motivate managers and reward them for performance as well as the way in which the accounting information is shaped in its use by the managers of the organisation themselves. In this respect it becomes impossible to separate accounting information from the decision-making process and both of these from the power relationships which exist in all organisations. These are all points which we will be considering in greater details in subsequent chapters.

It is therefore apparent that both the behaviour of managers and the way in which accounting information is used in organisations are factors which prevent organisations operating efficiently as resource allocators. These arguments support the problems of organisations which have been identified in the Organisational Failure Framework itself.

Inefficiencies in the market

Economic theory focuses upon the market as a means of exchange between different individuals or organisations, with the assumption that one party to the exchange offers goods or services while the other offers money in payment. These exchanges take place in the market. The market, therefore, is a shorthand expression for the process by which consumers of goods and services decide upon their needs and the suppliers of those goods and services decide upon what to provide. The mediating mechanism which reconciles the demand and supply for any particular good or service is that of price. There is an implicit assumption that each party to a transaction will behave rationally in seeking to maximise their utility and that in the long term the free operation of the price mechanism will be sufficient to determine a price at which supply and demand are brought into equilibrium. These assumptions, however, only apply in a situation of perfect competition and in reality such competition never exists. In reality, therefore, the market is affected by the respective power of various competitors in the market, the actions of the firm itself in the market, government regulation of the market, and the expectations of the various actors in the market concerning both the present and the future. Thus it can be argued that an equilibrium price never actually exists, or at least never exists for more than a brief period of time.

Thus one of the basic assumptions of economic theory, as far as the operations of markets is concerned, that equilibrium is a natural state can, be seen not to apply and this is the basic problem with market efficiency and the price mechanism for transaction mediation. The actions of the firm in determining its operational processes and seeking to minimise its transaction costs depend, however, upon a stable equilibrium in the market in order to make the necessary planning for operational activities. It therefore follows that the market too is problematical as far as the allocation of resources for the minimisation of transaction costs is concerned.

Thus, although it seems that Transaction Cost Theory provides a means for focusing upon the transformation process within the firm as a basis for managerial decision making and transaction cost minimising as a basis for profit maximisation, it can be seen that this would imply a restructuring of the way in which accounting information is collected and utilised within organisations. We can see, however, that there are practical problems with the application of the theory as far as ongoing decision making within organisations is concerned. Unfortunately, therefore, we must conclude that the theory has little practical application for organisations other than to provide a means to focus upon different aspects of the organisations transformational and operations processes.

Resolving Conflicts and Aligning Interests

Both Agency Theory and Transaction Cost Theory have been developed from the Organisational Failure Framework of Williamson. Both seem to offer some pointers as to how firms can be managed better but both have problems as far as their practical application is concerned. It is important to recognise, however, that although both develop the theory of the firm and its decision-making processes and show these to be more complex than might at first appear, they are both still based upon one key assumption. This assumption is that every party to a transaction acts in a rational manner in order to maximise their utility. This assumes, of course, that the evaluation of utility undertaken by every individual can be precisely calculated and thus that the same decision would always be made by the same individual in exactly the same set of circumstances – an obvious problem.

It is commonly understood that one of the main purposes of Agency Theory is to bring about the alignment in objectives between the principal and the agent. Much attention has therefore been focused upon rewards structures designed to do this, and there has been a gradual development and refinement of such structures to increasingly focus upon the long term as well as the short term and upon such non-financial aspects such as social responsibility in addition to profit and/or share price. The other main focus of attention has been upon the agency problem in terms of information asymmetry. In the investigation of these topics there has normally been an implicit assumption that these are problems which can be solved and the debate has focused upon how best to solve them.

More recently, however, it has become generally accepted that the information asymmetry which inevitably exists in this situation cannot readily be overcome and so attention has been devoted to the minimisation of any risk associated with the asymmetric information. In the past this has been attempted by attempting to ensure the alignment of objectives through manipulations of the rewards structures, but many would argue that this has merely resulted in increasing information asymmetry and the passing of control – and an element of ownership – to the managerial hierarchy. However viewed, the desired results have not been achieved. More recent attempts, therefore, have been concerned with procedural changes through the development of strong systems of corporate governance. Such systems of governance have become enshrined in codes with universal application but cannot be considered to be fully effective and are under continual development and modification.

The Anglo Saxon Model of Governance

The Anglo Saxon model of governance is, of course, familiar to most readers of this book. It is founded on rules which must be codified and can therefore be subject to a standard interpretation by the appropriate adjudicating body. It has a tendency to be hierarchical and therefore imposed from above; and along with this imposition is an assumption of its efficacy and a lack, therefore, of considerations of alternatives. In this model, therefore, the issues of governance, politics and power become inseparably intertwined.

The abuses which have been revealed within this system of governance have exposed problems with the lack of separation of politics from governance. This has led to the suggestion that there should be a clear distinction between the two. The argument is that politics is concerned with the processes by which a group of people, with possibly divergent and contradictory opinions, can reach a collective decision which is generally regarded as binding on the group, and therefore enforced as common policy. Governance, on the other hand, is concerned with the processes and administrative elements of governing rather than its antagonistic ones (Solomon, 2007). This argument of course makes the assumption that it is actually possible to make the separation between politics and administration. For example, both the UK and the USA have governance procedures to make this separation effective for their national governments – and different procedures in each country – but in both countries the division is continually blurred in practice. Many would argue, and we concur, that the division is not possible in practice because the third factor of power is ignored whereas this is more important. Indeed it is our argument that it is the operation of this power in practice that brings about many of the governance problems that exist in practice. We discuss this in greater detail later in the chapter but part of our argument is that theories and systems of governance assume that power relationships, while not necessarily equal, are not too asymmetric. If the relationship is too asymmetric then the safeguards in a governance system do not operate satisfactorily whereas one of the features of globalisation is an increase in such power asymmetries. We will return to this later.

As we have already identified, the Anglo Saxon model is hierarchical but other forms of governance are allowed and even encouraged to operate within this framework. Thus the market form features prominently in the Anglo Saxon model while the network and consensual forms can also be found. It is therefore apparent that it is not the form of governance which epitomises the Anglo Saxon model; rather it is the dependence on rules and adjudication which distinguishes this system of governance.

The Combined Code

At the present time, for example, all companies which are quoted on the London Stock Exchange, whatever their country of domicile, are required to comply with The Combined Code on Corporate Governance, which came into effect in 2003.[15] An investigation of the FTSE100 – the 100 biggest firms quoted on the London Stock Exchange shows that fully 30 per cent of the firms consider that their governance is adequate because they comply with The Combined Code on Corporate Governance. Of course, all firms reporting on the London Stock Exchange are required to comply with this Code, and so these firms are doing no more than meeting their regulatory obligations as the other 70 per cent also do in complying with the code. So 30 per cent are seeking to make a virtue out of a necessity. A further 24 per cent regard corporate governance as simply a part of investor relationships and do nothing more regarding such governance except to identify that it is important investors/potential investors and to flag up that they have such governance policies. In effect, therefore, 54 per cent of these firms merely consider governance in terms of issues mentioned within the Combined Code.

This, therefore, leaves only 46 per cent who recognise that there is a relationship between governance and other aspects of corporate activity. Thus 27 per cent of firms recognise that there is a clear link between governance and corporate social responsibility[16] and make efforts to link the two. Often this is no more than making a claim that good governance is a part of their Corporate Social Responsibility (CSR) policy as well as a part of their relationship with shareholders. And of course there are a lot of vague comments about firms doing their best[17] to behave sustainably, without any precise indications of what is meant by such a claim. Some firms do, however, go further then this and make clear links to specific action. Thus five per cent recognise the relationship to financial sustainability through an understanding of the relationship between governance and risk. Similarly two per cent relate governance to community relations; four per cent to ethical behaviour towards employees; three per cent to environmental policy and behaviour; and one per cent to their commitment to sustainable growth. Despite these seemingly

---

15   The Code was based upon the previous Cadbury and Greenbury Reports and has been subsequently revised during 2006. It deals with such issues as Board composition and remuneration, relationship with shareholders and investors, composition of the Audit Committee and so on.

16   The terms used include corporate social responsibility and corporate responsibility.

17   Often the phrase used includes something like 'within reason' or 'in the light of circumstance' as a way of obviating any real commitment to any particular sort of action.

dispiritingly small numbers though it is encouraging that seven per cent of firms recognise the relationship to all the aspects of sustainability which we have identified and clearly spell out this relationship in their corporate activity.

This can all be summarised in the Table 13.1

Table 13.1 Relating Governance and CSR

Type of relationship recognised/action undertaken/commitment made	Firms recognising the relationship %
Comply with code only	30
Related to investor relations only	24
Related to CSR policy	27
Community relations	2
Ethics	4
Environmental policy	3
Sustainable growth	1
Risk	5
Full connection to sustainability	7

Source: From Aras and Crowther, 2008.

The Relationship Between Corporate Social Responsibility and Business Financial Success

Often the more significant the power that multinational corporations and some groups of stakeholders in a firm have, the more is spoken about corporate social responsibility. Thus, a concept that was some kind of luxury some years ago, nowadays has reached the top of the public opinion discussion. Some steps taken in the corporation's development, in the environment and in the human values can be the guilty causes of this CSR fashion. If in the beginning firms were small and there was no distinction between ownership and management, the economic development meant that there was a necessity to join more capital to set up bigger enterprises. Thus, there were owners, who gave the funds, and experts in management, who managed the company and were paid by the owners. Agency Theory establishes this relationship between the principal, the shareholder, and the agent, the manager, bearing in mind that the goals of the shareholders must be reached through the management of the agents. Furthermore it is assumed, unquestioningly, that the shareholders' overriding objective must be to increase the enterprise value through the maximisation of profits.[18]

---

18   It is of course recognised that long-term and short-term value maximisation are based upon different strategies and much work has been done to manage this conflict. It is therefore recognised that the maximisation is often a compromise of long and short-term strategies for value maximisation.

But a company's structure is nowadays more complex than before and there have appeared other people, not owners, directly or indirectly implied in the company's operations – known as stakeholders. Multinational corporations have sometimes even more power than governments in their influence, and stakeholders have gained more power through the media and public opinion in order to require some kind of specific behaviour from companies. Within this new environment, although explained in a very simple way, the primary objective of the company has become wider. Although, generally speaking, the assumption may be that the first goal is to achieve financial performance in the company, after it the next step will be to comply with other socially responsible policies. That is because to pay attention to social objectives, or to show an orientation to multiple stakeholders group, could be considered a luxury, because it must have meant that the other basic company's goal had been met.

Conclusions

Business ethics is characterised by conflicts of interests. Businesses attempt to maximise profits as a primary goal on one hand while they face issues of social responsibility and social service. Business ethics is the honest, respectful and fair conduct by a business and its representatives in all of its relations. To talk about integral ethics and acquire common ethical values, individuals, businesses and existing system must act in compliance with ethical rules. Existence of a system governed by ethical rules in the framework of the manners and methods followed by individuals and businesses to acquire their goals is very important. Therefore, ethics is needed by individuals, organisations and systems to maintain their activities in cases when there are no legal regulations or existing regulations are not sufficient in contemporary economic order. In business lines, ethical principles have been set forth with a view to minimising uncertainty and developing an atmosphere of confidence in a web of emerging complex relations. With the impact of these developments, it is very important for financial markets and the organisations operating within these markets to accommodate and implement ethical rules. The reason for this is the quality of transactions and instruments in the financial sector. This area contains riskier transactions and complex instruments. The uncertainty created by this situation makes it difficult for organisations to create confidence on the segments concerned. Obviously, these markets and organisations are successful to the extent they secure confidence. Legal provisions and control mechanisms and sanctions introduced by them alone are not sufficient to ensure sound operation of the system and create confidence. Therefore, introduction of ethical rules and principles aims at increasing compliance with legal provisions and creating an atmosphere of confidence by securing interests of parties.

References

Akerlof, G.A (1970); The market for lemons; *The Quarterly Journal of Economics*, 84, 488-500.

Aras G & Crowther D (2008); Governance and sustainability: An investigation into the relationship between corporate governance and corporate sustainability; *Management Decision*, 46 (3), 433-448.

Becker L C (1992); Placed for pluralism; *Ethics,* 102, 707-719.

Berle A & Means G (1932); *The Modern Corporation and Private Property*; New York; Commerce Clearing House.

Briers M & Hirst M (1990); The role of budgetary information in performance evaluation; *Accounting, Organizations & Society,* 15 (4), 373-398.

Caves R E (1980); Industrial organization, corporate strategy and structure; *Journal of Economic Literature,* XVIII, 64-92.

Child J (1974); Managerial and organisational factors associated with company performance - part 1; *Journal of Management Studies,* 11, 73-189.

Child J (1975); Managerial and organisational factors associated with company performance - part 2; *Journal of Management Studies,* 12, 12-27.

Coates J B, Davis E W, Longden S G, Stacey R J & Emmanuel C (1993); *Corporate Performance Evaluation in Multinationals*; London; CIMA.

Crowther D (2000); Corporate reporting, stakeholders and the Internet: mapping the new corporate landscape; *Urban Studies,* 37 (10), 1837-1848.

Crowther D (2002); *A Social Critique of Corporate Reporting*; Aldershot; Ashgate.

Donaldson, T (1982); *Corporations and Morality,* Englewood Cliffs, NJ; Prentice Hall.

Donaldson, T (1989); *The Ethics of International Business*; New York; Oxford University Press.

Donaldson, T and Preston, L E (1995); The stakeholder theory of the corporations: Concepts, Evidence and Implications; *The Academy of Management Review,* 20 (1).

Eisenhardt, K M (1989); Agency theory: An assessment and review; *Academy of Management Review,* 14, 57-74.

Emmanuel C R, Otley D T & Merchant K (1985); *Accounting for Management Control*; London; Chapman & Hall.

Etzioni, A. (1998); A communitarian note on stakeholder theory; *Business Ethics Quarterly,* October, 8 (4), 679-691.

Fitzgerald L, Johnston R, Brignall S, Silvestro R & Voss C (1991); *Performance Measurement in Service Businesses*; London; CIMA.

Goodpaster, K E (1991); Business ethics and stakeholder analysis; *Business Ethics Quarterly,* 1(1), 53-73.

Hasnas, J (1998) The normative theories of business ethics: A guide for the perplexed; *Business Ethics Quarterly,* January, 19-42.

Herremans I M, Akathaparn P & McInnes M (1992); An investigation of corporate social responsibility, reputation and economic performance; *Accounting, Organizations & Society,* 18(7/8), 587-604.

Hirshleifer, J (1977); Economics from a biological viewpoint, *The Journal of Law and Economics,* 1-52.

Honore, A M (1961); 'Ownership', in A. G. Guest (ed.), *Oxford Essays in Jurisprudence,* 107-147, Oxford; Clarendon Press.

Jensen, M. and Meckling W (1976); Theory of the firm: managerial behavior, agency costs, and ownership structure; *Journal of Financial Economics* 3, 305-360.

Kant, I (1804/1981) *Grounding for the Metaphysics of Morals,* trans. by J. W. Ellington, Indianapolis, In.; Hackett Publishing.

Kay J (1998); Good business; *Prospect,* 28 (March), 25-29.

Lambert, R. A. (2001); Contracting theory and accounting; *Journal of Accounting and Economics,* 32, 1-87.

Marens, R and Wicks, A (1999); Getting real: Stakeholder theory, managerial practice, and the general irrelevance of fiduciary duties owed to shareholders; *Business Ethics Quarterly*, April, 9(2), 273-293.

McKean, R.N (1975); 'Economics of Trust, Altruism, and Corporate Responsibility', in Phelps, E.S. (ed.) *Altruism, Morality, and Economic Theory*, 29-44, New York; Russel Sage Foundations.

Myners P (1998); 'Improving Performance Reporting to the Market', in A Carey & J Sancto (eds), *Performance Measurement in the Digital Age*, 27-33; London; ICAEW.

Noreen, E. (1988); The economics of ethics: a new perspective on agency theory; *Accounting Organizations and Society*, 13(4), 359-369.

Pejovich, S (1990); *The Economics of Property Rights: Towards a Theory of Comparative Systems*; Dordrecht, The Netherlands; Kluwer Academic Publishers.

Rappaport A (1986); *Creating Shareholder Value*; New York; The Free Press.

Sen, A. (1987); *On Ethics & Economics*; Oxford; Blackwell.

Smith, H J and Hasnas, J. (1999); Ethics and information systems: the corporate domain; *MIS Quarterly*, March, 23 (1), 109-127.

Soloman J (2007); *Corporate Governance and Accountability*; Chichester; Wiley.

Sternberg, E (1994); *Just Business: Business Ethics in Action*; Little, Brown and Company; London.

Sternberg, E (1998) *Corporate Governance: Accountability in the Marketplace*; London; The Institute if Economic Affairs.

Stewart G B III (1991); *The Quest for Value*; New York; Harper Collins.

Tinker T (1985); *Paper Prophets: A Social Critique of Accounting*; London; Holt, Rinehart & Winston.

Vickers, J S and Yarrow, G K (1988); *Privatization*; Cambrdge, MA; MIT Press.

Williamson O E (1970); *Corporate Control and Business Behaviour*; New York; Prentice Hall.

Williamson, O E. (1985); *The Economic Institutions of Capitalism*; New York; Free Press.

KEY REFERENCES FOR FURTHER READING

Aras G (2008); 'Corporate Governance And The Agency Problem In Financial Markets'; in D Crowther & N Capaldi (eds), *The Ashgate Research Companion to Corporate Social Responsibility*; Aldershot; Ashgate; 87-96.

Aras G & Crowther D (2007); 'Is the global economy sustainable?'; in S Barber (ed.), *The Geopolitics of the City*; London; Forum Press; 165-194.

Baums, T and Scott, K E (2005); 'Taking shareholder protection seriously? Corporate governance in the U.S. and Germany'; *Journal of Applied Corporate Finance*, 17 (4), Fall, 4-7.

Jensen, M and Meckling W. (1976); Theory of the firm: managerial behavior, agency costs, and ownership structure, *Journal of Financial Economics* 3, 305-360.

Williamson O E (1975); *Markets and Hierarchies: Analysis and Anti-trust Implications*; New York; The Free Press.

Williamson, O. E. (1985); *The Economic Institutions of Capitalism*; New York; Free Press.

14 *Auditing, Product Certification and Corporate Social Responsibility*

CHARLES ELAD

Introduction

The past decade has witnessed a proliferation of product certification and labelling schemes that are designed to signal to consumers that goods have been produced in a sustainable manner. These social and environmental audit assurance schemes were developed by a diverse group of Non-Governmental Organizations (NGOs) in response to anxieties over the pervasiveness of risk in modern society and the failure of the state to protect citizens against what Beck (1992, p. 21) called 'hazards and insecurities induced by modernization': for example, the potential hazards of genetically engineered food, global warming, tropical deforestation, and environmental degradation. Indeed, Beck coined the phrase 'risk society' to describe this contemporary preoccupation with risk and its management, which is also a major theme of a recent book by Power (2007). The latter is essentially an extension of Power's seminal work entitled 'The Audit Society'[1] in which he cited the rise of a variety of non-financial auditing and product certification initiatives as contributing to an audit explosion at the turn of the twenty-first century (Power, 1999).

The aim of this chapter is threefold. First, we review the development of audit certification schemes by the Fair Trade Labelling Organisation (FLO) and the Forest Stewardship Council (FSC) in order to set the scene for an assessment of their role as tools for managing stakeholder dialogue and corporate social responsibility.

Second, we examine the concept of corporate social responsibility, and the extended theoretical conceptualization of corporate citizenship by Matten and Crane (2005), along with their operationalization in the context of the FSC's certification system.

The final objective of this chapter is to highlight some of the contrasts between financial audits and the audit certification models established by the FSC and the FLO, and their implications for corporate governance. In particular, although this chapter argues

---

1   This title is an obvious play on Beck's 'Risk Society'.

that the audit certification schemes of the FSC and the FLO are, in essence, blueprints for corporate social responsibility and corporate citizenship, it also presents a real-life case study that vividly illustrates the way in which unscrupulous managers use these schemes as part of a strategy to defend their company's enlightened self-interests, or to deflect undesirable stakeholder demands.

The Development of Auditing Standards in the Forestry Sector

In the late 1980s, sustained pressure from stakeholder advocacy organizations that are committed to socially responsible environmental stewardship, and increased consumer awareness and concern about the degradation and destruction of the world's forests, resulted in a multiplicity of dubious eco-labels and misleading claims regarding sustainability within the timber trade. For example, an authoritative study by the Worldwide Fund for Nature (WWF, 1994, p. 2) indicated that, out of a sample of 80 different environmental claims found on wood and paper products, only three could even be partially substantiated.

In order to protect consumers from deceptive advertising and misleading labelling practices, the Forest Stewardship Council was established in 1993 as an all-encompassing private sector body for accrediting third-party forest auditors. It was founded by a broad-based coalition of environmental organizations, timber trade associations, indigenous peoples' representatives, academia and NGOs from 25 countries. According to its mission statement, the FSC seeks to promote good forest management throughout the world, based on a set of principles designed to ensure that forests of all types are managed in ways that are environmentally appropriate, socially beneficial and economically viable (WWF, 1994, p. 12).

The FSC planned to achieve these goals by establishing auditing standards and by evaluating and accrediting forest management auditors worldwide (Hansen, 1997, p. 20). Shortly after it was created, the FSC embarked on a two-year consultative process, involving large-scale questionnaire surveys and interviews, carried out in several countries around the world, which led to the establishment of ten principles and criteria for sustainable forest management applicable to natural forests (temperate, tropical or boreal) and plantations as summarized in Figure 14.1. Representatives of social constituencies such as governments, forest owners and managers, academia, environmental campaigners and indigenous NGOs were involved in the consultative process (WWF, 1994, p. 12; Upton and Bass, 1996; Hansen, 1997, p. 20). The broad, ambitious and very demanding nature of the ten principles summarized in Figure 14.1 can be explained in terms of the need to accommodate the requirements of all the key stakeholders in order to achieve a consensus.

Nonetheless, it is important to point out here that the product certification schemes which were formulated by the FSC and the FLO are modelled on the long-established traditions of statutory financial audit (see, for example, Swift et al., 2000). The main similarities and differences between financial audits and forest stewardship audits are outlined in Figure 14.2. In particular, it is noteworthy that, in financial audits, the audit report is the primary tool for communication with stakeholders whereas in forest stewardship audits, any of the eco-labels shown in Figure 14.3 can be used, in addition to audit reports, to signal clean audits to stakeholders.

- **Principle 1: Compliance with Laws and FSC Principles**
  Forest management shall respect all applicable laws of the country in which they occur and international treaties and agreements to which the country is signatory, and comply with all FSC Principles and Criteria.

- **Principle 2: Tenure and Use Rights and Responsibilities**
  Long-term tenure and use rights to land and forest resources shall be clearly defined, documented and legally established.

- **Principle 3: Indigenous People's Rights**
  The legal and customary rights of indigenous peoples to own, use and manage their lands, territories and resources shall be recognized and respected.

- **Principle 4: Community Relations and Workers' Rights**
  Forest management operations shall maintain or enhance the long-term social economic well-being of forest workers and local communities.

- **Principle 5: Benefits from the Forest**
  Forest management operations shall encourage the optimal and efficient use of the forest's multiple products and services, in order to ensure economic viability and a wide range of environmental, social and economic benefits.

- **Principle 6: Environmental Impact**
  Forest management operations shall maintain the critical ecological functions of the forest and minimize adverse impacts on biological diversity, water resources, soils, non-timber resources and unique and fragile ecosystems and landscapes.

- **Principle 7: Management Plan**
  A management plan consistent with FSC Principles and appropriate to the scale of the operations shall be written, implemented and kept up to date, clearly stating the objectives of management, and the means of achieving them.

- **Principle 8: Monitoring and Assessment**
  Regular monitoring should be conducted that assesses the condition of the forest, yields of forest products, chain of custody, and management operations and their social and environmental impacts.

- **Principle 9: Relations Between Natural Forests and Plantations**
- Primary forests, well-developed secondary forests and sites of major environmental, social or cultural significance shall be conserved. Such areas shall not be replaced by tree plantations or other land uses.

- **Principle 10: Plantations**
  Plantations shall be planned and managed in accordance with Principles and Criteria 1–9. While plantations can provide an array of social and economic benefits, and can contribute to satisfying the world's needs for forest products, they should complement the management of, reduce pressures on, and promote the restoration and conservation of natural forests.

Figure 14.1 Summary of the Forest Stewardship Council's principles

Financial Audits	Forest Stewardship Audits
Audit reports indicate whether or not financial statements portray a true and fair view	Forest stewardship audit reports indicate whether or not forests are well managed
Presumption that compliance with generally accepted accounting principles means financial statements portray a true and fair view	Presumption that compliance with FSC principles means that a forest is well managed
Audit report is primary tool for communication with stakeholders	Eco-labels used, in addition to audit reports, to signal clean audits to stakeholders
Auditor not responsible for preparation of financial statements	Auditor prepares corporate social report
Mandatory for listed companies	Generally voluntary and market-driven but increasingly recommended to tropical countries by the World Bank as a condition for structural adjustment assistance

Figure 14.2 Similarities and differences between financial audits and Forest Stewardship audits

Figure 14.3 Some Eco-labels used by Forest Stewardship Council-accredited auditors

Furthermore, in FSC-based audits, the notions of 'auditing' and 'corporate social reporting' are conflated in the sense that audit reports that comply with FSC principles are essentially detailed corporate social responsibility accounting documents which encompass a wide range of disclosures relating to: protection of the customary rights of indigenous people, environmental impact assessment, long-term land tenure and other matters set out in Figure 14.1.

Forest Stewardship Council Principles, Corporate Social Responsibility and Corporate Citizenship

Corporate social responsibility (hereafter, CSR) has been defined in terms of the economic, legal, ethical and philanthropic expectations placed on organizations by society (Carroll and Buchholtz, 2000, p. 35). Essentially, this four-part definition of CSR, illustrated in Figure 14.4, suggests that society not only requires organizations to earn a fair return for investors (economic responsibilities), and to comply with the law (legal responsibilities), but it also expects them to meet their ethical responsibilities. Moreover, although the philanthropic responsibilities shown at the top of Carroll's pyramid in Figure 14.4 are not mandatory, they are desired by society.

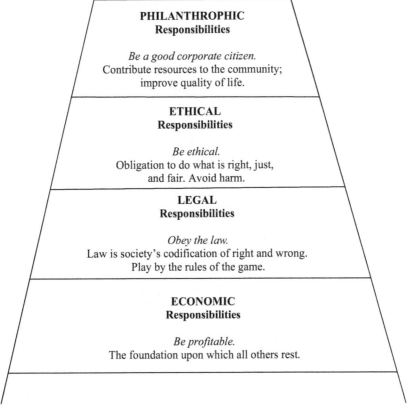

Figure 14.4 Carroll's Pyramid of Corporate Social Responsibility

Source: Carroll (1991, p. 42).

It is contended here that the FSC's auditing scheme in Figure 14.1 constitutes a framework for CSR because it meets the criteria set out in Carroll's four-part definition of the concept. For example, Principle 5 in the FSC model is in line with Carroll's 'economic responsibilities' since it specifically requires forest managers to ensure that their entities are economically viable. Similarly, Principles 1–4 address legal responsibilities and the rights of different stakeholders, thus fulfilling Carroll's second criterion. Also, companies that voluntarily implement all the FSC's principles in good faith are actually demonstrating a commitment to ethically sound environmental stewardship in conformity with Carroll's 'ethical responsibilities'. Finally, the 'philanthropic responsibilities' in Carroll's model fall within Principles 4 and 5 of the FSC's framework.

However, more recently, the concept of corporate citizenship was introduced into CSR discourse and has, over the past decade, gained international currency in both academic and practitioner circles. Indeed, as Kell (2005, p. 69) points out, the recent emergence of a global corporate citizenship initiative can be traced to a plenary address to the World Economic Forum in 1999, entitled 'The Global Compact', by Kofi Annan (then Secretary General of the United Nations).

The Global Compact was formally launched under the aegis of the United Nations in 2000, and, as of July 2008, had more than 5,500 signatory companies despite the fact that 630 companies were delisted in June 2008 for failure to provide progress reports which cover the ten principles of the initiative.[2] Companies that sign up to the Global Compact are required to report annually to stakeholders the progress made in implementing all the principles of the compact.

Although there is currently no universally agreed definition of corporate citizenship, three different perspectives on the concept have emerged in the literature (see, for example, Matten and Crane, 2005; Crane and Matten, 2007, p. 71), namely: (i) the 'limited view' which simply equates corporate citizenship with strategic corporate philanthropy; (ii) the 'equivalent view' which equates corporate citizenship with CSR and (iii) the 'extended view' which acknowledges the extended political role of the corporation in society.

Whereas the limited view and the equivalent view suggest that corporate citizenship is simply another label for CSR, the extended view, which was developed by Matten and Crane (2005), opens up a new theoretical approach that focuses on the social role of the corporation in administering citizenship rights for individuals (that is, civil rights, political rights and social rights). In this regard, Matten and Crane (2005, p. 173) offer the following definition: 'corporate citizenship defines the corporate function for governing citizenship rights for individuals'. This new conceptualization de-emphasizes the idea that the corporation is a citizen in itself and instead sees the corporation in terms of its role in administering some of the social, political and civil rights of individuals. As such, the corporation is thought of as a medium for providing social rights, enabling/ disenabling civil rights, or channelling/blocking political rights as illustrated in Figure 14.5.

It is argued here that the FSC's scheme is a blueprint for corporate citizenship in the sense that it enhances the capacity for an organization to administer citizenship rights

---

2   For further details, see: http://www.unglobalcompact.org/NewsAndEvents/news_archives/2008_06_25.html (accessed July 2008).

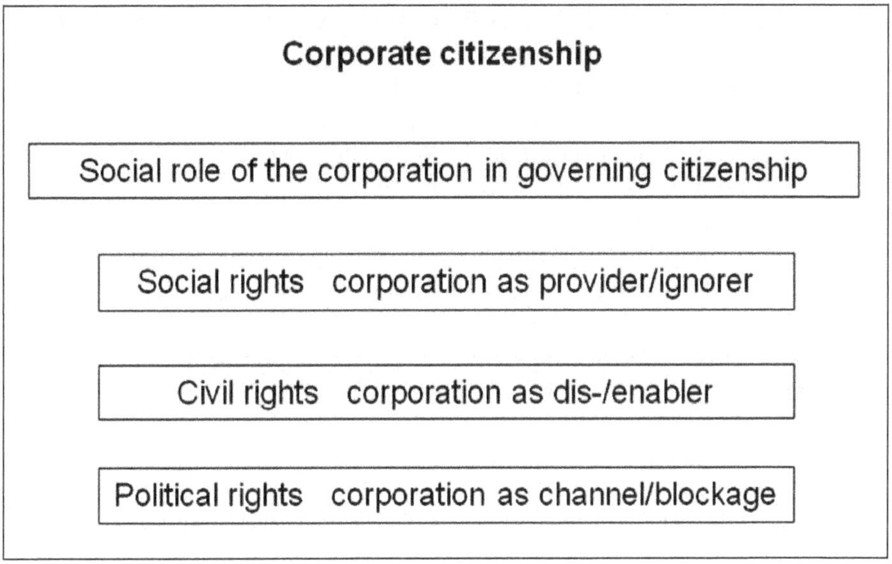

```
┌─────────────────────────────────────────────────────────────┐
│                 Corporate citizenship                        │
│                                                              │
│   ┌──────────────────────────────────────────────────────┐  │
│   │  Social role of the corporation in governing citizenship │
│   └──────────────────────────────────────────────────────┘  │
│                                                              │
│      ┌───────────────────────────────────────────────────┐  │
│      │  Social rights   corporation as provider/ignorer   │  │
│      └───────────────────────────────────────────────────┘  │
│                                                              │
│      ┌───────────────────────────────────────────────────┐  │
│      │  Civil rights   corporation as dis-/enabler         │  │
│      └───────────────────────────────────────────────────┘  │
│                                                              │
│      ┌───────────────────────────────────────────────────┐  │
│      │  Political rights   corporation as channel/blockage │  │
│      └───────────────────────────────────────────────────┘  │
│                                                              │
└─────────────────────────────────────────────────────────────┘
```

Figure 14.5 Components of corporate citizenship

Source: Crane and Matten (2005, p. 173).

for individuals. For example, a company that secures a clean FSC-based audit report and eco-label is deemed to have adequately protected the following rights of an individual as stated in Principles 2–4 in Figure 14.1:

- **Principle 2: Tenure and Use Rights and Responsibilities**
  Long-term tenure and use rights to land and forest resources shall be clearly defined, documented and legally established.
- **Principle 3: Indigenous People's Rights**
  The legal and customary rights of indigenous peoples to own, use, and manage their lands, territories and resources shall be recognized and respected.
- **Principle 4: Community Relations and Workers' Rights**
  Forest management operations shall maintain or enhance the long-term social economic well-being of forest workers and local communities.

In particular, compliance with Principle 4 indicates that the company is a provider of social rights of individuals. Similarly, companies that comply with Principle 3 are assuming an enabling role in securing some of the civil rights of indigenous people (for example, the right to own property).

But the role of the corporation as a conduit for the exercise of the political rights of citizens is more complex and will be considered later here in the context of protests by stakeholder advocacy groups and consumer boycotts aimed at companies that engage in unethical or unsustainable operations.

Fair Trade Labelling Schemes and Corporate Citizenship

Fair trade labelling initiatives also offer a useful framework for operationalizing the extended view of corporate citizenship developed by Matten and Crane (2005) because they enhance the role of the corporation in administering citizenship rights.

The Fairtrade Foundation is the most prominent advocacy group that seeks greater equity in international coffee trade not only by arguing that world market prices do not reflect the real value of the commodity but also by launching campaigns that have compelled the world's leading coffee sellers, such as Starbucks and Procter & Gamble, to consider ethical coffee brands that guarantee a minimum 'fair trade' price (as established by stakeholder advocacy groups) of 126 cents per pound to coffee farmers (Raymond, 2003, p. 1):

> *Small-scale coffee farmers around the world scored a victory this week when Procter & Gamble (NYSE: PG), the largest seller of coffee in the U.S., announced that it would introduce Fair Trade Certified™ coffee products through its specialty coffee division, Millstone.*

The announcement comes in response to dialogue with shareholders about the company's practices, as well as pressure from consumers, people of faith, human rights activists and humanitarian organizations. With P&G's announcement that it will offer Fair Trade Certified™ coffee through Millstone, the advocacy groups have agreed to suspend their campaigns against the corporation and the shareholders have withdrawn the resolution they had filed on the issue.

'With world market prices as low as they are right now, we see that many coffee farmers cannot maintain their families and their land anymore. We need Fair Trade now more than ever,' says Jerónimo Bollen, Director of Manos Campesinas, a Fair Trade Certified™ coffee cooperative in Guatemala. Over the past three years, the price of coffee has fallen almost 50 per cent, and now hovers near a 30-year low. This has resulted in a widespread humanitarian crisis for 25 million coffee-growing families in over 50 developing countries. Unable to cover their costs of production, small farmers cannot earn the income necessary to feed their families, send their children to school, purchase essential medicines and stay on their land.

The graph in Figure 14.6 illustrates the contrasts between world market coffee prices that fell dramatically below production costs over the past decade, ruining the lives and livelihood of peasant farmers, and the minimum 'fair trade' price of 126 cents per lb. Farmers who want to sell their coffee beans at the fair trade price (that is, at least 126 cents per lb), as opposed to the relatively low and volatile world market price, would have to comply with a set of very detailed standards established by the Fairtrade Labelling Organisation that cover *inter alia*:

- membership of democratic co-operative organizations;
- non-use of child labour in coffee farms;
- non-use of forced or slave labour;
- non-use of pesticides and fertilizers that contribute to environmental degradation, and so on (see Fairtrade Labelling Organisation, 2003, for details).

Figure 14.6 World Market price for Arabica coffee: 2000–2002

Compliance with these criteria is ascertained by way of a third-party audit of farming operations carried out by accredited coffee auditors under the fairtrade labelling scheme, the modalities of which are broadly similar to those of other audit assurance schemes established by the Forest Stewardship Council. Furthermore, part of the fair trade premium (referred to as the social premium) is earmarked for socio-economic development (for example, healthcare facilities, clean water supply, education, sanitation and other community projects) and spending decisions are made under the auspices of farmers' cooperative organizations. This means that, in principle, the premium over conventional market price will, at least, make a modest contribution toward the internalization of some externalities, poverty alleviation and protection of the environment.

As such, companies that promote the fair trade agenda are not only providers of social rights of individuals in coffee producing countries, or enablers of some civil rights, but they also play a channelling role as conduits for the exercise of the political rights of citizens. For example, the consumer boycotts and anti-corporate protests which compelled major coffee sellers, such as Starbucks and Procter and Gamble, to adopt fair trade brands, encapsulate this point.

Similarly, in the context of FSC-based audits, a more comprehensive case study of a forestry company (Leroy Gabon) will be used to illustrate the role of the corporation as a conduit for the exercise of the political rights of individuals in the next section of this chapter. However, it is important to point out that, thus far, we have only provided practical illustrations of Matten and Crane's descriptive conceptualization of corporate citizenship. We have not considered the reasons why companies might embrace the corporate citizenship agenda. This point will be taken into account later in this chapter when we analyse implications of the Leroy Gabon.

Case Study on the implementation of the FSC's Auditing Scheme in Leroy Gabon

Leroy Gabon is a subsidiary company of Isoroy, a French company owned by a German conglomerate known as Glunz AG. Leroy's logging concession in Gabon is located at the heart of the Congo basin rainforest which harbours a large diversity of flora and fauna including substantial populations of primates, elephants and other large animals. According to Knight (1997), this forest ranks alongside those of the Amazon as some of the most biologically diverse in the world (further details on this case study can be found in Elad, 2000, chapter 5).

In response to consumer demands in the European plywood market, the company invited Société Générale de Surveillance (SGS), an FSC-accredited auditor, to audit its forest management practices with a view to securing the right to use an eco-label that would enhance marketability of its wood products. SGS audited Leroy's operations in *La forêt des Abeilles*, an area of primary rainforest of extremely high biological value, and subsequently issued a certificate that would warrant Leroy Gabon to use an FSC-backed eco-label. This move infuriated domestic stakeholders and also sparked widespread outrage amongst environmental pressure groups and NGOs who fiercely contested the issuance of the eco-label.

The following passages from a communiqué captioned 'Good Intentions Betray Gabon Rainforest' that was issued by the Rainforest Action Network[3] encapsulate the key issues at stake:

> An African rainforest that is home to scores of endangered species, including the rare lowland gorilla, is about to be logged mercilessly with the approval of the world's largest certifier of 'sustainable' timber.

> ... logging is about to begin with the blessing of an organization that should be preventing it. The Forest Stewardship Council (FSC) was established in 1993 to help ensure the protection of the world's remaining primary forests through timber certification programmes. The FSC accredits auditors around the world, who in turn examine logging operations and determine if they can be called 'certified'. Principle 9 of the FSC guidelines indicates that to be considered 'certified', a logging operation must not destroy primary forest. Yet the FSC-approved certifier, SGS, has given Leroy the green light to log, even though much of the planned logging will take place in primary forest.

The approval process for Leroy Gabon has been clouded by sloppy accounting and conflict of interests from the very beginning. Even though FSC rules require a certification programme to be independent from the rest of the forest industry, SGS has other divisions that stand to profit from contracts with governments and multinational corporations.

---

3   This communiqué was published at the Rainforest Action Network website http://forests.org/gopher/africa/gabongoo.txt (dated 11th September 1997).

Despite this, FSC Executive Director Tim Synnott dismissed international outrage over the certification, embracing the Leroy logging as 'good forest management'.

However, following intense lobbying and sustained pressure from campaigns launched by a number of environmental activist groups spearheaded by Friends of the Earth (UK) and Rettet den Regenwald (Germany), the FSC finally yielded. In an unprecedented development, the FSC certification (and thus eco-label) awarded to Leroy Gabon was initially frozen, then subsequently suspended and revoked. These episodes in the Leroy Gabon case are now considered.

On 15 August 1996, Friends of the Earth (UK) and Rettet den Regenwald (Germany) wrote to Dr Tim Synnott, Executive Director of the FSC, requesting that the certification of Leroy's operations in *La forêt des Abeilles* by SGS be forestalled because at least three major FSC principles were violated. The first infringement was that the company was logging in a primary rainforest of exceptionally high biological value (that is, violation of FSC Principle 9). Secondly, it was noted that the clean audit report and resultant certificate that SGS intended to issue would cover the company's proposed logging in a protected area known as the Lope Reserve which was illegal under Gabonese law (that is, violation of FSC Principle 1). The third infringement of FSC principles related to a lack of information on the impact of the company's operations outside the Lope Reserve where one scientific study had indicated an 80 per cent drop in chimpanzee populations in the five years since logging started (that is, violation of FSC Principle 6 and Principle 8).

Friends of the Earth articulated these and other concerns in a number of protest letters and faxes to the FSC Executive Director from August 1996 to November 1996. In February 1997, five Gabonese NGOs pointed out in a series of press conferences and communiqués that the audit of Leroy's operations carried out by SGS manifested major infringements to FSC regulations (Kiekens, 1997, p. 19). These NGOs claimed that at least five out of the nine FSC principles were glaringly violated. Accordingly, they went on to press for: (i) revocation of Leroy's audit certificate, and (ii) loss of accreditation of SGS from the FSC.

In response to these impassioned demands, the FSC Secretariat announced a freeze on Leroy's certification pending further investigations. Following these investigations, the Secretariat issued a document entitled 'FSC Evaluation of Complaints against SGS Forestry Certificate issued to Leroy Gabon' (hereafter, the Evaluation Report) which formed the basis for a subsequent ruling that Leroy's certification be de-frozen. This new development incensed many stakeholders and environmental activist organizations who once again embarked on a fierce and well coordinated protest (see, for example, Figure 14.7) which raged for several months until the FSC was finally compelled to revoke the certificate and provisionally suspend SGS.

The following environmental activist organizations and NGOs around the world vigorously denounced the Secretariat's Evaluation Report and called on the FSC board to decertify Leroy Gabon immediately: Friends of the Earth (UK), Rettet den Regenwald (Germany), Greenpeace (Switzerland), Reforest the Earth (UK), CIAJE (Gabon), Greenpeace International (Holland), FERN (UK), Rainforest Action Network (USA), Environmental Defense Fund (USA), Greenpeace (Germany) and Rainforest Information Centre (Australia).

On 21 July 1997, these complainants criticized Leroy's certification in a joint protest letter to FSC board members, pointing out that it violated Principles 1, 5, 6, 7, 8 and 9. There was considerable disagreement within the FSC membership as to how Principle 9

Dear Ms Erwin

I am writing to express my dismay over the Forest Stewardship Council's approval of the Leroy logging concession in Gabon, an operation that independent agencies show will destroy primary forest. By allowing the certification of this cutting, FSC will be giving its blessing to a project that will imperil endangered species, including the lowland gorilla. Calling such a venture "sustainable" lets deforestation pass as environmental action. The FSC should withdraw its support from Leroy in its current form.

I urge you to pass this information on to the FSC board, and to take a stand as FSC's US representative to end this wasteful, destructive venture.

Sincerely,

Figure 14.7 Sample protest letter recommended by the Rainforest Action Network

Source: Rainforest Action Network website.

should be interpreted. Furthermore, SGS conceded in its audit report that adequate data on the growth and structure of the forest did not exist, thus endorsing the complainants' charge that environmental impact assessment was not carried out as required under Principle 6. Also, according to Friends of the Earth, the research station that produced much of the data that Leroy Gabon uses to justify its operations was supported by the company itself, and thus raises serious questions regarding its independence.

In view of the issues outlined above and other infringement of FSC principles that were clearly articulated in protest letters, the FSC board finally ruled in favour of the complainants on 2 October 1997. The board decided that: (i) Leroy Gabon's certificate and right to use an FSC-backed eco-label for marketing its wood be revoked immediately; (ii) SGS should be publicly sanctioned for performance not in compliance with FSC principles; and (iii) the Chair of the FSC Board of Directors review its procedure for handling complaints with the assistance of an outside consultant.

Some Implications of the Leroy Gabon Case for Corporate Social Responsibility and the Extended Theoretical Conceptualization of Corporate Citizenship

This case study provides another illustration of the role of the corporation as a conduit for the exercise of the political rights of individuals as suggested in the extended theoretical conceptualization of corporate citizenship by Matten and Crane (2005). For example, it is likely that some individuals who, for whatever reason, do not participate in national politics might be willing to participate in political action aimed at corporations rather than at governments, such as consumer boycotts and anti-corporate protest.

In the Leroy Gabon case, it was noted that green consumers, environmental campaigners and many NGOs around the world actively used a failed FSC audit as a platform for launching anti-corporate protests which finally halted the unsustainable operations of the company.

The role of NGOs in championing anti-corporate protests aimed at biodiversity conservation and environmental protection, in the public interest, indicates that some of the traditional functions of the State are now undertaken by private sector entities. In general terms, this declining role of the State was described by Beck (1996) as the rise of subpolitics – that is, forms of politics outside and beyond the representative institutions of the political system of nation-states (see, for example, Holzer and Sørensen, 2003).

In the case study, the environmental campaigners, NGOs and green consumers, want to protect the environment. Leroy Gabon wants to maximize its profit by pursuing its enlightened self-interest. The government of Gabon wants to increase the revenue it receives from timber exploitation. These conflicting stakeholder interests suggest different expectations regarding forest stewardship audit. Indeed, some stakeholders have even challenged the credibility of the FSC's auditing guidelines, thus revealing a number of areas where the institutional arrangements that currently exist for financial audits are remarkably similar to those which have evolved in forest stewardship audits. In particular, many of the problems associated with financial audit procedures (for example, establishment of auditing standards, qualifications in audit reports, expectations gap, problems of independence and so on), and their organizational impact (for example, in relation to corporate governance) also arise in the context of forest stewardship audits.

The FSC's formalized auditing procedures embodied in its principles and criteria constitute a social construction of auditability in line with Hines (1989) and Power (1997). For example, Power (1997, p. 309) notes:

... not only do audits create and reinforce the conditions for their own functioning, but they seek to do so by creating a new bureaucratic 'surface' or social reality which is highly standardized and which represents the auditee for the purpose of the audit.

This social constructivism could, to some extent, explain the major dispute regarding interpretation of FSC principles in the Leroy Gabon case from the standpoint of forest auditors (SGS), stakeholders (for example, Friends of the Earth, Rainforest Alliance and other environmental campaigners), and the FSC itself. Furthermore, it not only suggests an implicit 'expectations gap' between the social and environmental objectives of stakeholders and those that are achievable via FSC-based audits, but also portrays the kind of ambiguity associated with the 'true and fair view' audit qualification.

In order to define the phrase 'well managed', a series of public consultations was initiated by the FSC in 1993 that included formal hearings in Malaysia, Sweden, Peru, the United States and six other countries (Upton and Bass, 1996). In addition, FSC working parties comprising experts in economic, environmental and social issues, from both industrialized countries and less developed countries, carried out a large-scale questionnaire survey and subsequently convened on a number of occasions to revise draft 'principles' based on the information received. At least one of these principles was revised over nine times before being overwhelmingly approved by a formal vote in 1994. The broad range of countries and social constituencies represented in the FSC General Assembly – producers, traders, retailers, consumer groups, indigenous peoples, environmentalists and so on – highlight the social construction of auditability here.

Some interest groups (for example, the Timber Trade Federation, American Forest and Paper Association and small forest managers) have developed their own forest auditing standards, with different definitions of 'well managed', in order to avoid the perceived undesirable economic consequences of the FSC approach (see, for example, Urry, 1997). For example, WWF (1994, p. 19) explain:

> One might think that moves to improve the sustainability of forestry and timber trading would have been joined wholeheartedly by the trade and their representatives. However, in general the timber trade is a proud and deeply conservative business, and has not taken kindly to criticism. The frustration felt by environmentalists who have seen the horrors of unsustainable logging has increasingly led to acrimony and, on occasion, diversion from the most important issues.

Although the lack of agreement or consensus over the definition of 'well managed' has led to a proliferation of eco-labelling and certification schemes, the FSC model is currently the only one recommended by WWF, the World Bank and the European Union. The social constructivist nature of these forest auditing schemes might suggest that they portray a form of ideological 'green washing' and also present some of the problems associated with financial audits identified by Power (1995, pp. 320-321):

> With the possible exception of statistical sampling, auditing does not seem to have a knowledge base. ... Thus, the consensus of 'more experienced' auditors in performing an audit task which is well defined in the professional literature merely tells us that they are capable of reproducing officially sanctioned programmes based upon prescribed procedures. If we have doubts about the knowledge system which is constituted by these accepted procedures, then such a consensus is of little value. Indeed in such circumstances, it may be the minority dissenting judgements which deserve intellectual attention.

Conclusion and Implications

This chapter has demonstrated that the product certification schemes instituted by the Fair Trade Labelling Organization and the Forest Stewardship Council are essentially blueprints for corporate social responsibility and corporate citizenship. In particular, the way in which consumer-driven audits sanctioned by the FSC can be used to operationalize the extended theoretical conceptualization of corporate citizenship by Matten and Crane (2005) was explained. Nonetheless, it was also noted that the FSC's scheme can be used to defend a company's enlightened self-interest or to manage stakeholder relations.

Furthermore, although we have argued here that these audit assurance initiatives are frameworks for corporate citizenship, this does not necessarily mean that companies that engage in corporate social responsibility activities orchestrated by ethical investors and stakeholder advocacy organizations are actually demonstrating a genuine commitment to the public interest. Indeed, as Fridell (2006, p. 11) observes, many multinational coffee retailers have devoted only an insignificant percentage of their turnover to fair trade brands in order to secure positive publicity whilst continuing to carry on business-as-usual in the vast majority of their other operations.

But Elad (2007) used the Marxist notion of commodity fetishism, which refers to one aspect of ideology in capitalist societies, namely the tendency for social relationships (for example, the labour of coffee farmers) to appear as relationships between things (that is, reification), to analyze the potentially positive role of the product certification initiatives of the fair trade movement. In this context, social relations at the level of production appear to be imperceptible whereas the everyday phenomena of market-mediated commodity exchanges are clearly visible. However, the mission of product certification and labelling organizations is to subvert the reification of commodity fetishes by making the social and environmental conditions under which commodities are produced a visible part of the products. For example, the fair trade movement makes a modest contribution in helping to reduce alienation by bringing the plight of peasant farmers in far-flung corners of the globe to the attention of altruistic consumers in industrialized countries who demonstrate empathy and solidarity by their willingness to pay a price premium to alleviate the inequities of free trade.

References

Beck, U. (1992), *Risk Society: Towards a New Modernity*. London: Sage.

Beck, U. (1996), 'World Risk Society as Cosmopolitan Society? Ecological Questions in a Framework of Manufactured Uncertainties', *Theory, Culture & Society*, 13:4, 1-32. Carroll, A.B. (1991), 'The pyramid of corporate social responsibility: toward the moral management of organisational stakeholders', *Business Horizons*, August, 39-48.

Carroll, A.B. and Buchholtz, A.K. (2000), *Business & Society: Ethics and Stakeholder Management*. Cincinnati: South-Western College Publishing.

Crane, A. and Matten, D. (2007), *Business Ethics: Managing Corporate Citizenship and Sustainability in the Age of Globalization*, 2nd Edition. Oxford: Oxford University Press.

Elad, C. (2000), *Environmental Accounting for Sustainable Development*. London: Chartered Institute of Management Accountants, CIMA publishing.

Elad, C. (2001), 'Auditing and Governance in the Forestry Industry: Between Protest and Professionalism', *Critical Perspectives on Accounting*, 12:5, 647-671.

Elad, C. (2007), 'Fair Value Accounting and Fair Trade: An Analysis of the Role of International Accounting Standard No. 41 in Social Conflict', *Socio-Economic Review*, 5:4, 755-777.

Fairtrade Labelling Organisation (2003), *Standards and Certification* posted at http://www.fairtrade.net/ (accessed, May 2007).

Fridell, G. (2006), 'Fair Trade and Neoliberalism: Assessing Emerging Perspectives', *Latin American Perspectives*, 33, 8-28.

Hansen, E. (1997), 'Forest Certification and its Role in Marketing Strategy', *Forest Products Journal*, 47:3, 16-22.

Hines, R. (1989), 'Financial Accounting Knowledge, Conceptual Framework Projects, and the Social Construction of the Accounting Profession', *Accounting, Auditing and Accountability Journal*, 2:2, 72-92.

Holzer, B and Sørensen M. (2003), 'Rethinking Subpolitics: Beyond the "Iron Cage" of Modern Politics?', *Theory, Culture & Society*, 20:2, 79-102.

Kell, G. (2005), 'The Global Compact: Selected Experiences and Reflection', *Journal of Business Ethics*, 59, 69-79.

Kiekens, J.P. (1997), 'Certification: International Trends and Forestry Trade Implications', Study Presented by Environmental Strategies Europe to the Ministère de l'Environnement des Ressources Naturelles et de l'Agriculture de la Région Wallone, Brussels.

Knight, D. (1997), 'Forest Council Takes Actiuon Against Logging Company in Gabon', InterPress Service, Internet posting, 21st November.

Matten, D. and Crane A. (2005), 'Corporate Citizenship: Towards an extended theoretical conceptualization', *Academy of Management Review*, 30:1, 166-179.

Power, M. (1995), 'Auditing, Expertise, and the Sociology of Technique', *Critical Perspectives on Accounting*, 6, 317-339.

Power, M. (1997), *The Audit Society: Rituals of Verification*. Oxford: Oxford University Press.

Power, M. (1999), *The Audit Society: Rituals of Verification*, 2nd edition. Oxford: Oxford University Press.

Power, M. (2007), *Organized Uncertainty: Designing a World of Risk Management*. Oxford: Oxford University Press.

Raymond, N (2003), 'Advocacy Groups and Shareholders Persuade Procter & Gamble to Offer Fair Trade Coffee' *Oxfam America Press Release* posted at http://www.oxfamamerica.org/news/art6123.html (accessed September 2003).

Swift, T.A., Humphrey, C. and Gor V. (2000), 'Great Expectations?: The Dubious Financial Legacy of Quality Audits', *British Journal of Management*, 11:1, 31-45.

Upton, C. and Bass, S. (1996), *The Forest Certification Handbook*. London: Earthscan.

Urry, M. (1997), 'World Pulp and Paper: Sustainable Forests—Overcoming Growing Pains', *Financial Times*, December 8, 1997, p. 3.

World Wide Fund For Nature (1994), *Truth or Trickery? Timber Labelling Past and Future,* Godalming: WWF.

15 Decisive Risk Management for Corporate Governance

KURTAY OGUNC

Key Postulates

'Flexibility is not an option to be exercised; rather it is a must for survival!'

'Risk-taking and risk-accepting are distinct ways of capturing value.'

'Optionality is only a subset of flexibility.'

Introduction

For decades, risk management has mainly focused on the quantitative aspects of mathematical modeling due to the apparent need of corporations to minimize the probability of loss. The process of identifying and quantifying various types of risks in the areas of finance and manufacturing resulted in corporations reacting only when something is out of whack, rather than proactively going after uncertainties. There was no mechanism that helped decision makers exploit uncertainties in a proactive manner. In the process, executives have lost sight of the strategic realities, and concentrated on the tactical issues surrounding the operational side of the business. The mathematization[1] of risk management started naturally in the insurance field, which relies heavily on the correct pricing of risks. Other fields that adopted various modeling principles originated in insurance realized over the years that (i) quantification has its limits, (ii) data could be flawed or simply wrong and (iii) rare events are very difficult to predict.

Buehler and Pritsch (2003) argue that many companies have never articulated a *risk strategy*. Certain setbacks taught some business leaders to go back to the drawing board and start from scratch. It is difficult to argue with the following statement: If a corporation is more passive on *risk taking* than the competitors, it faces the inevitable risk of losing its competitive edge, which is very difficult to reverse once the downward spiral

---

1   The act of reducing to mathematical formulas. Gerard Debreu delivered a presidential address entitled 'The Mathematization of Economic Theory' at the 1990 AEA meeting.

takes place. More importantly, these early adopters realized that risk is not a by-product of the corporate decision making. Rather, it must be the starting point of the strategic management process. In other words, they accepted the fact that *risk taking* precedes *risk management*. There is a need to incorporate both the quantitative and qualitative aspects of corporate management and decision making. To this end, tools and techniques for proper risk taking should be built and implemented to yield a robust framework, in the form of a decisive risk management system. Lorsch and Clark (2008) raise excellent points regarding the responsibilities of directors of corporate boards. The following three quotes serve as a motivation of my proposals in this paper: (i) 'As directors have become more hands-on with compliance, they've become more hands-off with long-range planning, exposing shareholders to another kind of risk.' (ii) 'Most directors will say they squeeze some time into their meetings to discuss what they call "strategic matters." In most cases, however, they're actually talking tactics.' (iii) 'Directors must get serious about their role in ensuring the development of the next generation of senior leaders at their organizations.' They conclude the article by stating the obvious: '... to help their companies grow and prosper, not just in the next quarter but in the next decade and beyond.' I hope to start a discussion about the possible direction a company might take to bring corporate governance to a higher dimension.

I concur with Bowman and Hurry (1993) who argue that an organization can be viewed to function as a bundle of options for strategic choices. The strategic decision-making process should be based around a conceptually sound and analytical construct to integrate learning, risk taking, and timing for an effective synthesis between resource allocation and strategy development. The ability to properly assess the value of strategic investments has proven particularly useful for obtaining a sustainable competitive advantage. Corporations are facing intense competitive pressure and significant uncertainty in a chaotic business environment. What makes the business environment more chaotic and complex is the kind of uncertainty some scholars call endogenous. Kurz (1974) introduced the concept of endogenous uncertainty, which is propagated within a system by the beliefs and actions of agents rather than by exogenous forces. There is widespread evidence that exogenous sources of uncertainty do not account for much of market volatility. Kurz (1994) argues that correlation of heterogeneous beliefs is the essential cause of endogenous uncertainty and forms the basis for the theory of rational beliefs. Chichilnisky and Wu (2006) provide a model in which financial innovation directly produces further uncertainty and prevents the completion of the markets. Central to their analysis is the endogenous generation of uncertainty caused by default. More specifically, Chichilnisky et al. (1995) concludes that the introduction of mortgages and mortgage-backed assets causes endogenous economic uncertainty by altering the set of possible states, that is, the state space. The recent bailout of Bear Stearns by JP Morgan should be very telling about the challenges the economic system faces going forward. The formation of the real estate bubble was the result of some players in the economy taking advantage of the creative packaging of these loans. What is so surprising is the fact that Bear Stearns is believed to have one of the most sophisticated risk management systems in the market. How did this complicated system miss the increasing possibility of bankruptcy? The answer lies in the notion of endogenous uncertainty, which could not be properly priced to make sound decisions by the top management team. Board members could not envision the downward spiral effect of the tactical actions by the decision makers at Bear Stearns. In a completely different setting, Bak et al. (1988) demonstrates numerically that dynamical systems with extended spatial degrees of freedom in two or three dimensions naturally evolve into 'self-organized' critical states, which are robust to variations of parameters, specification of initial conditions and the presence of quenched randomness. I would argue that self-organized criticality is the essence of endogeneity, and it was the endogenous uncertainty that Knight (1921) was referring to when he outlined the differences between risk and uncertainty. Massey and Wu (2005) develop the so-called 'system-neglect hypothesis' in an attempt to correctly detect and respond to regime shifts. The postulate is that individuals react primarily to the signals they observe and secondarily to the environmental system that produced the signal. Their research suggests a very specific way in which individuals are quasi-Bayesian, and calls for greater attention to the precision of market information about valuation-relevant parameters as well as the stability of those parameters.

An Overview of Corporate Risk Management

On the 'operational' side of corporations, the computation of 'failure probability' has long been the cornerstone of modeling of technical risks as they pertain to failure of products, equipments, as well as infrastructure. Quality assurance and quality control techniques are designed to mitigate risks associated with product design and development, and minimize the probability of ending up with unsatisfied customers. Corporations have been aware of the significance and complexity of the 'demand process,' which embeds endogenous and exogenous features, and relied on risk reduction and mitigation strategies. This has led to prevalent methodologies such as Six Sigma, Lean Processes, Total Quality Management (TQM), and Statistical Process Control (SPC). The general idea is to eliminate as many disturbances as possible by a very rigorous approach and to define safety margins for variations which occur from pure randomness. This orientation is triggered by the concern of efficiency and competitiveness as it relates to different manufacturing processes, such as Just-in-Time, Push and Pull, Kanban Systems, Lean Processes, and so on. In this setting, supply chains are considered as value streams and these processes try to eliminate waste. Risks considered are those related to the variability of the service time, which affects the cycle time and the performance of the system. Reducing variability in the performance is addressed by Six Sigma and Quality Function Deployment methodologies, whereas SPC permits the detection of abnormal variability.

It is worthwhile to mention also the abundant literature available in civil engineering in the context of ruin of structures. It has a lot of similarities with technical risks considered in Operations Management, and also in the modeling of default of firms. Over the last decade, there has been a remarkable development of risk methodology with respect to the treatment of hazards (in particular seismic) that could result in serious consequences with respect to public safety. It is either structural, which relates to a building's ability to resist collapse, or non-structural, which includes falling hazards. Prediction of severity of earthquakes and their impact on infrastructure proves to be a fruitful area of research. It is interesting to note that the default of firms is modeled using techniques from reliability engineering and life data analysis, and more recently, Sornette (2003) tackles the issue of stock market crashes using techniques and models from the field of earthquake prediction.

Maintenance management is a related research topic. It can be complicated from lack of sufficient resources, as one cannot perform all desired maintenance actions simultaneously. The process should include the ranking of maintenance actions to implement an effective risk mitigation strategy. Despite the apparent complexities, maintenance management is vital in ensuring that corporate assets are handled in an optimal way, resulting in higher asset turnover ratios due to better asset utilization. Thornton (2004) argues that the traditional approach does not provide the necessary tools to create a coherent risk management platform. She proposes a new methodology, Variation Risk Management (VRM), which is based on two fundamental concepts: (i) a holistic view of variation, and (ii) the identification, assessment, and mitigation (I-A-M) process. VRM can be applied either proactively in the product development process or to an existing product. This new methodology requires the integration and participation of all functional groups that have influence over product quality, including design engineering, manufacturing, quality, system engineering, customers, procurement, and suppliers. In other words, the main deficiency is the lack of system approach. The complexity of systems is the major source of difficulties. The fact that parts of a system are performing in a satisfactory manner does not guarantee at all that the system will perform according to expectations.

Another main drawback of traditional approaches is that they do not take into consideration the level of risk aversion in a precise way. As an example in the domain of maintenance, Baker (2006) introduced the concept of a risk-averse maintenance policy. She applies principal-agent theory to the case of a maintenance engineer (the agent) who over-maintains equipment due to excessive risk aversion. She shows that incentives based on the total cost of maintenance and failures can reduce over-maintenance, and it may be optimal for management to pay such an incentive.

In view of the evolution of the supply chain organization, new types of risks have appeared and they are not addressed by traditional approaches. In particular, outsourcing has become a substantial part of the supply chain. Corresponding risks are underestimated by corporations. Uncertainties in availability and price of outsourced components should be tackled more systematically to eliminate unforeseen discontinuities in supply. Moreover, over the years, we have witnessed an increasing number of disruptions in supply and demand in the form of third-party interference, labor strikes, natural hazards, human errors, technological failures, terrorist attacks, and financial scandals. Lee and Wolfe (2003) suggest the following mitigation strategies for disruption risks: comprehensive tracking and monitoring, total supply network visibility, flexible sourcing strategies, and product and process redesign. Another way to reduce disruption risk is the formation of a supply alliance network, which is a collection of strategic alliances with other suppliers in different countries. Tang (2006) argues that these alliances can serve as a safety net for each member, who will receive help from other members if a disruption happens.

The decentralized treatment of the risk management process does not take advantage of dependencies among risk factors. In addition, it resulted in a reactive form of decision making, not enabling corporations to utilize risk management as a value-added tool. Over the last decade, many corporations have benefited from economically thoughtful processes that add more value to the bottom line than the risk they generate. Thus, treasurers and CFOs learned to consider the risk-adjusted return potential of an action they plan on taking rather than the traditional 'hedge away' as much risk as possible attitude. They are also learning that risk is bad if and only if it is mismanaged, misunderstood, or unintended. The fact that financial risks cannot be limited to purely external factors like interest rates or currency exchange rates has led to the concept of Enterprise Risk Management (ERM). It is intended to support strategic planning, to include risk avoidance as well as risk exploitation, to function in an integrated framework with consolidated reporting, and to provide open communication and continuous re-evaluation with responsibilities clearly defined at the outset. The integration and coordination of risk across various sources and domains has value-added implications for manufacturing firms as combining risk exposures and diversification among risk factors. However, this 'aggregation,' which arises in an effort to build integrated or enterprise-wide risk management systems within organizations is a hard task. There may be bad consequences resulting from inappropriate assumptions about risk factor dependencies. Mulvey and Erkan (2006) argue that centralized risk management in the form of ERM is impractical for large multinational corporations due to informational limits and complex local regulations within each country, making a division's optimal solution quite different than the solution of the enterprise-wide optimization problem. By utilizing the Conditional Value-at-Risk (CVaR) measure, they introduce a decentralized risk management strategy based on a stochastic optimization model with a particular emphasis on insurance companies.

The insurance problems have originated many models and concepts. The main issue now is to go beyond the sphere of 'insurable risks.' An important aspect concerns bundling insurance coverage into a single product, which hedges across a number of sources of risk. Inside corporations this concern has led to the idea of an 'insurance manager' with the responsibility of transferring, retaining, reducing, or avoiding risk to reduce the expected value of losses. The issue of insuring catastrophes originated from terrorism or natural hazards is now a big problem, for which few operational methods exist. A catastrophe can also come from changing behavior of consumers, aggressive competition, or globalization.

Decisive Risk Management

Various corporate scandals have led to the Sarbanes-Oxley Act of 2002 (SOX), requiring listed companies to use risk management systems for the understanding of questionable business activities, and thereby, minimizing the possibility of unforeseen events that might result in the possible bankruptcy of the corporation. Butler and Ribstein (2006) demonstrate that SOX has been a colossal failure since its enactment, imposing additional net losses to financial markets totaling $1.4 trillion. My proposals aim at resolving some of the issues that are said to lead to an unacceptable level of indirect costs, such as (i) diverting executives' attention from maximizing shareholder value, (ii) increasing risk aversion by decision makers, and (iii) distorting executives' and directors' incentives and investment decisions. Prudent corporate governance requires that there is intelligent risk taking by the C-level executives. The key for successful oversight and control begins with the evaluation of possible risk exposures that the corporation chooses to sustain its competitive edge in coming decades. After all, risk taking proceeds risk management. In other words, the wealth of shareholders is maximized, which is the main tenet of corporate governance, by taking on risks that are exploitable by the corporation and harnessing uncertainties in a proactive manner. I put 'decisive' in front of risk management to indicate the significance of decision making for corporate governance. The emphasis should be on building robust and flexible decision-making processes rather than putting all of our eggs into the basket of risk management. The recent collapse of Bear Stearns was an eye opener for many executives, who have been spending millions of dollars on risk management systems to adhere to SOX policies and to show that risks are under control. A political pundit recently offered the following comparison between the collapse of Bear Stearns and that of Enron: 'The fall of Bear Stearns will make the fall of Enron look like the fall of a lemonade stand!'

There are many methodologies and theories from various fields of knowledge waiting to be embraced by corporate decision makers. It is my belief that unless people who are responsible for corporate governance, namely board members, take a stand and demand for a transparent decision making platform, there will be no end to corporate scandals in all sectors of the economy. The complexity of decision making at the CEO level arises due to the fact that one should know simultaneously (i) how to diversify the bets taken, (ii) which risk factors to hedge, to mitigate or to accept, and (iii) how to manage a portfolio of real and shadow options. Moreover, some of these decisions are interrelated over time and space, as well as cover very distant domains and disciplines. Decisive Risk Management proposes a different organizational structure, which includes the Chief Flexibility Officer, who makes sure that the risk preferences of board members are embedded in the decision-making process. This individual should have a transdisciplinary mind and a transformative corporate management style.

Decisive Risk Management presents transdisciplinarity[2] to corporate executives and board members as an integrating mechanism to bring together disparate elements of knowledge in various disciplines. To that end, Manderson (2000) argues that the aim of bringing together diverse disciplines in a transdisciplinary project is not to transcend that knowledge base rather to transform it. I define transdisciplinarity to mean the conversion of information into knowledge through the mind traveling across various disciplines and reaching knowledge outside the disciplines. The fragmentation of knowledge by compartmentalizing it into 'disciplines' is an ineffective way to advance and unite knowledge within the social sciences. Disciplines, when left in isolation, cannot cope with the real world complexity, which requires a coherent framework to transform the boundaries between disciplines and beyond. There is a need for a progressive yet harmonious decision-making apparatus to deal with the chaotic and complex business environment. When we figure out how to efficiently integrate knowledge across disciplines, we could approach 'completeness' in the sense of mastering and harnessing knowledge. What makes transdisciplinarity unique and cohesive is the ability to simultaneously expand both the breadth and depth of knowledge. In one of the great books of the twentieth century, 'Consilience,' the Pulitzer prize-winning author, Edward Wilson (1998) makes the argument that social scientists spurn the idea of the hierarchical ordering of knowledge that unites and derives the natural sciences. By the same token, familiarity within a specialty makes them lose sight of the 'big picture' and leads to erroneous predictions as well as paradoxical conclusions within the discipline. Spiro et al. (1991) introduced the Cognitive Flexibility Theory to tackle the issues surrounding the deficiencies in learning. They cite oversimplification as a common thread that injects a reductive bias in the learning process. Specifically, they mention the additivity bias,

---

2   Basarab Nicolescu gives an extensive introduction to the subject matter in the 'Manifesto of Transdisciplinarity.' The term itself is believed to be first mentioned by Jean Piaget, the twentieth century Swiss psychologist.

the discreteness bias, and the compartmentalization bias. As far as I am concerned, the authors are in perfect harmony with transdisciplinarity.

The Evolution of Valuation Techniques

Discounted Cash Flow (DCF) analysis implicitly assumes a predetermined strategy that will not change over time. Yet strategic projects involve revisions of decisions as external and internal factors change the scope of the project. This dynamic nature of strategic planning makes it necessary to utilize Real Options Analysis (ROA). Real options allow the re-design of investment strategies along two key dimensions, time and scope. It has been argued that the main reason for the use of real options is the fact that managers can incorporate *flexibility* to make adjustments during the design, development, and implementation phases of a project. For instance, postponing costly investments, particularly related to projects involving a high degree of innovation, permits the corporations to acquire more information and thus mitigate *downside risk*. Having said that, I would like to caution that information must lead to learning and eventually to knowledge before there is a significant probability of limiting the downside risk. The flexibility gained is believed to be in the form of a wider array of choices for future decisions. Most scholars argue that flexibility can be explained by real options that bring to real projects and assets what financial options bring to financial securities and assets. Kulatilaka (1995) argues that incremental contribution of each additional option to project value can be attenuated by substitute options and/or enhanced by complementary options.[3] I would like to reiterate that it is not information per se that is a function of *value of waiting*; rather it is the integral of it, knowledge, which will trigger the second-round investment.

A support area within the organization, such as Risk Intelligence Unit, should be included as part of the corporate decision and risk analysis functions to process information efficiently and effectively. Brashers (2001) noted that *uncertainty management* can be complicated by the nature of information or the intrinsic complexity of information seeking and avoiding. Deloitte & Touche, in its 2006 publication 'The Risk Intelligent Enterprise: ERM Done Right,' proposes corporations to become Risk Intelligent Enterprises by embracing the following principles: (i) the risk management system should be built into decision making, (ii) there should be intelligent risk taking, (iii) conformance with ERM processes is incentivized, and (iv) it should be sustainable.

In the case of new technologies and highly-innovative industries such as biotechnology, aerospace, computers, and health sciences, decision makers immediately realized the limitations of DCF-based valuation methodologies and ventured into the realm of ROA. The ability to manage R&D initiatives has become a paramount task to sustain a competitive edge in these industries. ROA provides a framework to incorporate managerial flexibility into decision making by computing the value of embedded options independently from one and other. What options provide, whether they are financial or real, is the possibility of trading certain risks across investors and corporations that perceive or evaluate those risks in a different manner.

---

3   Substitute options are options to wait-to-invest and options to temporarily shut down, whereas complementary options are options to expand and options to temporarily shut down.

Problems with Real Options Analysis

Sanchez (2003) believes that option theory is useful for valuing the flexibility inherent in managers' investment decisions. However, option theory is only a convenient tool to assess the value of a 'particular form' of flexibility that could potentially be considered by the decision maker. The only way to cope with these issues is to learn to leverage uncertainty. Adner and Levinthal (2004) are concerned that ROA may lead to the underutilization of discoveries made in the course of exploration. More importantly, effective implementation of ROA requires a high degree of rigidity in the specification of the agenda of initiatives and the criteria for their success. It is important to examine what happens to the applicability of options logic as we move away from a world of *wait and see* to a world of *act and see* in which uncertainty resolution is endogenous to firm activity. They cite two main problems with ROA: (i) the impossibility of proving failure, similar to the Popperian argument, and (ii) the absence of formal expiration dates. I would argue that there is a need for some form of *non-classical/non-linear logic*, such as the organic logic of Heraclitus, the intuitionist logic, or the quantum logic, to better take advantage of the strategic and entrepreneurial opportunities and exploit Knightian Uncertainty. The thought process behind ROA relies on classical (linear) logic as articulated by Aristoteles, who formalized the views of Plato and Socrates in a simplifying manner.

The Nobel Laureate, Avinash Dixit, once stated that it is most important to regard the equilibrium of an industry as an organic process over time. He further postulated that drawing inferences from snapshots at particular instants can be seriously misleading. He went on saying that firms that refuse to invest even when the currently available rates of return are far in excess of the cost of capital may be optimally waiting to be surer that this state of affairs is not transitory. In this setting, the value of waiting has nothing to do with risk aversion. It is rather an intertemporal trade-off between present risk and future risk. The possibility of a downturn and the ability to avoid an action that could thereby prove to be a mistake is what makes waiting valuable.

It is important to differentiate innovations that are breakthroughs from existing technologies from those that are radical in nature, changing the whole dynamics of industries. Corporations need to be aware of the interplay between 'incremental' and 'radical' innovations. They have to learn to operate in the Mobile Disequilibrium™, which is a function of complex and highly interacting social, economic, and political factors within the context of bounded rationality, path-dependence, and moving targets. The Mobile Disequilibrium™ construct, closely related to the views by Dixit, enables decision makers to view the world from the perspective of multiple equilibrium constructs. The transitioning from punctuated equilibrium either to an equilibrium state that coheres with classical economic theory or to a completely new equilibrium state requires a more thorough modeling of flexibility. This is particularly important in the case of strategic decision making with regards to decisions surrounding mergers and acquisitions, venture capital investments, and divestitures. Learning has more value if corporations are aware of the particular equilibrium state they are in. This kind of learning results in value-added knowledge, and ultimately, provides a long-term competitive edge. The most successful companies are those that can build unique differential learning capabilities faster than the competition. Going forward, given the fact that most corporations pretty much can learn facts about the economic and business environment, there is a need for corporations to differentiate themselves in learning 'what's not obvious.' I argue that this is only possible if corporations embrace the Mobile Disequilibrium™ construct with intuition, disciplined imagination, and robust mathematical modeling as the main ingredients of the decision toolbox. In short, Mobile Disequilibrium™ incorporates dynamic complexity for making better strategic decisions to grow in a sustainable manner.

Bernanke (1983) came up with the *bad news principle*, which states that of possible future outcomes; only the unfavorable ones have a bearing on the current propensity to undertake a given project. In other words, the downside risk is the primary force governing optimal investment decisions when waiting is possible. ROA also suffers from the *economic hysteresis* as defined by Dixit to mean the failure of investment decisions to reverse themselves when the underlying causes are fully reversed. Moreover, ROA tends to ignore the potential of the firm to mold and enhance initiatives, learn about new opportunities and discover new possible initiatives not conceived at the time of the initial investment. *Endogenous discovery of opportunity structures* is the core challenge for ROA. I agree with Adner and Levinthal, who postulate that real options can only be used to incorporate risk, which is an uncertain realization from a well-specified probability distribution. The strategic environment, on the other hand, embeds the kind of uncertainty Frank Knight has defined in 1921; that is, *the future has no distribution!* The classical statistical estimation is only feasible when the future has a known or an unknown distribution. This important distinction is what makes ROA inadequate, or suboptimal, for strategic decision making.

Another weakness of ROA is that expected payoffs are exogenously determined. The game-theoretic nature of strategic management incorporates strategic interactions, where the actions of competitors have an effect on the decisions of the corporation. The value of waiting versus the strategic plans of competitors should be considered simultaneously as their interaction determines a significant portion of the flexibility value. Moreover, the timing of expiration cannot be specified ex ante. The discrete logical framework of ROA breaks down when target markets and technical agendas are constantly in flux a la Heraclitus.[4] Actors at different levels of the corporation have different perspectives on the attractiveness of a given opportunity due to differences in risk perception and risk-taking preferences. This requires the development of path-dependent processes to proactively capitalize on relevant, available, and unexpected opportunities and to create value-added synergies in a dynamic manner. One needs to go beyond ROA to fully take advantage of exogenous and endogenous opportunities, particularly when there is a high degree of uncertainty and complexity, in other words, when the exit criteria are not apparent.

In settings where the range of responses to the resolution of technical and market uncertainty is largely unconstrained, the utility of applying options logic is unclear. For such strategic investments, in contrast to financial options, exit criteria are not self-evident. Rather, in such circumstances it may be more useful to identify the possible sequence of experiments that will test the promising market and technical paths available to the firm. While real options logic may justify investments that would be rejected under the DCF methodology, these 'justified' investments may well destroy value when implicit assumptions about abandonment flexibility are wrong.

---

4   Around the fifth century B.C., Heraclitus offered the following proposition: 'You don't step into the same river twice.'

Flexibility Theory™ as a Meta-Process

Flexibility Theory™ offers the necessary conceptual framework to tackle the issue of option expiration due to exogenous as well as endogenous forces by building a typology of flexibility and providing a solution in a transdisciplinary manner. I believe that corporations have learned how to process and share information among functional and operational areas of business with the help of ERM. Going forward, they have to find systematic ways to transform information into knowledge, which serves as a prerequisite for wise decision making. The formation of sound belief systems and the issue of belief revisions should be handled within the context of Data-Information-Knowledge-Wisdom (DIKW) path. It was T.S. Eliot who first talked about the importance of this path in The Rock (1934). Unfortunately, most risk professionals and scholars are still working at the information level, and not paying enough attention to the question of what entails knowledge. That is, how can we have enough confidence that decision makers possess the kind of knowledge that is necessary to make wise decisions?

Sethi and Sethi (1990) called flexibility 'a complex, multi-dimensional, and hard-to-capture concept.' Bahrami and Evans (2005) use the term 'super-flexibility' to denote the multi-faceted (or what Sethi et al. calls hard-to-capture) meaning of the concept, from agility, versatility, and adaptability, to resilience, robustness, and malleability. They convincingly provide a case for the concept, yet fail to deliver a specific methodology or system as to how companies should build, manage, and take advantage of flexibility. A good starting point to tackle the concept of flexibility is to ask: What drives the value of flexibility? The most important factor is the level of uncertainty in the environment, particularly if it is of the endogenous kind. When uncertainty is large and chaotic, it is more likely that the project value will wander into the so-called flexible strategy region. The level of uncertainty depends on the opportunity at hand and the economic and business environment. To evaluate what kind of strategic options are necessary and available, one needs to understand the dynamics of the given opportunity. Thus, corporations should be involved in managing a portfolio of opportunities before they structure a portfolio of options to effectively take advantage of flexibilities provided by each project. The ability to ask relevant questions within the context of flexibility and optionality is the major determinant for success. The correct dimension includes discussions about which risk factors are driving the value of the project, how exogenous and endogenous uncertainties play a role in the further development and revision of opportunities, what kind of risks should be taken or accepted to enhance the value of the project or to reach the desired outcome.

One of the most important tasks decision makers face is the determination of when flexibility offers value. This issue is closely related to the identification of strategic inflection points, where flexibility offers the most value. It is also crucial to evaluate the value of flexibility within the context of overall optionality managed by the corporation, that is, the contribution of flexibility to the overall portfolio of options available to the corporation. ROA is a tool for corporations to value a project or a business that potentially offers a premium for optionality. The practice of equating ROA with flexibility does more harm than good because in so doing it ignores the real dynamics of flexibility, which requires a more sophisticated toolbox for decision making under Knightian uncertainty. Li et al. (2007) makes the ever significant point that although uncertainty is central to real options theory of investment, the theory itself does not specify the sources of uncertainty.

Flexibility Theory™ integrates the effects of competitive dynamics in the valuation of necessary flexibility to make effective investment decisions at the strategic level.

In the spirit of transdisciplinarity, Flexibility Theory™ does not limit itself to a particular field; rather, it combines the robust and complementary elements of various theories and methodologies to create a meta-process, a process of processes. It can be described as a meta-theory, which provides a framework to exploit uncertainties and help corporations manage strategic and entrepreneurial initiatives in a dynamic, real-time setting. Corporations will be able to continuously evaluate the trade-offs between avoiding false negatives, in which valuable opportunities are foregone and false positives that tie up resources that are better used elsewhere. It transcends ROA by creating a typology of *flexibility* and identifying key elements of decision making at the executive level in a *moving target* setting. Flexibility Theory™ addresses game-theoretic issues, such as the evaluation of options available to the corporation side-by-side the options available to the competition. The meta-process nature of Flexibility Theory™ enables corporations incorporate local, regional, and global competitive dynamics; manage a dynamic portfolio of options in real-time; separate risk taking, risk acceptance and risk reduction activities; and empower learning and information sharing among all functional and operational areas. The main goal is to find the most effective method from any discipline and the most qualified experts from the academia and industry to yield the best available 'optimal information' for each domain of uncertainty, and to provide efficient and sustainable solutions for corporations, governments and institutions.

Decision Making Toolbox: Promising Developments

The more intuitive, compact, and easy-to-understand decision trees and influence diagrams are said to improve on ROA. These graphical techniques provide an opportunity to describe relationships between variables in a decision problem with ease. Influence diagrams seem to be more tractable as they do not grow as much as a decision tree when more variables and time periods are added to the model. Moreover, they are better equipped to capture the *value of information* in the overall process. A fairly new concept of Dynamic Decision Networks (DDN), developed by Buede (2000), aims at building synergies between Bayesian networks and influence diagrams. Specifically, a DDN has three different parts, the decision sub-net, the data fusion sub-net, and the inference sub-nets, which are not constant with respect to time and the modifications between two subsequent time steps can be caused by external changes or by internal decisions depending on the value of information. DDNs are designed to solve complex, real-time problems with a non-constant number of time-evolving variables in a rule-based and probabilistic (subjective) system. For highly uncertain ventures and projects, another fruitful area of research is the application of extreme value theory as an extension to the standard ROA. Carlsson et al. (2007) introduce the so-called *fuzzy real option valuation* for giga-investments, which are large strategic projects with long life cycles. They argue that future uncertainty cannot be dealt with as a stochastic phenomenon in the case of giga-investments. To this end, *possibility theory* provides an alternative way to deal with uncertainty and the trade-off between precision and relevance.

Large innovative development programs in aerospace and defense are procured following spiral development principles, which started in software development due to

Boehm (1988). The terminology comes from a graphic representation of all development and implementation phases of a system. The successive phases expand like a spiral, not a purely sequential process. At each phase an analysis is conducted. Flexibility of choices is allowed at early stages. In the spirit of real option, it delays decision making and utilizes maximum flexibility. The original spiral model has difficulty determining the roots of elaborated objectives, constraints, and alternatives. Boehm (2000) introduced the WinWin spiral model to resolve this by adding three activities to the front of each spiral cycle: (i) identify the system or subsystem's key stakeholders, (ii) identify the stakeholders' win conditions for the system or subsystem, and (iii) negotiate win-win reconciliations of the stakeholders' win conditions.

As far as I am concerned, the most promising idea that fits with the conceptual development of Flexibility Theory is Risk-Constrained Optimization® (RCO), a patented system of planning under uncertainty, developed by Vladimir A. Masch. It aims at building a flexible and transparent decision-making platform to increase the quality of corporate governance, and hence, the probability of long-term sustainability of the corporation. To that end, RCO is an 'ensemble of technologies,' merging six fields, namely, Operations Research/Management Science, Scenario Planning, Decision Science, Risk Management, Utility Theory and Portfolio Theory. Masch (2004) explains the power of RCO coming, not from individual components, but from their combined impact within the process. I think he is on the correct path of creating a truly transdisciplinary decision making apparatus for decisive risk management. What I like the most about RCO is the fact that, as Masch puts it, RCO might provide the tools for implementing the uncertainty-centered decision systems of Keynes and Shackle (I would add Knightian uncertainty), and allows the transformation of standard tools into realistic customized models, even by executives who have no modeling skills. Other developments such as DDNs could act as complementary tools to make wise decisions.

The New Organizational Structure: A Modest Proposal

Vayanos (2003) postulates that risk management can be viewed as a hierarchical portfolio formation procedure, where each unit in a firm determines its portfolio of risky activities and then risk managers control the overall level of risk. He further notes that while risk managers set limits for the level of risk that each unit in a firm can take; they do not dictate the portfolio of a unit's risky activities, let alone the company as a whole. I would propose that a Chief Flexibility Officer (CFLO) can take on the role of managing the company as a portfolio of projects, businesses, activities, and units in real-time, and in so doing, provide the CEO the ever-needed strategic insight regarding the future of the corporation. The CFLO would also manage a paper portfolio of opportunities; for example, shadow options, to make sure the right ones will be included as part of the corporate portfolio down the road. There will be two executive level individuals reporting directly to CFLO, namely the head of ERM (in my proposal, the CRO function becomes redundant) and the head of Corporate Portfolio Management. It is the responsibility of CFLO to coordinate the risk management and portfolio management activities. In light of a key postulate, head of ERM is in charge of risk accepting (as well as risk mitigation and risk transfer), while the head of Corporate Portfolio Management deals with risk taking and opportunity development. The technical aspect of the job of a CFLO is making sure that risk accepting and risk taking bets are independent. Conceptually, this equates to managing a total risk budget, comprising of core and satellite risks. I would propose that the head of ERM handles the so-called core risks, which are a function of the core activities of the corporation, namely, operational, financial, and supply chain. On the other hand, the head of corporate portfolio management brings about satellite risks that would help the corporation grow in a sustainable manner, and hence, increase its competitive edge. Breene, Nunes, and Shill (2007) discuss a fairly new C-level executive position of Chief Strategy Officer (CSO), who bears the burden of strategy execution. The authors cite complex organizational structures, rapid globalization, new regulations, and the struggle to innovate as the challenges faced by CEOs, who are finding it harder than ever to be on top of everything. They describe CSOs to be seasoned executives with a strong strategy orientation who have typically led major initiatives or businesses and worn many operating hats before taking on the role of the CSO, but are not strategists per se. There is nothing new conceptually in the function and responsibilities of a CSO, whereas CFLO brings about new capabilities in an integrated framework to build the ever-needed flexibility for sustainable growth. In this sense, CFLO is the necessary C-level executive to help corporations become Risk Intelligent Enterprises, as proposed by Deloitte & Touche. Another intriguing C-level executive was proposed by Savage, Scholtes, and Zweidler (2006), namely the Chief Probability Officer (CPO). The authors correctly postulate that planning for an uncertain future calls for a shift in information management, from single numbers to probability distributions, to correct the 'flaw of averages.' In this spirit, the CPO is in charge of managing the distributions that underlie risk, real portfolios, real options, and many other activities in the global economy. Savage et al. offer 'interactive simulation' and 'stochastic libraries' as a way to balance the trade-off between complexity and practicality in business organizations. The CPO should have both statistical and managerial skills in building coherent network of models to illuminate enterprise-wide risks and opportunities. Within the context of my proposed C-level executive of CFLO, there would be a head of Probability Management, who would make sure that the right questions are being asked by the head of ERM and the head of Corporate Portfolio Management, and the various stochastic models are coherently integrated for the CFLO to properly assess the risk taking and risk accepting activities. The CFLO has the overall responsibility of understanding endogenous uncertainties and constantly maneuvering between strategic and tactical initiatives.

References

Adner, Ron, and D. A. Levinthal, 'What is Not a Real Option: Considering Boundaries for the Application of Real Options to Business Strategy,' *Academy of Management Review*, 2004, 29/1, 74-85.

Bahrami, Homa, and Stuart Evans, *Super-Flexibility for Knowledge Enterprises*, Springer, 2005.

Bak, Per, Chao Tang, and Kurt Wiesenfeld, 'Self-organized Criticality,' *Physical Review A*, 1988, 38, 364-374.

Baker, Rose, 'Risk Aversion in Maintenance: Overmaintenance and Principal-agent Problem,' *IMA Journal of Management Mathematics*, 2006, 17, 99-113.

Bernanke, Ben, 'Irreversibility, Uncertainty and Cyclical Investment,' *Quarterly Journal of Economics*, 1983, 98, 85-106.

Boehm, Barry, 'A Spiral Model of Software Development and Enhancement,' *IEEE Computer*, 1988, 21/5, 61-72.

Boehm, Barry, 'Spiral Development: Experience, Principles, and Refinements,' Special Report, CMU/SEI-2000-SR-008, Carnegie Mellon University, 2000.

Bowman, Edward H., and Dileep Hurry, 'Strategy Through the Options Lens: An Integrated View of Resource Investments and the Incremental-Choice Process,' *Academy of Management Review*, 1993, 18/4, 760-782.

Brashers, Dale, 'Communication and Uncertainty Management,' *Journal of Communication*, 2001, 51/3, 477-497.

Breene, Timothy S., Paul F. Nunes, and Walter E. Shill, 'The Chief Strategy Officer,' *Harvard Business Review*, October 2007, 84-93.

Buede, Dennis, *The Engineering Design of Systems: Methods and Models*, Wiley, 2000.

Buehler, Kevin S., and Gunnar Pritsch, 'Running with Risk,' *The McKinsey Quarterly*, September 2003.

Butler, Henry N., and Larry E. Ribstein, *The Sarbanes-Oxley Debacle: What We've Learned; How To Fix It*, AEI Press, 2006.

Carlsson, Christer, Robert Fuller, Markku Heikkila, and Peter Majlender, 'A Fuzzy Approach to R&D Project Portfolio Selection,' *International Journal of Approximate Reasoning*, 2007, 44/2, 93-105.

Chichilnisky, Graciela, and Ho-Mou Wu, 'Genereal Equilibrium with Endogenous Uncertainty and Default,' *Journal of Mathematical Economics*, 2006, 42, 499-524.

Chichilnisky, Graciela, G.M. Heal, and D.P. Tsomocos, 'Option Values and Endogenous Uncertainty in ESOPs, MBOs and Asset-Backed Loans,' *Economics Letters*, 1995, 48, 379-388.

Knight, Frank H., *Risk, Uncertainty and Profit*, University of Chicago Press, 1921.

Kulatilaka, Nalin, 'Operating Flexibilities in Capital Budgeting: Substitutability and Complementarity in Real Options,' in *Real Options in Capital Investment: Models, Strategies, and Applications*, ed. L. Trigeorgis, 1995, 121-132.

Kurz, Morcedai, 'The Kesten-Stigum Model and the Treatment of Uncertainty in Equilibrium Theory,' in *Essays on Economic Behavior under Uncertainty*, ed. M.S. Balch, D.L. McFadden, and S.Y. Wu, 1974, 389-399.

Kurz, Morcedai, 'On Rational Belief Equilibria,' *Economic Theory*, 1994, 4, 859-876.

Lee, Hau, and Michael Wolfe, 'Supply Chain Security without Tears,' *Supply Chain Management Review*, 2003, 7/1, 12-20.

Li, Yong, Barclay E. James, Ravi Madhavan, and Joseph T. Mahoney, 'Real Options: Taking Stock and Looking Ahead,' *Advances in Strategic Management: Real Options Theory*, 2007, 24, 31-66.

Lorsch, Jay W., and Robert C. Clark, 'Leading from the Boardroom,' *Harvard Business Review*, April 2008, 105-111.

Manderson, Desmond, 'Some Considerations about Transdisciplinarity: A New Metaphysics?,' in Transdisciplinarity: Recreating Integrated Knowledge, eds Margaret A. Somerville and David J. Rapport, EOLSS Publishers, 2000.

Masch, Vladimir A., 'Return to the Natural Process of Decision-making Leads to Good Strategies,' *Journal of Evolutionary Economics*, 2004, 14, 431-462.

Massey, Cade, and George Wu, 'Detecting Regime Shifts: The Causes of Under- and Overreaction,' *Management Science*, 2005, 51/6, 932-947.

Mulvey, John M., and Hafize G. Erkan, 'Applying CVaR for Decentralized Risk Management of Financial Companies,' *Journal of Banking and Finance*, 2006, 30/2, 627-644.

Nicolescu, Basarab, *Manifesto of Transdisciplinarity*, State University of New York Press, 2002, translated from French by Karen-Claire Voss.

Sanchez, Ron, 'Integrating Transaction Costs Theory and Real Options Theory,' *Managerial and Decision Economics*, 2003, 24/4, 267-282.

Savage, Sam, Stefan Scholtes, and Daniel Zweidler, 'Probability Management,' *OR/MS Today*, April 2006, 60-66.

Sethi, Andrea K., and Suresh P. Sethi, 'Flexibility in Manufacturing: A Survey,' *The International Journal of Flexible Manufacturing Systems*, 1990, 2, 289-328.

Sornette, Didier, *Why Stock Markets Crash*, Princeton University Press, 2003.

Spiro, Rand J., Paul J. Feltovich, Michael J. Jacobson, and Richard L. Coulson, 'Knowledge Representation, Content Specification, and the Development of Skill in Situation-specific Knowledge Assembly: Some Constructivist Issues as they Relate to Cognitive Flexibility Theory and Hypertext,' *Educational Technology*, 1991, 31, 22-25.

Tang, Christopher, 'Robust Strategies for Mitigating Supply Chain Disruptions,' *International Journal of Logistics: Research and Applications*, 2006, 9/1, 33-45.

Thornton, Anna C., *Variation Risk Management*, Wiley, 2004.

Vayanos, Dimitri, 'The Decentralization of Information Processing in the Presence of Interactions,' *Review of Economic Studies*, 2003, 70, 667-695.

Wilson, Edward O., *Consilience: The Unity of Knowledge*, Vintage, 1998.

KEY REFERENCES FOR FURTHER READING

Apgar, David, *Risk Intelligence: Learning to Manage What We Don't Know*, Harvard Business School Press, 2006.

Bahrami, Homa, and Stuart Evans, *Super-Flexibility for Knowledge Enterprises*, Springer, 2005.

Buede, Dennis, *The Engineering Design of Systems: Methods and Models*, Wiley, 2000.

Klein, Gary, *Intuition At Work*, Currency Doubleday, 2003.

Kurz, Morcedai, *Endogenous Economic Fluctuations: Studies in the Theory of Rational Beliefs*, Springer, 1997.

Marsch, James G., *A Primer On Decision Making: How Decisions Happen*, The Free Press, 1994.

Nicolescu, Basarab, *Manifesto of Transdisciplinarity*, State University of New York Press, 2002, translated from French by Karen-Claire Voss.

Raynor, Michael E., *The Strategy Paradox*, Currency Doubleday, 2007.

Russo, J. Edward and Paul J.H. Schoemaker, *Winning Decisions: Getting It Right The First Time*, Currency Doubleday, 2002.

Smith, Preston G. and Guy M. Merritt, *Proactive Risk Management: Controlling Uncertainty in Product Development*, Productivity Press, 2002.

16 Corporate Social Responsibility: A Broader View of Corporate Governance

GÜLER ARAS AND DAVID CROWTHER

Introduction

It is clearly accepted that good corporate governance is fundamental to the successful operation of any corporation; hence much attention has been paid to the procedures of such governance. Often, however, what is actually meant by the corporate governance of a firm is merely assumed without being made explicit; moreover it is assumed that the concept is simply connected to the management of investor relationships. Similarly corporate social responsibility is generally accepted to be fundamental to the continuing operating of any corporation, and is arguably the fashionable concept of the moment. While it is clear what is generally meant by corporate governance, it is much less clear what is meant by corporate social responsibility and we start by investigating this concept.

For two such fundamental concepts, however, it would seem that there should be a relationship between the two, although little work has been undertaken on exploring this relationship. We argue, however, that the two concepts are inextricably linked and that it is necessary to take a broader view of corporate governance which encompasses relationships with the whole stakeholder community and necessarily therefore incorporates the principles of corporate social responsibility. We argue that the more progressive corporations recognise this and use evidence from the FTSE 100 companies and their corporate governance policies to support our argument.

Every time society faces a new problem or threat then a new legislative process of some sort is introduced which tries to protect that society from a future reoccurrence (Romano 2004). Recently we have seen a wide range of problems with corporate behaviour, which has arguably led to prominence being given to corporate social responsibility (see for example Boele, Fabig & Wheeler 2001). Part of this effect is to recognise the concerns of all stakeholders by an organisation, and this has been researched by many people (for example, Johnson & Greening 1999; Knox & Maklan 2004) with inconclusive findings. Accordingly, therefore, corporations, with their increased level of responsibility and accountability to their stakeholders, have felt that there is a need to develop a code for corporate governance so as to guide them towards appropriate stakeholder relations.

A great deal of concern has been expressed all over the world about shortcomings in the systems of corporate governance in operation: Britain, Australia, most other Anglo-Saxon and English speaking countries, and many other countries, have a similar system of governance. Conversely Germany is a good example of where the distance between ownership and control is much less than in the United States, while Japan's system of corporate governance is in some ways in between Germany and the United States, and in other ways different from both (Shleifer & Vishny 1997). By contrast, in India the corporate governance system in the public sector may be characterised as a transient system, with the key players (namely, politicians, bureaucrats and managers) taking a myopic view of the system of governance. Such international comparisons illustrate different approaches to the problem of corporate governance and the problem of ensuring that managers act in their shareholders' interest. Recently of course much attention to this issue has been paid by institutional investors (Cox, Brammer & Millington 2004).

Good governance is, of course, important in every sphere of the society whether it be the corporate environment or general society or the political environment. Good governance levels can, for example, improve public faith and confidence in the political environment. When the resources are too limited to meet the minimum expectations of the people, it is a good governance level that can help to promote the welfare of society. And of course a concern with governance is at least as prevalent in the corporate world (Durnev & Kim 2005).

Corporate governance can be considered as an environment of trust, ethics, moral values and confidence – as a synergic effort of all the constituents of society – that is the stakeholders, including government; the general public and so on; professional/service providers – and the corporate sector. One of the consequences of a concern with the actions of an organisation, and the consequences of those actions, has been an increasing concern with corporate governance (Hermalin 2005). Corporate governance is therefore a current buzzword the world over. It has gained tremendous importance in recent years. Two of the main reasons for this upsurge in interest are the economic liberalisation and deregulation of industry and business and the demand for new corporate ethos and stricter compliance with the law of the land. One more factor that has been responsible for the sudden exposure of the corporate sector to a new paradigm for corporate governance that is in tune with the changing times is the demand for greater accountability of companies to their shareholders and customers (Bushman & Smith 2001).

Corporate Governance

One of the main issues which has been exercising the minds[1] of business managers, accountants and auditors, investment managers and government officials – all over the world – is that of corporate governance. Often a company's main target is to become global – while at the same time remaining sustainable – as a means to gain competitive power. But the most important question is concerned with what will be a firms' route to

---

1   The current time (June 2008) of economic recession brought about by the sub-prime lending crisis has once again focused minds on some of the significant issues of governance.

becoming global and what will be necessary in order to get global competitive power. There is more than one answer to this question and there are a variety of routes for a company to achieve this.

Probably since the mid-1980s, corporate governance has attracted a great deal of attention. The early impetus was provided by Anglo-American codes of good corporate governance.[2] Stimulated by institutional investors, other countries in the developed, as well as in emerging, markets established or adapted versions of these codes for their own companies. Supra-national authorities like the OECD and the World Bank did not remain passive and developed their own set of standard principles and recommendations. This type of self-regulation was chosen above a set of legal standards (Van den Barghe 2001). After the recent big corporate scandals the formalisation of corporate governance has become central to most companies. It is understandable that investors' protection has become a much more important issue for all financial markets after the tremendous, high-profile firm failures and scandals. Investors are demanding that companies implement rigorous corporate governance principles in order to achieve better returns on their investment and to reduce agency costs. Most of the time investors are ready to pay more[3] for companies to have good governance standards (Beiner et al. 2004). Similarly a company's corporate governance report is one of the main tools for investors' decisions. Because of these reasons companies cannot ignore the pressure for good governance from shareholders, potential investors and other markets actors.

At the same time, banking credit risk measurement regulations (Aras 2007a, 2007b) are requiring new rules for a company's credit evaluations. New international bank capital adequacy assessment methods (Basel II) necessitate that credit evaluation rules are elaborately concerned with operational risk which covers, inter alia, corporate governance principles. In this respect corporate governance will be one of the most important indicators for measuring risk. Another issue is related to firm credibility and riskiness. If the firm needs a high rating score then it will have to pay particular attention to corporate governance rules. Credit rating agencies analyse corporate governance practices along with other corporate indicators. Even though corporate governance principles have always been important for getting good rating scores for large and publicly-held companies, they are also becoming much more important for investors, potential investors, creditors and governments. Because of all of these factors, corporate governance receives high priority on the agenda of policymakers, financial institutions, investors, companies and academics. This is one of the main indicators that the link between corporate governance and actual performance is still open for discussion. In the literature a number of studies have sought to investigate the relation between corporate governance mechanisms and performance (for example, Agrawal and Knoeber 1996; Dalton et al. 1998; Bhagart & Black 1999; Coles et al. 2001; Gompers, Ishii and Metrick 2001; Bhagat and Jefferis 2002; Becht et al. 2002) Most of the studies have shown mixed results without a clear cut relationship. Based on these results, it seems that corporate governance matters significantly to a company's performance, market value and credibility, and therefore that every company has to apply corporate governance principles. But the most important point is that corporate governance is the only means for companies to achieve corporate goals and

---

2   The first such example is the Cadbury Report published in the UK in 1992. It has since been adapted and replaced – see later.

3   Such companies are perceived to be lower risk companies and this is reflected in a higher share price.

strategies. Therefore, companies have to improve their strategy and effective route to the implementation of governance principles. So companies have to investigate what their corporate governance policy and practice needs to be.

Corporate Governance Principles

Since corporate governance can be highly influential for firm performance, firms must know what the corporate governance principles are and how it will improve strategy to apply these principles. In practice there are four principles of good corporate governance, which are:

- transparency
- accountability
- responsibility
- fairness.

All these principles are related with the firm's corporate social responsibility. Corporate governance principles therefore are important for a firm but the real issue is concerned with what corporate governance actually is. Management can be interpreted as managing a firm for the purpose of creating and maintaining value for shareholders. Corporate governance procedures determine every aspect of the role for management of the firm and try to keep in balance and to develop control mechanisms in order to increase both shareholder value and the satisfaction of other stakeholders. In other words, corporate governance is concerned with creating a balance between the economic and social goals of a company including such aspects as the efficient use of resources, accountability in the use of its power and the behaviour of the corporation in its social environment (Sethi 2002).

The definition and measurement of good corporate governance is still subject to debate. However, good corporate governance will address such points as creating sustainable value, achieving the firm's goals and keeping a balance between economic and social benefit. Also, of course, good governance offers some long-term benefits for a firm, such as reducing risk and attracting new investors, shareholders and more equity.

DEVELOPING A FRAMEWORK FOR CORPORATE GOVERNANCE

In the UK there have been a succession of codes on corporate governance dating back to the Cadbury Report in 1992. Currently all companies reporting on the London Stock Exchange are required to comply with the Combined Code on Corporate Governance, which came into effect in 2003. It might be thought therefore that a framework for corporate governance has already been developed but the code in the UK has been continually revised while problems associated with bad governance have not disappeared. So clearly a framework has not been established in the UK and an international framework looks even more remote.

One of the problems with developing such a framework is the continual rules versus principles debate. The American approach tends to be rules based while the European approach is more based on the development of principles – a slower process. In general, rules are considered to be simpler to follow than principles, demarcating a clear line between acceptable and unacceptable behaviour. Rules also reduce discretion on the part of individual managers or auditors. In practice, however, rules can be more complex than principles. They may be ill-equipped to deal with new types of transactions not covered by the code. Moreover, even if clear rules are followed, one can still find a way to circumvent their underlying purpose – this is harder to achieve if one is bound by broader principles.

There are, of course, many different models of corporate governance around the world (see Aras & Crowther 2009a). These differ according to the nature of the system of capitalism in which they are embedded. The liberal model that is common in Anglo-American countries tends to give priority to the interests of shareholders. The coordinated model, which is normally found in Continental Europe and in Japan, recognises in addition the interests of workers, managers, suppliers, customers and the community. Both models have distinct competitive advantages, but in different ways. The liberal model of corporate governance encourages radical innovation and cost competition, whereas the coordinated model of corporate governance facilitates incremental innovation and quality competition. However there are important differences between the recent approach to governance issues taken in the USA and what has happened in the UK.

In the USA a corporation is governed by a board of directors, which has the power to choose an executive officer, usually known as the chief executive officer (CEO). The CEO has broad power to manage the corporation on a daily basis, but needs to get board approval for certain major actions, such as hiring the CEO's immediate subordinates, raising money, acquiring another company, major capital expansions or other expensive projects. Other duties of the board may include policy setting, decision making, monitoring management's performance or corporate control. The board of directors is nominally selected by and responsible to the shareholders, but the articles of many companies make it difficult for all but the largest shareholders to have any influence over the makeup of the board. Normally individual shareholders are not offered a choice of board nominees among which to choose, but are merely asked to rubberstamp the nominees of the sitting board. Diverse incentives have pervaded many corporate boards in the developed world, with board members beholden to the chief executive whose actions they are intended to oversee. Frequently, members of the boards of directors are CEOs of other corporations – in interlocking relationships, which many people see as posing a potential conflict of interest.

The UK on the other hand has developed a flexible model of regulation of corporate governance, known as the 'comply or explain' code of governance. This is a principles-based code that lists a number of recommended practices, such as:

- the separation of CEO and Chairman of the Board;
- the introduction of a time limit for CEOs' contracts;
- the introduction of a minimum number of non-executives Directors, and of independent directors;
- the designation of a senior non-executive director;
- the formation and composition of remuneration, audit and nomination committees.

Publicly-listed companies in the UK have to either apply those principles or, if they choose not to, to explain in a designated part of their annual reports why they have decided not to do so. The monitoring of those explanations is left to shareholders themselves. The basic idea of the Code[4] is that one size does not fit all in matters of corporate governance and that instead of a statutory regime like the Sarbanes-Oxley Act in the USA, it is best to leave some flexibility to companies so that they can make choices most adapted to their circumstances. If they have good reasons to deviate from the sound rule, they should be able to convincingly explain those to their shareholders. A form of the code has been in existence since 1992 and has had drastic effects on the way firms are governed in the UK. A recent study shows that in 1993, about ten per cent of the FTSE 350 companies were fully compliant with all dimensions of the code while by 2003 – when the Combined Code was introduced – more than 60 per cent were fully compliant. The same success was not achieved when looking at the explanation part for non-compliant companies. Many deviations are simply not explained and a large majority of explanations fail to identify specific circumstances justifying those deviations, although with the passage of time many more firms have become completely compliant. Thus the general view is that the UK's system works fairly well and in fact is often considered to be a benchmark, and therefore followed by a number of other countries.

Corporate governance principles and codes have been developed in different countries (see Aras & Crowther 2009b) and have been issued by stock exchanges, corporations, institutional investors or associations (institutes) of directors and managers with the support of governments and international organisations. As a rule, compliance with these governance recommendations is not mandated by law, although the codes which are linked to stock exchange listing requirements[5] will tend to have a coercive effect. Thus, for example, companies quoted on the London and Toronto Stock Exchanges formally need not follow the recommendations of their respective national codes, but they must disclose whether they follow the recommendations in those documents and, where not, they should provide explanations concerning divergent practices. Such disclosure requirements exert a significant pressure on listed companies for compliance.

In its Global Investor Opinion Survey of over 200 institutional investors first undertaken in 2000 (and subsequently updated), McKinsey found that 80 per cent of the respondents would pay a premium for well-governed companies. They defined a well-governed company as one that had mostly outside directors, who had no management ties, undertook formal evaluation of its directors and was responsive to investors' requests for information on governance issues. The size of the premium varied by market, from 11 per cent for Canadian companies to around 40 per cent for companies where the regulatory backdrop was least certain (for example, those in Morocco, Egypt or Russia). Other studies have similarly linked broad perceptions of the quality of companies to superior share price performance. On the other hand, research into the relationship between specific corporate governance controls and the financial performance of companies has had very mixed results.

The Development of Corporate Social Responsibility

There has been considerable debate about the relationship between corporate social responsibility and corporate governance but in recent years the term corporate social

---

4   The Combined Code on Corporate Governance.

5   Such as, for example, the UK Combined Code referred to earlier.

responsibility has gained prominence, both in business and in the press to such an extent that it seems to have become ubiquitous. There are probably many reasons for the attention given to this phenomenon, not least of which is the corporate excesses witnessed in recent years. For many people the various examples of this kind of behaviour – ranging from BCCI to Enron to Union Carbide to the collapse of Arthur Andersen – will have left an indelible impression among people that all is not well with the corporate world and that there are problems which need to be addressed[6] (Aras & Crowther 2008).

One of the implications of this current concern, however, is that this is a new phenomenon – one which has not been of concern previously. Issues of socially responsible behaviour are not, of course, new and examples can be found from throughout the world and at least from the earliest days of the Industrial Revolution and the concomitant founding of large business entities (Crowther 2002) and the divorce between ownership and management – or the divorcing of risk from rewards (Aras & Crowther 2007a). Thus, for example in the UK (where the Industrial Revolution started), Robert Owen (1816, 1991) demonstrated dissatisfaction with the assumption that only the internal effects of actions need be considered and the external environment was a free resource to be exploited at will. Furthermore, he put his beliefs into practice through the inclusion within his sphere of industrial operations the provision of housing for his workers at New Lanark, Scotland. Thus there is evidence from throughout the history of modernity that the self-centred approach towards organisational activity was not universally acceptable and was unable to satisfactorily provide a basis for human activity.

Since that time there has been a concern for the socially responsible behaviour of organisations which has gained prominence at certain times while being considered of minor importance at others. Thus during the 1970s, for example, there was a resurgence of interest in socially responsible behaviour, and especially environmental concern. This concern was encapsulated by Ackerman (1975) who argued that big business was recognising the need to adapt to a new social climate of community accountability but that the orientation of business to financial results was inhibiting social responsiveness. McDonald and Puxty (1979) on the other hand maintained that companies are no longer the instruments of shareholders alone but exist within society and so therefore have responsibilities to that society, and that there is therefore a shift towards the greater accountability of companies to all stakeholders. Recognition of the rights of all stakeholders and the duty of a business to be accountable in this wider context therefore has been a recurrent phenomenon. The economic view of accountability only to owners has only recently been subject to debate to any considerable extent.[7] Indeed the desirability of considering the social performance of a business has not always however been accepted and has been the subject of extensive debate.

Corporate Social Responsibility (CSR) therefore involves a concern with the various stakeholders to a business but there are several problems in identifying socially responsible behaviour:

- Research shows that the concern is primarily with those stakeholders who have power to influence the organisation. Thus organisations are most concerned with

---

6   Some would argue that these cases are related to corporate social responsibility failures, some to corporate governance failures, and some to both. Our view is that the two are too inter-related to separate.

7   See Crowther (2000) for a full discussion of these changes.

shareholders, less so with customers and employees and very little with society and the environment. CSR would imply that they are all of equal importance.

- The definitions imply that CSR is a voluntary activity rather than enforced though regulation whereas in actual fact it is an approach and the voluntary – regulated debate is irrelevant.
- Claiming a concern is very different to actually exhibiting that concern through actions taken (Crowther 2004).

Definitions of CSR abound but all can be seen as an attempt to explain and define the relationship between a corporation and its stakeholders, including its relationship with society as a whole. Many too are phrased in terms of the triple bottom line, in a way which, we argue, trivialises the concept. Because of the uncertainty surrounding the nature of CSR activity it is difficult to evaluate any such activity. It is therefore imperative to be able to identify such activity and Aras & Crowther (2007b) argue that there are three basic principles[8] which together comprise all CSR activity. These are:

- sustainability
- accountability
- transparency.

For a few years now the concept of CSR has gained prominence and is gaining increasing attention around the world among business people, media people and academics from a wide range of disciplines. There are probably many reasons (see Crowther & Ortiz-Martinez 2006) for the attention given to this phenomenon, not least of which is the corporate excesses which continue to become manifest in various parts of the world. These have left an indelible impression among people that all is not well with the corporate world and that there are problems which need to be addressed. Such incidents are too common to recount but have left the financial markets in a state of uncertainty and have left ordinary people to wonder if such a thing as honesty exists any longer in business.

More recently, the language used in business has mutated again and the concept of CSR is being replaced by the language of sustainability. Such language must be considered semiotically (Barthes 1973) as a way of creating the impression of actual sustainability. Using such analysis then, the signification is about inclusion within the selected audience for the corporate reports on the assumption that those included understand the signification in a common way with the authors. This is based upon an assumed understanding of the code of signification used in describing corporate activity in this way. As Sapir (1949: 554) states:

... we respond to gestures with an extreme alertness and, one might almost say, in accordance with an elaborate and secret code that is written nowhere, known by none and understood by all.

---

8   See Crowther (2002) and Schaltegger et al. (1996) for the development of these principles.

The Relationship Between Corporate Social Responsibility and Business Financial Success

In general, the more significant the power that some groups of stakeholders in a firm have, the more is spoken about CSR. Thus a concept that was perceived as a kind of luxury some years ago, nowadays is the focus of public opinion discussion. Some steps taken in the corporation's development, in the environment and in the human values can be the guilty causes of this CSR fashion. If in the beginning firms were small and there was no distinction between ownership and management, the economic development made it that there was a necessity to join more capital to set up bigger enterprises.[9] Thus, there were owners who gave the funds, and experts in management, who managed the company and were paid by the owners. Agency Theory establishes this relationship between the principal, the shareholder, and the agent, the manager, bearing in mind that the goals of the shareholders must be got through the management of the agents. But, which are the shareholders´ objectives? Obviously to increase the enterprise value through the maximisation of profits.

Of course, a company's structure is nowadays more complex than before and there have appeared other people, in addition to owners, directly or indirectly implied in the company's operations – known as stakeholders. Multinational corporations have sometimes even more power than governments in their influence, and stakeholders have gained more power through the media and public opinion in order to require some kind of specific behaviour from companies. Within this new environment, although explained in a very simple way, the primary objective of the company has become wider. Although generally speaking, the assumption may be that the first goal is to get financial performance in the company, after that the next step will be to comply with other socially responsible policies. This is because to pay attention to social objectives, or to show an orientation to multiple stakeholders group, could be considered a luxury, because it must have meant that the other basic goals of the company had been met. This argument is the basis of the first hypothesis about the relationship between CSR, linked to pay attention to stakeholders, and business success: 'Better performance results in greater attention to multiple stakeholders' (Greenley and Foxall 1997: 264). While the other hypothesis about this relationship will run in the opposite direction: 'that orientation to multiple stakeholder groups influences performance' (Greenley and Foxall, 1997: 264), which means to 'attend' to social policies in a better way.

This double-side relationship increases the difficulty to try to empirically prove it. Intuitively it seems as if there is a clear relationship between CSR and business success, but although the measurement of business success may be easy, through different economic and financial tools, such as ratios; the measurement of the degree of compliance of a company with social policies is really difficult. We can have in mind some kind of indicators, such as funds donated to charitable objectives, but a company can spend immeasurable quantities of money on charitable questions and have problems in the relationship with labour unions because of bad working conditions or low wages, for example. In this sense there have been, for many years, some companies whose objectives include philanthropic aims. We can cite examples of the Quaker companies – such as

---

9   Indeed many would argue that the Industrial Revolution and the development of transport infrastructure, in the form of canals and railways, without the combination of people with capital into joint stock companies.

Cadburys[10] and Rowntrees – which emerged in the UK Industrial Revolution or the Spanish saving banks, which emerged with the peculiar distinction of including in their aims charitable purposes. But finally, if they want to survive in the competitive market they have to bear in mind the conventional objective of profit maximisation. It may be understood as the initial values are ones, and then the market and the capitalism forces the firm to change them in order to survive in this maelstrom. Although at the same time the double-sided relationship operates, because people socially concerned bear in mind these basic aims and the image of such a company is improved, which provides a direct relationship with economic performance.

In this attempt to satisfy the necessities of the stakeholders there can appear other conflicts between the interests of the different groups included in the wider concept of stakeholders. Sometimes, due to this conflict of interests and to the specific features of the company, it tries to establish different levels between the stakeholders, paying more attention to those ones that are most powerful, but are there some goals more socially responsible than others? In the end the hierarchy will depend on the other goals of the company, it will give an answer to those stakeholders that can threaten the performance of the economic goals.

Relating Corporate Governance and Corporate Social Responsibility

It is of course no longer questioned that the activities of a corporation impact upon the external environment and that therefore such an organisation should be accountable to a wider audience than simply its shareholders. This is a central tenet of both the concept of corporate governance and the concept of CSR. Implicit in this is a concern with the effects of the actions of an organisation on its external environment, and there is a recognition that it is not just the owners of the organisation who are concerned with the activities of that organisation. Additionally there are a wide variety of other stakeholders who, justifiably, are concerned with those activities, and are affected by those activities. Those other stakeholders have not just an interest in the activities of the firm but also a degree of influence over the shaping of those activities. This influence is so significant that it can be argued that the power and influence of these stakeholders is such that it amounts to quasi-ownership of the organisation.

One view of good corporate performance is that of stewardship and thus, just as the management of an organisation is concerned with the stewardship of the financial resources of the organisation so too would management of the organisation be concerned with the stewardship of environmental resources (Aras & Crowther 2009c). The difference, however, is that environmental resources are mostly located externally to the organisation. Stewardship in this context, therefore, is concerned with the resources of society as well as the resources of the organisation. As far as stewardship of external environmental resources is concerned, then the central tenet of such stewardship is that of ensuring sustainability. Sustainability is focused on the future and is concerned with ensuring that the choices of resource utilisation in the future are not constrained by decisions

---

10   Interestingly Sir Adrian Cadbury who led the committee which established the first code of corporate governance is a member of this family – perhaps concern can be inherited.

taken in the present. This necessarily implies such concepts as generating and utilising renewable resources, minimising pollution and using new techniques of manufacture and distribution. It also implies the acceptance of any costs involved in the present as an investment for the future.

Not only does such sustainable activity, however, impact upon society in the future; it also impacts upon the organisation itself in the future. Thus good environmental performance by an organisation in the present is in reality an investment in the future of the organisation itself. This is achieved through the ensuring of supplies and production techniques which will enable the organisation to operate in the future in a similar way to its operations in the present and so to undertake value creation activity in the future much as it does in the present. Financial management also, however, is concerned with the management of the organisation's resources in the present so that management will be possible in a value creation way in the future. Thus the internal management of the firm, from a financial perspective, and its external environmental management coincide in this common concern for management for the future. Good performance in the financial dimension leads to good future performance in the environmental dimension and vice versa. Thus there is no dichotomy between environmental performance and financial performance and the two concepts conflate into one concern. This concern is, of course, the management of the future as far as the firm is concerned.

Similarly the creation of value within the firm is followed by the distribution of value to the stakeholders of that firm, whether these stakeholders are shareholders or others. Value, however, must be taken in its widest definition to include more than economic value as it is possible that economic value can be created at the expense of other constituent components of welfare such as spiritual or emotional welfare. This creation of value by the firm adds to welfare for society at large, although this welfare is targeted at particular members of society rather than treating all as equals. This has led to arguments concerning the distribution of value created and to whether value is created for one set of stakeholders at the expense of others. Nevertheless if, when summed, value is created, then this adds to welfare for society at large, however distributed.[11] Similarly good environmental performance leads to increased welfare for society at large, although this will tend to be expressed in emotional and community terms rather than being capable of being expressed in quantitative terms. This will be expressed in a feeling of well-being, which will, of course, lead to increased motivation. Such increased motivation will inevitably lead to increased productivity, some of which will benefit the organisations, and also a desire to maintain the pleasant environment which will in turn lead to a further enhanced environment, a further increase in welfare and the reduction of destructive aspects of societal engagement by individuals.

Relating Social Responsibility with Governance: The Evidence

There has been a variety of research over time investigating the relationship between the characteristics of a firm and its disclosure (for example, Cowen at al. 1987; Gray et al.

---

11   Essentially this is the Utilitarian argument, which we have expanded to take into account not just economic benefits but also welfare and spiritual benefits. We have argued elsewhere however (for example, Aras & Crowther 2009c) that the manner of distribution – and its concomitant equity – is crucial to any consideration of sustainable society.

2001) and equally there is research (for example, Burke & Longsdon 1996) showing the benefits of CSR. It is clear that these benefits are also directly related to the sustainability of a firm and that firm's success. It would seem apparent, therefore, that there should be some attention paid to social responsibility within the corporate governance of a corporation. It is therefore apposite to conduct an investigation as to what exactly is mentioned about CSR within such corporate governance. It is to be expected that good corporate governance will foster social responsibility in general.

There has been much work undertaken which investigates the failures of corporate governance and the ensuing problems which arise and this could be adapted to a consideration of our concern with the relationship between corporate governance and social responsibility. We argue however that this approach – akin to Popper's (1959) falsification theory – is not an appropriate methodology for this kind of research – companies which are not run perfectly are probably as common as black swans! Rather our starting assumption is that effective corporate governance will be largely unnoticed and that this will be manifest in examples of good practice rather than in the exceptional instances of poor practice. Our investigation therefore is based on exploring corporate governance in all the FTSE 100 companies – which are generally accepted to be examples of good practice in this respect. Our sample therefore consists of the 100 largest firms quoted on the London Stock Exchange[12] – so, whatever their country of domicile – they all comply with The Combined Code on Corporate Governance, which came into effect in 2003.[13] These firms obviously come from a variety of industrial sectors but in this analysis it is size rather than sector which has led to our choice of companies.

Although there is a clear link between good corporate governance and all aspects of a firm's performance, which will ultimately affect the sustainability of that firm's activity, our research does not show that this is at all clearly understood by many firms. Furthermore, although the majority of firms consider that CSR is important, they do not make any connection between this and corporate governance. They clearly do not understand the link between good governance, the management of all stakeholder relations, CSR and the longer-term economic performance of their company. Of the firms in the FTSE 100 it is clear that a majority do not understand this relationship – or do not think that it is important. Thus 30 per cent of the firms consider that their governance is adequate because they comply with The Combined Code on Corporate Governance, which came into effect in 2003. Of course all firms reporting on the London Stock Exchange are required to comply with this code, and so these firms are doing no more than meeting their regulatory obligations and the other 70 per cent also comply with the code. A further 24 per cent regard corporate governance as simply a part of investor relationships and do nothing more regarding such governance except to identify that it is important for investors/potential investors and to flag up that they have such governance policies. In effect, therefore, 54 per cent of these firms merely consider governance in terms of issues mentioned within the Combined Code.

---

12   Data was collected from the company websites during 2007 and therefore based upon what was stated in the latest annual report, produced in 2006 or 2007.

13   The Code was based upon the previous Cadbury and Greenbury Reports and was subsequently revised during 2006. It deals with such issues as Board composition and remuneration, relationship with shareholders and investors, composition of the Audit Committee and so on. We have therefore not considered these aspects of governance in our analysis.

This therefore leaves only 46 per cent who recognise that there is any kind of relationship between governance and other aspects of corporate activity.[14] Thus 31 per cent of firms recognise that there is a clear link between governance and CSR[15] and make efforts to link the two. Often this is no more than making a claim that good governance is a part of their CSR policy as well as a part of their relationship with shareholders. And, of course, there are a lot of vague comments about firms doing their best[16] to behave sustainably, without any precise indications of what is meant by such a claim. Some firms do however go further then this and make clear links to specific action, or recognise the relationship to specific parts of corporate activity. Thus five per cent recognise the relationship to financial sustainability through an understanding of the relationship between governance and risk. Similarly two per cent relate governance to community relations; four per cent to ethical behaviour towards employees; three per cent to environmental policy and behaviour; and one per cent to their commitment to sustainable growth. Despite these seemingly dispiritingly small numbers though it is encouraging that seven per cent of firms recognise the relationship to all the aspects of sustainability which we have identified and clearly spell out their relationship in their corporate activity.

An example of the most comprehensive statements is from BAT[17] which states:

> *The principle of Mutual Benefit is the basis on which we build our relationships with our stakeholders. We are primarily in business to build long term shareholder value and we believe the best way to do this is to seek to understand and take account of the needs of all our stakeholders.*

This can all be summarised in the Table 16.1.

Table 16.1   The recognised importance of CSR to Governance

Type of relationship recognised/action undertaken/commitment made	Firms recognising the relationship %
Comply with code only	30
Related to investor relations only	24
Related to CSR policy	31
Community relations	2
Ethics	4
Environmental policy	3
Sustainable growth	1
Risk	5

14   We recognize, of course, that there is always the possibility that companies do recognise this broader view of governance but do not report on it. We consider this unlikely however as most companies regard CSR as significant enough to feature prominently in other contexts.

15   The terms used include corporate social responsibility and corporate responsibility.

16   Often the phrase used includes something like 'within reason' or 'in the light of circumstance' as a way of obviating any real commitment to any particular sort of action.

17   From http://www.bat.com/oneweb/sites/uk – accessed on 12 June 2008.

It is tempting to try to undertake some analysis of sectoral differences in the approaches taken concerning governance practice, and from the evidence in the research there certainly are some differences. But we need to be realistic and state that, as we have only looked at the FTSE 100, our sample is too small (and probably unrepresentative) to undertake some reliable analysis of this nature. We therefore flag up this as further analysis to be undertaken in our project. So we simply turn to a consideration of what conclusions we can draw from this research.

Conclusions

It is clear that the definition of corporate governance has extended considerably beyond investor relations and encompasses relations with all stakeholders – including the environment. This is essential for the longer-term survival of a firm and is therefore a key component of sustainability. There is evidence that some firms understand this but they are in a minority. So it is possible to say that good corporate governance will address this but that not all firms recognise this. It is equally possible to state that a firm which has a more complete understanding of the relationship between social responsibility, sustainability and corporate governance will address these issues more completely. By implication a more complete understanding of the inter-relationships will lead to better corporate governance, and therefore to better economic performance.

The other tentative conclusion from this research is concerned with the extent of disclosure manifest through the reporting of such things as corporate governance and CSR, and is more in the nature of a prognosis. Crowther (2000) traces an archaeology of corporate reporting which shows that, over time, the amount of information provided – first to shareholders, then to potential investors (Gilmore & Willmott 1992), then to other stakeholders – has gradually increased throughout the last century, as firms recognised the benefit in providing increased disclosure. Similarly the amount of disclosure regarding CSR activity has been increasing rapidly over the last decade, as firms have recognised the commercial benefits of increased transparency. Therefore it is reasonable to argue – as we are doing – that the amount of information regarding the relationship between governance and social responsibility will also increase, not just as firms gain a clearer understanding of that relationship but also as they understand the benefits of greater disclosure in this respect. Thus we consider that this will become more apparent over time.

References

Ackerman R W (1975); *The Social Challenge to Business*; Cambridge, MA; Harvard University Press.

Agrawal A & Knoeber C R (1996); Firm Performance and Mechanisms to Control Agency Problems between Managers and Shareholders; *Journal of Financial and Quantitative Analysis,* 31(3) pp. 377–398.

Aras G (2007a); The Impact of the Basel II Banking Regulation on Real Industry Firms; Istanbul; Deloitte Academy Publication, *in Turkish*.

Aras G (2007b); The Road Map for SME's after Basel II Banking Regulation; Istanbul; Deloitte Academy Publication, *in Turkish*.

Aras G & Crowther D (2007a); Is the Global Economy sustainable?; in S Barber (ed), *The Geopolitics of the City*; London; Forum Press; pp 165-194.

Aras G & Crowther D (2007b); Sustainable corporate social responsibility and the value chain; In M M Zain & D Crowther (eds), *New Perspectives on Corporate Social Responsibility*; Kulala Lumpur; MARA University Press; pp 119-140.

Aras G & Crowther D (2008); Exploring frameworks of corporate governance; in G Aras & D Crowther (eds), *Culture and Corporate Governance*; Leicester; SRRNet; pp 3-16.

Aras G & Crowther D (2009a); Corporate Governance and Corporate Social Responsibility in context; in G Aras & D Crowther (eds), *Global Perspectives on Corporate Governance and Corporate Social Responsibility*; Aldershot; Gower, pp. 1-41.

Aras G & Crowther D (2009b); Convergence: a prognosis; in G Aras & D Crowther (eds), *Global Perspectives on Corporate Governance and Corporate Social Responsibility*; Aldershot; Gower, pp. 313-336.

Aras G & Crowther D (2009c); The Durable Corporation: Strategies for Sustainable Development; Aldershot; Gower.

Barthes R (1973); *Mythologies*; trans A Lavers; London; HarperCollins.

Becht M, Bolton P & Roell A (2002); *Corporate Governance and Control*; Working Paper, ECGI.

Beiner S, Drobetz W, Schmid M M & Zimmerman H (2004); An Integrated Framework of Corporate Governance and Firm Valuation – Evidence from Switzerland; *European Corporate Governance Institute Finance Working Paper* no 34/2004.

Bhagat, S. & Black, B., (1999); The Uncertain Relationship between Board Composition and Firm Performance, *The Business Lawyer*, 54(3) pp. 921-963.

Bhagat S & Jefferis R H (2002); *The Econometrics of Corporate Governance Studies*; Cambridge, US; The MIT Press.

Boele R, Fabig H & Wheeler D (2001); Shell, Nigeria and the Ogoni. A Study in Unsustainable Development: II. Corporate Social Responsibility and 'Stakeholder Management' versus a Rights-based Approach to Sustainable Development; *Sustainable Development*, 9, 121-135.

Burke L & Longsdon J M (1996); How Corporate Social Responsibility Pays Off; *Long Range Planning*, 29(4), 495-502.

Bushman R M & Smith A J (2001); Financial Accounting Information and Corporate Governance; *Journal of Accounting and Economics*, 32, 237-333.

Coles J W, McWilliams V B & Sen N (2001); An Examination of the Relationship of Governance Mechanisms to Performance; *Journal of Management*, 7, 23-50.

Cowen S S, Ferreri L B & Parker L D (1987); The Impact of Corporate Characteristics on Social Responsibility Disclosure: A Typology and Frequency-based Analysis; *Accounting, Organizations and Society*, 12 (2), 111-122.

Cox P, Brammer S & Millington A (2004); An Empirical Examination of Institutional Investor Preferences for Corporate Social Performance; *Journal of Business Ethics*, 52, 27-43.

Crowther D (2000); Corporate Reporting, Stakeholders and the Internet: Mapping the New Corporate Landscape; *Urban Studies*, 37 (10), 1837-1848.

Crowther D (2002); A Social Critique of Corporate Reporting; Aldershot; Ashgate.

Crowther D (2004); Limited liability or limited responsibility; in D Crowther & L Rayman-Bacchus (eds), *Perspectives on Corporate Social Responsibility*; Aldershot; Ashgate; pp 42-58.

Crowther D & Ortiz-Martinez E (2006); The abdication of responsibility: corporate social responsibility, public administration and the globalising agenda; in D Crowther & K T Caliyurt (eds), *Globalisation and Social Responsibility*; Newcastle, Cambridge Scholars Press, pp 253-275.

Dalton. D R. Daily, C M, Ellstrand, A E & Johnson. J L (1998); Meta-analytic Reviews of Board Composition, Leadership Structure, and Financial Performance; *Strategic Management Journal*, 19 (3), 269-290.

Durnev A & Kim E H (2005); To Steal or Not to Steal: Firm Attributes, Legal Environment, and Valuation; *Journal of Finance*, LX (3), 1461-1493.

Gilmore C G & Willmott H (1992); Company law and financial reporting: a sociological history of the UK experience; in M Bromwich & A Hopwood (eds), *Accounting and the Law*; Hemel Hempstead; Prentice Hall, pp 159-191.

Gompers P A., Ishii J L & Metrick A (2001); Corporate Governance and Equity Prices, *National Bureau of Economic Research,* Working Paper 8449.

Gray R, Javad M, Power D M & Sinclair C D (2001); Social and Environmental Disclosures and Corporate Characteristics: A Research Note and Extension; *Journal of Business, Finance and Accounting*, 28(3/4), 327-356.

Greenley, G E and Foxall, G R (1997); Multiple Stakeholders Orientation in UK Companies and the Implications for Company Performance; *Journal of Management Studies*, 34(2); pp. 259-284.

Hermalin B E (2005); Trends in Corporate Governance; *Journal of Finance*, LX (5), 2351-2384.

Johnson R A & Greening D W (1999); The Effects of Corporate Governance and Institutional Ownership Types on Corporate Social Performance; *Academy of Management Journal,* 42(5), 564-576.

Knox S & Maklan S (2004); Corporate Social Responsibility: Moving Beyond Investment Towards Measuring Outcomes; *European Management Journal*, 22(5), 508-516.

McDonald D & Puxty A G (1979); An Inducement-Contribution Approach to Corporate Financial Reporting; *Accounting, Organizations & Society*, 4(1/2), 53-65.

Owen, R (1816, 1991); *A New View of Society and Other Writings*, London, Penguin.

Popper K R (1959); *The Logic of Scientific Discovery*; London; Hutchinson.

Romano R (2004); The Sarbanes-Oxley Act and the Making of Quack Corporate Governance; *European Corporate Governance Institute Finance Working Paper* No 52/2004.

Sapir E (1949); The unconscious patterning of behaviour in society; in D G Mendelbaum (ed), *Selected Writings of Edward Sapir*; Berkley, CA.; University of California Press.

Schaltegger S, Muller K & Hindrichsen H (1996); *Corporate Environmental Accounting*; Chichester; John Wiley & Sons.

Sethi S P (2002); Standards for Corporate Conduct in the International Arena: Challenges and Opportunities for Multinational Corporations; *Business and Society Review*, 107(1), 20-40.

Shleifer A & Vishny R W (1997); A Survey of Corporate Governance; *Journal of Finance*, 52(2), 737-783.

Van den Berghe, L (2001); Beyond Corporate Governance; *European Business Forum,* Issue 5, Spring.

Applying Corporate Social Responsibility

There are many reasons for the current interest in Corporate Social Responsibility (CSR); it is a topic which is considered to be of particular importance at the present time and definitions of corporate social responsibility are many and diverse but one which has been created by the European Commission is

> *CSR is a concept whereby companies integrate social and environmental concerns in their business operations and in their interaction with their stakeholders on a voluntary basis.*

One which we prefer though was produced by Dahl in 1972. He stated that

> *...every large corporation should be thought of as a social enterprise; that is an entity whose existence and decisions can be justified insofar as they serve public or social purposes.*

CSR has been one of the most debated management issues, with both academics and practitioners trying to give proper meaning to the concept and justifying why corporations should adopt ethical and social responsible behaviour, yet there is lack of consensus on what the concept means, what it entails, why it should be embraced, how it should be operationalised, what its roles are in achieving organisational effectiveness or performance and lots and lots of issues bordering on the concept. At the same time the development of a theoretical underpinning for CSR has been given increased priority, with a critique of Utilitarianism and its antecedent, Classical Liberalism, featuring prominently.

Classical liberal philosophy places an emphasis upon rationality and reason, with society being an artificial creation resulting from an aggregation of individual self-interest, and with organisations being an inevitable result of such aggregations for business purposes. Thus Locke (1690) viewed societies as existing in order to protect innate natural private rights while Bentham (1789) and J S Mill (1863) emphasised the pursuit of human need. Of paramount importance to all was the freedom of the individual to pursue his[1] own ends, with a tacit assumption that maximising individual benefits would lead to the maximisation of organisational benefits and also societal benefits. In other words, societal benefits can be determined by a simple summation of all individual benefits. Classical liberal economic theory extended this view of society to the treatment of organisations as entities in their own right with the freedom to pursue their own ends. Such theory

---

[1] The use of the term *his* here is deliberate as these writers were only concerned with a certain section of society, who were of course all male.

requires little restriction of organisational activity because of the assumption that the market, when completely free from regulation, will act as a mediating mechanism which will ensure that, by and large, the interests of all stakeholders of the organisation will be attended to by the need to meet these free market requirements. This view, however, resulted in a dilemma in reconciling collective needs with individual freedom. De Tocqueville (1840) reconciled these aims by suggesting that government institutions, as regulating agencies, were both inevitable and necessary in order to allow freedom to individuals and to protect those freedoms.[2]

Thus classical liberal arguments recognise a limitation in the freedom of an organisation to follow its own ends without any form of regulation. Similarly Fukuyama (1992) argued that liberalism is not in itself sufficient for continuity and that traditional organisations have a tendency to atomise in the pursuance of the ends of the individuals who have aggregated for the purpose for which the organisation was formed to fulfil. He argued that liberal economic principles provide no support for the traditional concept of an organisation as a community of common interest which is only sustainable if individuals within that community give up some of their rights to the community as an entity and accept a certain degree of intolerance. On the other hand, Fukuyama considered the triumph of liberal democracy as the final state of history, citing evidence of the break up of the eastern block as symbolising the triumph of classical liberalism.[3]

Although this classical liberal/economic rationality view of organisations can be viewed as one paradigm representing the structure and behaviour of organisations, with consequent implications for the evaluating and reporting of performance within such an organisation, it is by no means the only such paradigm. An alternative paradigm, predicated in the stakeholder view of organisations and the dynamic disequilibrium existing within organisations, and brought about by the conflicting needs of the various stakeholders, is a pluralistic paradigm.[4] Such a paradigm views organisations not as entities acting for a particular purpose but rather as a coalition of various interest groups acting in concert, through the resolution or subsumption of their convergent interests, for a particular purpose at a particular point in time. This purpose changes over time as the power of the various stakeholders changes and as various stakeholders join, and influence, the dominant coalition while other stakeholders leave that coalition.

Most people initially think that they know what CSR is and how to behave responsibly – and everyone claims to be able to recognise socially responsible or irresponsible behaviour without necessarily being able to define it. So there is general agreement that CSR is about a company's concern for such things as community involvement, socially responsible products and processes, concern for the environment and socially responsible employee relations (Ortiz-Martinez & Crowther 2006). Issues of socially responsible behaviour are not of course new and examples can be found from throughout the world and at least from the earliest days of the Industrial Revolution and the concomitant founding of large business entities (Crowther 2002) and the divorce between ownership and management – or the divorcing of risk from rewards (Crowther 2004).

---

2   See Barnett & Crowther (1998) for a more detailed consideration and critique of classical liberalism.

3   Fukuyama presents these arguments as the end of history, which he does not celebrate. In actual fact it is his critique of classical liberalism which is the most significant contribution of his work. This aspect of his work is almost universally ignored in favour of his end of history argument.

4   Pluralism was of course one of the strands of classical liberalism which was written out of the discourse of liberalism during the late nineteenth century.

According to the European Commission, CSR is about undertaking voluntary activity which demonstrates a concern for stakeholders. But it is here that a firm runs into problems – how to balance up the conflicting needs and expectations of various stakeholder groups while still being concerned with shareholders; how to practice sustainability; how to report this activity to those interested; how to decide if one activity more socially responsible that another. The situation is complex and conflicting. In this part, therefore, the contributors are concerned with one of the most significant problems for business of theorising and implementing CSR in practice.

In the first chapter therefore Goergen and Renneboog focus upon the relationship between shareholders and other stakeholders. They focus upon ownership and consider that one of the reasons why ownership may have an impact on corporate social responsibility is that major shareholders are visible to outsiders and may therefore become the target of activists if they do not prevent their firm's management from making socially irresponsible decisions while another possible reason is that a high level of corporate social responsibility improves financial performance. Corporate social responsibility would then be one of the factors of good management that a major shareholder would enforce in their monitoring effort.

In the next chapter, Birch is concerned with what he considers to be a proliferation of external agencies offering advice, consultancy, guidelines, new principles and numerous CSR-related standards, indices, codes and performance indicators. In this chapter he examines some of those agencies and raises the question of whether such agencies are actually effective, not so much in helping the CSR agenda along (which it would seem they have done) but in actually enabling business to seriously embed new CSR policies and practices into their everyday business cultures. Given that even organisations such as GRI and AccountAbility seem to be trying to turn themselves into consultancies then this is a very pertinent issue.

In the next chapter, Ertuna and Ertuna are concerned with globalisation and how it is affecting CSR. In doing so they reflect on the possible challenges in the redefinition of the relationship between corporations and society. They state that corporations seem to assume that social responsibility is a means to achieve their objective of profit and value maximisation based on their self-interest rather than the promotion of common good. They note differences in the objective functions and the moral principles guiding corporations in the west and the east and suggest that this can provide opportunities for cross-fertilisation in the redefinition of corporate social responsibility. This redefinition may provide solutions to the pressing problems of globalisation.

Erden and Bodur focus upon the particular situation in a transitional society and consider social responsibility in the context of corporate social performance in such a society. Their concern is with Turkey but the issues, of course, are relevant to a large number of such transitional economies and are particularly relevant not just to managers of such firms but also to international investors and managers with an interest in doing business in such a transitional society. They argue that managers must make strenuous efforts in such a society to communicate their social responsibility policy and activity as this will increase employee commitment and, therefore, social performance for the firm.

In the following chapter, Ayupov and Komilova focus upon Uzbekistan and the social responsibility activities of SMEs in that country. This is interesting and important because it shows the ubitquity of the concept of corporate social responsibility and the fact that similar issues are relevant in every part of the world, albeit affected by cultural differences.

So they consider all stakeholders before concluding that, in such an economy, efforts that address the community are more effective than those directed at the environment. Their argument is similar to the previous chapter contributors, however, when they argue that for managers, efforts to publicise their CSR activities should be seen as an integral part of their CSR investments.

A different area of concern is expressed by Jallow in the subsequent chapter. Her concern is with education and its role in developing ethical and socially responsible behaviour. In her words, this chapter is concerned with some of the practical ways of engagement and the demystifying of ethics as an academic subject so that it can be part of a broader educational framework in which we see ethics as a means to guide our actions and understand our behaviour. She is essentially concerned with individual behaviour but this readily translates to a business environment where managers are regularly asked to make decisions which have an ethical component.

In the next chapter, Renneboog, Ter Horst and Zhang concentrate upon an area which is frequently highlighted in discussions of corporate social responsibility, namely that of socially responsible investment funds. There has been an explosive growth in such funds around the world reflecting the increasing awareness of investors to social, environmental, ethical and corporate governance issues. Views on such funds and their performance are mixed and so they start by reviewing the field. They conclude that the existing studies hint, but do not unequivocally demonstrate, that SRI investors are willing to accept suboptimal financial performance to pursue social or ethical objectives.

Tencati, in the subsequent chapter, provides a broad picture of the most important evaluation and reporting systems of corporate social, environmental and sustainability performance. The starting point of the analysis is the concept of *accountability* that directly derives from the notion of CSR: according to a stakeholder view of the firm, a company is held accountable for its actions to the different constituencies. He argues that companies increasingly need appropriate systems to measure and control their own behaviour in order to assess whether they are responding to stakeholder concerns in an effective way and to communicate the results achieved, and reviews the developments designed to assist managers to achieve these aims.

Another issue which is of growing importance to managers is that of corporate reputation, something which Brammer and Pavelin address in the next chapter in the context of corporate social responsibility. In this chapter they provide a coherent and critical introduction to research addressing the link between corporate reputation and social responsibility that may be of use to both researchers and managers, addressing the various strands of literature and research which currently exist. They point out that the study of changes in reputation has been largely restricted to the investigation of reputational fallout from crises of various forms. Leaving some gaps in our understanding which future research should address.

Another area of growing importance is that of rating systems for the evaluation of corporate social responsibility activity and this is a topic which Schafer addresses in the final chapter in this part. Almost all CSR ratings operate with international norms and conventions mainly adopted from Non-Governmental Organisations (NGOs). CSR ratings cover (big capitalised) companies listed on stock exchanges and represented in leading international stock indices. The ratings are provided for economic decision making and addressed mainly to capital market participants like asset managers. The different rating schemes are based on an individual self-understanding of CSR by the rating institution.

According to Schafer the most important challenges for CSR ratings might be their ability to cope with quality standards and transparency, the reaction of close competitors like credit rating agencies, and the power of ethical investors as the most important clients of CSR rating institutions.

References

Barnett N J & Crowther D (1998); Community identity in the 21st century: a postmodernist evaluation of local government structure; *International Journal of Public Sector Management*, 11 (6/7), 425-439

Bentham J (1789); *An Introduction to the Principles of Morals and Legislation*; many editions

Crowther D (2002); *A Social Critique of Corporate Reporting*; Aldershot; Ashgate

Crowther D (2004); Limited liability or limited responsibility; in D Crowther & L Rayman-Bacchus (eds), *Perspectives on Corporate Social Responsibility*; Aldershot; Ashgate; pp 42-58

Dahl R A (1972); A prelude to corporate reform; *Business & Society Review*, Spring 1972, 17-23

Fukuyama F (1992); *The End of History and the Last Man*; New York; The Free Press

Locke J (1690); *Two Treatises of Government*; many editions

Mill J S (1863); *Utilitarianism, Liberty and Representative Government*; many editions

Ortiz-Martinez E & Crowther D (2006); ¿Son compatibles la responsabilidad económica y la responsabilidad social corporativa?; *Harvard Deusto Finanzas y Contabilidad*, No 71 pp 2-12

De Tocqueville A (1840); *Democracy in America*; many editions

17 *The Social Responsibility of Major Shareholders*[*],[#]

MARC GOERGEN AND LUC RENNEBOOG

Introduction

There are two major reasons why ownership may have an impact on Corporate Social Responsibility (CSR). First, if CSR improves financial performance, CSR will be part of good management enforced by the major shareholder via their monitoring effort. Second, major shareholders are visible and can therefore become the target of activists. We distinguish between Stakeholder Management (SM) and Social Issue Participation (SIP). Using data on ownership and CSR for the Standard and Poors (S&P) 500 firms, we analyse whether a major shareholder increases the level of SM or SIP. We find that none of our ownership variables affects CSR, SM and SIP.

> *Did you ever expect a corporation to have a conscience, when it has no soul to be damned, and no body to be kicked?*

> (Edward, First Baron Thurlow 1731–1806)[1]

The focus of this chapter is on the responsibility of major shareholders towards the stakeholders of the firm. Berle and Means (1932) predicted that firms evolve towards a separation of ownership and control as they become larger. As a consequence, managers end up with high discretionary power over the firm and most shareholders will be too small to control the managers' actions (Roe 1994). In this kind of framework, there is an agency problem between the managers on one side and the shareholders and other stakeholders on the other side, as the former may not necessarily run the company in the interest of the latter two.

---

[*] This chapter is part of a project undertaken by the Institute for International Corporate Governance and Accountability (IICGA), Law School, The George Washington University, 720 20th Street N.W., Washington, DC 20052, USA. Both authors are Fellows of the Institute as well as Research Associates of the European Corporate Governance Institute in Brussels.

[#] We are grateful to Larry Mitchell and the other participants of the first conference (June 2001) of the Institute for International Corporate Governance and Accountability for valuable comments and suggestions. We would also like to thank Marina Martynova, Anna Meyer, Clemens Papaire, Peter Szilagyi and Chendi Zhang for interesting suggestions. Any remaining errors are those of the authors.

[1] Quoted in King (1977, p.1). Thurlow became a Solicitor in 1770 and Lord Chancellor in 1778 (during King George III's reign).

However, there is a vast body of empirical evidence (see, for example, Barca and Becht 2001) which suggests that not all firms experience the separation of ownership and control as predicted by Berle and Means. Even in Anglo-American countries where ownership concentration of listed firms tends to be low, there are certain types of shareholders that on average hold larger stakes than other types. For example, Goergen and Renneboog (2001) find that, for the case of the UK, institutional shareholders hold substantial minority stakes in most firms. McConaughy et al. (1998) report that, in over 20 per cent of the largest 1,000 United States' corporations, the founding family remains influential. To date, a lot of research has been done on the level of protection of minority shareholders in countries with different legal systems and corporate governance arrangements (see La Porta et al. 1997; 1998; and 1999). Although, all types of stakeholders are subject to expropriation by whoever controls the firm's decisions, most existing research has only concentrated on the potential expropriation of minority shareholders.

One reason why research has mainly focused on the possible expropriation of shareholders is that shareholders are considered to be more vulnerable as their investment is sunk into the firm and is relatively difficult to recoup (Shleifer and Vishny 1997). Conversely, the other stakeholders tend to be less vulnerable. For example, employees get paid by the month (or even by the week). They also have the option to change jobs if they are discontent with their employer. A similar argument applies to customers who can walk away from the firm and choose another supplier. We believe that this argument is not necessarily valid, as it is relatively easy for shareholders to diversify their investments and, as a result, face a lower risk of expropriation by specific firms. Conversely, it is difficult for employees to diversify their human capital. Further, they frequently make company-specific investments in terms of their human capital which may be very valuable to their firm, but may be worthless to most other firms. Similarly, customers do not always have the option to switch to another firm if the market is highly uncompetitive or switching costs are high.[2]

We propose to extend this research by looking at the interaction between ownership and corporate social responsibility. The definition used for corporate social responsibility is the one by Carter, Kale and Grimm (2000):

Social responsibility deals with the managerial consideration of non-market forces or social aspects of corporate activity outside of a market or regulatory framework and includes consideration of issues such as employee welfare, community programs, charitable donations, and environmental protection.

We define a major shareholder as a shareholder whose stake is large enough that it requires disclosure to the relevant stock exchange supervisory body. In the United States, the SEC requires all stakes in excess of five per cent to be disclosed.

On one side, the presence of a major shareholder can be beneficial as it may reduce the agency problem between the management and the stakeholders of the firm. If the major shareholder monitors the managers, then the latter may have less potential to expropriate the shareholders, as the major shareholder will ensure that the managers act in the interest of all the shareholders. In addition, the presence of a major shareholder may also prevent the management from expropriating stakeholders other than the shareholders.

---

2   One industry which has high switching costs is the retail banking industry.

There are at least two possible reasons why a major shareholder may be concerned about the relationship the firm maintains with the other stakeholders. First, the financial performance of a firm with a low level of social responsibility may be negatively affected, as, for example, customers may boycott the products of firms that soil the environment or employ child labour. Bad treatment of the firm's employees may also backfire in terms of a low employee productivity and morale. For example, Hillman and Keim (2001) argue that better relations with the employees will reduce employee turnover. Huselid (1995) analysed almost 1,000 United States' firms and found that policies such as pay-performance incentives, high employee involvement and training improved employee productivity and loyalty as well as firm performance.[3] However, Marchington and Wilkinson (2002), who surveyed the literature on the link between Human Resources Management (HRM) and performance, raised the point about what causes what. It may indeed be the case that HRM does not increase performance, but that profitable firms have more cash to spend on HRM. Second, the major shareholder is visible to the stakeholders and the control of the firm may be perceived to lie with him ultimately. Hence, the major shareholder of a firm with a weak level of social responsibility may be the ultimate target of criticism or may in extreme cases be targeted by activists. The recent case of Huntingdon Life Sciences in the UK supports this argument. Huntingdon Life Sciences was targeted by animal rights activists given its experimentation on life animals. As a result, some of Huntingdon's major British and American shareholders eventually sold their stakes in the company and made public statements that they had disengaged themselves from the company.[4]

On the other side, the major shareholder may create new agency problems, such as the expropriation of the minority shareholders and other stakeholders. The most famous case of expropriation of other stakeholders by a large shareholder is probably the Maxwell pension scandal in the UK. In 1991, a total of £440 million of the employee pension funds managed by various firms owned by Robert Maxwell disappeared. In this case, the presence of a major shareholder would reduce the corporate social responsibility of the firm.

To summarise, a major shareholder may either increase the firm's level of social responsibility via monitoring the management or decrease it by pursuing their own interests rather than those of the other shareholders or all the stakeholders. Neither theory nor empirical studies seem to agree on what effect is more likely to emerge or under what conditions large shareholders are detrimental/beneficial to the firm's other stakeholders (see Gugler 2001 for an overview of this issue). To our knowledge there are no empirical studies on corporate social responsibility that take into account the firm's ownership structure.

The remainder of this chapter is organised as follows. We review the studies on the link between financial performance and social responsibility. Next, we supplement existing research by studying the link between corporate social responsibility and ownership Before, finally, concluding this chapter.

---

3   Wood (1999) reviews the literature on the link between human resource policies and performance. More specifically, he addresses the question whether good human resource management – in isolation – influences financial performance or whether it should be seen as only one of a whole set of elements that form business strategy.

4   See, for example, the Financial Times of 10 January 2002, p.1: 'Huntingdon Life Sciences, the controversial drug testing company, has lost its biggest backer – the US bank Stephens Inc – after a wave of violent animal rights protests. [...] Warren Stephens, the bank president, saw his home in New York vandalised last week, and staff have been the victims of physical abuse for several months. Stephens is planning to end its relationship with HLS by the end of the month, marking a U-turn on its previous stance. [...]'

The Link Between Financial Performance and Corporate Responsibilities

The main reason why a major shareholder should be concerned with their firm's level of social responsibility is that a weak level of social responsibility may negatively affect the firm's value. There are only a few studies that analyse the link between financial performance and corporate responsibility. Some of these studies are subject to the same kind of criticism which applies to the earlier studies on the link between financial performance and ownership. The criticism refers to the implicit assumption made by these studies that the direction of causality is from ownership to profitability (see Chapter 2 of Goergen (1998) for a detailed discussion on the issue of the direction of causality).

Earlier studies found mixed evidence on the link between financial performance and corporate social responsibility (see Ullmann (1985) for an excellent survey of these studies). For example, Vance (1975) finds a negative link suggesting that corporate social responsibility is a cost for the firm and reduces its financial performance. Conversely, McGuire et al. (1988), Moussavi and Evans (1986) and Wokutch and Spencer (1987) find evidence for a positive relationship. A third group of studies do not detect a link between financial performance and social performance (for example, Alexander and Buchholz 1978). Apart from McGuire et al. (1988) – who find a link between both future financial performance and corporate social responsibility on one side and past financial performance and corporate social responsibility on the other side – none of these studies explicitly tests the direction of causality between the two variables.

Waddock and Graves (1997) and Renneboog et al. (2007) acknowledge the issue about the direction of causality: better financial performance may be caused by a higher level of corporate social responsibility and vice-versa. They argue that the relationship between financial performance and social performance will be negative, if social responsibility imposes a cost on the firm. The cost of being socially responsible (for example, by investing in pollution control) will make the firm less competitive, if its competitors decide not to incur this kind of cost. Alternatively, the link will be positive, if the benefits from being socially responsible exceed the costs.[5] Waddock and Graves give the example of positive employee policies. These policies tend to have low costs, but may substantially increase the motivation and the loyalty of the employees. In turn, this would have a positive effect on employee productivity. In addition, firms that have such policies in place may find it easier to recruit high quality employees.

Waddock and Graves advance two different arguments about the direction of the causality between financial performance and corporate social responsibility. The argument which advocates that financial profitability causes corporate responsibility is based on Jensen's (1986) free cash flow hypothesis.[6] Firms with excessive free cash flows[7] may divert some of these cash flows to social causes (such as the protection of the environment and contributions to charities). The argument which states that corporate

---

5   Waddock and Graves also reiterate an argument found in the earlier literature. This argument is as follows. Given that there is an interaction between so many socio-economic factors there should be no relationship between financial performance and the social responsibility of firms.

6   Waddock and Graves call it the 'slack resources' argument.

7   Free cash flow is defined as the total cash stock of a firm minus the cash component of working capital, minus cash necessary for all compulsory payments (debt, payables, taxes) and minus cash invested in positive Net Present Value (NPV) investments.

social responsibility influences financial performance is based on the rationale that a high level of corporate social responsibility is embedded in good corporate management. A high degree of corporate social responsibility will ensure good relationships with all the firm's stakeholders and thereby improve the firm's financial performance.

Waddock and Graves's measure of corporate responsibility is based on the Kinder, Lydenberg and Domini (KLD) ranking of the S&P500 firms according to five attributes of social responsibility.[8] Firms were ranked on a scale ranging from –2 (major concerns) to 0 (neutral) to +2 (major strength) according to the following five attributes: community relations, employee relations, workforce diversity, environment, and product quality and safety (see the Appendix for a definition of these attributes). Firms were also ranked from –2 to 0 for three negative screens (South Africa, military and nuclear power).

To test the validity of the alternative hypotheses, Waddock and Graves first regress the level of corporate social responsibility in 1990 on the financial performance of the previous year. They find that corporate responsibility is positively linked to their three measures of financial performance: the Return on Assets (ROA), the Return on Equity (ROE) and the return on sales. This validates the hypothesis of free cash flow. Second, they regress financial performance in 1991 on corporate social responsibility in 1990. They also find that corporate social responsibility increases the firm's performance when performance is measured by ROA and the return on sales. This gives support to the alternative hypothesis of good management. Waddock and Graves conclude that there is no evidence that corporate social responsibility always affects financial performance in a negative way, but that there may be cases where too many funds are diverted to activities of corporate social responsibility.

Based on the contradictory results obtained by previous empirical studies, Hillman and Keim (2001) formulate a model which explicitly allows for the possibility of having a negative or positive relationship between firm value and social responsibility. Hillman and Keim argue that there are two components of corporate social responsibility. One of the components refers to improving the relationships the firm has with its different primary stakeholders.[9] They call this Stakeholder Management (SM). Improving stakeholder relationships will have a positive impact on the firm's performance. The other component relates to the social issues that do not improve the relationships between the firm and its primary stakeholders. This component will reduce the firm's financial performance. They call this Social Issue Participation (SIP). Hence, Hillman and Keim's model includes both the good management hypothesis and the free cash flow hypothesis. They use the annual change in the Market Value Added (MVA)[10] (see Stern Stewart 1996) as well as ROE, ROA and the market-to-book-value ratio as performance measures. They regress current financial performance on their measures of SM and SIP for the previous year. They find that when current financial performance is measured by MVA, financial performance

---

8   During the period of study covered by Waddock and Graves (1997), the definition of the KLD index was different from the one which we use (that is, the definition for the year 2000) in the sense that it was based on only five attributes and three exclusionary screens. Firms operating in the gambling industry or producing alcohol were altogether excluded. As of the year 2000, there are now three additional attributes which are *non-US operations, product* and *other*. There are now five exclusionary screens including *nuclear power, military, alcohol, gambling* and *tobacco*. *South Africa* is now no longer an exclusionary screen.

9   Hillman and Keim adopt Clarkson's (1994) definition of a primary stakeholder. Primary stakeholders are the stakeholders that 'bear some form of risk as a result of having invested some form of capital, human or financial, something of value, in a firm' (Hillman and Keim's quote from Clarkson 1994). These include providers of finance, employees, suppliers, customers, community members and the environment.

10   There have been some criticisms about this measure of performance. See, for example, Brealey and Myers (2000).

depends positively on SM, and negatively on SIP. When either the current measure of SM or SIP is regressed on the previous year change in MVA, then the regression is not significant. This suggests that financial performance depends on social responsibility and not the other way round. Surprisingly, Hillman and Keim do not find that financial performance depends on either of the two components of social responsibility if the alternative measures of financial performance are used. Concerning the two components of social responsibility, they find corroboration of their two hypotheses: SM has a positive effect on financial profitability whereas SIP has a negative effect.

There are also a number of studies that concentrate on just one area of social responsibility such as environmental friendliness and charitable contributions. Klassen and McLaughlin (1996) develop a theoretical model on the link between financial profitability and environmental responsibility. They argue that good environmental management will have a positive effect on financial performance via increased sales and decreased costs. As a result of environmental friendliness customers will be more eager to buy the products of the firm. Environmentally responsible firms will also reduce future liabilities in the case of environmental accidents. Klassen and McLaughlin brush aside the issue of the direction of causality by arguing that the benefits from good environmental management always exceed the costs. They use the event study methodology applied to announcements by third parties of firms winning an environmental award or announcements about firms having caused environmental crises (such as oil spills). Klassen and McLaughlin find that shareholders of firms that earn awards realise excess stock returns (measured by the Cumulative Abnormal Returns (CARs)) that are positive and statistically significant. The excess returns for the three-day window centred on the event day are about 0.63 per cent. Stock markets react negatively to the announcement of environmental accidents with negative excess returns of –0.82 per cent. Klassen and McLaughlin also perform a regression analysis which measures the stock market reaction to the type of award. They include among others a dummy variable which is set to one if the firm is a first-time award winner and is zero otherwise, the pollution expenditure by industry and an interactive term of the former two. The only variables with coefficients that are significantly different from zero are the first-time award winner dummy and the above interaction term. They find that excess returns are five per cent higher on average if the firm is a first-time award winner. However, the coefficient on the interactive term is highly negative.

Depending on the magnitude of the pollution expenditures by the industry, the overall effect on the stock return then becomes negative for firms in relatively dirty industries, but remains positive for firms in relatively clean industries. Klassen and McLaughlin interpret this result by saying that '… first-time awards to firms operating in a dirty industry are treated with skepticism by the financial markets…'. An alternative interpretation of this result, which the authors of the paper fail to suggest, is that in certain industries the costs from good environmental management significantly exceed the benefits and therefore change the relationship from a positive one to a negative one.

The study by Carter, Kale and Grimm (2000) looks at the link between financial performance and environmental purchasing. The competing theoretical arguments for the sign of the relationship are similar to the ones for the link between firm value and overall corporate responsibility. The argument advocating for a positive link is based on the fact that consumers and other stakeholders can distinguish environmentally-friendly firms from less responsible firms via independent certification programmes and via ecological logos. Carter et al. measure good environmental purchasing by a qualitative index which is based on five different attributes. They find that their index is positively linked to net income, but is negatively linked to the cost of goods sold. Carter et al. conclude that their test confirms the theoretical model by Klassen and McLaughlin (1996).

To our best knowledge, the studies on donations by firms concentrate on the different motivations for making donations, but do not investigate the link between firm value and these donations. For example, Leclair and Gordon (2000) find that corporate donations to artistic and cultural activities are positively correlated to advertising expenditure, whereas donations to civic, health and educational causes are not. It would be interesting to extend this kind of research and test the Hillman and Keim (2001) model.

To summarise, earlier studies on the link between financial performance and corporate social responsibility have found mixed evidence. The relation was positive in some studies, and negative or neutral in others. Given that some of these earlier studies have not addressed the issue of the direction of causality, they may be subject to an endogeneity problem. The recent study by Hillman and Keim (2001) is based on a model which splits corporate social responsibility into two components, each of which is expected to have a different effect on financial performance. First, good SM is expected to have a positive impact on firm value. Second, participation in broader social issues is hypothesised to have a negative effect on corporate performance. Hillman and Keim find strong evidence for this. Hence, more recent studies suggest that it is in the interest of a major shareholder to ensure that their firm has good relationships with its stakeholders.

The Link Between Corporate Social Responsibility and Ownership

To our knowledge, there is no study which looks at how different ownership structures influence the level of corporate social responsibility. We propose to investigate this relationship. In line with the Hillman and Keim (2001) approach, we distinguish between SM and SIP.

We argue that, given that major shareholders are more visible to the general public than small shareholders and are also perceived to hold the ultimate control over the firm, the presence of a large shareholder should be associated with a higher degree of SIP. The competing hypothesis is that SIP is not in the interest of the firm and its direct stakeholders and therefore the firm should not engage in a high degree of SIP. If this is the case, a large shareholder may prevent the management from directing (excessive) corporate funds towards social issues that will not improve the wealth of the firm's direct stakeholders.

> Hypothesis 1a: Major shareholders, given their higher visibility, will come hand in hand with a higher degree of SIP.

> Hypothesis 1b: SIP is not in the interest of the firm's direct stakeholders. Therefore, a large shareholder will prevent management from diverting too many funds towards SIP.

In general, large shareholders should benefit from SM and the resulting improvement in corporate performance.[11]

> Hypothesis 2: Major shareholders will push for more SM as this improves the firm's financial performance.

The measures for SIP and SM are derived from the same source of data as the one used by most previous studies on corporate social responsibility, the KLD database. However, the format of the KLD data has now slightly changed. Instead of rating firms on a scale from –2 to +2 (or –2 to 0) for each attribute, KLD now present the data in terms of a number of individual strengths and weaknesses per attribute. KLD also rate firms based on five exclusionary screens. There are no positive ratings for these screens and ratings range from –2 to 0. The different attributes and exclusionary screens as well as the relevant strengths and weaknesses are listed in the Appendix. For example, the attribute *Community* has six different areas of strength (for example, support for housing) and four different areas of concern (for example, indigenous peoples relations). Each firm is attributed a value of zero or one in each area of strength or concern. A value of zero means that the area does not apply, whereas a value of one means that it does apply (see KLD 2001 and Johansson 2001). As the number of areas of strength and concern vary from attribute to attribute, a first step in treating the data is to standardise them so that they can be compared with each other. The usual way to do this is by transforming such data into a Z-score (see Johansson 2001).[12,13] Similar to Hillman and Keim (2001), for each firm, we then sum up the Z-scores obtained for the attributes relevant to SM to obtain SM. These attributes are *community, diversity, employee relations, environment* and *product*. SIP is obtained in a similar way by summing up the Z-scores of the individual attributes and screens relevant to SIP. They are: *non-United States operations, other* and the five exclusionary screens (*alcohol, gambling, tobacco, military* and *nuclear power*). We also added up SM and SIP to give us the level of overall corporate social responsibility.

The data on ownership, financial figures and SIC codes were extracted from the Worldscope database.[14] In our sample, no firm had more than seven major shareholders. The problem with the variable measuring the percentage of closely shares is that it does not include holdings by insurance firms and is computed by adding up shares across different classes of shares (including non-voting shares). We therefore decided to base

---

11   One can argue that if the large shareholder tends to keep their stake in the firm on a long-term basis, then they should be interested in SM. However, if the large shareholder has only a temporary stake in the firm, keeping good relationships with other stakeholders (for example, employees) is less of an issue. To the extreme, the large shareholder may even expropriate the other stakeholders. Hence, the sign of the relationship between ownership concentration and SM may be less obvious.

12   We are very grateful to Sandra Waddock for the suggestion to use Z-scores.

13   On the individual firm basis, for each attribute or screen, the areas of strength are summed up as well as the areas of concern. The difference between the two is then taken. This gives us the score a firm has achieved for a given attribute or screen. From this score, we then subtract the average score across the sample of firms. This difference is then divided by the standard-deviation – a measure of the spread – of the score across the sample. This yields a Z-score for a given firm by attribute or screen, that is, a standardised score which measures the distance of the firm's score from the sample average. The distance is measured in terms of the number of standard-deviations the firm's score is away from the sample's average score.

14   Worldscope provides information on the major shareholders (MajorShareholders) for each firm as well as a numerical variable (CloselyHeldSharesPct). For each year, Worldscope provides the list of the ten largest shareholders holding in excess of five per cent of a firm's common stock.

ourselves exclusively on the information on the major shareholders. The measures of ownership we used are as shown in Table 17.1

The thresholds of ten per cent and 20 per cent for the dummy variables were chosen in accordance with Becht (2001, p. 290) who reports that the SEC considers shareholders holding at least ten per cent or 20 per cent of the common stock to have a substantial level of control over the company.

Table 17.1 Measures of ownership

Large	The percentage holding of the largest major shareholder.
All	The sum of the holdings of all the largest major shareholders.
Herf	The Herfindahl index computed from all the largest holdings in each firm. The Herfindahl index measures concentration. The index will range from 0 for a firm with a highest possible dispersion of ownership to 10,000 for a firm which is 100 per cent controlled by a single shareholder.
$Major_1$, ..., $Major_7$	The percentage holding of each of the individual major shareholders.
Ten	A dummy variable[a] which is set to one, if the largest major shareholder controls more than 10 per cent of the firm's common shares, and zero otherwise.
Twenty	A dummy variable which is set to one, if the largest major shareholder controls more than 20 per cent of the firm's common shares, and zero otherwise.
Majority[b]	A dummy variable which is set to one, if the largest major shareholder controls more than 50 per cent of the firm's common shares, and zero otherwise.

[a]   A dummy variable is a binomial variable, that is, a variable that can only take on two values, 0 or 1. Examples of dummy variables are male versus female, smoker versus non-smoker and employed versus unemployed.

[b]   There is likely to be a bias on the measurement of the impact of this ownership variable on the corporate social responsibility measures SM, SIP and CSP, as KLD consider any firm, which is majority-owned by another firm, to be a division of the latter (see also the definitions for ownership strength/concern of *other* in the Appendix). By definition, firms that are majority-owned by other firms would have the same level of SM, SIP and CSP as their parent company. However, this would obviously not apply if the majority shareholder were a family or individual. Due to the latter and the small percentage of majority-owned firms in the sample, we decided to retain this dummy as a measure of ownership.

We used similar control variables in the regressions as the one used by Waddock and Graves (1997) and Hillman and Keim (2001): the size of the firm (measured by either the natural logarithm of sales (*LSales*) or employees (*LEmp*)), the percentage of debt in the capital structure (*Debt*), the firm's level of risk proxied by the beta factor from the Capital Asset Pricing Model (*Beta*),[15] the firm's financial performance (the return on equity per share (*ROES*), the return on equity per total dollar (*ROED*), or the return on assets (*ROA*)).

---

15   Beta measures the type of risk which cannot be eliminated by holding a well-diversified portfolio of investments. Beta is a measure of relative risk. Beta is measured relative to the market as a whole. A firm's expected stock return will be proportional to its beta. A firm with a beta of exactly one has a risk which is identical to the market as a whole. In this case, if the return on the whole market is ten per cent, the return on the firm will also be ten per cent (plus an error term). A firm with a beta of less than one is less risky than the market as a whole. Conversely, a firm with a beta in excess of one is more risky than the market as a whole. For example, a firm with a beta of 1.5 would have an expected return of 15 per cent (plus an error term), if the expected return on the market is 10 per cent (that is, 1.5 times ten per cent = 15 per cent).

Each model also includes seven industry dummies,[16] based on the first digit of each firm's primary SIC code. These dummies adjust for possible differences between the different industrial sectors.

The KLD database covers all the S&P500 firms as well as an additional 160 firms which are not included in the S&P500. As it is not entirely clear how these additional 160 firms were selected, our study only covers the S&P500 firms. We also exclude any foreign firms that are members of the S&P500 index. This leaves us with 485 firms. Table 17.2 shows the characteristics of the sample. On average, S&P500 firms have annual sales of US$10,826,000,000 million and employ about 43,000 employees. In terms of financial performance, their ROA averages eight per cent and their ROE is about 17 per cent. S&P500 firms typically have about a third of their capital structure made of debt and their beta is close to 1. The Herfindahl index – which can range from zero for a firm with no ownership concentration to 10,000 for a firm whose entire common stock is owned by a single shareholder – shows that on average ownership concentration is low in the sample firms. The largest major shareholder tends to hold on average nine per cent. There are 190, 31 and 4 firms with a shareholder holding in excess of ten per cent, 20 per cent and 50 per cent, respectively, of the common stock. In total, all the major shareholders hold about 16 per cent of the equity of the sample firms. The table also shows that the second major shareholder is relatively important compared to the first major shareholder. Conversely, outside the United States and UK, major shareholders normally do not face other major shareholders (see, for example, Goergen and Renneboog 2001). This suggests that there is a potential for coalition forming (we take this into account by using the measures *All* and *Herf*).

Table 17.3 provides information on the level of corporate social responsibility of the sample firms. Given the definition of the scores (that is, they are the relative deviation of a firm's score from the average score for the sample), the average for the sample is close to zero. About half of the firms have negative scores for corporate social responsibility and SIP. Conversely, only about 28 per cent of the firms have a negative score for SM. This suggests that on average firms are more concerned with their direct stakeholders than with general social issues.

Table 17.4 analyses the impact of ownership, measured by *Large*, *Herf* and *Ten*, respectively, on corporate social responsibility. The regressions also control for size, capital structure, risk and corporate performance. The control variables tend to have the expected sign and significance. For example, corporate social responsibility is significantly and negatively correlated with total sales. Similar to Waddock and Graves (1997), we find a positive and significant link between current corporate social responsibility and past financial profitability. However, none of the coefficients on the measures of ownership are significantly different from zero suggesting that firms with large shareholders do neither behave more responsibly nor less responsibly. Similarly, we find that ownership concentration does not influence the level of SM and SIP. The results are similar for the other ownership variables and the alternative firm size and performance variables. Hence, the results suggest that ownership does not have an impact on corporate social responsibility, SM (SM) and SIP (SIP).

The reason why we do not find a link between corporate social responsibility and ownership may be the high ownership dispersion of United States' firms. In most firms

---

16   In total there are nine different first-digit SIC categories. We had to drop the first category as it included only two firms. We also dropped category nine to avoid perfect multicollinearity.

Table 17.2 Characteristics of the 485 United States S&P500 firms for 1999

Beta is the firm's risk as measured by the CAPM beta. Large is the percentage holding of the largest major shareholder. All is the sum of the holdings of all the largest major shareholders. Herf is the Herfindahl index computed from all the largest holdings in each firm. Major1, ..., Major7 are the percentage holding of each of the individual major shareholders. Ten is a dummy variable which is set to one, if the largest major shareholder controls more than 10 per cent of the firm's common shares, and zero otherwise. Twenty is a dummy variable which is set to one, if the largest major shareholder controls more than 20 per cent of the firm's common shares, and zero otherwise. Majority is a dummy variable which is set to one, if the largest major shareholder controls more than 50 per cent of the firm's common shares, and zero otherwise.

Variable	Average	Median	Minimum	Maximum	Standard-deviation	Proportion equal to 1	Sample size
Sales (million USD)	10,826	5,275	1.07	176,558	18,491	–	484
Employees	43,067	19,595	17	1,140,000	76,535	–	476
Return on assets (%)	7.88	7.06	-198.24	52.98	14.43	–	483
Return on equity per share (%)	17.07	17.28	-336.57	130.89	29.07	–	475
Return on equity per dollar (%)	43.68	18.72	-2,116.55	12,033.33	559.47	–	478
Beta	0.91	0.73	-0.7	4.65	0.87	–	455
Debt ratio	34.89	34.89	0.00	213.84	24.01	–	484
Large (%)	8.96	8.40	0.00	95.00	10.13	–	481
All (%)	16.03	14.25	0.00	95.00	15.44	–	482
Herf	238.57	116.68	0.00	9,025.00	705.06	–	482
Major$_1$ (%)	8.89	8.36	0.00	95.00	10.13	–	482
Major$_2$ (%)	4.10	5.10	0.00	18.90	4.36	–	482
Major$_3$ (%)	1.95	0.00	0.00	14.89	3.24	–	482
Major$_4$ (%)	0.77	0.00	0.00	10.02	2.13	–	482
Major$_5$ (%)	0.25	0.00	0.00	8.53	1.21	–	482
Major$_6$ (%)	0.07	0.00	0.00	6.80	0.63	–	482
Major$_7$ (%)	0.01	0.00	0.00	5.40	0.25	–	482
Ten	–	–	–	–	–	39.42	482
Twenty	–	–	–	–	–	6.43	482
Majority	–	–	–	–	–	0.83	482

Source: Own calculations based on Worldscope.

Table 17.3 Corporate social responsibility of the 484 United States S&P500 firms

CSP measures overall corporate social responsibility and is the sum of the scores for SIP and SM for each firm. SM is the measure of SM. It is obtained by summing up for each firm the Z-scores obtained for the relevant attributes. These attributes are community, diversity, employee relations, environment, and product. SIP is obtained in a similar way by summing up the Z-scores of the individual attributes and screens relevant to SIP. These are non-United States operations, other, and the five exclusionary screens (alcohol, gambling, tobacco, military, and nuclear power).

Panel A: Non-standardised scores

	Average	Median	Minimum	Maximum	Percentage negative	Standard-deviation
SM						
Community [-4,+6]	0.20	0	-2	4	10.95	0.76
Diversity [-3,+8]	0.83	1	-2	6	12.19	1.37
Employee relations [-5,+5]	0.35	0	-3	4	16.32	0.96
Environment [-7,+6]	-0.27	0	-5	2	21.07	1.00
Product [-4,+4]	-0.30	0	-3	2	28.51	0.86
SIP						
Non-United States operations [-5,+3]	-0.08	0	-2	1	8.88	0.38
Other [-4,+3]	-0.63	-1	-3	1	56.82	0.65
Alcohol [-2,0]	0	0	-1	0	0.21	0.05
Gambling [-2,0]	0	0	-1	0	0.21	0.05
Tobacco [-2,0]	0	0	-1	0	0.21	0.05
Military [-4,0]	-0.13	0	-2	0	11.57	0.36
Nuclear power [-4,0]	-0.07	0	-2	0	6.61	0.27

Table 17.3 Concluded

Panel B: Z-scores

	Average	Median	Minimum	Maximum	Percentage negative	Standard-deviation
SIP	-0.07	0.01	-4.08	0.63	54.85	0.44
SM	-0.03	0.00	-1.64	2.12	28.45	0.57
CSP	-0.05	0.00	-2.45	0.89	47.84	0.36

Source: own calculations based on Worldscope.

Table 17.4 OLS regressions explaining corporate social responsibility

The dependent variable is CSR. The main independent variable is Large, the percentage holding of the largest shareholder holding more than five per cent of the common stock, Herf, the Herfindahl index, or Ten, a dummy variable set to one if the largest shareholder holds more than 10 per cent of the equity, respectively. Other independent variables are control variables used in previous studies as well as seven industry dummies (the latter are not reported here).

Variable	Coefficient	p-value	Coefficient	p-value	Coefficient	p-value
	Independent variable					
	Large		**Herf**		**Ten**	
	0.001	.694	0.000	.329	-0.007	.843
	Control variables					
Constant	0.443	.002	0.431	.002	0.448	.002
Lsales	-0.080	.000	-0.080	.000	-0.081	.000
Debt	-0.001	.220	-0.001	.227	-0.000	.229
Beta	-0.017	.440	-0.017	.450	-0.018	.422
ROES	0.000	.050	0.242	.048	0.000	.048
R^2	0.130		0.134		0.132	
Adjusted R^2	0.106		0.110		0.108	
p-value for F-test	0.000		0.000		0.000	
Sample size	449		450		450	

individual shareholders do not tend to be important enough in terms of their voting rights to influence the actions of the managers. Further, given the low incidence of firms with high ownership concentration (for example, there are only four firms in our sample with a majority shareholder), even if there is a link, it is unlikely that this link would be picked up by an econometric model. A way to solve this problem would be to run the model on a random sample of United States' firms, including smaller firms which are likely to have a

Table 17.5 Correlation matrix

	LSALES	LEMP	DEBT	BETA	ROES	ROED	ROA	LARGE	TEN	TWENTY	MAJORITY	HERF	ALL	CSP	SM	SIP
LSALES	1.000															
LEMP	0.826 ***	1.000														
DEBT	0.213 ***	0.197 ***	1.000													
BETA	−0.233 ***	−0.168 ***	−0.311 ***	1.000												
ROES	0.067 *	0.082 **	0.003	−0.013	1.000											
ROED	0.120 ***	0.125 ***	0.009	−0.021	1.000 ***	1.000										
ROA	0.187 ***	0.134 ***	−0.115 ***	−0.006	0.045	0.148 ***	1.000									
LARGE	−0.102 **	−0.017	−0.063 *	0.086 **	0.009	0.006	−0.025	1.000								
TEN	−0.163 ***	−0.029	0.011	0.085 **	0.059 *	0.049	−0.033	0.583 ***	1.000							
TWENTY	−0.016	0.026	−0.065 *	0.099 **	−0.013	−0.012	−0.034	0.684 ***	0.325 ***	1.000						
MAJORITY	0.006	−0.017	−0.035	0.016	−0.003	−0.003	0.016	0.721 ***	0.113 ***	0.349 ***	1.000					
HERF	−0.031	−0.017	−0.044	0.026	−0.008	−0.008	−0.002	0.879 ***	0.292 ***	0.542 ***	0.944 ***	1.000				
ALL7	−0.176 ***	−0.064 *	−0.047	0.077 **	−0.018	−0.019	−0.026	0.830 ***	0.621 ***	0.477 ***	0.456 ***	0.660 ***	1.000			
CSP	−0.216 ***	−0.179 ***	−0.125 ***	0.065 *	0.071 *	0.072 *	0.090 **	0.017	0.019	−0.023	0.005	0.009	0.011	1.000		
SM	0.014	−0.004	−0.122 ***	0.068 *	0.099 **	0.095 **	0.076 **	0.002	−0.020	−0.003	0.039	0.016	−0.045	0.718 ***	1.000	
SIP	−0.322 ***	−0.251 ***	−0.066 *	0.029	0.009	0.014	0.058	0.023	0.047	−0.030	−0.029	−0.002	0.058	0.764 ***	0.098 **	1.000

***, ** and * denote statistical significance at the 10%, 5% and 1% level, respectively.

higher ownership concentration. Our view is supported by the correlation between sales (*LSales*) and the percentage of shares held by the largest shareholder (*Large*) (see Table 17.5 opposite). Albeit small, the correlation is negative and statistically significant from zero suggesting that ownersthip of small firms is more concentrated. Unfortunately, the KLD database covers only the largest United States' firms.

Conclusion

This chapter has investigated the relationship between ownership and corporate social responsibility. One of the reasons why ownership may have an impact on corporate social responsibility is that major shareholders are visible to outsiders and may therefore become the target of activists if they do not prevent their firm's management from making socially irresponsible decisions. An alternative possible reason is that a high level of corporate social responsibility improves financial performance. Corporate social responsibility would then be one of the factors of good management that a major shareholder would enforce in their monitoring effort.

Similar to recent studies on the link between financial profitability and corporate social performance, we distinguish between two components of social responsibility: SM and SIP. Hillman and Keim (2001) find that the former has a positive impact on firm value whereas the latter has a negative impact. Using detailed ownership data and data on corporate social responsibility for the S&P500 firms, we analyse whether the existence of a major shareholder increases the level of SM or SIP. Although, we find similar signs and levels of significance to previous studies on the control variables in our regression, none of our ownership variables has an effect on social performance.

One of the reasons why we find no such link may be due to the fact that we focus on the S&P500 firms which tend to be large firms with low levels of ownership concentration. Future research should ideally look at a random sample of firms and not just at the largest ones. Although, we used numerous measures of ownership and control, we did not distinguish between the different types of shareholder. Ideally, future studies should also look at the identity of the major shareholder. For example, individuals who hold major stakes in a firm with a low degree of corporate social responsibility may be more visible and easier to target than a pension fund or a foreign investor.

References

Alexander, J. and R. Buchholz (1978), 'Research Notes Corporate Social Responsibility and Stock Market Performance', *Academy of Management Journal* 21, 479–486.

Barca, F. and M. Becht (2001), *The Control of Corporate Europe*, Oxford: Oxford University Press.

Becht, M. (2001), 'Beneficial Ownership in the United States', in: F. Barca and M. Becht: *The Control of Corporate Europe*, Oxford: Oxford University Press.

Berle, A. and G. Means (1932), *The Modern Corporation and Private Property*, New York: Macmillan.

Brealey, R. and S. Myers (2000), *Principles of Corporate Finance*, Boston: McGraw-Hill.

Carter, C., R. Kale, and C. Grimm (2000), 'Environmental Purchasing and Firm Performance: An Empirical Investigation', *Transportation Research Part E* 36, 219–228.

Clarkson, M. (1994), 'A Risk Based Model of Stakeholder Theory', *Proceedings of the Second Toronto Conference on Stakeholder Theory*, Centre for Corporate Social Performance and Ethics, University of Toronto.

Goergen, M. (1998), *Corporate Governance and Financial Performance: A Study of German and UK Initial Public Offerings*, Cheltenham: Edward Elgar.

Goergen, M. and L. Renneboog (2001), 'Strong Managers and Passive Institutional Investors in the UK', in Barca, F. and M. Becht: *The Control of Corporate Europe*, Oxford: Oxford University Press, 258–284.

Gugler, K. (2001), *Corporate Governance and Financial Performance*, Oxford: Oxford University Press.

Hillman, A and G. Keim (2001), 'Shareholder Value, Stakeholder Management, and Social Issues: What's the Bottom Line?' *Strategic Management Journal* 22, 125–139.

Huselid, M. (1995), 'The Impact of Human Resource Management Practices on Turnover, Productivity, and Corporate Financial Performance', *Academy of Management Journal* 38, 635–672.

Jensen, M. (1986), 'Agency Costs of Free Cash Flow, Corporate Finance and Takeovers', *American Economic Review Papers and Proceedings* 76, 323–329.

Johansson, P. (2001), 'The 100 Best Corporate Citizens for 2001', *Business Ethics Magazine*.

King, M. (1977), 'Public Policy and the Corporation', London: Chapman and Hall.

Klassen, R. and C. McLaughlin (1996), 'The Impact of Environmental Management on Firm Performance', *Management Science* 42, 1199–1214.

KLD Research & Analytics, Inc. (2001), *Inclusive Social Rating Criteria*, Boston: KLD Research & Analytics, Inc.

La Porta, R., F. Lopez-de-Silanes., A. Shleifer, and R.Vishny (1997), 'Legal Determinants of External Finance', *Journal of Finance* 52, 1131–1150.

La Porta, R., F. Lopez-de-Silanes., A. Shleifer, and R.Vishny (1998), 'Law and Finance', *Journal of Political Economy* 106, 1113–1155.

La Porta, R., F. Lopez-de-Silanes., A. Shleifer, and R.Vishny (1999), 'Ownership Around the World', *Journal of Finance* 54, 471–517.

Leclair, M. and K. Gordon (2000), 'Corporate Support for Artistic and Cultural Activities: What Determines the Distribution of Corporate Giving?', *Journal of Cultural Economics* 24, 225–241.

Marchington, M. and A. Wilkinson (2002), *People Management and Development*, 2nd edition, London: Chartered Institute of Personnel And Development (CIPD).

McConaughy, D, M. Walker, G. Henderson, and C. Mishra (1998), 'Founding Family Controlled Firms: Efficiency and Value', *Review of Financial Economics* 7, 1–19.

McGuire, J, A. Sundgren, and T. Schneeweis (1988), 'Corporate Social Responsibility and Firm Financial Performance', *Academy of Management Journal* 31, 854–872.

Moussavi, F., and D. Evans (1986), 'An Attributable Approach to Measuring Corporate Social Performance', mimeo, San Diego.

Renneboog, L., J. ter Horst and C. Zhang (2007), Socially Responsible Investments: Institutional Aspects, Performance, and Investor Behaviour, Discussion paper CentER, Tilburg University.

Roe, M. (1994), 'Strong Managers, Weak Owners: The Political Roots of American Corporate Finance', Princeton: Princeton University Press.

Shleifer, A and R Vishny (1997), 'Review of the Literature on Corporate Governance', *Journal of Finance* 52, 737–783.

Stern Stewart (1996), 'The Stern Stewart Performance 1000', New York: Stern Stewart Management Services.

Ullmann, A. (1985), 'Data in Search of a Theory: A Critical Examination of the Relationship among Social Performance, Social Disclosure, and Economic Performance', *Academy of Management Review* 10, 540–577.

Vance, S. (1975), 'Are Socially Responsible Corporations Good Investment Risks?', *Managerial Review* 64, 18–24.

Waddock, S. and S. Graves (1997), 'The Corporate Social Performance-Financial Performance Link', *Strategic Management Journal* 18, 303–319.

Wokutch, R. and B. Spencer (1987), 'Corporate Saints and Sinners: The Effects of Philanthropic and Illegal Activity on Organizational Performance', *California Management Review* 29, 77–88.

Wood, S. (1999), 'Human Resource Management and Performance', *International Journal of Management Reviews* 1, 367–413.

KEY REFERENCES FOR FURTHER READIN

Goergen, M. and L. Renneboog (2006), 'Corporate Governance and Shareholder Value', in D. Lowe and R. Leiringer (eds), *Commercial Management of Projects: Defining the Discipline*, Blackwell Publishing, 100-131.

Gugler, K. (2001), *Corporate Governance and Financial Performance*, Oxford: Oxford University Press.

Hillman, A and G. Keim (2001), 'Shareholder Value, Stakeholder Management, and Social Issues: What's the Bottom Line?' *Strategic Management Journal* 22, 125–139.

Renneboog, L., J. ter Horst and C. Zhang (2008), 'The Price of Ethics: Evidence from Socially Responsible Mutual Funds Around the World', *Journal of Corporate Finance*, forthcoming.

Renneboog, L., J. ter Horst and C. Zhang (2007), 'Is ethical money financially smart?', Discussion paper CentER, Tilburg University and European Corporate Governance Institute.

Waddock, S. and S. Graves (1997), 'The Corporate Social Performance-Financial Performance Link', *Strategic Management Journal* 18, 303–319.

Appendix: KLD's Social Rating Attributes as of 2000

STAKEHOLDER MANAGEMENT (SM)

Community: The six strengths are *generous giving* (the firm has been giving at least 1.5 per cent of its pre-tax profits over the last three years to charity), *innovative giving* (the firm has innovative giving schemes in place), *support for housing* (the firm supports social housing), *support for education* (the firm supports education for socially disadvantaged groups or supports on the job-training for young people), *indigenous peoples relations* (the firm respects the needs of indigenous peoples) and *other strengths* (the firm has other programmes in place that support the community). The four weaknesses are *investment controversies* (the firm is a financial institution which has earned a bad reputation in terms of its investment and lending policies), *negative economic impact* (the firm has in one way or another had major negative impacts on the community (for example, via pollution)), *indigenous peoples relations* (the firm has acted against the rights of indigenous peoples), and *other concerns* (the firm is involved in major conflicts with the community).

    Diversity: The eight strengths are *CEO* (the firm's CEO is female or from a minority group), *board of directors* (women and minorities sit on the board of the firm), *family benefits* (the firm has programmes in place that tackle work and family-related issues), *promotion* (there is evidence that the firm promotes women and minorities to key positions), *women/minority contracting* (the firm subcontracts or buys from women and minorities), *progressive gay & lesbian policies* (the firm offers to the partners of its gay and lesbian employees the same benefits it offers to the partners of its heterosexual employees), *employment of the disabled* (the firm employs and hires disabled people), and *other strengths* (the firm promotes diversity in other areas not included in the above areas). The three weaknesses are *controversies* (the firm has been successfully sued for controversial policies towards minorities), *non-representation* (there are no women on the firm's board or in other senior posts) and *other concerns* (there are other diversity problems).

Employee relations: The five strengths are *strong union relations, profit sharing for employees, employee involvement* (the firm promotes employee stock ownership and other types of employee involvement), *strong retirement benefits* and *other strengths* (for example, the firm has a good safety record). There are five possible weaknesses. They are *poor union relations, safety controversies* (for example, the firm has been successfully sued for violations against employee safety), *workforce reductions* (the firm has fired 15 per cent of its employees during the last year or a quarter of its employees during the last two years or is about to engage in such layoffs), *pension/benefits concern* (the firm operates an underfunded pension or benefits scheme), and *other concerns* (any other employee concern which does not fall under any of the previous concerns).

Environment: The six strengths are *pollution prevention* (the firm makes efforts to avoid or reduce pollution), *beneficial products and services* (a substantial percentage of the firm's sales are due to the sale of products or services that are beneficial to the environment), *recycling* (the firm uses recycled raw materials or recycles used materials), *alternative fuels* (the firm generates a significant revenue from alternative energy sources such as solar power), *communications* (the firm adheres to environmental codes of best practice (for example, CERES)), *and other strength* (the firm practices environmental policies not falling under any of the previous categories). There are seven possible concerns. They are *hazardous waste* (the firm has been fined for bad waste management or its liabilities for hazardous waste are in excess of US$50 million), *ozone depleting chemicals* (the firm is one of the largest producers of such chemicals), *substantial emissions* (the firm is one of the top polluters), *regulatory concerns* (the firm has violated the Clean Air Act, the Clean Water Act or other environmental rules), *agricultural chemicals* (the firm is a large producer of chemical pesticides or fertilisers), *climate change* (the firm produces energy from coal, oil and its derivatives or generates substantial income from these energy sources), and *other concern* (other environmental concerns not included in any of the previous categories.

Product: The four strengths are *quality* (the firm has had a long-term quality programme in place or its quality programme is considered to be among one of the best), *R&D/innovation* (the firm is recognised in its sector for its R&D), *benefits to economically disadvantaged* (the firm's mission statement refers to delivering products and services to the economically disadvantaged), and *other strength*. There are four concerns which are *product safety* (the firm has had problems or has faced fines for the low safety of its services or products), *marketing/contracting controversy* (the firm has been charged fines or is facing controversy for misleading advertising or government contracting), *antitrust* (the firm is facing antitrust action or has been fined for such antitrust violations), and *other concern* (any product concerns not listed above).

SOCIAL ISSUE PARTICIPATION (SIP)

Non-United States operations: The three strengths are *community* (the firm contributes to charities operating outside the United States), *indigenous peoples relations* (the firm respects the needs and interest of indigenous peoples in its operations) and *other strength* (the firm is known for its good relations with its overseas employees, communities, and so on). The five possible weaknesses are *Burma* (the firm operates in Burma), *Mexico* (the firm has been criticised for its treatment of employees or its environmental impact in Mexico), *international labour* (the firm has been criticised for its treatment of its employees outside the United States), *indigenous peoples relations* (the firm has violated the interests and needs of indigenous peoples), and *other concern* (any concerns relating to non-United States operations not covered by any of the previous categories).

Other: The three strengths are *limited compensation* (the CEO's total annual remuneration does not exceed US$500,000 and outside directors are not paid more than US$30,000 a year), *ownership strength* (the firm owns between 20 and 50 per cent of another firm which KLD considers to have a social strength; or the firm is owned by more than 20 per cent by a firm with social strengths; if a firm is majority owned by another one then it is considered to be a division of the latter) and *other strength*. The concerns are *high compensation* (the CEO's total annual remuneration is in excess of US$10 million or the total annual remuneration of outside directors is in excess of US$100,000), *tax disputes* (the firm is subject to tax disputes covering more than US$100 million), *ownership concern* (the firm owns between 20 and 50 per cent of a firm with social concerns or is owned more than 20 per cent by a firm with social concerns; firms that are majority owned by another firm are treated as divisions of the latter), and *other concern*.

Exclusionary screens: There are five exclusionary screens: ALCOHOL, GAMBLING, TOBACCO, MILITARY and NUCLEAR POWER. By definition, these screens have only concerns and no strengths. For alcohol the concerns are *substantial involvement* (a substantial percentage of the firm's income is generated by the sale of alcohol) and *other concern* (a substantial proportion of the firm's income is generated by activities related to the production of alcohol). For gambling and tobacco the concerns are similar to those referring to alcohol, but refer to gambling activities and tobacco products, respectively. For military, the four concerns are *substantial weapons contracting involvement* (during the most recent financial year, more than 2 per cent of the firm's sales or US$50 million were generated by activities related to weapons, or the firm earned more than US$10 million from nuclear weapons), *minor weapons contracting involvement* (during the most recent financial year, the firm earned between US$10 and US$50 million or 2 per cent of its sales were from conventional weapons; or it earned between US$1 and US$10 million from nuclear weapons), *major weapons-related supplier* (during the last financial year, the firm has been paid in excess of US$50 million by the Department of Defense for the provision of fuel or other supplies for weapons) and *other concern*. Nuclear power has four concerns: *derives electricity* (the firm owns a nuclear power station or generates electricity from nuclear power), *design* (the firm obtains a substantial part of its revenues from the design, but not the construction or maintenance, of nuclear power stations), *fuel cycle/key parts* (the firm obtains a substantial part of its revenue from selling key equipment for the generation of nuclear energy, or it mines, processes or enriches uranium, and *other concern*.

Source: Adapted from KLD Research & Analytics, Inc.

18 *External Agencies and Corporate Social Responsibility*

DAVID BIRCH

Introduction

In the last 20 years or so we have seen a major increase in the debates aimed at developing more effective Corporate Governance and Corporate Social Responsibilty (CSR) practices, although survey after survey seems to record that the pace is still relatively slow except where particular practices are mandated by legislation. Concurrent with this increase in debate has been a proliferation of external agencies offering advice, consultancy, guidelines, new principles and numerous CSR-related standards, indices, codes and performance indicators. This chapter examines some of those agencies and raises the question of whether such agencies are actually effective, not so much in helping the CSR agenda along (which it would seem they have done) but in actually enabling business to seriously embed new CSR policies and practices into their everyday business cultures.

In the December 2007 third biennial 'State of Corporate Citizenship in the U.S' survey[1] organized by the Boston College Center for Corporate Citizenship and The Hitachi Foundation, and conducted by GlobeScan, it was announced that, 'The gap between what companies say they value and what they actually do is the most important finding.' Bradley K. Googins, Executive Director of the Boston College Center for Corporate Citizenship, considered this to be a worrying trend asking why, presumably after what now amounts to a quite reasonable amount of time that CSR-related issues have been on a worldwide agenda, such a gap still exists and what can be done to 'help business leaders make the translation from rhetoric to actions that benefit both their businesses and society'.

As this chapter seeks to explore, there is no shortage of help out there for these business leaders, and while my main aim here is to outline some of the most important external agencies that have developed either a full or partial interest in CSR-related matters, this survey raises some very important issues about whether the work of such agencies is

---

1   www.corporatecitizen07.com. 751 executives were surveyed on line. Of these, 53 per cent were CEOs, 34 per cent vice presidents, 10 per cent directors and 3 per cent in other senior positions.

actually making much of a difference to actual CSR practice and cultural change in businesses on the ground.

Why is that while 60 per cent of the business leaders surveyed said that 'corporate citizenship is part of their business strategy to a large or very great extent,' only 39 per cent reported that 'it is part of their business planning process,' and only 25 per cent have an individual or team responsible for citizenship issues? Why is it that 76 per cent say corporate citizenship 'fits their companies' traditions and values', but only 36 per cent say they actually talk to staff in the company about corporate citizenship? Why is it that while 81 per cent say they value employees (one has to wonder about the remaining 19 per cent), only 46 per cent support work-life balance for all employees and only 31 per cent 'offer training and career opportunities for their own lower-wage employees'.

Why these results? Despite the fact that these issues stand at the heart of how many leading external agencies determine (and advise upon, often at considerable cost to many companies worldwide) what constitutes effective corporate social responsibility. why is it, after so many years of putting CSR onto global agendas, do only 41 per cent of these United States' business leaders consider that 'companies should be held responsible for improving the education and skills in the communities where they operate' and only 18 per cent offer job training 'to people in economically distressed communities', when these significant social issues are central to the many guidelines, frameworks and sets of CSR principles that have emerged over the last 20 years or so from a growing multitude of external agencies?

Corporate Social Responsibility Advocacy

One agency, for example, which many companies worldwide have used in their CSR-related journeys is The World Business Council for Sustainable Development (WBCSD).[2] This is a global association guiding companies with the relationship between business and sustainable development. The WBCSD 'provides a platform for companies to explore sustainable development, share knowledge, experiences and best practices, and to advocate business positions on these issues in a variety of forums, working with governments, non-governmental and intergovernmental organizations'. The Council's objectives are to:

- be a leading business advocate on sustainable development;
- participate in policy development to create the right framework conditions for business to make an effective contribution to sustainable human progress;
- develop and promote the business case for sustainable development;
- demonstrate the business contribution to sustainable development solutions and share leading edge practices among members;
- contribute to a sustainable future for developing nations and nations in transition.

As such, the WBCSD (in CSR-related matters) is probably one of the most widely cited agencies in the world, but the challenge of course is for companies to be able to embed the definitions they adopt from this Council into actual day-to-day practices. That is the

---

2   http://www.wbcsd.ch

more difficult part, and as such, is a challenge, for similar agencies like the United States-based Business Roundtable.

Corporate Social Responsibility Networks

The Business Roundtable[3] is an association of chief executive officers of leading United States' companies with (in 2007) US$4.5 trillion in annual revenues and more than 10 million employees. As its website announces, member companies 'comprise nearly a third of the total value of the United States stock markets and represent over 40 percent of all corporate income taxes paid'. These companies 'give more than US$7 billion a year in combined charitable contributions, representing nearly 60 percent of total corporate giving'. Perhaps this is how CSR is still being chiefly interpreted – *corporate philanthropy*, despite, as we will see, the much more wide-ranging guidance offered by a multitude of external agencies.

The member companies of this significant United States' Roundtable have signed up to a mission within this association that 'believes that the basic interests of business closely parallel the interests of the American people, who are directly involved as consumers, employees, shareholders, and suppliers'. But the survey cited above, and many others around the world, seems to suggest that business is, in fact, lagging behind what the public actually expects within CSR. Given the dominant economic focus of the Roundtable perhaps more could be done to bring its member CEOs into a more CSR-oriented frame of mind? In other words, an important question becomes: 'Do agencies like the Business Roundtable need also to reprioritize commitments to CSR, not simply as an expressed "interest", but as a serious business innovation?' If the balance between single bottom line economics and CSR is not right in such a powerful association of businesses, can it ever be so in its member businesses?

This is the challenge also facing the European Commission Brussels-based CSR Europe[4] established in 1995 as one of the leading European business networks for CSR. Its mission is to, 'Help companies achieve profitability, sustainable growth and human progress by placing CSR in the mainstream of business practice.' It seeks to do this by:

- connecting companies to share best practice on CSR;
- innovating new projects between business and stakeholders;
- shaping the modern day business and political agenda on sustainability and competitiveness.

In 2002, following a Green Paper on CSR in which CSR was defined as 'a concept whereby companies integrate social and environmental concerns in their business operations and in their interaction with stakeholders on a voluntary basis' The European Academy of Business in Society (Eabis),[5] was launched. Its mission: 'to be a world-class reference point for the integration of CSR into the mainstream of business practice, theory and education, and to enhance models for sustainable business success,' and in

---

3   www.businessroundtable.org

4   http://www.csreurope.org

5   www.eabis.org

2004 a *Roadmap on CSR* was produced, specifically designed to enable companies to better embed CSR thinking into business practice. In 2006 the European Alliance for CSR was launched together with a key policy document *Implementing the partnership for growth and jobs: making Europe a pole of excellence on corporate social responsibility on CSR*. The database of company activities is extensive, and many companies share information about their CSR activities.

Such sharing is not unusual, and indeed, is a common feature of many of the external agencies that have been set up to help companies. This is one way of keeping legislation in CSR at bay, by a public demonstration that companies are actually doing something voluntarily and hence don't require such activities to be mandated. Forming alliances and networks is becoming very common. For example The Corporate Responsibility Group (UK)[6] was set up in 1987 'by Corporate Responsibility (CR) practitioners to enable them to network and exchange information and ideas with their peers in different business sectors'. As such, 'CRG Member companies are committed to adopting a social, ethical and environmentally responsible approach to business practice.' Most of the UK's leading companies are members, many of whom use the standards established by the CRG developed through the London Benchmarking Group[7], in their CSR reporting and auditing.

Corporate Social Responsibility Alliances

It is clear that alliances like this, designed to create forums where companies can both share and gain CSR-based knowledge, are becoming more popular. But the emphasis still rests on *voluntary* participation and use of the knowledge gained, as it is, for example, in a United States-based major agency, The Conference Board.[8]

The Conference Board, established in 1916, considers itself to be 'the world's pre-eminent business membership and research organization'. It argues that, 'In an uncertain world of intense competition, increasing public accountability, and global risks, The Conference Board provides its members – top executives and industry leaders from the most respected corporations in the United States and around the world – with vital business intelligence and forward-looking best practices. At the same time, The Conference Board promotes confidence in the free enterprise system by shaping the values critical to ethical business performance.' As is often the case, ethics tends to come second to 'business intelligence'. Its mission re-affirms this:

'The Conference Board creates and disseminates knowledge about management and the marketplace to help businesses strengthen their performance and better serve society.' Rarely do we see 'serving society' as the prime aim of agencies like this.

The question, of course, is should we? At the heart of all the debates on CSR is a paradigm that positions business first – without profit there would be no business to 'serve' society at all. As a consequence, any agency attempting to influence CSR developments has to do so with a model of business economics that seems highly resistant to change,

---

6   http://www.corporateresponsibilitygroup.com

7   http://www.lbg-online.net/

8   http://www.conference-board.org

despite the efforts of organizations like the New Economics Foundation,[9] founded in 1986, for example, which seeks to 'challenge conventional wisdom and promote radical, but, practical economic alternatives giving consideration to social, ethical and environmental issues'. Agencies like this are given very little time in business debates about CSR, and this is perhaps understandable in the light of statements from powerful agencies like The Conference Board which seems to see CSR simply as 'new business opportunities' which 'are created by accelerating demand for sustainable products and services,' and going further by stating that, 'The question executives are now grappling with is not whether, but how, to convert citizenship and sustainability from a nice way of doing business into a source of real business value.' Little wonder, then, that surveys continually show business to be slow in embedding CSR into daily practice, if a dominant view is that corporate citizenship needs to be 'converted' into a product or service that returns business value. Clearly, not all companies will recognize the 'business opportunity' CSR provides.

Corporate Social Responsibility Priorities

But is this asking too much of an agency like this? Yes, if like many businesses worldwide, such an agency argues that CSR is not its *core* concern. No, if what constitutes that *core* starts to reflect a new economics more focused on multiple, rather than single, bottom lines.

For example, the Caux Round Table[10] announces itself as, 'A group of senior business leaders from Europe, Japan and North America who are committed to the promotion of principled business leadership.' It is administered through the Caux Institute for Global Responsibility Inc. in Waterville Minnesota, USA, and believes 'that business has a crucial role in identifying and promoting sustainable and equitable solutions to key global issues affecting the physical, social and economic environments'. To help business do that it has developed its *Principles for Business* for 'guiding best practice in these areas in business'. These began life as one of the very earliest CSR roadmaps developed in 1992 by a group of business leaders through the Minnesota Center for Corporate Responsibility 'to foster the fairness and integrity of business relationships in the emerging global marketplace'. The Minnesota Principles[11] of most relevance to CSR were as follows:

'We believe that as global corporate citizens, we have responsibilities in the communities in which we do business:

- to be a good citizen by supporting the communities in which it operates; this can be done through charitable donations, educational and cultural contributions, and employee participation in community and civic affairs;
- to respect human rights and democratic institutions;
- to recognize government's legitimate obligation to the society at large and to support public policies and practices that promote harmony between business and other segments of society;

---

9   http://www.neweconomics.org

10   http://www.cauxroundtable.org

11   www1.umn.edu/humanrts/instree/cauxrndtbl.htm

- to collaborate with less advantaged countries and areas in raising their standards of health, education, and workplace safety;
- to promote and stimulate sustainable development;
- to play a lead role in preserving the physical environment and conserving the earth's resources;
- to support peace, security, and diversity in local communities;
- to respect the integrity of local cultures.'

The current priorities of the Caux Round Table, which further developed these principles are, 'Good corporate governance, fiscal, environmental and ethical transparency and the essential conditions for increased responsible foreign investment and trade in order to create employment and to improve standards of living throughout the world.'

A key term in its understanding of what constitutes 'principled leadership' is *moral capitalism* through which 'sustainable and socially responsible prosperity can become the foundation for a fair, free and transparent global society'. This clearly goes well beyond a single bottom line approach to business. But the challenge, of course, is how to translate the rhetoric of its Principles for Business so that they can become 'the cornerstone of principled business leadership'. Believing, as the Caux Round Table does, that 'the world business community should play an important role in improving economic and social conditions' is one thing; enabling these principles to become a 'foundation for action' which will actually change business attitudes, culture and practice, is quite another. The real challenge is to move *aspirational* motivation to real change. How does an agency like this persuade business that the ethical ideals at the core of its principles for business – *kyosei* and human dignity are, in fact, good business?

How do you persuade a CEO under considerable pressure to meet ever-increasing economic performance demands, often on a weekly, let alone a quarterly basis, that the Japanese ideal of *kyosei* which 'means living and working together for the common good enabling cooperation and mutual prosperity to coexist with healthy and fair competition,' is worthy of significant capital, cultural and intellectual investment? How do you persuade the CEO that human dignity which 'refers to the sacredness or value of each person as an end, not simply as a mean to the fulfillment of others' purposes or even majority prescription' is good for business?

True, you can, as the Caux Round Table have laudably done, create a raft of codes and standards, guidelines and 'how-to' models, but, in practice, how many of these are management tools that significantly influence day-to-day decisions in business, beyond those, as in some areas of the environment and corporate governance, which are increasingly attracting mandatory legislative compliance? Attracting the attention of business to non-negotiable compliance is a relatively easy given, but not so the negotiable commitments to the less tangible aspects of *moral capitalism*. But many companies worldwide have begun what can be, for some, a quite difficult journey. One way of beginning that journey is to engage with the United Nations Global Compact.

Global Corporate Social Responsibility?

At the World Economic Forum in January 6 1999, United Nations Secretary-General Kofi Annan challenged world business leaders to help towards promoting and maintaining sustainability by disseminating good practices based on universal principles. The result, in July 2000 was the (then) nine Principles of the UN Global Compact,[12] drawn from a variety of UN documents, which business worldwide is invited to engage with and to integrate into their core business. Many have engaged, but it is unclear how many have actually embedded one or more of these principles into *every* business decision and action they take. By the end of 2007 over 5,000 organizations, including some cities, and some 3,600 businesses in 100 countries have engaged, and the nine principles have now become ten. This is not a regulatory instrument, but 'a tool designed to promote institutional learning'. As such, the UN, as a very powerful external agency, is seeking to influence business to 'use the power of transparency and dialogue to identify and disseminate good practices that are rooted in globally-acknowledged principles'.

We have to be cautious, though. Engaging with the Global Compact does not necessarily mean a company is going to change overnight, or indeed to radically alter any of its major business practices to ensure they are more CSR-oriented. With the dramatic rise of socially responsible investment pressures and global indices like the Dow Jones Sustainability Index[13] which 'scores' a company on whether it has engaged with the Compact, (amongst many other things) the pressure to engage is now high for many companies, but it is very early days yet to see whether engagement has made much of a difference in real business practice.

All that is required is for the CEO to write a letter to the United Nations Secretary-General, expressing commitment to the Compact. Once accepted all the company needs to do is to demonstrate, via the Global Compact website, how it has engaged with just *one* of the principles. There is, however, no guarantee in this demonstration that the company is reporting anything new as a result of its engagement with the Compact.

The ten principles cover some very significant universal issues and it may well be unfair to expect business to engage with more than just one of these with any serious commitment. Are we, in fact, asking business for too much? It is a relatively easy task to catalogue the myriad of guidelines, codes and frameworks that exist (and growing exponentially day by day worldwide), but what sorts of business decisions need to be taken in order to help a company determine which of the many they should apply to their own business practices? In the face of the numerous agencies out there offering advice and various CSR roadmaps, companies inevitably have to make a strategic decision about which ones they will engage with, either partially or fully, and which ones they will have to leave on one side.

Corporate Social Responsibility Principles

Five years later, the Reverend Leon Sullivan, in South Africa in 1997, developed what is now known as The Global Sullivan Principles.[14] They, 'Seek to support economic, social and political justice by companies where they do business; to support human rights and encourage equal opportunity at all levels of employment, including racial and gender diversity on decision making committees and boards; to train and advance disadvantaged

---

12   http://www.unglobalcompact.com

13   www.sustainability-indexes.com

14   www.globalsullivanprinciples.org/principles.htm

workers for technical, supervisory and management opportunities; and to assist with greater tolerance and understanding among peoples, thereby improving the quality of life for communities, workers, and children.' There are eight suggested principles for companies:

- Support universal human rights, particularly those of employees, the communities within which they operate, and the parties with whom companies do business.
- Provide equal opportunity for employees at all levels with respect to color, race, gender, age, ethnicity or religious beliefs, and prevent unacceptable worker treatment such as the exploitation of children, physical punishment, abuse of women, involuntary servitude or other forms of abuse.
- Respect employees' right to freedom of association.
- Provide compensation that enables employees to meet basic needs, and afford them opportunity to improve their skills and capabilities in order to increase their social and economic opportunities.
- Provide a safe and healthy workplace, protect human health and the environment, and promote sustainable development.
- Promote fair competition, respect intellectual and other property rights, and not offer, pay or accept bribes.
- Work with governments and communities to improve the quality of life – educational, cultural, economic and social well being – and provide training and opportunities for workers from disadvantaged backgrounds.
- Promote the application of these Principles by those with whom they do business.

Corporate Social Responsibility Aspirations

While these principles are voluntary (*aspirational* is a word commonly used), companies who engage are asked to report on their activities each year and to share their CSR (and related) experiences with others. This is true of all similar codes including very general ones like the Taskforce on the Churches and Corporate Responsibility Principles for Global Corporate Responsibility[15] which was developed in 1995 in Canada, the UK and the US by the Taskforce on the Churches and Corporate Responsibility (TCCR) in Canada; the Ecumenical Council for Corporate Responsibility (ECCR) in the UK, and the Interfaith Center on Corporate Responsibility (ICCR) in the US. The *Principles* are designed to create an ethical standard for global corporate social responsibility stemming from the joint belief of these three agencies that 'the community rather than the company is the starting point of economic life'. What that position does, somewhat controversially in many business quarters, is to refocus corporate priority, and that, to say the least, is a very contentious area.

Some agencies, however, like The Social Venture Network Standards of Corporate Social Responsibility[16] established in 1987 are very upfront about how they see the role of business in the community as 'a potent force for solving social problems' with a set of

---

15   http://www.web.net/~tccr/benchmarks/index.html. See also *An Interfaith Declaration: A Code of Ethics on International Business for Christians, Muslims and Jews* at http://www.iccr.org

16   http://www.svn.org/initiatives/standards.html

standards being developed in 1999 aimed at defining 'the landscape of corporate social responsibility and provide tools for organizations to make continuous improvement that is in concert with their overall business strategy.' There are nine non-binding CSR principles covering:

- ethics
- accountability
- governance
- financial returns
- employment practices
- business relationships
- products and services
- community involvement
- environmental protection.

Again the issue of the voluntary nature of these principles, like those for example developed as the now very widely used non-binding OECD Principles of Corporate Governance[17] surfaces.

Non-Binding Principles

The OECD Principles of Corporate Governance developed in 1998, 'are intended to assist efforts by Member and non-Member governments to evaluate and improve the legal, institutional, and regulatory framework for corporate governance'. They also provide 'guidance to stock exchanges, investors, corporations, and other parties that contribute to the corporate governance process' focusing upon:

- rights of shareholders;
- equitable treatment of shareholders;
- role of stakeholders in corporate governance;
- disclosure and transparency;
- the responsibilities of the board.

Similarly the OECD Guidelines for Multinational Enterprises,[18] which were established much earlier in 1976, 'are targeted specifically towards multinational enterprises from OECD member countries that adhere to the *Declaration on International Investment and Multinational Enterprises*. They provide multinational enterprises – defined here as "companies or other entities established in more than one country and so linked that they may coordinate their operations" – with voluntary, non-binding principles and standards of good business conduct. The *Guidelines* are intended to help these enterprises contribute to economic, environmental, and social progress, with a view towards achieving sustainable development.' Implementation is totally dependent upon 'the initiative of the individual companies,' as indeed it is with the many standards overseen

---

17   http://www.oecd.org/dataoecd/47/50/4347646.pdf

18   www.itcilo.it/english/actrav/telearn/global/ilo/guide/oecd.htm

by the 1969 founded Council on Economic Priorities (CEP),[19] which 'is a public service research organization, dedicated to the accurate and impartial analysis of the social and environmental records of corporations'and offering guidance in the following areas:

- strategic development of CSR and CC programmes;
- SIA and EIA – social and environmental impact assessment;
- SRI – strategies for social responsible investment;
- stakeholder brokering and management;
- dispute resolution and grievance management;
- ISO 14000, OHSAS 18001, SA8000, EMAS;
- preparing for oncoming ISO 26000;[20]
- good governance;
- strategic development of CSR and CC programmes.

This list of standards and 'components' of CSR-related activities has been steadily growing over the years and, as such, has opened up new consulting opportunities for hundreds of new agencies and organizations offering their expertise in helping companies make these decisions. One such agency is the Centre for Tomorrow's Company[21] a UK-based think-tank 'researching and stimulating the development of a new agenda for business'. At the heart of its thinking for the business of the future is a concentration on developing more *inclusive* stakeholder relations. Its vision is, 'To create a future for business which makes equal sense to staff, shareholders and society,' They do this by seeking to, 'Create value with our partners by building a mutually reinforcing link between ideas and implementation – between theory and practice. In so doing, we achieve our purpose of pushing the boundaries of thought leadership and business behaviour.' But just what is this likely to actually mean to a busy executive? In practice, the approach is a simple one. The *idea* of CSR, for example, needs to be implemented if it is to return any value. So, the *idea* needs a vehicle, and Tomorrow's Company's advice to business is that one effective vehicle is the management of 'stakeholder, reputational and regulatory pressures that are critical to achieving business success'. This then results in advice to 'help companies globally to make sense of what corporate responsibility and sustainability mean for areas susch as leadership, governance and reporting'.

Corporate Social Responsibility Consulting

A similar agency is Business in the Community (BITC)[22] which seeks to 'support and challenge companies to integrate responsible business through their operations in order to have a positive impact on society and therefore be of "public benefit"'. One way of doing that is through the Business in the Community's Awards for Excellence which is a peer-assessed 'endorsement of responsible business practice and a great way for you to share and celebrate the positive impact of your business on society'.

---

19   www.web.net/~robrien/papers/sri/players/cep.html

20   This is a new CSR standard to be launched in 2008, see www.iso.org/socialresponsibility

21   http://www.tomorrowscompany.com

22   www.bitc.org.uk

Effectively then, this positions an external agency, like BITC, (and others like The Corporate Citizen Company[23] which does similar things to BITC) in a very powerful position; but importantly it also distances the business itself from making *internal* decisions about how to implement the *idea* of CSR. Consultancies are a very effective source of advice and information to business worldwide, but they can also be a very effective mechanism for distancing executives from the responsibility for crucial strategic decisions. The relationship between the *power potential* of the external agency and internal management *responsibility* is an under-researched area and yet, for matters relating to CSR, it is a relationship that is, more often than not, a far more crucial one than in many other areas of business. For a business that is still coming to terms with whether full commitment to CSR is for them, external agencies can minimize risk to the executives making strategic decisions about new directions for a company. And that minimization is always going to be high on an executive's agenda.

Access to CSR information is no longer the problem it might once have been now that the Internet provides almost everything anyone could want. The problem for the busy executive is that no one has the time or the resources to sift through it all, especially as so few companies worldwide have dedicated CSR staff who can do it. This is where an external agency, like the United States-based Business for Social Responsibility (BSR),[24] for example, can be valuable. Founded in 1992, 'for companies seeking to sustain their commercial success in ways that demonstrate respect for ethical values, and for people, communities and the environment,' in 2007 it had a business membership base of more than 1,400 companies who have access 'to practical information, research, education and training programs, as well as technical assistance and consulting on all aspects of corporate social responsibility'. As such, 'BSR offers an informative library of reports, analysis, publications and news that focus on diverse aspects of corporate social responsibility (CSR), including the environment and climate change, human rights, governance and accountability, emerging economies and more.' But the offer of such information does not, of course, necessarily mean that the take-up of that offer necessarily translates into more effective CSR in business. There is interesting research to be undertaken in following up the many companies worldwide who pay membership fees to such agencies, or consultancy fees to others, to ascertain just to what extent external advice and information paid for has actually translated into significant (long-term) CSR changes.

Interestingly what constitutes 'consultancy' has also been changing as the CSR debate has deepened and developed. For example GoodCorporation[25] is a for-profit company owned set up in 2000 by a group of former partners and directors of KPMG Consulting 'who wanted to create a straight-forward and transparent method to help companies to measure their impacts in a credible way'. It argues that it is not a consultancy because it 'does not gain anything by identifying weaknesses in a client's business practices, other than helping the client to focus effort into areas where risks are present. By not providing consultancy services, we remove the risk of any conflict of interest, and allow the client to receive a genuinely impartial view of how the business is operating and where it needs to improve'. An interesting marketing device which seems to have developed specifically to suit the CSR agenda. Like other external agencies who have developed CSR-auditing

---

23   www.corporate-citizenship.co.uk

24   http://www.bsr.org

25   www.goodcorporation.com

standards and awards, there is now a GoodCorporation Standard (with 62 CSR-related management practices) which organizations are encouraged to use in order to develop their own codes of conduct covering:

- employees;
- customers;
- suppliers and subcontractors;
- community and environment;
- shareholders or other providers of finance;
- management commitment.

Corporate Social Responsibility Standards

Developing CSR-related standards and key performance indicators has been a major preoccupation of many external agencies, and probably the most successful to date has been the Global Reporting Initiative[26] developed in 1997 by the Coalition for Environmentally Responsible Economies (CERES),[27] 'with the mission of developing globally applicable guidelines for reporting on the economic, environmental, and social performance' of organizations. CERES was founded in 1989 (long before many companies starting to address CSR issues), with the aim of establishing 'a network of investors, environmental organizations and other public interest groups working with companies and investors to address sustainability challenges such as global climate change'. Its mission, simple but far-reaching: 'Integrating sustainability into capital markets for the health of the planet and its people.'

After the Exxon Valdez crisis, CERES developed the Valdez Principles (now known as the CERES Principles) to create a set of environmental (though voluntary) standards for business. The ten principles range from general commitments to protecting the biosphere, through energy conservation, stakeholder engagement and environmental reporting. At the heart of a company's endorsement of these principles is a central, underlying ethic: a *public* commitment to environmental protection. But relatively few companies worldwide have signed up. Like many of the growing number of external guidelines being developed, many companies pick and choose which of the principles are of strategic value to them. It is, perhaps, asking too much of a particular company to endorse them all. And it is often this failure of the recognition that business will make strategic selections that can frustrate many non-business CSR and environmental activists.

This act of strategic selection has proven to be the case in the way that many businesses use the 1997/1999 Global Reporting Initiative (GRI) standard for corporate reporting on environmental, social and economic performance (originally created by CERES and now recommended as the set of standards for reporting on a company's engagement with the UN Global Compact, amongst other things). This is undoubtedly now the most widely used sustainability reporting framework worldwide, setting out 'the principles and indicators that organizations can use to measure and report their economic, environmental, and social performance'. There have been continuous

---

26   http://globalreporting.org

27   http://www.ceres.org

revisions over the years – the G3 Guidelines on sustainable reporting in 2006 being the most recent (and publicly available) comprehensive changes. At the heart of the GRI is a belief that companies who are committed to effective sustainable reporting will, in effect, implement CSR change over time.

Well over 1,000 companies now use the GRI standards in fairly comprehensive ways, but many more are guided in various ways by some aspect(s) of the GRI. The challenge here, of course, is to find ways of ensuring that reporting guidelines and standards become more than just ticking off convenient performance boxes which satisfy ethical investment funds and the like but actually become a significant management tool that brings about a continual *process* of business-cultural *change*, not just the *product* of a self-satisfied set of reports at the end of each year. Capturing the extent to which CSR process becomes more embedded in a company than a preoccupation with the development of CSR products is not easy. But there is still a very dominant business culture, worldwide, which finds greater satisfaction in producing something tangible, like a CSR report, than in developing the more intangible processes of cultural change. Businesses like to be able to measure things, The GRI has enabled them to do that – but the extent to which the GRI standards are effecting significant *cultural* change within a business is more difficult to capture.

This last comment is not designed to be a negative statement about the impact of external agencies like CERES, and the GRI, but given the scope and often complexities of the various code and principles established by so many agencies, it might often be seen as too daunting a task for a company to engage when the risk of possible failure is so high.[28] It is often, therefore, easier to tick some selected boxes than it is to change policies.

One of the sets of boxes that are ticked more frequently than others is the now highly significant Social Accountability International: SA8000[29] developed in 1997 'to overcome the difficulties associated with monitoring internal corporate codes of conduct'. By establishing a standard and verification system, based on International Labor Organization conventions and United Nations human rights standards, for workplace conditions. Companies can apply to receive a certificate of compliance with SA8000, and as such, a standard like this paved the way for other more specifically CSR-related certification standards to be developed. Gaining certification is not easy, and neither is compliance to some CSR standards which have followed SA8000 like AA1000 developed in 1999 by the UK-based agency AccountAbility.[30]

AccountAbility is a very challenging external agency which seeks to hold 'those with power to account'. Its position is that, 'The *"civilizing of power"* is critical to reconciling conflict and mobilizing action, to address global challenges, from climate change to poverty and from HIV/AIDs to the needs of an aging population.' That sort of rhetoric is not always going to go well in some business circles, particularly those companies who do not rate well in the annual AccountAbility Rating,[31] which in 2007 found that:

- there has been an increase in the accountability of the G100;
- companies headquartered in Europe are the most accountable;

---

28   In 2007, for example, only 13 of the Fortune 500 companies had actually adopted the Ceres Principles.

29   http://www.cepaa.org/SA8000/SA8000.htm

30   http://www.accountability.org.uk/uploadstore/cms/docs/AA1000%20Framework%201

31   www.accountabilityrating.com

- automobile and oil and gas companies score well again in 2007;
- retail and FMCG sectors under-perform the average;
- accountability is becoming more strategic.

Companies need to be able to trick the 'right' boxes, of course, in order to be rated well in any of the multitude of CSR rating systems now in existence, and these boxes may not always suit all businesses all the time. Often, what we are seeing now as the result of the work of external agencies is not what an organization like Greenpeace,[32] for example, would like to see – overnight change – but a slow, gradual, awareness of the need for change, but, more importantly, we need to understand that that change will always be company-specific rather than emerging from some non-strategic adherence to so-called universal principles. If we have learnt anything in the last 20 years of CSR activity it is that business will resist universals unless they can be seen to apply to their particular business.

As a consequence, when Amnesty International[33] developed its Human Rights Principles for Business[34] in 1998 to 'help companies fulfill their responsibility to promote and protect human rights' it was never on the agenda (of business at least) that they would simply take on these principles in non-specific ways. The Principles call for companies to establish (1) an explicit human rights policy; (2) procedures to examine the human rights impact of operations; (3) safeguards to prevent employee complicity in abuses; (4) mechanisms to monitor compliance; and (5) a process to independently verify company compliance reports. But, as with many of these sets of principles, the responsibility rests upon the companies themselves to ensure 'compliance'. And companies will, more often than not, do this at their own pace. The reality is, is that there is not, as many NGO external agencies might like to see like, a one-size-fits-all CSR solution.

Company-Specific Corporate Social Responsibility

Recognizing the need for company-specific diversity and difference, for example, the Asia Pacific Economic Cooperation (APEC) Forum *Business Code of Conduct* developed at the 1999 APEC CEO Summit in Auckland, New Zealand, seeks to offer a set of seven behavioural standards which builds upon a company's existing code of conduct, 'To (1) encourage corporate transparency and predictability, (2) challenge APEC governments to maintain their commitment to enhanced transparency and predictability within the public sector, and (3) develop a better match between business practice and public expectations.' At the heart of this code is a recognition that the CEO of a company who signs up to the Code has *moral* obligations to international and local communities; to the laws and stakeholders of those communities; to the environment; fair competition, good governance and *licit* activities – all of which need to be a part of business thinking. But *how* the CEO implements this morality is deemed to be company specific.

This positioning of responsibility on the voluntary actions of management rather than on legislative demands is a major feature of many of the external agencies'

---

32   www.greenpeace.org

33   http://www.web.amnesty.org

34   www.amnesty.org.uk/business/

engagement with CSR-related issues. For example, the Ethical Trading Initiative,[35] which brings together business, NGOs and Unions 'was founded to promote "ethical sourcing", defined as "a company taking responsibility to work with its suppliers to implement internationally accepted labor standards in the workplace"'. The emphasis here is on the company taking responsibility itself, by using the Base Code or developing a company-specific one, and by sharing experiences on the implementation of international labour standards, with other members of this alliance.

The Base Code was developed in 1998, out of the ILO Conventions on worker and human rights,[36] but the ETI recognizes that 'some parts of the code may be (1) subject to constraints not controlled by the supplier, (2) in contravention of national laws, or (3) otherwise not realizable by the supplier'. In other words, compliance may not easily be universal, and companies themselves are in the best position to 'localize' such a code.

Emphasis on understanding 'local' conditions is also at the heart of The Fair Labor Association Workshop Code of Conduct[37] developed in the 1990s by the Fair Labor Association as an alliance of business, NGOs and other organizations to establish workplace standards in the garment and footwear industries, following often worldwide condemnation of some highly exploitative practices in developing countries by major global companies.

Corollary

It is often the establishment of codes like this, protecting the very basic rights of workers, but with an eye to highly specific local conditions, which, many then think, can then influence developments in CSR-related issues. Once a company gets used to working with codes and standards, say, in human rights and workers' conditions, the thinking might go, then it is more likely to be in an amenable frame of mind to using codes developed for CSR. There is an attractive logic to that kind of thinking, but given the proliferation of such external codes, standards and guidelines, there is also a great danger of companies developing *standards fatigue*. As this chapter seeks to demonstrate, there is no shortage of guidance available – others, over time, will better assess whether business is really taking any effective notice of that guidance. There is some interesting research waiting to be done on this.

Key References for Further Reading

Birch, David (2003) 'Corporate Social Responsibility: Some Key Theoretical Issues and Concepts for New Ways of Doing Business', *Journal of New Business Ideas and Trends*, 1/1, 1-19.
Cragg, Wesley (ed) (2005) *Ethics Codes, Corporations and the Challenge of Globalization*, Edward Elgar, LondonHabisch, Andre, Jan Jonker, Martina Wegner & René Schmidpeter (eds) (2004) *Corporate Social Responsibility Across Europe*, Springer, Berlin & New York.

---

35   http://www.eti.org.uk
36   http://www.ilo.org/public/english/standards/decl/declaration/text
37   http://www.fairlabor.org/all/code/

Hancock, John (ed) (2004) *Investing in Corporate Social Responsibility: A Guide to Best Practice, Business Planning and the UK's Leading Companies,* Kogan Page, London.

Hennigfeld, Judith; Manfred Pohl & Nick Tolhurst (2006) *The ICCA Handbook of Corporate Social Responsibility,* Wiley, New York.

Jonker, Jan & Marco de Witte (eds) (2006) *Management Models for Corporate Social Responsibility,* Springer, Berlin & New York.

Jonker, Jan & Marco de Witte (eds) (2006) *The Challenge of Organizing and Implementing Corporate Social Responsibility,* Palgrave Macmillan, Basingstoke.

Leipzigger, Deborah (2003) *The Corporate Responsibility Code Book,* Greenleaf Publishing, Sheffield.

19 How Globalization is Affecting Corporate Social Responsibility: Dynamics of the Interaction Between Corporate Social Responsibility and Globalization

ÖZER ERTUNA AND BENGI ERTUNA

Introduction

This chapter outlines the possible challenges in the redefinition of the relationship between corporations and society through a discussion of the dynamics influencing the current state of corporate social responsibility under the forces of globalization. Both corporate social responsibility and globalization are dynamic concepts which are interacting with each other in the process of continuous development. As globalization influences the role of corporations in society, redefinition of the rights and responsibilities of the corporation influences the outcomes of globalization. The objective functions and guiding moral principles of corporations are suggested to influence how societal aspirations are reflected into corporate social responsibility. At its current state of development, we observe a general acceptance of social responsibility by corporations. However, they seem to assume social responsibility as a means to achieve their objective of profit and value maximization based on their self-interest rather than promotion of common good. Differences in the objective functions and the moral principles guiding corporations in the west and the east are proposed to provide opportunities for cross-fertilization in the redefinition of corporate social responsibility. This redefinition may provide solutions to the pressing problems of globalization.

The purpose of this chapter is to discuss how globalization is affecting Corporate Social Responsibility (CSR) and to reflect on the possible challenges in the redefinition of the relationship between corporations and society. CSR is currently a very popular but vague and unresolved concept. There seems to be a general lack of consensus on the definition, motivations and mechanisms of CSR, both in theoretical constructs and empirical research. Similarly, globalization is a contemporary subject matter which involves conflicting analysis and findings. Lack of a general consensus on both is due to the fact that both globalization and CSR are complex issues that are interacting with each other in a process of continuous development. Developments in globalization have provided opportunities for corporations to increase their scope, influence, power and profits. To reap the benefits of these opportunities, corporations were quick to develop certain lines of conduct, which were considered to be socially unacceptable by individuals at large. People expected and demanded a better world from globalization. Opposition against the behavior of corporations and the process of globalization forced corporations to adopt better corporate behavior and assign higher respect to CSR. The developments in globalization and CSR are interacting and exercising great influence on each other.

In order to understand the development, the present state and the future of CSR better, we first attempt to explain the evolution of the corporation, since the corporation is both the subject of CSR and the main actor in globalization. In this section, differences in the evolution of corporations in the west and the east are outlined with respect to their objective functions, foundations and principles. Differences in moral foundations and principles are suggested to provide an opportunity for cross-fertilization within the framework of redefinition of corporation and globalization. Consequently, the next section concentrates on the CSR concept and globalization process together. Then, we explain the dynamic interaction between CSR and globalization, indicating the role of the common driving forces behind them. We also emphasize the role of people and the value structure of society in this process of dynamic interaction. After gaining an understanding of the dynamic nature of the evolution of CSR and globalization, we describe the current state of CSR and reflect on challenges in the redefinition of the relationship between the corporation and society. We propose a cross-fertilization of corporate principles of the west and the east in this redefinition. The chapter ends with a summary of conclusions.

Evolution of the 'Corporation' and its Moral Foundations

Societies need to establish systems to meet their aspirations to produce and to share the outputs of their production. The corporation is one of the social mechanisms designed to meet these aspirations. It is a mechanism for organizing production, creating income, sharing this income and creating means for consumption. That is, the corporation is one of the forms of organizing economic activity in societies. However, organization of economic activity took different forms in different periods in history and in different parts of the world. The forms of corporations have changed and are changing as the aspirations and the means of societies to realize their aspirations change.

The form, which evolved into the form that we denote today as corporations, can be considered the product of western societies. In its present dominant form, the corporation is an abstract legal structure, equipped with unique privileges and rights. It is its present unique legal structure that makes the corporation both a 'revolutionary idea' behind the contemporary technological and economic development (Micklethwait and Wooldridge, 2003) and a vehicle for 'pathological pursuit of profit and power' (Balkan, 2004). While corporations are among the major contributors to innovations, technological and economic development, at the same time they are also responsible for many of the pressing global problems of the capitalist economic system, such as environmental degradation, exploitation of resources and inequality in income distribution.

Corporations are equipped with all the rights of human beings. These rights are protected by laws. However, whether corporations also possess humanly values and responsibilities together with these rights is an issue of debate (Davies, 2003). This debate takes place along a continuum including value-free, self-interested corporation at one end and corporate-citizen with values, integrated into society at the other end. The outcome of this debate aims to define and resolve the social role of the corporation. But the resolutions are not static. They are dynamic, evolutionary, context dependent and are changing as the value structures of the societies change. Corporations in the west and the east evolved differently with respect to their objective functions and moral foundations.

WESTERN CORPORATIONS

During the evolution of the corporation into its modern form, the rights and responsibilities of the corporation have been continuously redefined. Micklethwait and Wooldridge (2003) provide a complete history of the evolution of the corporation in the west and illustrate the changes in the rights and responsibilities assumed by corporations. Throughout their evolution, corporations have both gained rights that supported self-interested corporate behavior and started assuming responsibilities at the same time. Whether they are value-free entities or corporate citizens, corporations in the west evolved to serve the parties providing their capital, mainly the shareholders. That is, corporations have assumed profit maximization as their basic objective. Within the free market capitalism, the sole responsibility of a coporation is assumed to be increasing profits for their shareholders while conforming to the rules and laws in society (Friedman, 1970). Specifically, corporations should be serving the shareholders who own the residual rights and thus, presumably, assume all the risk of the business. Accordingly, it is not the duty of the corporation to serve the interests of employees, suppliers, distributors, customers and community; that is the other social partners, or stakeholders of the corporation. Within this framework, the interests of other stakeholders are determined by contractual rights, which are protected by laws.

Consequently, during the evolution of the corporation in the west, the objective has been to increase profit or shareholder value, or in other words, serve the capital owners. Other stakeholders' interests have been incorporated as long as they enhanced the interests of the shareholders (Kolk and Pinkse, 2006). Serving social or humane interests has not been considered among the objectives of corporations. It has been believed that serving the shareholder interest would serve the general interests of the public better than in any other design. Mainstream economic and finance literature has argued that 'social welfare is maximized when all firms in the economy maximize the total firm value' (Jensen, 2002). As a matter of fact, the form of corporation, which evolved in west, contributed significantly to the economic and technological developments realized in recent periods.

NON-WESTERN FORMS

Economic forms that developed in other parts of the world, such as in Confucian and Islamic countries, have not been able evolve in a similar manner and contribute to economic development due to limitations shaped by geographic and cultural characteristics (Micklethwaith and Wooldridge, 2003). On the other hand, these Confucian and Islamic countries tried to develop economic models that will serve 'social good' more than the shareholder interest. Corporations in the east assigned different meanings to 'social good'. The social good concept in eastern culture is more than providing social rights and privileges protected by law. The system itself is built on principles of 'social good'.

As an example, in Islam all commercial relations among people are guided by the main principle of 'fairness' ('hak').[1] Only fair relations can lead to social good. Price in a trade relation has to be fair price. If a fair price is not charged in a trade transaction, one of the parties, either the seller or the buyer would be exploited. If committed, exploitation is a sin, which cannot be forgiven even by God himself. Thus, the exploiting person would have to be forgiven by the one exploited in their worldly life. The same principle applies to all prices, including wages. Wages have to be fair wages. Everyone has the 'right to claim' and receive a fair price or wage. The poor have a claim on the wealth of the rich. That is, the rich have a duty to share their wealth. If God has given wealth to the rich, it is given to fulfill their duty to share. The wealth mentioned here does not have to be only economic wealth; it may be intellectual capacity or ethical values.

Under these principles, the basic form of corporations in Islam is an agreement between financial and human capital to share the income generated according to pre-determined percentages. Namely, the capital is provided by 'rab-el mal' and the labor is provided by 'mudarib'. The contract, or the corporation in this case, is called 'mudaraba'. Under mudaraba contract, benefits and risks of the economic operation are shared by the providers of financial and human capital.[2] Another Islamic principle relates to the objective of the corporation and the conduct of this objective. Corporations should earn a fair profit, and in doing so, instead of competing with each other, they must compete in serving the society. Basing their discussions on a different set of principles, Williams and Zinkin (2005) also suggest that Islamic teachings on business ethics is very much in line with CSR agenda and in fact CSR can be a 'bridge between civilizations'.

Similar cultural characteristics are shared by eastern cultures. A recent trend in the United States is worth mentioning here: there seems to be an interest in learning about the way eastern philosophy may help to improve management philosophy. Swami Parthasarathy, one of the India's best-selling authors on Vadenta[3] has been giving conferences in United States' universities teaching about Karma Capitalism (Engardio and McGregor, 2006). Opposition to globalization shares most of the principles of the east and claims that what the world needs is 'fair trade' and not 'free trade' in order to eliminate exploitations.

Although the corporations in the east have not been able to spur innovation and economic activity, cross-fertilization between the western and eastern corporate principles may provide a chance to redefine the corporation in a way for it to meet the economic and social challenges of globalization. The new forms of corporation may provide mechanisms that both foster economic development and growth and also provide

---

1   'Hak' is a very broad concept in Islam. It is the creator Himself, according to the Koran, that requires fairness in all relations among people and not getting a share more than deserved. Islam itself is 'Hak' religion.

2   A brief definition of islamic terms can ben reached through Glossary of Islamic Terms, by Islamic Bank of Britain http://www.islamic-bank.com/islamicbanklive/IslamicTerms/1/Home/1/Home.jsp.

3   An ancient school of Hindu philosophy.

solutions to the current global problems, such as environmental degradation, poverty, unequal distribution of income and unemployment.

Whatever the origins and the locations of corporations are, in recent decades corporations are actually going through a significant transformation giving a new meaning to 'social good'. The main change is seen in the 'corporate social responsibility' dimension, which is very much influenced by the developments in globalization. While corporations are increasing their influence all around the world, concepts such as 'fair trade', 'equal treatment', 'environment-friendly production' and 'green consumption' are being integrated into the values of the corporation. The driving forces of this significant transformation are the changing aspirations of societies, enacted by better-informed consumers and investors with a long-term vision, who are empowered by advances in the information and communication technologies.

Corporate Social Responsibility and Societal Aspirations

Although corporate social responsibility theories started emerging in 1960s, the issue is not new. CSR represents the framework for the relationship between the corporation and society, which is dynamic and is still undergoing a complex process of development.

The CSR concept entails different issues and debates in different contexts and at different times. In its current state CSR evolves as society develops an understanding of how firms should behave and it expresses them as demands on the corporations. In his pioneering work, Carroll (1979) defined CSR according to the differences with respect to societal expectations from the corporation. He developed a hierarchical model of social responsibilities. These responsibilities include economic, legal, ethical and discretionary responsibilities. Similarly, Garriga and Mele (2004) identify four central themes in their review of 50 years of CSR research. The differing demands of society on corporations shape these central themes. They argue that society demands corporations to secure profits, to adhere to ethical values, to integrate social demands and to take a role in the community. These demands might either be in the form of demands to limit the negative impacts or demands to increase the positive impacts of corporations on society. The demands to limit the negative impacts arise from concerns for irresponsible corporate behavior and call for 'corporate responsibility', while demands to increase the positive impact of corporations call for 'corporate citizenship' (Van Der Putten, 2005).

The concept of social responsibility has developed following a hierarchical order. Initially, the sole responsibility of corporations was assumed to be to their shareholders. It was assumed that the duty of corporations was serving their shareholders. Some even claimed that it was unethical for corporations to serve any party other than the shareholders.[4] Following the employee movement and increase in the power of employees, responsibilities toward employees have come to be recognized later. It was not until recently that corporations recognized their responsibility to various stakeholders and to the society at large. In time, the experiences of the corporations have taught them that in their purchasing decisions, their customer base considered not only the attributes of

---

4   Friedman has written that 'few trends could so thoroughly undermine the very foundations of our free society as the acceptance by corporate officials of a social responsibility other than to make as much money for their stockholders as possible' as cited in Davis, 1973 (p. 133).

their products and services; but also the social behavior of the corporation. The advances in information technology made all actions of the corporation in any place in the world visible to the customers. Customers wanted the corporation to behave properly toward its suppliers, and their suppliers to treat their laborers fairly even in far distant lands. Corporations had no chance but to follow the aspirations of their customers and behave responsibly. They realized that this was the only way they could survive and enhance their commercial self-interest, and, in fact, increase their profits. Currently, social responsibility of businesses seems to be generally accepted. The issue now is not whether the corporations are socially responsible but it is how social responsibility will develop and how the demands of society will be reflected into corporate behavior (Economist, 2008).

It is still early days in the process of environmental issues entering the realm of corporate responsibility. Only in recent times have people become aware of the dangers confronting the planet we live on. Organizations like Greenpeace try hard to increase public awareness about the threats the world is facing.[5] The Kyoto Protocol, with the objective of reducing greenhouse gasses, only came into force in 2005.[6] The United States, although a signatory to the Kyoto Protocol, has neither ratified nor withdrawn from the Protocol.[7] Although corporate social responsibility to preserve the planet has a long way to go, there are corporations trying to benefit from the emerging public awareness on the subject.

Motivations to adopt socially responsible behavior have been investigated from various perspectives, however, why and how companies pursue corporate social responsibility still requires further analytical investigation (Margolis et al., 2007). In the adoption of social responsibility, an instrumental approach currently seems to prevail. Thus, socially responsible behavior of corporations seems to be motivated by economic reasons based on self-interest. Empirical research provides supportive evidence for this perspective. A recent worldwide survey of CEOs of companies participating in the United Nations Global Compact indicates that companies have a strategic motivation for attending to environmental, social and governance issues (Bielak et al., 2007). Companies are assumed to adopt socially responsible behavior in order to improve their reputation, satisfy their customers, attract talented employees and thus to increase the value of the company. At present, corporations seem to adopt the socially responsible behavior that increases their long-term economic performance. In order to comply with the objective function of the corporations as defined in the west, increasing long-term value of the firm seems to be the link between societal demands and CSR. Thus, another strand of research claims that socially responsible behavior leads to improved economic performance over the long term. However, the link between corporate social responsibility and financial performance is not so obvious. Margolis et al. (2007) report a positive but small effect of corporate social responsibility on financial performance as the result of a meta analysis

---

5 Greenpeace is present in 40 countries across Europe, the Americas, Asia and the Pacific. 'Greenpeace exists because this fragile earth deserves a voice. It needs solutions. It needs change. It needs action.' http://www.greenpeace.org/international/about.

6 The Kyoto Protocol is a protocol to the international Framework Convention on Climate Change with the objective of reducing greenhouse gases that cause climate change. It was agreed on 11 December 1997 at the 3rd Conference of the Parties to the treaty when they met in Kyoto, and entered into force on 16 February 2005. http://en.wikipedia.org/wiki/Kyoto_Protocol.

7 The signature alone is symbolic, as the Kyoto Protocol is non-binding on the US unless ratified. The US was, as of 2005, the largest single emitter of carbon dioxide from the burning of fossil fuels.

of 167 studies which were carried out between 1972 and 2007. Vogel (2006) claims that CSR 'gives an edge for competition but it does not guarantee business success'. Although the link is ambiguous, it is used as a means to justify CSR within the value maximization objective.

The question remains as to whether companies will incorporate dimensions of societal demands that do not necessary influence their economic performance. In other words, will companies move from self-interest to value-based socially responsible behavior that will consider the interest of the society at large and if yes, how? Recently, contributions from the east are being integrated into the development and formation of CSR concepts. An example is the 'Karma Capitalism' approach benefiting from ideas and principles in Bhagavad Gita. Karma Capitalism[8] claims that 'corporations can simultaneously create value and social justice'. What we need is 'balancing the compulsion to amass wealth with the desire for inner happiness' and executives who 'should be motivated by a broader purpose than money' (Business Week, 2006).

In summary, the literature on the dimensions of CSR indicates that the main factor influencing the way organizational responsibilities develop is through the aspirations and demands of the society at a given point in time. These aspirations and demands are dynamic and evolutionary in their nature.[9] They are very much influenced by the changes in environment and technology. Consequently, how demands of the society actually form and reflect into corporate behavior becomes a central question in understanding developments in CSR. Commercial self-interest and value maximization objectives seem to be the link between societal aspirations and CSR. Objective function and principles from the east offer an opportunity for CSR to address issues that do not reflect into profit and value. It can be argued that the interaction between the developments in Information and Communication Technology (ICT) and evolving social and environmental problems magnified by globalization trends are the current pressures that are influencing the evolution of the CSR concept.

Forces of Globalization

When the General Agreement on Trade and Tariffs (GATT) was signed and The World Trade Organization (WTO) was established in 1994, the globalization movement was assumed to provide a framework for global equality and integration (Stiglitz, 2003). But after a short period of implementation, globalization movement gained a bad reputation. Globalization called for the free trade of goods and services. The opponents called for fair trade carrying a banner: 'a better world is possible'. It is important to note the criticisms and suggestions of Joseph Stiglitz[10] on globalization. Stiglitz argues that globalization could help to reduce poverty and serve both the developed and developing countries if approached with an appropriate attitude. He also believes that the main requirement for the success of globalization is the 'establishment of an equitable playing field'.

---

8   The following link provides additional information on karma capitalism http://www.harekrsna.com/sun/features/10-06/features456.htm

9   Shermer (2004) provides a framework for the evolution of human values and aspirations.

10   Joseph Stiglitz is an eminent theoretical economist, the winner of the 1991 Nobel Prize, was once the Chairman of Bill Clinton's council of economic advisors and was Chief Economist at the World Bank. He wrote two books on globalization: Globalization and its Discontents (2002) and Making Globalization Work (2006).

Although the globalization literature is invaded by advocates and opponents with optimistic and apocalyptic perspectives, there are also valuable analytical studies. Whichever perspective is adopted, the inevitable nature of globalization seems to be acknowledged. Whether they are proponents, opponents or others, all the perspectives on globalization put pressure on the movement for change to serve all, to create a more equitable and enduring world. This can be considered to be imposing social responsibility on all players of globalization. As corporations are among the main agents of globalization, globalization also influences the societal demands on the corporations through an interactive process.

In fact globalization is not a new phenomenon. It started with ancient trade and developed parallel to the developments in transportation and communication opportunities. The industrial revolution is considered to have been the first phase of globalization. After the first phase of globalization, the early GATT was originally created by the Bretton Woods Conference as part of a larger plan for economic recovery after the Second World War. The GATT's main purpose was to reduce barriers to international trade. The accelerated speed of developments, starting in 1990s, may also be due to the phenomenal developments in the means of transportation and communication. The 1990s are recognized as the start of the second phase of globalization.

Since the Second World War, globalization discussions were carried out to remove the barriers to free trade under the GATT umbrella. The final Uruguay Round, which lasted for seven years (1986–93) resulted in an agreement and 125 countries signed a treaty in 1994, creating the WTO to enforce the GATT treaty. The GATT liberated trade and services, providing strong protection to patents, trademarks and copyrights (Trade Related Aspects of Intellectual Property Rights, also known as TRIPS). The WTO has promoted and developed the institutional foundations for 'free trade'. Free trade has important implications on the modes of production. It entails free movement of goods and services together with free movement of capital but not labor, creating immobile pools of labor and the split of the production operation into the production of physical product and the production of its brand image.

Current form of globalization entails three important elements that shape the production and sales of companies.

- companies can purchase their raw materials from any place in the world, wherever is the cheapest;
- companies can conduct the production of goods and services in any country wherever it is cheapest;
- companies can sell their goods and services in any country with their brand under the protection of intellectual property rights (TRIPS).

The purchase of raw materials from any place and the production of goods at any place split the production function in such a manner as to facilitate exploitation by corporations. While the first element enables exploitation of raw material sources, the second element facilitates exploitation of labor. Exploitation of raw material sources and labor have a negative impact on income distribution and environmental protection.

Operating in different countries with different raw material resources, human pools and markets, as well as societal structures and conditions, offers corporations both a challenge and an opportunity to increase their profits and power. In a free trade environment, these companies can easily impose their prices on the raw materials they purchase and wages on the labor they hire. Within this framework, as major agents of globalization, corporations increased their reach and potential and became supra-national powers. Functioning of the mechanism of 'free trade' has effectively increased global trade and global income but at the same time generated the painful consequences of exploitation of natural resources and labor, leading into environmental degradation and growing inequalities in income distribution. It is important to note here that as the corporations of developed countries moved their production to the countries with abundant cheap labor, laborers of the developed countries started losing their jobs, increasing unemployment, poverty and hunger in these countries. Before globalization, there were rich and poor countries. After globalization, income distribution in developed countries also suffered and developed countries also faced poverty problems.[11]

These negative consequences, which were not consistent with the aspirations of people and society, have generated a strong desire for 'fair trade' in global society, empowered by information and communication technologies. This desire for 'fair trade' translated into the realm of CSR, as redefinition of the 'corporation', in a way to secure society's resources by limiting the exploitation of people and the planet. People, desiring an end to environmental degradation, income inequality and poverty, called upon the companies to contribute to strucuring a better community.

Common Driving Forces and Interaction

Globalization and CSR have common driving forces. These common driving forces reshape both globalization and CSR, and also provide the means of interaction between corporations and society to give them a direction to change. The main common driving forces are the advances in ICT and developments in the means of transportation. These driving forces determine the nature of the evolution of globalization and corporate social responsibilities.

Crowther (2000) argues that social networks which are empowered by new ICT can change the power relations in the western world and can have revolutionary impact. Developments in ICT further facilitate the unbundling of the corporation and make them the main agents of implementing globalization. The spread of production and the consumption process globally has intensified the impact of corporations on society and the environment. Globalization powered by the advances of ICT and developments in the means of transportation provided new opportunities for and threats to corporations. To benefit from the opportunities provided, and to eliminate the threats, corporations have to take societal values into account. That is, the corporations have had to respect human behavior and values, social fabric, culture and environment.

At the same time, advances in ICT increased the visibility of the greater impact of corporations, eliminating the location differences in the world. The whole world, with its

---

11   In 2005, the (United States Census) Bureau found 37 million 'poor' Americans. Presidential candidate John Edwards claims that these 37 million Americans currently 'struggle with incredible poverty'. Edwards asserts that America's poor, who number 'one in eight of us... do not have enough money for the food, shelter, and clothing they need,' and are forced to live in 'terrible' circumstances. However, an examination of the living standards of the 37 million persons... reveals that American poverty might not be as 'terrible' or 'incredible' as candidate Edwards stated (Rector and Johnson, 2003).

joys and sorrows, has entered into our living rooms. The developments in the means of transportation brought variety of goods to our homes. The products and services we were consuming were produced in very diverse locations in the world by someone we have never thought of before. But, this increased the consciousness of the society about the welfare of those who produced the products and services we were consuming. Whenever someone is exploited in a far distant location in the world, we see it and we start to share their burden. The developments in communication and information technology made it possible for us to witness the environmental and societal impacts of the behavior of corporations in different parts of the world. Working conditions, consumption of natural resources and environmental pollution in different parts of the world are brought to the attention of the public through the developments in communications technology.

Not all the results of the increased impact of corporations are approved and accepted by the people. If the impact is not approved, corporations face the opposition of the people. On the other hand, corporations try to reshape the social values of the people using the means of information and communication technology to benefit from the opportunities created by globalization. This is an interactive process in which corporations influence the values of people and at the same time the value structure of the people influences corporations in the form of societal demands. Through this process CSR is developing and advancing and influencing the evolution of globalization. Then, interaction between corporations and society becomes an interaction between globalization and CSR. That is, globalization influences the role of the corporations in the society and redefinition of the rights and responsibilities of the corporation influence the outcomes of globalization.

Globalization has also altered the balance of power between governments (State), corporations and citizens (society). At the international level, the influence of governments decreased and multinational corporations have moved beyond the control of national governments. Formerly, citizens could influence the behavior of corporations through the political pressures they exerted on governments. Now, citizens have to develop new channels and means to influence the behavior of the corporation directly. Advances in communication and information technology have provided them the opportunity.

To summarize, advances in ICT stimulated globalization; and at the same time, the increased access of the general public to this technology has enabled the 'global society' to influence corporations. 'Global society' also emerged as a powerful stakeholder for corporations. Interaction between the 'global corporations' and the 'global society' is redefining the corporations in such a way as to include human aspirations and guiding corporations to assume global corporate citizenship. This redefinition of corporations can enable global society to reap the benefits of globalization.

Current State of Globalization and Corporate Social Responsibility

There is a growing mistrust for corporations both in developed and developing countries (Beschorner and Müller, 2007). Society is getting more critical of the behavior of corporations, especially of the global ones. Irresponsible behavior of various companies receives increased coverage in the media and attracts the increased attention of the public. The practices of many companies have come under close public scrutiny: use of child labor in suppliers' factories (Nike); production of unsafe products (Martel); unfair employee practices (Adidas); environmental pollution (Exxon, Shell).

In the initial stages of globalization, multinational or supra-national companies purchased their raw materials from the countries which sell them cheapest, produced the products they designed under the protection of TRIPS in the countries where the labor costs were the least and, adding their brand and image to the product, sold them in the markets where they can get the best price. This mechanism served them well them at first; their profits increased. But there soon came fierce opposition from two sides. The consciences of some were hurt by the human abuses and exploitation. Their common aspirations dictated fair price, fair wage and fair trade. Others, mainly the employees of the developed countries who lost their jobs, were the ones whose interests were hurt. The immediate results of globalization encouraged the cooperation of these two groups under the same banner: 'fair trade, and not free trade'. When the opposition gained strength by obtaining the participation of academics, clergyman and other uninterested parties, the banner was changed to 'A better world is possible'.[12] The opposition to the misbehavior of corporations under globalization has stimulated a vast group of intellectuals to search for a new definition of corporate objectives, a new definition of corporate behavior and a new definition of CSR.

Globalization has also given people the understanding that, in spite of the boundaries we live in, we are sharing a small planet and environmental problems are severe.[13] That is, we are to share the burden inflicted on the environment even if we do not cause it, directly or indirectly. People have been very sensitive to air pollution, the greenhouse effect and global warming. There is also increased public awareness of the wide variations in living standards, income inequalities and growing poverty in certain parts of the world. Living standards of rich countries as well as the poor countries in remote parts of the world can be obseoved by the public. This increased awareness is influencing consumption and investment patterns and will have significant influence on the redefinition of CSR.

Pressures from employees, consumers, investors and other stakeholders force companies to adopt socially responsible behavior. Results of a recent worldwide survey indicate that CEOs rank employees as the stakeholder group that has the greatest impact on social responsibility, while consumers as the second group. However, over the next five years, CEOs expect consumers to become the most influential stakeholder group, surpassing the impact of the employees (Bielak et al., 2007).

ROLE OF EMPLOYEES

When the production units were moved to the countries where labor is cheap, many laborers lost their jobs in the home countries. These lost jobs were named 'jobs stolen'. It was not difficult for labor unions to form a coalition with those whose aspirations were more equitable income distribution and 'fair wages and decent jobs'. Demand on the corporations for fair wages and good working conditions started to reshape CSR. Stakeholder concept had already imposed obligations on companies to their workforce. The

---

12   See The International Forum on Globalization (2002). A Better World is Possible: Alternatives to Economic Globalization. Also available as a summary in http://www.ifg.org/alt_eng.pdf.

13   Ecological Footprint (EF) measures how much land and water a human population requires under current technology to produce the resources it consumes and to absorb its waste. This measure increased 2.5 times in the period 1961 to 2001 and exceeded the sustainable levels as of 1980s (Malovics et al., 2007).

concept was expanded to include the foreign laborers in conformity with the aspirations sof public. Because of the new developments in ICT, a Chinese laborer is not considered any different than an American laborer. These impose redefinition of a corporation's responsibilities toward its employees. Present Non-Government Organizations (NGOs) and NGOs organized specifically for that purpose take an active role in this redefinition.

ROLE OF CONSUMERS

Another upheaval was much more peaceful. The companies themselves introduced the changes to expand their CSR. Some companies have discovered that consumers were willing to pay more for their products if their products do not exploit the producers of raw materials in distant locations around the globe. An example may be Simon Levelt, a Duch company selling roasted coffee beans. Since 1988, customers have been happy to pay more for their 'Max Havelaar' coffee brand knowing that Simon Levelt coffee farmers in South America are paid a 'fair' price. Consumers support companies that assume social responsibility (Sen and Bhattacharya, 2001). During the 1990s, consumer boycotts, ethical shopping guidelines, media campaigns and socially responsible competitors have forced companies to assume social responsibility.[14] Sales of goods with fair trade certification[15] have increased by 41 per cent and reached €1.6 billion in 2006 (Fair Trade Labeling Organization International, 2007). More and more companies are now complying with environmental, labor and developmental standards and certifying their products to satisfy the consumer demand for fair trade.

ROLE OF INVESTORS

Another influential group is the investors. Globalization has also helped the formation of global financial markets. Individual investors' desire to invest their money in companies which act in a socially responsible manner forced institutional investors to develop codes for socially responsible investing. The Socially Responsible Investment (SRI) movement is gaining in momentum and guiding the flow of capital to companies. In designing their portfolios, institutional investors are considering other dimensions other than mere financial performance. Alternative indices on social responsibility, such as the NPI social index, the Dow Jones Sustainability Index and the FTSE4 Good Indices (Sadler, 2002) aim to reflect the social responsibility level of companies. Increased sensitivity has put pressure on companies to revise their CSR policies. In order to attract external capital, companies needed to abide by the codes or guidelines developed by institutional investors. Socially responsible investing has also been facilitated by international organizations such as Global Reporting Initiative (GRI)[16] and Global Compact.[17]

---

14   This may be the reason why Paul Samuelson said 'a large corporation these days not only may engage in social responsibility, it had damn well better try to do so' (Samuelson, 1971, p. 24) cited in Carroll (1999).

15   Fairtrade certification enables customers to identify products that meet environment, labor and developmental standards.

16   GRI is a global multi-stakeholder network of experts which produces reporting guidelines on economic, environmental and social performance http://www.globalreporting.org/Home.

17   The Global Compact of the UN is an initiative to encourage businesses worldwide to adopt sustainable and socially responsible policies, and to report on them. http://www.unglobalcompact.org/.

ROLE OF GOVERNMENTS AND INTERNATIONAL ORGANIZATIONS

As mentioned above, globalization has reduced the power of national governments in favor of corporations. But as a parallel to this trend, international organizations have gained standing in shaping the new world. The WTO, which is the most authoritative institution of the globalization, imposes some rules of behavior to corporations and may facilitate the redefinition of corporations and CSR. Both governments and international institutions have started supporting CSR initiatives since the early 2000s. Government leaders have demanded greater environmental and social responsibility from corporations in the 2002 World Summit on Sustainable Development (UN, 2002). Similarly, the European Commission has issued a Green Paper on promoting a European framework for social responsibility (European Commission, 2001). As they have to meet the aspirations of their citizens, governments are shaping the values of the international organizations. The expanding power of international organizations may provide more efficient means to redefine the roles of corporations in global society and in CSR.

To summarize, globalization has created its 'discontents' (Stiglitz, 2002) and a search for 'Alternatives to Economic Globalization' (Koehler, 2002). This has forced people to search for a better and more respectable world. Since the main agent of globalization is the corporation, it has led to the questioning of the corporation. This questioning helped to strengthen the trend from stockholder to stakeholder concepts. The corporation was formed as an innovative mechanism of the capitalist system. It was an efficient way to accumulate capital for large investment projects. The goal of the corporation was the maximization of shareholder value. The only social responsibility of corporations was to maximize profits, abiding by the law and engaging in free competition (Friedman, 1970). Stakeholder concept, on the other hand, extends the responsibility of a corporation to its stakeholders; namely, the labor, customers, suppliers, the financial institutions, neighbors, environment and State. The change from shareholder concept to stakeholder concept is one of the major breakthroughs of the CSR understanding.

Triple Bottom Line and PPP (People-Planet-Profit) Principles

The current trends in CSR have added three new dimensions to the objectives and the assessment of the results of corporations. Formally, corporations sought to accomplish their financial objectives and their financial success was evaluated by comparing the outcomes against these objectives. The three new dimensions are environmental, social and economic dimensions, which are the same dimensions of the GRI. These three new dimensions are called 'triple bottom line'.[18] The triple bottom line concept reinforces the 'People, Planet, Profit' (PPP) principle. The PPP principle states that 'Corporate social responsibility is in fact nothing other than a business that behaves properly in relation to people and the environment'. It was previously assumed that 'a business earns its place in the world by making profit' and environmental measures and a good social plan eat into profits. But experiences in some countries have shown that a company can increase its profits by a good environmental and social plan (Reinders, 2003).

---

18   The concept was created in the late 1990s by Elkington (1997).

The PPP principles mentioned above clearly reveal the current state of CSR. The current state of the dynamic nature of CSR can be summarized as:

- people want a better world to live in;
- they believe in 'fair' relations and just and fair price. They believe that for a sustainable world better distribution of income and welfare are needed;
- in the newly developing globalization, customers can impose their aspirations on the corporations;
- corporations are aware of the fact that they have to obey customers' demands to reach their objectives;
- therefore, companies are trying to improve their CSR practices to reach their own objectives.

We need to underline a very important fact of the current state of CSR. At present, there have been very important developments in the definition of the role of companies and their social responsibilities, but, in its current state of development, corporations accept CSR as a means to reach the objective of maximizing profit or shareholder value. That is, in its current state, the better people and planet policies of the corporations are for the sake of profit. Serving people in ways consistent with their values and aspirations have not become the end or have not become the objective of the corporations yet. The current state of development is the product of western culture. If enriched with the other cultural endowments of the world, CSR may evolve to new forms. In its new form, societal values and corporate values may converge to the promotion of common good.

Challenges Ahead

Currently CSR practices and developments are viewed as means to improve profits or profitability. The challenge ahead is designing corporations for the sake of people and the planet, perhaps that is the necessary condition for a sustainable world. The question is, how can the aspirations of people become the focus of all the services of corporations?

Corporations, as social institutions, are capable of evolving and designing sustainable solutions. Currently, there seems to be an increased acceptance of the social role of the corporations. Motivations for adopting CSR can be commercial self-interest; expanded self-interest with immediate benefits; expanded self-interest with long-term benefits; and promotion of common good (Rondinelli and Berry, 2000). For the time being, the socially responsible behavior of the corporations still seems to be motivated by self-interest. The pressure from stakeholders has caused companies to assume social responsibility. Decreasing sustainability has reflected into increased consumer awareness and development of environmentally friendly technologies by companies, but the growth in the ecological footprint measure did not top, since consumption continued to grow exponentially. There seems to be a need for incorporating dimensions of social responsibility which do not increase profitability. In other words, the challenge is moving from 'self-interest' to 'common good' as the motivation for adopting CSR.

A related challenge is that there is the threat that CSR might become a way of building image and increasing competitive advantage for corporations rather than a tool for solving the pressing problems of society. Businesses perceive CSR as a business opportunity to enhance self-interest. Under the pressure of NGOs and the general public, corporations assume their responsibilities to various stakeholders and society in such a way as to ensure their viability, especially in the long term. A related challenge becomes striking a balance between the interests and demands of various stakeholders in such a way as to promote 'common good' for society.

Integration with the values of the east can contribute to the promotion of 'common good' as the motivation for the adoption of CSR by companies. However, there might be a danger of using the eastern values in a way to strengthen self-interests rather than promoting common good.

Corporations alone cannot address the issue of organizing economic function to achieve the common good for society. Society influences the social responsibility of businesses through consumers as they exercise their veto right, and socially responsible corporations can influence consumption patterns in society. Furthermore, CSR has limited impact under the current economic system, which depends on the growth of GDP and income. Together with corporations as economic actors, governments as the political actors and citizens as the social actors also have responsibility. Each actor has its own structural forms, strengths and competencies together with its weaknesses and limitations; such as citizens can reflect the society's values but they are atomistic, decentralized and heterogeneous (Waddell, 2000). For the promotion of common good, involvement and cooperation of the all of the major actors (governments, NGOs and citizens) seem to be necessary. One of the threats is that CSR might become a way for governments to shift their responsibilities to corporations (Economist, 2007) and leave important societal issues unattended. As corporations have social responsibilities, society has responsibilities to the corporations. The society and governments also have responsibilities toward the corporations. Addressing the pressing and urgent problems of globalization necessitates integrated responsibilities and coordinated action.

Conclusion

The significant advances in globalization and CSR took place during the recent decades. Yet, this is not just a coincidence. Both globalization and CSR positively influenced the developments in each other, while they were both influenced by the main driving forces of our period: the advances in ICT and the developments in the means of transportation.

Corporation is both the subject of CSR and the main player of the globalization. Initially the only responsibility of the corporations was toward their shareholders. The early stages of globalization presented opportunities to corporations: to produce cheap and sell expensive; that is, to increase their profits. Corporations got a chance to purchase their raw materials from anywhere in the world and get their goods produced in the countries where the labor is cheap. They would then sell their products in prime markets, adding their brand and design which were well protected by the new design. But this process of production and sale can easily mean exploiting the raw material producers and the laborers in under-developed regions which have a huge amount of unemployed labor. Taking the benefits of such opportunities created important threats to these supra-national companies. Both corporations and globalization itself faced the strong opposition of the public at large whose conscience was hurt. People demanded a fair price and a fair wage and good working conditions in those countries where the products were made. These developments called for redefinition of CSR. Soon corporations learned that they needed to conform to the values that society imposed on them.

Currently, CSR is widely accepted by corporations to help them reach their objective of securing profitability. But, the responsibility of corporations is widened to include all the stakeholders of the company. The responsibility of the company is increasing to include the preservation of the environment under 'triple bottom line' and PPP concepts. In spite of all the developments in CSR, corporations view CSR as a means to improve profitability. This may indicate that CSR is just a means of increasing profits and not yet a part of the value system of the corporation. That is, societal and corporate value systems are not in harmony yet. The future expectations may be the convergence of the societal and corporate values. Cross-fertilization of western and non-western business principles may facilitate this convergence in a way to achieve societal aspirations.

References

Balkan, J. (2004). Corporations: The Pathological Pursuit of Profit and Power. Free Press.

Beschoner, T. and Müller, M. (2007). 'Social Standards: Toward an Ethical Involvement of Business in Developing Countries', Journal of Business Ethics, 73, 11-20.

Bielak, D., Bonini, S.M.J. and Oppenheim J.M. (2007). 'CEOs on Strategy and Social issues', The McKinsey Quarterly, Web exclusive, October, accessed on 29.10.2007, <http://www.mckinseyquarterly.com/article_page.aspx?ar=2056&pagenum=7>

Business Week (2006). Special Report: Karma Capitalism, September 30, accessed on 22.12. 2007. <http://www.businessweek.com/magazine/content/06_44/b4007091.htm>

Carroll, A. (1979). 'A Three-Dimensional Conceptual Model of Corporate Performance', Academy of Management Review, 4(4), 500.

Carroll, A. (1999). 'Corporate Social Responsibility: Evolution of Definitional Construct', Business and Society, 38, 268-295.

Crowther D (2000). 'Corporate Reporting, Stakeholders and the Internet: Mapping the New Corporate Landscape', Urban Studies, 37(10), 1837-1848.

Davies, R. (2003). 'The Business Community: Social Responsibility and Corporate Values' in eds. Dunning, J.H., Making Globalization Good: The Moral Challenges of Global Capitalism, 301-319, Oxford University Press.

Davis, K. (1973). The Case For and Against Business Assumption of Social Responsibilities. Academy of Management Journal, 16, 312-322.

Economist (2007). 'In Search of Good Company', 384 (8545-September 8, 2007), 61-62.

Economist (2008). Special Report on Corporate Social Responsibility. 386 (8563-January 19, 2008), 1-22.

Elkington, J. (1997). Cannibals with Forks: The Triple Bottom Line of the 21th Century, Oxford.

Engardio, P. and McGregor J. (2006). 'Karma Capitalism', Business Week, October 19, http://www.businessweek.com/print/globalbiz/content/oct2006/gb20061019_650475.htm

European Commission (2001). Green Paper: Promoting a European Framework for Corporate Social Responsibility.

Fairtrade Labelling Organizations International (2007). www.fairtrade.net, accessed on September 15, 2007.

Friedman, M. (1970). 'The Social Responsibility of Business is to Increase its Profits', The New York Times Magazine, The New York Times Company.

Garriga, E. and Mele, D. (2004). 'Corporate Social Responsibility Theories: Mapping the Territory', Journal of Business Ethics, 53, 51-71.

IFG, The International Forum on Globalization (2002). A Better World is Possible: Alternatives to Economic Globalization. San Francisco, CA.

Islamic Bank of Britain. Glosssary of Islamic Terms, http://www.islamic-bank.com/islamicbanklive/IslamicTerms/1/Home/1/Home.jsp, accessed on January 4, 2008.

Jensen, M. (2002). 'Value Maximization, Stakeholder Theory and the Corporate Objective Function', Business Ethics Quarterly, 12, 235-256.

Koehler, B. (2002). Alternatives to Economic Globalization: A Better World is Possible, A Report of the International Forum on Globalization.

Kolk, A. and Pinkse J. (2006). 'Stakeholder Mismanagement and Corporate Social Responsibility Crises', European Management Journal, 24(1), 59-72.

Malovics, G., Csigene N.N., Kraus, S. (2007). 'The Role of CSR in Strong Sustainability', The Journal of Socio-Economics, Accepted manuscript.

Margolis, J.D., Elfenbein, H.A., Walsh, J.P. (2007). 'Does It Pay to be Good? A Meta Analysis and Redirection of Research on the Relationship Between Corporate Social and Financial Performance', November, Unpublished Manuscript, http://stakeholder.bu.edu/Docs/Walsh,%20Jim%20Does%20It%20Pay%20to%20Be%20Good.Pdf, accessed on January 21, 2008.

Micklethwaith J. and A. Wooldridge (2003). The Company: A Short History of a Revolutionary Idea, Modern Library Chronicles.

Rector, R.E and Johnson K.A. (2004). 'Understanding poverty in America', The Heritage Foundation, Backgrounder # 1713, http://www.heritage.org/Research/Welfare/bg1713.cfm

Reinders, T. (2003). 'Doing business in the Netherlands on the People Planet Profit principle', http://www.hollandtrade.com/dui/zoeken/ShowBouwsteen.asp?bstnum=156&location=&highlight, accessed on August 6, 2007.

Rondinelli, D.A. and Berry, M.A. (2000). 'Environmental Citizenship in Multinational Corporations: Social Responsibility and Sustainable Development – the Two Approaches of Sustainability Applied on Micro Level', European Management Journal, 18, 70-84.

Sadler, P. (2002). Building Tomorrow's Company: A Guide to Sustainable Business Success, Biddles Ltd.

Samuelson, P.A. (1971) Love That Corporation, Mountain Bell Magazine.

Sen, S. and Bhattacharya (2001). 'Does Doing Good Always Lead to Doing Better? Consumer Reactions to Corporate Social Responsibility', Journal of Marketing Research, 38, 225-243.

Shermer, M. (2004). The Science of Good and Evil: Why People Cheat, Gossip, Care, Share and Follow the Golden Rule. Henry Holt and Company.

Stiglitz, J.E. (2002). Globalization and its Discontents, W. W. Norton.

Stiglitz, J.E. (2003). 'We Have to Make Globalization Work for All', YaleGlobal, October 17, http://yaleglobal.yale.edu/display.article?id=2637, accessed on December 22, 2007.

UN (2002). Johannesburg Declaration, UN, NY.

Van Der Putten, F.P. (2005). 'A Research Agenda for International CSR', NRG (Nyenrode Research Group) Working Paper Series, November, No 05-09.

Vogel, D., (2006). Market for Virtue: The Potential and Limits of Corporate Social Responsibility, Paperback Edition, Brookings Institution Press.

Waddell, S. (2000). 'New Institutions for the Practice of Corporate Citizenship: Historical, Intersectoral, and Developmental Perspectives', Business and Society Review 105(1), 107–126.

Williams, G.A. and Zinkin, J. (2005). 'Doing Business with Islam: Can Corporate Social Responsibility be a Bridge between Civilisations?' (October 2005). Accessed on July 21, 2006, <http://ssrn.com/abstract=905184>

KEY REFERENCES FOR FURTHER READING

Baumol, W.J., Litan, R.E. and Schramm, C. (2007). Good Capitalism, Bad Capitalism, and the Economics of Growth and Prosperity, Yale University Press

Çizakça, M. (2000). A History of Philanthropic Foundations: The Islamic World From the Seventh Century to the Present, Bo aziçi University Press.

Ertuna, Ö. (2005). Kapitalizmin Son Direni i (Final Struggle of Capitalism for Survival), Alfa Yayınevi.

Frieden, J. (2006). Global Capitalism: Its Fall and Rise in the Twentieth Century, W.W. Norton.

Micklethwaith J. and A. Wooldridge (2003). The Company: A Short History of a Revolutionary Idea, Modern Library Chronicles.

Robbins, R. (2007). Global Problems and the Culture of Capitalism, 4th Edition, Allyn & Bacon.

Werther, W.B. and Chandler, D. (2006). Strategic Corporate Responsibility: Stakeholders in a Global Environment. Sage Publications, Inc.

Yao, S. (2002). Confucian Capitalism: Discourse, Practice and the Myth of Chinese Enterprise, Routhledge Curzon.

20 Responsibility and Performance: Social Actions of Firms in a Transitional Society

DENIZ ERDEN AND MUZAFFER BODUR

Introduction

This chapter describes awareness, motives, strategies and structures of social responsibility through which Corporate Social Performance (CSP) occurs within a transitional society context. Based upon stakeholder theory and principles-processes-performance paradigm, CSP is measured by the number of social activities directed at the employees, consumers and environment of firms. Results indicate that Corporate Social Responsibility (CSR) awareness, intense communications of CSR to employees, developing formal strategy and executing CSR through a department leads to higher social performance.

The increasingly unhindered flows of capital, information, and the ease in the transportation of people, goods and services impacted the key actors of the international system in differing ways. As major creators of technology and conduits for trade and investment, corporations became more powerful just as the authority of governments was receding. Controlling the bulk of a society's resources, business firms are now expected to address societal problems and assume social responsibilities. This is not surprising since a firm is embedded within a society and its decisions are not purely economic but also have social consequences (Mintzberg, 1983). In the final analysis, business derives its legitimacy from societal acceptance. A holistic approach to corporate sustainability would advise making links between the business purpose and the environmental and social performance (Schaefer, 2004). Concerned about their reputations, many companies try to fulfill the stakeholders' expectations with respect to their contributions to profit, planet and people in order to get a license to operate (Graafland, Eijffinger and Smid, 2004).

In the management literature the social responsibilities of firms to their various stakeholders are extensively studied mostly within a developed country context. However, there is recent work on corporate social responsibility in Asian developing countries (Chapple and Moon, 2005). The present paper studies the corporate social responsibility practices of large firms, including well-known multinational companies (MNC), operating in Turkey. Turkey is a transitional society on the periphery of Europe engaged in full membership negotiations with the European Union. The objective of the study is to identify the basic determinants of CSP of firms operating in Turkey by applying widely used explanatory variables enabling comparison with previous research. Examining the state of art of CSR, several discrete dimensions of the CSP construct are developed into an index which enables a more comprehensive assessment of a corporation's overall social performance.

A Selected Review of Literature on Corporate Social Responsibility, Corporate Social Performance and Stakeholder Management

There is a rich body of literature on the CSR of a firm although problems of definition abound (Clarkson, 1995). Waddock and Bodwell (2004) define CSR as the ways in which a firm's operating practices (policies, processes, and procedures) affect its stakeholders and the natural environment. Managers go through a process of corporate social involvement which incorporates the stages of a) awareness, b) analysis and plan, c) response policy, and d) implementation (Preston, 1978). The original model of Carroll (1979) and its further version by Wartick and Cochran (1985) rely on a triangular model composed of corporate social responsibility (principles), corporate social responsiveness (processes), and CSP (management of social issues). A firm's responsibilities can be categorized as economic, legal, ethical, and discretionary. Discretionary responsibilities would refer to community involvement and would include philanthropic activities. In terms of social responsiveness, Carroll identified reactive-defensive-accommodative-proactive strategies. According to Clarkson (1995) however, this model failed in research application. In real life, companies act parallel to stakeholder theory concepts rather than to corporate social responsibility paradigm (Clarkson, 1995). Firms have differing responsibilities to their shareholders, investors, employees, customers, suppliers, and the public, all of which constitute the firm's primary stakeholders. What is important is the performance data, what the firm is actually doing in relation to its various stakeholders. If there is no data, this is important for evaluating company strategy, for the absence of data means the issue is not being managed. Sethi (1995) concurs that society moved from the realm of corporate social responsibility and social responsiveness to the domain of CSP. Evaluating the principles-processes-performance model of corporate social performance, Wood (1991) notes that with motivations not being observable, and processes being observable by inference, outcomes are the only observable and assessable part of the model. A further refinement introduced by Wood is that performance can be decoupled. If a company does not have a formal policy to address social issues, she cautions us not to infer that no social performance exists. Furthermore, institutionalizing should not be idealized. Having formal social policies does not guarantee good social performance or responsible motives.

Within the firm, the Chief Executive Officer (CEO) plays a key role in the decision-making process leading to the formulation of a social program. Paying closer attention to it may help uncover the reasoning/motives that invoked action (Swanson, 1995). Managers do take into account ethical considerations in their ordinary, everyday decisions (Freeman, 1995). CEOs' 'thoughtful affirmation' is particularly important for building a quality program (Useem, 1988). On the other hand, the CEOs' functional background influences their perception of events in the environment with marketing specialized executives being more attuned to recognizing the multiple demands of their stakeholders as compared to the task-oriented approach of production and finance specialized CEOs (Thomas and Simerly, 1994). The last two authors also report that high CSP firms have CEOs with longer tenures in the company than their counterparts in low performance firms.

Hypotheses and Measures

CORPORATE SOCIAL PERFORMANCE INDEX (CSPI): DEPENDENT VARIABLE

In the present study CSP is measured in terms of the various actions/projects implemented by the company as regards its key stakeholders (Mitnick, 2000; Mattingly and Berman, 2006). The key stakeholders are studied in terms of those that are primarily associated with the production process representing the inner circle (internal) and those that are positioned within the immediate surroundings of the firm (external). The internal stakeholders are the employees and the customers, while the external stakeholders are represented by the natural environment and the social environment of the corporation. The CSP Index is constructed on the basis of the number of different projects/activities actually implemented by the firms geared toward these four key stakeholders (Mattingly and Berman, 2006). Numerous measures and scales have been used to operationalize the CSP construct. The Kinder Lydenburg Domini (KLD) Social Rating Data is regarded as the research standard (Waddock, 2003). There is currently no data basis available on the CSP of firms operating in Turkey. This is the first study to attempt to build a preliminary construct. It develops a model of CSP as a dependent variable (Husted, 2000).

The employees as internal stakeholders were studied in terms of the various social responsibility projects run by the corporation directed to its employees. These were composed of employee training and development projects, health care programs, compensation and reward mechanisms, career planning counseling, employee empowerment programs, retirement and termination counseling, and various assistance programs. The sum of these projects was calculated for each firm as a measure of the employee-related component of the CSP Index.

The second component of the internal stakeholders is customers. The social responsibility activities developed by each firm in relation to its customers included consumer complaint procedures, product usage/safety information, technical assistance and after sales service, total quality management, and consumer service units. The sum of these activities made up the consumer related component of the CSP Index.

The external stakeholders dimension included the physical environment of the studied corporations. This is operationalized by focusing on the firm policies indicating ecological responsiveness. The latter was defined in terms of: recycling, donations to environmental causes, solid waste/water treatment systems, a written record of toxic material release inventory, environmental impact study prior to major capital outlays, and networking with environmental interest groups. The sum of these policies defined the firms' environmental/ecological responsiveness.

Finally, society as an external stakeholder refers to various corporate activities/ programs directed towards the people residing in the social environment of the corporations. These included educational programs, sponsorship activities, philanthropic support, underwriting art, health-related projects, and various other fundings of sports and archeological projects. The total of such activities is the measure utilized for the society-related dimension of the CSP Index.

The development of the entire CSP Index is illustrated in Figure 20.1

DETERMINANTS OF CORPORATE SOCIAL PERFORMANCE INDEX (CSPI): INDEPENDENT VARIABLES

In this study awareness, motives, formal strategy, fixed budget, evaluation/monitoring mechanisms, communication and organizational structure are treated as the independent variables. Each is defined and interrelated to the CSP Index.

General awareness of corporate social responsibility

CSR awareness of the firm was assessed in terms of written and objective statements including code of conduct, mission statement, annual report, and website. Content analysis of annual reports and website reporting are frequently used means of measuring CSR (Clarkson, 1995; Wood, 1991; Chappel and Moon, 2005). Within the 'principles-embedding processes-actions' framework utilized, it is here implicitly assumed that principles refer to the presence of an awareness. At a more specific level, the existence of CSR awareness was related to the mention of social/environmental issues in such documents. To determine awareness in terms of a survey comprising four important firm documents rather than controlling simply one communication venue might be considered a more complete measurement (Abbott and Monsen, 1979). In this study CSR awareness is expected to be related to social responsibility performance as stated in:

H₁: Firms with higher levels of social responsibility awareness have higher CSPI score.

Motives in applying corporate social responsibility activities

An overview of the CSR motives literature indicates that motives range from ones that are primarily serving the interest of the company to those that consider public interest first (Caroll, 1979; Clarkson, 1995; Turban and Greening, 1997). The types of motives in applying CSR activities covered in this study are corporate reputation and image, well-being of society, governmental rules and regulations, recruiting high-quality employees and stakeholder pressure. Participants are asked to evaluate each motive in terms of its importance in applying CSR activities. Furthermore, it is expected that motives and CSP will be related.

H₂: Motives in applying CSR activities are related to CSP Index by varying levels.

Implementing formal strategy for Corporate Social Responsibility activities

Respondents are asked whether or not a formal strategy is exercised for planning and implementing their firms' CSR activities. Strategy formation is the interplay between the formal, intended strategies and informal, emergent strategies mediated by leadership

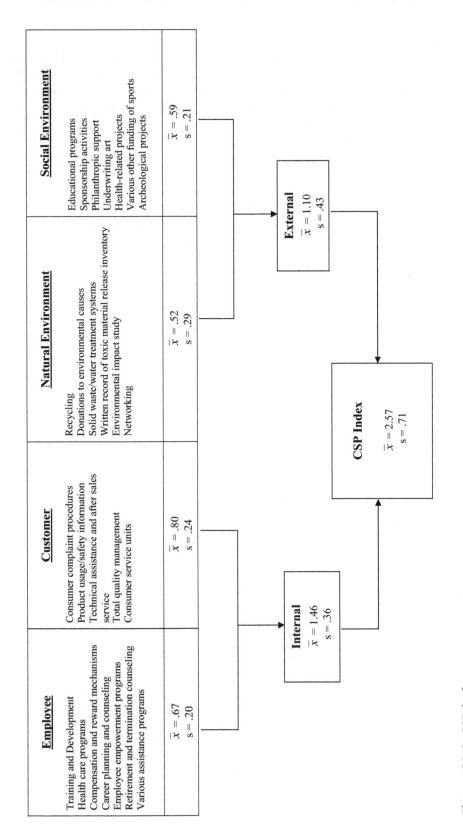

Figure 20.1 CSP index components

(Mintzberg, 1979). Since effective strategic management of a firms' social action must take place at the enterprise level (Freeman, 1984), the responding top managers were asked to indicate the CSR activities carried out under a formal strategy. For each firm a total formal strategy score is calculated by summing up the activities for which a strategy is implemented. Thus, the higher the score is, the more strategically oriented are the firms in implementing their CSR activities.

H_3: *Firms implementing a formal strategy are more active social performers.*

Furthermore, it may be argued that implementing a formal strategy for CSR activities may take some time. Initially, CSR may not be the top priority issue, but as the firms grow and penetrate into new markets, CSR may be viewed as an activity that requires formal strategy development. Therefore, as a sub-hypothesis for H_3, it may be stated that:

H_{3a}: *Firms with longer experience in CSR projects, apply formal strategies more frequently.*

Fixed budget and evaluation/monitoring mechanisms

The existence of a fixed budget and application of an evaluation/monitoring policy for CSR projects indicate a strong commitment on the part of the top management, reflecting the notion that only what is measurable can be managed. In this study, respondents were asked whether their companies devoted a fixed budget and whether an evaluation/monitoring mechanisms was applied for each CSR activity area (Burke, et al., 1986; Useem, 1988; Albinger and Freeman, 2000; Clarkson, 1995; Beliveau, et al., 1994). These areas range from cultural, sports, education to community, environmental, scientific issues, and to customer relations. A total score made up of number of activities for which a fix budget is devoted is calculated. A similar score is calculated for evaluation/monitoring mechanisms where the total number indicates that firm has higher performance evaluation/monitoring orientation. Based on this reasoning the following two hypotheses are formulated:

H_4: *Firms applying fixed budgets to their CSR projects are higher performers in social responsibility.*

H_5: *Firms applying evaluation/monitoring mechanisms for their CSR projects are higher performers in social responsibility.*

Communication of Corporate Social Responsibility activities to employees

Informing employees about the CSR activities carried out by the company is a measure of a company's commitment to CSR. Through this process, CSR is embedded in the mental agendas of the employees and its importance underlined. In this study respondents were asked to report the number of communication channels used to communicate their CSR activities to employees. It is expected that the more numerous channels used, the higher will be the company's CSR commitment. A total score of communication intensity is calculated for each company which is a summation of the number of different communication channels utilized. These channels included company intranet, bulletins, special announcement meetings and periodic reports (Weaver, Trevino and Cochran, 1999). Thus, it is expected that:

H_6: *Firms using more channels to communicate their CSR activities to employees are higher performers in social responsibility.*

Organizational structure for Corporate Social Responsibility activities

The type of organizational structure utilized by the firm to apply and coordinate its CSR activities is investigated with this variable. The structure is represented by a single manager, a committee, and a department in charge of CSR activities. One way of observing organizational complexity is via differentiation in structure, authority, and locus of control (Dooley, 2002). As more information and resources flow, comprehensibility of CSR issues may urge the company to move on from a single individual in charge to a committee and finally to a department utilization.

Execution of CSR activities by a department may be viewed as the most institutionalized structure. Committees may be set upon an ad hoc basis and thus represent an intermediate level of institutionalization. The third form of organizational structure, that is executing CSR activities under the responsibility of a manager, is considered the least institutionalized. Based on this conceptualization, a structural complexity score for each firm is calculated. It is expected that:

H_7: *Firms organizing their CSR programs through departments are higher performers in social responsibility.*

Additionally, implementation of a formal strategy and organizing CSR programs through departmentalization may suggest the most institutionalized form by which a fit between strategy and structure is obtained. Thus as a sub-hypothesis, it is suggested that:

H_{7a}: *Firms implementing a formal strategy for their CSR activities are more likely to use departments as organization structures.*

Sample and Data Collection

A sample of 50 firms are selected randomly from the largest 500 manufacturing and service firms operating in Turkey. The Chamber of Industry in Istanbul publishes a yearly listing of these companies, which provided the sampling frame for this study. All 500 firms were initially invited to participate in the study. After several follow ups 50 firms agreed to participate. The top level executive responsible for the CSR function was interviewed face to face, and asked to fill out a semi-structured questionnaire. Data collection instrument has been pre-tested with a representative group of respondents, and revisions in content, wording, and scales were made when necessary.

The final sample consisted of 28 (57 percent) firms with foreign capital affiliation, and 22 (43 percent) were owned by locals. Out of 50 firms, 29 (58 percent) were operating in manufacturing sector while 42 percent (n=21) were in services. The average firm age was

32.75 years reflecting a sample with considerable business experience. The mean firm size, as measured by number of employees, was approximately 1,000. Based on these characteristics it may be stated that the sample is representative of large and experienced firms in Turkey operating in both manufacturing and services sectors, and are either affiliated with a multinational company or are local.

Findings and Discussion

Data analysis yielded various descriptive and relational results. Table 20.1 presents the correlations among all the variables studied. In the following sections these results will be discussed for each component of the CSR process followed by a multiple regression analysis examining the overall model and its fit.

CORPORATE SOCIAL PERFORMANCE INDEX (CPSI)

For the sample at hand, the CSP Index mean is 2.57 (min: .86, max: 4) which corresponds to a mediocre performance record for the social performance of the corporations in general. It is also possible to observe from Figure 20.1 that the internal stakeholder dimension ($\overline{X}$ = 1.46) of the index is higher than the external stakeholder ($\overline{X}$ = 1.10) measurements (t=7.50; p<.000). That is to say, the studied firms engage more in internal stakeholder-oriented activities than in external ones. Furthermore, within the internal dimension, customer-related CSR projects ($\overline{X}$ =.80) are applied significantly more frequently than employee ($\overline{X}$ =.67) addressing projects (t=-3.299; p=.002). This leads us to conclude that for the studied firms CSR is regarded as a marketing tool geared towards customer relationships (Lou and Bhattacharya, 2006). However, there is no statistically significant difference between the natural and social environment related projects with respect to their application frequency.

The reliability of the CSP Index is indicated by a satisfactory level of Cronbach's alpha (.716). In other words, the developed index can be safely used in further analysis as the correlations among the four sub-dimensions as well as the dimensions to total scores are at acceptable level (see Table 20.1).

When company characteristics such as type (MNC versus local), sector (manufacturing versus services), firm age and size (number of employees) are analyzed with respect to CSP Index, no differences in mean number of CSR activities exist between MNCs and local ones. Similarly CSP Index does not vary with firm size but does vary with firm age; that is, older firms obviously are engaged in more activities. The sectoral positioning does result in differences in the number of CSR activities practiced where manufacturing companies are engaged in higher number of activities than the service firms (t=3.16, p=.002).

CORRELATES OF CORPORATE SOCIAL PERFORMANCE

Corporate Social Responsibility awareness

Table 20.2 indicates that among the various documents prepared by firms, websites and the mission statement are the most frequently utilized ones. In itself, that all firms have such documents suggest a high level of CSR institutionalization on the part of all firms. This may not be altogether surprising as the sample is composed of large, well-

Table 20.1 Correlations

	CSPI	Internal	External	Employee Projects	Customer Projects	Natural Environment	Social Environment	Awareness	Formal Strategy	Departmentalization	Fixed Budget	Evaluation/ Monitoring
CSPI												
Internal	.889**											
External	.885**	.596**										
Employee Projects	.694**	.829**	.422*									
Customer Projects	.736**	.772**	.543**	.285*								
Natural Environment	.865**	.628**	.810**	.454**	.560**							
Social Environment	.600**	.381**	.796**	.300*	.312*	.387**						
Awareness	.600**	.513**	.551**	.305	.550**	.565**	.313					
Formal Strategy	.415**	.269	.487**	.214	.217	.371**	.411**	.421*				
Departmentalization	.360*	.322*	.356*	.293*	.219	.240	.345*	.208	.343*			
Fixed Budget	.449**	.295*	.525**	.204	.273	.397**	.384**	.372	.723**	.450**		
Evaluation & Monitoring	.461**	.331*	.515**	.259	.273	.386**	.451**	.421*	.593**	.306*	.595**	
Communication	.538**	.361**	.610**	.204	.386**	.513**	.448**	.455*	.084	.077	.222	.328*

** p < .01   * p < .05

Table 20.2 Awareness and general principles

Documents	Presence (%)	Mention of Social/Environmental Issues (%)
Code of Conduct	87.2 (n=47)	68.3 (n=28)
Mission Statement	97.9 (n=48)	70.2 (n=33)
Annual Report	80.8 (n=47)	81.6 (n=31)
Website	97.9 (n=49)	83.3 (n=40)

known corporations. It can be noted, however, that these firms choose to utilize the full range of such documents within a developing country setting which does not have an overly-developed institutional heritage. Specific references to social and environmental issues were mostly done through the websites, followed by annual reports. Such specific references were the least observable in the corporate codes of conduct. This might raise the question of whether less emphasis is laid on embedding CSR awareness within corporate conduct. However, Wood (1991) cautions that the non-existence of codes of conduct does not necessarily mean a lack of CSR awareness.

The majority of firms refer to social/environmental concerns systematically through all basic documents reflecting high awareness of CSR issues.

Correlating the previously developed CSP Index with specific references to social/environmental issues shows that those firms with higher awareness level, are more active in CSR activities (r= .600; p= .001). This confirms our first hypothesis. In terms of the CSP Index dimensions, environmental issues/ecological responsiveness for external activities (r= .565; p= .003), and customer related ones for internal involvements (r= .550; p= .004) are at the forefront (see Table 20.1).

A question may arise as to whether the type of venue where the social concern is announced makes a difference on the performance level. Among the corporate documents, only mention of environmental/social issues in the mission statement (t=-3.04; p=<.004) and websites (t=-2.39; p=.021) make a difference in CSP Index whereas announcements in codes of conduct and annual reports make no such difference. If mission statements and websites are regarded as more easily revisable, this might suggest an element of dynamism. It is also possible to conjecture that mission statement references to CSR issues can be interpreted as a priori commitment whereas website references can be treated as post-facto mentions of CSR issues. As such website references indicate a more renewable concern.

When CSR awareness is examined with respect to firm characteristics, the only statistically significant finding is related to the sectoral distribution. There is a significant difference in awareness levels between service and manufacturing firms (t= -2.72; p= .012). The latter are more aware ($\overline{x}$ = 3.76) of CSR activities than service firms ($\overline{x}$ = 2.78). The reason may be related to the age of the firms in question. The surge in the establishment of the service firms in Turkey is a relatively more recent phenomenon (1980s) as compared to the real sector firms (1950s onwards).

Motives for applying Corporate Social Responsibility

Table 20.3 shows the importance of motives in applying CSR. Stakeholders' pressures seem to occupy the least importance as CSR motives. Rather, it is viewed as a vehicle to

Table 20.3 CSR motives

Motives	Mean*	s
Corporate Image and Reputation	4.32	1.11
Well-Being of Society	4.26	0.88
Governmental Rules and Regulations	4.14	1.10
Recruitment of Quality Employees	3.44	1.35
Stakeholder Pressures	3.39	1.20

* Scale values: 1 = not important   5= very important

improve the image and reputation of the firm and at the same time enhance society's well-being.

When motives are correlated with CSP Index, the only statistically significant relationship is obtained between enhancement of society's well-being and the social environment dimension (r= .316; p= .027). In other words, those who find enhancement of society's well-being important engage in more social-oriented projects. This finding reveals that H_2 is only partially supported and invites further research. At this point, one can note that except for the social well-being, all the other motives are in fact self-serving for the corporation. Engaging in projects enhancing the public good which is actually not a primarily economic and/or an immediate concern of the firm might be related to the cultural heritage of the social environment within which the firms are embedded (Chapple and Moon, 2005).

Further analysis of the most important CSR motive, the corporate image and reputation, across a set of firm characteristics, reveals that regardless of ownership structure, size, and age, the mean importance of image and reputation does not change by meaningful amounts except in the case of service firms. In other words, service firms ($\overline{x}$ = 4.67) perceive image and reputation as a more important motive than do manufacturing firms ($\overline{x}$ = 4.07; t=2.15; p=.03). The explanation may be related to the intangible nature of services delivered. Under such circumstances, the quality of the service is identical with the reputation of the corporation.

Implementing a formal strategy for CSR activities

Respondents are asked whether or not a formal strategy is exercised for planning and implementing their firms' CSR activities. Distribution of responses for each activity is given in Table 20.4.

Overall, it is observed that less than 40 percent of firms have a formal strategy for their CSR activities. A formal strategy is exercised most frequently for natural environmental issues. Out of 50 firms, 19 reported having a formal strategy for this activity. Sports is the activity area with the least strategic emphasis. Only 20 percent of firms reported execution of a formal strategy for this activity.

For each firm a total score for CSR activities exercised under a formal strategy is calculated. On average firms exercise a formal strategy for 2.14 activities, which is a relatively low mean as the range for this score is between 0–7. Later, a correlation between

Table 20.4 Formal strategy and CSR activity

CSR Activities	Formal Strategy	
	n	%
Natural Environment Issues	19	
Educational Issues	17	34
Social Environment Issues	17	34
Cultural Issues	15	30
Scientific Issues	15	30
Customer Relations	14	28
Sport Issues	10	20

having a formal strategy and the CSP Index was run in order to investigate whether or not those firms with more strategic orientation are more intensely involved in social responsibility activities. This hypothesis (H_3) is supported with a statistically significant correlation (r= .415, p=.003). Thus, it can be concluded that those firms implementing a formal strategy perform better in the CSP Index.

When sub-dimensions of the CSP Index are examined, it is found that having a formal strategy is correlated with external CSR activities (r= .487, p= .001), but not with the internal ones. Among the external CSR activities, those related to social issues have a stronger correlation with implementing a formal strategy (r= .411, p= .003) than natural environment issues (r= .371, p= .008). This finding indicates that exercising a formal strategy leads to higher CSP when CSR activities are in the areas of both the natural and social environment issues.

Publicizing CSR activities is another indication of firms' strategic orientation. Out of 50 firms, 41 (82 percent) publicize their CSR activities. In nearly 46 percent of the firms, media is used as the means for publicity. For 28 percent of firms such publicity is carried out via firm channels, while the remaining 26 percent include both media and firm channels. Firm channels include web pages, annual reports, announcements, brochures, and other company publications.

There is a definite difference in the level of the CSP Index between those firms which publicize their CSR activities and those that do not as seen in Table 20.5.

Those firms which publicize their CSR activities have a better performance in the overall CSP Index. When sub-dimensions of this index are examined, the statement is valid for the social environment component of the external CSP Index and the employee component of the internal CSP Index. It seems that publicizing does not help firms in raising their social responsibility performance in either natural environmental or in customer-related issues.

For exploratory reasons *history of CSR activities* was also correlated with formal strategy implementation. Nearly half of the firms have a history of more than ten years in practicing CSR activities. Those firms implementing such activities relatively recently (less than two years) make up nearly 15 percent of the sample. Remaining firms have been engaged in CSR either for two to five years (23 percent) or five to ten years (12

Table 20.5 Publicizing and CSP index

Index Dimensions	Firms Publicizing	Not Publicizing	t	p
Overall CSPI	2.68	2.07	2.48	.017
External CSPI	1.16	.84	3.52	.001
Social Environment	.63	.40	3.22	.002
Internal CSPI	1.52	1.23	2.32	.025
Employee	.70	.54	2.29	.026

percent). Another issue investigated is the relationship between implementing a formal strategy and history of CSR activities. Those firms which have a longer experience with CSR activities are indeed implementing a formal strategy for CSR management (r= 414, p= .003), thus supporting H_{3a}. This positive correlation implies that as experience in practicing CSR activities increases so does its institutionalization. This is manifested if the formulation of strategy is taken as an indicator of further institutionalization.

Fixed budget and evaluation/monitoring mechanisms

The existence of a fixed budget for CSR projects indicates a strong commitment on the part of the top management. Despite this strategic concern, the study finds that 55 percent of top managers do not think that CSR has led to financial benefits for their company. Fixed budgets for CSR may also be regarded as further institutionalization mechanisms. In this chapter, the existence of a fixed budget is traced in terms of the specific activity areas. Respondents were asked whether their company devotes a fixed budget and applies evaluation/monitoring mechanisms for each one of these areas. Table 20.6 illustrates the distribution of their responses.

Among the CSR activities, a fixed budget is devoted most frequently for educational activities, followed by cultural, environmental, and scientific issues, respectively. When probed about the application of an evaluation/monitoring policy, a similar pattern is observed whereby mostly educational and cultural activities are evaluated/monitored followed by customer relations. In another question, nearly half of the sample companies (56 percent) report to have CSR evaluation/monitoring mechanisms. This evaluation/monitoring mechanism is mostly in the form of surveys (73.6 percent), program reports (17.2 percent), and external coverage (9.2 percent).

Participating managers were asked whether they review and revise their CSR strategy on the basis of feedbacks from their CSR projects. They were further asked if they compare/benchmark their social performance with those of their competitors. A very high percentage (87.8 percent) of sample firms indicated that they periodically get feedbacks and review and revise their CSR strategies according to various information obtained. However, benchmarking is not as commonly used. In only half of the firms, a comparison of social performance with those of competitors is pursued.

Having a fixed budget and evaluation/monitoring mechanisms for CSR projects reflect a serious commitment of firm resources. Correlations between CSP Index and the presence of fixed budgets as well as evaluation/monitoring mechanisms are shown in Table 20.7.

Table 20.6 Fixed budget and evaluation/monitoring mechanisms by CSR activity areas

Activity Areas	Fixed Budget	Evaluation/Monitoring
Cultural issues	16 (32%)	18 (36%)
Sports	10 (20%)	11 (22%)
Education	20 (40%)	19 (38%)
Community relations	11 (22%)	16 (32%)
Environmental issues	15 (30%)	16 (32%)
Scientific issues	15 (30%)	11 (22%)
Customer relations	14 (28%)	17 (34%)

Table 20.7 Fixed budget, evaluation/monitoring mechanisms and CSP index

Index Dimensions	Fixed Budget	Evaluation/Monitoring
Overall CSPI	.449**	.461**
Internal CSPI	.295*	.331*
Employee	.204	.259
Customer	.273	.273
External CSPI	.525**	.515**
Natural Environment	.397**	.386**
Social Environment	.384**	.451**

$**\ p \leq .01 \quad *\ p \leq .05$

The number of CSR activities accomplished by a fixed budget is summed up for each firm in a total score of budget allocation practice. A similar calculation is done for the evaluation/monitoring mechanism measure.

As Table 20.7 reveals, a positive and significant correlation exists between the overall CSP Index and fixed budget allocation for CSR projects confirming H_4. When sub-dimensions of the index are investigated, it is further seen that a strong, positive correlation exists between fixed budget practice and the external activities. In other words, firms that are more active in natural and social environmental projects utilize fixed budgets.

Similarly, a strong and statistically significant correlation between evaluation/monitoring mechanisms and the CSP Index is observed; thus, H_5 is also supported.

However, the internal sub-dimensions of the CSP Index are not correlated either with a fixed budget allocation practice or with the mechanisms of evaluation/monitoring. The explanation may lie with the fact that employee-related social responsibility projects are run by the human resource departments, and customer-related social responsibility projects are carried out by the marketing departments. At this juncture, it seems that external activities directed towards the natural and social environments are left to be executed by the Corporate Affairs department.

Communication of Corporate Social Responsibility activities to employees

Informing employees about CSR activities is a manifestation of company's commitment to CSR. Almost all firms (98 percent) communicate their CSR activities to their employees. The most frequently used mode of communication is company intranet followed by bulletins and special announcement meetings with 67 percent and 66 percent, respectively. Communication by issuing periodic reports is practiced by half of the firms. Given that intranet and bulletin board announcements along with periodic reports are one-way communication means whereas special meetings are two-way, it is seen that one-way communication channels are used more often.

Mostly two channels of communication are used indicating a preference for multiple channels. On the average companies use 2.56 channels for communicating their CSR activities to their employees. When commitment to CSR is measured in terms of total number of channels of communication used to reach employees, there is a strong positive correlation between number of channels and CSP Index (r= .538, p< .000). Thus H_6 is supported. This correlation is stronger in external activities (r= .610, p< .000) than in internal activities (r= .361, p= .008).

Training of employees about CSR activities reflects a deeper commitment to social responsibility policies. In 52 percent of sampled firms, employees are trained about CSR activities. Whether or not training programs lead to higher CSP was investigated. Confirmation is obtained for overall CSP Index and for some of its sub-dimensions as shown in Table 20.8.

Organizational Structure for Corporate Social Responsibility Activities

The type of organizational structure utilized by the firm to apply and coordinate its CSR activities is investigated in this section. The structure is represented by a single manager, a committee, and a department in charge of CSR activities. Respondents are asked to report how their companies organize the CSR activities. It is to be noted that no firm in the studied sample has set up a separate CSR department leading us to deduce that the CSR function is not yet regarded as a strategic activity. Furthermore, outsourced structures are very rarely utilized while in-house implementation is favored. However, in only three

Table 20.8 Training and CSP index

Index Dimensions	Training	No training	t	p
Overall CSPI	2.82	2.29	2.81	.007
External CSPI	1.26	.94	2.82	.007
Internal CSPI	1.57	1.36	2.13	.038
Employee	.74	.60	2.53	.015

firms, CSR is carried out as the sole responsibility of an employee implying that in 94 percent of firms those conducting CSR activities are responsible for other functions as well. Distribution of alternative organizational structures is given in Table 20.9.

Among the listed CSR activities, the most frequently practiced ones are related to cultural and educational issues and customer relations. Table 20.9 shows that CSR activities are mostly executed by a department (except in the case of sports), then by a committee, and finally by a responsible manager. Thus, firms prefer to execute CSR activities mostly via departments.

Execution of CSR activities by a department may be viewed as the most institutionalized structure. Committees may be set up on an ad hoc basis and thus represent an intermediate level of institutionalization. The third form of organizational structure, that is executing CSR activities under the responsibility of a manager, is considered the least institutionalized organizational form. Based on this conceptualization, a structural complexity score for each firm is calculated where the mean number of CSR activities executed by a manager, committee, and a department are found as 1.14, 1.54, and 2.42 respectively. Table 20.10 presents the correlations of structural complexity levels and CSP Index.

Table 20.10 shows that highest positive and significant correlations are obtained with departmentalization, followed by committee use in applying CSR projects. Thus H_7 is supported. However, when a manager executes CSR activities, no relationships with CSP Index and its internal and external dimensions are observed.

It may also be possible that when firms develop a formal strategy for their CSR management, they will use departmentalization rather than a committee or a manager

Table 20.9 Organizational structure of CSR activities

Activities	n*		Handled by	
		Manager	Committee	Department
Cultural	43	9 (21%)	15 (35%)	19 (44%)
Sports	30	5 (17%)	15 (50%)	10 (33%)
Educational	42	10 (24%)	13 (31%)	19 (45%)
Community Relations	39	10 (26%)	11 (28%)	18 (46%)
Environmental	28	8 (29%)	9 (32%)	11 (39%)
Scientific	26	4 (15%)	9 (35%)	13 (50%)
Customer relations	42	11 (26%)	5 (12%)	26 (62%)

* n = number of firms engaged in each activity.

Table 20.10 Structure and CSP index

Index Dimensions	Manager	Committee	Department
Overall CSPI	.02 (ns)	.28 (p<.05)	.36 (p<.01)
External CSPI	.01 (ns)	.27 (p<.05)	.33 (p<.01)
Internal CSPI	.02 (ns)	.23 (p<.10)	.31 (p<.02)

for executing such activities. This is confirmed (H_{7a}) since the correlation between formal strategy implementation and departmentalization is positive and significant with a value of .343 (p= .02). On the other hand, no significant correlations are obtained between having a formal strategy and executing CSR activities by either a committee or under the responsibility of a manager. It seems that when institutionalization is considered, the simultaneous existence of a formal strategy and departmentalization of CSR activities may be interpreted as higher institutionalization.

In 28 out of 50 firms (56 percent) the CEO is found to be responsible for CSR decisions. However, when other sources of responsibility are considered, the Public Relations/ Corporate Affairs department plays a more dominant role (68 percent) than that of the CEO. The Human Resources Department occupies the third rank by 28 percent. These frequencies indicate that CSR is a shared responsibility among the CEO, Public Relations/ Corporate Affairs, and the Human Resources Department.

Keeping in mind that Public Relations/Corporate Affairs department carries more responsibility in CSR activities than the CEO, we then analyze the relationship between this department and the CSP Index. Bivariate analysis between placement of CSR at Public Relations/Corporate Affairs department and the CSP Index with all its sub-dimensions finds strong differences. Specifically, when CSR is the responsibility of the Public Relations/Corporate Affairs Department, the CSP Index is higher than when CSR is carried out by other departments and the CEO.

Table 20.11 shows that it is the Public Relations/Corporate Affairs staff that probably conceives of and certainly carries out the CSR projects. The internal sub-dimension of employees is left out of this table due to the insignificant relation with the Public Relations/Corporate Affairs department. In other words, betterment of the employee conditions is not in the domain of the Public Relations/Corporate Affairs department.

Table 20.11 CSPI index and public relations/corporate affairs

Index Dimensions	Placement of CSR		t	p
	Public Relations/ Corporate Affairs Department	Other Placement of CSR		
Overall CSPI	2.79	2.11	3.51	.001
External CSPI	1.23	.84	3.23	.001
Social Environment	.63	.49	2.29	.026
Natural Environment	.59	.35	2.87	.006
Internal CSPI	1.56	1.27	2.95	.005
Customer	.86	.65	3.11	.003

Chief Executive Officer responsibility for Corporate Social Responsibility

The CEOs in the sample are almost equally distributed between marketing (48 percent) and engineering (52 percent) backgrounds. The CEOs have been associated with these specific firms, on average for 13 years. In addition, they have been working in their current position for a mean of 4.5 years. In other words the CEOs have risen through the internal track allowing thorough familiarity with the company culture. In addition, they have had considerable experience in their current role.

An attempt to relate the background of the CEO with the level of CSP indicated that there is no statistically significant difference in intensity of CSR activities in relation to CEO background. In other words, whether the CEO has marketing or engineering formation does not make a difference in social responsibility performance. This holds true both on the general level and on the level of the sub-dimensions of the CSP Index.

MULTIPLE REGRESSION ANALYSIS

A series of regression analysis is conducted as presented in Table 20.12. Each column in this table represents the regression models with different dependent variables. Awareness of CSR activities and motives in applying CSR measures are excluded from this analysis simply for the reason that they are the prerequisites for strategy development and for organizing CSR activities. That is, when companies reach to a certain level of awareness and are motivated in achieving their social responsibility goals, then management will set formal strategies and use more sophisticated organizational strategies.

The first column of Table 20.12 shows that 47 per cent of variance in CSR performance is explained by strategy and structure variables. Among these, communication of CSR

Table 20.12 Multiple regression analysis results

Independent Variables	CSPI	Internal	Employee Projects	Customer Projects	External	Natural Environment	Social Environment	Total # of significant 'b's
Formal Strategy	.30**	ns	ns	ns	.44****	.33***	.38***	4
Departmentalization	.22**	.30**	.29**	ns	ns (.18*)	ns	ns(.11*)	3
Fixed Budget	ns	ns	ns	ns	ns	ns	ns	0
Evaluation/ Monitoring	ns	ns	ns	ns	ns	ns	ns	0
Communication	.50****	.34**	ns	.39***	.57****	.49****	.42****	6
Constant	8.47	6.30	.60	.58	4.43	.10	.31	
R^2	.47	.22	.09	.15	.56	.37	.34	
F	13.01****	6.25***	4.32**	8.05***	29.03****	13.30****	11.66****	

ns = not significant Values are standardized regression coefficients.

$*p < .10$ $**p < .05$ $***p < .01$ $****p < 0.001$

activities to employees, having a formal strategy, and a department which executes this strategy are the most important explanatory variables, respectively. In other words, when employees are informed about CSR activities communicated to them based on a well-grounded formal strategy within the domain of a department, corporations will engage in more CSR activities.

As seen from Table 20.12, regression models with the external dimensions of CSP Index have higher R^2 values than the models with internal dimensions ($R^2_{ext}=.56$ vs. $R^2_{int}=.22$). Standardized regression coefficients show that internal CSR performance increases at a lower extent with communication of CSR activities to employees and with departmental structures, whereas the same variables along with formal strategy have a greater influence on external dimensions of social responsibility performance.

Informing employees about CSR activities by multiple channels of communication is a powerful means of increasing firms' social responsibility performance. This variable appears to have the highest coefficient under each regression model except in the case when a employee-related project is taken as the dependent variable. This finding is due to the nature of employee-related projects which cover more self-centered health care and welfare programs rather than programs for raising awareness and commitment about external CSR issues.

Furthermore, having a formal strategy has a significant effect only in explaining external components of CSP Index. This finding may be interpreted as the need for developing formal strategies is stronger in the case when company's CSR activities are related to natural and social environmental issues. On the other hand, organizing CSR activities within a departmental structure explains social responsibility performance better in the case of internal components of CSP Index. Thus, it may be said that when CSR activities are organized as departments rather than committees or executed by a manager, internal components of the CSP Index, especially the employee-related projects, increases.

Finally, other strategic issues such as having a fixed budget and performance evaluation/monitoring mechanism do not contribute in explaining CSR performance as measures in this study. This finding consistently applies to all the regression models presented in Table 20.12. In the case of bivariate analysis, as reflected in Table 20.12, these two variables were found to be correlated to overall CSP Index and to some of its dimensions. However, with multiple regression analysis the same variables lost their significance due to multicollinearity. This conclusion leads us to revisit H_4 and H_5 and admit lack of support for them.

Conclusions

According to the World Bank's classification, Turkey is an upper-middle-income level developing country. It has a young population of 72 million and a GDP of $363 billion (2005). Insufficient accumulation of private capital necessitated a State-led economy relying on import substitution model of industrialization when the republic was established in 1923. Private firms emerged in the 1950s but their proliferation occurred only in the 1980s when the economy shifted to the export-led growth model accompanied by liberalization and privatization. Sociologically, Turkey is a typical transitional society where traditional as well as modern aspects coexist simultaneously (Lerner, 1964). With massive migration from the hinterland to the metropolitan areas, the social infrastructure, especially educational and health services, need to be boosted. Estimated on the basis of life expectancy (70 years), adult literacy (87 percent), and per capita income of $7,753, the Human Development Index (HDI) of the United Nations Development Program (UNDP) shows Turkey's rank as 92nd out of 177 countries (HDI, 2006).

Within this contextual framework, our study looks at a group of corporations to describe their awareness, motives, strategies, and structures of social responsibility through which CSP occurs. In general, when company characteristics are examined the manufacturing firms are more active social actors than service firms. Second, older firms engage in more social activities than younger firms. They also implement formal strategies more frequently. Third, there is no social performance difference between multinational companies and local firms. This is contrary to Chapple and Moon's (2005) finding of CSR in Asia. Fourth, there is no difference in social performance relative to firm size. Indeed, past research on the relationship between firm size and CSP has provided conflicting results (Wu, 2006).

The activity-based index finds a mediocre record. Firms direct their social activities more toward their employees and consumers (internal dimension) than toward their natural and social environment (external dimension). This supports Agle et al.'s (1999) finding that top managers assign more importance to those stakeholders that are primarily connected to the production process (employees, customers) than to community stakeholder groups. It is also in line with a study on the ethical judgments of Turkish managers (Ekin and Tezölmez, 1999). In fact, corporations are more concerned with their consumers than with their employees according to their CSP Index. On the external dimension, an almost equal weight is given to the natural and social environmental projects.

This article operationalizes the existence of principles (awareness) vis-à-vis specific references to CSR issues/projects in the communications venues utilized by the firm. As such, awareness is observed in each and every channel including codes of conduct, mission statements, annual reports, and websites. Social and environmental issues are mostly mentioned in company websites and annual reports probably because these two channels are updated more frequently than codes or mission statements. Significantly, firms with higher awareness levels are more active implementers of social projects.

The primary motive behind CSR is concern for corporate image and reputation. This is parallel with global trends whereby superior corporate reputation has become an important contributor to organizational performance (Lusch and Harvey, 1994). The second ranking CSR motive is a concern for the well-being of society. Furthermore, firms which find the well-being of society important, engage in more community-related social projects. This commitment may be related to well-rooted cultural community giving traditions. However, unlike the growing international practice, managers do not perceive CSR as a tool to attract qualified employees.

Implementing formal strategy is not a commonly used device by companies. It is practiced mostly for environmental projects. But when firms apply formal strategy, it clearly leads to higher levels of CSP in both community and natural environment projects. In other words, well-developed strategies addressing external stakeholders lead to higher scores in the CSP Index.

The majority of the corporations publicize their CSP through the media. This supports our previous finding that the primary motive behind CSR is image and reputation concerns. Those companies that publicize their CSP have also higher CSP Index scores especially for social environment projects.

Reflecting seriousness in commitment of resources, corporations resort to fixed budgets to run their educational activities and community projects. Application of fixed budgets leads to higher CSP. Evaluation/monitoring of CSP is also mostly geared to educational activities. The mechanism of choice is community surveys. Almost all firms engage in periodic review/revision based on feedback. Evaluation/monitoring processes are associated with higher CSP Index.

All firms communicate their CSR activities to their employees through a variety of means including the intranet, continuous bulletin postings, and special announcement meetings. In fact, the higher the number of communication channels used, the higher is the CSP Index. In our investigation of the circumstances leading to high CSP Index, the number of channels used in communicating the CSR commitment and the undertaken social projects to employees stands out as the variable with the most explanatory value.

Training programs on CSR is used only by half of the studied firms. However, training programs lead to higher CSP Index scores.

The corporations entrust their CSR activities to Public Relations/Corporate Affairs departments. This is a more institutionally complex mechanism as compared to assigning a single manager or a committee to the CSR function. The presence of formal strategies is also associated with the department structure. Employee-welfare projects are executed through departments whereas environmental projects are designated to committees.

The CEO chooses the CSR areas/projects but these projects are controlled and applied by the Public Relations/Corporate Affairs department.

Finally, multiple regression results indicate that strategy and structure variables have explanatory strength in explaining the CSP Index. Among these, communication of CSR to employees, developing formal CSR strategy, and executing CSR through a department are the most important explanatory variables. On the other hand, utilizing a fixed budget, or undertaking evaluation/monitoring mechanisms do not contribute to the CSP Index when considered together with other strategic and structural issues.

The CSR behavior of corporations operating in a transitional society shows similarities to those of their counterparts in developed, modern societies. The similarities can be listed as: 1) Employee and consumer-related CSR projects are more numerous than community and natural environment-related activities. 2) Corporate image and reputation are primary drivers of CSR. 3) Firms inform the public about their CSP. 4) Firms have departments in charge of CSP. 5) Firms provide their employees with a continuous flow of information regarding principles-processes-performance of CSR.

The behavioral differences are mainly that in Turkey: 1) Well-being of society is the second most important motive behind CSR. 2) There are no CSR departments per se. 3) Firms are aware of the marketing value of CSR but do not perceive it as a competitive tool in attracting and recruiting top quality people. However, recent intense corporate activity in underwriting public interest projects may be indicative of fast changing outlooks.

IMPLICATIONS

The present study is the first empirical work on CSP in Turkey. It incorporates the principle-process-performance framework and the stakeholder theory in raw data development. The survey explores whether firms that are more aware of and committed to CSR principles, and better embed them in their strategies and structure are more active social performers.

The study measures performance directly in terms of social activities. This is a contribution to the literature because 'motivations are not observable, and processes are observable only by inference' (Wood, 1991, p. 711). Secondly, it is a preliminary attempt to formulate a portrait of a corporation's overall social performance by identifying social action towards four stakeholders and compiling these in a single dimension as the CSP Index.

There are several limitations of the study. Measuring performance by the number of activities disregards the relative importance of each activity. Second, the CSP of firms need to be assessed by other stakeholders besides top managers representing the firms. Third, the small sample size hinders generalization of findings. Fourth, increased rigor can be achieved by studying CSP within a single industry. Finally, a longitudinal study would trace CSP development over time. These limitations in fact represent directions for future research.

Major structural reforms, high growth rates, and membership negotiations with the European Union have triggered considerable cross-border mergers and acquisitions. Foreign direct investment inflows increased by nearly 400 percent between 2000 and 2005 (WIR, 2006). Turkey sits at the core of the Eurasia region incorporating a potential market of 900 million people, and is assuming an increasing role as a transmitter of energy resources.

This study provides insights into social performance of firms operating in a transitional society. The most significant implication for managers lies in the finding that high social performance is strongly related to intense communications involving CSR to the employees. It seems that managers must utilize every means of informing their employees to raise their awareness and commitment to CSR issues.

The findings of the study provide guidance to international investors and managers with prospects of doing business in Turkey.

References

Abbott, W. F. and R. J. Monsen: 1979, 'On the Management of Corporate Social Responsibility: Self-reported Disclosures as a Method of Measuring Corporate Social Involvement', *Academy of Management Journal* 22(3): 501-515.

Agle, B. R., R. K. Mitchell and J. A. Sonnenfeld: 1999, 'Who Matters to CEO's? An Investigation of Stakeholder Attributes and Salience, Corporate Performance, and CEO Values', *Academy of Management Journal* 42: 507-525.

Albinger. H. S. and S. J. Freeman: 2000, 'Corporate Social Performance and Attractiveness as an Employer to Different Job Seeking Populations', *Journal of Business Ethics* 28: 243-253.

Beliveau, B., M. Cottrill and H. M. O'Neill: 1994, 'Predicting Corporate Social Responsiveness: A model Drawn from Three Perspectives', *Journal of Business Ethics* 13: 731-738.

Burke, L., J. M. Logsdon, W. Mitchell, M. Reiner and D. Vogel: 1986, 'Corporate Community Involvement in the San Francisco Bay Area', *California Management Review* 28(3): 122-141.

Carroll, A. B.: 1979, 'A Three Dimensional Conceptual Model of Corporate Performance', *Academy of Management Review* 4: 497-505.

Chapple, W. and J. Moon: 2005, 'Corporate Social Responsibility (CSR) in Asia: A Seven Country Study of CSR Website Reporting', *Business and Society* 44(4): 415-441.

Clarkson, M. B. E.: 1995, 'A Stakeholder Framework for Analyzing and Evaluating Corporate Social Performance', *Academy of Management Review* 20(1): 92-117.

Dooley, K.: 2002, *Organizational Complexity. International Encyclopedia of Business and Management*, N. Warner (Ed.) (London: Thompson Learning).

Ekin, M. G. S. A. and S. N. Tezölmez: 1999, 'Business Ethics in Turkey: An Empirical Investigation with Special Emphasis on Gender', *Journal of Business Ethics* 18: 17-34.

Freeman, R. E.: 1984, *Strategic Management: A Stakeholder Approach*, (Pitman, Marshfield, MA).

Freeman, R. E.: 1995, Stakeholder Thinking: The State of the Aart. In J. Nasi (Ed.), *Understanding Stakeholder Thinking*: 35-46 (LSR Publications, Helsinki).

Graafland, J. J., S. C. W. Eijffinger and H. Smid: 2004, 'Benchmarking of Corporate Social Responsibility: Methodological Problems and Robustness', *Journal of Business Ethics* 53: 137-152.

Husted, B. W.: 2000, 'A Contingency Theory of Corporate Social Performance', *Business and Society* 39(1): 21-48.

Lerner, D.: 1964, *The Passing of Traditional Society* (The Free Press of Glencoe Collier, Macmillan Limited: London).

Lou, X. and C. B. Bhattacharya: 2006, 'Corporate Social Responsibility, Customer Satisfaction, and Market Value', *Journal of Marketing* 70(4): 1-18.

Lusch, R. F. and M. G. Harvey: 1994, 'The Case for an Off-Balance-Sheet Controller', *Sloan Management Review* 35: 101-105.

Mattingly, J. E. and S. L. Berman: 2006, 'Measurement of Corporate Social Action: Discovering Taxonomy in the Kinder Lydenburg Domini Ratings Data', *Business and Society* 45(1): 20-46.

Mintzberg, H.: 1979, ,Patterns in Strategy Formation', *International Studies of Management and Organizations* 9(3): 67-86.

Mintzberg, H.: 1983, 'The Case for Corporate Social Responsibility', *The Journal of Business Strategy* 4(2): 12.

Mitnick, B. M.: 2000, 'Commitment, Revelation, and the Testaments of Belief: The Metrics of Measurement of Corporate Social Performance', *Business and Society* 39(4): 419-465.

Preston, L. E.: 1978, *Research in Corporate Social Performance and Policy, Vol. 1.* (JAI Press, Greenwich, CT).

Schaefer, A.: 2004, 'Integrating Environmental and Social Concerns', *Corporate Social Responsibility and Management Journal* 11(4): 179-187.

Sethi, S. P.: 1995, 'Introduction to AMR's Special Topic Forum on Shifting Paradigms: Societal Expectations and Corporate Performance', *Academy of Management Review* 20(1): 18-21.

Swanson, D. L.: 1995, 'Addressing a Theoretical Problem by Reorienting the Corporate Social Performance Model', *Academy of Management Review* 20: 43-64.

Thomas, A. S. and R. L. Simerly: 1994, 'The Chief Executive Officer and Corporate Social Performance: An Interdisciplinary Examination', *Journal of Business Ethics* 13: 959-968.

Turban, D. B. and D. W. Greening: 1996, 'Corporate Social Performance and Original Attractiveness to Prospective Employees', *Academy of Management Journal* 40(3): 658-672.

UNCTAD, World Investment Report 2006; Undersecretariat of Treasury, Central Bank of Turkey.

UNCTAD: World Investment Report 2006; FDI from Developing and Transition Economies, Implications for development, New York & Geneva: UNITED Nations.

United Nations Development Program: 2006, 'Human Development Index 2006', http://www.undp.org.

Useem, M.: 1988, 'Market and Institutional Factors in Corporate Contributions', *California Management Review* 30(2): 77-88.

Waddock, S.: 2003, 'Myths and Realities of Social Investing', *Organization and Environment* 16: 369-380.

Waddock, S. and C. Bodwell: 2004, 'Managing Responsibility: What can be Learned from the Quality Movement?', *California Management Review* 47(1): 25-37.

Wartick, S. L. and P. L. Cochran: 1985, 'The Evolution of the Corporate Social Performance Model', *Academy of Management Review* 4: 758-769.

Weaver, G. R., L. K Trevino and P.L. Cochran: 1999, 'Integrated and Decoupled Corporate Social Performance: Management Commitments, External Pressures, and Corporate Ethics Practices', *Academy of Management Journal* 42(5): 539-552.

Wood, D. J.: 1991, 'Corporate Social Performance Revisited', *Academy of Management Review* 16(4): 691-718.

Wu, M. L.: 2006, 'Corporate Social Performance: Corporate Financial performance and Firm Size: A Meta-analysis', *Journal of American Academy of Business* 8(1): 163.

21 Feasibility of Corporate Social Responsibility Activities Practiced by SME's in Uzbekistan: A Stakeholders' Perspective

BOKHODIR AYUPOV AND IRODA KOMILOVA

Introduction

The argument that the 'three most important things in business' are 'cash, cash, and cash' (Adcroft, 2002) would now be opposed by an increasing number of business owners. As the benefits of being socially responsible are recognized and the best practice of engaging in what is now called Corporate Social Responsibility (CSR) is disseminated in the business world, this party of 'not-just-profit' oriented entrepreneurs is likely to increase even more in the future.

At its most basic, CSR is about seeing business as an integral part of society, the global community and the environment that supports it. A business does not exist in isolation. It relies on a multitude of relationships with customers, employees, suppliers, communities, investors and others – in other words, stakeholders. This social interdependence of businesses and its stakeholders makes the need for businesses to engage in CSR activities even more essential. One way to understand the importance of this need is to look at what can happen when it is not done: customers see the firm as unresponsive to their needs; employees feel unappreciated; suppliers trust the firm less; communities dig in their heels; and investors get nervous (Industry Canada, 2007).

SMEs Defined

The size of a business is one of the important factors that determine both the type of CSR practices the businesses may engage in as well as the scale of these practices. There is substantial evidence to suggest that large corporations are more likely to run a socially responsible business than small and medium-sized enterprises (SMEs) (Fox, 2007). The most common barrier of SMEs to engage in CSR activities is the cost of implementing these practices when survival is often the greatest economic imperative. Other barriers usually include a lack of awareness of the business benefits with no or little understanding of the business case for SMEs, the absence of systematic incentives or frameworks for SMEs to engage with this concept, time and resource constraints which may mean a lack of affordable external support and resources, and the fact that existing CSR tools and guidelines are mainly geared towards large business (Niblock-Siddle et al., 2007).

The role SMEs play in community development often remains obscured by the informal nature of their actions – a phenomenon that is often called 'silent corporate social responsibility' (Medina Munoz and Medina Munoz, 2001). However, there is quantifiable evidence in a number of studies on small businesses, providing a sense of how important this sector is for sustainable development in emerging economies (Newberry, 2006). SMEs account for about 90 per cent of businesses worldwide and are responsible for 50–60 per cent of employment. As such, they play a fundamental role in society and can potentially have a huge impact on social welfare (Niblock-Siddle et al., 2007).

Many scholars take various perspectives in analyzing SMEs, and employ various characteristics of SMEs to base their researches on. However, difficulties in generalizing the findings of these researches are common. This comes as a result of differences in defining SMEs. For instance, Newberry (2006) defines SMEs as businesses that employ 10 to 100 people, while Burns (2007) classifies SMEs as firms with 0–249 people employed. According to the legislation of the Republic of Uzbekistan, there is no such term as medium-sized business. What would otherwise be called a SME is defined as micro- and small businesses. These would be those that employ up to 100 people, depending on the type of industry the businesses operates in (Presidential Decree, 2003). This chapter bases its primary object of analysis on SMEs in Uzbekistan, and will therefore employ the definition given in the Uzbekistan legislation.

Research Objective

Interestingly, many SMEs in Uzbekistan engaged in CSR one way or another label their actions in many ways but not as CSR. These may include providing excellent services and goods, establishing and encouraging a warm and friendly atmosphere at the workplace, or engaging with customers and other stakeholders. Peculiar is the fact that few of them would even be unaware of the long-term benefits that their activities may bring and are running their practices driven primarily by the religious and/or 'the right thing to do' factors. Generally, those SMEs that are not involved in CSR practices usually argue that these activities are extremely costly and therefore affordable only by their bigger counterparts (Niblock-Siddle et al., 2007). These arguments are amplified by the fact that they do not see the whole potential as well as the future returns of being socially responsible. What they don't understand is that implementation of CSR activities would often require more of a change in the companies' attitude rather than an additional investment (Carmona, 2007). And although financial commitments can almost never be eliminated from the CSR equation, entrepreneurs should therefore look for ways to find a balance between survival/profit and wanting to 'do the right thing' (EU Commission, 2007).

Even though the long accumulated pool of relevant researches outline a wide range of benefits of being socially responsible, they are of questionable relevance for Uzbekistan –

one of the countries in which the very concept of business is relatively new, let alone that of CSR. An entrepreneur intending to engage in CSR with a long- or short-term vision of returns will think twice before making a final decision. The questions that an entrepreneur may want to clarify are likely to be: 'How do these people respond to companies with good social intentions?', 'What stakeholders are likely to be more sensitive to CSR activities?', 'What kind of CSR activities would be the most or the least effective, given Uzbekistan's Soviet background, culture and values?'

The novelty of the idea of CSR in the business sphere of Uzbekistan is also proven by the absence of any research done around this concept. No light is shed:

- on the extent to which CSR is practiced in Uzbekistan;
- on the relevant expectations of business stakeholders as well as the possible nature of their reaction to and perception of CSR activities.

The first research project called 'Support for corporate social responsibility amongst SMEs in Uzbekistan' aimed at providing answers to the outstanding questions above, specifically the first one, was carried out by Westminster International University in Tashkent in 2006–2007. Based on some findings of this research, as well as taking into account the cultural features and historical background of the Uzbekistan nation, this chapter will attempt to reveal some answers to the second question by analyzing stakeholders' perspectives on CSR practices.

Stakeholders' Perspective

Zadek (2001) insists that CSR is based on the concept of 'stakeholder democracy', which is premised on the notion that organizations are made up of a number of different stakeholders with a multiplicity of interests, all of whom should have an influence over the organization's activities. This concept is supposed to preclude the privileging of any one interest above the rest. However, the question remains of how much influence different stakeholders will have in practice. Thompson and McHugh (1995) suggest that stakeholder democracy is fundamentally unrealistic about the distribution of decision-making power inside organizations, because it is the owners who hold the key 'stakes' in the organization and ultimately it will be their interests that predominate. Zadek (1993) also argues that shareholder interests are always likely to predominate, favouring financial over non-financial outcomes, with markets tending to reward bad rather than good behaviour, maximizing short-term profits and externalizing costs to individuals, the State and the region in terms of unemployment, poor working conditions, health and stress problems and pollution.

Rosemary (2004, p. 7) warns about the possibility of confusing CSR with philanthropy. He claims that, 'Corporate philanthropy is something corporations do because they want to, because they feel they should, and they expect no return. Corporate responsibility is about meeting expectations of your stakeholders so you can continue to have a contract to operate.'

The importance of being aware of a stakeholders' perspective on any CSR-related effort may be less obvious in cases when the business owner is driven by inner satisfaction and 'this-feels-right' reasons. However, when guided by Rosemary's (2004) definition of

CSR, entrepreneurs are at risk of underachieving in terms of their bottom-line long-term financial aims of their CSR activities if there is not a sufficient awareness of the possible ways stakeholders may perceive these efforts.

Some business- and management-related papers usually outline customers, employees, suppliers, competitors and government as the main stakeholders of business. But when the discussion is around the concept of CSR, competitors tend to drop out of this list and/or are replaced by the community, while suppliers tend to decrease in terms of their priority. On the other hand, the label 'main' is very subjective and often depends on the business nature as well as organizational values and visions. This chapter will follow the priorities presented by Industry Canada (2008) – customers, employees and community. Even though the environment is taken as another stakeholder in this chapter, it should be viewed as another means by which customers and community construct their impression about a business.

Corporate Social Responsibility to Customers

ENSURING QUALITY

One of the ways of ensuring CSR to customers is ensuring the quality of products and/or services a company produces. How quality sensitive is customer population in Uzbekistan? This should probably be the question to start with when wondering if this CSR practice is to prove itself as an effective one. During the Soviet era, prices were set centrally and economic activity was directed towards the achievement of certain prescribed targets as set out in 'five-year plans'. Profit was of limited importance and any losses experienced by the organization would be written off by the State. Accordingly, bureaucracy and power played a greater role in dictating the outcomes of economic activity than markets or profit motives (Crotty, 2004). The quality of products, even though fairly adequate and widely consistent, was of a lower priority compared to the availability of the product. The absence of competition was another factor: alternative products for customers to compare their purchase with were rarely available. The period of Perestroyka (rebuilding) amplified the problem of scarcity. Rarely would one see a customer waiting for their turn in a long queue and then leave without a purchase because of the bad quality. This was probably why low-quality Chinese products that flooded the Central Asian markets in the 1990s have been so successful – they were available and they were quite cheap. The last factor was of significant importance for the Uzbek population because of an extremely difficult economic situation in the country in that period.

With the competition being increasingly encouraged and with some conditions created for developing SMEs, the Uzbek population has started to become more and more quality sensitive.

MONITORING COMPLAINTS

Most of the organizations had some form of complaints procedure established. The most common way in which customers could express their dissatisfaction with a product or a service was recording the case in a special book called 'Kniga Jalob' (Book of Complaints) which was available to customers upon their request. Interestingly, this system, even though acted on internally, was mainly for administrative purposes and had little to do with satisfying the customer in question. Hence, Kniga Jalob was used by customers primarily with the intention of causing a reprimand for either the frontline personnel (by the management of the organization) or the organization providing the service or product (by the establishment overseeing it).

There is a strong sense in assuming that establishing a proper complaints handling system will be perceived by Uzbek customers positively. The primary reason for this assumption is the novelty of this practice, or to be more specific – the novelty of its nature. A complaints handling procedure which is aimed at satisfying the customer would be perceived by the Uzbek population as something new and unique. Yoswick (2001) argues that a well-handled complaint results in a loyal customer. Implications of this theory are believed to be more obvious in Uzbekistan than in countries where this system has been working properly for some time and is now perceived as something essential and is expected by customers to be operated by all businesses. Because the lack of this system in Uzbekistan has long been perceived as a norm, the presence of it now comes as a satisfier as explained in Herzberg's theory of motivation, rather than a hygiene factor (Workforce, 2002).

UTILIZING CUSTOMER FEEDBACK

What and how long does it take for a business to realize that utilizing customer feedback is more than many opinions aggregated in a big pile of paper? It has dual benefit: hints at ways in which the service or product can be improved as well as improving the relationship with a customer. Specifically it:

- increases the loyalty of customers;
- helps to identify those customers who are about to switch to another company. This is useful only if the company is ready to act on this signal and attempt to retain the customer;
- enables cross-selling of the firm's services. It is not unusual for customers' awareness to be limited just to the kind of a product or service they usually purchase. With a bit more of a thought, a feedback eliciting session could indirectly be used as a small promotional tool;
- discovers the clients' requirements and aids the development of new ideas for improved service. Customers may come as a strategic source of ideas for improvements because they take the time and make the effort to compare the service/product offered with those of competitors;
- finds out more about the way customers perceive the firm. Customers may therefore be used as an external eye on either the way the service is provided or the extent to which their products meet their expectations.

Customers seem to concur with the abovementioned benefits of utilizing customer feedback. One customer, for instance, recalls: '...I fondly remember the day representatives from Palo Alto, California-based Hewlett-Packard Co. visited me to discuss what would eventually become their scanner line – even though my small piece was simply interface and device drivers. I gave them all the time in the world, and probably too many secrets I had learned from other peripheral vendors. They listened. They asked questions. They took notes. They asked more questions and listened carefully. The rest is history' (Foden, 2003).

One of the interesting changes being observed in most of the Commonwealth of Independent States countries is the relationship between the clients and workers of companies. In Soviet times the lack of profit orientation combined with job security resulted in this relationship having a worker-centered nature. The psychological domination of a worker over a client during a transaction was a normally accepted event. A smile from a worker while providing a service could actually make the client's day – so rare were they. The new environment in which businesses fight for every customer requires a radical transformation of the worker-client relationship. With this transformation well in progress, every now and then one would still come across a worker with an old mindset. But then clients with similar mindsets who would still put up with an unwelcoming behaviour of a company worker are not rare.

This yet incomplete transformation of the worker-client relationship implies an embedded effectiveness of companies' efforts to elicit customers' feedback and utilize it. When a company expresses its interest in its client's opinion of the service experienced or a product purchased, the level of their satisfaction, or asks for suggestions for further improvement, this gives a client that rare feeling of importance in this relationship and comes across as something remarkable and outstanding for a customer. Even if a customer refuses to provide feedback, this unusually pleasant behaviour of a company will differentiate it from its competitors and result in a positive association with the company's image in the mind of a customer.

Some companies take this CSR activity as far as contacting customers regarding their feedback. Even though in countries where personal sales activities are common this effort may be a nuisance for some customers, for an average Uzbek customer who represents a culture with a relatively high level of collectivism this is likely to add a sense of a personal bond with a company.

Corporate Social Responsibility to Employees

Differentiation between large corporations and SMEs when discussing the CSR practices is vital when examining the employees' perspective. Employees in SMEs tend to have lower pay and less job security than in large firms (Burns, 2007). Workers in SMEs usually tend to be low-skilled (Newberry, 2006). This is often the main reason for the higher rate of staff turnover compared with large businesses. Staffing plays a significant role in achieving the major goals of a business. This is true in any business but employees in a small business are often a critical resource for the business's success and prosperity. As such, many small and medium-sized businesses emphasize increasing employee skills and work on motivating and building staff morale (Niblock-Siddle et al., 2007). An SMEs' decision to practice CSR increases the chances of recruiting specialists of the required qualification, and significantly contributes to the firms' staff retention rate. According to the 2003 CSR Monitor by GlobeScan, 70 per cent of North American students surveyed said they would not apply for a job at a company deemed socially irresponsible. What's more, the survey found that 68 per cent disagreed that salary was more important than social responsibility. A 2003 Stanford University study, 'Corporate Social Responsibility

Reputation Effects on MBS Job Choice', found that MBA graduates would sacrifice an average of $13,700 in salary to work for a socially responsible company (Fox, 2007).

GOOD WORKING CONDITIONS

The Stanford University study findings do not seem too surprising if one keeps in mind that CSR also includes the provision of good working conditions. Very high pay cannot compensate for poor working conditions. However, the opposite is true as well: the plushest office will not compensate for low pay. Striking the balance is what ensures the commitment of an employee to their company (Computer Daily, 2004). This type of CSR promotes a healthy lifestyle among staff members. It raises morale among workers, leading to higher productivity, lower staff turnover and consequently lower recruitment and training costs. Staff members are loyal to their employer, since they feel that the owners of the business take care of them.

Despite the fact that living conditions were generally mediocre, State ownership of all types of enterprises implied a wide responsibility of the USSR government for ensuring equally good working conditions. Most of the workers had, for instance, access to subsidized catering services, free medical support and specially assigned kindergartens for workers' kids. Those who worked in hazardous workplaces were offered additional allowances and bonuses, either financial or material. In Uzbekistan there was a general deterioration of working conditions that started in the late 1980s and got even worse in the first years of independence (after 1991). Although this was a natural result of the mass deregulation and privatization of enterprises, the population still expected adequate conditions in their workplace. Even though big corporations nowadays are able to meet its employees' expectations by offering a fair salary, various bonuses as well as necessary facilities, very few SMEs can afford to provide even the minimal working conditions to its employees. This results in a wide tendency for a highly qualified workforce to be inclined to apply for work in big corporations rather than small enterprises, causing a shortage of specialists in SMEs.

Based on these arguments it would make sense to suggest that a focus on CSR to employees in SMEs by creating a good working environment will be effective in attracting suitable applicants as well as keeping the current staff motivated. However, this CSR activity implies quite significant financial commitments. Given the current economic situation of Uzbekistan as well as the difficulties and various obstacles for SMEs' development in the country, there should be a limit to how much SMEs commit on this CSR activity: a wise strategy would be to ensure adequate working conditions to keep workers from being dissatisfied.

PROPER TREATMENT

Every now and then one comes across a phrase 'Soviet approach' when explaining certain decisions that have been made without involving other stakeholders and/or when changes are being implemented forcibly. An autocratic style of management has long been the dominant one. Most of the enterprises employed a bureaucratic organizational structure with a narrow span of control which usually made intra-organizational communication complicated and made an organization itself slow and unresponsive. An autocratic style of management has rarely been questioned by subordinates who in turn were used to it and did not expect to be involved in decision making by higher-level management. Work and social life were intertwined throughout the Soviet Union by virtue of the extended role played by the industrial organization in the life of the ordinary worker. This approach to economic organization involved the concentration of the specific branches of industry at different regional locations across the Union. Within these branches, large monolithic institutions were established, often employing tens of thousands of employees. Inside these institutions, a form of paternalistic management was employed. Within the context of the Soviet Union, this style of 'paternalistic' management organization has been summarized by The Samara Research Group (1995) as: charismatic leadership with strict managerial hierarchy and lack of information provided to workers; egalitarian principles of pay and distribution between shops/units; employee access to housing, cars, heating, holiday camps and other non-industrial goods and services through the factory; feelings of local patriotism among workers channelled into efforts to sustain and improve factory output (Crotty, 2004).

Even today most of the large State-owned corporations cannot be considered as having gone through major changes. Relatively participative and democratic styles of management can be observed primarily in multinational companies operating in Uzbekistan and some SMEs. Most of the workers who started their careers before 1990 still feel more comfortable being assigned their tasks and even feel unease when being given the freedom of autonomous decision making. This does not, however, apply to a younger generation. With a significant influence of western culture, and the emphasis on promoting and indoctrinating democratic values in the early 1990s, people exposed to it in their early lives were more absorbent because this time coincided with the period when the new generation's personality, viewpoints and beliefs were being shaped and established. This eventually resulted in a significant difference in the mentality of younger and older generations. Young people are now generally more determined, ambitious, less risk averse, more open to changes and more confident in independent decision making.

Therefore, even if there is an inclination by management for a participative approach, using it may not always be the best thing. The effectiveness of the democratic style of management is more obvious if the workers are the younger generation. Although this does not mean that it should not be used when a majority of staff is comprised of representatives of an older generation, doing this may require some adaptation in the form of briefings and necessary trainings. Analyzing this through a perspective of McGregor's theory of motivation, theory X would be more applicable for workers of an older generation, while for the new generation theory Y is more appropriate.

EQUAL OPPORTUNITY

'Svyazi na vostoke reshayut vsyo!' is a popular saying in Russian which means that 'in the East proper connections' can solve nearly any problem. These practices of inequality such as giving preference to relatives, friends and favourites when recruiting people or promoting employees are partially a heritage of the Soviet regime. It is also boosted by cultural peculiarities of Uzbek people such as the strong personal relations and bonds within the extended family. Yet whenever a certain company is known for being difficult to recruit a complete outsider, this significantly discourages people from applying to it. Internally, this also demotivates workers and causes a lack of belief that their efforts would be recognized, let alone their belief in being promoted.

Analyzed using Hofstede's explanation of cultural dimensions, Uzbek culture can be described as having a high level of masculinity. Uzbeks constitute a male-dominant society. Despite the recent various campaigns to fight for women's rights and introduce some changes in the current situation, the majority of Uzbek women still play a very submissive and passive role and are assigned with primary responsibility for looking after houses and bringing up their children. This state of affairs puts an enormous pressure on Uzbek men as they are almost always seen as and expected to be the primary source of a family's income. This explains the fact that Uzbek men are substantially more sensitive to their career progress. Consequently, more often than not male workers of a certain company get extremely demotivated when a female is promoted to a higher position above other male candidates.

One thing that makes it extremely difficult to establish an equal opportunities policy in companies is the question of maternity leave. Being part of a socially-orientated way of embarking on a market economy in Uzbekistan, the period of maternity leave according to local legislation is up to three years. Obviously, this is a substantial expense for any company employing a pregnant woman. As a result of this, it is very unlikely that a pregnant female applying for a position or promotion would succeed. The average age of getting married for Uzbek females is the early 20s. It is also a part of Uzbek culture to expect the first baby to be born within a year of marriage. These two factors decrease the chances of young mothers as well as single females in their 20s from progressing in their careers.

No matter how attractive promoting and maintaining policies of equal opportunity may seem to the management, actual implementation of it is a costly CSR activity. It is therefore likely to be practised in large corporations, either State owned or private, and multinational companies. An effort to establish and practice an equal opportunity policy in a small or medium enterprise would, therefore, by all means be a distinctive feature of the company, and attract highly qualified candidates as well as keep its workers highly motivated. But to make it even more effective, that is, to avoid the abovementioned risks drawn from the cultural aspects of Uzbeks, care should be taken to maintain an adequate gender balance.

Corporate Social Responsibility to the Environment

Would SMEs in Uzbekistan benefit from environmentally friendly activities? Should they commit their resources to these CSR activities? Even if ethical and moral factors would drive one to answer these questions otherwise, a manager conscious of the current environmental awareness of the Uzbek population is likely to give a negative answer. To put this straight and simple: the Uzbek population has not reached the stage when it is ready to pay even a bit more for the product produced by a company that uses an environmentally friendly production process.

On the other hand, the number and variety of environmentally- related efforts and campaigns of the Uzbekistan government contradict the previous statement and make the situation somewhat paradoxical. In cooperation with a number of Non-Government Oganizations (NGOs), the government of Uzbekistan has long been involved in various large-scale projects such as the establishment of the International Fund 'ECOSAN', developing and implementing different programmes on waste disposal, and protection of the environment.

This paradox can be explained by the inadequate attention to a vital effort – making the population assume the responsibility for improving the environment. Insufficient attempts to promote environmental concerns among the population as well as often practices of the government to force businesses to invest in greening – all point to the fact that environmental issues are being owned only by the government.

In countries where the dissemination of environmental issues, both local and global, is promoted in an effective manner (that is, considerable effort is made to ensure that these problems are owned by both the government and population) customers are demanding environmental and CSR credentials. For example, organizations are finding that without a proper environment policy in place they are not being included on tender lists (Taylor, 2007).

The general understanding of using 'recycled' resources is often associated with saving on quality or using resources of a lower quality. This is why, asked to choose between a product of an environmentally friendly producer and a product of the same price but produced by an environmentally unfriendly manufacturer, some customers would even go for the latter one. Those who are aware of environmental issues and recognize the benefits of recycled products are likely to look at their transaction from a 'why me?' perspective. All these point to a wide ignorance among the population about environmental issues.

Unless environmental issues and good practice are sufficiently promoted (rather than enforced) among the Uzbek population, any environmental CSR activity is likely to be a waste of effort and investment.

Corporate Social Responsibility to the Community

According to the findings of the recent research carried out by Westminster International University in Tashkent, CSR to the community is the most widespread and common CSR practice in Uzbekistan. When asked about their understanding of CSR, among the first examples given by representatives of most of the stakeholders were businesses contributing to improving the look of the local area, sponsoring some costly traditional ceremonies, such as weddings for underprivileged families or other religious ceremonies such as circumcision, and donations to orphanages. These practices also include renovations of local schools, cemeteries, kindergartens and so on.

Businesses are usually more inclined to engage in these activities because these are the ones that would enable them to most easily publicize their CSR activities and thus establish goodwill and improve their image in the eyes of a relatively wide public. Moreover, these activities also carry some promotional implications. For example, the fast food chain 'Multyashka' located in Tashkent provided free lunch for pensioners and old people every Sunday. By doing so, the owner of that business not only takes care of elderly people, but also created a positive image and increased sales figures.

Other factors of interest for businesses to engage in these types of CSR activities include some encouragement from the government. For instance, businesses that support underprivileged students by covering their tuition fees are entitled to a 1 per cent reduction of their profit tax. However, it is not unusual for some governmental encouragements to take the form of imposition. The year 2007 was announced as the year of social protection. Many businesses, both large and small, have been obligated during that year to sponsor various events and support their neighbourhoods.

The timing of donations and various other philanthropic campaigns of many SMEs in Uzbekistan coincides with the Eid-al-Adha and Eid-el-Fitr religious holidays. The best explanation for the decision of SMEs to schedule their community-related CSR activities is that the majority of the population of Uzbekistan is Muslim (about 88 per cent). Very smartly, SMEs try to adapt to this demographical situation: their CSR activities in these periods are considered to be Zakat (Alms), a form of giving to those who are less fortunate. It is obligatory for Muslims to give 2.5 per cent of their wealth and assets (although this proportions is not necessarily followed) each year (in excess of what is required) to the poor. Giving the Zakat is considered an act of worship because it is a form of offering thanks to God for the means of material well-being one has acquired. According to the Qur'an, only those who pay Zakat are in the 'brotherhood of faith' (SU: 9 103). The decision of SMEs to give their CSR activities a religious aura results in a significantly wider audience being affected rather than just those addressed directly, because Muslims, just like representatives of any other religions, have a very strong sense of solidarity (Kuroda, 2001).

Conclusion

The above discussion leads one to presume that unless a business owner is driven by philanthropic needs, engagement in CSR activities is a very daring decision. Not only does this decision take someone with a low level of uncertainty avoidance, but also a sound knowledge of Uzbek people with their traditions, views and values. The effectiveness of CSR efforts is likely to be increased with a good knowledge of local history as well as the current political and economic situation in the country.

The significant role of social bonds and the great value of the interpersonal communication of Uzbek people in all aspects of their lives suggests that businesses' efforts to establish and strengthen relationships with their customers is likely to be very effective both in the short as well as in the long run. This makes such CSR practices as establishing an effective complaints handling system and that of utilizing customer feedback to be particularly appropriate.

However, these CSR commitments cannot compensate for a low quality of goods and services offered by businesses. With the Uzbek population becoming more and more quality sensitive, ensuring the quality of products and services offered will be effective in the longer run. This CSR practice will even reinforce the effectiveness of the relationship-oriented efforts. These two types of efforts are therefore an optimal combination of CSR investments and can be seen as the best balance of period versus cost, making it most suitable for SMEs.

Even though the theoretical benefits can equally be expected from ensuring CSR to employees, the evidence suggests that given the economic and some legislative conditions of SMEs in Uzbekistan, maintaining the situation at or above status quo is often sufficient to keep the balance between employee satisfaction (or lack of dissatisfaction) and the expected returns of being socially responsible.

Without undermining the importance of the environment as one of the business stakeholders, it can be presumed that CSR efforts that address the community are more effective than those directed at the environment. Those businesses that engage in CSR and are driven by the potential gains of their efforts should, firstly, clearly distinguish between philanthropic activities and those of CSR. And secondly, efforts to publicize their CSR activities should be seen as an integral part of their CSR investments. Failure to do this is likely to diminish the purposefulness of their efforts, especially when CSR activities are aimed at being environmentally friendly.

References

Adcroft, A. (2002) *Corporate Strategy lecture*, University of Surrey

Burns, P. (2007) *Entrepreneurship and Small Business*, 2 edn, New York: Palgrave Macmillan.

Carmona, J. (2007) *Corporate Social Responsibility program for small businesses*, Caribbean Business, September 20.

ComputerWorld (2004) http://www.computerweekly.com/Articles/2004/07/08/203545/satisfied-staff-make-a-good-business-great.htm [last accessed 03.09.2009].

Crotty, J. (2004) *Transitions in environmental risk in a transitional economy: management capability and community trust in Russia,* Journal of Risk Research, 7(4), pp. 413-429.

European Commission (2007) *How to help more small businesses to integrate social and environmental issues into what they do,* Mutual learning meeting between projects co-financed by the European Commission, http://ec.european/enterprise/csr/ereb/mutual_learning_meeting2_may.pdf [last accessed on 18.02.2008].

Foden, A. (2003) *Customer-focused efforts require listening,* Marketing News, 37(5), pp. 56-56.

Fox, A. (2007) *Corporate Social Responsibility Pays pays off,* HR Magazine, 52(8), pp. 42-47, 6p.

Industry Canada (2008) *The Importance of stakeholder engagement,* part 3, http://www.ic.gc.ca/epic/site/csr-rse.nsf/en/rs00138e.html [last accessed on 20.02.2007].

Kuroda (2001) *Islamic Solidarity and Socio-Cultural Tradition. Japanese Institute of Global Communications.* http://www.glocom.org/opinions/essays/200111_kuroda_islamic2/index.html [last accessed on 18.02.2008]

Medina Munoz and Medina Munoz (2001) cited in Newberry D. (2006) *The role of small and medium-sized enterprises in the futures of emerging economies*, Earth Trends: Environmental Information (World Resource Institute).

Newberry, D. (2006) *The role of small and medium-sized enterprises in the futures of emerging economies,* Earth Trends: Environmental Information (World Resource Institute).

Niblock-Siddle, K. et al. (2007) *The importance of Corporate Social Responsibility for SMEs,* Australian Centre for Corporate Social Responsibility www.accsr.com.au, [last accessed on 20.02.2008].

Presidential Decree (2003) *Stimulating development of entrepreneurship and small businesses,* 30.08.2003 #UP-3305

Qur'an, SU, 9:103

Rosemary, R. (2004) *Community Support Pays off,* B&T, October 15, p. 7.

Samara Research Group (1995) Paternalism in Russian enterprises: our understanding, in S. Clarke (ed.) *Management and Industry in Russia: Formal and Informal relations,* London: Edward Elgar, pp. 102-48.

Taylor, C. (2007) *Why...the environmental and CSR are important,* Printing World, September.

Thompson, P. and McHugh, D. (1995) *Work Organizations: A Critical Introduction*. Basingstoke: Macmillan.

Workforce (2002) *Frederick Herzberg: Hygiene and Motivation*, 81(1), p. 33.

Yoswick, J. (2001) *Building Loyalty through Customer Service*, Automotive Body Repair News, 40(7), p. 20, 3p.

Zadek, S. (1993) *An Economics of Utopia*. London: Avebury.

Zadek, S. (2001) *The Civil Corporation: The New Economy of Corporate Citizenship*. London: Earth-scan Publications.

22 *Education for Ethics and Socially Responsible Behaviour*

KUMBA JALLOW

Introduction

In our largely technical world, ethical considerations are often subsumed into decision making at a level that is at best implicit and at worst ignored. Medical ethics are often the most newsworthy aspect of ethics, where moral responsibility and behaviour concern themselves with issues of life and death and the 'correct' ways of dealing with these huge (and basic) dilemmas. However, every day we make choices based upon some kind of ethical framework. What products do we buy, how do we do our jobs, how do we raise our children? Often these choices are made without a conscious debate about the morality of the outcomes, but most of us have an innate framework that tells us what is right and what is wrong.

What education can do is make these frameworks visible so that our decision making is justifiable (or not) and that we can understand why we make the choices we do. Behaviour can be analysed to understand the 'how' and 'why' of our actions. Education can also raise our awareness of our behaviour and its effects and so help us to recognise where change may be necessary.

Ethics as a subject can appear an abstract set of ideas, complex and obtuse. It has a long history and is often associated with philosophy and moral thinking, regarded as a theoretical and academic discipline not related to real life. However, teaching ethics is possible at any level and there are a number of approaches which can engage people at different levels. This chapter is concerned with some of the practical ways of engagement and the demystifying of ethics as an academic subject so that it can be part of a broader educational framework in which we see ethics as a means to guide our actions and understand our behaviour.

Ethical Frameworks

Ethics concerns behaviour and the ability to decide what the appropriate behaviour in a given situation is. 'Appropriate' is judged by comparison with a set of norms which themselves are determined by the framework underlying them. In order to incorporate ethics into teaching, consideration must be taken of the approaches to ethics that have been developed to provide an underlying ethical framework. Although categorised in a variety of ways, three main ethical strands have emerged: one with an emphasis on duties, rights and obligations (a deontological approach), one which examines the external consequences of the action (a teleological approach) (Drummond and Bain, 1994) and one which concentrates upon the actor's (rather than the action) motivation, character and intention (a virtue ethic) (Treviño and Nelson, 2007, Jones et al., 2005). However, this categorisation is not straightforward, and there is some overlap. Another way may be to look at the orientation of the ethical problem (Melé, 2004). This would result in four broad categories:

'*Profit-oriented*' ethics. This could also be described as enlightened self-interest. The ethics here are reduced to an adherence to legal and regulatory forces with some social constraints. Hence the making of profits (in a business sense) overrules any other consideration, which can lead to other damages such as to the environment or to human beings. Hence the use of child labour can be justified if profit is generated by this action.

'*Principle-oriented*' ethics. This form of ethics is based upon universal principles which are determined by reason and rationality. Hence reason determines what is the right (or wrong) action. Kant's 'categorical imperative' is often provided as a means of explaining this approach (Treviño and Nelson, 2007). Kant developed a set of maxims or prescriptions which are both universal and unchangeable. These are: that a person should act in such a way that the behaviour becomes a universal law, that human dignity is central and is an ends not a means, and that people act so that will becomes the universal determinant of right and wrong. This is the basis of the thinking around human rights, as outlined for instance, in the UN Declaration of Human Rights (UN, 1948). Hence a business will adopt corporate social responsibility principles by which it acts to carry on its business.

In contrast to Kant, but still within the principle orientation, is the theory of utilitarianism. This is often described by the rule 'the greatest happiness to the greatest number' and measures the consequences of an action in terms of the pleasure or pain in the outcome. This contrasts with the universal principle because it relates to the specific action and outcome and does not seek to make this universal. It is subjective and requires individual assessment, but it still retains the aspect of reason. This allows business to generate profits which benefit the greatest number of stakeholders, particularly where stakeholders who benefit are easily identified and those who do not are 'hidden'.

'*Agent-oriented*' ethics. This rejects the universality of the principle-based approach and regards the *actor* rather than the *action* as the prime consideration. In other words it is the attitudes, perceptions and feelings of the person carrying out the action which determines the ethical position taken. People have a 'moral impulse' (Melé, 2004) which allows them to respond and take responsibility for their actions. This position critiques both Kant, because it approaches ethics from an individual perspective, and utilitarianism, because this reduces the actor to a mere maximiser of utility. The actor/agent approach is also reflected in feminist ethics and ethics of care. First proposed by Gilligan (1982, in Melé, 2004) and others, feminist ethics recognises the interconnectedness of people in communities whose responsibility is to maintain proper care, and whose actions are therefore determined by feelings and intuition, not by principles and rights. Hence the social entrepreneurship movement will contain people who act in an agent orientation, wishing to benefit their communities as well as themselves through their business activities. However, this approach does not take into account the character of the actor, who is restricted to surrounding conditions, and may be influenced by, or subjected to claims by, stronger stakeholders (often closer in terms of spheres of influence) over weaker claims arising further away. Hence more powerful stakeholders – such a shareholders – may influence the agent to take certain actions which may be detrimental to those others less powerful – such as communities in resource-providing developing countries.

'*Human excellence-oriented*' ethics. This counters the criticisms of the above approach by taking into account the character of the actor/agent and seeks to advance the pursuance of excellence in communities (Melé, 2004). It represents an ethics of virtue. It is teleological – it recognises that a good person understands what is good. This enables the actor to overcome the sentimentality of feelings and intuition. Virtue leads to good behaviour and reinforces character qualities of truthfulness, loyalty, honesty and kindness. Individual characteristics can then be incorporated into organisational culture, and create the corporation as 'citizen'. It is not rationalist (that is, principles are not central) but there is a place for reason to allow reflection of one's actions. This approach is reflected in the recognition by some that business organisations, in order to be responsible for their actions, should act as citizens in the same way and for the same reasons as individual people (see, for instance, McIntosh et al., 2003).

This categorisation may be more useful in a pedagogic sense because students often consider themselves first and think about their own behaviour. Therefore it may be possible to begin with a consideration of the agent/actor responses before moving on to the action. This may be especially relevant in business ethics where often the action cannot be separated from the actor – here the business manager. Students are given scenarios which contain ethical dilemmas and their approach is often to ask: what would I do? It is often too difficult for students new to ethics to consider the action and its effects on other in isolation from their position as actors.

Hence any teaching of applied ethics (ethics as part of business and management, for instance) will take account of the various ethical frameworks outlined above. As these are complex and are often encountered for the first time by students it may be best to approach these by using examples from business practice, case studies and practical exercises using the 'lived' experiences of the students to link into the material. In other words, the educator can begin by allowing students to examine their own behaviour and establishing what the underlying framework is before applying it to the business situation. This form of teaching –'experiential learning' (Galea, 2007, p. 9) is appropriate because it brings live situations to an otherwise difficult and dry subject and allows students to explore the frameworks in a way that relates to their own experiences and gives them an insight into the world of business to which they aspire to enter.

Systems of Education and Training

Education can take place at both formal and informal levels. At the formal level, ethics can be part of all levels of the system from first years through to higher education. In this way ethical education may be stand-alone or integrated into other subject areas. Examples of early learning ethics may be in the ways in which pupils are encouraged to behave as part of a group and be considerate to each other; this may be extended later on to examine ways in which individuals are part of a global community and that we should consider the needs of people living in other parts of the world. Higher education may include specific modules of teaching ethics, either as study for its own sake, or where it is related to business studies.

Informally, ethical education – more correctly described as awareness-raising – can take place in the community in a variety of ways. Ethics can be seen as part of a wider educational initiative and may sometimes not be explicit in content. It may not even be regarded as education. Examples of this would be where the community campaigns on a particular issue – a local one such as the provision of a service (recycling, asylum services, childcare); a global one such as protest against poverty or war.

One way of developing formal ethical education is to consider programmes of work and how these may be integrated into the curriculum. The first question is whether ethics can be taught as a stand-alone topic or integrated into other subject areas. Where ethics is considered important as a means of providing a framework or where it is being taught as an academic discipline it makes sense to devote a complete course (or module and so on) to the underlying principles. However, for most purposes, ethics cannot be separated from the subject in which it is to become embedded, so it is more effective to teach ethics as part of a wider subject – medical ethics, business ethics, scientific ethics and so on. The methods are then chosen to be appropriate to the approach adopted.

Recent developments in Business School Curricula in higher education have seen the incorporation of ethics within teaching to address the wider societal concerns over business practice. This is by no means widespread, and often occurs where there are teaching staff who themselves are interested in the subject and who offer to develop the material. This has taken place alongside the developments in teaching Corporate Social Responsibility (CSR) and development. Both topics require a deeper thinking than the technical approaches often adopted in other business subjects such as accounting or marketing because they relate to questions of what ought to be happening – the 'right' approach to business activity. For instance, the profit motive (as outlined above) has been the main determinant of business activity and the justification given by managers for actions which society may disapprove. This has begun to change as issues such as climate change become more prevalent and pressing and are in society's consciousness. Managers can no longer blithely cite wealth creation for owners as justification for environmental damage – society demands greater protection. Managers therefore need to understand the underlying ethical principles so that they can 'do the right thing' and understand *why* this is right.

Examples of teaching experiences are now provided to show how ethics – particularly business ethics – can be incorporated into teaching at higher education levels.

Course Developments in a University Business School

MODULE 1: PERSPECTIVES ON ACCOUNTING AND SOCIETY

An undergraduate course for business students was designed and is run by a University Accounting Department. In order to present alternatives views of accounting and its effects, a module was designed which would place accounting in the context of its wider implications. In other words accounting was to be seen as a social construct. This would mean that it could not be regarded as merely a technical subject but one which was social, environmental, political and ethical. The aims of the module are shown in Table

22.1. These did not express explicitly the ethical content but used the subjects of CSR and sustainability as the means of exploring ethical thinking.

The course has an interdisciplinary content, including accounting and business, management, ecology, politics and ethics. Students therefore are challenged to look outside their normal programme subjects to areas that they may only have a negligible amount of prior knowledge. However, by embedding these other subjects within one with which they are familiar – accounting – unknown concepts become less alarming.

The course is offered to final year undergraduates who are taking accounting as a non-vocational subject. In other words, any student who has taken accounting subjects in the first and second year, but who is not following the programme resulting in an Accounting and Finance degree, is able to choose to take this course, or has to follow the course as part of their individual programme.

The content was designed to take aspects of accounting – seen in a framework of accountability – and make them transparent. One major aspect of this was the incorporation of CSR, which was regarded as a major element with which accountability could be delivered and with which accountants could and should be engaging. This is especially so through reporting mechanisms. This would also engage with ethical frameworks so that different justifications for the practice of CSR could be presented and discussed. In this way, CSR can be presented as an activity which can be placed upon a continuum from a managerial process to a moral imperative. The type of questions posed to the students is outlined in Table 22.2.

The module outlines the various ethical positions that society may take in determining what responsibilities are owed:

- The pristine capitalists, who feel that businesses operate to make a profit for their owners, and any activity which diverts from this (for instance greater environmental

Table 22.1   Module aims

Module aims
To allow business studies and accounting students to address the broader issues of Corporate Social Responsibility (CSR) through the examination of accounting and reporting models which move towards greater transparency and accountability
To develop a critique of current business practices to review the changes necessary to move towards sustainability
To review the contribution that the accounting profession can make towards the greening of business
To examine and critique current practice in corporate social reporting

Table 22.2 Considerations in CSR

Question
Is CSR another means of improving the bottom line?
Should we be concerned about the ethics of CSR?
What advantages are there to having greater responsibilities and to whom is this owed?
What are the disadvantages of being more responsible?
Should there be more or less CSR practice in our multinational companies?

costs incurred) is unreasonable. Hence CSR will only be tolerated if it does not interfere with income generation.

- The expedients, who recognise that enlightened self-interest will drive the CSR debate. In other words, if businesses ignore CSR, it may be imposed upon them by, for instance, the government. This position will result in the acceptance of minimal business 'ethics'.

- The proponents of the social contract propose that businesses exist at the will of society and therefore society can dictate what responsibility is owed to it. Business organisations must constantly legitimise their activities according to the demands of society.

- Those who recognise that business organisations may be responsible for the 'state of the environment', and that the economic system which has generated a poorer environment needs amending if human quality of life is to be improved. This is a human-centred approach to CSR.

- A socialist approach would suggest that restructuring the social, political and economic systems inherent in capitalist societies would be necessary to encourage greater CSR, and that changes in power and ownership structures will bring about changes which will improve social and environmental conditions.

- There is a more radical position which analyses the constructs implicit in business and accounting, and seeks to make transparent (and then challenge) the masculinity inherent in these constructs. Such masculine constructs as 'competition', 'success', 'control' are taken for granted as acceptable, but such drivers create the situation in which social and environmental damage can pass unnoticed.

- Even more radical still is the 'deep ecologists' position, which holds that humans are no more central to the environment than any other sentient or non-sentient being. Humans have no greater rights than these, and everything is connected in a 'web of life'. Hence the trade-offs in current economic systems between, say an environmental asset and an economic gain is morally not justifiable (Gray et al., 1996, Blair and Hitchcock, 2001).

These positions are often implicit, but in order to investigate corporate social responsibility, it is necessary to establish what positions lie behind the models and the mechanisms which are examined during the course. The positions largely equate to the profit-oriented ethics (above) – the first two in the list – or the principle-oriented ethics – the remainder in the list.

The course examines the damage caused to *the environment*. This relates to the impacts on the natural world through, for instance, resource usage, waste management and energy programmes, or habitat losses, and can be related to the concept of *eco-efficiency*. *Social* impacts may include human rights, employment issues and wealth distribution issues, which describe *eco-justice*. Hence by combining eco-efficiency and eco-justice the module arrives at the overarching concept of *sustainability*. This allows ethical decision-making to be considered in context.

The course is taught by a combination of lectures and tutorials. The lectures are formal dissemination sessions, covering one broad topic per lecture, and, if possible, outside speakers present at least one of the 12 lectures in the programme, to allow students to hear from an expert in the field and to learn about the latest thinking in practical circles. This gives an opportunity to compare the theoretical framework with the activities of organisations.

A separate tutorial programme links the broad ideas introduced by the lectures, and encourages greater debate and interaction. The tutorial programme links to the lecture subjects, and attempts to encourage students to examine the latest developments in corporate social responsibility in an interactive way. As the subject is dynamic, the content of the course has to be able to reflect the latest developments. However, the course maintains its overall integrity by ensuring that the different elements reflect or demonstrate accountability, relating this to corporate social responsibility.

Some examples of tutorial subjects covered

The Ecological Footprint   The ecological footprint is a measure of the amount of bio-productive land required to support human activity – at the global, national or local level it assesses what environmental impacts humans have as they go about their lives (Holland, 2003). It has been measured at the global level – to determine how much bio-productive land is available and what each person's share is – so that we can assess how far above or below our fair share we may be. It has also been calculated at the national level (for instance, Wales and Scotland in the UK), at the city level (Toronto and London both have well-established ecological footprint measurements) and at the business level (for instance, Anglian Water plc). It is a measure of environmental consumption and its measurement – and comparison – is a useful means of examining decision making from an ethical perspective (Wackernagel and Rees, 1996). For instance, students can compare their own country's ecological footprint with another, less developed country. This will reveal that richer more developed countries have a very high footprint compared with countries such as, say, Bangladesh. The ethical dilemma then becomes: how is it fair that some people live 'below' their fair share whilst others live 'above' theirs? The figures in Table 22.3 give some indication of 'shares'.

The ecological footprint exercise allows students to consider their own environmental impacts before relating these to the business scenario. Each student uses a website such as www.earthday.net/footprint/index.asp to assess their footprint and brings the score to the class. These are then collated so that the individual scores are displayed. (Some sensitivity is needed where individual scores are outside of the general range as embarrassment may be caused). Students can then see what impacts they have and what areas are most significant. They can then begin to assess what behaviour changes are necessary to reduce

Table 22.3   Ecological footprints around the World

Eco-capacity calculated at 1.5ha
Currently global EF is 2.9ha
German EF is 6.0ha
US EF is 12.5ha
UK EF is 6.3ha
Mexico EF is 3.1ha
Bangladesh EF is 0.6 ha

Source: redefiningprogress.org 2006

their footprints and how feasible these are. This links to ethics because students have to consider the consequences of their present actions and the effect of any proposed changes both on themselves and on others.

The footprint calculation centres on food, mobility, shelter and goods and services. These are relevant to individuals but students can also relate these to business activities. The exercise can then examine how businesses might measure their own ecological footprints and for what uses. Again the ethical aspect can be introduced as students can consider why a business may want to, or be required to, reduce its footprint. Hence different scenarios can be discussed whereby individual businesses can use the footprint methodology to become more environmentally responsible, to develop environmental management systems and to introduce environmental policies, and to report on their performance. Other scenarios can consider regulatory approaches to environmental performance in business, and the suitability of this approach.

Different eco-political frameworks   Another means of examining ethical positions in business is to assume that different structural frameworks are possible. These can then be used to assess where businesses currently are and whether any change is possible. The three frameworks used in the tutorial programme are eco-socialism, eco-radicalism and eco-modernity. Each is discussed in turn and critiqued. This is best done by attempting to apply each framework to a well-known business to see whether any alternative is feasible. So, for instance, the frameworks may be applied to a large supermarket, a bank or a software manufacturer. The 'dirty' industries such as chemicals, oil, pharmaceuticals and so on are deliberately not included as often the dilemmas are more obvious (although not easier to solve) and do not encourage deep thinking.

Eco-modernity   Eco-modernity combines business responses with regulation in an approach that is described as one of partnership to achieve environmental protection and economic growth. It encourages win-win situations and has some elements of centralisation (such as eco-taxes) but with industry cooperation and participation. It is concerned with processes in industry rather than end-of-pipe cleanup, and uses technological developments to solve environmental problems. This is the closest to giving a business case it is concerned with eco-efficiency and is process-orientated. This is often regarded as the position currently taken by business as a response to demands for greater CSR and is criticised by its opponents as a 'business-as-usual' approach. Hence students can use business paradigms and theories to explore this perspective.

A critique of eco-modernity   When students first examine the eco-modernity framework, they usually see no major problems and it often seems to them that this is the ideal situation and a means of protecting the environment without any major adjustments to economic systems. They are most comfortable with this framework, especially when they contrast it with the other two which have obvious drawbacks. Hence it is important to provide a contextual critique of this framework so that students can appreciate what the disadvantages to it are.

Proponents of the eco-modernity model cite the 1989 World Commission on Environment and Development (WCED, 1987) report as support for this, stating that eco-modernity flows directly from the recommendations that WCED put forward. Ward et al. (2004) suggest that eco-efficiency is the way forward for business. In other words, the business contribution to sustainability is via resource management and efficiency. Hence (in this understanding) business is delivering sustainable development. However the ways in which this is happening must be examined. Certainly if we consider that sustainability is concerned with the ways in which capital is utilised, developing a more efficient approach would seem to suffice. However, this cannot incorporate *eco-effectiveness* or *eco-justice*. Efficiency has its roots in traditional economic models of optimum allocation of resources, and these can be any type of capital, substitutable or critical. Indeed this has been taken further by such proponents as Weizsacker et al. (1997) who argue that by being more resource efficient, wealth can be increased. However, the question remains – wealth increases for whom? At what cost to those left behind? In order to increase wealth, demand must be maintained or even increased, and so limits to growth have to be set aside. It is also a model that suits the 'developed' or rich world very well, but ignores the needs of large parts of society to protect their own environment. It also has little if nothing to say about environmental justice (for instance, the right to use resources in different ways as appropriate to the needs of different parts of society) and it says nothing about social justice at all. If one takes the simplest model of sustainability – a combination of economic, environmental and social factors, eco-modernity addresses the first to the largest extent, the second to some extent and the third not at all. Eco-modernity will address some of the issues around the use, appropriation and substitution of *environmental* capital but cannot begin to (indeed ignores) the issues of *social* capital.

Eco-socialism   Eco-socialism combines the political structures of a socialist system with the concerns for environmental degradation. It is a centralised response to the factors of capitalism which are considered to have caused the environmental crises; it will also include a discussion of the social and democratic structures which bring about justice; the overall structure of the economy being interrelated units with central control. The ethical position is rights-based – and concentrates on human rights and justice, and so is *anthropocentric* – putting humans as the central concern. This allows the students to examine the concept of CSR from a political perspective.

Eco-radicalism   Stemming from deep green ecology, this is a rights-based ethic with an ideal world-view; concepts such as spirituality, communitarianism and harmony amongst the living and non-living world. It contains ideas such as bioregionalism, eco-anarchy and ecofeminism. Lessons can be learnt from indigenous peoples and alternative communities. In contrast to eco-socialism, which requires large state-controlled structures, this approach is local and small-scale. It has been termed 'ecological citizenship' and can be seen in the very recent 'transitions' movement in the UK in which towns and cities are attempting to respond to the joint crises of an oil-free future and climate change. Hence the ideas here allow students to examine what is a more ethical or moral set of concepts and to contrast them with the more overtly political approach of eco-socialism and the 'business-as-usual' approach of eco-modernity.

Having examined the three frameworks students begin to understand how to use the ideas in ethics to address the environmental and social concerns that CSR is supposed to capture and to begin to develop their own outlook and approach. Often students begin by rejecting the more 'radical' approaches of eco-socialism and eco-radicalism because these are far removed from their own experiences; however these can be used to examine what, if anything, are the failings of eco-modernity. A hybrid model can then be developed bringing together aspects of all three models into a 'super-model' where the ideal is created. The gap between where we are now and where this ideal would take us can then be explored and the ethical considerations needed to get there can also be identified. In this way students begin to understand how the business arena could function under changed conditions.

MODULE 2: BUSINESS ETHICS, ENVIRONMENT AND SOCIETY

This module is at postgraduate level and is offered to students taking International Business Master's degrees. It is a requirement for students who are studying the CSR programme and an optional choice for other International Business students. In this way the mix of students taking the module allows for wider debates within the classes, as students specialising in finance or management have also taken this course each time it has ran. It aims to integrate ideas about how businesses operate and should operate and incorporates aspects of environmental management, corporate governance and sustainability and examines what broader contexts these need to be placed in. Hence social and political systems are also examined, and international agencies such as those within the United Nations are used to show how businesses may be constrained by other supranational organisations or how their behaviour may be encouraged to change.

Postgraduate classes are run as blocks of teaching so that greater interaction between tutor and students is facilitated. Hence delivery is usually in the form of part formal lecture, part seminar. Scenarios and cases are provided to students to allow wider discussion of the issues after guidance from the tutor. Groups are generally smaller than for undergraduate classes and this enables deeper discussion and greater coverage of the issues. Because these groups of students tend to be international, they bring their own contexts to the discussions. Hence there may be different perspectives introduced as African, Asian and European students bring their own cultural experiences to the class. The tutor needs to be able to manage these processes and deal with potential conflicts which may arise out of cultural misunderstandings rather than ethical clashes. The tutor is acting as facilitator at this point to allow students to explore their personal ethics in a non-judgemental atmosphere.

Unlike the undergraduate module discussed above, this module does have an explicit ethics content and this is addressed at the start of the module. Individual ethical positions are explored first – for instance, the ways in which students approach their studies, the approaches to group work, problem-solving mechanisms and so on. This enables students to find their way around the ethical frameworks in a way that helps them to identify what exactly ethics as a subject is. This means that the teaching begins with considerations of personal ethics, as it is believed that without a more explicit understanding of one's own ethical framework, it is more difficult to understand organisational ethics. Hence the orientations outlined above can be a starting point to tease out an individual's position and then this can be used to broaden this to business ethics. A useful categorisation is given in Table 22.4.

Table 22.4 Business ethicists

Type	Focus	Concept of good	Hence orientation
Pragmatists: mix of theories with best elements	Legality: role of agent to apply rules	Wealth creation	Profit
Realists: look for best theory	Universal principles – no role for agent	Goodwill, fairness, peaceful settlement	Principles
Sceptics: no particular theory held	Agent has whole morality of situation	Responsibility towards others, harmonised human inter-relationships	Agent
Champions: hold one particular theory	Virtues of agent	Virtue in the community	Human excellence

Typical exercises in this module

Sustainability as described by the four capitals model   This is a means of examining both the individual elements of sustainability and the inter-relationships between them. First proposed by Ekins et al. (1992) the model analyses the way in which 'capital' contributes to sustainability and what it may need to improve (or what may reduce) conditions of sustainability. Fundamentally, capital of any kind should not be eroded if sustainability is to be maintained; this has its roots in economic theory which argues that capital provides interest and that it is this which should be consumed; any consumption of capital will reduce the amount of interest generated and therefore the ability to consume is also reduced. Capital maintenance is the key. Ekins et al. extended this idea to include natural (ecological) capital and human and social and organisational capital as well as economic (manufactured or financial) capital, as shown in Table 22.5.

Students are therefore presented with the four types of capital and it is their task to identify what the components of these may be and how they may be improved or eroded. This is first examined from a personal perspective before moving into a business scenario. They are required to examine whether it is the total of each capital which should be maintained and/or whether substitution between or within capitals is possible. For instance, if a school or factory is built, this increases manufactured capital but may erode ecological capital (if the building is using green space or replacing wildlife). Hence

Table 22.5 The Four Capitals model

Capital	Component	Ethical dilemmas
Natural	Resources Waste sinks services	Who has access? Where are these located? Population vs. consumption
Human	Individual labour Fulfilling work Health Education	Access to all? Who provides –public or private?
Social and organisational	Framework of human capital Community Relationships	Do different communities have different impacts?
Manufactured	Production Wealth creation	Externalities Whose economic benefits?

the total of all capitals has been maintained; however the loss of ecological capital may not be acceptable. The problem then becomes: if substitution is allowed, what ethical considerations are there?

In this way students begin to appreciate the interconnections between different aspects of sustainability and how complex it is. Capital substitution is seen from a variety of perspectives. For instance, there is a relationship between human and natural capital: poverty, for instance, may create environmental degradation and resource over-exploitation; this could also be seen in reverse. A degraded environment leads to poverty where people lack education and skills to prevent this (Veeman and Politylo, 2003). Education and skills development increases human capital (Ekins et al., 1992). It is considered that where there are high levels of human capital, reductions in environmental capital are less likely to be disruptive (Veeman and Politylo, 2003). For instance, people who have a high level of skills in the areas of environmental management and protection will be able to put processes in place to halt any further damage. However, in practice what often happens is that this compensatory activity displaces the environmental degradation to those areas which already suffer from it – the areas where human capital is also compromised. We can see this in the area of global climate change where developed countries are seen to export their own environmental damage to less developed areas – those which already struggle to develop either human or natural capital.

Related to this activity, students then examine significant business structures – Multinational Enterprises (MNEs). These are important because of their size, the amount of world resources they control, their political influence and the part they play in our everyday lives. Resource control obviously includes natural resources, and the MNEs' use of major non-renewable mineral and biotic resources can be associated with environmental impacts across their sphere of influence, which is global. This also includes human resources, and so issues of human rights, employee working conditions, and the effect on neighbourhoods and communities can be explored. These can all be related to the four capitals model which, when examined in this way, becomes more situated in real life and real experience rather than a model with theoretical content only. Students complete the exercise with a greater understanding of the interconnectedness of the world and the role of business in it; they also have the tools to assess the ethical dilemmas this role presents.

This is scene-setting for the next component, which is a more practical investigation of the manner in which businesses can express their social and environmental performance through their external reporting mechanisms. Most large companies now produce a document expressing their views on, and their performance of, corporate social responsibility, however they define this – environmental protection, social equity, issues of labour or human rights, sustainable development, the role of business ethics and so on. The definition can be expressed in the naming of the document – some use the term 'sustainability report', others refer to CSR or stakeholders – and the document itself can be extensive – many are 40–50 pages long in hard copy and may be boundless when viewed on-line. This document is separate from the annual report (which itself may have some CSR disclosure) and may be produced, variously, by the public affairs department, the corporate affairs department, the environmental management team, or in partnership with third-party organisations. The reports contain written text and graphics – pictures, photographs, graphs, cartoons, drawings and so on. The graphics combine with the written word to add to the audience's understanding of the message that the company wants to portray about its CSR performance. The volume of pictures in any given report is substantial and therefore these have an importance given by the producer of the image to the audience (although the importance to the audience may of course differ from that meant).

These reports are published separately from the annual report of companies. Disclosure can also take place in the annual report, and this has been the main focus of accounting research in this area; Unerman (2000) is an exception. There is a substantial body of published research discussing the meaning and content of the written part of the annual report (see, for instance Wiseman, 1982; Gray et al., 1995; Barlett and Chandler, 1997; Savage and Cataldo, 1999; Wilmshurst and Frost, 2000; Holland and Boon Foo, 2003).

Students are presented beforehand with the Holland and Boon Foo (2003) paper which gives a model for assessing content in reports from an environmental perspective. They are asked to consider the categories included here and to think about what further categories they may want to include in examining the content of reports which claim to be inclusive of social issues or sustainability. This is discussed in class and a consensus of content is reached. By this means each student has been able to consider what issues they would wish to see discussed and why. They are then each given a recent annual report and are required to assess the content using their revised categories. The results are then tabulated and presented to the class. These results can then form the basis of a discussion about reporting practices in general – whether the results are acceptable in terms of content, what information is missing and why this should be. This allows students to investigate the motives behind such reporting to establish the legitimacy of the process. They can then relate this to the ethical positions outlined at the beginning of the module – based upon the orientation frameworks outlined above – to assess the ethical position that such reporting practices take.

A similar exercise can be carried out on the stand-alone reports that companies produce. However, these are substantial documents and a full assessment of their content is very time-consuming. Therefore a more suitable approach can be to require students to read a selected report prior to the session (often downloadable form a company's website) and produce a summary for presentation to the class, again examining whether the report content is acceptable. The students have to justify their own assessment of the report so that they become aware of their own subjectivity in this exercise.

Further to this exercise, the images in a selection of stand-alone reports are examined separately. These can be projected in class so that all students are seeing the same image. The meanings of the images are then discussed and multiple meanings are thereby exposed. Again this allows the potential motives for the inclusion of particular images to be assessed and the value of communicating in this way can be discussed. There are several aspects that can be revealed by this process: what do companies want their audiences to think about them, what are they leaving out ('silences' as Chwastiak and Young, 2003, have discussed), does the audience share an understanding of the meaning of the image and why would these particular images reinforce the company's CSR message? Images are particularly interesting as they are often taken for granted in company communication, but much effort and expense goes into choosing them and therefore they have a great deal of influence on our understanding of the corporate message. Hence students begin to appreciate the role of images, not just in CSR communication, but in corporate message-making as a whole.

These exercises are therefore designed to develop an ethical appreciation in students of the actions of companies engaged in CSR activities. They are then equipped to analyse a company's actions and to decide for themselves how ethical a company is in relation to its CSR position.

Interestingly, this module's name has been regarded as off-putting by some students who feel that a module with 'ethics' in the title is too difficult, not relevant to their other subjects and likely to be too theoretical. Therefore many students who have the opportunity to study the module are choosing the more technical modules instead. The students who have taken the module, however, have always provided positive feedback about the module, its content and the experiences they have had. The tutors are at present considering whether the name of the module should be changed to remove the explicit reference to ethics and include a more general reference to management instead – itself an ethical dilemma which the tutors need to solve!

Final Thoughts

The information provided above has attempted to demonstrate how ethics can be taught to business students. It seems clear that ethics will be regarded as a difficult subject as long as it is taught separately from the topic in which it should be embedded. This is of course not to say that ethics should never be studied as an academic discipline in its own right. Rather, that there is a need for students studying business topics to assess the ethics implicit in every situation they come across, but that this integration is necessary for them to appreciate what the ethical position is or ought to be. Using frameworks which relate to real life and to personal experiences seems to be the most effective way to allow students to develop an ethical element to their studies, which then gives a richer dimension to their understanding. Business is not amoral and therefore ethics is, and should be, embedded in students' learning experiences.

References

Barlett, S.A. and Chandler, R.A. (1997) The Corporate Report and the Private Shareholder: Lee and Tweedie 20 Years on *The British Accounting Review* 29 pp. 245-261.

Blair, A. and Hitchcock, D. (2001) *Environment and Business* Routledge, London.

Chwastiak, M. and Young, J.J. (2003) Silences in Annual Reports *Critical Perspectives on Accounting* 14 pp. 533-552.

Drumond J. and Bain, B. (1994) *Managing Business Ethics* Butterworth Heinemann, Oxford.

Ekins, P., Hillman, M. and Hutchison, R. (1992) *Wealth Beyond Measure* Gaia, London.

Galea, C. (ed.) (2007) *Teaching Business Sustainability: Vol 2: Cases, Simulations and Experiential Approaches* Greenleaf, Sheffield.

Gray, R., Kouhy, R. and Lavers, S. (1995) Corporate Social and Environmental Reporting: A Review of the Literature and a Longitudinal Study of UK Disclosure *Accounting Auditing and Accountability Journal* 8,2 pp. 47-77.

Gray, R., Owen, D. and Adams, C. (1996) *Accounting and Accountability* Prentice Hall, London.

Holland, L. (2003) Can the Principle of Ecological Footprint be Applied to Measure the Environmental Sustainability of Business? *Corporate Social Responsibility and Environmental Management* 10 pp. 224-232.

Holland, L. and Boon Foo, Y. (2003) Differences in Environmental Reporting Practices in the UK and US: the Legal and Regulatory Context *The British Accounting Review* 35 pp. 1-18.

Jones, C., Parker, M. and ten Bos, R. (2005) *For Business Ethics* Routledge, London.

McIntosh, M., Thomas, R., Leipziger, D., and Coleman, G., (eds) (2003) *Living Corporate Citizenship: Strategic Routes to Socially Responsible Business* Financial Times/Prentice Hall, London.

Melé, D. (2004) Rival Philosophical Approaches to Business Ethics *Paper presented to the Inter-Disciplinary Conference on CSR Research,* Nottingham.

Savage, A. and Cataldo II A.J. (1999) A Multi-case Investigation of Environmental Legitimation in Annual Reports *Paper presented at American Accounting Association Annual Conference* 18 August.

Treviño, L.K. and Nelson, K.A. (2007) *Managing Business Ethics – Straight Talk about How to do it Right* John Wiley, MA.

Unerman, J. (2000) Methodological Issues – Reflections on Quantification in Corporate Social Reporting Content Analysis *Accounting Auditing and Accountability Journal* 13,5 pp. 667-680.

United Nations (1948) Universal Declaration of Human Rights, New York.

Veeman, T.S. and Politylo, J. (2003) The Role of Institutions and Policy in Enhancing Sustainable Development and Conserving Natural Capital *Environment Development and Sustainability* 5,3-4 pp. 31-332.

Wackernagel, M. and Rees, W. (1996) *Our Ecological Footprint: Reducing Human Impact on the Earth* New Society, BC.

Ward, H., Borregaard, W. and Kapelus, P. (2004) Corporate Citizenship: Revisiting the Relationship between Business, Good Governance and Sustainable Development in Bigg, T. (ed.) *Survival for a Small Planet* Earthscan, London.

Weizsacker, E. von, Lovins, A. and Lovins, L. (1997) *Factor Four: Doubling Wealth, Halving Resource Use* Earthscan, London.

Wilmshurst, T.D. and Frost, G.R. (2000) Corporate Environmental Reporting – A Test of Legitimacy Theory *Accounting Auditing and Accountability Journal* 13,1 pp. 10-26.

Wiseman, J. (1982) 'An Evaluation of Environmental Disclosures made in Corporate Annual Reports' Accounting, Organizations and Society 7,1 pp. 53-63.

World Council on Environment and Development (WCED) (1987) *Our Common Future* Oxford University Press, Oxford.

KEY REFERENCES FOR FURTHER READING

Bain, B. and Drummond, J. (1994) *Managing Business Ethics* Butterworth Heinemann, Oxford.

Blair, A. and Hitchcock, D. (2001) *Environment and Business* Routledge, London.

Jones, C., Parker, M. and ten Bos, R. (2005) *For Business Ethics* Routledge, London.

Treviño, L.K. and Nelson, K.A. (2007) *Managing Business Ethics – Straight Talk About How to do it Right* John Wiley, MA.

Gray, R., Owen, D. and Adams, C. (1996) *Accounting and Accountability* Prentice Hall, London.

23 *Socially Responsible Investment Funds*

LUC RENNEBOOG, JENKE TER HORST AND
CHENDI ZHANG*

Introduction

This chapter provides a critical review of the literature on Socially Responsible Investments (SRI). Particular to SRI is that both financial goals and social objectives are pursued. Over the past decade, SRI has experienced an explosive growth around the world reflecting the increasing awareness of investors to social, environmental, ethical and corporate governance issues. We argue that there are significant opportunities for future research on the increasingly important area of SRI. A number of questions are reviewed in this chapter on the institutional aspects of SRI, the risk exposure and performance of SRI funds, as well as fund subscription and redemption behavior of SRI investors. We conclude that the existing studies hint but do not unequivocally demonstrate that SRI investors are willing to accept suboptimal financial performance to pursue social or ethical objectives. Furthermore, the emergence of SRI raises interesting questions for research on corporate finance, asset pricing, and financial intermediation.

Over the past decade, SRI, frequently also called ethical investments or sustainable investments, have grown rapidly around the world. SRI is an investment process that integrates social, environmental, and ethical considerations into investment decision making. Unlike conventional types of investments, SRI apply a set of investment screens to select or exclude assets based on ecological, social, corporate governance or ethical criteria, and often engages in the local communities and in shareholder activism to further corporate strategies towards the above aims.

Following the rapid growth of the SRI industry, academic interest has emerged. The aim of this chapter[1] is to provide an overview of the state of the literature on SRI in order to summarize the main findings and to identify puzzles and interesting questions for further research. Although the literature on SRI is growing, a central question is whether or not the decisions of investors are affected by non-financial criteria.

*   Acknowledgements: We are grateful to Stijn Claessens, Cypriaan de Rore, Piet Duffhues, Marc Goergen, Kees Koedijk, Massimo Massa, Theo Nijman, Remi Rochefort, Peter Szilagyi, Gerard van Turnhout, and Bas Werker for their helpful comments as well as to the seminar participants at Keele, Sheffield, Tilburg, and Warwick Universities for their helpful comments. All remaining errors are our own.

1   This chapter is largely based on Renneboog, Ter Horst, and Zhang's (2008a) paper published by *Journal of Banking and Finance*.

If investors derive non-financial utility from investing in SRI funds or in companies meeting high standards of Corporate Social Responsibility (CSR),[2] then they care less about financial performance than 'conventional' (non-SRI) investors. Bollen (2007) argues that investors may have 'a multi-attribute utility function that is not only based on the standard risk-reward optimization but also incorporates a set of personal and societal values'. If such values matter to investors, we expect (i) further SRI growth even if the risk-adjusted SRI returns are lower than those of conventional investments, and (ii) less sensitive SRI money-flows to past performance. Consistent with the intuition that the socially responsible attribute smoothes allocation decisions, Bollen (2007) and Renneboog, Ter Horst, and C. Zhang (2005) find that volatility in SRI funds is lower than conventional funds flow volatility.

In parallel to investors' decisions on SRI, management makes decisions on whether or not to adopt CSR strategies, such as environmental sustainability or community involvement. Hence, closely related questions are whether CSR enhances shareholder value and whether investors are willing to pay for firms adopting CSR. If projects generate positive net present values to shareholders as well as positive externalities to other stakeholders (for example, a more healthy or safe environment or more social cohesion at the community level), the firm investing in such projects may have higher share prices which in turn translate into better SRI fund performance. The controversies emerge when there is a trade-off between the financial merits of a project and negative externalities (such as pollution). Specifically, SRI which *altruistically* exclude polluting firms or selects firms contributing to the local communities may have weaker financial performance (at least in the short run). However, some CSR studies argue that firms investing in CSR create shareholder value in the long run although stock markets undervalue CSR in the short run. Firms ignoring socially responsibility may destroy long-run shareholder value due to reputation losses and/or potential litigation costs.

In the first part of the chapter, we review the institutional aspects and recent industry trends related to SRI. In particular, we study the market development, the regulatory background, and the effect of investment screens employed by SRI funds. Second, we study whether SRI investors care less about financial performance than conventional investors by discussing the empirical evidence on the risk and return characteristics of SRI. For SRI mutual funds in the US and UK, there is little evidence that the risk-adjusted returns of SRI funds are different from those of conventional funds (see, for example, Bauer, Koedijk and Otten (2005)). However, SRI funds in Continental Europe and Asia-Pacific underperform benchmark portfolios (Renneboog, Ter Horst, and Zhang, 2008b).

Third, we discuss whether the investment behavior of SRI investors is different from that of conventional investors by reviewing the recent literature on the money-flows into and out of SRI funds. While SRI investors chase past performance, their decision to invest in or withdraw from SRI funds seems less affected by past negative performance than the decision of conventional fund investors (Bollen, 2007). Also, SRI investors base their investment decisions on different types of non-financial investment screens (Renneboog, Ter Horst, and Zhang, 2005; Zhang, 2006).

---

2   Henceforth, we define SRI as socially responsible investments made by individual or institutional *investors* in SRI funds or corporations. CSR (corporate social responsibility) refers to *corporate* decisions fostering social, corporate governance, ethical and environmental issues.

The main conclusion of this survey is that while some research has been performed on SRI, there are still a great many issues and puzzles that require further study. The emergence of SRI, combined with the behavioral differences between SRI and conventional investors, raises interesting questions related to asset pricing, corporate finance, and financial intermediation. For example, if a significant part of investors exhibits an aversion to corporate behavior that is not inspired by CSR, it is interesting to investigate whether investors require an additional return for investing in non-CSR firms and how this influences the cost of capital of firms as well as the investment and lending decisions of financial institutions. In addition, SRI portfolio managers pursue both financial goals and social objectives. This multi-task nature of SRI managers may weaken fund managers' incentives to pursue high risk-adjusted returns and hence increase potential agency costs. It would be interesting to examine the incentive structures in the SRI industry, and the impact of SRI on the investment and lending decisions of financial institutions.

The remainder of the chapter is organized as follows. The next section presents the institutional background of SRI. The following section introduces the empirical findings on the performance and money-flows of SRI, and the final section concludes and discusses a future research agenda.

Institutional Background of SRI

THE MARKET OF SRI

Over the past decade, SRI has experienced a phenomenal growth around the world. Table 23.1 presents estimates from the industry on the total Assets Under Management (AUM) of SRI portfolios in the US, Europe, Canada, and Australia, where portfolios are considered as SRI if they execute a strategy based on social screening, shareholder activism, or contributing to the community (see Section 2.4).[3] In the US, the professionally managed assets of SRI portfolios, including retail and (more importantly) institutional funds (for example, pension funds, insurance funds, and separate accounts), reached $2.3 trillion in 2005, growing by 1200 percent from $162 billion a decade earlier. Currently, SRI assets represent about 10 percent of total AUM in the US (SIF, 2005). Although the European SRI market is still in an early stage of development, it is also growing rapidly. In 2005, SRI assets in Europe amounted to $1.4 trillion, representing 10–15 percent of European funds under management (Eurosif, 2006). In addition, Canadian SRI assets have risen from $33 billion in 2000 to $55 billion in 2004 and in Australia SRI assets have also surged, rising almost five-fold in the period from 2001 to 2005 (SIO, 2004, and EIA, 2005).

If one focuses on SRI mutual funds available to retail investors, the market of retail SRI funds (which are mutual funds applying SRI screens in their investment process) is much smaller but is on the rise. From 1995 to 2005, the number of SRI mutual funds has grown from 55 to 201 in the US and from 54 to 375 in Europe (SIF, 2005, and SiRi,

---

3   The estimates from the industry on the SRI market size may be biased upwards due to this general definition of an SRI portfolio. If one adopts a more stringent definition of SRI, the estimates of SRI market size may be much smaller. For example, excluding portfolios using shareholder activism strategies only or simple negative screens (for example, divesting from tobacco and alcohol sectors; see Renneboog, Ter Horst, and Zhang, 2008a for details), the size of SRI market is $140 billion in Europe in 2005, or 1–1.5 percent of European assets under professional management (Eurosif, 2006).

2005). Table 23.1 shows that the AUM of SRI mutual funds reached $179 billion in US in 2005, and $30 billion in Europe. In a study of money-flows of SRI mutual funds around the world, Renneboog, Ter Horst and Zhang (2005) show that in almost all countries SRI mutual funds account for less than one percent of the domestic mutual fund market. In Europe, the Netherlands and UK are the countries with the highest percentage of SRI mutual funds.

Table 23.1 SRI Assets Under Management

Year	US		Europe		Canada		Australia	
	Total AUM ($b)	Retail AUM ($b)	Total AUM ($b)	Retail AUM ($b)	Total AUM ($b)	Retail AUM ($b)	Total AUM ($b)	Retail AUM ($b)
1995	639	12						
1997	1185	96						0.1*
1999	2159	154		11				0.2*
2001	2323	136		13	33*	6.6*	1	0.9
2003	2164	151	470	15	34*	6.7*	2	1.1
2005	2290	179	1400	30	55*	12.5*	6	

This table presents the total AUM (Total AUM, in billion US$) of SRI portfolios (including retail funds and institutional funds such as pension funds and insurance companies), and the AUM of retail SRI mutual funds (Retail AUM, in billion US$) in the US, Europe, Canada, and Australia, at year ends. Portfolios are counted as SRI if they use at least one of the social screening, shareholder activism or community investing strategies. Data in this table are collected from the following sources: US: SIF (1995, 1997, 1999, 2001, 2003, 2005); Europe: SiRi (2002, 2003, 2005), Eurosif (2003, 2005); Canada: SIO (2002, 2004); Australia: EIA (2001, 2002, 2003, 2005). Starred (*) numbers are taken from the previous year due to data availability.

In the foreseeable future, the growth of SRI assets is likely to continue worldwide. Issues like global warming, the Kyoto Protocol, emissions trading, corporate governance, community investing, and microfinance[4] have gained attention by governments and investors around the world. The 2007 Nobel Peace Prize was awarded to the UN Intergovernmental Panel on Climate Change (IPPC) and Al Gore for their work in increasing awareness on climate change. Some of the largest pension funds in the world have shown increasing interest in participating in SRI. The California Public Employees' Retirement System (CALPERS), the largest pension fund in the world, actively engages companies to promote socially responsible behavior and was one of the leaders of the tobacco divestment of the late 1990s. The Dutch Pension Fund for Public Employees (ABP), the largest pension fund in Europe, revised its Code for Prudent Investment Policy in 2000, which states that ABP will promote the integration of social, environmental, and

---

4   Microfinance refers to the practice of providing financial services, for example, tiny loans, to poor people. For example, the United Nations declared the year of 2005 as the International Year of Microfinance. In addition, Grameen Bank, a Bangladesh microfinance organization, and its founder, professor Muhammad Yunus, were jointly awarded the Nobel Peace Prize in 2006.

ethical criteria in its investment process. Mr. Jean Frijns, the former Chief Investment Officer of ABP Investments, regards sustainable investment as 'one of the most critical factors driving the future of fiduciary investment' (Financial Times, Jan. 26, 2003). In addition, the Dutch pension fund PGGM, which manages about €45 billion assets, applies two negative screens (weapons production and human rights violation) to all of its investment portfolios (Eurosif, 2003).

REGULATORY BACKGROUND

The growth of the SRI industry can be partly attributed to the changes in regulation regarding the disclosure of social, environmental, and ethical information by pension funds and listed companies. In this section, we review the regulatory SRI initiatives taken by national governments and summarize these in Table 23.2. Most of the SRI regulation is passed in Europe.

Table 23.2 SRI Regulations

Country	SRI-related regulations
Australia	In a 2001 bill it is stated that all investment firms' product disclosure statements should include a description of 'the extent to which labor standards or environmental, social, or ethical considerations are taken into account.' Since 2001, all listed companies on the Australian Stock Exchange are required to make an annual social responsibility report.
Belgium	In 2001, Belgium passed the 'Vandebroucke' law, which requires pension funds to report the degree to which their investments take into account social, ethical, and environmental aspects.
France	In May 2001, the legislation 'New Economic Regulations' came into force requiring listed companies to publish social and environmental information in their annual reports. Since February 2001 managers of the Employee Savings Plans are required to consider social, environmental or ethical considerations when buying and selling shares.
Germany	Since 1991, the Renewable Energy Act gives a tax advantage to closed-end funds to invest in wind energy. Since January 2002, certified private pension schemes and occupational pension schemes 'must inform the members in writing, whether and in what form ethical, social, or ecological aspects are taken into consideration when investing the paid-in contributions'.
Italy	Since September 2004 pension funds are required to disclose non-financial factors (including social, environmental, and ethical factors) influencing their investment decisions.
Netherlands	In 1995, the Dutch Tax Office introduced a 'Green Savings and Investment Plan', which applies a tax deduction for green investments, such as wind and solar energy, and organic farming.
Sweden	Since January 2002, Swedish national pension funds are obliged to incorporate environmental and ethical aspects in their investment policies.

Table 23.2 *Concluded*

Country	SRI-related regulations
UK	In July 2000, the Amendment to 1995 Pensions Act came into force, requiring trustees of occupational pension funds in the UK to disclose in the Statement of Investment Principles 'the extent (if at all) to which social, environmental, and ethical considerations are taken into account in the selection, retention, and realization of investments'. The Trustee Act 2000 came into force in February 2001. Charity trustees must ensure that investments are suitable to a charity's stated aims, including applying ethical considerations to investments. In 2002, The Cabinet Office in the UK published the Review of Charity Law in 2002, which proposed that all charities with an annual income of over £1m should report on the extent to which social, environmental, and ethical issues are taken into account in their investment policy. The Home Office accepted theses recommendations in 2003. The Association of British Insurers (ABI) published a disclosure guideline in 2001, asking listed companies to report on material social, environmental, and ethical risks relevant to their business activities.
US	Section 406 of the Sarbanes-Oxley Act, which came into effect in July 2002, requires companies to disclose a written code of ethics adopted by their CEO, chief financial officer and chief accountant.

This table summarizes the regulatory initiatives regarding SRI taken by national government in western countries.

UK

The UK was the first country to regulate the disclosure of social, environmental, and ethical investment policies of pension funds and charities. This has contributed considerably to the growth of the SRI industry. In July 2000, the Amendment to the 1995 Pensions Act was approved by Parliament, requiring the trustees of occupational pension funds to disclose in the Statement of Investment Principles 'the extent (if at all) to which social, environmental and ethical considerations are taken into account in the selection, retention and realization of investments.'[5]

The Trustee Act 2000, which came into effect in February 2001, requires charity trustees to ensure that investments are suitable to a charity's stated aims. According to the Charity Commission guidance, charities should include 'any relevant ethical considerations as to the kind of investments that are appropriate for the trust to make.' In 2002, The Cabinet Office in the UK published the Review of Charity Law in 2002, which proposed that all charities with an annual income of over £1 million report on the extent to which social, environmental, and ethical issues are taken into account in their investment policies. The Home Office accepted theses recommendations in 2003.

In addition, large organizations of institutional investors also have taken SRI initiatives. For instance, the Association of British Insurers (ABI), whose members invest

---

5   The SRI regulation has been introduced against a background of increasing pressure from governments, non-governmental organizations, and the general public on companies to improve their CSR. In 1998, the British Parliament incepted the All-Party Parliamentary Group on Socially Responsible Investment chaired by Tony Colman, which has played an important role in bringing about major developments for SRI regulations in the UK.

in about $1 trillion assets, published a disclosure guideline in 2001 suggesting that listed companies report on material social, environmental, and ethical risks relevant to their business activities.

Continental Europe

Over the past decade, some national governments in Continental Europe passed a series of regulations on social and environmental investments and savings. Since 1991, the Renewable Energy Act in Germany has given a tax advantage to closed-end funds investing in wind energy (Eurosif, 2003). In 1995, the Dutch Tax Office introduced the 'Green Savings and Investment Plan', which granted a tax deduction to investments in specific 'green' projects, such as wind and solar energy, and organic farming.

Following the British Amendment to the 1995 Pensions Act of 2000, four countries in Continental Europe (namely Belgium, Germany, Italy, and Sweden) have passed similar regulations requiring pension funds to disclose SRI-related information. In 2001, Belgium passed the 'Vandebroucke' law, which requires pension funds to report the degree to which their investments take into account social, ethical, and environmental aspects. In January 2002, Germany adopted a regulation requiring that certified private pension schemes and occupational pension schemes 'must inform the members in writing, whether and in what form ethical, social, or ecological aspects are taken into consideration when investing the paid-in contributions' (Eurosif, 2003). Sweden passed a regulation (effective since January 2002), requiring Swedish national pension funds to incorporate environmental and ethical aspects in their investment policies. In Italy, legislation was adopted in September 2004 demanding pension funds to disclose the effect of non-financial factors (including social, environmental, and ethical factors) that influence their investment decisions. All these initiatives have clearly had a positive impact on the growth of the SRI fund industry in Europe.

France is the first, and so far the only, country making social, environmental, and ethical reporting mandatory for all listed companies. In May 2001, the legislation 'New Economic Regulations' came into force: listed companies are to publish information on their social and environmental initiatives and investments in the annual reports.[6] Meanwhile, since February 2001, the managers of Employee Savings Plans are required to consider SRI issues when buying and selling shares.[7]

Outside Europe

Australia is the only country outside Europe that has adopted a regulation regarding SRI. In 2001, the Australian government passed a bill requiring that all investment firms' product disclosure statements include descriptions of 'the extent to which labor standards or environmental, social, or ethical considerations are taken into account.' Since 2001, all

---

6   Law No. 2001-420, Art. 225-102-1: '[The annual report] also contains information, the detail of which is being determined by a decree of the Council of State, on how the company takes into account the social and environmental consequences of its activities. The present paragraph applies only to (listed) companies [...].' (www.eurosif.org).

7   Law No. 2001-152, Art. 214-39: 'The [fund's] internal rules specify, if need be, the social, environmental or ethical considerations the fund management company must take into account when buying or selling securities, as well as when exercising the voting rights attached to the ownership of these securities. The fund's annual report reports on how these considerations have been taken into account, in terms defined by the Commission des Opérations de Bourse.'

listed companies on the Australian Stock Exchange are obliged to make an annual social responsibility report.

To summarize, we expect that the SRI industry will continue to soar as a response to the growing social awareness of investors and increasingly supportive regulatory environment.

INVESTMENT SCREENS

The investment screens used in SRI have evolved over time. Table 22.3 presents a summary of the SRI screens used by ethical funds around the world. Usually, SRI mutual funds apply a combination of the various types of screens. SIF (2003) reports that 64 percent of all socially screened mutual funds in the US use more than five screens, while 18 percent of SRI funds use only one social screen. These screens can be broadly classified into two groups: negative screens and positive ones.

First, the oldest and most basic SRI strategy is based on negative screening. These filters refer to the practice that specific stocks or industries are excluded from SRI portfolios based on social, environmental, and ethical criteria. The funds based on such screens account for $2.0 trillion out of the $2.3 trillion SRI assets in the US (SIF, 2003). A typical negative screen can be applied on an initial asset pool such as the S&P 500 stocks from which the alcohol, tobacco, gambling, and defense industries, or companies with poor performance in labor relations or environmental protection are excluded. Other negative screens may include irresponsible foreign operations, pornography, abortion, poor workplace conditions, violation of human rights, and animal testing. After performing a negative SRI screening, portfolios are created via a financial and quantitative selection. Some SRI funds only exclude companies from the investment universe when these firms' revenues derived from 'a-social or un-ethical' sectors exceed a specific threshold, whereas other SRI funds also apply negative screens to a company's branches or suppliers. A small number of SRI funds use screens based on traditional ideological or religious convictions: for instance they exclude investments in firms producing pork products, in financial institutions paying interest on savings, and in insurance companies insuring non-married people.

Second, SRI portfolios are nowadays also based on positive screens which in practice boil down to selecting shares that meet superior CSR standards. The most common positive screens focus on corporate governance, labor relations, the environment, sustainability of investments, and the stimulation of cultural diversity. Positive screens are also frequently used to select companies with a good record concerning renewable energy usage or community involvement. The use of positive screens is often combined with a 'best in class' approach. Firms are ranked within *each industry* or market sector based on CSR criteria. Subsequently, only those firms in each industry are selected which pass a minimum threshold.

Negative and positive screens are often referred to as the *first* and *second* generation of SRI screens respectively.[8] The *third* generation of screens refers to an integrated approach of selecting companies based on the economic, environmental, and social criteria comprised by both negative and positive screens. This approach is often called

---

8   For a more detailed description of the various generations of SRI funds, see: http://www.ethibel.org/subs_e/1_info/sub1_2.html

Table 22.3 SRI screens

Screens	Definitions	Type
Tobacco	Avoid manufacturers of tobacco products	-
Alcohol	Avoid firms that produce, market, or otherwise promote the consumption of alcoholic beverages	-
Gambling	Avoid casinos and suppliers of gambling equipment	-
Defense/Weapons	Avoid firms producing weapons for domestic or foreign militaries, or firearms for personal use	-
Nuclear Power	Avoid manufacturers of nuclear reactors or related equipment and companies that operate nuclear power plants	-
Irresponsible Foreign Operations	Avoid firms with investments in government-controlled or private firms located in oppressive regimes such as Burma or China, or firms which mistreat the indigenous peoples of developing countries	-
Pornography/ Adult Entertainment	Avoid publishers of pornographic magazines; production studios that produce offensive video and audio tapes; companies that are major sponsors of graphic sex and violence on television	-
Abortion/Birth Control	Avoid providers of abortion; manufacturers of abortion drugs and birth control products; insurance companies that pay for elective abortions (where not mandated by law); companies that provide financial support to Planned Parenthood	-
Labor Relations and Workplace Conditions	Seek firms with strong union relationships, employee empowerment, and/or employee profit sharing Avoid firms exploiting their workforce and sweatshops	+ -
Environment	Seek firms with proactive involvement in recycling, waste reduction, and environmental cleanup Avoid firms producing toxic products, and contributing to global warming	+ -
Corporate Governance	Seek companies demonstrating 'best practices' related to board independence and elections, auditor independence, executive compensation, expensing of options, voting rights and/or other governance issues Avoid firms with antitrust violations, consumer fraud, and marketing scandals	+ -
Business Practice	Seek companies committed to sustainability through investments in R&D, quality assurance, product safety	+
Employment Diversity	Seek firms pursuing an active policy related to the employment of minorities, women, gays/lesbians, and/or disabled persons who ought to be represented amongst senior management	+
Human Rights	Seek firms promoting human rights standards Avoid firms which are complicit in human rights violations	+ -

Table 22.3   SRI screens

Screens	Definitions	Type
Animal Testing	Seek firms promoting the respectful treatment of animals Avoid firms with animal testing and firms producing hunting/ trapping equipment or using animals in end products	+ -
Renewable Energy	Seek firms producing power derived form renewable energy sources	+
Biotechnology	Seek firms that support sustainable agriculture, biodiversity, local farmers, and industrial applications of biotechnology Avoid firms involved in the promotion or development of genetic engineering for agricultural applications	+ -
Community Involvement	Seek firms with proactive investments in the local community by sponsoring charitable donations, employee volunteerism, and/or housing and educational programs	+
Shareholder activism	The SRI funds that attempt to influence company actions through direct dialogue with management and/or voting at Annual General Meetings	+
Non-married	Avoid insurance companies that give coverage to non-married couples	-
Healthcare/ Pharmaceuticals	Avoid healthcare industries (used by funds targeting the 'Christian Scientist' religious group)	-
Interest-based Financial Institutions	Avoid financial institutions that derive a significant portion of their income from interest earnings (on loans or fixed income securities) (used by funds managed according to Islamic principles)	-
Pork Producers	Avoid companies that derive a significant portion of their income from the manufacturing or marketing of pork products (used by funds managed according to Islamic principles)	-

This table summarizes the investment screens used by SRI mutual funds. In the last column, the '-' refers to a negative screen, whereas '+' refers to a positive one. Data are compiled from Social Investment Forum (2003: 42) and the Natural Capital Institute (www.responsibleinvesting.org).

'sustainability' or 'triple bottom line' (due to its focus on People, Planet, and Profit). The *fourth* generation of ethical funds combines the sustainable investing approach (third generation) with shareholder activism. In this case, portfolio managers or the companies specialized in granting ethical labels attempt to influence the company's actions through direct dialogue with the management or by the use of voting rights at Annual General Meetings. Becht et al. (2006) show in a very interesting clinical study the activism of one of the Hermes investment funds. SIF (2003) reports that, in 2002, socially responsible investors in the US filed 292 shareholder resolutions on social, environmental, and ethical issues. The largest number of resolutions is on environmental issues, followed by issues on global labor standards and equal employment conditions.

Portfolio-level Analysis on SRI

Do investors base their decisions exclusively on risk-return characteristics or are they willing to tolerate suboptimal financial performance in order to satisfy their personal values related to social responsibility? This section reviews the theories and empirical evidence on a number of important issues on SRI, including the risk-return characteristics and money-flows of SRI.

SRI PERFORMANCE

The question as to whether SRI creates shareholder value is ultimately an empirical one. In this subsection we discuss the empirical findings on the risk-return characteristics of SRI. If investors derive non-financial utility from investing in SRI and care less about financial performance than conventional investors, we expect continued SRI growth even if their risk-adjusted returns are lower than those of conventional investments.

Evidence from the US and UK

There are several studies evaluating SRI fund performance in the US. Hamilton, Joe and Statman (1993) investigate the performance of 32 SRI funds and 320 randomly selected non-SRI funds in the US for the period of 1981–1990. The CAPM-based Jensen's alpha is measured against the value-weighted NYSE index. For the 17 SRI funds with a longer history, that is, established before 1985, the average alpha is –0.06 percent per month, which is higher than the average monthly alpha (–0.14 percent) of the corresponding 170 non-SRI funds. Meanwhile for the 15 SRI funds with a shorter history, that is, established after 1985, the average alpha is –0.28 percent per month, which is worse than the average monthly alpha (–0.04 percent) of the corresponding 150 non-SRI funds. Note that the differences between average alphas of SRI and of non-SRI funds are not statistically significant.

For the period of 1990–1998, Statman (2000) investigates the performance of 31 SRI funds in the US. The reference group contains 62 non-ethical funds with similar sizes as the ethical ones. The two groups of funds have similar average expense ratios: 1.50 percent for SRI funds and 1.56 percent for non-SRI funds. As there are no dead SRI funds in the sample period, the SRI fund sample is attrition free. Jensen's alpha is measured against the S&P 500 Index, but choosing the Domini 400 Social Index (DSI 400), one of the most well-known SRI indices, as a benchmark does not change the results. The average monthly alpha is –0.42 percent for SRI funds and –0.62 percent for non-SRI funds, but the difference is not significant (the t-statistic is 1.84). The finding suggests that the performance of SRI funds is not significantly different from that of non-SRI funds. In addition, the paper also documents that the DSI 400 index has a higher Sharpe ratio than the S&P 500 index (0.97 vs. 0.92), which indicates that a mean-variance optimizing investor should prefer investing in the former index.

Comparing the average performance of SRI funds to that of non-SRI funds does not necessarily provide useful information to an investor who can selectively invest in a subset of mutual funds. Unlike the above-mentioned studies, Geczy, Stambaugh and Levin (2006) investigate the diversification cost of an investor who invests in SRI funds but not in conventional mutual funds in the US for the period 1963–2001. This study reveals that there can be significant financial costs of imposing SRI constraints on mean-variance optimizing investors. To an investor who strongly believes in the CAPM and rules out stock selection skills, that is, a market index investor, the financial cost of the SRI constraint is just 5 basis points per month. The SRI constraint imposes large costs, more than 1.5 percent per month, on investors whose beliefs allow selection skills, that is, investors who rely heavily on individual funds' historical risk-adjusted returns to predict future performance.

A few studies investigate the performance of ethical funds in the UK. Luther, Matatko and Corner (1992) study 15 ethical funds in the UK for the 1984–1990 period. The Jensen's alphas of the ethical funds have a mean of 0.03 percent per month, which is not significantly different from zero. This implies that ethical funds have a similar performance as the benchmark assets. The authors also document that ethical funds have relatively high portfolio weights on small-cap companies. Luther and Matatko (1994) find that SRI portfolios are biased towards small-caps.

Whereas the above studies may have a benchmark problem, Mallin, Saadouni and Briston (1995) compare the Jensen's alphas of 29 ethical funds to those of 29 non-ethical funds with a similar fund size and age. The monthly alphas of ethical funds range from -0.28 percent to 1.21 percent, while 22 out of the 29 alphas are positive. The alphas of non-ethical funds, 23 of which being positive, range from -0.41 percent to 1.56 percent per month. There is no evidence that the two groups of funds have different risk-adjusted returns. Gregory, Matatko and Luther (1997) examine a subsample of 18 ethical funds for the 1986–1994 period. The reference group contains 18 non-ethical funds matched to the ethical funds by fund size, age, and investment area. To account for the small-cap bias, Jensen's alphas are calculated based on two factors, namely the FT All Shares Index and the Hoare Govett Small Cap Index. The alphas of ethical funds range from –0.71 percent to 0.24 percent per month, but most are not significant. The authors conclude that the difference in performance between SRI and non-SRI funds is not statistically significant.

International evidence

There are several recent studies also investigating the performance of SRI funds in countries other than the US and UK. For the short period of 1996–1998, Kreander et al. (2005) study the performance of 40 SRI funds in Europe using weekly data. The countries covered in the sample include Belgium (1 fund), Germany (4 funds), Netherlands (2 funds), Norway (2 funds), Sweden (11 funds), Switzerland (2 funds), and the UK (18 funds). The reference group to the SRI funds consists of 40 non-SRI funds from the same countries and with similar fund size, age, and investment universe as the SRI funds. The average Jensen's alpha of SRI funds and non-SRI ones are similar (0.20 percent vs. 0.12 percent per month, respectively). This finding is consistent with the results of previous studies for the US and the UK. In addition, the authors test the market timing ability of SRI and non-SRI fund managers, using the Henriksson and Merton (1981) model. The timing coefficients are also similar for the two types of funds (-0.29 vs. –0.28), and each of them is significant at the 95 percent level. Surprisingly, the signs of the timing coefficients are negative, which seems to signify that both SRI and non-SRI fund managers time the market in the wrong direction.

Large survivorship-free[9] samples of SRI funds (16 for Germany, 32 for the UK, and 55 for the US) and of non-SRI funds (4,384) are studied over the period 1990–2001 by Bauer, Koedijk and Otten (2005). Fund performance is measured by the Carhart (1997) model. As documented in previous studies, ethical funds have a smaller size and charge higher management fees than conventional funds. The average monthly alphas of SRI funds are 0.29 percent, 0.09 percent and –0.05 percent for German, UK domestic, and US domestic funds, respectively. The US domestic ethical funds significantly underperform conventional domestic funds, but the difference between the US international ethical funds and the US international conventional funds is insignificant. The UK ethical funds, both domestic and international funds, significantly outperform conventional funds, whereas the difference in average alphas between German SRI and non-SRI funds is insignificant. In summary, there is again little evidence that SRI funds significantly over- or underperform non-SRI funds.

Another international SRI performance study is by Schroder (2004) who examines 30 US funds and 16 German and Swiss ones. He applies a two-factor model with both a blue-chip index and a small-cap index as benchmarks to estimate the alphas which range from –2.06 percent to 0.87 percent. Thirty-eight out of the 46 alphas are negative, but only 4 are significant at the 5 percent level. This confirms that SRI funds do not significantly underperform the benchmark portfolio consisting of both large stocks and small stocks.

There are two studies investigating the performance of SRI funds outside the US and Europe. Both studies measure the risk-adjusted returns by the conditional version of Carhart (1997) model. Bauer, Otten and Tourani Rad (2006) find that, for the period of 1992–2003, Australian domestic ethical funds underperform their domestic conventional counterparts by –1.56 percent per year, while the Australian international ethical funds outperform their conventional peers by 3.31 percent per year. However, none of these differences are statistically significant. For Canadian SRI funds, Bauer, Derwall and Otten (2006) show that the difference in average alphas is insignificant between the eight SRI funds and 267 non-SRI funds (-0.21 percent vs. –0.18 percent per month). Hence, their findings suggest that SRI and non-SRI funds do not outperform or underperform in Australia and Canada.

Using a database consisting of 463 SRI mutual funds in the US, UK, Continental Europe, and Asia-Pacific, Renneboog, Ter Horst and Zhang (2008b) study the risk and return characteristics of SRI mutual funds around the world. They hypothesize that ethical, environmental, and social considerations influence stocks prices and that investors are willing to pay a price for ethics due to aversion to corporate behavior not complying to CSR standards. The authors also provide evidence in support of this hypothesis. SRI funds in many European and Asia-Pacific countries strongly underperform domestic benchmark portfolios by about 5 percent per annum. SRI investors are unable to identify the funds that will outperform in the future, whereas they show some fund-selection ability in identifying ethical funds that will perform poorly in the future. Finally, the screening activities of SRI funds have a significant impact on funds' risk-adjusted returns and loadings on risk factors.

To conclude, in this subsection we presented the empirical evidence of the performance. Although there is little evidence that the *average* performance of SRI in

---

9   Ignoring dead funds would overestimate the average returns of the non-SRI funds in by 0.01 percent, 0.02 percent, and 0.03 percent per month for respectively Germany, the UK, and the United States.

the US and UK is different from that of conventional funds (Bauer, Koedijk and Otten, 2005), restricting the investment universe to SRI can seriously limit the diversification possibilities and negatively influence the risk-return tradeoff (Geczy, Stambaugh and Levin, 2006). Despite the underperformance of SRI in Continental Europe and Asia-Pacific (Renneboog, Ter Horst, and Zhang, 2008a), SRI has experienced strong growth in these regions. This supports the hypothesis that investors are willing to accept suboptimal financial performance in order to satisfy their personal values related to social responsibility. When deriving non-financial utility from investing in firms meeting superior CSR standards, SRI investors may be content with a lower rate of return from ethical/socially responsible firms.

MONEY-FLOWS OF SRI

In spite of the fact that SRI funds experienced a tremendous growth in most developed economies around the world, little is known about how investors select funds with explicit non-financial attributes. The fact that SRI investors may have a different investment objective function is suggested by the SIF (2001) report: during the stock market downturn over the first nine months of 2001, there was a 94 percent drop in the money inflows into all US mutual funds, whereas the fall in net investments in socially screened funds amounted to merely 54 percent. The SIF (2003, p. 8) states, 'Typically, social investors' assets are "stickier" than those of investors concerned only with financial performance. That is, social investors have been less likely to move investments from one fund to another and more inclined to stay with funds than conventional investors.'

The first study on the determinants of money-flows in the SRI fund industry was conducted by Bollen (2007) who concentrates on money-flows and past returns for US SRI funds. This study shows that the volatility of money-flows in the US is lower for SRI funds than for non-SRI funds. Furthermore, money-flows of socially responsible funds are less sensitive to lagged negative returns than flows in conventional funds, but more sensitive to lagged positive returns.

Using a database consisting of 410 SRI mutual funds in 17 countries around the world, Renneboog, Ter Horst, and Zhang (2005) study the money-flows into and out of the SRI fund industry. They find that SRI investors chase past returns, past return rankings, and persistence in past performance, as do investors in conventional mutual funds. Unless a fund persistently underperforms, SRI investors care more about past positive returns than about past negative returns. In addition, the authors find that smaller, younger, or riskier SRI funds have higher money-flow volatility, partly resulting from the higher marketing efforts of these funds. Perhaps the most interesting finding of this study is that the money-flows and the flow-past performance relationship crucially depend on the types and intensities of SRI screening activities.

Taken together, the recent studies show that money-flows into and out of SRI are less sensitive to lagged negative returns than those of conventional funds (Bollen, 2007), and the flow-past performance sensitivity depends on the types and intensities of SRI screening activities (Renneboog, Ter Horst, and Zhang, 2005). This is consistent with the view that investors care about non-financial attributes of their investments.

Conclusions and Future Research Agenda

SRI has experienced rapid growth around the world, reflecting the increasing awareness of investors to social, environmental, and governance issues. In recent years, issues like global warming, the Kyoto Protocol, corporate governance, and community investing have gained significant attention by governments and investors around the world. In addition, governments in western countries have taken many regulatory initiatives to stimulate SRI. Given the growing social awareness of investors and the increasingly positive regulatory environment, we expect that SRI will continue their growth and relative importance as an asset class.

This chapter provides an overview of the state of the academic literature on SRI. The main conclusion of this survey is that while some research has been undertaken on SRI, there are still a great many issues and puzzles that remain to be resolved. The emergence of SRI, combined with the behavioral differences between SRI and conventional investors, raises interesting questions for research on corporate finance, asset pricing, and financial intermediation.

At the firm level, the question whether CSR is priced by capital markets is still an open one. Although CSR is found to be associated with higher shareholder value, there is no convincing evidence on the direction of causality. In addition, it would be a fruitful area of empirical research to investigate how CSR influences the cost of capital of firms and their investment decisions.

Furthermore, SRI may have important implications for asset pricing. For example, if investors exhibit preferences of 'aversion to unethical/asocial corporate behavior' in addition to the standard risk aversion, investors may require a lower rate of return from ethical firms than that suggested by the standard asset pricing models. However, the existing studies at the portfolio level hint but do not univocally demonstrate that SRI investment funds perform worse than conventional funds. In addition, it is a puzzle that investing in firms based on public information such as sound environmental performance or good corporate governance produces superior abnormal returns (as the CSR research shows). Further research remains to be conducted to investigate the anomaly.

Finally, the emergence of SRI also raises questions for financial intermediaries such as asset managers and banks. For example, SRI portfolio managers pursue both financial goals and social objectives. This multi-task nature of SRI managers may weaken fund managers' incentives to pursue economic efficiency, that is, risk-adjusted returns, and increase the agency costs. It would be interesting to examine the incentive structures in the SRI industry. In recent years, many banks voluntarily apply CSR screens in their lending processes. For instance, more than 50 banks around the world have adopted the Equator Principles, a set of principles committing the signatory banks to finance only projects meeting social and environmental criteria. Additional research is required to understand the impact of SRI on financial institutions.

References

Bauer, R., J. Derwall and R. Otten, 2006, The ethical mutual funds performance debate: new evidence for Canada, *Journal of Business Ethics*, forthcoming.

Bauer, R., K. Koedijk and R. Otten, 2005, International evidence on ethical mutual fund performance and investment style, *Journal of Banking and Finance* 29, 1751-1767.

Bauer, R., R. Otten and A. Tourani Rad, 2006, Ethical investing in Australia: Is there a financial penalty? *Pacific-Basin Finance Journal* 14(1), 33-48.

Becht, M., J. Franks, C. Mayer and S. Rossi, 2006, Returns to shareholder activism evidence from a clinical study of the Hermes UK Focus Fund, Working paper, European Corporate Governance Institute.

Bollen, N., 2007, Mutual fund attributes and investor behavior, *Journal of Financial and Quantitative Analysis*, 42, 683-708.

Carhart, M.M., 1997, On persistence in mutual fund performance, *Journal of Finance* 52, 57-82.

Ethical Investment Association (EIA), 2001, 2002, 2003, 2005, Socially responsible investments in Australia, available at http://www.eia.org.au.

European Sustainable and Responsible Investment Forum (Eurosif), 2003, 2006, 2008, Socially Responsible Investment among European institutional investors, available at http://www.eurosif.org.

Geczy, C., R. Stambaugh and D. Levin, 2006, Investing in socially responsible mutual funds, Working paper, Wharton School.

Gregory, A., J. Matatko and R. Luther, 1997, Ethical unit trust financial performance: small company effects and fund size effects, *Journal of Business Finance and Accounting* 24, 705-725.

Hamilton, S., H. Jo and M. Statman, 1993, Doing well while doing good? The investment performance of socially responsible mutual funds, *Financial Analysts Journal* 49(6), 62-66.

Henriksson, R. and R. Merton, 1981, On market timing and investment performance II statistical procedures for evaluating forecasting skills, *Journal of Business* 54(4), 513-533.

Kreander, N., G. Gray, D.M. Power and C.D. Sinclair, 2005, Evaluating the performance of ethical and non-SRI funds: a matched pair analysis, *Journal of Business, Finance and Accounting* 32(7), 1465–1493.

Luther, R. and J. Matatko, 1994, The performance of ethical unit trusts: choosing an appropriate benchmark, *British Accounting Review* 26, 77-89.

Luther, R., J. Matatko and D. Corner, 1992, The investment performance of UK ethical unit trusts, *Accounting, Auditing & Accountability Journal Review* 5, 57-70.

Mallin,C.A., B. Saadouni and R.J. Briston, 1995, The financial performance of ethical investment funds, *Journal of Business Finance & Accounting* 22(4), 483-96.

Renneboog, L., J. Ter Horst and C. Zhang, 2005, Is ethical money financially smart?, Working Paper, Tilburg University.

Renneboog, L., J. Ter Horst and C. Zhang, 2008a, Socially responsible investments: institutional aspects, performance, and investor behaviour, *Journal of Banking and Finance*, forthcoming.

Renneboog, L., J. Ter Horst, and C. Zhang, 2008b, The price of ethics and stakeholder governance: evidence from socially responsible mutual funds, *Journal of Corporate Finance*, forthcoming.

Schroder, M., 2004, The performance of socially responsible investments: investment funds and indices, *Financial Markets and Portfolio Management* 18(2), 122-142.

Social Investment Forum (SIF), 1995, 1997, 1999, 2001, 2003, 2005, Report on responsible investing trends in the US, http:// www.socialinvest.org.

Social Investment Organization (SIO), 2002, 2004, Canadian social investment review, http:// www.socialinvestment.ca.

Statman, M., 2000, Socially responsible mutual funds, *Financial Analysts Journal* 56 (3), 30-39.

Sustainable Investment Research International (SiRi), 2002, 2003, 2005, Green, social and ethical funds in Europe, available at http://www.avanzi-sri.org.

Zhang, C., 2006, Ethics, investments, and investor behavior, PhD Thesis No. 179, CentER, Tilburg University.

KEY REFERENCES FOR FURTHER READING

Bauer, R., K. Koedijk and R. Otten, 2005, International evidence on ethical mutual fund performance and investment style, *Journal of Banking and Finance* 29, 1751-1767.

Bollen, N., 2007, Mutual fund attributes and investor behavior, *Journal of Financial and Quantitative Analysis*, 42, 683-708.

Geczy, C., R. Stambaugh and D. Levin, 2006, Investing in socially responsible mutual funds, Working paper, Wharton School.

Hamilton, S., H. Jo and M. Statman, 1993, Doing well while doing good? The investment performance of socially responsible mutual funds, *Financial Analysts Journal* 49(6), 62-66.

Renneboog, L., J. Ter Horst and C. Zhang, 2005, Is ethical money financially smart?, Working Paper, Tilburg University.

Renneboog, L., J. Ter Horst and C. Zhang, 2008a, Socially responsible investments: institutional aspects, performance, and investor behaviour, *Journal of Banking and Finance*, forthcoming.

Renneboog, L., J. Ter Horst, and C. Zhang, 2008b, The price of ethics and stakeholder governance: evidence from socially responsible mutual funds, *Journal of Corporate Finance*, forthcoming.

Statman, M., 2000, Socially responsible mutual funds, *Financial Analysts Journal* 56(3), 30-39.

24 *Corporate Reporting Frameworks*

ANTONIO TENCATI

Introduction

This chapter provides a broad picture of the most important evaluation and reporting systems of corporate social, environmental and sustainability performance. The starting point of the analysis is the concept of *accountability* that directly derives from the notion of Corporate Social Responsibility (CSR): according to a stakeholder view of the firm a company is held accountable for its actions to the different constituencies. Therefore, if companies want to manage environmental, social and governance issues and obtain the trust of their stakeholders, they must not only communicate, but also give concrete evidence that they are committed to continual, long-term improvement. Thus, companies increasingly need appropriate systems to measure and control their own behaviour in order to assess whether they are responding to stakeholder concerns in an effective way and to communicate the results achieved. These new accounting and reporting systems have the purpose of broadening and integrating the traditional financial approaches to the corporate performance measurement, taking stakeholder needs into due account. The most advanced methodologies aim at monitoring and tracking from a qualitative and quantitative viewpoint the overall corporate performance according to a triple bottom line approach and/or a stakeholder framework.

Corporate Social Responsibility and Accountability

From the notion of CSR it is possible to derive the complementary concept of *accountability* (AccountAbility, 1999), which means that the company is held accountable for its actions. If companies want to manage CSR and sustainability issues and obtain the trust of their stakeholders they must not only communicate, but also give concrete evidence that they are committed to continual, long-term improvement. Therefore, a sustainability and responsibility-oriented company must define appropriate systems to measure, control and evaluate corporate performance. Over the years, many social and environmental standards and management solutions have been developed to evaluate and report the economic, social, environmental and sustainability performance of companies. These tools provide information of a qualitative, quantitative and economic nature and influence the interactions between a firm and its stakeholders (Table 24.1).

Table 24.1 Tools to measure, evaluate and report Corporate Performance

	The economic dimension	The social dimension	The environmental dimension	The sustainability dimension
Corporate performance management tools	Operating budget and annual report Return On Investment (ROI) Return On Equity (ROE) Leverage Current ratio Periodic performance measurement (*Economic Value Added*, EVA) (Stewart, 1991) Specific performance indicators (Marketing, Production, Logistics, R&D, Quality) Shareholder Value (Rappaport, 1986)	Social audit (Abt, 1977) and social report (Gruppo per il Bilancio Sociale, 2001) Social accounting (Zadek et al., 1997; Gonella et al., 1998) Socio-efficency Indicators (Schaltegger et al., 2002, 9) AccountAbility 1000 (AA1000) (AccountAbility, 1999). http://www.accountability21.net/ BS 8800 and Occupational Health and Safety Assessment Series Specification (OHSAS 18001). http://www.bsi-global.com Social Accountability 8000 (SA8000). http://www.sa-intl.org Ethical indexes (e.g. *Domini 400 Social Index, Citizens Index, Dow Jones Sustainability Indexes, Ethical Index Euro, FTSE4Good Index Series*) (Perrini et al., 2006, 81-82) Ethical and Social Rating (Goldman Sachs, 2006; Perrini et al., 2006, 82-84)	Environmental report and LCA (Hallay, 1990; Hallay and Pfriem, 1992; Beck, 1993) Environmental accounting (Bundesumweltministerium and Umweltbundesamt, 1995; Burritt et al., 2002) Ecolabels. http://www.eco-label.com Eco-efficiency Indicators (World Business Council, 2000) Performance Indicators (ISO 14031). http://www.iso.org/iso/en/iso9000-14000/index.html Environmental management regulations and standards (EMAS and ISO 14001). http://europa.eu.int/comm/environment/emas/index_en.htm; http://www.iso.org/iso/en/iso9000-14000/index.html Environmental communication (ISO 14063). http://www.iso.org/iso/en/iso9000-14000/index.html Greenhouse gases assessing and reporting (ISO 14064). http://www.iso.org/iso/en/iso9000-14000/index.html Carbon Disclosure Project. http://www.cdproject.net/	GRI. http://www.globalreporting.org Balanced Scorecard (Kaplan and Norton, 1992; Figge et al., 2002; Zingales and Hockerts, 2003) SIGMA Project. http://www.projectsigma.com Q-RES Project (2002; 2004) United Nations Global Compact. http://www.unglobalcompact.org/ ISO 26000. http://www.iso.org/sr; http://www.uni.com Other national initiatives, among which: CSR-SC Project (italy: Tencati et al., 2004; Perrini et al., 2006); SD 21000 (France: http://www.afnor.org/developpementdurable/normalisation/sd21000.html) The Prince's Accounting for Sustainability Project (UK: http://www.accountingforsustainability.org.uk/output/Page1.asp) ValuesManagementSystem (Germany: http://www.dnwe.de/dateien/wms.pdf) Sustainability Evaluation and Reporting System (SERS) (Tencati, 2002; Perrini and Tencati, 2007)

In the economic field a turning point was reached in 1986 with the definition of the shareholder value paradigm (Rappaport, 1986). The first social auditing systems were developed, between the late 1960s and early 1970s, in the United States and then in Europe and especially in Germany and France (Rusconi, 1988). The social reporting processes enter a new phase at the beginning of the 1990s through the initiatives developed mainly by the cooperative movement in Europe (Gonella et al., 1988). The first environmental reports were drawn up by research centres and companies in Germany, the Scandinavian and Anglo-Saxon countries in the late 1980s and coincided with the public's growing awareness of the importance of environmental issues (Hallay, 1990; Brophy and Starkey, 1996). Subsequently, this tool began to be commonly used even in the less aware countries from the ecological point of view (Bennett and James, 1999). The triple bottom line (also known as TBL) approach and the first attempts in the field of sustainability accounting were born in 1994 (Elkington, 1994), but a fundamental driver of their growth trend was the Global Reporting Initiative established in 1997.

In the next paragraphs we will examine some of the most important methods of *environmental, social and sustainability performance evaluation and reporting* which a company can adopt.

Corporate Social Performance Evaluation and Reporting

SOCIAL AUDIT

The success of the CSR concept modifies limits and opportunities within which a company operates. The mere pursuit of profits is no longer sufficient since the company has also to consider the needs of different stakeholders capable of influencing its own success. Therefore, it becomes crucial to measure the company's capacity to meet stakeholder needs, and to strike some sort of balance between what the company offers and what it receives from the social system. In order to address these issues, the first social auditing systems were developed, between the late 1960s and early 1970s, in the United States and then in Europe.

The many different approaches and the fact that it is generally a voluntary tool which measures the social results of companies – and thus subject to the influence of specific variables of a cultural, political and economic nature – has made it impossible to develop a generally accepted social reporting framework. The methods adopted diverge in content and final objective and so that the picture of the relationships between a company and society appears to be very distant one from the other. However, despite these divergences it is possible to formulate a definition of social auditing by combining the different experiences which have been developed up to now. To sum up, social audit can be considered as the control, at a given time, of the impact, which the activities of an organized system (in particular, a company) have on the well-being of the individuals that in some way interact with that organization (Bonal, 1982). In order to better explain the solutions companies adopt, it might be useful to see how the different approaches to accountability are classified (Table 24.2). They include different ways of measuring social impact and different ways of carrying out activities regarding *Social and Ethical Accounting, Auditing and Reporting* (SEAAR) (AccountAbility, 1999).

ACCOUNTABILITY 1000 (AA1000) FRAMEWORK AND SERIES

In order to overcome the above-mentioned problems and make the approaches to accountability more uniform so that information coming from different sources can be compared, in November 1999 AccountAbility (ISEA, Institute of Social and Ethical AccountAbility) published *AccountAbility 1000* (AA1000) (AccountAbility, 1999).

AA1000 is an *accountability standard* designed to ensure the quality of the *social and ethical accounting, auditing and reporting* process. It is a *foundation standard*, which can be used in two ways: as a tool to underpin the quality of specialized *accountability standards* (like the *Sustainability Reporting Guidelines* of the Global Reporting Initiative, *Social Accountability 8000* on *ethical sourcing*, the ISO standards on the development and certification of environmental and quality management systems); as a stand-alone system and process for processing and communicating social and ethical accountability and performance.

Table 24.2 Approaches to accountability[a]

Stated or 'named' approach	Examples of organizations using these approaches	Description
Capital valuation	Skandia	Regularly disclosed process to understand, measure, report on and manage various forms of capital (which could include intellectual, human, social, environmental, organizational, structural and financial capital)
Corporate community involvement reporting	BP, Diageo (Grand Metropolitan), NatWest Group	Description, illustration and measurement of community involvement policies and activities through occasional reports. This approach may also include benchmarking against other company performances
Ethical accounting statement	Sbn Bank, Scandinavian public sector	Regularly disclosed process, based on shared values that stakeholders develop through ongoing dialogue, aimed at designing future actions
Ethical auditing	The Body Shop International	Regular, externally verified process to understand, measure, report on and improve on an organization's social, environmental and animal testing performance through stakeholder dialogue
Social auditing	Ben & Jerry's Homemade, VanCity Credit Union, Black Country Housing Association, Co-op Bank	Regular, externally verified process to understand, measure, report on and improve on an organization's social performance through stakeholder dialogue
Social Balance	Coop Italia, Unipol	A regular reconstruction and aggregation of financial data across stakeholder groups which specifies financial costs associated with 'social activities'
Value-added statement	Credito Valtellinese, Telecom Italia, MPS, Acea, South African Breweries	Process to quantify the value-added generated by an organization and its distribution to stakeholder groups
Statement of principles and values	Shell International	Statement that develops and describes an organization's principles in meeting its financial, social and environmental responsibilities
Sustainability reporting	Shell, Baxter International, Procter & Gamble, Interface	Evolving reporting process that identifies ways forward and reports on progress against sustainability principles and targets

a   Source: Based on Gonella, Pilling and Zadek (1998, iv). In Bennett and James (1999, 55–56).

The principles of the AA1000 standard are organized according to a hierarchical order. The fundamental concept, found at the top of the pyramid, which regulates the SEAAR process is *accountability* defined as the capacity 'to explain or justify the acts, omissions, risks and dependencies for which an organization is responsible to people with a legitimate interest'. The principle of *accountability* means that a company is transparent, responsible and complies with agreed standards. *Accountability* generates the principle of *inclusivity*. *Inclusivity* is based on the remaining principles: *completeness, materiality, regularity and timeliness* regarding the scope and nature of the process; *quality assurance* (independent audit of the process), *accessibility* and *information quality* (implying that the information can be compared, is reliable, relevant and understandable) concerning the meaningfulness of the information; *embeddedness* (systems integration) and *continuous improvement* affecting the management of the process on an ongoing basis. Together with a set of user guidelines, AA1000 therefore provides a framework, which allows the company to effectively implement SEAAR processes and meet stakeholder needs. In fact, the main objective of the standard is to involve the interested parties. Only by building solid relationships with the stakeholders it is possible to define shared social and ethical objectives, improve the organization's capacity to respond by enhancing its corporate performance and thus contributing to sustainability.

In 2002 AccountAbility launched the new AA1000 Series, consisting of the AA1000 Framework and a set of specialized modules. The first module is the AA1000 Assurance Standard, issued on March 25, 2003 (AccountAbility, 2003)[1] and now under revision. The second edition should be published by October 2008. The second module is the AA1000 Stakeholder Engagement Standard, issued on September 1, 2005. The second edition of this document should be developed during 2008.

SA8000, THE NEW STANDARD FOR ETHICAL SOURCING

The *Council on Economic Priorities Accreditation Agency* (CEPAA)[2] has promoted the development of *Social Accountability 8000* (SA8000), a system which protects workers' rights by defining a set of auditable standards for a third-party verification. The CEPAA is an organization set up at the beginning of 1997 by the *Council on Economic Priorities* (CEP), one of the first institutions to deal with the issue of CSR. The CEPAA immediately set up an Advisory Board, which helped the agency draw up SA8000. This Board was originally made up of representatives from Non-Government Organizations (NGOs) such as Amnesty International and the Abrinq Foundation for Children's Rights (Brazil), consulting companies, auditing and certification bodies such as KPMG and SGS-International Certification Services, companies such as Avon, The Body Shop, Toys 'R' Us, Otto-Versand and Reebok, distribution companies, trade unions and universities, and so on. The SA8000 standard was officially launched on 15 October, 1997. A revised version was issued at the end of 2001 and the third edition is underway. Based on the International Labour Organization Conventions and other documents such as the Universal Declaration of Human Rights and the UN Convention on the Rights of the Child, SA8000 is a standard for companies, which aims to guarantee fundamental workers' rights. It is specific enough to be used to audit companies and suppliers in the same way

---

1   For further information see the website of AccountAbility, http://www.accountability21.net/.

2   *Social Accountability International* (SAI) is the new name adopted by the CEPAA in the summer of 2000.

in different sectors and countries. SA8000 represents a significant innovation since it is the first social standard whose application can be controlled by independent third parties. SA8000 basically provides a reference framework to control the ethical conditions of the production of all the goods manufactured by companies of all sizes throughout the world. This standard represents an important opportunity for companies to demonstrate their commitment to carrying out processes and products in a really ethical way. As of 30 June, 2007, the number of SA8000 certified organizations throughout the world (64 countries) totalled 1,373, with 626 facilities certified (45.59 per cent of total) in Italy. The first company to be certified in Europe against the standard was Coop Italia, the national consortium that carries out purchasing, marketing and quality control activities for the entire Coop system, the largest Italian retail chain, with a 17.1 per cent market share in the grocery market. Other certified organizations are: Avon Products (Suffern, New York) with the first site to be certified in the world, many Indian (217) and Chinese (159) factories especially producing toys, sportswear and sneakers, Celtipharm (France), Hoechst Marion (Turkey), Honda Logistic (Italy), and so on. The certified companies which meet the required standards are entitled to display the *SA8000 Certification Mark*. The certification is valid for three years with audits carried out every six months.

GBS PROPOSAL

Il Gruppo di studio per il Bilancio Sociale (the Study Group for Social Reporting)[3], also called GBS, held its first meeting on 15 October, 1998 in Milan. Many Italian universities, research institutes and consulting firms participate in GBS activities. In April 2001 GBS published the *Social Reporting Standards*.

According to the GBS proposal the Social Report has the following objectives:

- to provide all stakeholders with a comprehensive picture of the company's performance, establishing an interactive social communication process;
- to provide relevant information on the company's operations in order to broaden and improve stakeholders' awareness and ability to evaluate and make choices, also from an ethical-social standpoint (Gruppo per il Bilancio Sociale, 2001, 13).

Furthermore, the social reporting processes must comply with the following principles in order to ensure its quality: responsibility, identification, transparency, inclusivity, consistency, neutrality, accrual basis, conservatism, comparability, meaningfulness, clarity and intelligibility, verifiability of the information, reliability and true and fair presentation, third-party independence.

Finally, the social report is composed of the following three elements:

- the *corporate identity*, which comprises corporate structure, ethical values, mission, strategies and policies;
- the *creation and allocation of value-added*;
- the *social account*, which provides a broad picture of the outcomes achieved by the company through the implemented strategies and policies, and of the impacts

---

3   For further information, see http://www.bilanciosociale.it/gbs.html and the website of GBS, http://www. gruppobilanciosociale.org.

generated by its behaviour on the different stakeholder groups in relation to the adopted commitments.

In Italy, the GBS model is a point of reference for social reporting and it has been applied by private and public organizations.

Corporate Environmental Performance Evaluation and Reporting

CORPORATE ENVIRONMENTAL REPORTING

In general, the corporate *Environmental Report* is a tool a company uses to manage and control corporate activities and support communication with the stakeholders, especially those interested in environmental issues (Azzone et al., 1997). These groups include the following: employees and collaborators; clients/consumers; suppliers; local and/or national communities; the State, local bodies and the public administration; the mass media; special interested parties (consumer associations, environmental groups, and so on); banks; insurance companies; investors (individual shareholders, institutional investors, and so on). The perceived environmental risk of a company's activities can, in fact, influence the stakeholder attitude (either positively or negatively) towards the company. A careful communication strategy must, therefore, make the stakeholders aware of the degree of eco-compatibility of production processes and products and provide reliable and understandable information related to the company's current and future plans with regard to the environmental protection activities. In this sense, the environmental report, meaning the information system, which controls the company's ecological performance, has come to play a crucial and necessary role.

Drawn up mainly on a voluntary basis, the environmental report reflects the specific corporate, economic, legal and social context in which it developed. The first environmental reports were drawn up by research centres and companies in Germany, the Scandinavian and Anglo-Saxon countries in the late 1980s and coincided with the public's growing awareness of the importance of environmental issues. Subsequently, this tool began to be commonly used even in the less aware countries from the ecological point of view.

Due to the wide variety of methods and content and the complexity of the issue, a definitive and generally acceptable model of corporate environmental report is still not available. Therefore, there is no homogeneity among the data obtained by different companies and comparisons are very difficult. Because of this, many organizations[4] have drawn up guidelines for environmental reporting in order to help companies implement environmental accountability schemes. There are, however, at least two environmental reporting schemes worth analyzing in greater detail since they present important and interesting features: the framework of the Eni Enrico Mattei Foundation (Box 24.1); the IÖW framework (Box 24.2).

---

4   Some of these are: CEFIC-European Chemical Industry Council; CERES-Coalition for Environmentally Responsible Economies; GEMI-Global Environmental Management Initiative; PERI-Public Environmental Reporting Initiative; UNEP-United Nations Environment Program; WBCSD-World Business Council for Sustainable Development.

BOX 24.1   THE ENI ENRICO MATTEI FOUNDATION FRAMEWORK[a]

The Eni Enrico Mattei Foundation (FEEM), a research institute, which studies issues related to environment, energy and economic development, has defined a model of environmental report, which can be a useful management and information tool. The aim is to support companies through a reference framework which improves on the partial approaches adopted in the past and provides concrete information to help firms communicate better and make the right decisions regarding environmental management. The model suggested calls for building a complete accounting system which includes physical indicators and monetary measurements of the costs incurred to reduce or prevent pollution. The FEEM corporate environmental report is divided into three separate accounts: the resources account (input); the pollutants account (output); the environmental expenditure account. The model therefore consists of an input-output analysis together with the environmental expenditure. In this way, the environmental report becomes an intelligent container of environmental information since it adopts precise methods to gather and organize the basic data, which are fundamental for each subsequent elaboration. Since 1994, the Eni group has used this model to draw up its environmental reports.

[a] *Source*: Bartolomeo et al. (1995).

BOX 24.2   THE IÖW FRAMEWORK[a]

Between the autumn of 1987 and 1988 the Nordrhein-Westfalen region commissioned the Institut für Ökologische Wirtschaftsforschung (IÖW), in conjunction with Umwelt-future, (a German association of entrepreneurs) to develop and implement a new model of corporate environmental report. For this purpose, the Tecklenburg plant of the Bischof & Klein Company, which produces flexible packaging, was chosen. In 1987 the company employed over 2,000 workers and had a turnover in Germany of 400 million marks. The Tecklenberg plant employed 80 workers and manufactured bags and containers. The environmental reporting system developed by the IÖW (called *ecobalancing*) is made up of four elements: (1) corporate ecobalance or input-output analysis; (2) process ecobalances; (3) product ecobalances; (4) site assessment. The first element of the German model is the typical input-output analysis also found in the FEEM scheme, which considers the company or the plant analyzed as a kind of black box. The process ecobalances aim to audit the environmental impact related to the internal functioning of the black box not examined in the preceding phase. The production processes are subsequently subdivided according to criteria of space and time and inherent to the product. Each process thus identified is then analyzed by using a specific input-output matrix of the materials and energy flows. The product ecobalances coincide with the LCA (*Life Cycle Assessment*) of the company's main products and the site assessment represents a register of all the ecologically relevant aspects not included in the previous phases (need for reclaiming some sites, use of land, modifications in the landscape, and so on). In the German-speaking countries, the IÖW framework is considered a reference scheme used to draw up ecobalances and has been applied by many companies such as AEG Hausgeräte, (purchased by Electrolux in 1994), the Kunert textile company (the first German company to publish a complete environmental report in 1991), Siemens, Volkswagen, Allianz Versicherung, Sanyo and Novartis.

[a] *Source*: Hallay (1990); Hallay and Pfriem (1992).

ENVIRONMENTAL MANAGEMENT SYSTEMS

In the 1990s public opinion and companies became aware of the importance of environmental issues. As environmental awareness increased and companies began to include this variable in their corporate policies, standards to regulate environmental management systems were developed. In March 1992 the British Standards Institution (BSI) published the first environmental management systems' standard, which shares the same management principles as BS 5750 (subsequently replaced by the BS EN ISO 9001 standard) on quality assurance systems and represents a direct outgrowth in the area of environmental protection. The BS 7750 was tested over a two-year period and involved at least 500 participants including 230 companies. On the basis of the results obtained during this phase and the content of the new EMAS regulation, the modified and definitive version of BS 7750 was issued in January 1994. On June 29, 1993, the Council of the European Communities adopted the EEC Regulation No. 1836/93 allowing voluntary participation by companies in the industrial sector in a Community eco-management and audit scheme (EMAS). It was published on July 10, 1993, in the *Official Journal of the European Communities* and came into force in April 1995. As the first article of the regulation clearly underlines, EMAS is established for the evaluation and improvement of the environmental performance of industrial activities and the provision of relevant information to the public. EMAS aims to promote continuous improvements in the environmental performance of industrial activities by: the establishment and implementation of environmental policies, programmes and management systems by companies, in relation to their sites; the systematic, objective and periodic evaluation of the performance of such elements; the provision of information of environmental performance to the public through the environmental statement.

Many parts of the EMAS regulation coincide with BS 7750 and this demonstrates the influence the 1992 version of the British standard had on the new European regulation. In fact, at that time, the BS 7750 specification was the only tool which regulated environmental management systems. Only in September 1996, the standard ISO 14001:1996 Environmental Management Systems – Specification with guidance for use was published. It was largely based on the BS 7750 approach. In November 2004 the revised edition of ISO 14001 was issued.

Following a revision based on the experience acquired during the first five years it was applied, on 19 March, 2001 the European Parliament and the Council of the European Union adopted the EC Regulation No. 761/2001 allowing voluntary participation by organizations in a Community eco-management and audit scheme (EMAS II). The regulation came into force on April 27, 2001, and replaced the previous regulation. The main elements of the revised EMAS regulation are as follows: it applies to organizations; the adoption of ISO 14001 as the specification for the Environmental Management Systems Requirements; the promotion of organizations' participation, in particular of small- and medium-sized enterprises (SMEs); the strengthening of the role of the environmental statement to improve the transparency of communication of environmental performance between registered organizations and their relevant interested parties and the public. EMAS, therefore, is no longer exclusively applied to industrial sites but to all types of organizations according to the ISO 14001 standard. Moreover, the greater integration between EMAS and ISO 14001 makes it possible to better coordinate the European regulation and the international standard.

The advantages a company can obtain by introducing a management system, especially one which integrates quality, health, safety and environment (the Integrated Management System, IMS), are of an organizational, managerial and economic nature. The advantages include the following: clear and coherent definition of responsibilities and operating procedures; elimination of inefficient duplications and overlapping from the organizational point of view; one single file of records; full value given to in-company competence; improved evaluation of corporate risk profile and performance; better analysis, control and evaluation methods; better management of relationships with the different stakeholders; reinforcement of corporate image; greater compliance with regulatory standards; easier access to financial and insurance markets; reduction in management costs including auditing costs; more efficient use of raw materials and resources; fewer serious occupational accidents; fewer criminal lawsuits; minimizing hidden losses and liabilities. In short, management systems (and the related standards) are performance indicators since they point out companies which are active from the managerial viewpoint and pay close attention to developing and maintaining correct relationships with stakeholders. Moreover, they are tools for corporate performance measurement and evaluation since setting objectives and targets, which companies have to achieve, is part of them. Corporate performance is subsequently controlled through auditing procedures.

In more detail, ISO has issued other two standards related to environmental performance evaluation and reporting thanks to the efforts carried out by ISO Technical Committee ISO/TC 207 on 'Environmental Management':

- ISO 14031:1999, which provides guidance on environmental performance evaluation.
- ISO 14063:2006, which gives guidance on general principles, policy, strategy and activities related to both internal and external environmental communication.

Corporate Sustainability Performance Evaluation and Reporting

GLOBAL REPORTING INITIATIVE

The Global Reporting Initiative (GRI) is an international, long-term, multi-stakeholder project designed to develop, promote and disseminate a common framework for voluntary reporting of the economic, environmental and social performance of an organization (its activities, products and services). The *Sustainability Reporting Guidelines* provide this framework.

GRI is the result of a process begun in the autumn of 1997, which aimed to develop an international framework for environmental reporting. During the first meetings held at the beginning of 1998, GRI expanded its scope and decided to focus on defining guidelines for sustainability reporting, including not just environmental factors but economic and social ones according to the triple bottom line approach. In partnership with UNEP the GRI network includes the active participation of companies, entrepreneurs' associations, workers' associations, research institutes, universities, government representatives, NGOs, consulting firms, rating agencies, auditing firms and associations of chartered accountants. A provisional version of the Sustainability Reporting Guidelines was published in 1999.

After being tested in some companies, the revised, final version was issued in June 2000. For each dimension of sustainability (environmental, economic, social) the Guidelines include categories, aspects and indicators. After the guidelines were applied in an increasing number of companies,[5] in April 2002 a draft document containing the 2002 Sustainability Reporting Guidelines was released. The process of stakeholder consulting ended on 26 May and during the Johannesburg Summit the new guidelines were issued (Global Reporting Initiative, 2002). In the 2002 version, the performance indicators were revised, reorganized and integrated especially as regards the economic category and social ones (*labour practices and decent work, human rights, society* and *product responsibility*). In January 2006 the draft version of the *G3 Sustainability Reporting Guidelines* was issued for public comment (Global Reporting Initiative, 2006). After this engagement process, during the first Amsterdam Global Conference on Sustainability and Transparency, held from October 4 to 6, 2006, the new *G3 Guidelines* were officially presented and released. This third edition of the Sustainability Reporting Guidelines is characterized by a greater attention to the management approaches developed and adopted by a company to address the economic, environmental and social issues.

The guidelines represent an excellent tool to initiate a process, which will integrate economic, social and environmental reporting. In fact, they provide indicators to measure the performance of the organization in the three areas of sustainability and help enterprises draw up specific integrated indicators (*ratio indicators*). The GRI guidelines therefore provide an interesting *sustainability report* framework. Following the *social report* and the *environmental report* it represents the third phase in the development of control and reporting systems, which measure a company's corporate social and environmental performance.

BALANCED SCORECARD

Proposed by Kaplan and Norton in 1992, the *balanced scorecard* is a balanced measurement and management system, which evaluates corporate performance through a set of measures built around four perspectives: financial; customer; internal business processes; learning and growth (Kaplan and Norton, 1992; 1996). The balanced scorecard is a multi-dimensional model to monitor corporate performance. It aims to overcome the limitations of the traditional economic and financial measurements and integrate them with indicators of a quantitative and technical nature. This tool, thus, makes it possible to describe and explain what has to be measured in order to assess the effectiveness of strategies (Parker, 2000). These indicators furnish a balanced picture of the corporate dynamics since they also check the development of corporate competences and *intangible assets* (like the trust-based relationships with consumers) essential for the company's continual success. The balanced scorecard is a very important performance measurement

---

5   As of December 2007, more than 1,000 organizations from more than 50 countries adhered to the Guidelines including: Acea, Aéroports de Paris, AstraZeneca, AT&T, BASF, Baxter International, BC Hydro, Body Shop International, Bristol-Myers Squibb, British Airways, Buzzi Unicem, BT, Cable and Wireless, Canon, Chiquita Brands, Co-operative Bank, Cosmo Oil, Daikin, Danone, Enel, Eni, Electrolux, Fiat, Ford Motor Company, Fuji Xerox, General Motors, Henkel, Indesit Company, ING, Johnson&Johnson, J. Sainsbury, KLM, Matsushita Electric Group, McDonald's, Motorola, NEC, Nike, Nissan, Nokia, Novo Group, NTT, Pioneer Group, Polaroid, Procter & Gamble, Saint-Gobain, Shell International, South African Breweries, STMicroelectronics, Telecom Italia, Thames Water, Van City Savings Credit Union, UniCredito Italiano, Unipol Assicurazioni, Volkswagen, Volvo Car Corporation, Waste Recycling Group. For further information see the website of GRI, http://www.globalreporting.org.

methodology, which has been widely used by companies. However, the fact that it is not always applied properly has raised doubts as to whether the managerial tool is really effective. Moreover, Kaplan and Norton themselves proceeded to revise the system and drew up a *balanced scorecard strategy map* (Kaplan and Norton, 2000; 2004). In any case, due to its multi-dimensional features and flexibility, this evaluation system can also be oriented to control the sustainability performance of an organization through the introduction of elements of sustainability according to the triple bottom line approach. The *balanced scorecard* is therefore important for sustainability since it can be constructed to include economic-financial, social and environmental indicators in an organic way so that the real performance of an organization can be more closely evaluated.

SIGMA PROJECT

If companies have to contribute to achieving overall sustainability by modifying their policies and behaviours, management tools must be developed to help companies achieve this objective. The UK Sustainable Development Strategy called for a Government commitment to sponsor the creation of a *sustainability management system*. Thanks to the support and involvement of the Department of Trade and Industry, the Department of the Environment, Transport and the Regions, the SIGMA Project[6] (*Sustainability: Integrated Guidelines for Management*) was launched in July 1999. It aims to create a *strategic management framework for sustainability*, namely, a set of instruments and requirements for sustainable management, which might serve as an international reference standard. The pilot version of the *SIGMA Guidelines* was presented on May 31, 2001, and was available on the Internet until May 31, 2002, so that the interested parties could evaluate it. The new SIGMA Guidelines were launched on September 23, 2003. The Sigma Guidelines include (The SIGMA Project, 2003): (i) a set of Guiding Principles to help organizations understand and deal with the elements linked to sustainability. These Principles consist of two core elements: 1. The holistic management of five kinds of capital (Natural Capital, Social Capital, Human Capital, Manufactured Capital and Financial Capital) that reflect an organization's overall impact and wealth. 2. The exercise of *accountability*, by being transparent and responsive to stakeholders and complying with relevant rules and standards; (ii) a *management framework* which integrates sustainability into core processes and mainstream decision-making. It is basically a management system for sustainability which follows the traditional *Plan, Do, Check, Act* pattern; (iii) a series of instruments and approaches the organizations can use to implement effective strategies, initiate a cultural change, promote learning and reach their objectives. The *SIGMA Toolkit* includes well-known instruments like *benchmarking*, the balanced scorecard applied to sustainability (*sustainability scorecard*), environmental accounting, *stakeholder engagement* and the GRI guidelines. The Sigma Guidelines therefore represent an important effort to organize and synthesize all the best management proposals. The aim is to obtain a framework, which is really integrated, and goes beyond the partial approaches of the individual standards regarding quality (economic performance), safety (social performance) and the environment, and develops a new management paradigm.

---

6   The project resulted of a partnership between organizations with different expertise: BSI; AccountAbility; Forum for the Future.

This impressive contribution was used as the reference framework for the BS 8900 standard, which is a guidance for managing sustainable development and was issued by the British Standards Institution on May 31, 2006.[7]

Q-RES PROJECT

The Q-RES Project was conceived in September 1999 and launched in 2000 by CELE, the Centre for Ethics, Law & Economics of the LIUC University in Italy. It aims to develop *a management framework for the social and ethical responsibility* (RES) of corporations, based on the idea of the social contract between the firm and its stakeholders, by defining a new type of quality standard, externally certifiable.

The Q-RES model consists of an integrated and complete set of tools to introduce ethics into companies. It also defines excellence criteria in the management of social and ethical responsibility, taking into consideration emerging international standards and current best practices. The Q-RES management model includes six tools for managing the social and ethical quality of corporations (Q-RES, 2002 and 2004; Commission of the European Communities, 2004):

1. *Corporate ethical vision*: it defines and makes explicit the concept of justice of the company, from which the criterion to balance stakeholders' claims derives. The responsible behaviour that the company has to comply with in the relations with stakeholders is based on that concept of justice. The ethical vision expresses the concept of a social contract between the company and its stakeholders.
2. *Code of ethics*: it is the main tool to implement social and ethical responsibility within a business organization. Its function goes beyond the legal regulation.
3. *Ethical training and communication*: ethical training in a company is directed to the company employees and aims at enabling each organization member to apply moral reasoning tools to address ethical questions connected to corporate activities.
4. *Organizational systems of implementation and internal control:* they are the *ethical infrastructure* which is needed to support an effective implementation of corporate social and ethical responsibility.
5. *Social and ethical accountability:* the process of social and ethical accountability aims at broadening the perspective of corporate social communications from the relations between the firm and its shareholders to the relations among the company and all its stakeholders, in the social contract perspective.
6. *External verification:* it is the activity whereby a third party checks the consistency between the social and ethical responsibility tools adopted by the company and the excellence criteria defined by Q-RES. Therefore, external verification/certification provides trustworthiness to the company's declarations concerning its commitments on social and ethical responsibility.

Some Italian companies, professional associations, consulting firms and business organizations participate in the project through the Q-RES working Table. In Europe, a

---

7   For further information, see http://www.bsi-global.com/en/Standards-and-Publications/Industry-Sectors/Environment/more-products/BS-89002006-/.

constructive dialogue has been established with similar initiatives (such as The SIGMA Project in the UK and the ValuesManagementSystem in Germany) (Q-RES, 2005).

UNITED NATIONS GLOBAL COMPACT

In order to promote the idea of corporate citizenship and socially responsible behaviour, at the World Economic Forum in Davos on January 31, 1999, United Nations Secretary-General Kofi Annan challenged world business leaders to embrace and enact a Global Compact of shared values and principles in the areas of human rights, labour and the environment.[8] From an operational point of view, the initiative was launched on July 26, 2000, during a meeting at the UN headquarters in New York with the participation of leaders from business, labour organizations and civil groups.

The Global Compact is a voluntary initiative, open to the participation of companies and to the involvement of labour, human rights, environmental, development and academic organizations. It encompasses ten principles, drawn from the Universal Declaration of Human Rights, the ILO Declaration on Fundamental Principles and Rights at Work, the Rio Declaration on Environment and Development and The United Nations Convention against Corruption. If a company decides to participate in this initiative, the Global Compact asks that firms act on these principles in the fields of human rights, labour standards, the environment and anti-corruption in its own corporate domain. Moreover, the company commits itself to produce an annual Communication on Progress (COP) that the organization has made in implementing the ten principles in its business activities (United Nations Global Compact, 2007). Thus, the Compact promotes good practices by firms; it does not endorse companies. Some of the most important firms in the world are among the participating companies. They include ABB, Sanofi-Aventis, BASF, Bayer, BP, BT, Cisco Systems, Credit Suisse Group, Daimler, Deloitte Touche Tohmatsu, Deutsche Bank, Deutsche Telekom, DuPont, Enel, Eni, France Telecom, Ketchum, Nike, Novartis International, Rio Tinto, Royal Dutch Shell, SAP, Statoil, ST Microelectronics, Storebrand, Telecom Italia, UBS, Unilever and Volvo.

ISO 26000

The ISO 26000 process, started in March 2005 at the first World Meeting in Salvador, should be completed by 2010. The international standard that will be issued will provide Guidance on Social Responsibility to support not only the companies but all the organizations (including public authorities and NGOs) to address and manage social issues.

ISO 26000 is not a management system standard and is not intended for third-party certification. This is a radical innovation in the ISO panorama and points out how the social responsibility is increasingly recognized as a strategic perspective that cannot be reduced to a single managerial tool.

The drafting of the standard is still underway but the available documents confirm that accountability, transparency and stakeholder engagement are among the cross-cutting and characterizing principles. Therefore, also the reporting/communicating

---

8   Later an anti-corruption dimension was added.

activities of socially committed organizations will be comprised in this voluntary, and not legally binding, standard.

SUSTAINABILITY EVALUATION AND REPORTING SYSTEM (SERS)

As pointed out in the previous sections, in around 20 years many social and environmental standards and management solutions were developed and their number has been constantly increasing. This multiplicity, complexity and the absence of a clear reference framework generate undesired effects among companies and their own stakeholders (Italian Ministry of Labour and Social Affairs, 2003):

- confusion for companies and lack of management and organizational innovation;
- confusion and lack of clarity for the companies' stakeholders.

Thus, there is strong need for a clear and modular framework for a corporate sustainability performance evaluation and reporting system. This methodology should 'go beyond previous work on the "triple bottom line" and "balanced scorecard"' (Post et al., 2002, 25) in order to take into account, in an explicit and complete way, the different relationships which companies develop with their stakeholders.

With reference to the balanced scorecard, Paine (2003, 120) points out that some non-financial variables are important on their own terms and not only as means to financial ends and underlines that they may be critical success factors: 'Therefore, managers must care about them for the same reason they care about financial performance – because they are intrinsically important and part of what is expected of leading companies today... This expanded conception of corporate performance is implicit in the calls for corporate accountability that have become commonplace in recent decades...'. With regard to the triple bottom line, according to Elkington (2004, 16) '... the TBL agenda as most people would currently understand it is only the beginning. A much more comprehensive approach will be needed that involves a wide range of stakeholders...'. And the Global Reporting Initiative (2002, 9) adds, '... like any simplification of a complex challenge, this definition has its limitations... Defining sustainability in terms of three separate elements (economic, environmental, and social) can sometimes lead to thinking about each element in isolation rather than in an integrated manner'.

Therefore, it is crucial to work on managerial tools capable of monitoring and tracking, qualitatively and quantitatively, the overall corporate performance according to a stakeholder view of the firm (Clarkson, 1995; Post and Preston, 1995) and based on a flexible structure suitable for companies of different industries, sizes and countries.

On this topic a proposal – the *Sustainability Evaluation and Reporting System, SERS* – has been defined by SPACE (the Research Centre of Bocconi University on Risk, Security, Occupational Health and Safety, Environment and Crisis Management). This integrated approach derives from theoretical analyses and experiences that span more than 15 years of research into the management of sustainability and the evaluation of and reporting on social, environmental and sustainability performance in collaboration with companies and institutions (Perrini et al., 2006; Perrini and Tencati, 2007).

The SERS proposal aims to aggregate different management tools (for example, social reporting, environmental reporting and Key Performance Indicators (KPIs)) into a comprehensive model. The goal is to build an efficient and effective methodology for an overall assessment of corporate sustainability in order to support new accounting and reporting efforts (with a particular focus on SMEs), integrate financial and non-financial performance measures, improve the quality of decision-making processes and of the overall business management and strengthen corporate accountability and responsiveness towards the different stakeholder groups.

The SERS framework is composed of three modules (Figure 24.1):

- the Overall Reporting System (or the Sustainability Reporting System) which comprises:
  - the Annual Report;
  - the Social Report;
  - the Environmental Report;
  - a Set of Integrated Performance Indicators.
- the Integrated Information System;
- the KPIs for Corporate Sustainability.

The three modules have the following main characteristics:

- The *Overall Reporting System* is composed of the annual report, that comprises the profit and loss account, the balance sheet and the statement of cash flows; the social report, that includes the ethical policy, the value-added statement and the analysis of stakeholder relationships; the environmental report, that comprises energy and materials accounting and monetary environmental accounting. The Sustainability Reporting System allows a company to check and report its annual overall corporate performance. Its goal is to build a true and fair view of the business situation to

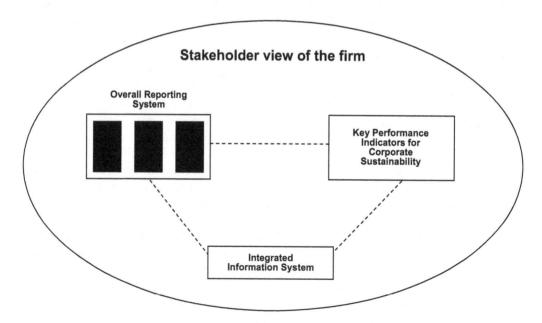

Figure 24.1 The Sustainability Evaluation and Reporting System (SERS)[a]

[a] *Source*: Perrini and Tencati (2007).

strengthen, improve and manage stakeholder relationships in a sustainable way. It is fundamental to the information needs of different stakeholder groups and corporate social accountability. Thus, in order to achieve a more complete picture of its behaviour, a company should also define and present a set of *integrated performance indicators,* that is, *cross-cutting indicators* (Global Reporting Initiative, 2002, 45 and 82-84). In general, cross-cutting indicators relate physical and technical quantities to financial ones (for example, an indicator could relate the total amount of waste generated during the year to the value added).

- The *Integrated Information System* is the core of performance evaluation and reporting processes. Based on the new ICT solutions, such as the Enterprise Resource Planning (ERP) systems, it enables an organization to collect, process and share physical/technical and financial data. Programmes to introduce environmental and social accounting systems to integrate and improve existing financial and cost accounting methodologies have to start from this level. The goal is to build a satellite accounting system (United Nations, 1993; United Nations et al., 2003) focused on social and environmental performance, capable of collecting and organizing all the relevant data (including financial) and connected with the other specific accounting/information systems.

- The *Key Performance Indicators for Corporate Sustainability* are specific indicators developed according to the corporate information requirements. The aim is to provide a tool to continually monitor an organization's performance trends. Number and types of measures should be defined on the basis of the real corporate needs. The KPIs thus represent a *Dashboard of Sustainability* (International Institute for Sustainable Development, 2001) supporting management decision-making processes. Sets of indicators proposed by many organizations, such as the Global Reporting Initiative (2002 and 2006), the World Business Council for Sustainable Development (2000 and 2003), Eurostat (2001a, 2001b and 2005) and European Environment Agency (2002 and 2003), can be used to draw up an organization's specific measurements, but they cannot limit its choices: every firm should build its own, specific set of indicators capable of providing the necessary information in order to support business management in an effective way. Indicators can focus on the financial, operating, marketing, environmental, social, cross-cutting aspects of business management. KPIs are also used in the Overall Reporting System, and in order to define them the company should carry on stakeholder engagement activities.

KPIs are the crucial element of the SERS methodology. SMEs would not have sufficient time and resources to define a long and complicated Sustainability Reporting System. But this kind of firm certainly needs a map for an ongoing assessment of its performance and of the related quality (that is, degree of sustainability) of the relationships with stakeholders. This map is really provided by a set of KPIs. And this consistent and clear dashboard of sustainability could also be used to communicate the information required by the different stakeholder groups. Therefore, this set of indicators must be the result of a process of stakeholder engagement, involving the different constituencies in the KPIs' definition. Moreover, in line with the adopted stakeholder view of the firm, the KPIs should be organized according to a stakeholder framework (Box 24.3).

BOX 24.3   THE ITALIAN CSR-SC PROJECT

One of the most important initiatives carried on during the last years in Italy in the CSR field was the Project called *Corporate Social Responsibility-Social Commitment* (CSR-SC), launched by the Italian Ministry of Labour and Social Affairs in June 2002. Bocconi University was involved in the Project by the Italian Ministry as a technical partner. The main aims that the CSR-SC Project pursued were as follows:

- promoting CSR culture among companies;
- defining a simple and modular tool that firms can adopt on voluntary basis in order to identify socially responsible behaviour;
- proposing a list of relevant performance indicators to measure the social performance of companies;
- guaranteeing citizens that the reporting of corporate social commitment by companies is true and not misleading.

Common elements of the proposal presented during the Third European Conference on Corporate Social Responsibility held in Venice on November 14, 2003, are the following:

- voluntary approach;
- corporate self-assessment:
- no traditional certification mechanisms;
- a set of performance indicators.

In particular, a set of performance indicators and a system of guidelines were provided in order to support companies in the self-assessment of their own social performance and in the reporting activities through an innovative tool called Social Statement. The Ministry of Labour and Social Affairs' proposal organizes the indicators according to a three-level framework (Global Reporting Initiative, 2002, 36-37):

- categories: stakeholder groups which are specifically affected by clusters of indicators;
- aspects: thematic areas monitored by groups of performance indicators related to a given category of stakeholders;
- indicators: measurements that supply information related to a given aspect. They can be used to check and demonstrate organizational performance. The information can be qualitative, quantitative (physical and technical) or economic-monetary.

The stakeholder categories identified are the following:

- human resources;
- members/shareholders, financial community;
- clients/customers;
- suppliers;
- financial partners;
- State, local authorities and public administration;
- community;
- environment.

The indicators were identified also through a broad stakeholder engagement process especially thanks to the establishment of a National CSR Multi-Stakeholder Forum called CSR Forum.

Source: Tencati et al., 2004; Perrini et al., 2006.

In conclusion, SERS goals are:

- to aggregate different management tools (for example, social reporting, environmental reporting and KPIs) into a comprehensive model – methodological integration;
- to supply information, which can be qualitative, quantitative (physical and technical) and economic-monetary, through the performance measurements – integration of data/information. These indicators build a sort of dashboard of sustainability, that is, an effective *Tableau de Bord*, which goes beyond the traditional financial data;
- to map and monitor the entire set of a company's stakeholder relationships – integration of different perspectives into the sustainability accounting system towards a *multiple bottom line* approach.

In this way, the SERS methodology enables a company and its management to manage stakeholder relationships and address the information needs and the economic, social and environmental concerns of various stakeholder groups. This point is crucial for every kind of firm and especially for SMEs, whose success is deeply rooted in stakeholder networks.

Moreover the SERS structure, composed of different modules (the Overall Reporting System, the Integrated Information System and the KPIs), is flexible enough to be used by businesses of different sizes operating in different sectors and countries.

However, further steps in the field of sustainability evaluation and reporting systems are expected: if stakeholder relationships are essential to the creation of sustainable wealth, not only the company-centred, but also the stakeholder-centred performance should be measured. In other words, for example, the degree of stakeholder trust and the stakeholder satisfaction generated by the corporate strategy and behaviour should be carefully evaluated (Ghoshal and Bartlett, 1999; Lev, 2001; Castaldo, 2007). This calls for the development of further methodologies that could broaden the available set of measures, but also problematize the use of specific performance indicators.

Therefore, if we adopt a stakeholder view of the firm to design sustainability accounting systems, we should also understand how the stakeholder relationships and the related engagement processes could impact the quantity and quality of indicators aimed at monitoring the corporate performance. This perspective could dramatically change the way managers and stakeholders assess firms, their success and their role in society.

REFERENCES

Abt, C.C. 1977. *The Social Audit for Management*. Amacom: New York.

AccountAbility (ISEA, Institute of Social and Ethical AccountAbility). 1999. *AccountAbility 1000 (AA1000) Framework: Standard, Guidelines and Professional Qualification*. AccountAbility: London. http://www.accountability.org.uk [August 24, 2005].

AccountAbility (ISEA, Institute of Social and Ethical AccountAbility). 2003. *AA1000 Assurance Standard*. AccountAbility: London. http://www.accountability.org.uk [February 10, 2008].

AccountAbility (ISEA, Institute of Social and Ethical AccountAbility). 2005. *AA1000 Stakeholder Engagement Standard. Exposure Draft*. AccountAbility: London. http://www.accountability.org.uk [November 14, 2005].

Azzone, G., Brophy, M., Noci, G., Welford, R., Young, W. 1997. A stakeholders' view of environmental reporting. *Long Range Planning* 30(5): 699-709.

Bartolomeo, M., Malaman, R., Pavan, M., Sammarco, G. 1995. *Il Bilancio Ambientale D'Impresa*. Il Sole 24 Ore Pirola: Milan.

Beck, M. (Ed.). 1993. *Ökobilanzierung im Betrieblichen Management*. Vogel Buchverlag: Würzburg.

Bennett, M., James, P. 1999. Key themes in environmental, social and sustainability performance evaluation and reporting. In M. Bennett, P. James (Eds). *Sustainable Measures. Evaluation and Reporting of Environmental and Social Performance*: 29-74. Greenleaf Publishing: Sheffield.

Bonal, J. 1982. Il bilancio sociale dell'impresa. In P. Schmidt Di Friedberg (Ed.). *L'impresa e l'ambiente*. Etas Libri: Milan.

Brophy, M., Starkey, R. 1996. Environmental reporting. In R. Welford (Ed.). *Corporate Environmental Management*. 177-198. Earthscan: London.

Bundesumweltministerium, Umweltbundesamt (Eds). 1995. *Handbuch Umweltcontrolling*. Verlag Franz Vahlen: Munich.

Burritt, R.L., Hahn, T., Schaltegger, S. 2002. Towards a comprehensive framework for environmental management accounting – Links between business actors and environmental management accounting tools. *Australian Accounting Review* 12(2): 39-50.

Castaldo, S. (Ed.). 2007. *Trust in Market Relationships*. Edward Elgar Publishing: Cheltenham.

Clarkson, M.B.E. 1995. A stakeholder framework for analyzing and evaluating corporate social performance. *Academy of Management Review* 20(1): 92-117.

Commission of the European Communities. Directorate-General for Employment and Social Affairs. 2004. *ABC of the main instruments of Corporate Social Responsibility*. http://europa.eu.int/comm/employment_social/soc-dial/csr/csr_abc.pdf [February 6, 2006].

Elkington, J. 1994. Towards the sustainable corporation: win-win-win business strategies for sustainable development. *California Management Review* 36(2): 90-100.

Elkington, J. 2004. Enter the triple bottom line. In A. Henriques, J. Richardson (Eds). *The Triple Bottom Line: Does it All Add Up? Assessing the Sustainability of Business and CSR*. 1-16. Earthscan: London.

European Environment Agency (EEA). 2002. *Environmental signals 2002. Benchmarking the Millennium*. Office for Official Publications of the European Communities: Luxembourg.

European Environment Agency (EEA). 2003. *Europe's Environment: The Third Assessment*. Office for Official Publications of the European Communities: Luxembourg.

Eurostat. 2001a. *Environmental Pressure Indicators for the EU*. Office for Official Publications of the European Communities: Luxembourg.

Eurostat. 2001b. *Measuring Progress Towards a More Sustainable Europe*. Office for Official Publications of the European Communities: Luxembourg.

Eurostat. 2005. *Sustainable Development Indicators*. http://epp.eurostat.cec.eu.int [June 2, 2005].

Figge, F., Hahn, T., Schaltegger, S., Wagner, M. 2002. The sustainability balanced scorecard – Linking sustainability management to business strategy. *Business Strategy and the Environment* 11(5): 269-284.

Ghoshal, S., Bartlett, C.A. 1999. *The Individualized Corporation: A Fundamentally New Approach to Management*. HarperBusiness: New York.

Global Reporting Initiative (GRI). 2002. *2002 Sustainability Reporting Guidelines*. Global Reporting Initiative: Boston. http://www.globalreporting.org [September 10, 2005].

Global Reporting Initiative (GRI). 2006. *G3 Guidelines*. http://www.globalreporting.org/ [January 20, 2008].

Goldman Sachs. 2006. *Portfolio Strategy: Capital Markets at the Crossroads, Sustainable Investing: Environmental Focus*. http://www2.goldmansachs.com/ideas/portfolio-strategy/portfolio-capital-markets.html [December 30, 2007].

Gonella, C., Pilling, A., Zadek, S. 1998. *Making Values Count: Contemporary Experience in Social and Ethical Accounting, Auditing, and Reporting*. Research rep. No. 57. Association of Chartered Certified Accountants/The New Economics Foundation: London.

Gruppo per il Bilancio Sociale – GBS – (Study Group for Social Reporting). 2001. *Social Reporting Standards*. GBS: Milan.

Hallay, H. (Ed.). 1990. *Die Ökobilanz. Ein betriebliches Informationssystem*. Schriftenreihe des IÖW: Berlin.

Hallay, H., Pfriem, R. 1992. *Öko-Controlling: Umweltschutz in Mittelständischen Unternehmen*, Campus Verlag: Frankfurt.

International Institute for Sustainable Development (IISD). 2001. *The Dashboard of Sustainability*. http://www.iisd.org [November 23, 2001].

Italian Ministry of Labour and Social Affairs. 2003. Project CSR-SC. The Italian contribution to CSR promoting campaign developed at European level. *European Conference on Corporate Social Responsibility 'The role of Public Policies in promoting CSR'*. Italian Ministry of Labour and Social Affairs: Rome.

Kaplan, R.S., Norton, D.P. 1992. The balanced scorecard: measures that drive performance. *Harvard Business Review* 70(1): 71-79.

Kaplan, R.S., Norton, D.P. 1996. Linking the balanced scorecard to strategy. *California Management Review* 39: 53-79.

Kaplan, R.S., Norton, D.P. 2000. Having trouble with your strategy? Then map it. *Harvard Business Review*, September-October: 167-176.

Kaplan R.S., Norton D.P. 2004. *Strategy Maps: Converting Intangible Assets into Tangible Outcomes*. Harvard Business School Press: Boston.

Lev, B. 2001. *Intangibles: Management, Measurement, and Reporting*. Brookings Institution Press: Washington DC.

Paine, L.S. 2003. *Value Shift. Why Companies Must Merge Social and Financial Imperatives to Achieve Superior Performance*. McGraw-Hill: New York.

Parker, C., 2000. Performance Measurement, *Work Study*, 49(2): 63-66.

Perrini, F., Pogutz, S., Tencati, A. 2006. *Developing Corporate Social Responsibility. A European Perspective*. Edward Elgar Publishing: Cheltenham.

Perrini, F., Tencati, A. 2007. Stakeholder Management and Sustainability Evaluation and Reporting System (SERS): A new corporate performance management framework. In S. Sharma, M. Starik, B. Husted (Eds). *Organizations and the Sustainability Mosaic: Crafting Long-Term Ecological and Societal Solutions*, Volume 4 in Edward Elgar Series 'New Perspectives in Research on Corporate Sustainability'. 168-192. Edward Elgar Publishing: Cheltenham.

Post, J.E., Preston, L.E., Sachs, S. 2002. Managing the extended enterprise: The new stakeholder view. *California Management Review* 45(1): 6-28.

Q-RES. 2002. *The Q-RES Project: The Quality of the Social and Ethical Responsibility of Corporations*. http://www.qres.it [February 6, 2006].

Q-RES. 2004. *Q-RES Standard and Guidelines for the Improvement of the Ethical and Social Performances of the Organisation*. http://www.qres.it [February 6, 2006].

Q-RES. 2005. *Contributing to the Convergence of CSR Management Standards in Italy, Germany, France and the UK by Developing and Promoting a Common CSR Framework, Terminology and Management Tools*. http://www.qres.it [February 6, 2006].

Rappaport, A. 1986. *Creating Shareholder Value. The New Standard for Business Performance*. The Free Press: New York.

Rusconi, G. 1988. *Il Bilancio Sociale d'Impresa. Problemi e Prospettive*. Giuffrè Editore: Milan.

Schaltegger, S., Herzig, C., Kleiber, O., Müller, J. 2002. *Sustainability Management in Business Enterprises. Concepts and Instruments for Sustainable Organisation Development*. Federal Ministry for the Environment, Nature Conservation and Nuclear Safety (BMU): Bonn.

Stewart, G.B. 1991. *The Quest for Value: A Guide for Senior Managers*. HarperCollins Publishers: New York.

Tencati, A. 2002. *Sostenibilità, Impresa e Performance. Un Nuovo Modello di Evaluation and Reporting*. Egea: Milan.

Tencati, A., Perrini, F., Pogutz, S. 2004. New Tools to Foster Corporate Socially Responsible Behaviour. *Journal of Business Ethics* 53(1-2): 173-190.

The SIGMA Project. 2003. *The SIGMA Guidelines. Putting Sustainable Development into Practice – A Guide for Organisations*. BSI: London. http://www.projectsigma.com [July 15, 2005].

United Nations. 1993. *Integrated Environmental and Economic Accounting*, United Nations: New York.

United Nations, European Commission, International Monetary Fund, Organisation for Economic Co-operation and Development, World Bank. 2003. *Integrated Environmental and Economic Accounting 2003. Handbook of National Accounting*. United Nations: New York.

United Nations Global Compact. 2007. *After the Signature. A Guide to Engagement in The United Nations Global Compact*, http://www.unglobalcompact.org/ [February 13, 2008].

World Business Council for Sustainable Development (WBCSD). 2000. *Measuring Eco-Efficiency. A Guide to Reporting Company Performance*. WBCSD: Geneva.

World Business Council for Sustainable Development (WBCSD). 2003. *Sustainable Development Reporting. Striking the Balance*. WBCSD: Geneva.

Zadek, S., Pruzan, P., Evans, R. (Eds). 1997. *Building Corporate AccountAbility: Emerging Practices in Social and Ethical Accounting, Auditing and Reporting*. Earthscan: London.

Zingales, F., Hockerts, K. 2003. *Balanced Scorecard and Sustainability: Examples from Literature and Practice*. INSEAD: Fontainebleau.

FURTHER READING

Commission of the European Communities. 2001. Commission Recommendation of 30 May 2001 on the recognition, measurement and disclosure of environmental issues in the annual accounts and annual reports of companies. *Official Journal of the European Communities* L 156 (June 13): 33-42.

De Silvio, M, Tencati, A. 2002. I costi della gestione ecologica: il caso della Centrale Termoelettrica Enel di La Casella. *Economia & Management* 3(May-June 2002): 107-122.

Elkington, J. 1997. *Cannibals with Forks. The Triple Bottom Line of 21st Century Business*. Capstone Publishing: Oxford.

Figge, F., Schaltegger, S. 2000. *What Is 'Stakeholder Value'? Developing a Catchphrase into a Benchmarking Tool*. Universität Lüneburg, Pictet & Cie, UNEP: Lüneburg.

Perrini, F., Tencati, A. 2006. Sustainability and Stakeholder Management: the Need for New Corporate Performance Evaluation and Reporting Systems. *Business Strategy and the Environment* 15(5): 296-308.

United States Environmental Protection Agency (EPA). 1995. *An Introduction to Environmental Accounting as a Business Management Tool: Key Concepts and Terms*. U.S. EPA Office of Pollution, Prevention and Toxics: Washington D.C. http://www.epa.gov [May 10, 1996].

25 *Corporate Reputation and Corporate Social Responsibility*

STEPHEN J. BRAMMER AND STEPHEN PAVELIN

Introduction

The increasing importance of both Corporate Social Responsibility (CSR) and corporate reputation has, in recent years, been recognised within the strategic management literature by a proliferation of conceptual and empirical work. The literature has paid particular attention to the relationships between one or other of CSR and reputation and such phenomena as corporate financial performance (Griffin and Mahon, 1997; Roberts and Dowling, 2002; Waddock and Graves, 1997), consumer perceptions of product quality (Milgrom and Roberts, 1986; Sen and Bhattacharya, 2001), employee morale, productivity, recruitment and retention (Moskowitz, 1972; Turban and Cable, 2003; Turban and Greening, 1996), company ownership characteristics (Johnson and Greening, 1999), and access to capital (Cochran and Wood, 1984; Hart, 1995). In spite of this burgeoning interest in both CSR and corporate reputation, there has been relatively little research of potential links between the two. However, in this chapter we will provide an overview of some notable contributions to our understanding of the nature and importance of this relationship.

In this chapter, we review the character and significance of research concerned with corporate reputation and social responsibility. In so doing, we identify the boundaries of current research, raise a number of issues concerned with this frontier and discuss possibilities for future work that would extend this frontier in productive directions. We intend to provide a coherent and critical introduction to research addressing the link between corporate reputation and social responsibility that may be of use to new researchers entering the field. Furthermore, our hope is that the review will also be valuable to experienced researchers who are interested in learning about the range of research in this area, perhaps to identify new research opportunities or to identify issues and approaches that relate to their current research. In the next section, we will discuss conceptual issues relating to the formation of corporate reputations and the role of CSR therein. We will then review key findings from the empirical literature before concluding with some thoughts on both lessons for managerial practice and an agenda for future research.

Theory

One avenue of enquiry within the burgeoning literature on corporate social responsibility relates to the mechanisms through which CSR might influence a firm's ability to amass economic rents through its business activities (McWilliams and Siegel, 2001; Jones 1995). The *stakeholder* model of the corporation has been forwarded as an organising framework to facilitate understanding of this potential influence. Within this approach, a firm's financial performance is dependent upon the character of its relationships with its stakeholders – typically conceived as various constituencies, such as customers, employees, shareholders, regulatory bodies, advocate groups and so on, and often defined as 'any group or individual who can affect or is affected by the achievement of the organization's objective' (Freeman, 1984, p. 46). The central idea here is that stakeholders impose contingencies upon these relationships, such that a stakeholders' willingness to participate in a firm's activities (customers' willingness to buy the firm's products; employees' willingness to work for the firm; and so on) is importantly determined by the degree to which the stakeholders' demands regarding the firm's behaviour and impacts are met.

Existing work has argued that social responsiveness can play a significant role in promoting favourable relationships with primary stakeholder groups. Stakeholders that view the firm as socially irresponsible may have the power to arrest power from managers, hamper the execution of corporate strategy or, by whatever means, bring a significantly deleterious impact on the financial performance of the company (Mitchell, Agle and Wood, 1997). If so, such stakeholder groups would demand attention from corporate management as there would be an economic imperative to demonstrate the firm's social responsibility as it would encourage constructive contributions from stakeholders.

Within this proposed *business case* for corporate social responsibility, corporate reputation plays a pivotal role – as the contingency of stakeholder behaviour is crucial and their behaviour is contingent upon the manner in which they *view* the firm. This leaves, among others, the following question: What is the influence of corporate social (ir)responsibility on corporate reputations held among stakeholder constituencies? This question relates to both the manner in which reputations are formed and the usefulness of CSR-related reputations for decision making. To address this question, we must first forward a view on the function of corporate reputations for stakeholders.

THE FUNCTION OF CORPORATE REPUTATION AND THE PROCESS OF REPUTATION FORMATION

The idea is that each stakeholder has a decision to make regarding its relationship with the firm – a customer must decide whether to buy the firm's product(s); an employee must decide whether to work for the firm and, if so, how much effort to deploy; investors must decide whether to buy and/or hold the firm's shares; and so on. The stakeholders have some information relevant for this decision, but not all the information they would like. There are attributes of the firm, its behaviour and performance that are deemed by stakeholders to be relevant for their willingness to participate in the firm's activities, which are nevertheless hidden. Therefore, each stakeholder has an incentive to impute these unobserved characteristics by, wherever possible, making appropriate inferences from observable characteristics. This implies some computation of the relevant information held by stakeholders and it is this computation that we will regard as the formation of a corporate reputation.

Given this, it is worth noting that one would expect the formation of corporate reputation to be guided by the use to which the reputation is to be put by the stakeholder. This is to say, each stakeholder would be expected to form a corporate reputation in a manner that best informs the decision(s) they face regarding their relationship with a firm. One would expect: a customer to form a corporate reputation that best informs their purchasing decisions; an employee to form a corporate reputation that best informs their career decisions; an investor to form a corporate reputation that best informs their investment decisions; and so on. Similarly, the key (at least partially) hidden corporate attributes would be expected to vary across stakeholders, for example, product quality for customers; job security for employees; financial soundness for investors. Accordingly, different stakeholder groups would be expected to employ different types of information for their reputational assessments, with each observable corporate characteristic emphasised according to its perceived usefulness as a signal of the particular hidden attribute(s) upon which each stakeholder group is focused.

Therefore, corporate reputation is fundamentally multidimensional, as it reflects: the various relationships that firms have with varied stakeholder groups; the variety of hidden corporate attributes that stakeholders regard as relevant for the decisions they face; and the various types of observable information that are deemed by stakeholders to be useful signals of these important unobservable corporate characteristics. A firm's overall reputation will be some amalgamation of various elements, such as their reputations for product quality, marketing effectiveness, innovativeness, quality of workforce and social responsibility. These reputations can, of course, have countervailing effects on the overall corporate reputation, such that a firm may be regarded as a provider of high-quality products but a poor marketer that lacks a capacity to innovate. Next, we will turn to the question mentioned previously.

WHAT IS THE INFLUENCE OF CORPORATE SOCIAL RESPONSIBILITY ON CORPORATE REPUTATIONS HELD AMONG STAKEHOLDER CONSTITUENCIES?

In a seminal contribution, Fombrun and Shanley (1990) argue that, 'perceptions of firms' concern for the wider society may influence judgments, with social responsiveness signalling that firms have achieved a mutualistic relationship with potentially powerful groups in their environment' (p. 239). Stakeholders do not have full information regarding a firm's regard for, and impacts on, social welfare, but do have some relevant information that they employ to assess the degree to which the company is socially responsible.

Regarding a potential for CSR activism to help a firm establish and maintain a good reputation, they note that, 'managers can signal their firms' social concern by contributing to charitable causes, developing non-polluting products, achieving equal opportunity employment, creating foundations, [or] placing women and minority members on boards...' (ibid). However, following Godfrey (2005), it may be that the ability of such activities to augment a firm's reputation is contingent upon stakeholders' perceptions of not only the resulting social impacts but also the underlying corporate motives.

Godfrey argues that, 'stakeholders assess interactions between the firm and stakeholders... that reflect some degree of "moral coloration" by individual actors, managers and leaders within the firm; from these morally colored activities and contexts, stakeholders impute moral values, principles and character elements that compose a moral reputation' (Godfrey, 2005; p. 783). In forming a moral reputation, Godfrey argues that stakeholders will ask the following question: 'Does the philanthropic activity at hand represent a genuine manifestation of the firm's underlying intentions, vision and character, or is the activity designed to ingratiate the firm among the impacted community?' In this connection, 'ingratiation is illicit and morally negative because it involves deception; honorable acts belie dishonorable motives and the goal of the ingratiator is to be seen as good without being good'. If so, CSR activism results in a positive reputational effect only if both the activity and the motive for the activity are positively viewed – and stakeholders perception of CSR are informed by not only a firm's CSR policies and their social impacts, but also the perceived motive for any investments in improved social performance.

The view that a perceived genuine regard for social welfare is quite so crucial is somewhat supported by the argument that a stakeholder's willingness to participate in a firm's activities is increased if that stakeholder perceives a good fit between their own values and those they perceive to be held by the firm (Dowling, 2004; Nelson, 2004). If one were to assume that a genuine regard for social welfare was a commonly held value among a firm's stakeholder constituencies, such an imperative for *value-alignment* would tend to increase customers' willingness to purchase the firm's products and employees' willingness to work for, and be loyal to, the firm and expend their best efforts while doing so. According to an alternative but similar view, individuals' behaviour is guided by a process of *self-actualisation* – whereby individuals view the things they do and have as determining the type of person they are (for example, stature, character) – implies that stakeholders will seek (avoid) associations with firms which, they perceive, hold those qualities to which stakeholders (do not) *aspire*. Corporate social responsibility may be regarded as reflecting attractive, aspirational qualities such as selflessness, generosity and/ or altruism, while corporate social irresponsibility may be taken to reflect unattractive qualities such as selfishness and/or sociopathic tendencies. If so, a firm's relationships with stakeholders may be made more beneficial by a corporate reputation for social responsibility, and be deleteriously affected were stakeholders to view the firm as socially irresponsible.

THE ROLE OF INDUSTRY AND THE IMPORTANCE OF FIT

Consistent with the view of reputation formation forwarded above, it has been argued that the relationship between CSR and corporate reputation is importantly moderated by industry environment (Brammer and Pavelin, 2004; 2006). Brammer and Pavelin (2006) argue that the 'strength and direction of the relationship between corporate reputation and social performance may be contingent upon the activity a company is engaged in since industry environments are correlated with significant pressure from institutional, and other, stakeholders' (p. 438). The reason for the moderating effect is systematic cross-industry variation environments in both the composition of stakeholder constituencies and the salience of particular social issues. As outlined previously, different stakeholder groups would be expected to differently form corporate reputations, as each employs information according to its perceived relevance for their particular interactions with firms. As industries tend to differ in the types of customers served, employees employed and regulators satisfied, corporate reputations may be differently influenced by corporate characteristics, including various observable aspects of CSR – such as charitable giving, environmental protection and health and safety policies.

In this connection, it is worth noting that the salience for each firm of particular aspects of CSR may be significantly determined by the perceived association between its industry and notable social issues – such as those between the oil and chemical industries and pollution, and between both tobacco and alcohol producers and health problems. It may be that corporate reputations relatively focus upon assessments of firms' positioning on any social issues perceived to be proximate to each company's core business activities. If so, there will be greater reputational rewards from improvements in social performance the more closely such improvements relate to social issues regarded to be highly salient in the industrial context. Conversely, a firm that invests in social performance that is perceived by stakeholders to be unrelated to any salient social issues will not be in receipt of as large a reputational dividend. Indeed, such CSR activism may damage the reputation of a firm if it is taken by stakeholders to reflect a wasteful discretionary act of management, perhaps born of a desire for self-aggrandisement (Bartkus et al., 2002; Navarro, 1988). In that case, CSR activities may either build or threaten a firm's reputation depending on the perceived degree of fit between the type of social investments made and those issues regarded as most relevant to the firm.

Empirical Evidence

In this section we review existing empirical evidence concerning the relationship between CSR and reputation. At the outset, it is important to recognise that such research is scarce and highly diverse, both in focus and in terms of methods employed. In part, this reflects the breadth and multidimensionality of the concept of CSR and the numerous ways in which it, or aspects of it, are operationalised.

Reviewing empirical research concerning corporate reputation and social responsibility necessarily requires some attention to be given to the measurement of corporate reputation. While a full review of the literature concerned with reputation measurement lies beyond the scope of this chapter, it is worth highlighting some of the key themes in this research. The most prevalent measures of corporate reputation in existing studies are those that attempt to provide a holistic index of a firm's reputation, usually through the means of a large-scale survey of senior corporate managers, investment analysts and industry experts. Among such measures, Fortune Magazine's *America's Most Admired Companies* (AMAC) ranking has attracted the most interest in existing research, largely because it has been consistently publicly available since 1983. Rankings generated by comparable methods have been produced for 38 countries including the United Kingdom in the form of Management Today's *Britain's Most Admired Companies* (BMAC) ranking, Germany, Spain, China and Brazil among others (Fombrun, 2007). Such reputation rankings have attracted considerable criticism, largely because the unidimensional measures that they produce are overly focused on, and related to, the financial performance of companies, and are derived from the opinions of a very narrow constituency of stakeholders (Chun, 2005).

Existing research relating to the link between corporate responsibility and reputation can usefully be thought of as being comprised of three types of study: (i) case study evidence, (ii) experimental evidence and (iii) large-scale statistical studies. For the remainder of this section, we reflect upon each of these groups of studies in turn.

CASE STUDY EVIDENCE

A significant group of studies explore the impact of corporate responsibility on reputation by adopting the case method. Often such research focuses on the impacts of behaviours or events that are, or could be, perceived by stakeholders as evidence of corporate irresponsibility. For example, studies have focused on the impact on reputation of the Valdez oil spill on Exxon (Tyler, 1992), involvement in the Ok Tedi mine in Papua New Guinea on the Australian company BHP (Hanson and Stuart, 2001), and of issues associated with corruption and illegal price setting in the Dutch construction industry (Kolk and Pinkse, 2006; Graafland, 2004). This research often has the advantage of being quasi-longitudinal in the sense that a given case is explored over a, sometimes lengthy, period of time and typically draws upon a range of sources including interviews with company executives and other key stakeholders and media coverage of events. The longitudinal aspect of much of this case study research enables an evaluation of the impacts on reputation of the ways in which companies manage these diverse situations.

Regarding the substance of this evidence, the state of a firm's reputation is captured in a variety of ways in existing case study research including the tone of media coverage relating to a company and proxies such as a firm's stock market price. With that in mind, looking across the studies available suggests that instances of corporate irresponsibility typically lead to significant and often longstanding declines in corporate reputation and to the subsequent development of improved CSR policies and practices. For example, Graafland (2004) highlights that the reputation of Heijmans, a large Dutch construction company involved in price-fixing allegations, declined significantly upon disclosure and that 'as new evidence about secret price agreements during the period from 1998 to 2001 is still coming out, the distrust of construction companies has not disappeared yet. For example, when on 14 February, 2004 new information was published about illegal price agreements, the stock value of Heijmans declined again by 4 per cent' (Graafland, 2004, 139). Similarly, Hanson and Stuart (2001) show that BHP's failure to effectively manage allegations of significant environmental degradation around its Ok Tedi mine contributed to a dramatic decline in its reputation.

Case study evidence has the capacity to reveal nuances within the relationship between CSR and reputation. Murray and Shohen (1992) highlight the impact of the Tylenol product tampering and poisoning crisis on Johnson & Johnson. They highlight that Johnson & Johnson's previously excellent reputation played an important role in shaping public perceptions of the crisis. Additionally, their study shows that companies that are perceived to deal with crises in a timely and honest manner can reduce damage to their reputation and rebuild relationships with stakeholders.

EXPERIMENTAL EVIDENCE

A second body of research examines the link between corporate responsibility and reputation using experimental methods. Typically, such research requires experimental subjects, most often graduate or undergraduate students, to evaluate and respond to hypothetical scenarios described in a series of vignettes. Respondents are provided with some initial information and are then asked to provide a reputational assessment. Reputational assessments are generally derived from a set of questions relating to the degree to which respondents like, admire, view positively or favourably particular companies. Experiments then provide subjects with further information concerning corporate actions and managerial responses to them after which respondents are asked to provide another reputational assessment. Compared with other research, this method has the notable advantage of permitting a wide range of experimental designs to be evaluated that are closely related to conceptualisations of how corporate reputations are formed. However, in practice, this research tends, like case study research, to focus on reactions to corporate wrongdoing.

Dean (2004) adopts a typical experimental design and focuses on the impact of a firm's prior reputation for social responsibility and a firm's approach to crisis management on the impact of a product harm crisis on its reputation. The hypothetical focal company (a fast food restaurant) was either described as a strongly community-oriented business with a significant philanthropic programme (to half of the subjects) or as a company that doesn't donate to local projects and challenges its tax assessments (to the other half). The results of this analysis suggest that (i) *bad* firms have worse reputations than *good* firms, (ii) that inappropriate responses (denying responsibility for a crisis) by good firms lead to a fall in reputation whereas the reputations of bad firms responding similarly were slightly enhanced and (iii) that firms of both types that are revealed to be responsible for the crisis event suffer declines in reputation.

A similar analysis conducted by Ruth and York (2004) explored how the presentation of performance information affects the reputational assessments of individuals within the context of attempts by the oil company Exxon to improve its reputation for environmental stewardship. In particular, their study investigated whether the type of information (numeric – for example, 20 per cent better than the industry average or verbal – for example, better than the industry average), and the reference point for the information (performance relative to the past or relative to competitors) affect individual's reputational assessments. Their findings suggest that the *consistency* between source and information type or reference point determines the impact on degree of attitude change and 'provide further evidence to support a consistency or *fit* approach to examining attitude change, and present direction for rebuilding reputation in the aftermath of a crisis' (Ruth and York, 2004, p. 19).

LARGE-SCALE STATISTICAL STUDIES

Perhaps the most numerous group of studies that explore the relationship between corporate reputation and social responsibility analyse the influence of indicators of CSR on widely known indices of reputation such as the AMAC and BMAC rankings. The other types of research discussed above lack generalisability and tend to be overly focused on instances of corporate irresponsibility. In contrast, the use of Fortune and other rankings have the notable advantage that these sources provide comparable data over long periods of time for large numbers of companies drawn from across the range of economic activity. Hence, such research gives us a much more general insight into how CSR might shape corporate reputations.

Fombrun and Shanley (1990) is the seminal empirical exploration of the influences on corporate reputations. Within their study of the drivers of corporate reputation, as captured by AMAC ratings in 1985, among 292 large United States' companies, they identify significant positive relationships between reputation and both a firm's rate of charitable giving (giving per dollar of sales) and the presence of a corporate foundation. These findings suggest that more socially responsible companies attract better reputational ratings. Karake (1998) explores the impact of social irresponsibility, as reflected in the presence of concerns relating to discrimination against employees on reputation, captured by Fortune's AMAC rating, within a sample of 178 large United States' companies between 1990 and 1992. Data on instances of discrimination were measured by the incidence of news stories regarding discrimination in the Wall Street Journal. Perhaps surprisingly, and in contrast to the case study evidence discussed earlier, no statistically significant relationship between corporate responsibility, thus captured, and reputation was identified. Taken together, these studies suggest that while there is some evidence that the level of a firm's social performance is related to its reputation, this is to some degree sensitive to the dimension of social performance being investigated.

More recently, several studies have examined the relationship between reputation and corporate philanthropy while paying attention to the interaction between a company's business context, its giving, and its reputation. Williams and Barrett (2000) explore the effect of corporate giving on the relationship between violations of environmental and occupational health and safety regulations and corporate reputation. Examining this link in the context of 184 firms continuously listed in the Fortune 500 between 1991 and 1994, their evidence suggests that firms involved in such transgressions have lower reputations while those that contribute to charities have enhanced reputations. Perhaps most significantly, corporate giving is found to significantly moderate the link between environmental and health and safety crimes and corporate reputations, indicating that investing in charitable giving can play an important role in protecting a firm's reputation in such circumstances. Similar evidence is provided for UK companies by Brammer and Millington (2005) which explores the relationship between the scale, composition and destination of corporate giving and corporate reputation captured through the BMAC rankings. Within the context of a sample of over 200 large UK companies in 2002, their evidence suggests that cash giving generates more significant reputational payoffs than does involving employees through matched giving or volunteering and that the relationship between giving and reputation is significantly stronger in industries that exhibit significant social externalities, such as the alcoholic drink and tobacco sectors than in other sectors.

Studies that examine the relationship between multiple aspects of CSR and corporate reputation are very rare. Two, Brammer and Pavelin (2004, 2006) examine the relationship between BMAC ratings and several aspects of CSR as measured by a social ratings agency. Their evidence, consistent with some of that discussed above, suggests that dimensions of CSR affect reputation differently. While strong community involvement activities benefit most firms' reputations, other aspects of CSR, such as environmental sensitivity and positive relationships with employees are less clearly related to reputation. Moreover, they show that a strong record of environmental performance may enhance or damage reputation depending on a firm's primary activity with good environmental performance only benefiting a firm's reputation in circumstances where the firm's activities 'fit' with environmental concerns in the eyes of stakeholders, such as in the chemicals and resource sectors. This suggests a need to achieve a 'fit' among the types of corporate social performance undertaken and the firm's stakeholder environment.

Until now, the research discussed in this section has focused on the relationship between social responsibility and a one-dimensional measure of corporate reputation. These general measures, as earlier studies have shown, are oriented towards the firm's reputation as a good investment. In contrast, a small number of studies have explored the influences on a firm's reputation as a responsible company. Toms (2002) explores the influences upon the reputation for community and environmental responsibility, one of the component elements of the overall BMAC rating, for a sample of 126 UK companies in 1996/7. His findings indicate that a firm's reputation as a socially responsible company is enhanced by implementation, monitoring and disclosure of environmental policies and their disclosure in annual reports. In a similar vein, Zyglidopoulos (2001) explores the influences upon the *community and environmental responsibility* component of the AMAC reputation ratings with a particular focus on the impact of various categories of industrial accidents. He shows that environmental damage does have an impact on the reputational scores for social performance but that accidents relating to human life (such as employee fatalities) do not. Moreover, where accidents were complex, in the sense that the causes of the accident were not transparent, the impact of accidents on reputation was reduced.

Some Thoughts on Managerial Practice and Future Research

In this section, we will consider the implications of the extant literature for both managerial practice and future research. Concerning implications for management, existing research offers a number of important lessons. First, research is reasonably unanimous in suggesting that there is a significant relationship between a firm's reputation and the extent to which that firm is perceived by its stakeholders to be behaving responsibly. When stakeholders perceive that a firm is socially responsible, its reputation is generally enhanced and when a firm is thought to be behaving irresponsibly, its reputation typically suffers. This suggests an imperative for firms to pay a significant amount of attention to propagating a view among stakeholders that the firm is a responsible organisation, either through highly visible philanthropic and charitable initiatives focused upon local stakeholder constituencies, or through other stakeholder engagement and communication activities.

Second, research offers the more subtle prescription that there are significant reputational payoffs to firms that tailor their CSR initiatives to the risks/threats that are perceived as being most salient by their stakeholders. Hence, rather than engaging in blanket CSR activities, companies ought to focus their CSR activities upon the most salient issues in order to maximise the return to themselves. Furthermore, this salience is greatly determined by the nature of the business activities in which companies are involved. Chemical and oil companies, mining companies and paper manufacturers all face significant environmental challenges and the evidence suggests that such companies should orient their CSR to addressing precisely these concerns. Other firms might face significant issues in the form of labour or human rights, product harm or diversity issues; in a similar vein, the CSR of these companies should be aimed at addressing these most salient challenges in order to generate, and help maintain, good corporate reputations.

Third, existing studies suggest that, particularly in the case of crisis events, the manner in which firms communicate with stakeholders plays a very substantial role in shaping the extent and longevity of reputational harm. Transparent, open and honest responses by companies that are not seen by stakeholders as attempts to deflect or avoid blame for particular events can, perhaps paradoxically, generate opportunities for companies to improve their reputations in the long run.

Regarding future research, there seems to be a distinct lack of longitudinal study, which is a somewhat surprising lacuna given the importance of dynamics for the processes through which corporate reputations are established, strengthened and weakened over time. The study of changes in reputation has been largely restricted to the investigation of reputational fallout from crises of various forms. Despite the sizeable and distinctive contribution of such studies – which offer valuable lessons concerning the contingency of a firm's financial success on the manner in which it is viewed by key stakeholders – it is not clear how relevant their findings are for the evolution of the reputations of companies that are not subject to some catastrophic event. Detailed investigation of these more subtle dynamic processes would be greatly informative.

References

Bartkus, B.R., S.A. Morris and B. Seifert (2002) 'Governance and corporate philanthropy: Restraining Robin Hood?' *Business and Society*, 41, 319-44.

Brammer, S.J. and S. Pavelin (2004) 'Building a *good* reputation.' *European Management Journal*, 22, 704-13.

Brammer, S. and A. Millington (2005) 'Corporate reputation and philanthropy: An empirical analysis.' *Journal of Business Ethics*, 61(1), 29-44.

Brammer, S.J. and S. Pavelin (2006) 'Corporate reputation and social performance: The importance of fit.' *Journal of Management Studies*, 43, 435-55.

Chun, R. (2005) 'Corporate reputation: Meaning and measurement.' *International Journal of Management Reviews*, 7(2), 91-109.

Cochran, P.L. and R.A. Wood. (1984) 'Corporate social responsibility and financial performance.' *Academy of Management Journal*, 27, 42-57.

Dean, D.H. (2004) 'Consumer reaction to negative publicity: Effects of corporate reputation, response, and responsibility for a crisis event.' *Journal of Business Communication*, 41(2), 192-211.

Dowling, G.R. (2004) 'Corporate reputations: Should you compete on yours?' *California Management Review*, 46, 19-36.

Fombrun, C.J. (1998) 'Indices of corporate reputation: An analysis of media rankings and social monitors' ratings.' *Corporate Reputation Review*, 1(4), 327-40

Fombrun, C. and M. Shanley (1990) 'What's in a name? Reputation building and corporate strategy.' *Academy of Management Journal*, 33, 233-58.

Freeman, R.E. (1984) *Strategic Management: A Stakeholder Approach.* Boston, MA: Pitman.

Godfrey, P.C. (2005) 'The relationship between corporate philanthropy and shareholder wealth: A risk management perspective.' *Academy of Management Review*, 30, 777-98.

Graafland, J.J. (2004) 'Collusion, reputation damage and interest in codes of conduct: the case of a Dutch construction company.' *Business Ethics: A European Review*, 13(2-3), 127-42.

Griffin, J.J. and J.F. Mahon (1997) 'The corporate social performance and financial performance debate: Twenty five years of incomparable research.' *Business and Society*, 6, 315-31.

Fombrun, C.J. 2007. 'List of lists: A compilation of international corporate reputation ratings.' *Corporate Reputation Review*, 10(2): 144-153.

Hanson D. and H. Stuart (2001) 'Failing the reputation management test: The case of BHP, the big Australian.' *Corporate Reputation Review*, 4(2), 128-43.

Hart, S.L. (1995) 'A natural-resource-based view of the firm.' *Academy of Management Review*, 20, 986-1014.

Johnson, R.D. and D.W. Greening (1999) 'The effects of corporate governance and institutional ownership types on corporate social performance.' *Academy of Management Journal*, 42, 564-76.

Jones, T.M. (1995) 'Instrumental stakeholder theory: A synthesis of ethics and economics' *Academy of Management Review*, 20(2), 404-37.

Karake, Z.A. (1998) 'An examination of the impact of organizational downsizing and discrimination activities on corporate social responsibility as measured by a company's reputation index.' *Management Decision*, 36(3), 206-16.

Kolk, A.J. and Pinkse (2006) 'Stakeholder mismanagement and corporate social responsibility crises.' *European Management Journal*, 24(1), 59-72.

McWilliams, A. and D. Siegel (2001) 'Corporate social responsibility: A theory of the firm perspective.' *Academy of Management Review*, 26, 117-27.

Milgrom, P. and J. Roberts (1986) 'Price and advertising signals of product quality.' *Journal of Political Economy*, 94, 796-821.

Mitchell, R.K., B.R. Agle and D.J. Wood (1997) 'Toward a theory of stakeholder identification and salience: Defining the principle of who and what really counts.' *Academy of Management Review*, 22(4), 853-886.

Moskowitz, M. (1972) 'Choosing socially responsible stocks.' *Business and Society*, 1, 71–5.

Murray, E. and S. Shohen (1992) 'Lessons from the Tylenol tragedy on surviving a corporate crisis.' *Medical Marketing and Media*, 27(2), 14-22.

Navarro, P. (1988) 'Why do corporations give to charity?' *Journal of Business*, 61, 65-93.

Nelson, K.A. (2004) 'Consumer decision making and image theory: Understanding value-laden decisions.' *Journal of Consumer Psychology*, 14, 28-40.

Roberts, P.W. and G.R. Dowling (2002) 'Corporate reputation and sustained superior financial performance.' *Strategic Management Journal*, 23, 1077-93.

Ruth, J.A., and A. York (2004) 'Framing information to enhance corporate reputation: The impact of message source, information type, and reference point.' *Journal of Business Research*, 57, 14-20.

Sen, S. and C.B. Bhattacharya (2001) 'Does doing good always lead to doing better? Consumer reactions to corporate social responsibility.' *Journal of Marketing Research*, 38, 225-43.

Toms, J.S. (2002) 'Firm resources, quality signals and the determinants of corporate environmental reputation: Some UK evidence.' *British Accounting Review*, 34(3), 257-82.

Turban, D.B. and D.M. Cable (2003) 'Firm reputation and applicant pool characteristics.' *Journal of Organizational Behavior*, 24, 733-52.

Turban, D.B. and D.W. Greening (1996) 'Corporate social performance and organizational attractiveness to prospective employees.' *Academy of Management Journal*, 40, 658-72.

Tyler, L., (1992) 'Exxon's ecological disaster and rhetorical response: Exxon's Communications in the wake of the Valdez spill.' *Journal of Business and Technical Communication*, 6, 149-71.

Waddock, S.A. and S.B. Graves (1997) 'The corporate social performance-financial performance link.' *Strategic Management Journal*, 18, 303-19.

Williams, R.J. and Barrett, J.D. (2000) 'Corporate philanthropy, criminal activity, and firm reputation: Is there a link?' *Journal of Business Ethics*, 26, 341-50.

Zyglidopoulos, S.C. (2001) 'The impact of accidents on firms' reputation for social performance.' *Business and Society*, 40(4), 416-41.

26 *Corporate Social Responsibility Rating*

HENRY SCHÄFER

Introduction

Over the last decade the rating of Corporate Social Responsibility (the so-called CSR rating) has evolved into well-established international information service markets. Widely common characteristics of CSR ratings are, amongst others, a focus on companies' relationships to stakeholders, the value chain of companies' economic activities and the life cycle of products. Almost all CSR ratings operate with international norms and conventions mainly adopted from Non-Governmental Organizations (NGOs). CSR ratings cover (big capitalized) companies listed on stock exchanges and represented in leading international stock indices.

The ratings are provided for economic decision making and addressed mainly to capital market participants like asset managers. The different rating schemes are based on an individual self-understanding of CSR by the rating institution. Four types of rating schemes exist in practice:

- Risk assessment approaches focus on how a company handles its specific environmental and social risks.
- Approaches of (sustainable) company value management assume that the concept of sustainable development can be transformed into company-specific strategies enabling a company to create excess returns.
- Innovator/pioneer approaches intend to identify companies which exploit extraordinary environmental and economical opportunities.
- Best practice approaches try to find out companies with a superior management of CSR issues.

The most important challenges for CSR ratings might be their ability to cope with quality standards and transparency, the reaction of close competitors like credit rating agencies and the power of ethical investors as the most important clients of CSR rating institutions.

The Emperors' New Clothes

Since the 1990s, stakeholders and NGOs have increasingly called for companies to act in a socially responsible way. Companies are no longer assessed solely on the financial gains achieved for shareholders but also on the contributions they make to stakeholders and societies. Consumers, employees, investors and others increasingly demand information about economical, environmental and social sustainability to control and sometimes discipline companies. Very often strong ties to the corporate governance of companies do exist. Those activities can be understood as an integral part of the new political concept of the 'civil society' as it was proposed in the 1990s by several politicians in industrialized countries (see, for example, Giddens, 1998). It has created a certain kind of demand for a completely new type of company-related information: Environmental, Social and Governance information (so-called ESG-information). Such a demand is very often not uttered by market participants, and challenges companies' managements to publish or deliver information based on the Triple Bottom Line accounting principle: Beyond a company's financial performance the management has to report on the company's environmental and social performance (see Elkington, 1999). Numerous companies around the world are nowadays documenting their performances and successes through environmental and social reporting. However, unlike financial reporting, which is based on uniform standards such as the International Financial Reporting System (IFRS) or US Generally Accepted Accounting Principles (US-GAAP) throughout much of the world, there exist no comparable standards for environmental and social reporting.

Even the financial standards mentioned above give management some degrees of freedom with regard to accounting and evaluation schemes and can result in residual informational gaps for stakeholders despite very explicit formulated reporting principles. In the case of triple bottom line reporting, this problem is intensified by the fact that triple bottom line reporting is voluntary and not standardized. And although NGOs like the Global Reporting Initiative (see their guidelines in Global Reporting Initiative, 2006) and others have undertaken initial steps toward triple bottom line standard setting, there is still a considerable deficit of the information that stakeholders need in order to assess a company's environmental and social performance (see Hawken, 2004).

At the beginning of the new millennium, the once separated objectives of financial reporting and triple bottom line reporting seem to need a convergence, particularly in corporate governance issues. The spectacular collapses of large companies like Enron, Worldcom and Tyco in the USA or Ahold and Parmalat in Europe brought about a new dimension to the corporate governance discussion. Ethical behaviour and the 'soft' factors of a management's quality have gained an unprecedented level of attention. The impact of management quality has been further increased since the implementation of 'new standards for credit rating' in banks and related financial institutions according to the Basle II Accord (see Basle Committee on Banking Supervision, 2001).

Communication and information about a company's performance largely reflect the work a company's management has carried out on the basis of the decision-making powers it has been entrusted with. Since companies are now commonly viewed as coalitions of various stakeholders (see Freeman, 1984), the management must provide stakeholders with reports on a regular basis. In this respect, stakeholders are usually considered as principals since they 'hire' the management as agents to carry out certain actions in the future and agree on compensation. Therefore one can say that corporate governance is tightly linked to triple bottom line reporting and ESG-information. Triple bottom line reporting then means the delivery of ESG-information to very different groups of stakeholders. And only in some countries is the management obliged by law to report on social and environmental issues (for example, in Germany) but the 'art of reporting' is left to the management.

The Actors on the Stage

As in many countries, the delivery of ESG-information by the management is done without strong legal obligations. The management would only deliver ESG-data (which is often inside information) voluntarily if it receives a monetary compensation from the counterparty (for example, a fee). But ESG-information is ultimately demanded by stakeholders who normally do not pay the management for the information delivery. Instead of a monetary compensation, stakeholders promise to grant or renew their licenses to operate or to cooperate for the company's management. The promise is in most cases based on implicit contracts: the management can neither enforce such licenses by law nor are the licenses exclusively written for a particular company. Therefore one can argue that the (private) ESG-information of companies is exchanged by the management against a fuzzy and foggy club good – the licenses granted by certain groups of stakeholders. It's noteworthy that these licenses are monitored in practice by NGOs, institutional SRI investors and sometimes by official institutions. Here CSR rating organizations come into play by their intermediary role as middlemen between the management supplying ESGinformation and the stakeholders demanding it.

From an economic point of view, CSR ratings are to be understood as the potential, process and output of an informational service production. Ratings record, evaluate and mark environmental, social and governance-related information of companies. Typically, such ESG-information is embedded in the ongoing process of worldwide discussions, initiatives and institutions attempting to enforce ethics and morality into daily business. CSR ratings therefore have to be understood as being a substantial part of business ethics and corporate citizenship. Many CSR rating organizations underline their strong ties to CSR and Corporate Sustainability (CS).

In many industrialized countries there are now self-contained markets for information services on CS or CSR, borne by several groups of agents (see SustainAbility/Mistra, 2004 and Schäfer, 2005):

- Rating Agencies: Like no other group, CSR rating agencies stand for the 'new' ESG-information service providers. Many of them offer their services to capital market participants and operate worldwide either on an individual basis or in networks. While the international market for credit rating services is oligopolized by three rating agencies (Standard & Poor's, Fitch IBCA and Moody's), the market structure for CSR ratings is far away from concentration.
- In-house research teams: Similar to credit ratings of banks assessing the credit worthiness of borrowing companies CSR ratings operated by in-house research teams of banks can be understood as to evaluate a company's 'CSR-worthiness'. Whereas the determination of the creditworthiness is common practice with banks and also mandatory and supervisory regulated (see Basle Committee on Banking Supervision, 2001), CSR ratings represent an extraordinary activity by banks without any official supervision.

- Another way to provide ESG-information is the service offered by the providers of stock exchange indices. Primarily such indices serve as indicators for the performance of a stock exchange segment or a specific group of securities. They fulfil an informational function within the scope of ethical or socially responsible investments if the composition of the index is based on compliance with certain social, environmental or ethical critical issues of a company's activities. Conversely a company failing to meet those standards would have to be excluded from the ethical or sustainability index.

- Another group encompasses NGOs. They materialize CS/CSR issues and insofar provide information services by collecting, evaluating and publishing data about activities of companies in their economic arenas and in societies. NGOs monitor corporate behaviour and sanction it. Apart from that, they do not only work on companies about the subject of CS/CSR, but often also collaborate with them. From their engagement and critical activism about and with different companies, many NGOs have, over their lifetime, gained a special kind of competence in social and environmental issues.

- Media play an important role for the diffusion of ESG-information. On the one hand they take on the role of an information provider by disseminating information about the behaviour of companies in CSR issues and by so doing provide others, for example, CSR rating organizations, with data for their work (vice versa the media sometimes distribute the results of the work of rating intermediaries). On the other hand, the media function as critical observers if journalists uncover unsustainable or unsocial behaviour of companies and present it to the wider public.

- Public authorities affect the market by setting mainly indirect CSR standards or incentives especially for companies (see, for example, European Commission, 2001). In some cases, public authorities can also influence intermediaries as with mutual funds' or pension funds' liability to account regarding compliance with certain sustainability criteria when investing for retirement provisions, for example, the UK Pension Act in 2000).

- Finally the management of companies, by attempting to deserve their social 'license to operate' or 'license to cooperate', contributes a significant amount of information necessary for evaluating a company's sustainability.

Corporate Social Responsibility Ratings – 'Big Brother's' New Screen

The rating models vary with respect to the complexity of the methods used and how their results are quantified. While capital market-oriented concepts of CSR ratings strive to achieve the greatest possible compatibility between their rating results and equity research, consumer and company-oriented concepts sometimes limit themselves to rough CSR ratings sometimes without any grading. Besides the 'grades' they give, ratings can also include or take the form of qualitative corporate profiles (rating reports), rankings that show an individual company's relative position with respect to its competitors and absolute universal CSR grades.

The methods currently being used for CSR ratings worldwide are also heterogeneous and lack standardizations. However, initial efforts between European rating institutions to reach agreement on a first standard (Corporate Sustainability and Responsibility Research Quality Standard, CSRR-QS) got underway in 2003 (see www.csrr-qs.org).

Several elements of existing rating schemes can be identified that recur in the various models (see Schäfer et al. 2006, p. 170). Many characteristics are shared across the schemes used in CSR ratings. It is common to distinguish in a first step between environmental and social ratings (see Figure 26.1) For example, the environmental rating models usually cover the companies' entire value chain, examining the entire life cycle of products and services, from R & D to physical destruction. The majority of the social rating systems are based on stakeholder models. Most CSR ratings merge the results of their environmental and social rating into a unique CSR rating expressing the overall CSR grade of a company.

When it comes to quantification, almost all of the CSR ratings comply more or less strictly with international standards and conventions such as the UN Declaration of Human Rights, the ILO Core Labor Standards, the OECD Guidelines for Multinational Enterprises, OECD Guidelines for Corporate Governance and fundamental environmental standards. To some extent, these international standards form the basis on which the institution-specific rating models are designed and implemented. Some rating schemes – in particular those from Scandinavia – are limited to verifying compliance with these norms and minimum standards (usually labour standards). They justify this with the universal validity and high level of acceptance of these standards. Individual weights and threshold are not considered (see Schäfer, 2005).

The fact that CSR ratings examine the effects of a company's behaviour on individuals – and sometimes only on critical stakeholders – is also characteristic of most CSR ratings.

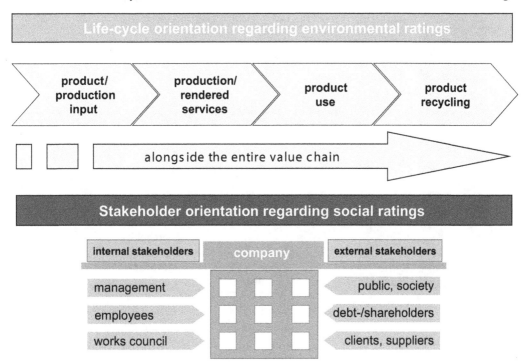

Figure 26.1 Environmental and social ratings – the two significant sub-models for the rating of a company's CSR

Almost all rating institutions emphasize the importance of business models and the level of transparency about the social and environmental effects of the company's behaviour as well as which stakeholders are affected. For this, the majority of CSR ratings conduct an integrated, systemic examination of the social, environmental and economic effects of the company's behaviour.

Long-term, forward-looking corporate strategies and the central role of crucial economic, social (and sometimes cultural) and environmental macro and micro trends in a company's overall range of activities are very significant in almost all CSR ratings. Sustainability and CSR are of primary concern throughout all management processes within the company, from strategy development, implementation and practical management to the real outcomes that are achieved in daily business. Rating models integrate various theories of causalities with some links to sustainability from numerous economic and non-economic models and heuristics such as the influence of unions on business success and customer-oriented management.

The subsequent Figure 26.2 gives an overview of the consideration and transmission of ESG criteria into a universe of companies leading in CSR/CS. Thus the selection of companies because of their shares fulfilling the sustainability/CSR criteria is a stylized process (see Schäfer et al., 2006, pp. 20-22).

The starting point of a model to identify company-specific sustainability is the specification, qualification and quantification of social and environmental issues into criteria. For this, almost all CSR rating systems rely directly or indirectly on the experiences

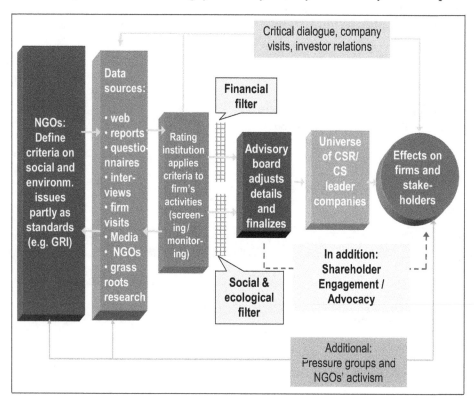

Figure 26.2 A general CSR rating model to identify sustainable/responsible companies

and CSR concepts of NGOs. The basis of these often normative criteria is the experience of NGOs in dealing with companies in specific areas of conflict between society and corporations (pressure group function, whistle-blowing and activism). The sources for the input data to feed the CSR rating models are dominated by questionnaires followed by web research and company-specific CSR/CS reports. Of only a minor importance are firm visits.

The main characteristic of rating institutions in this process is the development of a certain kind of 'production technology', with which sustainability/CSR-relevant information about particular companies or sectors is collected and bundled in a rating score. Depending on the design of the rating system, the selection of sustainable/ responsible companies is based on screens, which apply:

- either exclusively social and/or environmental criteria; or
- in addition, integrate financial criteria (here one can distinguish whether the financial screen is used prior to or after the social and environmental screen and whether they are equally weighted).

In most rating systems and organizations the final grading after the research analyst's work is done by an advisory board or commission. After the whole rating process is finished the rating reveals whether a company is sustainable/responsible according to the individual rating scheme of the analyzing institution.

Inside the Machine

CSR ratings generally cover companies and sectors. The dominating analytical approach today in almost all CSR ratings is called 'best in class approach'. In such approaches, a company's sustainability is defined in terms of its relative sustainability as compared with the sustainability of the sector as a whole. Only in a few cases is a company's CSR rating determined exclusively by negative, exclusionary and/or positive criteria. In Figure 26.3a, the best in class approach in CSR rating is demonstrated by an example of the Bank Sarasin from Switzerland whose research unit belongs to the leading CSR rating units in the world. As many other CSR rating institutions do, the in-house research department of Bank Sarasin, as a first step, assesses the individual degree of contribution a company makes to a single social and environmental item on a percentage scale. In Figure 26.3a this is demonstrated with the help of the Sarasin Sustainability-Matrix©, the bank's specific rating scheme. In the figure, the rating process is explained by an example comparing the Dutch-based food producer Unilever to the sector average. The box with the green bars mirrors the contribution of Unilever to the single items measuring the environmental issues in Bank Sarasin's rating scheme. The mentioned items indicate an environmental rating scheme which is life cycle-oriented. In the example, it is demonstrated that Unilever, according to the analysis of Bank Sarasin's research team, has been classified as above average in the environmental rating.

The same holds for the rating of social issues at Unilever which is depicted in Figure 26.3a in the second box below. Here the red bars representing the company's contributions to social issues underline again the above average performance of the company. The former two isolated ratings – environmental and social – are then merged and put into

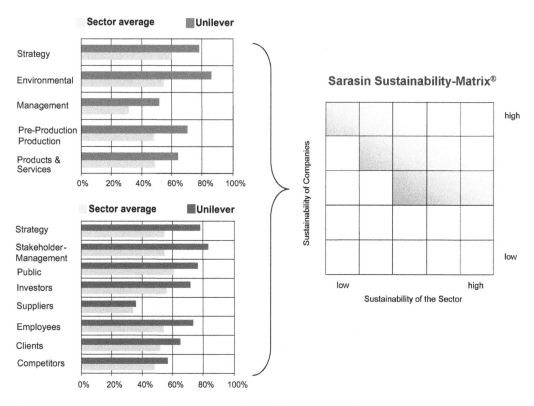

Figure 26.3a   Best in Class approach in CSR rating – Weighting of single items for a company

Source: Courtesy of Bank Sarasin, 2008.

a sustainability matrix (right box in Figure 26.3a). The matrix itself deserves a detailed explanation which will be illustrated in Figure 26.3b below.

The fusion of social and environmental rating at Bank Sarasin is expressed in the Sarasin Sustainability-Matrix©. Briefly explained, it is a comparison of the sustainability of individual companies with the sustainability of the entire sector in which the companies are operating. It is noteworthy that the definition of a sector depends on the notion of the research team and can therefore deviate from official definitions and the ones of other rating organizations. In the example the sector consists of food production and food distribution.

In Figure 26.3b it is stated on the x-axis that companies producing organic food contribute a relatively superior value to sustainability compared to producers of conventional food. That is the reason for the location of United Natural Foods in the eastern part of the matrix. Contrary to that position, Cadbury Schweppes's location in the matrix is in the south-west according to the company's production and distribution of non-organic food. The y-axis expresses the company-specific sustainability as measured by the social and environmental rating. Here we see Unilever as a company with company-specific sustainability that is above average, but with a relative low sustainability in the sector due to the broad range of non-organic food which the company offers. The label 'best in class', according to the Sarasin Sustainability-Matrix©, is deserved by all those companies located in the north-eastern region of Figure 26.3b (shown in light grey). Such

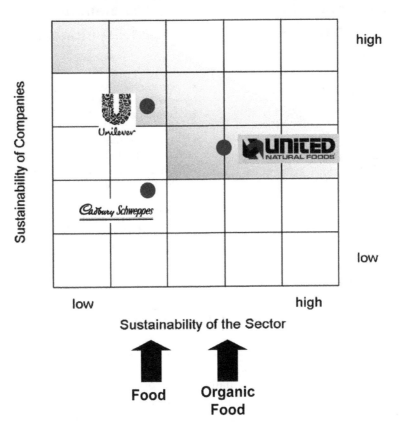

Figure 26.3b   Best in Class approach in CSR rating – Comparison of companies of the same sector

Source: Courtesy of Bank Sarasin, 2008.

companies are normally classified as CSR or sustainability leaders. Sustainability leaders are mature companies with a big market capitalization, a broad range of products and a global focus in their activities.

Besides the identification of sustainability leaders, many CSR rating schemes also analyze pioneers or innovators with respect to their contribution to sustainability or CSR. Such a group encompasses young, growth-driven companies that have implemented outstanding environmental and/or social innovations in their business models The following Figure 26.4 outlines the dichotomy between sustainability/CSR leaders and pioneers that often exists in practice with CSR ratings.

Depending on the provider, ratings may be available in the form of company profiles, rankings or database-supported tools with various selection options. A growing part of the rating institutions operates not only with traditional desk research and deliverance of special rating reports: complementary techniques and media are offered by web-based and electronic tools, like EIRiS's Ethical Portfolio Manager (EPM), SiRi's Pro (Profiles and Ratings Online) or KLD's Socrates. All those tools should allow stakeholders to carry out their individual determination and composition of ethical, responsible or sustainable

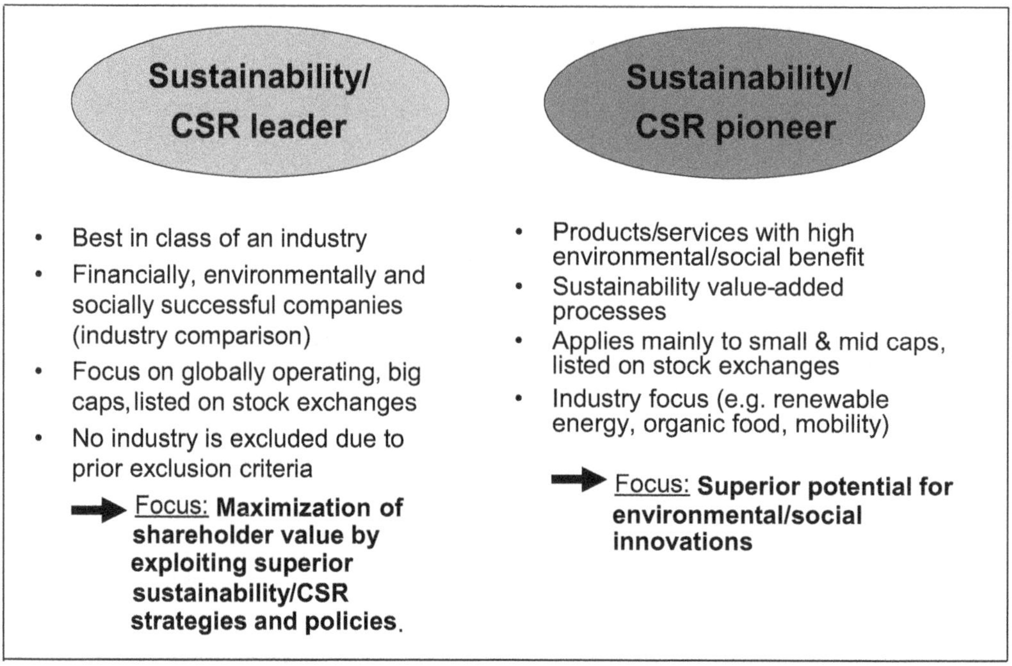

Sustainability/CSR leader

- Best in class of an industry
- Financially, environmentally and socially successful companies (industry comparison)
- Focus on globally operating, big caps, listed on stock exchanges
- No industry is excluded due to prior exclusion criteria

➡️ Focus: **Maximization of shareholder value by exploiting superior sustainability/CSR strategies and policies.**

Sustainability/CSR pioneer

- Products/services with high environmental/social benefit
- Sustainability value-added processes
- Applies mainly to small & mid caps, listed on stock exchanges
- Industry focus (e.g. renewable energy, organic food, mobility)

➡️ Focus: **Superior potential for environmental/social innovations**

Figure 26.4 Dichotomy between CS/CSR Leader and Pioneer/Innovator

companies according to individual 'tastes'. To an extent those tools can be interpreted as 'à-la-carte-approaches' to CSR ratings.

Beyond company ratings, additionally, many organizations offer CSR ratings of public institutions, supranational organizations and governments. Apart from ratings, most institutions also offer additional consulting services such as portfolio screening for institutional investors and assistance in creating SRI investment guidelines or exercising shareholder voting rights (engagement and advocacy approaches).

The bulk of current CSR ratings are offered as so-called unsolicited ratings. It means that users of CSR ratings, mainly capital market participants, buy the rating reports which are distributed through electronic channels of international leading providers of financial market data like Bloomberg and Reuters. The users of such CSR ratings pay by taking out a subscription with the rating CSR service. It is worth noting that a trend towards solicited ratings seems to be emerging and a few institutions (such as Vigeo) already specialize in solicited CSR ratings.

Roots and Branches of Corporate Social Responsibility Ratings

What is striking is that, in almost all countries, CSR ratings are predominantly information services that are provided by private, non-governmental institutions. Moreover, the providers are usually intermediaries and NGOs. Most of the CSR rating organizations originated in the 1970s. The first rating agencies in the United States (such as the United States-based International Responsibility Research Center, IRRC) were established to meet the needs of institutional investors (church-based institutions, charity organizations and pension funds), to exercise their voting rights in a socially responsible manner. In the

1980s, consumer-oriented systems among consumer and human rights organizations emerged to assess companies according to ethical, social and environmental criteria (for example, 'Shopping for a Better World'). In the UK, the founding of the Ethical Investment Research Service (EIRiS) in 1985 laid the cornerstone for the systematic ethical, environmental and social evaluation of companies for British investors. As in the United States, religious institutions in the UK (and in Continental Europe) initiated and encouraged this development.

In the 1990s, there was a surge in growth among capital market-oriented rating institutions worldwide, which are increasingly entering the market as independent financial intermediaries. This trend is accompanied by the involvement of banks and institutional investors which are developing rating schemes for the management of their own mutual funds or acquiring previously independent agencies (such as the United States rating organizations Vigeo and CoreRatings).

With respect to their economic orientation, rating institutions' activities can be classified along a continuum from non-profit organizations to private institutions that are explicitly established to maximize profits or are part of a profit maximizing entity like a bank. CSR ratings very often arose and remained as a by-product of existing information production technologies. Very specific categorizations can be made (see Schäfer et al., 2006, p. 166):

1. Rating institutions that conduct CSR research as an extension of existing research activities related to the capital markets make up the first group. They consist primarily of in-house research departments at banks and have to be understood in most cases as special branches of already operating securities research departments. Some new companies were established, for example, when employees of a bank (or other financial institution) left to set up their own independent CSR research and rating services. For example, Matthew Kiernan, co-founder of the World Business Council for Sustainable Development initiated Innovest, and the rating organization Kinder, Lydenberg, Domini (KLD) was co-founded by former stockbroker Amy Domini.
   This group also includes other financial intermediaries outside banks, who conducted related activities prior to taking up CSR research, including research institutions that had a link to companies managing mutual funds (such as CoreRatings).

2. Another category comprises CSR rating services that emerged as a reorientation of existing research-related activities without a direct link to capital markets. One such group comprises the research institutions that emerged from NGO activities. Examples include Belgian Ethibel, United States-based Co-op America and United States-based Verité. They have compiled databases on companies and their critical behaviour over time as part of their initial issues-based activism as NGOs. They have also developed special technologies for their rating work based on their experiences in critical communication with and activities related to companies. Such technologies provide them with special 'arts' of communication, data-gathering techniques and sanctioning potential.
   This category also includes specialized information service providers such as critical journalists who dealt with companies' triple bottom line in specific instances prior to their CSR rating activities. Much like the NGOs, these journalists developed specific communication channels by their investigations inside companies. As a by-product, they compiled databases that could later be used for CSR ratings. One such example is

the German firm oekom research, which evolved from the ökom publishing house. A third group that belongs to this category is dominated by research institutions whose original focus was not on CSR but in related issues. These include the Swedish Global Ethical Standard (GES) and the German Institut für Markt, Umwelt und Gesellschaft (imug).

3. Sustainability and CSR indices should also be taken into consideration because of the CSR ratings upon which they are based. These indices are a more recent trend, with the Domini Social 400 Index pioneering in this area when it was established in 1990 in the United States. It was ten years before the index had any competition. Today more than 20 socially and environmentally-oriented stock indices exist worldwide. Stakeholders have paid particular attention to index families such as the Dow Jones Sustainability Index (DJSI), the Financial Times Stock Exchange-Index (FTSE4Good) and the Ethibel Sustainability Index (ESI).

Although the 'by-product' hypothesis on the origins of many sustainability and CSR rating institutions may well be valid, there are also organizations with information production technologies that were developed independently. These include research institutions that were established specifically for the purpose of CSR rating, such as Britain's SERM Rating Agency or Italy's E.Capital Partners.

Workshops and Networks

The majority of the CSR rating institutions are headquartered in Europe. Most of them cover with their assessments companies all over the world. The staff size of such institutions varies between the organizations dramatically: they range from three to 70 employees. The most common size is between ten and 15 employees. It is important to note that the number of analysts working exclusively on the company analyses needed for rating can rarely be determined due to the lack of detailed information (see Schäfer, 2005).

Some rating institutions collaborate in a well-defined network. Horizontal networks allow individual rating organizations to stay independent but to exploit synergies from the experience, access and competences of different collaborators with often local or sector-specific knowledge. Two types of networks dominate here:

- The 'EIRiS-Network': In the last few years, the UK-based Ethical Investment Research Services (EIRiS) was successful in creating a network of other rating institutions to collaborate with. Besides divisions of labour in research activities, EIRiS' partners operate as distribution channels for some of EIRiS`s 'plug-and-play-rating services (for example, the Convention Watch tool).
- The 'SiRi-Network': On its website (www.siricompany.com) the Sustainable Investment Research International Company (SiRi Company) states that it is running a network with partners consisting of the leading SRI research organizations in major financial markets. The aim of the alliance is to combine resources and knowledge to provide extensive and high-quality research and advisory services.

Beside horizontal collaborations, vertically organized networks are also typical for the CSR rating services. A variety of cooperations among the rating institutions do exist here. Again, collaboration among such institutions serves mainly to allow them to cover locally the complex activities of corporations, the less transparent corporate activities, and the stakeholders they affect. For example, the Allianz-Dresdner Asset Management Group (ADAM) operates with a grassroots research network that allows utilizing the skills and knowledge of more than 300 researchers and more than 40,000 business contacts worldwide (see www.dresdnerrcm.co.uk/rcm/aboutus/05_grassroot/index.html).

Clusters of CSR Ratings

Several specific similarities, but also differences, among CSR ratings do exist. Despite the heterogeneous nature of the rating institutions, recurring model types can be identified. The clusters presented below illustrate the various archetypes among the existing rating schemes. However, in actual practice, these idealized approaches are seldom found in pure form. Usually, several approaches and/or models are combined.

Four important types of CSR rating models can be identified and are explained in the following bullet points (see also Schäfer et al., 2006, p. 174 and Figure 26.5):

*   Shareholder value type (also known as efficiency models, intangible value models and eco-efficiency models). This type of rating focuses on corporate management strategies and their orientation toward sustainability or responsibility. Identifying and implementing economic, environmental and social micro and macro trends early on should give management competitive advantages and increase shareholder value. In this way, stakeholders can benefit from rising company values, responsible production technologies and 'good' products.

Performance Type	Risk Assessment Type
→ Related to shareholder value	→ Risk of non-sustainability
• CS/CSR generate value drivers to create financial outperformance • Micro and macro trends in social and environmental issues count • High importance of intangibles for building long-term shareholder value	• Entire value chain of a company and management's collaboration with stakeholders matter ('license to operate', 'license to cooperate') • Additional focus on systemic and mega risks
Pioneer Type	**Business Case Type**
→ Focus on innovative/pioneering firms	→ CS/CSR as a benchmark for best practise management
• Environmental issues count • Processes and products are the foremost driver • Stakeholders only of minor imprtance • Focus on (listed) small and medium-sized companies	• Social and ecological issues are understood as dynamic capabilities and firm-specific core competences • Highly firm-specific • Integrated systems

Figure 26.5 Four clusters of CSR ratings

- Risk assessment type: The focus here is on analyzing how a company deals with the environmental and social risks it faces. This approach is based on the notion that a reduction of environmental and social risks (in the sense of reducing potential loss or damage) will result in increased financial success for a company. In a sense, a company's sustainable development means that it is able to prevent non-sustainability.
- Ratings focusing on 'innovator' and 'pioneer' companies. It is assumed that those companies can earn excess financial returns stemming out of the environmental and economic opportunities that arise from innovative products or productions. In some cases, the innovator analysis is limited exclusively to environmental aspects and does not take social issues into account. These 'eco-innovator models' are found primarily in CSR ratings in Continental Europe.
- The business type differs from the types above by seeking and prescribing more intensely what can be viewed as management`s best practices in terms of CSR rating issues. These models (particularly the one from Business In The Community, BITC) share some similarities with quality management models (for example, EFQM). Process elements such as strategy and planning, operational implementation, evaluation and reporting, as well as establishing stakeholder dialogue play a key role here.

The Neighbourhood of Corporate Social Responsibility Ratings

Beside CSR ratings, several systems or institutions can be identified which are operating with comparable techniques or with similar objectives. It can be summarized as follows.

- Integrators: Some institutions which are mainly addressing their services to capital markets are now also operating with schemes or issues similar to CSR ratings or are in a process of pondering how to cope with CSR ratings. The trend is twofold.
  - On the one hand, established credit rating agencies like Standard & Poor's are carefully observing tendencies in CSR rating (see Dallas, 2004). There might be a chance to enrich the traditional credit ratings by integrating such ingredients of CSR ratings that can help to gain new insights into certain kinds of risk sources like environmental or systemic risks (see WBCD, 2004). Besides capital market-oriented credit ratings, bank internal credit rating schemes, according to the supervisory guidelines for banks of the Basle II concordat, might be enriched by integrating CSR-related issues, for example, environmentally risky business practices.
  - On the other hand is standard investment research, where mainly equity research is becoming aware of the innovative attributes of CSR ratings. At the moment the most visible movement in that direction is the Enhanced Analytics Initiative (EAI. see www.enhancedanalytics.com). It was founded in 2004 and is an international collaboration between investors and asset managers aimed at encouraging a more sophisticated investment research. Organized as a network EAI seeks to address the absence of quality, long-term research which considers material extra-financial issues (EFI) and gives a commercial incentive to produce innovative and differentiated research.
- Standard setting institutions create guidelines to analyse CSR strategies and policies of corporations play a major role in CSR rating schemes. Beyond their usage in

CSR ratings, many of those guidelines have been successful in gaining awareness of companies and their management. A front-running guideline is processed by the Global Reporting Initiative (GRI). At the beginning of 2006 the third generation of GRI Guidelines (the 'G3') was presented to the CSR community as a draft (see http://www.globalreporting.org/ReportingFramework/G3Guidelines/). The G3 focuses on setting CSR reporting standards, definitions, indicators and CSR issues. Parallel to the GRI relaunch, the International Organization for Standardazation (ISO) has developed a new framework – the ISO 26000 – to set guidelines for Social Responsibility. As the ISO states on its website, 'the guidance standard will be published in 2010 as ISO 26000 and be voluntary to use. It will not include requirements and will thus not be a certification standard' (see www.iso.org/sr).

- Company reports on CSR issues have a strong link to CSR ratings. Usually they serve as sources for the desk research of rating institutions. Besides that usage, in general, stakeholders are the addressees of those reports. The reports can differ in their focus: Traditionally they have been developed as a source for a specific issue like environmental or social topics. Nowadays companies understand more and more that CSR and sustainability reporting requires an integration of economic, social and environmental issues. The publication of such sustainability or CSR reports has thus increased.
- Stock exchange services on CSR: The London Stock Exchange in cooperation with the British Social Investment Forum (UKSIF) has developed a Corporate Responsibility Reporting Tool, called Corporate Reporting Exchange (CRE). The CRE (Corporate Responsibility Exchange) is an online tool which should help companies to meet the demands of all major CSR rating systems, codes and fund managers in a single place (see www.londonstockexchange.com/en-gb/products/irs/cre/).

As Time Goes By...

It is apparent that CSR ratings have established an international market for specialized information services. Unlike credit ratings, no (quasi) monopolistic (supplier market) structure exists. A more and more vivid international and regional (for example, EU) competition among the CSR rating institutions does exist, whose structures resemble a polypoly rather than an oligopoly. It is evident that the majority of the CSR rating institutions apply economically-oriented concepts, primarily addressing financial markets and investors as stakeholders with their rating services. Much the same applies to the companies covered by the rating systems, as almost all of the companies covered are large enterprises that are listed on stock exchanges.

In addition, rating organizations usually share communication and information techniques with the companies they evaluate. Without doubt, such cooperation makes good sense from a quality perspective, that is, to ensure a high reliability and availability of information that is needed for a CSR assessment. However, if one considers that the current market structure for CSR ratings is characterized by sustainability and CSR paradigms that vary from one institution to another and by a broad diversity of methods and very different survey criteria, for companies a cooperation dilemma becomes apparent. For economic reasons, companies will inevitably not be able to provide all research and rating institutions with the information they need. Since the market for CSR ratings has taken only a few steps toward standardization so far, companies will seek to implement a process of selecting and focusing on certain rating institutions if they are not already doing so. In summer 2004, the 'Association for Independent Corporate Sustainability and Responsibility Research' (AI CSRR) was formally launched by 16 European CSR research institutions to achieve self-regulation in the sector of CSR research. One of the duties of the association will be to further develop and manage the Voluntary Quality Standard for Corporate Sustainability and Responsibility Research. This standard was founded in 2003 by several European CSR rating institutions. It comprises guidelines, rules, commitments and proofs on the transparency and quality of the processes involved in CSR research. A special focus lies on the accountability and verifiability of the rating processes in the field of CSR (see also www.csrr-qs.org/pdf/CSRR-QS_1_0_Pilot_Version.pdf).

This trend will inevitably cause significant changes in the market structure for CSR ratings. It is possible that provider structures similar to those known on the credit rating market will emerge. For example, it is conceivable that the value chains of CSR ratings could break open and vertical integrations with other information service providers would emerge.

Due to their intermediary nature, rating institutions will play a growing role in the formulation and assertion of stakeholder demands to companies. It is very likely that well-organized capital markets, in particular the securities exchanges and their most important participants (that is, institutional investors), will dominate these institutions more and more. In recent years the markets have been expanded by several newcomers and start-ups mainly driven by stock market index providers. On the other hand, some former rating institutions have abandoned their activities and left the market. Some of the first mergers and acquisitions have taken place – a reliable hint that a market is transforming into more established structures. Even conventional investment research and credit ratings have become aware of CSR rating schemes and efforts to integrate them into their standard research or into credit rating schemes are now underway. The management of high-quality research, more transparency and professional communication with the management of companies and stakeholders might be some of the most important challenges for CSR rating institutions in the short run. Whether they will survive in the stormy seas of international capital markets seems to depend mostly on the sustainability of socially responsible investments and the investors managing them.

References

Allianz-Dresdner Asset Management Group (ADAM), www.dresdnerrcm.co.uk/rcm/aboutus/05_grassroot/index.html

Basle Committee on Banking Supervision, 2001, The Standard Approach to Credit Risk, Consultative Document, Supporting Document to the New Basle Capital Accord, Basle.

CSRR-QS 1.0, 2003, Description of the Voluntary Quality Standard for Corporate Sustainability and Responsibility Research, http://www.csrr-qs.org/pdf/CSRRQS_1_0_Pilot_Version.pdf, accessed 01/2006.

Dallas, G., 2004, Nachhaltigkeit, Corporate Governance und Risikobewertung: Wo stehen die Vorreiter?, presentation at the Standard & Poor's conference "Risk & Opportunity. Best Practice in Non-Financial Reporting", 19.11.2004, Berlin.

Elkington, J., 1999, Cannibals with Forks: The Triple Bottom Line of 21st Century Business, Oxford (Conscientious Commerce).

European Commission, Directorate-General for Employment and Social Affairs, 2001, Promoting a European Framework for Corporate Social Responsibility. Green Paper, Brussels, Unit EMPL/D.1

Freeman, R.E., 1984, Strategic Management: A Stakeholder Approach, Boston, Mass.

Giddens, A, 1998, The Third Way. The Renewal of Social Democracy, London.

Hawken, P., 2004, Socially Responsible Investing. How the SRI Industry has Failed to Respond to People Who Want to Invest with Conscience and What Can be Done to Change it, Natural Capital Institute, Sausalito Cal., (http://www.naturalcapital.org/images/NCI_SRI_10-04.pdf) accessed 01/2008.

Schäfer, H., 2005, International Corporate Social Responsibility Rating Systems – Conceptual Outline and Empirical Results, Journal of Corporate Citizenship, Vol. 20, 2005, S. 107-120.

Schäfer, H./ Zenker, J., Beer, J., Fernandes, P., 2006, Who is Who in Corporate Social Responsibility Rating. A Survey of Internationally Established Rating Systems that Measure Corporate Social Responsibility, Research Report, http://www.bertelsmannstiftung.de/bst/de/media/Transparenzstudie2006.pdf, accessed 01/2008.

SustainAbility/Mistra, 2004, Values for Money. Reviewing the Quality of SRI Research, London/Stockholm.

IV Dealing with Stakeholders

One of the most significant areas of concern at the moment for any organisation is the management of its relationship with its whole stakeholder community. This is the focus of this part of the Handbook and is, of course, an extension of the last two parts, as both corporate governance and corporate social responsibility are increasingly concerned with the stakeholders of the organisation. Stakeholders can be considered solely in the context of people, or a broader view, encompassing the environment, can also be considered; this broader view is taken by some of the contributors to this part. The sustainability of the organisation (Aras & Crowther 2008a) itself depends upon the management of these relations and sustainability is also one of the most important concepts of organisational activity.

Not only does sustainable activity impact upon society in the future; it also impacts upon the organisation itself in the future. Thus, for example, good environmental performance by an organisation in the present is in reality an investment in the future of the organisation itself. This is achieved through the ensuring of supplies and production techniques which will enable the organisation to operate in the future in a similar way to its operations in the present, and so to undertake value creation activity in the future much as it does in the present. Financial management also, however, is concerned with the management of the organisation's resources in the present, so that management will be possible in a value creation way in the future. Thus the internal management of the firm, from a financial perspective, and its external environmental management coincide in this common concern for management for the future. Good performance in the financial dimension leads to good future performance in the environmental dimension and vice versa. Thus there is no dichotomy between environmental performance and financial performance and the two concepts conflate into one concern. This concern is, of course, the management of the future as far as the firm is concerned.[1] The role of social and environmental accounting and reporting and the role of financial accounting and reporting therefore can be seen to be coincidental. Thus the work required needs be concerned not with arguments about resource distribution but rather with the development of measures which truly reflect the activities of the organisation upon its environment. These techniques of measurement, and consequently of reporting, are a necessary precursor to the concern with the management for the future.

Similarly, the creation of value within the firm is followed by the distribution of value to the stakeholders of that firm, whether these stakeholders are shareholders or

---

1 Financial reporting is, of course, premised upon the continuing of the company – the going concern principle.

others. Value however must be taken in its widest definition (Aras & Crowther 2008b) to include more than economic value as it is possible that economic value can be created at the expense of other constituent components of welfare such as spiritual or emotional welfare.[2] This creation of value by the firm adds to welfare for society at large, although this welfare is targeted at particular members of society rather than treating all as equals. This has led to arguments by Tinker (1988), Herremans et al. (1992) and Gray (1992), amongst others, concerning the distribution of value created and to whether value is created for one set of stakeholders at the expense of others. Nevertheless if, when summed, value is created. then this adds to welfare for society at large, however distributed. Similarly good environmental performance leads to increased welfare for society at large, although this will tend to be expressed in emotional and community terms rather than being capable of being expressed in quantitative terms. This will be expressed in a feeling of wellbeing, which will of course lead to increased motivation (Aras & Crowther 2008c). Such increased motivation will inevitably lead to increased productivity, some of which will benefit the organisations, and also a desire to maintain the pleasant environment which will. in turn. lead to a further enhanced environment, a further increase in welfare and the reduction of destructive aspects of societal engagement by individuals.

Thus increased welfare leads to its own self-perpetuation. In the context of welfare, also, therefore. financial performance and environmental performance conflate into a general concern with an increase in welfare. It can, therefore, be argued that environmental and financial performance are not different dimensions of performance which must inevitably be in opposition to each other. Rather they are both facets of the same dimension of concern for the future. The conflation of financial and environmental performance into the same concept does not, of course, mean that environmental accounting becomes irrelevant. Rather it raises the profile of such accounting and places it at the centre of organisational accounting alongside management accounting. Furthermore, it means that more work is needed to develop the embryonic concepts of environmental accounting and make the quantification of environmental effect more effective and meaningful and comparative. Thus it becomes apparent that more work is needed in the area of environmental accounting but, moreover, it becomes apparent that this is work which is vital for the understanding of corporate performance and the future of that performance. Thus environmental accounting and performance must inevitably become the concern of corporate management.

In the first chapter of this part, therefore, Worthington takes a broad view by considering the environmental responsibility of business. He focuses on a number of issues related to the idea of the 'greening of business', beginning with an examination of the traditional model of business activity before moving on to explain how the adverse impacts of corporate activity can be linked to structural problems inherent in the system of market capitalism, not least the failure to take into account the negative externalities that arise as a consequence of economic behaviour. The focus then shifts to the organisational level and in particular to the question of how organisations can be encouraged to become more environmentally responsible, and concludes with a discussion of how researchers have characterised and modelled firm level responses to the various pressures on businesses to

---

2   See for example Mishan (1967), Ormerod (1994) and Crowther et al. (1998). This can be equated to the concept of utility from the discourse of classical liberalism.

become greener and comments on the utility of such approaches to understanding and conceptualising corporate environmental behaviour.

One of the main arguments against globalisation is that it has led to a global framework where companies can source globally while at the same time exploiting people and forcing down the level of environmental regulation. In the next chapter Heblich examines this supposition and shows that there are actually strong incentives for companies to act socially responsible – even in the absence of formal regulations. He argues that pursuing a corporate social responsibility strategy does not necessarily interfere with or hinder a firm's performance and can actually be regarded as innovation strategy that keeps a company competitive and thus contributes to its shareholder value. Effectively therefore the interests of many stakeholder grouping are in alignment rather than in opposition.

In the subsequent chapter, Vettori focuses upon the obligation which a company, as an employer, has towards its employees, one of the major stakeholders for any organisation. She argues that although there are three major sources of employer obligations: international law, common law and statute, all of these sources fundamentally require the same duties of the employer. At its simplest an employer has only one obligation towards its employees, which is to treat them fairly – but this obligation entails a myriad of employer duties. Ultimately of course an employee's dignity, privacy, right to property, quality of life and health must all be respected, which coincides with the corporate social responsibility ethos of behaving reasonably towards all stakeholders.

Vandekerckhove, in the next chapter, is concerned with an issue which can be very important for employees, namely that of whistleblowing. In this chapter he elaborates upon the relevance of whistleblowing for the business organisation at the present time. Rather than trying to justify circumstances in which whistleblowing is acceptable, he tells the story of how whistleblowing became an issue and why it still is. He emphasises that, although business organisations can clearly benefit from having internal whistleblowing procedures, managers should be aware that there are serious ethical risks involved in implementing such procedures, and also emphasises that despite procedures and legislation it actually remains an unpleasant business.

In the following chapter de Regil Castilla examines how stakeholders try to influence how business should conduct itself to become a socially responsible organ of society. His assessment is made in the context of society's pursuit of a holistic and democratic sustainability, encompassing its social, economic and environmental dimensions. He argues that there is no consensus about the responsibilities and areas of accountability of business and that this has engendered a permanent debate among different stakeholders with opposing views on the social responsibilities of business. He therefore provides an assessment of how interested stakeholders of civil society who want to change the current ethos try to influence corporate behaviour and that of other stakeholders opposing a binding framework.

In the next chapter, Wang and Wang are also concerned with environmental issues and with environmental management. They commence by stating that world wide environmental problems are making the whole of society – and hence all stakeholders – pay increasing attention to the Corporate Ecological Responsibility (CER), and to accountability for the need to protect the environment. For them it has become the core of Corporate Social Responsibility (CSR). For them to study CER from the perspective of Systematic and Dialectical Science (SDS) is to give insight into the evolutionary state of CSR in certain progress. The approach taken by them reflects the fact that they are

Chinese and their philosophical position is completely different to those in the West, something that they refer to several times in this chapter. This chapter has been included deliberately in order to show that in a significant part of the world understandings and ontologies are completely different, leading to different priorities, although, reassuringly, much that is argued is similar to that in Aras and Crowther (2009).

In the final chapter in this part Lau states that we often hear of corporations being socially responsible but non-profit organisations are also doing the same things, raising awareness of the same or similar social issues, but without the profit motivation. The non-profit sector deserves attention and non-profit organisations need to raise funds in order to conduct their business. In this chapter, therefore, Lau examines fundraising letters and their purpose and effectiveness to show that persuasion seems to lie in the cognitive interactions between writers and readers that could be modelled as a question-answer dialogue. Practically, the conceptualisation and fulfilment of readers' expectations is the crucial element in persuasion. This chapter is also different to most in the book and its inclusion is to show the extent and variety of issues which fall under the umbrella of CSR.

References

Aras G & Crowther D (2008a); Corporate sustainability reporting: a study in disingenuity?; *Journal of Business Ethics*, 87 (supp 1), 279-288.

Aras G & Crowther D (2008b); The social obligation of corporations; *Journal of Knowledge Globalisation* 1 (1), 43-59.

Aras G & Crowther D (2008c); Governance and sustainability: An investigation into the relationship between corporate governance and corporate sustainability; *Management Decision* 46 (3), 433-448.

Aras G & Crowther D (2009); *The Durable Corporation: Strategies for sustainable development*; Aldershot; Gower.

Crowther D, Davies M & Cooper S (1998); Evaluating corporate performance: a critique of Economic Value Added; *Journal of Applied Accounting Research*, 4 (3), 2-34.

Gray R (1992); Accounting and environmentalism: an exploration of the challenge of gently accounting for accountability, transparency and sustainability; *Accounting, Organizations & Society*, 17 (5), 399-425.

Herremans I M, Akathaparn P & McInnes M (1992); An investigation of corporate social responsibility, reputation and economic performance; *Accounting, Organizations & Society*, 18 (7/8), 587-604.

Mishan E J (1967); *The Costs of Economic Growth*; Harmondsworth; Pelican.

Ormerod P (1994); *The Death of Economics*; London; Faber and Faber.

Tinker T (1988); Panglossian accounting theories: the science of apologising in style; *Accounting, Organizations & Society*, 13 (2), 165-189.

27 *Business and Environmental Responsibility*

IAN WORTHINGTON

Introduction

The last two decades have seen the question of the adverse environmental impact of business emerge as a significant issue of public and political debate. In many corporate boardrooms, this rise in environmental awareness and concern has not gone unnoticed. Multinational enterprises, in particular, have been keen to demonstrate their environmental credentials to a wide range of stakeholders, via mechanisms such as environmental policy commitments, mission statements, environmental management systems and social and/or environmental reporting procedures. In an increasingly globalised and competitive business context, this activity itself has become highly competitive, with a growing number of organisations seemingly anxious to demonstrate higher levels of environmental responsiveness and performance than their nearest rivals in the market place.

In examining this aspect of corporate social responsibility, this chapter focuses on a number of issues related to the idea of the 'greening of business'. It begins with an examination and subsequent revision of the traditional model of business activity which tends to underplay (and frequently ignore) the impact of business operations on the natural world. The chapter then moves on to explain how the adverse impacts of corporate activity can be linked to structural problems inherent in the system of market capitalism, not least the failure to take into account the negative externalities that arise as a consequence of economic behaviour. The focus then shifts to the organisational level and in particular to the question of how organisations can be encouraged to become more environmentally responsible, through an examination of the key drivers of corporate ecological responsiveness. The analysis concludes with a discussion of how researchers have characterised and modelled firm-level responses to the various pressures on businesses to become greener and comments on the utility of such approaches to understanding and conceptualising corporate environmental behaviour.

Business and the Environment: The Traditional View

As economic organisations, businesses in market-based economies have often been portrayed as transformation systems which convert inputs into outputs for consumption purposes. Figure 27.1 below illustrates the basic model of business activity that has traditionally been used in university business and management schools when introducing students to the idea of 'business' and its generic processes (see. for example, Worthington and Britton, 2006; Wetherly and Otter, 2008). As the model indicates, at its simplest, business activity essentially involves acquiring and utilising a variety of inputs (for example, materials, labour, technology) to produce various outputs (for example, goods, services, information) which become available for consumption by individuals, groups or organisations. For commercial and industrial enterprises, the revenue derived from selling these outputs generates a stream of income for the business, some of which can be used to replenish its inputs and begin the cycle of transformation again.

This simple systems model of business activity is particularly useful in that it also draws attention to the idea of the organisation's 'environment', in essence the external context in which the whole transformation process occurs. Students of business are taught to see a firm's business environment as a key influence on its operations and decisions, including its corporate, business and functional strategies (see, for example, Johnson et al., 2005). As Figure 27.1 illustrates, this environment comprises a whole host of factors external to the organisation which can impinge upon its activities, from the acquisition and use of resources, through the conversion of these into outputs, to the sale and distribution of these outputs to intermediate or end consumers. Foremost among these variables are influences that emanate from the organisation's political, economic, social, technological, legal and ethical environments, usually referred to by the acronym the PESTLE factors. It is these and other external factors which some business theorists tend to emphasise when explaining the underlying forces that drive strategic change in profit-seeking organisations (Pettigrew, 1987).

This traditional view of business tends to stress the role of firms as legal/economic entities that pursue identifiable goals within a dynamic and changing external environment. For profit-making organisations, enhancing shareholder (or owner) value

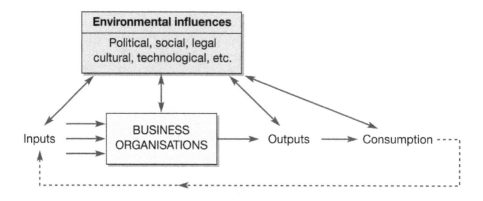

Figure 27.1 The firm and its environment

Source: Worthington and Britton (2006).

is seen as a primary concern, hence the tendency to emphasise organisational activities aimed at maximising revenue and/or minimising costs. In engaging in their day-to-day activities, businesses operate within a market-based economic system in which demand and supply (through 'prices') determine how both resources (inputs) and goods and services (outputs) are ultimately allocated. Moreover, since individuals gain satisfaction from consuming goods and services and firms (and their owners) gain revenue from selling them, implicitly there is a shared interest in increasing both production and consumption over time.

When examined more closely, it becomes evident that this model of business activity rests on a number of important assumptions. Shrivastava (1995) identifies them thus:

- a denatured view of the firm's environment – with a primary focus on the PESTLE factors and a tendency to ignore or downgrade the natural environmental consequences of economic behaviour;
- a bias towards production and consumption – with a stress on unconstrained consumption, cost minimisation, increased efficiency and shareholder value;
- a financial risk bias – with risk largely seen in terms of financial rather than social and environmental impact;
- an anthropocentric perspective – with an assumption of the superiority of the human species, with nature regarded as there to serve human needs and wants and a stress on activities which are thought to increase human welfare (for example, consumption).

In short, the culturally dominant ideology has tended to be one of constant economic growth and material well-being, with the natural environment seen as readily exploitable for human benefit and progress. As indicated in the introduction, this perspective has become increasingly challenged in recent years as exemplified by the emergence of concepts such as corporate social and environmental responsibility, corporate citizenship, sustainable development and the triple bottom line.

Business and the Natural Environment: Revising the Model[1]

The increased emphasis given to the impact of business on the natural environment is not simply a matter of morality or business ethics. As economists and others have recognised, the natural environment is a key part of a firm's business environment, providing three important economic functions that underpin the processes of production, consumption and distribution in the economy (Pearce and Barbier, 2001; Worthington, 2005). To ignore these functions puts at risk future economic prosperity and may ultimately threaten the ability of the economic system to carry out its tasks over the longer term.[2]

First, the natural environment is a provider of resources for firms in the form of inputs such as raw materials, land and water. While some of these resources can be consumed without running down stocks (that is, 'continuing resources' such as wind power, solar energy), and others can regenerate themselves naturally and therefore can

---

1   For a fuller discussion see Worthington (2005).

2   It has even been suggested that environmental degradation might ultimately result in the extinction of the human species.

be used without necessarily depleting the total stock (that is, 'renewable or flow resources' like fish stocks, forests), others are depleted through usage and will ultimately become exhausted (that is, 'exhaustible or stock resources such as oil, coal and iron ore). How these resources are exploited by businesses impacts therefore not only on current but also on future economic growth and prosperity.

Secondly, the natural environment acts as an assimilator of the waste products that are a consequence of economic behaviour. Examples include litter, packaging effluence and other forms of pollution. As the ongoing debate over climate change and ozone depletion illustrate, this function has a global as well as a national and local dimension. International borders offer no protection against greenhouse gases or chloroflorocarbons (CFCs) and economic activities in one part of the world can impact elsewhere on the planet, sometimes with potentially disastrous consequences.

Thirdly, the natural environment acts as a source of amenity value for individuals, providing, for example, access to enjoyable landscapes and space for recreation. While some of this attribute is provided as a 'free good' (see below), some incurs a price, as exemplified by the introduction of a system of charging for access to a national park or a nature reserve.

By incorporating these three economic functions into our original diagram (see Figure 27.2), we can gain an appreciation of how the natural environment contributes to business activity and to the operation of the economic system as a whole.

As the revised model illustrates, economic behaviour results not only in the production of 'goods' (that is, desirables such as products, services, employment), it also gives rise to what economists call 'bads', in effect the undesirable outcomes of economic behaviour. In addition to the depletion of the stock of some natural resources, business activity gives rise to the creation of 'residuals' (for example, waste products) which are often dumped in the environment and which can result in a negative impact on the natural environment's amenity function (for example, polluted beaches, ruined views). Notwithstanding the ability of the environment to absorb some of these outputs through natural processes, and opportunities for the recycling of some waste products, a limit exists to the ability of

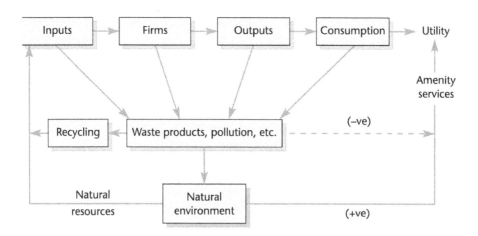

Figure 27.2 The firm and the natural environment

Source: Worthington (2005).

the natural world to act as a waste sink for economic bads. This is what environmentalists refer to as the 'carrying capacity' or assimilative function of the natural environment, which like any other finite resource can be used up by unfettered economic activity.

'Free Goods' and 'Externalities'

As the discussion above indicates, while the natural environment helps to support and sustain business activity, economic processes also help to create undesirable consequences which pose a threat to the future operations of the economic system. Put simply, no business activity can occur without causing some form of adverse environmental impact. The question then becomes, what lies at the root cause of environmental problems such as pollution and resource depletion?

Part of the answer lies in the economist's notion of 'free goods'. Whereas economic scarcity ensures that the majority of goods and services provided by the economy have positive prices and are traded in markets, some environmental resources and products are not relatively scarce and therefore do not command a price; they are effectively 'free' or 'zero-priced', as in the case of air, sea water and a fine view. Elementary price theory teaches us that as price declines more tends to be demanded and with zero-priced products demand is likely to significantly outstrip supply. As a result, overuse and exploitation tends to occur, as exemplified by the problems such as ozone depletion, carbon emissions and the decline of certain fish stocks.

It is worth noting that some of the examples given above also have another important characteristic that sets them apart from the majority of other goods and resources in the economy, namely that they are in common ownership in the sense that no-one owns the air or the sea. Since there are no private property rights, there is effectively no-one to prevent over-exploitation from occurring and there is no price mechanism to ration access to these environmental goods and services. The resultant free-for-all can mean that the environment can be seriously degraded or potentially destroyed on a local, national or even global scale, a situation that is sometimes described as the 'tragedy of the commons' (Hardin, 1968).

Even where the price mechanism operates, environmental problems can still occur because the market price does not usually reflect the full economic costs of production (Pearce and Turner, 1990; Worthington, 2005). For example, in the process of producing goods and services, firms may use up some of the natural environment (for example, when a company dumps waste products into a river rather than pays for them to be disposed of) and this represents a resource to the business for which it effectively pays nothing. In other words, whereas the true costs of production are the costs of the priced inputs (for example, labour, materials, energy) plus a number of un-priced environmental services, the market price only tends to represent the former, what economists call the 'private costs' of production. What has effectively happened is the firm has 'externalised' some of its costs and imposed these on individuals or on society generally as in the case of greenhouse gas emissions and some other forms of pollution. To the extent that these 'social costs' (or in some cases 'benefits') directly affect the welfare of others who are not party to a transaction, economists call these the 'externalities' or 'spill-over effects' of economic behaviour and portray them as an example of 'market failure'.

Drivers of Corporate Ecological Responsiveness

Given the current structure and operation of the market-based economy, one could be forgiven for assuming that businesses have every incentive to exploit the natural environment to its fullest potential and to ignore the negative externalities that arise as a consequence of economic behaviour. Business practice indicates, however, that firms often recognise that their actions and decisions can have an adverse impact on the natural environment and some businesses take active steps to improve on their environmental performance, even at an apparent or potential cost to the financial bottom line (Cairncross, 1995). How can we account for this tendency towards corporate ecological responsiveness on the part of some business organisations?

The literature of corporate greening suggests that firm-level responses in this area are shaped by four major influences: government decisions (especially regulation), market considerations, other stakeholder pressures and ethical motives (Bansal and Roth, 2000). Whilst these are not mutually exclusive categories, for ease of analysis they are depicted (see Figure 27.3) and examined separately below.

GOVERNMENT DECISIONS

As in other areas of 'market failure' (for example, monopoly), a government may decide to intervene in the workings of the economic system to achieve what it regards as desirable social and/or economic objectives such as the protection of the natural environment and the safeguarding of important natural resources and biodiversity. Such intervention takes a variety of forms from State direction to more persuasive approaches and involves the

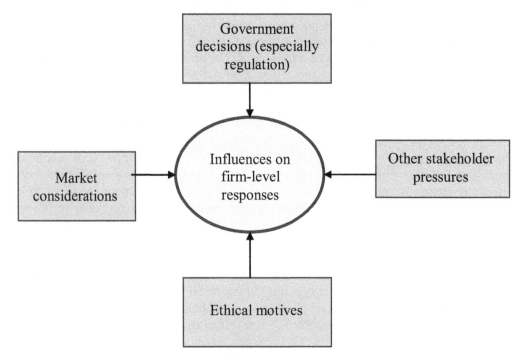

Figure 27.3 Drivers of corporate ecological responsiveness

use of different policy instruments aimed at shaping corporate environmental behaviour (Worthington, 2005). We examine three major approaches below.

Regulatory approaches

In the environmental sphere, legislation, regulations and directives are a familiar part of the architecture of government and have been an important influence in inducing corporate ecological responsiveness (Cairncross, 1995; Bansal and Roth, 2000; Patton and Worthington, 2003; Worthington, 2005). As the name suggests, this approach essentially involves using the law to instruct firms what to do either in detail or by setting a goal which they are required to pursue (Cairncross, 1995). In some cases a government may not only tell businesses what they have to achieve, but how they are to achieve it (for example, what technologies to use), an approach known as 'command and control' which involves the use of penalties or fines for non-compliance and the establishment of elaborate systems on inspection, monitoring and enforcement (for example, by an environmental agency) to ensure that firms meet their legal obligations.

Given that environmental problems occur at all spatial levels from the local to the global, regulatory solutions frequently involve different levels of governmental and/or intergovernmental response, what Roberts (1995) calls a hierarchy of environmental policy and law. Moreover, the outcomes of the regulatory process in different countries tend to be shaped by different traditions, styles, institutional settings and political imperatives (Kolk, 2000). The United States, for example, is said to be characterised by an adversarial regulatory environment which places emphasis on detail and uniformity and on suing firms for non-compliance, while European governments tend to take a more collaborative and consensual approach to regulation which involves negotiations with industry over policy and implementation (Kolk, 2000; Gunningham and Sinclair, 2002). That said we should not forget that differences in approach can also occur within as well as between countries, as illustrated by the recent decisions of some US states and cities to a take a different stance on carbon emissions from that of the federal government in Washington.

Market-based approaches

Whilst regulation has traditionally been the commonest tool of government environmental policy, market-based approaches have become increasingly fashionable, particularly in the developed economies (EEA, 1996; Pearce and Barbier, 2001). At their heart lies the idea that market forces can be used to induce changes in corporate behaviour that will begin to address the issue of market failure and the resultant negative externalities such as pollution and resource degradation. Pearce and Barbier (2001) define market-based instruments as those which 'explicitly affect the private costs and benefits reflected in markets so that any unaccounted social costs (and benefits) of environmental degradation can be internalized to ensure the desired environmental improvement' (p.173). Examples include environmental charges, taxes or fees, environmental subsidies, deposit refund systems, tradable emissions permits and a number of other approaches aimed at shaping corporate environmental responses through the market system. In this chapter we examine the two most significant policy instruments of this kind, environmental taxation and tradable emissions permits.

Environmental taxes (sometimes described as Pigovian taxes after the economist A.C. Pigou), essentially involve correcting false price signals in the market place that occur because the societal costs of pollution are generally externalised by firms when arriving at the costs of production (EEA, 1996). By adding an environmental tax to each unit of output to reflect (at least in theory) the costs imposed on society by the firm's activities, prices are effectively forced upwards and this should cause a reduction in demand for the polluting product. Since the tax is imposed on the firms responsible for the environmental damage, the 'polluter pays' for their behaviour (Pearce et al., 1994), although in practice some of the charge may be imposed on consumers in the form of a price rise. Firms wishing to avoid paying the tax have an incentive to find ways to reduce the environmental consequences of their activities, thereby benefiting both the firm and the environment simultaneously.

Whereas environmental taxation essentially involves using an 'administrative price' to influence corporate decisions, a tradable permit system (for example, the EU Emissions Trading Scheme) operates through an 'administered market' in which quantity rather than price is used to achieve the desired environmental outcome (Pearce and Barbier, 2001). Under such a system, the relevant authority (for example, national government or inter-governmental body) fixes an overall level of acceptable pollution then allocates property rights to specific firms or industries for a pre-determined yearly level (that is, quantity) of pollution (for example, carbon dioxide emissions) they are allowed to emit. The firm/industry is given permits which reflect this annual allowance and these permits have to be surrendered at the end of the agreed time period. Firms which exceed their permitted level of pollution have to enter the emissions trading market and buy additional permits from those who have not reached their own target level, the latter benefiting from controlling their emissions at the expense of the former who have failed to meet their target. In short, the system is designed to encourage firms to find innovative ways of reducing their environmental impact by providing financial incentives for responsible organisations within a framework which sets an upper (and potentially reducible) limit on the acceptable level of pollution emitted by businesses.

Voluntary approaches

Like market-based solutions, voluntary approaches to environmental protection have grown in popularity in recent years and are part of a package of new policy instruments used by governments to address the problem of environmental degradation caused by business activity (Jordan et al., 2003; Tews et al., 2003). Paton (2000) defines voluntary mechanisms as 'private or public efforts to improve corporate performance beyond existing legal requirements' (p. 328); this definition therefore covers a variety of responses from individual voluntary initiatives such as the establishment of an environmental management system within an organisation to different types of agreement between various parties including the government or one of its agencies. Of the latter, the three most prevalent types are unilateral commitments, negotiated agreements and public voluntary programmes (Gunningham and Sinclair, 2002).

Unilateral commitments are undertakings entered into by an industry acting independently of a public body, with firms in the industry deciding what to do and how to do it with regard to environmental protection. Such commitments often involve the development of a code of conduct or environmental charter (for example, the CERES principles) or may take the form of industry self-regulation in which the agreement is designed by the industry association (for example, the Chemical Industry's Responsible Care Program) which monitors individual business performance. While not strictly a direct form of government influence on business, unilateral commitments tend to be encouraged by the potential threat of regulation and/or other forms of state inducement (for example, lower taxes or increased subsidies). In effect they can help to fend off regulatory initiatives, as well as reducing the need for firms to become involved in lengthy and expensive battles to influence the regulatory process.

Negotiated agreements by contrast involve a commitment that is the result of a negotiation between an industry (or firm) and a public body such as an environment agency or government department. The agreement therefore is arrived at following a bargaining process and is frequently signed at a national level by the relevant parties. In the UK, for instance, the business community and government have negotiated agreements over energy-related targets as part of the government's attempt to tackle the issue of climate change and meet its Kyoto commitments on greenhouse gas emission reductions. Under this agreement, firms meeting their targets receive an 80 per cent discount in the Climate Change Levy, a tax imposed on business use of energy by the UK government.

With public voluntary programmes, the commitments to environmental protection are first devised by an environment agency and then individual firms are invited to participate. The commonest form is where the agency sets particular targets and firms are invited to sign up to the standards set by the programme which may include inducements for performance. Perhaps the two best known examples currently in operation are the US Environmental Protection Agency's 33/50 program aimed at reducing the release of toxic chemicals by United States' industry (Arora and Casson, 1995) and the EU's Eco-Management and Audit Scheme (EMAS), a voluntary standard indicating a participating firm's level of environmental management (Roberts, 1995).

MARKET CONSIDERATIONS

While governmental interventions tend to 'push' firms towards greater environmental responsibility, pressures in an organisation's market place can 'pull' it in the same direction. Market-related influences can affect both the demand and supply side of corporate activity and involve a range of stakeholders whose actions and decisions can impact on business revenues and/or costs and hence on corporate behaviour.

On the demand side, the response of customers to a firm's environmental performance can clearly affect its bottom line, particularly where a business has opportunities to exploit its green credentials (Azzone and Bertele, 1994; Bonifant et al., 1995). As Bansal and Roth (2000) have noted, the literature of corporate greening points to a range of potential benefits associated with corporate ecological activities including revenue growth through green marketing; the sale of waste products; outsourcing a firm's environmental expertise and rent-earning firm-based resources such as corporate reputation, enhanced learning capabilities and product quality (Hart, 1995; Russo and Fouts, 1997). Firms which exploit their environmental performance could be in a position to gain a competitive advantage over their rivals and this could be a spur to corporate action (Azzone and Bertele,

1994; Porter and van der Linde, 1995 and 1995a; Esty and Winston, 2006). Conversely, organisations which fail to meet customer expectations regarding their environmental behaviour might find themselves at a competitive disadvantage, especially where a firm's attitude to Corporate Social Responsibility (CSR) is an important influence on consumer behaviour.

Negative responses of the latter kind can also apply to organisational stakeholders on the supply side of business, potentially leading to a firm experiencing operational difficulties and/or increased costs of production that could have significant commercial and competitive implications. Organisations which are unable or reluctant to address their environmental impact could find finance and/or insurance difficult or more expensive to obtain and could face problems both up and down their supply chains, particularly where suppliers or corporate customers have a considerable degree of market power (Henriques and Sadorsky, 1999). Evidence from the CSR literature also suggests that a firm's overall social performance may impact on employee decisions and behaviour, including issues relating to employee recruitment and retention (Turban and Greening, 1997).

On the positive side, some businesses might achieve supply side benefits via gains in eco-efficiency that might accrue from environmental initiatives that involve energy or resource savings, materials substitution, product and/or process redesign or packaging reduction (De Simone and Popoff, 1997). Exploiting such benefits and/or managing supply side risks could prove an important stimulus to corporate ecological responsiveness, not least in organisations facing highly competitive market conditions and a challenging regulatory regime.

OTHER STAKEHOLDER PRESSURES

While market influences clearly act as powerful drivers for most private sector business organisations, other stakeholder pressures could prove instrumental in inducing beyond compliance environmental practices (Bansal and Roth, 2000). Environmental interest groups, other civic society organisations, the media and the local community generally can all encourage firms to consider their impact on the environment when making corporate decisions, if only to avoid the threat of public campaigns, direct action or adverse media publicity. Research suggests that stakeholder pressures can be linked to the formulation of corporate environmental plans and to the degree of proactivity in environmental management (Henriques and Sadorsky, 1996, 1999), with highly environmentally visible firms (for example, chemical and oil companies) likely to be more vulnerable to societal influences of this kind (Bowen, 2000).

ETHICAL MOTIVES

Firm-level environmental responses can also be linked to influences arising within the organisation, particularly the ethical stance adopted by senior managers and executives. As with CSR generally, some businesses might engage in environmentally responsible business practices because members of the top management team believe it is the 'right thing to do' (Bansal and Roth, 2000), with influential individuals acting as 'environmental champions' (Anderson and Bateman, 2000) in shaping corporate values and strategies. It has been suggested that while external factors create expectations and incentives for management action, organisational politics influences how managers interpret and act upon pressures arising within a firm's regulatory, market and social domains (Prakash, 2000). Under this perspective, beyond compliance environmental behaviour is basically explained by intra-firm dynamics, with 'power-based' and leadership-based' processes seen as central to understanding an organisation's response to demands for greater environmental responsibility (Prakash 2000, 2001).

Firm-level Responses to Environmental Protection

When faced with the kinds of pressures discussed above, businesses can respond in different ways, ranging from negative or fairly passive responses, through regulatory compliance, to what might be described as more proactive or advanced reactions to environmental protection. To analyse these responses, researchers have used a variety of lenses, including models derived from the fields of strategic management, corporate social responsibility/performance and corporate environmental management (Winn and Angell, 2000). In the CSR literature for example, Sethi (1987) has proposed a three-fold typology of business/society interaction in which he differentiates between 'social obligation', 'social responsibility' and 'social responsiveness'. Social obligation connotes a situation where the organisation uses legal and economic criteria to control corporate behaviour, with its strategy being essentially reactive and dependent upon change instigated by the market or through legislation. Social responsibility is defined as a situation where an organisation takes account of its impact on society – including the effect of its activities on the environment – and consequently acts in a way which accords with prevailing social norms, values and performance expectations. In contrast, social responsiveness signifies a situation where the firm pursues a proactive strategy and actively seeks social change by demonstrating and promoting socially responsible attitudes and behaviour (Worthington, 2005).

The use of classification systems to distinguish between different levels of organisational response is particularly prevalent in the literature of environmental management, with over 50 models appearing in the last 20 years or so (Kolk and Mauser, 2002). While some of these models are empirically-based, most tend to be conceptually-derived and are based on the experience and/or intuition of researchers in this field. At the risk of simplification, most of the models proposed fall into two main types: typologies and stage/phase/continuum models (Kolk and Mauser, 2002) Examples of each type are outlined below.

Following Doty and Glick (1994), Kolk and Mauser (2002) define typological models as those which do not provide decision rules for categorising organisational responses. Instead they propose multiple 'ideal types', each of which represents a unique combination of organisational attributes that are thought to determine the relevant outcome (p. 22). Steger (1993), for example, has put forward a two-dimensional or matrix model, where the axes represent 'corporate environmental risks' and 'market opportunities through environmental protection' and the scales are ranked small and large. The resultant two-by-two matrix identifies four possible generic environmental strategies which are described as: 'indifferent' (small risk; small market opportunities); 'defensive' (large risk; small market opportunities); 'offensive' (small risk; large market opportunities); 'innovative' (large risk; large market opportunities).

With models of this type – described by Hass (1996) as 'categorical models' – there is no assumption of progression in environmental protection, although movement between cells is theoretically possible. With stage (or phase or continuum) models by contrast, the notion of evolutionary progression is inherent in the model. Under this approach, firm-level responses are categorised into mutually exclusive and exhaustive sets, each with a series of discreet decision rules, such that firms are allocated to a specific category depending on their responses, attitudes and postures towards environmental protection across a range of parameters (Hass, 1996; Kolk and Mauser, 2002). Thus as an organisation's responses to protecting the environment develops, it can move along the continuum, indicating higher levels of corporate environmental performance.

Of the wide range of models of this type, two of the best known are those by Roome (1992) and Hunt and Auster (1990) who essentially classify firms according to their degree of proactivity in environmental management. Under the Roome model, companies are allocated to different categories on the basis of their strategic responses to external pressures, with five alternative forms of response identified:

- 'non-compliance' – a passive response linked to factors such as cost and organisational inertia;
- 'compliance' – a reactive and tactical response based on legislation;
- 'compliance-plus' – where the firm goes beyond legal compliance and proactively begins to integrate its environmental management systems into its business strategy;
- 'commercial and environmental excellence' – a proactive response involving value change in the organisation and acceptance that good environmental management is good management;
- 'leading edge' – a company at the leading edge in its sector, using state of the art management techniques.

Roome sees the first four responses as stages on a developmental continuum, whilst the last position defines the environmental leaders for a particular industry. According to Roome, the key factors affecting what choice a firm will make include the degree of environmental pressure faced by an organisation, the competence and knowledge of its management and the extent to which environmental values are embedded in the culture of the firm.

Like Roome, Hunt and Auster's model identifies five stages or categories of corporate environmental response, in this case based on considerations of risk reduction, commitment and programme design and a number of sub-criteria. The authors categorise the five stages as follows:

- 'beginner' – where there is no real protection against environmental risk and where environmental management is seen as unnecessary and minimal resource commitment takes place;
- 'fire fighter' – a situation of minimal protection, where environmental risks are addressed as necessary and resources committed as required;
- 'concerned citizen' – where the firm has moderate protection against risk, sees environmental management as worthwhile and has a consistent yet minimal budget to address environmental problems/risks;

- 'pragmatist' – where environmental management is seen as an important business function, protection against risk is comprehensive and sufficient funding is provided by corporate leaders;
- 'proactivist' – a situation of maximum protection, where environmental management is seen as a priority, funding is open-ended and the firm manages rather than reacts to environmental problems.

As Hunt and Auster (1990) note, each firm faces a unique set of circumstances in the field of environmental management that will shape its behaviour. That said, they argue that there appear to be a number of universal components of a proactivist environmental stance, including top level support and commitment, corporate policies which are designed to integrate environmental concerns, a high degree of employee awareness of and training on environmental issues and a strong auditing programme that facilitates problem identification and remedial action at the organisational level.

Interestingly, subsequent empirical testing of models such as these has tended to show contradictory findings. A study by Henriques and Sadorsky (1999) of Canadian firms was largely supportive of the above two models, whereas research by both Hass (1996) and Schaefer and Harvey (1998) calls into question their utility in interpreting firm-level responses. In Hass's study of Norwegian firms in two industries, she found the Hunt and Auster model inadequate as a research framework both in an operational and contextual sense and similar problems were evident in Schaefer and Harvey's testing of the two models in a UK context. As the authors point out, continuum models tend to imply linear and one-dimensional progression on all fronts, when in reality environmental responses tend to be more complex and multi-faceted. Thus, whilst models of this type can aid our understanding of the environmental management process and highlight the different reactions of corporate decision makers (Kolk and Mauser, 2002), we need to recognise their limitations, not least their tendency to over-simplify, to underplay the impact of both internal and external conditions on corporate responses and to treat environmental management as separate from considerations of business strategy as a whole, when in reality the two are often intertwined (Cramer, 1998; Schaefer and Harvey, 1998).

Concluding Comments

As the above discussion illustrates, environmental responsibility in business is a complex and multi-dimensional issue. Ultimately, how far firms will respond to the growing demands to become more environmentally responsible will depend upon a variety of internal and external influences operating within the organisation's regulatory, market and social domains. These include pressures from government and other stakeholders, market imperatives, institutional conditions, ethical considerations and managerial perceptions of risk and/or economic benefit from corporate ecological responsiveness. Given that the impact of these factors will differ both between organisations and over time, it is not surprising to find that levels of corporate environmental performance in practice can vary significantly between firms, even in the same sectors and industries. Some businesses clearly see environmental demands as a potential 'threat' to the firm's well-being and consequently their responses tend to be largely defensive and designed to minimise the impact on the organisation's bottom line. Others view being environmentally responsible as an 'opportunity' for creating organisational value and for enhancing the firm's competitive position vis-à-vis its rivals in the market place.

As with CSR generally, academics in this field remain divided over the question of whether being environmentally responsible 'pays off' (see, for example, Azzone and Bertele, 1994; Gallaroti, 1995; Maxwell, 1996; Porter and van der Linde, 1995 and 1995a; Walley and Whitehead, 1994). Proponents of the 'win-win' approach argue that both businesses and the environment can gain from firms becoming greener, with industrial and environmental performance seen as entirely compatible both in the short and the longer term (Rugman and Verbeke, 1998). In contrast, critics of this view maintain that any gains for the environment from higher levels of corporate ecological responsiveness are sometimes at the expense of the business, given that investing in environmental action tends to create 'losers' as well as winners, particularly at a time when environmental costs are growing substantially (Maxwell, 1996; Walley and Whitehead, 1994).

Current evidence suggests that among businesses themselves, many smaller and medium sized enterprises remain to be convinced that their activities can have a significant impact on the natural environment or that using resources to reduce their environmental footprint can benefit the organisation (Worthington and Patton, 2005). If sceptical businesses such as these are to accept that greening the firm creates rather than destroys organisational value, they will need to be persuaded of the merits of the business case for greater environmental responsibility. Only then are we likely to see a fundamental change in business culture, whereby environmental protection is seen as an inevitable part of doing business and as an essential component of organisational continuity and success.

References

Andersson, L. M. and Bateman, T. S. (2000) 'Individual Environmental Initiative: Championing Natural Environmental Issues in U.S. Business Organizations', *Academy of Management Journal*, 43(4), pp. 548-570.

Arora, S. and Casson, T. M. (1995) 'An Experiment in Voluntary Environmental Regulation: Participation in EPA's 33/50 Program', *Journal of Environmental Economics and Management*, 28(3), pp. 271-286.

Azzone, G. and Bertele, U. (1994) 'Exploiting Green Strategies for Competitive Advantage', *Long Range Planning*, 27(6), pp. 69-81.

Bansal, P. and Roth, K. (2000) 'Why Companies go Green: A Model of Ecological Responsiveness', *Academy of Management Journal*, 43(4), pp. 717-736.

Bonifant, B. C., Arnold, M. B. and Long, F. J. (1995) 'Gaining Competitive Advantage through Environmental Investments', *Business Horizons*, 38(4), pp. 37-47.

Bowen, F. E. (2000) 'Environmental Visibility: A Trigger of Green Organizational Response?' *Business Strategy and the Environment*, 9, pp. 92-107.

Cairncross, F. (1995) *Green, Inc.: Guide to Business and the Environment*, London, Earthscan.

Cramer, J. (1998) 'Environmental Management: from 'Fit' to 'Stretch'', *Business Strategy and the Environment*, 7, pp. 162-172.

De Simone, L. D. and Popoff, F. (1997) *Eco-efficiency: The Business Link to Sustainable Development*, Cambridge, Mass; The M. I. T. Press.

Doty, D.H. and Glick, W. H. (1994) 'Typologies as a Unique Form of Theory Building: Towards Improved Understanding and Modeling', *Academy of Management Review*, 19(2), pp. 230-251.

EEA (1996) *Environmental Taxes: Implementation and Environmental Effectiveness*, Copenhagen, European Environment Agency.

Esty, D. C. and Winston, A. S. (2006) *Green to Gold: How Smart Companies Use Environmental Strategy to Innovate, Create value and Build Competitive Advantage*, New Haven and London, Yale University Press.

Gallarotti, G. (1995) 'It Pays to be Green: The Managerial Incentive Structure and Environmentally Bound Strategies', *Columbia Journal of World Business*, 30(4), pp. 38-57.

Gunningham, N. and Sinclair, D. (2002) *Leaders and Laggards: Next-Generation Environmental Regulation*, Sheffield, Greenleaf Publishing.

Hardin, G. (1968) 'The Tragedy of the Commons', *Science,* 162, pp. 1243-8.

Hart, S. L. (1995) 'A Natural Resource-based View of the Firm', *Academy of Management Review*, 20, pp. 986-1014.

Hass, J. L. (1996) 'Environmental ('Green') Management Typologies: An Evaluation, Operationalisation and Empirical Development', *Business Strategy and the Environment*, 5, pp. 59-68.

Henriques, I. and Sadorsky, P. (1996) 'The Determinants of an Environmentally Responsive Firm: An Empirical Approach', *Journal of Environmental Economics and Management*, 30, pp. 381-395.

Henriques, I. and Sadorsky, P. (1999) 'The Relationship between Environmental Commitment and Managerial Perceptions of Stakeholder Importance', *Academy of Management Journal*, 42(1), pp. 87-99.

Hunt, C. B. and Auster, E. R. (1990) 'Proactive Environmental Management: Avoiding the Toxic Trap', *Sloan Management Review*, 31(2), pp. 7-18.

Johnson, G., Scholes, K. and Whittington, R. (2005) *Exploring Corporate Strategy*, 7th Edition, Harlow, Financial Times/Prentice Hall.

Jordan, A., Wurzel, R., Zito, A. R. and Bruckner, L. (2003) 'European Governance and the Transfer of 'New' Environmental Policy Instruments (NEPIs) in the European Union', *Public Administration*, 81(3), pp. 555-574.

Kolk, A. (2000) *Economics of Environmental Management*, Harlow, Financial Times/Prentice Hall

Kolk, A. and Mauser, A. (2002) 'The Evolution of Environmental Management. From Stage Models to Performance Evaluation', *Business Strategy and the Environment*, 11, pp. 14-31.

Maxwell, J. W. (1996) 'What To Do When Win-Win Won't Work: Environmental Strategies for Costly Regulation', *Business Horizons*, 39(5), September/October, pp. 60-63.

Paton, B. (2000) 'Voluntary Environmental Initiatives and Sustainable Industry', *Business Strategy and the Environment*, 9, pp. 328-338.

Patton, D. and Worthington, I (2003) 'SMEs and Environmental Regulations: A Study of the UK Screen-printing Sector, *Environment and Planning C: Government and Policy*, 21, pp. 549-566.

Pearce, D., Markandya, A. and Barbier, E. B. (1994) *Blueprint for a Green Economy*, London, Earthscan.

Pearce, D. and Barbier, E. B. (2001) *Blueprint for a Sustainable Economy*, London, Earthscan.

Pearce, D. W. and Kerry Turner, R. (1990) *Economics of Natural Resources and the Environment*, Hemel Hempstead, Harvester Wheatsheaf.

Pettigrew, A. M. (1987) 'Context and Action in the Transformation of the Firm', *Journal of Management Studies*, 24(6), pp. 649-670.

Porter, M. E. and van der Linde, C. (1995) 'Green Competitive: Ending the Stalemate', *Harvard Business Review*, September-October, pp. 120-134.

Porter, M. E. and van der Linde, C. (1995a) 'Towards a New Conception of the Environment-Competitiveness Relationship', *Journal of Economic Perspectives*, 9(4), Fall, pp. 97-118.

Prakash, A. (2000) *Greening the Firm: the Politics of Corporate Environmentalism*, Cambridge, Cambridge University Press.

Prakash, A. (2001) 'Why Do Firms Adopt Beyond-Compliance Environmental Policies?', *Business Strategy and the Environment*, 10, pp. 286-299.

Roberts, P. (1995) *Environmentally Sustainable Business: A Local and Regional Perspective*, London, Paul Chapman Publishing.

Roome, N. (1992) 'Developing environmental management strategies', *Business Strategy and the Environment*, 1(1), pp. 11-24.

Rugman, A. M. and Verbeke, A. (1998) 'Corporate Strategies and Environmental Regulations: An Organizing Framework', *Strategic Management Journal*, 19, pp. 363-375.

Russo, M. V. and Fouts, P. A. (1997) 'A Resource-Based Perspective on Corporate Environmental Performance and Profitability', *Academy of Management Journal*, 40(3), pp. 534-559.

Schaefer, A. and Harvey, B. (1998) 'Stage Models of Corporate 'Greening': A Critical Evaluation', *Business Strategy and the Environment*, 7, pp. 109-123.

Sethi, S. P. (1987) 'A Conceptual Framework for Environmental Analysis of Social Issues and Evaluation of Business Response Patterns' in Sethi, S. P. and Falbe, C. M. (eds), *Business and Society: Dimensions of Conflict and Co-operation'* Lexington Books.

Shrivastava, P. (1995) 'Ecocentric Management for a Risk Society', *Academy of Management Review*, 20, pp. 118-137.

Steger, U. (1993) 'The Greening of the Board Room: How German Companies are Dealing with Environmental Issues' in Fischer, K and Schot, J. (eds) *Environmental Strategies for Industry: International Perspectives on Research Needs and Policy Implications*, Washington, Island Press.

Tews, K., Busch, P-O and Jorgens, H. (2003) 'The Diffusion of New Environmental Policy Instruments', *European Journal of Political Research*, 42, pp. 569-600.

Turban, D. B. and Greening, D. W. (1997) 'Corporate Social Performance and Organizational Attractiveness to Prospective Employees', *Academy of Management Journal*, 40, pp. 658-72.

Walley, N. and Whitehead, B. (1994) 'It's Not Easy Being Green', *Harvard Business Review*, 72(3), pp. 46-52.

Wetherly, P. and Otter, D (2008) *The Business Environment: Themes and Issues*, Oxford, Oxford University Press.

Winn, M. I. and Angell, L. C. (2000) 'Towards a Process Model of Corporate Greening', *Organization Studies*, 21(6), pp. 1119-1147.

Worthington, I. (2005) 'Business, Government and the Natural Environment' in Worthington, I., Britton, C.B. and Rees, A. *Economics for Business: Blending Theory and Practice*, 2nd Edition, Harlow, FT/Prentice Hall, Chapter 14.

Worthington, I and Patton, D, (2005) 'Strategic Intent in the Management of the Green Environment within SMEs: An Analysis of the UK Screen-printing Sector', *Long Range Planning*, 38, pp. 197-212.

Worthington, I and Britton, C. B. (2006) The Business Environment, 5th Edition, Harlow, FT/Prentice Hall.

KEY REFERENCES FOR FURTHER READING

Bansal, P. and Roth, K. (2000) 'Why Companies go Green: A Model of Ecological Responsiveness', *Academy of Management Journal*, 43(4), pp. 717-736.

Cairncross, F. (1995) *Green, Inc.: Guide to Business and the Environment*, London, Earthscan.

Esty, D.C. and Winston, A.S. (2006) *Green to Gold: How Smart Companies Use Environmental Strategy to Innovate, Create value and Build Competitive Advantage*, New Haven and London, Yale University Press.

Kolk, A. and Mauser, A. (2002) 'The Evolution of Environmental Management. From Stage Models to Performance Evaluation', *Business Strategy and the Environment*, 11, pp. 14-31.

Pearce, D. and Barbier, E. B. (2001) *Blueprint for a Sustainable Economy*, London, Earthscan.

Porter, M. E. and van der Linde, C. (1995) 'Green Competitive: Ending the Stalemate', *Harvard Business Review*, September-October, pp. 120-134.

Prakash, A. (2000) *Greening the Firm: the Politics of Corporate Environmentalism*, Cambridge, Cambridge University Press.

Rugman, A. M. and Verbeke, A. (1998) 'Corporate Strategies and Environmental Regulations: An Organizing Framework', *Strategic Management Journal*, 19, pp. 363-375.

Russo, M. V. and Fouts, P. A. (1997) 'A Resource-Based Perspective on Corporate Environmental Performance and Profitability', *Academy of Management Journal*, 40(3), pp. 534-559.

Schaefer, A. and Harvey, B. (1998) 'Stage Models of Corporate 'Greening': A Critical Evaluation', *Business Strategy and the Environment*, 7, pp. 109-123.

Walley, N. and Whitehead, B. (1994) 'It's not easy being green', *Harvard Business Review,* 72(3), pp. 46-52.

Worthington, I. (2005) 'Business, Government and the Natural Environment' in Worthington, I., Britton, C.B. and Rees, A. *Economics for Business: Blending Theory and Practice*, 2nd Edition, Harlow, FT/Prentice Hall, Chapter 14.

28 *Corporate Social Responsibility in the Creation of Shareholder Value*

STEPHAN HEBLICH

Introduction

It is widely believed that globalization led to a global framework where companies can source globally and exploit people and force down environmental regulation. But, do they? In this chapter, it is shown that there are strong incentives for companies to act socially responsible—even in the absence of formal regulations. In fact, pursuing a Corporate Social Responsibility (CSR) strategy does not necessarily interfere with or hinder a firm's performance. Rather, it can be regarded as an innovation strategy that keeps a company competitive and thus contributes to its shareholder value. Two perspectives are relevant to this focus on innovation: (1) the within-firm innovative process and (2) the greater social environment outside the firm where knowledge can be gleaned as to what it is consumers, or more generally stakeholders, desire. Interaction with the firm's stakeholders reduces the risk of failure surrounding every innovation by making sure, in advance, that the innovation, whether it be product, service, or practice, meets their expectations—in terms of user value but also as to its environmental and social impact. Such sustainable innovations are a major driver of a firm's competitiveness and shareholder value as they are designed to fulfill consumers' practical *and* ethical/moral needs and desires.

In this period of globalization, it is widely believed that companies search out the cheapest production facilities in terms of labor costs and regulations. This is, indeed, partly true, at least to the extent that global competition has increased as a result of improved transportation and communication, increasing international capital mobility, and the reduction of trade barriers. New competitors have entered the marked and the resulting increased competition now puts pressure on all internationally competing companies. As general input factors such as unskilled labor and raw materials have become almost ubiquitously available, cost structures have started playing a more important role and companies now must focus on creating shareholder value as a way to survive the intense competition. Thus, companies use their connections and networks to shift labor-intensive production to areas of the globe that can offer competitive wages.

However, this does not necessarily mean that global sourcing companies sacrifice social and environmental standards for the sake of profit. In fact, I will argue that for a company to be truly successful, it cannot engage in a tradeoff between shareholder value and economic goals on the one hand and social or environmental goals on the other hand. Multinational companies can, of course, source globally and in the process exploit people and force down environmental regulation in those countries that are in need of foreign direct investment and thus have almost no bargaining power—there is no doubt about this. But, do they? This is the ultimate question.

To answer this question we need to investigate what really drives shareholder value. Basically, shareholder value reflects a company's expected future cash flow where costs and sales are major drivers. Global sourcing is one way to lower costs and thus to influence the cash flow. However, this strategy only works if sales stay at least constant. If cost reduction results in fewer sales, the company may, ironically, lose money by trying to save on costs. It is not too hard to imagine this scenario actually unfolding if, for example, consumers refuse to buy products produced under intolerable social and environmental conditions. Producers are the ones who initially decide what products to offer. But in the end, it is consumer behavior that determines the way of producing these goods and whether that decision will result in profit or loss. 'The direction of all economic affairs is in the market society a task of the entrepreneurs. Theirs is the control of production. They are at the helm and steer of the ship. A superficial observer would believe that they are supreme. But they are not. They are bound to obey unconditionally the captain's orders. The captain is the consumer' (Mises 1949: 265). Put another way, consumers vote with their pocketbooks: every purchase is like casting a vote for (or against) a particular product and thus consuming (and, by necessity, producing) becomes a democratic process. As a consequence, at least in a perfect world, firm behavior is completely determined by consumer choice and thus socially undesirable action is impossible. However, this is not a perfect world and one of its imperfections that is especially relevant to this topic has to do with information asymmetries. Consumers may be unaware of 'bad' corporate action taking place in some hidden part of the world. This is becoming less and less of a problem, though, due to the increased speed of information processing in today's world and the growing presence of Non-Governmental Organizations (NGOs) that act as global watchdogs. Thus, consumers do have at least some power to sanction corporate behavior.

Against this background, this chapter argues that companies have an incentive to act in accordance with society's demands, that is, to pursue CSR strategies—even in the absence of formal regulation. Pursuing a CSR strategy is a viable strategy for *increasing* shareholder value, not decreasing it as might be expected. If shareholder value depends on the firm's expected future competitiveness, CSR can be thought of as an investment in an intangible asset—the company's reputation—the returns on which can be measured as a company's goodwill. However, the level of return on this investment will depend on the number of firms pursuing the same strategy. As is true of every innovation, there is a pioneer rent for the first movers, but once a certain CSR strategy becomes common practice, rewards dwindle and, instead, *not* engaging in the strategy becomes punishable. Thus, the quest for consumer approval (and its tangible form, money) is a powerful driver of further innovation.

Along with this *direct effect* from a better reputation and greater consumer goodwill, there is an *indirect effect* from pursuing a CSR strategy, as it usually leads to the development or introduction of a new product, service, or practice that contributes to the firm's competitiveness. Examples include the creation of new energy saving technologies; relying on local suppliers as a way to save transportation costs and reduce pollution; increasing long-term productivity of the workforce by offering training; stimulating worker creativity by reducing stress through teamwork and a better balance between work and leisure; attracting highly qualified women by providing in-house daycare for children; and so on. Any innovation resulting from a CSR strategy is a win-win situation, in that both social and economic rent ensue. These are *sustainable innovations*, too, as integrating social and environmental demands into the company's product and image will meet with consumer approval and thus long-term economic success.

Against this background, CSR is introduced as an innovation strategy that keeps a company competitive and thus contributes to its shareholder value. Two perspectives are relevant to this focus on innovation: (1) the within-firm innovative process and (2) the greater social environment outside the firm where knowledge can be gleaned as to what it is consumers (ultimately, the firm's stakeholders) desire. Interaction with the firm's stakeholders will reduce the risk of failure surrounding every innovation by making sure, in advance, that the innovation, whether it be product, service, or practice, meets consumer expectations, not only in terms of user value but also as to its environmental and social impact.

This line of argumentation is developed within the following framework. To begin, the next section (Sustainable Innovations as a Major Driver of Shareholder Value) provides a more detailed discussion of a (sustainable) innovation-based shareholder value approach. The following section (CSR and Shareholder Value Across Time) provides an evolutionary perspective on the CSR concept, demonstrating how different perspectives on CSR in the creation of shareholder value have developed against the background of prevailing mainstream economic thinking. After this, 'Managing CSR Activities' looks at the creation of social innovations and how this process can be managed. 'Pursuing CSR as a Means of Becoming Socially Embedded' enlarges the within-firm process of innovating by taking the firm's environment into consideration. In doing so, this section merges the economic and social network surrounding a firm's production facilities, leading to a direct application of the stakeholder theory in the creation of shareholder value. 'Measuring the Impact of CSR on Shareholder Value' provides a short overview of common measures for the impact of CSR on firm performance. The final section concludes.

Sustainable Innovations as a Major Driver of Shareholder Value

Shareholder value reflects the market's expectations about the future productivity and competitiveness of a firm, reflected in its cash flow. In this regard, an expected positive cash flow means that the firm will earn profits in the future that can be distributed among shareholders. Accordingly, the discounted cash flow represents the firm's shareholder value today, where the discount factor is the opportunity cost of capital, that is, the return investors could achieve when investing in another project of similar risk.

One way of creating a future cash flow with a positive net present value is by way of constant and successful innovation. Following Schumpeter (1942: 85), 'it is not the kind of [price] competition which counts but the competition for the new commodity, the new technology, the new source of supply, the new type of organization (the largest-scale unit of control for instance)—competition which commands a decisive cost or quality advantage and which strikes not at the margins of the profits and the outputs of the existing firms, but at their foundations and at their very lives.' Accordingly, only those firms that innovate on a constant basis will survive and thus create shareholder value. The importance of constant innovation is further described by Aghion et al. (2006) in a model where technologically advanced entry creates a competitive environment that forces incumbents to innovate constantly. In this environment, each potential entrant arrives with leading-edge technology. If the incumbent is less technologically advanced, the entrant will replace the incumbent. If the incumbent is also employing leading-edge technology, it can use its reputation advantage and block entry. In short, an incumbent that is close to developing leading-edge technology has a strong incentive to continue to innovate and keep pace with technological progress as doing so can prevent entry of competitors. However, an incumbent whose technology is out of date—regardless of whether it innovates—will find it difficult to keep pace with technological progress and, presumably, will not be able to prevent entry of leading-edge competitors. Consequently, an incumbent that lags considerably behind the times is discouraged from innovating and will be forced out of the market. The main implication of this model is that the threat of technologically advanced entry (escape-entry effect) or of competition in an oligopolistic market (escape-competition effect) encourages innovation by incumbents already poised on the technology frontier (Aghion et al. 2001, 2005; Baumol 2002).

Taking a closer look at the innovation process itself, we can distinguish between different kinds of innovation. There are entrepreneurial innovations—revolutionary and heterodox contributions that are totally new to the market—and routinized innovations, which improve and extend on previous entrepreneurial contributions (Baumol 2002). This leads to the following categories of innovations likely to increase sales or cut costs and thus influence future cash flow.

1. Product innovations—that is, new products or services. These innovations increase sales.
2. Product improvements—that is, improvement or extension of existing products. These innovations increase sales.
3. Process innovations—that is, more efficient means of production. These innovations reduce costs.

These innovations initially create an economic rent as a new product or an improved process contributes to the firm's productivity and competitiveness. However, along with this direct effect, innovations may also create a social rent if the new product, process, or practice decreases environmental costs, for example, from pollution, or social costs, for example, by improving working conditions. Such *sustainable innovations* are the eventual result of a company's social embeddedness and its resulting ability to anticipate social demands, for example, for green products or socially responsible behavior in general. The sooner a company becomes aware of a new trend, the better its chances of improving its reputation as first mover. The company's reputation, in turn, may influence sales, for example, if consumers prefer Company A's products to Company B's products because Company A's practices guarantee higher social or environmental standards (Luo & Bhattacharya 2006). Furthermore, social innovations leading to an increase in reputation can also contribute to reducing (future) costs if they reduce the risk of damage to reputation. For instance, chemical companies cannot fully protect against accidents, but by constantly interacting with the local community and providing information about current activities along with having in place a proven catastrophe management plan, these companies build a stock of goodwill that can help them survive the negative effects that can occur in case of an accident.

Thus CSR can be regarded as an essential part of a sustainable R&D strategy where innovations create both economic and social rents. If CSR is viewed as a type of sustainable consumer research it becomes, in fact, the first step of the innovation process, where needs and thus emerging markets are discovered. With this knowledge, it then becomes possible to come up with an innovative product, process, or practice that meets consumer expectations and desires and leads to a pioneer rent. This, in turn, creates shareholder value. However, this nexus between CSR and shareholder value has not always been clear and it is therefore useful to take a look at the historical evolution of CSR and corresponding developments that have supported the idea that CSR strategy can create shareholder value.

Corporate Social Responsibility and Shareholder Value Across Time

The term CSR originated in the United States. It is generally assumed to encompass responsible corporate conduct that exceeds legal requirements. By engaging in CSR, enterprises will voluntarily compete in achieving social *best practices* and thus raise or improve standards in society (European Commission 2001).

Within the scientific literature, the term CSR was first formalized by Bowen (1953: 6), who argued in a normative way that 'it refers to the obligations of businessmen to pursue those politics, to make those decisions, or to follow those lines of actions which are desirable in terms of the objectives and values of society.' In the 1960s, several authors furthered developed the concept, including Davis (1960), Fredrick (1960), McGuire (1963), and Walton (1967).[1]

Remarkably, all these authors, like Bowen before them, refer only to 'businessmen.' In 1967, Davis finally enlarged the definition to include institutions and, thus, enterprises.[2] This was a crucial development because until that point, use of the term 'businessmen' implied that an enterprise's owner is also its manager and thus bears the cost of every social commitment personally. When, however, CSR is expanded to include enterprises in their own right as legal entities, the attribution of costs is not so simple. In the case of a manager-led enterprise, for example, the legal representative of the enterprise, the manager, does not bear the costs of social conduct; instead, the manager decides to take these actions in their role as agent of the principal. Friedman (1962, 1970) sees two problems with this, which ultimately cause him to fundamentally reject corporate social commitment.

---

1   Carroll (1999) provides a comprehensive overview of the development of the term CSR.

2   'Social responsibility moves one large step further by emphasizing institutional actions and their effect on the whole social system. Social responsibility, therefore, broadens a person's view to the total social system' (Davis 1967: 46).

First, managers in a free economic system are obliged by contract to maximize *shareholder value*: it is their primary task to maximize the value of the enterprise. To this end, resources should be put to their best possible use and employed efficiently, which, according to Adam Smith, best serves society as a whole. Managers' actions are bound only by institutional guidelines—the economic rules. Commitment beyond legal requirements[3] is in breach of this mandate as there are no corresponding gains and thus such commitment should not be undertaken. If managers want to work toward the betterment of society, they should do so as private individuals at their own expense, *not* as agents of their principals and at their principals' expense (Friedman 1970).

Friedman's (1962) second problem with management-invoked CSR is that he sees the financial commitment to social interests by managers as a threat to social freedom. Friedman believes that the identification and elimination of social nuisances are functions of the State. The State possesses adequate information and can effect an allocatively efficient distribution of funds via the tax system. Managers who, on their own authority, decide how much to spend and for what social interests, interfere with original functions of the State and run the risk of allocating funds inefficiently due to bounded information. Furthermore, Friedman fears that managers who act as civil servants rather than as the agents of their enterprises' owners will *de facto* increase governmental influence within the enterprises. In Friedman's eyes, this will induce a tendency toward collectivism, which he sees as a threat to social freedom.

Opponents[4] of this economic liberal position do not primarily view enterprises as auxiliary legal constructs that move like trains on tracks within the—best possible—established institutional framework. Instead, enterprises are viewed as a part of the society that legitimates their actions and on whose development they depend. A liberal society provides a favorable environment for enterprises and, in turn, enterprises are obliged to help develop and support the society,[5] especially in this day and age of increasing enterprise size, which only increases the level of social influence these enterprises can have.

Friedman is criticized for considering only the relationship between principals and agents and for choosing *shareholder value* as the only value to be maximized. An exclusive focus on shareholder value raises the worry that enterprises will neglect the (justified) interests of third parties and disregard external costs. However, as Friedman assumes the best possible institutional framework and, therefore, completely assigned property rights, external effects are ruled out *by definition*.[6] Therefore, the relevant question is not whether an enterprise behaves in socially desirable way, but whether existing institutions provide incentives that cause enterprises to so act. In other words, the important thing is not that

---

3   Friedman (1970: 33) speaks of 'general social interests.'

4   The most prominent of Friedman's opponents was another Nobel Prize winner, Paul Samuelson (1971: 24): 'A large corporation these days not only may engage in social responsibility, it had damn well better try to do so.' An extreme position was taken by Manne and Wallich (1972), who insisted that enterprises act as totally unselfish do-gooders in the sense of moral imperative.

5   'In its broadest sense, CSR represents a concern with the needs and goals of society which goes beyond the merely economic. Insofar as the business system as it exists today can only survive in an effective functioning free society, the CSR movement represents a broad concern with business's role in supporting and improving that social order' (Eells and Walton 1974: 247).

6   '[T]he enforcement of contracts voluntarily entered into the definition of the meaning of property rights [and] the interpretation and enforcement of such rights [in order to] prevent coercion of one individual by another' (Friedman 1962: 27).

enterprises or individuals *can* assume responsibility, but whether institutions have been designed to *cause* the desired conduct. We are thus dealing with a problem of institutions and not with a problem of individual or business ethics.

In fact, there are several factors that might hinder the accomplishment of a perfect institutional framework. To begin with, it must be understood that the design of current institutions is the result of a reaction to social needs, but the delay between a change in social preferences and a corresponding institutionalization creates a regulation gap.[7] Furthermore, due to increasing *global sourcing*, enterprises are confronted with various institutional frameworks—they are no longer subject to *just one* national regime. As there is no one-world government, much less one with adequate authority to sanction, there is no binding institutional framework at the supranational level. Therefore, global market failures—especially global external effects—can no longer be adequately internalized.

Under these conditions, enterprises—especially multinational enterprises—can contribute to closing this regulation gap. Such socially desirable conduct does not interfere with Friedman's presumption of profit maximization where (1) an enterprise's individual commitment may be assessed as a long-term investment, or (2) all enterprises agree on closing the regulation gap, making it a collective commitment. In fact, a company's active role in designing society's basic order leads to an adjustment of Friedman's implicit assumption of a perfect basic order. In reality, there are external effects that are not yet internalized and Freeman's stakeholder theory approach provides the theoretical framework to consider them.

The increasing credibility of the theory of stakeholders has made an enterprise's external environment a more important factor in its strategic decision making. Freeman (1984) finds that changing and ever-more complex requirements and the existence of new target groups, namely, stakeholders, makes this approach (that is, consideration of external environment) essential to successful business.[8] Anyone who might affect the business objective and anyone who might be affected by its realization is a *stakeholder* (Freeman 1984). Freeman believes that consideration of all stakeholders, including the shareholders, is critical for success and thus suggests establishing such consideration within the modern *theory of the firm* and including it in *management strategies*.[9] In Freeman's opinion, this is the only way to ensure current and future success (Freeman 1984).

Having this in mind, the next section practically applies stakeholder theory in the intra-firm context (Managing CSR Activities). 'Pursuing CSR as a Means of Becoming Socially Embedded' expands on this approach by focusing on the firm's social environment. Here, a firm's embeddedness in its social environment will lead to successful application of the stakeholder approach as, with time, the firm will become more aware of consumer needs and desires and be able to take advantage of clues about future trends and thus be able to come up with appropriate, and thereby profitable, innovations in a timely manner, leading to the capture of both economic and social rents.

---

7   Kofi Annan (2001) expressed this in a speech at the American Chamber of Commerce: 'Business is used to acting decisively and quickly. The same cannot always be said of the community of sovereign States. We need your help—right now.'

8   'Shifts in traditional relationships with external groups such as suppliers, customers, owners and employees, as well as the emergence and renewed importance of government, foreign competition, environmentalists, consumer advocates, special interest groups, media and others, mean that a new conceptual approach is needed' (Freeman 1984: 27).

9   In a comment to his book, Freeman (2004) highlights that his stakeholder approach was originally a strategic recommendation for managers and is thus to be understood as a strategy to maximize profit.

Managing Corporate Social Responsibility Activities

CSR can be used strategically to deal with identified stakeholder claims. Falck and Heblich (2007) introduce a concept for how management can use CSR as a prescriptive instrument in making plans that will satisfy both the stakeholder and shareholder approaches. They focus on the question of which stakeholders should be considered and, correspondingly, how much is at stake. These questions can be answered by employing a multi-stage process. As illustrated in Figure 28.1, the decision-making process is initiated by a social trend. At its inception, a trend is a social claim of unknown size. Thus the first task of strategic planning is to evaluate the trend. Is it merely the claim of a marginal group and liable to disappear quickly, or is it possibly a claim of great public interest that will become increasingly important? If government does not react to a trend of broad public interest, the company might be able to step in and address the public's concern. The decision as to whether the company should act must be based on an evaluation of the opportunities and risks involved. A cost-benefit analysis calculating the expected net present value of the future cash flow likely would be appropriate in making this decision. The following procedure is a template for the decision-making process.

First, are any of the company's stakeholders involved or interested in the trend? If not, the company should remain disengaged. However, if stakeholders are involved or interested, the claim could have either direct or indirect effects on the company, and management needs to deal with it, giving it the priority appropriate to the interested stakeholder's importance. Stakeholder importance is determined by the stakeholder's influence on the company's cash flow. To evaluate and thus be able to prioritize a stakeholder's importance, the influence of all known stakeholders needs to be mapped and thus, in a next step, all stakeholders are evaluated according to their potential to influence the company's cash flow. As illustrated in Figure 28.2, this leads to three different categories of stakeholders.

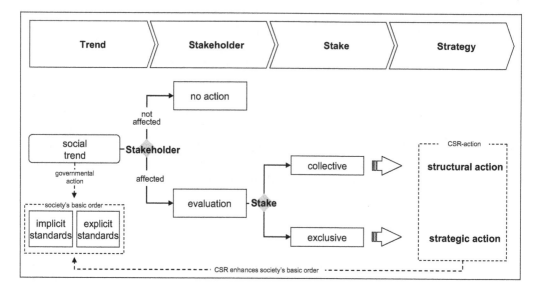

Figure 28.1 Planning process of strategic CSR action

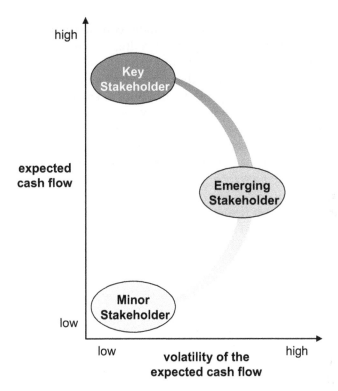

Figure 28.2 Management target priority

Stakeholders in the first category are the *Key Stakeholders*. This group includes all actors that have a direct connection with the company and can significantly influence the company's current and expected cash flow. Accordingly, these stakeholders need to be considered when calculating the expected net present value of the CSR action. Key Stakeholders are evaluated only once in a specific context, after which their status is fixed until the relationship changes fundamentally. The volatility of the Key Stakeholders' expected cash flow is low. This group includes, inter alia, the most important suppliers as well as major clients and crucial employees.

The second group is comprised of the *Emerging Stakeholders*. Currently, they do not have a direct connection to the enterprise's cash flow and do not influence the expected net present value. However, this situation can change rapidly, and management needs to keep an eye on this group in case some of its members suddenly become Key Stakeholders. The volatility of the Emerging Stakeholders' expected cash flow is high and thus this group must be evaluated regularly. This group includes, among others, suppliers that might gain influence in the future, NGOs dealing with sensitive issues, and politicians with the power to change the institutional framework.

Minor Stakeholders make up the third group. These stakeholders cannot interfere with the company's cash flow in the medium term and thus, although management needs to be aware of them, it does not have to pay them much attention. This group's expected cash flow volatility is low.

Management's decision criterion is the expected net present value of the social investment. If this value is positive, the investment should be made. As it might be possible to transfer Key Stakeholder contributions to the cash flow from one context to another and thus only the Emerging Stakeholder contributions need to be reevaluated, which should be done regularly in any case, making the investment decision concerning the new social trend will not take much time or incur much expense.

Depending on what is at stake, the investment can be either an individual or a collective commitment. The company should choose to make an individual commitment if the claim can be met by the company itself without any risk of opportunistic behavior by competitors. We call this an exclusive stake. This behavior is strategic because the goal is to attain a first-mover advantage (Jones 1995). The enterprise that leads the way as far as a socially desirable action goes can improve its reputation among customers and thus secure or expand its market share (Werther & Chandler 2005). The enterprise's action may also result in new social standards that turn out to be entry barriers for potential competitors. Migros, Switzerland's largest retain chain, is a good example of successful strategic action of the individual commitment type. Migros has supermarkets in Switzerland, France, and Germany and exports products to Austria, the United Kingdom, and the United States. In 2002, Migros committed itself to a standard for palm oil production. Palm oil is one of the most important oils on the world market and there is a steadily growing demand for it. It is an important raw material in the production of margarine, washing agents, soap, and cosmetics. Migros' palm oil production standard guarantees responsible sourcing because Migros will not buy palm oil produced from plantations that have been established at the expense of the rain forest. Introducing this standard paid off for Migros—twice! First, Migros won a UN award for its action. Second, and even more important, Migros became an outrider in the global consumer goods industry and thus gained influence. Migros initiated a Round Table on Sustainable Palm Oil (RSPO) and its standard has now become the global standard.

As a means of overcoming collective problems, a single enterprise's individual commitment is a risky investment that will be successful only if it does not lead to a competitive disadvantage in the long run. If the individual enterprise's activities weaken its competitive position, competitors will be quick to take advantage and, in the long run, the enterprise will either be forced to conform to the competitors' standard of behavior or leave the market. No social improvement will occur in this situation—collective commitment has to take the place of individual commitment.

Structural action should be undertaken when a collective commitment is required. It would not be rational for an individual enterprise to take action; rather, collective action is needed, something that is effected by and affects all competitors equally. The action could either lead to a concerted initiative to establish appropriate institutions or to a voluntary, collective commitment to a common code of conduct by several enterprises in the same market segment. Because all competitors (in the ideal case) are subjected to this code, there are no, at least no ruinous, distortions of competition. For example, take the case of corruption. If corruption (that is, bribery) is endemic in a certain industry, it would be nearly suicidal for a single company in that industry to commit itself to a code of conduct not permitting any use of bribery. Structural action would be needed to change this situation and make it possible for the industry as a whole to avoid great expense (that is, stop paying the bribes). According to the World Bank, corruption adds at least 10 percent to the common costs of doing business in many parts of the world. One of the most popular institutions supporting collective commitment is the UN Global Compact, by which enterprises commit themselves to respect ten rules in the fields of human rights, work, environment, and corruption. The free-rider problem, which is inherent in such situations, can be minimized by nonpolitical social organizations that monitor compliance with the code of conduct and thus act as watchdogs (Werther & Chandler 2005).

Structural and strategic action are both ways of practicing strategic CSR. If the actions move into the mainstream of society, they may become part of society's basic order, either as explicit, legal standards or as implicit, socially desired standards. Of course, it is possible that, over time, implicit social standards can become a part of the legal framework. Martin (2002) provides a detailed description of this process. Essential is that once an action becomes part of society's basic order, it is established in the public mind as such.

Hence CSR can be viewed as part of the dynamic process of discovery described by Hayek (1978). Society's basic order will always be imperfect, or incomplete, as it only reflects prevailing social opinion. Developments to come—the trends—cannot be foreseen and dealt with in advance. However, the way social trends are made a part of the social order, that is, by government intervention or by self-regulation, can be influenced and managed and it is in this aspect that companies have an opportunity to 'do well by doing good.'

Figure 28.3 is an illustration of how companies can temporarily bridge regulatory gaps by enacting a corresponding implicit institution.

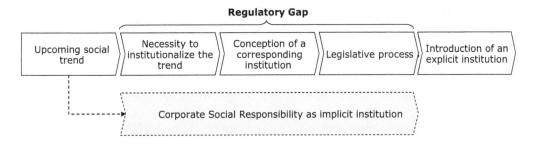

Figure 28.3 CSR as a way to bridge institutional gaps

Pursuing Corporate Social Responsibility as a Means of Becoming Socially Embedded

The discussion so far has made it clear that the type and amount of CSR activities should be determined by a firm's core business and also by its size. With this in mind, it is obvious that Multinational Enterprises (MNE) with many branches in various locations have to satisfy a much greater variety of stakeholders than do small and medium-sized companies located in only one region. However, this difference becomes smaller when adjusting the level of observation, that is, switching from the group level to the level of a MNE's local production facilities and its surrounding stakeholders. Regardless of their location, every single production facility of a MNE is located within one single region and within this region the production facility has to deal with the same set of stakeholders that are relevant to every Small and Medium-sized Enterprise (SME) operating in that same region. Both types of enterprise equally rely on the regional community, which encompasses both an economic and a social network that can hardly be separated out at this level: the economic network is embedded in the social network to such an extent that actions conducted within the economic environment cannot be separated from social life and vice versa. In this environment, every enterprise has an incentive to become socially embedded in the local community as a *corporate citizen* because doing so will ensure better access to the community's resources, for example, the regional labor pool, supporting institutions, and local suppliers, and also provide a window into local consumer desires and thus future trends (Kleinhenz, Heblich, & Gold 2006).

Accordingly, extending the stakeholder approach to interactions with local stakeholders would primarily require social embeddedness at the regional level where production initially takes place. Compliance with stakeholder demands may, for instance, include having employment policies that enhance the firm's status as good employer; environmental policies aimed at increasing the environmental friendliness of local production in support of the local quality of life; membership on regional university or school committees or in the local chamber of commerce; and contribution to local community development projects that are related to the firm's core business. In the case of companies that rely on a network of suppliers and thus cause a higher traffic volume, this could mean engaging in traffic planning projects. The social embeddedness resulting from pursuing CSR strategies in support of the community's long-term development eventually leads to a better understanding of consumer desires and thus provides information about upcoming trends and other important changes and developments in the 'real' world.

We can find support for the hypothesized positive effects of social embeddedness by drawing on the existing social network literature, a literature with a long tradition but one that has been based more in sociology than in economics. To take advantage of this research, it will be necessary to broaden our sights a little and embrace some sociological concepts, in particular the concepts of *social network* and *social capital*. Basically, a social network consists of a finite number of social entities (actors) connected by relational ties, where actors can be either discrete individuals at a micro level, or corporate and collective social units at an aggregated meso level (cf. Wassermann & Faust 1994). Analyses may focus on the locations and relations between single actors, between pairs of actors (Granovetter 1973; Burt 1992), or on the whole network and the institutions surrounding it, which institutions comprise the network's embedded resources (Scott 1988). The social network's outcome is usually referred to as social capital (cf. Bourdieu 1986; Coleman 1988; Putnam 2000; Lin 2001; for an economical approach, see Glaeser, Laibson, & Sacerdote 2002). An actor's incentive to participate in a social network, for example, to invest in social relations, is based in the expected returns from gaining access to the network's embedded resources, that is, social capital.

To become part of a social network, a certain initial reputation or status is required. Once achieved, the actor's status determines their networking possibilities and thus influences the production of further social capital. Following Burt's (1992) theory on structural holes, there may even be competition for new productive relationships, which makes the process self-enforcing. The actors become Schumpeterian entrepreneurs who constantly seek new and productive relational ties—so-called structural holes. Those actors who interlink crucial parts of the social network become 'gatekeepers' and thus pivotal within the social network. This role, in turn, increases the actor's networking power, which positions the actor to more successfully compete for additional gatekeeping functions and also increases the possibility of instigating certain changes in the actor's own favor. This self-enforcing process is a crucial part of the social network as it constantly enhances the social conduit system through which information flows.[10]

The basic idea of information flows in networks is that every single actor within the social network uses information provided by the network (input) to generate new information (output). In this course of information processing, the actor might enrich and also evaluate the initial information based on personal experience, a different perspective, or a different understanding. The interaction within the network eventually leads to a multiplication and valorization of embedded information for the benefit of all participants—they are all 'standing on each other's shoulders.' Thus, the network as a whole can deal with more complex problems than can individuals on their own and, furthermore, the social network acts as learning system as applied in neural network theory (cf. von Hayek 1945; Stokman & Zeggelink 1996). Research findings from epidemiology and the spread of diseases (cf. Bailey 1975) are useful in understanding the process of information diffusion within networks.[11] Two basic models have emerged that describe the diffusion of information in social networks. Granovetter (1987) and Schelling (1978) were among the first to create *threshold models*. These models are a way to describe collective action: an actor becomes active if a certain threshold number of neighboring actors is active. In contrast, *cascade models* focus on actors' relationships (Goldenberg, Libai, & Muller 2001). Whenever an actor adopts some information, there is a chance that their behavior will influence a neighbor to adopt it as well, that is, information is spread with a certain probability. Gruhl et al. (2004) expand the model with the concept of 'stickiness.' Hence, the probability that a topic might 'stick' to a neighboring actor depends on how interesting the topic is.

The role of relational ties in information diffusion is mainly based on Burt's (1992) theory of structural holes and Granovetter's (1973) fundamental theory of communication. Granovetter distinguishes strong relational ties from weak relational ties by the familiarity and trust between two actors. He argues for the importance of weak ties in the diffusion of fresh knowledge as these ties form a larger network. However, when dealing with relational ties in information diffusion, we need a more precise definition of the term 'information' as tacit knowledge comes into play (cf. Lundvall & Johnson 1994). Information can be codified, for example, in formulas, which makes it globally transferable; this sort of knowledge is available nearly everywhere instead of being a specific resource of a bounded social network. However, other types of knowledge, so called *tacit knowledge*, cannot be codified. This type of knowledge is transferred via direct interaction and thus cannot be dispersed in the absence of close spatial proximity (Anselin, Varga, & Acs 1997). It constantly circulates within a community's social network in the by way of regular face-to-face communication and informal meetings. The close interconnection

---

10   A network's superiority in information processing can be related to Hayek's (1937, 1948) idea of the superiority of decentralized information processing, that is, the division of knowledge as an expansion of Smith's argument on the division of labor. In his quest for a convenient economic order, Hayek (1948) comes to the conclusion that one major advantage of a free market society is prices developed within the system that contain a variety of information on scarcities and thus support efficient allocation. With regard to a social network, we can expand Hayek's argument. Within a social network, actors are interconnected by social ties and thus we do not necessarily need prices as a proxy for information transportation.

11   Classical disease-propagation models follow a cycle: a person is susceptible (S) to a disease and eventually infects other persons with a certain probability. Hence, the number of newly infected and thus infectious (I) increases. Depending on a disease's hazardousness, infected persons are either recovered (R) or, in a worse-case scenario, removed. Depending on whether individuals become immune (for example, chickenpox) or might be infected again (for example, influenza) involves SIR or SIRS models, respectively.

between the social and the economic network within a community (for example, friends who work for different firms) makes knowledge spill over (Saxenian, 1994)—it jumps, or runs, or 'spills' from firm to firm via the social network. Thus, a community's social life acts as a knowledge multiplier, increasing the pool of geographically bound knowledge. However, spatial proximity alone does not guarantee knowledge diffusion. The velocity and also the quality of the flow of regional knowledge further depend on an actor's social embeddedness (Gibbons 2005; Granovetter 2005).

The region's social capital—which is the outcome of effective network structures—is an intangible asset that supports every company's performance. On the one hand, being socially embedded contributes to a good reputation. Additionally, embeddedness is accompanied by increased access to information, which eventually leads to the emergence of productive networks as described in Porter's theory on economic clusters (Porter 1998). These clusters are comprised of a network of firms, along with their suppliers and supporting institutions, where social ties act as glue to stabilize the whole network. Being integrated in a network with its corresponding access to information additionally implies an *insurance function* that is closely related to the distinction between uncertainty and risk. According to Knight (1921), so-called objective probabilities cover *a priori* probabilities derived from given symmetries (as when throwing a die) and statistical probabilities as a result of analyzing homogeneous data. In contrast, subjective probabilities underlie an individual's estimate of proportions. Knight defines the former 'measurable uncertainty' as *risk* and the latter 'unmeasurable uncertainty' as *uncertainty*. With regard to business decisions, Knight characterizes them as 'situations which are far too unique, generally speaking, for any sort of statistical tabulation to have any value for guidance' (1921: 231). He believes that as it is far too complex to tabulate 'reality,' there will always be the problem of incomplete information to plague business decision making. Accordingly, gathering additional information is a way of decreasing uncertainty. This would seem especially important in the innovation process, which usually involves a certain degree of uncertainty with regard to the outcome. Knowledge concerning consumer desires and also about potential cooperation partners within the network can decrease innovation-related uncertainty.

Thus, to successfully pursue a stakeholder-oriented strategy, the company needs to meet the needs of both the economic and the social network. Embeddedness enables the firm to detect social and environmental externalities linked to the production process (that is, the firm's core business) that affect or might affect key stakeholders (an upcoming social trend) and thus should be taken into consideration. Taking action then has a twofold advantage. First, it is a signal of the company's willingness to interact with the social environment and meet its needs and/or desires. This contributes to the firm's reputation and thus increases its social embeddedness, which, in turn, leads to an increased flow of information, thus reducing uncertainty. The second advantage arises from the fact that having advance knowledge of social trends equals having information about an emerging market and makes it possible to come up with an innovation that can, at least temporarily, be the market leader and capture pioneer rent.

The previous sections have presented a theory on how reputation effects, along with the incentive to innovate, lead to an increased competitiveness and thus the creation of shareholder value. However, *knowing* this can occur is only one part of the story: actually *doing* it is it the other. Performance figures are regarded as major indicators of the efficiency of management strategies and thus can provide concrete evidence of the symbiotic relationship between CSR and profit. Therefore, the following section presents an overview of common methods for measuring the impact of CSR on shareholder value.

Measuring the Impact of Corporate Social Responsibility on Shareholder Value

The relevance of CSR for firm performance and thus shareholder value creation may be analyzed empirically by looking at the link between *Corporate Social Performance* (CSP) and *Corporate Financial Performance* (CFP), where CSP comprises the quality of stakeholder management evaluated by certain measures, and CFP is a measure of business success. This procedure is also described as *instrumental stakeholder* theory because the fulfillment of various stakeholder interests is seen as an *instrument* to augment the enterprise's performance.[12] According to Donaldson and Preston (1995), the instrumental stakeholder theory, along with *descriptive* and *normative* approaches, is one way of testing the 'true' impact of the stakeholder approach.

As early as the 1970s, several authors studied CSP's impact on CFP in the United States. Bragdon and Marlin (1972), using three different performance indicators, showed that in the paper and pulp industry, enterprises with the best records on pollution control and the environment were also the most profitable.

There are basically two approaches to empirical analyses: studies that measure the influence of CSR indicators on market data, and studies that relate CSP to accounting data (McWilliams & Siegel 2000). The first type often uses the event study method to document divergences from estimated development (abnormal returns), which may be viewed as reactions to CSR-relevant information that becomes known (see Stevens 1984; Klassen & McLaughlin 1996; Wright & Ferris 1997; Teoh, Welch, & Wazzan 1999). Among the studies that employ accounting data instead of market data, Bragdon and Marlin (1972), for example, chose the *average Return on Investment* (ROI), the *Return on Capital* (ROC), and the growth of *Earnings per Share* (EPS). Bowman and Haire (1975) chose the *Return on Earning* (ROE); Hart and Ahuja (1994), as well as Waddock and Graves (1997), chose the *Return on Sales* (ROS), the *Return on Assets* (ROA), and the *ROE* as measures of CSR influence. To measure CSP, indicators such as CSR announcements, environmental statements, or ratings have been used most often.

Margolis and Walsh (2001) made a detailed survey of 95 different research results from the period 1972 to 2000. The authors evaluated the studies by applying the vote-counting method (an analysis of frequency; see Hunter & Schmidt 1990; Light & Smith 1971) and found that most of the studies show a positive influence of CSP on CFP (53 percent) and a positive influence of CFP on CSP (68 percent). The event study methodology was used 16 times out of the 95 studies surveyed. Orlitzky, Schmidt, and Rynes (2003) are critical of these results as the applied frequency analysis does not properly consider sample and measurement errors and thus the conclusions might be erroneous (Hedges & Olkin 1980; Hunter & Schmidt 1990). They reevaluated many of the studies using the meta-analysis technique (Hunt 1997; Schmidt 1992). All in all, the results of all these studies on the

---

12   'In instrumental theory, statements are hypothetical—if X, then Y or if you want Y, then do X. In this sense, X is an instrument for achieving Y' (Jones 1995: 406).

relationship between CSR and financial performance are inconclusive (Margolis & Walsh 2003: 277).

Luo and Bhattacharya (2006) believe that these ambiguous findings relate to the design of the existing studies, in which CSR is generally rated based on backward-looking measures of firm profitability (ROI based on accounting figures) instead of on forward-looking measures like firm market value (Tobin's q). However, the concept of market value differs from ROI because 'accounting measures are retrospective and examine historical performance. In contrast, the market value of firms hinges on growth prospects and sustainability of profits, or the expected performance in the future' (Rust, Lemon, & Zeithaml 2004: 79). Accordingly, backward-looking measures based on accounting data may simply be too vague a proxy for financial performance.

Further, they suspect an omitted variable bias in these studies where underlying processes or contingency conditions remain unconsidered (Sen & Bhattacharya 2001). To test this second hypothesis, Luo and Bhattacharya propose a framework in which the relationship between CSR and firm market value is mediated by customer satisfaction. Building on previous work by Anderson, Fornell, and Mazvancheryl (2004) and Fornell et al. (2006) showing a positive relationship between customer satisfaction and market value, Luo and Bhattacharya add another stage to this framework by introducing CSR as a driver of customer satisfaction and provide some first empirical evidence for the existence of an indirect relationship between CSR and firm market value via customer satisfaction. Additionally taking into account that Luo and Bhattacharya find that firms with high innovativeness generate positive market value from CSR, these results support the current contribution's argument that CSR is a way to enhance reputation, obtain the knowledge necessary for sustainable innovation, and thus stay competitive.

Conclusions

This contribution's goal was to show that CSR strategies do not necessarily interfere with or hinder a firm's goal of increasing shareholder value. Indeed, quite the opposite appears to be true. Pursuing a CSR strategy has a reputation-enhancing effect that may affect the firm's future cash flow directly via increased goodwill. Furthermore, CSR has an innovation-triggering effect resulting in sustainable innovations. By sustainable innovation, I mean an innovation that involves a new or improved technology, process, or practice, thus generating economic rent, combined with desirable environmental or social behavior, thus generating social rent. Sustainable innovations are a major driver of a firm's competitiveness and shareholder value as they are designed to fulfill consumers' practical *and* ethical/moral needs and desires, thus creating a truly satisfied customer base that will lead to a truly 'happy' firm, too, that is, one with a promising future cash flow.

However, firms cannot innovate in a vacuum. Information about the world outside the firm and a head start on evolving trends are necessary prerequisites to successful innovation. Thus, a firm's interaction with its social environment is crucial. Against this background, pursuing a stakeholder-oriented strategy means direct interaction with stakeholders at the regional level where production takes place. The resulting social embeddedness grants access to an increased flow of information, enabling the firm to forecast and react appropriately to upcoming social trends.

In the case of multinational enterprises, social embeddedness does not and indeed, by definition, cannot, emerge from the top down. Rather, it starts at the regional level and works its way from the bottom up. If each separate production facility is socially embedded in its particular region, a diverse flow of information about stakeholder needs and desires will converge at the top, that is, at the group level. When the information reaches this top level, it then becomes the group management's task to evaluate the information and use it to devise a group strategy that will best meet the needs of all kinds of stakeholders—according to their priority. The MNE's strategy should include a general company-wide code of conduct that explicitly prohibits certain behavior at any time by any actor, a sort of 'Corporate Ten Commandments' if you will. However, the corporate policy must also ensure an appropriate amount of leeway so that region-specific customs and mores can be accommodated and the goal of social embeddedness furthered. For example, there could be a company-wide policy against being intoxicated on the job; however, in certain regions, a glass of beer at lunch would be tolerated, possibly even encouraged, because having a beer at lunch is local custom and *not* drinking would damage company reputation. This strategy of 'thinking global and acting local' can, when wisely employed, lead to an enhanced reputation and greater profit for the firm and, at the same time, make the world a little better place to live for the rest of us.

References

Aghion, P., N. Bloom, R. Blundell, R. Griffith, & P. Howitt (2005), Competition and Innovation: An Inverted-U Relationship, *Quarterly Journal of Economics*, 120, 701–728.

Aghion P., R. Blundell, R. Griffith, P. Howitt, & S. Prantl (2006), *The Effects of Entry on Incumbent Innovation and Productivity*, NBER Working Paper 12027.

Aghion, P., C. Harris, P. Howitt, & J. Vickers (2001), Competition, Imitation and Growth with Step-by Step Innovation, *Review of Economic Studies*, 68, 467–492.

Anderson, E. W., C. Fornell, & S. K. Mazvancheryl (2004), Customer Satisfaction and Shareholder Value, *Journal of Marketing*, 68, 172–85.

Annan, K. (2001), *Unparalleled Nightmare of Aids*, Address to the U.S. Chamber of Commerce. Washington, DC. Available at <www.un.org>.

Anselin, L., A. Varga, & Z. Acs (1997), Local Geographic Spillovers Between University Research and High Technology Innovations, *Journal of Urban Economics*, 24, 422–448.

Bailey, N. T. J. (1975), *The Mathematical Theory of Infectious Diseases and its Applications*, 2nd edition. London: Charles Griffin and Company.

Baumol, W. (2002), *The Free-Market Innovation Machine: Analyzing the Growth Miracle of Capitalism*. Princeton: Princeton University Press.

Bourdieu, P. (1986), The Forms of Capital. In J. G. Richardson (Ed.), *Handbook of Theory: Research for the Sociology of Education*: 241–258. Westport, CT: Greenwood Press.

Bowen, H. (1953), *Social Responsibility of the Businessman*. New York: Harper&Row.

Bowman E. & M. Haire (1975), A Strategic Posture Toward Corporate Social Responsibility, *California Management Review*, 18(2), 49–58.

Bragdon, J. & J. Marlin (1972), Is Pollution Profitable? *Risk Management*, 9–18.

Burt, R. (1992), *Structural Holes: The Social Structure of Competition*. Cambridge, MA: Harvard University Press.

Carroll, A. (1999), Corporate Social Responsibility—Evolution of a Definitional Construct. *Business & Society*, 38(3), 268–295.

Coleman, J. S. (1988), Social Capital in the Creation of Human Capital. *American Journal of Sociology*, 9, 95–121.

Davis, K. (1960), Can Business Afford to Ignore Social Responsibilities? *California Management Review*, 2, 70–76.

Davis, K. (1967), Understanding the Social Responsibility Puzzle: What Does the Businessman Owe to Society? *Business Horizons*, 10, 45–50.

Donaldson, T. & L. Preston (1995), The Stakeholder Theory of the Corporation: Concepts, Evidence and Implications. *Academy of Management Review*, 20, 65–91.

Eells, R. & C. Walton (1974), *Conceptual Foundations of Business*. Homewood, IL: Richard D. Irwin.

European Commission (2001), *Green Paper—Promoting a European Framework for Corporate Social Responsibility*. COM (2001) 366.

Falck, O. & S. Heblich (2007), Corporate Social Responsibility: Doing Well by Doing Good. *Business Horizons*, 50(3), S. 247–254.

Fornell, C., S. Mithas, F. V. Morgeson III, & M. S. Krishnan (2006), Customer Satisfaction and Stock Prices: High Returns, Low Risk. *Journal of Marketing*, 70, 3–14.

Fredrick, W. (1960), The Growing Concern Over Business Responsibility. *California Management Review*, 2, 54–61.

Freeman, E. (1984), *Strategic Management: A Stakeholder Approach*. Boston, MA: Pitman.

Freeman, E. (2004), The Stakeholder Approach Revisited. *zfwu*, 5(3), 228–241.

Friedman, M. (1962), *Capitalism and Freedom*. Chicago, IL: University of Chicago Press.

Friedman, M. (1970), The Social Responsibility of Business is to Increase its Profits. *New York Times Magazine*, September 13.

Gibbons, R. (2005), What is Economic Sociology and Should Any Economists Care? *Journal of Economic Perspectives*, 19, S. 3–7.

Glaeser, E. L., D. Laibson, & B. Sacerdote (2002), An Economic Approach to Social Capital, *The Economic Journal*, 112, 437-458.

Goldenberg J., B. Libai, & E. Muller (2001), Talk of the Network: A Complex Systems Look at the Underlying Process of Word-of-Mouth, *Marketing Letters*, 12(3), 211–223.

Granovetter, M. (1973), The Strength of Weak Ties. *American Journal of Sociology*, 78, S. 1360–1380.

Granovetter, M. (1987), Threshold Models of Collective Behavior. *American Journal of Sociology*, 83(6), 1420–1443.

Granovetter, M. (2005), The Impact of Social Structure on Economic Outcomes. *Journal of Economic Perspectives*, 19, S. 33–50.

Gruhl, D., R. Guha, D. Liben-Nowell, & A. Tomkins (2004), Information Diffusion Through Blogspace, Proceedings of the 13th International World Wide Web Conference (WWW'04), May 2004, 491–501.

Hart, S. & G. Ahuja (1994), Does it Pay to be Green? An Empirical Examination of the Relationship Between Emission Reduction and Firm Performance. *Business Strategy and the Environment*, 5, 30–37.

Hayek, F. A. von (1937), Economics and Knowledge. *Economica, New Series*, 4(13), 33–54.

Hayek, F. A. von (1945), The Use of Knowledge in Society. *American Economic Review*, 35(4), 519–530.

Hayek, F. A. von (1948), Individualism: True and False. In F. A. von Hayek (Ed.), *Individualism and Economic Order*: 1–32. Chicago: University of Chicago Press.

Hayek, F. A. von (1978), Competition as a discovery procedure. In F. A. von Hayek, *New Studies in Philosophy, Politics and Economics*: 179-190. London: Routledge & Kegan Paul.

Hedges, L. & I. Olkin (1980), Vote Counting Methods in Research Synthesis. *Psychological Bulletin*, 88, 359–369.

Hunt, M. (1997), *How Science Takes Stock: The Story of Meta-Analysis*. New York: Russell Sage Foundation.

Hunter J. & F. Schmidt (1990), *Methods of Meta-Analysis: Correcting Errors and Bias in Research Findings*. Newbury Park, CA: Sage.

Jones, T. (1995), Instrumental Stakeholder Theory: A Synthesis of Ethics and Economics. *Academy of Management Review*, 20, 404–437.

Klassen, R. & C. McLaughlin (1996), The Impact of Environmental Management on Firm Performance. *Management Science*, 42(8), 1199–1214.

Kleinhenz, G., S. Heblich, & R. Gold (2006), *Das BMW Werk Regensburg. Wirtschaftliche und Soziale Vernetzung in der Region*, Wissenschaftsverlag Richard Rothe.

Knight, F. H. (1921). *Risk, Uncertainty and Profit*. New York: Houghton Mifflin.

Light, R. & P. Smith (1971), Accumulating Evidence: Procedures for Resolving Contradictions Among Different Research Studies. *Harvard Educational Review*, 41, 429–471.

Lin, N. (2001), Building a Network Theory of Social Capital. In N. Lin, K. Cook, & R. S. Burt (Eds), *Social Capital: Theory and Research*: 3–30. New York: De Gruyter.

Lundvall, B.-Å., & B. Johnson (1994), The Learning Economy. *Journal of Industry Studies*, 1(2), 23–42.

Luo, X. & C. B. Bhattacharya (2006), Corporate Social Responsibility, Customer Satisfaction, and Market Value. *Journal of Marketing*, 70(4), 1–18.

Manne, H. & H. Wallich (1972), *The Modern Corporation and Social Responsibility*. Washington, DC: American Enterprise Institute for Public Research.

Margolis, J. D. & J. P. Walsh (2001), *People and Profits? The Search for a Link Between a Company's Social and Financial Performance*. Mahwah, NJ: Erlbaum.

Margolis, J. D. & J. P. Walsh (2003), Misery Loves Companies: Rethinking Social Initiatives by Business. *Administrative Science Quarterly*, 48, 268–305.

Martin, R. (2002), The Virtue Matrix. Calculating the Return on Corporate Responsibility. *Harvard Business Review*, 3, 69–75.

McGuire, J. (1963), *Business and Society*. New York: McGraw-Hill.

McWilliams A. & D. Siegel (2000), Corporate Social Responsibility and Financial Performance: Correlation or Misspecification? *Strategic Management Journal*, 21, 603–609.

Mises, L. von (1949), *Human Action*. London: William Hodge.

Orlitzky, M., F. Schmidt, & S. Rynes (2003), Corporate Social and Financial Performance: A Meta-Analysis. *Organization Studies*, 24(3), 403–441.

Porter, M. E. (1998), Clusters and Competition. New Agendas for Companies, Governments and Institutions. In M. E. Porter (Ed.), *On Competition*: 197–287. Boston: Harvard Business School Publishing.

Putnam, R. D. (2000), *Bowling Alone: The Collapse and Revival of American Community*. New York: Simon and Schuster.

Rust, R., K. Lemon, & V. A. Zeithaml (2004), Return on Marketing: Using Customer Equity to Focus Marketing Strategy. *Journal of Marketing*, 68(January), 109–124.

Samuelson, P. (1971), Love that Corporation. *Mountain Bell Magazine*.

Saxenian, A. (1994), *Regional Advantage: Culture and Competition in Silicon Valley and Rte. 128*. Cambridge, MA.

Schelling, T. C. (1978), *Micromotives and Macrobehavior*. New York: Norton.

Schmidt, F. (1992), What Do Data Really Mean? Research Findings, Meta-Analysis, and Cumulative Knowledge in Psychology. *American Psychologist*, 47, 1173–1181.

Schumpeter, J. A. (1942), *Capitalism, Socialism, and Democracy*. New York: Harper & Brothers Publishers.

Scott, A. (1988), *New Industrial Space: Flexible Production Organisation and Regional Development in North America and Western Europe*. London: Pion.

Sen, S. & C. B. Bhattacharya (2001), Does Doing Good Always Lead to Doing Better? Consumer Reactions to Corporate Social Responsibility. *Journal of Marketing Research*, 38, 225–244.

Stevens, W. (1984), Market Reaction to Corporate Environmental Performance. *Advances in Accounting*, 1, 41–61.

Stokman, F. & E. Zeggelink (1996), Self-Organizing Friendship Networks. In Wim B. G. Liebrand & David M. Messick (Eds), *Frontiers in Social Dilemmas Research*: 385–418. Berlin: Springer.

Teoh, S., I. Welch, & C. Wazzan. (1999), The Effect of Socially Activist Investment Policies on the Financial Markets: Evidence from the South African Boycott. *Journal of Business*, 72(1), 35–89.

Waddock, S. & S. Graves (1997), The Corporate Social Performance-Financial Performance Link. *Strategic Management Journal*, 18(4), 303–319.

Walton, C. (1967), *Corporate Social Responsibilities*. Belmont, CA: Wadsworth.

Wassermann, S. & K. Faust (1994), *Social Network Analysis. Methods and Applications*. Cambridge: Cambridge University Press.

Werther W. & D. Chandler (2005), Strategic Corporate Social Responsibility as Global Brand Insurance. *Business Horizons*, 48(4), 317–324.

Wright P. & S. Ferris (1997), Agency Conflict and Corporate Strategy: The Effect of Divestment on Corporate Value. *Strategic Management Journal*, 18, 77–83.

KEY REFERENCES FOR FURTHER READING

Carroll, A. (1999), Corporate Social Responsibility—Evolution of a Definitional Construct. *Business & Society*, 38(3), 268–295.

Donaldson, T. & L. Preston (1995), The Stakeholder Theory of the Corporation: Concepts, Evidence and Implications. *Academy of Management Review*, 20, 65–91.

Freeman, E. (1984), *Strategic Management: A Stakeholder Approach*. Boston, MA: Pitman.

Friedman, M. (1970), The Social Responsibility of Business is to Increase its Profits. *New York Times Magazine*, September 13.

Granovetter, M. (2005), The Impact of Social Structure on Economic Outcomes. *Journal of Economic Perspectives*, 19, S. 33–50.

Jones, T. (1995), Instrumental Stakeholder Theory: A Synthesis of Ethics and Economics. *Academy of Management Review*, 20, 404–437.

Luo, X. & C. B. Bhattacharya (2006), Corporate Social Responsibility, Customer Satisfaction, and Market Value. *Journal of Marketing*, 70(4), 1–18.

Martin, R. (2002), The Virtue Matrix. Calculating the Return on Corporate Responsibility. *Harvard Business Review*, 3, 69–75.

29 *Employer Duties*

STELLA VETTORI

Introduction

There are three major sources of employer obligations: international law, common law and statute. All of these sources require fundamentally the same duties of the employer. In terms of all these sources of law the employer is obliged to treat its employees fairly and to preserve the dignity of its employees. In terms of international law the International Labour Organisation (hereinafter the 'ILO') sets certain minimum standards which Member States are obliged to maintain. These standards are intended to be reflected in each State's national labour laws. The contract of employment, which is founded on common law principles, forms the basis of the employment relationship.

The International Labour Organization[1]

The ILO is one of the specialized agencies of the United Nations (UN) that serves to promote *social justice* for workers everywhere.[2] Historically, the ILO set its objectives as the promotion of rights at work, employment, social protection and social dialogue.[3] To achieve its objectives, the ILO formulates international policies to help improve working and living conditions; creates international labour standards to serve as guidelines for national authorities in putting these policies into action; carries out programmes of technical cooperation to help governments make these policies effective in practice; and engages in training and research to help advance these efforts.[4]

---

1   This section was written primarily by Prof McGregor of the University of South Africa.

2   The ILO originated from the aftermath of the Industrial Revolution in nineteenth-century Europe and North America (*The ILO What it is What it does* (2003) at 4). Although the revolution brought about economic development, this was at the cost of humans, and thus the idea of protective international labour legislation originated. Arguments in favour of international labour legislation basically included: (a) the necessity of improving the lot of the working masses; (b) the political importance of consolidating social peace in industrialized countries; and ©) the equalization of international competition (ibid). All of these, and the elimination of discrimination in respect of employment and occupation as a fundamental right, were written into the 1919 Constitution (later clarified in the Declaration of Philadelphia (1944)) when the ILO was officially established at the Peace Conference in Paris after World War I. At that stage, the ILO was associated with the League of Nations, the forerunner of the UN (*The ILO* at 4); *Basic Facts about the United Nations* (1995) 189; Paul Sieghart *International law of human rights* (1983) at 438; JG Starke *An introduction to international law* 6 ed (1967) at 517; 543-4). A supervisory system for the application of standards (a Committee of Experts composed of independent jurists) examines government reports on the application of Conventions ratified (later including also unratified Conventions and Recommendations) (*The ILO* at 5). It also presents its own report to the ILC annually.

3   ILO Report 'Decent work' op. cit. note 18 at 3.

4   Basic Facts about the UN op. cit. note 19 at 274.

The ILO has a tripartite composition, comprising of employers' organizations, unions and governments of its member States.[5] These parties participate with an equal voice in the International Labour Conference (ILC), which meets annually to discuss social and labour questions.[6] Currently, there are 174 member States.

ILO conventions which set international standards create binding obligations on Member States that ratify them, to put their provisions into effect.[7] Member States must periodically report on the measures taken to apply, in law and in practice, the Conventions ratified by them. These are intended to have a concrete impact on working conditions in workplaces all over the world.[8]

After the Second World War, the ILO adopted the Declaration of Philadelphia, reaffirming the fundamental principles on which the ILO is based, namely, that 'labour is not a commodity', 'freedom of expression and of association are essential to sustained progress', and 'poverty anywhere constitutes a danger to prosperity everywhere'.[9] These principles, to this day, constitute the main basis of the aims of the ILO.[10] The Declaration further holds that:

> *'All human beings, irrespective of race, creed or sex, have the right to pursue both their material well-being and their spiritual development in conditions of freedom and dignity, of economic security and equal opportunity.'* [11]

The ILO created certain basic international labour standards including the Forced Labour Convention,[12] the Convention on the Freedom of Association and Protection of the Right to Organize Convention[13] and the Right to Organize and Collective Bargaining Convention[14] and the prohibition of discrimination.[15] It adopted the Equal Remuneration Convention,[16] the Abolition of Forced Labour Convention,[17] the Discrimination (Employment and Occupation) Convention[18] and the Minimum Age Convention.[19] Membership grew rapidly in this period and the ILO took on a universal character.

---

5   *The ILO* op. cit. note 19 at 7.

6   Ibid.

7   *Basic Facts about the United Nations* op. cit. note 19 at 275. In addition to conventions, recommendations are found. These are non-binding instruments, which set out guidelines for national policy and action (*The ILO* op. cit. note 18 at 14).

8   *The ILO* op. cit. note 19 at 14.

9   Part I (a); (b); (c).

10   It is said that the Declaration anticipated and set the tone for the UN Charter and the Universal Declaration of Human Rights (*The ILO* op. cit. note 19 at 5).

11   Part II(a).

12   No 29 of 1930.

13   No 87 of 1948.

14   On 10 May 1944.

15   *The ILO* op. cit. note 19 at 6.

16   No 100 of 1951.

17   No 105 of 1957.

18   No 111 of 1958.

19   No 138 of 1973.

In 1998, the ILO adopted the Declaration on Fundamental Principles and Rights at Work, thereby reaffirming the obligation of Member States, to respect, promote and realize principles concerning fundamental rights, which are the subject of certain core Conventions, even if they had not been ratified.[a] These are the Forced Labour Convention,[b] the Convention on the Freedom of Association and Protection of the Right to Organize Convention,[c] the Right to Organize and Collective Bargaining Convention,[d] the Equal Remuneration Convention,[e] the Abolition of Forced Labour Convention,[f] the Discrimination (Employment and Occupation) Convention,[g] the Minimum Age Convention[h] and the Worst Forms of Child Labour Convention.[i] In addition there are *inter alia*, conventions regarding paid education leave, employment security, wages, working time, occupational safety and health, night work, social security, maternity protection and social policy. The Paid Educational Leave Convention of 1974, for example, provides for the obligation on each Member to formulate and apply a policy designed to promote, by methods appropriate to national conditions and practice the granting of paid educational leave for the purpose of training at any level, general, social and civic education and trade union education.[j] Article 2 of the Equal Remuneration Convention of 1951 provides for the application of the principle of equal remuneration for men and women workers for work of equal value. Provision is also made for effective equality of opportunity and treatment for men and women workers with family responsibilities in terms of the Workers with Family Responsibilities Convention of 1981. The Termination of Employment Convention of 1982 provides that 'the employment of a worker shall not be terminated unless there is a valid reason for such termination connected with the capacity or conduct of the worker or based on the operational requirements of the undertaking, establishment or service'.[k] The Convention then provides for appropriate procedures that employers should apply at the time of termination[l] and for the provision of procedures for appeals against terminations.[m]

---

a   *The ILO* op. cit. note 19 at 6.

b   No 29 of 1930.

c   No 87 of 1948.

d   No 98 of 1949.

e   No 100 of 1951.

f   No 105 of 1957.

g   No 111 of 1958.

h   No 138 of 1973.

i   No 182 of 1999.

j   Article 2.

k   Article 4.

l   Division B Article 7.

m   Division C, article 3.

At the end of the twentieth century, the ILO observed that globalization had (thus far) developed in an ethical vacuum where the attitude was one of 'winners take it all'. This, the ILO concluded had weakened the social fabric of many societies.[20] The ILO was particularly concerned about the unequal distribution of the gains of globalization between and within countries. In particular, it was concerned that the aspirations of

---

20   'Decent work and a fair globalization: national policy responses' An ILO Staff Seminar Turin, Italy 27–29/09/05 at 2-4. There is a direct link between decent work as a development agenda and the elimination of poverty (ILO Report 'Working out of poverty' op. cit. note 14 at 2).

workers and the unemployed had not been heeded.[21] The disparities in incomes, work and security worldwide were threatening the *legitimacy* of the global economy.[22]

The ILO began propagating a new 'global architecture' by adding a social dimension to globalization, that is, 'decent work' (referring to both employment and unemployment), for both women and men in conditions of freedom, equity, security and human dignity.[23] This was (and still is) perceived to be the most widespread need shared by people in every society and at all levels of development. A huge decent work deficit exists: there are not sufficient work opportunities; rights are denied at work; and an estimated 160 million people are openly unemployed in the world today.[24] Because whole families are affected, the figure affected is at least one billion.[25] Of every 100 workers worldwide, 16 are fully unemployed. Another 16 are unable to earn enough to get their families over the threshold of a minimum of $1 per person per day. Moreover, many more people work long hours at low productivity, are in casual employment, or are excluded from the workforce without being counted as unemployed.[26]

The ILO has developed a Global Employment Agenda, in terms of which the concept of decent work is of key importance.[27] In terms hereof, a rather wide definition of decent work was suggested:

- productive work in which rights are protected, which generates an adequate income, with adequate social protection; and
- sufficient work, in the sense that everybody should have full access to income-earning opportunities.[28]

The efforts of the ILO culminated in a 'blueprint' for globalization with a Report by the World Commission on the Social Dimension of Globalization (hereafter 'the Report').[29] In essence, the Report confirmed the unbalanced distribution of the benefits of globalization and held this to be morally unacceptable, politically unsustainable,[30] and a new version of earlier forms of domination and exploitation.[31] It stressed the fact that

---

21   ILO Report 'Reducing the decent work deficit' op. cit. note 14 at 13.

22   Ibid.

23   ILO Report 'Decent work' op. cit. note 18 at 3.

24   ILO Report 'Working out of poverty' op. cit. note 14 at 6.

25   ILO Report 'Decent work' op. cit. note 18 at 6.

26   ILO Report 'Reducing the decent work deficit 'op. cit. note 10 at 6.

27   'Decent work - the heart of social progress' http://www.ilo.org/public/english/decent.htm (12/05/06).

28   ILO Report 'Decent work' op. cit. note 18 at 13. Analyzing and interpreting this further, decent work then means: jobs of acceptable quality (that is constructive, profitable and gainful work) both within the formal and the informal sector; (the informal sector accounts for 60 per cent of Latin America's labour market and over 90 per cent of Africa's total employment (ILO Report 'Decent work' op. cit. note 18 at 4); decent remuneration (that is to fulfil basic economic and family needs); fair working conditions; fair and equal treatment at work (that is no discrimination); safe working conditions; protection in the case of unemployment; access to salaried jobs or self-employment (that is promoting entrepreneurship and supporting small businesses by providing access to credit, premises, management training, business advisory services, and so on);training and development opportunities; and job creation.

29   Report by the World Commission on the Social Dimension of Globalization 'A fair globalization: creating opportunities for all' (2004); Department of Labour 'International Labour Conference ends' 18/06/06; www.labour.gov. za/media/statementdisplay.jsp? _id=5331; Department of Labour 'South Africa accepts globalization report' 7/06/06; www.labour.gov.za/media/staement.jsp?statementdisplay_id=5348; 'South Africa accepts globalization report' 7/06/06.

30   ILO Report 'A fair globalization: creating opportunities for all' op. cit. note 31 at x.

31   ILO Report 'A fair globalization: creating opportunities for all' op. cit. note 31 at 5.

people are most directly affected by globalization through their work and employment. This is how people experience the opportunities and advantages, as well as the risks and exclusions. In order to distribute and share the gains of globalization widely, countries, enterprises and people 'have to be able to convert global opportunities into jobs and incomes'.[32]

Ideally globalization should encompass a strong social dimension. This should be based on universally shared values, and respect for human rights and individual dignity. The path to globalization should be fair, inclusive, democratically governed and should provide opportunities and tangible benefits for all.[33]

The main problems of globalization, the Report held, are not due to globalization as such, but rather its governance. Good governance is an essential ingredient for successful integration and for an equitable sharing of benefits.[34] Moreover, coherence between economic and social policies is essential.[35] Recognizing that each country has specific needs and conditions, the Report accordingly anchored its proposals at national level.

The major goals of decent work are to reduce unemployment and to rectify situations where people are fully employed but in unacceptable jobs, for example, in appalling conditions, at low productivity or subject to coercion, and at low wages.[36] Employment must be freely chosen and provide sufficient income to satisfy basic economic and family needs.[37] Three elements, namely respect for rights and representation, attainment of basic security through social protection and assurance of adequate conditions of work form the basis of decent work.[38]

The most obvious route to the creation of decent work lies in higher economic growth.[39] The Report found that problems of high or rising unemployment have been compounded by additional pressure on the quality of employment. Real wages and conditions of work have generally come under pressure due to labour market deregulation and the declining power of unions. And, an increase in contingent work and less secure contracts are commonly found due to technological developments which require greater flexibility.[40] In this regard, it has been suggested that balanced policies, taking into

---

32 ILO Report 'A fair globalization: creating opportunities for all' op. cit. note 31 at 64.

33 ILO Report 'A fair globalization: creating opportunities for all' op. cit. note 31 at x; 5ff.

34 ILO Report 'A fair globalization: creating opportunities for all' op. cit. note 31 at 7.

35 ILO Report 'A fair globalization: creating opportunities for all' op. cit. note 31 at xi; 2; 4; 7. Problems in this regard are that globalization has developed rapidly but without the necessary parallel development of economic and social institutions necessary for its smooth and equitable functioning. At the same time, there is concern about the unfair global rules on trade and finance, and their asymmetric effects on rich and poor countries. Market opening measures and financial and economic considerations appear to predominate over social ones. In this regard, the UN, the World Trade Organisation and other multi-lateral institutions are underperforming, lack policy coherence and are not sufficiently democratic, transparent and accountable. These are the result of global governance largely shaped by powerful countries and players. International policies have often been implemented without regard for national specifics. Developing countries have a very limited influence on global negotiations on rules and workers.

36 ILO Report 'A fair globalization: creating opportunities for all' op. cit. note 31 at 64.

37 Ibid.

38 Ibid.

39 Ibid. The key macro-economic issue is then whether a *focus on employment* calls for a different balance of *monetary policy*. For this to be adequately assessed, each country should adopt employment targets as part of their budgetary process; make an employment impact analysis an explicit criterion of macro-economic policy decision making; address gender issues through 'gender-budgeting' which examines the differential impact of macro-economic policy on women and men; obstacles to the creation of enterprises, particularly small and medium-sized, must be removed; and structural policies are needed to foster the growth of the economy.

40 ILO Report 'A fair globalization: creating opportunities for all' op. cit. note 31at 65.

account the interests of both workers and employers, based on a new *social contract*, are essential. This needs to include the following:

- commitment to social dialogue in the formulation of economic and social policies, especially from those affecting the reform of the labour market and social protection;
- recognition that the drive for greater efficiency and productivity must be balanced against the right of workers to security and equal opportunities; and
- a commitment to take the 'high road' of business-labour collaboration to achieve efficiency gains and to avoid the 'low road' of cost cutting and downsizing.[41]

To attain decent work, respect for core labour standards – the eight conventions mentioned earlier – is essential.[42] These constitute the minimum rules for labour in the global economy.[43] The core labour standards set in the 1930's and onwards is as valid today, in the era of globalization, as they were then. Further, the ILO pledged substantial cooperation programmes to assist countries to put such Conventions into effect. The role of the ILO and the value of ILO standards as a means to improve conditions of work worldwide, have been restated.[44]

The Common Law

Contract has always formed the basis of the employment relationship in the sense of bringing it into existence. Judges can and do make law. The adaptation of the common law principles in response to changing socio-economic exigencies is crucial to the development of a framework which is conducive to a measure of fairness. The fact that the basis of the relationship is embedded in contractual form allows the courts latitude in implying terms into the contract if there are matters that have not expressly been agreed upon.

Although English law has no general doctrine of good faith applicable to the law of contract,[45] the law of contract is characterized by the underlying principle that contracts should be fair. This truism is aptly expressed in the following *dictum* of Bingham LJ:[46]

In many civil law systems, and perhaps in most legal systems outside the common law world, the law of obligations recognizes and enforces an overriding principle that in making and carrying out contracts parties should act in good faith. This does not mean that they should not deceive each other, a principle which any legal system must recognize; its effect is perhaps most aptly conveyed by such metaphorical colloquialisms as 'playing fair', 'coming clean' or 'putting one's cards face upwards on the table'. It is in essence a principle of fair open dealing

---

41   ILO Report 'A fair globalization: creating opportunities for all' op. cit. note 31 at 64-5.

42   ILO Report 'A fair globalization: creating opportunities for all' op. cit. note 31 at 94. International institutions should take responsibility in promoting these core standards as part of a broader international agenda.

43   ILO Report 'A fair globalization: creating opportunities for all' op. cit. note 31 at 92.

44   ILO Report 'A fair globalization: creating opportunities for all' op. cit. note 31 at 92.

45   Roger Brownsword, 'Positive, Negative, Neutral: The Reception of Good Faith in English Contract Law', in Roger Brownsword, Norma Hird and Geraint Powell (eds), *Good Faith in Contract: Concept and Context*, (Ashgate, Dartmouth, 1998), p. 15.

46   *Interfoto Picture Library Ltd v Stiletto Visual Programmes Ltd* (1989) 1 QB 433 at 439.

... English law has, characteristically, committed itself to no such overriding principle but has developed piecemeal solutions in response to demonstrated problems of unfairness.

Unlike the Australian and English law of contract which recognize no general requirement of good faith in contracts, the law of contract in the United States of America does exactly that. Section 205 of the 'Restatement of Contracts Second'[47] of 1979 provides as follows: 'Every contract imposes upon each party a duty of good faith and fair dealing in its performance and its enforcement.' By the 1980s, given the considerable influence of this Restatement on the courts within the American states, the individual state courts 'had explicitly adopted or acknowledged a general obligation of good faith applicable to contractual relations...'[48] However, as is clear from the wording of the Restatement, there is no obligation on contractants to act according to the dictates of good faith at the negotiation stage. The Restatement therefore is only of relevance to substantive fairness. An aggrieved party wishing to set a contract aside on the basis of procedural unfairness will therefore have to resort to the common law remedies of misrepresentation, undue influence and duress. As far as duress is concerned, the long standing general rule is that any threat which undermines the free will of the other party constitutes duress.[49]

The principle of good faith is the underlying principle inherent in all contracts in South Africa and in civil jurisdictions. In *Meskin NO v Anglo-American Corporation of SA Ltd & Another*[50] Jansen J put it this way: *'It is now accepted that all contracts are bona fide* (some are even said to be *uberrimae fidei*). This involves good faith (*bona fide*) as a criterion in interpreting a contract and in evaluating the conduct of the parties both in respect of performance and its antecedent negotiation.'

The fact that the Australian and English law of contract recognize no general requirement of good faith in contracts is really immaterial with regard to contracts of employment specifically. The reason for this is that in both these countries and in South Africa, there is an implied term of mutual trust and confidence in every contract of employment. This term can be equated to a mutual duty to act in good faith. The need to strengthen, ameliorate and enforce individual rights has come to the fore. Recent court decisions in England and Australia (which are discussed below) have developed the common law by the use of implied terms, most notably the duty to maintain trust and confidence, in order to address the *lacunae* created by the de-collectivization of employment relations. The common law can therefore be used to introduce employer obligations to ensure fairness in the employment relationship.

---

47 A 'Restatement' is a type of law that is peculiar to the United States of America. Robert Summers, 'The Conceptualisation of Good Faith in American Contract Law: A General Account', in Reinhard Zimmermann and Simon Walker (eds), *Good Faith in European Contract Law*, (Cambridge, 2000), p. 119-120 explains: 'The American concept of a 'Restatement' is a very special type of "law". It is not statute law adopted by the state legislature or by Congress. Nor is it common law made by the highest court in any given state. It is not even an attempt to restate the actual case law of every state, state by state. Instead a Restatement constitutes an attempt by the American Law Institute, a private organization of scholars, judges and practitioners to formulate with some precision the leading rules and principles in major fields of American law, "in the aggregate", so to speak, as if the United States consisted of only one, rather that fifty state jurisdictions.'

48 Ibid., p. 120.

49 *Kaplan v Kaplan*, 25 Ill.2d 181,185,182 N.E.2d 706,709 (1962); *Austin Instrument, Inc. v Loral Ccorp.*, 29N. Y.2d 124, 130, 324 N.Y.S. 22, 25, 272 N. E. 2d 533, 535 (1971).

50 1968 (4) SA 793 (W) at 320 G-H.

A renewed importance of the common law in the contract of employment can be partly attributed to judicial acknowledgement of the relational nature of the employment relationship. This acknowledgement was succinctly articulated by McLachlin J in *Wallace v United Grain Growers.*[51] In this case the contract of employment was differentiated from 'a simple commercial exchange in the marketplace of goods or services' as follows: 'A contract of employment is typically of a longer term and more personal in nature than most contracts, and involves greater mutual dependence and trust, with a correspondingly greater opportunity for harm or abuse.'[52] In similar vein in *Johnson v Unisys*[53] Lord Hoffmann observed:[54]

> *Over the last 30 years or so the nature of the contract of employment has been transformed. It has been recognised that a person's employment is usually one of the most important things in his or her life. It gives not only a livelihood but an occupation, an identity and a sense of self esteem. The law has changed to recognise this social reality. Most of the changes have been made by Parliament ... And the common law has adapted itself to the new attitudes, proceeding sometimes by analogy with statutory rights.*

As a result of this transformation of the contract of employment there has been an 'increasing acceptance of the view that an employer's powers under the employment contract cannot be allowed to operate unfettered by the common law'.[55]

In the Australian case of *Gambotto v John Fairfax Publications Pty Ltd*[56] Peterson J stated the following with regard to the development of employment law in the twentieth century:

> *The notion of 'master and servant' relationship became obsolete. Lord Slynn of Hadley recently noted 'the changes which have taken place in the employer-employee relationship, with far greater duties imposed on the employer than in the past, whether by statute or by judicial decision, to care for the physical, financial and even psychological welfare of the employee: Spring v Guardian Assurance Plc. [1995] 2 A.C. 296, 335B.*

As far as the American judiciary is concerned one author has reached the following conclusion: 'In the past 30 or 40 years we have seen the judiciary attempt to fashion ways of tempering the injustices and economic inefficiencies of the at-will doctrine.'[57] In South Africa it is trite that the employment relationship is considered to be a relationship of the utmost good faith.[58] Judges have therefore made use of the principles of good faith to read employer obligations into contracts in the interests of fairness and reasonableness.

---

51   (1997) 152 DLR (4th) 1 at 46.

52   Other English cases where the 'relational' nature of the employment relationship is judicially recognized are *Spring v Guardian Assurance Plc* [1995] 2 AC 296; *Crossley v Faithful & Gould Holdings Limited* [2004] IRLR 377 (CA).

53   [2003] 1 AC 519.

54   At 1091.

55   Douglas Brodie, 'Legal Coherence and the Employment Revolution', *Law Quarterly Review*, 117 (2001): 604 p. 608.

56   [2001] NSWIRComm 87.

57   David Cabrelli, 'Comparing the Implied Covenant of Good Faith and Fair Dealing with the Implied Term of Mutual Trust and Confidence in the US and UK Employment Contexts', *International Journal of Comparative Labour Law and Industrial Relations*, 21 (2005): p. 445.

58   See *Carter v Value Truck Rental (Pty) Ltd* (2005) 26 *ILJ* 711 (SE) at 724; *Council for Scientific& Industrial Research v Fijen* (1996) 17 *ILJ* 18(A) at 26B-F; *Sappi Novoboard (Pty) Ltd v Bolleurs* (1998) 19 *ILJ* 784 (LAC) at par. 7.

The judiciary in England and Australia[59] has made use of the implied term of trust and confidence to create employer obligations in the interests of fairness. The implied term of mutual trust and confidence is perceived as a material term going to the very root of the contract,[60] as an incident of every contract of employment,[61] and it has been described as the 'implied obligation of good faith'.[62] Lord Steyn said in *Johnson v Unisys Ltd*: 'It could also be described as an employer's obligation of fair dealing.'[63] Similarly, in the Australian case of *Concut Pty Ltd v Worrel*[64] Kirby J observed: 'The ordinary relationship of an employer and an employee at common law is one importing implied duties of loyalty, honesty, confidentiality and mutual trust.'

The implied term of trust and confidence is the most influential of these implied terms in the context of the contract of employment. The acceptance of the term of mutual trust and confidence as a legal incident of the contract of employment has been described as forming the 'cornerstone of the legal construction of the contract of employment' and, being 'undoubtedly the most powerful engine of movement in the modern law of employment contracts'.[65] In similar vein Lord Hoffmann observed that: 'The contribution of the common law to the employment revolution has been by the evolution of implied terms in the contract of employment. The most far-reaching is the implied term of trust and confidence'.[66]

In short, the common law requires employers to treat employees in a fair manner. What this entails may differ from generation to generation. Ultimately, the mores of society and the general sense of fairness of the times as well as international standards as provided in terms of the ILO help judges give content to vague principles such as good faith and the term of mutual trust and confidence.

Legislation

The terms and conditions of the employment contract are not only determined by the common law, but also by legislation. Very often the content of these sources of law overlap. However, since in terms of the common law many of the employers' obligations are read into the contract as tacit terms, legislation may provide a more definitive and less vague source of employer obligations. Legislation may also serve as a basis to determine what constitutes fairness in terms of the common law.

The obligation to remunerate the employee for services rendered is the most obvious and important obligation. Although, clearly, also a right in terms of the common law, legislation often serves to determine the exact content of the obligation. For example, legislation sometimes provides for minimum wages prohibiting employers from paying

---

59   Stella Vettori *The Employment Contract and the Changed World of Work*, (Ashgate 2007) Ch 5.

60   *Courtlands Northern Textiles v Andrew* [1979] IRLR 84 (EAT) at 86.

61   *Malik v BCCI* [1997] 3 All ER 1 at 15.

62   *Imperial Group Pension Trust Ltd v Imperial Tobacco Ltd* (1991) 1 WLR 589.

63   Ibid., at 813.

64   [2000] HCA 64 at par. 52.

65   See Cabrelli, 'Comparing the Implied Covenant of Good Faith and Fair Dealing with the Implied Term of Mutual Trust and Confidence in the US and UK Employment Contexts', p. 451.

66   *Johnson v Unisys* (2001) 2 All ER 801 at 1091.

employees less than a certain amount for certain jobs. In addition legislation may also provide for matters such as the time and place of payment and the manner of payment Legislation usually provides for the number of ordinary working hours per week. Any work done beyond these hours constitutes overtime work. Legislation typically provides for more money to be payable for work done after hours, on public holidays and overtime work. This varies from a third more than normal remuneration to double the normal remuneration. It may also provide for the amount payable for 'danger pay' for certain jobs that may endanger the lives of employees.

Sometimes employers are obliged to provide work for employees. This is referred to as the right to work. This obligation also emanates from the common law. However, there is usually such an obligation in terms of the common law, in cases where this duty is not specifically agreed to in terms of the contract, if in the circumstances the arbitrator or judge is of the view that it would be fair or reasonable to imply such an obligation into the contract. This would be the case in the following instances: A sales representative who is paid commission based on the value or amount of sales, an actor who needs to build a name or reputation, an apprentice who needs to learn a trade by practical experience, or, an executive who needs to maintain contacts in the business and generally for reasons of the acquisition and maintenance of expertise. Since there is no *numerus clausus* as to the circumstances that would create a right to work in terms of the common law, it is sometimes difficult to predict with certainty under exactly what circumstances this would be the case. Legislation can specifically name these circumstances bringing more certainty to the employer obligation to provide work for its employees.

Although the content of labour legislation differs from country to country, there are certain employee rights (with corresponding employer obligations) which seem to be present in most legislative systems. Some of these rights are: the right to organize and associate, the right to render one's services in a safe working environment with safe machinery and equipment, the right not to be exposed to unnecessary dangers to one's life and health, the right to be compensated in case of job injuries and unemployment, the right not to be discriminated against on arbitrary grounds such as race or sex, the right to sick leave, vacation leave, maternity leave and family responsibility leave, the right to privacy, the right to fair procedures when disciplinary action is taken against the employee, the right not to be unfairly dismissed and so on.

The legislation in many countries provides for certain fringe benefits which are a form of social security to protect employees against in the event of certain contingencies materializing. These include pensions, unemployment payments, and benefits in case of illness or disability. The precise content of these employer duties differs from country to country.

Legislation sometimes also provides for employer obligations with regard to certain fringe benefits. The right to time off is an example. Reasons for time off may be study leave, family responsibility leave, trade union activities and so on. Other fringe benefits provided in terms of legislation for certain employees may be the right to transport and the right to board lodging and basic amenities.

Conclusion

An employer has one obligation towards its employees: to treat them fairly. This obligation entails a myriad of employer duties. Ultimately, an employee's dignity, privacy, right to property, quality of life and health must be respected. The obligation to treat employees fairly entails all the specific obligations provided in terms of all the sources of legal obligations discussed above. These three sources of obligations influence and reinforce each other. For example, if an obligation is provided for in terms of international standards or national legislation, it is likely that that obligation will be read into a contract of employment as a tacit term in terms of the common law. Conversely, what becomes customary in terms of practice will not only be read into a contract of employment as a tacit term but may eventually be adopted as legislation, since laws must reflect the mores and ethical standards of the society within which they operate. What is fair may differ from country to country and generation to generation. What is ultimately deemed to be fair and reasonable will be determined by the mores of society both national and international.

30 *Whistleblowing: Perennial Issues and Ethical Risks*

WIM VANDEKERCKHOVE

Introduction

This chapter sketches out today's relevance of whistleblowing for the business organisation. Rather than trying to convince the reader why the whistleblower ought to be protected or trying to stipulate criteria for justified whistleblowing, this chapter tells the story of how whistleblowing became an issue and why it still is. The first section gives some insight on the extreme positions on whistleblowing in the early 1970s. After that, a section is dedicated to a renewed attention for whistleblowing since the mid-1990s, which was induced by scientific research into the whistleblowing process and the shifting sense-making on what an organisation is and how one goes about organising. The third section informs the reader about current whistleblowing legislation around the world. Then, in a fourth section, I comment on four perennial issues involved in whistleblowing: loyalty, motive, right versus duty, and anonymous versus confidential whistleblowing. A fifth section emphasises that although business organisations can clearly benefit from having internal whistleblowing procedures, managers should be aware that there are serious ethical risks involved in implementing such procedures. I name a few of them and also advise on how to mitigate these risks. I close this chapter by explaining the ever remaining whistleblowing paradox.

How Whistleblowing Became An Issue

Although the activity we currently call whistleblowing must be much older, the term whistleblowing appeared around 1970, when Ralph Nader coined the term when he spoke at a number of conferences around the United States. Basically, Nader was lashing out at the dominant organisational culture of secrecy and their lack of accountability towards the public at large. Nader's charge was aimed at both government and business organisations. His 'call for responsibility' and 'encouragement to blow the whistle'[1] saw whistleblowing to mean the following:

---

1   Hartman (1971) attributes these words to Nader's speeches.

An act of a man or women who, believing that the public interest overrides the interest of the
organization he serves, blows the whistle that the organization is involved in corrupt, illegal,
fraudulent or harmful activity. (Nader et al. 1972, vii)

Nader's activism caught on, most probably because it was the right time to do that kind of stuff. Peters and Branch (1972), then-editors of the Washington Monthly, see whistleblowing as a new development in the history of American reform movements. David Vogel, a professor of business, describes advocating whistleblowing as one of the tactics of anti-corporate activity to put pressure on corporations. In more general terms, it seems that the end of the 1960s really was the end in the United States of the era of the 'organisation man'. Characteristic for that era was an employee who held an undivided loyalty to his employer. Linked to that is the Taylorist paradigm of the organisation, which makes a clear distinction between a small group doing the thinking and designing the production process and a larger group of workers who are supposed to follow orders and carry out the work without doing any thinking on what they are actually doing.

By the early 1970s feelings had changed considerably. Kerr (1964) had taken position against a society where people see their pattern of activities set for them by a single external institution rather than work with divided loyalties and set their own pattern of activities. The idea was that employees in a free society should not be obligated to restrict their loyalty to only one institution or cause. Hardt and Negri (2001: 261–74) analyse that period from a materialist perspective. They note a crisis of capitalist production in the late 1960s resulting mainly from an intense workers attack directed at the then dominant disciplinary regimes of labour – the 'organisation man'. Basically, that crisis was a bifurcation of the system of production. What this means is that the crisis is not caused by an external factor, but rather that the system comes into a crisis because it had worked so well. Hardt and Negri see the protests of the end of the 1960s and the refusal of work in general, and of factory work specifically, as an effect of the ideology of modernisation. Fordism – mass production and consumption of affordable luxury products – coupled with the Taylorist organisation of production had really paid off by the end of the 1960s. In the United States, life standards had increased considerably and the effect was that with this success came a new subjectivity, a new set of aspirations about life and corresponding desires.[2] However, the established relations of production – the Taylorist paradigm and the 'organisation man' – were no longer apt to manage these new aspirations and desires.

During the 1970s a response to the social struggles developed along two paths. The first was the further automation and increasingly also the computerisation of production. These took Taylorist mechanisms to its limits in the sense that these could no longer control the dynamic of productive and social forces (see also Sennett 1998). The second path was the one that, according to Hardt and Negri (2001), constitutes a paradigm shift in employment relations. In the sense that the new subjectivity was a struggle over the mode of life, within employment relations the notion of immaterial labour developed to contain that struggle and grasp its energy. This new subjectivity cracked the disciplinary regime of the 'organisation man':

---

2   For Hardt and Negri (2001), the sudden increase in the costs of raw materials, energy and certain agricultural commodities in the 1960s and 1970s is a symptom of these new desires.

The prospect of getting a job that guarantees regular and stable work for eight hours a day, fifty weeks a year, for an entire working life, the prospect of entering the normalized regime of the social factory, which had been a dream for many of their parents, now appeared as a kind of death. The mass refusal of the disciplinary regime, which took a variety of forms, was not only a negative expression but also a moment of creation [...]. (Hardt and Negri 2001: 273–74)

In this sense, Ralph Nader's whistleblowing activism was an exponent of a more general refusal of the disciplinary regime and a moment of creation. It emphasised the legitimacy of extra-organisational life and hence public interest in what goes on inside organisations. We can also read it as an expression of people's aspiration to be a whole person within the boundaries of the organisation. People aspired to be creative, responsible, challenged and problem-solving persons at work. Indeed, most of the human resources buzz-words of today have their ascension around the same time as the term whistleblowing started to be used in the context of organisations.

Hence it is no surprise that when sense-making about organisations – current understandings of what organisations are and of how to organise – is structured around terms like responsibility, flexibility, team work, human capital, knowledge workers, empowerment, trust, stakeholders and networks, that the issue of whistleblowing remains high on the agenda. In a sense, we can regard it as a necessary element of that sense-making (Vandekerckhove 2006).

Why Managers Started To Like Whistleblowing

In the 1970s, the attitude of management – in the private as well as the public sector – towards whistleblowing was rather hostile. Ravishankar mentions an arbitrator in a whistleblowing case from 1972 who told the employee that 'you cannot bite the hand that feeds you and insist on staying on for the banquet'. In 1971, James Roche, then Chairman of the Board of General Motors, warned against whistleblowing:

Some critics are now busy eroding another support of free enterprise – the loyalty of a management team, with its unifying values of cooperative work. Some of the enemies of business now encourage an employee to be disloyal to the enterprise. They want to create suspicion and disharmony, and pry into the proprietary interests of the business. However this is labelled – industrial espionage, whistle blowing, or professional responsibility – it is another tactic for spreading disunity and creating conflict. (Roche 1971: 445)

Today, management attitudes toward whistleblowing have somewhat changed. True, whistleblowers are still frequently bullied, sacked or even sued. However, whistleblowing procedures are advised for in corporate governance codes – for example, the Code Tabaksblat in the Netherlands and the UK Combined Code on Corporate Governance to name just two. Also, corporations have an increasingly vested interest in ensuring high ethical standards and conduct within their organisations (Olander 2004). Whistleblowing provisions are regarded an essential element in the detection of fraud (Arnold and Ponemon 1991, Ponemon 1994). There is a huge increase in auditing firms operating reporting hotlines for other corporations (Hassink et al. 2007). How might we explain this change? I see three reasons. The first is that research undertaken since the mid-1980s onwards has given us a different perception of who blows the whistle, why they do it and how they go about it. The second is that over time legislation protecting whistleblowers and requiring from organisation that they had internal procedures came about. The third reason is that the argumentation offering 'good reasons' to take whistleblowers seriously has shifted considerably towards a rationale that increasingly succeeds in grasping the interest of management and boards of corporations. Although these three reasons should not be seen separately, but rather reinforcing one another, I will not go into their mutual links but only briefly sketch out each of them.

From the mid-1980s onwards, academics researched the psychological characteristics of whistleblowers as well as organisational predictors of whistleblowing from a sociological perspective. This research shows that employees that have blown the whistle are loyal to the organisational goals and would rather have the wrongdoing corrected by raising the issue inside their organisation than cause a scandal by blowing the whistle externally (Dozier and Miceli 1985, Miceli and Near 1984, 1989, 1991, and more recently Chiu 2003). More important factors leading to acts of whistleblowing were found to be the perceived organisational disposition towards people raising concerns internally and the perceived seriousness of the malpractice (Miceli and Near 1985, Near and Miceli 1987, Callahan and Dworkin 1994).

Other important findings were that organisational retaliation against (internal) whistleblowers encourages further (external) whistleblowing (Miceli and Near 1992), that having internal whistleblowing procedures encourages internal disclosures but not external whistleblowing (Mathews 1987, Keenan 1990), and that formal organisational policies that support external whistleblowing are not a significant predictor of its occurrence but informal elements, on the contrary, such as supervisory support to do so, are more likely to lead to external whistleblowing (Sims and Keenan 1998).

Hence, towards the 1990s it became clear that whistleblowers were not really the 'rats', 'snitches' or disloyal employees management had thought them to be, but turned out to be people who cared about the professionalism of their organisation and who tried to raise their concerns inside their organisation first before disclosing to the media.

Interesting is an article in *Harvard Business Review* from 1975 (Walters 1975) advising managers to take those who raise concerns to them seriously in order to avoid whistleblowing. The tone of the article is that the future might very well bring laws protecting whistleblowers in private companies and recognising whistleblowing as an exemption from the employment-at-will doctrine. And indeed, whistleblower protection was legislated soon after.[3] In 1978, the US Civil Service Reform Act (amended in 1989 to the Whistleblower Protection Act) was the first statutory legislation explicitly offering protection for whistleblowers. Michigan, in 1981, was the first state to offer protection to whistleblowers in the United States. Today, in addition to the statutory laws at the federal level, nearly every state in the United States has legislation protecting whistleblowers. In the early 1990s, some Australian states passed whistleblowing legislation: South Australia in 1993, and the Australian Capital Territory, Queensland and New South Wales in 1994. Around the turn of the century, similar legislation was enacted in the UK in 1998, in New Zealand and South Africa in 2000, and in the remaining Australian States of Victoria in 2001, Tasmania in 2002 and Western Australia in 2003. The Sarbanes-Oxley Act passed by US Congress in 2002 is concerned primarily with restoring investor confidence but

---

3   See Vandekerckhove 2006 for an international assessment of whistleblowing legislation.

it also contains some whistleblower provisions. Similarly, the Corporate Law Economic Reform Program (Audit Reform and Corporate Disclosure) Act (CLERP9 Act), passed in 2004 in Australia, includes provisions protecting whistleblowers in the Australian private sector. In Japan, a law was passed at the end of 2004 offering whistleblower protection that covers the private and public sectors. In 2005, the Flemish Parliament in Belgium enacted whistleblower protection and so did the parliaments of Romania and Norway in 2007. Meanwhile, proposals for legislation to protect whistleblowers, have been tabled in Ireland, Canada, India and the Netherlands, while in many other countries discussion and lobbying are ongoing in order to protect whistleblowers in organisations.

There is also a significant shift to be noted in formulating good reasons to protect whistleblowers from retaliation. Basically, first attempts to formulate law proposals or advocate internal procedures use vague and unqualified arguments such as freedom of expression, corporate responsibility, stakeholder impact or business integrity. However, as the discussion within countries continues we see other arguments seeping in: organisational efficiency, risk management, accountability of and within organisations. It is striking that proposals from whistleblowing lobbying groups are only taken seriously by policy makers and business leaders when these additional arguments are made.[4] From the end of the 1990s and even more since the many Enron-like disasters of the early twenty-first century, discussions within society about whistleblowing have been formulated along the second stream of arguments, painting a picture of internal whistleblowing procedures as good management. Certainly, the research undertaken from the mid-1980s onwards, as well as the growing whistleblowing legislation worldwide, have added to that perception. But increasingly too, organisational decentralisation and flexibilisation have increased the importance of the human factor inefficiency. Organisational processes can be designed as very efficient but if they are not carried out properly by employees, this results in inefficiencies such as fraud and corruption. Also, as more discretionary power is dispersed over the organisation, there is a bigger risk of processes getting thwarted. At the same time, it becomes more difficult to detect where processes have gone wrong. In this context, internal whistleblowing procedures appear as the necessary governance mechanism, leaving enough flexibility whilst at the same time ensure the ability to detect wrongdoing.

Further, whereas whistleblowing originally referred to employees disclosing information about the organisation to entities outside of the organisation, since the mid-1990s the term has also been accepted to designate internal procedures allowing employees to raise concerns outside of the normal hierarchical line.[5] Hence, as management learned that 1) whistleblowers carry information that is quite often valuable to top management itself and 2) in general whistleblowers would prefer malpractice to be corrected in a strict internal way rather than through external disclosure, a consensus became possible between what whistleblowing activists wanted (societal control) and what managers were

---

4   See Vandekerckhove (2006) for an analysis of the shift in moral arguments for protecting whistleblowers from 1970–2004.

5   Jubb (1999) is an exception to this, although he acknowledges that there is significant debate about whether internally raising concern can also be called whistleblowing. Jubb develops a restrictive definition of whistleblowing only including external disclosures. However, current usage of the term whistleblowing also includes internally raising concerns. And as I argue, this shift is one of the reasons management in general has changed its attitude towards those who raise concern.

keen on (keeping internal matters from the public). The key to that consensus is the tiered recipient model as I will explain in the next section.

Current Legislation

A salient trend in whistleblowing legislation since the mid-1990s is that the protection of individuals is made conditional on raising the concern inside the organisation prior to external whistleblowing. Elsewhere, I have called this the 'tiered recipient' model (Vandekerckhove 2006). The term 'recipient' refers to the person, function or agency that receives the information or the concern of the whistleblower. Three subsequent tiers can be distinguished. The first is the internal tier. A number of people or functions can be designated and mandated to receive and register concerns about organisational malpractice. In the private sector these might be the ethics officer, head of department, internal audit, CEO or boards of directors. In the public sector this also includes any agency or office that is within the executive power of government, even mayors and ministers. The second tier is any function, office or agency that is set up or that we might regard as a proxy of society. For the private sector these are regulators, professional bodies or specific government agencies. For the public sector these are members of parliament or an ombudsman reporting to parliament. The third tier then is an open tier and includes anyone whom the whistleblower deems relevant or helpful in correcting the wrongdoing and includes Non-Government Organisations (NGOs) and media.

Most of the whistleblowing legislation includes the first two tiers. Sometimes a specific policy at tier one is demanded from organisations. On the other hand, little legislation includes a third tier, protecting the whistleblower when they finally disclose widely.

The point is that the 'tiered recipient' model, which is the dominant model for whistleblowing legislation since the mid-1990s, constitutes an important shift from the whistleblowing discussion in the early-1970s. Back in those days, whistleblowing and the protection of whistleblowers was discussed in terms of a conflict between organisation and society, or, between system and environment, inside and outside. What seems to have taken place since then is that the 'tiered recipient' model is containing and sort of neutralising that conflict. It is the second tier – the proxy of society – that contains the conflict between organisation and society. For example, the second tier stipulated in the New Zealand legislation is the Ombudsman, a parliamentary controlled agency dealing with allegations about public sector organisations from citizens and government employees – marks the border of the space in which the conflict is contained. Here, the Ombudsman is the mediator between executive power (public sector organisations) and controlling power (parliament as a proxy of society). Strangely enough, the New Zealand policy covers both public and private sector organisational malpractices. The conflict between society and private sector organisations (business) is also contained by the Ombudsman. This is a wider containment in the sense that it allows a proxy of society – not society at large – to control private sector organisational practices. The same goes for the UK Public Interest Disclosure Act legislation. There, a number of regulators have been identified as appropriate recipients for concerns about private sector malpractices. These regulators are appointed by government and in this sense they can be regarded as a proxy of society where private sector malpractice is concerned. Still, for the whistleblower, disclosing to a regulator is technically perceived as an internal disclosure. The idea is that concerns raised with a regulator will not be known to the public at large but the particular regulator is an authoritative function who can take up the issue with the manager to whom the malpractice pertains.

A 'tiered' whistleblowing policy prescribes a sequential order of recipients – for example, first head of department, then board of directors, then a specific government agency. There are many arguments in favour of tiered whistleblowing procedures. Besides having the advantage of recognising both organisational and societal interests, the most important argument is that it is in the interest of society that organisational malpractices get corrected, but not necessarily that the public knows about it. Whistleblowing to the media can cause a scandal, but it is not a guarantee that things will go right from then on. A committed CEO or audit committee can do much more than a newspaper. Therefore, it makes sense to expect from whistleblowers that they raise their concern inside the organisation first. Tiered whistleblowing policies allow organisations to bring or keep their organisational practices in line with the public interest. Hence, it is not society that takes control over organisational practices. However, when organisations refuse or when they appear to be unable to solve problems regarding their own practices, disclosures can then be made to a next-level recipient.

In short, whereas the original whistleblowing activism saw whistleblowing as a mechanism for holding executives from public and private sector organisations accountable to the public for what goes wrong inside their organisations, current whistleblowing discourse and policies amount to holding these executives accountable for not taking internal whistleblowers seriously and for not solving their internal problems adequately. In addition, management is starting to look at internal whistleblowing mechanisms as an important source of information for risk management on various issues.

This in no way implies that whistleblowing as an issue of organisation ethics is a resolved case. First of all, some issues appear to be perennial. I take some of these up in the next section. Second, with the shift in sense-making on whistleblowing arise a new set of ethical risks. One pertains to the role of labour unions in internal whistleblowing procedures. It is quite exceptional for a union to play a role in these. Yet strictly speaking, they are a good candidate as a second tier recipient. Another issue regards the subject of protected disclosures. Currently fraud, health and safety issues and illegal practices are covered by most whistleblowing procedures. However, raising concern about practices running counter organisational statements is almost never covered but might offer an organisation important information for managing its identity and branding (Vandekerckhove 2007). Finally, an ethical risk in general that comes with the current tendency in whistleblowing policy is that it is regarded too much as a panacea for anything that might go wrong in the governance of an organisation. The message that we can sleep safe because, as adequate internal procedures are in place, we can be assured that malpractices will be corrected, is a dangerous one. Not only is it naïve, it also tends to over-responsibilise the individual employee and turn every single employee into a safeguarding institution for the well-being of society (Tsahuridu and Vandekerckhove forthcoming).

Perennial Issues

In this section I discuss four perennial issues with regard to whistleblowing. I call them perennial because they continue to be the subject of scholarly research and judicial wondering.

A first issue pertains to loyalty and the extent to which employee loyalty allows whistleblowing. The second perennial issue regards the motive of the whistleblower. This qualification of whistleblowers plays an important role in offering protection to whistleblowers. A third issue treated in this section is how the right to blow the whistle differs from the duty to blow the whistle. Although this might seem trivial, ongoing research shows that the recognition of the right might imply accepting the duty. Finally, the fourth perennial issue pertains to the distinction between anonymous and confidential whistleblowing. Contrary to the right/duty distinction, this one is not that straightforward. Yet it is a very important distinction to make when designing internal whistleblowing procedures.

LOYALTY

The assumed loyalty an employee has towards their employer and the way this might interfere with whistleblowing has been debated as long as whistleblowing has been an issue. Various positions have been taken on that issue. Ralph Nader (see his definition earlier in this chapter) argued that the public interest overrides that of the organisation. James Roche (see the quote earlier) saw organisational loyalty as an important support of free enterprise and saw whistleblowers as troublemakers.

Given the whistleblowing climate of the 1970s, it is no surprise that business ethics scholars took up the issue as well. They formulate it as a dilemma for the potential whistleblower who, faced with the two morally obliging but contradicting options of remaining silent but loyal about a malpractice that harms society, or heroically blowing the whistle and warning society but being disloyal when doing so. One of the first important papers offering a way out of the dilemma is Duska (1988). Duska claims that employee loyalty to business organisations is a category mistake because business organisations are not proper objects of loyalty. He gives two reasons. First, loyalty to business requires granting business the status of a person. Second, loyalty depends on ties that demand self-sacrifice without expectation of reward. Now, Duska (1988) argues, since business does not deserve the status of a person and since employment relations imply a reward for made efforts, there is no such thing as a duty of loyalty to a business organisation. Thus, whistleblowers can go ahead. The dilemma they experience is but an error of mind.

The findings of the sociological and psychological research at the end of the 1980s and beginning of the 1990s show that the case is never that clear-cut. Although Duska's position has been reformulated recently from the perspective political philosophy (Lindblom 2007), we saw more nuanced positions being formulated in line with the renewed discourse on whistleblowing as it became a hot issue again at the turn of the century. Already at the end of the 1990s, De George (2006) had described Duska's position as recommendable but extreme because it implicitly denies any consideration of the harm that one's actions may do to those with whom one is associated. De George draws up three conditions that need to be fulfilled if whistleblowing is permitted: it must be about serious and considerable harm to the public, it must be done to the immediate superior first, all possibilities for internally raising the concern must be exhausted first.

Corvino (2002) has straightforwardly argued against Duska's analysis. Corvino refutes both of Duska's objections to loyalty to the organisation. First, business organisations are without doubt groups of persons. Second, the absence of reward cannot be a prerequisite for loyalty since relationships where Duska does see loyalty as appropriate – among sports team members, between friends, in family – always entail some expectation of reward. However, Corvino does agree that there is no conflict of duties between loyalty and whistleblowing. Corvino's way out of the dilemma is that loyalty is a virtue only to the extent that the object of loyalty is good. Surely loyalty to a business organisation will require some tolerance of shortcomings but this cannot mean absolute or complete tolerance. However, Corvino remains vague about just how tolerant one ought to be.

Vandekerckhove and Commers (2004) takes up Corvino's idea that the object of loyalty plays a crucial role in the whistleblowing dilemma. They introduce the notion of 'rational loyalty' to emphasise a rational deliberation concerning the object of loyalty. Vandekerckhove and Commers argue that with the rise of Corporate Social Responsibility it has become clear that there is an interdependence between civil society and business. Also, organisations increasingly make their goals, their procedures and the values by which they wish to operate explicit and public through mission statements, quality labels and reports. By doing this, business organisations acknowledge being part of society and point out in what way they contribute to society. Thus, for Vandekerckhove and Commers, the appropriate object of loyalty is not the physical aspects of a business organisation – buildings, executives, boards, hierarchies, colleagues – but rather the explicit set of mission statement, goals, value statement and code of conduct. The everyday practices within organisations can divert from that explicit set. In that case we say that a goal-displacement is taking place. Vandekerckhove and Commers assert that whistleblowers who disclose information about such goal-displacements are actually being loyal to the legitimate organisation – the organisation as it is represented by its explicit set.

Another important point made by Vandekerckhove and Commers (2004) rests on their analysis of loyalty as a bilateral attitude. Business organisations can only demand that kind of loyalty which they can reciprocate on. Hence, in the era of the 'organisation man', absolute loyalty could be demanded because business organisations implicitly guaranteed lifelong careers within their organisations. But as restructuring, outsourcing and flexibility become the norm, such guarantees can no longer be offered and thus absolute loyalty can no longer be demanded from employees. Organisations today can however demand rational loyalty from their employees, meaning that they demand from their employees to help them in avoiding goal-displacement. The implication is that organisations should implement adequate internal procedures for their employees to raise concern, or in other words, organisations must be willing to allow their employees to exercise rational loyalty. This re-conceptualisation of loyalty avoids the whistleblowing dilemma, is in line with the research on whistleblowing characteristics and also resonates with the potential of internal whistleblowing procedures to function as a mechanism for risk management (Vandekerckhove and Commers 2004, Vandekerckhove 2007).

MOTIVE

The motive of the whistleblower is a contentious issue more for policy makers than for scholars. Miceli and Near (1992) explain that they explicitly exclude the element of motive from their definition of whistleblowing because of research reasons, more precisely because of the impossibility of measuring motive. Jubb (1999) leaves it out of his restrictive definition in order to avoid vagueness, because motives may be mixed, misrepresented and very hard if not impossible to decipher. Nevertheless, time and time again policymakers have included a proper motive as a condition for protecting whistleblowers.

One reason for this might be that in the discussions leading up to law proposals, besides the universal counter argument that 'it is not in our culture to do that', the other universal objection raised is that whistleblowing protection schemes will be abused by disgruntled employees who are out for personal gains (Vandekerckhove 2006). Hence, introducing a moral motive as a condition for protection disposes that objection.

Still, it must be noted that business ethicists offer policy makers a lot of rationales for doing so. The general idea is of course that altruistic whistleblowing deserves protection – the whistleblower is the moral hero who saves society – while self-centred motivated disclosures do not. De Maria (1994) explicitly states that whistleblowing must have a moral motive. Bowie and Duska (1990), Chambers (1995) and Grant (2002) implicitly suggest it.

In this light, one particular piece of legislation deserves our attention here: the US False Claims Act. Amended in 1986, this remarkable legislation dates from 1863 and was originally enacted to protect the Union Arms against fraudulent suppliers who sold sawdust for gun powder during the American Civil War. Today it is known as a *Qui Tam* law and the idea is that any person assisting the United States' government to recover fraudulent money gets a percentage of that. The False Claims Act was hardly used until its revision in 1986, making it a very successful tool in recovering fraud. Since then, government's recoveries under the FCA have skyrocketed with the majority of qui tam cases being filed against those who do business in the healthcare industry.

Miceli and Near (1992) see the False Claims Act as a new approach to whistleblowing, valuing information over motivation. Indeed, the provisions of the False Claims Act are designed to meet the motivational criteria of a reward system. Hence it is not at all based on altruism. Still, there is no other country today with qui tam legislation such as the False Claims Act, paying for information. However, there might be soon.[6] The popularity of anti-corruption schemes and programmes to combat fraud pressure us to downplay the morals in favour of financial incentives in order to get the information so desperately needed.[7]

So what about moral objections to the False Claims Act? Carson et al. (2008) offer ethical arguments to defend the legislation. To the objection that this law is morally corrupting by introducing selfish motives for whistleblowing, they reply that having the right kind of moral motivation is not a necessary condition of morally justified whistleblowing. The example given is an employer involved in illegal and life-threatening activities and a whistleblower motivated by malice toward that employer. The malicious whistleblower will still save many lives. Further, although external incentives can alter a person's character, they can only do so when they are applied consistently and continuously. However, Carson et al. (2008) submit, it is unlikely that one person will blow the whistle more than one time in their careers. This consequentialist reasoning is new to the ethical debates on whistleblowing and I expect it to spur further debate among business ethicists.

---

6   For example, in a debate on 'public morality' in the Dutch Parliament (*Tweede Kamer*), combating fraud was explicitly mentioned as an exponent of public morality. Marijnissen (Socialist Party) and Halsema (Green Left) suggested offering whistleblowers financial rewards if they come up with hard evidence on big fraud cases.

7   Carson et al. (2008) calculated that for the period 1997–2001, the costs of False Claims Act for the United States' government were roughly $1.88 billion and the benefits were between $26.8 billion and $97.7 billion.

RIGHT AND DUTY

Although the loyalty dilemma was identified in terms of conflicting duties, whistleblowing legislation has up till now only recognised the right to blow the whistle. Some exceptions are important however. Specific 'gatekeeper' functions have been assigned the duty to report malpractice.

Recently, Boatright (2007) defined gatekeepers as intermediary parties – accountants, lawyers and bankers – whose cooperation is necessary for business organisations to function and who by withholding cooperation are able to prevent significant misconduct. Boatright (2007: 620) notes that although it is clear that an intermediary has a moral responsibility 'not to knowingly provide substantial assistance to a client's wrongdoing', it is far less clear to what extent an intermediary is morally obligated to determine whether a client is committing some wrong. In other words, gatekeepers should not participate or facilitate wrongdoing but what should they do – and to what cost? – to avoid such liability?

Tsahuridu and Vandekerckhove (forthcoming) examine the boundaries between the right and the duty to blow the whistle. They submit that if it is correct that internal whistleblowing procedures can be seen as institutional mechanisms supporting moral autonomy, then the successful implementation of such procedures theoretically annuls the distinction between right and duty. There then remains no excuse for not raising a concern. Hence, knowing about a malpractice but not speaking up makes one complicit to that malpractice.

All this might seem very academic humbug to the practitioner, were it not that some developments make this kind of work necessary. For example, the Sarbanes-Oxley Act does impose some liability on gatekeepers and Hassink et al. (2007) comment that the majority of the European organisational whistleblowing policies adopted a tone that was at least moderately authoritative, with codes speaking of a requirement or duty to report violations, and employees who 'must', 'should' or 'are expected to' report these. More importantly, Hassink et al. (2007) found that in 30 per cent of the policies reviewed, 'it was made clear that failing to report a violation (remaining silent about a breach or concealing information about one) is a violation in itself.' And although French and Belgian governmental privacy commissions have issued statements that whistleblowing schemes may not impose mandatory reporting on employees and that therefore, use of the reporting scheme must be optional, the whistleblowing policy of the European Commission, implemented after the Cresson crisis, maintains a mandatory disclosure procedure.[8]

ANONYMOUS OR CONFIDENTIAL

A final important remaining issue in whistleblowing policy pertains to the current confusion between anonymous and confidential reporting. The difference between anonymous and confidential reporting is quite simple. In anonymous whistleblowing, the recipient of the disclosure – to whom the whistle is blown – does not know who the whistleblower is. In confidential whistleblowing, the recipient knows the identity of the whistleblower, because the whistleblower must give that when raising the concern, but

---

8   Art 22a of the Staff Regulations of Officials of the European Communities, see OLAF (2005).

the recipient does not further disclose the whistleblower's identity during or after the investigation.

There are a number of arguments going for both options. Confidential whistleblowing had the advantage that the whistleblower can be contacted again to provide further details that might be necessary for the investigation. Also, in order to provide the whistleblower with any protection it is necessary that their identity is known. On the other hand, the possibility to blow the whistle anonymously entails a lower threshold for potential whistleblowers. Also, anonymous hotlines are easier and hence cheaper to operate because they require less administration and do not necessarily impose the burden of protection on the employer.

In 2005, two corporations implementing Sarbanes-Oxley requirements caused a row in France that sprawled across Europe. It had installed a telephone hotline where employees could anonymously report perceived malpractice. Unions took management to court, which ruled that the anonymous hotline was a breach of a European Directive on privacy. Basically the directive requires that data about someone cannot be stored without that person knowing about it. The court's interpretation implied that if I report an alleged wrongdoing by my boss, my boss has the right to know that I have reported on him. Of course, this makes both anonymous and confidential whistleblowing procedures impossible to implement.

The confusion is partly caused by an ambiguity in the Sarbanes-Oxley Act. Section 301 (4B) states that procedures must be in place for the 'the confidential, anonymous submission by employees of the issuer of concerns regarding questionable accounting matters.' The syntax suggests that there is no distinction between confidential and anonymous reporting, while of course both options differ substantially in their consequences.

In November 2005, the French data protection authority (CNIL) adopted a policy setting the framework for whistleblowing procedures in France. It was followed in 2006 by the Belgian privacy commission. Amongst other stipulations, this policy determines that hotlines should not be advertised as anonymous, that the identity of whistleblowers should be carefully protected and not communicated to the person accused of wrongdoing, that the data collected through a hotline should be recorded in an objective way and be limited to those details necessary for the case to be investigated in an efficient way, that the recipients must be professionals who are appropriately trained and who may be trusted to handle confidential information.

It is expected that this confidentiality position will be followed throughout Europe. However, as whistleblowing legislation takes further root and more business organisations adopt internal whistleblowing procedures, the anonymous/confidential issue becomes a very interesting research topic while it remains an unsolved puzzle for policy makers.

How To Mitigate Ethical Risks In Whistleblowing

The discourse on organisations that became dominant from the 1990s onwards – and that is based on procedural normative concepts like 'decentralisation', 'flexibility', 'network', 'corporate governance', 'integrity', 'trust', 'stakeholder' – implicates the necessity of gathering information outside of the hierarchical line about the production process. As a result, internal audits, board-disclosure and internal whistleblowing procedures are increasingly put forward as important corporate governance mechanisms.

Although this reformulated whistleblowing argumentation has been successful in the sense that significant progress was made on whistleblowing legislation worldwide, this reformulation – internal whistleblowing as a corporate governance mechanism – also entails new ethical risks (Vandekerckhove 2006, Tsahuridu and Vandekerckhove forthcoming). With ethical risk I mean that although internal whistleblowing is justified within the dominant organisational discourse – gathering information in this way is necessary in order to guarantee efficiency, risk management and good governance – these justifications entail particular modalities of implementation that ethically are not unproblematic. These ethical risks include the following:

- over-responsibilisation of the individual employee – institutionalisation of the employee into the guardian of organisational legitimacy;
- fading of the distinction between the right and the duty of an employee to report suspected wrongdoing;
- a shift from whistleblower protection as a means to hold organisations accountable for social responsibilities, to whistleblowing procedures as a mean to hold employees accountable for their performance and engagement. Characteristic for this shift is: absence of unions as recipients in internal whistleblowing procedures, restriction of subjects allowed to report on, the omission of external recipients in procedures communicated to employees, restriction of persons who can be recognised as whistleblowers to current employees;
- neglect of the necessity to protect internal whistleblowers against retaliation as a result of merely focussing on gathering information. Characteristic of this neglect is the preference of anonymous procedures above confidential procedures.

What these risks boil down to is that instead of providing organisational support for the moral autonomy of employees, internal whistleblowing procedures make employees liable both when they raise concern – for example when internal procedures are so complex the employee is bound to make mistakes – as well as when they remain silent while knowing what was going wrong.

Mitigating these risks is an important task for managers and policy makers if the full potential of whistleblowing policies for the well-being of business and society is to be realised. I see three areas of attention that can help mitigating these ethical risks. The first pertains to the distinction between concern and allegation, the second regards the recipients identified in the policy and the third concerns the importance of independent advice.

When making an allegation, one is convinced that there is wrongdoing. Allegations also include naming someone who is causing the wrongdoing – a colleague, a manager or 'the' organisation. Hence someone is being accused. If whistleblowing takes the form of an allegation and someone is being accused, all kinds of defence strategies are unlocked and there is a big chance that the messenger will get shot while the attention shifts from the alleged wrongdoing to the personal row which whistleblowing has then become. When whistleblowing takes the form of an allegation there is no way back. If the whistleblower was mistaken then false accusations have been made and a counter charge for defamation is likely to follow. It is obvious enough that no one benefits from this.

In contrast to that, raising a concern is articulating a worry. No proof is needed and no accusation is made. Rather, raising a concern is an invitation to look into the matter – 'I am not sure but something might be going wrong.' Raising a concern is much less charged than making an allegation. Moreover, concerns allow for a way back as it might be very reasonable for someone to have that particular concern in a given situation. Hence, if organisations could implement their internal whistleblowing policy in such a way that it invites employees to raise concerns rather than forces them to make allegations, much of the watchdog atmosphere and explosive rows around whistleblowing can be avoided. The difficulty is how to do this. Much has to do with building trust between employees and management. Hence it must be clear that it takes time for an organisation to realise a concern-raising-and-allegation-avoiding culture. What certainly helps this culture come about is clearly communicating to employees that raising concern is encouraged by management and is preferred to making allegations.

Another area of attention that concerns trust – and hence that can facilitate raising concern – is the identification of recipients within the organisation. The concept of internal whistleblowing rests on the idea that there might be good reasons for an employee not to raise a concern to the line manager or the direct superior. One reason might be that the concern pertains to possible wrongdoing in which the superior is involved. Another might be that previous concerns raised to that manager were not properly handled. In general, what holds employees from raising concern with anyone in particular is that there is a lack of trust. Whether this lack of trust is justified or not is of secondary importance to the organisation that might benefit from information about a possible malpractice. The issue of trust can be taken up later and in any case might be facilitated when a concern raised to someone else other than the line manager was handled adequately and the employee raising the concern is reassured about the professionalism of their organisation. Hence, when designing and implementing internal whistleblowing procedures, organisations should be careful about identifying a possible recipient with whom employees can raise a concern. As with many issues, a one-size-fits-all solutions cannot be provided (Kaptein 2002). However, it is advisable to keep three principles in mind. First, make sure the procedure identifies more than one recipient. Raising concern to the direct superior should be encouraged but certainly not be made mandatory. If your organisation has an ethics officer then of course this function must be one of the recipient – but certainly not the only one. The second principle is that the possible recipients must be persons whom can be expected to be trusted by employees. In this light, it is necessary to include recipients positioned at different levels. Make sure the CEO is one of them. The third principle to keep in mind is that trust is not the same as informal. An organisational whistleblowing procedure might gain substantial trust from employees when it allows – and explicitly states so – employees to get independent legal advice on how to raise a concern. This reassures the potential whistleblower that the organisation is capable and willing to play it fair. It also reassures the organisation that the employee gets competent advice on how to raise a concern – to whom, in what wording and with adequate care.

This brings us to the third area of attention when mitigating ethical risks, namely the importance of independent advice. Consulting a lawyer prior to raising a concern informs a potential whistleblower of their rights and duties. It gives them a clear image on where they stand. This is completely safe for the organisation – unless it intends to retaliate against the whistleblower – as the lawyer is bounded by confidentiality. It must be clear that getting legal advice should not be confounded with contacting a whistleblower organisation or self-help group. It must also be clear that external legal advice augments trust because the person giving the advice is in no way tied to the organisation. An exception to this is Public Concern at Work, a UK charity that is dedicated to offer free legal advice to potential whistleblowers. The charity also advises public authorities and policy makers in the UK and because it has done exemplary work also in the rest of the world. Some business organisations in the UK explicitly state in their internal whistleblowing policy that employees can get legal advice from Public Concern at Work. The charity nevertheless retains its independence because of its reputation built by its role as the forerunner of whistleblowing policy in Europe. No parallel to that organisation exists in any other European country. Perhaps in the United States, the GAP (Government Accountability Project) comes close, and in South Africa the ODAC (Open Democracy Advice Centre) might come close.

The Whistleblowing Paradox

Despite all the research into whistleblowing, all the whistleblowing legislation out there and all the good reasons for organisations to take their whistleblowers seriously, internal (let alone external) whistleblowing remains a difficult and at times a messy issue. Why? Perhaps I can best describe it with the following paradox. The kind of organisations that are able to implement internal whistleblowing procedures in a satisfactory way – they actually work and employees trust them – are the kind of organisations that strictly speaking do not need them, because they already have the organisational culture in which people do and are encouraged to raise concerns. On the other hand, the kind of organisations that really need internal procedures – because things are going terribly wrong and no one dares to speak out – are not capable of implementing them so that they will actually work, because no one trusts anything management does.

Hence the difficulty lies in changing an organisation that is incapable of making internal whistleblowing procedures work into an organisation that does not need them. Perhaps the best way to bring about that change is to start implementing one. Not just out of the blue but with knowledge of the research on whistleblowing, of the good reasons for doing so, while learning from others' experience in doing so and while carefully mitigating the ethical risks involved.

References

Arnold, D.F. and Ponemon, L.A. 1991. 'Internal Auditors Perceptions of Whistle-Blowing and the Influence of Moral Reasoning'. *Auditing* 10: 1-15.

Boatright, J.R. 2007. 'Reluctant Guardians: The Moral Responsibility of Gatekeepers'. *Business Ethics Quarterly* 17: 613-632.

Bowie, N.E. and Duska, R. 1990. *Business Ethics*. Englewood Cliffs: Prentice Hall.

Callahan, E.S. and Dworkin, T.M. 1994. 'Who Blows the Whistle to the Media, and Why: Organizational Characteristics of Media Whistleblowers'. *American Business Law Journal* 32: 151-184.

Carson, T.L., Verdu, M.E. and Wokutch, R.E. 2008. 'Whistle-Blowing for Profit: An Ethical Analysis of the Federal False Claims Act'. *Journal of Business Ethics* 77: 361-376.

Chambers, A. 1995. 'Whistleblowing and the Internal Auditor'. *Business Ethics: A European Review* 4: 192-198.

Chiu, R.K. 2003. 'Ethical Judgment and Whistleblowing Intention: Examining the Moderating Role of Locus of Control'. *Journal of Business Ethics* 43: 65-74.

Corvino, J. 2002. 'Loyalty in Business'. *Journal of Business Ethics* 41: 179-185.

De George, R.T. 2006. *Business Ethics*. Englewood Cliffs: Prentice Hall.

De Maria, W. 1994. *Unshielding the Shadow Culture*. Queensland: University of Queensland.

Dozier, J.B. and Miceli, M.P. 1985. 'Potential Predictors of Whistle-Blowing – A Pro-Social Behavior Perspective'. *Academy of Management Review* 10: 823-836.

Duska, R. 1988. 'Whistleblowing and Employee Loyalty' in Beauchamp, T.L. and Bowie, N.E. (eds) *Ethical Theory and Business*. Englewood Cliffs: Prentice Hall.

Grant, C. 2002. 'Whistle Blowers: Saints of Secular Culture'. *Journal of Business Ethics* 39: 391-399.

Hardt, M. and Negri, A. 2001. *Empire*. London: Harvard University Press.

Hartmann, D.P. 1971. 'Whistle Blowing'. *Computer* 4: 34.

Hassink, H., de Vries, M. and Bollen, L. 2007. 'A Content Analysis of Whistleblowing Policies of Leading European Companies'. *Journal of Business Ethics* 75: 25-44.

Jubb, P.B. 1999. 'Whistleblowing: A Restrictive Definition and Interpretation'. *Journal of Business Ethics* 21: 77-94.

Kaptein, M. 2002. 'Guidelines for the Development of an Ethics Safety Net'. *Journal of Business Ethics* 41: 217-234.

Keenan, J.P. 1990. 'Upper-Level Managers and Whistleblowing: Determinants of Perceptions of Company Encouragement and Information About Where to Blow the Whistle'. *Journal of Business and Psychology* 5: 223-235.

Kerr, C. 1964. *Labour and Management in Industrial Society*. Garden City: Anchor Books.

Lindblom, L. 2007. 'Dissolving the Moral Dilemma of Whistleblowing'. *Journal of Business Ethics* 76: 413-426.

Mathews, M.C. 1987. 'Codes of Ethics: Organizational Behavior and Misbehavior'. *Research in Corporate Social Performance and Policy* 9: 107-130.

Miceli, M.P. and Near, J.P. 1984. 'The Relationships Among Beliefs, Organizational Position, and Whistle-Blowing Status: A Discriminant Analysis'. *Academy of Management Journal* 27: 687-705.

Miceli, M.P. and Near, J.P. 1985. 'Characteristics of Organizational Climate and Perceived Wrongdoing Associated With Whistle-Blowing Decisions'. *Personnel Psychology* 38: 525-544.

Miceli, M.P. and Near, J.P. 1989. 'The Incidence of Wrongdoing, Whistle-Blowing, and Retaliation: Results of a Naturally Occurring Field Experiment'. *Employee Responsibilities and Rights Journal* 2: 91-108.

Miceli, M.P. and Near, J.P. 1991. 'Whistle-Blowing as an Organizational Process'. *Research in the Sociology of Organizations* 9: 139-200.

Miceli, M.P. and Near, J.P. 1992. *Blowing the Whistle: The Organizational and Legal Implications for Companies and Employees*. New York: Lexington Books.

Nader, R., Petkas, P.J. and Blackwell, K. 1972. 'Whistle Blowing: The Report of the Conference on Professional Responsibility'. New York: Grossman.

Near, J.P. and Miceli, M.P. 1987. 'Whistle-Blowers in Organizations: Dissidents or Reformers?' *Research in Organizational Behavior* 9: 321-368.

OLAF 2005. *OLAF Manual*. Brussels: OLAF.

Olander, S. 2004. 'Whistleblowing Policy: An Element of Corporate Governance'. *Management Quarterly*.

Peters, C. and Branch, T. 1972. *Blowing the Whistle: Dissent in the Public Interest*. New York: Praeger.

Ponemon, L.A. 1994. 'Whistle-Blowing as an Internal Control Mechanism. Individual and Organizational Considerations'. *Auditing* 13: 118-130.

Ravishankar, L. 2003. 'Encouraging Internal Whistleblowing in Organizations' *Business and Organizational Ethics Partnership*: Markkula Center for Applied Ethics.

Roche, J. 1971. 'The Competitive System, to Work, to Preserve, and to Protect'. *Vital Speeches of the Day*: 445.

Sennett, R. 1998. *The Corrosion of Character*. New York: Norton.

Sims, R.L. and Keenan, J.P. 1998. 'Predictors of External Whistleblowing: Organizational and Intrapersonal Variables'. *Journal of Business Ethics* 17: 411-421.

Tsahuridu, E.E. and Vandekerckhove, W. forthcoming. 'Organisational Whistleblowing Policies: Making Employees Responsible or Liable?' *Journal of Business Ethics*.

Vandekerckhove, W. 2006. *Whistleblowing and Organizational Social Responsibility. A Global Assessment*. Aldershot: Ashgate.

Vandekerckhove, W. 2007. 'Integrity: Talking the Walk Instead of Walking the Talk' in Carter, C., Clegg, S., Kornberger, M., Laske, S. and Messner, M. (eds) *Business Ethics as Practice*. Cheltenham, Northhampton: Edward Elgar.

Vandekerckhove, W. and Commers, M.S.R. 2004. 'Whistle Blowing and Rational Loyalty'. *Journal of Business Ethics* 53: 225-233.

Vogel, D. 1974. 'The Politicization of the Corporation'. *Social Policy* 5: 57-62.

Walters, K.D. (1975). 'Your employees' right to blow the whistle', *Harvard Business Review* 53: 26-34 cont. 161-162.

31 Framing the Social Responsibility of Business: The Role of Pressure Groups – Paradigmatic Feuds

ÁLVARO DE REGIL CASTILLA

Introduction

This chapter examines how stakeholders try to influence how business should conduct itself to become a socially responsible organ of society. The assessment is made in the context of society's pursuit of a holistic and democratic sustainability, encompassing its social, economic and environmental dimensions. I part from the premise that there is broad consensus that we must redress the postulates under which human activity takes place, for the footprint we are embedding on the planet is completely unsustainable. Thus, increasingly, we are coming to terms with the need to build a new culture for the sustainability of people and planet.

At the core of our consumer-society's structures is the market. Business, as the market's leading driver and with the largest sphere of influence on all dimensions of human activity, bears considerable responsibility for the current footprint and for the successful pursuit of a new sustainable ethos. Making it accountable for its performance, through a binding universal regulatory framework, is instrumental for building a truly sustainable paradigm.

Yet there is no consensus about the responsibilities and areas of accountability of business. This has engendered a permanent debate among different stakeholders with opposing views on the social responsibilities of business. This is an assessment of how interested stakeholders of civil society who want to change the current ethos try to influence corporate behaviour and that of other stakeholders opposing a binding framework.

A Global Capitalistic Ethos

Before addressing the different visions concerning the social responsibilities of business, it is necessary to describe the context upon which these visions are evolving and interacting, from the perspective of those stakeholders who want to change the current ethos.

The idea that business has to be socially accountable for the impact of its activity on societies and the environment is not a recent concept. The development of Corporate Social Responsibility (CSR) dates back to at least the 1970s when people began to question the business practices of well-known corporations. A boycott against Nestlé's infant formula was well known to consumers in Europe and North America during that decade, but its origins can be traced back to at least 1939 (Bromberg Bar-Yam: 1995). Yet it was with the transformation of many companies into truly global conglomerates, from the 1980s on, that questions about the negative impact of their activity, on all aspects of human life and the planet, began to be raised with increasing frequency.

This growing social concern for business practice carried a human rights undertone. Companies were being judged in relation to whether their activities respected human rights that were part of the rights of people, in democratic societies, ingrained in conventional wisdom, particularly among northern societies. It was also in the 1970s that work to control the impact of corporate behaviour on human rights began in the United Nations. The Transnational Corporations Commission, the Centre for Transnational Corporations and a Code of Conduct were created. Yet these organisms never fulfilled their original missions. The major economic powers were always adamantly opposed to the control of the impact of business practices (Teitelbaum: 2006). Three decades later, the social pressure to control corporate activity is far greater, and the debate is becoming increasingly polarised. Nonetheless, governments are even more adamant than before about imposing any legally binding framework enshrined in international law.

PARADIGMATIC SHIFT

Since the 1970s, capitalism was transformed, moving from demand-side to supply-side economics. Companies acquired far more power and governments abdicated from many of their most basic responsibilities. The Welfare State is in great decline and privatisation is on the rise. Some governments have even relinquished providing basic public services, such as water, a natural resource vital for life and a basic human right (UNDP: 2006), and have invited global corporations to take over and privatise the service in many cities (Lasserre and Rekacewicz: 2005).

In essence, governments have become promoters and protectors of neoliberalism. This so-called free market capitalism provides precedence to corporations over people. In this way, governments have worked in close connivance with business to promote the use of voluntary business codes of conduct. The implicit idea is to use CSR as an instrument for business to increase its intangible assets and gain market share by increasing the good will of its markets (White: 2006). This is how governments have supported the development of an array of principles and codes of conduct, strictly voluntary in nature. In great contrast with this trend, every time consumers are surveyed the response consistently favours a legally-binding framework to control the impact of business activity (de Regil: 2007). Yet, despite this dichotomy, governments consistently reject the demand for binding norms. This is possible because, the rules of the market have been imposed over people for the benefit of the owners of the market: the institutional investors and their corporations.

MARKET-DEMOCRACY

With the shift to supply-side economics, the support of governments radically shifted to benefit the welfare of business. Governments gradually moved from being regulators to becoming mere agents of the market. Instead of acting to reconcile the public with the private interest they have granted their acquiescence to the demands of business, heavily deregulating many areas of business and adopting a hands-off approach in support of the self-regulatory practices advanced by business.

Free trade rules, for example, have imposed in many countries an ethos that completely disregards the impact of trade agreements on societies and imposes no responsibilities on corporations (Oldenziel and Vander Stichele: 2005). By the same token, multilateral and bilateral investment agreements provide equal treatment status to global corporations vis-à-vis domestic corporations. They are given guarantees to protect their investments whilst there are no protections against the effect of these investments on communities within the sphere of influence of investors (Vander Stichele and van Bennekom: 2005). Such instruments are providing corporations unfettered access to labour, resources and markets.

With governments treading hard on their most basic democratic responsibility: *to procure the welfare of all ranks of society, especially of the dispossessed*, only the growing organised mobilisation of communities, both in northern and southern societies, has imposed limits to corporate demands. WTO's Doha Trade Round is now practically deemed irrelevant,[1] due to strong social pressure (Cassen: 2005), through mobilisation, and the refusal of many southern countries to further open their economies to the North's industrial goods and services, as long as the latter insist on maintaining their subsidies in agriculture.[2] It was social mobilisation as well that scuttled the Multilateral Agreement on Investment (MAI): an investment scheme advanced in the OECD intended to provide corporations with unfettered rights that would greatly limit governments' right and ability to regulate foreign investors and corporations. At its core, the MAI, inspired by the North American Free Trade Agreement (NAFTA),[3] included the right to sue governments over their laws, which could force them to pay damages or overturn their laws.

The WTO, MAI, NAFTA and other instruments of global capitalism, represent the primeval element of neoliberalism. It is the clearest expression of its philosophy, where capital takes precedence over States and civil societies, imposing rules that virtually destroy the concept of a sovereign State and of true democracy. The logic of the market is imposed over the rights of the State, people, workers, communities and the family (Bourdieu: 1998). Human rights and the social, economic and environmental responsibilities of business are rendered virtually irrelevant.

The origins of this development can be traced back to the fact that global untrammelled capitalism has overtaken the halls of government. Although financing political campaigns by private sources is not allowed in some countries, particularly in Europe, it is still prevalent in many more, including in the U.S (Nace: 2003). This is a major source of corruption, which allows corporations to set the public agenda in line with their very

---

1   El Fracaso de la OMC. La Jornada, Mexico City, 25 July 2006.

2   World Trade. Hard Truths. The Economist, 20 December 2005.

3   Álvaro J. de Regil. The Neo-Capitalist Assault in Mexico: Democracy vis-à-vis the logic of the market. A TLWNSI Issue Essay. The Jus Semper, Global Alliance, February 2004.

private interests. Once corporate candidates are in power, they draft policy to advance the interest of their corporate sponsors.

Despite the rhetoric and conventional wisdom, this is not a democratic ethos but a *marketocracy* where the rules of the owners of the market are being imposed over people and the planet. Public-policy-defining rules covering the entire spectrum of business activity, from trade, investment, development of genetically modified organisms, to patents, taxation and corporate governance, as well as areas indirectly related to business activity, such as health, education, infrastructure and public services, are all being heavily influenced by corporate interests. Consequently, corporate influence is having a profound effect on the development of criteria and of a framework to define the social responsibilities of business.

The Role of Pressure Groups Working to Maintain the Status Quo

It is in this context dominated by the interests of global capital that the debate over the social responsibilities of business is unfolding. We will first examine the groups that are working to define CSR from the same business-dominated environs currently in place. Examining their positions provides the context to convey how stakeholders, committed with changing the status quo, are working to overcome their arguments and influence their positions. These pressure groups are not composed exclusively of business, multilateral organisations, CSR consultants and the like. They also include a sector of organised civil society, mostly multi-stakeholder organisations in full allegiance with the market-driven ethos, and supporters, developers and promoters of a laissez-faire, voluntary, CSR practice.

LAISSEZ-FAIRE CORPORATE SOCIAL RESPONSIBILITY

In the same way that in the new heavily deregulated paradigm governments give their acquiescence to self-regulatory business practices, they support the development of self-regulatory CSR tools. The same vision is applied to corporate governance by encouraging companies to develop their self-defined ethical codes of conduct to eradicate internal corruption. Governments ought not to interfere with the so-called logic of the market. Their role should be to provide a level playing field that offers the best possible conditions for business to thrive, irrespective of the consequences, since it is assumed that the market will take care of the rest through the so-called invisible hand.

Such mind-set ensures that the criteria defining the social responsibilities of business –and how they ought to account for the impact of their activity in society and the environment– is to be defined by business itself. To be sure, governments encourage business to involve their stakeholders and establish a dialogue; but corporations are left in the driver's seat to define, implement and report on their activity according to their criteria and on a strictly voluntary basis. A laissez-faire hands-off approach that disregards societies' concerns and views has been adopted.

Lack of political will, on a global scale, to establish a binding CSR is very consistent with the low profile of neoliberal governments, renouncing their role of regulators and letting market mechanisms hold sway. The laissez-faire attitude of the European pharmaceutical industry's regulators, the 'drugs agencies', who do not carry out their own studies to ensure that new drugs actually bring real benefits to patients and not just extra profits to drug firms, ensure the very private welfare of the industry giants (Rivière: 2002). By the same token, in corporate governance, the Enron, Worldcom, Tyco and Parmalat financial scams, or the U.S. State Department demand to a U.S. federal court to dismiss a human rights lawsuit by Indonesian villagers against Exxon Mobile, saying a trial could harm U.S. economic and political interests in Asia,[4] clearly expose the mock democracy that the world endures.

CORE ARGUMENTS ON BEHALF OF A LAISSEZ-FAIRE CORPORATE SOCIAL RESPONSIBILITY

The business community, with very few exceptions, has staunchly opposed any form of legally-binding regulations controlling how their business has an impact on people and planet. Their entire position centres on maintaining a voluntary ethos concerning the accountability of business for its social and environmental impact. Its entire argumentation is that legal regulations hinder the competitive nature of business and, thus, impair businesses with their ability to make the best possible contributions to society and the planet. The more untrammelled their business environs remains, the greater possibility of thriving, and, thus, the greater possibility of giving back to the communities involved. A second major point against regulation falls directly in the realm of human rights: that protecting, promoting and respecting human rights are responsibilities of the State and not of business, or that the State is the primary bearer of these responsibilities (Leisinger: 2006).

Indeed, the main features of the international position of business regarding CSR can best be identified relative to human rights. This is the area that has generated the most contention and is being increasingly debated at the UN. In 2003 the UN Sub-commission on Human Rights submitted a draft set of standards proposed-to-be-adopted for further development to eventually becoming international law. This is the Draft Norms on business and human rights (E/CN.4/Sub.2/2003/12/Rev.1: 2003). The Draft is based on the International Bill of Rights, which consists of the Universal Declaration of Human Rights and the International Covenants on Civil and Political Rights and on Economic, Social and Cultural Rights. The draft also includes specific international covenants, such as the Convention on the Abolition of Slavery and the International Convention on the Rights of All Migrant Workers. Many of these covenants have become international law and have been ratified by many States, such as the core conventions of the International Labour Organisation.

In addition to proposing the Draft as a legal framework, the working group authoring the Draft proposed to subject corporations to monitoring and audits. As could be expected, this triggered a harsh rejection from major international business organisations,[5] specific companies, governments and from the UN itself.

A report of the High Commissioner on Human Rights incorporates the main arguments of these groups against the Draft (Commission on Human Rights: E/CN.4/2005/91:

---

4   U.S. Wants Suit by Indonesians Dismissed. Los Angeles Times, 7 August 2002.

5   The business organisations providing input in reaction to the draft of the UN Norms are: Bundesverband der Deutschen Industrie, Business and Industry Advisory Committee to the OECD, Confederation of British Industry, Confederation of Danish Industry, International Chamber of Commerce, International Organization of Employers, Netherland's Industry, United States Council for International Business.

2005). The groups considered that the Draft represents a major shift away from voluntary adherence by business to international human rights standards and that the need for this shift has not been demonstrated. It was argued as well that many norms have not been ratified by many States, and that the norms attempt to assign responsibilities to business that are the exclusive responsibility of governments under international human rights law. Other major negative arguments included:

- the implementation provisions of the Draft Norms are burdensome and unworkable;
- the Norms are more demanding on companies than on States;
- the Draft Norms duplicate other initiatives and standards;
- the imposition of legal responsibilities on business could provide a diversion for States to avoid their own responsibilities;
- the style of the Draft Norms is unduly negative towards business.

MARKETOCRACY IN PRACTICE

Essentially, the business community adamantly rejected developing a business and human rights framework designed to become international law. Given the *marketocracy* that we are enduring, these positions have heavily influenced governments and multilateral organisations. The system works very efficiently. The trade associations of the different business sectors in each country, many of which enthusiastically contribute to the campaigns of the politicians they favour in the different branches of government, convey their positions directly to their governments. Governments take the cue from business and subsequently act to fulfil the corporate demands either domestically or internationally.

A case with Starbucks is very illustrative of how corporations advance their interests. In 2005 Ethiopia applied with the U.S. Patents and Trademark Office (USPTO) to register three premium types of coffees. Such trademarks would enable Ethiopians to increase their price, which is vital for their sustainability, given that coffee accounts for 60 per cent of foreign exchange and ten per cent of government revenue, and it involves seventeen million Ethiopians. Ethiopia, one of the poorest countries of the world, has 80 per cent of Ethiopians living with less than $2 a day. However, Starbucks blocked the trademarks, despite Ethiopia proposing to sit down to establish an amicable licensing agreement by filing, at the same time as Ethiopia, for a trademark for a type of Ethiopian coffee and writing a letter to the National Coffee Association asking it to block Ethiopia's application with the USPTO. The action effectively resulted in the USPTO denial of Ethiopia's trademark registration (de Regil: 2007). Such behaviour comes from a corporation that signed up with the UN Global Compact (UNGC) only after it was heavily boiler plated through an agreement, after a three-year effort, between the UN and the U.S. Bar Association to protect U.S. corporations from being sued for not complying with the UNGC.[6] Yet Starbucks portrays itself as excelling in CSR practices (Starbucks: 2005).

This strategy is replicated systematically worldwide. Corporations act in a very unlevelled-playing field because of the very asymmetric conditions between the powers they can exert on governments vis-à-vis the powers that civil society can wield. If

---

6   The Economist. Corporate Social Responsibility. Bluewashed and Boilerplated, 17 June 2004.

the issue is being discussed at the UN, the OECD or other organisations, companies typically press their governments to advance their interests or approach the organisation directly.

Such is the case of the UNGC, a set of ten principles that reinforce the status quo by clearly reaffirming that globalisation is the driving force in today's societies, whilst failing to address critical issues such as fair labour endowments. Even more revealing is its conception exclusively incorporating the business perspective, strictly voluntary, and supposedly based on *public accountability, transparency and the enlightened self-interest of companies*.[7] The GC is widely perceived as a rhetorical posture given its already extremely business friendliness (Sanders: 2000). In this way, in a summit in the summer of 2007, the UNGC members announced the Geneva Declaration,[8] which proclaims their support for the current neoliberal globalisation and the voluntary ethos for the practice of CSR whilst concurrently demanding from governments to work to further open their markets with more guarantees and stability for business.

Another illustrative case of corporate power on governments is the Draft Norms, where one can clearly observe the position of the UN in favour of the business perspective, with the market reigning over people as the underlying context. In this case many companies approached the UN directly or through business umbrellas such as the International Chamber of Commerce, to influence the UN's position. In this way, in response to the submission of the Draft, the UN Human Rights Commission clearly affirmed that the document had not been requested; and asked for a report *in order to identify options for strengthening standards on the responsibilities of transnational corporations and related business enterprises with regard to human rights and possible means of implementation*.[9] In other words, it decided to strengthen the current human-rights ethos, which is not binding on corporations. The report recommends further evaluation of the topic. Yet its recommendation is clearly anchored in the context of the market as the central element ruling the lives of the members of society, supplanting a truly democratic ethos.

The other area where companies are increasingly active in the CSR arena is with the endorsement and promotion of voluntary multi-stakeholder initiatives such as the GRI, Social Accountability International and Accountability. These initiatives offer a natural environment for corporations to influence the development of CSR criteria. These initiatives have developed social responsibility norms, specific indicators and guidelines for best business practice. As could be expected, they all share the common characteristic of being strictly voluntary, which currently constitutes the only possible way of alluring corporations to take up their CSR tools and join their boards.

All of these, as well as the UN and OECD initiatives, principles and declarations provide their enthusiastic acquiescence to the untrammelled capitalistic ethos that engulfs the world. There is no obligation to abide by a set of specific norms encroaching the business environment. As a result, CSR practice is predominantly perceived by business as a tool to increase competitiveness (White: 2006).

---

7   See: http://www.unglobalcompact.org/AboutTheGC/index.html.

8   UN Global Compact. Business Leaders Adopt Declaration on Responsible Business Practices, 6 July 2007.

9   UN Human Rights Commission: E/CN.4/2004/L.11/Add.7: 2004, p. 81.

A MILD EXCEPTION

There is so far one mild exception to the rule, nonetheless. One group of well-known companies created the Business Leaders Initiative on Human Rights (BLIHR) to contribute to the development of a human rights and business framework. The group is formed by ABB, Alcan, AREVA, Barclays, Ericsson, Gap, General Electric, Hewlett-Packard, MTV Networks Europe, National Grid, Novartis, Novo Nordisk, Statoil, The Body Shop International and Coca-Cola.

The group clearly favours voluntary practice. One of their key arguments is their belief that some of the most effective and proactive contributions business can make should not be limited or enforced through regulation.[10] The BLIHR, in line with other supporters of a voluntary ethos, considers that governments are the primary bearers of the obligation to respect, protect and fulfil individual human rights. It argues that the overarching principle remains that States are primarily accountable to victims of human rights abuses and that businesses are accountable to States.[11]

However, the BLIHR, to the best of my knowledge, is the only business group willing to consider the possibility of a human-rights framework that includes both legally binding and voluntary standards. Moreover, in contrast with the dominant position in the business sector, which rejects the UN Draft of the norms, they decided to test it for a two-year period, in order to assess it objectively.

Such posture, which sets the BLIHR apart from the rest, has put it in a very influential position with the UN, establishing a close rapport with John Ruggie, the Special Representative for Business and Human Rights at the UN. This has generated strong affinity in their views. An important and shared position with Ruggie has been the argumentation in favour of three layers of human rights: essential, expected and desirable. The idea is that protection in a company's sphere of influence against human rights violations already part of international law should be considered essential. These would be the bare minimum standards with which business must comply. Expected rights are all the rights that many stakeholders expect business to satisfy voluntarily, beyond the bare minimum, for moral reasons. To be sure, the BLIHR is trying to appropriate the concept of human rights. Yet, perhaps sincerely, the BLIHR slightly opens the door to the development of future essential human rights by arguing that *expected behaviour today could become 'essential' behaviour tomorrow.*[12]

The Role of Pressure Groups Working to Build a New Ethos

The greater part of civil society represents a wide spectrum of social strata; mostly indirect stakeholders of the corporations, for most do not interact directly with business entities as employees or suppliers in the supply chains. They do interact, however, as consumers and, furthermore, consider themselves stakeholders who perceive their own lives negatively

---

10   Business Leaders Initiative on Human Rights. Report 3: Towards a 'Common Framework' on Business and Human Rights: Identifying Components. London, June 2006, p. 6.

11   Ibid, p.19.

12   Business Leaders Initiative on Human Rights. Report 3: Towards a 'Common Framework' on Business and Human Rights: Identifying Components. London, June 2006, p. 6.

affected in varying degrees by corporate activity. I will refer to them as the Alter-World Movement or AWM.

These pressure groups are the organised sectors of civil society who see global capital, ergo, the institutional investors and their corporations, as the overarching power dominating and determining the structures of society and the rapidly-diminishing prospects for enjoying progressive and sustainable development, materialised in a dignified quality of life. There is a clear perception that the current ethos has embarked the world on a trend consistently rendering diminishing returns for most people and the greatest benefit ever for a miniscule global elite.

BUILDING TRUE DEMOCRACY

This perception has greatly polarised the debate over the accountability of business before society. Large segments of the citizenry, both North and South, are increasingly opposed to what they perceive as an undemocratically imposed ethos that eliminated the rights of people and replaced them with the rights of corporations to profit over people and the planet. They share the conviction that society's democratic aspirations have been supplanted by market imperialism. In this way, they see the need for a coherent system regulating business practice that guarantees a minimum of democratic, transparent and participative processes (Rathgeber: 2006).

As a result, organised social mobilisation is on the rise with the conviction that true democracy must be built from the ground up as the core element sine qua non for building a new sustainable ethos. In several South American countries, namely Venezuela, Bolivia and Ecuador, the people have been able to organise and replace governments they perceived as being completely in partnership with global capitalism, and put in instead governments they perceive to be committed to fulfil the demands of the people by making radical changes in policy. In other countries with less radical approaches, such as Argentina and Brazil, new governments, under heavy social pressure, have paid off their debts with the IMF and the World Bank to put an end to the pressures to apply neoliberal policies. Indeed, Iberian America stands out for its growing grass roots mobilisation against the imposed order. In this way, Bolivians expelled their government for attempting to sell their energy resources to MNCs at dismal prices; Mapuche Indians in Chile blocked an energy contract awarded to a Spanish corporation; Argentineans formed cooperatives to re-start factories abandoned by owners; and Mexicans blocked the construction of a new airport on an ancient lake bed previously designated as a protected natural reserve (Cardozo and de Regil: 2006).

In northern countries the AWM has grown steadily not only to demonstrate during the summits of the leading powers or the leaders of global capital, but, especially, to organise in concrete actions to put in check policy making with governments as well as concrete corporate practices. People are organising to redefine the international financial system, to develop a people's fair-trade system, to build a new consumer culture anchored on sustainability. People are becoming aware about the close links existing between the problems endured by northern/southern societies. Global and regional summits of the people, such as the social forums that originated in Brazil, have now become a permanent event in direct opposition to the global capital summits.

The catalyst that these groups have for organising is the realisation that their aspiration for creating truly democratic and peaceful societies has been virtually cancelled by conscious and premeditated undemocratic decisions taken by governments in partnership with global capital. There is also a realisation that those who control power invest a great deal of energy in manipulating, coercing and controlling public opinion to make believe that this hoax is the ethos of truly democratic societies and that we are living the best of all possible worlds (Chomsky: 1999). In this way, the civil organisations that have chosen as their mission to develop a people and planet-centred framework for the social and environmental responsibilities of business generally see their work as an instrumental part of the new truly democratic paradigm.

CENTRAL GOAL OF PRESSURE GROUPS

The sectors of the AWM that have made it their mission to establish a new regulatory framework of business have set as their primary goal to harness the market to make it subservient to people and planet. This goal is anchored on the demand of developing a binding and universal regulatory framework that would strictly control business activity in the economic, social and environmental dimensions. The goal is to make this framework the overarching body of international and national laws controlling business practice on a global scale.

MAIN ARGUMENTATION

To advance this goal the AWM is developing a comprehensive and powerful body of knowledge that it deems critical for developing a strong argumentation capable of effectively challenging the position of governments and the market. This knowledge is intended to counter the arguments of the current paradigm, eliminate the myths and exhibit reality with hard facts. There are two major arguments encompassing the entire discourse used by the AWM against the current ethos:

- *Incompatibility.* The neoliberal ethos, *the dictatorship of the market's government,* (Bauman: 1999) is completely incompatible with the basic principles of true democracy and goes completely in the opposite direction of long-term sustainability. The current ethos is rendering a widening gap between rich and poor, growing job insecurity, large segments of society excluded from the formal economy, diminishing social protections and increasingly corrupt governments that do not fulfil their most basic responsibilities. Additionally, all natural resources and the sustainability of the planet itself are greatly in peril, to the point that current consumption levels may have crossed a threshold of no return in ecological unsustainability (Karliner: 1997). Consequently, there is no long-term viability for people and planet; and it is clearly perceived that the power of global untrammelled capitalism constitutes the core of the problem.
- *Injustice.* The current ethos is inherently unjust and subhuman. Even if we were living on a surreal planet that somehow had a plethora of resources that could never be exhausted, the current market-driven paradigm would still be a sheer generator of great injustice; for it is the antithesis of mankind's pursuit of a peaceful coexistence, which requires solidarity and respect of the wide diversity of cultures and ethnic groups that populate the planet.

MAJOR GROUPS – VARIATIONS IN THEIR STRATEGIC DEMANDS

The central demand of the AWM is to make business practice sustainable in a holistic sense. This implies broadly that the long-term sustainability of business must be anchored on the context of true democracy, harnessing corporate culture and the purpose of business itself, to the common good. In the social contract of truly democratic societies, the government's primeval responsibility is to procure and protect the welfare of all ranks of society. In this context all organs of society are obliged to contribute to this responsibility by not benefiting at the expense of others.

As could be expected, there is not a single set of visions and solutions shared by the entire AWM. There is diversity in the conceptualisation of key elements, such as sustainability, true democracy, sphere of influence, human rights, labour rights, dignified quality of life and living wage. Nevertheless, all share the conviction that corporate practice must be harnessed through a legally-binding framework, in full congruency with the aspiration to build a 'truly' democratic ethos. This movement shares the affinity that voluntary codes of conduct are largely discredited for they are a mockery of what business CSR should be, since they let the market regulate itself. However, there are two major groups of the AWM envisioning two distinctive approaches in which business practice should be reformed.

- *Legal framework without a new purpose of business.* These groups support a legal CSR framework to control corporations (CSR Worldwide Week Network: 2004). They support the enactment into laws of the International Bill of Rights. Although they believe in the need of a serious public policy agenda of regulations, which must underpin the fair and efficient working of markets (Tallontire and Vorley: 2005), they do not demand the replacement of capitalistic markets as the centre of social interaction. Alternatively, there is a belief that capitalism needs to be transformed to make it a sustainable and just means of socio-economic organising (Bendell et al.: 2005). This sector considers that, by establishing a universal and legally-binding CSR framework, we can make the market compatible with sustainability and democracy. In this sector's view, there is a need for another approach that recognises how a global market requires global rules on matters of human dignity and welfare (Bendel et al.: 2005). This sector encompasses a substantially greater portion of society than the second group.
- *Legal framework with a new purpose for business.* These groups advocate an entirely new paradigm anchored on long-term sustainability requiring the redefinition of business, its nature and purpose. They consider that the only way to make the market compatible with true democracy and sustainability is by changing the purpose of business from shareholderism to the social good (Corporation 20/20: 2006). This solution means that the reproduction of capital must occur without negatively influencing any stakeholders (Doane: 2005) within its sphere of influence. It also entails that the revenue generated must be distributed equitably among all direct participants in the company's activity. It means that companies must balance their shareholder with their social and environmental responsibilities, making the market subservient to democracy and long-term sustainability. In this sense, business practice must be humane and democratic, instead of autocratic, where decision making fully includes the participation of all stakeholders (Rathgeber: 2006). This change entails as

well a complete cultural change, diminishing as much as necessary our footprint on the planet by replacing our culture of consumerism with a culture of a balanced use of all resources. These groups are a small but rapidly growing segment, as more people become conscientious of the impossibility of reconciling amoral capitalism's fixation with profit with the need to achieve a holistic sustainability.

The essential difference between both groups is advocating a strong regulatory framework for business practice, within the capitalistic paradigm, vis-à-vis advocating a new paradigm anchored on sustainability and not capitalism. Moreover, albeit all want to broadly 'harness the market to serve the people and planet', there is an ample spectrum of variation in the intensity of this shared demand, even within the two major groups. Some want to confront the dominance of shareholderism rejecting its primacy (de Regil: 2006) whilst others want companies to give equal importance to stockholders and stakeholders (Kelly and White: 2007), including the planet, by developing the business practices necessary to maintain a permanent balancing act. Yet others only want to establish strict rules in corporate social responsibility (ActionAid: 2007) and corporate governance practices that guarantee a sustainable and democratic capitalistic market system. A good example of the middle approach advanced by a social network is its 'Core principles for corporate redesign':[13]

- The purpose of the corporation is to harness private interests to serve the public interest.
- Corporations shall distribute their wealth equitably among those who contribute to its creation.
- Corporations shall accrue fair returns for shareholders, but not at the expense of the legitimate interests of other stakeholders.
- Corporations shall be governed in a manner that is participatory, transparent, ethical and accountable.
- Corporations shall operate sustainably, meeting the needs of the present generation without compromising the ability of future generations to meet their needs.
- Corporations shall not infringe on the right of natural persons to govern themselves, nor infringe on other universal human rights.

MAJOR GROUPS – AFFINITIES IN THEIR STRATEGIC DEMANDS

Both groups consider that their demands can only take place gradually, and will take a generation or more to be accomplished. This means that some social groups consider their goals only of the first generation, which, once accomplished, should give way to the second generation. In this way, some groups' second-generation goals may converge with other groups' first-generation goals. This may be the result to some degree of greater differences in strategy and tactics than in concepts and long-term vision. Considering that completely replacing a paradigm, or even just revamping it, entails a major shift of social structures on a global scale, it would be unrealistic to expect these groups to share from inception a very cohesive vision of the major problems and solutions of the world's great diversity of cultures and experiences in life. For this reason, the differences

---

13   Corporation 20/20. Principles of Corporate Redesign. http://www.corporation2020.org/ November 2007.

notwithstanding, both groups share many demands concerning the social responsibilities of business. This is generating a cross-pollination of ideas that is allowing them to join efforts to exploit their synergies.

In broad terms, the following concepts that bear significant weight in framing a CSR practice, in the context of true democracy and sustainability, enjoy strong affinity among the different social groups who see themselves as part of the AWM. The development of these concepts is a critical activity for influencing the development of CSR. The following concepts, taken from an assessment in progress concerning business and human rights (Jus Semper: 2007), offer a good example of how organisations work to influence CSR development.

- *Holistic sustainability.* The reduction of our footprint to achieve the dignified sustainability of the planet by significantly decreasing consumption in the North while increasing consumption in the South to bring it to a sustainable balance. In this sense, efficiency and productivity must be directed to increasing the efficiency in the use of natural resources to consume less and preserve more, without a mercantilist criterion (Harribey: 2004).
- *Human rights.* Business must be responsible and directly accountable for its own actions, which has nothing to do with transferring State responsibilities to business.
- *Labour rights.* A living wage must be at the centre of labour rights for it bears the most direct influence in the access to a dignified quality of life; it is a basic human right and it is currently at the centre of the global system of exploitation.
- *Legally binding framework.* All rights regarding the social responsibilities of business must be enshrined in a universal legally-binding framework in order to become real rights and for governments and all organs of society to respect, protect and promote them.
- *Full inclusion of stakeholders.* The framing of the concepts and norms that will govern the social responsibilities of business must be done with the full and permanent participation of all direct and indirect stakeholders.
- *Sphere of influence.* Each company has a different sphere of influence, which must include all individuals and organisations with which the company has political, contractual, social, economic or geographic proximity, regardless of whether it has a direct or indirect relationship with them.
- *Stakeholders.* All people affected by a company's activity belong to the company's sphere of influence, and, thus, constitute the company's stakeholders.
- *Civil society's right to define.* In a democratically CSR framework, civil society should determine the sphere of influence as well as the stakeholders that belong to the area of responsibility of business instead of the company defining them unilaterally.
- *Complicity.* Companies are complicit of wrongful practices and violation of rights, particularly in the case of human rights, when the practices and violations would have not occurred without the company's participation, or when a company consciously profits from a violation made by another actor even if such violation would still take place regardless of the behaviour of the company.
- *Universal framework with punitive remedies.* A universal legally-binding CSR framework must have a penal code defining the elements of concrete violations and specifying the punishment and a remedy that is commensurate with the violation's negative effect on stakeholders.

- *Civil society's right to take legal action.* As in the case of the OECD's 'National Contact Points' (NCPs), civil society, and not just the States, is entitled to take legal action against any company violating any norm of the universal legally-binding CSR framework.

- *Reporting, monitoring and certification mechanisms.* Companies have a binding responsibility to report to States and civil society on their CSR performance vis-à-vis the universal CSR framework. A system of public monitoring, verification and certification mechanisms must be in place to validate their reports. Civil society's permanent and full participation in the management of these mechanisms must be instrumental for the credible certification and/or rejection of a company's CSR performance.

- *Applicable universally.* A universal and legally-binding CSR framework is applicable in every country, even in the case of weak States that are incapable or unwilling to take action. When necessary, civil society has the right to take legal action against a company, in accordance with the framework, before an international court.

SLOW-TRACK LONG-TERM STRATEGIES TO INFLUENCE CORPORATE SOCIAL RESPONSIBILITY DEVELOPMENT

Operationally, the basic strategy of the AWM to influence the framing of CSR is building critical mass. The more civil organisations joining a network, the more clout to influence actors defending the status quo.

Slow long-term strategies target primarily institutional actors (governments, EU, UN, OECD, ILO) and secondarily corporations as well as public opinion. The central purpose is to create opportunities, through pressure, to participate in the development of norms to regulate corporate practice by influencing the outcomes. Such was the case of the development of the draft of the UN Norms for Human Rights, where many civil organisations participated along with government and business representatives, and were able to include meaningful content that favoured the interests and vision of the AWM (Teitelbaum: 2006). The ultimate goal, to be sure, is to establish a legal CSR framework. This is a slow long-term strategy because it deals directly with the bureaucracies of States and multilateral organisations that normally move at a snail's pace and are staunch defenders of the status quo. This guarantees that the process will take decades. Despite the sluggish process, there is widespread agreement that civil society must maintain permanent pressure on these actors to eventually win the upper hand in the debate as part of the movement's effort to build true democracy. Four main strategic elements are used:

- *Content development.* Instrumental for successfully influencing institutional actors is the development of a body of knowledge, such as the previously illustrated examples, from diverse members of civil society, spanning from legal practitioners (ILRF: 2005) and scholars with expertise in the development of international law to testimonies provided directly by communities directly affected by corporate activity (Bogotá Declaration: 2007). Much of the content development comes about by cross-pollinating ideas. This content is used strategically, through diverse tactics, to influence, directly and indirectly, key actors. The development of content includes: position and seminal papers, first hand and secondary research on business practices, assessment studies on issues such as human rights, living wages, consumer responsibilities and rights, fair trade and impact assessment studies. Content is also critical to support the strategic elements.

- *Campaigns.* These actions target specific institutions such as the UN, the WTO, the OECD and the European Parliament. One typical tactic is to approach directly key actors in these institutions with the objective of influencing their work, by requesting to meet (ICCR: 2006), or through letters signed by hundreds of civil society organisations (ESCR-Net: 2007). These campaigns may also include street demonstrations and the use of alternative media and press releases to elicit public awareness and favourable public opinion.
- *Legal actions.* These are used to address concrete cases of corporate malpractice. For example, International Rights Advocates uses international human rights law in the U.S. court system and in those of other nations to defend individuals victimized by global corporations.[14] Another illustration is the work of OECD Watch, an international NGO network that has developed an extensive body of knowledge regarding the OECD Guidelines for multinationals and the specific use of the NCPs (OECD Watch: 2006), OECD's mechanism for NGOs against a specific corporation for alleged breaches of the OECD Guidelines.
- *Public opinion influence.* Influencing public opinion is surely the most critical strategic element in the effort to influence key institutions. This is achieved by reaching the general public with valuable, objective and well-documented information. Position papers, reports, newsletters and brochures are some of the typical vehicles used to reach the public using alternative radio, print newspapers, documentaries and the Internet. Events, such as the World and Regional Social Forum, are also valuable opportunities to reach the public, especially when they are able to receive mass-media coverage. Cross-pollination of content through scores of distribution points, from academic Internet portals to specific topic blogs increases reach and influence of the messages delivered. To be sure, publishing in academic and other institutional journals, newsletters and books further increases the influence on public opinion.

FAST-TRACK SHORT AND LONG-TERM STRATEGIES TO INFLUENCE CORPORATE SOCIAL RESPONSIBILITY DEVELOPMENT

These strategies are aimed at generating change in both the short and long-term. The primary target audiences are the citizenry in its consumer role and corporations to demand a universal and legally binding business regulatory framework. Besides influencing public opinion on behalf of the need to change the status quo, people are empowered to elicit change by leveraging their consumer power using the same logic of the market used by corporations.

This is a very powerful asset that increasingly is forcing change of corporate decision making in a very short period of time. It took mobilising 100,000 consumers to write to Starbucks to force it to stop blocking Ethiopia's coffees' U.S. patent registrations (Oxfam America: 2007). The consumer leverage of a student-run consortium of nearly 200 U.S. and Canadian universities has forced university administrations to develop a CSR code of conduct for their suppliers, which forces them to accept monitoring and inspection

---

14   See http://www.iradvocates.org/, November 2007.

of their supply chains, through a specialised NGO (Worker Rights Consortium: 2007) to ensure that they are conforming to the CSR code or suffer the cancellation of their contracts with the universities (USAS: 2007).

Ethical stockholders are also exerting pressure on corporations regarding CSR practice and corporate governance, such as in the case of Dutch supermarket chain Ahold.[15] The fair trade movement is also slowly but steadily influencing consumer behaviour to embed a sense of social responsibility in our consumer decisions, teaching us to become conscientious about the CSR record behind the brands we buy and to align our consumer habits with our social values to force change in business practices (de Regil: 2007).

Fast-track strategies are used to elicit change overtime with the goal frequently set to be accomplished in a generation or more. Yet tangible changes are achieved in the short-term as part of long-term goals. In the case of The Jus Semper Global Alliance, the project that I manage, our goal to achieve living wages in the South will take at least a generation. However, small changes, such as being able to sit down with international garment company 'American Apparel' and agree to make living wages a top priority of its CSR agenda, is a small step towards our long-term mission (de Regil: 2005). The results obtained through these strategies also positively influence institutional actors. Every time corporations are forced to change their decision making on specific CSR issues, institutional actors cannot avoid feeling a tangible increase in social pressure to respond to our social demands. The following points are the key strategic elements used in fast-track strategies.

- *Consumer campaigns.* Consumer campaigns – with consumer organisations naturally participating – are a strategy increasingly used to force rapid change in companies with consumer brands. Despite some critics regarding this tactic as politically incorrect, consumer boycotts are increasingly perceived as a consumer right. Indeed, in these times of Darwinian capitalism, consumer boycotts are the most politically correct and democratic exercise to vote our conscience with our consumer power; and surveys clearly attest to consumers' disposition to stay away from socially irresponsible brands (de Regil: 2004). Moreover, consumer boycotts have been showing that there is a positive trade-off for society as even the threat of a consumer boycott increases a company's willingness to cater to consumer demands (Haan: 2007).
- *Ethical stockholder initiatives.* Ethical investment is on the rise in Europe and North America (BSD: 2007). Investors are increasingly placing importance on ethical corporate governance and in socially and environmentally sustainable practices, incorporating these criteria into investment decision making and value considerations. Consumer campaigns and ethical investment are the two strategic elements that can elicit the most change in corporate practices in the short term.
- *Corporate practice monitoring.* Some NGOs monitoring global companies (Corporate Watch, Multinational Monitor, Sweatshop Watch, Transnationale) publicly denounce any irresponsible and unsustainable practices.
- *Fair trade development.* The fair trade movement is growing rapidly and is contributing meaningfully to create a new conscientious and socially responsible consumer culture. Fair trade is also the best source for alternative sources of consumption to replace predatory brands. Global corporations are feeling the pressure and have tried

---

15   Hans de Vreij, Risky business, risky pay. Radio Netherlands, 18 September 2003.

to neutralise fair trade by developing their own token fair trade programmes. Yet they have not been able to stop the market share growth of fully independent fair trade alternatives. Fair trade ground coffee, for instance, was already enjoying a 20 per cent share in the UK in 2004 (Krier: 2005). Albeit fair trade still has a long way to go in establishing norms that are truly sustainable and dignified, it is step in the right direction (de Regil: 2007).

- *Monitoring and social audits.* These actions are usually taken by broad national and international coalitions of NGOs, and typically use consumer boycotts to pressure companies to amend their business practices, particularly in their supply chains such as in the case of the college student networks. Most audits are used to demand compliance with the ILO's labour conventions and human rights international law.
- *Workers support and training.* A sector of NGOs supports workers in the supply chains of global corporations in the South. Networks such as the Coalition for Justice in the Maquiladoras in the U.S. and Mexico provides direct support to workers of in-bond plants in Mexico and other countries to enable them to organise and demand their labour rights. These networks also organise public relations and consumer campaigns to denounce corporate malfeasance and trigger positive corporate reactions.
- Obtaining and producing objective and meaningful information plays a fundamental role in the successful execution of these strategies to mobilise consumers and to prepare them to approach corporations. A successful consumer boycott must be supported by precise and accurate information or risk alienating consumers. Some of the information is obtained directly from corporations, especially in the case of investors, who have the right to demand specific information. When corporations refuse acting transparently, information is obtained through other sources, particularly the workers victimized by corporate malpractice, unions or other organisations in the movement with access to valuable first-hand information. Many of the content and media vehicles used to inform the public and consumers and execute campaigns are the same used in the slow-track strategies.

Corollary

This assessment finds that growing and substantial sectors of global civil society are immensely dissatisfied with the current structures that have been imposed on society. They share the conviction that the current paradigm of the imposed untrammelled Darwinian and predatory global capitalism is not sustainable and needs to be transformed and closely regulated, if not completely replaced by a new paradigm. Although there are differences relative to the intensity of the changes needed, all sectors share the conviction that business activity must be regulated through a universal and legally-binding regulatory framework. For this reason, these sectors are building an Alter-World Movement and mobilising to oppose the centres of global capitalism by influencing public opinion towards the need to harness business to make it subservient to people and planet.

To accomplish this, the AWM is developing a powerful body of knowledge to expose the truth, increase pressure and directly participate in the framing of the social responsibilities of business. Concurrently, it is building a socially and environmentally conscientious consumer culture to challenge corporations by using the very same logic of the market that they have imposed. Given the challenge at hand, these sectors are fully aware that successfully accomplishing their missions will take at least a generation. Yet the probability of success will largely depend on the continuation of the perverse pauperisation of billions of people and the depredation of the planet in as much as on the tenacity of society to put an end to *marketocracy*.

Bibliography

ActionAid. Who Pays? ActionAid, 2007.

Zygmunt Bauman. In Search of Politics. Stanford University Press, 1999.

Jem Bendell. Barricades and Boardrooms. A Contemporary History of the Corporate Accountability Movement. UN. Research Institute for Social Development, June 2004.

Jem Bendell, John Manoochehri and Shilpa Shah. Serving Systemic Transformations. The Lifeworth Review of 2005.

Pierre Bourdieu, The Essence of Neoliberalism. Le Monde Diplomatique, December 1998.

Business and Sustainable Development. www.BSDglobal.com

Naomi Bromberg Bar-Yam. The Nestle Boycott: The Story of the WHO/UNICEF Code for Marketing Breastmilk Substitutes. Mothering Magazine, Winter 1995.

Myriam Cardozo Brum and Álvaro de Regil Castilla. Non-Governmental Organisations and Corporate Social Responsibility in Iberian America. In Corporate Social Responsibility Volume 2. Performances and Stakeholders. Edited by José Allouche. Palgrave Macmillan, 2006.

Bernard Cassen. The Doha Round. The Great Trade Fair. Le Monde Diplomatique, December 2005.

Noam Chomsky. Profit over People. Neoliberalism and Global Order. Seven Stories Press, 1999.

Corporation 20/20. Creating the Vision and Charting the Course of the Future Corporation, 2006 Brochure.

CSR Worldwide Week Network. Netherlands, November 2004 Conference.

Deborah Doane. The Myth of CSR. Stanford Social Innovation Review, Fall 2005.

Declaration of the Social, Non-Governmental and Union Organizations and Indigenous and Affected Communities Convened at The Regional Consultation of the Special Representative of the Secretary General of the UN on the issue of Human Rights and Transnational and other Businesses Enterprises Bogotá, Colombia, January 18-19, 2007.

Economic, Social and Cultural Rights Network. Letter to John Ruggie of 25 October 2007.

Marco Haan. The Competitive Effects of a Consumer Boycott. University of Groningen. The Netherlands, May 2007.

Jean Marie Harribey, Do We Really Want Development? Growth, The World's Hard Drug, Le Monde Diplomatique, August 2004.

Interfaith Centre on Corporate Responsibility. Letter to John Ruggie of 10 October 2006.

International Labour Rights Fund. 2005 Annual Report.

The Jus Semper Global Alliance. The Living Wages North and South Initiative, March 2006.

Joshua Karliner. The Corporate Planet. Sierra Club, 1997.

Marjorie Kelly and Allen White. Corporate Design. The Missing Business and Public Policy Issue of our Time. Corporation 20/20, November 2007.

Jean Marie Krier. Fair Trade Europe 2005. FLO, IFAT, NEWS, EFTA.

Frédéric Lasserre and Philippe Rekacewicz. The Water Dossier. Blue Gold Rush. Le Monde Diplomatique, March 2005.

Klaus M. Leisinger. On Corporate Responsibility for Human Rights. Basel, Switzerland, April 2006.

Ted Nace. Gangs of America. The Rise of Corporate Power and the Disabling of Democracy. Berret-Koheler, 2003.

OECD Watch. Guide to the OECD Guidelines for Multinational Enterprises' Complaint Procedure. 2006.

Joris Oldenziel & Myriam Vander Stichele. Trade and the Need to Apply International Corporate Social Responsibility (CSR) Standards. SOMO Discussion Paper, 2 November 2005.

Oxfam America. Oxfam Celebrates Win-Win Outcome for Ethiopian Coffee Farmers and Starbucks, 20 June 2007.

Theodor Rathgeber. UN Norms on the Responsibilities of Transnational Corporations. Dialogue Globalization. OCCASIONAL PAPERS. N° 22. Friedrich-Ebert-Stiftung. Geneva, April 2006.

Álvaro J. de Regil. Consumer Power in the Logic of the Market: Real and Direct Democracy in Pursuit of CSR. A TLWNSI Issue Essay. The Jus Semper Global Alliance, December 2004.

Álvaro J. de Regil. How Sustainable is our Latte: An Assessment of Trends and Standards in Fair-Trade From the Perspective of a New Truly Sustainable People and Planet-Centred Paradigm. TLWNSI Issue Essay. The Jus Semper Global Alliance. May 2007.

Philippe Rivière. Drug deals in Europe. Le Monde Diplomatique, February 2002.

Bernard Sanders. Waking Up the Global Elite: Activism in the Streets Has Led to an Outpouring of Platitudes in the Suites. The Nation, 2 October 2000.

Starbucks Coffee. Beyond the Cup. Corporate Social Responsibility Fiscal 2005 Annual Report.

Myriam Vander Stichele and Sander van Bennekom. Investment agreements and Corporate Social Responsibility (CSR): Contradictions, Incentives and Policy Options. SOMO Discussion paper 1, November 2005.

Anne Tallontire and Bill Vorley. Achieving Fairness in Trading between Supermarkets and their Agrifood Supply Chains, p. 12. UK Food Group Briefing, September 2005.

Alejandro Teitelbaum. El Tema De Las Sociedades Transnacionales En La Onu, Agosto 2006.

UNDP. Human Development Report 2006. Beyond Scarcity: Power, Poverty and the Global Water Crisis, UN 2006.

Allen L White. Business Brief: Intangibles and CSR. Business for Social Responsibility, February 2006.

UN Commission On Human Rights Sub-Commission on the Promotion and Protection of Human Rights. Draft Norms on the Responsibilities of Transnational Corporations and other Business Enterprises with Regard to Human Rights E/CN.4/Sub.2/2003/12/Rev.1, 30 May 2003.

UN Commission On Human Rights. Report of the United Nations High Commissioner on Human Rights on the Responsibilities of Transnational Corporations and Related Business Enterprises with Regard to Human Rights. E/CN.4/2005/91, 15 February 2005.

UN Commission On Human Rights. Interim Report of the Special Representative of the Secretary-General on the Issue of Human Rights and Transnational Corporations and other Business Enterprises. E/CN.4/2006/97, 22 February 2006.

United Students Against Sweatshops. www.studentsagainstsweatshops.org

Worker Rights Consortium. Model Code of Conduct, November 2007.

KEY REFERENCES FOR FURTHER READING

Corporate Social Responsibility Volume 1. Concepts, Accountability and Reporting. Edited by José Allouche. Palgrave Macmillan, 2006.

Corporate Social Responsibility Volume 2. Performances and Stakeholders. Edited by José Allouche. Palgrave Macmillan, 2006.

Corporation 20/20 and Tellus Institute. Paper Series on Corporate Design, November 2007.

Gerard Fonteneau. Corporate Social Responsibility: Envisioning its Social Implications. A TLWNSI Issue Essay. The Jus Semper Global Alliance, October 2003.

Monica Prasad, Howard Kimeldorf, Rachel Meyer, and Ian Robinson. Consumers of the World Unite. Labor Studies Journal, Vol. 29, No. 3, Fall 2004.

Álvaro J. de Regil. Living Wages: The GRI's Missing Link. The New GRI's 'G3 Sustainability Reporting Guidelines' Continue to Avoid Living Wages, the Missing Link of Sustainability. A TLWNSI Issue Essay. The Jus Semper Global Alliance, March 2006.

Robert B. Reich. Supercapitalism. The Transformation of Business, Democracy and Everyday Life. Knopf, 2007.

32 Corporate Environmental Responsibility From the Perspective of Systematic and Dialectical Science

WANG HONG AND WANG XIAOLI

Introduction

Worldwide environmental problems are making the whole of society pay increasing attention to Corporate Environmental Responsibility (CER), the requirement to protect the environment. It has become the core of Corporate Social Responsibility (CSR). To study CER from the perspective of Systematic and Dialectical Science (SDS) is to give insight into the evolutionary state of CSR. The basic SDS views are the systematic point, the progressive point, and the time and space point. The fundamental laws of SDS refer to an emergent organizational law, different cooperative law, structural and functional law, class transferring law and integrity improving law. These views and laws are found to be an important vision and methodology to explore CER. Two empirical analyses on the investigation of auto enterprises are used to suggest a better interaction between Chinese government and automotive enterprises and more strict self-discipline in environment management.

Recently, with the advocacy of world organization and supra-national governments, has come a realization of the importance of CSR, which is becoming an indispensable notion relating to corporation governance and strategic management. It is widely accepted that enterprises shoulder social responsibilities in order to expand and correct their traditional objective of maximizing their benefit and shareholder's wealth. Also it will help to establish harmonious relations between enterprises and stakeholders, foster sustainable development and improve the benefit for the whole of society. This chapter focuses on the environmental aspect of CSR with the aim to introduce more valuable opinions in this research field.

Background and Significance

The following top ten environmental disasters of the twentieth century (see Table 32.1) are unprecedented:

Table 32.1   Top ten environmental disasters of the twentieth century

Year	Environmental Disasters	Country
1930	Fog Disaster of Meuse Valley	Belgium
1943	Smog Disaster of Los Angeles	USA
1948	Donora (Pennsylvania) Smog Disaster	USA
1952	Smog Disaster of London	UK
1953–1956	Mercury Disaster of Minamata	Japan
1955–1972	Bone Disease of Fuyama	Japan
1968	Rice Bran Oil Disaster	Japan
1984	Union Carbide Disaster of Bhopal	India
1986	Chernobyl Nuclear Plant Accident	USSR
1986	Toxic Pollution of Rhine River	Switzerland

Source: Chinese Youth, 6th January, 2000.

The environmental awareness and performance of enterprises greatly affects human safety and health. And the responsibility to protect the environment is becoming perceived as the core of CSR.

In China, on 13th November 2005, in the city of Jilin, an explosion happened in a petroleum factory causing a hundred tons of benzene to flow into the Songhua River, leading directly to severe pollution of the drinking water supplies of the major cities downstream. This was the greatest environmental pollution event since 1949, when the People's Republic of China was established.

Furthermore, the sea water deterioration in China (see Table 32.2) is alarming. The result shows that in 2006 the cleaner sea fields were less than that in 2003, due to the influence of the principal superscalar materials, such as inorganic synthesized material and phosphate. Meanwhile, the slightly polluted, medially polluted and seriously polluted sea fields were increasing between 2003 and 2006. If those polluting enterprises do not take care then the deterioration consequence will be much larger.

Table 32.2   The result of water evaluation of Chinese sea fields

Year and Pollution State	Cleaner Sea Fields	Slightly Polluted Sea Fields	Medially Polluted Sea Fields	Seriously Polluted Sea Fields
2003	8.05	2.20	1.49	2.40
2006	5.10	5.21	1.74	2.84

Number unit: 10 thousand square kilometers

Source: Chinese Statistics Bureau Website.

On the matter of CSR, there are a lot of controversies in western developed countries. However, as for the environmental problem, there is more agreement. Moreover, CER has been actually put into social and economic practice according to certain standards and regulations. At the World Economic Forum on 31st January, 1999, the UN Secretary-General Kofi Annan launched the Global Compact, which was formally initiated in the UN headquarters in July 2000. The requirement of protecting the environment is included. On 12th December, 2001, the Social Accountability International issued the first edition of SA8000 Standard–SA8000:2001, which concerned CER.

From 2006 to 2007, a questionnaire investigation was carried out by the authors in China (Shanghai and Beijing). Among nearly 100 different enterprises, it is found that most of them put CER at an important position within CSR, and quite a few placed CER at the top of priority list of CSR.

In short, CER is an increasingly important issue.

Vision and Methodology of Systematic and Dialectical Science

Despite the development of new theories and modern science, SDS is a science and philosophy based on Marxism. SDS aims to explain the dialectical development law of a systematic world in a scientific way. Deeply and completely, it uncovers the features and links of nature and human society as a systematic movement of the thinking field; it examines the life-cycle progress of systems and the dialectical relations both in and out of those systems.

As Hegel (1957), a famous German philosopher, pointed out, 'The element of truth is concept; the virtual state of truth is scientific system.' More specifically, Qian Xueseng (1987), a well-known Chinese space scientist, held, 'The system is regarded as fairly complicated research subject, that is the organic unity combined with several components, interacting and interdependent with each other, and this functional system itself is affiliated to a bigger system.' Consequently, CER is a complicated system, which is affiliated to the CSR system and is one of its important components. As an open system, the enterprise exchanges with the outer environment. It should firstly get the investment of human resource, capital, materials, technology, information and so on from the outer environment and then through the transferring system within the enterprise, the investment is changed into product, labor and reward. When the output leaves the enterprise system, the exchanging progress is finished. Therefore the living environment is essential to enterprise development. While making fine products and increasing benefit, one main task that CSR should undertake is to encourage clean manufacturing and reduce pollution. As one Dow Jones analyst puts it, those companies who enjoy the highest capital reward also perform better than their rivals in pollution governance and resource control; those who consider the society and their environmental influence, hold superior stock accomplishment than others. Undoubtedly, it is the combination of wealth and environmental responsibility that enables a modern enterprise, the open system, to develop continuously.

The basic SDS views are the systematic point, the progressive point, and the time and space point. The fundamental laws of SDS refer to organization-emerging law, difference cooperating law, structural and functional law, class transferring law and integrity improving law. These views and laws are found to be an important vision and methodology to explore CER.

Corporate Social Responsibility From the Perspective of Systematic and Dialectical Science

The systematic point explains that the system is the essential attribute of the material world, and the world itself is that material world of system. The systematic point mainly discovers the systematic link, existence, movement and development horizontally, whereas the progressive point refers to the systematicness of world historic development, the present progress and the development trend. Vertically, the progressive point discovers the progress and state of the world system. The time and space point means the existing state, relationship and development of the systemic world. The above three points are interdependent each with the others. Among them, the systemic point is dominant and takes the leading role (Wu Jie, 2003:38, 39).

Based on the above view points, we can use SDS to analyze CSR. Firstly, in the systematic point of view, CSR is composed of three core factors—elements, structure and function. The elements are the subjects of CSR, such as shareholders, employees, customers, commercial partners, community and environment. As for shareholders, the basic responsibility of an enterprise is to respect their rights regulated by law, keep the balance between the capital safety and benefit to them, and provide them with the true information of operations and investment, such as financial reports and company annual meeting amd so on. As for employees, the enterprise should provide a safe and healthy working environment first, then fair job opportunities, promotion opportunities and education opportunities, and finally, the opportunities of democratic participation and self-management. As for customers, enterprises should offer safe and reliable products and respect customers' right to know and to choose. As for commercial partners, enterprises can use contracts to compete fairly. In the community, enterprises should participate in local institutions. In order to be a 'social citizen', the enterprises may take advantage of product and technology to support educational causes, employ the jobless, help the homeless and so on. As for the natural environment, then CER is essential. Guided by green values, the enterprises should strengthen a green awareness, apply green management, and advocate green manufacturing and consuming. The green value is the new notion which aims at the harmony between man and nature, calling for respecting and protecting nature and refusing any opposite attitude and behavior. To cultivate green role awareness means that enterprises should hold an equal attitude toward environment responsibility and shareholder accountability. When enterprises make their investing and publicizing plan, the negative influence on the environment should be taken into consideration. Thus the technological process may be altered in order to raise technical content and reduce the polluting index. The financial department should design an effective evaluation system and calculate the potential cost of destruction to the environment. Similarly, the sales department should advocate the green consuming concept and lead customers in the way of proper, healthy, safe and economical consuming. In the work of green audit, enterprises should be strict with themselves in disciplining, monitoring and examining.

Figure 32.1 shows the pyramid structure of CSR created by Professor Archie B. Carroll. In his opinion, CSR refers to the economic, legal, ethical and altruistic expectations of

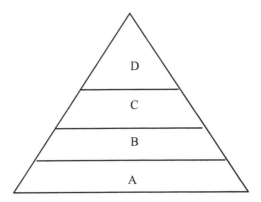

A: Economic Responsibility   B: Law-abiding Responsibility
C: Ethical Responsibility   D: Beneficent Responsibility

Figure 32.1 The pyramid mode of Corporate Social Responsibility

society from enterprises. Specifically, the economic responsibility involves not only the maximum profit but also productivity improvement, shareholder's wealth maintaining, more employment, fair payment and social welfare and so on. So it has the function of improving efficiency and fairness. The law-abiding responsibility is to legally maintain the basic social order with the highest ethical standard. Therefore, it is a compulsory restriction for the responsible undertaking. The ethical responsibility of an enterprise refers to other social expectations which have not become law. This is the self-discipline, or the internal, voluntary and active responsible alternative. This kind of 'soft restriction' is helpful to advocate high social standards. Voluntary responsibility means enterprises conduct additional activities according to some determined value and social expectation, such as supporting community projects and voluntary causes and so on. Such voluntary help can effectively improve social welfare. More or less, CER exists in every class of the above structure. Comparatively, there are more small- and medium-sized enterprises in A section (the bottom) and more large companies in D section (the top), where they are wealthy enough to shoulder more ethical and voluntary responsibilities.

Secondly, as the progressive point of SDS, CSR appears to be a dynamic changing process with the development of the enterprise life-cycle. As an individual in the social economic activities, an enterprise has its own life duration. Figure 32.2 shows that the scope and emphasis of CSR is ever adjusting with the life progress of the enterprise.

During the initial establishing period, CSR is focused on survival. Managers participate in the economic activities of minimizing cost and maximizing profit to raise the investors' benefit and gain more space for growing; during the developing period, the emphasis of CSR is put on the interest of employees and customers. Apart from the investors' interest, managers strive for human resources management and to link the enterprise development with employee improvement. With the continuously rising status in the profession and product share in the market, the cash flow and profit tend to be stable. Then enterprises begin to be customer-oriented, take part in the fair play in market, respect and maintain customer's rights and interests, provide fine quality goods and services at the most affordable price; during the gaining period when enterprise scope extends greatly, CSR aims at public welfare. Managers actively pursue social justice and voluntary causes by helping the weak and so on. As for the aspect of protecting

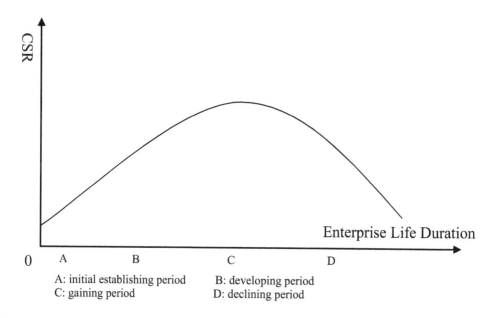

Figure 32.2 Social responsibility and enterprise life duration

Source: Made by the authors.

the environment, enterprises make a comprehensive use of resources and maintain the ecological balance. During the declining period, enterprises are likely to fade from market competition due to various reasons, and the aim of CSR lags behind the economic goal. Therefore, enterprise development is the base to shoulder CSR (Tian Hong, 2006:49, 50). Small- and medium-sized enterprises are existing in the first two periods. If properly guided, for example, supported by the government or cooperated with large enterprises, they will show great potential in environment protection. The large enterprises at the gaining period can make more contribution to the environment and this will keep them more competitive and dynamic.

Finally, in the time and space view of SDS, the social expectation and the requirements for contemporary enterprises are different due to various social systems. Thus the focus and scope of CSR are various with obvious national and epochal features. From the initial period of maximizing shareholders' interest, to the responsibility for employees, to the responsibility for the community and to the responsibility for natural environment, the enterprises experience an ever rising progress with more profit and stronger capability to reward the society. The improvements promote enterprise development from the newly emerging state to the continuously gaining state. Different history, culture and economic conditions are accountable for different values and systems.

Take China for example. To study the relationship between man and nature has been an excellent tradition since ancient times. Opposite to the notion, held by modern western philosophers, that man and nature are contrary to each other, most ancient Chinese thinkers adopted an integral attitude. They regarded man and nature as a whole which can not be divided. From the early Book of Changes (YiKing) and Book of HongFan, 'the Eight Diagrams (BaGua)' used eight things selected from nature to explain the origin of other things in the world. The eight things are the sky, the earth, the thunder, the fire, the wind, the pool, the water and the mountain. Among them, the sky and the earth are the general origin. They are the parents of the other six things. 'The Five Ingredients (WuXing)' regarded the five fundamental materials (gold, wood, water, fire, soil) as the essential components of various things in the world. This simple but systematic notion of 'interdependent link of man and heaven' is well established and long lasting. It emphasized the coordinated unity of man and nature. Man not only changes nature, but also obeys it; neither submits to the nature, nor destroys it. That is to say, man is not the owner of nature, or the slave, but the friend of it. It is human duty to take part in activities protecting nature and coordinating with it. This Chinese ancient notion enlightens enterprises to take CER seriously.

The Fundamental Laws of Systematic and Dialectical Science and the Enlightenment to Corporate Environmental Responsibility

The fundamental laws of SDS refer to organization-emerging law, difference coordinating law, structural and functional law, class transferring law and integrity improving law. The organization-emerging law discovers that structure and function have the instinct and tendency of systematic self-improvement and self-creation in orderly evolution. The difference coordinating law shows that in the integrity all kinds of differences between systems, system and elements, elements and structures appear to be in perfect coordination. This is result of the cooperation of sub-systems and elements within the system as the target of systematic integrity. The structural and functional law points out that consuming structure exists in open system and through the exchange of materials, energy and information with the outside, the structure of system will be more dynamic and superior. The class transferring law clarifies that the systematic world always moves in the way of class transferring: from the lower level to the higher level, and different from the inferior class, the superior class involves the basic difference of it. This makes the difference coordination of systematic integrity. The integrity improving law shows the tendency and direction of systematic movement with the internal elements interaction. All of these laws lead us to have an insight into CER.

CER is a subordinate system of CSR. It is the responsibility that enterprises should take in certain progress when the public require strongly, the government advocate greatly and the enterprises develop continuously for a better natural environment. Although the degree varies in different areas because of different political, economic and cultural conditions, CER turns out to be a healthy, stable and sustainable tendency (as Figure 32.3 shows). This also embodies a more superior spirit of the enterprises, from its resources and for the society. At this stage, beyond the economic and legal conditions, enterprises can ethically take shareholders' requirement into consideration and responsibly improve further environmental protection.

In the view of SDS, the restrictions of laws and regulations of developed countries, the entrepreneur and environment culture, and enterprise self-discipline play an important role in promoting the environment management of the whole enterprise system.

The German government has, for example, gradually solved the pollution problem in the industrializing process by means of issuing a series of laws and adopting a series of measures. Thus the transferring of economic development mode has been realized, the industrial structure has been adjusted, the manufacturing technology has been improved and energy efficiency has been raised. Especially in the aspect of waste disposal, the

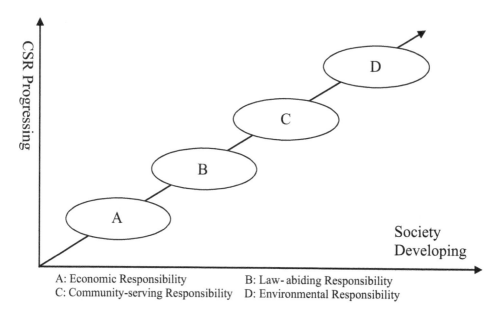

A: Economic Responsibility   B: Law-abiding Responsibility
C: Community-serving Responsibility   D: Environmental Responsibility

Figure 32.3 Sustainable improvement of CSR

Source: Made by the authors.

German government has already taken the leading role in the world. Since the mid-1920s, the discussion on the project of waste disposal in German has been scientific and practical. The ever-improving laws and regulations have relieved the conflict between industrial development and environmental protection. The waste has been eradicated by environment-friendly measures. The enterprise behavior has transferred from a focus on the previous end products to the whole process control. The negative influence of industrial manufacturing and consuming has been controlled and revised. This has helped material recycling and reusing and reduced the energy requirement of human society (Huang et al., 2007).

Japanese enterprises' spirit of innovation is very admirable. One example is Honda, the well-known international enterprise, which used to be a trivial small company. The success of Honda is closely related to the responsible awareness and innovation spirit, which is held by its founder Honda Soichiro. In Japanese, the original meaning of the word 'learning' is to 'imitate'. Therefore, Honda Soichiro led his enterprise to imitate advanced technology and practice persistently to improve. However, they didn't only keep imitating, but added their own ideas into reproducing at the same time (see Table 32.3).

Consequently, Honda developed from imitation to creation, combining its innate talent with acquired knowledge. The final product of Honda not only derives the essence of foreign goods, but also maintains its own characteristic and traditional integrity. The value of 'contribution to the society' influenced every employee and accumulated the enterprise culture. Now, one subordinate of Honda in China (Guangzhou province) has realized 'zero emissions', in addition to providing fine products to society. The practice embodies the ever-improving culture of Honda, which will become more dynamic with time. It is the key to survival in the face of severe competition and to becoming more prominent (Daxiayingzhi, 2005).

Table 32.3 Entrepreneur, philosophy and practice of Honda

Time	Details of Honda's entrepreneur, philosophy and practice
1951	Honda Soichiro instructed his apprentices that good repairing meant complete explanation of the repairing method to customers, cleaning the car and prompt delivering. It was far more than the repairing itself and formed an initial notion of Honda's social responsibility.
1960	He set up an innovation concept and stressed the idea to accelerate development with the establishment of Honda technical research institute.
1966	The Japanese Ministry of Transport issued restrictions for vehicle waste emission. At the same time, the Air Pollution Research Center had been set up to explore new engines according to the new rules.
1970	Japan issued the Masiji Act. The big three American auto manufacturers opposed this act, because they found it impossible to meet the restrictions for waste emissions. Starting from N600 engine, the Air Pollution Research Center reconsidered the design and undertook trials.
1971	The Honda technical research institute successfully developed the engine which met restrictions for waste emissions.
1972	The Honda technical research institute issued the content of Honda low-polluting CVCC engines and submitted successful standards documents to the U.S. Environmental Protection Agency. CVCC engine technology which met legislative standards gained praise at home and abroad.
1973	The 65-year-old founder expressed in his retirement speech that the auto manufacturers who produced waste emission should be responsible to society. He believed that the company would establish a new value, a new operating style and close relations between the enterprise and society to strengthen CSR and protect the natural environment.

Source: From the book of Ningen Honda Soichiro.

The American Xerox Company has carried out quite a few environmental controls. The environmental leading project is such an example for enterprises to take active measures without depending on government. The total quality management of Xerox encourages all employees to take part in selecting materials which are up to environmental protection standards, that reduce water emissions, use reproduced products and improve packaging to shoulder the responsibility of disposing waste. Such performance will increase costs, but will decrease the amount of dangerous waste and emissions of chemical products. In some cases, it can also save costs. The improved capital management is really economical. It is helpful to make continuous procedure improvement, realize better reproduction of instrument and component, put the useless capital in and out of sections of the company into play, and promote the effective delivery of products. 'We must protect the earth... This is also the safest and most reliable method to keep our profit continuously.' This decision comes from the top management that enabled Xerox to gain the gold reward of International Enterprise Environmental Achievement by the World Environment Center in 1993. Also, it is the internal motivation to strive for the target of zero waste (Reinhardt et al., 2000; 221-249.)

The development of the auto industry is a strong impetus to social progress and development of human civilization, but it also brings harm to the environment, including consumption of resources, atmospheric pollution, the greenhouse effect and traffic noise, and so on. According to the relevant statistics, in 1979 there were about 200 million vehicles around the world and the number rose to over 500 million in 2004. With the rapidly increasing number of motor vehicles, the environmental problem is becoming more serious. According to the statistics of 150 cities of the world in 1999, Beijing, Shanghai, Guangzhou, Xi'an and Shengyang are listed in the top ten of the most serious air pollution cities. Therefore, environmental protection, safety and energy saving have become the three major themes of technological progress for vehicle manufacturers in recent years. The following investigation and analysis, focusing on Chinese auto enterprises in environment management, has been conducted by the authors in China.

At the 9th International Automobile and Manufacturing Technology Exhibition (Auto Beijing 2006), we took 37 auto enterprises as our interview objects, including auto manufacturers, system suppliers and designing company. The effective questionnaires were found to be 35. Among them, the auto enterprises included: Dongnan Auto Company, Dibiya Auto Company, Chongqing Changan Lingmu Auto Company, Shengyang Huacheng Jinsong Auto Ltd, Dongfeng Electric Auto Ltd, Canghe Lingmu Auto Company, Leinuo Company, Beiqi Futian Auto Ltd, Beijing Auto Factory, and so on; the auto suppliers included: Kuodan-Linyun Auto Tyre Ltd, Panasonic Electric Company, Tangshan Aixin Cogwheel Ltd, and so on; the designing company was Wuxi Ruifeng Auto Designing Company. The relatitionship between 'the force of government pressing on the investigated companies in environment management' (F) and 'the influence from the investigated companies in environmental policy with the government' (I) is analyzed by SPSS (Pearson Correlation). Table 32.4 is the result.

Table 32.4 Relativity analysis between F and I

		F	I
F	Pearson Correlation	1	.192
	N	35	35
I	Pearson Correlation	.192	1
	N	35	35

Source: The investigation conducted in November, 2006.

The relativity analysis shows that the mutual link between our government and automotive enterprises in environmental management is hardly close. Pearson Correlation 0.192 proves that the cooperation between our government and auto enterprises in environment management remains in a low level, and is far from the international development tendency. Nowadays the European and American countries have entered into a more active stage. Business-led plan has promoted the self-management achievement. Practice shows that, based on mutual trust, the enterprises and government can make certain agreements, which helps the governors reduce executing cost and encourages the enterprises to apply more flexible and proper technologies to make greater innovation. On the one hand, the government, as one of the stakeholders, should make environmental laws and regulations to guide the behavior of the enterprises. On the other hand, its policy making and applying should also be influenced by the enterprises. The interaction will create the mutual benefit effectively. Therefore, the volunteer environment management can have inspiration for China.

Subsequently, the investigation was improved to focus on the enterprise environment performance. At the 12th International Automobile and Manufacturing Technology Exhibition (Auto Shanghai 2007), we took 30 auto enterprises as our interview objects, including Shanghai Huapu Auto Ltd, Tianjin First Auto Ltd, Dongfeng Nissan, Honda Technology Research, Tongji Tongjie Ltd and so on. Now 12 excellent state-owned auto enterprises and 12 world-famous non-state-owned auto enterprises are picked out to have a contrast analysis of automotive emission standards. Table 32.5 shows the result.

Table 32.5   Contrast analysis of automotive emission standard

	Euro II	Euro III	Euro IV
State-owned auto enterprises	1	9	2
Non-state-owned auto enterprises		4	8

Source: The investigation made in April, 2007.

The result shows that 75 percent state-owned auto enterprises have touched the Euro III emission standard, while 67 percent non-state-owned auto enterprises have been up to the Euro IV emission standard. Consequently, a big gap can be found. On 13 December, 2006, the European Parliament issued new vehicle emission criteria, Euro V and Euro VI, to restrict car emissions. According to the new standard, Euro will control the pollution emissions of local cars and imported cars strictly, especially the emission of nitrogen oxides. Euro V emission standard will be implemented from 1st September, 2009. Euro VI standards will be put into effect in September 2014, and it will help to improve people's health benefits by approximately 60–90 percent, compared with Euro V. So far, the emission standard of China has still been Euro I or Euro II, lagging far behind the advanced emission standard. And the time of applying the standard is at least seven years later than the European countries (Tong, 2006). Consequently, it is a timely corresponding strategy for the government to take effective measures to advance the regulations and laws and the enterprise to improve the technology.

From the perspective of SDS, the developed countries have gained greater achievement in environmental management. In the experience of enterprise environment governess, there is a large gap between developed countries and developing countries as far as time and space is concerned. The former one shows obvious leading advantage in development. On the one hand, it has set up a target for the latter one to catch on. On the other hand, some less successful experience in environmental management provides lessons for the latter one. One illuminative point for China is to have effective cooperation with developed countries, avoiding the way of 'governance after pollution'. Basing on the real condition and keeping good balance between economic development and resources effectiveness is the wise policy.

To summarize, CER, the environmental responsibility of enterprises, is a sub-system of the system of CSR. Enterprises should take economic influence on the environment into consideration and try to reduce the negative externalties as far as possible. Different from the previous perspectives, such as the principles of economics, management, sociology and ethics, this thesis discusses CER philosophically. The SDS provides the contemporary Chinese enterprises with their deep-rooted value of 'Man and Heaven—One Unity'. It requires them to learn the successful experiences of developed countries in environmental management, integrating with Chinese characteristics. It serves the mutual benefit of government, the public and enterprises with the aim to construct the harmonious society of 'Economical Resource and Friendly Environment'.

References

(Germany) Hegel, (1957), Speech on the Philosophy History, Beijing: Business Press.

Qian Xueseng, (1987), Science of Socialist Modernization and Systematic Engineering, Beijing: Chinese Communist Party Central School Press, pp. 221.

Wu Jie, (2003), Systematic and Dialectical Science, Beijing: Chinese Financial and Economic Press, pp. 38–39.

Archie B. Carroll, (1991), The Pyramid of Corporate Social Responsibility: Toward the Moral Management of Organizational Stakeholders. Business Horizons, July–August).

Tian Hong, (2006), Corporate Social Responsibility and the Advancing Mechanism, Beijing: Economic and Management Press, pp. 49–50.

Huang Haifeng, Liu Jinghui, et al., (2007), Recycling Economy in Germany, Beijing: Science Press.

(Japan) Daxiayingzhi, (2005), (translated by Wu Yaoming, Ningen Honda Soichiro, Hangzhou: Zhejiang People Press.

Forest Reinhardt, Richard Vietor, (2000), Business Management and the Natural Environment, Dalian: Dongbei University of Finance and Economic Press, pp. 221-249.

Tong Na, (2006), Running for the International Standard of Environmental Protection, Economic Daily, December 19, 2000.

33 Why People Do Good: Promoting Responsible Behaviours: The Myth or Reality of Persuasion in Fundraising Letters

CUBIE LAU

Introduction

Companies identify and solve social problems. They are change agents for building an ethical society. However, other stakeholders can also create value: Non-profit organizations. Corporate social responsibility usually talks about profit-making organizations. I think social responsibility should not be bounded by the nature of organizations. Non-profit organizations help make a better world, a more socially responsible society.

We often hear of corporations being socially responsible. For example, most people associate the name Body Shop with Corporate Social Responsibility (CSR). The Body Shop has vigorously worked on social issues, from worker and community betterment in Nigeria to animal testing and packaging waste. The Body Shop may be doing these things out of CSR, but many see a materialistic side here too. The company uses environmentalism to harness the power of persuasion. Customers buy its products believing that they are indirectly supporting those social causes (Lau, 2004). To make an analogy, non-profit organizations are doing the same things, raising awareness of the same or similar social issues, but without the profit motivation. The non-profit sector deserves attention. Non-profit organizations need to raise funds. But how?

One technique non-profit organizations use to obtain money is fundraising letters. While some work has been done on this genre of written communication, there is little information on what works. I use an ethnographic approach to see how practitioners from non-profit organizations move readers (donors) in fundraising letters. For this study, we look at fundraising letters used by Hong Kong non-profit organizations.

The fundraising world is extremely competitive. Charity organizations are inventing ways of increasing incomes through various channels, for instance, TV programmes hosted by celebrities, direct mail programmes, printed or electronic display advertisements in Hong Kong's Mass Transit Railway (MTR) cars and stations, or telephone solicitation.

Fundraising by direct mailing is extremely common in Hong Kong, as it can provide both regular and quick income (Clarke and Norton, 1997:190). As reported in 'Partners Express' of Oxfam, a total of HK$80,246,189 income was earned from the Hong Kong public in a typical year, where direct mailing is one of the major fundraising activities (Oxfam Editorial Committee, 2001). The amount is enormous, especially in times when Hong Kong was suffering from an economic downturn. This has aroused my interest in fundraising texts and in the kind of persuasive argument that influences the conduct of the donors. What is the persuading argument that generates funds for charitable causes?

My assumption is that fundraising texts are not significantly different from sales promotional texts written to sell goods or services. Readers are to be persuaded to tender money for some purpose. The service in this case concerns doing good, helping society. The charity organization offers the service of problem solving and appeals for financial contributions. A charitable request for donation is an argument for action to ameliorate a problem. In other words, argumentation is based on 'where a need or problem is posed, and the action needed to solve the problem is recommended ... and the ability of the agency sponsoring this advertisement to do the job' (Walton, 1989:113-114).

It is reasonable that the effect and the way a text is written are related. If people make donations, it is a response to the message(s) in the texts. However, it is unclear if the donation is a direct response to one particular convincing argument or to the whole of the text. Is it possible to dissect the text in relation to the types of arguments that shape the genre of fundraising texts? It is equally interesting to find out if it is possible to come up with a preferred argumentative move in the fundraising texts.

With this background in mind, I designed a study to learn more about what kinds of texts can encourage individuals to donate to charity. Although the focus is on individuals not corporations, even when there is corporate giving individuals make many decisions. This study will not answer all questions about what makes individuals and organizations do good, but it may help provide part of the answer.

The argumentative elements of fundraising texts are believed to be crucial factors that influence prospective donors. Argumentation is 'the art of influencing others, through the medium of reasoned discourse' (Rottenberg, 1988:9). The aim of this study is to explore argumentation by identifying the types of argument that shape the genre of fundraising texts and show how persuasion comes about.

Swales (1990) suggests that 'a genre comprises a class of communicative events, the members of which share some set of communicative purposes' (Swales, 1990:58). The common communicative purpose of asking for donations plays an important role in the genre of fundraising texts.

Texts which are meant to influence others have been termed 'hortatory'; hortatory discourse describes existing states of affairs and/or problems and their possible solutions, and induce the reader to take some action or to adopt an attitude or point of view. Examples of hortatory genres are political speeches, sermons, and letters to the editor (Martin, 1989:17). As for fundraising texts, 'hortatory texts aim to solicit contributions' (Mann et al., 1992:109).

In Longacre's (1992) view, hortatory genre has four deep structure moves: (1) establish authority/credibility, (2) present problem/situation, (3) issue command(s) and (4) create motivation. In his schema, (3) is basic to hortatory discourse. It is the move which aims to influence the conduct of readers. Longacre adds that there is necessarily some problem that provokes the command elements (Longacre, 1992:110). In addition, most hortatory discourse includes (4), that is, to create motivation by 'threats with predictions of undesirable results, and promises along with predictions of desirable results' (110). Lastly, unless the power of writer is incontestable, it is necessary for the writer to establish authority or credibility.

To look at arguments in hortatory genre is not an entirely new idea. In a paper entitled 'The Blending of Narrative and Argument in the Genre Structure of Newspaper editorials', Reynolds (2000) shows how argument dominates in the three assumed modes of narrative-description-argument. In a paper entitled 'Towards Classifying the Arguments in Research Genres', Shaw (2000) illustrates a regular spread of argument types in selected research genres. To apply argument types for analysis of fundraising texts has not been attempted yet to my knowledge. This suggests several questions. (1) What kinds of arguments are exhibited in the fundraising texts? (2) Is there a particular argument structure that underlies the discourse moves? and (3) Wherein lies the persuasion of these fundraising texts?

Literature Review

The purpose of fundraising texts is to ask for financial help by 'creating a sense of urgency' that gives the reader a reason to act now (Warwick, 1994:41). Similar to sales promotion letters, fundraising texts have the purpose to elicit a specific response or action from readers. Following Swales (1990), I suggest that both text types belong to the larger dimension of promotional discourse. By highlighting the differences between sales promotion letters and fundraising texts, a first attempt is made to describe how they can share features and be different at the same time. Fundraising texts appeal on the basis of benefits to donors, not their needs. Rather than satisfying their needs, donors give money because of mixed motives; they may receive in return for their contribution the benefits such as 'lives saved, or human dignity gained, or larger causes served' (Warwick, 1994:39). As for sales promotional letters, they are generally addressed to those potential customers who are known to have some need (immediate or future) for the product or service being promoted (Bhatia, 1993:46).

Communicative event or purpose is a key factor in identification of genre. Though fundraising letters and sales promotional letters share the same general purpose of soliciting a specific response from readers, unlike sales promotional letters, fundraising letters are specially designed to solicit money contribution from readers who give because of the associated benefits given to the needy rather than of satisfying their own needs. Thus sales promotion letters and fundraising texts both belong to promotional discourse, but are themselves different sub-genres. The following section describes how genres are identified according to structures of discourse moves.

Bhatia (1993) proposes that the structuring of genre is mainly cognitively motivated, which is reflected in its rhetorical move structures. He suggests that sales promotion letters have the following move structure, although not always in this order:

1. Establishing credentials
2. Introducing the offer:
   a) offering the product or service
   b) essential detailing of the offer
   c) indicating value of the offer

3. Offering incentives
4. Enclosing documents
5. Soliciting response
6. Using pressure tactics
7. Ending politely.

Other studies have focused on the move structure of the fundraising letter which addresses 'benefit', that is the need of donors. Mann and Thompson (1992) collected 11 diverse approaches to a single fundraising text 'Zero Population Growth (ZPG)'. For example, Longacre (1992) suggests that any genre is characterized by a particular configuration of deep structure moves (Longacre, 1992:110). In regard to fundraising texts, he calls this deep structure 'hortatory schema' (ibid.) whose purpose is 'to modify the conduct of the receivers of the text' (ibid.). As an instance of hortatory text, the ZPG letter aims to get the reader to send in donations essentially using the command move. The ZPG appeal letter usually 'starts with narrative and expository materials, warms up to an appeal via mitigated command elements, and finally graduates to an outright open appeal at its climax' (Longacre, 1992:124).

Lee, in his MA Dissertation 'Fundraising Text. A Discourse Description of Two Appeal Letters and Two Leaflets,' projects the problem-solving structure advocated by Hoey and Winter to four fundraising texts. He finds that fundraising texts could be viewed as a variety of problem-solving discourse with the move 'situation or problem' always placed in the beginning, followed by a combination of 'response, solution or problem' moves, and then concluded with 'response' move either in terms of the readers or the charity organizations (Lee, 2000:3).

Bhatia (1993), Longacre (1992) and Lee (2000) have labelled the textual segments, which can be observed mostly but not necessarily in linear sequence, as 'moves'. They can be viewed as discourse moves, such as offering, detailing not done by physical action, but by discursive moves. The question has to be asked how arguments fit in the picture. Is it possible to dissect the text in relation to the types of arguments used that shape the genre of fundraising texts? In what ways is argument the same, similar or different from established discourse moves? I hold with Reynolds that 'argument' permeates any discourse move.

Reynolds (2000) in 'The Blending of Narrative and Argument in the Generic Texture of Newspaper Editorials' suggests that all discourse takes a particular generic form, namely narrative, description and argument (Reynolds, 2000:25). Texture, in his view, is realized by both the language system and the socio-rhetorical action potential of genres, or in other words, is the 'linguistic structure and generic structure' (26). In his study, 'argument' provides the generic feature since it permeates both 'description' and 'narrative'. Argument, understood according to Toulmin's model, is said to be narrative 'narrative-cum-argument' and description 'description-cum-argument' (29). In arguing, 'we invariably mix fact and opinion, assumption and supposition. With narrative, too, there is always a narrator point of view may be seen as the link between narrative and argument' (ibid.).

Concerning the study of elements of arguments in genre analysis, Shaw in 'Towards Classifying the Arguments in Research Genres' refers to 'argumentative schemata as parallel to narrative schemata, seeing them composed of ordered sequences of elements like premises and conclusions' (Shaw, 2000:42). Shaw looks at argumentative elements in two academic genres dissertations and research articles. He gives a pilot classification of typologies of arguments according to linguistic forms, and then investigates the argument typologies. Shaw shows that there were 'no major differences between the types of argument in dissertations and articles'. However, the analysis revealed that there were significant differences in the frequency of use of several argument types, which might help to identify the difference between these two genres. For instance, 'justify method' arguments in dissertations had evaluative expressions in their premises like necessary or important. These arguments were not used in research articles.

Fundraising texts could be viewed to incorporate a hortatory schema of argument structure. Following Shaw's suggestion that different positions in a move structure draw in certain predominant argument types, I assume that the units that shape the genre of fundraising texts are arguments.

Argumentation is a complex process with many dimensions, and there is no consensus of how it should be described and explained. Some scholars are logicians who view arguments as based on the truth condition which stipulates 'true premises and sound reasoning' (Mills et al., 1968/69:260-7/55-60) (quoted in Inch and Warnick, 1998:11). Others argue that truth is not a logical given, but should be studied as 'a means of influence in the social and political marketplace' (Anderson and Mortenson, 1967:143-151) (quoted in Inch and Warnick, 1998:11). Still others suggest that 'the central focus of argumentation is on discovering and applying the general standards for determining what is true or reasonable' (Ziegelmueller et al., 1990:3) (quoted in Inch and Warnick, 1998:11).

After accounting for their differences, Joseph W. Wenzel (1990) summarizes the various perspectives on argument: logical, dialectical, and rhetorical (quoted in Inch and Warnick, 1998:11-12). The logical perspective views argumentation as addressed to rational audiences who are well informed on the topic of the dispute, where arguments are considered as statements connected by logical inferences.

Argumentation viewed from a dialectical perspective focuses primarily on the process of reaching the best conclusion. The assumption is that the best conclusion will be accepted if all viewpoints and issues have been comprehensively considered and discussed.

From the rhetorical perspective, arguments appeal to a particular audience in a social and political context in which they are likely to be influenced by the author's position. The rhetorical approach to argument emphasizes the effectiveness of arguments in persuading.

The view is shared that arguments are statements that include judgement of writers, backed up with reasons (premises), which are not always based on truth conditions. Valid argumentation consists of the movement from grounds (or premises) to the claim itself (or conclusion of an argument).

Fundraising texts are hortatory in nature. Believing that there are arguments in fundraising texts that persuade readers to send in donations, again we ask wherein lies the persuasion? Is it the whole of fundraising texts? Or is it the sum of sentences? Is it possible to use 'argument' as a unit of observation which interrelates sentences or the whole of a text?

Arguments are attempts to influence someone at various levels of belief, emotion and behaviour. An argument may be addressed to a specific group of an audience who supposedly share the same experience with the authors. On some occasions, however, it may address to a group of mass audience whose interest or attitudes are unknown.

Believing that audiences of argument in a particular situation will have special interests, values and attitudes, different authors have their own category scheme. Taking different contexts and particular situations into account, there is no wonder that work on arguments is not unified. Any proposition with any kind of perceived persuasion can be called an argument or a claim of some kind. The labels 'argument' and claim are interchangeable for most authors.

Some authors break proposition types into factual (including descriptive, relational, predictive or historical statements that reason from something that is known to something that is unknown), value and policy (137-140). Ramage et al, (2001) develop another category scheme that divides propositions into those of categorical, definitional, causal, evaluation and proposal (Ramage et al., 2001:183-187).

In this section, the most frequently used category schemes, and a list of representative sentential arguments will be introduced.

Inch and Warnick (1998) propose that each argument is a challenge; in a sense it attempts to change what people already believe or do. The arguer who advocates new ideas, therefore, should 'assume the burden of proof, which obligates arguers to provide good and sufficient reasons for changing what is already accepted' (137). That is to say, the arguer who advances a claim should be able to explain why, assuming audiences want to know what the issues are, why they are important and what is needed to resolve them. They follow 'the simplest and most frequently used category scheme which divides claims into categories of fact, value, and policy' (ibid.).

- FACTUAL CLAIMS: Factual claims 'make inference about past, present, or future conditions or relationships' (ibid.). The writer attempts to reason from something that is known or assumed to be true (evidence) to something that is unknown or disputable (claim).
- VALUE CLAIMS: Value claims assess 'the worth or merit of an idea' (ibid.). The writer attempts to influence the conception of audience that something is desirable or undesirable.
- POLICY CLAIMS: Policy claims 'call for a specific course of action' (140). Policy arguments 'ask audiences to make decisions about future actions' (288).

Inch and Warnick conclude that these three major types of claims, fact, value and policy are interdependent. Fact-based claims serve as the basis for both value and policy claims; and value claims assumes the existence of certain facts and serves as the basis for making policy claims (141).

Other authors categorize arguments in similar but not identical ways. Fraigley and Selzer (2000) categorize argument into six major types: definition, causal, evaluative, narrative, rebuttal and proposal argument. This categorization overlaps that of Inch and Warnick, for instance, causal and proposal, but some new terms are used, for example, narrative.

Narrative argument relies mainly on story telling or representative anecdotes, and allows readers to fill in the conclusion. Fraigley and Selzer remark, 'A narrative argument succeeds if the experience being described invokes the life experiences of the readers' (170).

Wood (1998) looks at categories of claims somewhat differently. Wood introduces the additional arguments of definition and cause. Cause statements establish the probability of a cause-and-effect relationship, by using factual data, analogies or induction (166).

It is apparent that argument category schemes are not unified across authors. However, it may be possible to look at fundraising arguments in a simplified way. Modalities like fact, value and policy can be the basis for a categorical entry, and logical relations like cause and condition as well. Another feature which makes the argument a difficult unit of observation is the fact that it can be presented in different syntactic shapes. Perhaps we can look for the common semantic core, propositions which are related as premises and conclusions. 'The semantic core is a set of propositions made up of one or more conclusions and some sets of premises' (Walton, 1989:114). Will a study of fundraising texts find this? To learn more, a study was conducted.

The Study

Initially, 17 texts from the following charity organizations were examined: Cedar Fund, Lifeline Express, Oxfam Hong Kong, Children's Heart Fund (abbreviated as CHF) Hong Kong, and Medecins Sans Frontieres (abbreviated as MSF) Hong Kong. After initial explorations, an in-depth study looked at six fundraising texts chosen from four charity organizations, namely ORBIS Hong Kong, MSF, Oxfam Hong Kong and World Vision Hong Kong. The six fundraising texts included four leaflets (or pamphlets) and two appeal letters.

Appeal letters and leaflets, though different in layout, serve the same purpose of making a request for donation. Unlike leaflets, appeal letters have the conventional style of letter writing, with the letterhead of the organization. Next usually comes the date of writing and the salutation, such as 'Dear supporter' or 'Dear friends'. After the salutation, the main message relating to the purpose of writing, the description of the problem or situation, the open appeal to donation will be given. Images or photographs representing the promoted causes are embedded. In the end, there is always a complimentary close with the handwritten signature and the professional role of the writer. For some appeal letters, there is an optional postscript repeating the request for contribution.

Leaflets, however, are usually written without any salutation; it mainly contains the main message that narrates the problem or situation leading to the appeal for donation.

Fundraising letters or leaflets can both be part of the direct mailing package. This usually consists of an outer envelope with a window that carries the name and address of the reply device; a letter introducing the purpose of writing or the fundraising events; a coupon or some reply device summarizing the appeal, giving examples of expected donation levels, or other references number or codes to keep track of responses; a reply envelope, usually postage free for returning the completed reply device; a brochure or leaflet that helps to provide additional information or illustrations of the need highlighted in the letter (Clarke and Norton, 1997:192).

Leaflets could be standalone or complementary information sent with an appeal letter. As standalone sweepers, they are either placed in shops of sponsors or sent with bank statements to the audience. According to Ms. Krim Chan, Communication Manager of World Vision, 'the leaflets of World Vision are usually standalone information placed in the outlets of sponsoring companies'.

Standalone leaflets are usually addressed to a *mass audience* who are free to pick up one anywhere. Different from leaflets, appeal letters are purposely sent to an *imagined or known audience* who may include potential donors. Anne Lung, Fundraising Officer of MSF Hong Kong, says that there is some informal market segmentation, which guides the sending of direct mailing package. For example, if the issue relates to children, the direct mailing will be sent to districts where young couples are known to live. If the needs of displaced refugees is promoted, the mailing is directed to an 'old' district with more elderly people who are supposed to have shared a similar experience.

The contents of appeal letters and leaflets are similar, because they serve the *same purpose of persuasion and communication; eliciting response* from readers. The content normally follows a structure, which aims to achieve four specific outcomes: 'attention, interest, desire, and action' (334). **Attention** refers to attract the readers' attention, **Interest** means to 'identify a reason for the reader to be personally interested' (ibid.), **Desire** refers the desire of readers to support the promoted cause, and **Action** is to get the readers to take action, that is to fill in the donation reply. A review of fundraising texts in this study revealed that 'personalizing' is often used to both attract attention and generate interest. For example, one often finds:

Seg. 3 *'I am writing from Angola, where I volunteer as a Medecins Sans Frontieres surgeon in Kuito Hospital. I arrived in Kuito...'*

Seg. 3 *'This is the first time I have written to you... I would like to take this opportunity to share with you two real-life stories on food and starvation. I hope these stories will arouse your concern about the problem of poverty on **our** planet. And I also hope that you will continue to support Oxfam in **our** fight against poverty.'*

Other texts are less personalized, using 'they' instead of referring to a specific individual.

Seg. 1–3 *'**Every child** is precious and unique. **Children** have the right to live, to be educated and to be loved. Poverty, war, famine, disaster and disease...make **millions of children** live in darkness'.*

Seg. 2 and 4 *'It is true The World Health Organisation predicts that if nothing significant is done, the number of blind people in the world will double in two decades....With no significant intervention, **these people**, both old and young will never see light, colour...'*

A review of texts suggests that letters, for example from MSF and Oxfam, show a high degree of personalizing (see Table 33.1).

In order to have in-depth knowledge about the writing process of the selected fundraising texts, three charity organizations: Oxfam Hong Kong, MSF Hong Kong and World Vision Hong Kong were interviewed. Issues relating to the process of writing and expected audience were discussed.

Practitioners of these three organizations point out that there is no manual guiding the writings of texts, but they acknowledge that there is a structural design that is commonly used. Ms. Maranda Wong, Senior Donor Development Officer of Oxfam, says 'for instance, regarding the leaflet 'I have a dream...', there are usually three essential ideas: *the genuine*

Table 33.1 Degree of personalizing by charity organizations

Type of texts	Degree of personalizing	Examples
Appeal letters	Personal letter writing	Oxfam Hong Kong (1), MSF Hong Kong (2)
	Narrative (or story telling)	CHF (1)
Leaflets/pamphlets	Narrative (or story telling)	World Vision Hong Kong (1), ORBIS Hong Kong (1), Oxfam Hong Kong (2), CHF (1)
	Factual reportage on a general cause	World Vision Hong Kong (1), ORBIS Hong Kong (1), Cedar (2), MSF Hong Kong (1), CHF (2), Lifetime Express (1)

*   The number in bracket represents the number of articles for the respective organizations.

needs of women in remote China; the *work done by Oxfam* emphasizing the before and after effect, and lastly *the call to action* indicating how and when to donate'. She explained that other than an open appeal for money, an effective fundraising leaflet should at least properly inform the prospective donors of the genuine reasons for donation, the usage of the fund and expected consequences.

Obviously fundraising texts aim at soliciting responses from prospective donors. There is always a final and central claim, a kind of exhortation that commands, suggests or urges some action. However, how exactly this happens in fundraising texts is not clear. Types of argument have been presented above. I have applied these ideas and developed a set of arguments found in fundraising texts. The argument which is always present is the proposal argument, that is, the discourse gesture which nudges the audience into the action of donating money. Other than the predominant claim, that is the proposal argument, more than one type of claim may be present in the texts. I add other types of argument, such as ability argument, which better represent the characteristics of fundraising text as a hortatory discourse.

In the following section, a set of argument types will be presented illustrated with examples from relevant data texts. Evidence for the classifications will be highlighted in *italics*.

- NARRATIVE-FACTUAL – is defined as a claim describing a situation or problem using story telling or experience supported by evidences such as statistics or reports.

    (1) Seg 1 'Dasongyuan, a mountainous are in Yunnan, has had a water shortage for a long time. People in that area, particularly women, have to collect water for the daily use. Like everyone else, Zhang Xiuzhen hopes that a water system can be built so that there will be safe water at the tap.'

    (2) Seg. 2 'Every year in Hong Kong more than 500 children are born with heart disease.'

- PROMISE – pledges the organization itself to the use the contribution sent in for the intended benefits, and is usually achieved by the use of modal verb 'will' (cf.

Longacre, 1992:123). Similarly, Jespersen (1924:320-1) suggests that the word 'will' serves the function as 'promissive' illustrated by the example 'I will go/It shall be done' (quoted in Palmer, 1986:10).

(3) Seg. 23 'Your donation will be an everlasting gift of hope and happiness in the life of a blind people.'

- CAUSAL – is the claim that indicates a causal or cause-and-effect relationship, which helps to point out the root of the problems.

  (4) Seg. 3 'Poverty, war, famine, disaster and disease...make millions of children live in darkness.'

- ABILITY – is the claim that emphasizes the possibility or ability of the prospective donors of achieving something valuable by doing. In other words, the argument highlights the importance of contributions, and is usually expressed by the use of modal verb 'can' (cf Longacre, 1992:121).

  (5) Seg. 8 'You can help provide the needy with basic care, education, safe water and nutrition.'

  (6) Seg. 41 'Without your support, my mission here would be impossible.'

- PROPOSAL – is a claim that serves the function of calling to an action to help the promoted cause. It is usually a mitigated appeal and may use the question form 'will you.../ could you...' or use an imperative such as 'donate'. Others may use the verb 'need' to expresses a lack of something (Longacre, 1992:119).

  (7) Seg. 29 'Please make cheque payable to ORBIS.'

  (8) Seg. 22 'Could you consider a gift to help the Children's Heart Fund?'

- JUSTIFY – is a claim consists of an action of the organization and an evaluation of the (desirable) consequences due to the action (cf. Shaw, 2000:48). It is mainly for justifying the proposed solution.

  (9) Seg. 11 'With our support, people's workloads have lightened and their livelihoods have improved.'

- PREDICTIVE – is defined by having in itself an attempt to use threat of negative (undesirable) outcomes if not taking actions to create motivation or exaggerates the adversity, and is usually taking the form 'if X is present, then Y will occur' (cf. Vestergaard, 2000:104).

  (10) Seg. 1 'If nothing is done to stop world blindness, the number of blind will double by the year 2020.'

- CREDIBILITY – is the claim that introduces the organization in terms of its goal or resources, states the plan of actions or the (culminated) achievements made up to date. It is normally used for building up its trustworthiness.

    (11) Seg. 6 'Since the day the Children's Heart Fund began at..., it has had one goal: to improve the lives of underprivileged children...'

- EVALUATION – is the claim about 'whether things, real or imaged, are good or bad, desirable or undesirable' (Vestergaard, 2000:104). It helps to bring out the promoted cause bearing the judgment of the writer (cf. Martin; 1989).

    (12) Seg. 6 'These people are the poorest of the poor.'

    (13) Seg. 21 'Every person deserves a chance at life, and a chance at light.'

- GAP – a claim that presents a gap between the existing state of affairs and the desired state of affairs, highlighting the (positive) negative consequences if (something) nothing is done. It can explicitly or implicitly suggests a (viable) solution.

    (14) Seg. 4 'The good news is that with proper care, 80 per cent of the world's blindness can be avoided.'

    (15) Seg. 4 'However, darkness doesn't have to last forever.'

Though these categories did allow the arguments in the text to be classified, there is sometimes no definite clear-cut type. For example, seg. 20 'the infant mortality is one of the highest in Africa, 120/1,000 births'. The claim may be classified as an evaluation or narrative-factual argument as it shares both characteristics representing the judgment of the writer 'highest' and the verifiable information '120/1,000'. As explained before, it is possible to 'mix fact and opinion, assumption and supposition' (Reynolds, 2000:29). I classify it as an 'evaluation'. Though these categories may not represent an exhaustive list, and are somewhat subjective in that they are tailor-made for hortatory discourse. Types of arguments are summarized in Table 33.2.

Six fundraising texts were carefully analyzed, phrase by phrase. Each text is segmented leaving out all the original formatting, such as bold-face, underlining and so on, and labelled according to a discourse move and an argument type, followed by a brief description of the information or message conveyed by writers as the one intended to be conceived by readers. The deliberate design is crucial as the last three columns from the left may provide important inputs to exploring the three research questions mentioned above. Evidence for the labelling of discourse moves and argument is highlighted in **bold and italics**, while key intended information is paraphrased and shown in **bold**. Assuming that the reply coupon plays a less important role in persuasion compared to leaflets or appeal letters, I disregard this coupon. In addition, the theme of the leaflet and the headline of individual paragraphs in shown underlined, and is excluded from the analysis, since headlines summarize which is not a proper function of argument. A sample analysis in table form is shown in Table 33.3.

Table 33.2 Functions of arguments in fundraising texts

Type of Argument	Functions
NARRATIVE-FACTUAL	Presents a situation or problem with verifiable evidences, or serves as some supporting.
PROMISE	Provokes readers to help by promising some expected benefits.
CAUSAL	Indicates cause-and-effect relationship.
ABILITY	Assures the importance of donors of achieving something valuable by doing.
PROPOSAL	Calls to readers' actions.
JUSTIFY	Justifies the works of the charity organization(s).
PREDICTIVE	Attempt to use threat of negative (undesirable) outcomes if nothing is done.
CREDIBILITY	Builds up the trustworthiness of the charity organization(s).
EVALUATION	Expresses writers' attitude or judgment to some issues as important or unexpected.
GAP	Explicitly or implicitly suggests a solution.

Table 33.3 Analysis of 'Darkness doesn't last'

Segments	Discourse Moves	Type of Sentential Arguments	Intended information conceived by readers
Theme: Darkness doesn't last... Child Sponsorship light up their lives, and yours (A summary of the effectiveness of the proposed solution).			
Headline 1: Will you bring light and hope to a needy child? (A mitigated command supported by a summary of some intangible benefits)			
Seg. 1 Every child is *precious* and *unique*	Evaluation of a situation	Evaluation	Brings out the promoted cause that is '**child is precious and unique**'
Seg. 2 Children have the *right to live*, and *to be educated* and *to be loved*	Elaboration of a situation	Evaluation	Elaborates on seg. 2 that '**children/child should be entitled some basic rights**'
Seg. 3 *Poverty, war, famine, disaster and disease...make* millions of children *live in darkness*	Presentation of problem	Casual	Identifies the causes leading to '**the problem of children living in darkness**'
Seg. 4 *However, darkness doesn't* have to *last forever*	Propose solution	Gap	Rebuts the problem of 'darkness' stated in seg.3, but implicitly suggests that there is **a solution to end the 'darkness'**

An aggregated analysis showing the position and all types of arguments used in sequence is presented in Table 33.4. For ease of reference, the six texts are abbreviated: (1) leaflet 'Darkness Doesn't Last' by World Vision Hong Kong (=WW), (2) leaflet 'Double or Nothing: It's Up to You' by ORBIS (=O1), (3) appeal letter by Medecins Sans Frontieres (=MF), (4) appeal letter by Children's Heart Fund Hong Kong (=CF), (5) leaflet 'I Have a Dream...' by Oxfam Hong Kong (=OM), and (6) leaflet 'What Would You Pay for to be Able to See?' by ORBIS (=O2). It is evident that there is always a proposal argument, which calls for actions, most often placed in last position. The table also shows other types of arguments, which lead up to the proposal argument.

Table 33.4 Flow of Arguments (combined)

WW	O1	MF	CF	OM	O2
EVALUATION	PREDICTIVE	CAUSAL	NARRATIVE-FACTUAL	EVALUATION	EVALUATION
CAUSAL	EVALUATION	EVALUATION	NARRATIVE-FACTUAL	CREDIBILITY + JUSTIFY	EVALUATION
GAP	PREDICTIVE	NARRATIVE-FACTUAL	GAP	JUSTIFY	GAP
PROPOSAL + PROMISE	CREDIBILITY	NARRATIVE-FACTUAL	CREDIBILITY	PROPOSAL + ABILITY	CAUSAL
PROMISE	CREDIBILITY	NARRATIVE-FACTUAL	CREDIBILITY	NARRATIVE-FACTUAL	CREDIBILITY
CREDIBILITY	CREDIBILITY	CREDIBILITY	JUSTIFY	NARRATIVE-FACTUAL	NARRATIVE-FACTUAL
ABILITY	JUSTIFY	NARRATIVE-FACTUAL	NARRATIVE-FACTUAL	NARRATIVE-FACTUAL	NARRATIVE-FACTUAL
PROMISE	EVALUATION	NARRATIVE-FACTUAL	NARRATIVE-FACTUAL	GAP	NARRATIVE-FACTUAL
PROPOSAL + ABILITY	EVALUATION	NARRATIVE-FACTUAL	NARRATIVE-FACTUAL	CREDIBILITY	NARRATIVE-FACTUAL
PROMISE	EVALUATION	JUSTIFY	PREDICTIVE	JUSTIFY	CREDIBILITY
EVALUATION	PREDICTIVE	NARRATIVE-FACTUAL	NARRATIVE-FACTUAL	PROPOSAL + ABILITY	JUSTIFY
PROMISE	CREDIBILITY	NARRATIVE-FACTUAL	CREDIBILITY	PROMISE	NARRATIVE-FACTUAL
PROPOSAL + PROMISE	EVALUATION	NARRATIVE-FACTUAL	JUSTIFY	NARRATIVE-FACTUAL	NARRATIVE-FACTUAL
	CREDIBILITY	NARRATIVE-FACTUAL	JUSTIFY	NARRATIVE-FACTUAL	NARRATIVE-FACTUAL
	CREDIBILITY	EVALUATIOIN	CREDIBILITY	NARRATIVE-FACTUAL	NARRATIVE-FACTUAL

Table 33.4 *Concluded*

WW	O1	MF	CF	OM	O2
	JUSTIFY	EVALUATION	JUSTIFY	CREDIBILITY	NARRATIVE-FACTUAL
	JUSTIFY	NARRATIVE-FACTUAL	ABILITY	JUSTIFY	EVALUATION
	PROPOSAL + ABILITY	NARRATIVE-FACTUAL	EVALUATION	PROPOSAL + ABILITY	EVALUATION
	PROPOSAL + ABILITY	CREDIBILITY	PROPOSAL + PROMISE	CREDIBILITY	EVALUATION
	EVALUATION	JUSTIFY + PROMISE	PROPOSAL	JUSTIFY	NARRATIVE-FACTUAL
	PROPOSAL + PROMISE	EVALUATION	PROMISE	EVALUATION	EVALUATION
	PROMISE	CREDIBILITY	PROMISE	EVALUATION	JUSTIFY
		EVALUATION	NARRATIVE-FACTUAL	CREDIBILITY	CREDIBILITY
		NARRATIVE-FACTUAL	PROPOSAL + ABILITY	PROPOSAL + PROMISE	CREDIBILITY
		CREDIBILITY		PROPOSAL	CREDIBILITY
		CREDIBILITY			PROPOSAL + ABILITY
		JUSTIFY			PROPOSAL + PROMISE
		JUSTIFY			PROPOSAL
		JUSTIFY + PROMISE			
		JUSTIFY			
		CREDIBILITY			
		CREDIBILITY			
		CREDIBILITY			
		PROPOSAL			
		PROPOSAL			
		PROPOSAL + ABILITY			
		ABILITY			

As a further overview, Table 33.5 provides the frequencies of the ten argument types. The counting represents the number of argument types only, not the flow of arguments. The overall frequencies indicate that in particular, five types of arguments: promise, ability, proposal, credibility and evaluations are most frequently used.

Table 33.5 Frequencies of arguments

Types of Argument	WW	O1	MF	CF	OM	O2
Narrative-factual	0	0	14	8	7	10
Promise	6	2	2	3	2	1
Causal	1	0	1	0	0	1
Ability	2	2	2	2	3	1
Proposal	3	3	3	3	5	3
Justify	0	3	6	4	5	2
Predictive	0	4	0	1	0	0
Credibility	1	6	8	4	5	5
Evaluations	3	6	5	1	3	7
Gap	1	0	0	1	1	1
Total: (173)	17	26	41	27	31	31

The comparative data reveals variations of types of arguments used. There is heavier use of 'narrative-factual' arguments in both MF and O2, while there is none in WW and O1. A closer look at the findings in Table 33.4 shows some interesting patterns. Almost all texts start with either 'narrative-factual' or 'evaluation', except the 'predictive' in O1, and followed by further evaluations or a 'gap' argument in WW, CF and O2.

After the introduction of the problem and solution, the arguments of 'credibility' and 'justify' usually follow. 'Credibility' is related to building the credibility of the organizations, and 'justify' highlights the achievements and justifies the work carried out by the organizations.

The overall data not only shows a perfectly well-matched projection onto discourse move, but also indicates a preferred pattern of arguments in particular discourse moves (see Table 33.6). It is not at all uncommon that 'evaluations' or 'narrative-factual' arguments are predominately used in 'problem-solving' move, 'credibility' and 'justify' are frequently found in 'credibility building' move; 'ability' and 'promise' are very often used in 'motivation creation' move. 'Proposal', 'promise' and 'ability' are to solicit responses by emphasizing the expected benefits. They indeed reflect the crucial elements in the persuasion process, which are to construct a mutually-agreed and significant cause, explain what and how both readers and writers should respond to it, and finally to provoke an action.

Table 33.6   The arguments by discourse moves (combined)

Sequential Arguments	Narrative-factual	Promise	Causal	Ability	Proposal	Justify	Predictive	Credibility	Evaluation	Gap
Discourse Moves										
Problem solving										
Presents situation/problem	15		3							
Evaluates as a problem									13	
Elaborates problem/situation	16								2	
Proposes solution										4
Establish Credibility										
Introduces organization's mission or background								15		
Introduces plan of action or work undertaken								10		
Highlights achievement/justifies work	7					20	1	4		
Create Motivation										
Creates urgency							4		2	
Highlights ability				12						
Gives promises (to donors of expected benefits)		6								
Gives promises of its commitment to achieving something valuable by organization		10								
Appeals to value or emotional feelings	1								6	
Issue Command					20					
Total: (173)	39	16	3	12	20	20	5	29	25	4

It is worth mentioning that there is often mixed arguments in one sentence. This kind of combination is particularly evident in the case of a 'proposal' argument, which may have 'ability' and/or a 'promise' arguments.

Discussion

Arguments are present in all fundraising texts, albeit in different combinations. The differences may be related to the 'degree of personalizing'. In general, fundraising texts in the form of story telling or personal recount exhibit a higher proportion of 'narrative-factual' arguments. The intention of writers to reflect the 'true reality' to readers leads them to the presentation of facts. As Anne Lung suggests, a personal experience of a volunteer in the field is convincing as it lets the readers know the reality of the promoted cause. While differences in types of arguments are found in individual texts, the results do reveal that there are several commonly shared arguments; they are 'evaluation', 'credibility', 'proposal', 'ability' and 'promise'. The pattern of use of these arguments is in agreement with the discourse moves: 'present problem', 'establish credibility', 'create motivation' and 'issue command', and confirms that there are arguments at work behind the moves.

The parallel patterns of sentential argument exhibited in individual moves also suggest that these regularities shape the genre of fundraising texts. To elaborate on the pattern as highlighted in findings, it is apparent that 'credibility' and 'justify' are the two most predominant arguments in the 'establish credibility' move. There are altogether a total of 49 out of 57 sentences related to this move, while there is one 'predictive' and seven 'narrative-factual' arguments. The seven 'narrative-factual' arguments altogether are a personal narrative of a beneficiary who tells how delighted she has been helped by ORBIS. In other words, they serve actually the function of 'justify' too.

In the beginning, I asked 'What kind of arguments are exhibited in fundraising texts?', and 'Is there a particular argument structure that underlies the discourse moves?' I have answered these questions by dissecting the texts according to a scheme of argument categories which I adapted from other available schemes.

My last question 'Wherein lies persuasion?' is not yet answered. I will reflect on this question by considering aspects of the writer-reader interaction. 'Whenever we read a sentence it sets up expectations in our mind and those expectations shape our interpretation of what comes next' (Hoey, 2001:22). For fundraising texts to be effective and to persuade, it seems that they have to be written in the structure which I have revealed. This structure must match the one expected by readers.

Obviously, there is a structure that is a necessary condition for persuasion to happen. If readers 'are surprised or disconcerted by the direction a text takes' (Hoey, 2001:23), it will not have the desired effect.

Hoey and Winter show the interaction between writers and readers as a question-answer sequence. 'A monologue, written or spoken, may be regarded as a dialogue in which the reader/listener's questions or comments have not been explicitly included but which retains clear indications of the assumed replies of the reader' (Hoey, 1994: 29). How then can a dialogue be assumed for a fundraising text? Another look at the World Vision 'Darkness Doesn't Last' text helps show how questions can be inferred, making a monologue into a dialogue.

While the text being analyzed does not include questions one to seven below, they can be imagined by the reader. The text provides arguments responding to these unasked questions.

Q1: WHY IS THERE A NEED?

*A1: (1) Child is precious and unique (**Evaluation**), (2) children have the right to live ... (**Evaluation**), (3) poverty, war ... make millions of children live in darkness (**Causal**).*

Q2: IS THERE A SOLUTION?

*A2: (4) Darkness doesn't last forever (**Gap**).*

Q3: WHAT IS THE EXPECTED RESULT?

*A3: (5) When you become a World Vision Child Sponsor ... have personal satisfaction of knowing that you have helped change the life of a child ... (**Proposal + Promise**) (6)... two lives will be changed (**Promise**).*

Q4: HOW CAN WORLD VISION CHILD SPONSORSHIP HELP A NEEDY CHILD?

*A4: (7) It is a child-focused programme (**Credibility**), and (9) it will help improve the economic conditions of the child's family ... enabling the child to lead a healthy life (**Promise**).*

Q5: HOW CAN I HELP A NEEDY CHILD?

*A5: (8) You can help provide the needy child with basic medical care, education ... (**Ability**).*

Q6: HOW MUCH AND HOW OFTEN DO I NEED TO GIVE TO HELP THEM?

*A6: (10) For just HK$200 month, you can bring light and hope to a needy child ... (**Proposal + Ability**).*

Q7: WHY SHOULD I BELIEVE IN IT?

*Q7: (11) When you become a child sponsor, you will receive, a photo and a personal profile of your sponsored child ... (**Promise**).*

Q8: WHY SHOULD I ACT NOW?

*A8: (12) Being a World Vision Child Sponsor is an enriching experience (**Evaluation**).*

*(13) When you write to your sponsored child ... you will see for yourself how your love helps light up a needy child's life (**Proposal and Promise**).*

The projected question-answer dialogue shows clearly how persuasion works out in anticipating and meeting expectations of readers. The dialogue also reveals some similar patterns, which correspond closely to the 'hortatory schema' and the rephrased argument structure as shown above.

To summarize, arguments in these texts characterize a unique genre of fundraising texts. This argument structure reflects schema believed to be persuasive to readers. The study suggests that persuasion works in a virtual question-answer dialogue between writers and readers, in which readers' expectations are formulated and fulfilled.

Conclusion

In this study, we explore argumentative elements which suggest that fundraising texts are a particular genre, with persuasive effect. I have shown above that there is an argument structure that shapes the genre of fundraising texts, though not necessarily arranged in a strict sequence. This study is a first step in examining the argumentative elements in fundraising texts. The classification may not capture the full complexity and variation of argument structures. It provides, nevertheless, a useful representation of this genre.

The study also aims to show what argument structure underlies individual moves. The projection on to hortatory schema confirms that there is a parallel pattern of arguments in individual moves.

Concluding with my last question, 'Wherein lies the persuasion?', the study reveals that persuasion seems to lie in the cognitive interactions between writers and readers that could be modelled as a question-answer dialogue. Practically, the conceptualization and fulfilment of readers' expectations is the crucial element in persuasion. People, and people in organizations, can be persuaded to do good things. And ideally this small study of selected fundraising texts helps shed light on this process.

References

Activity Report (2000). Belgium: Medecins Sans Frontieres – International Office.

Bhatia V. K. (1993). Analysing Genre: Language Use in Professional Settings. London: Longman.

Clarke S. and Norton M. (1997). The Complete Fundraising Handbook. London: Directory of Social Change.

Fraigley L. and Selzer J. (2000). Good Reasons. USA: A Pearson Education Company. Ch.5–Ch.10.

Hoey, M. (1994). 'Signalling in Discourse: A Functional Analysis of a Common Discourse Pattern in Written and Spoken English' in Coulthard, Michael (ed.). Advances in Written Text Analysis. London: Routledge.

Hoey, M. (2001). Textual Interaction: An Introduction to Written Discourse Analysis. London and New York: Routledge.

Inch E. S. and Warnick B. (1998). Critical Thinking and Communication: The Use of Reason in Argument. USA: Simon and Schuster.

Lau, C. (2004). Unpublished MBA Dissertation in The Power of Environmentalism: A Case Study of the Body Shop. United Kingdom: University of Kent at Canterbury.

Lee C.W. (2000). Unpublished MA Dissertation in Fundraising Text. A Discourse Description of Two Appeal Letters and Two Leaflets. Hong Kong: Hong Kong Baptist University.

Mann, W.C. and Thompson, S.A. (eds) (1992). Discourse Description. Diverse.

Linguistic Analysis of a Fund-Raising Text. Amsterdam/Philadelphia: John Benjamins.

Longacre, R.E. (1992). 'The Discourse Strategy of An Appeals Letter' in W.C. Mann and S.A. Thompson (eds), Amsterdam/Philadelphia: John Benjamins.109-130.

Martin J. (1989). Factual Writing. Oxford: Oxford University Press.

Oxfam Editorial Committee (2001). Partners Express. Hong Kong: Oxfam.

Palmer F. R. (1986). Mood and Modality. Cambridge: Cambridge University Press.

Ramage D, Bean J and Johnson J. (2001). Writing Arguments. USA: Person Education.

Reynolds M. (2000). The Blending of Narrative and Argument in the Generic Texture of Newspaper Editorials. International Journal of Applied Linguistics 10(1):25-39.

Rottenberg A. T. (1988). Elements of Argument: A Text and Reader. New York: St. Martin's Press.

Shaw P. (2000). 'Towards Classifying the Arguments in Research Genres' in Trosborg A (ed.) Analysing Professional Genres. Amsterdam: John Benjamin.

Swales J. (1990). Genre Analysis. Cambridge:Cambridge University Press.

Vestegaard T. (2000). 'Persuasive and Expository Genres In The Press' in Anne Trosborg (ed.) Analysing Professional Genres. Amsterdam: John Benjamin.

Walton D. N. (1989). Informal Logic: A Handbook for Critical Argumentation. Cambridge: Cambridge University Press.

Warwick M. (1994). How to Write Successful Fundraising Letters. Berkeley: Strathmoor Press.

Winter, E. (1994). 'Clause Relations as Information Structure: Two Basic Text Structures in English' in Coulthard, Michael (ed.). Advances in Written Text Analysis. London and New York: Routledge.

Wood N. V. (1998). Perspectives on Arguments. New Jersey: Prentice-Hall.

V Experience in Practice

According to Crowther (2002), although organisational performance is normally presented as a dialectical performance along the two incompatible dimensions of financial performance and social/environmental performance, this is in fact a false dialectic. Although the annual reporting of organisations presents it as such, empirical evidence demonstrates that organisations actually perform equally well along both dimensions. Thus that dialectic is a construction inherent in annual reports which is created and maintained through the semiotic of these reports, to such an extent that the perception of the dialectic as extant is generally accepted within the discourse of both corporate reporting and of accounting theory. Thus the dialectic appears in a form which is believed so absolutely that an alternative becomes inconceivable; it has, therefore, assumed the mantel of a myth (Cassirer 1946, Miller 1992). Indeed the proponents of environmental accounting and reporting found their analysis upon the existence of this dialectic. It therefore becomes necessary to consider why, if this dialectic does not in fact exist, it is created through the semiotic of the corporate annual reporting mechanism.

If the dialectic does not exist in corporate performance itself then its creation in the annual report must be undertaken by either the authors of the script of that report or by the readers of that reporting script. Although it has been argued that the semiotic is created by the reader of the report based upon their understanding of the contents of that report, the implication of this is that each person produces an interpretation based upon the linguistic, social and environmental experiences which underpin any understanding. Thus each person creates an individual semiotic (Habermas 1971) from the information available to them but moreover seeks to create a semiotic understanding based upon the intentions of the group which holds power (Lakoff 1975). That group is, of course, the authors of the script who are at the same time the managers of the organisation.[1] For that semiotic to be created, however, in such a way that the dialectic between the internal (or traditional accounting) and the external (or social) perspectives upon corporate performance is understood to exist, it is of course necessary that sufficient signals are created within the text for the semiotic to be extracted as a general interpretation. It is in this method that the author's meaning is reinstated in the text (Gadamer 1975). The only people with the power to achieve this are, of course, the authors of the text. Hence it must be concluded that the dialectic of corporate reporting is both created and maintained by the managers of the organisation. It therefore becomes necessary to consider why this might be so.

---

1   More specifically it is the dominant coalition of managers.

The management of an organisation tends to be treated as a discrete entity[2] but it is important to remember that this entity actually comprises a set of individuals with their own drives motivations and desires. Thus every individual has a desire to fulfil their needs and one of these is self-actualisation (Maslow 1954). This need is the one at the top of Maslow's hierarchy of needs and consequently, perhaps, the one most considered in terms of motivation. The next two most important needs – the need for esteem (as reflected in self-respect and the respect of others) and the need for love and belonging (as reflected in the need for being an integral part of a community) – are, however, more important for the understanding of the behaviour of the members of the dominant coalition of management within an organisation. These two needs help explain why managers, in common with other individuals, need to feel important, skilled and essential to organisational performance.

In the previous parts of this book we have considered a variety of theoretical and practical issues concerning the operation of corporate governance and/or corporate social responsibility in an organisation. This final part of the book is devoted to some case studies of actual organisations and their experiences. It is intended through these case studies to highlight actual implementation issues and difficulties and benefits in ways which will provide practical guidance to managers to supplement the knowledge transmitted in the previous chapters and at the same time to give an indication of possible areas for further research to academics and researchers.

In the first chapter, therefore, de Jong, DeJong, Mertens and Roosenboom consider the case of Royal Ahold, a company which was based in The Netherlands, and was formerly one of the world's largest international retail grocery and food service companies, prior to its collapse in 2003. In this chapter de Jong et al. analyse the role of corporate governance mechanisms in Roval Ahold's operations and show how, initially, a family and later professional management exploited the intent of the law and existing regulatory structures to maintain absolute control of the company. In doing so, they analyse in detail the applicable governance mechanisms of Ahold that were designed to hold the self-interest of the parties in check.

Peddle, Rosam and Castka are interested in systems thinking and use their case study presented contribution to demonstrate how the System Thinking approach can be applied and used within a real organisation. They show how organisations can bring Corporate Social Responsibility (CSR) to life as a part of an existing management system and demonstrate that a process-based management system supports CSR implementation and how individual processes, sub-processes and procedures contain CSR elements as a natural part of business activities. They argue that a System Thinking approach to CSR promotes the interdependence of different functions in organisations, recognising that action in one part of the organisation always has an effect in most others. Moreover, it assumes that successful and sustainable CSR significantly impacts on a wide variety of organisational planning and management.

Earlier de Jong et al. considered the problems in one of the largest companies in the world; in the next chapter Wagner looks at the opposite extreme and considers Istiqibol Dilnoza, a small start-up company based in Tashkent, Uzbekustan. In his analysis he concentrates primarily upon the corporate social responsibility issues facing the company and their response to those issues. The contrast in terms both of size and of business

---

2   Or rather a coalition which acts in unison.

environment serves to emphasise the ubiquity of the concepts and their relevance to all businesses and their managers, and hence also to researchers. Wagner also illustrates some of the problems in adopting CSR when he acknowledges that there are so many contextual factors that influence a micro or small business's ability to be successful or to implement a CSR strategy, and so it is not easy to definitively state one or even a couple of recommendations that would have the same positive affect each time used. Nevertheless, this chapter focuses upon some significant issues.

The following chapter takes a different perspective as Goetz considers sustainability from a public sector perspective when she analyses the sustainable business programme developed by the Washington State government in the USA. In the chapter she makes a distinction between sustainability and corporate social responsibility – a distinction with which many people would concur – but regards them as inextricably related. Her analysis focuses upon the issues involved in developing the Washington programme and in maintaining the relationships with the businesses in the state to foster the necessary sustainability programme. This chapter therefore raises some key issues which are important both for business managers and for managers in the public sector and in Non-Government Organisations (NGOs) seeking to interact on issues of governance, social responsibility and sustainability.

In the next chapter a different perspective is taken and a company in the North East of England is the subject. Esh Group is the largest indigenous construction group in the region and currently employs over 1,000 people and, in the last five years, turnover has more than doubled to over £150m for fiscal year end 2007. The group is committed to the local economy and the community which provides its direct workforce. The company is very conscious of the impact it has on both the natural environment and its local community and as such, takes its corporate responsibilities seriously. The company has an active policy of procurement in the North East and adjacent regions, recognising the impact this has on the local economy, not only in terms of employment but also in relation to the environment and reducing its carbon footprint. CSR activity is high on the company's strategic agenda with firm commitment from the very top level of the organisation downwards. 'Esh Added Value', a collection of varied and innovative award winning CSR initiatives and programmes, has been an integral part of the Group ethos and culture for years. This chapter chronicles the CSR journey of the company.

In the next chapter Shaw takes a different perspective by looking at an industry rather than a company. She has chosen the tobacco industry – a regular shibboleth of the CSR researchers – which enables her to raise the important issue of socially responsible activities versus the social responsibility of the product, or service, itself. The analysis enables her to raise a variety of issues which are relevant to other managers, and to researchers, and also raises the ethical question central to the analysis, thereby highlighting that at the end of the day we all have an ethical position which affects our opinions and actions. This case also highlights an issue which has been raised many times during this book – namely the inexact nature of our definition of what constitutes socially responsible behaviour.

References

Cassirer E (1946); *Language and Myth*; trans. S K Langer; New York; Dover Publications.
Crowther D (2002); *A Social Critique of Corporate Reporting*; Aldershot; Ashgate.

Gadamer H G (1975); *Truth and Method*; trans. G Bardent & J Cumming; London; Sheed & Ward.

Habermas J (1971); *Knowledge and Human Interests*; trans. J J Shapiro; Boston, Mass.; Beacon Press.

Lakoff R (1975); *Language and Woman's Place*; Cambridge; Harper & Row.

Maslow A H (1954); *Motivation and Personality*; New York; Harper & Row.

Miller D F (1992); *The Reason of Metaphor*; London; Sage.

34 Royal Ahold:* The Role of Corporate Governance

ABE DE JONG, DOUGLAS V. DEJONG, GERARD MERTENS
AND PETER ROOSENBOOM

Introduction

Royal Ahold (*Koninklijke Ahold NV*) was one of the major success stories in the 1990s and suffered a complete meltdown in 2003. This chapter analyzes the role of Ahold's corporate governance mechanisms. and illustrates how initially a family, and later professional management, exploited the intent of the law and existing regulatory structures to maintain absolute control of the company. It analyzes in detail the applicable governance mechanisms of Ahold that were designed to hold the self-interest of the parties in check.

The rise and fall of Royal Ahold is an important event in corporate governance. Headquartered in The Netherlands, Ahold is one of the world's largest international retail grocery and food service companies. At its peak in 2001, Ahold's reported sales and profits were €66.6 billion and €1.1 billion and it operated 5,155 stores in 27 countries with nearly a quarter of a million employees. Ahold began as a family firm in 1887 and went public in 1948. Ahold was a family-controlled business under the Heijn family, operating primarily in the Netherlands for over 100 years. In 1989, Ahold underwent a transition from a family-controlled to a management-controlled firm. Following this transition, Ahold experienced a remarkable period of success. It generated over a 1,000 percent return for its shareholders and had a market capitalization of €30.6 billion by November 2001. In 2003, Ahold suffered a complete meltdown. The ensuing period found a firm in complete disarray: a failed strategy, an accounting scandal, the firing of professional management and litigation filings from all parts of the world. Shareholders lost most of their returns generated since 1989.

The fall of Ahold sent shock waves through the corporate governance landscape. Since the initial public offering in 1948, the family had used Dutch corporate law and a small blockholding to control Ahold with a dispersed ownership structure. The transition to professional management in 1989 left Ahold with dispersed shareholders but no major blockholder. When professional management raised capital from institutional investors, management denied them their voting rights by exploiting regulations that allow Dutch

---

* This chapter is based on our paper 'Investor relations, reputational bonding, and corporate governance: The case of Royal Ahold', *Journal of Accounting and Public Policy* 26 (2007), 328-375.

companies to issue non-voting certificates rather than voting shares. Thus, blockholders were not able to supplant the role of the family as a monitor of professional management. With a dispersed ownership structure and weak minority rights, management was unconstrained. The surprising aspect of the Ahold saga is that it is unclear why the family and professional management should have done anything differently or that we would have expected them to do anything differently. The exploitation of regulatory structures is not unique but rather a general characteristic with implications beyond Ahold. This chapter provides insights on how family and management's objectives interact with (and within) the constraints of outside regulations and their consequences. Our evidence is particularly relevant to Europe where a common characteristic of firms is their majority and/or family control structure without blockholder monitoring or disciplining by the market for corporate control. The general concern is that these ownership structures often hinder the performance of publicly traded firms (Faccio and Lang, 2002).

For regulators, Ahold shattered the illusion that corporate governance was a United States' problem; Ahold became 'Europe's Enron' (*The Economist*, March 1, 2003). It caused Dutch and European policymakers to rethink their approach to corporate governance. In The Netherlands, a committee on corporate governance was installed on March 10, 2003 (Tabaksblat Committee, 2003) to restore confidence in public companies. In the United States, the Public Company Accounting Oversight Board (PCAOB) that regulates the accounting profession under the Sarbanes-Oxley Act used Ahold as an example to successfully negotiate the extension of its oversight to European accounting firms working in the United States or working on foreign companies listed in the United States (*Wall Street Journal*, March 5, 2003). First principles of corporate governance are generally understood in the academic literature and in the policy arena (Demsetz, 1983, Hart, 1995 and Agrawal and Knoeber, 1996). We use the Organization for Economic Co-operation and Development's (OECD) Principles of Corporate Governance, the international standard by which corporate governance codes are often measured, to illustrate first principles. We then analyze in detail the applicable governance mechanisms of Ahold that were designed to hold the self-interest of the parties in check.

After our discussion of the governance structures of Ahold in period 1989–2003 (Ahold's corporate governance structures), we describe the course of affairs which led to the firm's failure (Ahold's strategy and Ahold's failure). We focus on the strategic and accounting issues. In our accompanying paper (De Jong et al., 2007) we describe these issues in more detail.

Ahold's Corporate Governance Structures

FRAMEWORK: CODE OF CORPORATE GOVERNANCE

In this section, we analyze Ahold's corporate governance structure and ask what went wrong. First principles of corporate governance were generally understood in the academic literature (Hart, 1995) and in the policy arena where corporate governance codes addressing best practices appeared in the 1990s. Because best practices are generally accepted and commonly known, they form a benchmark for evaluating Ahold's corporate governance. We use the OECD Principles of Corporate Governance (1999) as our benchmark, see

Table 34.1, the standard by which other international codes are compared.[1] Shareholder rights, the role of supervisory boards (and non-executive directors in unitary systems), and disclosure and transparency are important aspects of the OECD code. For example, shareholders are to be informed and have the right to elect members of the board, vote on fundamental corporate changes, and vote in general shareholder meetings (in person or in absentia). The market for corporate control should function without anti-takeover devices. General and institutional shareholders should consider the implications of their votes. The board should exercise objective judgement independent of management and devote sufficient time to the firm. The board's functions include guiding corporate strategy, ensuring the integrity of financial reporting, disclosure and communication, and selecting, overseeing and compensating key executives.

Table 34.1 OECD principles of Corporate Governance

Corporate governance should protect shareholder rights

- Basic shareholder rights include the right to elect members of the board.
- Shareholders have the right to participate in decisions concerning fundamental corporate change (amendments to governance, authorization of shares, sale of the company).
- Shareholders vote in general shareholder meetings (whether this is in person or in absentia).
- Capital structures and arrangements that give certain shareholders a disproportionate degree of control should be disclosed.
- Market for corporate control should be allowed to function without anti-takeover devices.
- Shareholders, including institutional investors, should consider the costs and benefits of their votes.

Corporate governance should ensure equitable protection of all shareholders, including minority and foreign shareholders

Corporate governance should recognize the rights of stakeholders as established by law and encourage the active co-operation between the corporation and stakeholders

Corporate governance should ensure that timely and accurate disclosure is made on all matters regarding the corporation (including financial, performance, ownership and governance)

Corporate governance should ensure the strategic guidance of the company, the effective monitoring of the management by the board, and the board's accountability to the company and shareholders

Board should act on a fully informed basis with due diligence and in the best interest of the company and shareholders.

Board should treat all shareholders equally.

---

1   The OECD code was established in 1999 and updated in 2004. The ideas reflected in the code are already present in the 1992 Cadbury report. In 1996, the Dutch corporate governance code was released by the Peters Committee (De Jong et al., 2005). Regarding the supervisory board, the Dutch code recommendations address independence, conflicts of interest and multiple board memberships.

Table 34.1 *Concluded*

Board should ensure compliance with the law.

Board should fulfill certain key functions, including:

- Reviewing and guiding corporate strategy; setting performance standards; monitoring implementation and corporate performance; overseeing major capital expenditures, acquisitions and divestures.
- Selecting, compensating, monitoring and when necessary, replacing key executives and overseeing succession plans.
- Reviewing key executive and board remuneration, and ensuring a formal and transparent board nomination process.
- Monitoring and managing potential conflicts of interest of management, board members and shareholders.
- Ensuring the integrity of the corporation's accounting and financial reporting systems.
- Monitoring the effectiveness of its corporate governance practices.
- Overseeing the process of disclosure and communication.
- Board should exercise objective judgment on corporate affairs independent, in particular, from management
- Board should consider assigning non-executive members to tasks where there is the potential for conflict of interest.
- Board should devote sufficient time to their responsibilities.

Board should have access to accurate, relevant and timely information

---

Note: Table summarizes the OECD's Principles of Corporate Governance authored by the Ad Hoc Task Force on Corporate Governance in 1999.

We evaluate Ahold's management board, supervisory board, ownership and control structure and incentive compensation. We also consider the traditional gatekeepers in the financial markets, financial analysts and Ahold's house bank.

MANAGEMENT BOARD

Prior to 1987 the management board consisted primarily of the two sons of Jan Heijn, Ab Heijn, CEO, and his younger brother Gerrit Jan Heijn. Given the firm's growth, the lack of a long-term family heir and the need for professional management, the Heijn brothers expanded the board to seven members by 1987, see Table 34.2; we focus on two, Cees van der Hoeven, CFO, and Pierre Everaert, responsible for foreign activities. The transition to professional management was accelerated by the kidnapping and murder of Gerrit Jan Heijn in late 1987 and early 1988. Gerrit Jan was expected to succeed Ab and keep the firm under family control for another three years. Ab wanted to continue as the CEO when he reached mandatory retirement in 1989, but this plan was voted down by the other members of the management board (Smit, 2004, p.98-99). Ab Heijn retired in 1989 and moved to the supervisory board.

There were two management board members who were candidates for the CEO position. Cees van der Hoeven was the company's CFO with 15 years experience with

Table 34.2 Ahold's management board

Name	Nationality	Started	Ended	Expertise	1987	1993	1998	2002	2003	Employment/affiliations
A. Heijn	Dutch	1962	1989	Retail	C					Heijn family
C.H. van der Hoeven	Dutch	1985	2003	Finance	M	C	C	C		Former Royal Dutch/Shell; later in supervisory board Stroeve bank, ABN-Amro and KPN
P.J. Everaert	U.S.	1985	1993	Marketing	M					Former Goodyear, General Biscuits
P.J. van Dun	Dutch	1980	1997	Organization	M	M				Former SHV
F.I. Ahlqvist	Sweden	1981	1998	Marketing	M	M	M			Former Mölnlycke
G.J. Heijn	Dutch	1962	1988	Retail	M					Heijn family
R. Zwartendijk	Dutch	1981	1999	Production	M	M	M			Former Mölnlycke
J.G. Andreae	Dutch	1997	2004	Retail			M	M		Former Albert Heijn and since 1979 Ahold
A.M. Meurs	Dutch	1997	2003	Finance			M	M		Former ABN-Amro; since 1992 Ahold; also supervisory board Van der Hoop bank
E.S. Moerk	Norway	1994	1998	International business			M			Former Canada Dry, Pepsi and Campbells' Biscuits
M.P.M. de Raad	Dutch	2001	Present	Retail				M	M	Former SHV, Metro AG, CSM and Hagemeyer
W.J. Grize	U.S.	2001	Present	Retail				M	M	Management Stop & Shop
J.L. Miller	U.S.	2001	Present	Retail				M	M	Management U.S. Food Service
A.S. Noddle	U.S.	1998	2001	Retail						Management Giant Food Stores
P. Wakkie	Dutch	2003	Present	Legal					M	Former De Brauw Blackstone Westbroek
A. Moberg	Sweden	2003	Present	Marketing					C	Former Ikea
H. Ryopponen	Finland	2003	Present	Finance					M	Former Ikea
D. Eustace	U.K.	2003	Present	Finance					M	Former CFO Philips

Note: Table shows the development of the management board of Ahold from 1987 to 2004. C denotes CEO and M denotes management board member. Data is collected from annual reports and REACH database.

Royal Dutch Shell. His opponent, Pierre Everaert, was an engineer with international experience at Goodyear and Générale Biscuit before joining Ahold. Cees van der Hoeven won the vote for CEO within the management board. However, members of the supervisory board and Ab Heijn preferred and appointed Pierre Everaert as CEO in September 1989. In December 1992, Everaert announced his departure to Philips, the large Dutch consumer electronics firm. Choufoer, Chairman of Ahold's supervisory board, agreed that van der Hoeven would not only become the new CEO but also retain his CFO position. With Evereart's resignation, van der Hoeven became both CEO and CFO. This is a breakdown in controls. By 1998 van der Hoeven had surrounded himself with managers who were loyal to him. Van Dun had retired. There were three additions, one insider Andreae from Albert Heijn for his retailing experience, and two from the outside, Meurs from ABN-Amro, the CFO in waiting, and Moerk for his international business background.

Over the four year period, 1998 to 2002, there was a 50 percent turnover in the management board. Van der Hoeven (now only CEO), Andreae (Albert Heijn) and Meurs (CFO) were still on the board. New members were de Raad (formerly of SHV and German retailer Metro), Grize (management from Stop & Shop), and Miller (management from U.S. Food Service). In addition, Noddle, management from Giant Food Stores, came on and went off the board during this time period. The presence of former management of recent acquisitions, Grize, Miller and Noddle, promoted loyalty, because these managers were promoted to the board of a much larger firm in a very uncertain situation. Further, these board members monitored the subsidiaries they previously managed. Though consistent with Ahold's strategy of keeping acquired management, it represents poor internal control over management.

The management board was not effective for two reasons. First, all members owed their positions to van der Hoeven. After a period of high turnover, the board consisted of people internally promoted from subsidiaries (Grize, Miller, Noddle and Andreae) or staff functions (Meurs). The second characteristic is van der Hoeven's personality. Van der Hoeven is described by Smit (2004) and Ab Heijn (De Jager, 1997) as a strong and persuasive personality. In addition to several awards for Ahold (Dutch investor relations, worldwide retailer), van der Hoeven also received personal awards, like 'CEO of the year' (Het Financieele Dagblad, January 12, 2000). The combination of van der Hoeven's power in the management board, his successes in the 1990s and his personality had a major impact on Ahold's strategies.

SUPERVISORY BOARD

The supervisory board failed to adapt to a professionally managed firm with a dispersed ownership structure. The OECD structure and responsibilities for supervisory boards imply that the problems documented for Ahold are primarily the board's responsibility. Supervisory board members must be independent, capable and devote sufficient time to the firm (John and Senbet, 1998). The supervisory board is especially important in the Netherlands, where either by Dutch law or by company statutes in the case of Ahold after 2001, key decision rights of shareholders were transferred to the supervisory board, see Table 34.4. Ahold's supervisory board was not independent due to the presence of former managers and supervisors with conflicting interests with other stakeholders. Moreover, many board members were overcommitted.

Members of Ahold's supervisory board with their relevant professional experience are detailed in Table 34.3. Independence from the management board is limited when former

Table 34.3 Ahold's supervisory board

Name	Nationality	Started	Ended	Expertise	1987	1993	1998	2002	2003	Employment/affiliations
J. Kreiken	Dutch	1969	1990	Business	C					Nationale Investeringsbank, chair until May 1987
D. Vethaak	Dutch	1981	1987	Finance	M					Was in management board from 1959-1981
A. Spaander	Dutch	1981	1993	Unknown	M	M				
A.J. Kranendonk	Dutch	1985	2000	Business, Finance	M					Former diary cooperation Friesland, also on supervisory board of Athlon, also on DNB
J.H. Choufoer	Dutch	1985	1996	Business	M	C				Former RD/Shell, also on supervisory board of RD/Shell, ING, Hoogovens and Pakhoed
G. van 't Hull	Dutch	1972	1988	Unknown	M					Former KLM, also 18 other supervisory directorships
J.F.A. de Soet	Dutch	NA	1988	Marketing	M	M				
R.J. Nelissen	Dutch	1981	2001	Finance, Politics	M	M	M			Former ABN-Amro, DNB, parliament and minister, also 18 supervisory directorships including Deloitte, GTI and ABN-Amro
N. Rempt-Halmmans de Jongh	Dutch	1979	1992	Politics	M					Member of parliament
R.J. Bogomolny	U.S.	1992	1998	Retail		M	M			Former CEO of First National Supermarkets
A. Heijn	Dutch	1990	1997	N.A.		M				Family; was in management board 1962-1989; also supervisory director at Athlon, Randstad, Reesink, ABN-Amro
J. de Koning	Dutch	1991	1994	Politics		M				Member of parliament and minister (died in 1994)
R.F. Meyer	U.S.	1988	2000	Academic		M	M			Finance professor at Harvard Business School
H. de Ruiter	Dutch	1994	2003	Business			C	C		Former RD/Shell, also 17 supervisory directorships including RD/Shell, Heineken, Hoogovens/Corus, Pakhoed
J.A. van Kemenade	Dutch	1996	2001	Politics, Academic			M			Former parliament and minister, mayor, chaired university, DNB
M. Perry CBE	U.K.	1997	Present	Business			M	M	M	Former Unilever
L.J.R. de Vink	Dutch	1998	Present	International business				M	M	Former Warner Lambert
R. Fahlin	Sweden	2001	2003	Retail				M		Management ICA
C.P. Schneider	U.S.	2001	Present	Academic				M	M	Art professor, former U.S. ambassador in the Netherlands
R.G. Tobin	U.S.	2001	Present	Retail, Marketing				M	M	Management Stop & Shop, was in management board 1998-2001
C. Boonstra	Dutch	2001	2002	Marketing						Former Philips
J. Hommen	Dutch	2003	Present	Finance					M	Former Philips
K. Vuursteen	Dutch	2002	Present	Business					C	Former Philips and Heineken

Note: Table shows the development of the supervisory board of Ahold from 1987 to 2004. C denotes Chairman and M denotes supervisory board member. Data is collected from annual reports, REACH database, and www.parlement.com.

Table 34.4   Takeover defences and shareholder rights at Ahold

Takeover defense	Years	Description
Founder or priority shares	1948–1979	The founder shares entitled the Heijn family to make binding nominations for all the members on the management board and one member on the supervisory board. The founder shares also entitled them to a part of the excess profit. In 1979 the founder shares were stripped of their right to make binding nominations for board positions.
Structured regime	1972–2001	The structured regime is a legal requirement for large domestic Dutch companies. The regime transfers several decision rights from the shareholders to the supervisory board such as the right to appoint and dismiss members of the management board, to adopt the annual accounts and the election of the supervisory board itself, called co-optation. Multinational Dutch companies (defined as companies with more that 50 percent of their work force outside the Netherlands) are exempt from this regulation. But, because a multinational Dutch company typically starts out as a large domestic company under the structured regime, such companies are allowed to voluntarily keep the structured regime. Ahold which was organized as a domestic company under the structured regime could therefore have left the regime in the 1990s, when it met the multinational requirement. As a defense against proposed legislation that would have required that labor constitute 1/3 of the members of the supervisory board, Ahold abolished the structured regime in 2001, which exempted Ahold from the proposed legislation (simultaneously Ahold introduced binding nominations).
Preferred shares	1973–now	The foundation *Stichting Ahold Continuïteit* (SAC) is an anti-takeover defense. The foundation is a separate legal entity with board members typically aligned with the interests of the current management and supervisory board. The foundation owns an option to call preferred shares with voting rights that equal the voting rights of the outstanding current shareholders. In case of a takeover threat the foundation will exercise the option and keep or place the preferred shares – of which only 25 percent has to be paid – among friendly parties. This will dilute the stake of a hostile bidder.
Certificates of preferred shares	1996–now	Certificates of preferred shares have been stripped of their voting rights with the voting rights under control of a second Ahold-related foundation *Stichting Administratiekantoor Preferente Financieringsaandelen Ahold* (SAPFA). This foundation, friendly to incumbent management, casts the votes on the certificates of preferred shares held by the institutional investors at the general meeting of shareholders.
Binding nominations	2001–now	Ahold introduced into its corporate charter a right for the supervisory board to nominate all supervisory and managerial board members. The nominations are binding and can only be rejected with a 2/3 majority representing at least half of the voting rights.

Note: Table shows Ahold's takeover defenses. Data is collected from annual reports, newspapers and De Jager (1995, 1997).

managers become supervisors. The 1987 board had former CFO Vethaak as a member and former CEO Ab Heijn was a member from 1990 to 1997. The role of Heijn was very passive. Starting in 1993, supervisory board members were recruited from the management of acquired firms: Bogomolny was the former CEO of First National Supermarkets. In 2001, Fahlin (former ICA) entered the board, as did Tobin. Tobin was the former manager of Stop & Shop and had been in Ahold's management board starting in 1998.[2]

Several board members had ties with institutions related to Ahold, which led to conflicts of interest with these stakeholders. As detailed earlier, Nelissen, a board member from 1987 to 2001, is particularly interesting; he was the CEO of Amro, one of Ahold's main banks. When Amro and ABN merged in 1990, Nelissen became CEO of the combination until his retirement in 1992. After retiring he became a member of the bank's supervisory board. Nelissen was also on the board of Ahold's auditor, Deloitte. Through Kreiken and Choufoer, Ahold had interlocking directorates with two other Dutch financial institutions, Nationale Investeringsbank and ING. Choufoer was also from Royal Dutch Shell, van der Hoeven's employer for 15 years. Sir Perry was the former CEO of Unilever, a major supplier of consumer goods to Ahold.

The board members were generally qualified based on experience and background. One exception should be noted. Several politicians served on Ahold's board: Rempt-Halmmans de Jongh, de Koning, van Kemenade and Schneider. While there were no conflicts of interest with other businesses, their business expertise was most likely less than other members.[3]

Ahold had board members with enormous board portfolios, which limited their commitment to the firm. For example, in 1987, five of the nine board members served on other companies' supervisory boards, three are overcommitted: Choufoer (with four additional supervisory board positions), de Soet (with 18) and Nelissen (with 18). In 1998, four of the seven supervisory board members are overcommitted. The new chairman, de Ruiter, had 17 other supervisory board positions including Royal Dutch Shell.[4]

There is very little information on committees and their membership. The 1997–2001 Dutch annual reports indicate that the supervisory board had a functioning audit committee, a remuneration committee and a selection and nomination committee. However, no members were listed.[5]

Evidence suggests that the management board had significant influence over supervisory board appointments and its decisions, dating back to the Heijn family who controlled the supervisory board by its grandfathered members and the co-optation under the Dutch company law that allowed the supervisory board to effectively choose its own members. Professional management continued this tradition in which Ahold's management board provided the nominations for the supervisory board.

---

2   Though Tobin owns no shares in Ahold, he had 278,000 options, which were awarded when Tobin was on the management board.

3   According to Smit (2004, p.268), Schneider, an art professor and former U.S. ambassador to the Netherlands, was given an internal introduction into U.S. and Dutch GAAP and mentions not to have understood the issue. In a radio interview shortly after the events in February 2003, she states 'I don't feel responsible. I am not a business person.' (Danko, 12 June 2003).

4   Both in 1998 and 2001 *Elan*, a Dutch magazine for board members, announced that on the basis of board positions, de Ruiter was the most powerful supervisory board person in the Netherlands. Ferris, et al. (2003) find that in 1995 3,190 U.S. firms with assets over $100 million have 23,673 directors. Less than 0.5 percent of these directors have more than four positions. The authors find no relation between multiple directorships and firm performance.

5   The only additional information from the 20-F's was the remuneration committee members for 2001, H. de Ruiter, R.J. Nelissen, and M. Perry. De Ruiter and Nelissen were chair and vice-chair of the supervisory board and Nelissen has been discussed.

For example, when Ab Heijn retired in 1997, 'the supervisory board asks the management board to think about the nomination of new members. This is the habit in Ahold. The management board determines the composition of the supervisory board, because normally their nominations are followed' (Smit, 2004, p.175). Other examples illustrating this relationship are de Ruiter's argument with van der Hoeven about the takeover in Brazil. In the end, de Ruiter agreed (Smit, 2004, p.165). De Ruiter argued with van der Hoeven about the 15 percent growth promised. Van der Hoeven replied: 'I promised it and did it' (Smit, 2004, p. 195).

OWNERSHIP AND CONTROL STRUCTURE

The role of shareholders in Ahold depends on the ownership structure, that is, ownership distribution and legal constructions that limit shareholder influence. Beginning in 1948 with the family through 2001 with professional management, the family and management adopted all the defenses available to Dutch companies to obtain and maintain complete control of Ahold: founder/priority shares, preferred shares with the option to dilute 100 percent in case of a hostile takeover, the structured regime, binding nominations and certificates (see Table 34.4).[6] These defenses negate the ability of shareholders to monitor management on a day-to-day basis by depriving shareholders of their voting rights and the ability of the market for corporate control to discipline management via a takeover. The legal structures and takeover defenses introduced under the Heijn family and later capitalized upon by van der Hoeven to maintain control of Ahold undermined the disciplining power of the market for corporate control, prevented blockholder monitoring by denying institutional shareholders their voting rights and transferred decision rights from shareholders to the supervisory board. In the remainder of this subsection we will summarize Ahold's ownership structure and the obstruction of shareholder influence, which stands in a sharp contrast to its investor relations image.

Prior to the addition of professional management on the management board in 1989, the Heijn family used all legal means at their disposal to maintain control of the company. The firm Albert Heijn, Ahold's predecessor, was listed in Amsterdam in 1948 with the two sons of Albert Heijn, Gerrit and Jan Heijn, only holding 50 percent of the outstanding shares (De Jager, 1995, p. 108). In the public offering, the two sons received founder shares, also referred to as priority shares (see Table 34.4), which gave the sons the right to make binding nominations for all the members on the management board and one member on the supervisory board.

In the early 1970s, two legal constructions were adopted by Ahold. First, a major revision of Dutch company law superseded the founder shares and required Ahold to organize under the 'structured regime' in 1972. This regime weakened the powers of shareholders by assigning the following responsibilities to the supervisory board, see Table 34.4: the establishment and approval of the annual accounts, the election of the management board, and the election of the supervisory board itself (called co-optation). The supervisory board also has authority over major decisions made by the management board. The law prescribes

6   Voogd (1989) documents that in 1988, 51 percent of the Dutch listed companies examined had 'defensive' preferred shares, 44 percent was under the structured regime, 32 percent had certificates and 49 percent had binding nominations. De Jong and Röell (2005) find that the priority shares are present in 28 percent of the firms in 1958 and 43 percent in 1993. Priority shares are often found in family firms; in 1958 45 percent of the family firms had priority shares, while only 22 percent of the other firms used this measure.

that the supervisory board be 'independent' and serve the firm's interest. However, the family effectively controlled Ahold via the grandfathered management board, which consisted of the two sons of Jan Heijn, Ab and Gerrit Jan, and the grandfathered supervisory board, previously controlled by the family via founder shares.

The second construction was adopted in 1973 when Ahold set up the *Stichting Ahold Continuïteit* (SAC, Foundation Ahold Continuity), which is an anti-takeover defense. This foundation owns an option to call preferred shares with voting rights that equal the voting rights of the outstanding current shareholders.[7] In case of a takeover threat the foundation exercises the option and places the preferred shares – of which only 25 percent has to be paid – with friendly parties. This dilutes the stake of a hostile bidder, see Table 34.4. SAC is friendly to incumbent management; the defense has no effect until the option is exercised.

By 1989, when professional management took over the positions of the Heijn family in the board, family ownership had declined to 7.3 percent (see Table 34.5, which details Ahold's major blockholders starting in 1989). In 1993, several Heijn family members needed funds for other ventures. To keep control over Ahold, van der Hoeven convinced the family to have ABN-Amro purchase the shares instead of an anonymous United States' investor, De Jager (1997, p.239). ABN-Amro, then placed the shares with institutional investors to ensure a dispersed ownership structure without blockholder monitoring. In 1996, van der Hoeven again avoids blockholder monitoring in the dissolution of Ahold's co-operative venture, European Retail Association (ERA).[8] This involved the sale of Ahold's stakes in its partners Argyll and Casino. Argyll and Casino also sold their respective stakes in Ahold by placing them with four institutional investors, pension fund ABP and bank/insurance companies Achmea, Fortis, and ING.

In 1996, simultaneously with the sale of the Argyll and Casino stakes, van der Hoeven announced the issuance of preferred financing shares, a type of security not used before; €59.4 million was raised from friendly institutional investors Achmea, Aegon, Fortis and ING in June 1996. The investors qualified for tax exemption because they each owned more than five percent stakes in Ahold. By 1997, 34 percent of Ahold's shares were owned by institutions with holdings in excess of five percent, see Table 34.5.[9] Van der Hoeven avoided blockholder monitoring by the institutional investors via certification of the preferred shares. Certificates of preferred shares were stripped of their voting rights, with the voting rights under control of the foundation *Stichting Administratiekantoor Preferente Financieringsaandelen Ahold* (SAPFA). This foundation is not related to the SAC foundation mentioned earlier. These institutional investors agreed with this construction because they

---

7   Under Dutch law, preferred shares can be designed to provide a much larger ratio of voting power to paid-in capital than ordinary shares. The foundation can even be set up to be self-financing: it can borrow the amount required for the paid-in capital, receive dividends on the preferred shares that are tied to the required interest on the loan, and with cumulative preferred rights, the foundation can be assured of meeting its obligations (Voogd, 1989).

8   With the inception of the European Union in 1992, an overriding concern in 1989 was competition policy and the integration of EU markets. The European retail grocery industry was anxious about the threat of further consolidation in the manufacturing portion of the food industry and its adverse consequences for the retail chains and independent stores. Cooperative arrangements across countries were a potential way of mitigating this threat. In 1989, Ahold formed an alliance with Argyll (UK) and Casino (France) called the ERA or the European Retail Alliance. In order to strengthen the ties among the three companies, Argyll and Casino each bought four percent of Ahold's shares, see Table 34.5. Due to the reporting date (May of each year), Argyll's and Casino's stakes are first reported in 1990. Ahold bought about 1.5 percent of Argyll's shares and 3.4 percent of Casino's.

9   The stakes in Table 34.5 are the sum of ordinary shares and the certificates of preferred shares. Dutch ownership notification regulation does not allow a differentiation between classes of shares.

Table 34.5 Ownership structure of Ahold

Shareholder	Description	1989	1990	1991	1992	1993	1994	1995	1996	1997	1998	1999	2000	2001	2002	2003
SHV	Non-listed family firm	12%														
Heijn family	Family	7.3%	7.3%	7.7%	7.7%											
ASKO	Retail firm		15%													
Argyll*	Retail firm		4%	4%	4%	4%	4%	4%								
Casino*	Retail firm		4%	4%	4%	4%	4%	4%								
ABP	Pension fund								5.4%	5.4%	5.4%					
AEGON**	Insurer									6.1%	6.1%	6.1%	6.1%	6.1%	6.1%	6.1%
Achmea**	Insurer									7.2%	7.2%	7.2%	7.2%	7.2%	7.2%	7.2%
ING**	Bank/Insurer									7.4%	7.4%	7.4%	7.4%	7.4%	7.4%	7.4%
Fortis**	Bank/Insurer									8.0%	8.0%	8.0%	8.0%	8.0%	8.0%	8.0%
Aviva plc	Insurer													5.1%	5.1%	5.0%
Eureko	Insurer														4.9%	4.9%
U.S. institutional investors										0.5%	0.5%	0.6%	0.6%	1.1%	0.9%	1.9%

Note: Table shows the ownership structure of Ahold in May of each year. Before 1992 ownership stakes are taken from an annual stock market guide *De Omzetcijfers* published by Het Financieele Dagblad. After 1992 ownership stakes, other than the ownership of Argyll and Casino, are based on the notifications under the Act on Disclosure of Holdings in Listed Companies (*Wet Melding Zeggenschap*). Starting in 1997, the stakes are the combination of the ordinary shares and the certificates of preferred shares. Ownership stakes for United States' institutional investors are taken from the Thomson Financial Spectrum database, which compiles this information based on SEC rule 13(f); this database does not contain information for Ahold before 1997.

* Members of the European Retail Alliance with Ahold.
** Friendly institutional investors who purchased the €59.4 million issue of preferred preference shares from Ahold.

had little incentive to monitor Ahold as the preferred cash dividends secured their yearly returns.[10] SAPFA was set up by management to control the votes tied to the certificates of preferred shares held by the institutional investors, see Table 34.4, via the board of SAPFA.[11] The workings of SAPFA are best illustrated by the first annual shareholder meeting held after the refinancing on May 6, 1997. In the 1997 meeting, there were 823 shareholders present, representing 63 million shares. SAPFA controlled 63 percent of the votes with its 40 million preferred shares cast by the chairman of the foundation. During the meeting the chairman explained that the board of the foundation in a meeting held before the annual meeting decided to vote favorable on all management proposals.

Finally, in the shareholders' meeting of May 15, 2001, Ahold abolished the structured regime, Het Financieele Dagblad (May 16, 2001).[12] Ahold changed its statutes and included so-called binding nominations, which implies that the supervisory board does all the nominations and these can only be rejected with a two-thirds majority representing one-half of the voting rights. By eliminating the structured regime and adopting the new statute, Ahold eliminated supervisory board nominations from the workers (a possibility under proposed legislation) and increased the threshold for rejecting supervisory board nominations.

INCENTIVE COMPENSATION

Option-based incentive schemes align interests and encourage professional managers to behave in the interest of shareholders. Executives at the level of Ahold's management board negated the long-term incentive effects of ownership by exercising their options and immediately selling the shares. This represents a stark breakdown in an incentive structure (overseen by the supervisory board). If management had any doubts about an acquisition or accounting policy, the compensation incentives (bonuses and stock options based on earnings growth) certainly appeased those doubts.

We focus on stock options at the executive and board level for two reasons: aggregate stock option information is available and reliable and for Ahold, stock options were an integral part of its incentive structure. Table 34.6 details Ahold's stock option information from 1987 through 2003. For each year when available, the information includes the beginning number of options outstanding, options granted, exercised and cancelled, average

---

10   The academic literature argues that dividends and leverage are corporate governance mechanisms (for example, Jensen, 1986, Easterbrook, 1984). Ahold's management successfully circumvented the potential role of dividends on ordinary shares as a disciplining device. Until 1989, Ahold paid cash dividends. Beginning in 1989, it initiated a choice dividend (for example, in 1989, investors received an interim dividend of fl 0.50 + $ 0.05 and a year end choice dividend of fl 1.10 + $ 0.20 or 2 percent in shares). The ratio of shares to cash could be set such that shareholders chose the stock dividend (of course, tax issues are important here). Beginning in 1990, interim dividends were also choice dividends. Choice dividends allowed management to influence the cash outflow, without announcing a dividend reduction. If van der Hoeven wanted to keep cash he could make stock attractive; if he wanted fewer shares; he could favor cash dividends. The debt levels and the interest coverage ratio in Table 34.5 show that until 2002 the coverage was always well above twice the interest payments, while debt levels were relatively high in 2000.

11   In annual reports, no information is disclosed about the board of the SAPFA. In 1997, Dutch Chamber of Commerce filings indicate that the board consisted of Choufoer (former supervisory board Ahold), Bergsma (former AKZO), Heida (investment manager at ING) and Schaafsma (De Brauw Blackstone Westbroek, Ahold's attorneys) and Cram. In the 2001 shareholders meeting, Brüggeman was appointed and shareholders asked him to step forward. He was not present and no vita was available. In response to an individual request, Ahold provided the members per April 18, 2002: Bergsma, Schaafsma, Bouma (finance professor, supervisory board SNS Reaal, Dutch bank-insurer, and member of board of a foundation holding shares of Aegon), Izerda and Brüggeman.

12   Firms with more than half of the workforce outside the Netherlands are not required to adopt the structured regime. Thus, Ahold had the right to abolish the regime already in the mid-1990s. It was a custom among Dutch multinationals to keep the regime on a voluntary basis even if they were no longer legally required to adopt it.

exercise price of the options exercised, the exercise price range of the options outstanding at year's end, the average market price of the stock, and the number of employees under the plans (in the note below Table 34.6). Compensation (salary, bonus and pensions, excluding stock options) is presented in the second and third columns of the table, broken down by supervisory and management board. To provide a perspective on the potential influence of the options, the last two columns present the net proceeds from the options exercised and the percentage of the net proceeds to the management board's cash compensation.

Through 2001, bonuses and options were based on annual income per share growth (Form 20-F, 2002). Starting in 2002, the bonuses were based on improvement in Economic Value Added (EVA). For the Dutch management board members, the target was based on improvement in EVA for the overall company. For the United States' management board members, their target was weighted 10 percent on improvement for Ahold over all and 90 percent on improvement for their respective United States' areas of responsibilities. The bonus paid for meeting the targets was 125 percent of the base salary. Stock option awards were still based on growth in basic net income after deducting preferred dividends (Form 20-F, 2002).

In 2002, the management board held about 2 million options; van der Hoeven had about half of those options. However, the management board owned very few shares, 188,000, and van der Hoeven ranked a distant third among the management board with 34,000 shares. In June 2002, the management board announced their intention to purchase shares in order to support and improve the stock price. As of September 2002, only de Raad, Andreae and Meurs had bought shares. The supervisory board held 5,200 shares with Fahlin, ICA management, holding 2,000 of those shares.

If managerial ownership with its long-term incentives was the goal of the stock option plan (overseen by the remuneration committee of the supervisory board), it was not working for top management at Ahold. Management essentially sold the shares obtained from these plans, which placed additional pressure on management to maintain liquidity and support the stock price via its investor relations (Bushee and Miller, 2005). A simple measure to gauge the incentive effects of the options exercised is the percentage of the net proceeds from the exercised options compared to the management board's other compensation (salary, bonus and pensions).[13] During the 1987 to 1997 period (Table 34.6), a period when options were available to only a relatively few in the company, this percentage for 1988 was ten percent, from 1989 to 1995 it ranged from 69 percent to 162 percent, in 1996 and 1997 it was 662 percent and 758 percent respectively.[14]

FINANCIAL ANALYSTS AND THE ROLE OF INVESTOR RELATIONS

With the analytical skills necessary to evaluate Ahold's strategies and provide objective information to market participants, financial analysts are one of the traditional gatekeepers to the financial markets. Thus, financial analysts are critical to maintain the demand for Ahold shares and enable Ahold's management to pursue its aggressive growth strategy via acquisitions. Because Brennan and Tamarowski (2000) argue that much of the investor

---

13   Net proceeds from the option exercises are based on the options exercised by all employees (not only board members). The percentage is therefore only an approximation of the percentage between the net proceeds board members received from exercising their options and their cash compensation.

14   The formula for the annual percentage is [(average monthly stock price minus average exercise price of options exercised) times (number of options exercised)] divided by [management board compensation]. Also recall that there are 150 members of the firm under the option plan from 1987 to 1997.

Table 34.6 Ahold's Board compensation and stock options

Year	Management board compensation (€thousands)	Supervisory board compensation (€ thousands)	Stock option plans									
			Number of options at the beginning of year for board and top management (thousands)	Number of options for board members (thousands)	Number of options granted (thousands)	Number of options exercised (thousands)	Number of options cancelled (thousands)	Average exercise price of options exercised (€)	Exercise price range of options outstanding at year end (€)	Average monthly stock price during the calendar year (€)	Net proceeds (average stock price - average exercise price)*number of options exercised (€thousands)	Net proceeds/ Management board compensation (%)
1987	2,643	316	0	NA	1,013	-	-	-	3.95	3.44	0	0
1988	2,501	418	1,013	NA	1,726	328	-	2.23	2.23 - 3.95	3.00	252	10
1989	2,561	270	2,412	NA	2,021	2,146	-	3.36	2.23 - 3.95	5.13	3,798	148
1990	3,178	281	NA	NA	NA	NA	-	NA	NA	4.94	NA	NA
1991	3,192	324	6,352	NA	3,242	1,826	-	4.06	2.17 - 5.05	5.99	3,523	110
1992	4,015	326	7,768	NA	2,878	1,717	-	4.19	3.28 - 6.42	6.22	3,486	87
1993	3,933	289	8,928	NA	3,481	2,149	124	4.87	4.88 - 7.35	7.02	4,621	117
1994	3,923	255	10,260	NA	3,794	1,246	23	5.27	8.12 - 4.85	7.43	2,692	69
1995	4,050	248	12,785	NA	3,928	2,318	136	5.79	9.91 - 4.82	8.63	6,583	162
1996	4,789	241	14,289	NA	4,325	3,848	293	5.30	5.81 - 16.33	13.54	31,705	662
1997	6,814	248	14,473	NA	4,861	3,134	206	5.82	14.43*	22.31	51,675	758
1998	6,014	222	15,995	NA	5,768	3,794	190	9.60	20.50	28.47	71,589	1,190
1999	6,304	238	17,778	2,048	5,745	1,912	146	10.90	23.36	32.87	41,012	650
2000	10,210	272	21,465	2,346	8,662	3,097	825	13.48	27.81	30.11	51,504	504
2001	18,658	257	26,205	3,050	9,111	3,160	495	17.87	30.03	33.82	50,397	270
2002	20,345	278	22,742	2,027	8,292	393	4,083	16.01	29.00	20.27	1,672	8
2003	10,532	1,662	27,186	758	8,979	92	3,498	10.07	25.19	6.60	0	0

Note: Table shows information on board compensation (salary, bonus and pensions) and stock option plans from 1987 to 2003. Data is collected from Dutch annual reports during 1987–1990. The annual report of 1990 does not contain information about the stock option plan. From 1991 onwards the data comes from form 20-F filings with the SEC. About 150 employees qualify for stock options in the period 1987–1997. 820 employees have been granted stock options in 1998–1999. In 2000 there are 5,000 employees that have been granted stock options. This increases to 6,700 employees in 2001. Number of options has been adjusted for 1 for 2 stock split in 1993 and 1990 and a 3 for 1 stock split in 1997. *From 1997, the annual reports disclose the average excess price of the options outstanding instead of the excess price range of options outstanding. The last three columns report the average monthly stock price during the calendar year, the net proceeds from the options exercised, and the percentage of the net proceeds to the management board's other compensation (salary, bonus and pensions). Stock price data is from Datastream and adjusted for stock splits. NA denotes not available.

relation effort is directed at analysts because of their role in information dissemination to shareholders, we first discuss Ahold's investor relations efforts and then describe the role of financial analysts.

Investor relations are crucial to convince investors of Ahold's growth strategy and analysts to follow the company. The start of a publicity offensive, part of a broader campaign to improve investor relations, was initiated by Everaert in 1990 (*Het Financieele Dagblad*, October 6, 1990). As the new CEO in 1992, Cees van der Hoeven became the driving force behind Ahold's efforts to have the best investor relations. A former Royal Dutch Shell executive, he was responsible for Shell's investor relations in London for a two year period. When Cees van der Hoeven signed his first annual report as the CEO in 1992, the corporate policy explicitly considered the return earned by shareholders. When there were significant announcements made by Ahold, van der Hoeven explicitly set aside the day to react to inquires by the investment community. 'Each Ahold executive spent the equivalent of three weeks per year visiting investors' (van der Hoeven, *Het Financieele Dagblad*, September 7, 2001). An investor relations consulting firm was retained, Rematch, the same investor relations firm that conducts the annual survey to determine the firm with the 'best investor relations' in the Netherlands.

The Rematch survey queries Dutch professional portfolio managers, analysts/advisors, financial press and private investors. The main factors comprising the scores from the different user groups are: (i) Assessment of the firm's strategy: respondents are asked whether they believe the strategy is credible/reliable, ambitious, challenging for management; (ii) Disclosure/openness: does the firm provide its (potential) investors enough information about the strategy, operations and investment decisions; (iii) Timeliness of the information.

Over the ten year period, 1992 to 2001, Ahold was ranked number one for nine years by portfolio managers, for nine years by analysts and advisors, for ten years by the financial press and for five years by private investors. While 1999 marked the pinnacle of Ahold and van der Hoeven's overall rankings, both were number one (Rematch, 1999), Ahold was never ranked lower than number three by any group over the ten year period. Similar results are obtained for 2002. To illustrate Ahold's success, in 2001, Ahold raised 2.2 billion euros within 24 hours without pre-announcements or road shows '...thanks to 16 years of investing a lot of time in investor relations' (Meurs, *Het Financieele Dagblad*, September 7, 2001). After the exposure of the accounting manipulations and fraud, 2003 and 2004, Ahold's ranking dropped substantially.

Clearly, Ahold has devoted much attention to their investor relations policy. The next question to address is how analysts perceived Ahold's strategy. For domestic and international analysts included in IBES/First Call, Figure 34.1a and 34.1b graph their recommendations for Ahold from 1993 to 2003. To facilitate a comparison with the Rematch investor survey results, we compare analyst recommendations for Ahold to the average recommendation for Dutch firms in the AEX/AMX index, Figure 34.1a. We also compare analyst recommendations for Ahold to its chosen international peer group, Carrefour and Wal-Mart, in Figure 34.1b. There were 490 recommendations for Ahold during this period. Supporting the investor relations survey results, analysts were generally optimistic about Ahold until October 2002, when on average analysts downgraded Ahold. This downgrade was before the fraud and matched Ahold's abandonment of its 15 percent growth target and its first losses in 30 years. A similar conclusion holds for analysts' recommendations for Ahold compared to its international peer group. Not surprisingly, the most positive recommendations came from ABN-Amro, Ahold's house bank, even after the bitter end, Figure 34.1a. This is in line with the multiple relations the bank had with Ahold.

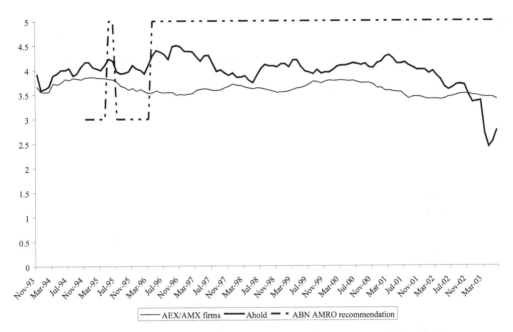

Figure 34.1a   Analyst recommendations of Ahold versus AEX/AMX firms

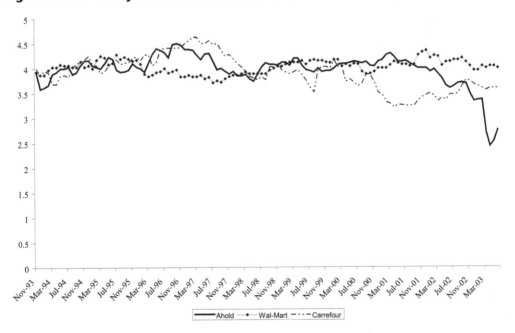

Figure 34.1b   Analyst recommendations of Ahold versus Carrefour and Wal-Mart

Note: Figure 34.1a shows the average analyst recommendation per month (5 = strong buy, 4 = buy, 3 = hold, 2 = sell and 1 = strong sell) of Ahold and other firms that were part of the AEX/AMX index. The graph shows that the average analyst opinion was positive until 2003 (with the average score above 3). The coverage begins in November 1993 and our data ends in June 2003. For ABN-Amro (the bank with the most optimistic forecasts in the IBES/First Call database) coverage starts in November 1994 and ends in May 2003. Figure 34.1b shows the average analyst recommendation per month for Ahold, Carrefour and Wal-Mart.

THE HOUSE BANK

Ahold used ABN-Amro as its main bank. The bank played an important role in sustaining Ahold's investor image via its analyst recommendations, Figure 34.1a, and financing. Nelissen, past CEO of ABN-Amro and supervisory board member, was on Ahold's supervisory board. Meurs, Ahold's CFO, was a former employee of ABN-Amro. In 1997, van der Hoeven was appointed to the supervisory board of ABN-Amro and in 2001 to its audit committee. Among Meurs, Nelissen and van der Hoeven, strong personal relations were present at the highest levels. ABN-Amro's 2002 annual report disclosed that van der Hoeven had a personal loan of 5.088 million euro with this bank (*Het Financieele Dagblad*, March 31, 2003). More importantly, ABN-Amro frequently participated in the bridge financing of Ahold's acquisitions and the debt and equity offers ultimately used to finance those acquisitions.[15]

Ahold's Strategy

Over three generations of the Heijn family, Ahold evolved from a single grocery store in 1887 to a food company with a dominant position in the Netherlands. In 1989, when family management was supplanted by professional management, Ahold was the largest food retailer. Ahold included the Albert Heijn supermarket chain and a franchise, Schuitema, supplying independent groceries. Specialty stores include Etos, a chain of drug stores, and Alberto, a chain of liquor and wine stores. Combining grocery and specialty chains, Ahold had a total market share of about 45 percent in the Netherlands. Ahold had a solid base of operations in the United States that contributed significantly to Ahold's overall sales and profits, and a small number of other European activities. Ahold operated its foreign store chains under their own name, management and local identity.

Starting in 1989, Ahold's ambition under professional management was to be in the same league as Wal-Mart and Carrefour, the number one and two internationally ranked retail companies. Figure 34.2 presents a comparison of Ahold, Carrefour and Wal-Mart's stock price performances. Ahold planned to accomplish this ambition by maintaining its dominant position in the Netherlands, developing a critical mass in the United States in order to establish synergies at the widest possible level within Ahold USA, and considering other international opportunities (Rabattu, Aubin and Botteri, 1997). Specifically, Ahold's strategy was growth via acquisitions of store chains and then continuing to operate these chains under their own name, local management and local identity.

Under CEO Pierre Everaert, the first professional manager appointed CEO in 1989, Ahold's growth objective was a ten percent annual growth in earnings per share. He also announced plans to double profits and sales every five years (*Het Financieele Dagblad*, September 9, 1992). Under Cees van der Hoeven, the second professional CEO appointed in 1992, this was increased to a 15 percent annual growth in earnings per share, 10 percent from internal growth and 5 percent from external growth (*Het Financieele Dagblad*, March

---

15   SDC New Issues Database contains data on gross spreads for 28 out of Ahold's 46 debt and equity issues. A total of $384.2 million was paid out in the 16 debt and equity issues lead managed by ABN-Amro It is plausible to assume that ABN-Amro earned a significant part of these gross spreads.

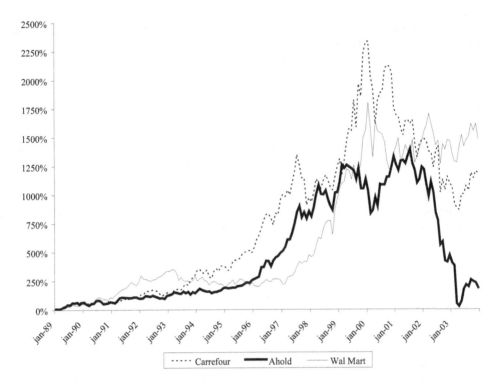

Figure 34.2 Ahold's Stock Price Performance

Note: Figure shows the buy-and-hold returns of Ahold, Carrefour, and Wal-Mart from January 1989 to December 2003. Data is collected from Datastream.

19, 1994).[16] Neither the growth rate implied by Ahold's stock price nor van der Hoeven's stated annual earnings growth rate of 15 percent was sustainable without significant acquisitions (Rabattu et al., 1997, HSBC James Capel, September 15, 2000, and Coriolis Research, 2001).

With dominance in its domestic market, Ahold pursued its growth strategy by focusing mainly on the United States with the announced objective of being the largest supermarket chain on the East Coast. In the period 1977–1995 Ahold made several medium-sized United States acquisitions: BI-LO, Giant Food Stores, First National Supermarkets, Tops Markets, Red Food Stores and Mayfair Supermarkets. In 1996 Ahold made its largest acquisition so far, Stop & Shop Companies, Inc., the largest chain in New England. With the Stop & Shop acquisition, Ahold was the fifth largest supermarket chain in the United States and close to its goal of being the largest chain on the East Coast. Continuing to implement its successful growth strategy, Ahold made its largest United States' acquisition up to that point, the publicly traded Giant Food, a Maryland-based chain, in 1998. Then, in 1999 due to concerns about potential market concentration, the Federal Trade Commission blocked Ahold's acquisition of Pathmark, a store chain in New Jersey, New York, and Delaware. This set back was a blow to Ahold's strategy of becoming

---

16   Van der Hoeven is always somewhat vague about his definition of earnings and earning per share (analysts are also confused about his definition). A working definition is one based on Dutch generally accepted accounting principles (earnings excluding goodwill amortization).

the largest chain on the East Coast. In 2001, Ahold moved south with the acquisition of Bruno's Supermarkets in Florida, Mississippi, Georgia and Alabama.

While Ahold was the dominant player in the Netherlands, it was almost impossible to penetrate the large European markets, UK, Germany or France (Perkins, 2001, and Wrigley, 2002). Europe was a gaping hole in Ahold's strategy, as it was not among the top then European retailers by sales (HSBC James Capel, November 12, 1999). When the two French retailers Carrefour and Promodès merged in 1999, more analysts started to question Ahold's fragmented European operation. Nevertheless, continuing its inclination towards fragmented and large acquisitions, Ahold Europe purchased a 50 percent stake in ICA, Norway and Sweden, in 1999 and a 100 percent stake in Superdiplo, Spain in 2000.

The developing world of Asia and Latin America provided opportunities for high growth; however the operating environment differed substantially from the United States and Europe (Coriolis Research, 2001). Beginning in 1996, Ahold expanded outside of the United States and Europe (Table 34.3). Ahold entered Latin America for the first time through a joint venture in Brazil. Ahold also entered Asia for the first time, China, Malaysia and Singapore in 1996, and Thailand and Indonesia in 1997.

Asia was by far the largest and most fragmented international market, with most food sales occurring outside supermarkets. It is unclear what Ahold's Asian strategy was. Carrefour was the top ranked supermarket chain in Asia.[17] Carrefour was the only profitable firm in this region among its international peer group (Wal-Mart, Ahold and Carrefour), which competed with Ahold in each of the countries Ahold entered (Coriolis Research, 2001). Ahold's growth strategy in Asia failed, because the short-term focus on earnings conflicted with the long horizon required to successfully enter this part of the world. Ahold withdrew from China and Singapore only three years after entering these markets in 1996, as it did not anticipate an acceptable return in the near future.[18] Ahold's remaining Asian operations suffered from the after shocks of the Asian financial crisis.

In sum, Ahold was largely unsuccessful in its global retail grocery expansion with the exception of the United States. Although Ahold operated in four continents by 1999, it was predominantly a United States and Dutch-based retailer, with 57 percent and 31.2 percent of its total sales from the United States and the Netherlands, respectively. Analysts questioned whether the fractured acquisitions in Europe, the international acquisitions in Asia and Latin America and the constraints placed on Ahold's East Coast strategy in the United States were sufficient to sustain the 15 percent growth target.

Despite the challenges it faced, Ahold turned its main attention to the food-service industry in the United States. It was a $200 billion industry that was less consolidated than the supermarket industry, with Sysco Corporation and U.S. Food Service, the top two companies, controlling less that 20 percent of the $160 billion restaurant business, the largest single segment in the industry.

Ahold entered the United States' food-service market in March 2000 with its purchase of U.S. Food Service (Maryland-based with sales of $7 billion). In December 2000, it purchased PYA/Monarch (South Carolina-based with sales of $5 billion) and in November 2002 Alliant Exchange (Illinois-based with sales of $6.6 billion). Ahold's sudden move into

---

17   We exclude Japanese chains in this ranking; while larger, they have not been successful in exporting their business model outside of Japan.

18   One analyst described this move as: 'entering in haste and then repenting later when they go wrong' (HSBC James Capel, March 20, 2000).

the foodservice industry was generally not well understood. One analyst writes: 'While this move [in the food-service industry] does open a new growth avenue for Ahold, it is a significant change in strategic directions and as such is unexpected' (HSBC James Capel, 20 March 2000). By 2002, 74 percent of Ahold's sales came from the United States, 21.9 percent from Europe, 3.4 percent from Latin America and 0.7 percent from Asia.

Ahold's Failure

In 2002 and 2003, the firm faced three violations of accounting regulations: hidden contractual obligations, manipulation through the consolidation of joint ventures and a fraud with vendor rebates.

In 2002, Ahold admitted that the firm had not disclosed several material off balance sheet obligations relating to its joint ventures. The joint venture partner in Disco, the Peirano family, was having financial problems. In 2002, the chairman of ICA Ahold went public with the shareholder agreement that showed Ahold was obliged to buy him and ICA Förbundet, the other partner, out in April 2004 for an estimated price of €2.5 billion. The annual report of 2001 did not mention this obligation of Ahold (*Het Financieele Dagblad*, October 8, 2002).

In the conference call covering 2002 first quarter results (Fair Disclosure Financial Network, June 6, 2002), van der Hoeven reported and forecasted 'pro forma' earnings growth of 22 percent and pro forma earnings per share growth of ten percent for the year. In the second quarter (Fair Disclosure Financial Network, August 29, 2002), van der Hoeven reported Ahold's first quarterly loss in 29 years and confirmed the July 17th profit warning, expected earnings per share growth would be between 5–8 percent. Finally, for the third quarter (Fair Disclosure Financial Network, November 19, 2002), van der Hoeven announced another quarterly loss and the failure of the 15 percent growth rate.

On Monday, February 24, 2003, Ahold announced that net earnings and earnings per share under Dutch GAAP and U.S. GAAP would be significantly lower than previously indicated for the year ended 2002. At issue were vendor rebates, also known as promotional allowances. Food vendors, such as Sara Lee Corp. and ConAgra Food Inc., paid rebates to U.S. Food Service for selling certain amounts of their products. U.S. Food Service booked these rebates early resulting in inflated promotional allowances. Ahold's press release gave a preliminary estimate of the effect this had on operating profits for 2001 and 2002, an overstatement of €466 million. In the end, the number was €820 million over the three year period, 2000 to 2002. The overstatements required the restatement of Ahold's financial statements for fiscal years 2000 and 2001 and the first three quarters of fiscal year 2002.

In addition, the company announced that four current joint ventures (ICA, Bompreço, Disco, Jerónimo Martins Retail) and one former joint venture (Paiz Ahold) should not have been fully consolidated in its financial statements. The full consolidation of these joint ventures was based on letters stating Ahold had control over these joint ventures. With stated control, Ahold recorded 100 percent of revenue and expenses of the joint venture and 100 percent of the net income under Dutch and U.S. GAAP, which boosted Ahold's sales and earnings (Ahold's objective was doubling sales every five years). The problem was the existence of secret side letters, known as comfort letters, nullifying the control letters. These side letters stated that Ahold was not in control of the joint ventures and were meant to 'comfort' the other joint venture partners by ensuring them that their shares would not be worth less due to the loss of control to Ahold. Commencing fiscal year 2002, Ahold was forced to proportionally rather than fully consolidate these joint ventures under Dutch GAAP and U.S. GAAP.[19]

Dutch GAAP earnings in 2000 started at €1,116 million, restatements reduced this number to €920 million and reconciliations to U.S. GAAP reduced earnings to €442 million. For 2001, earnings started at €1,114 million, restatements reduced earnings to €750 million, and U.S. GAAP reconciliations resulted in a €254 million loss. Finally, for 2002, loses started at €1,208 million and ended with a €4,328 million loss under U.S. GAAP.[20]

The supervisory board announced the resignations of CEO, Cees van der Hoeven, and CFO, Michael Meurs. The chairman of the supervisory board was given responsibility for the conduct of the management board and the affairs of the company. The company deferred its announcement of the full year results for 2002. Ahold's auditors suspended the 2002 year audit pending completion of its investigations.

Subsequent market reactions were violently; Figure 34.2 documents the drop in equity prices. The abnormal return on the day of announcement was -59.4 percent. The bond market reacted in a similar manner; in the sterling market Ahold's bonds dropped 28.3 percent and in the euro market, the bond prices decreased 27.4 percent. Standard & Poor's responded immediately by downgrading Ahold's credit rating from BBB to junk. The next day Moody's downgraded Ahold from Baa3 to B1.

The forensic audit of PriceWaterhouseCoopers documented lax internal controls and poor financial and accounting practices on the part of Ahold in the United States. A total of 275 out of 470 accounting irregularities could be related to weak internal controls. The forensic audit also showed that throughout Ahold there was a lack of knowledge about Dutch GAAP and U.S. GAAP and the consequences of management's activities as more accurately reflected in the U.S. GAAP numbers.

Deloitte & Touche, Ahold's auditor detected the problems at U.S. Food Service at an early stage. Deloitte conducted a due diligence investigation at the time of the acquisition of U.S. Food Service, 2000. Deloitte reported that the system used to record vendor allowances at U.S. Food Service was very opaque (Smit, 2004, p.261). Deloitte also uncovered the scale of Ahold's accounting irregularities as part of its 2002 year-end audit. Moreover, Deloitte & Touche was not informed about the conflicting comfort letters; they were only shown the side letters that stating Ahold had full control over the joint ventures.

Conclusions

Ahold's strategy, in combination with its weak corporate governance had a significant impact on the firms' accounting policies and its fraud. Beginning with the family and

---

19   The company also announced that it has been investigating, through forensic accountants, the legality of certain transactions and the accounting treatment thereof at its Argentine subsidiary Disco.

20   For 2001, there was a €588 million reduction in earnings under U.S. GAAP to reflect the difference between the share in the loss of joint ventures under Dutch GAAP and U.S. GAAP. This difference primarily relates to a goodwill impairment loss of €505 million in Disco; the €505 million impairment was reclassified by Ahold from the goodwill adjustment in the original statements to the joint venture adjustment in the restated numbers. There was a further €311 million reduction in restated Dutch GAAP earnings due to U.S. GAAP reporting requirements for Ahold's sale and leaseback, derivatives and options transactions. For 2002, there was a €3.2 billion charge to earnings under U.S. GAAP due to goodwill amortization and impairment with €1.85 billion from U.S. Food Service.

continuing under professional management, the family and management adopted all the defenses available to Dutch companies to obtain and maintain complete control of Ahold. The CEO, van der Hoeven, eliminated family oversight by convincing the family to sell its holdings to institutional investors. Van der Hoeven negated blockholder oversight by choosing a financing method that put voting control of the institutional investors' holdings in a foundation, whose board was strongly influenced by Ahold's management. These explicit manipulations of Ahold's corporate governance by management negated the ability of blockholders and other shareholders to monitor management on a day-to-day basis and the ability of the market for corporate control to discipline management. Again, the emphasis on management control is in stark contrast to Ahold's investor relations and its emphasis on shareholders.

This control allowed management to capture the supervisory board, which was the last institution that stood in the way of management's complete control of the company. With the dominant tradition of the management board and the supervisory board's over commitments and conflicts of interest, the supervisory board failed in its transition to a professionally managed firm with dispersed ownership. Van der Hoeven then had control of the management board, the incentive compensation system and the firm. Since management held very little of the company's stock, the incentive compensation plans with their emphasis on earnings growth aggravated the other shortcomings.

References

Agrawal, A., Knoeber, C., 1996. Firm performance and mechanisms to control agency problems between managers and shareholders. Journal of Financial and Quantitative Analysis 31, 377-398.

Brennan, M., Tamarowski, C., 2000. Investor relations, liquidity and stock prices. Journal of Applied Corporate Finance 12, 26-37.

Bushee, B., Miller, G., 2005. Investor relations, firm visibility and investor following. Working Paper, Harvard Business School.

Cadbury Committee, 1992. The Financial Aspects of Corporate Governance. Burgess Science Press, London.

Coriolis Research, 2001. Retail Supermarket Globalization: Who's Winning? Coriolis Research, Auckland.

Danko, Q., June 12, 2003. Talmende toezichthouders. Intermediair 24, 34-37.

De Jager, J., 1995. Arm en Rijk kunnen bij mij hun Inkopen doen; De Geschiedenis van Albert Heijn en Koninklijke Ahold. Tirion, Baarn.

De Jager, J., 1997. Albert Heijn; De Memoires van een Optimist. De Prom, Baarn.

De Jong, A., DeJong, D., Mertens, G., Wasley, C., 2005. The role of self-regulation in corporate governance: evidence and implications from the Netherlands. Journal of Corporate Finance 11, 473-503.

De Jong, A., Röell, A., 2005. Financing and control in the Netherlands: an historical perspective. In The History of Corporate Ownership Around the World: Family Business Groups to Professional Managers. R. Morck. (ed.), NBER, 467-515.

DeJong, D., De Jong, A., Mertens, G., Roosenboom, P.G.J., 2007. Investor relations, reputational bonding, and corporate governance: The case of Royal Ahold. Journal of Accounting and Public Policy 26, 328-375.

Demsetz, H., 1983. The structure of ownership and the theory of the firm. Journal of Law and Economics 26, 375-390.

Easterbrook, F., 1984. Two agency-cost explanations of dividends. American Economic Review 74, 650-659.

Faccio, M., Lang, L.H.P., 2002. The ultimate ownership of Western European corporations. Journal of Financial Economics 65, 365-395.

Fair Disclosure Network, June 6, 2002. Royal Ahold (AHO) Q1 2002 (conference call transcript), 1-16.

Fair Disclosure Network, August 29, 2002. Royal Ahold (AHO) Q2 2002 financial release (conference call transcript), 1-22.

Fair Disclosure Network, November 19, 2002. Royal Ahold (AHO) Q3 2002 financial release (conference call transcript), 1-18.

Ferris, S., Jagannathan, M., Pritchard, A., 2003. Too busy to mind the business? Monitoring by directors with multiple board appointments. Journal of Finance 58, 1087-1111.

Hart, O., 1995. Corporate governance: some theory and implications. The Economic Journal 105, 678-689.

Het Financieele Dagblad, October 6, 1990. Ahold relations.

Het Financieele Dagblad, September 9, 1992. Ahold ziet verdubbeling omzet, winst.

Het Financieele Dagblad, March 19, 1994. Sterker Ahold houdt vast aan hoog groeitempo.

Het Financieele Dagblad, October 29, 1999. Beleggers koesteren hun favoriet: Ahold.

Het Financieele Dagblad, January 12, 2000. Topmanager 1999 opnieuw een man.

Het Financieele Dagblad, May 16, 2001. Beleggers krijgen niet meer greep op Ahold.

Het Financieele Dagblad, September 7, 2001. Ahold haalt euro 2,2 mrd op in amper 24 uur.

Het Financieele Dagblad, October 8, 2002. Beleggers nemen Ahold onder vuur.

Het Financieele Dagblad, February 26, 2003. De val van het solide volksaandeel Ahold.

Het Financieele Dagblad, March 31, 2003. Ahold-topman fors in het krijt bij ABN Amro.

HSBC James Capel, J., November 12, 1999. Ahold: Strategically Challenged. HSBC James Capel, London.

HSBC James Capel, J., March 20, 2000. Ahold: Buying into a New Strategy. HSBC James Capel, London.

HSBC James Capel, J., September 15, 2000. Ahold: Addicted to Shopping – Acquisition of Superdiplo. HSBC James Capel, London.

Jensen, M., 1986. Agency costs of free cash flow, corporate finance, and take-overs. American Economic Review 76, 323-329.

John, K., Senbet, L., 1998. Corporate governance and board effectiveness. Journal of Banking & Finance 22, 371-403.

Organization for Economic Co-operation and Development, 1999. OECD Principles of Corporate Governance. OECD Publications Service, Paris.

Perkins, B., 2001. The European retail grocery market overview. British Food Journal 103, 744-748.

Peters Committee (Corporate Governance Committee), 1997. Corporate governance in the Netherlands: forty recommendations. Corporate Governance Committee, The Hague.

Rabattu, D., Aubin, E., Botteri, X., December 5, 1997. European Equities Food Retailing. Deutsche Morgan Grenfell.

Rematch, 1999. Investor relations in Nederland; een kwestie van geloofwaardigheid. Rematch BV report.

Smit, J., 2004. Het drama Ahold. Balans, Amsterdam.

Tabaksblat Committee (Corporate Governance Committee), 2003. The Dutch corporate governance code; principles of good corporate governance and best practice provisions. Corporate Governance Committee, The Hague.

The Economist, March 1, 1993. Europe's Enron: Ahold. 366, 63.

The Wall Street Journal, March 5, 2003. The economy: U.S. oversight board proposes to register foreign accountants.

Voogd, R., 1989. Statutaire Beschermingsmiddelen bij Beursvennootschappen, Ph.D. dissertation, University of Nijmegen.

Wrigley, N., 2002. The landscape of pan-European food retail consolidation. International Journal of Retail & Distribution Management 30, 81-91.

35 Embedding Corporate Social Responsibility into the Day-to-Day Life of Organisations: A Practical System Thinking Approach*

ROB PEDDLE, IAN ROSAM AND PAVEL CASTKA

Introduction

Corporate Social Responsibility (CSR) has become an often discussed topic of many managers in recent years. After the initial confusion of what CSR means and encompasses, a general consensus seems to emerge: that CSR is concerned with the impacts that the activities of an organisation have on the social, environmental and economic environment in which it operates. This understanding seems to set the direction for the first CSR initiatives in organisations and also for further fine-tuning of the meaning of CSR. Indeed, since 2005, a group of over 300 experts from over 50 countries have jointly worked on the international standard for social responsibility – ISO 26000 – using this understanding.

The fine-tuning of CSR, through the development of an international standard, is inarguably an important next step to enhance our understanding about CSR. Yet even without this, many organisations have decided to address and implement CSR in their own way. These implementations took different routes. Some organisations have chosen to set-up projects to address various elements of CSR (that is, philanthropy in third world countries; accounting for and offsetting carbon emissions). Other organisations targeted CSR as a strategic initiative and have chosen to profile their business in a specific market niche (that is, producing only fair trade or bio products). Yet not every organisation

---

* The material in this chapter is based on the previous work of the authors (Castka et al., 2004; Rosam and Peddle, 2004). The reader is encouraged to study this material for further examples and discussion of the approach that is outlined in this chapter.

wants to (or in fact cannot afford to) run a specific project. And not every organisation can operate in a market niche that values CSR products. What can other organisations do? Are there common things they all can do?

In this chapter we will present the case of an organisation that operates successfully yet wants to enhance its business and everyday operations by applying some focused elements of CSR; an organisation that does not necessarily want to introduce new CSR products or services and profile itself in a CSR market niche – simply an organisation that wants to do good by doing well – every day. An organisation that realises that CSR cannot be applied in isolation of the rest of the organisation. An organisation that demonstrates what we call a System Thinking approach to CSR.

The System Thinking approach to CSR promotes interdependence of different functions in organisations – action in one part of the organisation always has an effect in most others. It assumes that successful and sustainable CSR significantly impacts on, or be impacted by:

- the way the organisation understands the market and business environment in which it operates;
- the way it plans its future activity;
- the way it develops products, services, partnerships and acquisitions;
- the way it communicates to customers and other stakeholders about the way it operates;
- the way it understands its true performance and uses this to define where and how this will be improved;
- or even the way it ensures it has the right resources in the right place at the right time;
- how it works to balance the effect of customer service on the organisation's other stakeholders;
- the culture, beliefs and value systems that really determine what happens and the behaviours at all levels in the organisation.

The case study presented in this chapter will demonstrate how the System Thinking approach can be applied and used within a real organisation. We will show how organisations can bring CSR to life as a part of an existing management system. We will furthermore demonstrate that a process-based management system supports CSR implementation and how individual processes, sub-processes and procedures contain CSR elements as a natural part of business activities.

Case Study Organisation

Palmer and Harvey (P&H) are a logistics and distribution company operating solely in the UK with a turnover of approximately £4 billion with 12 sites across the country. The management system has not been subject to any specific CSR review or built to meet the principles outlined above. The system has therefore been built to help the organisation manage and control its key business processes and improve the results they achieve. The system is outlined in Figure 35.1.

| Home | Achievements | Business Management | Calendar | Documents | Policies | Request a change? | Updates | Help |

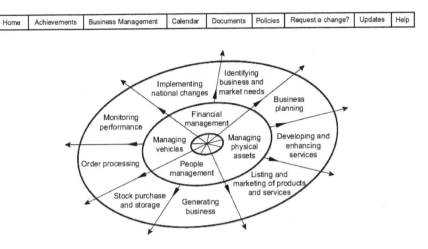

Figure 35.1 Palmer and Harvey (P&H) Management System

The management system is constructed following the best practice used to create a process-based management system. The system is made up of 13 key business processes that run across all sites including Head Office and include the activities and responsibilities of all people irrespective of level or job, from Board members to drivers to HR professionals to the Finance Director. The management system operates by focusing on these key processes:

- understanding and prioritising the needs of the different stakeholders;
- using this information to define business objectives;
- developing the required products and services;
- seeking business and creating sales;
- delivering these services;
- reviewing performance;
- learning lessons;
- implementing changes.

The processes shown at the centre of the system (Figure 35.1) define how resources are acquired, managed, used and eventually disposed of. They provide 'support' to the delivery of every process in the outer circle.

It should be noted that the management system has not only been built on best practice but also meets the requirements of ISO 9001:2000. Because of this and the fact that the system describes the whole business, not just the customer facing elements of many poorly designed ISO 9001:2000 systems, meeting CSR requirements can be straightforward. It is unfortunate that many ISO 9001:2000 systems have not been implemented effectively and best practice principles adopted for management system design, as this prevents their relatively straightforward extension to include CSR requirements.

Corporate Social Responsibility Requirements to be Applied

There are many and varied CSR requirements and technical frameworks that management need to ensure they and their organisation adhere to. The list for each individual organisation will be different, and it is the role of the senior management to define what is applicable to their operations, by reference to their stakeholder requirements.

It is not unusual for these requirements to be treated in isolation from each other, each with its own 'system' to manage, control and deliver. However, what actually ties them into the organisation are the real business processes that make up the management system. The process-based management system should bring them alive, as it does for any other standard, model or framework. The system makes them real so that all managers are capable of understanding exactly where and how the issues are addressed within the organisation and alongside all other standards or frameworks that the organisation chooses to apply. The management system should be an interpretation of the organisation and how it delivers its required results, including CSR results.

To outline how this works three example CSR requirements have been selected and applied to the P&H management system outlined above. The three requirements applied are:

- Higgs Report: which specified changes in CG based on this review.
- GRI (Global Reporting Initiative Guidelines) – a globally used tool for reporting of economic, environmental and social dimensions of performance.
- SA 8000 – a Social Accountability standard.

Applying the Provisions of all Three Requirements

It may seem a strange place to start the case study but it does prove a valuable point in understanding system thinking and how it is applied to CSR.

To demonstrate this we will look at the first requirement in each document. Each of these will then be applied to the management system to show how the requirement could be covered. The first major points made in each document are listed in Table 35.1.

Having listed the main points, the next stage is to see where these areas may or may not be being addressed in the P&H management system.

Lets Start with the Higgs Report

The Higgs requirement is that 'every listed company should be headed by an effective Board'. In the P&H system there is a process for business planning. A closer look at this process, an extract of which is shown below, shows the responsibilities of the Board in the context of the overall business planning process. The organisation does not just have a Board for the sake of it – it is there for a reason. By inserting the Board's activities into the process, which is the reality anyway, the source of the information used by the Board (inputs) and where the decisions and actions go to (outputs or outcomes) can be seen. The extract from the process is illustrated in Figure 35.2.

Table 35.1 Examples of criteria from various CSR frameworks

Higgs Report	GRI: Global Reporting Initiative Guidelines	SA 8000 requirements
Principles of good governance, Section 1 Companies, point 1 – The Board Every listed company should be headed by an effective Board. The Board is collectively responsible for promoting the success of the company by directing and supervising the company's affairs.	Economic criteria (simplified) EC1: Net sales EC2: Geographic breakdown of markets EC3: cost of all goods, materials and services purchased EC4: Percentage of contracts that were paid in accordance with agreed terms, excluding penalty arrangements. EC5: Total payroll and benefit (including wages, pension, other benefit, and redundancy payments) broken down by country or region. EC6: Distributions to providers of capital broken down by interest on debt and borrowings and dividends on all classes of shares with any arrears of preferred dividends to be disclosed. EC7. Increase/decrease in retained earnings at end of period. EC8.Total sum of taxes of all types paid broken down by country. EC9. Subsidies received broken down by country or region. EC10. Donations to community, civil society and other groups broken down in terms of cash and in-kind donations per type of group. EC11. Supplier breakdown by organisation and country. EC12. Total spent on non-core business infrastructure development. EC13. The organisation 's indirect economic impacts.	1. Child labour 1.1 The company shall not engage in or support the use of child labour as defined above. 1.2 The company shall establish, document, maintain, and effectively communicate to personnel and other interested parties policies and procedures for remediation of children found to be working in situations which fit the definition of child labour above, and shall provide adequate support to enable such children to attend and remain in school until no longer a child as defined above. 1.3 The company shall establish, document, maintain, and effectively communicate to personnel and other interested parties policies and procedures for promotion of education for children covered under ILO Recommendation 146 and young workers who are subject to local compulsory education laws or are attending school, including means to ensure that no such child or young worker is employed during school hours and that combined hours of daily transportation (to and from work and school), school, and work time does not exceed 10 hours a day. 1.4 The company shall not expose children or young workers to situations in or outside of the workplace that are hazardous, unsafe, or unhealthy.

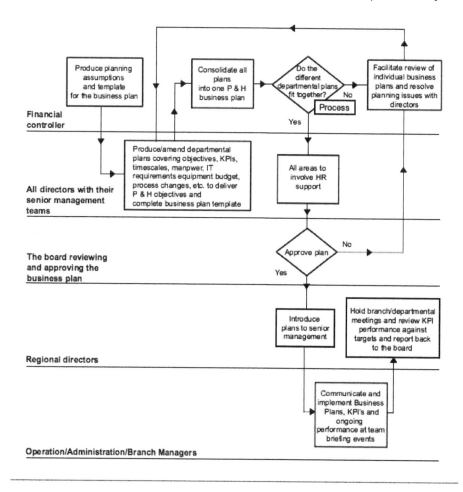

Figure 35.2 P&H Management System Extract (1)

The requirement of the Higgs Report calls for an 'effective Board' not just that one exists. To cover this point the system contains several items:

- there is a defined set of measures and KPIs linked directly to this process. The performance of the process can therefore be seen, and providing appropriate items are defined for these measures and KPIs, than effectiveness can certainly be understood and displayed;

- a monitoring performance process is also defined within the management system, which includes activities that describe how the system and its processes are audited for compliance and effectiveness. As part of this audit (of the business planning process) the auditors would check that the Board activity actually took place (compliance) and how well these activities were in 'directing and supervising the affairs of the company' (effectiveness). This auditing should not only be directed to the Board, but critically also to those who it affects. Of course how auditors do this or how well they do it is another issue but this first example does show how at least one of the requirements of the Higgs Report could be met.

So What About the Global Reporting Initiative Guidelines

The first point to make regarding these measures is that they are just measures, the results achieved from applying business processes and the activities they contain. Some are more strategic in nature and show how the system (the organisation) is performing, others are more tactical in nature and determine how, perhaps, an individual process or even sub-process is performing.

The method that was used before can be used to identify within the management system where the:

- measures originate, that is, the needs of stakeholders and other interested parties;
- measures link to the processes that deliver them;
- measures are linked to the objectives of the business;
- measurement actually takes place and is used;
- information is reported internally to initiate change and externally to show how the needs and requirements of all stakeholders are being met.

As can be seen in Figure 35.3, individual processes provide the starting point from which the performance required will be produced and hence the places to measure, based upon the needs of stakeholders. It should be noted that the GRI measures also come from the needs of stakeholders, so they are merely specific requirements defined within that

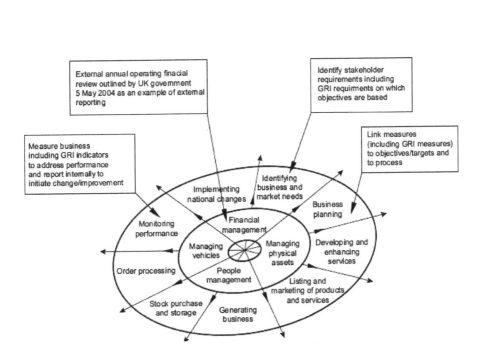

Figure 35.3 P&H Management System Extract (2)

framework and are no different from other stakeholder needs. Having set objectives and implemented activities to meet them, the performance of the organisation is measured against targets. They are then reported internally, to stimulate change, and externally to report on overall business performance to those that have a stake in the business, who may be investors, customers, suppliers and supply chain regulators. GRI measures are just like any other measure and incorporated into any other part of normal business activity. But what about something like child labour?

The SA 8000 Social Accountability Standard

The SA 8000 Social Accountability standard outlines requirements concerning how the organisation engages with potential risks associated with child labour and if it does, for example by accident, how it addresses any issues raised. The first point is that the organisation should not support child labour. If it is to be effective, this policy declaration should be part of the same strategy process that creates and deploys any policy, and not a separate unlinked statement. It should just be one of the items that the Board declares is important in the way the organisation will operate.

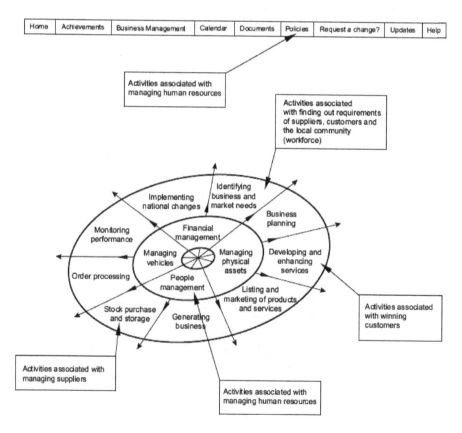

Figure 35.4 P&H Management System Extract (3)

The section of the standard then moves on to define how child labour should be handled. For P&H this could include:

- How suppliers are appointed to ensure that child labour issues have either been addressed or where they are known that the supplier has a policy in place for handling the situation in the longer term. This requirement not only relates to direct suppliers but also to second- and third-tier suppliers, that is, the whole supply chain. In some cases, this will mean tracking the supply chain across countries, continents and many organisations. As P&H are involved in the distribution of food products that originate from around the world, this is an area that certainly needs to be covered. The process that is most likely to cover this area is the one that deals with supplier appointment and evaluation, and the requirements should be embedded into the appropriate parts of this process, together with relevant measures to ensure that it is effective.
- How customers are won, which is mainly in the UK in the instance of P&H. Is child labour being used? If so to what extent and is it within the regulations laid down in terms of hours to be worked (that is, schooling requirements and other factors). These areas may well be covered as part of the process associated with sales, and checked through the auditing activities included within the monitoring performance process.
- How P&H use children, if they do (as defined locally), as part of their own workforce. In the P&H system this would be covered by policies and procedures associated with the human resource activity and embedded within the people management process.

Implementing Other Corporate Social Responsibility Requirements

The same approach can be taken with other requirements of the three documents. The system should be examined to identify where the requirement should be addressed. The process(es) should then be checked to determine whether or not it/they need(s) to be amended. Some more examples are listed in Table 35.2.

Lessons learnt

From carrying out the case study the following lessons have been identified. Firstly, if a management system is to be extended to include CSR requirements as part of its natural everyday activity, then it must be built on best practice design. It must be built from the first principle that organisations deliver their results by optimising their cross-functional process performance. Secondly, CSR requirements are built into the management system and they do not stand-alone. It is the most effective way to deliver the requirements, demonstrate the extent to which the requirements are being met and identifying gaps in performance. Thirdly, assessing CSR effectiveness should be subject to the normal business processes that describe how the system and its processes are audited. Of course, whether the internal or external auditors have the necessary skills is another matter, but auditing will be critical. Similarly, reporting against CSR requirements and the results achieved is a natural consequence of monitoring/measuring process performance and defining how

Table 35.2   Examples of process investigation requirements

Requirement	Covered in process	Questions to ask about the process and its activities
Higgs Report		
Financial reporting 1. The Board should present a balanced and understandable assessment of the company's position and prospects.	Financial management process where a sub-process addresses the need for annual reporting.	Does the annual report cover the GRI measures or those required by the UK Government requirements for a 6-monthly Operating Financial Review?
Dialogue with shareholders 1. Companies should enter into a dialogue with shareholders based on the mutual understanding of objectives.	Understanding business and market needs process where the needs of all stakeholders are sought and prioritised. In some cases, it may be decided that ongoing shareholder communication is so critical that there may even be a specific process devoted to this activity.	How are the different needs actually prioritised? Which method is used? Does a dialogue really happen with all stakeholders including those in the supply chain?
Board balance and independence 3. The Board should include a balance of executive and non-executive directors (including independent non-executives) such that no individual or small group of individuals can dominate the Board's decision making.	Business planning process where the Board's activities are carried out. Also the monitoring performance process in which auditing is carried out to assess whether any one individual is indeed dominating the Board's decision making. In the managing people process, there may even be some guidelines about recruitment of Board members and their training.	Is this defined anywhere? Do P&H have the auditing capability to assess the areas to address?
GRI – Sustainability Reporting Guidelines		
Environmental indicators	Included in the business planning process as part of objective setting and the Understanding Markets process as part of gathering information on what stakeholders require.	Are the measures highlighted part of the Key Performance Indicator reporting mechanism that is being used?
Social Accountability SA 8000		
Management Systems Policy 9.1 Top management shall define the company's policy for social accountability and labour conditions to ensure that it: includes a commitment to conform to all requirements of this standard; includes a commitment to comply with national and other applicable laws, other requirements to which the company subscribes and to respect the international instruments and their interpretation (as listed in Section II); includes a commitment to continual improvement; is effectively documented, implemented, maintained, communicated and is accessible in a comprehensible form to all personnel, including; directors, executives, management, supervisors, and staff, whether directly employed, contracted or otherwise representing the company; is publicly available.	The business planning process should include some policy decision making. This is the place in the system to promote all policies to all managers and staff. It may also appear in the people management process, as defined elements of induction and refresher training. The monitoring performance process covers auditing which assesses the effectiveness of policies in their implementation. The whole system is based on continuous improvement and the business processes describe how this is achieved.	Does such a policy exist or are the requirements built into an existing policy? Is the policy part of the auditing and internal communication regime? Is it publicly available? Does the management system cover all the areas highlighted in the SA 8000 standard.

this information is used to improve performance. And finally, if the management system has been built on the basis of key business processes, covering the whole organisation, then it should be possible to see from the system where the different CSR requirements could be embedded.

References

Castka, P. Bamber, C. and Sharp, J.M. (2004), *Implementing Effective Corporate Social Responsibility and Corporate Governance – A Framework*, British Standards Institution, London.

Castka, P. and Balzarova, M.A. (2008), 'ISO 26000 and supply chains – on the diffusion of the social responsibility standard', *International Journal of Production Economics,*, Vol. 111 No 2, pp.274-286.

Castka, P. and Balzarova, M.A. (2007) 'A critical look on quality through CSR lenses – key challenges stemming from the development of ISO 26000', *International Journal of Quality and Reliability Management*, Vol. 24 No. 7, pp.738-752.

Higgs, D. (2003), *Review of the Role and Effectiveness of Non-Executive Directors*, Department of Trade and Industry, London.

Peddle, R. and Rosam, I. (2004), 'Finding the balance', *Quality World,* Vol. 16, pp.18-26.

Rosam, I. and Peddle, R. (2004), *Implementing Effective Corporate Social Responsibility and Corporate Governance – A Guide*, British Standards Institution, London.

Rosam, I. and Peddle, R. (2006), *Auditing for the 21ˢᵗ Century*, British Standards Institution, London.

36 Istiqbol Dilnoza: A Corporate Social Responsibility Study of a Micro/Small Business in Tashkent

ROWAN E. WAGNER

Introduction

The company Istiqibol Dilnoza (ID) was born out of a catering business plan for the Young Entrepreneurs program at Westminster International University in Tashkent (Uzbekistan) developed by Dilnoza Wagner during the summer of 2006. Two weeks prior to graduating from the program, Ms. Wagner received her first major catering job with the National Training Business Center in Tashkent, which provided the capital and clients she needed for the initial startup of her catering service.

Over the following months, with support of family in the form of dishes and service ware, Dilnoza's Catering grew rapidly, averaging at least one event per week for 50 plus people. Bootstrapping the profits into new equipment, service sets and staff uniforms, and focusing the menu and sector on halal niche events such as coffee breaks for conferences, small local gatherings and, at times, wedding celebrations, she built a stable, small family-oriented business. However, responding to positive legal changes in support of small enterprises and the need to find a less physically labor-oriented business, she opened a small holding company (Istiqbol Dilnoza) using the profits from the catering service to pay the registration fees and to build a treasure chest for her next enterprise venture; selling cosmetics. One day she noticed that there was a very popular Turkish Cosmetics line (Golden Rose) being sold in almost every bazaar (market) by people with no understanding of the product and no customer service orientation and she came upon the idea of opening a small shop that would be customer focused in terms of product knowledge, friendliness and access to samples, something no other cosmetic shop or bazaar vender in Tashkant offered. On November 10, 2006, Dilnoza opened the first Yasmeen Cosmetics, carrying primarily one line (Desert Rose) of decorative cosmetics and other beauty items such as facial sponges, clippers and tweezers. By the February of 2007, the shop had expanded to include three lines of beauty products: Desert Rose (Turkey),

Black Pearl (Russia) and Lander (USA). However, in March of 2007, the landlord of the shop decided to break the one-year contractual agreement and pressured the company to either purchase an alternative shop located next to the current shop (owned by the same landlord), seek alternative premises in a different part of the district or close down. Not having the ready capital to purchase the larger place, an alternative smaller location was found to reduce the held inventory and to keep the established client base. The landlord sold the larger shop and occupied the smaller shop with his own drug store. After negotiating with the new owner of the larger shop, Yasmeen was reopened, and the small shop was closed. The shop began adding newer product lines to meet customer demands and the new operation costs, as well expanding the services to include an onsite cosmetologist, a manicurist and two hair stylists.

Like most micro and small business operating in Uzbekistan, Istiqbol Dilnoza's community support or social responsibility was not an inherent activity beyond Islamic traditions such as feeding the poor or doing some good work during the period of Ramazan (Ramadan), meeting obligations to the Mahalla (community association) (Animova 2007), or supporting the local Akim's (mayor's) office's presidentially-decreed theme (such as 2007 being the 'Year of Social Protection'). However as the business began going through various stages of growth and challenges, the need to establish better control of resources use and brand identity emerged. With the realization that no strategy and no real control of the business could occur without truly defining the business through a vision, mission and values framework, Istiqbol Dilnoza began the process of developing these critical frameworks with the participation of all staff members. This was a very hard process because micro and small businesses in Uzbekistan do not understand the need for these key business tools, and do not engage employees in the process of defining the business unless they are key (normally male) family members, so initially the staff was reluctant to fully engage in the process as they had very little understanding of the importance. However, with persistence, coaching and drive, a mission, vision and value statement which incorporated core elements of what both the staff and management saw as the business now and in the future was developed.

VISION STATEMENT

Our vision is to be one of most successful agents of change through delivering the best quality health, beauty and food products in the markets we serve, in a manner that proactively balances the human, financial and environmental needs of present and future generations.

MISSION STATEMENT

Istiqbol Dilnoza mission is to be positive agent of change through:

- dedicating our business to the pursuit of social and environmental change;
- creatively balancing the financial and human needs of our stakeholders, employees, customers, franchisees and shareholders;
- proactively ensuring that our business is ecologically sustainable, meeting the needs of the present without overly compromising the future;

- meaningful contribution to local, national and international communities in which we trade, by adopting a code of conduct which ensures caring, honesty and justice;
- tirelessly working to narrow the gap between principle and practices especially in areas dealing with equity and the rights of women and children;
- actively engaging our workplace, employees in the creation where fun, passion and caring a part of our daily lives in the execution of our business.

VALUES STATEMENT

We believe that it is the responsibility of every individual to actively support those who have human rights denied to them or those that have been marginalized.

We believe that a business has the responsibility to protect the environment in which it operates locally and globally and to support the growth of local low-impact producer communities who supply use with natural ingredients and accessory products.

And our company aims to ensure that these values are inclusive in all policies and actions of our employees regardless of location globally.

(Istiqbol Dilnoza 2007)

Based upon the values, mission and vision, and operating under the basic premise that Istiqbol Dilnoza is not just a small enterprise but a 'political citizen' in the community, which implies active participation in making a positive difference (Drucker 1993, p.155), there are four basic focuses of the current Corporate Social Responsibility (CSR) strategy; governance, employees, customers and community.

Governance

There is often a big discrepancy among small business and regulators in Uzbekistan in the area of transparency in conducting business according to local and national legislation. A case in point is the use of the bank transfer for conducting payments to suppliers, venders and others. Uzbek law stipulates that all major payments to raw material and product suppliers to business must be done via bank transfer, minor payments of less than five minimum salaries (about US$54) may be made in cash (Law on Currency Regulation 2004). This does not provide a lot of flexibility for most micro and small businesses to operate legitimately, especially when you factor in low levels of trust in the banking sector by most people due to problems of delayed payment processing and the general perception by many people that the government can confiscate 'at will' funds deposited in any Uzbek bank. Though this had occurred in the past, it was mostly to large-scale businesses and very little evidence exists to indicate that this practice has been used against micro and small businesses.

To be both in compliance with government regulations and ensure that venders are paid in a timely matter; Istiqbol Dilnoza has taken proactive measures to build transparency and compliance into its supply chain. This is done by firstly selecting only companies that are willing to provide products and receive payment via bank transfer. This was initially very difficult as many venders wanted only a cash payment plan and those venders who did do business via bank transfer had too general a product line or required a minimum order that was beyond most small business's operating budget. But, over time and through building trust with venders, as well as the increased pressure of the Uzbek government through legal action against non-compliant businesses and better laws that made the transfer system more business friendly (such as a three-day maximum transfer processing time limit and insurance mechanism), more venders, with a larger range of better quality products that fitted within the brand image and values of Istiqbol Dilnoza, became available. Also, the company worked with its local bank and venders to develop simpler and more transparent mechanisms that increased efficiency thus reducing processing costs for the businesses and increased business for local banks as other businesses became aware of the services offered. The result was a win-win situation for all: businesses saved money that could help buffer their small profit margins against swings in business cycles (as in our case) and inflation, and the bank increased both its reputation and service portfolio of business.

Another aspect of good governance was to ensure that the government tax inspectors and monitoring government bodies adhered to the laws as well. The presumption of Istiqbol Dilnoza was that if it complied with the laws then the representatives of the government must as well. Knowing that predatory practices can undermine a business and ultimately the community it operates in as resources are wasted in the form of lost revenue diffusion (taxes and lost jobs crated by the business and through its value chain), the founding management developed strong links to mid-level and senior government employees in several key ministries and local government. This was done knowing that predatory practices often occur at a low level where official pay is sub-par and that because of silo effects between government offices and between levels of government administration, key decision-makers are often unaware of problems and victims of such practices do not want to voice problems for fear of retribution or fear of having their illegal activities exposed, such as selling of contraband or unregistered goods.

In addition to maintaining good relations with key government officials, the management team is proactive in environmental scanning. This is done through reading biweekly updates of tax and custom codes, watching local business news programs and engaging in the local chamber of commerce activities such as round-tables, trade shows and monthly meetings. It was through these activities that a hotline was set up to the Akim's office to report offenses committed by rogue inspectors, the staff used in the early days of operations. Upon reflection this was actually very risky because in the beginning many people thought the hotline would be just a façade and that those reported may inflict retributive damage upon the person or business who reported them. The first use of the hotline was when an attempt was made by a local inspector to extract an illegal fine. The inspector was reminded of the process, shown the codes that must be adhered to when inspecting (a copy of all essential laws are kept on the store premises as are the appropriate operating certificates). The inspector pressed on with the request for unofficial remuneration. The inspector was informed that the sum of money requested was not available at this time and after a heated discussion the inspector relented vowing to return the next day to receive the money or else there would be problems. After an intense internal discussion it was decided to use both the hotline and bring this matter up with other people in both the Akim's office and the Department of Tax Inspections within the Ministry for Foreign and Economic Affairs. For the safety of the employees it was decided that, until the issue was resolved, the store would be closed and each employee given an equivalent of a weeks' pay, to help them out over the following days.

The call was made and a formal report was filed against the tax inspector. To prevent any serious damage the store was cleared of high-end items and all the windows and doors were double locked. The following day the management received a call to come to the local tax office with our financial documents. Fearing that a process was started that would lead to losing the store, there was a brief fit of frantic activity and some last minute calls to inform ministry contacts but the management was reassured that everything would be alright. Upon arriving to the local tax office, the management team was met by the inspector, his supervisor, a representative from the Akim's office and a representative from the Ministry for Internal Affairs. Everyone assembled in a small conference office and, in view of all, the store documents were reviewed by both the local inspector and his supervisor. During the review several questions were asked of the management team on specific entries, which the management team answered, often quoting a current tax code book that they brought with them. After three hours, the officials declared no discrepancy could be found and asked the Istiqbol Dilnoza management if they wanted to press formal charges against the local inspector. After a discussion with all parties, the management team decided not to press formal charges, however an official letter about the offense was written and placed in the local inspector's work file.

Though the incident ended further attempts by the local tax inspector and other local government inspectors, for several months following the incident unfounded rumors about the quality of the products or that the store was closing permeated throughout the neighborhood, resulting in a short-term loss of some of the customer base and of a key employee.

Employees

With the understanding that in a service-oriented business sales staff are critical in all aspects of ensuring customer satisfaction and loyalty, ensuring that the employees are treated with fairness and are given opportunities to share in the rewards generated by their efforts is essential. Added to this understanding is the reality that, in micro and small businesses, human resources budgets are often very limited or non-existent and many micro/small business owners become virtual prisoners in their business. This can ultimately impede the development of the business or may degrade the owner's quality of life resulting in health problems or a loss of will to keep the business going. Istiqbol Dilnoza, from its inception, has looked to build into its culture the practice that employees should not be hired for the job that currently needs to filled, but for their potential to take on greater responsibility and gain greater rewards as the business grows and that every employee has worth and should be valued within the organization. Added to this is one of the key missions of the company to address equity imbalances that currently exist for women in terms of their economic viability, potential for rewarding careers and recognition of their contribution to their families and communities. When recruiting, the company actively looks to employ women who been denied these opportunities because of limited access to higher education, early forced marriages or the loss of economic support due to divorce or spousal neglect. Once employed these women are given not only a fair base wage, but are given opportunities to earn bonus money on a daily basis (depending on the gross daily sales) and on-the-job and formal training in workplace skills such as communication, critical thinking, teambuilding, conflict management and good business practices. These are not normal practices for micro and small business in Central Asia who often see employees a means to an end for profit making,

Istiqbol Dilnoza does this for two reasons. The first is that these activities directly contribute to the financial income of the business, because these are the activities that build better customer relations and add flexibility and fun to the organization. The second is that these skills improve their future marketability should they decide to leave or if the company should fail in the future, making it less likely that they would regress into their former lifestyles that add burdens to their families, communities and society as a whole. The negative risks in this practice is that the return on investment in terms of time and effort can be very limited since those employees who gain these skills and a higher level of self-efficacy can (and some have) move on to other jobs, which creates more costs in terms of the hiring process. However, even with the loss of some employees, including one key management trainee, these activities have added to the growth of the business in terms of client loyalty and a relatively stable core staff that has contributed with new ideas to improve operational efficiency and the viability of building the first local master franchise model in Uzbekistan.

In addition to fair pay and training, the company provides either a free or subsidized on-site lunch for the staff, which is a custom of most business operating in Uzbekistan. Because customer flow cannot be determined and due to the fact that the shop has a relatively small staff, having a ready meal is a low-cost solution that meets the needs of both staff and clients and allows for team building and organizational culture.

Lastly, on issues related to pay, having an employee payroll is a priority even if it means management receives less or no pay after operational expenses and other financials commitments are settled. Though this scenario has not yet occurred, it does reinforce the long-term company commitment to the employee which has been reciprocated in terms of motivation and commitment, and in reality has not affected the management as the key members of the management team have a secondary source of income or substantial financial reserves.

Customers

The health and safety of our clients is paramount. This is not just common sense good business practice, but also because key founding members of the company have medical backgrounds and have personally had bad experiences with poor quality personal hygiene products sold in the region, and also because an effective consumer safety system does not exist in Uzbekistan at present. So every product which is sold in Yasmeen World of Beauty or ingredient used in Dilnoza's Catering products is purchased through venders that have some level of basic safety testing and governmental approval, and all products and ingredients are randomly tested using lot quality assessments and a reliable private laboratory. Though this has added significant costs and burdens on the management and staff, it has allowed the company to weed out venders whose products could damage the image of the company and affect the customer loyalty base which has an inherent belief that the products sold to them will not cause them harm. To offset the costs associated these activities; the store has added some of the costs on to the price of the higher-end products aimed at clients who are not price sensitive and has worked with larger venders to make it their best practice in terms of being more competitive and building longer-term store/clients bases. In the cases where the company has discontinued selling products due to potential quality assurance concerns and there is a strong customer demand, the staff of Yasmeen's World of Beauty consult and educate the customer base about potential health risks and provide sources of reliable information for the customer to explore, such as consumer and scientific research organizations within Central Asia and the former Soviet Union and in some Western countries as well. This helps the customer build better consumer decision-making skills and reinforces the customer service commitment of the organization. This has resulted in the slow but steady migration from customers buying our low-end products to buying more higher-end products with the knowledge that some of the cost includes ensuring their health and safety.

Community

As mentioned earlier, community-oriented CSR is based primarily on religious and political imperatives, often with no linkages between what a business does and what type of community activity it is involved in. These activities are often focused on roads, community meals or sports. However, in Istiqbol Dilnoza, the company has worked with both religious and community leaders in order to identify activities that are linked with its primary customer base, namely women and to some extent children. Taking a cue from major cosmetics brands, the company has purposely chosen to provide limited material support (such as cosmetics and toys) to women and children undergoing cancer treatment and also works with causes that are helping to improve the treatment process for women and children in Uzbekistan. This is done to both promote the connection of the service and products of the company and because this area of medicine is one of the most under supported in the country.

Cancer treatment can be a harsh and disfiguring process for the patients and often disheartening to their families who must watch loved ones suffer, often in poorly kept and understaffed facilities that contain only the bare essentials. So, any material support, whether it is a television, a VCR, radio or personal gift to a patient is well received by all. By linking company CSR activities, such as giving beauty baskets to women undergoing chemotherapy or toys and bath products to children undergoing treatment, to key religious or government holidays such as Ramadan or Women's Day, it meets both a community-felt need and the company brand-building objective with very little upfront cost. And this can bring in long-term rewards such as increasing the customer base from the recipients, their families, medical facility staff and their friends who have received word-of-mouth marketing; a positive moral feeling for the employees involved in the activity, which strengthens and reaffirms the company's values and their commitment to the company; and the management's feeling of self-worth within the community. All of this has been observed during the last year through the motivation and commitment of employees and also through new customer surveys.

Recommendations for Others

Given that there are so many contextual factors that influence a micro or small business's ability to be successful or to implement a CSR strategy, it is not easy to definitively state one or even a couple of recommendations that would have the same positive affect when used each time. This is true especially in the context of Uzbekistan which has many of the characteristics left over from the Soviet period, such as a highly regulated society and a focus on centralized systems and bureaucracy; creating a culture where having the right documents is more important than actually executing any policy. This has led to large gaps between having laws and regulations that support business and actually allowing business to work effectively in providing goods and services that are in demand by the local population. This often creates barriers to enterprise development or going beyond trying to survive because the gap creates an environment where predatory practices such as rent seeking, protection racketeering or anti-business practices such as over-regulation and red-tape can thrive, thus reducing any incentive for individuals to become entrepreneurs.

However, having said this, currently no business, including Uzbek businesses operating in today's highly competitive and globalized world, can afford not to have a CSR strategy in order to be really successful, especially micro and small businesses which work at the community level. This is because consumers now have access to more information and choices in terms of products and service and are willing to exercise their right to buy elsewhere or not buy at all. Elements of the strategy should include activities and processes such as good governance that both increase efficiency in operations, which leads to lower costs, and building better relations with external stakeholders, such as local government and/or customers. Activities undertaken should be linked to what the business does in terms of services and product, building in benchmarks that can help identify the effectiveness of the activities in terms of the benefits received by the business and the group or individuals the CSR activity is aimed at assisting.

References

Animova, M. (2007) Aspects of CSR SMES and Other Business Practices in Mahallyas of Uzbekistan (unpublished paper, Westminster International University in Tashkent).
Drucker, P. (1993) Post Capitalist Society (Oxford, Butterworth-Heinnman).
Istiqbol Dilnoza (2007) Company HR Manual (Tashkent, Uzbekistan).

37 *Lessons Learned from Washington State's Sustainable Business Program*

KIMBERLY GOETZ

Introduction

Fifty years ago, it was possible to own and operate a profitable business without giving any thought to sustainability. Fifty years from now, that will not be true anywhere in the world. Businesses today have started to pay attention to the connection between sustainable practices and their company's long–term health and profitability. To assist businesses in our state improve their environmental, economic, and social performance, the Washington State Department of Ecology spent considerable time, money, and staff resources to create the 'Sustainable Washington' program.[1] This case study reviews the impetus for creating a new program, some of the program development challenges, and an explanation of how and why Ecology staff made some key decisions.

Background

Ecology is the state agency responsible for enforcing Washington's environmental laws. Beginning in 2001, Ecology adopted a new strategy for reducing hazardous and solid waste in Washington State. The agency's '30-Year Vision for Beyond Waste' states, 'We can transition to a society where waste is viewed as inefficient, and where most wastes and toxic substances have been eliminated. This will contribute to economic, social and environmental vitality.' (Ecology 2004, 3). While Ecology understands that we can never truly eliminate waste from human society, the Beyond Waste Vision reminds us that significant reductions are possible.

---

1   'Sustainable Washington' is a working title for the program. A final name will be chosen after the pilot program is complete.

Sustainability and Corporate Social Responsibility

'Sustainability' and 'Corporate Social Responsibility' ('CSR') are terms that are sometimes interchanged. However, we view them as slightly different concepts: CSR is a subset of sustainability and is the means by which we attempt to measure sustainable practices. The impacts of sustainable practices are expressed in terms of the 'three legs of sustainability': environmental, economic, and social effects. CSR is the method by which those effects are quantified and reported.

The differences between sustainability and CSR might best be explained through an example. Say a land mine manufacturer stops using toxic chemicals in its manufacturing process and final product. The company writes and distributes the appropriate reports about that improvement. The company might 'score' well from a CSR perspective: both the new manufacturing process and use of the final product will have a smaller effect on the environment. However, the production of land mines, toxic-free or not, is not a sustainable process because it has significant negative social and economic effects.

This is why we view CSR and sustainability as two sides of the same coin: related but not identical. A business can adopt sustainable practices but fail to quantify the effects of those practices through the appropriate CSR tools. A business can also fulfill all its CSR reporting obligations while still being involved in unsustainable practices. To date, our focus at Ecology has been on sustainability first and CSR second. While both are important, we believe changing behavior by encouraging sustainability is the most essential activity.

Development of a Sustainable Business Program

In 2004, Ecology adopted an extensive Beyond Waste plan incorporating five separate waste reduction initiatives and 64 specific recommendations (Ecology 2004, 57–9). To implement part of this plan, Ecology's Hazardous Waste and Toxics Reduction Program began to develop a program to help businesses be more sustainable. The intent was to develop a program that would provide financial incentives and technical assistance to participating businesses. Ideally, the program would be equally attractive and helpful to all businesses in the state regardless of business size, industry, or location. A team of Ecology staff convened, assigned areas of responsibility, and engaged the assistance of environmental consultants.

Ecology's team members reviewed information on 35 environmental programs and research from across the United States and the European Union.[2] After reviewing the information collected by staff and contractors on each program, we realized programs fell into two categories: programs emphasizing regulatory compliance and programs focused on going beyond regulatory requirements. Both approaches have merit. A compliance-centered program would help keep the agency's focus on its primary purpose: to enforce the state's environmental regulations. In contrast, a 'beyond compliance' approach might be more effective at protecting the environment. Getting businesses to do more than is legally required could help avoid future problems. However, this type of program would

---

2   Ecology staff performed the EU research and focused on academic research and papers related to small businesses and corporate social responsibility issues.

exceed the agency's legal authority and could only work on a voluntary basis. While environmental leaders might enroll in a voluntary program, those businesses with the highest environmental risk probably would not.

When faced with the question of which type of program to create, the Ecology team came up with what we believe is a new approach: do both. Ecology's program would use existing authority to establish a new compliance-based program. As a business successfully completes the compliance portion of the program, it can easily transition into the 'beyond compliance' portion of the program, the initial stage of which would require just a little more work than is already required by law. The second stage would also offer incentives for doing that extra work.

To create this new combined program, Ecology originally decided to follow an existing compliance-based model known as the 'Environmental Results Program' ('ERP'). The state of Massachusetts developed ERP to address industry sectors that are low enforcement priorities: industries with large numbers of small businesses, each producing a relatively small amount of waste (such as dry cleaners or photo processors). Following this model, Ecology would develop and mail informational materials to all businesses in a selected industry. The materials would explain (in plain English) what the law requires and how the business can implement 'Best Management Practices' ('BMPs'). Each business would review the materials and either (1) certify that it is 'in compliance' with the applicable environmental regulations, or (2) submit a 'Return to Compliance' plan explaining how and when it will fix its problems. Instead of visiting—or attempting to visit—all businesses in a given sector, regulators would choose a statistically significant sample for random spot checks. This approach has seen impressive results and has expanded to 15 other states addressing 17 different industrial sectors (Dyke-Redmond 2006, 4). Although ERP addresses the needs of small businesses, we hoped it could be adapted to meet the requirements of large businesses as well.

For the beyond compliance portion of the program, we felt none of the programs currently in existence addressed our specific vision for the program. One voluntary program we looked at closely was 'EnviroStars.' Started in King County, Washington in 1995, this program has since expanded and is currently active in five counties surrounding Puget Sound (EnviroStars 2008). The program has over 600 participating businesses in a variety of industries, each recognized for their environmental performance using a rating system of two to five stars. The EnviroStars program has been successful, but some aspects of the program made it inadequate for Ecology's purposes. Of primary concern was that the EnviroStars program is only available to businesses that generate hazardous waste. We specifically wanted to design a program that would be available to all businesses, not just those that use toxic chemicals.[3] Another concern was that the EnviroStars model requires an on-site inspection prior to a business being enrolled in the program—a requirement far beyond Ecology's workload constraints, even with significant additional funding and legislative authority. Finally, we were concerned that the various EnviroStars recognition levels did not have many associated incentives. To a large extent, doing well in the EnviroStars program must be reward enough because there are few if any financial incentives. Given these limitations, we kept the EnviroStars model in mind, but began to develop a new program instead.

---

3   In fact, the Bill & Melinda Gates Foundation at one time inquired about EnviroStars certification, but was turned away because it did not meet the program's requirement of being a generator of hazardous waste.

Because the Beyond Waste plan heavily emphasized financial incentives, we knew that had to be a significant focus of the program. However, we were consistently challenged by the question, 'Incentives for what?' In other words, how do we logically tie a specific financial incentive to a corresponding environmental outcome? Other important questions we asked included, 'How do we know we aren't rewarding businesses for taking actions they would take even if there were no incentive? And how do we ensure participating businesses continue to make environmental progress?' The last thing we want to do is inadvertently create a negative inducement—that is, making an incentive so attractive that a business will allow its environmental performance to worsen in order to later 'improve' and receive a reward for that improvement.

To address these issues, the team designed a voluntary program containing five leadership 'tiers.' Each tier requires an increasing level of environmental performance but offers more financial incentives. The exact nature of the environmental improvements we were seeking was relatively vague at this point, but we hoped our stakeholders would help us refine the program.

Stakeholder Involvement

After the team finished an initial draft of the program, the next step was to convene a stakeholder advisory group. The group contained representatives from environmental advocacy groups; business advocates; local, state, and federal government entities; and representatives from small, medium, and large businesses. The advisory group initially recommended reducing the number of leadership tiers from five to three, suggested Ecology look to the EnviroStars program as a possible program model, and encouraged Ecology to consider that a single program would be unable to meet the differing interests and needs of both large businesses and small businesses.

After the first meeting of the stakeholder advisory group, the Ecology team worked with contractor staff to conduct additional research. Two of these research activities proved to be the most informative: a survey of Washington residents regarding hazardous substances and a series of small focus group meetings. Both of these investigations provided tremendously valuable information.

In February and March 2007, a research firm conducted a telephone survey of Washington State residents about their knowledge about toxic chemicals. Respondents were asked a series of questions about their attitudes, beliefs, and awareness of toxic chemicals. We found the following results surprising:

1. When asked, 'What kinds of concerns (about toxic chemicals) have you had?' the most popular response was 'Animals/pets ingesting; getting sick' at 21 percent of respondents; the second most popular response was 'Children ingesting; getting sick' with 18 percent (Jull 2007, 19). While we were unable to reach any conclusion about why more respondents were concerned about their pets than their children, the concerns about accidental exposure and poisoning were clear. We believe this information could help us find new ways to motivate business owners to change their behavior by emphasizing the health aspects of pollution, instead of just the environmental effects.

2. When asked where they might find information about hazards related to lead (especially lead-based paint), there were clear economic and social differences.

Respondents who classified themselves as 'white' and those reporting high incomes were more likely to rely on the Internet for information or not seek information at all about lead-based paint. In contrast, respondents who did not classify themselves as 'white' or who reported lower incomes favored talking with a store clerk or asking a government agency for information (Jull 2007, 29). These differences between social and economic groups helped team members understand that we might need to adopt a variety of communication techniques in order to reach everyone in our target audience.

3. While we expected to see some differences between cultural groups, we were surprised by some of the survey's findings.

Latinos and Spanish-speaking respondents were much more likely to agree that 'concerns about the dangers of toxic products are exaggerated.' In fact, 67 percent of Spanish-speaking respondents and 48 percent of Latino respondents *somewhat* or *strongly* agreed with the statement. By comparison, 15 percent of non-Latino respondents agreed with the statement, as did 25 percent of non-Spanish-speaking respondents (Jull 2007, 32).

This result further confirmed that there are sometimes significant differences between social, economic, and ethnic groups. In order for a new statewide environmental program to be successful, it must include strategies for reaching all potential program members and communicating with them in a way that speaks to their concerns in a culturally sensitive manner. It must also incorporate research about cultural beliefs and attitudes in the program design phase.

The focus group data also proved unexpected and informative. Participants were selected from auto body shops, cabinetmakers, and painters—industries that use large quantities of spray paint. Participants were randomly chosen from a list of businesses and assigned in groups of approximately six people. Unlike previous stakeholder outreach efforts, the focus groups took place without Ecology staff present. Only the consultants knew who participated and what each respondent said. There was no direct link to any participant, so they would feel free to discuss their true opinions (including any environmental problems they have) without fear of inspections or penalties from Ecology. The contractor paid each participant $100 for their time.

The most common concern expressed by focus group participants was about exposure injuries to themselves, their workers, and their family members. More than one participant shared a personal story about how they were injured by toxic chemicals. Each of the focus groups expressed a consensus that avoiding injuries to their workers was of primary importance. This was very helpful information for Ecology to have and confirmed the results of the telephone survey.

The contractors were also pleased with an unexpected outcome of these focus group meetings. They observed industry competitors discussing their mutual problems and concerns. With no direction from the group facilitator, participants would share information and discuss various products and techniques. Many participants expressed their need for these types of discussions with others in their industry in order to learn about better products and techniques. To paraphrase the message that emerged from multiple focus groups: 'I'd use the best product for the environment if I knew what it was. But I don't have time to figure that out. Just tell me what I should use and I'll use it.'

In addition to information about specific environmental programs, contractor staff also researched various possible financial incentives and, to a lesser extent, non-economic incentives. The list of possible incentives that Ecology might offer includes:

- reduced or refunded fees;
- reduced regulatory requirements;
- an expedited permitting process;
- being assigned a single contact person at Ecology (instead of separate contacts in each program area);
- a grant or low-interest loan program;
- training;
- networking opportunities;
- reduced insurance premiums;
- employee discount incentives (such as membership fee waivers at a local gym).

It is important to remember that even 'non-economic' incentives are inherently financial. Training, networking opportunities, and research into environmentally preferred products are services that can be provided by government for a relatively small investment. If a small business tries to obtain those same services in the private sector, they will likely find them cost prohibitive. While we may not traditionally think of training or a networking breakfast as an 'economic incentive,' it may prove invaluable to participating business owners.

After all this research and analysis and two more stakeholder advisory group meetings, Ecology finally had a basic program design. The program would have two phases: an 'ERP' phase focused on compliance and an 'EnviroStars' phase based on leadership. Both the ERP and EnviroStars models would be adapted to fit Washington's needs. Training, technical assistance, and other 'non-economic' benefits would be offered for the ERP phase of the program, while financial incentives would be reserved for businesses going beyond compliance. While the program would be open to all businesses, it would be tailored to the needs of small and medium-sized businesses.

Key Challenges

All organizations face limitations on available resources, trouble gaining support for new ideas, and unexpected setbacks. The Ecology team experienced all of these challenges when it began to implement the Sustainable Washington program. We believe the following challenges were the most significant and informative.

The first challenge the development team encountered was resistance to setting up the stakeholder advisory group. Ecology usually tends to make decisions based on consensus, but some people involved in the process were uncomfortable relying on outsiders to achieve that consensus.

The team took two steps to overcome this discomfort. First, we emphasized that this group was an 'advisory' group. The fact that the group only had the authority to recommend—not make binding decisions—helped alleviate fears that Ecology was abdicating too much control over the development process. Second, we recruited a wide range of stakeholders to be part of the advisory group, including many members who were personally known to Ecology. The team made sure that environmental groups, business advocates, business owners, and government officials all had a seat at the table and were equal members of the advisory group. The inclusion of strong environmental advocates helped alleviate concerns that business representatives would design a program that would do little other than reward participating businesses.

The second key challenge encountered during the development process was identifying which industry sector or sectors would be best for testing the new program. This was especially challenging because there were competing priorities for which sector deserved attention first. The team considered the following options:

1. *Should we focus on a sector with a large number of facilities or a small number of facilities?* Picking a sector with a large 'universe' might make it easier to detect environmental changes due to program participation, but picking a sector with a small universe will make it easier to involve stakeholders and provide personal assistance to program participants. A smaller universe might have a better chance of producing positive results, but might be harder to prove those results. Unfortunately, without substantial evidence of the program's worth, it would likely be discontinued.

2. *Should we focus on a sector that is a significant contributor to environmental problems?* It would be ideal if we could determine which chemicals are polluting Puget Sound so we could focus our attention on the sector or sectors that use those chemicals. Unfortunately, we found that the data regarding which chemicals are present in our ecosystem are either not available or are insufficient for decision-making purposes. We also found that regulators generally lack knowledge about which industries use which types of chemicals.

3. *Should we focus on a sector that has already been addressed in another state?* Dry cleaners, photo processors, and auto body shops are all examples of industry sectors where similar program materials already exist. It would require minimal work to customize the materials produced by other state governments and make them applicable to businesses in Washington State. However, many of the sectors where materials already exist are those with large numbers of facilities (like dry cleaners and photo processors) or those where Ecology has already done extensive outreach (like auto body shops).

Finally, the third key challenge encountered during the development process was gaining sufficient internal support. This was of special concern when beginning the site visit process for the ERP phase of the project. Many Ecology stakeholders were adamantly opposed to the original inspection methodology. The original method required more than 400 random baseline site visits and a second round of 400 random visits approximately a year later, after the facilities have returned their certification forms.[4] Even though Ecology staff weren't performing the inspections, managers expressed significant concerns related to workloads. The managers asked the program development team to make sufficient alterations to the program to result in 150 site visits in each round of inspections.[5]

Eventually, we decided to focus on auto body shops for our pilot project. This gave us a universe of 975 facilities in the pilot project, an industry with a pre-existing level of trust, good connections with trade groups, and a direct impact on the environment.

---

4   At a 95 percent confidence level and margin of error of five percent.

5   The team will accomplish this by reducing the confidence level and increasing the margin of error.

This sector also gave us an excellent opportunity to evaluate worker health issues. Auto body shops have high numbers of workers injured due to isocyanates exposure. 'Isocyanates are the raw materials that make up all polyurethane products' and are a cause of occupational asthma and other exposure disorders (OSHA 2006). Implementation of BMPs at participating auto body shops should not only reduce the environmental harm from these chemicals, but should also result in fewer workers being injured by these chemicals.

Program Evaluation

The ultimate success or failure of the pilot project may lie with the final program evaluation. Ecology is not unique in its need to prioritize budgets and workloads based on which programs produce demonstrable results. When making decisions about which programs will receive priority, real outcomes are only as good as the proof they rely on. Ecology needs to measure the 'real world' success of the pilot. To determine what data could be used to evaluate whether the program was successful, we asked two questions: 'If I am a small business owner, what sort of data do I have easy access to?' and 'If I am a legislator, what questions do I want answered before I agree to fund this program?' Data that did not answer one or both of those questions did not receive further consideration.

The team determined there were three criteria for program measures. First, data must be easy to obtain, either for a business owner or for Ecology staff to gather directly from the source. Second, measures must provide meaningful information about the 'real world'; theoretical and extrapolated data should be kept to a minimum and actual measures should be used whenever possible. Finally, measures must be requested in just a few questions. Ecology will use the information provided by firms and collected by project staff to evaluate whether the program's achievements are sufficient to justify the expense involved with implementation. The specific categories of data to be analyzed include:

1. *Workers' compensation rates.* 'Workers' compensation' is a state-run insurance program that covers workers injured during the course of their employment, irrespective of whether they have other health insurance coverage. To verify that BMPs have a beneficial effect on worker health, we plan to review accident rates and workers' compensation premium ratings for the auto body industry in Washington State. To date, we have been unable to find any similar environmental program that uses worker injuries as a performance measure. We believe this will be a powerful evaluation tool and is well worth the effort needed to obtain the data. It will be very persuasive to decision-makers and stakeholders, telling us about both the economic and human effects of the program in very real terms.
2. *Pollution released to the environment.* Like other environmental programs, the primary focus of the Sustainable Washington program is the amount of pollution discharged to the environment. Firms participating at higher levels of the program will report which BMPs they implement and the amount of wastewater and stormwater runoff they discharge each year. From this information, Ecology will estimate the firm's reduction in air and water pollution. Firms may also be required to report expenses for mitigation and conservation activities (such as the cost of installing low-flow restroom fixtures). While extrapolating program effects is a less-desirable method

than direct measurement, we believe it will be too onerous for businesses to try to measure their contribution to water pollution. In this case, we placed a higher priority on information that businesses could easily obtain. Avoiding extrapolation was less important.

3. *Waste generated.* Washington law requires Ecology to work to reduce the production of both solid and hazardous waste in the state. The Sustainable Washington team believed reducing the amount of waste generated was a logical extension of that requirement. Both solid and hazardous waste are of significant concern to the long-term health of our environment. Hazardous waste requires special handling and treatment and poses a significant danger to the environment and to human health. Solid waste not only requires careful long-term management, it is also resource-intensive. We are rapidly running out of landfill space, and incinerators are not always a safe option.

   Participants in the Sustainable Washington program will be required to report the amount of solid and hazardous waste they generate each year. We expect that businesses implementing BMPs will report decreases in both types of waste because BMPs should help participating companies be more efficient. However, it is possible that we will see participating firms actually *increase* the amount of solid waste generated. Depending on the specific BMPs implemented, participants may initially reduce their generation of hazardous waste by changing products or methods to eliminate toxins, but not reducing the waste generated during the business activity in question. While the total amount of waste generated may be similar, we may initially see a transfer from the 'hazardous waste' category to the 'solid waste' category. Our data analysis techniques will need to consider this possibility and, if it occurs, we will need to carefully and clearly explain why an increase in solid waste generation actually demonstrates program success.

4. *Resources consumed.* Today, more than ever, it is vital that each of us be more aware of the amount of resources they consume. This is especially important in the United States with its disproportionately high rate of resource consumption. Current state law does not restrict any company's use of natural resources, including energy. As is typical in the United States, resource consumption is controlled by the market. However, there is a growing understanding that we live in a world of finite resources which must be managed and used efficiently. We believe it is important that Ecology take the lead in emphasizing the need to use less, utilize wisely, and recycle what's left. In the leadership portion of the program, we plan to examine consumption rates for raw materials (especially energy), recycling rates for wastes generated, and business expenses for mitigation, such as installation of low-flow bathroom fixtures, biofuel conversion costs, or purchase of carbon offset credits.

5. *Facility compliance.* While the Sustainable Washington pilot program is voluntary, its initial focus is on regulatory compliance. Even if the final program is unable to demonstrate a direct benefit to the environment, it might still be successful if it helps businesses achieve regulatory compliance. A firm that properly manages its hazardous waste, minimizes its stormwater runoff, and installs the proper equipment on its air emissions equipment is less likely to have a serious environmental accident. Compliance rates are also a 'hard' number that agency decision-makers and legislators can quickly understand and evaluate. It is important to not view compliance rates as the sole important measure, but instead to remember that compliance rates are an indirect measure of environmental performance.

Finally, although not part of the initial pilot program, Ecology hopes to collect data in the future that demonstrate the relationship between sustainable practices and profitability. Many businesses, both small and large, are interested in the 'triple bottom line' approach to accounting. We believe that we may be able to incorporate this type of program measure in the future, after we have substantiated the program's worth through other metrics.

Recommendations

Based on the research and work done over the last two years, I would make the following final recommendations to anyone developing an environmental or CSR program for small businesses:

1. *Human health effects may be the most effective motivation for behavior change.* Business owners who are unconcerned about sustainability and CSR issues might alter their behavior in order to prevent illness or injury to themselves, their employees, their family members, or their pets. As noted above, the primary concern of both survey respondents and focus group participants was avoiding injury. Although information about human health effects is not typically part of environmental programs, it may be this information that will persuade a business owner to change their behavior when other information fails to persuade them.
2. *Programs to change behavior must be appropriate and relevant to the target audience.* Regulators and other organizations must give special consideration to ethnicity, socioeconomic status, business size, and typical industry practices. It is vitally important to remember that not all audience members are concerned about the same things or will be persuaded by the same arguments. For a program to be successful, it has to communicate to its audience in a way that the audience is predisposed to understand. This might require preparing materials and conducting workshops in multiple language or defining problems and solutions very broadly so that many cultures and socioeconomic groups can find common ground.
3. *Sustainability and CSR tools currently available are practical only for larger businesses.* There are a number of CSR and sustainability programs currently in existence that are designed to meet the needs of large businesses. Ecology spent substantial time reviewing programs like USEPA's Performance Track, various private-sector programs, and the Global Reporting Initiative and Facilities Reporting Project. Unfortunately, we found that all of these programs fell short when it came to addressing the needs of small and medium-sized businesses. Small and medium-sized businesses do not possess the time, resources, or expertise to utilize these tools and programs. Small business owners may be experts in their field, but very few of them are in the field of environmental consulting. Firms that are large enough to have dedicated environmental and CSR staff typically don't need government assistance in these areas. The type of businesses Ecology specifically tried to target is those firms that might like to improve their sustainability and be better corporate citizens: the businesses that can't use the tools currently available. The owner who is struggling to make ends meet and is spending each night after supper at the kitchen table trying to pay bills is a person who does not have time to develop an Environmental Management System.

In many respects, it is that well-meaning small business owner who may pose the greatest environmental risk because they lack the planning and resources on-hand to deal with an unexpected crisis.

4. *Internal communication and consensus is vital to program success.* While this may seem like an obvious point, it should not be underestimated. Any program of similar magnitude will undoubtedly involve numerous staff members, possibly from different sections or units of an organization. It is easy for details to 'fall through the cracks' and for misunderstandings to arise. Establish a clear communication plan from the very beginning and make sure you follow it.

Conclusion

If I could give environmental regulators just one lesson about the businesses they regulate, it would be that businesses aren't *trying* to pollute our environment. Pollution is an unintended byproduct of the system in which we live. Business owners are just like everyone else. They breathe the same air, drink the same water, and want the best for their children. They don't get up in the morning trying to think of new ways to poison our ecosystem.

What they do think of when they get up in the morning is, 'How am I going to make payroll this week?' If you can't help them answer that question, they probably don't have time to deal with you. If you want them to do something or change their behavior, make it fast and easy to understand what you want and why it's important. Sometimes that means doing some of the work for them up front; but in the end, you'll spend less time fixing the mess.

References

'About the EnviroStars Cooperative.' *EnviroStars Cooperative* [website], <http://www.envirostars.org/about.cfm>, accessed 20 May 2008.

Dyke–Redmond, T. (13 November 2006), *Technical Research for Ecology's Toxics Reduction Incentive Program (TRIP): Review of Environmental Results Programs.* Boston: Industrial Economics, Incorporated. Unpublished.

Jull, P.M.M. et. al. (April 2007), *Department of Ecology Reducing Toxic Threats Statewide Household Survey.* Bellingham, Washington: Applied Research Northwest, LLC. Unpublished.

'Safety and Health Topics: Isocyanates.' *U.S. Department of Labor Occupational Safety and Health Administration ('OSHA')* [website], (updated 22 November 2006) <http://www.osha.gov/SLTC/isocyanates/index.html>, accessed 9 May 2008.

'Summary of the Washington State Hazardous Waste Management Plan and Solid Waste Management Plan (Publication No. 04–07–022).' *Washington State Department of Ecology* [website], (November 2004) <http://www.ecy.wa.gov/pubs/0407022.pdf>, accessed 17 May 2008.

38 Esh Added Value: A Case Study in Indigenous Corporate Social Responsibility

RIHAM RIZK AND SUZANNE GREGORY*

Introduction

Esh Group is one of the largest construction groups operating in the North East of England. Their headquarters are situated within a few miles of their original home in the village of Esh Winning, County Durham, with numerous offices throughout the North East region and Leeds.

Strongly committed to the local economy and the community which provides its direct workforce, 'modern-day' Corporate Social Responsibility (CSR) activity has been on the company's agenda since its inception over three decades ago. The company has always had an active policy of procurement in the North East and adjacent regions, recognising the impact this has on the local economy, the natural environment and its own bottom line. With increased interest and awareness in corporate responsibility and citizenship from a variety of stakeholder groups, 'Esh Added Value', the Group's collection of varied and innovative community schemes, have gained notoriety and strategic importance.

This unique case study chronicles the CSR journey of a home grown Small and Medium-sized Business (SME). Data has been compiled from a number of corporate documents and communications as well as interviews conducted with senior personnel at Esh Group, providing a rare look into the motivations, expectations and experiences of a local organisation on the road to sustainable development.

THE REGION

The North-East of England is one of the nine official regions of England and comprises the combined area of Northumberland, County Durham, Tyne and Wear and Tees Valley.

* The authors gratefully acknowledge the access granted to employees, resources and facilities at Esh Group and the financial support of the Department of Business Enterprise and Regulatory Reform (BERR) through the Knowledge Transfer Partnership scheme, without either of which, this project would not have been feasible.

The principal city is Newcastle-upon-Tyne, with the largest city in terms of population being Sunderland. As well as its urban centres, the region is also noted for the richness of its natural beauty, which includes National Parks and coastline, as well as its historic importance and two World Heritage Sites.

With a regional economy of £38.8bn, the North-East has the lowest GDP/capita in England. With a per capita GDP at 80 per cent of the EU average, the North East of England is particularly challenged by the decline of traditional industries and a weak enterprise base. On 10 December 2007, the European Commission approved a Regional Operational Programme for the North East of England for the period 2007–13. The Operational Programme falls within the framework laid out for the Regional Competitiveness and Employment Objective and has a total budget of around €750 million. Community investment through the European Regional Development Fund (ERDF) amounts to some €375 million, which represents approximately 3.5 per cent of the total EU investment in the United Kingdom under the Cohesion Policy 2007–13 (European Commission, 2007).

The shipbuilding and coal mining industries that once dominated the area suffered a terrible decline during the second half of the twentieth century. With the help of the EU's Operational Programme, as well as national schemes and programmes, the area is now re-inventing itself as an international centre of art and culture, scientific research, technology and popular nightlife. Northumberland and County Durham, both being largely rural, base much of their economies on farming and tourism. These programmes aim to make a difference by enhancing competitive and innovative businesses, supporting the research base and helping enterprises to exploit the scientific strength of the regional research institutions. The programme aims equally to enhance the economic performance of the weakest communities in the region.

THE COMPANY

In the 1970s, three enterprising men founded new businesses in the village of Esh Winning in County Durham. Tony Carroll and Jack Lumsden formed Lumsden & Carroll Construction and Michael Hogan formed Deerness Fencing. By the 1990s, Jack and Tony had recruited Brian Manning (now Chief Executive), Andrew Pickett (now Finance Director), Fred Gressman and Steve Bass. In the mid-1990s, the businesses were merged to create what has become 'the largest indigenous construction company operating in the North East of England' – the Esh Group.

Although not explicitly a corporate mission, 'Leading the Way in Constructing the Region' is at the heart of the Esh culture. It is a statement repeated in various forms of corporate communications and features prominently and prevalently on the website. Similarly, 'the largest indigenous construction group operating in the North East of England', pride in their local beginnings, is reiterated throughout.

> Our roots are firmly in the region. Group headquarters are sited within a few miles of our original home in the village of Esh Winning. Our founder directors continue to be actively involved and we have a rich tradition of 'growing our own'; many of our senior team first joined as trainees and apprentices and we continue to recruit and nurture young people.
>
> (Brian Manning, CEO)

The Esh vision statement echoes the same message of responsibility and commitment and identifies their key stakeholder priorities.

We see construction as dynamic, exciting and rewarding. We are passionate about continuing to progress and develop; delivering satisfaction and reward to our clients, our people, the public we serve and the region in which we live, work and play.

(www.eshgroup.co.uk)

Esh Group currently employs over 1,000 people and in the last five years, turnover has more than trebled to over £150m in 2007. In keeping with their stated commitment to the local economy, Esh Group spent over £109 million with suppliers and staff in the North East region (£87 million supplier spend), with over £51 million within County Durham (£40 million supplier spend).

It is not surprising then, that in 2003, when the Group left their humble beginnings in the village of Esh Winning and relocated to their new corporate headquarters, Esh House in Bowburn, that they felt a sense of responsibility to the community they were leaving behind, as one of its largest employers.

The Initiatives

COMMUNITY

Esh has continued their sponsorship of Esh Winning Football Club, as a means of maintaining commercial and social links with their home village of Esh Winning for the five years since the move. Esh's first non-philanthropic CSR initiative, 'Fit for Employment', was launched in 2004. It is a work-related learning programme for young people about to leave school. The scheme was launched at a local school, Deerness Valley Comprehensive, with a larger than average number of graduates falling into the NEET group (not in further education, employment or training). The programme provides meaningful work experience to Year 10 and 11 students and is designed to get them 'work ready', with the promise of a full-time job to 20 per cent of the participants if they complete the entire programme and achieve five GCSEs. To date, since its inception, 70 young people have been employed on a full-time basis by Esh Group and over 600 students have participated in the intensive work experience programmes.

Anne Lakey, Head Mistress of Deerness Valley, now called Durham Community Business College, talks passionately about the impact the Fit for Employment scheme has had on her school.

Initially, there was some resistance from the School, as it is actually quite disruptive to timetabling to have different groups of 10 students out of classes for one week at a time and there was a fear that it would negatively affect student performance. On the contrary, it has had the exact opposite effect! At our school, truancy has almost ceased as young people see real value in attending. GCSE results, measured by both quantity and quality of grades achieved, have improved by over 10 per cent. The percentage of students staying in education and training or gaining proper employment has risen from 75 per cent to a staggering 98 per cent; that means the horrendous percentage of 25 per cent of students who 'dropped out' has been reduced to barely two per cent, in just three years. One senior member of staff still refers to it as 'the magic dust that was sprinkled on our students'.

In 2005, having become involved with the Government's agenda on 'worklessness', Esh developed 'Fit for Employment Again'. Worklessness, a term that applied to a range of people with a range of issues, is often associated with disadvantage, and costs the North East alone approximately £2.5 billion per year (Office for National Statistics, 2008). To date, Esh Group has worked exclusively with those with multiple disadvantages. The programme started with over 40 participants – ex offenders, ex-drug users, long-term unemployed and those with a combination of these and other personal issues.

The concept was simple. Esh Group wanted a new NVQ Level 2 (equivalent to five GCSEs) in conjunction with a regional college, to be delivered in 26 weeks, rather than the standard two years, to the participants, in order to get them 'work ready', that is, qualified, trained and motivated. This required engagement with and support from a variety of stakeholders of the various local councils, the North East Employers Coalition and in particular, Job Centre+, who were required to exercise discretion and flexibility with the Benefits System.

After an induction period, the numbers were reduced to the 16 who started their NVQ. Ten eventually completed the course and qualified, obtaining CSCS cards, which allowed them access to employment on construction sites across the country. seven of these were employed by the Esh Group.

The following year, Tyneside Cyrenians, a charity that provides shelter and support for homeless people, needed an extension to their premises in Newcastle. Esh bid for the construction work on these premises, and then offered to reduce the tendered amount if the Cyrenians provided some of their people to carry out the works. In addition to being paid for the work, they would also be offered training and mentoring to enable them to complete an NVQ Level 2 similar to the Fit for Employment Again scheme.

13 candidates started the programme which created so much local interest that it was featured on the BBC's Look North programme three times as it followed the progress of the candidates. By Esh standards of delivering tangible results, the scheme was another success story. The Cyrenians have their building; seven 'self-builders' completed the scheme and qualified; two 'graduates' were employed by the Esh Group. Five 'graduates' were subsequently employed by Tyneside Cyrenians as the maintenance team for their property portfolio.

The project aimed to give service users real work experience and a life changing opportunity. The skills developed by the participants proved to be the key to a new life and helped them to 'get back on track' by giving them a sense of pride, raised self-esteem and a realistic chance of future employment. Tyneside Cyrenians have since established their own training centre to develop further clients and continue training for their 'graduates'.

Future Business Magnates

As a result of the close relationship with Durham City Local Strategic Partnership and Brian Manning's Chairmanship of the Economic Regeneration Group, 'Future Business Magnates' was born. This year-long competition, the first year of which was launched by Sir Bobby Robson in September 2005, involved eight schools in and around Durham City.

Each school worked closely with a different company based nearby in a competition to find the 'Future Business Magnates' of the North East.

A team from Esh Group worked with a group of Year 8 students at Fyndoune Community College on their plans to create a healthy eating retail operation and campaign. Regional newspaper, The Northern Echo, ran updates on the challenges facing the teams and printed League Tables after each submission was judged. The competition has fired young peoples' imaginations, encouraged competitiveness between the schools, fostered great links between them and the businesses involved and raised awareness among parents and staff of the opportunities of enterprise and business. The Fyndoune Community College Team, mentored by Esh Group, were the first winners of this competition in 2006. This innovative project has now completed its third year and a team from Dunelm Property Services, is currently partnered with pupils from Park View School in Chester-le-Street.

ESH CHARITABLE TRUST

In November 2005, the Esh Group announced it had established a Charitable Trust worth £1million. 'The Esh Charitable Trust' would run for at least five years during which time the Group intended to donate approximately £200,000 annually into the Charity. The Trust was intended to reflect the culture and values of the company; that of a local business which cares about its people, its community, its marketplace and its region. Given that reinvestment, in the North East was a long-standing principle at the Esh Group, it was now putting its money where its mouth was.

The specific objectives of the Charity would be to fund 'good causes' in the North of England such as:

- environmental work – including protection, education and awareness;
- provision of skills and training to young people and disadvantaged people;
- supporting local communities.

A range of different awards values have been made annually since the Trust's establishment. To date (2007), the Trust has awarded £274,377 [£117,452 (2006) £136,925 (2007)] in support of a number of projects throughout the North East.

Austin Donohoe, non-executive chairman of the Esh Group, explained the motivation:

> The Trust is a structured way of reinvesting in the community – a fulfilment of the vision and commitment we have, both as a business and as individuals, for our region. Our ambition is that this Charitable Trust will underpin and further the efforts of those who share our ideals and principles. Construction is not usually regarded as glamorous – but we at Esh know how essential, exciting and rewarding our efforts can be. It would be nice to think that this character could be reflected in the projects which are chosen for support by the Trust – a champion for unsung heroes perhaps?

Grow with Esh

In 2007, the Trust launched a flagship project designed to instigate a wide range of positive outcomes using the focus of a horticultural project in schools across the region. Through

'Grow with Esh', £20,000 was distributed between 20 middle and secondary schools from Northumberland to Teesside and westward towards Hexham and Weardale, and £5,000 prize money was shared between the four prize-winning schemes.

The scheme was a great success: innovative school learning was promoted, derelict school environs were rejuvenated, community links were forged and commercial social enterprises established. In early 2008, the project was promoted to over 800 primary schools in the region, with the competing cohort of 20 schools based as far afield as Cornhill on Tweed in the North and Saltburn on Sea in the South.

ENVIRONMENT, HEALTH AND SAFETY

Prior research into social and environmental reporting suggests that industry membership appears to be significantly related to the type of disclosure, with employee information being most important in industries where health and safety considerations have traditionally been issues of concern, that is, cement and ceramic production (see, for example, Belal, 2001; Rizk et al., 2008), with employee assistance programmes, absenteeism and turnover, and health promotion all being significantly related to industry membership.

It is also noted by the literature (for example, Imam, 2000; Deegan, 2002) that environment-related disclosure tended to be concerned with favourable social performance, such as energy conservation and recycling rather than with activities detrimental to the environment and organisational legitimacy, that is, pollution emissions and governmental fines or non-compliance penalties. Furthermore, 94 per cent of disclosure was purely descriptive and six per cent was non-financially quantified. No disclosure was financially quantified. As suggested by Ingram and Frazier (1983) and supported over the years by numerous empirical studies, descriptive information is monitored and controlled less rigorously than financial information, indicating that managers have considerable choice as to the environmental information they wish to disclose.

The following section briefly overviews a few Environmental, Health and Safety initiatives at Esh.

Environmental Policy

Esh are currently working towards the achievement of the stringent environmental standard of ISO 14001 for all companies within the Group. Several employees have achieved NVQ Level 4 in Environmental Management and every aspect of the business and operations are continuously being examined. Purchasing and operational strategies and policies for both site and office activities are scrutinised and amended as necessary; waste management, energy and resource utilisation are rigorously reviewed and revised in light of the stated commitment to the objectives of long-term sustainability and carbon neutrality.

Bardon Esh Recycling, a joint venture company, ensures that 80 per cent of waste materials from the various Esh sites are recycled, as well as recycling 70,000 tonnes from other construction companies across the region. The recycling plant is located on Teesside, where materials are sorted then re-used directly or recycled and used in new processes. The volumes of green waste which Sones Landscaping generates are composted and re-used on landscaping projects.

Introduction of Sustainable Energy Companies

Esh Energy was launched in early 2008 as a joint venture company between Michael Hogan and Esh Group. The business will explore and develop opportunities for sustainable energy generation. The formation and development of a company which focuses on wind power energy generation, Pure Renewable Energies, at the beginning of 2008 is a key first move in this strategy. Green Energies, a specialist plumbing company involved in developing green technology and installing environmentally-sound systems, joined the Group in 2008 as a subsidiary of Bartram Walker.

The new national standard for sustainable design and construction of new homes was launched in December 2006. The code rates the home as a whole by measuring its sustainability against nine categories of design. The code uses a one to six star rating system to communicate the overall sustainability performance of a new home and sets minimum standards for energy and water use at each level. It is intended to provide information to home buyers and to offer developers a tool with which to measure performance.

Mindful of the changing marketplace, green agenda and energy supplies and pricing, we will be seeking considerable synergy throughout the Group between Esh Energy, Green Energies and Dunelm Homes' sustainable housing project and beyond.

Health and Safety Policy

Throughout the Esh Group, the management of risk, the prevention of accidents and the avoidance of ill health are crucial. Promoting and disclosing safe working practices and the maintenance of a safe working environment at all times, is paramount in this industry sector. Esh have developed a measure of health, safety and environmental Key Performance Indicators (KPIs) using a scoring system from one to five. This is derived from site inspections and differs from the three core areas of construction activities, supporting documentation and environmental issues. Site inspections measure how well project teams are implementing health and safety management as the inspections are based on observations of what is physically happening on site. The three reporting areas are maintained separately to ensure that any weaknesses are recognised immediately and that effort and resources are directed to where they are required.

In 2006, Esh Group were awarded the Young Apprenticeship pilot programme to develop the new BTech qualification in Construction and the Built Environment. Esh has delivered new insights into the process as the first organisation which is not a school, college or training provider to be awarded this type of scheme. CITB Construction Skills and the Health & Safety Executive have also supported the programme, helping to find practical solutions for young people experiencing real situations in a hazardous industry.

The Motivation

It is a matter of debate as to whether the policies in place at Esh regarding the Environment and Health and Safety are truly voluntary. The industry is a highly regulated one with stringent standards in regards to environmental management and employment standards. There is little disagreement, however, that the community-based initiatives and schemes developed by Esh are as innovative and commendable as the statistics are sobering: 4.35m people in workless households, including 1.8m children. Is that the motivation...simple altruism? Not according to senior executives at Esh.

> *Let's consider the industry we are in..Construction – not a sexy industry, not the industry you want your child to join, perhaps? Well it's a wide and diverse industry with lots of opportunities and a great many career paths available. Some of these paths do not require 'brain surgeons' and do not require qualifications that are beyond the reach of many ... the industry needs leaders, professionals, senior and junior managers, craftsmen/tradesmen, labour and support staff. Like most industries, it has high qualifications at one end and lower qualifications at the other end. And from the work we have done on Fit for Employment Again, it is clear that a mixture across the spectrum, that for a multitude of reasons, have ended up 'labelled'. So perhaps there is something here for our industry, not to provide the main source of new recruits, but another net to cast. I'm not going to pretend it is easy, I don't think it's for every contractor, certainly at this time it may limit a company's work opportunities. It is only one of a number of ways you can recruit. Probably one of the hardest, but worklessness is a societal issue, an expensive one that requires the support of many different groups and organisations if we are going to tackle it.*

> (Phil Young, Director of Customer Services)

Reiterating the message of the 'business case' or enlightened self-interest, Brian Manning, CEO adds:

> *It's not altruism. We are acutely aware of our responsibilities to our employees and our region, but there are commercial reasons why this makes sense for us. It works both ways. We seek to empower individuals so that they work confidently to support our corporate aims and objectives and that they in turn are fulfilled and invigorated by association with our company.*

> (Brian Manning, CEO)

Awards and Awareness

The unique range of heartfelt, home grown CSR initiatives, collectively termed 'Esh Added Value', quickly caught the attention of a wide range of organisations from academia and business to government and media. In 2005 alone, Esh Group received two Big Tick Awards from Business in the Community (BiTC), media coverage on the BBC and local press and an awards ceremony dinner at 10 Downing Street for the work done with Fit for Employment, referred to by then Prime Minister Tony Blair as 'the mother of innovation' in CSR schemes.

Since its inception, Esh Group has had an active policy of procurement in the North East and adjacent regions, recognising the impact this has on the local economy, not only in terms of employment, but also the size of its carbon footprint. It is widely held that in a rural county, such as Durham, local trading and CSR have significant regional economic impact, but it is a matter of academic and practitioner debate as to what that impact is and how best to measure it (see, for example, Sacks, 2002; MMU, 2004). In 2007, wanting to maintain and develop further its position as a leader in local trading and CSR assist other companies in following suit, Esh embarked on a two-year research project in conjunction with Durham Business School. The project aims to develop and implement a model for business engagement and to demonstrate the value of trading locally, encompassing public and private sector procurement and corporate social responsibility via:

- auditing public sector and other large customer procurement practices;
- reviewing tendering processes at Esh Group;
- liaising with local organisations on the development and progress of the LM3 North East Delivery Programme including work with Durham City Council on defining the local multiple;
- investigating the role of CSR locally, it's contribution to the local economy and how to influence others to adopt best CSR practices;
- benchmarking Esh Group against other comparable organisations (CSR and LM3);
- developing, piloting and implementing a replicable model for local procurement;
- working with supply chain to introduce best practices;
- providing evidence of the local multiple.

It is anticipated that the project will result in the following tangible benefits for the Group:

- increased business from local sources through partnership working;
- improved assessment of local economic impact through use of LM3;
- improved understanding of local authority procurement practices;
- increased understanding of the benefits of CSR;
- efficient tendering processes to be developed;
- improved relationships with supply chain and customers;
- improved company profile through increased recognition for CSR initiatives and local leadership on CSR.

The Challenges Ahead

Construction in the UK accounts for just over five per cent of UK Gross Value Added (GVA). In 2002, output from the industry in the UK was estimated at £83.6 billion according to the DTI. The output of new work and repair, maintenance & improvement (RM&I) is divided into ten key sectors. New work accounts for 53 per cent of construction with RM&I the remaining 47 per cent. The largest type of construction work is commercial activity which accounts for 19 per cent of output, followed by private housing RM&I and private non-residential RM&I. Public sector construction activity accounts for 24 per cent of output whilst housing related activity accounts for 36 per cent.

Looking at new work specifically enables a breakdown of activity by three sectors – residential building, non-residential building and civil engineering. Non-residential activity accounts for 56 per cent of new work and was valued at £22.6 billion in 2001. Residential activity accounts for 26 per cent and was valued at £10.2 billion and civil engineering accounts for 18 per cent and valued at £7.1 billion. Total employment in the construction industry was 1.537 million in 2001 of which, just under 1 million workers, or 63 per cent were employees with the remaining third self-employed (Blake et al., 2004).

There were 168,123 contractors operating in the construction industry in 2001 according to the DTI. The majority of firms in the industry are extremely small. Forty six per cent of contracting firms have one employee while 75 per cent of firms have three employees or less. Britain, by developed country standards, has a relatively small number of construction firms operating in the industry. It is worth noting that this is a slight underestimate as the DTI includes only those companies registered for VAT. The ABI, which covers firms registered for VAT and PAYE, estimated there were 192,400 firms in 2001. The industry is characterised by a large number of small firms and very few large firms, with around 90 per cent of firms classed as micro, employing less than ten workers, as shown in Table 38.1 below. While micro firms account for the majority of enterprises, they typically account for around a third of employment. Large firms in the UK, on the other hand, account for 20 per cent of employment.

The DTI makes an adjustment for sub-contracting to ensure no double count in calculating output shares by organisation size. In 2001, the share of output accounted for by micro firms in the UK was 26 per cent compared with a 34 per cent share of employment. This suggests that micro firms are less productive than large firms.

Table 38.1   Size of UK construction firms

Number and % of Contractors by Employment Size Band in 2001		
Employment Band	Number	%
1	77,926	46.35
2-3	50,653	30.13
4-7	22,455	13.36
8-13	8,044	4.78
14-24	4,920	2.93
25-34	1,782	1.06
35-59	999	0.59
60-79	354	0.21
80-114	304	0.18
115-299	433	0.26
300-599	129	0.08
600-1199	68	0.04
1200 and over	56	0.03
Total	**168,123**	**100**

Source: adapted from Blake et al. (2004); DTI Construction Economics and Statistics.

Gross output data breaks new construction activity into three main sectors – residential, non-residential and civil engineering. UK construction is much less dependent on housing activity than its European counterparts, such as France and Germany. Conversely, non-residential building which includes commercial, industrial and public (non-housing) construction is relatively more important in the UK, accounting for 56 per cent of new work. In France, for example, non-residential construction accounts for around a third of construction output. Over the past 20 years the share of new non-residential work of total new work for the UK has varied from 42 per cent to 60 per cent. The rise and fall in the non-residential sector's share is a function of a number of factors – the health of the economy at large and thus demand for the three main types of building in the private commercial sector – offices, retail, and leisure, government investment in public buildings such as health and education facilities, and the strength or otherwise of the housing sector (Blake et al., 2004). Civil engineering output accounts for around a fifth of construction in the UK.

'Esh Added Value', with all the innovative schemes that it encompasses, was furthered and promoted for all the right reasons, long before anyone at the Esh Group had heard the term CSR. It is core to their business, true to their vision and it made financial sense. The raised profile and increased awareness, combined with the challenges of surviving the current economic climate in one of the hardest hit sectors will be the true test of just how committed to the CSR agenda the Esh Group really is. In hard times, if forced to choose between bottom line and virtue, which will win out? Only time will tell.

References

Belal, Ataur Rahman (2001); *'A Study of Corporate Social Disclosures in Bangladesh'*; *Managerial Auditing Journal*; Vol. 16 No. 5; pp 274-289.

Blake, Neil, Jane Croot and James Hastings (2004); 'Measuring the competitiveness of the UK Construction Industry'; DTI; Construction Economics and Statistics; Volume 2.

Deegan, Craig (2002); *'The Legitimizing Effect of Social and Environmental Disclosures'*; *Accounting, Auditing and Accountability Journal*; Vol 15 No.3; pp 282-311.

European Commission; Operational Programme: North East England 2007–2013 available at http://ec.europa.eu/regional_policy/country/prordn/details_new.cfm; [Accessed on 10 September 2008].

Esh Group; http://www.esh.com.uk

Imam S (2000); Corporate Social Performance Reporting in Bangladesh; *Managerial Auditing Journal*; Vol 15 No. 93; pp 133-142.

Ingram R W and Frazier K B (1983); Narrative Disclosures in Annual Reports; *Journal of Business Research*; Vol 11 No. 1; pp 49-60.

Manchester Metropolitan University International Centre for Research and Consultancy; *West Somerset Railway:Local Economic Impact Study;* February 2004; available at http://www.hollings.mmu.ac.uk/faculty/fcthm/industry/report.pdf [Accessed 4 August 2008].

Office for National Statistics; *'Work and Worklessness Among Households'*; August 2008.

Rizk, Riham, Rob Dixon and Anne Woodhead (2008); Corporate Social and Environmental Reporting: A Survey of Disclosure Practices in Egypt; *Social Responsibility Journal*; Vol 4 No 3, pp. 306-323.

Sacks, Justin (2002); The Money Trail: Measuring your impact on the local economy using LM3; New Economics Foundation and The Countryside Agency; Available: http://www.neweconomics.org/gen/uploads/The Money Trail.pdf [Accessed 12 April 2008].

Appendix: Esh Group Timeline

Source: www.eshgroup.co.uk

LUMSDEN & CARROLL – **1971** ▪ Lumsden & Carroll formed

DEERNESS – **1976** ▪ Deerness Fencing formed

1993 ▪ Partnership between Lumsden & Carroll & Deerness Fencing, the Esh Partnership

DUNELM – **1995** ▪ Dunelm Castle Homes formed
▪ 2006 - re-branded to Dunelm Homes, Move to Esh Business Park at Newton Aycliffe

WILKINSON ▪ David Wilkinson Building Contractors Ltd formed

ESH GROUP – **1999** ▪ Esh Partnership formalised into the Esh Group

SONES ▪ Sones Landscaping becomes part of the Group

NECT – **2000** ▪ NECT formed

MECHPLANT – **2002** ▪ Mechplant North East formed

DUNELM ▪ Dunelm Property Services formed

BARTRAM WALKER – **2003** ▪ Move to Bowburn HQ

▪ Bartram Walker formed

BARDON ESH ▪ Bardon Esh formed

ESH DEVELOPMENTS – **2004** ▪ Esh Developments formed

ACORN – **2005** ▪ Dunelm Acorn Homes formed
2006 - re-branded to Acorn Homes

ESH CHARITABLE TRUST – **2006** ▪ Charitable Trust formed

DUNELM ▪ Dunelm Lifestyle Homes formed

STEPHEN EASTEN ▪ Stephen Easten Building formed

ESH EDUCATION – **2007** ▪ Esh Education formed

▪ Esh Communities formed

ESH COMMUNITIES ▪ Dunelm Facilities Services formed

DUNELM ▪ Esh Space formed

ESH SPACE

39 A Case Study on the Tobacco Industry, Social Responsibility and Regulation

JULIA J. A. SHAW

Introduction

The detrimental effects of smoking are well documented yet there are 1.3 billion smokers throughout the world; of those, 84 per cent live in developing and transitional economies. The World Health Organisation (WHO) recently claimed that tobacco products, which 'contain and emit many noxious substances and known carcinogens hazardous to human health when burnt', result in an estimated 5.4 million deaths annually due to tobacco-related diseases. New research has revealed that some people have an inherited susceptibility to lung cancer which makes them more vulnerable to the damaging effects of tobacco.[1] Tobacco use is so harmful to the human body that it is a risk factor for six of the eight leading causes of death in the world.[2] The 2008 WHO report is the first comprehensive worldwide study of tobacco use and attempts at controlling, what it refers to as, a 'devastating global tobacco epidemic'. It is clear therefore from the outset, that the tobacco business and ideals of corporate social responsibility are mutually exclusive.

The tobacco industry is one of several key business enterprises, including nuclear power, defence and oil, which have been accused of ruthless profiteering and exploitation by a range of interest groups and agencies. In the last decade, however, the industry has tried to reinvent itself as socially responsible by becoming involved with various social and environmental initiatives; it has given financial backing to projects such as small business programmes in Kenya, promoted crime prevention in South Africa, folk culture preservation in Venezuela, offered medical treatment and flood relief in Pakistan. With a view to adding an intellectual gloss to pro-smoking arguments, tobacco companies have focused many of their Corporate Social Responsibility (CSR) activities on education in the form of scholarships and grants; for example in 2000, British American Tobacco

1   A. Burton, 'Smoking out genetic components of lung cancer', *The Lancet Oncology*, Vol. 9(5), pp. 417-418.

2   WHO Report on the Global Tobacco Epidemic, February 2008 - The MPOWER package; http://www.who.int/tobacco/mpower/mpower_report_full_2008.pdf

(BAT),[3] the world's second largest cigarette manufacturer, spent £3.8 million on funding Nottingham University's International Centre for Corporate Social Responsibility (ICCSR) – a contentious move as UK researchers, a large number from the charity 'Cancer Research UK', immediately transferred their research teams from Nottingham University to other institutions because of a policy which prohibits on ethical grounds 'working in such proximity to others supported by tobacco industry funding'.[4]

In an age where the provision of goods, services, job creation and payment of taxes are no longer sufficient as a company's sole contribution to society, to protect their core business brand, CSR programmes are set up which address popular social and environmental issues. Whatever the motivating factor(s) however, the fundamental social issue with the tobacco giants is the product itself; tobacco products, whilst legal, are lethal. Controversially, tobacco is the only available consumer good responsible for the deaths of approximately one-half of its regular users. As such, the corporate nature of tobacco companies presents a structural obstacle to reducing the harm caused by tobacco use. Privately-owned companies have a fixed and predictable order of priorities; being primarily accountable to their shareholders on the assumption that what is good for shareholders is also good for other stakeholders and society at large.[5] This is problematical reasoning in the case of tobacco, as shareholders derive benefit from the sale of cigarettes but many smokers pick up various associated health and poverty problems for which society picks up the ensuing medical and social costs.

To discover the extent to which the tobacco industry is genuinely committed to CSR in its well-planned and efficiently-managed philanthropic gestures, it is first necessary to evaluate the success of past and present legal and non-legal controls over this controversial industry, and the actions and reactions of the tobacco industry to criticism. The wider role of national and international regulatory bodies will be examined as to the difficulties inherent in balancing public health issues concerning the use of a highly dangerous product, tobacco, against the demands of a free market built on the ruling principle of consumer choice. Trial testimony from recent legal landmark cases and in-house CSR initiatives will also be appraised in order to expose the current strategies employed by the largely American tobacco industry. Finally, the role of law and legislation will be evaluated in terms of its actual performance and its potential to protect the vulnerable against unconscionable corporate behaviour.

Key Stages in the History of Tobacco

In 1604 King James wrote an anti-tobacco treatise, blaming the 'Indians' for bringing tobacco into Europe, warning of 'dangers to the lungs', criticising tobacco's odour as

---

3   BAT received an overall 94 per cent score and was awarded a 'gold' ranking in the latest Business in the Community (BITC) Corporate Responsibility Top 100 most responsible '2007 Companies that Count' list, *The Sunday Times*, 6 May 2007.

4   Pre-empting the industry's tactical avoidance of tobacco control initiatives by assuming the cloak of social responsibility, in 1998 Cancer Research UK developed a Code of Practice for University Funding, together with the Committee of Vice-Chancellors and Principals of UK Universities. The Code prohibited research teams who were in receipt of tobacco industry grants from applying for support from the charity. Most recent amendment, 2004 Cancer Research UK Code of Practice on Tobacco Industry Funding to Universities: http://info.cancerresearchuk.org/images/pdfs/codeofpratice.pdf

5   'When commercial interests and broader social welfare collide, profit comes first', *The Economist*, 22 January 2005, p. 4.

'hateful to the nose' and even commenting on the dangers of second hand smoke and its negative effects.[6] His disproval failed to affect the popularity of tobacco and in 1607 the London Virginia Company set up in the United States producing cash-crop tobacco for export back to England. At the time, there was a widely-held belief that tobacco was perhaps the most important discovery in human history; a plant allegedly capable of curing virtually any human illness. The colonists' decision to pursue tobacco cultivation had far-reaching consequences and adversely affected the indigenous population. This also signalled the birth of slavery in the United States, enslaving African 'indentured servants' who were originally brought in to work the plantations and whose labour enabled Jamestown, and ultimately America, to flourish.

In the nineteenth century, mechanisation of cigarette production led to falling manufacturing costs, lower consumer prices and a corresponding boom in sales. The twentieth century witnessed a rise in anti-tobacco sentiment but medical evidence wasn't available to support such objections and during the First World War, soldiers were routinely allocated cigarettes in their rations. In the mid-1920s tobacco consumption had become commonplace and even women had begun to take up smoking. Having just won the right to vote in the United States, women were encouraged to see cigarettes as symbolic 'torches of freedom', claiming for themselves equal access to a phallic symbol previously enjoyed exclusively by men. Described as a feminist promotion of the emancipation of women, this was in reality a public relations ploy by Edward Bernays, who had been retained by the American Tobacco Company to open a new market for tobacco by getting women addicted to cigarettes (Shaw & Shaw, 2005). During the Second World War once again the armed forces became the distributor of free cigarettes, and tobacco use proliferated whilst governments continued to act in a manner which was, if anything, counter-productive to public health requirements.

During this time both the British and American Medical Associations were silent on the matter of smoking and in the early 1960s anti-cancer groups in the United States and the UK called for the setting up of a Commission to investigate any harmful effects. As a result of lobbying, in 1962 and 1964 the London-based Royal College of Physicians and the US Surgeon General released landmark reports documenting the causal relation between smoking and lung cancer.[7] During the next 25 years, extensive research confirmed that smoking affects almost every organ. The history of research on passive smoking followed a similar route, as the US Surgeon General's 1982 report on smoking and cancer reviewed the first epidemiological studies published on the relation between passive smoking and lung cancer and found an increased risk of lung cancer in non-smoking women whose husbands smoked.[8] By 1990, the US Surgeon General concluded that 'smoking represents the most extensively documented cause of disease ever investigated in the history of biomedical research'.[9] The next defining moment was publication of the 1993

---

6   King James I, 'A Counterblaste to Tobacco', published in 1672.

7   Royal College of Physicians, 'Summary and Report of the Royal College of Physicians of London on smoking in relation to cancer of the lung and other diseases', Pitman Publishing, 1962; and US Department of Health, Education, and Welfare, 'Report of the Advisory Committee to the Surgeon General of the Public Health Service', Centre for Disease Control, 1964 (PHS Publication No 1103).

8   US Department of Health and Human Services, 'The health consequences of smoking: cancer', 1982. (DHHS Publication No (PHS) 82-50179).

9   US Department of Health and Human Services, 'The health benefits of smoking cessation', A report of the Surgeon General [Preface]', Office of Smoking and Health, Rockville, 1990, (DHHS Publication No (CDC) 90-8416).

US Environmental Protection Report on environmental tobacco smoke. By this time, eight countries had conducted 30 epidemiological studies on passive smoking and lung cancer, of which 24 had evidenced a positive association. The Environmental Protection Agency (EPA) classified environmental tobacco smoke as a known human carcinogen, to which it attributed 3,000 lung cancer deaths annually in United States non-smokers.[10]

Effectiveness of Recent Tobacco Control Measures

There is a long history of the tobacco industry's ambivalence towards smokers' health; smoking kills over half a million EU citizens per year and in the UK alone, tobacco illnesses cost the NHS £1.7 billion in 2006. Tobacco advertising has traditionally showed that it was smart to smoke, but in recent times there have been new restrictions on smoking on an almost annual basis, including health warnings, restrictions on sports sponsorship, banning of all advertising and, of course, most recently the ban on smoking in public places and a future plan to put gruesome pictures of tarred lungs on cigarette packets in the UK. Other countries have not been so strict or diligent and in order to lay the basis for a global tobacco control effort, WHO enacted the 2005 Framework Convention on Tobacco Control (FCTC), in order to encourage signatories from the international community to implement national measures. These include, for example, imposing restrictions on tobacco advertising, sponsorship and promotion; establishing new packaging and labelling of tobacco products; establishing clean indoor air controls; and strengthening legislation to clamp down on tobacco smuggling. During discussions in May 2001, Philip Morris Companies Inc demanded 11 provisions be deleted from the draft FCTC treaty, of which ten deletions were supported. United States government negotiators also objected to a provision that warning labels on cigarette packages be printed in the main language(s) of the country of sale and have since continued to oppose important public health provisions. In November 2001, the United States delegation again insisted successfully that trade principles ought to override public health concerns (FCTC Negotiations, 2002). Not only was the tobacco industry deeply concerned about the impact of the FCTC on its profits and plans for expansion, but it would also appear that the United States government fought the FCTC at every opportunity whilst publicly claiming support. Of course there are huge gains to be made from taxation revenue, direct and indirect, for example during the financial year 2000–2001 the UK Treasury earned £7,648 million (ex VAT) in excise duty (Shaw, 2004). During the period 2006–2007 this figure had risen to £8,149 million (ex VAT) and, anticipating an initial decline in tobacco sales following the July 2007 public smoking ban, revenue of £8,107 million (ex VAT) is forecast for the period 2007–2008.[11] A pack of 20 premium brand cigarettes currently costs around £5.50 of which £4.40 (80 per cent) is tax. Similarly in the United States, federal tax on tobacco stands at 39 cents per 20 unit pack and about $7.2 billion was generated for the United States

---

10   US Environmental Protection Agency, 'Respiratory health effects of passive smoking: lung cancer and other disorders', Washington, (Publication EPA/600/6-90/006F); see also California Office of Environmental Health Hazard Assessment, 'Health effects of exposure to environmental tobacco smoke' Sacramento Environmental Protection Agency, 1997.

11   HM Revenue and Customs Annual Receipts, October 2007: http://www.hmrc.gov.uk/stats/tax_receipts/table1-2.pdf

Treasury in 2005. In addition States also tax cigarettes at rates ranging from $2.58 cents a pack in New Jersey to 7 cents a pack in South Carolina[12] and with the price of a pack of cigarettes costing around $4.30 for 20, this amounts to a considerable gain. It is unsurprising therefore that at the Intergovernmental Working Group meetings in June 2004 and February 2005, the United States government continued to engage in obstructionist tactics especially in relation to treaty funding. Progress has been slow and it has been suggested that there is a clear pattern in recent history of the United States negotiating down to the lowest common denominator, then failing to support environmental, human rights and other treaty agreements.[13] However the purpose of the recent 2008 WHO initiative is to expand and expedite the FCTC treaty provisions by outlining six proven strategies to assist Member States in reducing tobacco use in their countries, namely:

- monitor tobacco use and tobacco-prevention policies;
- protect people from tobacco smoke in public places and workplaces;
- offer help to people who want to stop using tobacco;
- warn people about the dangers of tobacco;
- enforce bans on tobacco advertising, promotion and sponsorship; and
- raise tobacco taxes and prices.

It remains to be seen how effective this FCTC upgrade proves to be. In the meantime, legislation protecting the rights of non-smokers has been enacted, to a greater or lesser extent, in many US states and throughout the developed world. Many countries have enacted tobacco advertising prohibition rules, making it more difficult for tobacco companies to promote their products. In the UK and other EU countries, smoking bans, raising the minimum smoking age and anti-smoking incentives have increased, for example, insurance companies offering non-smoker rated policies, which will be discussed later. Even so, people continue to smoke[14] and the tobacco industry has continued to deny liability and to date ensures it wins all litigation. Repeated attempts are made to undermine regulation by routinely refuting and obfuscating the findings of legitimate research bodies, as discussed later. One example involved a comparison of the dangers of second-hand smoke with the 'risks' associated with drinking milk and biscuit consumption (Davey-Smith & Phillips, 1996).

Although advances have been made in recognising and addressing the public health risks associated with tobacco use, it is noteworthy how much of this awareness is due to the efforts of a small number of individuals from the private and public sectors, as opposed to a coordinated and sustained legislative/executive initiative. For example the above-mentioned US Surgeon General, Luther Terry, was a key figure in pioneering the original 1964 Report and was assisted not by an appointed government body, rather by a group of academic lawyers from the public interest sphere who also published influential educative papers.

---

12   US Department of the Treasury, Alcohol and Tobacco Tax and Trade Bureau; http://www.ttb.gov/tobacco/tobacco_stats.shtml.

13   'Global Tobacco Treaty Action Guide', *Corporate Accountability International Report*, September 2005.

14   For example, despite the UK being more hostile to tobacco than any other European country, some 22 per cent of British adults continue to smoke daily; *The Economist*, 29 March 2008.

In view of the inherent incompatibility between the objectives of the tobacco industry and aim of the state in promoting public health, it would appear that government and international agencies have been largely negligent in their duty to implement successful tobacco control policies, relying on soft law options. Following on from ratifying the FCTC, the US 2005 Family Smoking Prevention and Tobacco Control Act gave the Food and Drug Administration (FDA) limited authority to regulate cigarettes to 'protect the public health' but this didn't go far enough. In July 2008 the United States House of Representatives approved a bill which would allow the FDA the necessary and broad authority to regulate the manufacturing, marketing and sale of tobacco products and impose specific restrictions on tobacco advertising that appeals to children and further restrict tobacco marketing. It remains to be seen if the Bill becomes law, and what restrictions are imposed on the FDA.

Other countries have promoted anti-tobacco strategies, for example between 1996 and 2006 the UK Department of Health spent £96.6 million on advertising the dangers of smoking and most recently, the Health Act, which bans smoking in all enclosed workplaces received Royal Assent in July 2006 and came into force in July 2007.

Although this sort of measure is a step in the right direction, experience shows that such legislation is unlikely to substantially reduce smoking or related deaths since tobacco companies are among the world's most sophisticated and successful marketers and will not tolerate any curb on their sales figures. On numerous occasions they have used their substantial resources to bury such policies, dilute them when they cannot halt implementation, and undermine their enforcement when protective measures are passed. More invidious strategies have included establishing inappropriate relationships with WHO staff members to influence policy, payment of WHO consultants and advisors for inside information or services, employment of former WHO officials or use of similar inducements to elicit the support of current WHO officials.[15]

Assisted by years of public indifference, tobacco companies have enjoyed decades of unrestrained influence in which they have developed a range of subtle and aggressive methods of promotion, especially in the developing world and to young people. The 2008 WHO report outlines the tobacco industry's strategy to target young people and adults in the developing world, where 80 per cent of the more than 8 million annual tobacco-related deaths projected by 2030 are expected to occur. Young women are another group highlighted as one of the 'most ominous potential developments of the epidemic's growth'.[16] The tobacco industry is one of the most lucrative and is constantly seeking to develop new markets. Resistant to proposals for control, the scale and intensity of the industry's often deceptive yet successful strategies have assumed many forms.

---

15   T. Zeltner, D.A. Kessler, A. Martiny, F. Randera 'Tobacco Company Strategies to Undermine Tobacco Control Activities at the World Health Organisation' Report of the Committee of Experts on Tobacco Industry Documents 2000; http://www.who.int/tobacco/en/who_inquiry.pdf

16   See note 1 *supra*.

Strategic Manoeuvres Promoting Tobacco Use

EMOTIONAL MARKETING

Marketing science has developed an impressive body of evidence on the efficacy of linking functional utility to emotional need in successfully promoting a product. Positive-image enhancing tactics have traditionally focussed on incisive advertising campaigns in order to target a particular demographic and reinforce brand awareness. Aggressive use of emotional marketing has been used to give the cigarette a socially-structured significance which has served to weaken and overcome any pre-existing resistance (Shaw & Shaw, 2005); see Table 39.1.

A growing number of consumer studies have emerged in the last few years which scrutinise implicit brand attitudes, which are capable of being activated automatically and outside conscious awareness. Even incidental exposure to an advertisement, whilst engrossed in a primary task, for example reading a newspaper article, increases brand familiarity and probable inclusion in the consumer's 'consideration set' (Shapiro, 1999; Bargh, 2002; Maison, Greenwald & Bruin, 2004). Marketing science continues to evolve increasingly sophisticated techniques of persuasion designed to appeal to particular groups. The R.J. Reynolds Tobacco Company launched its latest cigarette in the United States in 2007 with the catchy slogan "light and luscious', accompanied by glossy magazine ads featuring floral designs and lace in 'fuchsia' and 'teal'. They hosted promotional events offering makeovers including free cigarettes; even the product's name 'Camel No. 9' has subliminal associations with a young person's fragrance marketed by the famous French perfume house.

Although Reynolds claimed their campaign targeted only established adult female smokers it hoped to entice away from other brands, other parties disagreed pointing to the detail of the campaign focussing on the aspirational wants, narrative and visual style designed to appeal to teenagers and young women in general. The American Legacy Foundation, an anti-smoking organisation established with the money tobacco companies have had to pay in settling state lawsuits, claims that the tobacco industry always seeks new smokers in order to replace those who die or manage to quit. Its Chief Lawyer recently claimed, referring to the industry's tactics, 'there's nothing new in the universe of tobacco companies' but warned '80 per cent of new smokers (in the United States) are under the age of 18', which means one-third of teenagers now smoking will eventually die from the habit; she concluded 'no matter how you look at [the 2007 Camel No. 9 campaign] it's extremely troubling especially as the target audience is young women'.[17]

Lung cancer is the biggest cause of death amongst women, overtaking deaths from breast and gynaecological cancers, and whilst more men die from the disease than women new research has shown that women may absorb more cancer-causing chemicals from cigarettes than men and become ill after smoking less.[18] New research has found that the presence of oestrogen is a likely trigger for the onset of cigarette smoke-related lung

---

17   M. Cocco 'Light & Luscious' Carcinogens?, *The Washington Post*, 20 February, 2007; Marc Longpre 'ALF pressures R.J. Reynolds to end Camel No. 9', *PR Week*, 16 Aug 2007.

18   UK Lung Cancer Mortality Statistics Aug 2006; www.info.cancerresearchuk.org/cancerstats/types/lung/mortality/ ?a=5441; see also http://www.cbsnews.com/stories/2006/05/29/ap/health/mainD8HTK0OG0.shtml

cancer; in light of this discovery it seems morally indefensible to support the use of a campaign designed to attract particularly young women to becoming dependent on a product which may lead to their death (Henschke, Yip & Miettinen, 2006). Nicotine tends to be an appetite suppressant and women are a particularly susceptible group where image consciousness is concerned, and as Terrazzano points out 'I wonder if a teenager or a 20-something woman reading the magazines has the willpower to stay away from cigarettes, as she is simultaneously bombarded in neighbouring pages with messages about being thin and how to lose fat'.[19] This is just one example of how the tobacco giants have been deceptive and insidious in their approach to advertising. Over the years, women's ambitions, attitudes, insecurities and fears have been meticulously researched and exploited in order to sell them cigarettes, which has resulted in a history of distinctive female brands with inspirational imagery and subliminal messages calculated to stimulate and nurture specific emotions in women, such as independence, achievement, desire, femininity and social acceptability.

Social commentators such as Galbraith and Packard have maintained that manufacturers produce goods and then apply 'ruthless psychological pressures' through clever advertising techniques to generate demand for them (Galbraith, 1958). Vance Packard accused marketers of implementing 'an increasingly precise method of manipulation that can circumvent the conscious mind, influencing consumers without their awareness' (Packard, 1957). In upholding a ban on TV advertisements for cigarettes, United States Federal Judge Bazelon referred to the insidious implementation of subtle commercial advertising, 'It is difficult to calculate the subliminal impact of this pervasive propaganda ... but it may reasonably be thought greater than the impact of the written word.'[20] Table 39.1 opposite lists a small number of hugely successful campaigns which have often cleverly coincided with some contemporaneous societal development.

MEDIA MANIPULATION

Tobacco companies are adept at influencing the media. It can be argued that they seek to cultivate relationships with journalists so as to gain positive media coverage of the tobacco industry by both tone and content of their editorial, and have used intimidation tactics to stifle bad press. A 2008 study by the *American Journal of Public Health* found tobacco companies have suppressed research and information on the presence of the dangerous radioactive poison, polonium 210 (PO-210) in tobacco and tobacco smoke. This is the same poison used in the 2006 murder of former KGB agent and Russian dissident Alexander Litvinenko, however the industry has so far suppressed information about PO-210 out of concern that it would cause public relations and litigation problems and to avoid 'waking a sleeping giant', as one industry official stated.[21] Tobacco companies have used lawsuits and threats of litigation to suppress unfavourable results. For example, an editor of Psychopharmacology requested revisions of a paper entitled 'Nicotine as a positive reinforcer in rats' submitted by three authors employed by the Phillip Morris

---

19   L. Terrazzano, 'Life with Cancer', *Newsday*, 31 January 2007.

20   Banzhaf v. F.C.C. 405 F2d 1082, 1100-1101 (D.C. Cir. 1968) quoted in C.B.S. v. Democratic National Committee 412 U.S. 92, 128 (1973). Also cited in US District Court NewYork v James Alexander et al., (2007) Case 5:07-CV-0118.

21   M.E. Muggli, J.O. Ebbert, C. Robertson, R.D. Hurt, 'Waking a Sleeping Giant: The Tobacco Industry's Response to the Polonium-210 Issue', *American Journal of Public Health*, Vol.98(9), September 2008.

Table 39.1 1918–2007: Cigarette brand promotion using emotional marketing techniques in order to target women

Year	Slogan	Cigarette Brand	Link to Particular Emotional Need	Target Age Group
1918	I wish I were a man (so I could smoke)	Lucky Strike	Freedom and empowerment	18–35
1928	Reach for a Lucky instead of a sweet	Lucky Strike	Weight-conscious, self-image insecurity	18–60
1929	Light up a torch of freedom	Lucky Strike	Feminist idealism: women's emancipation	25–55
1933	I really don't know if I should smoke...	Chesterfield	Empowerment: equality with men	25–55
1968–1986	You've come a long way baby...	Virginia Slims	Independence and peer group assimilation	18–50
1998	B Kool	Brown & Williamson	Teenage/youth appeal; contemporary	18–25
1999	Find your voice	Virginia Slims	Multicultural female solidarity; assertiveness	18–60
2007	Light and Luscious	Reynolds	Lifestyle, youthful elegance, allure	16–35

Source: Author's Research 2008.

Research Centre. In response, the authors withdrew the manuscript, and later stated Phillip Morris issued an injunction against publishing the article (Barry, 2006). Tobacco companies have also taken over ownership, either directly or indirectly, of media outlets so as to control the content of the media. Sponsored media symposia, training sessions and all-expenses paid trips have all been arranged to promote their company during which tobacco-related issues are 'discussed' in a favourable light.[22]

EXERCISE OF POLITICAL INFLUENCE

The tobacco industry is also skilled at exerting political and financial power to influence tobacco policy. In 2004 for example, tobacco manufacturers including BAT spent approximately US$87,000 to take Nigerian MPs on a 'workshop break' to Mombassa to discuss and foster support for amendments to weaken the Tobacco Products Control Bill, which would 'provide a legal framework for the manufacture, sale, promotion and use of tobacco products' including banning outdoor tobacco advertisements. Although a Bill

---

22   R. Davis, E. Gilpin, B. Loken, K. Viswanath, M. Wakefield, 'The Role of the Media in Promoting and Reducing Tobacco Use', *NCI Tobacco Control Monograph Series*, Vol. 19, National Cancer Institute, US Dept. of Health and Human Services, National Institutes of Health, 2008. See also Pan American Health Organization (PAHO), 'Profits over People: Tobacco Industry Activities to Market Cigarettes and Undermine Public Health in Latin America and the Caribbean', Pan American Health Organization, Washington, DC: 2002; http://www.paho.org/English/HPP/HPM/TOH/profits_over_people.pdf

demanding health warnings and a ban on public smoking was passed, BAT complained that the 'regulations were untenable because of the company's lack of involvement in the law-making process' and attempted to delay enactment.[23] The Kenyan ban on smoking in public places, whilst vigorously enforced initially, had slackened noticeably during 2007. In Nigeria, although cigarette advertising is banned on billboards and only allowed on TV after 10pm, local celebrities have been employed by the tobacco companies to glamourise smoking; free cigarettes have been handed out to cinema-goers and little is done to prevent minors buying cigarettes. Consequently the Nigerian government begun a £22bn lawsuit in 2008 against three multinational cigarette manufacturers, accused of trying to push tobacco to young Africans. Tobacco companies have been accused of obstructing control efforts by influencing Nigerian MPs to keep tobacco sales largely unregulated.[24]

FRAUDULENT RESEARCH

It is widely known that the tobacco industry has funded scientific research to discredit established knowledge of, and to maintain controversy over, the dangers of tobacco use. Economists, philosophers and sociologists were bankrolled by tobacco companies to produce articles in scientific literature down-playing the risks, and in mainstream media in order to undermine popular understanding of the hazards of smoking whilst also claiming that smokers are well-informed about risk.[25] Industry documentation shows that in the 1970s seven major players including Philip Morris, BAT and Rothmans got together to present a 'united approach' against an increasing body of evidence exposing the medical and social impact of smoking, which is when the industry began bankrolling academics.[26] For example, tobacco companies recruited scientists in Germany to bolster their credibility, to contradict tobacco control scientists and improve their image. Research results that were potentially harmful to the industry were suppressed and genuine anti-tobacco science was diluted with pro-tobacco 'science'. Rather, research was produced, published and presented which focussed on other possible causes of illness rather than smoking, whilst these scientists concealed their links to the tobacco industry (Grüning, Gilmore and McKee, 2006). Associates for Research In the Science of Enjoyment (ARISE) was created by the tobacco industry in 1988 and described itself as 'a worldwide association of eminent scientists acting as independent commentators' showing how 'everyday pleasures, such as eating chocolate, smoking, drinking coffee and alcohol, contribute to the quality of life'. Lead by the Head of Psychopharmacology at the University of Reading[27] and Senior Editor of the Psychopharmacology Journal, ARISE remained active until 2004, and between 1989 and 2005, in excess of 846 articles appeared in the European, Australian and United States media alluding to ARISE, its

---

23   Namunane B. 'Threat to Tobacco Firms Plan, *The Nation*, 22 Nov 2004; also 'Kenyan smokers win new court reprieve from puffing ban', Agence France Presse, 20 June 2006.

24   C. McGreal 'Nigeria takes on big tobacco over campaigns that target the young', *The Guardian*, 15 January, 2008, p. 23.

25   G. Monbiot, 'Exposed: the secret corporate funding behind health research', *The Guardian*, 7 Feb 2006.

26   Big Brains bought by big tobacco, *New Scientist*, 16 February 2008.

27   The University of Reading claimed it had received over £300,000 in research monies from ARISE, also Professor Warburton and the University of Reading were in receipt of BAT research funding between 1995 and 2003; see G. Monbiot, 'Exposed: the secret corporate funding behind health research', *The Guardian*, 7 Feb 2006.

members or its activities. Many of these emphasised two recurring themes, that smoking was a healthy 'pleasure' and health promotion recommendations such as cessation, were stressful and injurious. Few articles contained either responses from other health advocates or criticisms of claims made by the tobacco-funded ARISE scientists (Smith, 2007). The tobacco, sugar and monosodium glutamate industry have all set up 'expert' sites to convey conflicting messages which serve to undermine any real debate and deny any actual medical or scientific research (Shaw & Shaw, 2005). The Deputy Director of the Medical Research Council and Chair of the committee drawing up the UK's first national dietary guidelines, referring to tactics employed by sugar companies, said 'the sugar industry has learned the tricks of the tobacco industry. These are firstly, confuse the public and then produce experts who disagree, try to dilute any health message, by indicating that there are extremists involved in public health'.[28]

Since the US Surgeon General concluded in 1964 that cigarette smoking causes lung cancer, tobacco companies responded to the health issues he raised in his report by introducing 'light', 'filtered', 'low tar', and 'ultra low tar' brands and set about marketing these as less dangerous than regular cigarettes. In 1967, low-tar cigarettes constituted two per cent of the market and by 1997, half of all tobacco advertising revenue was dedicated to promoting low-tar products so that by 2005, these products held 83.5 per cent of total market share.[29] R.J. Reynolds markets one of these 'safer cigarette' brands, 'Eclipse', which heats and vaporises tobacco rather than burns it. They have used their own researchers and independent scientists to push the potential health benefits of switching to Eclipse cigarettes, making various health claims based on important scientific advances, including an allegedly rigorous four-step verification process. Charles Blixt, Executive Vice President and legal attorney for Reynolds commented, 'The scientific data we have clearly leads us and our panel of independent scientists to conclude [changing to Eclipse cigarettes] might lead to less cancer, bronchitis, emphysema.' The US Department of Justice determined that 'all R.J. Reynolds did was look at all of the work it already had done to evaluate Eclipse to date, categorize it, and retroactively dub it a four step methodology'.[30] Interestingly, the head of the 'independent' scientific team reviewing Eclipse received more than $1.5 million from Reynolds. In July 2005 nine States and the Columbia District brought legal action accusing the tobacco company of making misleading claims that its Eclipse brand of cigarette carries less risk of cancer and other health ailments. As of February 2006, 1,280 tobacco-related cases were pending against Reynolds Tobacco or its affiliates; of these 1,270 are in the United States, five in Puerto Rico; four in Canada and one in Israel.[31] However consumers are still deceived by inaccurate and invalid health claims and this cigarette continues to be sold as a 'safer alternative'.

The simple truth is that we do not know enough about the relationship between the specific components of tobacco smoke, their amounts and interaction, and the development of disease to be able to conclude that reducing the amounts of certain

---

28   Barton, L., 'A Spoonful of Propaganda', *The Guardian*, p.7, 12 April 2002.

29   Federal Trade Commission Cigarette Report for 2004 and 2005, issued 2007; http://www.ftc.gov/reports/tobacco/2007cigarette2004-2005.pdf

30   The Lessons of 'Light' and 'Low Tar' Cigarettes: Without Effective Regulation, 'Reduced Risk' Tobacco Products Threaten the Public Health, US House of Representatives, 30 December 2007; http://ideas.repec.org/p/cdl/ctcres/1034.html

31   Litigation Affecting the Cigarette Industry, 22 February 2006; http://sec.edgar-online.com/2006/02/27/0000950144-06-001530/Section3.asp

smoke components is going to prevent disease, reduce deaths and improve public health. However it is evident that research funded by a private company 'invariably contains the seeds of direct or indirect profit motives' and calls into question the reliability of that research (Batra, 2007). Furthermore, not releasing or manipulating data which contains significant health implications is against the wider public interest.

The Efficacy of Tobacco Industry Corporate Social Responsibility Policies

There are four established principles of good corporate governance aligned with social responsibility; namely, fairness, accountability, responsibility and transparency (Aras & Crowther, 2008). When corporate goals are not aligned with society's best interests then CSR needs to be an integral part of corporate strategy and by reviewing recent developments within the tobacco industry it is possible to determine whether there is evidence of any fundamental change in their objectives or practices. The evolution and public embrace of IT has meant the Internet has been a key catalyst for progress, exposing the activities of unpopular industries on a constantly updated and monitored world stage so there is nowhere left to hide (Shaw, 2008, p. 22). Therefore new philanthropy projects have been pursued by much-criticised industries in recent years, as the realisation has dawned that they need to be seen to be taking steps to address any adverse impact on society in areas like, for example, health, employment practices, human rights and the environment. The recently rebranded Altria, parent company of the Philip Morris Group, reassuringly identifies the 'twin pillars of Integrity and Responsibility' as being at the heart of their organisational operations.[32] Aware of public concern over a spate of high-profile legal cases, they claim, 'We have been researching and seeking to develop products that have the potential to reduce harm. We have knowledge, we have scientific expertise, and we want to share our knowledge and expertise to reach a better understanding of how products can be made less harmful.'[33] To incentivise tobacco companies to conduct their operations in a responsible manner so as to reduce harm is a worthy goal however the question persists, can a company whose very existence depends on addicting customers to its deadly products really be a responsible corporate citizen?

The question as to whether a company which produces and promotes products proven to kill can ever be socially responsible was answered by the Vice-President of Philip Morris International whilst sharing a conference platform with the Group Director of Corporate Affairs at British Nuclear Fuels 'Business in the Community' (BITC) Annual Conference 2004 – A Better Way of Doing Business. Having conceded that 'Our product is not safe; our product causes disease', he then continued, perhaps missing the point, 'the product cannot be the determinant of whether your company is socially responsible; behaviour is'.[34] BAT,

---

32   L.C. Camilleri, Chairman and CEO of Altria Group, quoted in Altria's 'Code of Conduct for Compliance and Integrity; http://www.altria.com/responsibility/4_0_responsibilityover.asp

33   D. Davies, Senior Vice President, Corporate Affairs -Philip Morris Inc., 'The politics of harm reduction: A perspective on public policy approaches to a controversial industry and product', 23 March 2005: http://www.philipmorrisinternational. com/PMINTL/pages/eng/press/speeches/DDavies_20050323.asp

34   'No place to hide: How companies respond to social challenges around controversial core business', Philip Dewhurst – Group Director Corporate Affairs, BNFL; D. Davies, Vice President, Philip Morris International; Business In the Community Conference Annual Conference, 6 July, 2004. See also http://www.ethicalcorp.com/content. asp?ContentID=2345

the world's most international tobacco group, is a leader in reputation management and has even devised its own 'Framework for Corporate Social Responsibility', outlining 'five core beliefs' under the headings of 'The Principle of Good Corporate Conduct' and 'The Principle of Mutual Benefit'. Under the heading 'The Principle of Responsible Product Stewardship', BAT acknowledges that 'smoking is a cause of diseases such as lung cancer, cardiovascular disease and respiratory diseases like chronic bronchitis and emphysema' also that 'smoking is addictive'. Downplaying such social costs of its increasing sales, the statement continues 'Tobacco products are legal and we believe it is for informed adults, balancing the pleasures and the risks, to decide whether to consume tobacco products or not.' Under the mutual benefit principle, BAT present themselves as a champion of consumer rights by asserting, 'Tobacco products are legal, significant demand for them exists and seems likely to continue and informed adults have rights to consume them and to choose the brands they prefer.'[35] The website contains descriptions of various global projects, which all tend to distract from the hard ethical questions posed by their core activities. For example, the BAT website fails to mention that the company is actively offering funds to right-wing think tanks committed to blocking health and environment legislation.

Tobacco companies attribute customer expectations as the main driver for their company's CSR agenda.[36] It follows that this newly heightened sensitivity to environmental, social and ethical issues has come about primarily because consumers are more aware of the CSR performance of companies from which they buy their goods and services, and are more likely to change their shopping habits as a result. Companies are therefore under economic pressure to behave in a socially and environmentally sustainable manner in order to maintain profits and even improve their 'brand identity'. The power of naming is significant when creating brand image. Within the corporate organisation, language is used as a signifying mechanism; it is capable of 'creating reality which then becomes truth' (Crowther & Gomez, 2007: 113). In 2003 the Philip Morris Group adopted the new name 'Altria' from the Latin *altus*, meaning 'high'. An interesting choice given the connotations of high standards, high ideals, high levels of product safety; this could be seen as yet another public relations contrivance designed to disassociate themselves from earlier negative publicity and clean-up their brand image. Other tobacco giants have similarly greenwashed their image and filled their home pages with references to good corporate governance, social investment and news of the latest CSR accolade. In recognition of a 2007 BITC Corporate Responsibility Index award, BAT's Director of Corporate and Regulatory Affairs boasted. 'This [award] recognises our commitment to the corporate responsibility issues that particularly affect our industry, such as harm reduction, conservation of natural resources and biodiversity, and our approach to appropriate marketing of our products.'[37] Yet, in spite of their gongs, promises and pledges the evidence of bad corporate citizenship in the tobacco industry continues to mount. There remains a seemingly unbridgeable gap between discourse and practice, the rhetoric

---

35   http://www.bat.com/oneweb/framework.nsf/F/MB1?opendocument British American Tobacco's website 'Business Principles and Framework for CSR, 7 January 2008.

36   A Benjamin, 'Fags and fiction: That a US tobacco giant should be courting the idea of ethical trade beggars belief', *The Guardian*, 8 July, 2004.

37   M. Prideaux, 'Companies that Count' and 'Business in the Community Big Tick award' on BAT's web pages, 31 October, 2007; http://www.bat.com/group/sites/uk__3mnfen.nsf/vwPagesWebLive/DO732CMH?opendocument&SKN=1 &TMP=1

and reality, as the act of promoting sale and use of tobacco products can be viewed as antithetical to social responsibility.

Tobacco Regulation and the Law

Since 2000 there has been a raft of high-profile United States High Court decisions relating to the contrivances employed by the tobacco industry to push their lethal product. In 2004 the United States Massachusetts High Court ruled in favour of a class of cigarette purchasers who alleged they had been misled by 'low tar' claims on their cigarette packs.[38] In a 2006 landmark case, a United States trial judge issued a final opinion asserting that the defendants, a number of tobacco companies, had over the course of 50 years 'devised and executed a scheme to defraud' and had deceived the American people about the dangers of smoking and 'distorted the truth about low-tar and light cigarettes [and their addictive properties] … in order to achieve their goal – to make money'. Judge Kessler's ruling affirmed, not that the tobacco companies are criminally culpable villains but rather, that in marketing a legal product they merely engaged in misleading advertising and other questionable business practices. Although the judge ordered some important remedies, for example, prohibition of brand descriptors such as 'light' and 'ultra light' and disclosure of future disaggregated marketing data, she was legally constrained from implementing other key remedies that would, in her own words, 'unquestionably serve the public interest'. Judge Kessler was further restrained by the narrow standard outlined in the Appeal Court's opinion, limiting remedies to those preventing and inhibiting *future* violations of the 1970 Racketeer Influenced and Corrupt Organizations Act (RICO). Significantly the trial judge found it 'exceedingly clear' that 'defendants have not … ceased their wrongdoing or … undertaken fundamental or permanent institutional change' and that '[t]here is a reasonable likelihood that defendants' RICO violations will continue in most of the areas in which they have committed violations in the past'.[39] Clearly some other measure is needed to ensure that the industry's racketeering misconduct does not continue.

The tort system often plays a key role where there is, for example, a significant health risk (Brownsword, 2006). Gostin suggests the enormous potential for using tort litigation as an effective tool to reduce the burden of injury and disease by awarding compensatory damages. This form of civil litigation is capable of redressing many different kinds of public health harms, including environmental damage, exposure to toxic substances, unsafe pharmaceuticals, vaccines, or medical devices, defective consumer items and hazardous products such as tobacco (Gostin, 2000). In support of this view, one way of discouraging and punishing producers and marketers of dangerous goods like tobacco has been by means of excessive punitive damages, which has also generated considerable media attention. With levels reaching hundreds of millions of dollars and beyond, such awards impose sizeable economic costs, for example, in the United States individual cigarette smoker cases have generated punitive damages amounts of $28 billion, $3 billion and $150 million. Tobacco class actions have generated punitive awards of $145

---

38 Aspinall v. Philip Morris Cos., 442 Mass. 381 (2004).

39 US v Philip Morris USA, Inc., et al., No. 99-CV-02496GK (U.S. Dist. Ct., D.C.) Final Opinion, 17 August, 2006; http://www.tplp.org/doj

billion and $7.1 billion. With an estimated 400,000 United States' smokers dying each year from smoking-related illnesses, these stakes could become quite substantial and in a few cases, may even threaten the economic viability of the defendant (Kip Viscusi, 2005). Yet in February 2007 this particular form of aversion therapy was defeated as the £40.6m punitive damages awarded to Mrs Williams against Philip Morris in 1999 on the tobacco-related death of her husband, were overturned in the United States Supreme Court. In a landmark decision, the court decided that a jury can only 'punish for harm done to the plaintiff and not the harm caused to strangers'.[40] Although overturned on a legal technicality and not the question of excessiveness of damages, this was viewed as a victory for big business. The tobacco industry has long argued that the size of punitive damages should be restricted, as they are designed to punish criminal behaviour, not to compensate a victim; and now a heavier burden is placed on plaintiffs to make a strong case for large punitive damage awards. The New York Times criticised the ruling as 'a win for corporate wrongdoers' and that the United States Supreme Court 'is more concerned about, and more willing to protect, the powerful than the powerless'.[41]

It would seem that the regular legislative route is not always the most effective regulatory strategy. If regulators and policy makers want to reduce, on health grounds, the amounts of alcohol and tobacco consumed, they might better advance their strategy, not with law, but with a campaign designed to cultivate a culture that treats binge-drinking and smoking as anti-social (Scott, 2004). Such campaigns have been and continue to be advanced in the UK along with statutory provisions. The 2006 Companies Act became law in October 2007 and, for the first time, makes it a legal requirement that all company directors take into account the interests of their staff, their suppliers and customers, also the community and the environment. For quoted companies a business review must be produced which sets out the company's policies in relation to these interests and their practical effectiveness. For larger companies, key performance indicators must be set in order to help analyse this non-financial information. Such endeavours are welcome and this is a positive development, however it is necessary for any social responsibility strategies to extend beyond the usual window dressing. Even after the legal issues are resolved, serious concerns regarding the moral and ethical dimensions of tobacco promotion and sales remain unresolved in the United States and the UK and significantly, are also unaddressed in relation to accelerated consumption in other parts of the world.

Conclusion

Cigarette smoking takes a staggering toll on human health robbing people of years of life expectancy and attracts considerable public health attention, yet the past 500 years of tobacco control efforts demonstrate that nicotine prohibition is a practical impossibility for a variety of reasons, state revenue being one of them. Facilitation of trade and economic considerations have traditionally trumped the need for legislation, resulting in a dearth of effective socio-legal measures necessary for ensuring the safety of people coming into contact with harmful products. Also despite the tobacco industry's thinly-disguised attempts to gain respectability and claims to have transformed their practices,

---

40   Philip Morris USA, Inc., v Mayola Williams, Case No. 05-1256, (US Supreme Court), 20 February 2007.

41   Editorial, 'Shielding the Powerful', *The New York Times*, 21 February, 2007.

it is evident that they continue to use a vast assortment of unethical and irresponsible strategies in continuing to promote their lethal products, expand markets, develop new markets and increase profits.

As evidenced many times, corporate self-policing has failed to make an impression and state regulatory bodies have had little restraining influence (Shaw, 2004). There is plenty of evidence to suggest that voluntarily assuming the mantle of social responsibility has in reality had little practical impact on a company's overall behaviour or on its more unsavoury activities. In support of this view, it is has been suggested that, 'short of a backlash against globalisation, states will have little choice but to pool their sovereignty to exercise public power in a global environment now mostly shaped by private actors' (Reinicke & Witte, 1999).

Legal measures holding the tobacco industry accountable, the provision of funding for tobacco use prevention and cessation programmes are essential to ensure that developing countries can implement the WHO proposals in order to halt the tobacco pandemic. The Framework Convention needs to counter the root of the problem, namely the tobacco industry itself; 'Tobacco use is unlike other threats to global health. Infectious diseases do not employ multinational public relations firms. There are no front groups to promote the spread of cholera. Mosquitoes have no lobbyists.'[42] In summary, the evidence presented from various sources suggests that tobacco is a unique case, and that overturning its oppressive burden on global health will come about not only by understanding addiction and curing disease, but just as importantly, about overcoming a determined and powerful industry.

References

Aras, G. & Crowther D. (2008) 'Exploring Frameworks of Corporate Governance', in *Culture and Corporate Governance*; G. Aras & D. Crowther (eds), Social Responsibility Network Research Series.

Bargh, J. (2002) 'Losing consciousness: automatic influences on consumer judgment, behaviour and motivation', *Journal of Consumer Research*, Vol. 29(2), pp. 280-85.

Barry, H. (2006) 'Censorship by a tobacco company', *Psychopharmacology*, Vol. 84(3-4), p. 273.

Batra, A. (2007) 'Funding support – cui bono?' *Addiction*, Vol. 102, pp. 1034-1040.

Brownsword, R. (2006) 'Public health, private right, and the common law', *Public Health*, Vol. 120, Supp. 1, pp. 42-50.

Davey-Smith, G & Philips A.N. (1996) 'Passive smoking and health: should we believe Philip Morris's experts', *British Medical Journal*, Vol. 313, pp. 929-33.

Galbraith, J.K. (1958) *The Affluent Society*, Houghton Mifflin, New York.

Gomez A.M.D. & Crowther, D. (Eds) (2007) *Ethics, Psyche and Social Responsibility*, Ashgate Publishers, Aldershot.

Gostin, L.O. (2000) *Public Health Law*, University of California Press, Berkeley, p. 270.

Grüning, T., Gilmore, A.B. & McKee M. (2006) 'Tobacco industry influence on science and scientists in Germany', *American Journal of Public Health*, Vol. 96(1), pp. 20-32.

---

42   Thomas Zeltner, David A. Kessler, Anke Martiny, Fazel Randera 'Tobacco Company Strategies to Undermine Tobacco Control Activities at the World Health Organisation' Report of the Committee of Experts on Tobacco Industry Documents 2000; http://www.who.int/tobacco/en/who_inquiry.pdf

Henschke, C.I., Yip, R., & Miettinen, O.S. (2006) 'Women's susceptibility to tobacco carcinogens and survival after diagnosis of lung cancer' *Journal of the American Medical Association*, Vol. 296, pp. 180-184.

Kip Viscusi, W. (2005) The Blockbuster Punitive Damages Awards, *Harvard Law School Discussion Paper Series*, No. 473.

Maison D., Greenwald A.G. & Bruin R.H. (2004) 'Predictive validity of the implicit association test in studies of brands, consumer attitudes and behaviour', *Journal of Consumer Psychology*, Vol. 14(4), pp. 427-42.

Packard, V. (1957) *The Hidden Persuaders*, Pelican, London.

Reinicke, W.H. & Witte J.M. (1999) 'Interdependence, globalisation and sovereignty: The role of non-binding international legal accords', *The Role of Non-Binding Norms in the International Legal System*, Oxford University Press, Oxford.

Scott, C. (2004) 'Regulation in the Age of Governance: The Rise of the Post-Regulatory State', in *The Politics of Regulation*; J. Jordana, D. Levi Faur (eds), Edward Elgar, Cheltenham, p. 145.

Shapiro, S. (1999) 'When an ad's influence is beyond our conscious control: perceptual and conceptual fluency effects caused by incidental ad exposure', *Journal of Consumer Research*, Vol. 26(1), pp. 16-36.

Shaw, H.J. (2008) 'Resisting the hallucination of the hypermarket', *International Journal of Baudrillard Studies*, Vol. 5(1), pp. 1-30.

Shaw, H.J. & Shaw, J.J.A. (2005) 'Resisting Reification: free market or free citizens', *Social Responsibility Journal*, Vol. 1(1/2).

Shaw, J.J.A. (2004) 'Giants and Freaks: Understanding the Challenges of Social Responsibility in a Context of Oppression', in *Stakeholders and Social Responsibility*; D. Crowther and K.Tunca Caliyurt (eds), Ashgate Publishers, Aldershot.

Smith, E.A. (2007) 'It's interesting how few people die from smoking': Tobacco industry efforts to minimize risk and discredit health promotion, *European Journal of Public Health*, Vol. 17(2), pp. 162-170.

Index